Egypt

Revolution, Failed Transition and Counter-Revolution

Egypt

Revolution, Failed Transition and Counter-Revolution

Azmi Bishara

I.B. TAURIS
LONDON • NEW YORK • OXFORD • NEW DELHI • SYDNEY

I.B. TAURIS
Bloomsbury Publishing Plc
50 Bedford Square, London, WC1B 3DP, UK
1385 Broadway, New York, NY 10018, USA
29 Earlsfort Terrace, Dublin 2, Ireland

BLOOMSBURY, I.B. TAURIS and the I.B. Tauris logo are trademarks of Bloomsbury Publishing Plc

First published in 2016 in Lebanon as *The Great Egyptian Revolution* (in two volumes)
by the Arab Center for Research and Policy Studies
First published in Great Britain 2022
This paperback edition published 2024

Copyright © Azmi Bishara, 2022

Azmi Bishara has asserted his right under the Copyright, Designs and Patents Act, 1988, to be identified as Author of this work.

Cover image © Godong / Alamy Stock Photo

All rights reserved. No part of this publication may be reproduced or transmitted in any form or by any means, electronic or mechanical, including photocopying, recording, or any information storage or retrieval system, without prior permission in writing from the publishers.

Bloomsbury Publishing Plc does not have any control over, or responsibility for, any third-party websites referred to or in this book. All internet addresses given in this book were correct at the time of going to press. The author and publisher regret any inconvenience caused if addresses have changed or sites have ceased to exist, but can accept no responsibility for any such changes.

A catalogue record for this book is available from the British Library.

A catalog record for this book is available from the Library of Congress.

ISBN: HB: 978-0-7556-4590-9
PB: 978-0-7556-4594-7
ePDF: 978-0-7556-4591-6
eBook: 978-0-7556-4592-3

Typeset by Deanta Global Publishing Services, Chennai, India

To find out more about our authors and books visit www.bloomsbury.com and sign up for our newsletters.

Contents

List of illustrations   vi
List of abbreviations   ix

Introduction   1

Part I   From July Republic to January Revolution

1. Historical background in brief   9
2. Economic liberalization and political authoritarianism   80
3. Deconstructing the myth of acquiescence: A short history of protest in modern Egypt   110
4. From protest to revolution   166
5. Revolution in the provinces   269
6. Revolutionary youth in numbers   305
7. Who took part in the revolution, and can revolutions be predicted?   322

Concluding remarks: Part I   342

Part II   From Revolution to *Coup d'État*

1. In lieu of an introduction   351
2. The army's return to politics: Neither a conspiracy nor just a contingency   378
3. The lost opportunities and the deepening rift   411
4. Sectarian strife, social protest and fears of instability   450
5. The Selmi Document, the events of Mohammed Mahmoud 1 and parliamentary elections   460
6. The Constituent Assembly, presidential elections in a chaotic climate and the elected president   487
7. The deterioration: Unlike a Greek tragedy, it was not fate but politics   517
8. The coup   548
9. Egyptian public opinion during the transition and after the coup   590
10. International reactions from the fall of Mubarak to the coup   617

Final observations   671

Bibliography   680
Index   706

Illustrations

Figures

I.7.1	Sufficiency of income for basic needs (all respondents to AOI)	324
I.7.2	Sufficiency of income for basic needs (Egyptian respondents to AOI)	325
I.7.3	Attitudes towards Mubarak's ouster	329
I.7.4	Did you participate in the revolution?	332
II.9.1	Attitudes towards the Arab revolutions and the Arab Spring (2012, 2014, 2015)	592
II.9.2	Views on the future of the Arab Spring (2014, 2015)	596
II.9.3	Attitudes towards the 25 January revolution and the removal of Hosni Mubarak (2011)	598
II.9.4	The best system of government for Egypt (2012, 2014, 2015)	603
II.9.5	Attitudes towards the civil and religious state (2015)	612

Maps

1	25th January 2011, Greater Cairo Demonstration, Giza and Cairo City	179
2	28th January, 2011, Greater Cairo Demonstration	180
3	28th January, 2011, Greater Cairo Demonstration, The Giza Routes	181
4	28th January 2011, Greater Cairo Demonstration, The Cairo City Route	182

Tables

I.3.1	Development of Peaceful Protest (2001–8)	134
I.6.1	List of Revolutionary Youth Who Participated in the 2011 Revolution	306
I.6.2	Revolutionary Youth by Gender	318
I.6.3	Revolutionary Youth by Profession	318
I.6.4	Revolutionary Youth by Political Affiliation	320
I.6.5	Activists after the Revolution	321
I.6.6	Attitudes to the Coup	321
I.7.1	Causes of the Revolution	330
I.7.2	Causes of the Revolution by Gender, Age, Education, Residence and Income	330
I.7.3	Participation by Revolutionary Activity	334

I.7.4	Participation in Revolutionary Activity by Gender, Age, Education, Residence and Income	335
I.7.5	Wages and Benefits as a Share of GDP (%)	339
I.7.6	Income Distribution	340
II.6.1	Final Results of the First Round of the Presidential Election, 2012	498
II.6.2	Final Results of the Presidential Runoff, 2012	498
II.6.3	Comparison of Votes Cast	499
II.6.4	Final Results of the Presidential Runoff, 2012, by Governorate and Urban Population	500
II.7.1	Per Capita Income: Investment and Savings (2010–14)	530
II.7.2	GDP Growth (%)	531
II.7.3	GDP and Expenditure at Current Rates	532
II.7.4	Population Growth and Labour Force	533
II.7.5	Import Coverage of Exports (million USD)	533
II.7.6	Foreign Reserves (billion USD)	534
II.7.7	Tax Burden	535
II.7.8	National Budget Deficit	535
II.9.1	Attitudes towards the Arab Revolutions by Age, Education, Rural/Urban Residence and Religiosity (2015)	593
II.9.2	Reasons Cited for Positive View of the Arab Revolutions (2012, 2014, 2015)	594
II.9.3	Reasons Cited for Negative View of the Arab Revolutions (2012, 2014, 2015)	595
II.9.4	Top Three Reasons the Arab Revolutions Stalled and Failed to Meet Their Aims (2015)	597
II.9.5	Most Important Condition to Consider a Country a Democracy (2011, 2012, 2014)	599
II.9.6	Attitudes towards Anti-Democratic Sentiments (2011, 2012, 2014, 2015)	600
II.9.7	Attitudes towards Democracy (2011, 2012, 2014, 2015)	600
II.9.8	Attitudes towards the Infringement of Human Rights for the Sake of Security (2012, 2014, 2015)	601
II.9.9	Views on the Appropriate System of Government for Egypt (2012, 2014, 2015)	602
II.9.10	The Best System of Government for Egypt, by Gender, Age, Educational Attainment and Rural/Urban Residence (2015)	604
II.9.11	Evaluation of Guarantees for Political and Civil Liberties (2012, 2014, 2015)	606
II.9.12	Assessment of the Freedom to Freely Criticize the Government (2012, 2014, 2015)	607
II.9.13	Assessment of the Application of the Principle of Equal Citizenship (2012, 2014, 2015)	608
II.9.14	Attitudes towards Governance by Various Political Parties	609
II.9.15	Attitudes towards the Rising Influence of Islamist Political Movements (2012, 2014, 2015)	610

II.9.16	Reasons for Concern about Islamist Political Movements' Rise to Power (2015)	610
II.9.17	Attitudes towards the Rising Influence of Non-Islamist Political Parties (2014, 2015)	611
II.9.18	Reasons for Concern about Non-Islamist Political Movements' Rise to Power (2015)	612
II.9.19	Attitudes towards the Civil and Religious State by Gender, Age, Education and Urban/Rural Residence (2015)	613
II.9.20	The Definition of a Religious State (2015)	614
II.9.21	The Definition of a Civil State (2015)	614

Abbreviations

ACA	Administrative Control Authority
ACRPS	Arab Centre for Research and Policy Studies
AIPAC	American Israel Public Affairs Committee
AKP	Justice and Development Party (Turkey)
AmCham	American Chamber of Commerce in Egypt
ANHRI	Arabic Network for Human Rights Information
AOHR	Arab Organization for Human Rights
AOI	Arab Opinion Index
ASU	Arab Socialist Union
BDP	Building and Development Party
CA	Constituent Assembly
CAO	Central Auditing Organization
CAPMAS	Central Agency for Public Mobilization and Statistics
CBE	Central Bank of Egypt
CDB	China Development Bank
CIA	Central Intelligence Agency (US)
CIHRS	Cairo Institute for Human Rights Studies
CSA	Supreme Council of Antiquities
CSF	Central Security Forces
DFP	Democratic Front Party
EAEF	Egyptian-American Enterprise Fund
EBDA	Egyptian Business Development Association
EBRD	European Bank for Reconstruction and Development
ECES	Egyptian Center for Economic Studies
ECESR	Egyptian Center for Economic and Social Rights
EFP	Egyptian Food Bank
EGP	Egyptian Pound
EIB	European Investment Bank

EIJ	Egyptian Islamic Jihad
EIPR	Egyptian Initiative for Personal Rights
EMC	Egyptian Movement for Change (known as Kefaya)
EOHR	Egyptian Organization for Human Rights
ERTU	Egyptian Radio and Television Union
ESCWA	Economic and Social Commission for Western Asia
ESDP	Egyptian Social Democratic Party
ETUF	Egyptian Trade Union Federation
EU	European Union
FDEP	Front for the Defence of Egyptian Demonstrators
FGF	Future Generation Foundation
FJP	Freedom and Justice Party
GCC	Gulf Cooperation Council
GDP	Gross Domestic Product
GIS	General Intelligence Service
HADITU	Democratic Movement for National Liberation
HASHD	Popular Democratic Movement for Change
IAEA	International Atomic Energy Agency
IBRD	International Bank for Reconstruction and Development
ICJ	International Court of Justice
IDF	Israel Defense Forces
IDSC	Egyptian Cabinet's Information and Decision Support Center
IG	Islamic Group (al-Gama'a al-Islamiyya)
ILO	International Labour Organization
IMF	International Monetary Fund
IPCC	Inter-Party Coordination Committee
JDP	Justice and Development Party (Morocco)
KGB	Committee for State Security (USSR)
MEDO	Middle East Defence Organization
NAC	National Association for Change
NASL	National Alliance to Support Legitimacy and Reject the Coup (or the Anti-Coup Alliance)
NCHR	National Council for Human Rights

NCHRL	National Community for Human Rights and Law
NDC	National Defence Council
NDP	National Democratic Party
NFC	National Front for Change
NIR	Net International Reserves
NPUP	National Progressive Unionist Party (commonly referred to as the Tagammu)
NSA	National Security Agency
NSF	National Salvation Front
NSPO	National Service Projects Organization
NSS	National Security Staff (US)
OIC	Organization of Islamic Cooperation
OneWay ANOVA	One-way Analysis of Variance Test
PCC	Popular Campaign for Change (Freedom Now)
PPC	Political Parties Committee
PYC	Progressive Youth Coalition
QIZ	Qualifying industrial zones
RCA	Revolution Continues Alliance
RCC	Revolutionary Command Council
RDP	Reform and Development Party
RYC	Revolutionary Youth Coalition
SCAF	Supreme Council of the Armed Forces
SCC	Supreme Constitutional Court
SJC	Supreme Judicial Council
SMEs	Small and medium enterprises
SPAP	Popular Socialist Alliance Party
SPRING	Support for Partnership, Reform and Inclusive Growth
SSIS	State Security Investigations Service
SSRN	Social Science Research Network
UAE	United Arab Emirates
UAR	United Arab Republic
UK	United Kingdom of Great Britain and Northern Ireland (or Britain)

US	United States of America
USAID	United States Agency for International Development
USSR	Union of Soviet Socialist Republics or the Soviet Union
WINEP	Washington Institute for Near East Policy
YJF	Youth for Justice and Freedom

Introduction

In writing this book, I have sought to produce a study of the 2011 Egyptian revolution, the initial transition to democracy and its ultimate defeat by the coup within the context of modern Egyptian history. The first part of this book traces the background of the revolution from the July Republic through to its historic crisis at the end of Hosni Mubarak's tenure. The second part assesses the developments that culminated in the mass demonstrations against President Mohamed Morsi on 30 June 2013 and the subsequent military putsch.

This project has required taking a fresh look at various aspects of twentieth-century Egyptian history in the light of developments since January 2011. This sort of reconsideration – of economic and social conditions, of the role of the army and its relationship to the presidency, and the history of protest in Egypt – is crucial not only to understanding the revolution itself but also to the events that have followed it.

Writing an introduction to the Egyptian revolution is a daunting task. Academics, historians, journalists, travellers and politicians (in their autobiographies) have all written extensively on Egyptian modern history (see Chapters 1 and 2). Given its importance, Egypt has often been the subject of comparative studies in relation to other Arab countries and to the developing world more broadly, especially in the study of Islamist movements. Adequately covering such a wide range of sources is thus a challenge. Moreover, the prospective author of such an introduction must choose a chronological starting point and justify that choice. With some hesitation, I decided to begin with the events leading up to the coup of 1952, which, with the transition to a republican form of government and the revolutionary changes to the prevailing social and economic relations that accompanied it, came to be popularly perceived as a revolution.

Having reviewed the historical background and the economic and social conditions on the eve of the January revolution in Chapters 1 and 2, Chapters 3 and 4 move on to a discussion of the history of protest through to the qualitative leap that occurred after 25 January (and particularly 28 January). Here I concentrate in particular on the events leading up to 11 February 2011, taking a 'direct history' or 'current history' approach, which requires detailed documentation and analysis of the revolutionary movement. Since one of the purposes of this book is to serve as a reference, whether for interested citizens or for researchers, the process is equally concerned with documentary and analysis.

The study looks at the structure of the Egyptian regime on the eve of the revolution and the hidden fault lines that served as the seeds of internal conflict: the relationship between the presidency and the army, the rise of the president's family and the regime's increasing reliance on a new circle of influential businessmen. It then analyses how these conflicts played out during the revolution, emphasizing in particular the army's decision not to defend the Mubarak regime by confronting the revolutionaries, a decision that was interpreted as sympathy for the revolution itself. The second part argues that the real agenda of the army was, in fact, to prevent radical change as a first priority, preserve and expand its own privileged status, and even to govern the country itself if conditions allowed – or at the very least to impose its own vision of how it should be governed by leading from behind.

Writing the history of a revolution as an exceptional event or series of events in which mass popular forces seize the tiller of history in order to change the system of government becomes even more complex if the author begins to write in the immediate aftermath, when the story itself is as yet incomplete. One of the downsides of this proximity is that all the relevant information is not yet available; the author should therefore be careful in drawing conclusions. Rational speculation does not compensate for vital information that could include the irrational human motivations, decisions and attitudes. Another obstacle is that it is easy to be influenced by one or another of the forces or parties to the struggle. The author must be aware of this temptation and resist it insofar as is possible by means of that awareness. But this does not mean suppressing moral sympathy for human dignity and freedom or for justice more generally – the desire for which is the essence of any revolution against injustice. It simply means that value judgements and political opinions must not skew the collection of data or the documentation and analysis of events.

So long as the author bears this in mind, temporal proximity to the revolution is an advantage. Writing contemporary history at this point means getting ahead of distorted versions of events or narratives told from the exclusive perspective of institutions or new political forces – or, subsequently, the forces of the counter-revolution or ruling regimes. Documenting the tumult of events as it happens, directly experiencing the atmosphere and context, and then crosschecking these initial impressions against new data once a reasonable window of time has elapsed are all sources of strength for a study. This way, details are recorded before subsequent developments make one more important and another less so, before one person's role is elevated and another's marginalized. The main weakness is simply that some information remains hidden, and, without the benefit of hindsight, the study may end up exaggerating or underestimating the significance of particular factors.

Documentation here is different from press coverage. It is not intended for publication as an individual story or investigation, but instead collects and compares data methodically, returning to it later to verify and analyse it critically. It looks closely at context – the social and economic background and analyses of the political forces that are party to events. Over the last five years, I have developed a theoretical approach to revolutions that sees them as mass popular movements seeking to change a political system from outside, thereby distinguishing them from both military coups originating within the regime (which is not to say that they cannot subsequently lead to revolutionary change in political and social relations) and pure protest movements pursuing particular aims, which, although they are external to the regime, do not seek to change it (although these, too, can become revolutions). This distinction is important, not only because it allows us to differentiate between these three phenomena but also because it lets us identify the point at which one transforms into another. It also means that we can identify synthetic phenomena: the 1952 coup became a revolution, for example, unlike that of 2013, whose aim was the restoration of the pre-revolutionary regime; the 2011 revolution was a reformist revolution because it did not aspire to take power itself. Instead, it demanded the president's abdication and regime change, but without calling on a specific political or social force to seize power – demands that were interpreted as calling for democratic transition.

In the same five-year period, I methodically documented the progress of the Egyptian, Syrian and Tunisian revolutions. I used the resulting documentary base as one of several sources in the writing of a contemporary history, alongside local and international statistics from official bodies, opinion surveys conducted by the ACRPS, and existing secondary and theoretical literature. My method has been to treat a social phenomenon as a historical one, with various dimensions that require the historian's attention: economic, political, social, historical and discursive, among others. In all my writings on the Arab revolutions, I have sought to adopt an interdisciplinary approach, combining economics, political science, history and sociology. I believe that this approach, the tentative beginnings of which can be seen in *Understanding Revolutions: Opening*

Acts in Tunisia,[1] reached maturity in *Syria 2011–2013: Revolution and Tyranny before the Mayhem*,[2] which covered the first two years of the Syrian revolution before its transformation into a civil war, and in this book on the Egyptian revolution. Part I of this book concludes with some theoretical suggestions drawing on research data regarding the socio-economic structure of participants in the revolution and the debate over the circumstances under which revolutions take place.

Part II documents the period from President Hosni Mubarak's resignation to the military coup of 3 July 2013 and attempts to explain why the democratic transition grounded to a halt. Like the first part, it takes a contemporary history approach to the phenomenon as a whole, taking into account not only socio-economic structures and political forces but also cultural factors. The content of Part II is discussed in more detail in a separate introductory chapter.

This study does not rely solely on a critical study of books and publications but also includes data collected through methodical field investigation from a variety of sources. The work of a team of research assistants, led by Hani Awwad and Nerouz Satik and guided by the author, who conducted individual and group interviews with a number of activists, has proven indispensable. Interviews were also conducted throughout Egypt by another team of Egyptians led by Ahmed Abd Rabou. The use of focus groups helped to reduce the effect of individual biases; over the course of lengthy sessions conducted by the teams or by me, activists often corrected or acted as a check on one another. Nonetheless, individual interviews were also used where necessary. At a fairly late stage of the process, we were joined at the ACRPS by an Egyptian research assistant, Abdo Moussa, whose knowledge of the local context, the functioning of Egyptian NGOs and the use of torture by the Egyptian regime was invaluable when reviewing and verifying information.

Help with sources on the historical and economic background of the revolution was provided by Huda Hawwa, Jamal Barout, Zoheir Hamedi and Samir Seifan, all of them colleagues at the ACRPS. The section on the day-to-day development of the revolution was reviewed by Hany Mahmoud, Abdelrahman Fares and Khaled Elsayed, all of them members of the RYC. Hany has been blessed with an archival memory and, even in exile, has kept hold of many important documents that provide information on this period; Abdelrahman provided access to

---

[1] Azmi Bishara, *Understanding Revolutions: Opening Acts in Tunisia* (London and New York: I.B. Tauris, 2021).
[2] Azmi Bishara, *Syria 2011–2013: Revolution and Tyranny before the Mayhem* (London and New York: I.B. Tauris, 2022).

a network of contacts among the young people that participated in the revolution; and Khaled showed an incredible knowledge of details. I enjoyed our sessions immensely: each of them has a different political background, and in the course of their discussions they often reminded or corrected one another regarding particular details, enriching their common narrative. The AOI project team furnished me with the opinion data that appears in Part II. The Egyptian academic Seif al-Din Abdel Fattah reviewed both parts and provided many helpful observations. Part I was also reviewed by Jamal Barout and Part II by Khaled Elsayed and Mohamed Naim, all of whom likewise gave valuable feedback.

It was not possible, of course, for us to cover every aspect of the revolution and its context or to interview most of those who led it (not to mention activists or participants). I apologize to all those whom we did not have the opportunity to speak to, pleading in my defence the limited capacity of both humans and of any research project: any book must have an end. The documentation process, however, continues – and others who did not get their chance in this book will fill in the gaps left by this work.

A few books on the Egyptian revolution have been published in foreign languages, some journalistic, others more academic, but none of them presenting Egyptian history and the history of its revolution in context. Many Egyptian activists and intellectuals with direct experience of the revolution have also documented its progress from their own perspectives. Most of these works are tendentious or impressionistic, but I have nonetheless benefited from them to a limited extent.

This book is distinct in that it looks at the revolution itself, at both the micro and macro levels, using an interdisciplinary methodology that combines a relatively broad vision of modern Egyptian history spanning the second half of the nineteenth century and the twentieth century with a 'direct history' reading of events up to the 2013 coup.

Readers will notice that the closer the book gets to the events of January 2011, the more it drills down into the day-to-day detail. As previously noted, this is because it is intended to serve both as an analytical and as a self-consciously archival and reference work. The ultimate fate of the revolution and the young people who organized it has only made the need for such a reference work more pressing. Those who have an interest in forgetting this remarkable moment in the history of Egypt and the Arab World cannot be allowed to misrepresent it or to disregard those who seized the reins of history. The Egyptian revolution, a revolution fought against despotism and for 'bread, freedom, social justice' and human dignity was one of this nation's finest moments.

Finally, I want to thank my friends and colleagues who worked with me on the English version of the book, which I did my best to update, taking into consideration that the original Arabic version appeared in Beirut in 2016. I express my gratitude to Chris Hitchcock, who translated Part I; Peter Daniel who translated Part II along with Mandy McClure, who also edited both parts.

Part I

From July Republic to January Revolution

1

Historical background in brief

I The road to July

When Egyptians first rose up against foreign occupation in the late nineteenth century, their slogan was 'Egypt for the Egyptians'.¹ More than a hundred years later, the same slogan is an apt encapsulation of the goals of the 2011 January revolution, albeit this time in the full and positive sense of a state belonging to all its citizens and not simply an end to foreign interference. Citizenship is the real internal manifestation of sovereignty.

In January 2011, Egyptians revolted against the political system established in 1952, which grew out of a century and a half of dramatic social and economic change. During the nineteenth century, the Muhammad Ali dynasty had laid the foundations of a modern Egyptian state, efforts that reached their peak under the ambitious Khedive Ismail (r. 1863–79). The non-Muslim poll tax (*jizya*) taken in lieu of military service had been abolished, and Copts were admitted into the senior ranks of the civil service and, after 1883, served in government – both major steps towards the emergence of a concept of citizenship.² The new atmosphere of openness brought an influx of foreign migration: by 1870, the population of Alexandria had risen to 130,000, including 50,000 Europeans. Cairo was extensively redeveloped, and its population swelled as well, from 263,000 in 1798 to 374,000 in 1882, including some 19,000 foreigners.³ Egypt's economy was bolstered by the booming cotton trade and the completion of the Suez Canal. And under Ismail, Egypt had participated actively in

---

[1] The phrasing is closely associated with Mustafa Kamil (1874–1908), founder of the National Party and editor-in-chief of the newspaper *al-Liwa*.
[2] This development can be seen even earlier, under Muhammad Ali (r. 1805–48), who abolished sumptuary discrimination against Copts and allowed the renovation of churches. Military service was imposed and the poll tax abolished under Khedive Ismail. For a more detailed review of these developments, see: Azmi Bishara, 'Can We Speak of a "Coptic Question" in Egypt?', *Arab Centre for Research and Policy Studies*, May 2011, Available online: https://bit.ly/3A2rM45 (accessed 25 October 2021).
[3] Jacques Berque, *Egypt: Imperialism and Revolution* [French] (Paris: Gallimard, 1967), 78, 87; Sophie Pommier, *Egypt: Behind the Scenes* [French] (Paris: Editions la Découverte, 2008), 33.

international military campaigns, contributing forces to the Ottoman side in the Crimean War (1853–6) and to the French intervention in Mexico (1861–7).

While the system created by Muhammad Ali resembled that later established in the Ottoman Empire by the Tanzimat reformers, the Egyptian national identity that began to crystallize in the nineteenth century brought together a clearly Arab-inflected Islamic reformism with liberal thought, influenced by the cultural revival (*nahda*) in the Levant and the widespread translation of books from European languages. A flourishing Arabic language press developed, with two of its flagship papers – *al-Ahram* and *al-Hilal* – founded by Levantine émigrés.

Like their counterparts in Tunisia and the Ottoman Empire, Egyptian reformers were to discover that the drive for modernization – of the military, infrastructure and the educational system – ran up against the country's limited financial resources. The Egyptian state thus increasingly turned to borrowing from Europe, with disastrous consequences. In 1874, Ismail was forced to sell Egypt's share in the Suez Canal Company, and in 1876 the European powers imposed a Public Debt Administration run by representatives of France, the UK, Italy and Austria and installed foreigners in key Egyptian ministerial portfolios. When Ismail resisted these dictates and attempted to dismiss these ministers in 1879, he was deposed and replaced by his son Tawfiq.[4] Resentment at this new, foreign-dominated order was the main driver of the military revolt led by Colonel Ahmed Urabi (1841–1911) in 1882. The UK intervened directly to put down the mutiny, initiating an occupation that would last in various forms until 1956.

The purported aim of the British occupation of Egypt in 1882 was to ensure the payment of Egypt's debts and protect the Khedive Tewfik Pasha (r. 1879–92) from the Urabists. Broader imperial objectives also underlay British actions, most importantly securing the Suez Canal (the way to

---

[4] Between 1876 and Ismail's deposal, some five committees were appointed to inspect Egyptian debt, all of them, including the Public Debt Commission, controlled by the debtor countries, specifically Britain and France. The task of the foreign employees attached to these committees – which eventually rose to some 1,300 people – was to 'restructure the Egyptian economy'. See: Roger Owen, *The Middle East in the World Economy, 1800–1914*, rev. edn (London and New York: I. B. Tauris, 1993), 130–6.

The Ottoman Empire likewise faced official bankruptcy twice in the course of the later nineteenth century: once in 1875, less than a year before Abdulhamid II took the throne (31 August 1876), and again in 1879 (just after the Empire's defeat in the Russo-Turkish War (1877–8) and the loss of most of its European provinces), when around 80 per cent of its annual revenue went to service the debts taken on after the Crimean War. After the second bankruptcy, the state's finances were placed under foreign supervision. See: Philip L. Cottrell, 'A Survey of European Investments in Turkey, 1854–1914: Banks and the Finance of the State and Railway Construction', in *East Meets West: Banking, Commerce and Investment in the Ottoman Empire*, ed. Philip L. Cottrell, Monica Pohle and Iain L. Fraser (Aldershot, Hampshire, UK: Ashgate, 2008), 80–1.

India and the Indian Ocean) and establishing a foothold in the Arab region during a time of Ottoman weakness. Achieving all of these aims meant imposing a colonial order in which Britain was permanently at odds with the Egyptian army. After directly intervening to save the khedive from his own troops, the occupying forces followed a deliberate policy of keeping the military weak and small. The Egyptian economy was similarly subordinated directly to the needs of the colonizing power. The production of cotton for British cotton mills became a major priority, particularly due to the fall-off in cotton production in the United States during the American Civil War (1861–5), a process that damaged Egyptian subsistence agriculture and food production and resulted in a weak industrial bourgeois in contrast to an emboldened and influential landowner class.[5]

In December 1914, after the Ottoman Empire sided with Germany in the First World War, Britain made Egypt an official protectorate and the khedive became a sultan, emphasizing the break with the Ottomans. Egypt's changed status entailed a concomitant transformation of the British contingent in Egypt, who turned from debt collectors into fully fledged colonists backed by thousands of soldiers and civil servants. Slowly but surely, a fissure began to emerge between the monarchy and this British presence.

The British presence did not, however, put a stop to the evolution of social interactions and national consciousness that had been underway since the nineteenth century. The social contradictions to which these developments gave rise exploded in the mass demonstrations of the 1919 revolution, led by Saad Zaghloul (1859–1927), who represented the liberal-nationalist wing of the landowning class in alliance with an ascendant bourgeoisie and intelligentsia alongside elements of the new bureaucracy. The mass uprising set off a string of events and negotiations that ultimately led to the end of the British Protectorate on 28 February 1922, albeit with extensive privileges reserved for the UK, including the right to 'protect minorities', retain the security of imperial communications, maintain the security of the Suez Canal and protect its interests in Sudan. In practice, this meant colonial oversight of an autonomous Egyptian 'state', in which Egyptian institutions, including the army, functioned under Egyptian control, but within the limits set by the colonial power. This pseudo-independence birthed a new pluralist, partisan politics. The constitution promulgated in 1923 created a limited constitutional monarchy that would struggle constantly to avoid becoming a fully constitutional monarchy. As a result,

---

[5] Hazem Kandil, *The Power Triangle: Military, Security, and Politics in Regime Change* (Oxford and New York: Oxford University Press, 2016), 231.

an uneasy balance of power was established between the palace, the British authorities and Zaghloul's Wafd Party.[6]

The interwar period also saw a new industrial and financial capitalism emerge from within the merchant and landowning class, exemplified by the founding of Banque Misr by the industrialist Talaat Harb (1867–1941). The nascent conflict between traditional society and modern urban society overlapped with conflict between the new classes produced by this capitalist transformation (wage labourers, capital, the new bureaucracy, the middle class), giving rise to new contradictions that manifested most clearly in new political currents outside the hegemony of the liberal Wafd led by Zaghloul and later Mustafa al-Nahhas (1879–1965). Communist and nationalist opinion, influenced by European socialist and national movements respectively, became popular, particularly among minorities and later within a broad swathe of the working class. An Islamist current also appeared, giving expression to parts of a traditional lower-middle class whose way of life and economic status had been undermined by modernization and for whom religious identity was a realm of stability and intimacy in the midst of rapid, alienating changes. Although it drew on the reformist legacy of the nineteenth century that endeavoured to purify Islam from tradition to prove that there is no contradiction between the fundaments of Islam and modernity, the new Islamist activism that developed after the great disappointments of the Anglo-French partitioning of the Middle East (1920–3) and the dismantling of the Caliphate (1925) was less interested in reconciling religion with the challenges of the modern age than with using religious rhetoric to challenge the modern age itself. The Muslim Brotherhood, founded in 1928[7] by Hassan al-Banna, initially took the form of resistance to missionary activity and changes in customs (e.g. gender mixing) brought about by modernization and ideological compensation for the disappearance of the Ottoman Empire.

The military establishment, however, had been more or less totally excluded from politics since the defeat of the Urabi revolt.[8] It took no part in the suppression of popular movements or demonstrations, whether

---

[6] Wafd meaning 'delegation'. The party was so named because it had initially sought to act as the Egyptian delegation to the Paris Peace Conference.

[7] Hassan al-Banna (1906–49) was the product of a religious-reformist upbringing in Mahmoudiyya, Alexandria. He began his work in Ismailia, which was a centre of foreign settlement in Egypt thanks to the presence of several British companies and garrisons, as well as a major missionary hotspot. In 1934, the Brotherhood's new Executive Committee drew up a comprehensive 'Islamic' plan for society, politics and the economy. Like many contemporary parties, it had its own youth wing, the Rover Scouts (founded in 1937), as well as an armed wing, the Secret Apparatus (1940), which was involved in attacks on cinemas and police stations, and assassinations of foreigners and political figures.

[8] Which is not to say that individual soldiers, particularly officers, were not involved in politics – quite the contrary.

in the liberal period or even under the rule of the pro-palace parliamentary minority (especially from 1930 to 1934). Although the monarchy sometimes sought its help with logistics and supply during times of national crisis, both army recruitment and military hardware were strictly limited.

Under Zaghloul's successor Mustafa al-Nahhas, the Wafd Party found itself trapped between the realities of governing in a country dominated by a foreign power and the strong anti-colonial sentiment that had provided its raison d'être. During this period, partisan factionalism was rife, and there was a constant tug of war between the palace, the Wafd (the majority party) and the British. As prime minister in 1935, Nahhas oversaw the signing of the unpopular Anglo-Egyptian Treaty on 26 August 1936, which reaffirmed many of Britain's privileges and left some 10,000 British soldiers on Egyptian territory, most of them garrisoned around the Suez Canal.

Something of a cultural renaissance also took place at this time, although it was limited to major urban centres. An urban civil service and educational establishment developed, as did a class of middle-class professionals and unions – all supported intellectually by an active press. The social base of the army's leadership was changing as well. From 1936, the number of middle-class youths who were allowed to join the military college due to a Nahhas reform – and thus came to occupy senior military positions – grew steadily.[9] Most of the Free Officers who took part in the 1952 coup belonged to this generation of middle-class officers whose careers had been made possible by the exigencies of war.

Looking at the wider society, however, the majority of the population still toiled in poverty and ignorance in the countryside, where social relations were subordinated to a system in which landowners controlled poor farmworkers. Before the 1952 coup and the expansive revolutionary mobilization that preceded it, 0.5 per cent of Egyptians owned 35 per cent of agricultural land,[10] while eleven million agricultural labourers owned no land at all – whence the term 'half-per cent society' often used to characterize this period.

In 1942, amidst the Second World War battles in Egypt's Western Desert, Nahhas agreed to form a pro-British ministry forced on King Farouq (r. 1936–52) at gunpoint after British tanks surrounded Abdin Palace – a humiliation that few would forget, least of all in the army, to whom it was a slap in the face.[11] This seems to have been a formative experience for many

---

[9] Ahmad Abdullah, 'The Armed Forces and the Development of Democracy in Egypt' [Arabic], in *The Army and Democracy in Egypt* [Arabic], ed. Ahmad Abdullah (Cairo: Sina Publishing, 1990), 10.

[10] Joel Beinin, *Workers and Peasants in the Modern Middle East* (Cambridge: Cambridge University Press, 2001), 118.

[11] Mohamed Naguib (1901–84), leader of the Free Officers, says in his memoirs that the humiliation drove him to submit his resignation to the king, who refused to accept it. See: Mohamed Naguib, *I*

young officers, who developed a marked hostility to the British.[12] However, British backing ultimately damaged the Wafd, most apparent in 1944 when the king dismissed the Nahhas government that had been forced on him by the British only two years before.

Among the beneficiaries of the Wafd's decline were the ideological movements that had begun to emerge after the First World War. Movements and parties across the political spectrum – from the communist factions to the Muslim Brotherhood to Wafd splinter parties and fascist-influenced youth movements – actively vied for power and public influence. Some, like the fascist-inspired Young Egypt and the Muslim Brotherhood, established paramilitary youth wings similar to those common in Europe at the time. The Brotherhood's 'Rover Scouts' (*gawwala*) were exempted from a government ban on such organizations issued by the Mohammed Mahmoud government (formed on 27 April 1938) on the grounds that they were a purely religious and not party-political organization.

By the 1940s, many of these parties had become mass movements, with the Brotherhood boasting hundreds of thousands of members.[13] None of them, however, could aspire to the sort of vote share that the Wafd had enjoyed at its height.

In the immediate aftermath of the Second World War, the UK reneged on its promise to leave Egypt. In response, on 9 February 1946 students staged a mass protest against Britain that ended in bloodshed in what became known as the Abbas Bridge Massacre, setting the stage for a new phase of resistance to the British occupation and prompting the National Workers and Students' Committee to organize a general strike in April.

This period of heightened social mobilization also witnessed rising political violence. By the late 1940s, the Brotherhood and others accused of belonging to secret youth organizations had been implicated in a string of bombings of cinemas and commercial establishments, as well as the assassination of prominent public figures like Prime Minister Ahmed Maher (24 February 1945), the Wafdist minister Amin Othman (5 January

---

Was a President of Egypt [Arabic] (Cairo: al-Maktab al-Misri al-Hadith, 1984), 60–1.

[12] See: Khaled Mohieddin, *And Now I Speak* [Arabic] (Cairo: Ahram Centre for Translation and Publishing, 1992), 34–45. Mohieddin says that the experience was a formative one for Nasser as well.

[13] This figure is contested, but the most conservative estimates suggest hundreds of thousands of members. It is worth noting that the exact number of Brothers has been exploited as part of the struggle for power in Egypt, and very different figures have been floated – some dramatically exaggerated and others played down for political effect. At the end of the 1940s, there were barely a quarter as many Egyptians as there are today, with only very few active in politics: politics remained an elite pursuit and social development and education were still limited. Mitchell suggests a figure of half a million members on the cusp of the 1950s, while Pommier estimates 100,000–500,000 active members. See: Richard Paul Mitchell, *The Society of the Muslim Brothers* (New York and Oxford: Oxford University Press, 1993 [1969]); Pommier, *Egypt*, 224.

1946) and Judge Ahmed al-Khazindar (22 March 1948). Things came to a head on 28 November 1948, when the government of Mahmoud Fahmi al-Nuqrashi (1888–1948) issued a military decree dissolving the Brotherhood branches in Ismailia and Alexandria, claiming the group was plotting a revolution. On 28 December, Nuqrashi himself was killed by a veterinary student accused of membership in the Brotherhood, sparking massive reprisals that ended with the organization's dissolution in November 1948,[14] the arrest of some 4,000 Brothers and Banna's assassination a few months later.[15]

The only party that came out of this chaotic period unscathed was the army; it was the only 'force [which] was still in the field, its mass proudly deployed and surrounded by respect and popular sympathy, which regarded it as Faruk's victim'.[16] The army of this era no longer resembled its predecessor of 1882, which had been comfortably controlled by the king. Starting in 1936, the army launched a recruitment drive, ostensibly to meet Egypt's military obligations under the Anglo-Egyptian Treaty, opening up the military college to middle-class youths.[17] The number of men under arms thus grew precipitously – from 30,000 to 100,000 men over the course of the 1940s – as did the number of middle-class officers.[18] The middle-class officers in general were to prove particularly open to certain kinds of radical and mass politics, and the expanding social base of the army – as well as its relative isolation from the increasingly sordid world of civilian politics – contributed to a general belief in its integrity as an institution.

The British occupation managed to survive these successive waves of dissent, especially once the public was distracted by Egypt's military intervention in Palestine in 1948. But the failure of that intervention was to have fatal consequences for the parliamentary system. Those who had fought against the Zionists came back 'disillusioned and defeated' – or 'full of rage and set on vengeance'[19] – convinced that 'treacherous politicians' had sold them out. Clandestine cells proliferated within the army, which was in any case still smarting from the Abdin Palace affair of 1942.[20] Most were linked to the traditional parties, but the one that was to play the key

---

[14] At this point, the Brotherhood was still fighting in Palestine, and Egypt had not yet signed a ceasefire with Israel, which it did on 24 February 1949.
[15] The immediate pretext for the dissolution was the alleged discovery of an arms cache and plans to overthrow the government put together by the Brotherhood's armed wing, the Secret Apparatus.
[16] Anouar Abdel-Malek, *Egypt: Military Society; the Army Regime, the Left, and Social Change under Nasser*, trans. Charles Lam Markmann (New York: Random House, 1968 [1962]), 44.
[17] Ibid.
[18] Abdullah, 'The Armed Forces', 10.
[19] Mohieddin, *And Now I Speak*, 75.
[20] Hazem Kandil, *Soldiers, Spies, and Statesmen: Egypt's Road to Revolt* (London and Brooklyn, NY: Verso, 2012), 10–1.

role in the events of 1952, Gamal Abdel Nasser's Free Officer Command Cell, was independent.

The Free Officers quickly built up connections with other political movements and cells, some of whose members later joined them in an individual capacity.[21] Nasser himself, reeling from the 1948 war and sick of the corruption of palace and political life, established contact with parties like the Wafd, the Brotherhood[22] and the communist HADITU.[23] Some of the five officers who made up the first Free Officer Command Cell had been members of the Brotherhood's Secret Apparatus between 1944 and 1945.[24] Nasser's links to the parties, however, seem to have been entirely pragmatic, in the sense that he wanted to win their support or at least guarantee their neutrality; he had no intention of supporting them in turn, their own members and ideologues' misconceptions notwithstanding.[25]

The Command Cell first met in the second half of 1949. This was not the only cell within the military; other groups included HADITU's Gamal Mansour Group, Mustafa Kemal Sidqi's Iron Guard (directed from the palace by Youssef Rashad, a navy doctor) and the Hussein Tawfiq Group, which

---

[21] Abdel Latif Boghdadi, *Memoirs of Abdel Latif Boghdadi* [Arabic], vol. 1 (Cairo: al-Maktab al-Misri al-Hadith, 1977), 12–13.

[22] Hussein Ahmed Hammouda, one of the Free Officers, claims that after being introduced to members by Abdul Munim Abdul Rauf, Nasser had joined the Brotherhood along with four other officers in 1946, swearing an oath on a Quran and a pistol. Nasser is also alleged to have provided weapons training to Brotherhood members and to have helped put together plans for the Brotherhood's guerrilla campaign against the British between 1946 and 1947. See: Hussein Muhammad Ahmed Hammouda, *Secrets of the Free Officers Movement and the Muslim Brotherhood* [Arabic], 2nd edn (Cairo: Zahra Arabic Media, 1985), 150.

Khaled Mohieddin states, more accurately, that Nasser was one of the military men who contacted Mahmoud Labib (an officer who was a member of the Brotherhood) via Abdul Munim Abdul Rauf and that the Brotherhood pinned their hopes on this group, treating them as an autonomous but subordinate squadron. He claims that they met Hassan al-Banna multiple times. While Mohieddin leaned to the left, Nasser sought to establish relations with the Brotherhood, although he remained suspicious of them. This did not prevent the two men from joining the Brotherhood's Secret Apparatus, however, and Mohieddin claims that both he and Nasser swore an oath of allegiance to the group. See: Mohieddin, *And Now I Speak*, 43–5. Neither Mohieddin nor Nasser ever officially resigned from the Brotherhood, although their positions subsequently diverged: Mohieddin objected to the Brotherhood's decision to stand against the National Workers and Students' Committee during the student and worker revolt and cooperate with Wafdist prime minister Ismail Sidqi (1875–1950), while Nasser felt that the Brotherhood used officers for their own ends rather than those of the nation (Mohieddin, *And Now I Speak*, 47). This proved to be characteristic of Nasser's position on political parties more broadly.

[23] Mohieddin, *And Now I Speak*, 289.

[24] Ibid., 44, 63. It is also worth noting that a battalion of Brotherhood members fought in El Arish during the 1948 war under the command of an army officer, Ahmed Abdel Aziz, alongside others who would later join the Free Officers, including Kamal el-Din Hussein and Salah Salem. While the Brotherhood's contribution to the war was far from decisive, it provided an important boost to morale and to the image and self-image of the Islamist movement in the region. Indeed, the intervention of the entire Egyptian army did not prove decisive in settling the war one way or another. Steven A. Cook, *The Struggle for Egypt: From Nasser to Tahrir Square* (Oxford and New York: Oxford University Press, 2013), 35.

[25] Mohieddin, *And Now I Speak*, 68, 81, 107.

brought together civilians and military men – including future president Anwar Sadat – and carried out terrorist operations. Another group of air force officers, active since 1940, had been in contact with German military command during Erwin Rommel's campaign; Sadat was also a member of this group.[26] These and other officers were inspired by Field Marshal Aziz al-Misri, a former Ottoman general who had been much impressed by the assassinations conducted by Bulgarian nationalists and now recommended the same strategy against the British. Some members of HADITU's group subsequently joined the Free Officers as individuals.[27]

There were two main reasons for the proliferation of these cells within the army. The first was the officers' growing resentment at British tutelage. The humiliating experience of 1942 had been enough to trigger a meeting of 400 officers hostile to Britain,[28] which proved a formative experience for many of those who organized as the Free Officers after 1948, including Mohamed Naguib.[29] The second was the disastrous defeat in Palestine. Egypt's senior military and civilian leadership (including Naguib himself) had initially opposed intervention on the grounds that the army, deliberately kept weak by British policy, was not battle-ready, but Farouq insisted on sending troops.

After a Wafd landslide in the 1950 elections, Nahhas returned to power and formed a new government. He immediately ended martial law and released political prisoners, and in October 1951 he withdrew from the 1936 Anglo-Egyptian Treaty, transforming British troops into an illegal occupation force overnight. This immediately galvanized popular opposition to the British occupation, resulting in guerrilla attacks in the Suez Canal zone as well as broad popular strikes and demonstrations in support of the government, actions which continued right up to the 1952 Cairo fire.[30]

The tension continued to mount with military reprisals around the canal. In December 1951, British troops destroyed the village of Kafr Abdou, claiming that it had been harbouring guerrillas, while in January 1952 they occupied Ismailia, culminating in a desperate defence of the police station by Egyptian policemen on 25 January (subsequently commemorated as National Police Day, the national holiday that provided the occasion for the

---

[26] Boghdadi, *Memoirs*, 12–13.
[27] Ibid., 68.
[28] Mohieddin, *And Now I Speak*, 35–6.
[29] Kandil, *Soldiers, Spies, and Statesmen*, 10–11.
[30] Tarek El-Bishry summarizes this period as follows: 'The 1936 agreement was terminated by decree in October 1951, and a common armed struggle began. When popular mobilization was unable to secure the revolution's demands as articulated between 1951 and 1952, the revolutionary blow was struck instead by the young men of the army on 23 July 1952.' See: Tarek El-Bishry, *Pages from the January 25 Revolution* [Arabic] (Cairo: Dar Shorouk, 2012), 23.

first protests of the 2011 revolution). The next day, an organized group of unknown assailants began a riot in downtown Cairo, an area hosting many foreign businesses and residents. Soon enough, downtown was in flames, leaving forty-six people dead and millions of pounds worth of property destroyed.

The last six months between the Cairo fire and the July military coup were chaotic ones. Against a backdrop of constant popular protest and public disorder, no less than four governments were appointed and collapsed. The short-lived premiership of Hussein Sirri, the thirty-fifth of pre-revolutionary Egypt, was to be its last. The three poles of Egyptian politics until that point – the palace, the Wafd and the British – had reached a dead end. The opposition parties, too, had lost popular confidence after squandering their own opportunities to govern.

Alongside this political volatility, a struggle was being waged over the army that could be traced back to 1950, when the Wafd government had refused to cede its constitutional right of control over the army.[31] The king had immediately appointed his brother-in-law as commander-in-chief, an appointment much resented by the officer corps; this resentment was on display in the elections for the head of the Officers' Club, where the king's appointee (Hussein Sirri) was roundly rejected in favour of Mohamed Naguib. The king responded by dissolving the club's board and replacing it with a temporary alternative. The king's move was consistent with his attempts to use the army in the political rivalry. It is reported that the palace used the Iron Guard organization to conduct a campaign of political violence against its enemies.[32]

During this revolutionary period, the defeat in Palestine became a patriotic Egyptian narrative that placed the blame firmly at the feet of the ruling parties, the king and the British; the army, meanwhile, were cast as the heroic victims of a great betrayal.[33] Within our theoretical framework, it is thus possible to analyse the events of this period as a revolution culminating in a military coup against the regime.

---

[31] An investigation into faulty equipment initiated by the last Wafd government was terminated by the public prosecutor, who was afraid that it would implicate the king. See: Naguib, *I Was a President of Egypt*, 91–2.

[32] Mohamed Naguib claims in his memoirs that the Iron Guard was established by the palace and its members chosen by the naval doctor Youssef Rashad in order to monitor nationalist army officers. He also says that Anwar Sadat was a member. See: Naguib, *I Was a President*, 67, 69.

[33] The stab-in-the-back myth is far from unique to Egypt or the Arab world. Such myths have proven central to nationalist mobilization around armies and against politicians after traumatic military defeats.

The stage was now set for a change: a military coup. At 3.00 am on 23 July, forces led by Youssef Mansour Seddik[34] occupied the headquarters of the general staff in Kobri al-Qubba. Luckily for the coup plotters, Seddik found almost all the army's senior leadership already gathered there, ending any possibility of resistance in a single stroke. Three days later, Farouq was in exile and the Free Officers were in power.

The Free Officers' coup should be understood analytically as the culmination of an ongoing revolutionary mobilization, and may in fact have stolen a march on a popular revolution. It brought the curtain down on the so-called liberal era, a period that had seen the development of a genuinely pluralistic party system, free expression and a diverse press alongside major leaps forward in art and education. But the liberal era had also witnessed an incessant conflict between the king, the parliament and the British and the emergence of an anti-liberal populism with little respect for institutions. With violence playing an ever-greater role in political life and a regime incapable of solving the enduring agrarian problem, dealing with rural poverty or building a modern army, the situation had quickly degenerated into chaos. The events of 1952 constituted, indisputably, a classic military coup,[35] but one that was made possible by public distrust in the regime. In this context, the army – which had refused to embroil itself in the liberal era's internecine conflicts – had maintained a consistently patriotic and anti-British stance. Many of the Free Officers came from a nationalist or Islamist background, and some of them had been members of the Brotherhood at different points in their lives or affiliated with leftist groups. With its broad middle-class base and connections to a range of political movements, the army seemed to be the only force with the integrity needed to run the country.

The military proclamation that announced the coup, however, gave no hint of any specific vision for the future of Egypt; its content was largely restricted to the need to hold the corrupt regime to account for its

---

[34] Youssef Mansour Seddik subsequently submitted his resignation from the Revolutionary Command Council (RCC) when it was decided that elections would not be held and when officers from the 35th Artillery were arrested for criticizing RCC members' behaviour in January 1953. Although the RCC declined Seddik's resignation, it imprisoned him before later forcing him to leave the country for Switzerland in March 1953. He was repeatedly accused of being a communist.

[35] According to Naguib, 'We were all accustomed to calling [it] a coup. "Coup" was the term that we used. We weren't afraid of it – it was a description of reality. "Coup" was the term used in the initial negotiations and the messages I exchanged with the government discussing a return to the barracks. Then when we wanted to speak directly to the people and win them over, or at least make sure that they wouldn't stand against us, we called it a "movement" or "operation" [*haraka*], which was a more refined, softer way of saying "coup" – and at the same time, a uniquely elastic and nebulous word without a clear meaning in the political lexicon. And when we sensed that the masses were behind us, we added the adjective "auspicious" [*mubaraka*], and started talking about the "army's auspicious operation" in our communiqués and press statements.' See: Naguib, *I Was a President*, 145.

'betrayal' of those who had fought in Palestine.³⁶ The Free Officers' aim was to free Egypt from British occupation and to bring about change within the army itself. Patriots were undoubtedly seeking a strong, independent and modernized Egypt, but they had no comprehensive plan for social and political revolution. They did not even initially plan to overthrow the monarchy – in fact, for several months they were to rule as regents of the infant King Ahmed Fouad (r. 1952–3), in whose favour Farouq had been forced to abdicate. Even the decision to mount the coup seems to have been prompted by the discovery of their plans and the risk of immediate arrest.³⁷ But as time went on, the officers led by Nasser came to see the coup as a first step towards something else: a comprehensive top-down revolution that would target not only the British but also the landowners and the palace, creating a regime that could modernize both society and the economy. From 1953 onwards, they began to refer to what they had done in July 1952, and everything that followed it, as a 'revolution'.

II The July Republic and the Nasser era

After the success of their coup, the Free Officers set about installing an authoritarian regime that would remain in place, in various forms, until 2011. Of course, this regime evolved over the years, in part in design and in part in response to domestic, regional and international events. In the first two or three years, the situation was especially fluid, and the Free Officers often seemed to act based more on trial and error than in accordance with a defined plan. This is understandable considering the

---

[36] It is worth noting that the first statement made by the military plotters after 23 July – many of whom had fought in Palestine, including Mohamed Naguib, who had been injured twice in combat there – condemned the 'treacherous politicians' responsible for the catastrophe.

[37] Nasser and Abdel Hakim Amer decided to act after being informed that the palace had a list of the Free Officers' names and was planning to arrest them. See: Ahmed Hamroush, *The Story of 23 July Revolution* [Arabic], 3rd edn (Cairo: Madbouli, 1983), 192–3. Naguib states in his autobiography that he suggested bringing the coup forward for similar reasons, prompting Nasser to suggest the night of 4–5 August; the actual date was chosen because Naguib was aware of a late-night meeting of senior commanders to be held by Chief of Staff Hussein Farid at Army HQ on 22 July (*I Was a President*, 109). However, Youssef Mansour Seddik, who commanded the unit that seized Army HQ on the night of the coup, states that he only discovered that the meeting was being held when he surrounded the building. In a separate account given to Hamroush, Naguib states that the date was chosen on the night of 18–19 July, when the plotters were told that the Ministry of War had uncovered their plans. See: Ahmed Hamroush, *Witnesses to the July Revolution* [Arabic], 2nd edn (Cairo: Madbouli, 1984), 224. Mohieddin gives the same account (*And Now I Speak*, 132), adding that this was the moment that an attempt to take control of the army became a coup against the government, although he does not explain what prompted the change. Sadat's account states only that he received a message from Nasser on 21 July telling him to make his way to Cairo with all haste because the coup was to take place between 22 July and 5 August. See: Anwar Sadat, *In Search of Self: My Autobiography* [Arabic] (Cairo: al-Maktab al-Misri al-Hadith, 1978), 119.

social and political circumstances. The Free Officers came to power at a moment of exceptional political mobilization and had to contend with the Muslim Brotherhood, multiple communist factions, and vibrant student and labour movements. The coup took place in a Cold War context and while Egypt was still under partial British occupation. Finally, the Free Officers were not a homogeneous group, and the power struggles within it – some ideological, some personal – would in part determine the trajectory of the July Republic and the shape of the regime to come. The political and ideological commitments and affiliations of the broader officer corps were equally diverse.

Just as in its final years, the emergent July regime was far from hostile to the United States, whose government had come to the conclusion that independent countries under authoritarian leadership would provide the best guarantee against the spread of communism. Indeed, the Free Officers had already established a relationship with Kermit Roosevelt, the representative of US intelligence in the region,[38] and they had assured the United States that they would protect American interests. Accordingly, Nasser had asked air force intelligence officer Ali Sabri to inform the US embassy about the coup before it happened, which he did the night before it took place.[39]

In the course of the coup, King Farouq had sought assistance from the United States because his relationship with the British was, at that point, strained. But the United States had no interest in supporting Farouq, and even went a step further and pressured the British not to intervene. When Farouq ultimately contacted Anthony Eden to request his support after the coup, the British took no action. US ambassador Jefferson Thomas Caffery advised Farouq to surrender and attended the king's departure on 26 July 1952 alongside Naguib and new prime minister Aly Maher. Soon after, Caffery attended a dinner held by in the home of one of the officers,[40]

---

[38] Miles Copeland, *The Game of Nations: The Amorality of Power Politics* (New York: Simon and Schuster, 1970), 51–3. Although Roosevelt never denied having been in contact with the Free Officers, Copeland notes that there is no evidence of any direct contact between him and Nasser. The meetings are corroborated by the Free Officer Hassan Ahmed Hammouda, who says that he and Nasser met the US military attaché on multiple occasions between 1950 and 1952 to discuss the communist threat to the Middle East. According to Hammouda, the United States supported a prospective coup because it felt that the status quo risked encouraging communist revolution, and it offered the Egyptian army extensive training opportunities after the revolution (*Secrets*, 88–91). Sadat also notes, 'While the English were still trying their best to work out who was behind the revolution, the American ambassador had already invited us for dinner at the embassy, and all of us – all the members of the RCC – accepted the invitation.' See: *In Search of Self*, 121.

[39] Ali Sabri seems to have established connections within the US government while on training courses in the United States. The fact that he had to hastily call up the embassy on the night of the coup, however, is in itself clear proof that there was no pre-planning with the Americans.

[40] The dinner was held at the home of Lt Col Abdel Moneim Amin, who had been made a member of the RCC on the day of the coup.

organized to show goodwill towards the American. The United States believed that the British presence in Egypt and elsewhere was unhelpful to the struggle with communism. It preferred this struggle to be fought by independent countries under a modernizing authoritarian leadership that would begin by fighting communism at home.

The United States was interested in modernizing Egypt, seeing the traditional agrarian system and widespread resentment among farmers as reminiscent of the ground in which Maoism took root in China, and it believed that the army was up to the task.[41] In August 1952, the State Department sent a telegram to the embassy in Cairo informing the new leadership that the United States was prepared to support agrarian reform. On 3 September, the US secretary of state welcomed positive developments within Egypt, and expressed his support for the programme of agricultural reform and his respect for the efforts of Aly Maher and the officers – now constituted as the RCC – in dealing with domestic challenges.[42] It is likely that Nasser was reassured by these guarantees. RCC member Abdel Latif Boghdadi certainly was, and said as much at a meeting held at the home of fellow RCC member Hassan Ibrahim.[43] In this atmosphere, and as a message of goodwill to the United States, the RCC had also decided not to task the Egyptian legal scholar Abdel Razzaq al-Sanhuri with forming a government, specifically because he had been a signatory to the Stockholm Peace Appeal of 1950, and to adopt a political discourse hostile to communism.[44]

During an official visit in 1953, Secretary of State John Foster Dulles voiced his support for a free Egypt and said that the United States would never support British imperialism. According to State Department documents, Nasser stated that the United States and Egypt shared the same basic aims and that Egypt was also interested in establishing a MEDO, but that this would have to be preceded by British withdrawal from Suez.[45]

From 23 July onwards, US relations with Egypt were determined not by the nature of the political system, but by its aspiration for a MEDO to encircle the Soviet Union (USSR). In fact, researchers have found evidence

---

[41] Kandil, *Soldiers, Spies, and Statesmen*, 25.
[42] 'Press Conference Statement by Secretary Acheson', *Department of State Bulletin* 27, no. 690 (July/September 1952): 406, Available online: https://bit.ly/3jkcpMH (accessed 25 October 2021).
[43] Mohieddin, *And Now I Speak*, 121–2.
[44] A telegram on 8 September 1952 from the US ambassador confirms that this was the reason that Sanhuri was not appointed. See: US Department of State, 'The Ambassador in Egypt (Caffery) to the Department of State', *Foreign Relations of the United States, 1952–1954, The Near and Middle East, Volume IX, Part 2*, Document 1006, Available online: https://bit.ly/3niahs2 (accessed 20 December 2014).
[45] US Department of State, 'Memorandum of Conversation, Prepared in the Embassy in Cairo', *Foreign Relations of the United States, 1952–1954, The Near and Middle East, Volume IX, Part 1*, Document 5, Available online: https://bit.ly/32gc0ok (accessed 20 December 2014).

that the United States opposed Mohamed Naguib's calls for pluralist democracy, preferring to work with a more predictable group of organized officers.[46] This was in line with Cold War policy and theory which saw Third World societies as culturally and economically unprepared for democracy – disregarding Egypt's rich experience of liberal democracy, which might have been developed further.

1 Containing social mobilization

On the domestic front, curtailing the economic and political influence of the major landowners and distributing their land to the peasantry was one of the Free Officers' most important goals. Prime Minister Aly Maher disagreed with the proposed maximum amount of land it should be legal to own, which the Free Officers had set at 200 *feddans*.[47] He resigned on 7 September 1952 and was replaced by Naguib,[48] who formed a government on 9 September. The next day, agricultural reform was enacted alongside the new parties law.[49]

This newly formed government dissolved all political parties except the Muslim Brotherhood – seeking to avoid a confrontation with the organization, the Free Officers did not classify it as a party – and ordered them to re-register with the Interior Ministry by 7 October. Nasser also offered the Brotherhood three ministries in the new government, although the organization's leadership rejected the offer because they did not want to legitimize a government they did not control and which did not govern according to their interpretation of Shari'a. Nonetheless, Nasser went ahead and appointed a Brotherhood member, Sheikh Ahmed Hassan El-Bakoory, as the minister of endowments (*Awqaf*) without the consent of the leadership. This was the first of many crises with the Brotherhood.

Shortly after Naguib's appointment as prime minister, a constitutional drafting committee made up of fifty legal and political figures was announced. Meanwhile, the decrees came ever thicker and faster. On 1 December the 1923, the constitution was abrogated, and on 16 January 1953 all political parties banned – days after the Wafd Party had appealed the Interior Ministry's decision not to grant it a licence. On 23 January, the Liberation Rally was established as a national body intended to replace political parties. It was announced that there would be a transitional period

---

[46] Kandil, *Soldiers, Spies, and Statesmen*, 26.
[47] A *feddan* is equivalent to 4,200 square metres or 1.037 acres.
[48] The US ambassador wrote at the time that Maher did not understand the nature of the developments going on around him and was dismissed for dragging his feet on agricultural reform. US Department of State, 'The Ambassador in Egypt (Caffery) to the Department of State'.
[49] Cook, *The Struggle for Egypt*, 45–6.

of three years, during which, according to a new temporary constitution, the RCC would exercise full sovereign power in Egypt.[50]

The Liberation Rally did not, however, win wide popular support. The students of Cairo University, who had been central to the revolutionary mobilization prior to the coup, were polarized between the Brotherhood and the Wafd, leaving little space at the university for the Liberation Rally. Seeing it as a vehicle to replace or co-opt the Brotherhood, General Guide Hassan al-Hudaybi was deeply opposed to the Liberation Rally, disappointing those Brotherhood voices who had advocated working within it.[51] Hudaybi was well aware that the Free Officers aimed to gain total control of political life and marginalize the Brotherhood. Not that the Brotherhood had registered any opposition to the dissolution of political parties – they had a long-standing antipathy towards party politics dating back to Banna's famous *Epistles*, an antipathy that aligned closely with the Free Officers' position. But they were opposed to the Liberation Rally, which they saw as an alternative to themselves.

The Brotherhood leadership initially managed to convince themselves that the Free Officers were loyal allies and that the Brotherhood would be their party; after all, they had close ties with some individual officers, and they reasoned that even if the officers did not consult them on everything, they would coordinate major political action with the general guide. But the Brotherhood failed to understand the nature of the regime. The final break between them came when the RCC dissolved all political parties and refused to give the Brotherhood any special privileges.

The workers, meanwhile, leaned leftwards, particularly since the rise of communism after the Second World War. The communists were suspicious of the motives of the Free Officers and the Americans, particularly in the newly polarized atmosphere of the Cold War, but the communist movement was itself divided into many smaller groups and sects. HADITU supported the army's actions, while the Egyptian Communist Party deemed their actions as fascist and the Workers' Vanguard slammed them as a pure 'military coup'.

The communists and the left more generally (with the early exception of HADITU) initially denounced the Free Officers as agents of imperialism. Even the pro-regime left was often sharply critical, particularly when it came to the regime's relationship with the United States (at a time when the USSR was hostile to Egypt's new regime). The left was also suspicious of the new regime's decision to raise the limit on foreign ownership of Egyptian

---

[50] Mohieddin, *And Now I Speak*, 219–25.
[51] Ishaq Mousa al-Husseini, *The Muslim Brotherhood: The Largest Modern Islamic Movement* [Arabic], 2nd edn (Beirut: [Dar Beirut], 1955), 302.

companies from 49 to 51 per cent on the grounds that this would encourage foreign investment, and of its apparent antipathy to democracy.[52] This set the stage for a state crackdown. In August 1952, hundreds of striking workers were arrested in Kafr al-Dawwar, and two of them were hanged the following month. By the end of 1953, a sweeping campaign of arrests had put many leftists behind bars, including some former Free Officers and a number of prominent intellectuals. Most HADITU leaders were held at the military prison, where they were tortured. Nasser himself was very suspicious of members of parties, including those who had supported or even led the coup. He expected absolute loyalty to the Free Officer leadership – or more accurately, absolute loyalty to himself.[53]

After concluding an arms deal with the Czech Republic in 1955 and nationalizing the Suez Canal in 1956, however, Nasser began to enjoy a certain amount of support within leftist circles. His nationalization policy spurred a debate among imprisoned communists about how to characterize these steps: Were they socialist, or state capitalist? This question was ultimately to prove far more important than it seemed at the time, not only for Egypt but for the socialist countries of Eastern Europe, too. Ultimately, the beleaguered communist organizations announced their support for Nasser's nationalizations, and their members were released en masse. When Egyptian-Syrian unification was announced on 22 February 1958, however, a new wave of debate and persecution began, particularly after Syrian communists refused to dissolve their parties as ordered and presented a proposal on 14 December 1958 to turn the UAR into a federation.[54]

The contention mounted when a military coup led by Abdul Karim Kassem succeeded in overthrowing the Iraqi monarchy on 14 July 1958; the Iraqi communists backed Kassem and opposed Iraq joining the UAR. Nasser subsequently launched a new campaign against communists in Egypt and Syria, beginning with a speech on 23 December 1959 (which notably avoided any direct criticism of the USSR). The initial pretext was the refusal of *al-Masa'* newspaper headed by former RCC member Khaled

---

[52] Mohieddin, *And Now I Speak*, 290.
[53] Ibid., 97–100.
[54] The document proposed a loose federation in which the responsibilities of the central government would be limited to national defence and foreign policy. The ostensible aim of this programme was to 'reinforce the idea of Arab unity [. . .] and strengthen the ties of brotherhood and cooperation with the Republic of Iraq, for the betterment of all Arabs'. In fact, however, it belied Syrian communists' opposition to unity with Egypt and their preference for the sort of alliance that had prevailed between the Iraqi Communist Party and the regime after the Revolution of 1958 in Iraq. See: Hanna Batatu, *The Old Social Classes and the Revolutionary Movements of Iraq* (Princeton: Princeton University Press, 1978), 861–2.

Mohieddin – founded by the state in 1956 as a platform for socialist views – to condemn Kassem and Iraqi communists.[55]

In April–May 1964, as Egypt grew closer to the USSR and construction began on the Aswan Dam, Nasser ordered the release of many communist prisoners shortly before an official visit by Nikita Khrushchev. Many communists found employment in various branches of the Egyptian media, where they would subsequently help to frame the regime's narrative. HADITU dissolved itself in March 1965, followed shortly by the Egyptian Communist Party. When new communist formations began taking shape in October 1966, they were slapped down.[56] The official Egyptian communist line, as in other Arab countries, was now the Soviet theory of non-capitalist development: Third-World authoritarianism was justifiable because it spurred development according to a non-capitalist model and because it was 'anti-imperialist'.

Between repression and persecution on the one hand and self-dissolution and identification with regime discourse on the other, the left was never able to regain its lost vigour. Nationalist media also managed to successfully cast communists as agents of a foreign power hostile to religion, the family and the motherland.

The Free Officers were unwilling to accept any sort of loyalty to a political party, seeing themselves as the embodiment of national unity, which is incompatible with partisanship. Nasser had no interest in sharing political power even with Naguib, never mind the Brotherhood or the communists. The disputes among the officers themselves between 1952 and 1954 boiled down to the question of whether to pursue anti-democratic measures and whether to stay in power or return to the barracks. Officers with partisan loyalties were purged fairly early on, leaving the remainder to fight a battle for power that had become personal, even if it took the form of disagreements over domestic policy and global alliances.

2 Consolidating power within the Free Officers

In the immediate wake of the coup, the Free Officers were more afraid of the army than any other institution, a lesson learned from their own experience as well as that of recent coups in Iraq and Syria. Using the army to govern without it devolving into factionalism was thus a major challenge. Indeed, shortly after Naguib became prime minister, Nasser ordered that a list of army officers be drawn up, ranking them by political reliability, and

---

[55] Ramzi Mikhail Jayyed, *The Crisis of Democracy and the Dilemma of the 'Nationalist' Press, 1952–1984* [Arabic] (Cairo: Madbouli, 1987), 54–5.
[56] Mohieddin, *And Now I Speak*, 297–8.

those suspected of hostile ideological sympathies or political ambitions were either cashiered or transferred to civilian positions.[57] Nasser was particularly attuned to the threat of internal divisions because he was aware of partisan 'inclinations' within the officer corps.[58] In addition to his long-standing relationship with the Brotherhood, Nasser remained very close to Khaled Mohieddin, who had represented the left current in the original Command Cell. HADITU, meanwhile, had been printing Free Officer leaflets since early 1950, anonymously delivering them to the homes of officers, and had also drawn up the Free Officers' programme in September 1951.[59]

The Free Officers needed time to win the army's loyalty: they were mid-ranking officers who had not been among its senior command before the coup. A conflict erupted when Naguib, the highest ranking of the officers, took his rank and presidential functions too seriously and refused Nasser's request to appoint Abdel Hakim Amer as commander-in-chief.

During the struggle for power, Naguib never took a consistent position. He supported the RCC taking over the government so long as he could remain president, but he was also quick to advocate real representative mechanisms as an aim of the revolution. Although this was very similar to the stated position of Nasser's faction, the latter justified the officers' continued hold on power by pointing to the common deceit and untrustworthiness of politicians: 'so we have decided that this country should not be ruled by a class of political mercenaries.'[60]

In June 1953, Egypt officially became a republic. Naguib became the president (remaining prime minister as well), and Nasser became his deputy and interior minister (a position which subsequently went to Zakaria Mohieddin, the founding father of the new state intelligence apparatus). In the same month, the Republican Guard was founded with the explicit mission of protecting the new regime from dangers within the army. In September, a new revolutionary court was established. Headed by military judges, including Anwar Sadat, the ostensible purpose of the People's Court was to stamp out corruption, but in fact it spearheaded the purge of

---

[57] Abdallah Imam, *Memoirs of Salah Nasr* [Arabic], vol. 1 (Cairo: Dar al-Khayal, 1999), 156, 180.
[58] For example, Khaled Mohieddin says that he was initially a supporter of Young Egypt, then established Brotherhood connections in 1944, then in 1947 joined Iskra, a communist organization. See: Hamroush, *Witnesses*, 144–5. In the same book, Youssef Mansour Seddik informs the interviewer that he was in contact with the communists during the second half of the 1940s and later became a member of HADITU (478). Abdel Latif Boghdadi, meanwhile, says that he was a member of the Brotherhood, alongside Abdel Rahman Anan and Abdul Munim Abdul Rauf (218).
[59] Abdul Qader Yassin, 'Nasser and the Egyptian Communist Movement', [Arabic], in *Gamal Abdel Nasser and His Age* [Arabic], intro. Adel Hassan Ghunaym (Cairo: Dar al-Ma'arif, 2013), 288–9; Mohieddin, *And Now I Speak*, 69–70.
[60] Abderrahman al-Rafi'i, *23 July 1952 Revolution: Our National History in Seven Years 1952–1959* [Arabic], 2nd edn (Cairo: Dar al-Ma'arif, 1989), 53–4.

ancien régime loyalists and opposition figures. Early defendants included Ibrahim Abdel Hadi, who had led the police crackdown after Nuqrashi's assassination (he was sentenced to death, subsequently commuted to life imprisonment with hard labour) and Fouad Serageddin, the leader of the Wafd Party (sentenced to fifteen years, subsequently released under house arrest). In October, the National Guard was founded, providing training to citizens in case a general mobilization was required 'to protect the revolution'.

On 23 February 1954, Naguib resigned, triggering major protests, including among members of the artillery corps who supported Naguib. Nasser was forced to accept his return as president two days later due to Naguib's popular support among Egyptians. But at the same time, he planned reprisals against the mutinous artillery officers, arresting them on 29 March 1954, two days after releasing imprisoned Brotherhood members in an attempt to win the group's favour.[61]

In addition to their other disagreements, there was no consensus among the Free Officers on the question of democracy. Some were veritable Jacobins, radicals intent on following the revolution through to its end who insisted that the coup leaders should remain in charge as revolutionaries rather than politicians (i.e. that there was no need for elections).[62] Their dispute with Nasser was not about democracy, but whether the regime would be led by a group or one man – an oligarchy or autocracy? They imagined that the RCC would rule as a democratically run conciliar body, rather than being sidelined in favour of autocratic rule by Nasser.[63] The leftist Khaled Mohieddin (backed by his armoured units) was a more persistent advocate for democracy, and as a result was removed from the RCC early on. But given the choice between autocracy (Nasser) and democracy, most of the Free Officers came down in favour of the former, whether because they believed this better served the goals of the revolution or because of their preference for strongmen.[64] Nasser's ability to politically outmanoeuvre both enemies and friends was unmatched by any of his peers among the Free Officers. He understood power clearly from the very beginning, both within and outside the RCC.

Meanwhile, the political forces surrounding the coup plotters – including the Brotherhood – initially encouraged the RCC to remain

---

[61] Hammouda, *Secrets*, 100–2.
[62] See, for example, Gamal Salem's suggestions regarding potential enemies within and beyond the army (Boghdadi, *Memoirs*, 59–60, 182) and his suggestion that Naguib be assassinated (Mohieddin, *And Now I Speak*, 254). This spirit is also pervasive in the first volume of Boghdadi's memoirs.
[63] See Mohieddin's discussion of Boghdadi's ideas (*And Now I Speak*, 335).
[64] Anwar Sadat, for example, was a particularly early proponent of transferring all power to Nasser, on the grounds that strongman rule was both successful and well-suited to 'Oriental countries'. See: Boghdadi, *Memoirs*, 240, 245.

in power. A revolutionary constitutional jurisprudence was developed, hostile to democracy and capable of justifying authoritarian measures from a revolutionary perspective. The Brotherhood hoped that the army would wipe out the partisan competition, allowing them to co-opt the Free Officers.[65] Even Naguib was opposed to any movement in the direction of democracy when he felt that his position at the head of the revolution was secure.[66]

The desire to hold on to power ultimately meant restrictions on freedom and the extensive surveillance of society. Nasser presented the RCC with a choice between the anarchy of absolute freedom and the unswerving determination of autocracy, between democracy and development.[67] He was far from alone in doing so.[68] The logic was clear: the Free Officers, lacking a popular base, could not compete in an election,[69] but by the time they acquired a popular base, they had consolidated their power to the point that they no longer needed to give the issue any thought. Having come of age intellectually during the decadent final years of the liberal period under the hegemony of the landowning aristocracy, the king and the British, many of them were hostile to democracy and party politics, which had proved unable to solve the country's social problems. Whenever democracy was presented as a possible solution, it was immediately cast aside, as in the famous 1954 decision to abolish all political parties in accordance with 'the popular will, which has expressed itself clearly'.[70] Once the two institutional pillars of the new regime were in place – developmental/productive and repressive/disciplinary – all talk of democracy as a political system stopped.

There were various reasons for this: an unwillingness to trust any other political force with the revolution and a belief that the people were either ill equipped for democracy and freedom, ingrates, gullible or greedy.[71] The RCC mobilized the masses against democracy,[72] paying unions to strike in at

---

[65] Mohieddin, *And Now I Speak*, 208.
[66] Ibid., 213.
[67] Boghdadi, *Memoirs*, 148, 171; Mohieddin, *And Now I Speak*, 206.
[68] Huntington argues that the priority in developing states should be state stability and institution building and that the enemy is political mobilization and chaos. See: Samuel P. Huntington, *Political Order in Changing Societies* (New Haven: Yale University Press, 1968).
[69] Boghdadi, *Memoirs*, 171–2.
[70] Mitchell, *The Society of the Muslim Brothers*, 133.
[71] See Nasser's speech to the mutinying tank officers: 'The transitional period is essential and cannot be dispensed with. Our people cannot [learn to] identify their real interests this quickly – three years may not be enough. Our people cannot manage the responsibility of liberty. Feudalists have been known to buy electors' votes.' And: 'A people who cannot manage the responsibility of liberty cannot enjoy liberty.' See: Mohieddin, *And Now I Speak*, 272.
[72] Boghdadi, *Memoirs*, 157–8, 167, 169. The State Council once objected strongly to the RCC's alleged incitement of protesters, to which the government diplomatically responded that it was 'awaiting the results of the investigation'.

least one case[73] and providing transport to take workers to anti-democracy demonstrations. This negative attitude to the masses easily mutated into a romantic idealization of them in populist discourse, combined with suspicion towards elites, especially intellectuals and university students.[74] Putative foreign conspiracies against the revolution were cited to discredit democracy, pluralism and freedom of expression. To promote a popular acceptance of authoritarianism, Mohieddin writes that Nasser engineered six bombings at civilian installations in Cairo on 19 March 1954; though they caused little material damage, they did scare the populace. Fathi Radwan, meanwhile, says that after Naguib's dismissal Nasser went to the radio building with Salah Salem and requested all the tapes containing recordings of speeches by the leaders of the revolution and ministers from 26 July 1952 to October 1954, in addition to speeches by King Farouq and other pre-1952 political leaders, in particular those of Wafd leader Nahhas. He then erased them.[75] The Free Officers were not the first revolutionaries, of course, to try to erase the past.

Although Nasser maintained in his *Philosophy of the Revolution* that the officers' mission had a definite time limit, he also consistently characterized them as a vanguard leading the people, emphasizing that the only route was 'political and economic freedom', which to him meant not a liberal economy but freedom from poverty through the provision of basic needs, protected temporarily by the officers. Egyptian society, he said, was culturally immature and 'still taking shape'.[76] After the old elites regrouped and aligned themselves with the regime, perpetuating the Free Officers' hold on power, he found many more reasons for them to continue their 'temporary' mission. In fact, as is typical of populist rhetoric, an indisputably patronizing and paternalistic tone can be observed in all the Free Officers' statements on society, coupled with statements that extol the people and their purity. When the RCC got rid of Naguib in March 1954, the United States supported the move because it preferred an authoritarian government to a democratic one.

---

[73] According to Boghdadi, one of the various complaints he made to Nasser at an RCC meeting held on 11 April 1954 was that Sawi Mohammad al-Sawi, head of the Cairo transport union, had been paid 4,000 Egyptian pounds to encourage his members to go on strike after the pro-democracy rulings of 25 March 1954 were issued. Nasser responded that he was simply making sure he got there before Mohieddin did (*Memoirs*, 181). Mohieddin himself reports that when he met with Nasser years later, the president told him with 'unusual honesty' that he had paid 4,000 Egyptian pounds to prevent the rulings going any further (*And Now I Speak*, 298).

[74] Boghdadi, *Memoirs*, 164; Mohieddin, *And Now I Speak*, 314.

[75] Adel Hassan Ghunaym, 'The Other Face of Gamal Abdel Nasser' [Arabic], in *Gamal Abdel Nasser and His Age* [Arabic], intro. Adel Hassan Ghunaym (Cairo: Dar al-Ma'arif, 2013), 267–79. See also: Boghdadi, *Memoirs*, 144; Mohieddin, *And Now I Speak*, 305.

[76] Gamal Abdel Nasser, *The Philosophy of the Revolution and the Pact* [Arabic] (Beirut: Dar al-Qalam, 1970), 55, 69–70, 75–6.

Nasser's personal popular appeal was bolstered still further after an attempt on his life on 26 October 1954 in Manshiyya Square in Alexandria, allegedly orchestrated by the Brotherhood. This ushered in a new open confrontation with the organization, and the People's Court returned to work, this time with Anwar Sadat, Salah Salem and Hussein el-Shafie sitting in judgement. Some 2,000 activists and members of the Brotherhood were arrested. Naguib, accused of conspiring with them, was placed under house arrest, where he remained until his death in 1984.

Despite initial promises to dissolve the political police, the Free Officers actually strengthened and expanded it. Zakaria Mohieddin set up the Internal Security Directorate and reconstituted the Secret Section (the monarchy-era political police) as the GIS, which in 1971 was renamed the SSIS.[77] Mamdouh Salem, a career secret policeman who became director of the Alexandria Investigations Bureau after the revolution and ultimately interior minister under Sadat, is exemplary of the continuity between the old and new regime in this respect. US reports indicate that immediately after the 1952 coup, Washington provided $1 million for surveillance and anti-riot equipment for the police. US mediators also put the Egyptian political police in touch with former German officers who were able to help with planning and training.[78]

Salah Nasr tells us that after a month spent studying intelligence services around the world, he came up with a blueprint for an agency suitable for Egypt, closely modelled on the US CIA:[79]

> The specific task of the General Intelligence Service was to provide political and economic intelligence. [. . .] Military Intelligence was split off and placed under the commander-in-chief of the armed forces, while the General Investigations Service was to report to the minister of the interior and have a domestic remit, taking responsibility for armed groups, political party activity, organized labour, the press, student activism, etc. – that is [. . .] domestic political security.[80]

One of the new GIS's early achievements was to expose Mossad attacks on US businesses in 1954, which were intended to undermine relations with Washington (the Lavon affair, after then Israeli defence minister Pinhas Lavon).

---

[77] Prior to 1952, Egypt's Military Intelligence Service oversaw both military and general intelligence; the political police was subordinate to the Ministry of Interior. It was only after the coup that the GIS was separated from Military Intelligence. Imam, *Memoirs*, 53.
[78] Owen L. Sirrs, *A History of the Egyptian Intelligence Service: A History of the Mukhabarat, 1910–2009* (Milton Park [England] and New York: Routledge, 2010), 33.
[79] Imam, *Memoirs*, 53–8.
[80] Ibid., 65.

On 23 June 1956, a referendum was held on the new constitution and Nasser's presidency. Both were approved with more than 98 per cent of votes. This came on the heels of the 'press purge' decree, as well as another decree forbidding some thirty-nine former ministers from holding public office or exercising political rights.[81] With the nationalization of the Suez Canal and the defeat of the joint British-French-Israeli invasion in 1956, the Nasserist period had truly begun, bringing the curtain down for good on the liberal period and the chance of any kind of democratic transformation.

Many of those who sing the praises of the liberal era forget that the cultural revival of that period benefited only a very small elite of landowners and urban bourgeois, while the majority of the Egyptian people continued to toil the land in ignorance, poverty and illness. Because of its particular structure, the liberal regime was unable to solve many pressing social problems – above all, the issue of land reform (a capitalist, modernizing process undertaken by many Western countries, not a socialist policy in the narrow sense of socialism). The Free Officers, however, were able to solve this problem in one go with a single top-down decree.

No historical period is monolithic, and the Free Officers indisputably achieved great things with the tools available to them: mass education, an invigorated public sector, the Nile Dam, land reform. These were major historical accomplishments by any measure, even if they came at the expense of the ascendant urban culture, political pluralism and the elitist education of the liberal period. That said, many of those who fondly remember the 1960s as a time when bareheaded women smoked cigarettes at Umm Kulthum concerts likewise forget this era's darker side. Yes, the 1960s saw mass education, the nationalization of the country's resources, attempts at industrialization and leadership of an Arab political project, but they also saw the creation of a security regime that ruled by fear, a regime that valued political loyalty above ability and an obscurantist populism that produced the defeat of 1967. The Nasserist regime had two faces: nationalizations, wealth redistribution and new economic infrastructure were accompanied by a police state, populist rhetoric, contempt for alternative opinions and exaggeration of the country's achievements and capabilities – and, later, declining institutional performance and educational achievement.

At first, the Free Officers were preoccupied with building a republic. To them, this was synonymous with national unity and an end to partisan politics, and as such all political parties were dissolved under Law 179/1953.[82] The interwar liberal elite were replaced by those who were politically reliable, and, often, those who were reliable were not

---

[81] Boghdadi, *Memoirs*, 182–3, 187.
[82] The decree dissolving the Muslim Brotherhood was issued on 14 January 1954, a year later.

particularly knowledgeable or experienced. Loyalty and populism became the prevailing values of public administration. But this was concealed by policies that were indeed patriotic and popular – policies that destroyed the old liberal elite.

At first, Nasser sought to translate the Free Officers' warm relations with the United States into military and economic support, requesting some $100 million in aid. This, however, was opposed by the UK, which believed that aid should be a bargaining chip in the ongoing negotiations over the future of the British presence in the Suez Canal zone. Dwight Eisenhower seems to have been influenced by this attitude,[83] leading Egypt to reconsider its position on 'positive neutrality'.[84] At the same time, Egypt concluded defence treaties with Syria, Saudi Arabia and Yemen against the Baghdad Pact, as well as signing a trade agreement with the USSR in April 1955 followed by an arms deal with Czechoslovakia the following month. Panicking, the United Kingdom informed the United States that it had decided to overthrow the governments of Syria, Saudi Arabia and Egypt because they threatened British interests in the region.[85]

After a long struggle and much bargaining, British forces finally withdrew from the Canal Zone. The first signs of an impending clash with the West came when Cairo refused to join the Baghdad Pact (including Turkey, Iran, Pakistan and Iraq), which Nasser saw as an attempt to isolate Egypt. The United States had refused to arm Egypt or stand by it in the face of Israeli reprisals against guerrilla activities in the Gaza Strip between 1955 and 1956, in particular Operation Black Arrow (1955), which left thirty-eight Egyptian soldiers dead. It was after Operation Black Arrow that Egypt signed the Czech arms deal.

According to Owen Sirrs, there is a general impression that Nasser's turn to the Non-Aligned Movement can be traced to a 1955 Israeli raid on Gaza, the establishment of the Baghdad Pact and his refusal to join it, and the unwillingness of the United States (and the West generally) to sell weapons to Egypt. But he adds another reason: Nasser's belief, shared by some of his supporters, that US intelligence wanted to get rid of him.[86] This may well

---

[83] Cook, *The Struggle for Egypt*, 65. For more on Nasser's changing relationship with the United States, see: Jon B. Alterman, 'American Aid to Egypt in the 1950s: From Hope to Hostility', *Middle East Journal* 52, no. 1 (Winter 1998): 51–69.

[84] Meaning neutrality between the two Cold War camps.

[85] Ali Muhafaza, *Britain and Arab Unity 1945–2005* [Arabic] (Beirut: Centre for Arab Unity Studies, 2011), 168–9; Abdelazim Ramadan, *The Story of Abdel Nasser and the Communists* [Arabic] (Cairo: Egyptian Book Authority, 1998); Gamal Shaqra, 'The Modern State in Egypt (3) (1952–1970)' [Arabic], in *The Reference for Egypt's Modern and Contemporary History* [Arabic], ed. Yunan Labib Rizq (Cairo: Higher Council for Culture, 2009), 577–658; John W. Copp, 'Egypt and the Soviet Union: 1953–1970' (PhD diss., Portland State University, Portland, 1986).

[86] Sirrs, *A History of the Egyptian Intelligence Service*, 51.

be true, but it cannot be separated from the aforementioned analysis: any plan to oust Nasser was certainly derived from the political positions that he had taken, and not the other way around.

In response to the Baghdad Pact, Cairo signed a separate defence treaty with Saudi Arabia, which had its own reasons to be suspicious of the pact alliance (in particular its rivalry with the Hashemites). In 1956, the IBRD granted preliminary approval to an Egyptian request for $200 million to build the Nile Dam, for fear that the USSR would provide the funding instead if it refused. The IBRD attempted to impose very strict political and economic conditions on Egypt, which refused, accepting only some limited conditions to ensure that the debt would be paid. In February 1956, the bank announced that it would loan Egypt 70 million Egyptian pounds,[87] but the United States and the United Kingdom subsequently withdrew their support for funding after Egypt recognized the communist government in China in order to guarantee delivery of the Czechoslovakian arms. Nasser then announced the nationalization of the Suez Canal along with fifty-five British and French companies.

After the United States withdrew its offer to fund the Nile Dam, Nasser granted himself wide-ranging presidential powers under a new constitution approved in 1956 by a popular referendum. On 26 July 1956, he went to Manshiyya Square, where he had almost been assassinated two years previously, and announced to a crowd that the Suez Canal would be nationalized. This was a major step for the Egyptian popular psyche: maintaining the canal was one of the main justifications for the British presence in Egypt, meaning that foreign domination was linked closely to the Suez Canal in the popular consciousness. Nationalizing it thus carried huge emotional weight for Egyptians.

Nationalization was followed by the Tripartite Aggression. Paris justified its participation by citing French citizens' ownership of shares in the Canal Company and claiming that Egypt was involved in hostile activities in Algeria and other Maghreb countries. Amin Howeidi argues that the real reason was Egypt's decision to break the West's monopoly on arms supplies by purchasing Czech and Soviet weapons. The immediate cause cited by all was the nationalization of the Suez Canal, but it was the arms deal, not the nationalization, that threatened the Cold War balance of power in the region.[88] It was French prime minister Guy Mollet who initiated preparations for the attack with Israel – the same French administration that helped Israel to develop nuclear weapons.

---

[87] Boghdadi, *Memoirs*, 314.
[88] Amin Howeidi, *Lost Opportunities: The Resolute Decisions in the Attrition War and October* [Arabic] (Beirut: Matbu'at Publishing and Distribution, 1992).

The Tripartite Aggression, launched on 29 October 1956, sought to oust Nasser. It lasted for a week and included strikes on airports and various areas in Cairo. French and British paratroopers landed in Port Said on 5 November. The secret policeman Zakaria Mohieddin led the resistance in the Canal Zone. The aerial assault was followed by Soviet warnings and US pressure on Britain forcing it to withdraw. Immediately after the crisis, international emergency forces were deployed to keep the Tiran Straits (the gateway to the Red Sea) open and ensure freedom of navigation towards Israel.

As Nasser's approach became clearer, various powers came together to oppose it. These different powers had different motivations. France feared that Egypt would play the same role in Algeria as China had in Vietnam, galvanizing opposition to the French presence. Britain wanted to prevent nationalization of the Suez Canal and was also concerned about Nasser's activities in Jordan, Yemen, the Gulf and other regions of British influence. Israel disliked Nasser's regime because of its hostility to Israel and because it allowed Palestinian guerrilla activities in Gaza.

Although the Nasser regime was defeated militarily, it won a major political victory – perhaps the first time in Arab political history that the expression 'a military defeat but a political triumph' was used (and latter so often misused). The USSR and the United States opposed the intervention of the fading colonial powers. The Arab peoples, too, supported Egypt, which now became a true Arab and Third World power. Israeli forces withdrew from Sinai, and Israel itself was shown to be a regional partner of old imperialist powers.

These developments set the country on a political path that defined the Nasser era. Egypt turned its face to the Arab world as a strategic space, particularly Arab public opinion (firmly behind Egypt during the Suez crisis), and the country sought alternative international alliances that would support its developmental policies, nationalizations and purchase of arms. The Egyptian military regime thus sought to establish alliances between the army and local financial institutions – Banque Misr, for example – to encourage them to invest in development and industry. This was a Bonapartist regime, in which the bourgeoisie were expected to be content with investment in industry, leaving political power in military hands, although the state quickly abandoned this approach in favour of exclusively state-driven industrial development.

Egypt's relationship with the USSR continued to develop steadily. One of the curious paradoxes demonstrating that the alliance was a purely foreign policy decision for both sides is that the persecution of communists within Egypt actually intensified during this period: at the height of the security forces' crackdown on communists in 1958, the director of Nasser's office visited Moscow to facilitate the training of those same security forces by the KGB. According to Sirrs, in March 1957, after CIA-Egyptian relations had broken off, Eisenhower again considered overthrowing Nasser and discussed the matter with the director of the CIA.[89] At that point, however, the Nasser regime uncovered British and Saudi conspiracies to oust it, and Nasser became very suspicious of Egypt's neighbours and ultimately of Egyptian society too.

3 Arab socialism and high Nasserism

In 1962 the ASU was established. The purpose of the ASU was to act as a popular vehicle for the regime, giving it a civilian façade that would reduce its dependency on the army (and thus on Abdel Hakim Amer). It was presented not as a ruling party but as 'an alliance of the toiling forces of the people'. The Arab socialism it embodied was ideologically hostile to communism, Marxism and the concept of class struggle. Despite borrowing elements from the Islamic past, it was also hostile to Islamism, although it accommodated popular religiosity and co-opted religious institutions and Sufi orders so long as they were willing to support its modernizing policies (e.g. women working outside the home and gender mixing). The positive content of Arab socialism largely consisted of generic nationalist slogans and the person of Nasser himself, which in the absence of a systematic ideology served as the basis for popular mobilization. It also espoused an idea similar to the theory of non-capitalist development articulated by Soviet theorists to explain their political and economic influence in the so-called popular democracies (i.e. populist authoritarian regimes): the Nasser regime would bypass capitalism and go straight to socialism via state-driven, non-capitalist modernization made possible by Soviet technical and economic assistance. After the new land reform launched in July 1961, the regime pursued a series of full and partial nationalizations (including in Syria, the 'northern region' of the UAR) targeting manufacturing and foreign trade. The state seized most of the capital of those firms that were not nationalized, and in 1961 socialist laws were passed, laying the groundwork for a command economy. The press had already been nationalized by this point.

Land reform benefited many peasants and produced an agrarian middle class able to put their children through formal education, allowing them to enter public life and influence it. It was these young people who formed

---

[89] Sirrs, *A History of the Egyptian Intelligence Service*, 59.

the backbone of both the ASU and the July Republic's new bureaucracy. Nasserist policies also laid the groundwork for new middle-class constituencies in the barracks and the civil service.

Land reform was not easy. In many cases, old landowning families collaborated with the security forces and sometimes the local ASU branch in order to prevent redistribution of their lands and send misleading reports back to Cairo. This led to clashes with peasants.[90]

Industrialization, infrastructure building, land reform and public sector expansion all led at first to rapid economic growth, but public sector development quickly ran up against the law of diminishing returns in the form of declining marginal productivity, requiring a shift from quantitative to intensive qualitative investment. State revenues could not keep up with an expanding bureaucracy and its huge modernizing projects. In the first decade of the July Republic, workers and civil servants saw their income double and educational opportunities for the poor increased dramatically. But by 1966, the first signs of an impending crisis had appeared, caused by a fundamental disconnect between public sector spending and the productivity and financial capacity of the economy.

This problem was exacerbated by the interminable military intervention in Yemen launched in 1962. Cairo had not expected a long war in Yemen, but ended up bogged down in the country for most of the decade: at one point, there were as many as 70,000 Egyptian soldiers in the country, 26,000 of whom were killed in five years. The last Egyptian soldier only left in December 1967. As well as the enormous burden it placed on the budget, the Yemen War dealt a serious blow to the morale of the Egyptian army and its battle readiness.

The regime's pan-Arab ambitions were disproportionate to Egypt's military and economic resources – and even those of its intelligence forces. This was demonstrated clearly by the withdrawal of Syria from the UAR and military failure in Yemen, although Nasser blamed these disappointments on Abdel Hakim Amer, which, according to former defence minister Mohammed Fawzi, was the beginning of the covert rivalry between the two.[91]

The years from 1961 to 1964 saw major nationalizations. In exchange for new educational and material benefits for labourers, union activity disappeared completely, political freedoms were strictly delimited and university life, academic research and student activism were placed under extensive surveillance. A Ministry of National Guidance, responsible for

---

[90] One particularly famous case being the Kamshish uprising, discussed later in the chapter on the history of protest.
[91] Mohamed Fawzi, *The Three-Year War 1967–1970: Memoirs of Former Minister of Defence General Mohamed Fawzi* [Arabic], 5th edn (Cairo: Arab Future, 1990), 23.

censorship and propaganda, had already been established in 1952, headed by Salah Salem.

The emergency law (Law 162/1958) granted the government sweeping powers to close newspapers and restrict political and union activity; State Security courts, whose rulings were not subject to appeal, were set up to enforce its provisions. Applied more or less continuously from 1967 to the January 2011 revolution, the emergency law sanctioned various measures restricting freedoms, banning strikes and major gatherings, and imposing censorship on the press. At around the same time, the regime entered a near-existential struggle with the Muslim Brotherhood, which played a significant role in its transformation into a security regime. This struggle was to produce major shifts in the thinking and organization of the Brotherhood, as well as various splinter groups radicalized by repression and isolation from the people, who showed little sympathy for them; in the long term, these groups were to have a significant effect on the trajectory of political Islam.

This period was also a major turning point for politicized religion, which turned increasingly towards extreme thought and a position deeming society as a whole to represent a 'new Jahiliyya' or pre-Islamic paganism – a position which naturally implied social isolation and alienation in preparation for jihad and a mission to spread Islam from scratch. This change in direction is inseparable from the Brotherhood experience of imprisonment, torture and lack of political options, which left Islamists disconnected from the status quo and often willing to sweep it away in its entirety. With the flight of many of those influenced by Sayyid Qutb to Saudi Arabia – a US ally hostile to the rising tide of pan-Arabism – Brotherhood thought came into extended contact with Wahhabi Salafism. This meeting of ideologies was to have a significant role in producing the jihadi Salafism that we know today.

From 1955 to 1966, Brotherhood members were imprisoned in droves for conspiring to overthrow the government, with several prominent members – including the ideologue Sayyid Qutb – sent to the gallows. It is still unclear whether a Saudi-backed coup was actually in the works as alleged. Some US intelligence reports suggest that there was a plot in place,[92] while some Egyptians have claimed that the United States itself was involved in the plot.[93]

The period leading up to the 1967 war was marked by a particularly violent conflict between the so-called 'progressive' and 'reactionary' forces in the Arab world, often referred to as the Arab Cold War. Cairo broke

---

[92] Sirrs, for example, is certain that a coup was to take place (*A History of the Egyptian Intelligence Service*, 89).
[93] Ibid., 89–90.

off diplomatic relations with London in protest over Rhodesia; the United States stopped providing Egypt with wheat; and Nasser announced that $150 million had been put aside to purchase essential food for the country. In 1967, Egypt consumed some 4 million tons of wheat and produced only 2.5 million tons, importing the rest. In June 1966, the United States suspended the Food for Peace programme.[94]

After reports spread of an Israeli force massing on the Syrian border on 8 May 1967 – reports confirmed (mistakenly, it turned out) by the USSR – Egyptian forces were deployed throughout Sinai, with a speed that left their logistics in complete disarray. Various sources, including the then chief of staff Mohammed Fawzi, state that there was no evidence of any Israeli mobilization on the Syrian border[95] or even of Syria itself mobilizing; this is confirmed by the then head of Military Intelligence, Mohamed Sadek,[96] and likewise Amin Howeidi.[97] When Fawzi was ordered to ask peacekeeping forces to withdraw from their positions, they understood that they were being asked to leave Sinai entirely, and the Egyptian forces entered Sharm El-Sheikh. The situation became even tenser when Egypt closed the Straits of Tiran to Israeli shipping. This escalation seems to have been the result of brinksmanship and miscalculation on the part of the Egyptian authorities.

The memoirs of various writers who held positions of responsibility at the time claim that the events of 1967 were the result of an international conspiracy. Fawzi's letter to UN secretary general U Thant requested only a partial withdrawal from specific positions, notably excluding particular hotspots like the Gaza Strip and the Sharm El-Sheikh area,[98] and the military and political leadership were well aware of the dangers involved in closing the Straits of Tiran. Salah Nasr claims that Thant interpreted Fawzi's letter as a request for total withdrawal from Gaza and Sinai, offering the Egyptian leadership a choice between rescinding its request and accepting the full withdrawal of all peacekeeping forces. Nasser chose the latter.[99]

Fawzi states that prior to 1967, Nasser and Amer were actively looking for an international or regional opportunity to secure the withdrawal of peacekeeping forces, which they considered a holdover from the Tripartite Aggression. The opportunity came when the Syrian minister of defence informed Amer that some eleven to thirteen Israeli battalions were massing on the Syrian border[100] (this contradicts Sadek and Howeidi's reports).

---

[94] Imam, *Memoirs*, 202–3.
[95] Fawzi, *The Three-Year War*, 71.
[96] Sirrs, *A History of the Egyptian Intelligence Service*, 98.
[97] Howeidi, *Lost Opportunities*, 70.
[98] Fawzi, *The Three-Year War*, 76–9.
[99] Imam, *Memoirs*, 202–3.
[100] Fawzi, *The Three-Year War*, 69.

Cairo had declared that it would consider any attack on Syria equivalent to an attack on Egypt itself, citing invasion threats made by senior Israelis, including Yitzhak Sharon.

In any case, while dispensing with the peacekeepers had been a national objective since 1957, Nasser was not so set on it that he wanted to go to war – unlike Amer, who according to Fawzi was quite happy with the idea of a short conflict.[101] The different narratives all suggest that Egypt simply overplayed its hand, engaging in a war of words with Saudi Arabia that ultimately drove it into an actual war with Israel. The internecine disputes between Arab powers and the media brinkmanship that accompanied them are an embarrassing chapter in the history of Arab politics, demonstrating the immaturity of the political elites in charge at the time. The Israeli army was looking for a pretext for war, and it would be unreasonable to expect the enemy to play by rules set by the Egyptian leadership. (We will return to this point later in our discussion of the army.)

On 23 May, with the Gulf of Aqaba closed to Israeli shipping, Lyndon Johnson called for both sides to respect the ceasefire, promising Nasser that the United States would support Egypt in the event of hostile action against it and suggesting that the shipping issue be referred to the ICJ. In reality, however, the United States was backing Israel: on 27 May, the USSR informed the US government that Tel Aviv was planning an attack on Egypt, but Johnson took no action.[102] In late May, the Israeli foreign minister visited Washington DC and received assurances that the Johnson administration was behind his government. Israel took this as a green light for military action, supporting the position of the generals.[103]

The problem for the sort of political system that Egypt had at that time is that if the leader adopts a tactic, the whole governing establishment enthusiastically embraces it as if it were a strategy, and this problem recurs down the chain of command: any error of judgement on the part of the leader is made considerably worse when the government comes to implement it. With no freedom of expression, there is no channel for feedback from below; criticism or alternative opinions are seen as disloyalty. Amer's order to redeploy to the Israeli border thus went uncontested, and the National Assembly likewise meekly assented to a law giving Nasser the power to rule by decree in matters of relevance to national security – as well as supporting the withdrawal of the peacekeepers and the closing of the Straits of Tiran. The same applied to the Higher Executive Committee of the ASU.[104]

---

[101] Ibid., 70.
[102] Wm Roger Louis and Avi Shlaim, *The 1967 Arab-Israeli War: Origins and Consequences* (Cambridge: Cambridge University Press, 2012), 9.
[103] Fawzi, *The Three-Year War*, 141–3.
[104] Howeidi, *Lost Opportunities*, 68.

On 30 May, King Hussein of Jordan arrived in Cairo to sign a mutual defence agreement with the UAR. On 4 June, the Iraqi prime minister did the same. Nobody in any of the meetings held by the Joint Defence Council objected to Egypt's inexorable drive towards war. The only criticism came from Ali Amer, commander-in-chief of the United Arab Command, who warned that war risked the destruction of Arab air power and the capture of strategic areas by Israel that could then be used as bargaining chips to force its own resolution to the Palestinian issue.[105] In the event, Amer turned out to be right: if there was to be another war (a necessity David Ben Gurion was always convinced of), Israel was sure to use it as another opportunity to present the Arabs with a fait accompli of occupied Arab territories, which would force them to make peace without resolving the question of Palestine.[106]

Nasser predicted that Israel would launch a pre-emptive air attack on 5 June, but the Egyptian air commander Sedky Mahmoud was convinced that 80–90 per cent of his forces would survive it.[107] In fact, they were wiped out within hours of the first bomb falling. Syria, Jordan and Egypt sustained a humiliating and avoidable defeat, with Egyptian forces retreating in disarray from Sinai and large portions of Arab territory falling under Israeli occupation. Egypt immediately agreed to a UN ceasefire resolution, which, unusually for such resolutions, did not stipulate that the occupying forces should withdraw.

The 1967 defeat was a turning point for the pan-Arab project led by Egypt. The occupation of areas of Palestine that had remained under Arab administration, as well as other portions of Arab territory, opened up the possibility of trading land for peace with Israel. It also ushered in a distinct popular ambivalence towards the Nasser regime. Yes, that regime had raised the hopes of the masses and boosted Egyptian and Arab national pride, but it had also overseen the most humiliating defeat in Arab history. Yes, it was a proudly patriotic regime willing to go to war with Israel, but it had bungled that war disastrously. And yes, it represented emancipation and the fight against colonialism, but it was also responsible for extensive violations of human rights and restriction of freedoms.

The outcome of the war came as a total shock – a sort of civilizational trauma, a psychological rout with long-lasting effects on all Egyptians and Arabs as well as on pan-Arab thought. In Egypt it opened the door to a Brotherhood resurgence and provided new ammunition for critics

---

[105] Ibid., 71.
[106] Azmi Bishara, *From the Jewishness of the State to Sharon: A Study on the Contradiction of Israeli Democracy* [Arabic], 2nd edn (Cairo: Shorouk, 2010), 96.
[107] Sirrs, *A History of the Egyptian Intelligence Service*, 99–100.

of Nasserism everywhere. This ammunition would be put to use after Nasser's death.

Immediately after the defeat Nasser tendered his resignation, but withdrew it in the wake of massive demonstrations. Nonetheless, Nasserism had sustained a major defeat. A new era had begun – one in which nationalist regimes that had lost much of their legitimacy would rely ever more heavily on security crackdowns to maintain their grip on power. At the same time, their political and economic visions tacked more consistently towards socialism, drawing on ideas of a 'people's war' in an attempt to bolster the defeated Arab sense of self using radical rhetoric.

In 1968, demonstrators protested against the light sentences handed down to the commanders of the air force (these protests will be discussed in more detail later). The first signs of a growing impatience with authoritarianism can be discerned in these protests. The regime had lost its lustre and much of its legitimacy, and nationalist slogans were no longer capable of hiding the parlous state of the economy. In 1969, the Judges Club elected a new committee critical of despotism. Nasser's response was to dismiss hundreds of judges, in an action known as the 'massacre of the judges'. Many intellectuals were also arrested, charged and harshly sentenced, including the singer Sheikh Imam.

Hostilities resumed between Egypt and Israel on 1 July 1967, setting off the War of Attrition. A Soviet-Egyptian rapprochement bore fruit with the installation of Soviet missile systems to protect Egypt from Israeli air raids. In his memoirs, Fawzi states that at one of a series of meetings conducted during the War of Attrition, Nasser threatened to resign if the USSR refused to provide Egypt with defence systems; according to Howeidi, he specifically threatened to resign in favour of Zakaria Mohieddin, who would be able to come to an agreement with the United States.[108] A subsequent meeting was decisive: Soviet military advisers were sent to Egypt.[109]

During the War of Attrition, US secretary of state William Rogers presented a plan for a lasting settlement between Israel and Egypt. In its basic outlines, it entailed an Egyptian-Israeli agreement on a timetable for the withdrawal of Israeli troops from Egyptian territory; the termination of the state of war; the establishment of demilitarized zones and the recognition of freedom of navigation for all states, including Israel, through the Tiran Straits; and mutual recognition by Israel and Egypt of one another's sovereignty, political independence and right to live in peace within secure borders.

---

[108] Howeidi, *Lost Opportunities*, 187.
[109] Fawzi, *The Three-Year War*, 347–59.

Israel rejected the initiative the day after its announcement on 10 December, as did the USSR, which rejected any unilateral attempt by the United States to act as mediator. The second Rogers Plan in June 1970 proposed a three-month ceasefire, which was agreed upon in August of the same year and continued until the Yom Kippur War of 1973.

This episode showed just how closely senior figures' opinions were tied to Nasser's: although the ASU Executive Committee initially opposed the second Rogers Plan because they expected Nasser to dismiss it, they quickly fell in behind it once they realized he supported it.[110] The ceasefire provided an opportunity for Egypt to set up rocket batteries around the Suez Canal unmolested by Israeli fire, rocket batteries which were subsequently to provide much-needed cover to Egyptian ground forces during the 1973 war.

At the same time, Henry Kissinger encouraged Israel not to keep to the terms of the Rogers Plan: he had a personal rivalry with Rogers and was opposed to any settlement with Egypt as long as the USSR retained a presence there. Ultimately, Israel refused to cooperate with the UN special representative, and any chance of the Rogers Plan serving as the basis for a comprehensive peace agreement was scuppered.

4 Nasser's legacy

On 28 September 1970, Nasser died. Around seven million Egyptians participated in his funeral procession, and millions of Arabs across the region mourned the loss of a charismatic father figure – including those who had suffered personally because of his regime's policies. It was the physical end of a period that had already come to its political end with the defeat of 1967.

Much of the literature on the Nasserist period repeats the narrative dominant in Western academia: this was a regime that restricted political activity, monopolized power and drove the Islamists and other parties underground. There is also a general conviction that the Free Officers' modernization projects bankrupted Egypt.[111] What many of these foreign observers are unable to grasp is that Nasser's popularity cannot be reduced to his populist policies. More than that, it was about a modernizing state project that opened up new horizons for huge numbers of Egyptians, whose better quality of life and new opportunities for advancement increased their expectations – expectations that were later to become a driver of protest in times of crisis. For the Arab world more broadly, the policies of the Nasser

---

[110] Howeidi, *Lost Opportunities*, 189.
[111] See, for example, Daniel Kurtzer and Mary Svenstrup, 'Egypt's Entrenched Military', *The National Interest*, no. 121 (September/October 2012): 40.

regime represented their aspirations to achieve political unity and move past the colonial legacy. It is this that distinguishes the Nasserist period from later stages of the July Republic that suffered from the same problems.

Samir Amin characterizes the Nasserist period as 'the final chapter in a long list of struggles that began with the 1919–20 revolution', whose aims were to achieve 'democracy, national independence and social progress'.[112] Under Nasser, these aims were articulated in a centralized, authoritarian form in the name of the 'masses', and political mobilization was remoulded into a top-down affair. The Nasserist model was based on a command economy: it sought to accelerate industrial development and improve economic infrastructure and social integration, founded on the ideal distribution of income and participatory control in which various social groups were active in the political fabric (without providing any space for political pluralism per se). The popularity and populism of the regime were not enough, however: the regime always required the iron fist of the security forces to impose its authority.

The Nasser regime's policies – land reform, planned industrialization, import substitution and free education – were heavily influenced by development models in Eastern Europe and the Third World. These have come in for a great deal of criticism, much of it tendentious smears and some of it objective. But criticism notwithstanding, these were the policies that made modern Egypt and produced a new kind of Egyptian people. They effected a shift away from a project of national awakening that benefited only a tiny urban elite, and to which the vast majority of Egyptians were considered at best marginal, to a society in which workers, peasants and junior bureaucrats were the source of the regime's legitimacy.

The main driver of the economy during the Nasserist period was the state. But there was a historic shift in its economic policy as the regime moved into its second decade. During the first ten years, all the way up to the great nationalizations, the state supported and accelerated the development of manufacturing, and it experienced dramatic growth as a result. But in subsequent years, the effects of a bloated civil service based on the principle of job creation rather than efficiency – and an inability to fund it thanks to the simultaneous financial requirements of development and army reconstruction – began to be felt.

State intervention in the economy developed gradually after the 1952 coup in order to stimulate higher growth rates, as part of a national project whose aim was to rid Egypt of the holdovers of British colonialism, the monarchy and the magnates' control of land through a package of

---

[112] *al-Hiwar al-Mutamaddin*, 12 December 2015, Available online: https://bit.ly/3EcuXZd (accessed 20 November 2020).

policies: land reform, integration of the peasantry into public life, mass education and modernization to 'catch up' with more developed countries. The land reform law of 6 September 1952 struck at the heart of the social and political power of the agrarian aristocracy and laid the foundations of a new social base for the regime among the peasantry and a new rural middle class. It also created a fairer distribution of wealth by putting a ceiling on landownership, controlling rents and prohibiting the eviction of tenants except in exceptional circumstances.[113] The state gradually took control of production, pricing and distribution through an expanding network of cooperatives. At the same time, new industries – cement, fertilizer, iron, steel – were set up in Helwan, in the suburbs of Cairo, and the state took control of domestic and foreign trade.

The nationalization of the Suez Canal in 1956 marked a decisive shift in the state's role in the economy. With the private sector unwilling to invest in industry, the state increasingly took on this role itself, encouraged by the successes of the first three years, when industrial investment rose from 2 million Egyptian pounds in 1957 to 49.3 million in 1960.[114] Nasser's manufacturing programme was entirely in keeping with his strategy of restructuring production in Egypt away from agriculture and towards industry, itself central to state-driven import substitution, which was the philosophy of development in vogue at the time. At a time when the Third World seemed to be resurgent, Nasser saw rapid industrial development as inseparable from economic and national independence.

The state also sought to put in place more developed infrastructure, pursuing a series of five-year plans to this end. The first of these plans (1960–5) took on a more statist aspect with the beginning of massive nationalizations, driven primarily by political concerns resulting from the failure of the UAR in 1961. With this, the public sector became the uncontested engine of industrial development, accounting for almost all investment in industry and some 70 per cent of GDP. By the mid-1960s, industry accounted for 20 per cent of GDP. The Nasserist era may have begun with a plan limited to getting rid of colonialism and the monarchy, but it ultimately acquired a much more radical economic outlook. This supported the new military political elite, who needed to establish a social base and integrate it within corporatist structures in order to retain its loyalty.

---

[113] Ahmed al-Sayyed al-Naggar, 'Socialist Experiments in Egypt, the Impact of Egypt's Turn to Market Policies, and the Impact of Globalization and Structural Adjustment' [Arabic], in *The Social Welfare State and Discussion of the Seminar Organized by the Centre for Arab Unity Studies in Cooperation with the Swedish Institute in Alexandria* [Arabic] (Beirut: Centre for Arab Unity Studies, 2006).

[114] Nadia Ramsis Farah, *Egypt's Political Economy: Power Relations in Development* (Cairo: American University in Cairo Press, 2009), 35.

The Egyptian political elite was heterogeneous. Over time, loyalty to the leader substituted for any kind of intellectual homogeneity. The messages adopted by the elite in order to cultivate a social base changed from period to period depending on the struggles they were facing, ultimately arriving at the 'union of popular productive forces' as a slogan intended to mobilize peasants, workers, intellectuals and the so-called national bourgeoisie simultaneously, through representation in the corporatist parliament or centralized labour organization.[115] This was coupled with social policies intended to cultivate a fairer distribution of wealth: free education, social security, a minimum wage and labour legislation protecting workers' rights. There was something in it for businessmen, too: public sector contracts and commerce remained potential sources of income.

The state's economic policies, in particular those relating to industry, quickly ran out of steam. By the second half of the 1960s, growth was in decline, and its rewards were in any case largely redirected towards the insatiable demands of the bureaucracy and military, particularly during the protracted conflict in Yemen. In Egypt as in other countries, it became clear that while the public sector could jolt the economy into rapid growth, this growth would not last long in an atmosphere marked by the absence of competition, underemployment, a persistent need for imports to meet the needs of industry, financial difficulties resulting from a swollen state budget, and an inability to keep up with people's changing and diversifying needs.

When import substitution policies based on redirecting investment away from agriculture fail, the negative effects are doubled. On the one hand, rather than economic independence, they lead to greater dependence, especially if they depend on intermediate products made from imported inputs. At the same time, they have deleterious effects on the agricultural sector: Egypt became a net importer of food. After the defeat of 1967, the costs of rebuilding the army placed enormous pressure on the budget, and there was a pressing need for wheat imports after the suspension of shipments provided by the United States under the Food for Peace programme. Overcoming financial problems and regaining lost territory became more important than social and economic transformation, and economic and foreign policy became two sides of the same coin, both more closely tied to – and more dependent on – the international environment. This became obvious with the economic liberalization that began in the 1970s under Sadat.

---

[115] For more on the centralization of union activity under Nasser, see: Agnieszka Paczyńska, *State, Labor, and the Transition to a Market Economy: Egypt, Poland, Mexico, and the Czech Republic* (University Park, PA: Pennsylvania State University Press, 2009), 86–7.

Parallel with these developments, a bureaucratic elite emerged that accumulated wealth from bribery, graft and the manipulation of public sector assets. Soon numerous channels of corruption and misappropriation linked the private and public sectors. Those active in these channels were able to make huge profits from black marketeering and as state contractors.[116] This phenomenon began under Nasser, facilitated by the lack of transparency and accountability and the valuing of loyalty over competence and professionalism, the politicization of government procedure and law, the ever-narrower margin available for criticism and free expression, and the absence of an independent judiciary. But under Nasser it was the exception; under Sadat, it was to become the norm.

III Choices of the July Republic and the growing power of the presidency

There are many continuities between Nasser's tenure and those of Mubarak and Sadat – the structure of the state, the domination of the security regime, a ruling party overlapping with the state bureaucracy – that allow us to see them all as a single republic: the July Republic.[117] Most of the political elite that emerged under Nasser remained active well into Mubarak's time, including prominent personalities closely involved in decision making. Almost every major figure in the Mubarak regime had a background either in the ASU or the security forces under Nasser or Sadat. But this is only one indication of continuity. The real proof is in the structure of the regime, the role of the army and the security forces, and the powers of the presidency. The structure of the regime remained the same throughout: a bureaucratic-authoritarian regime headed by the president and rooted in the army and security forces, the single-party system and a government that managed the economy. The only thing that changed was policy.

Nasser's policies created an economic system based on state-driven development, infrastructure building, industrialization and intensive protectionism, requiring an enormous bureaucracy far out of proportion to Egypt's economy and its productive capacity. Sadat's tenure, on the other hand, was characterized by economic liberalization or 'opening up' (*infitah*). But Sadat continued to rely heavily on the public sector, keeping the security forces, the bureaucracy and the ASU as he had inherited them from Nasser. The same applies to Mubarak, who completed the transition to capitalism that had begun under Sadat. The 'deep state' is not only deep

---

[116] Farah, *Egypt's Political Economy*, 38.
[117] Now resurrected by Abdel Fattah El-Sisi.

in space but also in time – that is, it has built up over many, many years, and its depth consists of historical strata built up over those years.

Of course, this does not mean that there were not essential differences between the different presidents' eras, which make it necessary to subdivide the July Republic into at least two periods. Indeed, Egypt has been a pioneer in several respects: it was the first 'public sector state' in the Arab world and also the first to set out on a programme of privatization and economic liberalization driven by realignment towards the United States.[118] Sadat's assassination on 6 October 1981 had no effect on the latter development.

After taking over from Nasser in 1970, Sadat set about purging the traditional Nasserists in what he referred to as the 'May Movement'. Although he was keen to market this as a 'corrective movement' within the July regime itself, he was moving quickly towards a break with the Nasserist period – but without giving up any of the constituent elements of Nasser's political system. To these he added a limited party pluralism – a 'state liberalism' to accompany his state capitalism. But this was a liberalism based not on citizens' rights and freedoms but on a margin of freedom determined entirely by the authoritarian state. Economic liberalization brought into being a new class of business magnates, who under Mubarak were to take their place alongside the army and security forces and the party as one of the three central pillars of the regime.

Nazih Ayubi argues that Egypt's open-door policy 'developed under the impact of the state bourgeoisie opting for alliance with international capital, more than it has under any pressure from the local industrial capitalists'.[119] While the term 'state bourgeoisie' adds nothing to the analysis here, he is right that economic liberalization was a political decision taken by a near-absolutist presidential regime; in this case, politics is the key to understanding economic decisions and not the other way around. As yet, there was no Egyptian capitalist class with the economic or political weight required to influence the president's decisions.[120] It was not until the

---

[118] Nazih N. Ayubi, *Over-stating the Arab State: Politics and Society in the Middle East* (London and New York: I.B. Tauris, 2001), 339.

[119] Ibid., 340.

[120] Some theories explain this transition by reference to a hidden capitalist class without making it clear which capitalists are supposed to have acquired sufficient clout to influence these decisions. Others point to Egypt's weak position in the international division of labour, arguing that such a transition was thus inevitable. The only tangible explanation, however, is that of a state attempting to maintain its economic position in society, citing justifications rooted in ideological currents that had existed within the regime for decades. For more on this transformation, see: Nazih Ayubi, *The Centralized State in Egypt* [Arabic] (Beirut: Centre for Arab Unity Studies, 1989), 143–50. Note that rather than shrinking, the public sector grew larger under the open-door policy, with annual government expenditure rising from 1.658 billion Egyptian pounds at the end of the 1960s to 5.395 billion at the beginning of the 1980s (Ibid., 153–4).

later Mubarak period, during Ahmed Nazif's time as prime minister, that private capital was able to exercise this kind of influence.

Nasser's regime had been based on sovereignty and comprehensive national development, incorporating the most marginalized parts of the population – particularly the peasantry – through land reform and mass education. Sadat's realignment towards the West, his pursuit of economic liberalization and his policy of peace with Israel thus represented a dramatic volte-face.

In November 1970, only a few weeks after Nasser's death, Moshe Dayan suggested reducing the number of Egyptian and Israeli troops stationed on each side of the Suez Canal as a prelude to reopening it to international shipping. He hoped that if the Egyptian regime could be encouraged to build along the canal, within easy range of Israeli weapons, this would be an incentive to maintain the ceasefire. Cairo relayed its interest in the scheme via the US embassy, and on 4 February 1971, President Sadat – without consulting any state institutions, but as part of a plan and with the support of some of his allies – announced in the People's Assembly an initiative that included preparations to reopen the Suez Canal, a six-month extension of the ceasefire agreement and a restoration of the relations between Cairo and Washington DC if Israel withdrew its troops and some Egyptian forces were allowed to cross to the eastern side of the canal. Under pressure from the United States, Israel expressed interest in the initiative.[121] On 8 July 1972, Sadat expelled the Soviet advisers – a dramatic move intended to keep the Americans happy.

Although Sadat was seen as a weak figure who had spent his political life nestled under Nasser's wing, no sooner had he taken power than he began to foreground the power of the president and underscore its independence from the ASU Executive Committee. Some members of the regime's old guard have claimed that he was chosen to succeed Nasser precisely because of his relative weakness and lack of influence. A quick review of Nasser's tenure, however, shows that although he may have been an opportunistic sycophant, he was also a consistent member of the close-knit circle of officials around the president. In any case, the powers of the presidency gave him strength, irrespective of his personality. He considered the course he pursued in 1971 to be necessary to right the ship – similar, perhaps, to the 'corrective movement' undertaken by Hafez al-Assad in Syria. He purged the so-called centres of power (specifically the triumvirate of Ali Sabri, Sharawi Jum'ah and Sami Sharaf), who were suspicious of his intentions, particularly towards Israel.

---

[121] Howeidi, *Lost Opportunities*, 247–8.

During his initial struggle with the Executive Committee of the ASU, Sadat made overtures to the leftists: Ismail Sabri Abdullah was appointed minister of planning and the strong relationship with the Soviets was emphasized, despite the plans already set in motion to re-establish relations with the United States. Although Sadat had few pan-Arabist inclinations, he took steps to establish a new Arab union with Syria and Libya without consulting the ASU, forcing it to object to pan-Arabist measures and so driving a wedge between the organization and its Nasserist base.[122]

From 15 to 17 April 1971, Interior Minister Sharawi Jum'ah effectively barred Sadat from addressing the Egyptian people by deploying the security forces around the TV and radio building. At the same time, Minister of War Mohammed Fawzi deployed units throughout Cairo. This was interpreted as preparations for a coup, although it may have been simply a show of force on the part of the 'centres of power', who were worried that Sadat would sideline them. On 2 May, Sadat dismissed Ali Sabri, the vice-president. Sabri's allies did not raise any objections, showing that there were disagreements among the power centres themselves. On 13 May, Sadat dismissed Gomaa, replacing him with Mamdouh Salem, director of the Alexandria Investigations Directorate and a veteran of the Farouq-era secret police. He also dismissed intelligence chief Ahmed Kamel for 'failing to uncover the conspiracy', replacing him with Ahmad Ismail. Gomaa, Sami Sharaf and Ali Sabri were all sentenced to death before their sentences were commuted to life imprisonment with hard labour.

Sadat portrayed all these actions as reform of the 'intelligence state'. He ended the practice of bugging telephones without a court warrant, released many political prisoners and took various steps to 'liberalize' political life. A veritable flood of literature was published condemning the excesses of the security forces under Nasser, including Naguib Mahfouz's *Karnak Café* and Gamal al-Ghitani's *Zayni Barakat*. Other media, including films like *Dawn Visitors*, also provided opportunities to settle scores with Nasser.

Having defeated the centres of power and the ASU, Sadat set about establishing a new balance of political power, allowing the Muslim Brotherhood to return to limited public activities and to publish a newspaper (albeit without any legal legitimacy). In September 1971 he began to talk about 'state of institutions'. In the same year, he announced that this would be the year in which Sinai would return to Egyptian control. In fact, he was preparing for a military conflict, an extension of Nasser's own plans

---

[122] Sadat states in his memoirs that he presented the plan for a federation of Arab republics to the ASU Executive Committee and it was rejected; he then presented it to the Central Committee, where it won unanimous approval. He considered this a victory against the 'centres of power' (*In Search of Self*, 231–2).

after the War of Attrition, while simultaneously seeking a political solution that would involve Israeli withdrawal from Sinai. He concluded that war was inevitable after exhausting all possible peaceful alternatives, having presented various ideas for a solution with US mediation. Kamal Adham, the head of Saudi Intelligence and a friend of Sadat since the 1950s, played a major role in the Egyptian-Saudi rapprochement that took place during this period as well as attempts to mediate between Egypt and the United States.[123] Some have claimed that Sadat had been the recipient of Saudi gifts – and US phone calls – since the 1960s.[124]

In January 1972, student protesters demanded an immediate declaration of war and democracy as a means of strengthening Egypt against Israel. By this point, many intellectuals had become convinced that dictatorship was a main cause of the defeat of 1967. An attempt by the security forces to break up the protests on 24 January led to a two-day sit-in in Tahrir Square. Throughout the academic year, demonstrations would die down in one university only to break out in another.

Sadat allowed Islamist groups to operate under his watch and released many Brotherhood members from prison as a counterweight to nationalists and leftists, in particular the remaining Nasserists. Islamist groups were particularly active in the universities, where they made strong showings in student union elections, taking full advantage of the religiosity of society, reactions to the 1967 defeat and the willingness of the Sadat regime to accept criticism of the Nasserist period. They found a willing social base among those who had suffered under Nasser as well as those who had benefited from the social mobility afforded by his regime and migrated to the cities without becoming fully urbanized. (In fact, the margins of the city had been 'ruralized' and developed into extensive poverty belts.) Public religiosity became more prominent, with religious programmes more common on TV and preachers far more active in society. Just as the transistor radio had brought Nasserism into every provincial home, the cassette tape now facilitated the spread of Islamist discourse.

Mass religiosity began to take hold. A more rigid, less diverse phenomenon than urban and rural folk religion, it emerged after the development of mass society and the atomization of individuals in response to the loss of community in a faceless urban environment. It furthermore served as fertile ground for *political* religiosity. As mass religiosity spread, it came to colour the reaction to any modernizing or liberalizing measure taken by Sadat. An amendment to the personal status law that allowed a woman to divorce her husband and retain possession of the marital home

---

[123] Sirrs, *A History of the Egyptian Intelligence Service*, 123.
[124] Kirk J. Beattie, *Egypt during the Sadat Years* (New York: Palgrave, 2000), 14.

and custody of the children if he took a second wife without her consent triggered a storm of protest. This period also saw a marked uptick in sectarian tensions and attacks on Christians, beginning with the Khanka incident in 1972; similar events in al-Zawiya al-Hamra in June 1981 left some eighty-two Egyptian Copts dead.

The military's successful crossing of the Suez Canal in the October 1973 war was central to the Sadat era. But his subsequent management of the war squandered this remarkable achievement, allowing the Israelis to cross to the western side of the canal and encircle the Third Army. This led to negotiations that ended with a separation of forces agreement signed on 18 January 1974. (I will return to this topic in the chapter on the army.)

On 9 November 1977, Sadat announced in the People's Assembly that he intended to travel to Israel and give a speech in the Knesset, a radical step that would completely change the trajectory of both the Arab-Israeli conflict and Egypt. After prolonged negotiations mediated by Jimmy Carter, on 26 March 1978 Sadat and Menachem Begin signed the Camp David Accords, which set out principles for a permanent solution to the Arab-Israeli conflict as well as a temporary settlement for Palestine. This began a process of normalization, with ambassadors exchanged between the two countries on 26 January 1980.

Sadat's withdrawal from the united Arab front – and by extension, to a remarkable extent, from the Arab political scene as a whole – constituted a veritable coup against the pan-Arab project and the central place that Egypt had occupied within it. It ushered in a political and cultural emphasis on a distinct Egyptian identity historically separate from its Arab environment, a cultural movement motivated by a decision taken at the very top of the political hierarchy. It brought about a massive rift in Egyptian political society, with a powerful opposition coalescing around rejection of the Camp David Accords. Despite Sadat's attempts to cast himself as a devout president, demonstrated most clearly in the new constitution's designation of Shari'a as the main source of legislation, the Brotherhood members that he had released at the beginning of his tenure now acted decisively against him. He walked a very narrow tightrope, encouraging Islamist discourse and even Islamist student activism against the Nasserists and the left while at the same time allying with the United States and suppressing Islamist opposition to his Israel policy.

With the Israeli threat apparently neutralized and the main problem now lying with domestic opposition, the importance of Military Intelligence declined precipitously in favour of the SSIS, which grew more powerful after Sadat's assassination and during the Islamist insurgency in the 1990s under Mubarak.

Sadat's move away from the socialist model built on the foundations laid by Nasser himself after the 1966 economic crisis, when the state had begun to gradually ease restrictions on the private sector and set up commercial and development banks to provide loans to businesses. After the October War, Sadat accelerated this process, particularly after the publication of the 'October Paper' in March 1974 and the issuance in June of Law 43/1974 incentivizing Arab and foreign investment in Egypt, which allowed free trade areas to be set up in Alexandria, Suez and Port Said. As in many other Third World countries setting out on the path of economic liberalization, people let their imaginations run away with them, envisioning high-tech production zones modelled on Japan. In fact, these areas ended up serving primarily as zones for warehousing and tax evasion. The only actual increase in state revenue came from oil exports, which grew markedly in this period, and from the Suez Canal, whose revenues increased 12 per cent year-on-year between its reopening in 1974 and 1980. This money was used to fund an expanding trade deficit, driving inflation and price increases and forcing the government to raise subsidies on essential products. When these subsidies were abruptly rescinded in 1977 as part of efforts to secure support from the IMF, leading in some cases to overnight price hikes of 45 per cent, it triggered a massive wave of protests known as the Bread Uprising.

After the 1970s oil boom, the number of Egyptians working abroad in the Gulf, Iraq and Libya rose precipitously – from 58,000 in 1970 to 5,000,000 in 1980. Returning expatriates invested their money in Egypt, providing a significant boost to business, property and commerce. Migration absorbed many of the vast army of Egyptians left unemployed by liberalization, as well as graduates unable to find suitable employment in the public sector. All this helped drive liberalization forward, as well as creating closer ties between Egypt's economy and those of the oil-producing countries.

The Mamdouh Salem government was the main instrument of liberalization under Sadat. The problem with the open-door policy was that most of the foreign money invested in Egypt went not to productive sectors but into property, services, commerce, speculation or construction. Industrialization suffered a serious setback during this period, with the economy increasingly reorienting itself towards imports. In the year that Nasser died, 1970, Egypt did not have a single millionaire (more accurately, not a single *declared* millionaire). By 1980, it boasted some 17,000, most of whom had made their money through speculation. A wealth gap emerged comparable to that which had existed on the eve of the 1952 coup – that is, before the development of a mass society and a regime that claimed to speak in its name in the language of social justice. In the second half of the 1970s, as part of attempts to encourage domestic and foreign tourism and investment in property development, 53.3 per cent of public land on the Mediterranean seaboard was transferred to private ownership free of charge (it was later sold on the private market for some 4 billion Egyptian pounds). And although one of the reasons for economic liberalization had been financial shortfalls, under Sadat the public debt increased tenfold. Three-quarters of this debt served to finance consumption, not production.[125] This period also saw the creation of a private banking sector, with the number of banks jumping from zero in 1974 to fifty-six in 1980. Many of these were branches of US banks, which facilitated capital flight: by 1985, $9.9 billion was held by Egyptians in foreign currency deposits, most of which was transferred abroad.[126] And although as much as 50 per cent of the Egyptian workforce was employed in agriculture, by the early 1980s Egypt was importing some 60 per cent of its food.[127]

In January 1976, Sadat created 'political platforms' for the left, right and centre within the ASU. Law 40/1977 transformed these platforms into fully fledged parties. In 1978, a new PPC was established to register new party organizations, headed by the NDP, which replaced the now-dissolved ASU, inheriting some six million of its members. The NDP essentially represented the alliance of the bureaucracy, the business sector and the regime's rural strongmen. It formed a social base for the regime rooted in employment opportunities and material interests linked to the bureaucracy and the new business magnates.

In 1979, after peace was concluded between Egypt and Israel, the US Congress approved approximately $2.5 billion in annual aid for Egypt, with some $1.5 billion earmarked as military aid for the purchase of US weapons.[128] Some 82 per cent of the non-military aid went to the oil sector, and only 4 per cent to industry. Between 1974 and 1980, the United States provided some $15 billion of aid and loans to Egypt. In 1981, Sadat himself set up the American Chamber of Commerce in Egypt (known as AmCham), which helped to create a lobby of businessmen pushing privatization and liberalization. AmCham was later to serve as one of Gamal Mubarak's biggest lobbying organizations, playing a major part in the campaign to secure US approval for a father-son transfer of power.

On 6 October 1981, Sadat was assassinated by Khaled Islambouli, a member of the EIJ. His death brought the curtain down on an age of dramatic transformations in which his own oversized and melodramatic personality

---

[125] Kandil, *Soldiers, Spies, and Statesmen*, 161–2.
[126] Kandil, *The Power Triangle*, 296.
[127] Kandil, *Soldiers, Spies, and Statesmen*, 202.
[128] Jeremy M. Sharp, 'Egypt: Background and U.S. Relations', *CRS Report for Congress*, 27 May 2020, 30, Available online: https://bit.ly/33nAfAk (accessed 25 October 2021).

had played a central role. He was succeeded by his deputy, Hosni Mubarak, consolidating the tradition of presidential inheritance begun by Nasser. This strengthened the position of the presidency itself, since new presidents were made not by elections or even coups but by their predecessors.

During Sadat's tenure, the regime party became the *president*'s party. It was run by the close circle of political elites that surrounded his person, and those who joined it did so because they wanted to be close to the centre of economic and police power – the president. This development continued, and intensified, under Mubarak. And when the office of the president began to extend to his family, it became the party of his family too.

1 The presidential system and the president's party

Mubarak wanted to establish a base of legitimacy for himself, and thus tried to reconcile the contradictions that had brought an end to his predecessor. He respected the peace agreement, but declined to visit Israel, and insisted that every last square metre of Sinai be returned – finally achieved in 1989 with the withdrawal of Israeli forces from Taba, which had been the subject of international arbitration after the Camp David Accords. In 1982, after Fatah fell out with Syria, Yasser Arafat returned to Egypt, allowing Egypt to resume a legitimate role in Palestinian affairs; support provided to Iraq during its war with Iran heralded its return to Arab affairs. In 1990, the Arab League – which had expelled Egypt after Camp David and relocated to Tunisia – returned to Cairo. From then on, Egypt sought to keep the United States happy by maintaining an untroubled peace with Israel, while at the same time avoiding anything (Knesset visits, for example) that might provoke a public more interested in spectacle than reality. The death of the architect of peace with Israel seemed to mean that the issue was settled: the possibility of annulling the agreement was no longer taken seriously in the Egyptian or broader Arab media. The accords survived their maker.

The Mubarak era began with a sort of political relaxation driven by two factors. The first was the political crisis that had marked the end of Sadat's tenure in 1981, when the president ordered a wave of arrests sweeping up hundreds of politicians and activists. Mubarak was keen to avoid the same fate as his predecessor and thus acted very cautiously, avoiding any measures that might set large portions of Egyptian society against him – abolishing subsidies on essential products, for example, which had resulted in the bread riots of 1977. The second factor was a rise in oil revenues in the early 1980s, which meant that the regime was relatively flush with cash and able to pursue popular policies. Overall, however, this move towards openness was driven less by a reformist impulse than caution, underpinned by a structural trend towards stagnation.

Mubarak followed Sadat, building a powerful presidency supported by a fragile political body and a wobbly economy made up of a dilapidated public sector and a private sector expanding rapidly in all directions. Unable to dispense with the state of emergency, the regime continued to renew it regularly.

The political dynamics of the Nasser era and the institutional and corporatist channels through which they flowed never produced as autocratic a presidency as developed under Mubarak. Nasser was always obliged to consider many different stakeholders: the army command, the Free Officers and the ASU leadership, although towards the end of his tenure the presidency had become more influential. Sadat had built on this development by bringing the ASU and the army to heel, and Mubarak inherited a presidential office whose authority was unchallenged by any other force within the regime. This omnipotence, as elected president Mohamed Morsi was later to discover to his detriment, risked becoming impotence when a regime outsider assumed the office. But so long as a figure acceptable to the regime held the position, the president enjoyed absolute power; no matter how weak he may have been personally, his office made him powerful.

The 1956 constitution had transferred most of the responsibilities of the RCC to the president, which allowed Nasser to transfer many ministries from military to civilian control and thus granted him extensive powers to appoint and dismiss ministers, draft policy, issue emergency laws and administrative orders, and veto legislation.[129] The constitutional amendments of 1958, 1962 and 1964 left these powers almost entirely unchanged, although the latter did provide for a succession mechanism: presidents would be chosen by a two-thirds majority vote in the People's Assembly before being confirmed by the people in a simple yes-no referendum, without any alternatives being provided (making the referendum meaningless, since a 'no' vote did not mean a vote for another president).[130]

In 1971 a new constitution was promulgated which was to remain in force until the January 2011 revolution. This constitution, whose drafting was overseen personally by Sadat, was decisive in both entrenching and expanding the dictatorial position of the president, with some thirty-five of its fifty-five articles concerning the powers of the presidency.[131] It made the

---

[129] Ninette S. Fahmy, *The Politics of Egypt: State-Society Relationship* (London and New York: Routledge, 2012), 45.

[130] The 1964 text granted members of the ASU the right to stand for the presidency. See: Maye Kassem, *Egyptian Politics: The Dynamics of Authoritarian Rule* (Boulder, CO: Lynne Rienner Publishers, 2004), 19–17.

[131] Fahmy, *The Politics of Egypt*, 45.

president 'an arbitrator between state authorities, allowing him to control and head the government and make policy' and granting him a raft of exceptional powers set forth in the infamous Article 78.[132] He could now issue laws by presidential decree on economic matters and arms purchases, declare a state of emergency, appoint and dismiss governments at will, overrule the legislature by calling a referendum to dissolve it, appoint and set the salaries of judges, and determine the judiciary's budget. He also retained various other powers established in the Nasser era, including financial oversight of the police and army and the ability to establish state security courts.[133] Although the 1971 constitution provided for term limits, Sadat had this section removed in 1980.[134] The constitution also changed the official name of the country from the 'United Arab Republic' to the 'Arab Republic of Egypt' and added a provision making the principles of Shari'a a primary source of legislation, amended in 1980 to make Shari'a *the* primary source. This was a sop to Islamist groups, albeit one that did not prove sufficient to save Sadat's life.

This entrenchment and expansion of the powers of the presidency under the 1971 constitution was the most important aspect of Sadat's regime restructuring. But the new regime was indisputably the child of the old, and its aim was not to abolish or dismantle it but to bring together all of its different parts. The pan-Arab ASU was divided into three distinct political 'platforms' in 1975 and then into parties, with the president's party (the NDP) retaining a permanent two-thirds majority of the People's Assembly (the majority required to elect a new president or renew his term) and the others permitted to exercise a limited oppositional function.

The government continued to rely on the army and the security forces as the regime's main guarantor, but the judiciary was given a greater margin of independence in order to secure investor confidence. The retreat from Nasserist corporatism was the inevitable result of socio-economic transformation within the regime, but the shift towards capitalism involved no concurrent changes to the presidency, which retained its position through clientelism. Capital did not compete with the government but satisfied itself with Bonapartism.[135] The influence of capital gradually increased inside the regime through the NDP itself, particularly after Mubarak ascended to the presidency as reshaped by Sadat. Unlike Nasser

---

[132] Tarek El-Bishry, *Egypt: Between Insubordination and Disintegration* [Arabic], 2nd edn (Cairo: Shorouk, 2010), 85.
[133] Kassem, *Egyptian Politics*, 24–5.
[134] Fahmy, *The Politics of Egypt*, 45.
[135] Bonapartism is an absolutist – but not totalitarian – system in which capital is willing to accept a (usually military) leader controlling political life as long as he protects its interests.

and Sadat, Mubarak, who sought stability and not change, did not have to confront any threats from within the regime.[136]

The 1971 constitution was amended in 1980, 2005 and 2007, each time further centralizing power in the hands of the president, generally at the expense of the legislature.[137] Under Mubarak, the People's Assembly consisted of 454 deputies elected for 5 years, 10 of whom were appointed by the president (as were a third of their colleagues in the Shura Council). The 2007 amendments expanded the Shura Council's powers somewhat, but membership remained in practice a reward for regime loyalists. The president was still responsible for appointing and dismissing the prime minister and the cabinet as well as the heads of the military and the GIS, provincial governors and chancellors of universities.

The president used his People's Assembly appointments to give seats to women, Copts and others that the NDP shied away from nominating. The NDP, always catering to popular prejudices, showed little interest in encouraging social integration or representation of this kind – despite its disingenuous attacks on the Muslim Brotherhood's positions on religious minorities and the rights of women. The regime's artificial attempts at bringing about integration via top-down appointments, however, only deepened resentment and division, as recognition of the rights of Christian citizens and women was framed as an act of charity from the president.

Until 2005, the president was elected (formally) by a two-thirds majority in the People's Assembly and then presented to the people in a simple yes-no referendum in which he would typically win more than 90 per cent of the vote. Under pressure from the neoconservative administration in the United States, however, a constitutional amendment was pushed through that modified Article 56 to allow for competitive direct popular elections, albeit within limitations so strict that the outcome was a foregone conclusion. In elections held that September, Mubarak took 88.6 per cent of the vote, while the nominees of the Ghad Party (Ayman Nour) and the Wafd (Noaman Gomaa) took 7.6 per cent and 2.9 per cent respectively. US pressure to expand the margin of political activity led to a rash of analyses in the official press claiming that Washington was conspiring with the Muslim Brotherhood.

Under Mubarak, three key elements of the Egyptian regime were consolidated. The powers of the president saw a near-constant expansion and entrenchment, with the office itself free of scrutiny or accountability.

---

[136] Tarek Osman, *Egypt on the Brink: From Nasser to Mubarak* (New Haven: Yale University Press, 2010), 170.
[137] Raymond A. Hinnebusch, 'The Formation of the Contemporary Egyptian States from Nasser and Sadat to Mubarak', in *The Political Economy of Contemporary Egypt*, ed. Ibrahim M. Oweiss (Washington, DC: Centre for Contemporary Arab Studies, Georgetown University, 1990), 194–7.

The state relied more heavily than ever on the security forces, which saw a concurrent growth in their numbers and their influence. And the ruling party was converted into the *president's* party, bringing together a coalition of state bureaucrats, the ascendant bourgeoisie and the rural notability.

IV Transformations within the Egyptian army

In the absence of a strong, organized middle class with its own ideology, after 1952 military men were to take on the historical vocation of that class, reshaping agrarian relations, pushing aside the rural aristocracy and taking a stand against British tutelage and royal corruption. Coming to power in the wake of a mass movement composed of labour, student and urban middle-class elements, manifested in various popular uprisings, the Free Officers presented themselves as representatives of national unity and protectors of the nation. Was the military coup, then, the culmination of a popular revolution or did it prevent a true popular revolution from happening? However we decide to answer this question, the army's actions exemplified the widespread claim in the Third World that the army is the only force capable of taking the reins of development.[138] Between the 1950s and the 1970s, it was common to see the army as a uniquely organized, uniquely patriotic, progressive force with a unique sense of duty towards the nation. Armies themselves tended to share this view, forming closed fraternities that saw their own modern military discipline as indisputably superior to the 'chaos' and 'backwardness' of civilian life. In this section, we will discuss the development of the military establishment and its relationship to politics and society over three main stages.

Stage 1: Military hegemony and the overlap of army and president

Of the eighteen governments formed between 1952 and 1970, only the first – which lasted a mere two months – was headed by a civilian, Prime Minister Aly Maher. With the exception of a brief period under Mohamed

---

[138] This is quite different from the model in which the army acts as an *obstacle* to development, as happened after the January revolution. In that case, it was not patriotic junior officers with modernizing ambitions, but high-ranking figures who had risen to their positions under the old regime, and they only made their move once numerous civilian forces had made it clear that they were capable of bringing the state administration to a grinding halt. Neither the Egyptian army nor Egyptian society is the same as they were in 1952. We must always bear in mind the important difference between a military coup carried out by officers from the top of the military hierarchy to prevent democratic transition (2013 in Egypt, 1973 in Chile) and a coup carried out by junior officers with radical aspirations (1952).

Naguib, all Egyptian governments during this period included significant numbers of officers (36.6 per cent of ministerial positions on average), with military men invariably holding the more important portfolios.[139]

Nasser did not intend to set up a military dictatorship. He wanted to create a populist republic supported by the army. Because he knew from his own personal experience how important the army was politically – and recognized the danger of coups – he sought to distance the army from direct intervention in politics. He asked those Free Officers who were active in the political sphere to take off their army uniforms and put on civilian clothes. Unlike Naguib, however, he had no intention of leading a full-scale return to barracks and handing over power to a representative civilian administration. This has been the central contradiction of military politics in Egypt since the July revolution: the politicians are soldiers in civilian clothes, while the army is expected not to intervene in politics – in fact, to evince total loyalty to these former soldiers as the main guarantor of regime stability.

Nasser rooted his legitimacy in social achievements, a nationalist discourse vis-à-vis the UK and Israel and, later on, a pan-Arab discourse based on the broad sense of solidarity that many Arabs felt with Egypt after the nationalization of the Suez Canal. He relied on military men in both of these spheres, with officers taking senior positions in government and the economy.

The regime sought to create a popular base for itself outside the army – a sort of regime party. The first of these was the Liberation Rally, which was replaced in 1957 by the National Union and in 1962 by the ASU. These were all regime parties and mechanisms for social mobilization, discipline and surveillance.

As commander-in-chief, Abdel Hakim Amer appointed Salah Nasr (later head of the GIS) director of the Office of the Commander-in-Chief for Political Guidance, a department which continued to function until the 1967 defeat. The purpose of this office was to spy on the officer corps: those who had seized power in a coup had no desire to be the victims of one. Military appointments were made above all else on the basis of loyalty, which trumped ability.

Military men were very well represented in the diplomatic corps and the security services, in state companies and in local government. Amer himself acquired a vast portfolio, overseeing Sufi orders, the Nuclear Energy Organization, the National Research Centre, the Cairo Public Transport Authority and the Football Association, as well as chairing the

---

[139] Imad Harb, 'The Egyptian Military in Politics: Disengagement or Accommodation?', *Middle East Journal* 57, no. 2 (Spring 2003): 278.

Supreme Council for Public Companies and the Supreme Council for the Dissolution of Feudalism.[140] As the Egyptian economy, and particularly the public sector, developed, bringing with it the rise of a technical and administrative class, officers entered universities and competed with technical experts there.[141] This tendency still exists today.

In order to fill the upper ranks of the army hierarchy after a coup led by junior officers, a national Defence Academy was set up, which allowed for a significant increase in the number of senior officers – with the addition of a new rank, lieutenant general, allowing for the promotion of more major generals and brigadiers. Most of the new officers came from the middle class, and alongside junior civil servants and technocrats they were to form the new national elite. Slowly but surely, this elite displaced the old gentleman soldiers and elite graduates of the interwar period, although some remained in place – in teaching positions, ministries or law – until the 1970s.

National service was made compulsory for all Egyptians in 1955, alongside an expanded campaign of specialist recruitment that produced a core of professional soldiers. The 1967 defeat, however, showed the limits of their professionalism and training, and this led to another recruitment campaign targeting university graduates, which was to be central to the subsequent development of the Egyptian armed forces.[142] On the eve of the Six-Day War, fewer than one in every sixty officers held an undergraduate degree. Only six years later, the figure was three in five. Alongside better training and armament, this helped the army to make a better showing in 1973.[143] Promotion depended on an officer's politics and social background. Subsequent developments, particularly Sadat's assassination by a team of soldiers, led to a much more selective recruitment policy.

Nasser emphasized that while he did not want any politics in the army, he *did* want the army in politics.[144] Politics in the army meant the threat of another coup, the dangers of which the Free Officers knew better than anyone. The army in politics, however, meant that the army should be the foundation of the regime's security and one of its key social constituencies, with a group of officers bound together by personal ties and hierarchical

---

[140] Ayubi, *The Centralized State*, 117–18.
[141] Abdullah, 'The Armed Forces', 12.
[142] Magdy Hammad, 'The Military Establishment and the Egyptian Political Regime, 1952–1980' [Arabic], in *The Army and Democracy in Egypt* [Arabic], ed. Ahmed Abdullah (Cairo: Sina Publishing, 1990), 32.
[143] Joseph Kechichian and Jeanne Nazimek, 'Challenges to the Military in Egypt', *Middle East Policy* 5, no. 3 (September 1997): 126.
[144] In Nasser's speech to mark the tenth anniversary of the revolution: *Bibliotheca Alexandria*, 22 July 1962, Available online: https://bit.ly/32rVG3W (accessed 6 November 2014).

discipline ruling the country. The 'new sociopolitical doctrine' cited to justify this position was articulated by Mohamed Hassanein Heikal:

> Under the conditions that are typical of the class struggle in the underdeveloped countries, and bearing in mind the feeling of the general public that the leaders in power represented only interests which by their very nature are opposed to those of the masses, the popular revolutionary movement has no choice but to base itself on the army in order to pave the way for the revolution.[145]

This confidence in the army – and lack of confidence in the people or in civilian leadership – was central to the discourse of many intellectuals and journalists surrounding the officers. This elite remained loyal to this position even after the 2011 revolution, ultimately trusting the army to end the 'chaos' of the transitional period.

Officers were appointed to censor the press after it was nationalized. They also took most of the important positions in the Foreign Ministry: in 1962, 72 per cent of senior jobs in this field were held by officers, including the post of ambassador to the United States. They dominated the popular organizations, holding a majority of seats in the ASU secretariat general throughout the 1960s,[146] as well as becoming provincial governors and directors of public companies. The steady penetration of the state bureaucracy by retired officers, from local government all the way up to the office of the prime minister, continued throughout the July Republic period.

Those officers who remained in military service, first among them Abdel Hakim Amer, gradually came to form a network of loyal supporters around Amer himself. Supporting his personal ambitions and his struggle for influence within the state, they turned a blind eye to his arbitrariness and lack of professionalism, both of which were cast into humiliating relief more than once. The decline in military ethics and accountability became particularly marked after the Yemen campaign, which gave the army 'an inflated sense of pride in non-existent victories [. . .] a lethal arrogance and a baseless self-confidence' that led them to fatally underestimate the Israelis.[147] Exchanging a uniform for civilian clothes does not always make officers immune to this tendency, as Abdel Fattah El-Sisi and his many military appointees demonstrate clearly.

Fawzi writes that the presidential council set up in 1962 after the UAR collapsed to establish the powers and responsibilities of the political leadership served as a de facto legislature until the ratification of the new

---

[145] Abdel-Malek, *Egypt: Military Society*, 345–6.
[146] Harb, 'The Egyptian Military in Politics', 279.
[147] Fawzi, *The Three-Year War*, 26.

constitution in 1964 and the election of the first National Assembly.[148] In the same year, Decree 2878 made Abdel Hakim Amer deputy commander-in-chief, making him responsible to the president and the presidential council for all military affairs – thereby removing them from the direct control of the president.[149] During this period, Nasser attempted to bring senior military appointments under the control of the Presidential Council, but was forced to make a volte-face when Amer threatened to resign.[150] Under Decree 162/1962, the army was given a separate budget independent from that of the Ministry of War[151] transforming the minister himself into a sort of aide-de-camp of the commander-in-chief. Indeed, Presidential Decree 1956/1966 stipulated that 'the minister of war [. . .] shall assist the commander-in-chief of the armed forces in the exercise of his powers, and shall be responsible to him for whatever administrative or military aspects of the affairs of the armed forces that [the commander-in-chief] may delegate to him'.[152] A close organizational relationship developed between the minister of war, the various intelligence organizations and the Ministry of Local Government, allowing for the imposition of military control in the provinces. A similarly close relationship developed between the Ministry of War and many other parts of the state on the pretext of benefiting from officers' expertise: public companies, for example, and embassies. Fawzi even claims that the army took control of secondary schools and university faculties by appointing members of the National Guard as de facto political commissars.[153] The president had a say only in the promotion of generals and lieutenant generals; all other appointments were the exclusive purview of Amer and the minister of war.

Amer was vice-president of the republic (a political position), general commander and deputy supreme commander of the armed forces. He was personally responsible for Decree 367/1966, which set out the powers of the minister of war.

In 1966, Law 25/1966 on military service was introduced, which among other things empowered the military police to arrest any civilian involved in a dispute with a soldier and refer him to a military court for trial. Even before that, in 1965, the army had used all of its resources – including the

---

[148] Ibid., 32.
[149] Ibid., 36.
[150] Hamroush, *Witnesses*, 229, from the testimony of Abdel Latif Boghdadi. Sadat claims that at the same time, Nasser flirted with the idea of removing Amer from direct command of the army, but that Amer rejected this proposal out of hand and Nasser was forced to reconsider (*In Search of Self*, 172–3).
[151] The Ministry of War became the Ministry of Defence in 1979, after the peace deal was signed with Israel.
[152] Fawzi, *The Three-Year War*, 37–8.
[153] Ibid.

Military Criminal Police, which had branches in most governorates – to conduct judicial investigations into the Muslim Brotherhood, which the minister of war oversaw personally.[154] After the 1967 defeat, however, the Military Criminal Police were abolished and the military courts' jurisdiction over civilians removed in an amended version of the law.

The exclusive club to which army officers belonged saw its fair share of internecine strife. Many of the officers' memoirs describe a struggle between Nasser and Amer for control of the state, with each side trying to demonstrate the other's incompetence and expose counter-revolutionary conspiracies. The Military Intelligence Service, for example, uncovered an ostensible Brotherhood conspiracy against the regime, which it used as proof of the incompetence of the General Investigations Service, which did not answer to the army and was run by 'civilian' officers.[155] Some 30,000 Islamists were rounded up, 250 of whom died under torture. This entire period, it is generally agreed, saw a massive expansion of arbitrary detentions, repression and torture, whether in military prisons or elsewhere.

Another feature of this struggle was Amer's success in 1966 in pressuring Nasser to replace Prime Minister Zakaria Mohieddin with Sedki Sulayman, in whose government the number of officers rose from around one-third to more than half of the cabinet. Mohieddin had warned Nasser that 'in Egypt there are two states: the army and the government'.[156]

The rivalry between Nasser and Amer also appeared in the build-up to the Six-Day War. It was Amer who gave the order to mass troops in Sinai on 14 May 1967; naturally inclined towards brinksmanship and escalation, he was also desperate to improve both the image of the army (after its conduct in Yemen) and his own image (after the collapse of the UAR, for which he was often blamed domestically). Salah Nasr, generally defensive of Amer, says that troops were mobilized at random, with the main object being a display of force for domestic consumption.[157] He also says that Amer had been planning to close the Gulf of Aqaba since 1966. Fawzi agrees that the closure of the Straits of Tiran and the military escalation were Amer's idea, running directly contrary to Nasser's promises to U Thant that commercial shipping would not be harmed. He also claims that while Nasser was convinced that an Israeli attack would take place on 5–6 June at the latest, Amer was unconvinced, going ahead with his plan to visit Sinai during that period and ignoring the risk of an offensive.[158] Howeidi, meanwhile, says that the so-called Taher Plan for war with Israel existed

---

[154] Ibid., 42.
[155] Kandil, *Soldiers, Spies, and Statesmen*, 75.
[156] Ayubi, *The Centralized State*, 118.
[157] Imam, *Memoirs*, 205.
[158] Fawzi, *The Three-Year War*, 122–4.

only on paper: the Egyptian army had not been trained to carry it out, and it was not based on any credible Military Intelligence.[159] Egypt was not set up to receive Military Intelligence, in fact, even from the early warning station in Ajloun, in Jordan, which alerted Cairo to the incoming Israeli fighters. The Israeli attack on 5 June destroyed 85 per cent of Egypt's fighter planes and most of its air defence capacity. By 8 June, Gaza and Sinai were under Israeli occupation, as were the West Bank and the Golan Heights.

The crushing defeat and the chaotic retreat from Sinai came as a complete shock to the Egyptian public. The war had not only revealed shortcomings in the army's command structure, planning and organization.[160] It had shown the weakness of the regime itself and the hollowness of its slogans. This was traumatic, not only for Egyptians but for the Arab world as a whole.

Nasser's dramatic decision to tender his resignation, and his equally dramatic withdrawal of that resignation under popular pressure, was followed immediately by a crackdown on the army. The SCAF was dissolved and its members fired along with eighteen other senior officers. Nasser placed responsibility for the defeat with the officer corps, and in particular Amer.

Amer refused Nasser's suggestion that he become vice-president and step down from his military role. On 25 August, as part of a coordinated plan between Nasser, Interior Minister Shaarawi Gomaa, Secretary to the President for Intelligence Sami Sharaf and new minister of war Amin Howeidi, Amer was summoned to Nasser's house in Manshiyya, where he was detained and placed under house arrest. He committed suicide the next day. The heads of the three service branches then submitted their resignations to Nasser, who accepted them immediately. Other senior officers were cashiered off. According to Salah Nasr, the task of purging any remaining supporters of Amer from the army was entrusted to Fawzi, Zakaria Mohieddin and Sami Sharaf.[161]

Howeidi identifies the night of Amer's arrest as the beginning of Sadat's campaign against the 'centres of power'. When Sadat took over the presidency, he remembered the conspiracy against Amer and perhaps feared that they would do the same to him – he had, after all, been present at the meeting where Amer was arrested. Howeidi further claims that Sadat was the only person saddened by Amer's fall, since 'he was the only member of the RCC who socialized with Amer, and received large quantities of money from him in secret'.[162]

---

[159] Howeidi, *Lost Opportunities*, 75.
[160] In this context, Fawzi wrote that the many of the Egyptian officers were in key positions based on loyalty and not on merit. Fawzi, 53.
[161] Imam, *Memoirs*, 174.
[162] Ibid., 120–31.

After 1967, Nasser criticized the 'intelligence state' and blamed it for the defeat.[163] Salah Nasr, head of the intelligence apparatus, was sentenced to life imprisonment for conspiring against the regime with Amer (as well as a separate fifteen-year sentence for abuse of power). Sadat was later to release him. In fact, Nasser was seizing the opportunity to take control of and depoliticize the army, which under Amer had been a consistent thorn in his side. This was not democratization: there was no concurrent strengthening of civilian institutions or the rule of law. The only effect of his critique of the intelligence state was to bring it, and all other institutions, under the control of the presidency, where it would become even stronger.

Howeidi, who after a brief spell as minister of war became head of GIS, describes the brief transitional period between the 1967 defeat and Nasser's death in bleak terms:

> I saw for myself how big a catastrophe the country was facing. [...] The military had been operating outside the borders and framework of the state, with no oversight. [...] The defeat was a defeat of military leadership and not at all of the army itself. [... The army] had involved itself in other things far beyond its purview.[164]

The essential structural problem was lack of political oversight, in addition to corruption and outmoded practice and equipment.

The 'corrective' measures taken under Sadat, however, not only failed to separate the army from the political leadership (the president and the minister of war). In fact, they brought the military completely under political control, and not only in the sense of being subordinated to the political echelon; political considerations also beginning to obstruct the professionalism of the military, interfering in decisions of an entirely operational character. In 1967, Nasser had shied away from challenging Amer and allowed the military to slip out of civilian control. In 1973, on the other hand, the conduct of the war was to be entirely dependent on amateur decisions made by Sadat.[165]

Stage 2: The army subordinated to the president

On 20 January 1968, shortly after his appointment as commander-in-chief, Mohammed Fawzi was also named minister of war (replacing Amin Howeidi). For the first time, the minister of war was to be more than just head of the commander-in-chief's clerical staff. At around the same time,

---

[163] Kandil, *Soldiers, Spies, and Statesmen*, 43.
[164] Howeidi, *Lost Opportunities*, 9.
[165] Ibid., 11.

Law 4/1968 set out the new (and still extant) structure of the Egyptian armed forces. After the president and the NDC, the minister of war and the SCAF were now at the top of the military hierarchy – above the general staff. This system was to continue until after the January 2011 revolution.

The new army command was made up of a generation of men who had not been involved in the Free Officer movement – professionals, not revolutionaries. A new strategic partnership was established with the USSR, which involved both close cooperation and military support (weapons, training and advisers). The Soviet presence jumped from 3,000 technical advisers in 1967 to 15,000 in 1970 and 20,000 in 1972.[166] The army was being rebuilt in readiness for the coming battle for Sinai.

In 1968, the lenient sentences handed down to the commanders of the air force (after an official campaign of criticism, bordering on incitement, that found them responsible for the defeat) triggered a wave of protests. Armament workers in Helwan and students in Cairo and Alexandria poured out onto the streets, first in February and again in November. While the students were certainly influenced by the student revolution then ongoing in Europe, their main grievance was the defeat of 1967; they wanted accountability for those responsible – including the security state – and democracy. Sadat, then speaker of the People's Assembly, invited student representatives to a meeting, but those who attended and expressed their views were arrested as soon as the meeting concluded, despite promises of a safe forum to air their opinions.

On 30 March, Nasser issued a statement that marked a sea change in official political discourse, adopting a reformist tone and criticizing previous mistakes. But the 99.98 per cent of votes that this statement received in a subsequent referendum showed that beyond adopting a language rooted in people's aspirations, little had changed within the structure of the regime. While using democratic language, the state still condemned anyone who sought actual democracy.

In 1969, a NDC was set up, consisting of the president, the interior and foreign affairs ministers, the heads of the intelligence agencies and other strategic bureaucrats. On 3 March, Nasser announced the fall of the intelligence state: from now on, the different intelligence and security agencies would stick to their respective jurisdictions (domestic or foreign). There were to be no essential changes to surveillance or the restriction of freedoms. The ASU was given control over appointments to 367 public companies formerly dominated by Abdel Hakim Amer.[167]

---

[166] Kandil, *Soldiers, Spies, and Statesmen*, 95.
[167] Ibid., 92.

In the same year, the CSF were set up under the Interior Ministry to deal with 'rioting', allowing the military to distance itself from repression. The CSF was made up of the least-qualified army conscripts and would later start taking on those who had been rejected by the army. It soon became an army in its own right, with 100,000 recruits by the beginning of Sadat's tenure, and grew continuously. And it was a cheap army: its members were poorly paid and often unable to make ends meet.[168] Alongside the CSF and other official organs, the Ministry of Interior came to rely more and more heavily on informers and petty thugs (*baltagiyya*), some of whom were paid employees. In the countryside, where the police had less of a presence, it relied on a system of village headmen ('*umdas*), who linked the state and the various administrative structures ordering daily life, particularly conscription.

Sadat continued the process of 'demilitarizing' the state after the fall of Amer and his officers. If we look at the history of the July Republic from this perspective, we find that the transition from one stage to another is often marked by a change in the relationship between army and presidency. Under Mubarak, this can be observed through reading the balance between the army and presidency in light of the growing power of other influential forces – businessmen, the Interior Ministry's security forces – and interpreting the army's behaviour on the eve of the 2011 revolution through this lens.

One way of looking at modern Egyptian history is to see it as a struggle for influence between different institutions, in particular the army.[169] Hazem Kandil explains Sadat's behaviour through his desire to maintain and bolster political authority vis-à-vis the army, since he complained that under Nasser a new coup attempt was discovered every six months. He extends this to the army's behaviour during the January revolution, which he sees as an attempt to restore its influence after its long attenuation under Mubarak. This interpretation has been repeated by many authors.

Raymond Hinnebusch says that of the core of the Nasser-era ruling elite, only some eight former officers remained in place under Sadat.[170] The

---

[168] It is difficult to precisely estimate the number of CSF personnel. Mansour el-Essawy, a minister of interior after the January revolution, claimed in a TV interview that some 290,000 conscripts were 'borrowed' from the army and spread out across the CSF and other units, with only 118,000 going to the CSF specifically. See the interview posted on *YouTube*, 23 February 2012, Available online: https://bit.ly/32rDY0E (accessed 25 October 2021). The same figure was given by former interior minister Habib el-Adly at his trial in June 2020. See: *Al-Masry Al-Youm*, 2 June 2012, Available online: https://bit.ly/30Azlms (accessed 17 October 2021). AbdelLatif El-menawy, meanwhile, claims that the CSF had 175,000 conscripts at its disposal, but that Adly liked to encourage misconceptions and exaggerations. See: AbdelLatif El-menawy, *The Last Days of Mubarak's Regime: 18 Days* [Arabic] (Cairo: al-Dar al-Misriyya al-Lubnaniyya, 2012), 124.

[169] Kandil, *Soldiers, Spies, and Statesmen*, 156.

[170] Abdullah, 'The Armed Forces', 13; Raymond A. Hinnebusch, *Egyptian Politics under Sadat: The Post-Populist Development of an Authoritarian-Modernizing State* (Cambridge, Cambridgeshire;

number of military men also decreased noticeably in Sadat's cabinets.[171] But this did not mean that civilians were becoming more powerful – only that the president's own influence was growing at the expense of the army.

Sadat's expulsion of the Soviet advisers in July 1972 was followed by his dismissal of then Minister of War Mohamed Sadek on 26 October 1972. This was a year before the war, and ushered in a period of intense suspicion of the army during its preparations for battle.[172] Sadek was replaced by Ahmad Ismail, and Ahmed Tawfiq Ismail was appointed as head of the GIS. The army command was repeatedly changed during the period leading up to and immediately following the war. Once he was sure of Ismail's loyalty, Sadat excluded Saad El Shazly, who had become very popular after leading the crossing of the canal. After Ismail's death in late 1974, he appointed Abdel Ghani al-Gamasy to replace him. When the impending Camp David Accords required a more flexible leadership, he replaced him again with Kamal Hassan Ali.

By declaring war on Israel, Sadat hoped to force it to accept a peace initiative that would include withdrawal from Sinai. This meant that the war was, in effect, a question of crossing the Suez Canal. This limited war goal made it possible for the Israeli forces to cross to the western side of the canal. Despite an ineffectual air attack, however, the army managed to take the canal and secure the Bar Lev line.[173]

In the case of Anwar Sadat, the personal factor played a fundamental role, and at the beginning of his tenure he retreated from Nasser's inclinations even before his shake-up of political organizations and institutions. The best example of this was his famous 1971 peace initiative,[174] which would have involved the reopening of the Suez Canal to shipping and Israel's withdrawal a few kilometres to the east, with a few symbolic Egyptian troops stationed on the eastern bank. A situation of this kind was ultimately the aim of the October War. Sadat intended to start negotiations from an advanced position, where he expected Israeli forces to stop. But the latter did not comply with Sadat's plan, and took advantage of US information

---

New York: Cambridge University Press, 1985), 94–5.
[171] Mark Cooper provides statistics on this in Mark Cooper, 'The Demilitarization of the Egyptian Cabinet', *International Journal of Middle East Studies* 14, no. 2 (May 1982): 210.
[172] Sirrs, *A History of the Egyptian Intelligence Service*, 126.
[173] In the course of 1973 war, it is worth mentioning that the Egyptian forces stopped 10–12 kilometres east of the Suez Canal on 8 October. Israel launched a counteroffensive on the Syrian front, meaning that the Egyptian pause took place at the worst moment for the Syrian front. When Egyptian forces resumed their offensive on 14 October, it was too late, and the chance of surprise had been dashed. Strangely, Egypt informed the United States of its plan to stop the attack, and there is no doubt that the United States passed this information on to Israel, which facilitated its plans on the northern front, knowing that it was fighting at the time on one front.
[174] Howeidi, *Lost Opportunities*, 32.

about the limited war to launch a counterattack once the Egyptian offensive was halted.

In the Aswan negotiations on 11 January 1974, Sadat agreed to the disengagement and separation of forces agreement. The agreement was signed on 17 January and implemented on 25 January.[175] The Suez Canal opened to navigation on 5 June 1975, diplomatic relations between Washington and Cairo were restored, and, in 1976, the United States allowed its companies to resume arms sales to Egypt.

Here is not the place to discuss the planning and consequences of the 1973 war in detail. What is important to us here is, first, that the canal crossing restored the army's lost prestige without restoring its direct political role, and second, that Sadat took the opportunity this presented to ally with the United States and come to a separate peace with Israel in order to take back Sinai. A great deal of financial and cultural capital was invested in populist propaganda doubling down on a chauvinistic Egyptian identity distinct from other Arabs, emphasizing the Pharaonic past alongside an Islamic element introduced by Sadat. After the 1973 war, other populist aspects were added that exploited Egypt's glories rhetorically to brand regime critics as traitors to Egypt itself. Disappointments and failures were consistently papered over by this hollow discourse of greatness.

At Camp David, too, Sadat offered concessions, driving three foreign ministers in four years to resign in protest at his conduct and his way of managing the relationship with the United States and the peace negotiations. Zbigniew Brzezinski believes that Sadat's main motivation was his personal image in Washington.[176]

After 1973 there were no more wars between Arab countries and Israel because of the separate peace signed by Egypt: all subsequent wars took place between Israel and Arab resistance movements, not states. Without Egypt, an Arab war was impossible. The peace was thus of great strategic importance to Israel, even putting aside the significance of official recognition from an Arab state – something Tel Aviv had been unable to secure after the 1948 war.

Drawing back for a moment from the details of Sadat's disputes with the officer corps over his military policies and his approach to negotiations and look at the big picture, it is clear that he systematically sidelined the generals who participated in the war. Indeed, on the eve of Camp David, not a single one still held a command. Shazly's calls for the army to 'rise up against the dictator' met with silence within the armed

---

[175] Ibid., 425.
[176] Kandil, *Soldiers, Spies, and Statesmen*, 153–6.

forces.[177] With the marginalization of Abdel Ghani al-Gamasy and his colleagues two weeks after the signing of the accords, the face of the army was completely changed. None of the generals were present at the signing of the peace treaty.

These continuing changes further weakened the army and its position, precluding any possible transformation of the army into a political force within the regime. Sadat worked to marginalize the army and the officers in ministerial appointments, too, with the number of officer-ministers markedly reduced during his tenure. The military budget was also slashed after 1973, especially after the peace agreement with Israel. This trend was to continue under Mubarak: in 1976, the defence budget stood at 13 per cent of GDP, but by 2009 it was only 2 per cent.[178]

Presidential Decree 35/1979 granted all officers who had participated in the 1973 war military privileges as advisers, though it also retired them from military service and barred them from party politics. With Law 127/1980, Sadat also reduced the military service obligations of Egyptians with postgraduate degrees to a single year in order to encourage them to enter the labour market (as opposed to one to two years for those holding undergraduate degrees and around three for those with no education or qualifications).

After the reduction of the military budget and the shift in the army's doctrine, the regime allowed the army to engage in new functions (including income-generating business activities) that would allow it to maintain its strength and privileges. A new minister of defence was appointed, former military attaché in Washington Abdel Halim Abu Ghazala. Abu Ghazala would oversee a massive expansion in the army's civilian and economic activities as well as an unprecedented hike in salaries.

Some academics consider this a positive development; from their perspective, the army's financial independence is a major achievement. After the signing of the peace accords, the army faced two thorny problems: it needed to reduce its numbers and change its doctrine, and it also needed to maintain its prominent role in the relationship between state and society. The first problem was solved by technological and organizational innovations imported from the West. The second involved the integration of the army into the state's development initiatives. The minister of defence was made part of the Higher Policy Committee, and the army was given the

---

[177] Saad El Shazly, *The October War* [Arabic] (Paris: Arab Nation Foundation, 1980), 101.

[178] Under Sisi, military spending has continued to fall, from 1.7 per cent of GDP in 2015 to 1.24 per cent in 2018. See: Stephen H. Gotowicki, 'The Military in Egyptian Society', in *Egypt at the Crossroads: Domestic Stability and Regional Role*, ed. Phebe Marr (Washington, DC: National Defense University Press, 1999), 116–17; *World Bank*, 'Military expenditure (% of GDP) – Egypt, Arab Rep.', Available online: https://bit.ly/32baaoT (accessed 15 September 2020).

right to open private bank accounts to deposit income from development projects, gradually assuming responsibility for the implementation of a range of different projects.[179] Officers also retained significant positions in other state bodies, including those of local government.

The influence of the Interior Ministry also rose steadily under Sadat and Mubarak. Particularly prominent under Sadat were Mamdouh Salem and Al Nabawi Ismail, policemen who became interior ministers. Nonetheless, the security forces were never able to secure decisive victory in major crises on their own. During the January 1977 uprising, the army agreed to intervene. It was this experience that produced the CSF plan for dealing with major unrest, the same plan that was used (unsuccessfully) in January 2011.

After the peace agreement, the interior minister became the number one domestic strongman after the president, a tendency that only increased under Mubarak, when the state became a security state. But this was only the case because the regime had succeeded in ousting the army from politics, or striking a deal with it to keep it out of politics. The army remained the major force in the state, but it was a force that was politically inactive. Its strength was made clear every time that the internal security services failed to suppress unrest on their own: 1977, 1986 and 2011. Once granted financial independence and various privileges by Mubarak, the military was happy to leave politics to others. The space it left behind was filled by the security forces and the NDP, which increasingly came under the influence of businessmen; the ruling family was the link that bound them all together.

Stage 3: Historic pact and independent army

In 1972 Mubarak was commander of the air force and deputy minister of war. Sadat chose him to be his deputy in 1975 because he was level headed and had no designs on the presidency. Minister of Defence Abdel Halim Abu Ghazala, on the other hand, was a powerful and active figure who had improved the army's pay and uniforms. Despite having played an important role in bringing Mubarak to power, his relationship with the future president was a tense one.

In 1983, after becoming president, Mubarak embarked on a reshuffle of senior military positions without consulting Abu Ghazala. In 1984 he banned officers from joining political parties, possibly to preclude Abu Ghazala from becoming an influential member of the NDP. The defence

---

[179] Gihad Ouda, 'The Military Establishment and Foreign Policy under President Mubarak, 1981–1987' [Arabic], in *The Army and Democracy in Egypt* [Arabic], ed. Ahmad Abdullah (Cairo: Sina Publishing, 1990), 57–78.

minister was a prominent public figure, regularly appearing in the media and taking pains to present himself as a pious man during interviews.

The army continued to be excluded from politics until 1986, when the regime found itself in pressing need of its support during a CSF mutiny, which the army suppressed quickly and violently. For a while, it looked as if Abu Ghazala might be about to mount a coup,[180] and indeed, the minister seemed – right up until his dismissal – like an unstoppable force. He had close ties to the United States, where he had served as military attaché, and at the same time was popular with Islamists because of his apparent conservatism (and his wife never appeared in public without her headscarf).[181]

But Abu Ghazala did not seize the opportunity to launch a coup. In fact, the exact opposite happened: Mubarak effectively carried out a coup against his minister of defence. In 1989, after the Israeli newspaper *Yedioth Ahronoth* published a story about Abu Ghazala's possible prosecution in the United States for smuggling missile parts out of the country, Mubarak promptly dismissed him from his position and made him a presidential aide, a position with no power or influence from which he was to resign in 1993.

After a two-year spell under Youssef Sabri Abu Taleb, the ministry was taken over by Field Marshal Mohammed Hussein Tantawy, whose equanimity and dislike for the spotlight made him the polar opposite of Abu Ghazala. Tantawi was to remain in his post until after Morsi's election. This long tenure is indicative of the army's status and its relationship to the presidency, which combined loyalty with relative independence. Abu Ghazala laid the foundations of this relationship.

In 1987, Abu Ghazala set forth the army's basic strategic principles: maintaining 'military balance in relation to surrounding countries and deterrence' in order to 'preserve the independence of the state, the safety of its territory, and the security of its borders, coasts, territorial waters and economic interests'.[182] Eight years later, Tantawi added 'protection of the domestic front' and dealing with natural disasters.[183]

In the mid-1970s, the military budget was some 33 per cent of GDP, but by 1980 it had fallen to 19.5 per cent, then to 11 per cent by the mid-1990s and a mere 2.2 per cent by 2010. Early on in this process, the army started

---

[180] Robert Springborg, 'The President and the Field Marshal: Civil-Military Relations in Egypt Today', *MERIP* 17, no. 147 (July/August 1987).
[181] For example, in the newspaper *al-Shaab*, 14 October 1984, Mohamed Abd Elkodos complains that TV stations have refused to air an interview with Abu Ghazala affirming the importance of faith in the army and refusing to attack Islamists. Ironically enough, many of the traits that won Abu Ghazala the support of the Islamists – pious language, prayer, a wife who wore a veil – were subsequently to endear Abdel Fattah El-Sisi to President Morsi, and seem to have encouraged the latter to appoint Sisi as minister of defence.
[182] Kechichian and Nazimek, 'Challenges to the Military in Egypt', 128.
[183] Ibid.

looking for new ways of funding itself in order to guarantee a suitable lifestyle for its officers. Abu Ghazala's tenure saw the armed forces become more and more involved in civilian economic activity, ostensibly because it was contributing to the state's development plans.

In 1986 the Egyptian media saw a heated debate, lasting more than two months, over the role of the army and the military budget. Despite Mubarak personally intervening in defence of the army, it was difficult to believe that a debate of this kind could have gone ahead without the president's tacit support, likely to pressure Abu Ghazala by reducing his budget.[184]

The presidency continued to encourage opposition voices to criticize certain influential figures within the regime, allowing a broader margin of expression to do so – not for democratic reasons, but because Mubarak wanted to get rid of or indirectly show his displeasure with these figures. Generally speaking, the critics themselves did not know why they were suddenly allowed to voice their complaints, although in some rare cases there was direct collaboration.[185] Some criticized the army's attempts to independently meet officers' housing, health and education needs by expanding into the construction sector, while others defended it on the grounds that it contributed to development and insulated the army from market pressures.[186] The existence of a special military public sector was thus justified with socialist language even as the state itself was moving towards market capitalism. But in truth there was no contradiction between the capitalism of the state elite, and the 'socialism' of the military: behind the socialist rhetoric was nothing but the corporate privileges of a segment of the ruling elite. And this 'private public-sector' would soon acquire a near monopoly over the capitalist marketplace, using its political and symbolic capital to acquire vast amounts of property and take over a broad swathe of the consumer trade not just of the armed forces, but society as a whole.

Steven Cook argues that in Egypt, as in Algeria and Turkey, the army's core interests are the economy, foreign and security policy, the political and state apparatus, and nationalism. In all three countries, the army has emphasized economic independence as a path to growth and state-driven development. When each country began to liberalize its economy in the 1970s, however, its army showed more concern for its own economic

---

[184] Ibid., 134.
[185] It was therefore not surprising to have heard so many fervently patriotic voices expressing ardent concern about the democratic transition and elected bodies after the January revolution only to have it revealed after the 2013 coup that they were collaborating with the security services. Such people were instruments deployed in the regime's factional conflicts and to cast aspersions on adversaries' objectives by accusing them of foreign collaboration and the like.
[186] Cf. an article by Ahmed Fakhr in *al-Gomhuria*, 2 January 1985.

interests than for development itself.[187] In all three states, the army has maintained strong ties with the United States.

Under Mubarak, a major accommodation was reached that made the minister of defence the strongman exclusively within the army. Officers developed as a political entity whose purpose was to preserve the army's privileges and economic interests and the many government offices held by retired officers. The business of governing the country in cooperation with the security forces and the other domestic institutions was left to the president. None of this meant that the army was no longer the dominant power. It was still capable of making major shows of force when necessary and remained very popular with the public precisely because of its non-involvement in politics – which, along with the veil of secrecy that covered its operations, allowed it to present itself (somewhat disingenuously) as a 'clean' alternative to the security forces, the ruling family and the NDP. It was generally considered very unlikely that the army would make any attempt to seize power, in part because 'it was already at the top' in real terms.[188] This was not quite right: there is a difference between being powerful and influential and governing. When it looked like a coup was in the works in the late 1980s, Ahmad Abdullah wrote that most Egyptians would have been willing to accept a military autocracy capable of achieving a degree of discipline and order because 'the democratic experience did not rest on a broad base. The [real] political force was a group of elites absorbed in a battle of political slogans [. . .] which the vast majority of the population had no time for.'[189] As long as a political accommodation allowed it to maintain its privileges, the army had no interest in launching a coup, but if it had, Egyptian society would have been willing to accept it, because Egyptians were living under an autocratic regime anyway. The limited intra-elite pluralism permitted by the regime had neither expanded rights and freedoms nor improved participation in decision making, nor driven human development and social justice. Under such conditions, much of society – suffering as a result of the regime's policies – may come to prefer the sort of organized authoritarianism produced by a military coup to a more fragile authoritarianism providing an ineffectual and discredited margin of pluralism.

Cook repeats the claim that the army had no need to intervene because it was the real power in the country even if it did not govern directly. He says that this was the case in Egypt, Algeria and Turkey until the turn of the twenty-first century.[190] This conclusion is not quite right: from the

---

[187] Steven A. Cook, *Ruling but not Governing: The Military and Political Development in Egypt, Algeria, and Turkey* (Baltimore: Johns Hopkins University Press, 2007), 19.
[188] Abdullah, 'The Armed Forces', 24–5.
[189] Ibid., 26.
[190] Ibid.

1967 defeat onwards through Sadat's tenure, the government had total control over the army. Under Mubarak, a settlement was reached that reordered the relationship between them. The army was granted extensive privileges and functions in order to keep it content and out of politics.

Mubarak was genuinely very careful to maintain this relationship with the army. Even when Abu Ghazala's power was at its height, Mubarak retained control of senior military appointments. He was forced to make concessions after the CSF mutiny, dismissing Abu Ghazala's rival Ahmed Rushdi from the Interior Ministry, but he quickly followed this up by dismissing Abu Ghazala himself.

For the same reasons, Mubarak was careful to preserve the army's image. After the special forces' disastrous showing in the 1985 EgyptAir hijacking led to the death of half the hostages, Minister of Information Safwat El-Sherif worked hard to downplay the deaths and cast the botched operation as a victory, drawing on a mixture of spin and the pious patriotism often invoked under Mubarak. The Mubarak-era media establishment proved adept at casting any criticism of the regime as an attack on the national achievements of the Egyptian people – an approach that was briefly exposed and defanged by the January revolution before its enthusiastic readoption with the army's return to power.

Robert Springborg notes the massive scope of the army's commercial projects, which enjoyed such extensive government support that they came to represent a burden on the state budget, particularly after the broad liberalization initiatives of 2003.[191] The army seems to have been concerned that a wealth gap might develop that could be exploited by forces like the Muslim Brotherhood to stoke resentment against the regime.[192] The expansion of the armed forces' economic activity placed them in direct competition with the urban bourgeoisie, whom economic liberalization had allowed to expand into areas traditionally dominated by the public sector. Soon enough, however, this competition was checked by a growing network of common interests bringing together the two sides, including army tenders offered to private companies and full-scale partnerships.

The process that had begun with Abu Ghazala under the pretext of alternately protecting the army from the fluctuations of the market and contributing to national development thus ended with the establishment of a fully fledged parallel community, the so-called Officers' Republic. By the 2010s, the army's activities were estimated to account for some

---

[191] Springborg, 'The President and the Field Marshal', 148.
[192] Cook, *Ruling but Not Governing*, 89.

10–15 per cent of the $210 billion Egyptian economy.[193] According to a 2012 statement by Mahmoud Nasr, undersecretary to the minister of defence for financial affairs and a member of the SCAF, the size of the army's financial activities in 2011 stood at around $1 billion.[194] The actual figure is definitely much higher.

After the 25 January revolution, there was a risk that these privileges would be subject to parliamentary scrutiny. The military thus sought to retain its position above the law in order to preserve its influence and privileges, exploiting differences between the forces competing for power to avoid this eventuality. In the two rounds of discussion on the post-revolutionary constitution, the army sought to ensure that it contained articles providing not only for its privileges but its de facto independence from political oversight.

The Officers' Republic came to exercise exclusive control over the defence budget, US military aid and its own companies. It is important to note that this 'republic' was headed by a small clique of senior officers. The Egyptian military comprises about a million active duty conscripts and a half million reservists, and plays a key role in the formation and social integration of young Egyptian men, training about 80,000 new soldiers every year who remain in the reserves for nine years after completing their national service.[195] Although it has shrunk considerably since the peace accords, it remains a large army: in 1997, there were 440,000 Egyptians in active service with another 254,000 in reserve.[196] A source from 2020 suggests a total force of 468,500 men, including 45,000 officers.[197]

In contrast, by the end of the Mubarak era, the security forces (police, GIS, SSIS, CSF) employed a remarkable 1.5 million people, and the Interior Ministry had an annual budget almost three times that of the Defence Ministry.[198] Under Tantawi, the longest-serving defence minister in Egyptian history, the security forces emerged as a more important political player than the army. Tantawi's lengthy tenure was, of course, due to his loyalty to Mubarak and his preservation of the army's corporate interests. Yezid Sayigh suggests that the decision to keep Tantawi and other members of the SCAF in place long after they had passed retirement age was 'a

---

[193] Ivan Ivecovic, 'Egypt's Uncertain Transition', in *Egypt's Tahrir Revolution*, ed. Dan Tschirgi, Walid Kazziha and Sean F. McMahon (Boulder, CO: Lynne Rienner Publishers, 2013), 181. See also: Yezid Sayegh, 'Above the State: The Officers' Republic in Egypt', *Carnegie Endowment for International Peace*, 1 August 2012, Available online: https://bit.ly/3CmtHSI (accessed 12 November 2014).
[194] Kandil, *Soldiers, Spies, and Statesmen*, 183.
[195] Gotowicki, 'The Military in Egyptian Society', 107–9.
[196] Kechichian and Nazimek, 'Challenges to the Military in Egypt', 127.
[197] *Global Fire Power*, Available online: https://bit.ly/3heIpA5 (accessed 9 September 2020).
[198] Sayegh, 'Above the State'.

matter of regime stability – and the stability of what many have called the "Officers' Republic".[199]

After Sadat's assassination, both because of his conciliatory leanings and because his own legitimacy was rooted in his military service, Mubarak allowed the army more power – but this was social and economic, rather than political power. After 1991, he found himself expanding Abu Ghazala's approach, allowing the army to take an ever-larger role in the economy and society. He also made a habit of providing officers who had reached retirement age with comfortable civilian employment, allowing former military men to permeate almost every sphere of Egyptian life. Under Nasser, officers had been concentrated in the top jobs, but with Mubarak they began to proliferate at every level of the civil service and the private sector. Sayegh notes that as well as providing a regular income, this gave the army a degree of control over local government and the security forces without needing to dominate the cabinet. These appointments also gave senior officers control over the ACA, the agency responsible for rooting out corruption within the civil service.[200] This, alongside the invisible sources of income that appointments elsewhere offered, made retired officers a key part of a network of corruption that cut across the state and public sector.

From 1991 onwards, Tantawi oversaw the establishment of some twenty 'military cities' to house the officer corps, built by army companies far away from the hustle and bustle of overcrowded Cairo, setting off what was to become a trend among the entire Egyptian middle class. Officers' associations became de facto clubs offering a range of services and privileges to their members, with many of them providing retail space. The military acquired a vast empire of hotels, resorts and shopping centres serving the army and the upper classes.

The military also produced domestic appliances (including washing machines and heaters), stationery, food items, haulage trucks, helicopters and radar equipment – alongside weapons, which it made a lot of money exporting to Iraq during its war with Iran (1980–8). By the turn of the millennium, its manufacturing centres employed some 100,000 people and accounted for $500 million of Egypt's GDP. Its agricultural arm has sought to make the army 100 per cent self-sufficient with regard to agricultural production. Its income goes directly into the army's bank account; Law 39/1979 made military factories independent of the state budget, allowing them to set up independent accounts in commercial banks.[201]

---

[199] Ibid.
[200] Ibid.
[201] These figures were published in a study from 2003. See: Harb, 'The Egyptian Military in Politics', 285–6. Egypt's military commercial projects fall under three main bodies: the Ministry of Military Production, established by Nasser in 1954 to help Egypt achieve self-sufficiency in arms

The military economy and the Officers' Republic are all that remains of the once-extensive public sector state – a state within a state that no longer intervenes directly in politics and leaves the business of government to civilians. But the extreme economic liberalization that began in the second period of Mubarak's rule, particularly with the rise of Gamal Mubarak and his circle of businessmen and economists, led to a covert and then overt battle between two economies, two visions, two elites: the army-dominated 'public sector' and the economic liberalism championed by a new stratum of businessmen loyal to the ruling family and influential in the NDP.

Hazem Kandil argues that the Mubarak regime underwent a transformation from a military regime to a police or security state and that this explains some of the success of the January revolution, which the army refused to crush.[202] I would argue that the failure of the democratic transition in Egypt can be attributed to the same factor: that rather than competing with other institutions, the army threw in its lot with the judiciary and the security forces to prevent the consolidation of an elected regime that might usher in a new elite and bring these institutions firmly under civilian control.

Many failed to predict a revolution in Egypt because they believed that the army ruled the country. The reality was that by 25 January 2011 the army had been excluded from the government, but remained a powerful (if politically quiescent) part of the state enjoying near-total autonomy. Despite many claims to the contrary, the regime was not homogeneous. For example, the intense privatization that took place under the influence of an ascendant Gamal Mubarak had begun to undermine the Egyptian military economy and the interests of the army elite more generally. The deleterious effects of neoliberal policy and fear of a clique of businessmen running the country hand in hand with the security forces produced a great deal of resentment within the military. It is thus no surprise that it refused to ride to Mubarak's rescue as he faced down a popular revolution in January 2011.

---

production, which oversees the management and operation of twenty companies; the Ministry of Defence, which controls dozens of companies; and the Arab Manufacturing Authority, founded in 1975, owned by the Egyptian government and responsible for about a dozen companies that manufacture mechanical and electronic products. Estimates vary on the size of the military's role in Egypt's economy, with some economists estimating it at around 3 per cent of GDP. The World Bank estimated that Egypt's GDP was about $332.92 billion in 2016 and $303.175 billion in 2019. Sisi claims that the military's share of national production is only 2 per cent. But some estimates place it much higher. See: *Reuters*, 16 May 2018, Available online: https://reut.rs/3ht2i6p (accessed 16 September 2020).

[202] Kandil, *Soldiers, Spies, and Statesmen*, 4.

2

Economic liberalization and political authoritarianism

I Mubarak: From a policy of appeasement to authoritarianism and economic liberalization

The three decades between the initial 'opening up' (*infitah*) of the Egyptian economy and the liberalization of the early twenty-first century are marked by such continuities that it is worth treating them as a single period, notwithstanding the changing domestic and international factors that influenced policy in the 1990s, such as the Gulf War, and during Mubarak's last years in power.

The *infitah* represented a retreat from three principles central to the Nasserist project: economic independence via the domestication of economic activity; ambitious five-year plans to develop the economy; and the redistribution of income and wealth by the state.[1] It began with a political and economic gamble that opening up to (and allying with) the United States would secure peace and the return of occupied Egyptian land and that opening the door to foreign and Arab capital would put an end to the regime's economic woes. Having liberalized the foreign investment regime under Law 65/1971, the government made its hopes for this wager clear in the priorities it set out in Law 43/1974: attracting Arab and foreign capital, incentivizing private–public partnerships with foreign investors and integrating Egypt into the world economy.

None of this was to be subordinated to higher development goals – improving industry and agriculture, for example, or any other development plan that might have incorporated foreign investment. Capital was to go wherever the winds of profit blew, even if that meant making a quick buck by semi-legal means at the expense of the broader economy and the public interest. Foreign investment thus remained limited, and the lion's share

---

[1] Galal Amin, *Egypt and the Egyptians under Mubarak, 1981–2011* [Arabic], 2nd edn (Cairo: Shorouk, 2011), 39.

went to the service sector or to manufacturing consumer products: of the 5 billion Egyptian pounds invested between 1974 and 1982, only 16 per cent of total investment came from outside the Arab world, rising to 33 per cent within the tourism sector.² A capitalism dependent on import–export offices and commercial agents soon emerged.³

The *infitah* coincided with a period of rising oil revenues after the 1973 war, and Egypt was thus able to export some of its social problems to the oil-producing countries via labour migration to the Gulf, Iraq and Libya. This helped, albeit unintentionally, to keep the steadily rising unemployment figures in check, with jobs abroad taking the place of those lost to privatization and a new rentier economy springing up around labour remittances. The projects established under Law 43, meanwhile, provided new jobs for less than 1.5 per cent of the workforce.⁴

Nor did economic liberalization succeed in solving the public sector's financial problems. In fact, it exacerbated them: in 1976, the government was forced to request debt rescheduling from the IMF, which was made conditional on restructuring measures, including an end to subsidies on essential goods.

When Mubarak came to power in 1981, oil revenues were at their height, and at first he took full advantage of this fact to pursue a more conciliatory policy. Domestic politics had been febrile since the uprising of 1977, and he hoped to still the troubled waters by distributing rents more widely (without any real retreat from the open-door policy pursued by his predecessor) and allowing a margin of political freedom (without any meaningful change to the authoritarian nature of the regime).

The changes that followed the 1977 uprising have been described as 'gradual and, in many cases, covert, particularly as regards the public sector and state subsidies'.⁵ The government promulgated laws only to reverse them, *said* but did not *do*. In early 1985, as oil prices fell and the fiscal crisis worsened, the government passed laws that were intended to cut imports, but only a few months later, it reversed the measure.⁶ Anticipated annual revenues from partial privatization never materialized. The whole period was characterized by 'a very gradual approach to any new decision that might disturb the [regime's] equilibrium, which sometimes meant

---

² Farah, *Egypt's Political Economy*, 38.
³ In 1974, the first year of the *infitah*, there were some 500 commercial agents representing foreign companies in Egypt. See: Izzeddin Abdelfattah, *Workers and Businessmen: Transformations of Political Opportunities in Egypt* [Arabic] (Cairo: Centre for Political and Strategic Studies, 2003), 43.
⁴ Farah, *Egypt's Political Economy*, 40.
⁵ Ibrahim al-Isawi, *The Egyptian Economy in Thirty Years: An Analysis of Macroeconomic Developments since 1974 and a Discussion of its Social Repercussions with an Alternative Development Outlook* [Arabic] (Cairo: al-Maktaba al-Akadimiyya, 2007), 104.
⁶ Ibid., 91.

reducing the pace of change and sometimes reversing decisions that had already been taken'.[7]

But by the late 1980s, with persistent structural problems and declining oil revenues exacerbating its foreign obligations, Egypt was forced to seek debt rescheduling from international organizations. Mubarak's short-lived policy of conciliation and equivocation was now replaced by creeping economic liberalization. In the twenty-first century, with the rise of Gamal Mubarak's neoliberal 'young wolves' within the NDP, this process would accelerate dramatically.

Mubarak's more generous distributive policy was accompanied by efforts to strengthen the security forces and cast his clientelist net wider, drawing the various wings of the elite more closely into the NDP. The Muslim Brotherhood was permitted to field slates of candidates in the elections (especially in the 1985 elections, the most 'open' of all those that took place under Mubarak) and to operate freely within the professional syndicates.

Mubarak took pains to keep the political elite happy. During his first two decades, he made very few changes even within his cabinet – far less than Nasser and Sadat, both of whom had been great reshufflers. His prime minister, Atef Sedky, remained in place from 1986 to 1996, the longest premiership since Egyptian independence. But when he felt that a minister represented a challenge to his authority, he did not hesitate to get rid of them, as we saw in the case of Abdel Halim Abu Ghazala.[8] In his early years, Mubarak sought to establish a broad power base within the NDP, disposing of powerful figures inherited from the Sadat era (especially the sleazier characters) and promoting conservative Nasserists and new men from the bureaucratic bourgeoisie to counterbalance the pro-Sadat faction.[9] He also reversed controversial laws from Sadat's final years in power, released thousands of prisoners, allowed professional syndicates and an ever rising number of NGOs to play a more active role, and reduced press censorship, allowing journalists to criticize senior officials, though the president remained a red line.

Although the ready availability of oil revenues in the first half of the 1980s made it possible to inaugurate 'a plethora of economic initiatives and programmes, most devoted to upgrading the country's ailing infrastructure',[10] these initiatives did not form part of a broader strategy for building a national economy. When Egypt was forced to accept IMF restructuring in the 1990s, it became obvious that Egypt had no national

---

[7] Abdelfattah, *Workers and Businessmen*, 47.
[8] Kassem, *Egyptian Politics*, 28.
[9] Fahmy, *The Politics of Egypt*, 64.
[10] Osman, *Egypt on the Brink*, 182.

programme of its own.¹¹ It had become a dependent country in both its foreign policy and economy.

Mubarak had no personal charisma. Instead, he relied on the security forces and on his policy of appeasement. The NDP continued to be central as a forum for regime stakeholders and as a link – via a complex web of interlocking rural and urban interests – between the regime and broader society.

The NDP had no clear and independent ideology. It was not a ruling party, but the party of the ruler, the president's party. It brought together a mixture of Nasserists (public sector technocrats and bureaucrats), Sadatists (open-door and private sector technocrats) and opportunists.¹² Throughout Mubarak's tenure, the party was pulled back and forth between forces seeking to accelerate liberalization and others desperate to protect the public sector.¹³ The regime itself vacillated under various domestic and international pressures, but ultimately the weakening of the public sector simply empowered crony capitalists, whose moment came in 2002 with the creation of the NDP Policies Committee headed by Gamal Mubarak. While the NDP had no ideology, no clear social base and no electoral legitimacy, what it did have was an extensive network of patron–client relationships. This network was particularly important in the countryside, where most wealthy smallholders, major landowners and village headmen were members of the NDP.¹⁴

The only organized competitor to the NDP, particularly in the countryside and the provincial cities, was the Muslim Brotherhood. During the second half of the 1980s, the Brotherhood was allowed to increase its presence both in the parliament and in the professional syndicates. In one of the strange paradoxes of the Mubarak regime, in the 1990s this relative weight forced a reversal of the earlier relaxation in security policy. Kassem argues that this drove many of the Islamist movements to adopt a terrorist strategy during this decade.¹⁵ It is important to note, however, that during this period many Islamist movements were moving towards violence anyway, driven by specific internal dynamics as well as regional developments, such as the return of the Afghan Arabs, the Gulf crisis and the Islamist revival.

In 1984, the Brotherhood won ten seats in the parliament in the freest and fairest elections to date. As a result, they began to focus more on electoral politics, advocating for an independent electoral commission.

---

[11] Ibid., 183.
[12] Fahmy, *The Politics of Egypt*, 65.
[13] Hisham D. Aidi, *Redeploying the State: Corporatism, Neoliberalism, and Coalition Politics* (New York: Palgrave Macmillan, 2009), 104.
[14] Fahmy, *The Politics of Egypt*, 65.
[15] Kassem, *Egyptian Politics*, 145.

By securing as much parliamentary representation as possible, they hoped to bolster their political legitimacy as well as influence decision making insofar as that was possible. But in 1990, the opposition boycotted the elections, and turnout fell below 20 per cent and even 10 per cent in some areas. The brief focus on national elections was redirected towards social action and professional syndicates.

The dismissal of Interior Minister Ahmed Rushdi in May 1986 and the appointment of Assiut governor Zaki Badr to replace him ushered in a much harsher policy on Islamists. This policy saw its fair share of violent reactions: Badr himself faced an attempt on his life in 1989, and the speaker of the People's Assembly, Rifaat el-Mahgoub, was assassinated a year later. Groups like EIJ and IG were already clashing with the security forces and carrying out violent actions in the late 1980s. But the broad campaign against tourists, secular intellectuals, Copts and politicians only began in earnest in 1992. In 1993, assassination attempts were made against the interior minister and the prime minister, with the latter taking the life of a primary school pupil. Targeted attacks on tourists reached their peak in 1997 with the killing of fifty-eight foreign visitors in Luxor.

The reform efforts that began in the mid-1980s, and the attempt to contain the Brotherhood between 1985 and 1988, thus ended with the resurgence of the security state. The limited margin of media freedom never developed into political liberalism or democracy, and reforms remained a matter of government fiat, to be advanced or rolled back whenever it suited its interest.[16] The regime did not fracture due to reforms from above as predicted by the models of democratic transition studies. It is worth noting, given everything that has happened since the January revolution, that the regime's retreat from reform dealt a serious blow to the current within the Brotherhood that favoured a more open-minded attitude, allowing the conservatives and the hardliners within the group to regain the initiative. After the death of the relatively pro-reformist General Guide Omar el-Telmesany in 1986, his successors Muhammad Hamid Abu al-Nasr (1986–96) and Mamun al-Hudaybi (2002–4) proved far more supportive of the conservative current,[17] and by January 2011, conservatives were firmly in control of the Brotherhood. We might also add that politically quiescent Salafist groups willing to defer to the regime became much more numerous during this period.[18]

---

[16] I have discussed this elsewhere at length in *The Arab Question: Introduction to an Arab Democratic Declaration* [Arabic] (Beirut: Centre for Arab Unity Studies, 2007), 219–42, in particular 232–3.

[17] Khalil al-Anani, 'The Muslim Brotherhood in the Post-Morsi Peiod' [Arabic], *Siyasat Arabiya*, no. 4 (September 2013): 17–23.

[18] Khalil al-Anani and Maszlee Malik, 'Pious Way to Politics: The Rise of Political Salafism in Post-Mubarak Egypt', *Digest of Middle East Studies* 22, no. 1 (Spring 2013): 60.

At the same time, the social base of jihadi Salafism, which had produced Sadat's assassins, was becoming more entrenched. Jihadi Salafists were contemptuous of other Salafists, accused secularists and even other Islamists of apostasy, and advocated overthrowing the regime, unlike quietist Salafists, who were happy to agitate against Christians and secularists and work towards the 'Islamization' of social life according to their understanding of Islam. Towards the end of Sadat's tenure and up to the end of the 1980s, Egyptian intelligence had encouraged Islamists to go off and fight in Afghanistan.[19] In the 1990s, however, they were forced to reap what they had sown when hundreds of 'Afghan Arabs' returned to Egypt with a new mentality and new organizational skills acquired from extensive field experience fighting against the Soviets.

The first signs of a change in attitude came in 1986, when increased restrictions were placed on mosques in Upper Egypt and attempts were made to break up the enthusiastic crowds that gathered to hear extremist sheikhs preach; some of the latter were placed under house arrest. But in the summer of 1987, the state launched what Kassem describes as an 'irrational' confrontation with the Islamists, arresting some 3,000 people, including many non-activists and women.[20] State measures only intensified in subsequent years, with Omar Abdel-Rahman, the leader of the Gama'a al-Islamiyya, deported in 1989 and a campaign of assassinations conducted against senior activists throughout 1990. All told, violent operations conducted by extremist Islamist organizations and by the state throughout the 1980s and 1990s left around 1,200 Egyptians and scores of foreign tourists dead. Victims included prominent cultural figures like the intellectual Farag Foda, who was killed by the Gama'a al-Islamiyya in 1992, and the renowned novelist Naguib Mahfouz, who was left permanently disabled by a failed assassination attempt in 1994. In the wake of a failed attempt on Mubarak's life in Ethiopia in 1995, the GIS become a far more central part of the security state, and Omar Suleiman, who had headed foreign intelligence during the 1991 Gulf War, became head of the agency.[21]

In the aftermath of the Luxor massacre in 1997, public opinion turned decisively against the armed Islamist groups, whose activities had undermined tourism and, in turn, the incomes of millions of Egyptians. This ultimately spurred a process of revision within some Islamist groups, and in March 1999 a unified declaration of Gama'a Islamiyya leaders abroad and in prison called for a ceasefire.

---

[19] Sirrs, *A History of the Egyptian Intelligence Service*, 140–1, 154.
[20] Kassem, *Egyptian Politics*, 151–3.
[21] Unlike the Interior Ministry's security forces, the GIS reports directly to the president and enjoys a close relationship with the CIA.

In July 1992, amendments were introduced to the Penal Code and the State Security courts law, which made it easier to hand down death sentences and introduced a very loose definition of terrorism, defined in part as 'any act of force or violence or threat or intimidation [...] thereof' that might 'impede public authorities' in the exercise of their powers. The government was now able to brand anyone who objected to its activities a terrorist and prosecute them – if necessary before a military court, since the pre-existing state of emergency gave the president the right to refer any criminal case to a military tribunal, a right reaffirmed by the SCC in 1993. By 2001, between 15,000 and 20,000 Islamists were being held in Egyptian prisons.

Throughout the confrontation, the government maintained an ambivalent attitude to the Brotherhood, which was vocally opposed to attacks on tourists and civilians as well as political assassinations. In 1995, the Brotherhood was allowed to field some 150 candidates in the legislative elections. By the time of the elections, however, sixty-four of them had been detained and referred to military courts, and only one Brotherhood candidate was ultimately elected after an extensive campaign of voter fraud and suppression.

George W. Bush's victory in the 2000 presidential election ushered in a period of sustained pressure on US allies to introduce democratic reforms, particularly after 11 September 2011, a message that Mubarak received in no uncertain terms during his humiliating visit to Washington DC in spring 2004. A series of conferences, including one in Alexandria, brought Arab leaders together to hold forth on the importance of democratic and economic liberalization. These conferences were largely hot air, performances intended to appease the United States. They also allowed regimes to reconcile with prominent cultural figures and liberals genuinely eager for reform. In February 2005, Mubarak introduced a freer electoral system, allowing the Brotherhood to win eighty-eight seats in the 2005 People's Assembly elections despite allegations of widespread fraud and intimidation. But in 2007, with the neoconservatives on their way out, judicial oversight of elections was rolled back, and there was nothing to stop the NDP from fixing the next round of voting in 2010.

All this exemplifies the paradox that I have alluded to elsewhere: Arab regimes have been rolling out tactical, top-down reforms on a regular basis since the mid-1980s, *without ever losing the initiative or the ability to reverse these reforms*, as is required by at least one major model of democratic transition. One of the most important reasons for this, in my view, is the fact that in regimes of this kind (usually called bureaucratic-authoritarian systems), elites simply cluster around the individual ruler, rather than forming distinct, stand-alone groupings of a kind that could split into camps of moderates and hardliners. With the repeated failure of reform, the river of change was ultimately redirected towards revolutionary action.

Some writers have characterized the January revolution as a mass movement seeking to accelerate the pace of reforms already initiated by Sadat and then Mubarak, following well-known models of democratic transition.[22] I disagree. The reforms did not split the ruling elite or give rise to a democratizing faction within the regime that relied on popular pressure to support its cause. In fact, reform entrenched a new kind of authoritarian regime, economically 'liberal' and offering citizens an elastic margin of political freedom that stretched or contracted as suited the regime's needs.

II State and society: From corporatism to clientelism

Clement Henry and Springborg characterize the Mubarak regime as a 'bully praetorian state', with loyalists tied to the regime by patron–client relationships based on the distribution of rents and an elite drawn from diverse social backgrounds. Because of its dependence on the state itself, it had little need to build broad social coalitions, but it also found it very difficult to pursue privatization.[23] But as a result of widespread privatization initiatives and Gamal Mubarak's alliance with capital outside the direct control of the security forces, this system was shaken to its core, leaving a marked imbalance in the regime and its established way of operating.

The regime allowed a restricted party pluralism and a certain kind of economic liberalism that functioned under the aegis of the authoritarian state, a market allied to the state – what I have already described as 'state liberalism'. Many of those who benefited from the market economy were part of the state apparatus. The freedom of the market was not based on civil or political rights rooted structurally in civil society and its relation to the state. Nor did it generate such rights. The elastic margin of rights and

---

[22] See, for example, Amel Ahmed and Giovanni Capoccia, 'The Study of Democratization and the Arab Spring', *Middle East Law and Governance* 6, no. 1 (2014): 20, 26–7. Compare with the pessimistic attitude of a contemporary observer of the reforms, who did not believe that they were likely to lead to democratic transition: Emad El-Din Shahin, 'Democratic Transformation in Egypt: Controlled Reforms . . . Frustrated Hopes', in *The Struggle over Democracy in the Middle East: Regional Politics and External Policies*, ed. Nathan Brown and Emad el-Din Shahin (London and New York: Routledge, 2010), 117–19.

[23] Clement M. Henry and Robert Springborg, *Globalization and the Politics of Development in the Middle East*, Contemporary Middle East, 2nd edn (New York: Cambridge University Press, 2010), 162–3.

freedoms allowed by the state could be stretched as far as was necessary to calm domestic tensions or mollify international pressure.

Scholars interested in the mid-twentieth-century shift towards modernization in Arab countries often use Weber's concept of the neo-patrimonial state, defined by Hafez Abdelrahim as 'a state model that, although it seeks to dispose of traditional leadership, replaces it with a personalized-privatized authoritarian alternative, thereby preventing any genuine movement towards the modern state'.[24] In a neo-patrimonial state, hierarchical authority operates on the principle of personal loyalty, whether on the political or the economic plane, and in fact separating these two is very difficult.[25] Patron–client relationships based on this principle extended to the most quotidian spheres of life, to the point that they are necessary even 'to guarantee access to essentials such as food, work, health and education'.[26] The state bureaucracy thus took the place of the pre-revolutionary notability, and the merchant class failed to evolve into a capitalist bourgeois independent of the state, in part because of the military regime and in part because of nationalization programmes. Even with the advent of economic liberalization, this class was unable to develop in this direction because it was inextricably linked with government contracting, corruption networks and relationships of personal loyalty to the state bureaucracy.

Some analyses have argued that for many reasons the new Arab bureaucracies cannot be described as 'rational'.[27] This is something of an exaggeration of what Weber meant by rational bureaucracy; moreover, although Arab bureaucracies subsequently became bloated and sluggish, they once spearheaded a thoroughgoing modernization of state and society. The problem of the authoritarian regime in Egypt as elsewhere is not that it was 'irrational' per se but that its authoritarian approach sometimes involved using tools that sat uneasily with bureaucratic rationality. Bureaucratic rationality is instrumental and has no necessary connection to democracy. Nevertheless, even according to its narrow definition as an approach to maximize efficiency, it is incompatible with relationships of personal loyalty.

Left critiques have often argued that privatization was the central problem of the Sadat era, but this is incorrect. Even in privatization, the

---

[24] Hafez Abdelrahim, *Political Clientelism in the Arab Society: A Socio-Political Reading of the National Structure in Tunisia* [Arabic] (Beirut: Centre for Arab Unity Studies, 2006), 257.
[25] Ibid., 260.
[26] Ibid., 264.
[27] Palmer et al.'s study of the Egyptian bureaucracy shows many of its institutional shortcomings. See: Monte Palmer, Ali Leila and El Sayed Yassin, *The Egyptian Bureaucracy* (Syracuse, NY: Syracuse University Press, 1988), 93–6, 109–14, 148–51.

regime relied heavily on the existing economic and security agencies and on the tangled web of patronage that had grown up between state and citizen. A similar web of patronage was established between the bureaucracy and the new capitalists, who depended on government contracting and licensing. The privatization initiatives of the twentieth century had very little effect on this dispensation, which remained in place well into the Mubarak era. It was not until the extensive privatizations of the early twenty-first century, driven by Gamal Mubarak's NDP Policies Committee, that the equilibrium was broken and discontent began to spread within certain parts of the regime.

Mubarak's tenure can be split into two periods. The first begins with his appointment to the presidency and ends at the beginning of the 1990s. The second comprises the rest of his time in office, from the 1990s to his resignation.

It was clear from very early on just how fragile economic liberalization would be under the public sector. Foreign debt dwarfed rentier income, a problem exacerbated by falling oil prices in the mid-1980s; towards the end of the decade, Egypt was forced to default on its debts. In fact, from the late 1980s, resort tourism on the Red Sea coast of Sinai developed rapidly, becoming a major source of foreign currency. As part of Mubarak's first five-year plan (1982–7), new laws were passed and new government entities set up to encourage the development of infrastructure in these areas, following through on many ideas dating from the final Israeli withdrawal from Sinai in the early 1980s. The financial crisis of the mid-1980s was exacerbated by this development plan. In 1989, full foreign ownership was made legal in some sectors, and in 1991 an office was set up specializing in tourism investment.[28] Ahmed Nazif, then the minister of communications and technology, was working very hard to improve communications infrastructure in the country, including internet infrastructure, and the Egyptian communications market registered the greatest growth of any in the Middle East.

At the same time, the political activities – and relative electoral successes – of the Islamist opposition, and its competing social support schemes, alarmed the regime and precipitated a return to a policy of confrontation beginning in the late 1980s. The rising influence of the Muslim Brotherhood in parliament and the professional associations, where they were particularly active, was a source of real concern for the government. At one point in the early 1990s, the Brotherhood held fourteen of the twenty-

---

[28] Thomas Richter and Christian Steiner, 'Politics, Economics and Tourism Development in Egypt: Insights into the Sectoral Transformations of a Neo-Patrimonial Rentier State', *Third World Quarterly* 29, no. 5 (2008): 948–9.

five seats on the board of the Egyptian Bar Association.[29] The concurrent bloody confrontation with the armed Islamists provided a pretext for reversing the policy of 'tolerating' the Brotherhood that had characterized the 1980s, and a wave of arrests followed. The regime's clashes with radical Islamists were invariably used to justify cutting an ascendant Brotherhood down to size. The limited electoral freedoms of the 1980s were replaced by police crackdowns at electoral junctures, banned and disqualified lists and candidates, and, ultimately, falsified results. Attempts to contain the different elites petered out, and repression and despotism became the refuge of a regime with only a tenuous social base, lacking any broad societal coalition to shore up its power, with the exception of the authoritarian and self-interested alliance between the civilian bureaucracy, the army leadership (itself increasingly coming to resemble a *military* bureaucracy) and disparate cliques of businessmen and traditional rural strongmen.

The first period of Mubarak's tenure came to an end with this resurgence of the security state and the implementation of IMF diktats. The IMF bailout of 1991 was made conditional on extensive structural adjustment measures (privatization and stabilization) accepted without modification by Cairo. A full half of Egypt's foreign debt burden was forgiven as a reward for siding with the United States during the Gulf War[30] and to encourage further economic liberalization and fiscal austerity.[31] Something of an economic boom followed, giving the regime a new lease on life, but this was due to the debt settlement rather than any growth in production. Even during this period, rents from the Suez Canal, oil and gas, and the sale of land to investors remained the basic sources of income for the economy. In order to bring Egypt into line with the IMF's conditions, the state pursued austerity policies targeting social security benefits and transfers, and health

---

[29] After the Brotherhood's strong performance in the professional associations, Law 100/1993 guaranteeing democracy in professional bodies imposed judicial oversight on association elections and set a lower limit of 50 per cent participation for results to be valid; if in a second round of voting 33 per cent of members did not participate, then the positions would be filled by judicial fiat. The Brotherhood's victories in the engineers' and pharmacists' associations (1987 and 1990) and the Bar Association (1992) had all been won in elections where less than 30 per cent of members voted. Other measures targeted the labour movement, making it impossible to establish a local union branch with less than 250 members – which more or less prevented the unionization of private sector workers, 96 per cent of whom worked in businesses with less than 250 employees. Eberhard Kienle, *A Grand Delusion: Democracy and Economic Reform in Egypt* (London and New York: I. B. Tauris, 2001), 85, 78–9.

[30] Former prime minister Kamal Ganzouri claims that Abu Ghazala played a central role in convincing the US administration to push for half of Egypt's debt to be forgiven. See: Kamal Ganzouri, *My Way: The Years of Patience, Confrontation and Solitude: From the Village to the Premiership* [Arabic] (Cairo: Shorouk, 2014), 80.

[31] Egypt's foreign debt reached $14.2 billion, $3.4 billion of which was forgiven in 1991. Any further forgiveness was made contingent on reforms: an end to fuel subsidies, a unified exchange rate, depreciation of the pound and reductions in the deficit. Egypt was unable to meet these conditions, but after many years of negotiation, the remainder of the debt was written off. Ibid., 81–5.

and education spending, leading to an unprecedented deterioration of public services. More than 75 per cent of subsidies on basic goods were abolished overnight. This fuelled growing resentment among the middle and lower classes.

A former US ambassador to Egypt says that although Mubarak succeeded in reconciling the Egyptian economy to IMF and World Bank conditions and made a great deal of headway in infrastructure (electricity, communications and transport), he failed to deal with three major holdovers from the Nasser era. The first was persistent military hostility to the Muslim Brotherhood, which meant that the regime retained its generally authoritarian character, the narrow margin of freedom provided early on in Mubarak's tenure notwithstanding. This was most marked in widespread electoral fraud and the free hand given to the security services in dealing with the populace, as well as the later move towards dynastic succession. The second was the regime's failure to turn growth into development and distribute its benefits fairly. The third was allowing the military to establish an economic–military nexus and granting it special privileges.[32]

The 1990s ushered in the second period of Mubarak's tenure. The policy agenda of this era was twofold: in the security sphere, the regime pursued an ever-harsher crackdown on political freedoms,[33] while in the economic sphere it sought to reduce spending on education and medical care (i.e. on human development). Privatization accelerated the break-up of the old corporatist system and drove the emergence of a new business class. The state relied more heavily on strong-arm security tactics and patron–client relationships, the main beneficiaries of which were crony capitalists. Corruption ran rampant, and wealth disparities increased enormously as the mass of the poor got poorer and a small minority got much, much richer. This process was redoubled after 2003, when Gamal Mubarak's clique entered centre stage and figures from the new business class took over various political offices, in both the executive and legislative branches. Privatizations were expedited and corruption worsened, and with both the middle and working classes increasingly dissatisfied, the government was haemorrhaging legitimacy by the day. This broad dissatisfaction began to be expressed, in this period, through protest movements and strikes.

---

[32] Kurtzer and Svenstrup, 'Egypt's Entrenched Military', 41.
[33] Between 1993 and 2002, the PPC accepted only a single application for registration: the National Accord Party. One of the most significant parties to be refused registration was the Wasat (Centre) Party, which continued to submit applications until its eventual success after the 2011 revolution. See: Kienle, *A Grand Delusion*, 68–9. In 2002, Law 84 on civic associations was issued. With wording kept deliberately vague and ambiguous, it was easily used to place limits on association activity. All Egyptian associations were obliged to re-register after its issue.

Another development of the 1990s was the replacement of oil exports – Egypt now imported more oil than it exported – with natural gas, production of which developed rapidly along with various dependent industries like petrochemicals, steel and iron. By the late 2000s, these developments resulted in a natural gas boom, reflected in a rise in GDP.

When Egypt accepted the IMF's conditions in the 1990s, it ushered in a period of not only economic but also social, political and cultural restructuring. An IMF report in the early 2000s listed Egypt as the fourth-biggest privatizer in the world after Hungary, Malaysia and the Czech Republic.[34] Under the pretext of a 'participatory' approach, the privatization programme integrated decision-makers – that is, the upper reaches of the state bureaucracy headed by NDP secretary general Yousef Wali – with the business elite, a process provided with consistent US support in the form of USAID and World Bank funding. The result was a complex network of overlapping interests binding these two groups together; politicians and senior bureaucrats became businessmen, and businessmen became crony capitalists whose ability to make money was dependent on their relationships with the government.[35] Alongside newer arrivals, there were several familiar faces who had made their fortunes securing imports and military equipment for the Sadat regime.[36]

With neoliberalism in the ascendant worldwide, Egypt's liberalization programme became a poster child for international financial institutions, alongside the 'Tunisian miracle' of Zine al-Abidine Ben Ali. The Egyptian economy, it was said, had achieved annual growth of more than 5 per cent throughout the 1990s. The private sector now accounted for two-thirds of GDP. Dollar reserves had seen 'enviable' growth. All this has now been thoroughly refuted, most prominently by Ahmed al-Isawi, who attributes growth primarily to investments in oil. These investments had no effect on the lives of everyday citizens, and their profits generally flowed abroad even as unemployment grew steadily at home, the

---

[34] Timothy Mitchell, *Rule of Experts: Egypt, Techno-Politics, Modernity* (Berkeley, Los Angeles and London: University of California Press, 2002), 279–80.

[35] As well as Yousef Wali, politicians prominent in this process included Fouad Sultan (minister of tourism), Maher Abaza (minister of energy) and Amal Othman (minister of social affairs and labour). Prominent businessmen included Hussein Sabbour (president of the Egypt-US Business Council), Farid Khamis, Omar Mehanna (head of the Misr-Iran Development Bank) and Taher Helmy (founder of a major corporate law firm). See: Ayubi, *Over-stating the Arab State*, 350; Mahmoud Abd al-Fadil, *Crony Capitalism: A Study of Social Economy* [Arabic] (Cairo: Dar al-Ain, 2011), 11.

[36] This group included figures such as Ahmed Bahgat, Mohammed Mansour, Safwan Thabet (Arabian International), Osman Ahmed Osman and Naguib Sawiris (Orascom). See: Mitchell, *Rule of Experts*, 282.

dubious figures of the government statistics agency notwithstanding.[37] More importantly, this period saw an explosion in the consumption of luxury products, including private healthcare and education; even as the consumption of products accessible to the working classes fell, food prices spiked and the quality of drinking water and sanitation deteriorated.[38] In the 'dual economy' of twenty-first-century Egypt, the vast majority of the population did not experience the effects of growth; class divisions widened and discontent grew.

From a purely economic standpoint, the obsession with these indicators reflected adherence to the cult of growth and trickle-down economics and a conviction that growth automatically reduces poverty. But what the neoliberals missed was that although growth is a precondition of development, it does not automatically fuel development and in fact may be a bubble driven by monopolistic competition between members of the bureaucratic and economic elite.[39] It may be a deceptive sort of growth based on remittances from a migrant workforce, or growth that accelerates consumption without developing the structure of the economy, and it may come at the cost of state services, increasing people's willingness to protest.

This is exactly what happened in Egypt, where increasing growth rates disguised a bubble, giving rise to what Timothy Mitchell called 'Dreamland'.[40] Growth in real estate far outpaced agriculture, displacing it as the third most popular non-oil investment sector. Exemptions and incentives offered by the state to 'fatten up' the business sector led to the emergence of a new class, whose attempts to imitate a Hollywood lifestyle in 'smart cities' and luxury housing developments were a key part of the restructuring-era speculative bubble.[41]

The Egypt of this era, more than any other reforming state in the region, was selling off the state. Around 40 per cent of the income from privatizations was used to pay off bad debt, essentially functioning as

---

[37] Ibrahim al-Isawi, *Social Justice and Development Models: With Special Attention to Egypt and its Revolution* [Arabic] (Beirut: ACRPS, 2014), 248.
[38] Ibid., 250.
[39] This description is taken from Abd al-Fadil, *Crony Capitalism*.
[40] Dreamland was one of the first luxury property developments established by Ahmed Bahgat, a businessman with close ties to the regime who made a fortune through government-backed loans (some 7 billion Egyptian pounds in one decade, according to one estimate). The trajectory of the court case brought against him by the banks that had loaned him this money itself points to the sorts of pressure that could be exerted in intra-regime conflicts. After the revolution, the dispute was brought to an end via commercial litigation. The court ruled that the development should be sold and the proceeds given to the banks, who also received the majority of the shares in the companies and hotels at the centre of the dispute. Mitchell dedicates a whole chapter of his book to corruption in the loan sector and its ties to privatization and the rise of the businessmen (*Rule of Experts*, 272–303). For a brief summary of the settlement, see the report on: *Bawaba News*, 28 March 2014, Available online: https://bit.ly/35uRYbP (accessed 25 October 2021).
[41] Mitchell, *Rule of Experts*, 272–5, 279–80.

a cash gift to banking elites, one of the most prominent strata of the government-allied business elite. The fire sale of government property was accompanied by widespread corruption, contributing to the formation of a new class of parasitical *nouveaux riches*. Since economic liberalization took place in a quasi-authoritarian environment, the fruits of the much-celebrated growth went, of course, to the powerful: the bureaucracy and the new business class.

The 'invisible hand' in this case belonged less to the market – since a free market cannot exist under a clientist regime – than to the authoritarian alliance of bureaucracy and business. It was the bureaucrats who handed out fee exemptions and tax holidays, government contracts, commercial licences and planning permission; it was they who guaranteed stability and prevented popular unrest with the state of emergency. There is nothing at all strange about the fact that even as the regime was engaged in extensive economic restructuring and free-market reform, its grip on the public sphere grew ever tighter.

The relationship between political repression and economic liberalization is exemplified by the capitalization of agriculture. Wealthy landowners – a demographic which, incidentally, included Yousef Wali, the minister of agriculture and NDP secretary general – mobilized the media to agitate for changes to the land law, supported by members of the religious establishment who cited Shari'a provisions on the illegality of contracts in perpetuity. Soon enough, a raft of government decrees were issued that essentially reversed Nasser's land reforms. Most significantly, Law 96/1992 stipulated that after a grace period of five years, farm tenancy contracts dating to the Nasser period that barred the eviction of tenant farmers and set a fixed, low rent would be terminated and the land would revert to its owners. As the eviction date approached, the atmosphere in the countryside grew tense, snowballing into major unrest between 1997 and 1999.[42] The government responded with a security crackdown, in the course of which some 66 people were killed, 1,161 injured and 3,160 arrested, after which the tenants' cause gradually faded from public view.[43]

The fig leaf of formal party pluralism may have made it seem otherwise, but the limits of the public sphere under Mubarak were always set by the interests of the authoritarian regime and the alliance between the bureaucracy (including the security forces), the NDP and the new business magnates. These interests were defined over a complex web of relations and via overlapping and at times contentious channels, but ultimately the

---

[42] Ibid., 265.
[43] *Shorouk*, 22 June 2014, Available online: https://bit.ly/3kgkF0p (accessed 14 December 2014). The author, oddly, says that the crisis passed 'relatively quietly'!

process was the same: the experts drafted the necessary bills, the NDP-dominated parliament signed them into law, and the security forces dealt with popular pushback, detaining protesters and shuttering any newspaper that dared support them.

During the twenty-first century, economic growth continued to be driven primarily by rents, which became more prominent as a percentage of foreign trade. Government neglect and exposure to competition from international firms took their toll on productive sectors, and the country did not develop any real savings capacity. The new capitalists invested in rentier reproduction – a source of resentment for those parts of society excluded from this process. The state's increasing reliance on domestic borrowing strengthened the role of society, which inevitably had repercussions in the political sphere.[44]

The privatization process was checked by the regime's awareness of the dangers of reform and austerity. But after 2003, when a new neoliberal government was formed, it came back with a vengeance. It was accompanied by a new economic-political alliance with an increasingly dynastic vision for the future of Egypt – that is, that the presidency should pass to Gamal Mubarak, who sat at the centre of a remarkable network of contacts between elites from the political and security spheres and monopoly capitalists. This government and its alliances and policies left society with only one option: direct confrontation. In the course of this confrontation, a new kind of protest force was to crystallize.

In general, throughout the Mubarak era there was a thoroughgoing effort to modernize Egypt's infrastructure. In 2000, there were only 300,000 mobile phone users in the country.[45] From 2007, however, when Egypt acquired its third mobile phone operator, mobiles became an essential part of daily life for Egyptians of all social classes,[46] and by 2010, 72 per cent of all Egyptians owned one, with ownership almost universal among the twenty-five to thirty-five age group.[47] This development was not only important economically, but mobiles also had major implications for lifestyles, needs, expectations, engagement with civil society and new social movements – and later, for state surveillance.

Under Mubarak, Egypt experienced a period of growth, beginning with conciliatory policies soon reversed by the regime. Despite periods of

---

[44] Samer Soliman, *The Autumn of Dictatorship: Fiscal Crisis and Political Change in Egypt under Mubarak*, trans. Peter Daniel (Stanford, CA: Stanford University Press, 2011).

[45] Linda Herrera, *Revolution in the Age of Social Media: The Egyptian Popular Insurrection and the Internet* (London and New York: Verso, 2014), 12.

[46] According to the World Bank, by 2019 this figure stood at 95 per cent. See World Bank, 'Mobile Cellular Subscriptions (per 100 People)—Egypt, Arab Rep.', Available online: https://bit.ly/3iannTq (accessed 25 October 2021).

[47] Herrera, *Revolution in the Age of Social Media*, 10.

intense economic activity, however, the wealth gap widened enormously. In the decade leading up to the 25 January revolution, the effects of this on the regime itself began to appear. Presidential succession seemed to be all people could talk about. At one point, it seemed to have been settled in favour of Gamal Mubarak – to the point that the whole thing seemed to be an 'artificial problem'. As one writer said, 'There was much speculation over what would happen when King Hassan II of Morocco died, then King Hussein of Jordan, and then Hafez al-Assad in Syria. The reality is that none of these deaths resulted in the sort of political upheavals that have been predicted. More importantly, the transfer of power in Egypt is going to be smooth.'[48] But this particular analyst failed to consider the differences between different authoritarian regimes: a republic is not a monarchy, and Syria – whose regime was entirely closed and afforded no margin for political activity – was not Egypt.

1 The regime and the businessmen

Economic liberalization happened gradually over the course of the Sadat and Mubarak eras, beginning with the famous 1974 law and continuing with the partial liberalization of commerce (1975),[49] the foreign currency law (1976),[50] the exemption of private sector businesses from labour laws (1977), the investment and free trade zones law (1989), and finally – with the influx of businessmen into ministerial positions and the upper reaches of the NDP – full liberalization and the fire sale of state property through privatization.

The price at which the regime bought the loyalty of the new capitalists was a high one. The bureaucracy was steeped in graft, enmeshed in a complex network of corruption, kickbacks and dubious campaign financing schemes between the state and the new class. Over time, the loyalty of the businessmen to the regime became increasingly reciprocal, but the political decision-makers, whose power guaranteed the loyalty of the army and the security forces and their willingness to accept alliances of this kind, always retained the upper hand.

Egypt's big businesses had a deeply dynastic quality until the end of the 1980s, their various parts held together by 'ties of blood, shared ancestry

---

[48] *Al-Masry Al-Youm*, 4 June 2009, Available online: https://bit.ly/3p9g31G (accessed 17 October 2021).
[49] Ending the state monopoly on imports with the exception of eighteen strategic commodities.
[50] Granting any legal person the right to hold foreign currency and use it directly for import purposes without reference to the Banking Organization. The private sector used this opportunity to hoover up Egyptian expatriates' savings abroad and buy black market currency.

and marriage' and the close association between money and government.⁵¹ Osman Ahmed Osman was a prime example of the overlap between these two forces: a close friend of Sadat's, his business successes were inseparable from his penetration of the ruling elite. Businessmen were dependent on the state, and this relationship stayed stable throughout the 1970s because the majority of businessmen worked in import-export and relied on the government for licences and tenders.⁵²

In the 1980s, new business associations began to appear outside the existing frameworks, with the earliest being the American Chamber of Commerce in Egypt (AmCham), founded in 1981 (with personal approval from Sadat). AmCham was important not so much in its own right, but for the interface it provided between various other organizations and as a vehicle for US-Egyptian commercial relations. Other institutions included the Egyptian Business Association (given state approval in 1979), which helped stymie government efforts to crack down on black marketeering in the mid-1980s. A government business committee was set up featuring major business figures, and in 1983 the Alexandria Businessmen's Association was established.⁵³ The reshuffle of the Ali Lotfy cabinet in the mid-1980s was also indicative of a greater closeness between the government and businessmen. And while the ABA itself was not part of any political organization, it shared a large portion of its membership with the NDP, facilitating contact with the government.⁵⁴

From the mid-1980s, Mubarak began to appoint figures from, or supportive of, the private sector to ministerial positions, and it became increasingly common for the government to draft economic laws in consultation with business associations.⁵⁵

During this period, Egyptian capital began to organize itself into associations and organizations with specific goals and the plans and strategies to achieve them – in other words, a lobby. This lobby was able to exercise considerable influence over a state bureaucracy that seemed to have lost all sense of direction and socio-economic vision. It was now the business class that was influencing the bureaucracy and not the other way around. This change was embodied in new patronage relationships. For example, businesses began hiring former bureaucrats as consultants to

---

[51] Abdelfattah, *Workers and Businessmen*, 233.
[52] Ibid., 243.
[53] Ibid., 172.
[54] Ibid., 170–1.
[55] Ibid., 377.

provide expert insight into the workings of the state and how best to shape its decisions.[56]

Under Law 203/1991, the public sector was restructured into 314 holding companies slated for privatization. By 1999, the government had sold 124.[57] With subsidy cuts and privatization between 1991 and 2001, the state's budget deficit fell from 15.3 per cent of GDP to 3 per cent. The fruits of privatization went, of course, to the businessmen.

Between 1982 and 2002, the public sector's share of GDP and investment fell from 54 per cent to 20 per cent and 70 per cent to 44 per cent, respectively, with a particularly sharp fall after 1990. From 1992 to 2002, domestic debt rose from 67 per cent to 90 per cent of GDP. In 2003, economic decision-makers, supported by Gamal Mubarak, advocated floating the Egyptian pound. The result was a tanking currency and rising prices, including those of basic foodstuffs, stoking popular resentment at a time of positive growth rates and higher expectations of better living standards coupled with an expanding wealth gap.

In 1998, Gamal Mubarak founded the FGF, whose purpose was to encourage a culture of private sector initiative and give a voice to young businessmen. As well as various ministerial positions, members of the FGF's board of directors were soon ensconced in influential positions at the ECES and AmCham, and graduates of its training programmes became ubiquitous in private and public sector organizations. In the 2004 government reshuffle, no fewer than seven of the fresh-faced cabinet members were close associates of Gamal Mubarak, including the minister of education and the minister of youth.

This period was indisputably marked by the rise of the businessmen (alongside certain liberal intellectuals), who permeated the government and parliament and owned numerous media outlets. This was to become very important during the January revolution and the reaction against it. Egyptian businessmen enjoyed a wide network of contacts in the deep state and used their newspapers and television stations to market their projects and ideas. These same outlets helped create a sense of chaos and longing for stability after the revolution, which was exploited by the army with its coup.

Gamal Mubarak's efforts to establish a socio-economic base within the NDP were just another product of the marriage of bureaucracy and business. His problem was that this third pole of politicians and businessmen could not break the army–presidency duopoly. He was unable to protect himself

---

[56] Samir M. Youssef, 'The Egyptian Private Sector and the Bureaucracy', *Middle Eastern Studies* 30, no. 2 (1994): 371–2.
[57] Kandil, *Soldiers, Spies, and Statesmen*, 206.

or the business class from a popular uprising or the military's turn against his father and the dynastic succession project.

Gamal Mubarak joined the NDP in 2000. Two years later, he was the driving force behind the establishment of its Policies Committee, which included various figures from the ECES, founded in 1992 to serve as the business lobby's main think tank. The committee itself was responsible for maintaining the neoliberal alliance of businessmen within the NDP and for the extensive privatizations of the 2000s. After his election as NDP assistant secretary general in 2007, Mubarak *fils* began to be seen as a possible candidate to succeed his father to the presidency, and ambitious politicians of the younger generation naturally sought an appointment on the committee to secure their political future. Failing to secure such a position on the committee – and therefore in Gamal Mubarak's inner circle – drove some businessmen to adopt a temporarily critical attitude towards the government. Although these attitudes were essentially born of anger at being excluded, they sometimes looked like genuine opposition and would later be depicted as 'revolutionary' sentiments.

Alongside businessmen, the Policies Committee also incorporated a few 'liberal' intellectuals willing to defend the regime's more repressive policies. Friendly academics, journalists and political figures were often rolled out by lobby shops for interviews with the US media,[58] being well qualified to address the US public, promote Gamal Mubarak's programme and warn of the dangers lurking behind the sort of democratic reforms proposed by pressure groups like the Working Group on Egypt.

In the 1995 parliament, 37 of the 454 representatives were businessmen; in the 2000 parliament, this figure rose to 77.[59] With Gamal Mubarak's star in the ascendant, however, they dominated the NDP and, through it, the country's economy. Their companies served as a breeding ground for a new generation of experts and managers, who left Cairo in droves for new luxury neighbourhoods beyond the urban sprawl, adding a spatial dimension to the existing class divide. These neighbourhoods, along with the extensive new tourist developments that sprang up along Egypt's coastline, were built on land sold by the state at a pittance to companies owned by families close to the regime. The corruption involved in the sale of state land did not go unnoticed by Egyptian citizens.

Ahmed Ezz, who acquired a monopoly on steel production in Egypt by buying up state factories, is an exemplar of the corrupt, political businessmen so prominent under Mubarak. It was Ezz, acting in his capacity as the NDP's

---

[58] Mohammed al-Manshawi, *America and the Egyptian Revolution from 25 January to 3 July and Beyond: Testimony from Washington* [Arabic] (Cairo: Shorouk, 2014), 67–8.
[59] Fahmy, *The Politics of Egypt*, 172.

organizational secretary, who introduced Gamal Mubarak in the last party conference in 2010 as 'the leader of the modernization revolution'.

With these policies came systemic, institutional corruption – grand larceny when placed against the petty bribes citizens paid daily for basic government services.[60] The extent of the problem showed how far the regime had moved away from its origins in the July revolution. While petty graft was visible under Nasser, structural corruption was limited and served political purposes beyond simple personal enrichment. Under Mubarak, however, corruption was institutionalized and systemic. The public was generally aware of this fact, if not the details of it. They knew, for example, that the likes of Mamdouh Ismail, whose ferry company caused the deaths of hundreds of Egyptians through negligence, or Agriculture Minister Yousef Wali, who was accused of importing carcinogenic pesticides, had got where they were not by personal effort but because they were part of the regime – and that they could not be held to account for the same reason. Wali's protestation that he was not responsible because 'ultimately, all of us are just secretaries to the president'[61] became emblematic of the period.[62]

Some outside observers trumpeted Egypt's economic miracle under Mubarak. David Ottaway, the former Cairo bureau chief for the *Washington Post*,[63] argues that the ascendancy of the Gamal Mubarak clique – whom he compares to Russian oligarchs – brought about a dramatic economic revival. By 2008, growth had reached 7 per cent, and from 2004 to 2009 GDP more than doubled, climbing from $78 billion to $162 billion.[64] But most people did not benefit from this remarkable growth. Nor was it translated into the development of services or infrastructure. In Mubarak's last decade in power, the fusion of business and power was so obvious that

---

[60] On this topic, see: Ismail al-Shatti et al., *Corruption and Righteous Governance in Arab Countries* [Arabic] (Beirut: Centre for Arab Unity Studies, 2004).

[61] Yousef Wali made his famous statement that ministers were mere 'secretaries' carrying out the orders of the president as part of testimony given to the Public Prosecution in a case concerning some 100,000 acres of land given to Alwaleed bin Talal's Mamlaka company by Mubarak in the late 1990s. Having bought the land on the pretext of an agricultural reclamation project, the company only completed the reclamation of a few hundred acres, and was accused of buying and deliberately leaving the land unused in order to sell it and benefit from rising property prices. Wali maintained that he had only signed off on the contract because the president and the prime minister had expected him to. This seems to have satisfied the public prosecution, which released him without charge. See an interview with one of the journalists who uncovered the story: *Al-Masry Al-Youm*, 17 March 2011, Available online: https://bit.ly/3ASCB94 (accessed 17 October 2021).

[62] *Youm7*, 11 February 2010, Available online: https://bit.ly/3bPGl0n (accessed 5 November 2014).

[63] David B. Ottaway, 'Egypt at the Tipping Point?', Woodrow Wilson International Centre for Scholars, Middle East Program Occasional Paper Series, Summer 2010, 4, Available online: https://bit.ly/33CzLGX (accessed 20 December 2014).

[64] Menawy, *The Last Days*, 54.

it became a common source of stories and novels. As novelist and essayist Alaa Al Aswany put it:

> Article 158 of the Egyptian constitution stipulates that no minister in Egypt can engage in commercial business during their tenure, in order to preclude a conflict of interest between his ministerial position and his business interests. [. . .] But the regime in Egypt respects neither the constitution nor the law, and in the last reshuffle many ministries were handed over to assorted middlemen and merchants. [. . .] It's like the whole of Egypt is a company owned by Mubarak and Sons, Inc. Mr Mansour-Chevrolet [i.e. Mohamed Mansour, the local partner of General Motors] is now minister for transport; the owner of Garana Tours is minister for tourism; and Dr Hatem El-Gabaly – part-owner and director of Dar al-Fouad Hospital, the Cairo Scan radiology centre, and various pathology labs and hotels for tourists – has overnight been transformed into a minister of health.[65]

The rich and the powerful came together in order to manage the two elites' common interests. This was the first time in modern Egyptian history that the rich intervened in government, in this case in an attempt to ensure Gamal Mubarak's succession to the presidency.[66]

III Deteriorating social conditions under Mubarak

Poverty alone does not lead to protest – that requires a general state of discontent generated by rising expectations and a growing wealth gap. In the same way, abstract economic data does not generate the overwhelming resentment from which the will to revolt is born. Rather, a climate conducive to rebellion grows out of the conjunction of a general state of frustration and depression at social and economic conditions, awareness of relative deprivation and/or humiliation, and a sense of long-term stagnation driving a desire for change.

Within the last decade of Mubarak's tenure, life for many in Egypt had become intolerable. The lower middle classes had been particularly badly hit by socio-economic developments, making them both angrier and less self-confident – a cocktail of feelings that can manifest alternately as desperation, a sense of impotence or a desire to rise up or take revenge. The dramatic decline in conditions and the growing sense of resentment were obvious even to the casual observer, notwithstanding popular claims

---

[65] Alaa Al Aswany, *Essays by Alaa Al Aswany* [Arabic], 2nd edn (Cairo: Shorouk, 2010), 20.
[66] Stephan Roll, 'Gamal Mubarak and the Discord in Egypt's Ruling Elite', *Carnegie Endowment for International Peace*, 1 September 2010, Available online: https://bit.ly/3iypiEy (accessed 16 December 2020).

that Egyptians had become inured to pollution, poor public services and police abuses. After so many years under Mubarak, and with the president himself exercising his functions largely from the resort town of Sharm El-Sheikh, the regime seemed decrepit and the country broken; the prevailing sense was that Egyptians were living in an era of stagnation. The regime's popularity tanked, to the point that one retired Egyptian general told the *New York Times* that he doubted the army would be willing to fire on the public to protect it.[67] In January 2011, he was to be proven right.

Given poverty, overcrowding, uncertainty and the disappearance of the welfare state established by the 1952 regime – for most citizens, the state's only concrete manifestations were in repression and its labyrinthine, maddening bureaucracy – it was only natural that there were negative effects on individuals' nature. In both its repressive and bureaucratic guises, the state prefers the individual to be obsequious, obedient and a collaborator. The market, meanwhile, wants energetic consumers and the cheapest possible labour. Fixers and wheeler-dealers proliferated, when doing things the right way meant failure and might be made right. This was a natural response to the very public example set by the rich and the powerful in a society already predisposed to a strict hierarchy of classes determining social status.

Growth rates rose because of elevated oil prices from the mid-1970s onwards, as well as increased remittances from Egyptians working abroad, especially in the Gulf. Although Egypt was no longer a subsistence economy, according to the Egypt Human Development Report of 2010, more than 20 per cent of the population still lived below the poverty line.[68] Indeed, despite the growth of per capita GDP between 2008 and 2010, poverty had actually risen from 19.6 per cent to 21.6 per cent over the same two-year period. In 2008, some 1.7 million people (2 per cent of the population) were living in 'extreme' poverty.[69] The poorest decile of Egyptian society accounted for only 4 per cent of spending, while the richest accounted for 28 per cent.[70] Healthcare spending, one of the three key traditional measures of human development, fell from 3 per cent of GDP in 1997 to 2.2 per cent in 2005 and 1.7 per cent in 2007.[71]

There are many ways to define relative poverty within Egypt. But many of those considered middle class (junior civil servants and teachers, for

---

[67] *New York Times*, 3 July 1995, A1 and A9.
[68] Heba Handoussa et al., *Egypt Human Development Report 2010: Youth in Egypt: Building our Future* (Cairo: UN Development Programme, 2010), 5.
[69] Ibid., 109–10.
[70] Ibid., 108.
[71] Shadi Abdel Karim et al., *Potential Risk: Corruption in Egypt* [Arabic], ed. Said Abdelhafiz (Cairo: Multaqa al-Hiwar li'l-Tanmiya wa-Huquq al-Insan, 2007), 27.

example) were certainly poor inasmuch as they struggled to make ends meet and were forced to reduce their expectations and accept housing well below the standard required for dignified living. That a fifth of the population was living in absolute poverty does not mean that those families whose daily incomes exceeded $2 were middle class.[72]

Rising levels of consumption were coupled with rising levels of poverty. In 2006, a Cairo University study showed that mobile phone purchases were growing at a rate unmatched anywhere else in the world – 35 per cent annually (compared with 30 per cent in China). The number of internet subscribers shot up from 654,000 in 1999 to more than 6 million in 2006.[73] Higher consumption on lower incomes meant the impoverishment of the working classes, and this dragged down the country's productive capacity. This all took place against the backdrop of ongoing economic liberalization, which produced a puerile capitalism concerned primarily with consumption rather than production, and with over- or under-consumption without regard for broader social and economic conditions.[74] This expanding consumerism without a concurrent rise in income made people more aware of poverty, feeding into a growing sense of resentment.

Growth resumed after 2003, particularly between 2006 and 2008, when it stood at an impressive 7 per cent according to the World Bank. These figures are attributable above all to natural gas production and subsidiary industries as well as a boom in tourism: in 2008 alone, some 12.8 million tourists visited Egypt.[75] There were optimistic hopes that Egypt could use the windfall – comparable to the high oil revenues of the 1970s – to transform itself into a flourishing market economy. Cash from growth strengthened dollar reserves and stimulated commercial banking and investment loans to business magnates, and even to small and medium business owners.

Of course, as Isawi points out, it is important to recognize the limitations of GDP in reflecting the actual situation on the ground, as there is a large informal sector in Egypt whose scope is difficult to calculate or estimate given ever more pervasive underreporting. This raises the problem of nominal growth versus actual growth, especially given national planners' common bureaucratic habit of overestimating, or at least leaning towards

---

[72] Some 47 per cent of Egyptians surveyed for the 2011 Arab Opinion Index, which was conducted four months after the revolution, stated that they could not afford basic essentials on their current salary and had to borrow money to make ends. See: The Arab Opinion Index, Arab Centre for Research and Policy Studies, Available online: https://bit.ly/3r6tCh6 (accessed 17 December 2020).
[73] Ayman Zohri, *Conditions of Egyptian Society* [Arabic] (Shibin al-Kom, Egypt: [self-published], 2006), 11.
[74] Thana Fuad Abdullah, *The Future of Democracy in Egypt* [Arabic] (Beirut: Centre for Arab Unity Studies, 2005), 172.
[75] Henry and Springborg, *Globalization and the Politics of Development*, 177.

the higher bound of estimates. Estimating actual growth, as well as its effect on prices and inflation, is a perennial problem.[76] In 2008, during this period of putative growth, Egypt experienced a sudden bread shortage, apparently because the government was selling subsidized flour to private bakeries – yet another example of endemic corruption. Protests and strikes grew ever more common.[77]

Between 2002 and 2008, the state's absence and its unwillingness to take basic remedial measures were cast into sharp relief by a series of crises, leaving citizens to sink or swim. Deteriorating infrastructure caused several major accidents on Egypt's trains, still the most common form of transport in the country: on 19 February 2002, around 400 people died on an Upper Egyptian railway line when several third-class carriages caught fire. The dilapidated state of second- and third-class carriages, invariably overloaded and posing a serious fire hazard, does not do justice to the proud history of Egyptian railways and is the product of long neglect of public services and corruption.[78]

A plague of building collapses also began after the 1992 earthquake, which legislative efforts proved incapable of checking due to pervasive local government corruption.[79] On 5 September 2005, forty-seven people, including actors and critics, were killed when the Beni Soueif cultural centre burned down. In January 2004, 135 French tourists died along with aircrew when a Boeing 737 operated by an Egyptian tourist company crashed into the Red Sea. And on 3 February 2006, the ferry *Boccaccio al-Salam* – owned by one of Mamdouh Ismail's companies – sank, taking with it 375 of its 1,400 passengers and crew. Family members looking for news of their loved ones at the dock were dispersed brutally by the security forces, and Ismail himself fled abroad.

In September 2008, 100 people died in a landslide in the Cairo neighbourhood of Duweiqa, an informal slum neighbourhood under the cliffs of the Al-Mokattam plateau. Help was slow in coming, and they were unable even to look for survivors under the rubble of their houses. Former residents were made homeless and promises to rehouse them went unfulfilled. In such a dangerous location, the government should have sought recommendations from expert bodies. But the absence of the state, its bloated and byzantine bureaucracy, and the spectre of corruption and cronyism meant that reports were simply shelved and no action taken. With

---

[76] Isawi, *The Egyptian Economy*, 55, 59.
[77] Henry and Springborg, *Globalization and the Politics of Development*, 178.
[78] *Al Jazeera*, 20 February 2020, Available online: https://bit.ly/3bReBbD (accessed 17 December 2014).
[79] Some of the most significant such incidents are discussed in a report in *Al-Masry Al-Youm*, 11 August 2014, Available online: https://bit.ly/35uyvrH (accessed 13 October 2014).

class divides being what they were, the state saw no value in intervening actively in unplanned neighbourhoods so long as the demographics that it really cared about lived a safe distance from them.[80]

Rigid, class-based geographic segregation and the regime's willingness to tolerate appalling conditions in poor neighbourhoods reached such heights that some neighbourhoods were essentially left to their own devices, with crime, violence and religious extremism allowed to proliferate freely. So long as violence was directed inwards, or at Copts in the same area, the state was not concerned. It was only when violence threatened to escape the confines of the neighbourhood that it would intervene.

All this meant that people did not feel the effects of rising growth rates. That is, it was growth without development, growth comparable, in fact, to the growth of the unregulated slums themselves. Crises and disasters added to the sense that the country had stagnated politically under Mubarak while the socio-economic order had become a near jungle. Poverty and slum neighbourhoods were the other face of this growth, the product of the inequitable distribution of wealth, bad policymaking and economic neoliberalism. They showed that the businessmen's grand projects had failed to absorb the waves of unemployed people entering the job market, particularly young people, at a time when the average age of the population was falling thanks to a high fertility rate.

Difficulties in obtaining bread are a quintessential example of Egyptians' plight under Mubarak. Shortages of bread, as well as propane for cooking and other basic goods, caused more than one lethal altercation between citizens. The housing crisis, meanwhile, was a constant burden in citizens' daily lives because of a lack of affordable accommodation. Housing became a central concern and a major talking point for society as a whole, even litterateurs and artists. Having to look for shelter in an informal neighbourhood was an ever-present possibility for Egyptians.

The growth of unplanned slum neighbourhoods in Egypt in general, and Cairo in particular, was one of the most visible consequences of the socio-economic policies of the *infitah* era. The massive urban bloat was due in part to rapid population growth completely disproportionate to the country's habitable areas, estimated at a mere 7 per cent of its total territory. In 2011, Egypt's eighty million inhabitants were almost all housed within 35,000 square kilometres of land along the banks of the Nile and in the Nile Delta, producing one of the highest population densities in the world at 1,700/square kilometre.[81] In some working-class districts, this figure rose

---

[80] Amnesty International, "'We Are Not Dirt': Forced Evictions in Egypt's Informal Settlements', 23 August 2011, 1–2, Available online: https://bit.ly/2Z6kgbI (accessed 17 October 2021).
[81] Pommier, *Egypt*, 177.

to 35,000/square kilometre. Such extraordinary levels of overcrowding exacerbated economic and social difficulties.[82]

By 2005, the percentage of the population who had received a school education had risen to 76.9 per cent, and the literacy rate among over-fifteens stood at 71.4 per cent; 95.9 per cent of girls had received a primary school education, compared to 57.4 per cent in 1961.[83] Rising levels of education combined with population growth, a housing crisis (meaning the prospect of marriage receding into the far-distant future for many young people) and high unemployment to produce a generational time bomb: the January revolution would be driven by millions of frustrated young people without any dependents or family responsibilities. More education also meant higher status and job expectations – expectations the Egyptian economy was unable to meet, feeding discontent.

One particularly important sign of the limits of economic growth was the high level of unemployment, a significant driver of internal and external migration (Egypt is a major exporter of labour to the Gulf countries in particular). Some 20 per cent of those who left their home regions between 1996 and 2006 cited a lack of jobs as their reason for moving.[84] Internal migration was also a contributing factor in the development of slum neighbourhoods.

The reversal of the Nasser-era land reform in 1997 affected some 432,000 peasants, almost half as many as the original programme had helped in 1952 (around 905,000). Evictees were left, quite simply, without any land.[85] Although we have no exact figures for how many of them ended up living in urban slums, this measure is a good example of policy decisions elsewhere driving rural outmigration to cities, which were socially and economically incapable of absorbing them in such numbers. According to the CAO, 79.8 per cent of villages countrywide – home of 25.5 million Egyptians, or 17.7 per cent of the population – lacked basic sanitation services.[86]

---

[82] Zohri, *Conditions*, 40. According to the latest figures from Egypt's statistical agency, there are now more than 100 million Egyptians. The National Housing Council estimates that 77 per cent of the country's population lives in only 6 per cent of its area, with the habitable regions having an average population density of 1,422/square kilometre, up considerably from 1,109/square kilometre in 2014. See the population clock maintained by the Central Agency for Public Mobilization and Statistics (CAPMAS), Available online: https://bit.ly/3lMsOgr (accessed 17 October 2021); Hussein Sayed, *Review of the Executive Plan 2015–2020 in the Context of the National Population and Development Strategy 2015–2030* (Cairo: UNFPA, August 2020), Available online: https://bit.ly/3p0K9B9 (accessed 17 December 2020).

[83] Ibid., 199.

[84] Muhammad Ahmad Ali Hassanein, *Internal Migration in Egypt: a Study in Human Geography* [Arabic] (Beirut: Centre for Arab Unity Studies, 2010), 264.

[85] Mitchell, *Rule of Experts*, 265.

[86] Ali Leila, 'Why Did the Revolution Break Out? A Study on the Status of State and Society' [Arabic], in *The Egyptian Revolution: Motivations, Trends and Challenges* [Arabic], ed. Aya Nassar et al. (Beirut: Arab Centre for Research and Policy Studies, 2012), 37–8.

By 2011, according to government statistics, there were 12.2 million Egyptians living in unregulated slums – 16 million according to the World Bank.[87] Some estimates placed the number of slum dwellers in Cairo at 46 per cent of the total population of the city,[88] with around one million living in cemeteries.[89] The housing shortage meant that many middle-class people – junior civil servants, low-income families, even junior officers – ended up in these neighbourhoods, which were some of the most impoverished both in purely monetary terms and in terms of human development. Poverty in slum neighbourhoods leads to family breakdown and undermines social solidarity, making these areas the main source of Cairo's two million 'street children', whose ages range from eight to eighteen.[90] One study suggests that 80 per cent of girls on the street have been victims of sexual assault, while 70 per cent of them have not received any schooling.[91]

The Egyptian slums are a vast reservoir of human vulnerability. They are home to the most marginalized members of society, who – packed in like sardines – live difficult and precarious lives that can be completely derailed by the slightest tremor. A yawning gulf separates them from the neighbourhoods where their better-off compatriots live, a gulf made wider by psychological, social and class distance. They are dogged by feelings of alienation, aimlessness, anxiety, insecurity and marginalization. They have the highest rates of elementary school attrition in the country, and are very likely to work poorly paid, stigmatized and irregular jobs. In short, they are the city's dark underbelly, the poorest of the urban poor. As the director Daoud Abdel Sayed puts it:

> They have no stable way of making money, are entirely excluded from production. [...] Life for them is constant toil or marginalized dreams. But in spite of all that, they are always trying to snatch moments of joy, no matter how brief, from the jaws of a very harsh life, with all the excitement and clamour that such short-lived and infrequent moments deserve.[92]

Neoliberal-authoritarian socio-economic policy is necessarily governed by a dynamic of polarization. Comparative study of models of this kind shows that the security forces can only perform their disciplinary functions so long as the victims of these policies continue to express their aspirations

---

[87] Abd al-Fadil, *Crony Capitalism*, 28.
[88] This figure is from 1993, when it was estimated that 84 per cent of all new buildings in the city were constructed without planning permission. The numbers today are likely to be considerably higher. See: Abdullah, *The Future of Democracy*, 167.
[89] Said Ismail Ali, *Culture of the Oppressed* [Arabic] (Cairo: Alam al-Kutub, 2008), 45.
[90] Ibid.
[91] Ibid.
[92] Abd al-Fadil, *Crony Capitalism*, 29–30.

within the conventional political frameworks provided by the regime. Collapse is only possible when a challenge shakes the security forces' belief in their own omnipotence and omniscience. This is what happened in Sidi Bouzid in Tunisia and Deraa in Syria – both towns characterized by a high degree of rural in-migration – when people began to protest, first against humiliating treatment and then unaccountable killing. It was akin to thousands of Noras slamming the door on an autocratic Doll's House. Dignity is no less important than bread and freedom, even if it cannot be measured quantitatively – although of course they are inseparably linked, as one cannot have the former without the latter.

In Egypt, socio-economic polarization had grown worse and worse. The cities of the rich were differentiated starkly from the slums of the poor on every level – semiotically, sociologically and economically. The story of Cairo in this period is not so much a tale of two as three cities: the wealthy 'upper city' west of the Nile, the medieval 'lower city' to its east and the vast periphery of unregulated, unplanned slums that Abd al-Fadil calls the 'hinterland'. These three cities coexisted only 'with difficulty, amid an array of social and behavioural tensions and architectural contradictions'.[93]

A fourth Cairo had developed in the previous two decades as well: a Cairo of gated desert communities straight out of a Florida real estate ad. Having failed to develop or modernize the existing urban core, or even to establish wealthy footholds protected from the endless sprawl of unregulated slums, the business establishment retreated from the city altogether and escaped to a 'West' of its own design. As if this was not enough, the president himself abandoned the capital, conducting the business of government primarily from his resort in Sharm El-Sheikh. Class and social segregation took on a quasi-racial colouring, with the poor existing in an entirely different world seen through the lens of a real contempt for their culture.

According to the sociologist Sameer Naim, it came as a surprise to many when the poor threw their weight behind the revolution because of the prevailing belief in an impending 'revolution of the hungry', when slum dwellers would maraud and loot neighbouring areas. But in fact, Naim says:

> They worked day and night to protect everyone who participated, forming popular committees [to that end]. They are unjustly seen as dangerous, and we cannot deny that some of them have behaved badly because the *ancien régime* denied them the opportunity to live like human beings. [. . .] If the men of the slums, the heroes of the revolution, had not turned out, then it would not have succeeded. They

---

[93] Ibid., 30.

rebelled against injustice, and if the revolution should be subverted, it is they who will right its course. They are capable of sacrifice because they have experienced real hunger.[94]

Subsequent events have shown that these comments were a romantic exaggeration: while it is true that the revolution would not have succeeded without them, the men of the slums did not protect the revolution when it was 'subverted', nor did they produce a politically conscious leadership. At first, the marches and the demonstrations on Tahrir Square provided a space where they could make their voices heard, and they provided a powerful base for the demand that Mubarak should stand down. In other words, they managed to transform their aspirations into politics. There was no random looting of wealthy areas, as often happens during widespread social unrest. Their anger was directed at the government. But when their most pressing, everyday demands were not met quickly enough after the revolution and disagreements split the revolutionary camp, they quickly became disillusioned. With the revolutionaries unsure of how to retain their loyalty, during the immediate post-revolutionary period the forces of the old regime managed to win some of them over, whether through media demagoguery or bribery.

---

[94] See the interview with Sameer Naim in: Abdullah, 'The Armed Forces'.

3

Deconstructing the myth of acquiescence

A short history of protest in modern Egypt

In this chapter, we will take a brief, non-exhaustive look at the history of protest in Egypt. As in the previous chapter, the closer we get to 2011, the more detailed our analysis will be. This is not because of a lack of interest in or disregard for the movements of earlier periods, but rather because the revolutionary wave of January 2011 is directly linked to the protests of the late Mubarak era. Since the purpose of this study is to understand the January revolution, it is inevitably the events that constitute its immediate context that we will look at most closely.

Early examples of protest in Egypt include resistance against Napoleon led by the students and faculty of al-Azhar (1798–1801); the rebellion against the Ottoman governor Hurshid Pasha (1805); and, in particular, the events that laid the foundations of a modern Egyptian national identity, the Urabi revolt (1881–2)[1] and the 1919 uprising. Some of the first organized labour mobilizations took place during the same period, including the Port Said coal heavers' strike of 1882 and the subsequent Cairo cigarette rollers' strike of 1899, events which paved the way for the establishment of labour unions a few years later.[2] By the early twentieth century, students had emerged as a major player in resistance to colonialism. During the

---

[1] The term *thawra* ('revolution') was not used by contemporaries, even by Urabi, who used the word 'revival' or 'resurgence' (*nahda*) instead. None of its spokesmen – neither Abdullah al-Nadeem, its major orator, or its great poet Mahmoud Sami al-Baroudi – described the Urabi revolt as a revolution. Disinterested observers, including Muhammad Abduh, referred to it as a 'movement', while conservatives used the term 'unrest' (*hawja*). This latter designation remained common in government propaganda after Urabi and his companions were exiled, and appears in the writings of the then British agent Lord Balfour, as well as intellectuals close to the palace (including the poet Ahmed Shawqi), who took it upon themselves to popularize it. The Western press referred to it as an 'insurrection' or 'rebellion', while contemporary Western historians called it a 'movement'. It was only against the backdrop of the 1919 revolution that historians and propagandists began to describe it in revolutionary terms, some eight years after Urabi had returned to Egypt. Urabi himself did not live to see the 1919 revolution.

[2] Fares Oshti, 'Historical Roots of Social Movements in Arab Countries' [Arabic], in *Social Movements in the Arab World: Egypt, Lebanon, Bahrain* [Arabic], ed. Amr El-Shobaki (Beirut: Centre for Arab Unity Studies, 2011), 91.

1919 revolution, which culminated in limited Egyptian independence (see Chapter 1), it was students that initiated and kept up the energy of the constant demonstrations and protests[3] demanding national independence, self-determination and the right to establish an elective constitutional monarchy.[4] They were joined by tram workers, railwaymen, printers and the employees of the national gas company, as well as peasants, who went on strike to protest the UK's refusal to allow an Egyptian delegation to attend the Paris Peace Conference.[5]

Another major milestone came with the protests against Prime Minister Ismail Sidqi. Sidqi's People's Party came to power in 1930 with British support, and within a short amount of time he had abolished the constitution and created a semi-dictatorial regime that granted sweeping powers to the king.[6] These actions outraged the nationalist movement, leading to condemnation by the Wafd – which called for mass demonstrations against his policies – and widespread civil disobedience coordinated by student committees, followed by a violent government crackdown.[7] The students, however, were unshaken. On 13 November 1935, after the UK announced that it would not agree to a treaty providing a roadmap for independence, schools and universities throughout the country went on strike, and massive demonstrations were staged in Ismailia Square (today's Tahrir Square) and neighbouring governorates.[8] British forces clashed with students at Cairo University, and a congress held at the Faculty of Medicine announced that demonstrators would be going on strike until the 1923 constitution was restored and the government pursued anti-colonial policies.[9] The Young Egypt Society, an

---

[3] Mohammed Hafez Diab, *Uprisings or Revolutions in the Modern History of Egypt* [Arabic] (Cairo: Shorouk, 2011), 161–72.

[4] Khaldoun Hasan al-Naqib, *The Authoritarian State in the Contemporary Arabian East: A Constructivist Comparative Study* [Arabic], 3rd edn (Beirut: Centre for Arab Unity Studies, 2004), 74.

Azharite sheikhs and Coptic priests marched at the front of these demonstrations carrying placards that showed the cross and the crescent together, and priests chaired meetings held in mosques and vice versa. This was intended to refute Britain's attempts to present itself as the protector of religious minorities, a role it had enshrined in various agreements with Egypt and laws passed within the country. The Egyptian elite managed to prevent any reference to Britain's role as protector being included in the 1923 constitution. See: Tarek El-Bishry, *Muslims and Copts in the Framework of the National Community* [Arabic], 4th edn (Cairo: Shorouk, 2004), 164.

[5] Oshti, 'Historical Roots', 97–8; Abderrahman al-Rafi'i, *The 1919 Revolution: The National History of Egypt from 1914 to 1921* [Arabic], 4th edn (Cairo: Dar al-Ma'arif, 1987).

[6] Eric Davis, *Challenging Colonialism: Bank Misr and Egyptian industrialization 1920–1941* (Princeton, NJ: Princeton University Press, 1983), 139.

[7] Ali Shibli, *The Crisis of the Global Great Recession and its Repercussions for Rural Egypt, 1929–1934* [Arabic] (Cairo: Shorouk, 2006), 154–7.

[8] The area surrounding the square was originally known as 'Ismailia' after Khedive Ismail and became a rallying point for the national movement after the 1919 revolution. It was officially renamed Tahrir ('Liberation') Square after 1952. See: Aya Nassar, 'The Symbolism of Tahrir Square' [Arabic], in *The Egyptian Revolution: Motivations, Trends and Challenges* [Arabic], ed. Aya Nassar et al. (Beirut: Arab Centre for Research and Policy Studies, 2012).

[9] Diab, *Uprisings or Revolutions*, 172–3.

organization with Arab-Egyptian nationalist leanings, played a prominent role in organizing the protests[10] alongside the Wafd, the communists and the liberal constitutionalists.[11] The Wafd's student committees also proved crucial to extending protests beyond the capital.[12] This series of events ultimately led to the return of the Wafd to power in 1936.

By 1946, ten years later, the Marxist left, and the student and worker left more broadly, were emerging as the key players in post-war nationalist politics. In February of that year, dozens of leftist students who had attended a general congress at Cairo University before a planned march on the Abdin Palace died trying to escape police gunfire on the Abbas Bridge, triggering a wave of popular outrage that spread rapidly to other cities. On 17 February, shortly after the massacre, representatives of all the major left movements and the newly founded Workers' Committee for National Liberation formed the National Workers' and Students' Committee,[13] which promptly announced a general strike for independence; on 21 February, massive demonstrations took place throughout Cairo, with fierce resistance from the police.[14] In response, the committee declared another general strike and day of mourning for 4 March. Newspapers suspended publication, and shops, coffee houses, schools and factories were shuttered. The committee managed to bridge the gap between the different parties, which put aside their differences in order to pursue popular demands for liberation and national independence within a non-partisan framework. The events of 1946 were indisputably a popular uprising, in the full sense of the word. And although the immediate effects were limited, a rising tide of national fervour encouraged Nahhas's Wafd government to withdraw from the 1936 Anglo-Egyptian Treaty in 1950, setting off a campaign of guerrilla warfare and protest against colonialism that was only brought to a decisive end by the July revolution.

I After 23 July

The popularity of the Nasser regime – and of Nasser personally – prevented the crystallization of any organized or even spontaneous form of protest.

---

[10] Ibid., 274.
[11] Oshti, 'Historical Roots', 99.
[12] For more details, see: Hamada Ismail, *The 1935 Uprising between the Rise of Cairo and Outrage of the Provinces* [Arabic] (Cairo: Shorouk, 2005).
[13] The Muslim Brotherhood were hostile to the committee, and on 28 February set up an alternative bringing together representatives from Young Egypt, the National Party and young members of the Constitutional Party, the socialist Falah Party and Aly Maher's Egyptian Front.
[14] For more details, see: Isamuddin Galal, *The National Street: The School and Model, 1924–2008* [Arabic] (Cairo: Merit, 2009), 191–273. Cf. Tarek El-Bishry, *Political Movement in Egypt, 1945–1952* [Arabic], 2nd edn (Cairo: Shorouk, 1983), 108–9.

The regime dominated the public sphere culturally and politically, and its security forces were on hand to suppress and dissuade potential opposition. As a result, this period saw almost no open popular protests of a nationalist or even economic nature. There were only two exceptions to this general trend: the labour mobilizations in Kafr al-Dawwar and the demonstrations that followed the lenient sentences handed down to members of the air force command after the 1967 war. In the first of these incidents, in August 1952, workers at Misr Spinning and Weaving in the industrial city of Kafr al-Dawwar marched to demand better conditions; their protests were broken up ruthlessly, and two workers were executed. In the second incident, protests were organized in universities and industrial areas throughout the country to demand more appropriate punishments for those deemed responsible for the defeat,[15] and student demonstrations lasting an entire week called for an end to the military and security state. These protests, too, were suppressed violently using live ammunition, leaving 21 dead, 472 injured and around 1,100 arrested on the charge of being foreign agents.[16]

Under Sadat, there were more outpourings of public discontent. Before his regime had established its legitimacy, a wave of strikes and sit-ins swept the country in 1971 and 1972 demanding the liberation of Sinai, against the backdrop of frustration with the 1967 defeat and the continuing occupation of Arab territories despite the president's repeated promises to settle scores with Israel. The largest of these demonstrations was a student occupation of Tahrir Square in February 1972, which lasted several days and saw more than 1,000 students arrested.[17] These actions were organized by the student left and the Nasserists, who, during this period, were hostile to Sadat, and the leaders of this era of protest would later serve as an inspiration to the revolutionaries of 2011. Islamist students, who considered the left their mortal enemies, were generally opposed to the demonstrations and were given carte blanche to act against them by the regime. During this period, the student movement included a broad range of ideological groups: leftists and pan-Arabists, Islamists, and supporters of Sadat's domestic and foreign policy innovations,[18] but the pan-Arabist element remained, for the moment, dominant.[19]

---

[15] Ahmad Bahauddin Shaaban, 'Lucky Is He Who Lives the Moment of Revolution!' [Arabic], *al-Adab* 59, no. 4–6 (April/June 2011): 11–15.
[16] Kandil, Soldiers, Spies, and Statesmen, 96–7.
[17] Diab, *Uprisings or Revolutions*, 209.
[18] Ahmed Al Tuhami, 'Youth and Politics: Experience of Student Activism' [Arabic], in *The Future of Society and Development in Egypt: Youth Perspective* [Arabic], ed. Abdel-Aziz Shadi (Cairo: Cairo University Faculty of Economics and Political Science, 2002), 364.
[19] Personal interview with Abou Elela Mady, conducted by Nerouz Satik and Hani Awwad, Doha, 6 October 2012.

While the battle drums fell silent in the wake of the 1973 war, economic crisis soon took their place as a driver of protest. Sadat's policies – in particular the decision to increase and then abruptly abolish subsidies for basic goods – were widely seen as a deliberate retreat from the lifestyle that Egyptians had enjoyed under the Nasserist socialist state. In January 1977, these tensions exploded in the famous Bread Uprising, a response to the lifting of subsidies and subsequent price hikes of a long list of basic goods.[20] On the same morning that the measure was announced, demonstrations began with workers from Misr Helwan Spinning and Weaving, who were quickly joined by workers from other factories. By noon, students from Ain Shams University's Faculty of Engineering were marching on the People's Assembly and Ataba Square. Demonstrators attacked businesses, public transport infrastructure, police stations, department stores and casinos, and in Giza and Alexandria there were wildcat strikes, riots and clashes with the security forces.

Protests ultimately spread to nine of Egypt's twenty-seven governorates, with the majority taking place in low-income areas; wealthy neighbourhoods did not participate. Seventy-nine people were killed and 214 injured. Although the protests had been sparked by a deterioration in economic conditions, demonstrators' slogans included political demands. The acts of violence committed by workers, students or the apolitical masses targeted the markers of prosperity[21] – luxury cars and department stores, for example[22] – and their chants, too, showed a real rage at manifestations of economic disparity.[23] Once again, the Muslim Brotherhood remained hostile to the demonstrations; it was much closer to the regime, which had recently released many of its members and allowed them a certain amount of freedom of action, than they were to the contemporary leftist and nationalist opposition. This partisan attitude remained characteristic of the Brotherhood's approach to protest throughout the period: although they did not and do not consider themselves a political party, their behaviour is the most partisan of all the political movements.

As soon as calm was restored, the regime launched a propaganda campaign to undermine this mass movement, with Sadat himself branding it a 'thieves' uprising'. It was claimed that those who had participated were members of illegal 'communist' organizations, and thousands were

---

[20] Isawi, *The Egyptian Economy*, 94.
[21] Islamists also participated in these demonstrations in a personal capacity. See: Hossam Tammam, ed., *Abdel Moneim Aboul-Fotouh: A Witness to the History of the Islamic Movement in Egypt, 1970–1984* [Arabic], intro. Tarek El-Bishry (Cairo: Shorouk, 2010), 59.
[22] Diab, *Uprisings or Revolutions*, 216.
[23] For some of these slogans, see Shaaban, 'Lucky Is He'. Shaaban was sixth on a list of 176 individuals charged in the aftermath of the protests.

arrested, with 176 activists subsequently charged. The majority were acquitted at trial, with the exception of a small group who had been caught red-handed distributing revolutionary pamphlets. Sadat also sought to contain the political and social forces behind the protests by meeting personally with committees representing them. One such meeting held with a student union delegation was broadcast live on radio, with two students – the Nasserist Hamdeen Sabahi and the Islamist Abdel Moneim Aboul-Fotouh – engaging in a fiery exchange of words with the president.[24]

In 1976, a new set of university regulations was released establishing the Federation of Egyptian Students as an independent body. Elections were held the same year, bringing an ideologically diverse crop of leaders to the fore including Sabahy and Aboul-Fotouh as well as Essam el-Erian and Ziyad Ouda.[25] This marked the beginning of a new wave of Brotherhood successes in student union elections. Within a year, they had seized control of eight of Egypt's twelve union boards,[26] replacing the nationalists as the largest force in the student movement.[27]

In 1979, after the signing of the Camp David Accords with Israel, Sadat dramatically restricted student activism through another new set of student regulations. The federation's powers and ability to act were much reduced, and other student organizations were banned irrespective of their character. Student unions were made answerable to faculty administrations, which were given the right to veto their decisions and agendas. University security was dramatically increased.[28] The accords prompted a wave of strikes and demonstrations, and many of the student leaders were arrested, including the young Islamist Abou Elela Mady, later founder of the Wasat (Centre)

---

[24] Tammam, *Abdel Moneim Aboul-Fotouh*, 59–61. An audio recording of the exchange can be heard on *YouTube*, 4 December 2012, Available online: https://bit.ly/3itaR2G (accessed 7 February 2014). Both Sabahy and Aboul-Fotouh ran for the presidency after the 2011 revolution. It has been my long contention that if they had run together, or if one of them had stood aside in favour of the other, then the fate of the revolution would have been quite different. Many of the student activists of the 1970s ultimately became prominent academics, media figures or politicians, and many of the fierce personal rivalries between them today can be attributed at least in part to the skirmishes of those early days. After 2011, these rivalries – which often played out in ways that more closely resembled student union elections, or battles for control of professional associations, than mature and responsible government – prevented the sort of intra-opposition coordination that was so crucial to the success of the revolution that their children had made. Democratic transition is a collective responsibility; partisanship is the province of a consolidated democracy, not a democratic transition.

[25] Diab, *Uprisings or Revolutions*, 210–1.

[26] Manar al-Shourbagi, 'Kefaya: Redefining Politics in Egypt' [Arabic], in *The Return of Politics: New Social Movements in Egypt* [Arabic], ed. Dina Shehata (Cairo: Ahram Centre for Political and Strategic Studies, 2010), 118.

[27] Abou Elela Mady, personal interview.

[28] Dina Shehata, 'Youth Protest Movements: Youth for Change, Tadamon, and 6 April Youth Movement' [Arabic], in *The Return of Politics: New Social Movements in Egypt* [Arabic], ed. Dina Shehata (Cairo: Ahram Centre for Political and Strategic Studies, 2010), 249–50.

Party.²⁹ Nonetheless, protest continued in various forms, including the establishment of organizations that agitated against normalization with Israel and activism within professional associations.

Anger with Sadat and his policies was at its height on the eve of his assassination. The president's response – which demonstrated the extent to which he had become politically isolated – was to launch a campaign of arrests that swept up 1,563 political figures and activists from across the political spectrum.

1 Protest under Mubarak

Mubarak's era began with an attempt to contain the anger unleashed by Sadat's policies. He released all of those detained during September 1981, seeking to present himself as more moderate and tolerant of opposition than his predecessor. This period saw an unexpected, spontaneous social protest by the CSF, the instrument of regime suppression itself, when on 25 and 26 February 1986, tens of thousands of angry CSF conscripts took to the streets to protest their living conditions.

The incident began at two CSF camps, one on the road between Cairo and Fayoum and the other on the road between Cairo and Alexandria, after a rumour spread that the government was about to extend CSF conscripts' compulsory service from three to four years while cutting their pay. The next day, protests spread to six other camps around the country. Conscripts vandalized hotels and shop fronts, clearly indicating their resentment at the markers of prosperity and consumption that they were expected to protect. But with the proclamation of a state of emergency and the deployment of the army, the mutiny was soon quelled.

The CSF revolt was the culmination of years of pent-up anger at the mistreatment of conscripts, most of whom were and are from impoverished rural backgrounds due to the regulations governing military service.³⁰ According to official figures, some 107 people, most of them conscripts, were killed (104 of them in Cairo and the other 3 in Assiut), and another 719 were injured; some unofficial counts put the number in the thousands. Thousands of CSF conscripts were detained, along with other homeless or marginalized young men who had joined in with the attacks on luxury facilities. Some 21,000 conscripts were discharged. The traditional

---

[29] Abou Elela Mady, personal interview.
[30] Ibrahim al-Sahari, '25 and 26 February 1986: Twenty Years after the CSF Uprising' [Arabic], *Centre for Socialist Studies*, 2006, Available online: https://bit.ly/32qa6BL (accessed 17 February 2014).

opposition (the Wafd, the Labour Party, the NPUP[31] and the Liberals) all supported the regime's policy.[32]

2 Protest in Mubarak's last decade and the rise of the new social movements

In later decades, a pan-Arab sensibility was an essential factor in bringing Egyptians out to protest political conditions. Similar motivations were behind the massive demonstrations held in solidarity with the Second Intifada in 2000, which came after years of citizen disinterest in politics and alienation from Arab realities. It is worth noting that because of the regime's disagreements with Israel's approach to Yasser Arafat and the intifada, it permitted demonstrations and even encouraged secondary schools to organize protests; the official media provided almost propagandistic levels of support.

Demonstrations against regime positions – whether on Palestine after Camp David, on Iraq during the Kuwait War or the US invasion in 2003, or on the gas deal signed with Israel – generally acted as a sort of safety valve for opposition forces to express various social and political demands. The Palestinian cause in particular, which enjoyed a unique legitimacy among struggles against injustice, was the opposition's greatest weapon (even if it was not the consensus issue that it was in other Arab countries because of the regime's involvement in the peace accords, its emphasis on the burden Egypt had shouldered by confronting Israel and its partial success in promoting an Egyptian nationalism, instead of the pan-Arabism of Nasser's era).

The Second Intifada was a political awakening for the generation born in the 1980s. Time after time in the interviews that I conducted for this book, activists involved in the 25 January revolution told me that they had first become politically aware or active with their involvement in the Palestinian solidarity movement during that period. Wearing a Palestinian *keffiyeh* became a symbol of revolutionary politics among young Egyptians.[33]

These solidarity demonstrations were not limited to Cairo. Similar events took place in the governorates of Alexandria, Aswan and Suez. In the latter governorate, for example, the Bar Association called for a demonstration that ultimately attracted the largest number of people of any outside Cairo. Many of the secondary school pupils who participated

---

[31] Ibid.
[32] The NPUP is commonly referred to as the Tagammu.
[33] Various interviews conducted by ACRPS personnel with activists from diverse political and intellectual backgrounds.

en masse were arrested by the police but were released after their families threatened to continue their protest unless they were freed. During protests against the People's Assembly elections of the same year, American and Israeli flags were burnt on an almost daily basis,[34] a linkage of domestic and pan-Arab issues that can be attributed to a local political culture rooted in ideological diversity and a long history of resisting occupation.[35] Demonstrations and spontaneous walkouts took place at every Egyptian university, particularly al-Azhar and Cairo University in the capital. Protesters universally demanded that the Israeli ambassador be expelled and the embassy closed down.

In February 1997, some twenty years after the Bread Uprising of 1977 and twenty-five years after the student uprising of 1972, the Mahrousa and Elgeel centres[36] called a meeting that attracted around 1,000 attendees.[37] The meeting provided a space for activists from the left, liberal and nationalist movements and the Islamists of the Wasat Party to conduct in-depth discussions on how to bring about political change, ultimately producing two books on the subject:[38] *Debates* and *The Future*.[39] On 13 October 2000, a few days after the Second Intifada began, the Egyptian Popular Committee to Support the Palestinian Intifada was founded on the initiative of similar groups.[40] Regular popular demonstrations were held in solidarity with the intifada, the largest taking place in Tahrir Square on 10 September 2001.[41]

Protests intensified after the battle of Hebron in 2002, with an almost unparalleled wave of demonstrations sweeping the country. The largest of these, which took place in front of Cairo University on 1 April 2002, culminated in clashes between demonstrators and security forces, which were concerned by its proximity to the Israeli embassy.[42] Further intensification accompanied the 2003 invasion of Iraq. On 20 and 21 March

---

[34] Ahmed El-Kelany (member of the NAC General Secretariat and the Karama Party), personal interview, conducted by Ahmed Abd Rabou, Suez, 17 November 2011.

[35] Abdullah El Tahawey (Egyptian journalist raised in Suez), personal interview, conducted by Nerouz Satik and Hani Awwad, Doha, 8 October 2012.

[36] The Mahrousa Centre is a publishing and journalism organization run by Faried Zahran. The Elgeel ('Generation') Centre is a research body concentrating on youth and social issues, founded by the late Ahmed Abdalla Rozza.

[37] Farid Zahran, *The New Social Movements* [Arabic] (Cairo: Cairo Institute for Human Rights Studies, 2007), 46–7.

[38] Abou Elela Mady, personal interview.

[39] Zahran, *The New Social Movements*, 48.

[40] Ibid., 31. See also: Ala al-Din Hilal, *The Egyptian Political System: Between Past Legacy and Future Prospects, 1981–2010* [Arabic] (Cairo: al-Dar al-Misriyya al-Lubnaniyya, 2010), 458.

[41] Mohammad El Agati, 'Protest Movements in Egypt: Phases and Evolution' [Arabic], in *Social Movements in the Arab World: Egypt, Lebanon, Bahrain* [Arabic], ed. Amr El-Shobaki (Beirut: Centre for Arab Unity Studies, 2011), 204.

[42] Ibid., 205.

2003, some 40,000 demonstrators prevented from gathering in front of the US embassy regrouped in Tahrir Square,[43] where they were brutally beaten by the security forces; 800 of them were arrested.[44] It was in these protests that emails and mobile phones were used for the first time to mobilize demonstrators. They also midwifed the leftist 20 March Movement.[45]

This activism, particularly within the popular Palestinian solidarity committee, was largely led by veteran opposition activists who had cut their political teeth in the 1970s. At around the same time, twenty-two of these activists held a series of meetings to discuss the possibility of putting democratic change on the common agenda of demands, thereby undercutting the regime's attempts to play on Western fears of movements focusing on Iraq and Palestine.[46] In September 2004, these meetings produced the EMC, known universally as Kefaya ('Enough!').

Kefaya maintained that any attempt to address national and pan-Arab issues had to begin with political and social reform.[47] At its founding, it comprised four main groups. The first three represented small but organized political parties: Abou Elela Mady's Islamist Wasat Party; the left-Nasserists of the Karama (Dignity) Party, led by Hamdeen Sabahi and Amin Iskander; and the Islamic Labour Party headed by Magdy Ahmed Hussein and Magdy Qorqor. The fourth group consisted of prominent independents from a range of ideological backgrounds,[48] who had perhaps the greatest influence on the character of the new group.

Kefaya was able to achieve such prominence because its founders realized that the established channels of political activity were either stacked against them or incapable of absorbing demands for change. As such, it refused to become a single-issue group, instead adopting a range of political and social demands.[49] Its first protest took place in front of the High Court in downtown Cairo on December 2004. An advert placed in *Egypt Today* brought some 1,000 people out to join the organizers – and about twice that number of CSF.[50] Nonetheless, attendees made the daring

---

[43] Ibid., 206.
[44] Mohammad El Agati, 'The Left and Protest Movements in Egypt: Ajeej – Popular Committee for Supporting the Uprising – March 20 Movement' [Arabic], in *The Return of Politics: New Social Movements in Egypt* [Arabic], ed. Dina Shehata (Cairo: Ahram Centre for Political and Strategic Studies, 2010), 80–1, 85.
[45] Abou Elela Mady, personal interview.
[46] George Ishaq, personal interview, conducted by Islam Hegazy, Cairo, 22 May 2012.
[47] Hilal, *The Egyptian Political System*, 460–1.
[48] Zahran, *The New Social Movements*, 48–9.
[49] Shourbagi, 'Kefaya', 116.
[50] The CSF was established by ministry resolution no. 1010 of 1969. It was established as highly-trained specialized forces, tasked with confronting riots, disturbances, violence, and any other activity threatening the security and safety of Egypt's internal front, as well as any acts that the police were unable to confront. See: Muhammad Al-Gawadi, *Police Commanders in Egyptian Politics 1952–2000* [Arabic] (Cairo: General Egyptian Book Organization, 2008), 67.

decision to attack the president directly, with activists waving placards explicitly rejecting any extension of Mubarak's term or familial succession project; this was the first occasion on which the chant 'down with Hosni Mubarak' was ever recorded in Cairo (similar words had, however, been used at labour mobilizations in Mahalla Al-Kubra in the 1980s).[51] Many passers-by indicated their support by making the victory sign.[52]

Over the next few years, Kefaya actions fostered the development of a protest culture, and its list of demands steadily expanded, with demonstrations targeting unemployment and corruption. At the same time, it acquired an unprecedented degree of organizational complexity, with sectoral branches like Journalists for Change, Doctors for Change, Artists and Authors for Change, and Students for Change representing the desire for political change among youth and the middle classes. The movement soon began to influence bloggers and human rights organizations,[53] whose younger employees were drawn to Youth for Change, which was set up to push Kefaya leftwards. By 2005, Youth for Change included some 200 activists from Palestine solidarity and anti-globalization groups.[54]

Kefaya intensified its activities after February 2005, when Mubarak announced his intention to amend the constitution, and in March and April of that year organized significant protests outside the capital. A massive demonstration held on 25 May showed the success of its cumulative approach, but also triggered a brutal response from the security forces, who beat up and arrested protesters as well as harassing female participants.[55]

Another major force that emerged around the same time as Kefaya was the PCC. The PCC took longer to get off the ground, with its ideologically diverse make-up causing early organizational problems, and ultimately restricted its membership to individuals in a personal capacity, changing its name to the PCC (Freedom Now). It subsequently operated more or less as a coalition of leftist figures, most of whose members had also participated in the Palestine solidarity committee. It was distinguished from Kefaya by the early adoption of the slogan 'no military rule!' alongside more conventional attacks on Mubarak's attempts to engineer additional terms or pass the presidency onto his son, as well as its attempts on at least three occasions to move beyond non-elite protest by organizing in poorer neighbourhoods.[56]

[51] George Ishaq, personal interview.
[52] Abou Elela Mady, personal interview.
[53] Ahmed Menissi, *New Social Movements in the Arab Region: The Egyptian Case* [Arabic] (Abu Dhabi: Emirati Centre for Strategic Studies and Research, 2010), 128–9.
[54] Shehata, 'Youth Protest Movements', 255.
[55] Agati, 'Protest Movements', 215–6.
[56] For more, see: Zahran, *The New Social Movements*, 55–8.

Other single-issue groups also appeared during this period, including the 9 March Independent Universities Movement[57] and Engineers Against Receivership.[58] Whatever their precise character, however, the new social movements[59] shared two key features: they had emerged outside established partisan and institutional frameworks, and, unlike older movements that had avoided direct criticism of the president himself, all rejected any extension of Mubarak's presidency or dynastic succession. The political veterans of the 1970s played a pioneering role in building coalitions that cut across ideological lines and were able to attract and politicize a new generation of young activists.[60]

II Social protests

Various protests within specific social sectors or professions have taken place in Egypt over the years, generally motivated by low wages, poor public services such as water and bread shortages, or motorway accidents. In most cases, the main driver was mounting either economic burdens or the positively scandalous level of government and economic corruption,[61] and the demands were for higher wages or social security provision. While these actions were given extra impetus by the success of the new social movements in reviving a culture of protest, the forces behind these strikes and labour mobilizations had almost no connection whatsoever to the traditional partisan and political structures – though party activists may have taken part in them – or even to Kefaya and the other new movements. The state's response was typically to try and isolate them from the rest

---

[57] Established in 2003 by university professors, the 9 March Movement held its first conference in 2004 after a long conflict with Cairo University authorities. From its founding, it participated actively in protest activities, opposing the privatization of education, student fees and the Interior Ministry's campus security. Its name refers to the 1932 resignation of the then rector of the Egyptian University, Ahmed Lutfi el-Sayed, in protest against the minister of education's decision to reassign the academic and public intellectual Taha Hussein away from the university without his permission. See: *al-Araby al-Jadid*, 4 March 2014, Available online: https://bit.ly/2FFQ4tV (accessed 19 July 2014).

[58] Founded in 2003 with the aim of restoring the Engineers' Association's corporate rights and holding free and fair elections for a new board (as well as subsidiary demands concerning wages and other similar issues). See: *al-Wafd*, 5 November 2011, Available online: https://bit.ly/2ZAGNut (accessed 17 December 2014).

[59] I use the term 'social movements' to distinguish these groups from parties on the one hand and non-governmental organizations on the other. Social movements operate as organizations that mobilize their bases with the aim of accomplishing various sociopolitical objectives, and are not limited to a particular party or ideology.

[60] This point comes out clearly in various sources, including Dina Shehata, 'Introduction: The New Protest Movements in Egypt' [Arabic], in *The Return of Politics: New Social Movements in Egypt* [Arabic], ed. Dina Shehata (Cairo: Ahram Centre for Political and Strategic Studies, 2010), 12–18.

[61] Agati, 'Protest Movements', 226.

of society, to incite popular opinion against them as 'divisive' and self-interested, or even to accuse them of undermining national security and aiding the country's enemies – a 'securitization' of political discourse.[62] In order to better understand the sectional nature of these demonstrations, we will look in some detail at four protests that served as stepping-stones on the way to further protests: the uprising by textile workers in Mahalla Al-Kubra, the property tax clerk demonstrations and various violent uprisings in impoverished areas of the Egyptian countryside, Sinai and the urban hinterland.

1 Misr Spinning and Weaving strike, Mahalla Al-Kubra

Although workers had participated actively in the 1919 revolution and the 1935 uprising, it was only with the 1946 workers' and students' uprising that they began to take part in protests as an essential social force. Prior to the Second World War, workers had occupied a relatively weak position in Egypt's socio-economic structure. But as importing from Europe became difficult and domestic production was ramped up to meet the shortfall, their numbers increased and this position rapidly improved. In 1942 the Wafd government granted workers the right to organize in unions, and with the war over, much of Egyptian industry was brought to a grinding halt, including most of the new manufacturing sector that had emerged during wartime.[63] There had been labour mobilizations before in Cairo and elsewhere, some of them closely associated with establishment power struggles.[64] But the strikes at Misr Spinning and Weaving in 1946 and 1948 were the first ever in Mahalla Al-Kubra and were so large that British armoured cars were sent in to suppress them.[65]

Nasser's socialist policies – which included the nationalization of major companies and worker representation on boards – afforded workers the opportunity to participate in governance and to improve their lot, and other than the Kafr al-Dawwar incident, there was no major labour unrest during his tenure. But under Sadat, it returned with a vengeance. On 21 March 1975, a wildcat strike took Mahalla by storm, sparked not by party

---

[62] The term 'securitizing' used here comes from the Copenhagen school's critique of classical security theory, which has focused exclusively on warfare. See: Janicke Stramer-Smith and Ian M. Hartshorn, 'Securitising the New Egypt: Partisan vs. Revolutionary Demands', *The Journal of North African Studies* 26, no. 1 (April 2020): 2.
[63] Diab, *Uprisings or Revolutions*, 182.
[64] Oshti, 'Historical Roots', 101.
[65] Fathy Abdelhamid (member of the General Federation of Pensioners board of directors in Mahalla Al-Kubra), personal interview, conducted by Ahmed Abd Rabou and Islam Hegazy, Mahalla Al-Kubra, 19 December 2011. See also: Rabab Mahdi, 'The Workers of Mahalla: The State of a New Labour Movement' [Arabic], in *The Return of Politics: New Social Movements in Egypt* [Arabic], ed. Dina Shehata (Cairo: Ahram Centre for Political and Strategic Studies, 2010), 157.

activists and experienced labour leaders but a group of ex-conscripts who had returned from the 1973 war to find a desperate economic situation and a government with little regard for the sacrifices they had made.[66] After an attempt by the security services to storm the factory left seven strikers dead and seventy others injured, an enormous demonstration was held calling for the dismissal of the interior minister. The factory ultimately remained closed for several days.[67]

In 1977, a group of labour leaders who had first met at the 1975 demonstrations – Nasserists and leftists hostile to Sadat's foreign and domestic policies – set up a committee to represent Mahalla's weavers. The committee soon announced fresh demonstrations, set to coincide with the Arab-African summit to be held in Cairo in March of that year. Their hopes of embarrassing Sadat in front of sixty-something delegates of Arab and African countries, however, were dashed by the security forces, who detained the leaders for several months before transferring them to various other factories in order to keep them apart.[68]

Increased pressure from the security forces and the dispersal of the leadership was a major blow to the labour movement. A new round of protests in 1986 restricted itself to purely social demands, such as overtime pay on Fridays and holidays. Nonetheless, some 170 protesters were detained by the security services for 30–60 days. In 1988, the committee managed to organize a second demonstration, and this time participants paraded around a coffin with Mubarak's name written on it. Once again, the leaders were rounded up and moved to different factories after their release.[69]

In 1986, railway workers went on strike; a group of political activists who had spoken up in support of them were detained by the security forces immediately afterwards. In 1989, stoppages were organized by iron and steel workers, and in 1995 textile workers in Kafr al-Dawwar went on strike, too.[70] All of these movements were violently suppressed by the security forces.[71]

On 7 December 2006, the Mahalla weavers went on strike again, this time to demand two months' worth of bonuses promised them by the prime minister. The leaders this time were veterans of the actions of the 1980s,[72]

---

[66] Fathy Abdelhamid, personal interview.
[67] Ibid.
[68] Ibid.
[69] Ibid. This group consisted of Magdy Hussein, Mohammad El Sheikh and Shawqi al-Shaykh.
[70] Mahdi, 'The Workers of Mahalla', 146.
[71] Ibid., 156.
[72] Kareem el-Beheiri, personal interview, 3 January 2012. On union organizing after the Mahalla strike, see: Joel Beinin and Hossam el-Hamalawy, 'Strikes in Egypt Spread from Center of Gravity', *MERIP*, 5 September 2007, Available online: https://bit.ly/35yjzJb (accessed 25 October 2021).

with women workers the first to move, leading their male co-workers to demonstrate outside the company headquarters on Talaat Harb Square.[73] On previous occasions, stoppages had lasted only a few hours, but on this occasion around 10,000 workers went on strike for three whole days, even setting up a committee to coordinate their activities.[74] As a result, they were able to secure a bonus equivalent to forty-five days' wage from the authorities.

In March 2007, 5,000 employees resigned their membership of the Weavers' Union to protest its failure to support the strike. In December, they downed tools for another six days – this time to make sure that the promises made in 2006 were kept. By the end of this strike, they had won 70 days' additional pay, which subsequently increased to 130. At Misr Spinning and Weaving's general assembly meeting on 17 February 2008, about a month and a half before the 2008 uprising, the entire board of directors tendered their resignations.[75]

The Mahalla strike galvanized workers and precipitated a string of labour mobilizations throughout the public and private sectors, in other textile companies, cement factories and railway yards and on the metro. These demonstrations were so large that the police were unable to respond to them with violence.[76]

These mobilizations showed that workers were willing to fight, but they did not necessarily indicate any real level of political awareness. They were typically driven by the results of neoliberal policy and strengthened by the Mahalla workers' long tradition of protest – many participants had parents or relatives who had taken part in the protests of the 1970s.[77] These were local strikes rooted in social demands, without any significant contribution from political parties despite the latter's attempts to establish a presence.

Workers continued to organize, and in February 2007 strikers demanded a minimum wage. As demonstrators chanted 'down with Mubarak', the security forces sought to pen them inside the factory, threatening to open fire if they attempted to leave.[78] As we will see, attempts to expand the scope of the strike to include political demands and use it as a springboard to a general strike – the great hope of the 6 April Movement – ultimately failed. But in Mahalla itself, workers began to see their struggle as more than just

---

[73] Mahdi, 'The Workers of Mahalla', 152.
[74] Kareem el-Beheiri, personal interview.
[75] Mahdi, 'The Workers of Mahalla', 152.
[76] Abdel Ghaffar Shokr, *The Struggle for Democracy in Egypt* [Arabic] (Cairo: Centre for Arab and African Research, 2009), 272.
[77] Mahdi, 'The Workers of Mahalla', 155–7.
[78] Kareem el-Beheiri, personal interview.

bread-and-butter demands, part of a bigger struggle against the Mubarak government.[79]

Law 35/1976 on Egyptian labour syndicates had deprived unions of various rights that they should have enjoyed under the international agreements to which Egypt was a signatory. The Ministry of Labour was granted broad powers to suppress unions, including the right to object to the formation of new unions and demand the dissolution of elected boards or set prerequisites for membership. Moreover, extensive procedural regulations effectively allowed the ministry and the security forces to control the results of union elections, and stack boards and committees with figures more loyal to the regime than to workers' interests.[80] With union leaders repeatedly refusing to back workers' calls for strikes or protests, it is no surprise that the two groups became steadily more estranged.

One of the largest legal obstacles to workers exercising their right to organize was a provision restricting union membership to full-time workers, totally excluding temporary workers, who constitute a significant portion of those employed in the private sector and the new investment projects. As a result, official unions represented only a minority of Egypt's workers, around 1.5 million out of a total workforce of 19 million.[81] Workers were forced to establish their own unofficial organizations to fill the gap, including the Centre for Trade Union and Workers Services, the Labour Rights and Freedoms Coordinating Committee, and the Labour and Unions Observatory.[82]

2 The property tax clerks' strike and the first independent union

Workers' successes in using protests and strikes to wrest back certain rights encouraged other social groups to follow their lead. One of the most successful such groups was the property tax clerks, whose strike ultimately produced the first independent union in Egypt – as well as securing them better wages and working conditions and their reassignment from the Ministry of Local Government to the Finance Ministry, as had been the case before 1974.

Representatives from property tax offices throughout Egypt first came out to protest in October 2007. When the government failed to meet any of their demands, they decided to escalate, launching simultaneous strikes at almost 500 sites across the country (440 tax offices and 50 local government

---

[79] Stramer-Smith and Hartshorn, 'Securitising the New Egypt', 5.
[80] Shokr, *The Struggle for Democracy*, 203.
[81] Ibid., 204–5.
[82] For more on these organizations, see: Ibid., 202–20.

branches); in total, these sites employed some 50,000 workers.[83] On 3 December 2007, they began an eleven-day sit-in in front of the People's Assembly and the Finance Ministry. After negotiations between the government and the strike committee, the clerks succeeded in winning all their demands.

This committee operated on a democratic basis: most of its decisions were taken by a simple vote, and both the central committee and its branches in the governorates were elected by strikers.[84] Although many of the strikers had clear political leanings – Kamal Abou Eitta, for example, was a veteran Nasserist activist who had cut his teeth in the 1970s – they kept political demands out of the strikes, allowing for straightforward, demand-based negotiations to be conducted with the government. The security forces acted as the mediator between the strikers and the government, employing carrot or stick as the trajectory of the protests required:[85] negotiations when strikers behaved as they wanted them to, detention and accusations of collaborating with Israel or the United States when they did not.[86]

The network of strikers and the strike committee itself concluded that they needed a union independent of the pro-government official syndicate, as provided for by both local and international law. Their opportunity came when Minister for Manpower Aisha Abdel Hady met with a delegation from the ILO to discuss union freedoms in Egypt. Protesters gathered outside the ministry building, chanting demand after demand until delegates heard them and an embarrassed Abdel Hady was forced to meet them and officially accept their application to establish a union.[87] According to the syndicates' law, a union acquires juridical personality from the date on which its incorporation papers are deposited, and the administrative body shall lose its right to object one month after the date of deposit.[88] The ILO provided further backing, writing to Mubarak specifically to express its support for the founding of an independent union.[89]

With a new union established, members abandoned the official union in droves,[90] with some 47,000 switching their membership over – a

---

[83] Kamal Abou Eitta, interview, conducted by Islam Hegazy, Cairo, 12 April 2012. Abu Eita was the president of the Egyptian Federation of Independent Unions and a member of the Karama Party.
[84] Ibid.
[85] Amr El-Shobaki, 'The Property Tax Collectors' Protests: From Sectional Strike to Independent Union', in *The Return of Politics: New Social Movements in Egypt* [Arabic], ed. Dina Shehata (Cairo: Ahram Centre for Political and Strategic Studies, 2010), 182–5.
[86] Kamal Abou Eitta, personal interview.
[87] Ibid.
[88] Cairo Institute for Human Rights Studies, *Bastion of Impunity, Mirage of Reform: Human Rights in the Arab Region, Annual Report 2009* (Cairo: CIHRS, 2009), 123, Available online: https://bit.ly/3Ecbpo0 (accessed 1 October 2021).
[89] Shobaki, 'The Property Tax Collectors' Protests', 194.
[90] Ibid., 189–90.

remarkable number, given that membership was entirely voluntary.[91] Following a complaint from the head of the ETUF, proceedings were launched against its elected president, Kamal Abou Eitta, who was accused of establishing an illegal union.[92] Nonetheless, the clerks' victory had shown the way: hundreds of independent unions sprouted up across various different sectors.

3 Provincial protest

Before the 1952 revolution the large landowners had controlled every aspect of life in the countryside, treating the peasants that worked their vast estates like serfs. Their close links to the provincial state apparatus allowed them to circumvent the law and cover up dubious and even criminal practices. Politically and socially, landowners were a conservative force that functioned as a bulwark against change to the prevailing social order; the idea of peasants' children receiving an education – and the possible changes that this might bring about in the way that they saw the world and their own circumstances – caused them a great deal of anxiety.[93]

Perhaps the most famous collective act of resistance against the dominance of the landlords is that of the people of Kamshish, a small village in the Nile Delta governorate of Monofiya. Resistance against the local landowning family, the Fiqqis, began in the immediate aftermath of the 1952 revolution. Led by Salahuddin Hussein, a young, educated leftist, the villagers even engaged in armed clashes with the Fiqqis' men. Although the uprising spurred Nasser to intensify implementation of his land reform programme, the repeated failure of the July regime to deliver on its promises meant that the struggle continued intermittently for over a decade. After Hussein's assassination in 1966, Kamshish became an icon of the global struggle between landlords and peasants, receiving stopovers from Jean-Paul Sartre, Simone de Beauvoir and Che Guevara when they visited Egypt. Kamshish returned to the news in the 1990s after Law 96/1992 effectively reversed the land reform and allowed the mass eviction of tenant farmers.[94]

---

[91] Kamal Abou Eitta, personal interview.
[92] Cairo Institute for Human Rights Studies, *Bastion of Impunity*, 123.
[93] Assem Desouky, *Large Landowners and Their Role in Egyptian Society, 1914–1952* [Arabic] (Cairo: Shorouk, 2007), 259–76.
[94] One side of this story can be found in the defence drafted by the leftist lawyer Nabil al-Hilali on behalf of Shahenda Maklad, peasant organizer and wife of Hussein, in petition no. 11807/2005, filed with the Nasr City Misdemeanour Court. See: *Muntada al-Mohamoon al-'Arab*, 27 March 2012, Available online: https://bit.ly/3AHozav (accessed 17 October 2021). See also: Mitchell, *Rule of Experts*, 169–71; Yassin Taha, 'The Socialism of 23 July and the Battles of Small Landholders in Kamshish' [Arabic], Centre for Socialist Studies, September 1997. Archived copy available online:

Under Sadat and Mubarak, protests in the countryside generally took one of two forms: peaceful protests against the unavailability of basic agricultural necessities (fertilizer, water, seeds)[95] or violent clashes with landowners attempting to reappropriate land distributed to peasants under Nasser's reforms.[96] Clashes of the latter kind were commonplace in many parts of the countryside between 2004 and 2010, as efforts to evict tenant farmers with the support of the police and the judiciary met with fierce resistance.[97] Take, for example, the small rural settlement of Sarando. In February 2005, Salah Nawwar – whose family had owned extensive estates in the area as long ago as the Ottoman period – attempted to seize villagers' land, supported by the security forces and hired toughs. When the villagers resisted, the local police chief rounded up the village women, hoping to force their menfolk to surrender; one woman was so badly beaten that she died.[98] Collective punishment of this kind was a regular response to resistance by landless farmers.[99]

4 Protests on the periphery

Violence and law breaking are manifestations of indirect – and sometime unwitting – protest by the marginalized. The negative relationship of marginalized, peripheral regions with the centre accounts for a great deal of the violence witnessed by those regions. Sometimes this violence takes political forms, whether religious or otherwise, while at other times it manifests as a refusal to obey laws imposed by the centre or to abandon local custom.

Ever since its liberation from Israel in 1982, the Sinai Peninsula has been seen as a 'land without a people'. Cairo has treated it less as an integral part of Egypt finally restored to the motherland than as a massive tract of land ripe for commercial development – irrespective of the desires or aspirations of the local population, who have been ignored or even excluded entirely from the process. This has resulted in a steady build-up of resentment among the local population. This resentment finally found its voice in 2004, when

---

https://bit.ly/2ZDmmA7 (accessed 28 October 2021). For more detail on the Kamshish uprising, see: Shirin Abu al-Naga, *From the Papers of Shahenda Maklad* [Arabic] (Cairo: Merit, 2006).

[95] Various demonstrations of this kind are mentioned in the reports of the Egyptian Organization for Human Rights (EOHR).

[96] Many incidents of both peaceful and violent forms of rural protest are documented in: Sayyed Ashmawi, *Peasants and Power in Light of the Egyptian Peasants' Movement* [Arabic] (Cairo: Merit, 2000), 225–48.

[97] Atef Shehat Said, *Torture in Egypt, 1981–2008: A Crime Against Humanity* [Arabic] (Cairo: Dar al-Iltizam, 2010), 75–8.

[98] 'Nafisa al-Marakibi: A Farmer Who Paid Her Life to Defence of Her Land', *al-Ard*, no. 7 (April 2010): 17.

[99] Said, *Torture in Egypt*, 78–82.

the indiscriminate arrest of as many as 6,000 people in the aftermath of the Taba bombings[100] provoked outrage across the peninsula.[101] Protest has been a regular part of life in Sinai ever since, intensifying as locals have abandoned their fear of the security forces. The city of El Arish in particular became famous for the demonstrations held in its central square every week after Friday prayers between 2004 and 2007,[102] in which local Tagammu activists played a central role.[103] Another city, Sheikh Zuweid, was the scene of violent clashes between local protesters and the security forces in 2004, with protesters repeatedly blocking the main road.[104] As men were often subject to harsh security measures, women have played a key role in demonstrations.[105] Sinai's tribal culture fostered a degree of solidarity among protesters that should not be underestimated.[106]

The We Want To Live movement was established in 2007 to demand development in the region; it brought together the various tribes living along Egypt's Sinai borders with some inhabitants of the city of El Arish.[107] In 2005, activists in the countryside set up the Land Reform Peasants' Solidarity Committee to fight for the rights of rural workers.[108]

As part of its ongoing war on insurgent groups in Sinai, the regime has employed particularly harsh measures against the inhabitants of the desert region, refusing to recognize property rights, forcibly halting land reclamation projects and excluding them from the development of major tourist centres. This, alongside the broader economic problems and sense of marginalization felt throughout Sinai, led many locals to take up arms on several occasions from 2004 onwards. The policy of arbitrary security harassment naturally resulted in more frequent clashes between resentful citizens and the state. By 2010, some border areas were entirely 'liberated'

---

[100] A series of bombings took place on 9 October 2004 in two Sinai resort towns close to the border with occupied Palestine, resulting in thirty-four deaths.
[101] Mostafa Singer, personal interview, conducted by Ahmed Abd Rabou, Ismail Alexandrani and Aly El Raggal, Sheikh Zuweid, 22 October 2011. Singer was an activist and journalist formerly involved with the Tagammu Party and later a member of the Socialist Revolutionary Movement.
[102] Salah El-Buluk, personal interview, 21 October 2011.
[103] Mostafa Singer, personal interview.
[104] Ashraf Alanany (poet and blogger from Sheikh Zuweid), personal interview, conducted by Ahmed Abd Rabou, Aly El Raggal and Ismail Alexandrani, Sheikh Zuweid, 22 October 2011.
[105] Salah El-Buluk, personal interview.
[106] Sa'id Uteil, personal interview, conducted by Ahmed Abd Rabou, Aly El Raggal and Ismail Alexandrani, Sheikh Zuweid, 22 October 2011. Uteil is a left-wing activist and member of the RYC in Sheikh Zuweid.
[107] According to Salah El-Buluk, the most important founders included Salah Buluk, Yahya Abu Nusseira, Mohammad al-Mani'i and Massaad Abu Fajr, a novelist detained for some two years before being released only months before the revolution and who founded the We Want To Live blog.
[108] Bashir Saqr, 'News Report on Farmers' Movements in Egypt in Recent Years' [Arabic], *Contemporary Worker Research Centre*, 3 May 2009, Available online: https://bit.ly/32BsHed (accessed 23 July 2014).

from any police presence, and in a few cases of role reversal locals ended up detaining policemen.[109]

This phenomenon predates the involvement of extreme Islamist groups in the peninsula like al-Tawhid wa'l-Jihad from 2005, and more recently Ansar Bait al-Maqdis, which in 2015 announced that it had joined ISIL. Sinai natives' great bitterness at being excluded and treated as an obstacle to commercial development did not by any means translate into a warm reception for terrorist movements among the mass of the population, but a small number of locals were sympathetic, and the collective punishment meted out by the state does not distinguish between collaborators and non-collaborators. Just as they have in other countries, these extremist movements have steadily overshadowed the sociopolitical issues that initially drove protest, subsuming a local battle into the global War on Terror. This point was reached in Egypt with the military coup of 2013.

III Palestine and protest

Pan-Arab causes have enjoyed a unique ability to bring together different political forces in Egypt, and this is particularly true of the Palestine issue. Egypt's role in the Gaza blockade and the regime's collaboration with Israeli aggression against Gaza in 2008 contributed to a growing sense of bitterness and anger among many Egyptians. As already noted, the Palestine issue provided much of the impetus for the formation of the new social movements that, after twenty-three years of stagnation, were now leading a new wave of protests. How the security forces dealt with these protesters shifted markedly, however, when they began to turn their attention to the sufferings of the Gaza Strip.

The first demonstration against Egypt's decision to participate in the Gaza blockade by closing the Rafah border crossing took place on 23 January 2008, when the Popular Committee to End the Blockade organized a peaceful gathering in front of the Egyptian Bar Association. On this occasion, demonstrators were surrounded by a huge security force cordon intended to prevent them from leaving the area. The next day, Kefaya and various political parties organized a demonstration in Tahrir Square, which was followed on 3 March by a sit-in, again in front of the Bar Association. In both cases, protesters were the victims of considerable CSF violence.

---

[109] Salah El-Buluk, personal interview.

On 1 September of the same year, the 6 April Movement, along with Nasserists and Islamists, organized another gathering in front of the State Council, this time to protest the new gas export treaty with Israel; they met with harassment from the security forces. On 24 November, the ongoing blockade and the refusal to allow humanitarian aid to enter Gaza as well as the gas treaty were the target of yet another protest, this time involving thousands of students from universities across Egypt.

When Israel launched its attack on Gaza on 28 December 2008, the popular belief that Egypt was collaborating directly with Israel sparked simultaneous demonstrations across the country;[110] some 3,000 people in the governorate of Fayoum, for example, came out to protest the Israeli assault. Professors and students organized protest vigils and demonstrations on their campuses, with the biggest taking place not in Cairo but at Assiut University in Upper Egypt. Members of the People's Assembly occupied the parliament building and demanded the expulsion of the Israeli ambassador. All of these demonstrations saw a major security presence intended primarily to prevent demonstrators from moving freely and turning their protest into a march.[111]

On 29 December, thousands of students at Ain Shams University came out to protest, accompanied by almost the entire faculty. Vigils were organized by the Doctors' Syndicate, the Aid Committee, the Shari'a Association, opposition and independent members of the People's Assembly, and representatives of the Red Crescent. In Giza, staff and students from Cairo University organized a demonstration that attracted more than 3,000 people – and thousands more attendees from the security services, who prevented them from taking their protest off campus and onto the streets.[112] Other actions were organized by activists, opposition parties and the new social movements. On 31 December, more than 100 activists who had participated in the Tahrir Square sit-in were detained by the police.[113]

---

[110] On 25 December 2008, the then Israeli foreign minister Tzipi Livni visited Cairo and met with Mubarak, even holding a joint press conference with her Egyptian counterpart, Ahmed Aboul Gheit. Livni took the opportunity presented by the press conference to warn Hamas that Israel was about to change things in Gaza, saying that their control of the Strip would not be allowed to continue and that the resistance's rocket fire would soon be silenced. During her visit, the Egyptian state newspaper *al-Ahram* ran a front-page story accusing Hamas of preventing the entry of humanitarian aid. See: 'Palestinian Sources to Ahram: Hamas prevents the delivery of Egyptian Aid to Gaza Strip, 26 December 2008', [Arabic] *Palestine Today: Alzaytouna*, no. 1273 (2008).

[111] Nashwa Nashat, ed., *The State of Human Rights in Egypt: Annual Report 2008* [Arabic] (Cairo: Egyptian Organization for Human Rights, 2008), 234–5.

[112] Ibid., 236–7.

[113] Sayyid Fawzi Abu'l-Ala, *Charged with Supporting Gaza* [Arabic] (Cairo: HIsham Mubarak Law Centre, 2010), 79–80.

On 17 January 2009, more than 10,000 citizens gathered in Cairo's Ramses Square to protest the Israeli attack on Gaza and demand an immediate end to gas exports to Israel. This demonstration was broken up by the security forces using truncheons, and dozens of participants were detained.[114]

On 24 March, when students at Fayoum University organized a 'Victory for Gaza' festival, two faculty administrations turned their own students in to the police; a third, the Faculty of Agriculture, suspended seven of its students for a week for participating in a sit-in.[115] At least three activists who had crossed into Gaza itself to express solidarity with its inhabitants were arrested and tried by military courts, receiving prison terms of one to three years alongside heavy fines for crossing the Egyptian border illegally: Ahmed Douma, a law student in Tanta and coordinator of the 'Angry Ones' youth movement; Magdy Hussein, the secretary general of the Islamic Labour Party; and Kamal Abdel Al, a young man from Upper Egypt.[116] Douma was later to play a significant part in the January revolution.

In the same year, the security forces also cracked down on the football Ultras firms, conducting operations on the eve of matches to prevent any pro-Palestinian chants at the stadium. The hard core of the Ahlawi and White Knights firms – associated with Cairo's most prominent teams, Ahly and Zamalek – were detained on the eve of a major showdown, after a previous game against Ismaili where fans from both sides had shouted pro-Palestinian slogans.[117] Ultra activity, formerly a matter of tribal support for clubs that served as proxy homelands, was beginning to take on the character of protest.

Various human rights reports[118] attest to the Egyptian regime's violent police crackdown on those who protested the Gaza blockade, not to mention those who attempted to run the blockade and deliver humanitarian aid to Gazans themselves. This approach contrasts directly with the relative tolerance shown to protests demanding better socio-economic conditions.[119] Ironically, the Mubarak-era regime had not been at all tolerant of the limited socio-economic protest of the 1980s and 1990s,

---

[114] Nashat, *The State of Human Right in Egypt*, 237.
[115] 'Behind the Walls of Fear: Police Siege on Fayoum Governorate' [Arabic], *Arabic Network for Human Rights Information (ANHRI)*, 3, Available online: https://bit.ly/3ixHYSN (accessed 5 October 2014).
[116] On the trials, see: Abu'l-Ala, *Charged*, 53–66.
[117] Mohamed Gamal Beshir, *The Ultras: When the Masses Challenge Nature* [Arabic], 4th edn (Cairo: Dar Dawwen, 2012), 65–6.
[118] In particular, the 2008 and 2009 reports of the EOHR; the 2009 and 2010 reports of the CIHRS; the AOHR's 2009–2010 report on the state of human rights in the Arab world; and the ANHRI.
[119] *Human Rights in the Arab World: Report from the Arab Organization for Human Rights on the State of Human Rights in the Arab World, Annual Report 2009–2010* [Arabic] (Beirut: Centre for Arab Unity Studies/Arab Organization for Human Rights (AOHR), 2010), 225; Cairo Institute for Human Rights Studies, *Bastion of Impunity*, 126.

but in the new millennium, with attracting foreign investment now the overriding concern of the regime and its circle of businessmen, it wanted to cultivate an image of a 'politically open' Egypt. It was thus willing to take a more restrained approach so long as demonstrators avoided directly political demands. Pro-Palestine demonstrations, however, were brutally crushed. The main determinant of the regime's behaviour towards protest activity was the all-important relationship with the United States, and Western powers had no objection to repressive action in defence of Egypt's relations with Israel. Pro-Palestine protests thus suffered the same fate as demonstrations with political demands.

IV Escalation in the last years of Mubarak

In the final years of Mubarak's tenure, a diverse group of political and social forces began to converge around a single goal: the end of his presidency, with no extension of his terms and no dynastic succession within his family. The effects of this convergence began to be felt with the formation of new broad-base social movements serving as a broad umbrella for joint activity between diverse groups, a development that provided a major boost to the wave of protest sweeping the country.

The figures below show that between 2001 and 2008 there was a dramatic jump in the number of peaceful demonstrations in Egypt. The objects of these protests ranged from the general to the very specific and sectoral, from great national causes to quotidian problems, from union mobilizations to demonstrations of solidarity, whether with the poor and deprived or with political prisoners.[120]

Sectoral strikes doubled over a five-year period, with twenty-four recorded in 2008. Work stoppages became a weapon used by all sorts of groups, from doctors and pharmacists to drivers and teachers.[121] More dramatically, from 2007 to 2008 the number of sit-ins and occupations

---

[120] Nashat, *The State of Human Right in Egypt*, 219–20. Nariman al-Sayyed gives higher figures, claiming that between 1998 and 2004 there were as many as 1,000 demonstrations in the country, largely of a socio-economic character but occasionally demanding political change. She says that this figure continued to rise after 2005. See: Nariman al-Sayyed, 'The New Media and Opportunities for Democratization of Authoritarian Regimes: A Study of the Vision and Practices of Politically Active Youth, the Case of Egypt' [Arabic], in *The Egyptian Revolution: Motivations, Trends and Challenges* [Arabic], ed. Aya Nassar et al. (Beirut: Arab Centre for Research and Policy Studies, 2012), 270–1.

[121] This figure does not include individual hunger strikes as a form of protest. The EOHR suggests that these, too, increased some six times over between 2007 and 2008. See: Nashat, *The State of Human Right in Egypt*, 238–43.

Table I.3.1 Development of Peaceful Protest (2001–8)

Year	2001	2002	2003	2004	2005	2006	2007	2008
No. of demonstrations	19	6	12	24	20	27	14	94

Source: Nashat, *The State of Human Rights in Egypt*, 219–20.

increased seven times over, with forty-two examples representing all the different social groups that participated in demonstrations or strikes.[122]

To gain a clear understanding of the nature of the protest movement in this period, however, we must take a closer look at where these actions were taking place between October 2005 and January 2009. Coverage of peaceful protest activity in this period from three newspapers of quite distinct political and ideological leanings (*Elbadil*, *Al-Masry Al-Youm* and *al-Dostor*)[123] shows that protests were not confined to the capital. Quite the contrary: protests took place in every single governorate, despite the security forces' tight grip on these regions and their ability to freely engage in abuses that would have been sure to attract media attention in Cairo. Some 58.6 per cent of protests occurred outside Cairo and Alexandria, showing just how far the culture of protest had spread within Egyptian society.[124] The single-most common object was to secure economic and social rights, with approximately half of demonstrations taking place for this purpose. Opposition to corruption or torture came in second place, while demands for political rights came in third.

Popular protest was thus a fixture of the landscape in the years leading up to the revolution. Nary a day passed without some sort of protest or strike, the majority of which had specific sectional demands. For the most part, the regime responded to these protests without using force, the aforementioned exceptions aside. Its main concern was to clamp down on any attempt to articulate demands for political change, and in these cases it was willing to use force wherever necessary.[125]

A fresh crop of social actors joined protest activity in 2010 off the back of particular social demands. These demands included some of particular relevance to Egypt's Coptic Christians: a unified law on the establishment of places of worship, for example, allowing for the construction and

---

[122] Ibid., 249–57.
[123] These figures correspond closely with statistics compiled by various human rights organizations, including EOHR and CIHRS.
[124] Imad Siyam, 'Map of Peaceful Protests in Egypt: Preliminary Indications of the Emergence of a New Kind of Civil Society' [Arabic], in *The Return of Politics: New Social Movements in Egypt* [Arabic], ed. Dina Shehata (Cairo: Ahram Centre for Political and Strategic Studies, 2010), 49–76.
[125] Gamal Zahran, 'Regional Trends in Egypt and their Relations with the Center' [Arabic], in *The Egyptian Revolution: Motivations, Trends and Challenges* [Arabic], ed. Aya Nassar et al. (Beirut: Arab Centre for Research and Policy Studies, 2012), 139.

renovation of churches. At the same time, working-class and lower-middle-class anger was increasingly expressed not in socio-economic demands but sectarian violence, encouraged by the media and a small group of Muslim and Christian preachers. In early 2010, for example, a widely circulated rumour that a Christian man had raped a Muslim woman resulted in attacks on several church properties. Sectarian tensions and violence against Copts had been rising gradually since 2002 – a development in which the security forces likely played no small part – but they reached a violent climax on 7 January 2010, in the city of Nag Hammadi, where eight Copts and a policeman were killed[126] in an attack whose motives remain unknown (although accusations were made against a local NDP grandee).[127] On 14 February, in direct response to this incident, a massive demonstration was held in Tahrir Square to call for reform of the church construction law and other legal measures to ensure equality between Muslims and Christians in a range of fields.[128] In November of the same year, three demonstrators were killed in violent confrontations with the police after thousands of Copts came out to protest restrictions on church building in Giza.[129] Protests of this kind culminated in the vast anti-sectarian rallies organized by Egyptians of all religions in the aftermath of the Church of the Saints bombing on New Year's Eve 2010 (we will return to this event shortly).

V The Brotherhood and the new movements

The first decade of the new millennium saw a sea change within the Egyptian opposition, which ceased to be the exclusive preserve of the parties and movements that had developed in the early years of Mubarak's tenure. Walid Kazziha identifies two major currents within the pre-2010 opposition: one, represented by the likes of Kefaya and the NAC, which rejected any prospect of reform under the existing regime; and another, comprising party groups like the Brotherhood or the Wafd, which continued to exploit the margin of freedom provided by the regime and shied away from demanding political change.[130] The distinction here is not so much

---

[126] Cairo Institute for Human Rights Studies, *Roots of Unrest: Human Rights in the Arab Region, Annual Report 2010*, 149, Available online: https://bit.ly/3vHGY5R (accessed 1 October 2021).
[127] Some footage of the events can be viewed on *YouTube*, 8 January 2010, Available online: https://bit.ly/3iuT5Mv (accessed 20 July 2014).
[128] Footage of an earlier demonstration is available on *YouTube*, 3 January 2011, Available online: https://bit.ly/3kjVUQG (accessed 20/12/2014).
[129] Cairo Institute for Human Rights Studies, *Roots of Unrest*, 150.
[130] Walid Kazziha, 'Egypt under Mubarak: A Family Affair', in *Egypt's Tahrir Revolution*, ed. Dan Tschirgi, Walid Kazziha and Sean F. McMahon (Boulder, CO: Lynne Rienner Publishers, 2013), 30.

between different parts of the protest movement as between the protest movement and the traditional parties. But while there is much truth to this distinction, it lacks important nuance. Both Kefaya and the NAC drew heavily on party forces at their formation. These forces had been searching for alternatives to the traditional alliances and counterbalances of partisan politics, and the new social movements – which had a very different character due to the involvement of prominent independents, including academics and media figures – provided a solution. Moreover, the Muslim Brotherhood in particular can be distinguished from the other parties.

On the one hand, the Brotherhood had greater numbers and organizational capacity; on the other, the margin of freedom it enjoyed was much narrower. Unlike other parties, its members were often hounded by the security forces, and its offices and branches shut down. The regime took great pains to prevent it from translating its popular clout into political clout, whether at the ballot box or elsewhere. And after its many 'ordeals', as the organization refers to the recurrent bouts of persecution throughout its recent history, many Brothers were wary of a full-on clash with the regime. The Brotherhood's decision not to pursue the revolutionary option was thus, in part, the product of pragmatism among its members.

Brothers had participated in various protests of a pan-Arab character as part of the new wave of demonstrations that had swept Egypt. Particularly notable was a demonstration against the Iraq war held at Cairo Stadium on 27 February 2003, organized by the Brotherhood with the permission of the Interior Ministry – an event followed only a week later by a similar NDP demonstration at the same venue, featuring speeches from Gamal Mubarak and party chairman Safwat El-Sherif. During this period, the regime was willing to provide an outlet for political movements to express their dissatisfaction with American neocons' policy.

The Mubarak-era Brotherhood thus generally operated within the margin of freedom afforded it by the regime, particularly after 2002. It avoided confrontation in the hope that it would be able to secure a gradual expansion of this margin. It did not become an official part of Kefaya, precisely because the latter's willingness to attack the presidency directly was at odds with this strategy. It knew very well that any moves in that direction would see the regime's forbearance immediately withdrawn – that it would not even enjoy the limited tolerance otherwise granted to Kefaya. The moment the Brotherhood showed itself willing to raise issues like presidential term extensions or the succession project, the regime would see it as a threat.

Nonetheless, from 27 March 2005 – the date of a demonstration in front of the High Court downtown and in Ramses Square – Brotherhood members did begin to participate in Kefaya actions. Coordination between the two movements was a sensitive issue for both parties. The Brotherhood was anxious to avoid a direct confrontation with the regime and thus took part within carefully defined limits intended to avoid provoking the government. Kefaya, on the other hand, did not want their protests dominated by Brotherhood elements.

By the 2005 elections, the occupation of Iraq had brought with it US pressure to expand the margin of permitted political activity, and the Brotherhood ran a campaign of unprecedented daring and scope, fielding around 400 candidates. Under the usual slogan, 'Islam is the solution,' it mobilized almost every last member in massive rallies held throughout the country. In the first round of voting, it secured 34 out of 164 available seats, nearly twice the 18 won by the non-Islamist opposition. The prospect of losing the two-thirds majority required to push through constitutional amendments, however, alarmed the regime. The head of the SSIS, Major General Hassan Abdel Rahman, met with the Brotherhood's General Guide Mahdi Akef and his deputy Khairat el-Shater and demanded that they reduce the number of candidates they were set to run in the second and third rounds or else face arrests and police action. The negotiations were sufficiently stormy that Akef himself withdrew and left the process to his deputy, but the Brotherhood ultimately agreed to field few enough candidates that they would not be able to repeat their performance in the first round. This meant convincing a number of candidates who had already begun campaigning to withdraw. Shater promised to take responsibility for this difficult task in order to convince the general guide to throw his weight behind the move.[131] But despite Akef's backing and the extensive powers he was granted to this end, Shater was largely unsuccessful. The regime then followed through on its threat, arresting some 800 Brotherhood members and engaging in brutal voter suppression in much of the country. Nonetheless, the Brotherhood managed to win another forty-two seats, bring its total to seventy-six. In the final round, the regime simply shuttered many polling stations and falsified the results, and NDP thugs were set loose on the electorate. The final count left the pro-regime bloc holding 330 of the 445 seats, the Brotherhood with 88 and the remainder of the opposition with a paltry 12. Under the constitution then in force, the final ten representatives were appointed directly by Mubarak.

---

[131] Interview with a former Brotherhood member who asked to remain anonymous for personal reasons, 22 November 2012.

Between the second and third rounds of voting, intelligence chief Omar Suleiman had several meetings with Israeli officials.[132] It was commonly believed in Israel that Egypt was hoping Tel Aviv could convince US policymakers that the prospect of a Brotherhood victory was dangerous enough to justify turning a blind eye to any repressive measures taken by the regime.[133]

By the time the 2010 elections came round, however, pressure from the neoconservative administration in the United States had receded, and the regime dispensed with any pretence of fairness whatsoever. The security forces wasted no time on negotiations. Police initiated an arrest campaign, 30 of the Brotherhood's 100 candidates were disqualified on dubious grounds, and results were simply falsified in many cases to preclude Brotherhood victories. As hundreds of Brothers protested the conduct of the election outside polling stations in Alexandria and Cairo, only a single Brotherhood candidate was elected.[134]

The flagrant manipulation of the electoral results was the source of much bitterness for younger members of the Brotherhood as well as the opposition more broadly, which served as the impetus for the establishment of a 'shadow' opposition parliament. Intergenerational tensions within parties – and a sense among younger members that the boundaries of traditional partisan political action dictated by the leadership were insufficient and needed to be left behind – had been building since the beginning of the decade. These young people had already begun to challenge the established balance between the Brotherhood and the regime, even if this meant disregarding ideological and tribal barriers. Many of them participated in the sectoral actions discussed earlier in this chapter. In February 2009, for example, Brotherhood members participated in a demonstration at Cairo University demanding higher education reform alongside students from a range of other movements and parties. In September 2010, a Brotherhood contingent joined members of the NAC, the 6 April Movement and other groups at a protest against the prospect of Gamal Mubarak's succession to the presidency. In an individual capacity, young Brothers were also

---

[132] Omar Suleiman was made head of the GIS in 1993, and from 2000 he began to become a public figure, first appearing in the spotlight alongside Mubarak at the funeral of Syrian president Hafez al-Assad. He subsequently appeared regularly in the media to discuss Sudanese and Palestinian issues. In 2003, he was tipped to be a possible successor to Mubarak in the Western press. This possibility was a topic of much discussion within Egypt.

[133] Wikileaks subsequently showed that although Suleiman did meet with Israeli officials in September 2005, the topic of discussion was actually how to prevent a Hamas victory in Palestinian elections, which the regime feared would strengthen the Brotherhood's hand in Egypt. See: *The Jerusalem Post*, 11 February 2011, Available online: https://bit.ly/3c1V08D (accessed 24 October 2021). Suleiman also visited Ramallah on 20 December, the day before the third round of voting in Egypt.

[134] BBC Arabic, 29 November 2010, Available online: https://bbc.in/2DXTYhk (accessed 20 December 2014).

present at most of the vigils for Khaled Saeed, whose death we will return to shortly.[135]

The Egyptian Brotherhood had always placed a premium on the political, organizational and religious education of the younger generation. Young Brothers thus played a prominent part in efforts to push the boundaries of political activity. They were enthusiastic participants in almost any protest action at a time when demonstrators were beginning to call for political change. Although this placed Brotherhood leadership in a hugely difficult position, General Guide Akef – who, unlike most of the members of the Brotherhood's most senior body, favoured the society's reformist current – gave them support and encouragement. In fact, Akef repeatedly circumvented established decision-making protocols to the benefit of younger members.[136] By 2010, the growing disconnect between the Brotherhood and its younger members had reached such a pitch that they were threatened with expulsion, having sided with Abdel Moneim Aboul-Fotouh and Essam el-Erian's reformist current during the group's Consultative Council elections in 2009 and criticized the leadership's decision to break the opposition boycott of the December elections.

The founding of the Brotherhood-led Free Union of Egyptian University Students provided an important forum for cooperation with left and liberal students from other movements and backgrounds.[137] Although these young people were part of the Brotherhood organization, the leadership were willing to allow them a certain degree of freedom to operate alongside other youth groups and help organize demonstrations. Although the Brotherhood itself did not participate in the 25 January protests or the 'Friday of Rage' in any official capacity, Brotherhood members were present in large numbers. Young Brothers also became famous for their Facebook activism, publishing posts under their real names and engaging in continuous debate with those of other political persuasions. Unlike older generations of the organization, closely bound by the authority of the office of the General Guide, they had no central hierarchy.

Hozaifa Aboul-Fotouh, a former Brotherhood activist, offered an extensive breakdown of the reasons for the intergenerational gap within the organization's ranks. Most important, he says, was the sense that the leadership were complacent and happy with the status quo, while younger members were attracted to revolutionary causes and wanted to reconsider

---

[135] Hozaifa Aboul-Fotouh, interview, conducted via Skype with ACRPS staff, 6 February 2014, supplemented by Khaled El-Sayed, personal interview, 10 November 2015.
[136] Islam Lotfy, personal interview, conducted by Nerouz Satik and Hani Awwad, Doha, 9 October 2012. Lotfy is a former Brotherhood activist, member of the RYC and the coordinator of the Egyptian Current Party, created after the revolution.
[137] Ibid.

the Brotherhood's approach to the government. Moreover, they chafed at the strong centralization of authority and the unwillingness to allow others to express their opinions. This exclusivism and a refusal to accept criticism had led to political and intellectual stagnation. As Aboul-Fotouh put it: 'You can express your opinion, so long as you can tolerate paying the price and being marginalized later, but in the end whatever [the leadership] says goes. [They] know best, they are best equipped to judge, they have the most informed view of the situation – not to mention the security precautions that need to be taken.'[138]

The first step in the 'soft exclusion' of a member who repeatedly objected to the leadership's decisions was to pass them over for any organizational responsibilities, restricting their participations to basic meeting attendance. Those who were particularly rebellious and wanted change were branded 'troublemakers' and marginalized or even accused of disloyalty. Only rarely was anyone actually expelled. It was more common for dissidents to be 'hounded out', to be isolated and excluded until they left of their own accord, leaving many of them with a deep-seated hostility to the Brotherhood – or, more accurately, its leadership. Moreover, as is often the case in centralized parties of this kind, the leadership often privileged reliability over ability. Deputy leader Khairat el-Shater, who had held responsibility for both the financial and organizational affairs of the Brotherhood since his release from prison in 2000, had used his uniquely powerful position to replace much of the Brotherhood's leadership with his own favoured candidates, beginning with the all-important middle leadership but eventually working his way down to the smallest units of organization, the individual branches and the cells known as 'families' (*usar*). The appointment of unqualified candidates to lead individual families was the subject of a great deal of resentment among members, particularly a younger, bolder generation more concerned with issues of national concern than internal politicking.

This general sense of alienation encouraged some young Brothers to dedicate more of their time to other protest movements or their activities than they did to the Brotherhood. More and more young members found themselves agreeing on a number of key points – that the Brotherhood had ceased to be an appropriate, or at least sufficient, framework within which to pursue their common vision; that remaining within the organization meant missing out on more open and more developed ways forward; and that reform from within was no longer a satisfactory prospect. These young people began to pursue their own initiatives.

---

[138] Hozaifa Aboul-Fotouh, personal interview.

Husam Tammam conducted a comprehensive review of the Brotherhood's attitudes towards the protest movements, analysing their behaviour through the lens of the political opportunities available in Egyptian society. He argues that changes in these attitudes were closely linked to the degree of political openness present in the political system at any given time, as well as the organization's own internal distribution of roles and available resources.[139] Throughout much of the later twentieth century, the Brotherhood had become institutionalized as part of the Egyptian political fabric, and as a result its leadership had become somewhat tribal, looking down on other, 'weaker' political parties. In the last decade of Mubarak's rule, moreover, it suffered from an inability to understand the new mechanisms for change that had developed within Egyptian society, mechanisms neither it nor any other traditional party could control.[140]

The problem for the Brotherhood was ultimately that its greatest strength was also its greatest weakness. It was a substantial, well-organized force with an ability to put boots on the ground unmatched by any other non-state force in the country. Maintaining this position required it to operate as a single, closed, homogenous mass, and the intellectual and social uniformity necessary to achieve this effectively transformed it into a sort of community – the group's official name is the Society of Muslim Brothers, after all – distinguished even from a more general popular religiosity by its peculiar lifestyle and language, as if it were a sect. As a result, regardless of the organization's numerical strength, it was easy to cordon it off from the rest of society, especially when relations with the regime were in crisis – under Nasser, for example, or when its competitors formed a united front against it with the state apparatus in the build-up to the 2013 coup. Although the Brotherhood enjoyed an unparalleled capacity to organize, mobilize and provide services, it also constituted a closed, all-encompassing community with a single position on every issue. Members were expected to submit to this community completely, whether in how they lived their lives or the smallest particulars of their political opinions. Other groups were judged solely by how closely they conformed to the Brotherhood. This is the key to understanding the Brotherhood's relations with other figures. An ally that had outlasted his usefulness could become an enemy at the first whiff of disagreement.

---

[139] Hossam Tammam, *The Muslim Brotherhood: Before the Revolution* [Arabic] (Cairo: Shorouk, 2012), 54.
[140] Ibid., 62–3.

VI The labour movement and the new social movements

In 2006, the political parties of Mahalla Al-Kubra agreed to establish a joint coordinating committee, which by 2007 was fully operational. The committee included activists of all different political persuasions, including communists, Nasserists, Brotherhood members and representatives of a few local liberal parties.[141] Activities were coordinated from the headquarters of the DFP,[142] located a convenient distance from Shoun Square in the heart of the city. The mass demonstrations organized by the committee have already been discussed elsewhere. Kareem el-Beheiri's *Workers of Egypt* blog, with its constant flow of pictures and video clips from local protests, became an important source for journalists, intellectuals and opposition activists.[143] Labour leaders, for their part, sought to capitalize on the relative success of strike actions in 2006 and 2007 by building ties with workers at other companies and in other cities, hoping that by increasing the pressure on the Egyptian government they could make as many gains as possible. But these attempts bore very little fruit, other than the Mahalla Weavers' Association, which brought together Beheiri with the veteran leftist Gehad Tahhan and the Democratic Workers Party activist Kamal El-Fayoumi.[144] The association, which also cooperated with other such leaders,[145] agitated for wage increases, greater labour freedoms and better housing and healthcare.[146]

On March 2008, *Voice of the Mahalla Workers* announced an impending strike, without giving a date.[147] The *Workers of Egypt* blog likewise published a statement exhorting workers to 'put a nail in this corrupt regime's coffin'.[148] This was enough to alarm the regime, and the security forces promptly occupied the city, detaining workers at the factory or in their homes. Some labourers felt that the more politicized leadership had undermined their attempts to secure their more local demands with their imprudent communiqués.[149] In a press statement on the eve of the strike, the Brotherhood expressed its reservations about the 'chaos' that a new action

---

[141] Alaa Bhlawan (DFP in Mahalla), personal interview, conducted by Ahmed Abd Rabou in Mahalla Al-Kubra, 19 December 2011.
[142] A liberal party established in May 2007 and absorbed by the Liberal Party on 21 December 2013. Its most prominent member and leader was Osama El-Ghazali Harb.
[143] Kareem el-Beheiri, personal interview. For more, see his blog *Workers of Egypt*, Available online: https://bit.ly/3mo8lgf (accessed 24 October 2021).
[144] Ibid.
[145] Ghada Ragai, *Report on the Conditions of Workers in Spinning, Weaving, and Garment Manufacture* [Arabic], Land Centre for Human Rights, November 2008.
[146] Ibid.
[147] Ibid.
[148] Kareem el-Beheiri, personal interview.
[149] Mahdi, 'The Workers of Mahalla', 165.

might cause.¹⁵⁰ Both the Wafd and Tagammu likewise voiced misgivings, citing the failure to coordinate with traditional forces and the unknown provenance of the calls to strike.¹⁵¹ Although none of these groups rejected the right to down tools in principle, they were unwilling to hitch their carts to a movement they had no part in and did not know the origins of.

Naturally enough, given the broad popular sympathy for the people of Mahalla, there were efforts to reproduce the experience in Cairo and thereby escalate the challenge to Mubarak's government. Activists, among them Ghad Party activist Esraa Abdel Fattah, set up a Facebook page titled 'No Surrender: Egypt's Youth Will Take It Back', which called for a general strike on 6 April encompassing both industry and public sector workers throughout the country. Within three days it had around 77,000 subscribers.¹⁵² Mobile phones, messages, emails and posts on social media were used to promote the action.¹⁵³ On 6 April, the media descended on Mahalla, where the security forces attempted to prevent the foreign press from covering the event.¹⁵⁴ Various opposition activists were also there, waiting with bated breath for the workers to come out to strike. But the security forces managed to scotch the timing by taking workers out of the city centre en masse via circuitous routes a few hours earlier, making it very difficult for them to get to the protest on time.¹⁵⁵ A group of young protesters gathered on Bahr Street with the intention of joining demonstrations, which quickly escalated when the police assaulted an elderly woman, dragging in passers-by who had initially had no intention of participating. As more and more people joined the protests, swelling their numbers to the tens of thousands, more and more security officers were brought in as reinforcements.¹⁵⁶ One group of protesters cut off the railway line, and power cuts and communications blackouts occurred across the city. The security forces were able to take back control of the city overnight,¹⁵⁷ but on the following day protesters came out in even greater numbers than before. When night fell, they attempted to round up activists. Fires and

---

[150] Ibid., 164.
[151] 'Politicians and Activists: 6 April created a new Political Map in Egypt', [Arabic] *Cairo Institute for Human Rights Studies*, 23 April 2008, Archived Copy Available Online: https://bit.ly/3JW867h (accessed 25 October 2021).
[152] Mahmoud Afifi, personal interview, conducted by Islam Hegazy, Cairo, 14 April 2012. Afifi was the media spokesman for the 6 April Movement and founder of its Qalyobiya branch.
[153] Shehata, 'Youth Protest Movements', 261.
[154] Kareem el-Beheiri, personal interview.
[155] Alaa Bhlawan, personal interview.
[156] Ibid.
[157] An example of such random arrests can be seen on *YouTube*, 7 April 2008, Available online: https://bit.ly/2Ftl80n (accessed 21 July 2014). In his interview, Kareem el-Beheiri claimed that the security forces set fire to several schools in order to portray the protesters as rioters. I have been unable to verify this claim.

violent confrontations swept the whole of Mahalla, and the protest saw its first casualty: a secondary school student on the balcony of his home.[158] He was quickly followed by three others.[159]

After this high point, the demonstrations sputtered out. Demonstrators' chants had focused on high prices and poor living conditions. But it was clear that this was no normal labour protest focused on day-to-day concerns: protesters tore down a huge picture of Mubarak from a billboard in Shoun Square and stamped all over it, giving vent to broader resentment towards the regime. However, the mass of the workers had not participated – not only because of the security forces' ruse but also because the minister of labour hurriedly conceded to some of their demands[160] and because they were warned that politicization would harm their cause. We ought to add the caveat that many individual workers and their families must inevitably have taken part, since in an industrial city like Mahalla it would be impossible for a major demonstration to take place without some worker support. But the fact remains that this was a classic case of workers rejecting attempts to politicize a strike action for fear that it might undermine their own struggle. Management are generally able to come to an understanding with their employees before the strike's energy can be redirected towards broader political aims. In a sense, of course, this means that the action has succeeded, in that is has forced employers to give in to demands in order to avert this intersection of labour agitation and political activism.

In the aftermath of the uprising, the head of the city council was dismissed and replaced with the head of the local SSIS. A security clampdown followed: some forty-nine citizens were prosecuted on various charges.[161] There was a coda to the story: on 9 April, some 200 people held a vigil outside a police station in the city, demanding the release of detainees.[162] Similar vigils were held in February 2009 outside the courts to call for the release of twenty-two people who had received prison sentences of between three and five years.[163]

---

[158] Alaa Bhlawan, personal interview.
[159] Personal interviews with Abdelmonem Emam (3 January 2012) and Kareem el-Beheiri.
[160] Personal interviews with Fathy Abdelhamid (19 December 2011).
[161] Nashat, *The State of Human Right in Egypt*, 220.
[162] Ibid., 226.
[163] Ibid., 239.

VII The 6 April Movement and the general strike

The many strikes that took place during the last few years before the revolution had been enough to convince young Egyptians that if the many disparate and angry forces arrayed against the regime could be brought together under a single movement, this would be sufficient to challenge the systematic despair cultivated by Mubarak. But this was rooted in a failure to understand the true nature of the sectional protests. No single movement emerged capable of channelling the energies of all the protesters, and the much-anticipated general strike failed to materialize. As a political action, a general strike is more than the aggregate of various smaller strikes. Nonetheless, the movement which had crystallized around the idea of a general strike, the April 6 Movement, was to lay much of the groundwork for the revolution, creating a revolutionary mood in the country and encouraging democratic political discourse.

We are dealing here with a protest movement of a new kind, a new social movement. Unlike older protest movements, it was not built around a single specific issue, and unlike an NGO, it sought to establish a broad social base. Founded after a series of discussions and meetings between young activists involved in the events in Mahalla, its purpose from the very beginning was to change Egyptian political and social realities. In late June 2008, a press conference was held at the Journalists' Syndicate by a small group of young people (five from Mansoura, two from Alexandria and the remainder from Cairo) to announce its establishment.[164] Alongside its media department, it boasted an organizational committee, a trustees' committee responsible for collecting member dues (20 Egyptian pounds a month) and a dedicated mass action group that was to oversee its protest activities.[165]

The founding of the 6 April Movement was a clear manifestation of the growing role of young people in political activism and their attempts to chart a different course from the veteran activists who had come of age in the 1970s. Most of its members had cut their political teeth as part of Kefaya, within the Youth for Change movement, but had become disillusioned because of security breaches or disagreements over organization.[166] It owed its rapid growth to technological advancement and the fresh hope for real change engendered by the Mahalla uprising. Like other new youth movements, it was unique in that it emphasized action, cut across ideological lines and was active in the new spaces provided by the

---

[164] Mahmoud Afifi, personal interview.
[165] Ibid.
[166] George Ishaq, personal interview.

internet and social media.¹⁶⁷ Its first action, on 27 April 2008, was typically innovative: protesters sang patriotic songs while flying kites emblazoned with the Egyptian flag.¹⁶⁸ Influenced by anti-authoritarian movements in other countries, its members showed a keen interest in revolutions in Eastern Europe and Latin America as well as other political and social issues in their online debates. At the same time, they were constantly organizing new demonstrations and actions.¹⁶⁹ Their activities provided an infusion of new energy to the protest movement throughout Egypt.

The movement's annual calls for mass demonstrations, sent out every 6 April on the anniversary of the Mahalla uprising, have led some writers to misidentify it as a labour movement and thus to make misguided claims about subsequent events.¹⁷⁰ But in fact, the 6 April Movement was not a labour movement. From its founding it was involved in a range of political-democratic and social struggles with a human rights dimension – the fight against torture, for example. And the 25 January revolution itself, whose immediate trigger was the abuses of the security forces, was a political movement relying on mass popular participation from the very beginning.¹⁷¹

In the run-up to 6 April 2009, the movement called for fresh strikes to commemorate the Mahalla uprising. Exhortations were published online and in pro-reform newspapers, with emphasis placed on the peaceful nature of the protests (as much for the Interior Ministry's benefit as anyone else's).¹⁷² The four demands – a minimum wage of 1,200 Egyptian pounds, wage increases linked to prices, an elected constituent assembly to draft a new constitution guaranteeing political and labour freedoms and placing a two-term limit on the presidency, and an end to gas exports to Israel – linked the political to the social. This daring manifesto laid the groundwork for the sort of demands that would subsequently be set forth

---

[167] Shehata, 'Youth Protest Movements', 247–50.

[168] Mahmoud Afifi, personal interview.

[169] Amr Salah (RYC and human rights activist), personal interview, conducted by Islam Hegazy, Cairo, 7 May 2012; Mahmoud Afifi, personal interview.

[170] Sean McMahon, for example, claims that the 6 April Movement was at heart a labour movement, or at the very least a working-class movement. He argues that the January revolution began as a workers' revolution with social demands, but that it was subsequently hijacked and these demands jettisoned by those with a more political agenda. Sean F. McMahon, 'Egypt's Social Forces, the State, and the Middle East Order', in *Egypt's Tahrir Revolution*, ed. Dan Tschirgi, Walid Kazziha and Sean F. McMahon (Boulder, CO: Lynne Rienner Publishers, 2013), 151–72.

[171] There is a great deal of division over how to characterize the events of January 2011: where secularists see a secular revolution, leftists see a left-wing revolution and Islamists see a revolution to topple a secularist regime. This in itself is evidence of the fact that the nature of the revolution was not determined by any ideological position on the part of its leadership. Its true nature can be discerned from the slogans that were employed and the social make-up of the protesters.

[172] See the movement's blog, *Shabab 6 April*, 11 March 2009, Available online: https://bit.ly/33qJY9b (accessed 21 July 2014).

by the revolutionaries of January 2011 and the political language that they shared. The movement was building on the extensive experience of protest that Egyptians had built up over the last few years.

The attempt to reproduce the Mahalla uprising by announcing a general strike was a failure. On 6 April 2009, after protesters managed to push their way into Tahrir Square, the security forces detained dozens of members of the movement, Kefaya, the Ghad Party and the Brotherhood student movement, among others.[173] A year later, in 2010, more than 150 young people were arrested, some 96 of whom were held at the CSF's infamous Salam Camp;[174] they had attempted to turn a march into a sit-in in front of the Interior Ministry, in an early application of the 'snowball' strategy that would later prove so successful during the January revolution.[175] The leaders of these protests subsequently formed the core of the YJF movement, whose organizational efforts were key to the 25 January protests.

The Mahalla uprising of 2008 saw young people standing shoulder to shoulder with the masses, confronting the security forces for a whole two days far away from the capital. The same applies to the call for strikes on 6 April 2009. All these demonstrations represented a new phenomenon. The identity of the organizers, the fearless language, the mass gatherings in the squares, the efforts to draw on the experience and bravery built up over years of protest – none of it differed from the events of 25 January. The behaviour of those who advocated a general strike was rooted in the mentality of a protest movement. Rather than planning to bring the country to a halt and thereby seize power, they were content to announce strikes and trust that they would spontaneously develop in the right direction. The same is true of 25 January: the structure, language and preliminary demands of the protests were those of a protest movement. The main difference was simply that in January 2011 the recent success of revolutionaries in nearby Tunisia and organizers' greater experience with new media encouraged broader popular participation and a greater degree of optimism. It was this that made the revolutionary slogans and the unprecedented success of 25 January possible.

---

[173] Cairo Institute for Human Rights Studies, *Bastion of Impunity*, 121.
[174] Khaled El-Sayed, personal interview.
[175] Alaa Bhlawan, personal interview. In 2009, pro-opposition papers were optimistic about the prospects for a broad popular escalation: *Shorouk*, for example, published a daily front-page update on the calls for a strike, hoping that it would be possible to reproduce the Mahalla uprising across Egypt (*Shorouk*, 2–7 April 2009). In 2010, however, the paper was much more circumspect, providing only brief coverage (*Shorouk*, April–May 2010).

1 Youth for Justice and Freedom (YJF)

The pan-ideological model established by veteran activists in Kefaya was soon reproduced by the younger generation in a variety of new social movements. The priority for these movements was to spur political and social change by building a more daring coalition across party lines, using the new tools available to them and acting more quickly and flexibly than Kefaya could. This did not end with the 6 April Movement. In 2010, disillusioned members of 6 April joined newly politicized activists to form YJF.[176]

In both its ideas and its activities, YJF sought to link political rights and regime change on the one hand to popular demands of a socio-economic character – particularly labour demands – on the other.[177] Its members believed strongly that if they were to succeed in changing the political system, their struggle needed to incorporate poorer demographics by speaking to the socio-economic issues that mattered to them. They made great efforts to convince the older generation of activists that the revolutionary option was feasible and that more serious and radical methods of mobilization aiming to attract the broader population were needed if the protest movement was ever going to be more than an elite struggle between the regime and a handful of opposition figures and intellectuals.[178] In this sense, it was a truly novel phenomenon and might be described as a revolutionary movement.

YJF tried to overcome traditional ideological sensitivities by emphasizing that if the regime was to be overthrown, unity was paramount. Its founders consciously spurned the problematic legacy of the opposition political elite, reaching out to young members of the Brotherhood and organizing joint protests and demonstrations. In the interests of furthering this new entente between the Brotherhood and the rest of the opposition, in the 2010 legislative elections YJF endorsed a Brotherhood candidate alongside a leftist and a liberal.[179]

In cooperation with other political forces, over the course of 2010 YJF participated in a range of demonstrations against Mubarak's

---

[176] Gamal Zahran describes YJF as 'a group [. . .] characterized by its hard-line positions after the wave of protest that followed the killing of Khaled Saeed in Alexandria, and whose most important demand was the total overthrow of the regime. YJF were in the vanguard of the youth movement calling for a revolution against the regime after the parliamentary elections of November 2010'. See: Zahran, 'Regional Trends in Egypt and their Relations with the Center', 148.

[177] YJF were close to the Socialist Renewal movement and often coordinated its activities with the latter. For this reason, many people have categorized YJF as a leftist organization.

[178] Mohamed Salah (a founder of YJF), personal interview, conducted by Mohammad Abbas, Doha, 23 January 2014.

[179] Ibid. The first joint protest took place when a member of campus security assaulted a young woman who was a member of the Brotherhood.

dynastic plans, as well as providing support to protests by workers and those on the edges of society.[180] They played an active role in the Alexandria protests that followed the death of Khaled Saeed in custody in 2010 and after the Church of the Saints bombing in early 2011.[181] They also organized protests against the law restricting church building and the strict provisions of the country's personal status laws, attempting to make the bombings part of a national issue of equality before the law and redirect sectarian resentment towards the regime.[182] It is worth noting, too, that New Year's Day 2011 saw the first demonstration by Copts *qua* Copts in Egypt's modern history, in which they were not only defending themselves against sectarianism or calling for the right to build churches but demanding full civic equality. Moreover, these demonstrations won an unprecedented amount of sympathy among the Egyptian public, and in the week after the bombings, hundreds of Muslims turned out to protect Christians celebrating Coptic Christmas.

VIII Bloggers and the technological upsurge

From 2000 onwards, the rapid expansion of internet access and the rash of websites and blogs that it brought with it (and later social media) provided a digital space capable of circumventing the barriers put up by the security forces in the real world – a space for the free expression of opinions and discussions between different intellectual currents. This digital space allowed for the fast, cheap and unfettered audiovisual transmission of protests as well as rapid communication between citizens.[183]

The effects of this change first became clear during protests against the undemocratic constitutional amendments in the early 2000s. As usual, demonstrators gathered in Tahrir Square and outside the Journalists' Syndicate and were quickly set upon by regime thugs and CSF personnel. But this time, pictures of the beatings and assaults inflicted on protesters were quickly uploaded to various blogs and picked up by Dream TV, an Egyptian satellite channel.

Bloggers began to cover political issues in 2004, at around the same time that Kefaya was organizing its first demonstrations, followed by a veritable boom in political blogging in 2005 thanks to elections and a series of high-

---

[180] Ibid.
[181] Ahmed Iraqi Nassar, personal interview, conducted by Islam Hegazy, Cairo, 24 April 2012. Nassar was a member of the RYC in Alexandria, the 'We Are All Khaled Saeed' movement and the 6 April Movement.
[182] Mohamed Salah, personal interview.
[183] Hilal, *The Egyptian Political System*, 469.

profile corruption scandals.[184] One such blog was *Egyptian Consciousness*, edited by Wael Abbas, which focused on exposing torture in regime prisons using documents and tapes leaked by security officers; it also covered police abuses during the constitutional referendum. Another blogger, Kareem el-Beheiri, provided live footage of worker sit-downs in Mahalla straight from his mobile phone.[185] And in his *We Want To Live*, Massaad Abu Fajr focused on Sinai Bedouins' fight against discrimination.[186]

In 2004, Egypt had around forty blogs; by July 2008, it had about 160,000.[187] About 70 per cent of these blogs published exclusively in Arabic, another 20 per cent in Arabic and English and another 10 per cent only in English. Their authors were generally between twenty and thirty years old, with slightly more than a quarter of them being women.[188] By 2010, there were just short of 200,000 blogs, mostly run by young people in their late teens and twenties.[189] Of course, many of these were fairly obscure and had little influence on public opinion, but some of them had substantial audiences and served as a forum for complex, nuanced debates on public affairs. As well as regular harassment and surveillance, many political bloggers faced police action. In 2006, more than 100 of them were arrested, including Abdel Kareem Soliman (known online as Kareem Amer) – who was sentenced to four years imprisonment for disseminating material against the regime and Islam – Karim Al Shaer, Hossam el-Hamalawy and Mohamed El Sharqawy, who was tortured in police custody.

The remarkable rise in blogging activity was attributable in large part to the massive expansion of communications infrastructure and computer usage overseen by the Ahmed Nazif government.[190] But it brought with it a concurrent rise in new ideas, projects and initiatives that sought to translate digital debates into manifestos and plans for real political change. The *Children of Egypt* website, for example, which covered a range of political and social issues at all levels of Egyptian society, was founded

---

[184] Sheima Abdelsalam and Hoda Salaheddin, *Blogs* [Arabic] (Cairo: International Centre for Future and Strategic Studies, 2010), 10.
[185] Menissi, *New Social Movements*, 115.
[186] Nadim Mansouri, *Sociology of the Internet* [Arabic] (Beirut: Muntada al-Ma'arif, 2014), 71.
[187] These figures are from an Egyptian Cabinet's Information and Decision Support Center (IDSC) report cited in: Open Net Initiative, 'Internet Filtering in Egypt', 2009, Available online: https://bit.ly/3kVcIxI (accessed 20 January 2020).
[188] Mohammed el-Nawawy and Sahar Khamis, *Egyptian Revolution 2.0: Political Blogging, Civic Engagement, and Citizen Journalism* (New York: Palgrave Macmillan, 2013), 77–8.
[189] Diab, *Uprisings or Revolutions*, 227.
[190] Amal Hammad, '25 January 2011: Leader, Agent, Regime' [Arabic], in *The Egyptian Revolution: Motivations, Trends and Challenges* [Arabic], ed. Aya Nassar et al. (Beirut: Arab Centre for Research and Policy Studies, 2012), 103. For more, see: Naeem Saad Zaghloul, 'Digital Media in Egypt: Reality and Challenges' [Arabic], Egyptian Cabinet's Information and Decision Support Center (IDSC), February 2010. See also: Herrera, *Revolution in the Age of Social Media*, 10.

in this period by a group of fifteen young activists from various political backgrounds. The contents of the blog were later published as a series of books titled 'Project for a Nation', and in late 2008 some of the founders established their own small press, appropriately named Dawwen ('take this down!' or 'blog it!').[191] Significantly, blogs were one of the main forums in which younger Brotherhood members began to break with the party line in 2009-10.

IX The National Association for Change (NAC) and the broadening of political participation

The emergence of groups like the 6 April Movement and YJF was not the only change that took place on the Egyptian political scene between 2008 and 2009. In August 2009, the émigré diplomat Mohamed ElBaradei, whose term as head of the IAEA was soon to come to an end, gave an interview to Egyptian TV in which he discussed the country's domestic problems at some length. Within days, a Facebook page calling for a Baradei bid in the 2011 presidential election had been set up by an economics student at Cairo University; the page quickly acquired a thousand supporters.

This attempt to put Baradei forward as a credible alternative to Mubarak was not lost on the regime, and it soon launched an extensive smear campaign, accusing him of having helped build the case for the 2003 invasion of Iraq while director of the IAEA. As a civilian enjoying diplomatic immunity and a Nobel Prize winner (along with the IAEA), Baradei represented a formidable challenge to the regime. Unlike Ayman Nour, for example, who had run against Mubarak in the 2005 election, it could not simply fabricate a criminal case against him.

Various people active on the Facebook page, meanwhile, had begun to reach out to one another, and work soon began on a campaign to promote Baradei as a consensus candidate for the opposition. In September 2009, an organized 'popular campaign' was set up. No contact was made with the man himself until members of his family joined the group, and Baradei told a US media outlet that he had 'heard the voices of the Egyptian people' despite his only contact with the group itself being a single email sent to the official address of the IAEA.[192]

The campaign quickly acquired an organizational structure and a website allowing visitors from all over Egypt to learn about it and to sign up. At first, it had no more than fifteen members. In response, several of

[191] Hammada, '25 January 2011', 106.
[192] Ibid.

the small sham parties within the regime's orbit[193] launched a counter-campaign 'to protect Egypt from Baradei', claiming that the presidential bid was 'a plot by the Zionists and Americans' intended to 'undermine national security'.[194] Having previously lauded Baradei as an internationally successful Egyptian – in 2006, Mubarak had inducted him into the Order of the Nile, Egypt's highest civilian honour – the regime now intensified its efforts to discredit him.

In 2011, Wael Ghonim set up a Facebook page to support the Baradei bid. In his book, he says that while he was not a very political person, the idea of a Baradei presidency gave him a glimmer of hope that change was possible. Criticism of Mubarak was often met with questions about the alternative. By setting up the page, he hoped to show that there *was* an alternative.[195]

The campaign began to plan activities on the ground. The first step was to organize a huge rally at the Cairo airport to welcome Baradei back to the country and announce his presidential candidacy. In cooperation with the 6 April Movement, they were able to publicize the event on social media as well as in some traditional media outlets. The campaign against Gamal Mubarak's succession also agreed that some of its prominent members would put in an appearance, including Hassan Nafaa and George Ishaq. When Baradei's plane touched down on 19 February 2010, he was met by a crowd of 3,500 people carrying placards emblazoned with the words 'Baradei for president!'[196]

Baradei was an academic and international technocrat with little experience of politics, whether in government or opposition. Nonetheless, after discussions with various prominent figures in Egypt and the young people who had put the campaign together, he agreed to participate. The campaign became better organized and better structured, training its members in techniques of achieving peaceful change and drawing on the lessons of international non-violent protest movements. It acquired some 10,000 volunteers, who canvassed support for Baradei across the country. As well as engaging in traditional protest activities, it came up with innovative new ways of expressing dissatisfaction: 'beep for Baradei', for example, involved racing down a street honking your horn before making

---

[193] Specifically, the Homeland Party, the Democratic Peace Party, the People's Party, the Arab Egypt Party, the Democratic Federation Party, the Free Republican Party and the Egyptian Liberal Party.
[194] *Al-Masry Al-Youm*, 1 March 2010, Available online: https://bit.ly/2RsxQ1Y (accessed 20 December 2014).
[195] Wael Ghonim, *Revolution 2.0: If, One Day, the People Wanted to Live* [Arabic], 2nd edn (Cairo: Shorouk, 2012), 57.
[196] Video footage of Baradei's arrival as attendees sing the national anthem can be seen on *YouTube*, 19 February 2010, Available online: https://bit.ly/2ZzN2yy (accessed 25 October 2021) and on *YouTube*, 20 February 2010, Available online: https://bit.ly/35AFbEU (accessed 23 July 2014).

yourself scarce to avoid the long arm of the security forces. The movement also began to receive funding from businessmen outside the narrow circle of magnates close to the regime.[197]

In October 2010, the campaign made plans to hold extensive demonstrations in front of the various 'tombs of the unknown soldier' scattered around Egypt's different governorates. Part of the plan involved Baradei writing an article for *Dostor* titled 'a message to the armed forces', but in the event the security forces blocked publication of the article and forced editor-in-chief Ibrahim Eissa to resign. Activists received anonymous phone calls from private numbers threatening them with arrest and warning them of very harsh treatment if they went ahead, forcing them to call off the demonstration.[198] The regime was unwilling to accept any attempt to speak directly to the army or even to discuss its relationship with the regime – especially when the person speaking was presenting himself as the alternative.

The Baradei campaign ultimately became bogged down in internal divisions and disagreements, reducing its effectiveness. But in the course of the interviews conducted for this book, many of the newly politicized activists who played a part in the revolution made it clear that for them, Baradei's return was a symbol of hope, of the possibility of bringing about change. They needed an alternative to Mubarak capable of convincing the man on the street. This was not about his qualifications – there were many people more qualified than both Mubarak and Baradei. It is never a question of qualifications. It was a matter of finding someone who seemed like they might be able to take power. Baradei was that someone.

'But what is the alternative?' is a question commonly asked in dictatorships – rhetorically, as if there could be no possible alternative to the one-in-a-million dictator. This is the wrong question to ask: by definition dictatorship brooks no alternative. The right question is how to get rid of the dictator. With the dictator gone, a whole range of alternatives will suddenly become possible – too many alternatives, in fact. The problem is not finding an individual alternative to the ruler but coming up with an alternative political system. It is thus better to concentrate on the alternative system that will provide space for various competing figures. To propose an alternative to the dictator is simply to operate within the confines of the authoritarian regime. But Baradei, as a person, was important inasmuch as he embodied the possibility of change in a person who, thanks to his international credentials, could not easily be imprisoned or punished by the regime.

---

[197] Abdelmonem Emam, personal interview.
[198] Ibid.

In late February 2010, after extensive meetings between political and intellectual representatives of various political forces, the NAC was established.[199] The NAC incorporated the Brotherhood; the DFP, Wasat, Karama, Labour and Ghad parties; the Popular Campaign to Support Baradei; the Revolutionary Socialists and the Egyptian Communist Party; and the 6 April Movement and Egyptian Women for Change. The traditional opposition – the Wafd, Tagammu and the Nasserists – were notably absent.[200] Baradei was chosen as head and Hassan Nafaa as the first general coordinator; he was subsequently replaced by Abdel Galil Mustafa.[201]

The NAC demanded the creation of a democratic system via constitutional amendments and legal changes that would guarantee free and fair elections:[202] ending the state of emergency; empowering the judiciary to oversee the electoral process; allowing civil society groups and international organizations to act as electoral observers; guaranteeing equal media coverage for all candidates, particularly in presidential elections; providing voting infrastructure at embassies and consulates so as to allow expatriates to exercise their electoral rights; guaranteeing the right to stand in elections without arbitrary limitations, in line with the various international agreements to which Egypt was a signatory; instituting a two-term limit for presidents; and conducting the vote using national ID numbers. Without these conditions, Baradei did not think it was worth standing.

The NAC quickly set up branches across Egypt as well as abroad. It organized protests, such as the attempt to muster a million signatures demanding that its reform demands be met (the 'banging on the doors' campaign). But its rallies, demonstrations and vigils remained dependent on the willingness of its constituent forces to participate and showed a distinct lack of coordination.[203]

In the years leading up to the revolution, coordination offices intended to bridge the gap between different political forces sprang up all over

---

[199] These figures included the following: Hassan Nafaa, coordinator of the campaign against the Mubarak succession; Mohamed Saad Elkatatny, a Brotherhood representative; Osama El-Ghazali Harb, head of the DFP; Mamdouh Qenawi, head of the Free Constitutionalist Party; Ayman Nour, founder of the Ghad Party; Mustafa al-Tawil, from the Wafdist campaign against the Mubarak succession; Hamdeen Sabahi of the Karama Party; Essam Sultan of the (at this point still unofficial) Wasat Party; Judge Mahmoud Khudairi; Kefaya leaders George Ishaq and Karima Hefnawy; People's Assembly member Gamal Zahran; and various cultural figures, including the author Alaa Al Aswany.

[200] *Al-Masry Al-Youm*, 25 February 2010, Available online: https://bit.ly/35EFbDJ (accessed 4 June 2013).

[201] Abdelmonem Emam, personal interview.

[202] *Al Jazeera*, 7 February 2011, Available online: https://bit.ly/3mfrSj7 (accessed 23 July 2014).

[203] Ibid.

Egypt. These offices brought together prominent figures from across the political spectrum, including the new generation of activists and political parties. More ideological individuals also took part, although generally in a personal capacity; this tendency was particularly marked in the case of the Muslim Brotherhood. But while those involved in these initiatives came from a diverse range of backgrounds, they were giving expression to a more general, national feeling, a feeling channelled by local elites aware of both the urgent need for change and their own role in bringing it about.

In Cairo, in the aftermath of the Mahalla uprising, a group of lawyers and activists set up the FDEP, which provided legal support to those detained for participating in protests.[204]

In 2010, the Rasd network of election observers was established in anticipation of the fraudulent parliamentary elections of that year.[205] In the same year, the Hisham Mubarak Law Centre began to coordinate its efforts with the FDEP, 6 April, the We Are All Khaled Saeed campaign, and the Brotherhood youth,[206] hoping to help protect human rights protesters. The Brotherhood also organized several joint protests at Cairo University with My Right, a leftist group.[207] Even the Tagammu youth managed to break free of the party's cautious senior leadership, coordinating efforts with 6 April and holding meetings at party HQ in the guise of youth-wing workshops.[208] The youth movements themselves also joined forces for the 2010 parliamentary elections, organizing the 'Day of Rage: Make a Commotion' campaign two days before the polls opened. Successful protests took place in fourteen of Egypt's twenty-seven governorates, with broad participation.[209]

The spirit of inter-party cooperation was particularly strong in Alexandria, where political forces sought to ramp up the pressure on the regime. Here, additional impetus was provided by a series of high-profile cases of torture, above all the case of Khaled Saeed. The Coordination Office in Alexandria was set up in late June 2010, two weeks after Saeed's death. But although it began as no more than a body for organizing protest, it ultimately became a forum for discussion between intellectuals from a range of political backgrounds.[210] Nine different political forces

---

[204] Taher Abu'l-Nasr (FDEP), personal interview, conducted by Yusra Taha, Cairo, 21 April 2012.
[205] Amr Farrag (Rasd), personal interview, conducted by Yusra Taha, Cairo, 12 April 2014.
[206] Ahmed Ragheb (Hisham Mubarak Law Centre), personal interview, conducted by Yusra Taha, Cairo, 19 April 2012.
[207] Ammar El-Beltagy, personal interview, 9 October 2019.
[208] Khalid Tallima, personal interview, conducted by Nihal Ragab, Cairo, 2 May 2012. Tallima was secretary of the Tagammu youth wing and later a member of the Constitution Party.
[209] Abdelmonem Emam, personal interview.
[210] Mohamed Samir (Baradei campaign coordinator), personal interview, conducted by Ahmed Abd Rabou and Aly El Raggal, Alexandria, 7 December 2011.

were represented in the office, with their participation in any given action entirely voluntary.²¹¹ When the office organized a protest in response to the detention and torture of two Muslim Brothers, the Brotherhood participated in an official capacity.²¹²

X The death of Khaled Saeed

On 6 June 2010, a young man sitting in an Alexandria cybercafé was suddenly set upon by police and brutally beaten in the café, his head smashed against a piece of marble. He was dragged to a nearby building entrance, thrown against the staircase and beaten to death. This young man was Khaled Saeed, and when pictures of his disfigured corpse – which had clearly been subject to torture – were disseminated on social media, it galvanized local public opinion in Alexandria almost overnight. Activists organized actions across the city. A vigil outside the police station on 9 June was ruthlessly broken up by the security forces.²¹³ More protests followed, some in Manshiyya Square and some in front of the city court buildings, demanding justice for Saeed's killers. The biggest of these protests, on 25 June, attracted thousands of people – and almost as many security officers, who set up checkpoints to prevent more people from joining the demonstrations and ensure that it did not turn into a march through the city.²¹⁴

At first, the demonstrations were dominated by the political parties active in Alexandria. But subsequent protests held in front of Saeed's house on Cleopatra Street attracted many locals, both men and women,²¹⁵ who were heard shouting 'down with Hosni Mubarak' as they joined the demonstrators. Alongside the actions organized by existing movements, the We Are All Khaled Saeed Facebook page played an important role, organizing regular vigils every Friday on the seafront and elsewhere in Alexandria. The local protests against Saeed's killing resembled those that were to take place in the Tunisian city of Sidi Bouzid after Mohamed Bouazizi set himself on fire in January 2011. As in Sidi Bouzid, political

---

²¹¹ Ibid.
²¹² Ahmed Fahmy (6 April coordinator in Alexandria), personal interview, conducted by Ahmed Abd Rabou and Aly El Raggal, Alexandria, 7 December 2011.
²¹³ Ahmed Iraqi Nassar, personal interview.
²¹⁴ For footage, see *YouTube*, 25 June 2010, Available online: https://bit.ly/3hzRbIR (accessed 20 July 2014).
²¹⁵ Video filmed in front of Khaled Saeed's house, *YouTube*, 20 July 2010, Available online: https://bit.ly/3ijbXhp (accessed 26 January 2021); *YouTube*, June 2010, Available online: https://bit.ly/2ZoCSAE (accessed 26 January 2021). These videos show both the extent of participation and the local character of the protests.

activists tried to appropriate the tragedy in order to build an anti-regime movement around it.[216] But in the event, they had to wait more than six months for a real popular uprising against the security forces' abuses – after the revolution in Tunisia.

Protests were accompanied by an extensive social media campaign. Mahmoud Sami, administrator of the My Name Is Khaled Saeed Facebook page and a member of the 6 April Movement, was subsequently to play a prominent role in organizing the 25 January demonstrations.[217] The We Are All Khaled Saeed page, meanwhile, was set up by Wael Ghonim and Abdelrahman Mansour – part of the team behind the Popular Campaign to Support Mohamed ElBaradei, whose experience seems to have given them a very good idea of the mobilization possibilities offered by Facebook.[218] By 2011, We Are All Khaled Saeed had some 390,000 members, 70 per cent of them under twenty-four and 40 per cent of them women, and was receiving nine million hits a day.[219] This page did a great deal to force police torture and violence onto the media agenda in the face of attempts to turn a blind eye or parrot the standard official line (smearing the victim and making excuses for his death).[220] It also, along with pages run by the 6 April Movement, organized numerous successful demonstrations and vigils attracting participation from outside the narrow circles of regular protesters. Although the main focus was on Khaled Saeed, the admin team[221] also highlighted other torture and sexual assault scandals as well as other examples of criminal behaviour or corruption, including the Church of the Saints bombing.[222] Many young activists first became interested in politics through We Are All Khaled Saeed.

Despite this ferment of protest and social media activity, however, torture and violence remained commonplace in Egyptian prisons and police stations. In fact, it became worse. On 13 November 2010, We Are All Khaled Saeed published the story, complete with video evidence, of a nineteen-year-old boy who had been detained and tortured for several

---

[216] Azmi Bishara, *The Glorious Tunisian Revolution: The Structure and Unfolding of a Revolution through Its Daily Happenings* [Arabic] (Beirut: ACRPS, 2012), 199–212.

[217] Ghonim, *Revolution 2.0*, 140.

[218] Abdelrahman Mansour and Ahmed Saleh (We Are Khaled Saeed), personal interview, conducted by Yusra Taha, Cairo, 24 April 2012.

[219] Herrera, *Revolution in the Age of Social Media*, 5. As of September 2020 (the last time the author accessed the page before it was shut down), the page had more than 3.5 million followers and 3.4 million likes. See: *Facebook*, Available online: https://bit.ly/2EDhIHU (accessed 28 September 2020). Today 3.5 million does not seem particularly impressive, but in 2011, 390,000 followers was a major achievement.

[220] By early 2010, Facebook had some 4.3 million users in Egypt, meaning it had supplanted blogs as the most popular form of social media.

[221] The initial founders, Ghonim and Mansour, were later joined by Ali Ahmed Saleh. Saleh had worked alongside Ghonim and Mansour on the Baradei campaign.

[222] Personal interviews with Abdelrahman Mansour and Ahmed Saleh.

days at the Sidi Gaber police station after arguing with a security officer in the street. After the boy succumbed to his injuries, his body was dumped in the Mahmoudiyya canal.[223]

After the Church of the Saints bombing on New Year's Day 2011, the security forces rounded up young members of the Alexandria Salafist movement. One of those arrested, Sayed Belal, was summoned to Old Security Directorate by the SSIS. A few days later, his family were instructed to come and pick up his body. They were told that Belal had already been dead when he arrived, brought in by two unknown persons, but the corpse had severe bruising and showed clear signs of torture.[224] We Are All Khaled Saeed published pictures of the young man as well as details that refuted official claims about his fate; the officers responsible were ultimately put on trial after the 25 January revolution. It is worth noting, however, that the Salafist movement refused to participate in the protests against his killing.[225] In his press statement, the movement's official spokesperson Abdel Moneim el-Shahat expressed scepticism about the protesters' motives, warning that they would bring ruin on Egypt and the Salafists. The Salafists continued to be hostile to the revolutionaries throughout the first week of the revolution.[226]

XI The Judges' Club and the independent judiciary movement

Before moving on, let us take a moment to consider the Judges' Club protests that took place during Mubarak's final years in power. These protests were unique by any standard. The Egyptian judiciary is a conservative institution, not a revolutionary one, and undemocratic almost by definition.[227] For judges to come out to protest suggests a profound crisis of trust between the institutions of the state. Before discussing the protests themselves, it seems only appropriate to give a brief history of the Judges' Club. Readers should approach this section as part of both the history of protest and the struggle between the different institutions of the state discussed in Chapter 1.

---

[223] We Are All Khaled Saeed page, *Facebook*, 13 November 2010, Available online: https://bit.ly/3mnDkt5 (accessed 23 July 2014). To listen to the testimony of the victim's relatives, see: *YouTube*, 13 November 2010, Available online: https://bit.ly/2RsK7mO (accessed 26 January 2021).
[224] *al-Ahram*, 19 February 2012, Available online: https://bit.ly/3lOGGXz (accessed 17 October 2021).
[225] Anani and Malik, 'Pious Way to Politics', 60.
[226] Ibrahim El Houdaiby, 'Islamism in and after Egypt's Revolution', in *Arab Spring in Egypt: Revolution and Beyond*, ed. Bahgat Korany and Rabab El-Mahdi (Cairo and New York: The American University in Cairo Press, 2012).
[227] The Egyptian judiciary is a more or less a closed shop, and judgeships are essentially inherited. This applies even to the leaders of the Judges' Club protests.

Despite everything, the judiciary remained loyal to the regime from the moment that the Nasser government finally curtailed its independence in 1969. For the most part, it was hostile even to the January revolution, even if it objected to the diminished role it was forced to play towards the end of Mubarak's tenure. But although it was not a protest or social movement in any sense of the word, the judges' protest contributed to the general pre-revolutionary ferment, and for that reason it is worth thinking about here.

The Judges' Club was established in 1949. Although membership is not compulsory, almost all members of the Public Prosecution's judicial staff, as well as regular judges and retirees, are members: in 2005, the figure stood at around 90 per cent.[228] It is the equivalent of the professional associations or syndicates associated with other occupations.

The July regime's approach to the judiciary's authority was to 'outflank and chip away at it, without resorting to direct control or outright annexation'.[229] It contained the judiciary by excluding it from areas that might impinge on policy,[230] without this directly affecting the independence that judges had enjoyed prior to 1952. This meant that they posed no threat to the government. In any case, the steady flow of new legislation employed by the July regime naturally reduced the impact of judicial rulings.

In 1962, the ASU was set up to replace the National Union as a single ruling party intended to represent the 'forces of the working people'. The ASU had branches in various state institutions, but not in the judiciary – despite the best efforts of the state, which only intensified after the 1967 defeat.[231] In response, those judges who were unwilling to countenance further restrictions intensified efforts to expand their narrow purview.[232] Those opposed to incorporation in the ASU and in favour of an independent judiciary won a decisive victory over pro-government candidates in the 1968 board elections, and in March the association released a statement refusing outright to join the ASU.[233]

---

[228] Atef al-Shahhat, 'The Role of the Judges' Club in Strengthening Judicial Independence and Political Reform' [Arabic], in *Judges and Political Reform* [Arabic], ed. Nabil Abdel Fattah (Cairo: Cairo Institute for Human Rights Studies, 2006), 353. Special associations exist for members of the SCC (50–75 judges) and the State Council (500–600 judges). The regular Judges' Club has around 8,000 members.

[229] Tarek El-Bishry, *The Egyptian Judiciary between Independence and Containment* [Arabic], 2nd edn (Cairo: Shorouk, 2006), 14.

[230] Ibid., 61.

[231] Ahmed Mekki, 'The Clash between Judges and the Nasserist Regime' [Arabic], in *Judges and Political Reform* [Arabic], ed. Nabil Abdel Fattah (Cairo: Cairo Institute for Human Rights Studies, 2006), 93. It was also proposed that court benches should include citizen representation, producing a 'popular judiciary' that would have resembled the Agrarian Dispute Resolution Committees. This was rejected out of hand by the judiciary.

[232] Bishry, *The Egyptian Judiciary*, 18.

[233] For more, see: Mekki, 'The Clash', 95.

In late August 1969, however, the executive issued a raft of judicial reform legislation that set off a thoroughgoing purge: among those fired were the chief judge of the Court of Cassation and the deputy chief judge of the State Council. A puppet Supreme Court was set up to restrict lower courts' ability to intervene on constitutional matters.[234] The Judges' Club board was dismissed and its premises in Cairo and Alexandria shuttered until 1977.[235] Yahya El Rifai, a leading light of the pro-independence judges, has this to say:

> It came into force on 21 August 1969, and those who were removed included the chief judge of the Court of Cassation and more than half its judicial staff. Around 200 of the judges purged should only have been dismissed for disciplinary reasons by law. [. . .] Some of those in the judiciary and the State Council wrote secret denunciations of their colleagues to the political leadership, telling them about what was being said at the Judges' Club and the various judicial boards. [. . .] This was the first time that anything like this had happened in the history of the Egyptian judiciary, from its establishment to this catastrophic event – an event which came to be known as the 'massacre of the judges'.[236]

After Nasser's death, Sadat overturned the previous rulings and the independent-minded judges[237] regained their influence.[238] But Law 46/1972 soon put the old approach to containing the judiciary back on the table, granting the executive control over the judiciary's budget[239] and moving much of the work of the judiciary outside the Ministry of Justice by setting up the SJC.[240] Nonetheless, the Judges' Club managed to reassert its right to elect its president, and in 1978 the first ballot in ten years was finally held.[241]

During the 1990s, the judiciary's political role became more marked. As the regime's legitimacy deteriorated and its reliance on repression and the state of emergency grew, it found itself in need of legal backing to imbue

---

[234] The establishment of a supreme court should have been a major step forward, but the way it was set up and the provisions governing it show that the purpose was simply to prevent lower civil and administrative courts from raising constitutional issues in their judgements. Judge Zakaria Abdel-Aziz, personal interview, conducted by Hani Awwad and Nerouz Satik, Cairo, 30 November 2012.
[235] Mekki, 'The Clash', 21.
[236] *FJP Portal*, 28 February 2020, Available online: https://bit.ly/33f6stz (accessed 10 September 2020).
[237] The basic demands of this group were: recognition of the club as the legitimate representative of the judiciary; guarantees for the independence of the judiciary; full oversight of elections; and an end to the state of emergency.
[238] Ahmed Abdelhafiz, 'The Judiciary and Political Reform in Egypt' [Arabic], *Kirasat Istratijiyya* (Cairo) 17, no. 181 (November 2007): 23.
[239] Mahmoud Khudairi, 'How Does Law 46/1972 on the Judicial Authority Legitimize the Infringement of Judicial Independence?' [Arabic], in *Judges and Political Reform* [Arabic], ed. Nabil Abdel Fattah (Cairo: Cairo Institute for Human Rights Studies, 2006), 103.
[240] Bishry, *The Egyptian Judiciary*, 23.
[241] Zakaria Abdel-Aziz, personal interview.

its controversial economic reforms with legitimacy. While these reforms bolstered the regime's authority in many respects, they also created the basis for a new societal interaction between the regime, the judiciary and civil society.[242]

Sadat's judicial reforms helped to facilitate capitalist transition and strengthen the position of the new political and economic groups. These reforms took place at a time when the sorry effects of the hostility to independent legal institutions shown by Nasser in his later years were becoming clear.[243] Most significantly, reforms in 1972 and 1984 increased the relative power and independence of the administrative courts vis-à-vis the government bureaucracy, and Law 48/1979 established the SCC. Tamir Moustafa argues that the new SCC enjoyed far more independence from regime interference than its predecessor and was able to adjudicate even the most sensitive political and economic cases.[244] But the state's main motivation was to encourage private and foreign investment by creating a safe investment climate, protecting private property and facilitating dispute resolution, and it was on this basis that the legislation was drafted.[245] Under Mubarak, the SCC was to play an important role in establishing private owners' rights to previously nationalized property.

The court's commitment to restoring property rights was the subject of its first and most important review in 1981, but it also took this opportunity to show that it operated outside the regime. Its ruling declared Laws 150/1964 and 69/1974 on expropriation of private property and the 1961–3 laws on industrial nationalization and agrarian reform unconstitutional. This opened the door to hundreds of compensation lawsuits. In the 1990s the court reviewed other issues of relevance to private property, including tax law, landlord–tenant relations and the public sector.[246]

In political and constitutional matters, the court's first intervention concerned the electoral system of proportional representation, which it deemed 'prejudicial to independents' (1986); in 1990, it ruled it

---

[242] Tamir Moustafa, *The Struggle for Constitutional Power: Law, Politics, and Economic Development in Egypt* (New York: Cambridge University Press, 2007), 6.
[243] Ibid., 65.
[244] Although in principle the chief justice of the SCC was appointed by the president, in practice they succeeded by seniority, and this became the established custom of the court. Other checks preventing government interference in the court's functioning were also provided: although judges were forced to retire at the age of sixty-six years, they could not be dismissed; the only body capable of disciplining the court was the court itself; and the court enjoyed full control over its financial and administrative affairs. Ibid., 78–9.
[245] Law 34/1971 abolishing the government's right of expropriation and Law 65/1971 extending guarantees against government property seizures, as well as the provisions of the 1971 constitution on private property and nationalizations (which from now on were only to be conducted where there was a clear public interest and with compensation). Ibid., 69–71.
[246] Ibid., 91–3.

unconstitutional. From the mid-1980s onwards, the administrative courts began to review allegations of electoral fraud, regularly ruling to annul the results in individual constituencies – although in the 1987 elections, the People's Assembly only accepted the annulment of seven of the eighty-seven constituencies whose results had been challenged. All this formed the kernel of a new struggle between institutions, which would take particularly stark forms in the future.[247] Under Mubarak, the regime regularly refused to enforce judicial rulings, making judicial independence something of a paper tiger. What use is an independent judiciary whose orders are not implemented?

On the other hand, the SCC of the 1980s accepted the constitutionality of the State Security courts in a historic ruling issued in 1984. The rulings of these courts, which were staffed by military personnel and selected judges, could not be appealed, and with the state of emergency still in effect, they had become a de facto parallel judiciary. The SCC, however, insisted that they were legitimate and rejected dozens of cases appealing their rulings on jurisdictional grounds.[248] In 1993, when the battle between the Islamists and the regime was at its height and new legislation had been introduced allowing for terrorism charges on the most dubious grounds, the SCC once again upheld the president's right to refer any crime to a State Security court.

In 1984, Mubarak reinstated the SJC, which had been abolished during the judges' massacre of 1969. In 1986, judges held the first ever Justice Conference, with Yahya El Rifai, by now head of the Judges' Club, calling for the state of emergency to be terminated. Rifai paid the price for this act of defiance in the form of a two-year suspension, but the pro-independent judiciary faction still managed to re-elect him to the club, giving him another full year in office before his retirement.[249] From 1991, however, regular meddling in its elections meant that the Judges' Club remained overall loyal to the regime for some ten years.[250] The independents regained control of the association in June 2001 with the election of Zakaria Abdel-Aziz.[251] Abdel-Aziz remained in post until February 2009, when a sustained campaign by the NDP and the security forces installed pro-Mubarak candidate Ahmed Al-Zend,[252] who was to be a major counter-revolutionary figure after January 2011.

---

[247] Ibid., 98.
[248] Ibid., 104–6.
[249] Ibid.
[250] Abdelhafiz, 'The Judiciary and Political Reform', 23.
[251] The regime attempted to overturn the results of these elections by disregarding the three-year election cycle, but Abdel-Aziz managed to win a second time.
[252] Zakaria Abdel-Aziz, personal interview.

Deconstructing the Myth of Acquiescence 163

So how did the judges' movement begin?

The 11 September attacks and the rise of the neoconservatives in the United States meant that Arab regimes friendly to the United States came under greater pressure to pursue political liberalization, particularly after the occupation of Iraq in 2003. As a result, many of them loosened their grip on certain aspects of public life. The Egyptian regime itself adopted a series of carefully calculated reforms that allowed the development of a manageable form of political mobilization. It was in this context that the Judges' Club, already led by independents, was able to transform itself into a sort of authority on the issue of free and fair elections.

As noted earlier, the first round of the 2005 elections saw unprecedented successes for the Muslim Brotherhood.[253] The regime sought to prevent a repeat performance in the second and third rounds by violently suppressing turnout and colluding with judges acting as observers to fix individual races. The most egregious example of this took place in Damanhur, in the El-Beheira governorate, where the NDP candidate Mostafa El Feki (a close Mubarak ally and, for a long time, his minister of information) beat the Brotherhood candidate Gamal Heshmat thanks to extensive ballot rigging.[254] The extent of the electoral fraud was exposed in large part thanks to the bravery of judge Noha el-Zeini, who wrote an open letter to *Al-Masry Al-Youm* stating flatly that 'indications from the branch committees suggest that Gamal Heshmat took at least 25,000 votes, while Mostafa El Feki received at most 7,000'.[255] Zeini soon received the support of the independent judges.

The first real mobilization within the Judges' Club, however, began in 13 May 2005. Members held a conference to discuss the upcoming constitutional referendum on direct presidential elections and the subsequent presidential elections themselves, which judges were supposed to oversee. They agreed that if the government refused to implement various legislative amendments facilitating full oversight of the elections, they would refuse to participate.[256] When this demand was stonewalled by both the legislature and the executive, they decided to escalate, announcing at the club's general assembly that they would be boycotting the referendum until changes were made to the judiciary law.[257] Although judges soon

---

[253] Mohammad Gamal Heshmat, *Rigging Is a State Crime and an MP's Experience* [Arabic] (Tanta: Dar al-Bashir li'l-Thaqafa wa'l-'Ulum, 2011), 168–70.

[254] Ibid., 71–183.

[255] For the open letter in which Zeini set out the details of the ballot rigging, see: *Al-Masry Al-Youm*, 25 November 2005, Available online: https://bit.ly/3pDuafU (accessed 25 October 2021).

[256] 'The Judges' Statement: Eventful Days and a New Ministry' [Arabic], *al-Qudah* 21 (April–September 2006): 1–5.

[257] In order to avoid a repeat performance of the sham oversight they had provided in the 2000 legislative elections, the first in Egyptian history to have judges acting as observers.

changed their minds, not wanting to miss the opportunity to secure direct presidential elections,[258] at an extraordinary general assembly meeting in September, the association announced that if its conditions were not met – most importantly, the presence of observers from civil society organizations at the vote and the count – it could not take any responsibility for the results of the elections. In November, during the regime's campaign to subvert the second round of the legislative elections, the club called on the armed forces to intervene and protect judges carrying out their oversight functions.[259] It seems unlikely that anyone took this demand seriously, but it is worth noting simply as evidence of the widespread belief, even among judges, that the army might serve as an effective counterweight to the NDP and the security forces.

After the elections were over, the Judges' Club released a report detailing various breaches of the law documented during the voting and arguing that the turnout rate was no more than 5 per cent – a far cry from the claim of 50 per cent circulated by the regime. In response, 1,500 judges were barred from acting as observers in the legislative elections two months later, elections which the club also criticized harshly. The government brought disciplinary cases against two judges, Mahmoud Mekki and Hisham Bastawisy (deputy chief justices of the Court of Cassation).[260] To protest the move, the Judges' Club announced an open sit-in at its headquarters, which was accompanied by demonstrations at the disciplinary court and – from 18 April 2006 – solidarity actions by Kefaya and the Brotherhood.[261]

On the morning of 19 April, a group of young activists and intellectuals joined the sit-in, handing out fliers and waving placards supporting the action and calling on others to join in. Most of these new additions were members of the Kefaya-linked Youth for Change or the 9 March Independent Universities Movement.[262]

On 24 April, a mass of security officers surrounded the headquarters of the Judges' Club. Some of the approximately thirty young activists present at the time were arrested. More shockingly, when a group of judges attempted to leave the association, they were set upon by security officers and beaten.[263]

---

[258] Menissi, *New Social Movements*, 99.
[259] Natalie Bernard-Maugiron, 'Evolution of the Relationship between Judges and Human Rights Organizations during 2005' [Arabic], in *Judges and Political Reform* [Arabic], ed. Nabil Abdel Fattah (Cairo: Cairo Institute for Human Rights Studies, 2006), 466.
[260] Ibid., 100.
[261] Shehata, 'Youth Protest Movements', 253.
[262] Discussed earlier in the text.
[263] During this period, various activists and intellectuals attended demonstrations carrying pictures of the detained judges, including the prominent poet Ahmed Fouad Negm in Tahrir Square.

The judges received a great deal of support from political forces and unions across Egypt. Despite the intense security presence, judges – accompanied by demonstrators from the Journalists' Syndicate and the Bar Association – managed to pull off a second protest march to the Court of Cassation on 27 April, the first day of Mekki and Bastawisy's trial.[264] Another march took place on 18 May, this time accompanied by Brotherhood MPs, who gathered around the court buildings wearing sashes bearing the slogan 'the people's representatives support Egypt's judges'. The defence team, made up of protesting judges, managed to refute the charges legally and constitutionally, and the accused were acquitted on the same day.[265]

Some judges continued to fight for an independent judiciary. But with the February 2009 board elections, the pro-regime faction led by Ahmed Al-Zend regained control of the Judges' Club. When revolution finally came in January 2011, the association was to play a thoroughly reactionary role.

[264] Nagi Dirbala [et al.], 'Diary of a Sit-in' [Arabic], *Qudah* 21 (April–September 2006).
[265] Ibid.

4

From protest to revolution

I Preparing for the 25 January demonstrations

The date of 25 January in Egypt is National Police Day, and 2011 was not the first time that activists had called for protests to mark the occasion. Indeed, protests had become such a routine part of this national holiday that many anticipated nothing out of the ordinary, and most of the activists that we interviewed for this book dismissed the idea that the revolution was planned in advance as an oversimplification of a very complex issue. But in fact, this year was to be very different. As a precaution, the regime had rescheduled the official ceremony attended by Mubarak to 24 January. Interior Minister Habib el-Adly took the opportunity to smear those calling for protests, linking them to the perpetrators of the Church of the Saints bombing and thereby drawing on the familiar Mubarak-era discourse of anti-terrorism.[1]

The We Are All Khaled Saeed campaign – whose explicit purpose was, after all, to 'keep track of Egyptian police abuses'[2] – had agreed with various other activists that National Police Day should see a 'major mobilization' to demand an end to torture and the dismissal of the interior minister. According to Abdelrahman Mansour, 'We were always looking for holidays to organize our protests and mobilizations on, and I happened to find out that there had been annual protests every 25 January for the past two years. So, I suggested that we take advantage of the day to organize something, a protest or a video screening.'[3] On 28 December 2010, the page called

---

[1] Adly's speech focused on the various recent achievements of his ministry and its security forces, in particular their success in apprehending the Church of the Saints bombers, who he claimed were members of an al-Qaeda-linked Palestinian group called the 'Army of Islam'. This claim was later proven entirely false – in fact, no such group exists. But it was entirely in keeping with the Mubarak regime's disingenuous anti-terrorism rhetoric, which typically conflated Palestinians and Islamists and alluded constantly to a grand conspiracy to sabotage Egypt's future.

[2] As described by one of its founders, Abdelrahman Mansour. See: Ahmed Abdelhamid Hussein, *Diary of the Egyptian Revolution, January 2011* [Arabic] (Doha: Al Jazeera Institute for Studies, 2011), 44.

[3] Personal interviews with Abdelrahman Mansour and Ahmed Saleh.

for a mass demonstration to protest police brutality and the abuses of the Interior Ministry. Various demands were laid out, most importantly the dismissal of Habib el-Adly, the dissolution of the parliament produced by the fraudulent elections of 2010 and the implementation of a minimum wage. Two days later, on 30 December, the page wrote: '25 January is a national holiday, National Police Day. I think they've done quite a lot over the last year that's worth celebrating – in our own way, of course.'[4]

On 14 January, eleven days before the protest, Zine al-Abidine Ben Ali had been forced to flee Tunisia – a country he had ruled for three decades – in the face of unrelenting popular protests. According to Mansour, the activities organized in Egypt in response were still 'very simple – nowhere near as organized as they seemed'.[5] But activists had now seen that if they acted en masse against oppression, it was possible for a people to bring down a regime and that young people were critical to any such mobilization. Moreover, Tunisia had shown that even in a state with a formidable security apparatus, it was possible to mobilize popular feeling to the point that even the smallest demonstrations would enjoy a degree of protection. Activists' greatest anxiety was always that people would not come out to join their protests, leaving them to face the massed ranks of the security forces on their own, with predictable results. Of course, daring actions of this kind had initially done much to break the barrier of fear among the public, but by now, protests were routine events organized by political forces simply to declare a stance.

As events escalated in Tunisia, a fierce debate erupted around the possibility of achieving the same thing in Egypt. Members of the elite rolled out all sorts of elaborate explanations to downplay any similarity between the two cases, repeating again and again that 'Egypt is not Tunisia'.[6] Other citizens, meanwhile, sought to demonstrate the opposite through individual protests inspired by the Tunisian street vendor Mohamed Bouazizi. On 17 January, Abdo Abdel Moneim attempted to set himself on fire in front of the parliament building in Cairo, and over the next eight days some 251 threats of self-immolation were recorded throughout the country, including dozens of street peddlers in Aswan and Kom Ombo protesting against a decision to clear their stalls off the streets.

There were many separate plans to protest on 25 January. Because nobody was aware that Ghonim and Mansour were the admins of the We Are All Khaled Saeed page, however, they had not been invited to

---

[4] *Youm7*, 15 January 2012, Available online: https://bit.ly/3DRGPQ6 (accessed 17 October 2021).
[5] Personal interviews with Abdelrahman Mansour and Ahmed Saleh.
[6] Activist Amr Salah told us that the efforts to emphasize differences between Egypt and Tunisia 'in themselves made the whole thing seem more serious and gave it a big boost among the population'.

any of the meetings and were only aware of the locations that had already been announced publicly.[7] After making some phone calls to prominent activists and polling group members, Ghonim eventually settled on the densely populated neighbourhoods of Shubra and Imbaba, where he had previously been out demonstrating during the Church of the Saints protests.[8] Until as late as 20 January, however, he remained uncertain. A phone call to Ahmed Maher of the 6 April Movement encouraged him, however: 'The thing about this moment', Maher said, 'is that the security forces are uncertain too.'[9]

Young activists had no misgivings about working alongside the political parties. It is interesting to note that Ghonim says that he hoped that the Muslim Brotherhood would participate, because of their organizational skills and their numbers. Omar El-Qazzaz, one of the admins of Rassd News Facebook page, told him that individual Brothers would be participating, but when Ghonim tried to coordinate efforts, he was told that the Brotherhood refused to coordinate with an unknown quantity.[10] Here we see the difference between organized party thinking, always focusing on those behind initiatives and their possible consequences, and the way that the young activists thought, concerned above all with action now. Young people consistently worked to achieve concrete objectives though without any overarching strategy. This was a strength in the field, but ultimately become a source of weakness after the revolution when parties turned to more organized politics removed from the sphere of youth political action.

Many of those who have written about the revolution have viewed various training programmes on non-violent action and organization as akin to a conspiracy, drastically exaggerating the importance of the citizen journalism programmes organized by the International Federation of Journalists or Freedom House courses.[11] These workshops were doubtless important, but it was the drive to action by groups like YJF or 6 April that was the key.

Until approximately ten days before the revolution, We Are All Khaled Saeed remained for the most part a sort of virtual media outlet, receiving and publishing videos and other documentary evidence from activists and encouraging protest. But as 25 January drew near, the page admins decided to coordinate with other young activists.[12] Mahmoud Sami of 6 April acted as the point of contact.

---

[7] Ghonim, *Revolution 2.0*, 170–2.
[8] Ibid., 175.
[9] Ibid., 176.
[10] Ibid., 195.
[11] Menawy, *The Last Days*, 68.
[12] Personal interviews with Abdelrahman Mansour and Ahmed Saleh.

Sami, 6 April's mass action coordinator, called for a meeting to translate digital action into reality, and on 15 January just such a meeting was held at the YJF headquarters close to Abdel Moneim Riad Square. Along with several YJF representatives, there were two young activists from 6 April, a member of Kefaya and a representative of the Baradei campaign in attendance. Sami set out a plan for what he called a 'snowball' demonstration. Rather than heading for a single fixed point immediately, they would start off by marching through densely populated working-class areas, chanting slogans focusing on basic economic demands calculated to draw in local residents. The idea was to keep the protest 'snowballing' until it was big enough that the security forces were powerless to stand in its way. Everyone in attendance approved the plan, but it was clear that it would only work so long as the wider public was willing to participate. Just how willing they proved to be – after so many years of growing resentment against the Mubarak regime, and with the success of the Tunisian revolution fresh in their minds – surprised all those involved.

On two separate dates, Sami scouted out the areas in question, sketching out a route from Nahia Street down to Tahrir Square via Arab League Street. This route was ideal because it ran through a densely populated area full of winding side streets that could provide cover from the prying eyes of the security forces:[13] Nahia Street itself is one of the busiest thoroughfares in Cairo, and many of the alleyways that branch off it are no more than two to three metres wide. Because it is cut off from central Cairo by a railway line and the only way across is via a footbridge connecting it directly to Arab League Street, this footbridge was chosen as the initial assembly point. Everyone involved was aware that if the security forces found out about this bottleneck in advance, it would spell disaster for the demonstration.[14]

This was far from the only plan being put together in the days before 25 January. Many other youth movements had already responded to the call for demonstrations by coming up with their own ideas for protests, most of which ultimately fed into and became part of a single main plan. It is perhaps for this reason that so many groups were subsequently to claim that the plan originated with them before being 'stolen' by others, producing all sorts of tensions (as had happened earlier on in the Mahalla uprising). During the transitional period, as young activists were torn between the various political forces vying for power and failed to organize as a single

---

[13] Information from various interviews with: Zyad Elelaimy (Baradei campaign), conducted by Mohammad Abbas over Skype, 11 May 2014; Sally Touma (Baradei campaign), conducted by Mohammad Abbas over Skype, 21 May 2014; and Mohamed Salah (YJF). Also an eyewitness account given by Mahmoud Sami (6 April/RYC) in an interview with the Egyptian newspaper *Shorouk*, 24 January 2013, Available online: https://bit.ly/35x1w6h (accessed 7 April 2014).

[14] Moaz Abdelkarim, personal interview, conducted by Umaima Abdellatif, Doha, 2 May 2011.

unified force, these tensions resurfaced on several occasions, including during the election and subsequent ouster of President Mohamed Morsi. These activists failed to recognize that revolution is a matter of sustained, relentless work to change the political system. To reduce it to a two-week occupation of Tahrir Square – and to say romantically that this or the other person has 'stayed loyal' to it or 'betrayed it' – shows a serious misunderstanding of this revolutionary process, which should culminate in a change in regime and not simply the resignation of a president.

The revolutionary ferment in the years leading up to 25 January was felt by young people across Egyptian society. In fact, the opposition and its parties had witnessed a veritable youth revolt, or a revolutionary change in their cultural outlook. The revolution was not stolen from anyone. It is no one's 'intellectual property' to steal. I have thus chosen to concentrate on the ebb and flow of events and their internal logic rather than on every group of young people who came up with an independent plan prior to the coordinated action that ultimately took place. The success of the call to protest was ultimately less about the call itself or who sent it out than the fervour generated by the victory of the revolutionaries in Tunisia, the unexpected mass participation, the confused response of the regime and the build-up of anger and other factors. Events have shown that whose idea it was is less important than how it happened, which in turn is less important than which forces were (or were not) capable of organizing it, leading it and bringing it to a successful conclusion by effecting regime change – and whether they managed to do so. The call for protest could have led to a mass demonstration and ended there; its transformation into a political revolt that called for regime change was not predicted beforehand.

In any case, a group of young Brotherhood activists heard the call to protest, and on the evening of 18 January a closed group was set up on Facebook: 'A true word to an unjust sultan (Brotherhood youth participating in 25 January).' Around 250 young Brothers joined the group, which was managed by Mohammad Abbas and Taha Mohamed. The group was established before any Brotherhood members were made aware of the coordination efforts between other political forces,[15] and while Brothers were later to join the revolution in droves, at this point the Brotherhood contingent was no bigger than any other.

On 20 January, Abbas spoke to Abdelrahman Fares, a Kefaya activist and a former member of 6 April, to coordinate their plans for the demonstration. Khaled Elsayed, a leftist activist, also took part in this meeting. Another meeting was then held with Fares, Mohammad Abbas, Nasser Abdel

---

[15] Mohammad Abbas, personal interview, 9 October 2012.

Hamid (NAC), Mahmoud Sami and Amr Ezz (6 April) to prepare the ground for another, broader, planning meeting to be held on 22 January. The upshot of all this was that a group of Brotherhood activists became fully incorporated into the overall coordination effort and attended the lectures put on by 6 April and YJF with the Hisham Mubarak Law Centre. (Most protests were preceded by some instruction on the law surrounding protest and how to interact with the police or prosecutors and another on what protesters should carry with them.)

On the evening of 24 January, a final meeting was held at the headquarters of Socialist Renewal,[16] with Abdelrahman Fares, Khaled Elsayed, Khaled Abdel Hamid (YJF/Socialist Renewal), Mohammad Abbas and Moaz Abdelkarim (Brotherhood) in attendance. At this meeting, the details of where each group would go and what they would do were finalized. Mostafa Mahmoud Square was chosen as the 'public' meeting point for demonstrators, while other groups were to try and mobilize passers-by around Nahia Street. For security reasons, only forty people were to know in advance that the real plan was to meet in Nahia. It was also agreed that no partisan slogans or chants would be heard at the demonstrations, that placards would be signed with the name 'Free Youth of Egypt' and that each group would contribute 500 pounds towards materials.[17] After attracting as much support as possible, the protest was to make its way down to Mostafa Mahmoud and – if all went well and they had sufficient numbers – occupy the square. In the event that the plan to reel in passers-by failed, the protest would simply go ahead as announced: marchers would set off from Mostafa Mahmoud at 2.00 pm led by Basem Kamel (Baradei campaign) and a group of YJF activists led by Waleed Abd Elraouf.[18]

The coordination between young Brothers and representatives of other youth movements was a major achievement. It was agreed that Brotherhood members would not be present at Mostafa Mahmoud Square and that they would concentrate their efforts around Nahia Street. Mohammad Abbas says that this decision was the result of long experience of 'failed coordination with other political orientations, which fell through because the Brotherhood had always insisted on controlling everything because there were so many more of them'.[19] The self-awareness that the young Brothers were showing here was far ahead of the Brotherhood

---

[16] Socialist Renewal was a group that split off from the Revolutionary Socialists in 2010. It has a blog: *Revolutionary Socialists*, Available online: https://bit.ly/3hvTOve (accessed 25 October 2021).
[17] Personal interviews with Zyad Elelaimy, Moaz Abdelkarim, Mostafa Shawky (4 May 2014), Mohamed Salah, Mahmoud Sami (23 March 2014) and Khaled Abdel Hamid (27 May 2014).
[18] Mahmoud Sami interview in *Shorouk*; Mohamed Salah, personal interview.
[19] Mohammad Abbas, personal interview.

organization itself, which stuck to its 'sectarian' attitude all the way into the transitional period.

The details of the agreement were relayed back to the young Brothers' Facebook group, and the members began dividing up responsibilities. They took extensive precautions, buying group leaders new phones in order to avoid being tracked by the security forces. On the evening of 24 January, the Brothers who had attended the coordination meetings contacted the Brotherhood's Student Bureau and let them in on the plan. The bureau had long experience coordinating protests with students of other political backgrounds and could mobilize large numbers of young Brotherhood activists. As a result, various new faces joined the protest, including Mohamed Al-Qasas and Islam Lotfy.[20]

In order to further confuse the security forces, YJF organized a second demonstration in Shubra, another densely populated area with a high percentage of Christian inhabitants. This demonstration was led by three activists with close ties to the local community, most prominently Mina Daniel (who was later killed in the Maspero massacre after the revolution), and included members of the Karama Party, Kefaya, the Revolutionary Socialists and the Tagammu Party youth wing.[21]

Although activists were still very unsure how many people would respond to the call to protest, there was an implicit agreement that if large numbers did turn out then the plan would be to stay on the street, although there was no universally accepted idea of what this meant. Was the plan to begin an open sit-in? An extra-long vigil? Or something else? But what was clear was that after the remarkable success of the Tunisian revolution, everyone involved was hoping for a new kind of protest, a break with the established routine of an afternoon's demonstrating and home-in-time-for-tea. On social media and in the blogosphere, expectations were running high and activists were already using the word 'revolution' (after the momentous events in Tunisia). But this was tempered by a heavy dose of irony: there was still no certainty that 25 January would end up being anything more than another small escalation in the gradual progress of the protest movement.

Organizers expected the day to go as follows: two small elite demonstrations of the usual kind would take place outside the Journalists'

---

[20] Islam Lotfy, personal interview.
[21] The Revolutionary Socialist Movement was established in the early 1990s with the aim of rebuilding an independent revolutionary left that saw the USSR not as a model for socialism but a form of despotic state capitalism. See: *Revolutionary Socialists*, Available online: https://bit.ly/3miUKqB (accessed 8 August 2014). The Union of Progressive Youth is a leftist youth group and the de facto youth wing of the Tagammu party. It was established on 10 October 1976. See: their page on *Facebook*, Available online: https://bit.ly/3OgPTUQ (accessed 8 July 2014).

Syndicate and the Doctors' Syndicate, which would inevitably be surrounded by a dense security cordon. At the same time, around 400 marchers would set off along Nahia Street, heading for the 'public' demonstration on Mostafa Mahmoud Square where a few dozen activists would already be present – along with the security forces, of course. The hope was that by the time the Nahia Street march met up with the demonstrators at Mostafa Mahmoud, enough passers-by would have joined them that they would be able to break through the security cordon. The most optimistic estimates placed the maximum size of the demonstration arriving at the square at around 5,000 people, and the organizers anticipated that it would remain in Mostafa Mahmoud until around 5.00 pm, calling for nothing more than an end to the state of emergency, the dismissal of the interior minister and fresh elections, which at the time seemed like ambitious demands.[22]

The traditional opposition parties were even less optimistic. There was a general consensus that the day would end with a traditional 'vigil of conscience' in front of the High Court. The president of Tagammu, Refaat El-Saeed, declared on 21 January that it was wrong to politicize National Police Day (in an earlier statement he had called on all Egyptians to take the occasion to express their appreciation for the hard work of their police force) and so his party would not be participating.[23] The Nasserists made it known that they would be boycotting the event because the party could not simply 'fall in behind a protest when no-one knows who its real organizers are'.[24] Brotherhood spokesman Essam el-Erian[25] agreed, and said that since it had not been invited to any specific event, the call to protest had to be interpreted as a call 'to the people as a whole'. Nonetheless, he added that 'anyone who wants to take part can take part' – that is, while the Brotherhood would not be participating in an institutional capacity, it signalled to its members that they could join the protest if they so desired.[26] One young brother who was part of efforts to get the leadership to change their position says that they were still very wary of tying themselves to any protest that might subsequently be used to justify punitive measures against the Brotherhood.[27]

Egypt's cultural and media elite, meanwhile, had been busy since the fall of Ben Ali telling anyone who would listen about the differences between Egypt and Tunisia. The national papers *al-Ahram* and *al-Akhbar* largely

---

[22] Personal interviews with Zyad Elelaimy, Moaz Abdelkarim, Mostafa Shawky, Mohamed Salah, Mahmoud Sami and Khaled Abdel Hamid.
[23] *al-Ahram*, 21 January 2012, Available online: https://bit.ly/3kf3I6q (accessed 5 May 2014).
[24] *Dotmsr*, 26 January 2016, Available online: https://bit.ly/3AOWfmo (accessed 17 October 2021).
[25] Erian died in his cell at the maximum security Aqrab Prison in August 2020 after being detained by the Sisi regime. His family have yet to receive his body.
[26] *Shorouk*, 20 January 2011, 4.
[27] Islam Lotfy, personal interview.

ignored the issue. But the editorial columns of privately owned outlets like *Shorouk*, *Al-Masry Al-Youm* and *Dostor* showed a great deal more interest, generally playing down comparisons while warning the regime that if serious reforms were not forthcoming, the Tunisian 'contagion' might well spread further afield. On 16 January, future MP Amr El-Shobaki informed readers of *Shorouk* that Tunisian society was more 'rational' and 'educated' and the Tunisian state more dictatorial than their Egyptian counterparts.[28] Five days later, Galal Amin wrote that while the populations of both countries had been immiserated by neoliberal economic policy and systematic corruption – and that in fact, Egyptians had 'other grounds for resentment' not shared by Tunisians, including attempts to engineer dynastic presidential succession – revolutionary change was 'ultimately not a matter of simple addition and subtraction, but of unquantifiable psychological factors [...] and foreign support for the rebels'.[29] Wael Kandil warned that ministers were walking 'blindly' into a 'major conflagration',[30] adding in another article published on the same day that 'Egypt will lose nothing by allowing thousands of digital activists to come out onto the street on 25 January and give vent to [...] their legitimate aspirations for a better life'.[31] Amr Hamzawy remained confident that the Egyptian regime would be able to defang and depoliticize social protests, alluding to various factors that ostensibly distinguished Tunisia from other Arab countries, in particular a thriving middle class and a politically neutral army.[32] Waheed Abdel-Mageed argued that events in Tunisia should give the complacent rich cause for concern,[33] while Mohamed Aboulghar warned that 'nobody knows if such a thing could happen in Egypt, and if it could, when it will happen', citing various grounds for resentment among the population.[34] Mahmoud Emara predicted that 2011 would be the year of the 'revolution

---

[28] *Al-Masry Al-Youm*, 16 January 2011, Available online: https://bit.ly/35Ch20C (accessed 2 November 2015).

[29] *Shorouk*, 21 January 2011, 20. Amin's comments were divorced from reality: there was no foreign support for the spontaneous and organized protests that shook the country only a few days later.

[30] *Shorouk*, 22 January 2011, 4.

[31] *Shorouk*, 23 January 2011, 4.

[32] *Shorouk*, 23 January 2011, 13. In reality, Egypt and Tunisia were very similar on these and other metrics. The issue of army neutrality was decisive in the transitional period. The fate of each country's democratic transition was ultimately decided by very different factors: the culture of the political elite, the extent to which they had a shared vision of democracy, the political ambitions of the army and the role played by external factors. In 2011, just before each country's revolution, there was less than a 5 per cent difference in how much of the population lived beneath the poverty line, while the size of the two middle classes as a portion of the population according to income scale differed less than 1 per cent. See: Azmi Bishara, *The Issue of Democratic Transition: A Comparative Theoretical and Applied Study* [Arabic] (Beirut: ACRPS, 2020), 530–4.

[33] *Al-Masry Al-Youm*, 21 January 2011, Available online: https://bit.ly/3BefJ3Y (accessed 25 October 2021)

[34] *Al-Masry Al-Youm*, 23 January 2011, Available online: https://bit.ly/3EgQIqL (accessed 25 October 2021)

of the hungry', calling for a two-term limit on the presidency and imploring Mubarak not to stand again in the next round of elections.[35] Ammar Ali Hassan concluded his own article, published on 25 January, saying:

> Everyone in Egypt is carefully weighing up the situation, even if the government and the institutions of the state are trying to make it seem that the opposite is true. The new political movements and the masses uniformly support and celebrate events in Tunisia. Now suffused with broad hope, they are saying openly: 'They think it's far away, we know it's just around the corner.'[36]

Perhaps the strangest analysis of all came from Mohamed Hassanein Heikal, who predicted in an interview with Al Jazeera, 'The Western response to events in Tunisia will occur in Lebanon [...] we must keep one eye on Tunisia, and the other on Lebanon.'[37] All of these figures – from very different political and ideological backgrounds – were to play prominent roles during the transitional period. Some were elected to parliament, while others backed regime figures in the presidential elections. None of them predicted what actually happened, but they were all aware that something had changed in the aftermath of the Tunisian revolution. It is also worth noting the relative freedom with which they were able to speculate about the future of the regime and changes to the constitution – which shows how much the margin of freedom had expanded under Mubarak alongside the spread of social media.

It is unlikely that the Mubarak regime underestimated the importance of the Tunisian revolution and the ouster of Ben Ali. But with the passing of time, regimes often become fixed in their ways. Mubarak seems to have believed that he had made all the reforms that were possible without ushering in the end of his regime. He believed he could rely on Western fears of Islamist rule and the Obama administration's apathy towards regime change in light of bitter experience in Iraq. More importantly, he believed he could rely on the security forces – and, if all else failed, that the army would step in to protect him, just as it had during the CSF mutiny in 1986. It never occurred to him that it might not.

On 22 January, a video was uploaded to YouTube reassuring prospective demonstrators worried about police violence that they would have some muscle on their side, too. The video showed the Ahly and Zamalek Ultras in a series of recent confrontations with the police – one of them only days

---

[35] *Al-Masry Al-Youm*, 24 January 2011, Available online: https://bit.ly/3mapn3m (accessed 25 October 2021).
[36] *Al-Masry Al-Youm*, 25 January 2011, Available online: https://bit.ly/3GjUhhW (accessed 25 October 2021).
[37] *Shorouk*, 22 January 2011, 1.

before, when fans had chanted in support of the Tunisian revolution.[38] The Ultras had a long-standing vendetta with the security forces, but this was the first sign that they would take part in the coming demonstrations. They were ultimately to play a very important role in the clashes with the CSF on 25 January and in subsequent days.

On the eve of 25 January, young activists from 6 April and YJF went around Nahia Street distributing thousands of flyers about the socio-economic state of the country and police brutality, and to remind people of the torture of a local man (Emad el-Kabir) by the police.[39] In order to mislead the security forces, 6 April also announced that demonstrators would be setting off from four different areas – the Arab League building, the Shubra roundabout, Matariyya Square in north-eastern Cairo and Cairo University – and converging on the Interior Ministry, where they would arrive at 5.00 pm. The announcement was picked up by the media and published by *Al-Masry Al-Youm* the day before the protests.[40]

By the evening of 24 January 2011, various political forces had thrown their weight behind the demonstrations against the state of emergency, set to take place in front of the High Court – most importantly, the DFP, Labour, Ghad and Karama parties, as well as Kefaya, the Revolutionary Socialists, the HASHD and NAC.[41] A senior Brotherhood figure, Mohamed El-Beltagy, had also announced that members of his organization would be present as part of the NAC and shadow parliament contingents.[42] Another leadership figure, Essam el-Erian, told *Al-Masry Al-Youm* that the Brotherhood would be represented at the protest and that its younger members had 'the right to engage', particularly given that plans had originated online.[43] This shift in the Brotherhood's attitude reflected the enormous pressure that younger members with ties to the new social movements had been able to bring to bear: the Guidance Office had finally been induced to permit all those under the age of thirty years to take part.[44] The Wafd also decided to join planned protests in various governorates almost at the last second via its younger members, whom the party was to provide with 'all necessary

---

[38] Beshir, *The Ultras*, 70.
[39] Personal interview with Zyad Elelaimy, Moaz Abdelkarim, Mostafa Shawky, Mohamed Salah, Mahmoud Sami and Khaled Abdel Hamid.
[40] Neil Ketchley, *Egypt in a Time of Revolution: Contentious Politics and the Arab Spring* (Cambridge: Cambridge University Press, 2017), 23–4.
[41] *Shorouk*, 24 January 2011, 1.
[42] The 'shadow' parliament was set up by opposition forces in Egypt in December 2010 in response to widespread ballot fixing during the 2010 elections. It convened at the headquarters of the Ghad Party in central Cairo. Some referred to it as a 'parallel' parliament. See: *Al-Masry Al-Youm*, 16 December 2010, Available online: https://bit.ly/32rJUXw (accessed 15 November 2014).
[43] *Al-Masry Al-Youm*, 24 January 2011, Available online: https://bit.ly/2RtG9dR (accessed 15 November 2014).
[44] Islam Lotfy, personal interview.

support'. In their case, it was the secretaries and members of provincial youth committees who put pressure on the leadership, bringing about 'a qualitative shift in the party's behaviour after the approach that it had taken for thirty years reached a dead end'.[45] Tagammu's Refaat El-Saeed, meanwhile, continued to reject participation, although this did not stop younger members, who were set on taking part even if this meant defying the leadership.

Prominent figures in the Salafist movement, most significantly Yasser Borhamy, told their members not to join the protests. In one statement circulated online, Borhamy told an audience at a mosque in Alexandria that his organization, the Salafist Call, rejected the protests because they served 'the interests of [our] enemies, whose aim is to spread unrest'.[46] In the years leading up to the revolution, the Salafists had been dealt with leniently by the regime, which saw them as a counterweight to the Brotherhood and allowed them to operate with relative impunity. Most Salafist sheikhs were supportive of the regime and preached that it was a sin to rebel against a political leader. Initially hostile to protests, they then tried to maintain a studied neutrality, but they were ultimately forced by events to allow some of their representatives to join demonstrations and sit-ins over the following fortnight.[47]

Most church leaders did not express an opinion on the protests,[48] although *Shorouk* reported that some churches were telling their congregations not to take part. Anba Morqos, the bishop of Shubra al-Kheima, was reported as saying, 'We don't know the purpose of these protests [. . .] our children should think carefully about participating, because we reject acts of deliberate destruction.' Andrea Zaki, the president of the Coptic Evangelical Organization, meanwhile, rejected the protests outright. Kamal Zakher of the Secular Copts – although adamant that the church should not express a position on the protests – described them as 'suspicious' and 'incendiary'. Abdel Maseeh Basset, priest of the Church of the Virgin Mary in Mostorod, told Christians they would do better to spend the day in prayer and contemplation than go out to protest.[49] This was very much a traditional response: Christian leaders knew from bitter intergenerational experience that political unrest could have disastrous consequences for a minority that was made to believe that it depended on the state for protection. But many Christians nonetheless took part in

---

[45] *Shorouk*, 25 January 2011, 5.
[46] *Shorouk*, 25 January 2011, 5.
[47] Hammada, '25 January 2011', 110–11.
[48] Nagi Muris, pastor at the Qasr al-Dobara evangelical church, personal interview, conducted by Amal Hamada, Cairo, 25 April 2012.
[49] *Shorouk*, 24 January 2011, 5.

the demonstrations, and the patriotic mood in Tahrir Square cut across differences of religious background.

During this period, a new generation of political activists were finally making their presence felt. This generation were not only digitally and technologically literate in a way that their predecessors were not. They also saw political action not just as a matter of 'standing up to be counted' but of achieving specific goals. And unlike previous generations, they did not accept that the security forces were omnipotent. They had decided to capitalize on the successes of the Tunisian revolution – not only symbolically but practically as well.

Apart from the day-to-day problems of Egyptian citizens and the other political issues discussed in the media, Egyptian public opinion in the years leading up to the revolution had been focused on what seemed to be a naked attempt by Mubarak to pass the presidency to his son Gamal. It was a widely held belief that the army and many within the security forces were unhappy with this prospect.

One of the side effects of this process was that intra-generational tension developed between the people who were part of Gamal Mubarak's circle and the NDP Policies Committee and those who were not, either because they had not been given the opportunity or because they had refused to join on principle (it was not a capital offence to reject the Gamal Mubarak phenomenon out of hand). This tension fuelled many intellectuals' resentment of the regime, making them seem like regime critics at the time, although they would ultimately revert to fundamentally conservative or even pro-regime positions as soon as Mubarak was gone. The distinction between those with a genuine commitment to democracy and others who merely held a personal vendetta against the regime only became clear much later.

The Interior Ministry and the security forces underestimated the 25 January protests. Holding an exaggerated faith in their deterrent capacities compared to their counterparts in Tunisia, all police plans and contingencies assumed numerical and organizational superiority over protesters. In an interview with *al-Ahram* on 23 January, and in the speech given on the same day, Habib el-Adly seemed untroubled by the prospect of serious political unrest. The United States seems to have shared this misplaced confidence, and only began to pay attention once it became clear just how many people had come out to demonstrate. As Hillary Clinton put it in a press conference on 25 January, 'Our assessment is that the Egyptian government is stable and is looking for ways to respond to the legitimate needs and interests of the Egyptian people.'[50]

---

[50] *Reuters*, 25 January 2011, Available online: https://reut.rs/3cSbdQd (accessed 8 February 2021).

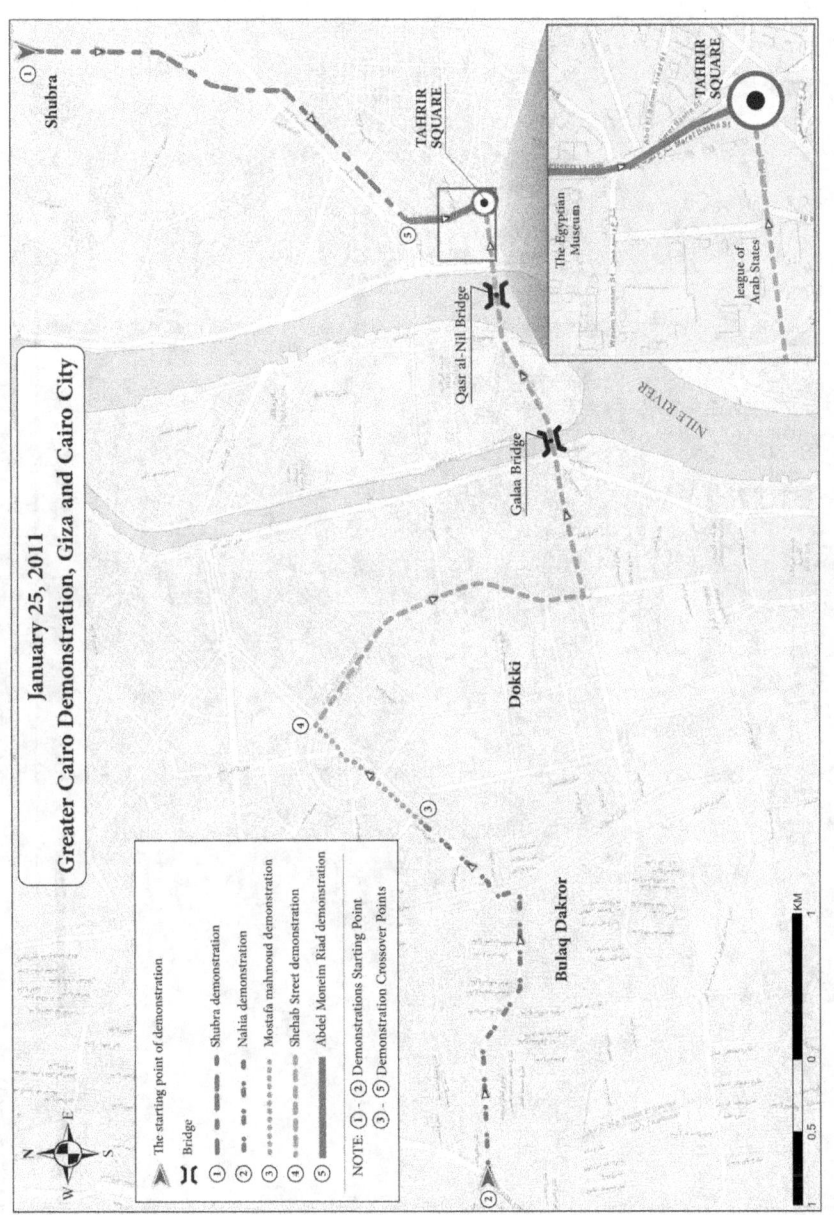

Map 1 25th January 2011, Greater Cairo Demonstration, Giza and Cairo City.

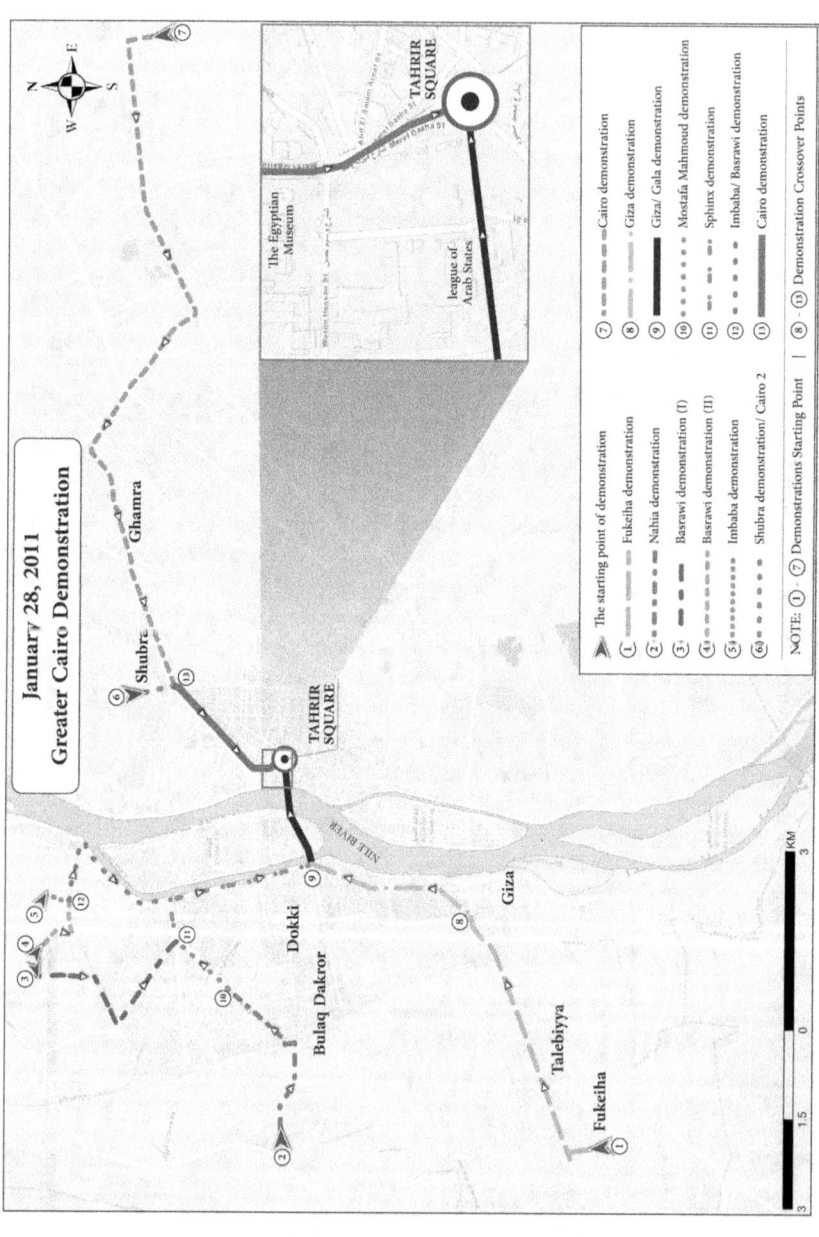

Map 2 28th January, 2011, Greater Cairo Demonstration.

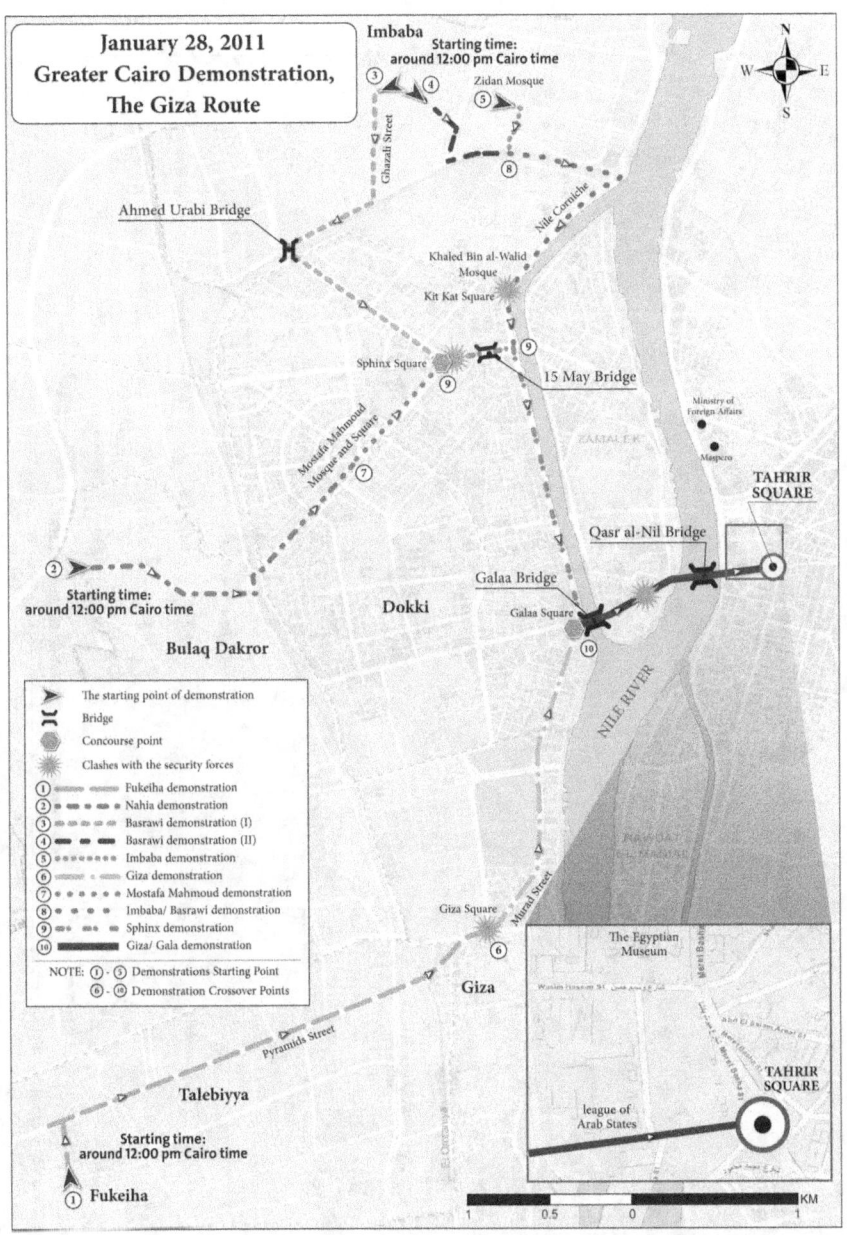

Map 3 28th January, 2011, Greater Cairo Demonstration, The Giza Routes.

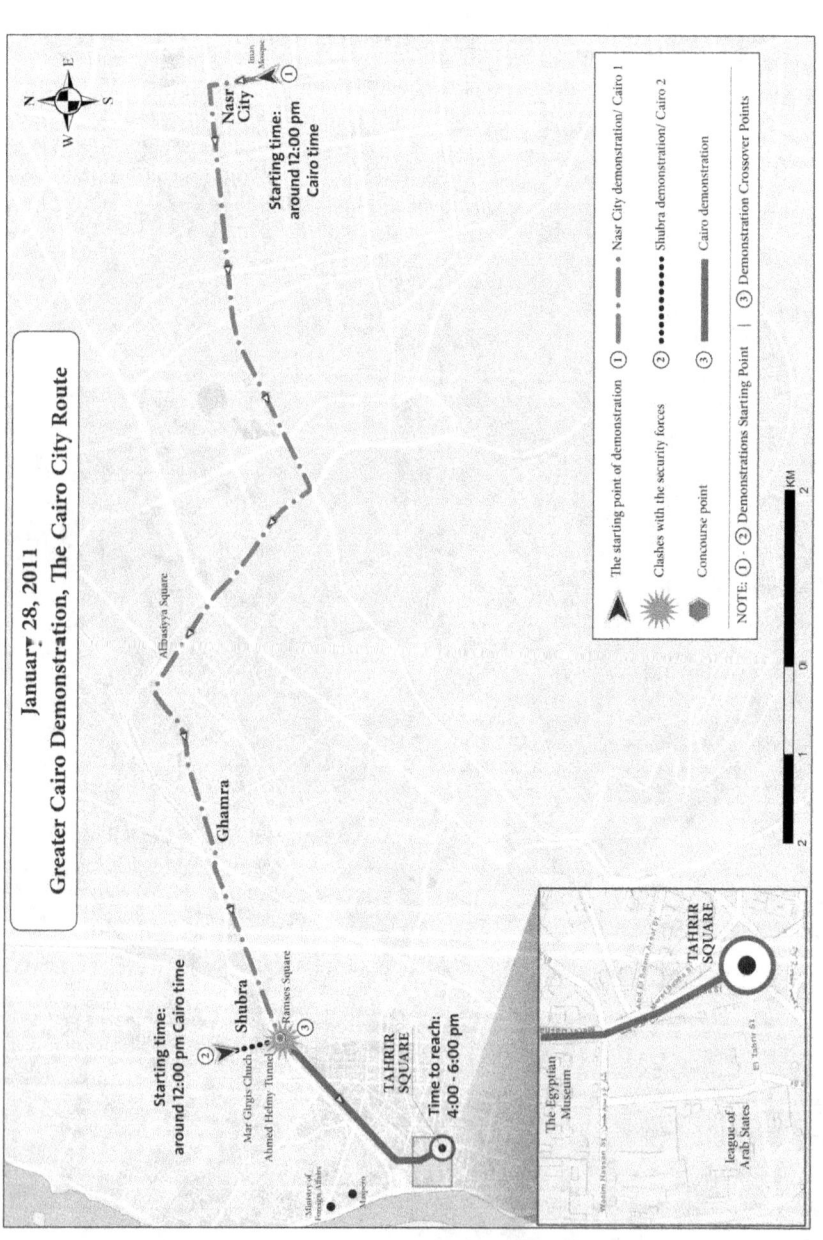

Map 4 28th January 2011, Greater Cairo Demonstration, The Cairo City Route.

II The day of 25 January

On the morning of 25 January, Egyptians woke up to headlines downplaying the significance of the call to demonstrate. *Al-Ahram* featured a dismissive interview with Interior Minister Habib el-Adly in which he sarcastically encouraged prospective protesters and promised them protection so long as they left public and private property alone. He also made it clear that if demonstrators did break the law, he had total confidence in his forces' ability to suppress it.[51] But by this point, the glimmer of hope produced by the success of the Tunisian revolution had spread far and wide among a deeply discontented Egyptian population antipathetic towards Mubarak and his sclerotic regime. Young people from better-off sections of society, in particular, had taken the call to protest very seriously indeed.

A few unlucky encounters hint at how politicized these upper reaches of society had become. At dawn on 25 January, the security forces arrested Halem Henish and Wesam Atta, both Revolutionary Socialist members of YJF, at a press in Mahalla printing pro-demonstration leaflets.[52] A few hours later, however, they were released. Half an hour before protests were set to begin, the police picked up a group of young people who had gathered at Café Cilantro in Mostafa Mahmoud Square to make placards, many of which called for Mubarak's ouster or condemned the Interior Ministry.[53] These were individuals or groups acting independently on their own initiative who did not anticipate any reaction from the security forces. The fact that there were so many spontaneous meetings of this kind is indicative of the general political atmosphere.

This is not to say that the youth movements themselves were not busy. Quite the contrary: they were buzzing with activity. There was a general feeling that they were about to do something very daring, a feeling that was only reinforced by the posting of sentries to observe the security forces' movements. Each of the forty or so activists aware of the real starting point of the demonstration on Nahia Street was put in charge of a group of no less than ten other young people, who would make their way there separately. One group was to stay on Nahia Street itself to make sure that the others managed to find the demonstration, while the others were to drum up support in the surrounding area.[54] Young people thus managed to

---

[51] *al-Ahram*, 24 January 2011, https://bit.ly/32v6Rc9 (accessed 15 May 2014).
[52] Khaled Elsayed, personal interview. See also: *Shorouk*, 6 May 2012, Available online: https://bit.ly/3maQYRY (accessed 25 October 2021). Hanish was in the fourth year of his law degree at the time. He was arrested again during the Abbasiya protests in May 2012.
[53] Mohammad Abbas, personal interview.
[54] Personal interviews with Mohammad Abbas, Abdelrahman Fares (24 February 2014), Moaz Abdelkarim, Mahmoud Sami and Mohamed Salah.

keep the actual starting point of the demonstration a secret and retain the element of surprise. The demonstration was led by Khaled Elsayed of YJF, joined later by Mohamed Al-Qasas and Mohammad Abbas of the Muslim Brotherhood. Abbas was in charge of adding the different groups to the demonstration and controlling its direction.[55]

1 The Nahia demonstration: Mass participation

The Nahia demonstration kicked off with chants inviting local residents to come out to protest: 'Join us, people, throw in your lot, we've got to get rid of all the rot.'[56] Other slogans linked their day-to-day sufferings with participation in the protests: 'Come out, come out – we're here to claim your rights'; 'why so silent, no ballyhoo? Already got your rightful due?'; 'sugar's up, oil's up, tomorrow we'll all be belly up'; 'diesel and gas go higher and higher, we're still here stuck here in the mire' – all mixed in with patriotic shouts of 'long live Egypt!' and the simple mantra of 'bread, freedom, social justice'. These were all chants that resonated in a working-class area like Nahia.

At first, groups of demonstrators drummed up support in specific areas close to Nahia Street, hoping to get as many people out as possible before wending their way towards the railway bridge connecting Nahia with Arab League Street. The outcome exceeded their wildest dreams. Within half an hour, according to one participant, the demonstration had swollen to more than 15,000 demonstrators.[57]

Demonstrators quickly realized how unambitious their plans had been. They had expected that on their arrival in Mostafa Mahmoud, they would be pinned down by the usual security cordon and prevented from moving elsewhere. They were thus planning to continue the protest until 5.00 pm and then head home. But the sheer size of the crowd bearing down on the square meant that any thought of stopping was quickly cast aside. The security forces were quickly overwhelmed, and despite repeated attempts to prevent demonstrators breaking through, the two protests met up at the corner of Arab League Street and Shehab Street. Plan A seemed to have come off without a hitch, and there was no reason to stick around in Mostafa Mahmoud. They now had to quickly work out what to do next.[58]

---

[55] Mohammad Abbas, personal interview.
[56] Amr Guevara (6 April), personal interview, conducted by Amal Hamada, Cairo, 23 April 2012.
[57] Personal interviews with Abdelrahman Fares, Moaz Abdelkarim, Mahmoud Sami, Mohamed Salah, Khaled Abdel Hamid, Zyad Elelaimy and Amr Guevara.
[58] Personal interviews with Mohamed Salah, Mahmoud Sami, Waleed Abd Elraouf (24 June 2014), Islam Lotfy, Mohammad Abbas and Amr Guevara.

So, it was that demonstrators made the fateful decision to continue their march in the direction of Tahrir Square, apparently without any previous planning.[59] Amidst sally after failed sally by the security forces, their horizons seemed to suddenly and dramatically broaden. For the first time, activists felt safe – this was no longer an elite protest. Their spirits rose. This was a game changer.[60]

The protest wound its way along Arab League Street to Ahmed Abdel Aziz Street and down to Dokki Square. From here, it made its way along Tahrir Street to the square itself, crossing the Nile via the Galaa and Qasr al-Nil bridges. Organizers chose this route deliberately to avoid potential chokepoints, sticking to built-up areas to make it as difficult as possible for the security forces to stop them. Pushing past the checkpoints and barriers thrown up hastily in their path, their numbers – and morale – grew steadily as more passers-by joined the protest. Those joining were encouraged by the security forces' unwillingness to use their firearms.

It took the protest almost two hours to reach the entrance to Tahrir Square, which they found blocked by yet another line of security officers. But the protesters were not to be deterred: photos and videos from the event show them charging the cordon head-on, displaying considerable individual heroism. By around 3.30 pm, demonstrators had forced their way onto the square. Despite their unprecedented numbers, however, they now found themselves filling only one small part of its vast open space. The protest that had seemed so impossibly huge in Nahia Street suddenly looked quite inadequate.

While all this was going on, the security forces had, as anticipated, formed a cordon around the official demonstration held by the opposition party leaders outside the High Court downtown. While demonstrators here numbered in the hundreds, there were nonetheless signs that a new cultural and political elite had come of age, an elite to whom the old boundaries between parties and organizations meant little. One of the speakers at that event, Abdel Moneim Aboul-Fotouh, perhaps put it best: 'To our young brothers and sisters, I say: only you can save Egypt. Do not make the mistake of relying on the frail and sclerotic generations that preceded you. Only you can bring Egypt through. Make freedom, justice and development your watchwords. There can be no more party slogans

---

[59] Mohammad Abbas said in personal interview that the decision to head for Tahrir was entirely spontaneous. Khaled Elsayed, however, recalls people chanting, 'Anyone who wants change, come with us to Tahrir', implying that this was one of the slogans chosen in advance as part of the planning.
[60] Personal interviews with Mohammad Abbas and Khaled Elsayed.

after today.'⁶¹ As he uttered these words, the Nahia demonstration was just about to reach Tahrir.

2 Shubra: Confrontation and challenge

The Nahia demonstrators were soon joined by another, smaller march of no more than 2,000 people, which had been making its way from Shubra to the High Court protest. This march included various nationalist and Islamist figures from the NAC and former Brotherhood parliamentarians. When it changed direction and tried to move towards Tahrir, it met with a brutal response from the security forces, and protesters scattered before regrouping at Abdel Moneim Riad Square. This group then engaged in running battles with the CSF until it succeeded in pushing through onto Tahrir Square via the metro station. Orders not to use lethal force again played in the protesters' favour (Muammar Gaddafi and Bashar al-Assad were to learn from this 'mistake', making a point of using lethal force from the moment that demonstrations first began).⁶²

The Shubra demonstrators were the first to use fists and stones against the security forces, a phenomenon which was to intensify over the next two days and result on 28 January in their exhausted withdrawal from the area. If the Friday of Rage's overwhelming force of numbers echoed the spirit of the Nahia protest, then the twenty-four hours of street fighting on 26 and 27 January was an extension of the Shubra demonstration. These two models – extended clashes with the security forces versus mass gatherings that the security forces avoided – were to complement each other right up to the fall of Mubarak and, indeed, throughout the transitional period.

The security forces were ill prepared to take on gatherings of this size. The Interior Ministry was paying a high price for its dismissive attitude. Only 4,000 officers had been deployed in downtown Cairo, an unusually small number that would not have been up to the task.⁶³ It is thus no surprise that they were unable to stop protesters crossing the bridges or forcing their way onto Tahrir. There was an attempt to address these failures on 26 and 27 January, with far more boots on the ground in Cairo. But this was to precipitate clashes with the inhabitants of many of the working-class districts in the area, most of whom had nothing to do with the planned demonstrations. In turn, these clashes exhausted the security

---

[61] Video clip available on *YouTube*, 23 March 2012, Available online: https://bit.ly/3mkpqHT (accessed 1 October 2021).
[62] Abdulrahman Gadd, personal interview, 13 May 2012. Many of those who were present recalled that senior officers stepped in to prevent clashes with demonstrators.
[63] Ketchley, *Egypt in a Time of Revolution*, 26.

forces' energies in the two days leading up to the Friday of Rage while turning much of society decisively against them.

The Shubra demonstrators put up such fierce resistance that many officers lost helmets, truncheons or shields, and the security forces were eventually forced to fall back towards Mohammed Mahmoud Street. Attempts to close off the square then led to fresh clashes[64] interspersed with acts of remarkable bravery, most famously Osama el-Mahdy's attack on an armoured car that had been bombarding protesters with a water cannon.[65] One participant described it like this:

> We'd been in the square less than five minutes. The main body of the protest had come down from the Arab League Building and entered from the Tahrir Street side, and protesters were spreading out in every direction. Just as the demonstration got to the middle of the square, an armoured car came out of nowhere, drove right into the mass [of protesters] and started firing its water cannon. Osama ran up, clambered up to the turret using the protective shield over the windscreen. It was absolutely heroic – he leapt on the guy on the cannon and dragged him down off the car.[66]

Demonstrators' success in breaking through the cordon around Tahrir Square inspired many others – from all sorts of social backgrounds – to find ways around the security forces and join them. Despite orders to prevent any such eventuality by force, the security forces' truncheons proved ineffective, and the protest grew.

3 'The people want to topple the regime'

By around 5.00 pm, thanks in large part to judicious use of paving stones, the demonstrators had occupied Tahrir Square. Despite the tear gas still hanging in the air, an atmosphere of relative calm prevailed. The security forces dug in around the parliament building on Qasr al-Aini Street, where they were rumoured to be stopping ambulances and arresting those inside on suspicion of being injured in the fighting. In response, protesters set up the first of the revolution's field hospitals,[67] staffed by doctors and pharmacists who had attended the protest; a whip-round provided the

---

[64] Abdulrahman Gadd, personal interview.
[65] A video of the scene is available on *YouTube*, 22 November 2011, Available online: https://bit.ly/3bZX013 (accessed 8 May 2014). Another famous incident saw a young man blocking the path of an armoured car on Qasr al-Aini Street, forcing it to come to a halt. His identity remains unknown. See: Ghonim, *al-Thawra 2.0*, 212.
[66] Hany Mahmoud, personal interview, conducted by the author, 5 and 15 September 2015, Doha.
[67] Ibid.

cash for bandages, disinfectant and basic medicine. In subsequent days and throughout the transitional period, hospitals of this kind were to become one of the hallmarks of protest, symbolic of the role played by doctors and medical students.

The more than 50,000 people that soon found their way to Tahrir defied all expectations. The organizers had never dreamed of such numbers and found themselves yet again faced with the fundamental question of what to do next. A meeting was swiftly convened by young activists to discuss prospective scenarios. Some suggested that they should quit while they were ahead, taking advantage of what was by any previous standard an extraordinary victory to send a stark message that the regime could not ignore. Others wanted to stay put, hoping that once news spread of the demonstration even more people would want to join in.[68]

It was decided that the protest would continue, at least until it was clear whether this extra support would materialize, and that more donations should be collected to buy food for those already in the square. Food committees were set up to distribute meals. But these attempts were quickly stymied by the security forces, who arrested one YJF member (Halem Henish) who had volunteered to go on a food run and confiscated everything he had bought. Instead, protesters were forced to rely on deliveries by relatives or friends or from the various human rights and legal organizations headquartered close to the square.[69] Blankets originally intended for use by striking workers were provided by the Hisham Mubarak Law Centre.

In the meantime, the demonstrators were preparing themselves for all eventualities, including the possibility of staying in the square.[70] They set to work coming up with innovative ways of resisting assaults, including using fizzy drinks and vinegar to counter the effects of tear gas and a shift system allowing those defending the protesters to take breaks.[71] At 9.00 pm, thanks to a megaphone, they were finally able to address the assembled crowd as a whole, directing, deciding, warning and alerting demonstrators with a single voice. By this point, the first physical symbols of the nascent gathering – tents, the field hospital – were starting to go up, reinforcing

---

[68] Personal interviews with Khaled Abdel Hamid and Mostafa Shawky.
[69] Ibid.
[70] This meeting was attended by many of the younger demonstrators as well as Ibrahim Eissa, Osama El-Ghazali Harb (head of the DFP) and Kamal Abou Eitta. Harb and Abu Eita encouraged those present to carry on with the demonstration, warning them that if they left the square there would be no coming back (Mohammad Abbas, interview). Of course, neither Abu Eita nor Harb were suggesting that they should stay there for two weeks – nor did the young activists they were speaking to yet have any thought of doing so.
[71] Abdulrahman Gadd, personal interview.

the message.⁷² Organizers had also started leading roving protests in the vicinity of the square, which would go and come back in the hope of raising morale.⁷³

At the same time, something else was going on that had very little to do with the organizers and activists or with politics more generally. A spirit of solidarity and conviviality, of warm mutual feeling, was starting to grow up among those present. Egyptians from all sorts of backgrounds were getting to know one another – a sort of mass family reunion between relatives who had never met. The pictures from the square that found their way into the media the next day were enough to show everyone watching, whether in Egypt or beyond, that something unique was happening – something that people wanted to engage with or trust in as a snapshot of a brighter future. Groups of Ultras from the Ahly and Zamalek firms were present, setting off fireworks and banging drums.⁷⁴ (Although the media only became aware of their role after the major clashes of 28 January,⁷⁵ they were already there in force on 25 January, and, in fact, had coordinated their involvement in advance with organizers.⁷⁶) Not only were the revolutionaries protesting, they were learning the principles of protest, pooling their knowledge and experience to ensure the success of their efforts.⁷⁷ The security cordon and the communications blackout imposed on downtown from 9.00 pm onwards only increased demonstrators' determination to finish the journey they had started in the square.⁷⁸

This was a crucial moment. Demonstrators now needed to decide what the aim of their protest was. Meeting after meeting was held between the members of the various protest movements.⁷⁹ Some suggested occupying the parliament building and forcing the government to negotiate, a proposal that was ultimately discarded because it would have made it easier for the regime to portray them as rioters. By 7.00 pm, plans were being made on the assumption that the regime would not allow them to remain in the square overnight. There were worries that if the Tahrir protest were dispersed, then the newfound sense of strength and confidence would be lost. One

---

72 Ahmed Abu Khalil, personal interview, 6 April 2014.
73 Personal interviews with Mohammad Abbas and Mohamed Salah.
74 Personal interviews with Islam Lotfy and Abdulrahman Gadd.
75 Amal Hamada, 'Defiers of Authority: The Ultras as a Force for Redefining the Relationship between the Street and State' [Arabic], *al-Siyasa al-Duwaliyya* (supplement on theoretical trends), 187 (January 2012).
76 The author learnt from Khaled Elsayed that leading figures in some Ultras firms had spoken to activists in the lead up to 25 January and that their members were present in large numbers on the first day, teaching other demonstrators many of the 'techniques' involved in fighting the security forces, in particular how to break through cordons.
77 Amr Guevara, personal interview.
78 Islam Lotfy, personal interview.
79 Hany Mahmoud, personal interview.

group suggested that they should issue a list of demands at midnight and then head home after announcing fresh protests for the following day, earning them a stream of invective from those sitting nearby. At that exact moment, people began to chant: 'The people want to topple the regime!' At the next meeting, held at 8.00 pm, it was decided that they would be staying in the square.[80]

There was now another change in atmosphere. Young people gathered around the entrances to the square, calling out to passers-by: 'Off home? Bored, are you? We're just getting started – it's a long road to freedom, you know!' Across the square, the chant rang out: 'The brave soul has pluck and the coward's a wuss, and we, brave fella, are gonna stay put!'

Zyad Elelaimy, Kamal Abou Eitta, Mostafa Shawky, Islam Lotfy and Sameh al-Barqy had begun putting together a manifesto demanding an end to the state of emergency, the dismissal of the Nazif government (including the interior minister), fresh legislative elections and a guarantee that Mubarak would not pass the presidency on to his son. Although this manifesto seemed ambitious by the standards of the moment, the spontaneous chants demanding the fall of the regime and Mubarak personally[81] – which came as such a surprise that some believed that a conspiracy was afoot[82] – rendered it totally obsolete, and it was torn up. The spontaneous escalation of the protest had raced ahead of all the activists' plans and expectations and opened up new horizons no less ambitious than those of their Tunisian neighbours. The new manifesto that they set about writing was to bear the title *Down with the Regime!*[83] As yet, there was no clear organizational structure – the meetings brought together activists from a range of groups who happened to be in the same place – but a seed had been planted, already visible in the burst of activity leading up to 25 January. A few days before Mubarak's resignation, this seed would grow into the RYC.

That evening, a noticeably flustered Adly gave a recorded statement on national Egyptian television. The patronizing confidence of his last interview was gone: he now railed against 'intellectuals', who he accused of hating him for 'protecting Egypt'. But the mask of bravado and contempt was starting to slip. The Interior Ministry had been taken completely by surprise.[84]

---

[80] Ibid.
[81] Islam Lotfy, personal interview.
[82] Menawy, for example, claims that the chant was 'linguistically' foreign to Egypt and – since it was an entirely novel phenomenon in Egyptian protests – could not have been spontaneous (*The Last Days*, 90–1).
[83] Personal interviews with Islam Lotfy and Mostafa Shawky.
[84] Mohamed Naim, a written personal interview sent to the author. Naim is a leftist activist who participated in the protests.

4 After the surprise: Coordination with the Brotherhood

The Brotherhood was slow to realize exactly what was happening. There had been almost immediate attempts to make contact by the activists in Tahrir: Hany Mahmoud had phoned Essam el-Erian in the immediate aftermath of Osama el-Mahdy's assault on the armoured car and tried to impress upon him that something unprecedented was happening:

> 'What's happened? I was at the High Court protest and I've only just got back,' Erian said. So I told him, 'Doctor, today is something else entirely – it's nothing like the High Court thing. I've never seen a demo like the one we've just been in [. . .] the numbers, the distance, the spirit of the demonstrators.' And he said that he'd speak to the Brothers in the [Guidance] Bureau. He took a while getting back to me, so I asked Ahmed Nezeily to ring his dad – one of the Society's older leadership figures, who was in charge of the Giza administrative office. And he told [Ahmed] to carry on doing what he was doing and let them carry on doing what they were doing. He was talking like he was worried that his phone was bugged![85]

The young Brothers in the square did not give up. They arranged a meeting with members of the Guidance Bureau, including Mohamed Morsi, Mahmoud Ezzat and Mohamed El-Beltagy, hoping to bring large numbers of Brothers out in support. But other than Beltagy, who backed the young activists, the leadership was wary of involving the organization in a new kind of event whose consequences could not be predicted. According to Islam Lotfy, Morsi himself was particularly keen on establishing the exact number of demonstrators already present: 'Are there a lot of you? How many are we talking about?'[86] By this point, the Interior Ministry had already issued a statement accusing the Brotherhood and 6 April of subverting the demonstrations and announcing that it was mobilizing more than 10,000 CSF personnel for an attack on the square.[87] The activists argued that since the regime had already decided the Brotherhood were responsible, the organization was going to face consequences no matter what it did – so it might as well take part. They asked the bureau to prepare for another massive gathering on 28 January and to appoint leaders to act on their behalf on the ground – leaders who would be able to make independent decisions without constantly consulting their superiors.[88] Mahmoud Ezzat's response was that the protest had started

---

[85] Hany Mahmoud, personal interview.
[86] Islam Lotfy, personal interview.
[87] *Youm7*, 25 January 2011, Available online: https://bit.ly/33vFG02 (accessed 11 May 2014).
[88] Personal interviews with Hany Mahmoud and Islam Lotfy.

as a popular protest and should stay a popular protest, and that while it was infeasible for the Brotherhood to take part now, they could try and coordinate with other political forces for the Friday protest. Mahmoud Ghozlan told them that the Brotherhood was too large and unwieldy an organization to mobilize within such a short period of time and proposed 5 February as the earliest that Brothers could be expected to come out en masse.[89] The activists responded by asking for the downtown Cairo branch to provide logistical support and for a prominent Brotherhood figure to make an appearance at the square alongside the representatives of other political movements already present. The bureau agreed to send Beltagy, who on the way there told activists that he had been 'trying to convince them to let me go to the square since the moment I got back from the High Court – but they wouldn't listen'. Beltagy was subsequently to play a key role in expanding Brotherhood participation in the protests beyond younger members. In the meantime, the media had announced that the riot squad was about to disperse protesters.[90] Within moments of Beltagy's arrival in Tahrir, the attack had begun.

5 After midnight: The revenge of working-class districts

By the time that the CSF moved in at around 2.00 am, there were around 20,000 demonstrators in the square,[91] whom they immediately set upon with truncheons and tear gas. So much gas was deployed that it became impossible to see anything, and many of those there attest that the attackers were using live ammunition.[92] Many of the demonstrators in the square put up fierce resistance,[93] but eventually the sit-in was dispersed, breaking up into dozens of small protests that retreated into the surrounding areas. The CSF and police continued to hound these protests until daybreak,[94] leaving a haze of tear gas floating over central Cairo's working-class neighbourhoods. Security cast its net wide, detaining more than 1,000 young men and women in a campaign of random arrests that kept various human rights organizations busy all day long.[95] But the gas and the noise and the unfamiliar presence of battalions of uniformed men were to produce a counter-reaction in the neighbourhoods, and those activists

---

[89] Ibid.
[90] Personal interviews with Islam Lotfy, Mohammad Abbas, Mostafa Shawky, Mohamed Salah and Mahmoud Sami.
[91] Ibid.
[92] Personal interviews with Amr Guevara, Mohammad Abbas and Mohamed Salah.
[93] Personal interviews with Mohammad Abbas, Islam Lotfy, Moaz Abdelkarim, Khaled Abdel Hamid, Mostafa Shawky, Mohamed Salah, Zyad Elelaimy and Sally Touma.
[94] Ibid.
[95] Personal interviews with Ahmed Ragheb and Taher Abu'l-Nasr.

who had evaded arrest the night before were to have the satisfaction of witnessing a full CSF rout – of seeing the same police personnel who had pursued them keeling over from exhaustion.[96]

The call for fresh protests disseminated via the various forms of new media – Facebook, Twitter, even SMS text messages – had already met with an even bigger response than that of the day before. But the real difference came not from the established networks of protesters but from the so-called popular districts – working-class neighbourhoods – whose inhabitants were to play an ever-greater role in events over the coming days. The inhabitants of these areas were not Facebook users and had no connection with the young demonstrators who had organized the activities of the day before. But they were hostile to the government and police, whose brutal practices they had had plenty of opportunity to witness over the years leading up to the revolution. Above all else, it was this hostility that brought them out in such large numbers to confront the security forces. They sought only to give those who had beaten, tortured and terrorized them a bloody nose, a taste of their own medicine – to take advantage of an opportunity for revenge. Over the next two days, these protesters were to fight the CSF to an exhausted standstill, setting the stage for the defeat of the Interior Ministry on 28 January (the Friday of Rage).

The involvement of these demographics brings us back to a question discussed earlier and later in the final chapter: the social make-up of the protests and the role of the internet. This is particularly important because many have described the revolution as a 'digital' or 'Facebook' revolution. According to official statistics,[97] by May 2011 there were twenty-five million internet users in Egypt, including those who accessed the internet from their phones – sixty times the number of users in 2000. But internet use was unevenly spread across different demographics. One survey[98] found that 29 per cent of Egyptian adults generally had internet access at home. Those who did not have personal access, however, likely had access via friends and relatives, at least in Cairo.[99] A survey conducted by BBC Media Action in March–April 2010 suggested that 55 per cent of Egyptian internet users did not know how to use a computer and that 43 per cent could not buy a private computer – that is, they used the internet only on their phones.[100]

---

[96] Mohamed Salah, personal interview.
[97] Ministry of Communications and Information Technology and UNCTAD, 'ICT Policy Review, Egypt', 2011, Available online: https://bit.ly/3uLXLWL (accessed 25 October 2021).
[98] International Republican Institute, 'Egyptian Public Opinion Survey April 14–April 27, 2011', Available online: https://bit.ly/30ctO2s (accessed 25 October 2021).
[99] Xiaolin Zhuo, Barry Wellman and Justine Yu, 'Egypt: The First Internet Revolt?', *Peace Magazine* (July/September 2011): 7.
[100] See: Socially Responsible Media Platforms in the Arab World, [An initiative by BBC Media Action] *BBC*, 13 February 2012, Available online: https://bbc.in/3ElP7jG (accessed 28 October 2021).

The internet was certainly an important opposition tool:[101] internet use and computer ownership among the hard core of protesters and the inner circles of those who responded to call for protest were certainly higher than the average. But while pages like We Are All Khaled Saeed attempted to translate digital action into demonstrations and protests, the effects only extended to a relatively narrow circle of people – the first 'circle' of people attending demonstrations. The mass of those who joined the protests between 25 and 28 January did not join because of the internet, but because of socio-economic conditions, political grievances and the behaviour of the security forces, as well as the excitement generated by the Tunisian revolution and the events of 25 January that they heard about on TV.

Unofficial networks of friends and relatives were also important in spurring and maintaining protest. One survey[102] showed that 72 per cent of respondents heard about 25 January from social networks of this kind, with only television (97 per cent) more important. Text messages (28 per cent), Facebook (15 per cent), internet news (13 per cent), email (2 per cent) and Twitter (1 per cent) played far less important roles.[103]

III 26–28 January: The race

The next day, 26 January, provided an opportunity to regroup and to assess the first day of the revolution. A unique spontaneity gripped the country. There were repeated reports of unplanned protests – some real, some imaginary – in almost every part of Greater Cairo (and in other governorates as well). Despite their exhaustion, the protesters of the day before were determined to maintain momentum.

The security forces, meanwhile, were trying to play whack-a-mole, wearing themselves out racing from reported protest to reported protest in an effort to prevent another major mobilization. The police and CSF also had to deal with surging unrest in the working-class areas around Tahrir Square, whose inhabitants attacked a number of government buildings and even stormed the Interior Ministry.[104] Mubarak's security forces had rarely policed these areas directly – preferring to cooperate with networks of local strongmen (*baltagiyya*) run by businessmen linked to the

---

[101] Tim Eaton, 'Internet Activism and the Egyptian Uprisings: Transforming Online Dissent into the Offline World', *Westminster Papers* 9, no. 2 (April 2013): 8.
[102] International Republican Institute, 'Egyptian Public Opinion Survey'. See also: *Daily News Egypt*, 7 June 2011.
[103] Zhuo, Wellman and Yu, 'Egypt: The First Internet Revolt?', 7.
[104] Personal interviews with Mohammad Abbas; Mohammad Badawi (YJF), personal interview, conducted by Mohammad Abbas via Skype, 21 February 2014.

regime – and the mere presence of large numbers of CSF men was felt in itself to be a provocation. These attacks were demonstrations, but not of a demand-oriented or political character: the perpetrators were giving vent to years of pent-up rage without any direction from parties or political movements.[105] Nonetheless, the smaller activist protests that took place at the same time outside the Bar Association and Journalists' Syndicate – despite their merely circumstantial link to the unrest – received much the same brutal treatment.

Until the afternoon, activists were unsure exactly who was leading or participating in the demonstrations. The popular mobilization in Cairo (and even more so places like Alexandria) spread rapidly and erratically, with new focal points emerging constantly without any coordination or direct link with other areas or with organizers. This was its strength – and after Mubarak's fall, its weakness. Aly El Raggal, who took part in demonstrations on Alexandria, says that the spread of protest was 'horizontal' rather than top-down, but was 'not chaotic' and this is what allowed the revolution to move beyond existing hierarchical structures like political parties and state institutions: neither leftist nor secularist nor Islamist nor even 'third way', it was a decentralized revolution without a clearly defined single leadership, ideology or identity, and this was the secret to both its rapid spread and its staying power.[106]

It is worth emphasizing this point because even after Mubarak's fall it has often been claimed that the 26 January demonstrations were led by the various protest and political movements. This misconception was shared by the regime, which at the time believed that these demonstrations were a continuation of the events of the day before. By 27 January the regime claim that Brotherhood members had 'hijacked' the revolution by turning up with chains and bricks was everywhere. The media was full of 'reports' that foreign Brotherhood cadres from Yemen, Gaza and Sudan had infiltrated the country as *agents provocateurs* (media employees have since described how 'senior government figures' got in touch with producers and presenters, who proved very willing to push their line[107]). The regime

---

[105] Ibid.
[106] Ali Raggal, 'A Revolution Patterned after Others: An Attempt to Understand the Nature and Type of the Egyptian Revolution' [Arabic], in *The Egyptian Revolution: Motivations, Trends and Challenges* [Arabic], ed. Aya Nassar et al. (Beirut: Arab Centre for Research and Policy Studies, 2012), 65–78.
[107] Menawy, *The Last Days*, 109. Lt Gen Sami Anan made similar claims in his memoirs, published in 2013: on the second day of the revolution, Brotherhood members 'took control', 'taking advantage of loyal youth and revolutionary slogans as a justification for bringing down the state'. See: *al-Watan*, 28 September 2013, Available online: https://bit.ly/3m8IxEX (accessed 12 May 2015). There are many other similarities in the narratives given by Anan – who during the revolution was chief of staff – and Menawy. Menawy promotes similar claims in his book (105–8), claiming that the protesters were all Brotherhood members ordered in advance to avoid religious or Islamist chants and slogans.

itself seems to have believed many of these claims, which would later be repeated in court by its intelligence chief, Omar Suleiman.

Around midday, El-Sayyid el-Badawi, the leader of the Wafd, made a statement to the press in which he demanded the dissolution of parliament and the formation of a national unity government (a 'government of national salvation'), saying that the 'street' had spoken.[108] Badawi was well aware that Egyptian governments were impotent entities; he knew that power in Egypt rested with the president and that this had been the case since 1952. So, this was hardly a revolutionary demand.

At the same time, the leaders of the protest movements were holding fresh meetings. It was clear that the revolution had begun to snowball. The different groups were instructed to avoid downtown Cairo until the nature and size of these disorganized demonstrations had become clear. There was a real sense that something qualitatively different was happening[109] – a sense apparently shared by the security forces, which took the unprecedented step of firing directly at people's faces and chests.[110] As Mahmoud Sami puts it, 'I realized that there were demonstrations and marches developing spontaneously everywhere out of small groups and that nobody, neither the security forces nor the activists, would be able to control or direct them. And that made me happy. At last, the people were mobilizing!'[111]

In the evening, activists heard that demonstrations in Suez had left several people dead. This news sent shockwaves through the revolutionary movements, whose leaders quickly agreed to schedule mass demonstrations for Friday 28 January.[112] The various organizations set about the urgent tasks of planning and preparation. The 6 April Movement, for example, held a meeting at the Egyptian Centre for Social and Economic Rights to decide who would do what, while the young Brothers renewed their attempts to pressure the organization into participating.[113] It was to be a 'Friday of Rage'.

At around 8.00 pm, the youth movements decided that after the deaths in Suez there could be no going back on the demands made in the square. The regime had to go. Safe entrances and exits from Tahrir Square were identified. It was proposed that various marches be launched from different spots around Greater Cairo, forcing the CSF to divide their energies between several different places. Activists also agreed that they would attempt to reproduce the successes of the Nahia protest, holding unannounced

---

[108] *Alwafd*, 25 January 2011, Available online: https://bit.ly/3aN6KvU (accessed 17 October 2021).
[109] Personal interviews with Khaled Abdel Hamid and Mohamed Saleh.
[110] Khalid Tallima, personal interview.
[111] *Shorouk*, 24 January 2014, Available online: https://bit.ly/33qnd5c (accessed 15 November 2014).
[112] Khalid Tallima, personal interview.
[113] Mohammad Abbas, personal interview.

demonstrations in working-class districts to whip up popular support.[114] When the moment of truth came and they were forced into confrontation with the hundreds of thousands of CSF personnel in central Cairo, they would respond Palestinian-style, using bricks and stones. A unit was set up to pick up and throw back the tear gas grenades used by the police. Shields were improvised from plastic barrels, and if the police used live ammunition, protesters agreed that they would respond with Molotov cocktails.[115]

As night fell, We Are All Khaled Saeed, 6 April and Rassd published the times and starting points of the various demonstrations on Facebook. Mass text messages also helped spread the word. Activists got in touch with their Tunisian counterparts to ask for their advice on dealing with police tactics.[116] When an internet blackout was imposed, Al Jazeera Mubasher – with its text-in ticker tape – filled the void.

IV 27 January: The elite mobilize

The day of 27 January began with the arrest of Wael Ghonim, one of the admins of We Are All Khaled Saeed, at a restaurant in Zamalek; he had just finished a meeting with Google executives who had warned him that the government was desperate to find out who he was. Ghonim's arrest was to galvanize public sympathy (especially middle-class sympathy) for the revolution.[117]

The same morning, Mohamed ElBaradei touched down in Cairo airport, where he announced that he had come back to Egypt to take part in the Friday of Rage. His first order of business was to meet with Abdelmonem Emam, Abdel Rahman Youssef and Mostafa Alnagar from the Baradei campaign. They were joined by several figures from the NAC, including the Brotherhood leaders Essam el-Erian and Mohamed Saad Elkatatny. Those present agreed that all available energies had to be thrown behind the Friday of Rage. Where the various prominent opposition figures would be positioned on the day had already been decided at an NAC meeting at 3.00 pm at the DFP headquarters attended by Abdel Galil Mustafa, Ahmed Darrag, Osama El-Ghazali Harb, Sekina Fouad, Shahenda Maklad, Hany Mahmoud (attending on behalf of Mohamed El-Beltagy), Yasser El Hawary

---

[114] Personal interviews with Moaz Abdelkarim and Khaled Abdel Hamid.
[115] Moaz Abdelkarim, personal interview.
[116] Personal interviews with Mohammad Abbas, Islam Lotfy, Moaz Abdelkarim, Khaled Abdel Hamid, Mostafa Shawky, Mohamed Salah, Zyad Elelaimy and Sally Touma.
[117] An interview with Ghonim after his release can be seen on *YouTube*, 8 February 2011, Available online: https://bit.ly/35yXIkL (accessed 11 May 2014).

(a representative from the Ghad Party) and others. They had chosen the Istiqama Mosque in Giza, on the west bank of the Nile, as their meeting point, which was to remain secret. They had also arranged a way to keep in touch with one another during a communications blackout, agreeing that they would use landlines to provide regular updates to an operations room throughout the day. The various tasks were parcelled out to different groups, and the limited media tools available to the opposition were used.

The Brotherhood agreed to participate. Baradei, too, would join the demonstration proceeding from the Istiqama Mosque and be accompanied by Katatny[118] in a show of Brotherhood support for the demonstration. Activists of Christian backgrounds also held a meeting with Coptic leaders at a priest's house, managing to extract a public statement expressing understanding for the demonstrators' demands for 'natural human needs and necessary social values: God wants man to enjoy a dignified life'.[119]

The young activist coordinating groups – what I have called 'revolutionary movements' – met again at the house of Zyad Elelaimy's mother in Agouza to map out Friday's protest. The planners picked out twenty mosques around Cairo, as well as a single church in Shubra, to serve as the jumping-off points; these were duly publicized on social media. It had already been agreed that three other marches – which, like the Nahia protest, would not be made public – would set off from mosques in the working-class areas of Imbaba, the Al-Haram area and Basateen. Route planning fell to the Brotherhood members, whose experience with electoral rallies had given them a very good idea of how to avoid confrontations and bottlenecks, along with Basem Kamel (Baradei campaign), who was put in charge of the march from Basateen.[120]

At 7.00 pm, the young Brothers launched two demonstrations, one in Talebiyya and the other in Nasr City. One of the leaders told me:

> Our group agreed that I would be responsible for organizing the Talebiyya demonstration since I lived in Omraniyya, which is nearby, and since I had an organizational relationship with many of the guys there and knew the streets well. I visited the area on Wednesday (26 January) and met some of the Brotherhood guys there. I asked them to help organize a route for the demonstration that would stick to alleyways and side streets rather than main roads. I made it clear to them that this was not a Brotherhood event and that I wasn't there in my organizational capacity but was asking them for help for purely patriotic reasons – that they could

---

[118] Abdelmonem Emam, personal interview.
[119] Nagi Muris, personal interview, 24 April 2012.
[120] Khaled Abdel Hamid, personal interview.

refuse or ask their Brotherhood superiors if they wanted, but that I hoped they would participate and lend a hand. And they did.[121]

The gathering began in Talebiyya with about twenty people chanting against unemployment and high prices. They moved through side streets and back alleys for about two hours, gathering some 2,000 demonstrators. When Islam Lotfy tried to bring the demo to a close after the organizers heard that the police and the local *baltagiyya* were on their way, the locals refused to leave – in fact, they stormed a police station on Talebiyya Street and burned it down.[122] The protest continued until dawn on Friday.[123] The Nasr City protest was smaller and was quickly dispersed by the CSF; its leader Anas al-Sultan was arrested.[124]

At a meeting at Zyad Elelaimy's house late in the evening of 27 January, the members of the coordinating committee, which now included DFP members Shadi Ghazali Harb, Ahmed Eid and Amr Saleh, were surprised to hear that Baradei had announced that he would set off from the Istiqama Mosque, located on Giza Square halfway between Talebiyya and Tahrir Square. His decision to do so threw something of a spanner in the works, because wherever Baradei was the CSF would be too – and this was the area on which most of the young activists had arranged to converge. The organizers had already decided to change the site of the main protest to a mosque in Imbaba that sat in the middle of one of the biggest food markets in Giza.[125] They were now in a race against time to tell everyone about the new location. This task was made much easier because of the absence of any police in central Cairo; they were recovering after days of exhausting street fighting. The revolutionaries were also lucky that most of the groups were staying overnight in or near to the relevant spots, making it easier to speak to them face to face or get in touch via landline.[126]

The regime's preoccupation with quashing the spontaneous demonstrations of 26 and 27 January thus gave the revolutionaries the opportunity to regroup, take stock and plan for Friday in relative peace. They were so surprised at the complete absence of the police that they thought it was a sign of some kind of plan. It never occurred to them that the security forces were human too and had a limited amount of energy. All the regime was able to do, meanwhile, was block Facebook and YouTube

---

[121] Hany Mahmoud, personal interview.
[122] Ibid.
[123] Islam Lotfy, personal interview.
[124] Ahmed Abu Khalil, personal interview.
[125] Khaled Elsayed, personal interview. Other accounts placed the change of location at the same meeting, but during a three-way discussion between Abdelrahman Fares, Hany Mahmoud and Khaled Elsayed, all three participants agreed that the change was made beforehand.
[126] Mohamed Salah, personal interview.

for a few hours, a measure easily overcome by means of proxy servers. The rapid course of events, and in particular the unexpected popular reaction to them, afforded a historic opportunity for people to pull ahead of their government and get a better idea than the security forces of what was happening on the ground. All this meant propitious circumstances for the Friday of Rage, which would see the birth of the 'million-man march' (*milyoniyya*) and mark the definitive storming of the public sphere.[127]

It is clear from Wael Ghonim's account of his interrogation – described in detail in his book – that the security services were convinced of their own conspiracy theories. His interrogators were very interested in calls he had made to Google about a prospective job, which they described as 'communication with foreign parties'. Certain that the Brotherhood was pulling the strings, they could not give Ghonim's spontaneous and apolitical patriotism any credence despite his full confession (not only of what he had done but also of what he had *thought*).[128] The regime and the security forces would later try to make a self-serving distinction between the honest, good-hearted young people with their legitimate demands on one hand and the local and foreign political forces that exploited them on the other, identifying them as 'conspirators', 'terrorists', Iran, Hamas, Hezbollah, America or simply 'them'.[129]

No regime can continue to function if its employees are no longer convinced of the rightness of their actions. It does not matter whether those at the head believe in the regime's slogans and conspiracy theories, but the lower levels must believe, at least in part, in the accusations directed at the regime's enemies. At the very least, they must buy in to an 'us vs them' mentality that allows them to imagine conspiracies and bad intentions on the part of the other and justifies coercing confessions or framing suspects.

State audiovisual media ignored what was going on.[130] The private media, meanwhile, was split: channels like ONTV were sympathetic to the

---

[127] There was a great deal of talk surrounding these 'million-man marches', but Ketchley claims that the numbers involved were exaggerated and that no single protest attracted a million Egyptians until the 11 February demonstration that finally toppled Mubarak (*Egypt in a Time of Revolution*, 19).

[128] Ghonim, *al-Thawra 2.0*, 228–32. There were of course many people far more political than Ghonim involved in the organizing of demonstrations, but discontented, apolitical, patriotic young people were also an important part of the phenomenon.

[129] On 25 January, the Ahram Centre's Mohamed Abdel Salam appeared on Egyptian TV to give a somewhat different analysis: that Egypt was witnessing its own May 68 and needed to approach it with understanding. Although he did not make an explicit distinction between 'sincere' young people and sinister political forces, his reasoning formed the foundation of such distinctions.

[130] *al-Ahram*, for example, limited its front-page coverage of the protests on 27 January 2011 to the following brief item: 'Four dead, 118 citizens and 162 policemen wounded, 100 arrested in Cairo and the governorates.' Elsewhere, it described the protests as riots and anarchy. See: *al-Ahram*, 27 January 2011, Available online: https://bit.ly/33BRFJN (accessed 14 June 2014). Another item noted fresh demonstrations in Suez and attempted to smear the protesters by focusing on looting, ignoring the demands made by protesters.

protests, while others were more hostile. The latter camp included channels owned by regime-linked businessmen such as Hassan Rateb's Mehwar and Wafd president El-Sayyid el-Badawi's AlHayah network.[131]

On the evening of 27 January, the NDP leadership held a meeting attended to discuss the possibility of organizing pro-Mubarak demonstrations. But the Interior Ministry objected to the plan, saying that it would be unable to both protect these demonstrations and squash the revolutionaries' protests at the same time.

The regime leadership were convinced that Al Jazeera was helping to inflate the size of the protests on Thursday and Friday after it broadcast pictures and news from the Tuesday demo.[132] But Al Jazeera's importance was ultimately the product of the local media's behaviour: if the latter's coverage had been less wildly inaccurate, then no foreign media outlet would have been able to transform itself into a major source of news for Egyptian viewers, who were historically very loyal to their national media. Accusations against Al Jazeera have continued to be central to regime propaganda against mass mobilization, and while the network certainly took far more interest in the protests than other Gulf-owned media outlets or indeed Egyptian outlets, it did not fabricate the events. The regime was living in denial, and continued to do so until the protesters came knocking at its door directly.

V 28 January: The Friday of Rage

From 10.00 am on 28 January, internet and mobile phone services were cut off across Egypt. Plans for such a contingency had been in place since 23 January, but this was the first time they had been deployed.[133] The intention

---

[131] Albert Shafik, the head of the ONTV network, personal interview, conducted by Maria Adeeb, Cairo, 9 April 2012.
[132] Menawy, *The Last Days*, 119–22.
[133] According to a fact-finding commission set up under the post-revolutionary caretaker government: 'Dr Amr Badawy (chief executive, National Telecom Regulatory Authority), when asked, attested that on 23 January 2011, representatives of the security forces invited him to a meeting attended by representatives of the three mobile phone companies. In light of the urgent threat to national security, an Emergency Command Centre was set up to control the activation and deactivation of communications networks, pursuant to Article 67 of the communications law. At 10.00 am on 28 January, the ECC ordered the networks shut down. It did the same at 9.30 am on 29 January. Internet access, meanwhile, was suspended on 28 January and only restored on 5 February. [Dr Badawi] explained that these shutdowns had no effect on police communications because they operate on a different frequency and an independent system. He added [...] that this was the first time any such blackout had been imposed anywhere in the world, that it had had a negative impact on Egypt's international standing and that the mobile phone companies had suffered losses in the course of it.' See: 'National Fact-Finding Commission Summary Report on the Events of the 25 January Revolution' [Arabic], Available online: https://bit.ly/3BPS8Id (accessed 17 October 2021).

was to leave demonstrators in the dark and prevent communication among organizers. The effect, however, was to announce to Egyptians up and down the country that something big was happening – in fact, to encourage them to go outside and see what was going on for themselves. That morning, millions of Egyptians made their way to local mosques for Friday prayers. That week there was a much greater variety of sermons than usual. Some preachers, of course, supported the demonstrations, but others were hostile, accusing protesters of unlawful rebellion or of 'spreading strife'. In a sign of how much momentum the revolutionary wave had gained, many of these pro-regime preachers were pulled down from their pulpits or thrown out of mosques.[134] Meanwhile, security forces deployed en masse around the protest locations that had been announced publicly the previous day. The stage was set for a fresh, perhaps decisive confrontation – a confrontation that would usher in a new chapter in Egypt's history.

1 March A, Giza: The western bank of the Nile

a Imbaba and Talebiyya

By this point, young activists were very comfortable with the 'Nahia approach', and the huge crowds they managed to mobilize in the working-class neighbourhoods of Imbaba and Talebiyya were to set the rhythm of the protests as a whole: the demonstrators that followed this route were among the first to get to Tahrir. As they made their way along the long and circuitous route, chosen deliberately to avoid the security cordons around the publicly announced protests – in particular Giza Square, where Baradei was to make an appearance – they were to draw in dozens of smaller spontaneous marches setting off from mosques all around the neighbourhood.

The Imbaba demonstration began immediately after Friday prayers had finished.[135] Activists from YJF and 6 April, accompanied by members of Ultras firms,[136] had already begun whipping up support in nearby thoroughfares, blowing whistles and waving red cards to symbolically 'send Mubarak off'. Yet another protest, meanwhile, had started to move out from Basrawi towards the Nile, clashing with police in Kit Kat Square (one of the protest locations announced the day before). Although

---

[134] Personal interviews with Mohammad Abbas, Islam Lotfy, Moaz Abdelkarim, Khaled Abdel Hamid, Mostafa Shawky, Mohamed Salah, Zyad Elelaimy and Sally Touma.
[135] Ibid.
[136] The Ultras had continued their clashes with the CSF even on 26 and 27 January in some areas, and in Alexandria the Ultras Devils and White Knights Alex firms had played a role in clashes around Qaed Ibrahim Square. They were also active in Suez, where one of their number (Mohammad Mikwa) was the first martyr of the protests. See: Beshir, *The Ultras*, 71.

organizers managed to redirect the protest up the Nile in order to get around the CSF, by the time they arrived at Ghazali Street – one of the area's longest and most densely populated – they were no longer in control. All they could do was try to keep marchers to the established route while continuing to chant.[137]

Less than two hours after Friday prayers had finished, tens of thousands of demonstrators had come out of Imbaba shouting anti-regime slogans and 'bread, freedom, social justice!' Just as anticipated, the march had snowballed. The sight of so many people making their way over Ahmed Urabi Bridge seemed almost fantastical and came as a shock even to the demonstrators themselves. There was a sense that everything was spontaneous and yet, at the same time, moving according to some vast plan.

The demonstrations that had been announced publicly, meanwhile, had also attracted thousands of people, and although they had been intended largely as a distraction, those present took them very seriously indeed. The unsung heroes who gathered at the twenty points around Greater Cairo, and in particular those in the Nahia area, helped to galvanize protest and engaged in running battles with the CSF. By the time that the vast wave of protesters arrived from Imbaba, marchers from Nahia had already worn down the CSF forces on 15 May Bridge.

b Galaa Bridge: 'Keep it peaceful!'

The other 'unannounced' demonstration began further south in Talebiyya, one of the most densely populated areas in Giza, and was the responsibility of the young Brotherhood members.[138] Beginning from Fukeiha in the heart of Talebiyya, it adopted much the same style as the Imbaba demonstration: organizers roamed the backstreets trying to attract as many demonstrators as possible. This demonstration, too, soon began to snowball and found its way out onto Al-Haram Street, where it quickly broke through a security cordon set up around the Al-Haram Tunnel.[139] This brought them down to Giza Square, where clashes broke out between protesters and police. Baradei, who as previously noted was present at an official protest in the square, left the area as soon as the police attack began.[140]

---

[137] Personal interviews with Mohammad Abbas, Islam Lotfy, Moaz Abdelkarim, Khaled Abdel Hamid, Mostafa Shawky, Mohamed Salah, Zyad Elelaimy and Sally Touma.
[138] Mohamed Al-Qasas (former member of the Brotherhood and the executive bureau of the RYC), personal interview, conducted by Mohammad Abbas over Skype, 14 February 2014.
[139] One of the main arterial roads leading through Giza to the Nile.
[140] Mohamed Al-Qasas, personal interview.

At around 3.30 pm, after fierce fighting, the CSF commander in Giza Square surrendered to the demonstrators, handing over his firearm (whose ammunition had been used up in the battle) and allowing them to pass.[141]

The march moved on and shortly thereafter met up with the Imbaba demonstration at Galaa Bridge. Here, the two marches formed an unstoppable mass of people that quickly overcame the CSF troops stationed around the bridge despite heavy use of gas and buckshot.[142] But as officers and conscripts fled before protesters or cowered in their vehicles, rings of demonstrators formed around them to protect them, and a remarkable chant went up: 'keep it peaceful!' (*Silmiyya!*). CSF men were stripped of their guns and uniforms, which were immediately thrown into the Nile,[143] but they were not harmed. So, it was that the famous slogan was born – from a position not of weakness but of strength, after the protesters had the defeated CSF at their mercy.

One participant described the events as follows:

> I was on a march that set off from Mostafa Mahmoud. When I got there before prayers, the mosque was packed – the streets were full of people waiting to pray. The first thing I noticed was that young men and women were praying alongside one another. This was an odd sight, and I got the sense that it was going to be an unusual day. No sooner had the imam finished leading the prayers and said 'peace be upon you' than people started chanting 'the people want the fall of the regime'. The sound was incredible. And then a march started – the biggest march I'd ever seen, by pre-25 January standards. At least 25,000 people started to move, with the actor Amr Waked at the front chanting. It took a real effort to keep the movement of the march organized and make sure that it stayed connected, because we weren't used to marching in such huge numbers. All the way along Arab League Street people kept joining us. [. . .] At Galaa Bridge there were violent clashes, which made it clear to me that the security forces were completely confused – and that we were, too. [. . .] Ultimately the CSF retreated to Qasr al-Nil Bridge, where they were soon caught up in a fresh confrontation with the vanguard of the protesters arriving from Giza.[144]

---

[141] Ibid.
[142] Personal interviews with Mohammad Abbas, Islam Lotfy, Moaz Abdelkarim, Khaled Abdel Hamid, Mostafa Shawky, Mohamed Salah, Zyad Elelaimy and Sally Touma.
[143] Ibid.
[144] Mohamed Naim, written personal testimony. Naim links the confusion of the officers to the central role played by the middle class in the protests: 'Many of the CSF officers saw among the demonstrators gatherings of people from the same demographic, people who, "like them" (i.e. like the officers), deserved to be described as "citizens". This raised questions about the legitimacy of using extreme force against them – after all, for these officers there was the possibility that they might have relatives or friends among the demonstrators. One senior CSF officer that I met by chance in Al-Mokattam on 8 February told me, in an excitable and high-pitched attempt to justify the police's retreat, "I couldn't fire on them with live ammunition [. . .] the people I was facing were

The battle for Qasr al-Nil Bridge was the fiercest of the day. The scenes – broadcast in detail on international media – were to become a symbol of endurance and challenge. The CSF used all available means to break up the demonstration, beginning with water cannon and volleys of rubber bullets. In epic scenes, protesters set fire to armoured cars, acting as human shields for one another.[145] At 6.00 pm, an exhausted CSF retreated with its tail between its legs, and the victorious demonstrators poured into Tahrir Square.

The defeat on Qasr al-Nil was the first domino to fall in what would quickly become a total rout of the security forces. Interior Minister Habib el-Adly informed Mubarak that his forces were no longer capable of confronting demonstrators and asked him to order the military out on to the streets.[146] At exactly 5.00 pm, the Republican Guard surrounded Maspero, the state TV building, and Mubarak announced a curfew from 6.00 pm to 7.00 am the next day.

That Friday also saw the first appearance of military equipment when demonstrators were crossing the area between Galaa Bridge and Qasr al-Nil Bridge. Demonstrators were alarmed to see military armoured cars heading towards the bridge. But they simply passed through the CSF checkpoint and moved on before the CSF renewed their attack on demonstrators.

2 March B, Cairo, eastern bank of the Nile: Revenge on the police

While on the Giza side of the river protests followed the Nahia pattern, in western Cairo it was the Shubra model that prevailed. No sooner had marchers poured out of Friday prayers than they were caught up in brutal clashes with the security forces. The latter did not hesitate to use lethal force, particularly when demonstrators began taking out years of pent-up resentment on local police stations. All eyewitnesses agree that there were dozens killed and wounded in the course of these clashes, particularly in the working-class areas of Matariyya and Sayyida Zeinab.[147] After nightfall, demonstrators were to attack police stations across the whole of

---

like you, or like Kamal. [. . .] How could I shoot someone like that with live ammunition?" The phrase "like you" or "like so-and-so" here refers to a shared social background.' But this officer's characterization of the CSF's behaviour is not entirely accurate: they *did* fire on, and kill and injure, middle-class demonstrators, and CSF conscripts sometimes specifically targeted intellectuals or middle-class people when doing their job gave them the chance to vent class resentments. In my view, this account may apply only for an individual case or two.

[145] Mohamed Salah, personal interview.
[146] Menawy, *The Last Days*, 153. See also: *Al-Masry al-Youm*, 28 January 2011, Available online: https://bit.ly/3iwAkbt (accessed 25 October 2021).
[147] Mohammad Awwad (YJF), personal interview, conducted by Mohammad Abbas over Skype, 2 May 2014.

Greater Cairo, blurring the distinction between the two kinds of protest. But in any case, even when the difference was obvious, the two types of protest naturally complemented one another, allowing for a more effective confrontation with a regime determined to stop the revolution.

Most of the demonstrations that began in the Cairo governorate on the eastern side of the river were spontaneous and lacked any political organization, with the notable exceptions of the relatively organized (and relatively small) marches that set off from Nasr City and Shubra.[148] The security forces' response was remarkably violent: according to the website WikiThawra, more than 150 people died in these demonstrations, accounting for more than half the deaths recorded countrywide in the 28 January protests. But demonstrators' successful attacks on police stations throughout the capital were the final nail in the coffin for the Interior Ministry. With its forces in retreat and its precincts set ablaze, its omnipotence and omniscience had been exposed as a myth.

Police stations had been burning in Suez since 25 January, as we will see later when we return to developments in the provinces. But on 28 January this phenomenon spread to the rest of the country,[149] contributing to the general paralysis of the Interior Ministry and the police. In any revolution, it is common for violence and non-violence to complement one another. When we say that a revolution was peaceful, we are talking about two things: first, its general character is peaceful, and, second, it is not armed struggle. Violent incidents did take place during the Egyptian revolution, including the burning down of police stations. This phenomenon ultimately contributed to the success of the Tahrir Square occupation, since it diverted the attentions of thousands of policemen away from demonstrators. The CSF were far better prepared on 28 January than they had been three days earlier, and far more willing to use force.

Let us return to the trajectory of the Cairo demonstrations. These demonstrations were concentrated around two major hotspots (as well as many smaller points largely coalescing around police stations): one march that began at the Iman Mosque on Makram Ebeid Street in Nasr City, and another that set off from the Mar Girgis Church in Shubra. Compared to

---

[148] Ahmed Abu Khalil, personal interview.
[149] Ketchley, *Egypt in a Time of Revolution*, 19–21, 29. Including the first incident in Suez, eighty-four of the republic's police stations (about one-quarter) were burned down within the two weeks of the revolution. The CSF and police also lost thousands of cars. This was not the first time that police stations had been burned down. Locals had occasionally responded in similar ways to previous police killings. On 10 January, for example, the inhabitants of Giza's Warraq neighbourhood attacked a police station for precisely this reason. Even during the revolution, demonstrators concentrated their efforts on those stations with particularly bad reputations for torture.

the Giza protests, the coordinating protest movements were much less involved, which perhaps accounts for the ensuing chaos.[150]

The Nasr City march, made up of about 100,000 demonstrators, made its way across Abbasiya Square and through Ghamra before running into a CSF contingent around Ramses Square. At the same time, the Shubra march was making its way towards the same area via the Ahmed Helmy Tunnel, engaging in running battles with the CSF as it went. By 4.00 pm, the CSF positions in Ramses Square – one of the main routes into Tahrir Square – were besieged by demonstrators from both marches, as well as a number of other smaller demonstrations that had joined them.[151]

Ahmed Abu Khalil, who had joined the Nasr City march, provided a lengthy description of the scene in Ramses Square:

> The CSF cars were parked in a line no more than 50 metres away from the Fateh Mosque, and between them and where I was standing there were thousands of people, dozens of formations and gatherings. Every five minutes a group would retreat carrying its injured, only to be replaced by another, bigger group. The sound of the tear gas grenades was constant, and the police sirens were echoing all around the square. [You could see] the flames and the smoke coming off the police shelters around the bottom of the bridge, and there were burnt-out barriers among the lines. The chants were mixed in with shouts and screams, and the ground was covered with endless numbers of people. Ramses Street was still heaving with an unbroken flow of people, packed together like sardines but moving steadily. We'd started in Nasr City, but others had come from Almaadi, Al-Mokattam, Gisr Suez, Zeitoun and dozens of other neighbourhoods and areas – some taking half a day to get there.[152]

The CSF cordon between Ramses Square and Tahrir fought on until around 6.00 pm, when they finally beat a retreat. The symbols of the regime set alight, the police stations and NDP buildings gutted by fire – all this had an almost surreal quality about it. Greater Cairo was in chaos. By 7.00 am the next day, with protesters successfully ensconced in Tahrir Square for the second time, the protest had been transformed into a broad-based popular revolution demanding that Mubarak leave within two weeks and his regime be dismantled. Of course, the demonstrators had not given much thought to the exact meaning of this latter demand. They believed that the regime was unjust, and they were angry. They imagined that changing the regime meant changing the president. By the time that the revolutionary

---

[150] Ahmed Abu Khalil, personal interview.
[151] Ibid.
[152] Ibid.

forces had managed to put together a more far-reaching programme of what should come next, this idea had become embedded in the popular consciousness.

VI Questions about the defeat of the security forces

The withdrawal of the CSF contingents and their declining firepower confused the revolutionaries. One activist suggested that they must have received an order to retreat or used up all their ammunition. Then they began to move out of the way to allow demonstrators to pass,[153] and it became increasingly clear that they had completely abandoned the main streets and redeployed around Simon Bolivar Square and Mohammed Mahmoud Square, close to the Interior Ministry. They seemed to be recognizing that their mission had failed. No orders had been given, and no trap had been set. The CSF had simply shown that the rot that had spread across Egypt's neglected public institutions over the last few years had not spared them either. Although some find it genuinely difficult to believe, a security force is an institution just like any other – an institution that can be inefficiently managed, or eroded by inaction, maladministration, a lack of incentives and a search for personal benefit. The CSF had come up against something far beyond all their predictions, and all their plans had been made obsolete. Inefficient, slow, lacking in clear structure – combine these with a corrupt leadership, and it is no surprise that they were unable to stand in the demonstrators' way. But this does not explain why the police withdrew entirely from the civilian sphere, abandoning their traditional social function. That was a decision. The only explanation is that the regime decided that by removing the police from the equation, it would open the door to chaos and lawlessness of a kind that might persuade the armed forces to intervene on its behalf.

Personal testimony and investigations carried out later confirm that the massive popular response to the Friday of Rage simply overwhelmed the CSF, which lacked the means to deal with a revolution of this size. Communication broke down between the field commanders and the senior leadership at the Interior Ministry. When on 30 January the Interior Ministry ordered the CSF back out onto the streets, these orders simply were not obeyed. The security forces had collapsed in on themselves.

After the revolution, the media reported that the plan for the protests – finalized on 24 January at a meeting between Habib el-Adly and his security

---

[153] Personal interviews with Mohammad Abbas, Islam Lotfy, Moaz Abdelkarim, Khaled Abdel Hamid, Mostafa Shawky, Mohamed Salah, Zyad Elelaimy and Sally Touma.

chiefs – had been for the CSF to police the protests 'as its chief considers appropriate', to make as little use of firearms as possible and to show restraint in order to prevent an escalation. Events in Tunisia were still fresh in everyone's minds.[154] This strategy was the polar opposite of that later chosen in Syrian by Bashar al-Assad, who resolved to learn the lessons of Egypt and Tunisia and deploy lethal force from the very first moment. But the security forces were nonetheless responsible for the deaths of around 800 people over the two weeks of the revolution, and some 900 over the year as a whole.[155]

It does not seem that the authorities planned for the possibility that the CSF might lose control of the demonstrations or that demonstrators might outnumber the police. When questioned on the issue of the killing of demonstrators by the public prosecution, Habib el-Adly was later to concede that this was due to an 'underestimation' of the size of the protests, but that this was because 'the 25 January demonstrations were bigger than anybody had predicted – nobody in Egypt expected so many demonstrators would come out'.[156]

According to the judgement ultimately handed down by the Administrative Court on the management of the protests, the Interior Ministry set up an operations room in Ramses telephone exchange, staffed by representatives of the relevant authorities, to deal with 'agitators' and the use of text messages and the internet to 'foment anarchy'. The means at their disposal gradually expanded to include IP tracking and the interruption of internet services. Pursuant to a decision issued by a committee headed by Ahmed Nazif (which included the communications, interior, defence, foreign and information ministers as well as Samy Saad Zaghloul, the secretary general of the cabinet), Adly was empowered to identify threats to national security; it was he who took the extreme step of ordering the communications shutdown.[157]

Orders came down from Adly to his four deputies, the heads of SSIS, the General Security Division, the CSF and the Cairo security chief. During questioning, he maintained that other than four cases in Suez, he

---

[154] Amnesty International report shows a detailed data on the main arms supplies to Egypt. The data is of the main generic types of weaponry, munitions and related equipment examined in the report, namely small arms; smooth-bore weapons over 20 millimetres; ammunition; bombs, rockets, missiles and explosives; armoured vehicles; and toxic agents between 2005 and 2010. Amnesty International, 'Arms Transfers to the Middle East and North Africa: Lessons for an Effective Arms Trade Treaty', 2011, 8–9; Available online: https://bit.ly/3nC0BJ3 (accessed 25 October 2021).
[155] *Guardian*, 14 March 2013, Available online: https://bit.ly/2DReobY (accessed 10 September 2020); Amnesty International, 'Egypt Rises: Killings, Detentions and Torture in the "25 January Revolution"', 19 May 2011, 28; Human Rights Watch, 'World Report 2012: Egypt - Events of 2011', Available online: http://bit.ly/2CyCR4r (accessed 25 October 2021).
[156] *al-Ahram*, 28 March 2011, Available online: https://bit.ly/2FGtod8 (accessed 15 November 2014).
[157] *Youm7*, 7 August 2011, Available online: https://bit.ly/2Zv3wet (accessed 25 October 2021).

was unaware of any deaths among the demonstrators, and that he still did not know how or why there had been other deaths. Saying that he had been in continuous communication with his deputies up to 31 January, he dismissed the possibility that the police could have used live ammunition so long as nobody was engaging in 'terrorism', claiming that he was unaware of any incidents in which the police had used live ammunition against peaceful protesters. He asserted that the CSF's orders were to use water cannons, truncheons and tear gas. He also claimed that it is the CSF chief alone who decides whether a situation warrants opening fire. These desperate attempts to avoid responsibility were based on the knowledge that the deep state had not changed and would not abandon him, and he was ultimately proved right. Since CSF officers in the field could not have opened fire without permission from their superiors, and since no permission had been given, the shootings could not have happened. As a result, nobody would be held accountable.

1 Testimony of field officers

Officers questioned by the investigators, however, tell a different story. They say that they consulted the interior minister, who had resolved to prevent citizens from gathering in Tahrir Square or any other public square on 28 January at all costs, although they 'decided to use force against demonstrators without consulting the commanders'. (Lt Colonel Essam Hassan Abbas of the General Administration for Conscript Affairs contradicts this account, maintaining that the interior minister's security deputies gave orders over radio sets and that the quartermaster's books prove that the units policing the protests were equipped with automatic weapons, shotguns and rubber bullets, although this is denied by Adly.)[158] Adly and other senior figures seem to have decided that more force was needed after the failure to contain the 25 January demonstrations, but lethal force failed too.

Inspection of the operations room's event logs for 28 January shows clearly that the deputy minister did order the CSF to provide their units with automatic weapons, shotguns and ammunition and that the officer responsible for protecting the Interior Ministry gave a direct order to fire on demonstrators, despite his subsequent denials.[159]

---

[158] Amnesty International, 'Egypt Rises: Killings, Detentions, and Torture in the "25 January Revolution"', 19 March 2011, 93–4, Available online: https://bit.ly/3lLX9fi (accessed 17 October 2021).

[159] *Youm7*, 9 September 2011, Available online: https://bit.ly/3iyLKv6 (accessed 5 June 2014).

In his testimony to the court on the killing of protesters, CSF Major Mohamed Galal Abdel Rahman attested that on 28 January he did witness use of weapons around the Interior Ministry, but that he was unable to determine the number of dead or wounded. He said that there were snipers from SSIS's international terrorism unit stationed on the roof, who got their orders directly from Adly. He blamed the security forces' failure to exercise restraint on the poor judgement of the ministry leadership, by which he meant the minister himself and his deputies.[160] Bassem al-Oteifi, who was in charge of intelligence coordination, confessed that he had written up Item 244/28 Jan in the operations room event log, which released firearms to CSF units and ordered them to fire on demonstrators under the authority of the deputy minister.[161]

As far as the retreat of the CSF and the police was concerned, Adly initially claimed in testimony to the Military Prosecution that with the police clearly unable to control such large numbers of protesters, 'circumstances forced' him to order a withdrawal, since the only other option was to order the use of live rounds and oversee a massacre.[162] During his subsequent prosecution in the case of the dead protesters, however, he denied ever giving such an order, instead pointing to the police's 'total exhaustion' after four days of constant action as well as disagreements between the different agencies responsible for operations of this kind, in particular the CSF and the General Security Forces. He argued that they lacked the workforce to police such large numbers of protesters, and that in the face of orders not to use live ammunition despite constant attacks on policemen, many of them had simply abandoned their posts. He also claimed that with the armed forces now apparently in the field, many of the police felt that they were no longer needed, and this led to a collapse in morale and widespread absenteeism.[163]

The picture that emerges from all this is of a security force taken completely off guard by the events of 25 January (when lethal force was not used) and left exhausted by the street fighting of 26 and 27 January (when several demonstrators died in Suez and elsewhere). Although they were finally given permission to use lethal force in the capital on 28 January, they were tired out and overwhelmed by unprecedented numbers of demonstrators. They thus withdrew from the field out of exhaustion and in the hope of precipitating intervention by the armed forces.

---

[160] *Youm7*, 21 August 2011, Available online: https://bit.ly/3C4cXzT (accessed 17 October 2021).
[161] Ibid.
[162] *Christian Dogma*, 11 February 2011, Available online: https://bit.ly/3E89r7S (accessed 25 October 2021).
[163] *Khaberni*, 28 March 2011, Available online: https://bit.ly/3vmrS5z (accessed 17 October 2021).

With the police off the streets, furious demonstrators descended on police stations throughout the country. In Cairo, the attackers were the inhabitants of the informal slum areas ringing the capital, the victims of long years of arbitrary detention, torture and extortion by the police. Armouries were robbed, detainees were freed and documents were burned – just as they had been at the court complex in Galaa. Cairo slid towards anarchy, even after the deployment of the army. Mahmoud Wagdy, interior minister in the post-revolutionary caretaker government, estimated that the police lost some 2,000 vehicles and 90 stations. In the ensuing security vacuum, the only serious body attempting to maintain order was the set of popular committees set up by citizens.

VII The Egyptian army deploys

1 The army and the revolutionaries

Even as the security forces beat a hasty retreat, military vehicles were making their way towards key government buildings in the capital: the major ministries, the parliament, the state broadcaster and various institutions of relevance to the army.[164] Nobody was sure whether the military was there to protect the regime or to support the revolution. While some revolutionaries welcomed the prospect of a military intervention, others already had their doubts, especially when the rumour spread that the soldiers were there to reinforce the flagging CSF. The famous chant that 'the army and the people stand hand-in-hand' was an attempt to contain the scattered clashes that broke out between demonstrators and army units as a result of these rumours.

The army had deployed, in fact, on the orders of the president. But demonstrators were unable to shake the feeling that events in Tunisia were being repeated in exactly the same form in Egypt: that Mubarak, like Ben Ali before him, might have already fled the country and the army was there simply to maintain order. Most Egyptians had a positive view of the army, generally rooted in patriotism.[165]

---

[164] Amr Guevara, personal interview.
[165] There is a big difference between this assertion and the overgeneralizations of scholars like Ali Leila, who claims that the Egyptian army has allied itself with the people in every revolution in the country (1805, 1882, 1919, 1952, 2011) and that Egyptians know that it will always stand with them. See: Leila, 'Why Did the Revolution Break Out?' 27–8. The revolution of 1919 was not the product of an alliance between the army and the people, since the army was then busy in Sudan, while that of 1952 began without popular support, only winning such support after the success of the military coup. Civilian revolutions, of course, cannot succeed when the army stands united against them: the army must either remain neutral or support the revolutionaries, or be split. On 25 January, the

Demonstrators continued to swing between fear that the army would crush the protests and the hope that it would stand with them. The announcement of a curfew was generally well received – there was an expectation that the army would put an end to police brutality. The first army vehicle to arrive in Tahrir Square was applauded by many of those present, who gave way to allow it to pass. But once the convoy had crossed the square, the police resumed their attack. Now demonstrators began to suggest that the army had tricked them and was delivering ammunition to the Interior Ministry. A solitary tank stationed outside the Egyptian Museum was attacked and set on fire, and when a second convoy of armoured cars attempted to cross the square, it met a similar fate. 'A lot of demonstrators clambered up on the tanks and cars,' says Hany Mahmoud, continuing:

> And what I saw was, it wasn't that they were celebrating the army's arrival – it was more an attempt to keep demonstrators safe from the army 'stabbing us in the back', as more than one person who sat on the top of an army vehicle put it. Some of them even tried to get on the barrels of the guns mounted on top. The soldiers inside were swearing that they weren't going to use their weapons [. . .] all so the people would get down off their guns.[166]

Some scholars have described this as a 'fraternization' strategy intended to de-fang the army, but this strategy was not prepared in advance. It developed spontaneously, through physical contact, discussions, tellings-off, even hugs.[167] The slogan proclaiming that 'the army and the people stand hand-in-hand' – scribbled in moments of excitement even on the side of military vehicles – was not so much a political pronouncement as an attempt to impose this sense of fraternity on the army.[168] And while this may have allayed some fears, the many photos of revolutionaries sleeping in tank tracks bear witness to an ongoing worry that the army might move to support the regime at any moment.

The young revolutionaries had no in-depth knowledge of the army or its relationship with the regime. By law, military affairs were kept out of all public and media discourse, and they were thus very suspicious of the army's intentions, particularly after a rumour spread that demonstrators

---

Egyptian army chose the first option, later pressuring Mubarak to step down in order to preserve the regime. But its motives would not become clear until much later.

[166] Hany Mahmoud, personal interview.
[167] Ketchley, *Egypt in a Time of Revolution*, 51.
[168] The army was later to co-opt this slogan and put it to use in its communiqués during the transitional period and its suppression of revolutionary mobilizations after the coup. There it was used to mean that the army acts in the *name of the people* even as it crushes *the people themselves*.

had found a stash of gas canisters hidden in an army jeep.[169] In the following days, these suspicions turned out to be entirely justified.

2 Official responses

The Friday of Rage protests had left the regime in a state of total confusion, and, as a result, it was almost midnight before Mubarak appeared on state TV to give an official response. In a speech that attempted to balance freedom of expression against the threat of anarchy (as witnessed in unnamed 'other countries'), he claimed to recognize the 'legitimate demands' of protesters – an end to unemployment and corruption and improved living standards – but emphasized that these would only be achieved through economic reform and a fuzzy, ill-defined process of 'national dialogue'. This was accompanied, predictably, by dire warnings of agitators and fifth columnists among the protesters whose aim was to sabotage the economy in pursuit of their own agenda (i.e. the Brotherhood, a well-established regime bogeyman). These mysterious saboteurs were to be a regular theme of speeches throughout the transitional period.

In the face of mass protest, all despotic regimes display a magnanimous desire to understand social demands, in particular those that concern the standard of living. This allows them to appear fair and balanced even as they condemn any demands that concern the nature of the regime. They assume that political demands are parasitic on social demands – which, unlike political demands, can be broken up into chunks and negotiated safely under the existing regime. They make every effort to drive a wedge between 'the masses' and the activists (the 'infiltrators'). The activists, they say, could not care less about the real concerns of the people; they are only interested in scoring political points or making 'the masses' unwitting accomplices to foreign conspiracies. They assume that 'normal' people have no truck with politics, that their sole concern is their own individual conditions rather than any general notion of justice. At the same time, they evoke the spectre of anarchy, of unpredictable change in the absence of any alternative. Fear of anarchy and unrest is a tried-and-true justification for authoritarianism.

Mubarak's decision to address the country in person seemed to suggest that the revolution was heading in the right direction. Tunisians had been able to observe the steady collapse of the regime in real time through the speeches given by Ben Ali in the lead up to his departure. The long delay

---

[169] Personal interviews with Islam Lotfy and Mohamed Salah.

that preceded the speech was also taken as an indication of confusion within the regime over how to respond.

Also on 28 January, US president Barack Obama gave a speech in which he asserted that Mubarak's speech meant in practical terms a transition to democracy. He said that he had told Mubarak that it was impossible to rule by coercion. Throughout the long sit-in in Tahrir Square, the United States maintained constant pressure on the regime, but never directly demanded that Mubarak step aside. As the revolution gained pace, the United States began to advocate a transitional government. US press statements called on 'both sides' to show restraint and told the government not to diverge from the path of reform.

In her memoirs, secretary of state at that time Hillary Clinton relays a meeting on 28 January with the national security team in the White House Situation Room, in which Obama asked for recommendations on how to handle the events in Egypt. The debate, Clinton summarizes, revolved mainly around how the United States can 'balance strategic interests against core values?' and how successfully they can influence the internal politics in Egypt, taking into consideration the 'negative unintended consequences?' Lastly, 'what does it mean to be on the right side of history?'[170] While Clinton states that she shared the feeling of support for the young Egyptian protesters along with other White House staff, she also said that her concern, which was shared by Joe Biden, Robert Gates and Tom Donilon (the National Security Adviser), was for the United States 'not to be seen as pushing a longtime partner out the door, leaving Egypt, Israel, Jordan and the region to an uncertain, dangerous future'.[171]

Clinton questioned the US influence on the events in Egypt even if they decided to do the right thing and support the people of Egypt. She writes,

> What if we called for Mubarak to step down, but then he refused and managed to stay in power? What if he did step down and was succeeded by a lengthy period of dangerous disorder or by a successor government no more democratic and actively opposed to our interests and security? Either way, our relationship would never be the same and our influence in the region would erode.[172]

Clinton stated in a press conference, on 30 January, that the administration hoped to see a 'peaceful, *orderly* transition to a democratic regime' in Egypt.[173] She stressed that she intentionally chose the word 'orderly' rather

---

[170] Hillary Rodham Clinton, *Hard Choices* (New York: Simon and Schuster, 2014), 339.
[171] Ibid., 340.
[172] Ibid.
[173] Ibid., 341.

than 'immediate' even though it was unpopular choice among some of the White House staff, especially some on the president's team who wanted to foreshadow or even call for Mubarak's departure.[174] According to Clinton, Obama's administration was split between those who sided with 'Obama's idealism' – that he should declare that he was done waiting for Mubarak to do what was right – and the senior cabinet officials, including herself, who were in support for being cautious in dealing with the situation. With all that, Obama stated that 'what is clear – and what I indicated tonight to President Mubarak – is my belief that an orderly transition must be meaningful, it must be peaceful, and it must begin now'.[175] With all that, Obama stated that 'what is clear – and what I indicated tonight to President Mubarak – is my belief that an orderly transition must be meaningful, it must be peaceful, and it must begin *now*'.[176] When asked at a press conference what Obama meant by 'now', Robert Gibbs, the press secretary, answered, 'now means yesterday'.[177]

Obama and Secretary of State Hillary Clinton saw the demonstrations as an opportunity for the Egyptian government to address domestic problems and respond to the public's demands. And although Obama wanted Mubarak to step down, this remained the official US position until 9 February, the sixteenth day of the revolution, when White House spokesman Robert Gibbs said that he was unaware of any message demanding that Mubarak step down in spite of his 'now means yesterday' comment a week earlier.

Mohamed ElBaradei consistently rejected the US stance in his interviews with American media, dismissing as nonsensical the idea of a dictator who had been in power for thirty years leading a process of reform. Speaking on behalf of the NAC, he also rejected Mubarak's speech, saying that the only way that the Egyptian regime could survive was if Mubarak stood down. This was a marked escalation on his first speech on 26 January, when he had said that Mubarak should not stand again in the next presidential elections (as well as demanding a new constitution and an end to the state of emergency).[178] In the absence of any organized revolutionary leadership, Baradei's comments took on additional importance as representative of developments on the ground.

The mass popular upheaval of the Friday of Rage also spurred most of the traditional political forces to finally come out in support of the protests

---

[174] Ibid., 341.
[175] Ibid., 342–3. See also: 'Press Briefing by Press Secretary Robert Gibbs, 2/2/2011', *The White House*, 2 February 2011, Available online: https://bit.ly/3pZ00E7 (accessed 11 November 2021).
[176] Ibid., 343.
[177] Ibid., 344.
[178] *Al Jazeera*, 25 January 2011, Available online: https://bit.ly/3mYN664 (accessed 17 October 2021).

and announce their participation in an official capacity, most significantly the Muslim Brotherhood. As previously noted, Brotherhood members, including some senior figures, had already been present on the ground in large numbers, and the organization's leadership had publicly given them the green light to take part in the Friday of Rage as individuals. But now the Guidance Bureau announced that the Brotherhood backed the protests officially. This is a very important point that requires careful consideration if we are to draw the necessary conclusions. The traditional parties had initially been very wary of the Friday of Rage, but when they saw how successful the popular mobilization had been, they rushed to take advantage of it. At first, they hoped only to extract some concessions vis-à-vis the role of political parties. When their bases (and popular opinion more broadly) began to decry anyone who turned their back on the revolution, however, their support quickly became much more full-throated.

With the success of the Friday of Rage, the Brotherhood had to make a decision. If it committed to the revolution, there would be no going back; if it failed, the Brotherhood would suffer the consequences. When the organization chose to support the revolution, it went all in.[179] The Wafd, meanwhile, were forced to participate by their youth wing. The first statement on the revolution made by any traditional party came from El-Sayyid el-Badawi, who called for a transitional government, elections and a constitutional amendment limiting the number of presidential terms to two terms of six years each (with Mubarak to remain in post until the end of his current term). At the time, this was widely viewed as an attempt to exploit the revolution to reiterate old reformist demands, and as a sign of the parties' inability to understand that the revolution was an extraordinary event, more than just an opportunity to offer 'advice' to the regime.

The leadership of the leftist Tagammu had expressed its opposition to the protests on 25 January, as we have already seen, despite large numbers of their members participating. It began to moderate its response slightly in the run-up to the Friday of Rage, when its Secretary General Sayed Abdel Aal announced that 'although the party did not receive any invitation to participate in the Friday of Rage, it will not prevent any of its members from participating, and will participate itself in memory of the martyrs of 25 January'. The same applied to the Nasserists, whose press statement did no more than condemn excessive violence against demonstrators.

These positions are best analysed as the product of a cost–benefit analysis on the part of the parties. The Wafd, for example – so ideologically divided that its leaders were almost totally disconnected from their young

---

[179] *Al-Akhbar* (Lebanon), 22 February 2011, Available online: https://bit.ly/3iqGzgO (accessed 15 November 2014).

base – had been trying desperately to find a way out for the regime, and these efforts intensified after the Friday of Rage. The traditional parties had reconciled themselves to their established role as eternal opposition. They had become part of the regime, active on its margins while never participating in government. In the aftermath of the revolution, they were never quite at home in the new atmosphere of political freedom, and in 2013, when a military coup gave them the chance, they eagerly resumed their well-worn position of handmaidens to the regime.

The events of the day had left the country reeling, and the various political forces needed time to work out what had happened. The Friday of Rage was a turning point in modern Egyptian history. The shock sustained by the political, cultural and economic elite was more violent than any since the defeat of 1967. They now began to prepare themselves for the post-Mubarak era.

The first indication that this era was around the corner was the emergence of the square's moral authority. From Friday onwards, Egyptian TV channels began to broadcast events in the street. NDP figures began to publicly criticize the party and Ahmed Ezz's secretariat. By the evening, it was clear that some at least had begun to abandon Mubarak's ship.

This stage of the revolution had several characteristic features. Firstly, young activists interacted closely with the community in Cairo's working-class districts, whose inhabitants proved themselves quite willing to clash with security forces if they opened fire on demonstrators or entered their neighbourhoods in large numbers 'without permission'. This interaction produced demonstrations that the police were simply not prepared to deal with. Here we note the dialectical relationship between the organized and the spontaneous in actual reality – the real answer to the theoretical question about the nature of the protests. While much of the activity was spontaneous – and without the spontaneous element demonstrations would never have reached the scale that they did – a good part of it involved organized groups. While for the organizers, organization seemed to be crucial, the Facebook and text message campaigns only accounted for a part of the massive response. Even in the protest locations that were intended as decoys, huge crowds gathered far beyond expectations. This is without going into the massive protests of 26 and 27 January. Secondly, the young people interacted very closely with the newer political parties (as well as the Muslim Brotherhood), as distinct from those parties that had become de facto parts of the regime; indeed, the leadership of the newer parties was often more or less indistinguishable from the leaders of the youth movements.

Drawing on an article by Eric Trager in *Foreign Affairs*, Cherif Bassiouni has claimed that the Brotherhood waited to see whether the army would object before throwing its weight behind the 2011 revolution; it was only on

28 January, once they saw that the army had no objection, that it encouraged those who attended Friday prayers to join the demonstrations.[180] There is no evidence whatsoever to support this claim. For one thing, on 28 January the army's position was still very much unclear, despite its deployment following the defeat of the CSF. For another, the Brotherhood did not announce its official support – all it did was encourage individual members to participate if they wanted to. The Brotherhood is a broad-base organization accustomed to both repression and being held responsible for any popular mobilization. As such, it was perhaps not unreasonable for it to exercise a degree of caution with regard to the demonstrations. But young Brothers participated actively from the very beginning, and on the Friday of Rage some of the organization's leaders also joined in symbolically. And despite the fact that the organization only came down conclusively on the side of the revolution after the Friday of Rage, that evening most of its leaders were arrested, including Mohamed Morsi.

With the traditional parties in crisis and the youth groups taken by surprise, Baradei was thrust into the limelight as the spokesman of the revolution, though he lacked any serious revolutionary credentials. Despite his good intentions, his limited organizational skills, hesitant relationship with the masses and apparent lack of revolutionary ambition meant that he was ultimately unable to fill this important gap. Moreover, many of the political parties, including the Brotherhood, were hostile to Baradei from the beginning because they considered him a threat to their own popularity, and he was in turn unwilling to confront them. Once a prospective opposition candidate, he now became an advocate for Mubarak's immediate resignation. As an international figure of good repute, he helped win the sympathy of the Western media – especially when he took the time to warn Western countries that they were losing their 'credibility' by continuing to support the regime.

On Saturday, the army released a statement attributed to Field Marshal Tantawi, the minister of defence, in which it appeared to demand that demonstrators hand over lawbreakers to the armed forces. It subsequently became clear that Mubarak had offered Tantawi the position of vice-president and, when he refused, had tried to dismiss him. Tantawi had then ignored Mubarak's orders and returned to the general staff building, where Mubarak – realizing that the army held all the cards – subsequently sought him out and apologized to him. This was the source of a widely disseminated clip showing the president with senior military officials.

---

[180] Cherif M. Bassiouni, 'Egypt's Unfinished Revolution', in *Civil Resistance in the Arab Spring: Triumphs and Disasters*, ed. Adam Roberts et al. (Oxford: Oxford University Press, 2016), 64; *Foreign Affairs*, September–October 2011, Available online: https://bit.ly/34iktaG (accessed 25 October 2021).

Mubarak seems to have been playing for time, having concluded (wrongly) that Sami Anan's return from the United States would improve matters and allow him to sideline the ponderous and conciliatory Tantawi. In the event, Anan, who seems to have decided that the only way to save the regime was to get rid of Mubarak, proved even less willing to take orders than Tantawi. Tantawi visited Maspero and was photographed shaking hands with officers and talking to demonstrators. He avoided being photographed with his host, Information Minister Anas El-Fiqqi, clearly striving to seem independent.[181]

It is important to note that the contacts between the US military establishment and the Egyptian army leadership may have been crucial in understanding the army's attitude. According to Obama, the security establishment in the United States 'remained uncomfortable with the prospect of an Egypt without Mubarak'. However, they had 'more impact on the final outcome in Egypt'. With a military-to-military outreach, the Pentagon and the intelligence community kept a daily contact with high-ranking Egyptian officers in both the military and intelligent services. The United States sent them a message that cracking down the protests by the military would sever the US-Egyptian relationship. This outreach had a clear warning message; as Obama puts it, 'U.S.-Egyptian cooperation, and the aid that came with it, wasn't dependent on Mubarak's staying in power, so Egypt's generals and intelligence chiefs might want to carefully consider which actions best preserved their institutional interests.'[182] Secretary of Defense Robert Gates, who belonged to the conservative camp in the administration supported Mubarak, and opposed a transitional period without him, contacted Tantawi, to urge him 'to ensure that the army would exercise restraint in dealing with the protesters and to support political reforms'. Tantawi assured Gates in this regard.[183]

VIII The Republic of Tahrir

1 29 January

On the morning of Saturday, 29 January, the country awoke still reeling from the shock of the Friday of Rage. The regime, political parties and youth movements, regional powers and international organizations – all were desperately trying to understand exactly what was going on. The second week of the revolution began with the revolutionaries ensconced in

---

[181] Menawy, *The Last Days*, 222–4.
[182] Barack Obama, *A Promised Land* (New York: Viking, Penguin Books, 2020), 650.
[183] Robert M. Gates, *Duty: Memoirs of a Secretary at War* (New York: Alfred A. Knopf, 2014), 505.

Tahrir Square. It was to end with the regime making a last-ditch attempt to draw them into 'national dialogue'.

Over the course of this week, there were many important developments. Egyptians, especially those young people on the front lines of the revolution, got to know one another in an unprecedented way. Perhaps the most famous product was the spirit of the square itself. Though it barely had time to develop, the young revolutionaries were to make constant, though unsuccessful, attempts to keep it alive and politically salient throughout the following year before it finally dissipated in the face of the putschists and the traditional parties. The army, meanwhile, was to remain on the edge of things, a silent third-party independent of both regime and revolution. The Brotherhood was to have its first taste of legitimacy in the form of a seat at the national dialogue table, while the other parties were forced to contemplate for the first time a future in which the map of legitimacy had totally changed. As for the elite surrounding Mubarak, although the decisive break did not yet come, they began to differentiate themselves from the president.

a Ahmed Ezz, the scapegoat

On the morning of 29 January, Mubarak tasked Ahmed Shafik, minister of civil aviation under Ahmed Nazif, with forming a new government. In an attempt to redirect popular anger by putting paid to any suspicions of dynastic succession, Omar Suleiman was appointed vice-president – the first ever of the Mubarak era. Suleiman had previously been tipped as a possible successor, particularly during Mubarak's visit to Germany for medical treatment in 2010. His appointment was welcomed by the United States as sufficient evidence of a genuine commitment to a transition of power, and he was rewarded with a congratulatory call from then vice-president Joe Biden. Shafik, meanwhile, was presented as the ideal of the respected military man, a new face and a successful administrator. But the actual change in personnel was far more limited than it may have appeared. Despite apparent attempts by both the army and the intelligence services to convince the president to expand its scope, Mubarak remained wary of serious change.[184]

The most notable thing about the Shafik cabinet, whose formation was officially announced on 31 January, was that it left Gamal Mubarak's men (the former ministers of trade, agriculture, housing, health and tourism) out in the cold, along with the IMF-linked finance minister Youssef Boutros Ghali. Ahmed Ezz, the NDP secretary general, was also unceremoniously

---

[184] Ibid., 253–4.

ditched from all his positions. According to Ali al-Din Hilal, a prominent NDP figure, 'In a meeting of the secretariat staff held on Thursday, 27 January, which lasted from 10.00 am to 6.00 pm, serious accusations were made about the results of the 2010 parliamentary elections. I said that the party was only reaping what it had sown during the elections – and this set off an enormous row with Secretary-General Ahmed Ezz.'[185] Helal was not alone: many other regime figures pinned responsibility for the build-up of popular resentment behind the demonstrations on Ezz's mismanagement of the vote. AbdelLatif El-menawy, for example, stated, 'The most recent parliamentary elections, which were overseen by Ahmed Ezz and Gamal Mubarak – in that order – were the trigger for the explosive events that Egypt has seen since then.'[186]

Mubarak seems to have left the management of domestic politics to his son in the years leading up to 2011, a decision which greatly exacerbated the tendency in government circles to underestimate the opposition and the general population. Gamal Mubarak himself famously responded to the founding of the shadow parliament after the 2010 elections with a contemptuous 'ah – let them have something to keep themselves entertained!'[187] In his memoirs, Sami Anan claims to have had misgivings about the barefaced ballot-stuffing in the 2010 elections, but when Omar Suleiman and Tantawi made these concerns known to Mubarak, he told them not to worry because 'Ahmed Ezz has sorted everything out.'[188] The president thus had a great deal of confidence in the group of policymakers around Gamal Mubarak and supported their actions in principle.

The revolutionary activists saw the appointment of Suleiman and Shafik as the first of many likely concessions to be put forward by a regime on the back foot, and this encouraged them to keep going. Many of the traditional parties, meanwhile, continued to use the language of reform and conciliation, but some of them were beginning to realize that this was a historic moment that demanded more than just cosmetic changes. The Wafd, for example, issued a joint declaration with the NAC in which Badawi called for the founding of a single national front that would demand a new government and a constituent assembly to draft a new constitution providing for a genuine transfer of power.[189] Abu Al-Izz Al-Hariri, meanwhile – a member of the shadow parliament for Tagammu – broke with his party's official

---

[185] Ali al-Din Hilal (former NDP media secretary), personal interview, conducted by Amal Hamada, 8 May 2012, Cairo.
[186] Menawy, *The Last Days*, 43.
[187] Ibid., 49.
[188] *al-Watan*, 28 September 2013, Available online: https://bit.ly/3m8IxEX (accessed 12 May 2014).
[189] *Shorouk*, 30 January 2011, 2.

line[190] by saying openly that a national unity government should take over the country and that Mubarak should stand down and be put on trial along with the rest of the NDP Policies Committee for their mismanagement of the country over the last thirty years.[191]

After Omar Suleiman had been sworn in, and despite the curfew, Baradei made his way to Tahrir Square and joined protesters there, telling journalists that 'a new era has begun. There is no going back for the revolution!' and emphasizing that the fundamental demand was for 'the end of the regime'.[192] These statements were particularly significant because Baradei's NAC had been one of the forces that had called for protests on 25 January. His decision to stress the 'end' of the regime was a response to Mubarak's latest manoeuvre of appointing Suleiman.

On the evening of the same day, it was reported that Omar Suleiman had narrowly escaped an assassination attempt that had claimed the life of his bodyguard. Since it was his official car that had been attacked and nobody other than the president's office knew the kind of car he drove, the rumour mill naturally went into overdrive.[193] The incident was quickly forgotten thanks to the machine-gun pace of events, but after the revolution Mubarak's foreign minister Ahmed Aboul Gheit told journalists that he had witnessed the attempt on Suleiman's life personally.[194] In a subsequent TV interview, he hinted that senior army figures unhappy with Suleiman's appointment might have been behind the incident.[195] Jihad al-Khazen, a journalist close to Suleiman, later revealed that Suleiman himself suspected Gamal Mubarak.[196] The truth of the matter remains clouded in mystery, however, since there was no serious investigation, and it is still unclear whether the assassination attempt was politically motivated or the result of the breakdown of law and order.

On the international level, France and the UK issued an evasive, joint statement in which they demanded Mubarak take whatever measures necessary to avoid using violence. Sweden's foreign minister Carl Bildt was

---

[190] Hariri subsequently resigned from the Tagammu after the revolution and was one of the founders of the Popular Socialist Alliance party (SPAP).
[191] *Asharq al-Awsat*, 5 September 2014, Available online: https://bit.ly/2Ypdspx (accessed 7 November 2021).
[192] *BBC Arabic*, 31 January 2011, Available online: https://bbc.in/2RpXeVX (accessed 15 May 2014).
[193] Suleiman was not the only one to suggest that someone close to Mubarak might have been behind the attempt on his life. *Youm7*, 15 April 2012, Available online: https://bit.ly/3kgEgNQ (accessed 9 July 2014). Note that this newspaper was and still is linked to the Egyptian security forces and has been used in the past to plant rumours.
[194] *Shorouk*, 23 February 2014, Available online: https://bit.ly/3jbge8P (accessed 17 October 2021).
[195] *Al-Arabiya*, 28 March 2014, Available online: https://bit.ly/3khnq1w (accessed 9 July 2014).
[196] Khazen initially refused to give a specific name, but later pointed the finger at Gamal Mubarak during an interview with *Al-Masry Al-Youm*, 28 July 2012, Available online: https://bit.ly/33rmQHI (accessed 15 November 2014).

clearer and more principled, making it clear that Egypt needed a political initiative that would result in democratic elections that same year. But generally speaking, international positions were marked by ignorance and lack of clarity, and tended to equate the regime and the demonstrators. Despite the 'deep concern' that the United States evinced towards the regime's response, it also warned demonstrators to avoid violence in much the same tone.[197] Western countries were clearly nonplussed by what was going on. After the neoconservative debacle in Iraq, they were very wary of any attempts to 'export' democracy to the region. At the same time, with Tunisia fresh in their minds, they were worried about the consequences of supporting the regime. Unsure who to side with, they fell back on formulaic 'concern' and fence-sitting.[198]

By rushing to make concessions that had seemed unimaginable before the revolution, the Mubarak regime played its last remaining cards. After the Friday of Rage, its willingness to meet such limited demands had very little value. Every concession met with fresh chants calling for the fall of the regime. This insistence that the regime itself had to go was the clearest expression of the fact that this was a revolution. In Tahrir and in other squares and public spaces across the country, there was an awareness of this, which manifested time and time again in the refusal to accept half measures. When a revolutionary mood seizes the popular consciousness, concessions are no longer enough. In fact, they were seen as signs of weakness.

b Funeral processions for the martyrs

The evening of 28 January was simultaneously confusing and alarming for many. Law and order seemed to have broken down: department stores were looted and cash machines robbed. While Mubarak's speech presented Egyptians with a choice between the regime or anarchy, the latter seemed to already be rearing its ugly head on Egypt's streets. Moreover, many of those who had participated in the Friday of Rage were spent, and the ongoing communications blackout made it difficult for them to maintain contact. It was a stressful evening, and nobody knew what the next day was going to look like.

---

[197] *Telegraph*, 28 January 2011, Available online: https://bit.ly/3hvBvGD (accessed 13 May 2014).
[198] Former US secretary of defence Robert Gates claims in his memoirs that the United States was surprised by the revolutions in Tunisia and Egypt. Gates says that Obama first commented on events in Tunisia on 14 January and that in his State of the Union speech on 25 January 2011 he said only that he supported democratic aspirations. See: Gates, *Duty*, 503. Gates says that most of the senior figures in the administration (himself, Biden, Clinton, Mullen) were very concerned about the prospect of Mubarak being toppled and the possible repercussions of a Brotherhood government in Egypt for peace with Israel and the stability of the region generally. Obama, meanwhile, came to favour a more positive public position on the revolutions (504–5).

The key question for those who were able to speak to one another on the morning of 29 January was how to get people back on the street given popular anxieties about the consequences of making political demands. When they learnt of the death of Mostafa El Sawy, a Brotherhood member killed in demonstrations in Agouza, they decided to regain the initiative by organizing a mass funeral procession.

The plan, put together by Mohamed Al-Qasas, was for the procession to make its way to Tahrir. There attendees would stop to pray before heading towards the graveyard where Sawy was to be buried. A confrontation was narrowly avoided outside the Dokki police station thanks to the bravery of mourners, who prevented an officer from firing his gun, and by the time it reached the square the procession was far too large for the police to control.[199] As it moved towards the graveyard, however, the police opened fire, killing eight people. The pallbearers just about managed to get the body onto Falaky Street from the direction of the AUC library, but in the meantime protests had broken out in Mohammed Mahmoud Street, Falaky and Bab al-Louq. Large numbers of policemen took up positions on the roofs of nearby buildings and began firing down into the crowds. Enraged, demonstrators turned away from their original route and set off for the Interior Ministry, where Adly soon found himself trapped. Security forces now loaded their guns with live rounds and attacked the funeral procession. Thirteen people were killed, but their funerals, too, would turn into massive demonstrations.[200] Confrontations pitting bullets against Molotov cocktails continued through to the next day, when the army intervened and drove Adly away in an armoured car.[201] The Interior Ministry was now under military control.

Could the first wave of the revolution have succeeded if the army had not remained (relatively) neutral? Many have attempted to answer this question. Hazem Kandil, for example, rejects the hypothesis that regimes never fall so long as their repressive organs are willing and able to quash rebellions, arguing that the behaviour of the Egyptian army shows this hypothesis to be untrue.[202] He is wrong here, insofar as the Egyptian army was not *willing* to put down the revolution. (Kandil in fact accurately describes the army as an independent entity, not simply the iron fist of the regime.) No peaceful revolution can succeed if the army as a whole falls in behind the regime and is willing to use violence. The Syrian and Libyan revolutions, both of which devolved into civil wars, demonstrate

---

[199] Hany Mahmoud, personal interview.
[200] Personal interviews with Moaz Abdelkarim, Khaled Abdel Hamid and Islam Lotfy.
[201] Personal interviews with Waleed Abd Elraouf and Mohamed Salah.
[202] Hazem Kandil, *Soldiers, Spies, and Statesmen*, 2.

this point. In the face of such a development, the only options available to revolutionaries are to go home or turn to armed action.[203] An unarmed people cannot defeat an army willing to bring its full military might to bear.

The revolutionaries had realized by now that it was crucial to maintain a presence in Tahrir Square, that space in the heart of Cairo. Three young Brotherhood members went to buy speakers, and various revolutionaries came together to build the first 'stage' in the square, responsibility for which was given to YJF.[204]

Saturday also saw the first tensions between the revolutionaries and the leaders of new political parties, some of whom, including Ayman Nour (Ghad Party) and Hamdeen Sabahi (Karama Party), attempted to give speeches.[205] Activists had begun to realize that they were overseeing a revolution, and they were wary of its appropriation by partisan political forces – a wariness that would later transform into a sort of obsession during the transitional period, with adverse, if not disastrous, consequences.[206]

With security forces still entirely absent (with the exception of the contingent protecting the Interior Ministry), law and order seemed to have broken down, particularly after hundreds of prisoners managed to make their escape from various prisons around the country. At the time, many believed that the disorder was deliberate and intended to encourage demonstrators to stay at home and protect their property from the predations of thugs and other criminal elements.[207] The response was to set up popular committees. Mostafa Shawky says:

> We held a quick meeting in Tahrir, and it was agreed that we would form popular committees to protect [people's] houses. It turned out that before we'd even thought about it, the different regions of Greater Cairo had already set up their own committees spontaneously. We received dozens of calls from our home neighbourhoods telling us our houses were safe and that we should carry on doing what we were doing.[208]

---

[203] Even when revolutionaries organize themselves into armed militias, they will struggle to defeat an army unless they are united, organized and capable of putting in place an alternative strategy.
[204] Islam Lotfy, personal interview.
[205] Personal interviews with Mohamed Salah and Khaled Abdel Hamid.
[206] Young activists failed – or did not have enough time – to organize themselves into a clear political alternative, while remaining mistrustful of the existing political parties. This ultimately allowed the traditional parties to regain their strength. During the transitional period, every party was able to wheel out its own 'revolutionary youth'. The same was true of both private and public media. All this, as well as their lack of political maturity, resulted in the steady deterioration of young activists' public image, making it easier to attack them. And while some did emerge as individual figures with political ambitions, the military coup cut them down to size.
[207] Personal interviews with Islam Lotfy, Mohammad Abbas, Mostafa Shawky, Mohamed Salah and Mahmoud Sami.
[208] Mostafa Shawky, personal interview.

There was broad awareness of the absence of the police, and also a sense of the sometimes-aggravating role they had played in the crisis:

> Based on my own personal experience of putting together and taking part in popular committee patrols in Al-Mokattam, the main thing was the sense of hostility to the police. The immediate feeling when we saw a car that was going too fast or a car whose passengers were firing guns out of the window, whether to scare people or as a joke, was that they were behaving like the police.[209]

The popular committees played a very important role in this stage of the revolution, and they deserve to be studied in much greater detail from many different angles: their social implications, the effect of the rapidity with which they arose, people's readiness to engage with them to protect their neighbourhoods and undermine the plan to create anarchy and the different stages of their development, as well as the state's exploitation of this form of popular mobilization in later stages (in some cases, the state designated local gangsters 'popular committees' and used them as police reinforcements).

Rumours of total anarchy, meanwhile, had spread to residential areas and villages across the country, and demonstrators began to receive calls and messages from their families reporting gunfire and looting, in many cases based on nothing but rumour. The regime assumed that demonstrators hearing this news would leave the square to protect their homes. But in fact the sense of anarchy spreading across Egypt was not an individual but a collective problem, and the people of every area found their own solutions to it. In 6th October City, for example, where released prisoners from Fayoum reportedly went on a rampage, locals formed popular defence committees which continued to operate effectively through to 8 February, when people began to get used to a life without police. This case may be one in which some escaped prisoners did commit crimes, but overall there was very little documented 'rampaging' by escaped prisoners, despite the media frenzy and insane rumours. On the contrary, many prisoners were shot down in prisons across the country or left to fend for themselves when prison guards deserted their posts.[210] When they did escape, they were often molested and beaten by people who had been driven into paranoid hysteria about hardened criminals looting the country.

---

[209] Mohamed Naim, personal testimony.
[210] Human rights organizations subsequently documented some of the state violence against prisoners during the revolution and urged the authorities to launch official investigations. See, for example, *Egyptian Initiative for Personal Rights*, 7 March 2011, Available online: https://bit.ly/3CcfVCj (accessed 25 October 2021); *Egyptian Initiative for Personal Rights*, 24 August 2011, Available online: https://bit.ly/3vFqBHf (accessed 1 October 2021).

With the first stage set up in the square[211] and demonstrators determined to stay in place until Mubarak was ousted, the 'Republic of Tahrir' was born, a republic whose basic features were to take shape over the following days. The Republic of Tahrir was to become the only body with the legitimacy to respond to the regime's political proposals.

On the evening of the same day, the armed forces issued a statement, copies of which were distributed near to the Interior Ministry, announcing:

> For the good of the country, we are here with you to realize your ambitions. Let us stand together to preserve the safety of the nation and prevent the actions of saboteurs. The armed forces are here to keep you safe and to make sure some of your demands are met. We are here to protect your property and prevent rioting, vandalism and violence. It is your right to express your opinions and demands in a civilized fashion.

The statement also warned that demonstrators risked being held responsible for destruction of property, alluding to infiltrators who sought to 'destroy our history, our civilization, our culture and our economy and prevent them from functioning properly'. In another press statement, the army reiterated that it had put in place a curfew from 4.00 pm to 7.00 am.[212]

As yet, it was still unclear exactly what the position of the military establishment really was. The army had said quite clearly that it was there to make sure *some* of the demonstrators' demands were met, but at the same time it was alluding to 'infiltrators' among the revolutionaries. This lack of clarity was to remain a consistent feature of the army's statements for a long time yet.

2 30 January: The sit-in continues

The revolutionaries stayed in the square overnight, donating whatever money they had with them to buy bedding, blankets and food. Some of them slept without covers. With security forces still largely out of the picture, a steady flow of people continued to make their way onto the square, where they quickly became demonstrators. On the Mohammed Mahmoud side, clashes continued all the way up to Bab al-Louq Square and beyond, where the buildings around the Interior Ministry were bristling with snipers.[213]

The day of 30 January witnessed a mass breakout by political prisoners from Wadi Natroun Prison, including the Brotherhood members

---

[211] The materials for which were all purchased by the businessman Mamdouh Hamza.
[212] *Shorouk*, 30 January 2011, 4.
[213] Personal interviews with Islam Lotfy, Mohammad Abbas, Mostafa Shawky, Mohamed Salah and Mahmoud Sami.

detained three days earlier.²¹⁴ The breakout, while quite understandable in the prevailing atmosphere, was nonetheless to be cited as evidence against President Morsi. The fact that escaping from a Mubarak-era prison during the revolution was couched as a crime after his overthrow in 2013 is one of the most decisive pieces of evidence that the coup against Morsi was counter-revolutionary in nature. The testimony of prison guards shows beyond a shadow of doubt that the detainees were only able to escape because some local Bedouins whose relatives were also inside stormed the prison to set them free. Many prisons, in fact, witnessed similar scenes during the revolution, albeit generally involving non-political prisoners. But the fact that there were two Hamas members among the escapees allowed coup plotters to accuse Morsi of collusion with the Palestinian group.

Morsi himself, speaking to Al Jazeera via satellite telephone, denied that he or anyone else had escaped from the prison, claiming that the doors had been left open; he then gave his location and invited the police to come and rearrest him if necessary.²¹⁵ The prison warden was later to claim that armed men had assaulted the prison before heading straight for wings two and seven, which were used to hold members of local jihadi groups and common criminals.²¹⁶

In any case, the escaped Brotherhood leaders now had an opportunity to clarify their position on the events of the last few days. Naturally enough, they adopted a fairly open attitude: one member of the Guidance Bureau, Mohamed Saad Elkatatny, stated that the Brotherhood trusted Baradei to speak on behalf of the revolutionaries.²¹⁷ This was a transparent attempt to avoid taking centre stage and take cover behind Baradei's international respectability. It was not to last long after the revolution, when the Brotherhood not only rejected the idea of a Baradei presidency but even the prospect of his appointment as prime minister.

Discussions about partisan representation began very early on in the revolution. But it is clear that neither the Brotherhood nor their younger members were inclined – never mind able – to monopolize leadership of the revolution. In fact, many senior Brotherhood figures remained sceptical about the wisdom of throwing the organization's weight behind the uprising. The Brotherhood youth, meanwhile, were deeply involved in all sorts of alliances and partnerships on the ground.

---

[214] *Sama News*, 1 February 2011, Available online: https://bit.ly/3Gv0WpB (accessed 25 October 2021).
[215] The interview with Morsi can be viewed on *YouTube*, 2 February 2014, Available online: https://bit.ly/3bZMyqz (accessed 25 October 2021).
[216] *Shorouk*, 9 June 2013, Available online: https://bit.ly/2E5uLlm (accessed 6 July 2014).
[217] *Deutsche Welle Arabic*, 30 January 2011, Available online: https://bit.ly/3jBuYhz (accessed 25 October 2021).

a) The problematic Brotherhood declaration

The Brotherhood released a declaration congratulating the Egyptian people on their uprising and making a series of demands: a coalition government excluding the NDP, an end to the state of emergency and dissolution of the parliament. There was no mention of ousting Mubarak or the regime itself, suggesting that many senior Brothers saw this simply as an opportunity to eke out concessions. This approach was only to be expected from a popular broad-based movement that had learnt its caution the hard way. The Brotherhood was not a revolutionary movement – indeed, its characteristic approach was based on the gradualist reform of society.

The declaration was issued even as those in the square were shouting 'the people want the butcher to be executed' in response to the massacre on Mohammed Mahmoud Street (the chant spurred the army into removing Adly from the Interior Ministry building for his own protection). It was distributed on the square despite prior agreement by all political forces to avoid partisan slogans and material. Moreover, its content was less an expression of the demands being made by protesters across Egypt than of the traditional party lines.

The declaration caused a great deal of resentment on the square, where young people were alarmed by the prospect of a schism among protesters. A group of younger Brothers called a meeting and agreed that they would stop members from handing out the leaflets, and they began destroying those leaflets that had not yet been handed out. Hany Mahmoud and Ahmed Nezeily, meanwhile, went to speak to Mahmoud Ezzat,[218] a member of the Guidance Bureau and deputy supreme guide, to explain how damaging the declaration had been and ask the bureau to think of some way of reassuring non-Brotherhood forces of their good faith. They warned Ezzat that the declaration had made many people anxious that the Brotherhood was hoping for a deal with the regime, whereupon it would simply withdraw all its forces from the field. Although Ezzat attempted to defend the declaration, he eventually gave way, suggesting that the Brotherhood would release a press statement affirming that it was fully committed to whatever demands were made by the revolutionaries.[219]

---

[218] Ezzat was arrested on 27 August 2020 during the preparation of the English edition of this book, having gone into hiding in Egypt after the coup.

[219] The first declaration is available in full at: *Ikhwan Wiki*, 30 January 2011, Available online: https://bit.ly/3iyMQqP (accessed 25 October 2021); the second is available at: *Ikhwan Wiki*, 31 January 2011, Available online: https://bit.ly/2Rn0UrA (accessed 25 October 2021).

b) Free Egyptian Youth

On the evening of 30 January, representatives of youth movements met at the headquarters of Socialist Renewal, affirming their demands for the total overthrow of the regime and the call for a 'million-man march' for Tuesday, 1 February. The addition of certain new prominent faces gave this meeting particular importance. Khaled El-Sayed (YJF) proposed the *milyoniyya*, the call for which was made in a proclamation signed by 'Free Egyptian Youth' sent to the media.[220] This declaration was the first document to give official expression to the entity of the Tahrir revolutionaries. The time spent by the representatives of the youth movements in the square gave them greater confidence in one another and improved their relationships. This was also the first time that the term *milyoniyya* had been used in the call for demonstration. The term itself indicated something unique about the exaggerated descriptions of demonstrations during both the revolution and the counter-revolution. The negative side of this began to become clear when people started to look down on any demonstration that failed to muster less than hundreds of thousands of people, regardless of how just its demands were.

The revolutionaries' growing esprit de corps was strengthened by a sense that the road might be a long one. Just before this meeting, propaganda footage had been broadcast of Mubarak visiting the armed forces command centre – accompanied by Suleiman, Tantawi and Anan – and listening attentively to an officer explain what appeared to be operational plans set out against a map of Egypt. It was not exactly difficult to see that the president was trying to demonstrate that the army was an inseparable part of the regime and that the regime was thus in full control of the country.[221] The next day, however, the head of the army's Morale Department was to state on TV that the army 'had not and would not' use violence against demonstrators with legitimate demands. The repeated broadcasts of this message on the eve of the first *milyoniyya* doubtless encouraged greater participation in that demonstration.

The Brotherhood, meanwhile, began to take a more strident tone. Mohammed Ali Beshr, a member of the Guidance Bureau, gave a statement to the effect that not only should prominent regime figures stand down and leave politics; they should also be put on trial and held to account for their actions while in power, while also reiterating that the organization had no

---

[220] Personal interviews with Khaled Abdel Hamid, Mostafa Shawky and Mohammad Abbas.
[221] *Al Jazeera*, 11 February 2011, Available online: https://bit.ly/3iBTMn1 (accessed 6 July 2014). It later became clear that the army was quite capable of stringing the different sides along even as it was making plans to undermine them. Consider, for example, the footage of General Sisi applauding Morsi's speech on 30 June 2013 only three days before he overthrew him.

interest in taking over the demonstrations and wanted only to participate. This marked a decisive break with the regime. The following day, the Guidance Bureau accepted Ossama Yassin[222] as their point of contact with activists, finally granting those in the square what amounted to total independence from the leadership.[223]

At a meeting at its downtown headquarters, the shadow, people's parliament pinned full blame for the chaos on the regime and set up a National Crisis Management Committee representing most of the opposition parties.[224] It also called for the formation of a presidential council, to be made up of two judges and a military man, to assume charge of the country. The opposition's enthusiasm for a traditional government made up of judges and army officers[225] as well as the hostility of the traditional parties towards both the Brotherhood and non-partisan figures such as Baradei – according to *Shorouk*, Brotherhood General Guide Mohammed Badie walked out, while others objected strongly to Baradei's name being included in the list of signatories – were early indications of dynamics which were to prove deleterious during the transitional period.[226]

The Muslim Brotherhood is often blamed for the failure of the transitional period, but it was not only their behaviour and mistakes that paved the way for the regime's triumphant return on 3 July 2013. All the opposition parties had their own prejudices, ambitions and self-interested reasons for riding the revolutionary wave – in particular, their fear of being outmanoeuvred by their opponents. Another indication of this also appeared around this time: the phenomenon of the token 'youth activist', through which parties attempted to co-opt the young revolutionaries for their own ends. Some of the more political revolutionaries were to make an early effort to resist these attempts on 31 January, when Ahmed Maher, coordinator of the 6 April Movement, announced that his organization and the NAC were willing to discuss the formation of a national unity government with the president and the army in order to facilitate the transfer of power to demonstrators.[227]

---

[222] Yassin was a Brotherhood leader and secretary general of the Freedom and Justice Party (FJP) who subsequently became president of the youth committee of the dissolved 2012 People's Assembly and later minister of youth in the Qandil government.
[223] Islam Lotfy, personal interview.
[224] The members of this committee were Mahmoud Khudairi (Judges' Club), Abdel Galil Mustafa (Kefaya), Ayman Nour (Ghad), Hamdeen Sabahi (Karama), Osama El-Ghazali Harb (DFP), Abdel Halim Qandil (journalist), Abu Al-Izz Al-Hariri (Tagammu), George Ishaq (Kefaya) and Magdy Hussein (Kefaya), as well as an anonymous judge and a representative of the young activists on Tahrir.
[225] They did ultimately get a government of this kind, albeit after the counter-revolution.
[226] *Shorouk*, 31 January 2011, 12.
[227] *Revolutionary Socialists*, 6 February 2011, Available online: https://bit.ly/2XiiLX4 (accessed 17 October 2021). See also: *Asharq Al-Awsat*, 11 February 2011, Available online: https://bit.ly/2Rn18yW (accessed 16 March 2016).

In any case, various prominent figures were busy coming up with possible compromises to resolve the crisis. Omar Suleiman made a number of proposals: the prospect of a Gamal Mubarak presidency would be taken off the table for good, businessmen would be excluded from government, the constitution would be amended, those guilty of 'misconduct' would be held to account and Mubarak would step down from the NDP presidency. Parliamentary Speaker Fathy Sorour announced that he would respect any ruling ordering the dissolution of the People's Assembly so long as the Court of Cassation, Egypt's highest judicial body, accepted its legality. Pope Shenouda III, meanwhile, told Mubarak in a telephone call that he approved of his decision to appoint Suleiman vice-president,[228] showing the church's continuing preference for gradual reform over regime change and the social and political upheaval it might bring.

Shenouda's was not the only telephone call that Mubarak received that day. President Obama also spoke to his Egyptian counterpart, urging him to hand over power and not to fire on demonstrators. At the same time, Secretary of State Clinton told Fox News that the US administration supported an organized transition to democracy in Egypt, adding that there was no Brotherhood conspiracy and that large parts of Egyptian society were participating in the protests. Mubarak was not pleased, and TV channels were ordered by the Ministry of Information to drop Obama's call down to the end of the list, after the messages of solidarity he had received from Libya's Colonel Gaddafi, King Abdullah of Saudi Arabia and King Hamad of Bahrain.[229]

3 31 January: The creation of the Republic of Tahrir

With the army in control of the Interior Ministry, the confrontations around Mohammed Mahmoud Street petered out. The army may have surrounded the square and put up barbed wire, but it was the revolutionaries themselves who now began to secure the borders of their little republic, well aware of the risk of neighbourhood thugs infiltrating the demonstrations and causing problems.[230] They organized committees to defend the entrances to the square, with the already-well-organized Brotherhood playing a major part. Some committee members checked the ID cards of those entering, while others searched them for weapons.[231] In response to the regime's attempts to market Omar Suleiman as an alternative to Mubarak, new and

---

[228] *Shorouk*, 31 January 2011, 2.
[229] Menawy, *The Last Days*, 195.
[230] Personal interviews with Islam Lotfy, Mohammad Abbas, Mostafa Shawky, Mohamed Salah and Mahmoud Sami.
[231] Personal interviews with Islam Lotfy and Mohamed Salah.

inventive slogans and chants emerged, many of which were subsequently to become iconic. Revolutionaries began to explore drama and music. Two new stages went up in the square and the Bedaya movement put up a huge screen to broadcast news from Al Jazeera.

The media blackout imposed on the square intensified on 31 January. Police raided Al Jazeera's Cairo bureau and confiscated all of its equipment, while the local channels focused all their attention on the Nile Corniche, broadcasting scenes of sunny normality and calm streets. The revolutionaries were very aware that this would make it easy to disperse the protest without the Egyptian public even realizing. Setting up some kind of direct broadcast from Tahrir itself thus became a major priority (another outlet for the new atmosphere of creativity and joint effort between those with no previous connections). A call went out for engineers and technicians with relevant expertise, and after a meeting held outside the Tahrir Square KFC, they split up into two groups to work out whether it would be possible to set up a closed network broadcasting to the surrounding areas.

At around the same time, Hany Mahmoud received a phone call from an unknown number, which turned out to be Ahmed El Tafahny of Al Jazeera Mubasher. Tafahny explained that during the raid on Al Jazeera's premises he had managed to conceal a camera and some broadcasting equipment, which he was willing to place at the revolutionaries' disposal. Mahmoud and a group of young activists went to pick up the equipment before asking Ahmed Zein, to phone up other friends of his at Al Jazeera and get them to bring down any other necessary equipment and start broadcasting from the square, where they were promised protection. In the meantime, they set about finding a suitable spot to film from, settling on a huge billboard in front of the Omar Makram Mosque. All that remained was for Tafahny to set up the camera and the first live broadcast from Tahrir Square could begin – just in time for another Al Jazeera technician to arrive with extra equipment. The camera would be moved several times over the next few days, with more than one attempt made to arrest the team.

This day also saw a new series of demands drawn up by the youth movement: Mubarak out, a new government, fresh legislative elections, a new public prosecutor, no more state of emergency, a restructured Interior Ministry and trials for the leading regime figures.[232] These seven demands were written out on an enormous placard hung on a building overlooking the square, which stayed in place until Mubarak's resignation many days later and soon became iconic and a mainstay of international TV coverage.

[232] Personal interviews with Islam Lotfy, Mohammad Abbas, Mostafa Shawky, Mohamed Salah and Mahmoud Sami.

Despite the curfew, a steady flow of new demonstrators continued to make its way onto the square.

The army released a statement affirming that it would not use violence against Egyptians, stating that it was aware of the legitimate demands raised by 'upstanding citizens' and that it would act as the guarantor of their freedom of expression and protect any peaceful protest as provided for by the constitution, while issuing a warning to any lawbreakers who sought to 'intimidate citizens and undermine their security'.[233] That these statements used very different language from that of the regime, and addressed citizens directly, signalled a change that would not be easily reversed. The army was demonstrating that it was an independent actor within the regime and sought to differentiate itself from the president – it might even be said to have carried out a soft coup against him. Soon enough, prominent regime personalities like Amr Moussa, secretary general of the Arab League, were advocating a handover. They could see which way the wind was blowing.

At 10.00 pm, Omar Suleiman made his first public appearance as vice-president, informing the nation that Mubarak had tasked him with opening a dialogue with all 'political forces' to discuss fundamental issues of political and democratic reform. No timeline was given. He also said that Mubarak had impressed on him the importance of respecting the Court of Cassation's judgements in the electoral fraud cases of a year earlier and promised that the new government's priority would be to fight corruption and unemployment.[234]

The most notable elite development of the day, however, was the establishment of four new parties and a cross-party alliance, the Popular Coalition for Change, bringing together the Wafd, Tagammu, Nasserists, Ghad Party and various public figures like lawyer and intellectual Ahmed Kamal Abul-Magd and the Nobel Prize-winning scientist Ahmed Zewail. Wafd chair El-Sayyid el-Badawi described the PCC as an attempt to fill the 'political vacuum' that had arisen in the wake of the protest movement, saying that 'after the demonstrations and protests deprived his regime of legitimacy, President Mubarak must respond to popular demands and step down from his position as president'.[235] This marked the first attempt by the opposition parties to organize within the framework of the revolution, a point we will return to when we discuss its first steps on 2 February.

Meanwhile, the White House said that it was reassured by the self-control shown by the army towards the demonstrators. It revealed that there had been constant calls between the two governments over the

---

[233] *Reuters*, 31 January 2011, Available online: https://reut.rs/2ZwBfUp (accessed 25 October 2021).
[234] *Shorouk*, 1 February 2011, 1.
[235] *Shorouk*, 1 February 2011, 3.

course of the week, but refused to say what it thought should happen to Mubarak, stating that this was a choice for the Egyptian people and not the US government.[236] US officials also alluded to 'talks' between Robert Gates and Chairman of the Joint Chiefs Mike Mullen and their Egyptian counterparts Tantawi and Anan.[237] Frank Wisner, former US ambassador to Cairo and a personal friend of Mubarak's, was sent to talk to Mubarak directly. Wisner subsequently told the administration that it was vital that Mubarak remain in post; years later, it was revealed that he was already on the Egyptian government's payroll as a lobbyist.

Ahmed Ezz also seems to have sent out orders to provincial NDP officials telling them to arrange pro-Mubarak demonstrations as quickly as possible. Over the next few days, Mostafa Mahmoud Square saw repeated gatherings by pro-regime demonstrators, including the infamous march that made its way to Tahrir Square during the 'Battle of the Camel'.

4 1 February

Although 1 February was a Tuesday – right in the middle of Egypt's working week – the revolutionaries managed to muster crowds characteristic of a Friday. Vast numbers of demonstrators responded to the call for fresh protests broadcast in international Arab media. The national channels, for their part, pulled out all of the stops to prevent any major gathering. Footage of empty streets was accompanied by a parade of prominent figures, wheeled out to bewail the 'chaos' on Egypt's streets and its deleterious effects on the economy or to accuse the revolutionaries of being 'agents' of foreign powers or Islamist agitators. Al Jazeera played a central role in refuting this propaganda, assisted by some of the braver independent Egyptian channels, such as ONTV.

An unprecedented number of spontaneous marches set off from every part of Cairo. This time, despite the regime closing down much of the national railway network, there was also significant representation from the governorates – Egyptians knew that the contest would be decided in the capital.[238] The sheer scale of the demonstrations far outstripped all expectations, including those of the organizers. Military planes made many low-altitude sweeps of the square, reminding protesters of the attempts made to intimidate participants in the 1986 CSF mutiny. This

---

[236] 'Remarks by the President on the Situation in Egypt', *The White House*, 1 February 2011, Available online: https://bit.ly/3EF6Bb5 (accessed 25 October 2021).
[237] *Shorouk*, 1 February 2011, 14.
[238] *Shorouk*, 2 February 2011, 8.

time, however, the response was simply the derisory chant, which went up again and again every time a helicopter went over: 'Hosni's gone mad!'

a) The army and the people

The new confidence and sense of power produced a sort of carnival atmosphere in the square. As some participants worked to set revolutionary chants to music, street peddlers began to appear among the demonstrators, signalling the total normalization of the demonstrations. Many Egyptians generally not at all interested in protest made their way out onto the streets to observe or to take part. This phenomenon also sent a message to the international community: even those who joined in simply to have some fun unintentionally deepened the impression that the revolution was civil and peaceful and undermined the regime's attempts to misrepresent it.

Sami Anan met secretly with the deputy ministers of defence and members of the SCAF – Tantawi was not present, to avoid giving the wrong impression, but was fully aware of the meeting – to draft a statement in which the armed forces declared that they 'sided with the people'. When the statement was read out in the square, it was applauded. Mubarak then summoned Tantawi and Anan and asked them outright, 'So, you've decided which way you're going, Hussein? [. . .] I remind you that it is your duty to protect the legitimate government.'[239] It is worth noting that Anan claims in his autobiography that he had already proposed the idea of a soft coup and a SCAF transitional presidency to Tantawi upon his return from the United States on 28 January, but that Tantawi had asked him not to raise the subject again.[240]

b) The emotional speech

Mubarak now decided to give a public speech, scheduled for 9.00 pm but ultimately broadcast at midnight. He spoke emotionally about his long history of fighting for Egypt and his desire to die on Egyptian soil, promising that he would not run for president again and asking the parliament to amend the articles of the constitution regulating presidential terms. He swore that he would spend the rest of his term making sure that the government provided for a peaceful transfer of power, calling for a full investigation into the breakdown in law and order and the prosecution of those responsible. He offered the people, once more, a choice between

---

[239] Published as a series in *al-Watan* newspaper. See: *al-Watan*, 28 September 2013, Available online: https://bit.ly/3EaITD6 (accessed 12 May 2014).
[240] Ibid.

stability and chaos, pointing to his efforts to open a dialogue with the opposition, which had been stymied by 'certain political forces'.[241]

Despite the concessions that it contained, this speech proved to be a very effective weapon. Contemporary observers all agreed that it struck a particularly sensitive chord, buttressed by a subsequent wave of emotional appeals from pro-regime media figures asking demonstrators to give the misunderstood president a second chance. Many of the demonstrators cursed the president for manipulating people's emotions; those who were watching the speech in cafés near to the square rushed back to redouble their protest. But others responded quite differently. For the first time, the protesters found themselves divided. A significant number began to argue that there could be no harm in letting Mubarak serve out the last six months of his term. The revolutionary movements, meanwhile, maintained that evacuating the square would give the regime a chance to regroup before initiating reprisals against all of them, with no guarantee that they would be able to revive the popular anger that had made the revolution possible.[242]

At more or less every entrance to Tahrir, people from the surrounding neighbourhood gathered to discuss the usefulness of staying in the square with demonstrators. Again and again, as if they had been told what to say in advance, they pleaded with the revolutionaries: 'Let's just let him finish his term – he's like a father to us!' In fact, it seemed very much like the regime was cooking up a plan for a counter-spectacle, a demonstration that would parallel the revolutionary scenes in Tahrir. The demonstrators asked soldiers to prevent regime supporters from entering, but were told that the army could not prevent them from exercising their right to free expression 'just like you'.[243] At the same time, Mubarak's supporters began to organize demonstrations in Mostafa Mahmoud Square, announcing a march on Tahrir Square for the following day.[244] Mubarak's speech gave the NDP its first opportunity to muster counter-protests. Well aware of the great efforts being made by NDP grandees to drum up hoodlum support for Mubarak's cause, the revolutionaries began to take far more stringent precautions.[245]

While demonstrators on the street were dealing with divisions of an entirely spontaneous kind, the opposition elites were repositioning, trying to strike a balance between those popular demands they considered realistic and those regime concessions they thought were serious. At this

---

[241] *Shorouk*, 2 February 2011, 1. A video of the speech is available on *YouTube*, 31 August 2013, Available online: https://bit.ly/3vFpzuG (accessed 25 October 2021).
[242] Personal interviews with Islam Lotfy, Mohammad Abbas, Mostafa Shawky, Mohamed Salah and Mahmoud Sami.
[243] Hany Mahmoud, personal interview.
[244] Personal interviews with Khaled Abdel Hamid, Mohamed Salah and Islam Lotfy.
[245] Khaled Abdel Hamid, personal interview.

point, sitting down to negotiate with the regime still seemed a worthwhile possibility. Even Baradei – who in an interview with Al-Arabiya dismissed the speech as a 'trick' and maintained that the only guarantee of a stable Egypt was for Mubarak and his regime to go – was willing to consider talks with Omar Suleiman, and missed no opportunity to mention his conversations with the army. His proposed solutions remained limited to either a presidential council made up of two civilians and a military man or an Omar Suleiman caretaker presidency that would stay in place until the new constitution had been ratified and elections could be held.[246]

For the most part, the various joint statements issued by the opposition parties did take a fairly radical tone; the popular parliament, for example, rejected the speech out of hand and made any dialogue conditional on Mubarak's exit.[247] In the rough-and-tumble of the drafting process, with each party trying to outdo the others in the knowledge that the statement would not be attributed to any one of them in particular, they were willing to be very bold. But in their individual statements, they were far more cautious, particularly those parties that had had decades to settle into their role as a perennial opposition. Hamdeen Sabahi's central objection to Mubarak's speech was that it did not guarantee that Article 88 of the constitution would be amended to allow for full judicial oversight of elections,[248] while the Wafd demanded respect for the head of state and his history, arguing only that his reforms had not gone far enough. One traditional opposition group stood out: in a statement signed by General Guide Mohammed Badie, the Muslim Brotherhood rejected any prospect of negotiations with 'a regime that has lost all legitimacy: its president, its parliament, its party and its government', demanding that a provisional government should be put in place pending a new constitution and fresh elections.[249] This revolutionary attitude was not to last long once the Brotherhood were offered a seat at the table, as we will see.

In any case, the regime took full advantage of the mixed feelings of the public and immediately set about trying to contain the revolution. Newly appointed prime minister Ahmed Shafik made the rounds of the local media, telling Egyptian state TV that the government was willing to meet the demands of the vast majority of people and that he was willing to go personally and talk to the demonstrators in Tahrir Square. He also condemned the attacks on Mubarak himself, dismissing demands for

---

[246] *Shorouk*, 2 February 2011, 2.
[247] *Youm7*, 2 February 2011, Available online: https://bit.ly/2FErPMF (accessed 7 July 2014).
[248] *Shorouk*, 2 February 2011, 1.
[249] *Shorouk*, 2 February 2011, 2.

him to step down or forgo another term as 'unconstitutional'.[250] Even as Mubarak himself was promising that he had no intention whatsoever to stand for president again, the regime was preparing for a possible future U-turn.

That evening, the media reported that Obama had once again called Mubarak to tell him that the process of handing over power had to begin now, without explicitly saying that this meant Mubarak had to step aside. This call coincided with the arrival of the US envoy on Egyptian soil, where he was to conduct meetings with a series of senior leadership figures.[251]

From around midnight, many demonstrators who did not belong to the hard core of the protest movement began to trickle away, some because of exhaustion, some alarmed by the growing numbers of regime supporters circling the square and some influenced by Mubarak's speech. Regime intellectuals lined up to accuse 'the Brotherhood' of trying to force demonstrators to stay and showing a complete 'disregard for the country's stability'.[252] The revolutionaries seemed to have lost the initiative. In fact, the whole revolution seemed to be in peril. If the demonstrators all went home, then what guarantee did they have that even Mubarak's limited concessions would actually be enacted? But the next day, the regime's soft efforts to gently contain the revolution would come to an abrupt and unexpected end, pushed aside by a not at all gentle attempt to completely crush it, taking advantage of the revolutionaries' reduced numbers.

IX The Battle of the Camel (2–3 February)

The day of 2 February was a turning point for the revolution in almost every sense imaginable. Domestically, it snuffed out any willingness that the general population had to take the regime's promises of reform at face value. Internationally – as the surreal and primitive scenes of men on horse- and camelback charging demonstrators in Tahrir appeared on TV screens around the world – it gave the distinct impression that the regime had unintentionally signed its own death warrant.

There were fewer demonstrators in Tahrir on 2 February than there had been the day before, and the regime seems to have regained some of its self-confidence as a result. With pro-Mubarak demonstrations planned for several locations across Cairo, internet and mobile service was restored.

---

[250] *RT Arabic*, 3 February 2011, Available online: https://bit.ly/3jLbyXs (accessed 25 October 2021); *Al Bawaba*, 3 February 2011, Available online: https://bit.ly/3mkpNo6 (accessed 25 October 2021).
[251] *Shorouk*, 2 February 2011, 2.
[252] Sami Anan repeats this accusation in his memoirs, published in *al-Watan*.

The idea of a pro-Mubarak march ending in Tahrir itself had already been proposed the day before. Groups of regime supporters had gathered in the area around the square, and some of them joined the sit-inners with the aim of making trouble. This sort of agent provocateur or false flag operation was a well-worn tactic seen many times before during elections, when NDP grandees would pay local thugs to cause disturbances and provide pretexts for shutting down particular polling stations.

AbdelLatif El-menawy believes that it was Gamal Mubarak and his associates who directed the pro-regime demonstrators towards Tahrir with the explicit aim of causing a riot. The minister of information, a Gamal Mubarak associate, told Menawy to announce that it was now 'safe' to enter the square, and around 3.00 pm, thousands of pro-Mubarak demonstrators flooded into the area. Among these demonstrators, many of them riding camels or horses, was a group from Nazlet al-Semman, an area of Giza close to the Al-Haram whose inhabitants mostly worked as tour guides.[253] It was thanks to them that the day would become known as the 'Battle of the Camel', an allusion to a seventh-century battle fought between the early Muslims. Menawy, a senior TV executive, recalls that a senior security officer called him to request that a team be sent down to film a major demonstration 'that had been organized by businessmen'.[254]

It is unclear exactly how many anti-regime demonstrators were out in the square at this point. Menawy claims that there were no more than 10,000, three-quarters of them 'Islamist extremists' and 'Brotherhood members' who had prevented others affected by the speech from going home.[255] But the various interviews conducted for this book from those who were there completely contradict this account: they all agree that there were far more than 10,000 people there and that while the Brotherhood, thanks to its pre-existing organization, was certainly a prominent part, there was still a great diversity of participants similar to that seen in previous demonstrations.

In any case, according to both accounts given by revolutionaries and the conclusions of an inquiry conducted under the Sharaf government, senior NDP figures summoned groups of local thugs carrying knives and clubs from the poor neighbourhoods in which they enjoyed influence.[256] The NDP leadership drew on its established networks in the ETUF, which was typically used to sabotage elections, to muster a small army of thugs, and that the president of ETUF, the minister of labour and several of their subordinates were all seen in the company of these thugs near

---

[253] Menawi, *The Last Days*, 295–6.
[254] Ibid., 301.
[255] Ibid., 291.
[256] According to the interviews, most of the groups that moved towards Tahrir came from Sayyida Zeinab, the old city and the slum districts, and had close links to NDP members.

to the offices of *al-Ahram*. Mortada Mansour, a regime-linked lawyer, and Mubarak business crony Mohamed Abou El Enein were also seen organizing the attack.[257]

These groups made their way across 6 October Bridge, given free passage through the army positions around the TV building and the road towards Tahrir. This naturally added to anxieties that the army were coming down on the side of the regime. One army officer had told the demonstrators in the square earlier in the day that they should go home because 'you've made your point'.[258] Another, according to Brotherhood leader Mohamed El-Beltagy, had warned him personally of the likelihood of bloodshed if the demonstrators were still there when the pro-Mubarak marchers arrived, and offered to guarantee them safe passage if they left in the morning.[259]

Menawy recalls that around 7.15 pm Egyptian state TV received a message from the armed forces (attributed to a security source) that demonstrators were now obliged to evacuate the square. Another security source informed them that 'Brotherhood elements' were throwing firebombs at those in the square in order to cause a riot.[260] It was decided to send in more thugs and policemen dressed in civilian clothing (including snipers) to mop up what remained of the protesters using bullets and Molotov cocktails. A media team filmed the chaos, accusing the Brotherhood of causing it. Similar operations would precede the coup of 3 July.

The army did not involve itself directly in these developments, allowing the regime the opportunity to crush the revolution if it was able. Once it became obvious that the regime was *not* able to do so, the army took a very different position. For the time being, however, it seemed to have promised to take no action to impede the attack on the revolutionaries – quite the opposite, in fact. It sought to position itself above the conflict, much as it was to do two and a half years later when demonstrators massed outside Morsi's presidential palace. In this way, it was able to present itself as the adult in the room, the only force capable of ruling the country.

At 10.00 am on 2 February, the army released a statement read by the official spokesman of the Defence Ministry, Ismail Etman, who warned state TV viewers of the dangers of instability and asked demonstrators to leave the square 'because their demands have been understood and their voices heard'.[261] The counterattack against the demonstrators had begun. General and Military Intelligence started rounding up foreign journalists

---

[257] Kamal Abou Eitta, personal interview.
[258] *Shorouk*, 3 February 2011, 1.
[259] *al-Ahram*, 11 June 2012, Available online: https://bit.ly/2Fx54dI (accessed 7 July 2014). Beltagy revealed this in an interview on *Ten PM*, [TV programme] Dream 2, 10 June 2012.
[260] Menawy, *The Last Days*, 307.
[261] *al-Ahram*, 2 February 2011, Available online: https://bit.ly/3kleAjl (accessed 13 April 2014).

and opposition figures as evidence of a 'foreign conspiracy' to undermine the country. It seems clear that the army's statement was coordinated both with Mubarak's speech and with the attack on Tahrir.

The attack began around 2.00 pm. The assailants quickly broke down the fortifications that demonstrators had erected around Tahrir the day before. Those approaching the square from Talaat Harb Street were driven back by the brave individual actions of army officer Maged Boulos, known later as 'the Lion of the Square', who fired his weapon above their heads to drive them back.[262] At the other entrances, however, hundreds of pro-regime thugs were able to force their way onto the square: the same army that had refused to let supplies through for the demonstrators gave way to armed men on horses and camels.

As soon as those in the square realized what was going on, they launched a counterattack with clubs and stones. Showing remarkable bravery, they quickly managed to regroup. Young women used their bags and scarves to collect the stones,[263] and those on the stage – an elevated vantage point equipped with loudspeakers – helped coordinate their efforts, warning of gaps in the defences and pointing out attackers.

At around the same time, the Brotherhood issued an official statement saying that they would be withdrawing from the square. Rashad Bayoumi contacted the young activists and told them that people were saying that the Guidance Bureau, the Brotherhood's central building and the headquarters of its parliamentary bloc had all been attacked or surrounded by 'citizens' and policemen. They thus concluded that the state had decided to wipe out the Brotherhood. Mahmoud Ezzat later claimed that the statement was written after they had received word that the protest in the square had already been broken up, although one young Brotherhood leader contradicts this narrative. Within three hours the Guidance Bureau had decided to reverse the decision.[264] In any case, nobody on the ground had paid it any heed whatsoever: the Brothers in the square played a key role in repelling the attack.

The battle for the square continued intermittently for some twelve hours. Ultimately, the demonstrators, armed with Molotov cocktails, were able to win the day. Pro-regime thugs occupied many of the surrounding buildings and continued to bombard them with pieces of rock and marble, but demonstrators were eventually able to dislodge them.[265]

---

[262] Interviews with various young demonstrators who protected the entrances to the square. Brotherhood members were responsible for Abdel Moneim Riad Square, YJF activists for Mohammed Mahmoud Street. The Ultras played a central role in protecting those on the square.
[263] Interviews with Khaled Abdel Hamid, Mohamed Salah and Islam Lotfy.
[264] Islam Lotfy, personal interview.
[265] Waleed Abd Elraouf, personal interview.

The revolutionaries set up a temporary jail in Tahrir metro station. Two Brotherhood leaders, Mohamed El-Beltagy and Safwat Hegazy, helped to bring in reinforcements from Shubra al-Kheima.[266] Appeals broadcast by Al Jazeera's team from the square itself – the only media team to cover the events directly – also contributed to the return of thousands of protesters who had left the previous evening. With their arrival at around midnight, the scales tipped decisively in favour of the demonstrators, who hounded the attackers until dawn. This, despite the use of live ammunition, which resulted in the deaths of three demonstrators on 6 October Bridge.[267]

After more than twelve hours of the most brutal fighting seen during the revolution, the attackers had been driven back. Ten demonstrators had been killed. Over the next two days, another three would die as a result of their injuries. But for the regime, it had been a disaster. Not only did the assault on Tahrir precipitate an outpouring of international sympathy for the revolutionaries, the army had almost been dragged into direct confrontations with protesters. From now on, it would try much harder to differentiate itself from the presidency and Mubarak.

It is still unclear why NDP grandees acted with such monumental stupidity and short-sightedness. Their approach was completely at odds with Mubarak's emotional speech and his attempts to contain the revolution more gently. It is my belief that they were attempting to act unilaterally, without Mubarak's knowledge, in order to forestall attempts by the regime to scapegoat them. A regime of the Egyptian kind, when faced by a crisis, is inclined to sacrifice some of its middling elites in order to placate popular anger. Many of those within the NDP had seen this happen to their predecessors during the rise of the Gamal Mubarak clique,[268] and they had no interest in allowing the same thing to happen to them. The group led by Safwat El-Sherif probably hoped to use their tried-and-tested methods to crush the revolution entirely, precluding the need for the regime to make concessions.

Unfortunately for them, they were not wrong about the regime's intentions. The next day, Public Prosecutor Abdel Meguid Mahmoud announced that several senior NDP figures had been arrested, including Ahmed Ezz, Zoheir Garana, Ahmed El Maghrabi and Habib el-Adly; they were banned from leaving the country and their accounts were frozen.[269] It is nevertheless important to reiterate that the army and the security forces were most certainly aware of the plan to attack Tahrir.

---

[266] Amr Guevara, personal interview.
[267] Personal interviews with Khaled Abdel Hamid, Mohamed Salah, Islam Lotfy and Moaz Abdelkarim.
[268] Joshua Stacher, *Adaptable Autocrats: Regime Power in Egypt and Syria* (Stanford, CA: Stanford University Press, 2012), 98–103.
[269] *Youm7*, 3 February 2011, Available online: https://bit.ly/2ZwZ6Rh (accessed 7 July 2014).

In particular, it is worth noting that a certain Abdel Fattah El-Sisi, head of Military Intelligence since January 2010, undeniably had advance knowledge of the attack.

The regime's official response was to deny all responsibility. Ahmed Shafik made an official apology for the assault on Tahrir and promised that it would not happen again and that an investigation was underway, all while maintaining that he had had no foreknowledge of it whatsoever.[270] The rector of al-Azhar (and senior NDP member), Ahmad al-Tayyeb, made an appearance on state TV to tell protesters to put an end to these 'tragic confrontations' by going home, warning that they were threatening national unity.[271] Omar Suleiman, meanwhile, condemned those who had attacked demonstrators and swore to hold them to account,[272] while continuing his somewhat desperate efforts to induce opposition parties into a national dialogue.

Internationally, the events of the Battle of the Camel drew condemnation from all corners. Hillary Clinton decried violence against the opposition and journalists, demanding that the Egyptian government and army step in to protect demonstrators and calling for 'serious negotiations' to begin at once on a peaceful and orderly transition of power.[273] Catherine Ashton, the European Union (EU) high representative for foreign affairs, said that Mubarak should move as quickly as possible to meet the protesters' demand for a political transition,[274] while German foreign minister Guido Westerwelle announced that he had spoken to Baradei directly to ask whether the Egyptian government understood what it needed to do.[275]

In Tahrir, meanwhile, hundreds of thousands of demonstrators once again gathered to demand that Mubarak step down and leave the country. This was a direct and unequivocal response to the events of the previous day. The core group of young activists (6 April, YJF, Brotherhood, Baradei campaign, DFP and various independents) made a statement to the press in which they announced a *milyoniyya* for 3 February.[276]

Various prominent figures now made their way down to the square to talk to protesters, and in response, State Security men in civilian clothes began to attempt arrests against possible leaders as they left and entered the square. The army maintained its cordon around the square, preventing

---

[270] *Shorouk*, 5 February 2011, 1.
[271] *Youm7*, 2 February 2011, Available online: https://bit.ly/3ixyGpN (accessed 7 July 2014).
[272] *Shorouk*, 4 February 2011, 1.
[273] *BBC Arabic*, 11 February 2011, Available online: https://bbc.in/3jcCEXl (accessed 17 October 2021).
[274] *Youm7*, 2 February 2011, Available online: https://bit.ly/2ZDmRHo (accessed 7 July 2014).
[275] *Youm7*, 2 February 2011, Available online: https://bit.ly/3kjZ3QS (accessed 7 July 2014).
[276] Mohamed Salah, personal interview.

the entry of food or medical supplies. On Qasr al-Nil Bridge, police personnel in civilian clothes accompanied by neighbourhood thugs were seen confiscating food and medicine from passers-by; forty demonstrators from the square eventually saw them off. The revolutionaries also redoubled their efforts to put pressure on the army, whether by sleeping in tank tracks to prevent them from moving or engaging officers in long conversation.[277]

For the second day in a row, the regime continued its attempts to spin its way out of the crisis. In an interview with the US-based ABC channel, Mubarak denied any responsibility for events in the square, claiming that he had set up a 'safe zone' for demonstrators and offering Obama the choice between his presidency and 'anarchy'.[278] The NDP itself likewise condemned the attack on Tahrir, conceding in an official statement that 'Egypt is not the same as it was before 25 January' while maintaining – to widespread ridicule – that there was 'enough space' in the country's squares for both pro-regime and anti-regime demonstrators to protest peacefully. It also warned, once again, of sinister elements 'parachuting' in and taking over a revolution that had filled 'all Egypt with joy', especially now that the revolutionaries had made their point.[279] The difference in tone was marked: after the Battle of the Camel, the regime seemed to have decided against attacking the revolutionaries directly, a strategy that would take on a new importance after the fall of the regime.

Omar Suleiman spent a busy day giving interviews, perhaps the most important of which was his appearance on state TV (at his own request). Here he conceded the legitimacy of the demonstrators' demands while expressing his regret that 'less upstanding elements, elements with their own agenda that may be linked to foreign agendas or domestic special interests, have infiltrated [the protests] with the aim of spreading fear and causing unrest'. He maintained that Mubarak had responded to all the demands, but that the government would need at least 200 days to make amendments to the constitution and organize new elections. In fact, he said, the demands were contradictory in this regard: if the parliament were dissolved, there would be no body capable of considering the amendments.[280] But even as he emphasized procedural detail and alluded to possible deals with the opposition at home, he was speaking to the international community in a very different language, bringing out all the old canards about how the

---

[277] Personal interviews with Khaled Elsayed, Khaled Abdel Hamid, Mahmoud Sami, Islam Lotfy and Mohammad Abbas.
[278] *ABC News*, 3 February 2012, Available online: https://abcn.ws/2ZwZHCv (accessed 20 December 2014).
[279] *Youm7*, 3 February 2011, Available online: https://bit.ly/2FCE3W6 (accessed 7 July 2014).
[280] *Youm7*, 3 February 2011, Available online: https://bit.ly/3hvHifB (accessed 7 July 2014).

absence of a 'culture of democracy' meant that any move in that direction would simply hand the country over the Islamists.[281]

Studies of democratic transition generally suggest that a transition begins with the split of the regime into hardliners and moderates, divided on their attitudes towards reform. But this is not what was happening in Egypt. Omar Suleiman was not a reformer nor was he speaking for reformist moderates willing to cooperate with their counterparts among the revolutionaries in order to bring about a democratic transition. He was simply playing for time, hoping that if the revolutionaries could be induced to go home, the regime could regroup and reassert itself – with or without Mubarak.

Suleiman claimed that the initial spontaneity of the demonstrations had given way to conspiracy: the demonstrations of 25 January were genuine and had legitimate demands, but subsequent events – particularly after Mubarak's speech – were the product of foreign, Brotherhood, 'partisan' or business interests,[282] and while the initial demands had been legitimate, they had also been met. However, he said, 'The idea of [Mubarak] leaving office is alien to the ethics of the Egyptian people. We all respect our father and leader President Mubarak and his service in the armed forces and as president of Egypt. When he leaves office it will happen naturally, in a few months.' He added that 'no member of his family' would be standing for president, hoping to counter fears of a Gamal Mubarak bid.[283]

In previous years, the opposition parties – and even the youth movements – would have considered the suggestion of a 'normal' exit from office for Mubarak more than satisfactory. Even two days earlier, Mubarak's emotional speech in the same vein had been enough for many of those who had come out to demonstrate. But as soon as those won over by his tearful promises not to run again had gone home, regime supporters had stormed the square and tried to drive out the remaining demonstrators by force. It was becoming clear that those demanding change had no real institutional representatives and that there was no one within the regime who genuinely supported their demands. In the face of empty promises and attempts to play for time, they realized that their only option was to continue their protest.

---

[281] See Suleiman's interview with *YouTube*, 6 February 2011, Available online: https://bit.ly/2Pk5eu2 (accessed 29 March 2021).
[282] As described by Menawy, who conducted the interview and was sympathetic to Suleiman. See: *The Last Days*, 329–30.
[283] Ibid.

X National dialogue, first round

1 The parties

Initially, Brotherhood leaders rejected Suleiman's blandishments out of hand. Mohamed Morsi and Abdel Moneim Aboul-Fotouh, for example, maintained that the Brotherhood denied any possibility of dialogue with an 'unconstitutional, illegitimate' regime that had already been 'toppled' by the people. For them it was not a question of 'legitimate demands made by patriotic forces' but of a regime that wanted 'to trample all over the people's interests and the constitution, throwing under the bus the millions of people who have come out onto the streets to say that they do not want Mubarak'.[284] This was also the initial position of the majority of opposition parties, including the Wafd, Tagammu and the DFP, as well as Mohamed ElBaradei. There was general agreement that national dialogue could only take place if the demands of the people were met – that is, if Mubarak was stepping down.[285]

In response, Suleiman organized a meeting with representatives of some twenty-one small opposition parties (many of them complete unknowns, politically speaking) and the NDP, accusing those parties that did not attend of 'irresponsibility'.[286] The army, it seems, was not particularly impressed. Sami Anan was later to say that in such a pressured atmosphere, and given that 'experience shows that the political parties in Egypt are exceedingly weak and flimsy, and have no popular base capable of exercising influence', dialogue was very unlikely to succeed.[287]

It is worth noting that even as it was supposedly seeking a constructive national dialogue, the regime's security forces were rounding up human rights activists from the Egyptian Center for Economic and Social Rights (ECESR) and the Hisham Mubarak Law Centre as well as representatives of Amnesty International and Human Rights Watch.[288] These organizations not only agitated for the release of detainees and documented abuses against the revolutionaries; they had also, on many occasions, provided them with direct logistical support.

---

[284] *Youm7*, 3 February 2011, Available online: https://bit.ly/2ZBBZVv (accessed 7 July 2014).
[285] *Youm7*, 3 February 2011, Available online: https://bit.ly/3iHLZE8 (accessed 7 July 2014). See the Baradei statement in *al-Wafd*, 3 February 2011, Available online: https://bit.ly/3AOZ6fc (accessed 17 October 2021).
[286] *Al-Masry Al-Youm*, 4 February 2011, Available online: https://bit.ly/3mYUHBv (accessed 17 October 2021).
[287] Anan's memoirs, *al-Watan*.
[288] *al-Wafd*, 3 February 2011, Available online: https://bit.ly/3vmAKbK (accessed 17 October 2021).

2 A covert struggle between two elites

Whether or not the president and his government had foreknowledge of the attack on Tahrir, the Battle of the Camel was disastrous for the regime. The opposition adopted a much more strident rhetoric, shaming those opposition parties that had already agreed to participate in the national dialogue (the Nasserists, for example) into making a volte-face.[289] Figures that belonged to no party or movement but enjoyed connections with both the regime and the opposition began to organize, hoping to play a role in ongoing developments. Perhaps the most prominent of these efforts was the group of intellectuals, politicians and businessmen who announced the formation of the 'Committee of Wise Men'.[290] The committee released a statement making five demands: a transitional period during which the country would be run on Mubarak's behalf by Omar Suleiman, fresh parliamentary elections, an amended constitution, an independent technocrat government and an end to the state of emergency. They also demanded that 'those responsible for terrorizing Egyptians' be held accountable and that demonstrators throughout Egypt be protected from retributive attacks.[291]

The members seem to have wanted to present themselves as the 'adults in the room'. Some of them later maintained their liberal integrity against the military coup. In any case, the committee – its intellectual and political diversity notwithstanding – gave expression to a new, 'non-partisan' political elite, which seemed to have no objection to Omar Suleiman – the head of intelligence, no less – taking power so long as his government was made up of technocrats. Some of this elite were doubtless more sensitive than others to questions of rights and freedoms, but the general attitude was one of distaste for parties, including the NDP, and willingness to work with an 'enlightened' dictator. One section of this elite in general served the SCAF government, the Morsi government and the coup plotters without reservation. They were not opposition figures but former officials and intellectuals from outside the political parties who wanted to play a role.

In opposition to this group stood a second elite made up of members of the Popular Coalition for Change (established on 31 January), an alliance of several officially registered parties (the Wafd, Tagammu, Nasserists and Ghad Party) that likewise sought to establish itself as the representative of the opposition. Fairly quickly, the PCC beat a hasty retreat from its initial position that any national dialogue that did not assume a Mubarak exit

---

[289] *Youm7*, 2 February 2011, Available online: https://bit.ly/2ZAzWkP (accessed 7 July 2014).
[290] The main members of this committee were Ahmed Kamal Abul-Magd, Nabil Elaraby, Salama Ahmed Salama, Ibrahim El Moallem, Abdul Aziz Al Shafei, Amr El-Shobaki, Gamil Matar, Safwan Thabet, Nabil Fahmy, Mervat Tallawy, Ali Mashrafa, Naguib Sawiris and Amr Hamzawy.
[291] *Youm7*, 2 February 2011, Available online: https://bit.ly/309gmz0 (accessed 1 October 2021).

was simply impossible, citing the need to preserve national security and law and order. But it nonetheless maintained that all the popular demands must be met and that Mubarak must resign, adding that a total separation had to be enforced between the NDP and the presidency during the transitional period. The coalition also rejected 'any foreign interference in internal affairs'.[292]

The willingness to accept dialogue with the assumed president-in-waiting was rooted in the traditional parties' desire to secure themselves a place in the new regime. The representatives of the non-partisan elite had already explicitly demanded that power be handed over to Suleiman, and although for the moment the party elites did not join them, they would fall into line quickly enough once the Brotherhood announced its intention to run a presidential candidate in mid-2012. Both sets of elites were also very wary of activists. Baradei was willing to reach out to the young people, but even his political proclivities aligned closely with those of the Committee of Wise Men: at a meeting with a youth delegation held at his house on the Alexandria Road, he supported those activists who argued that the demonstration had served its purpose and that Suleiman's appointment and Mubarak's promise to step down at the end of his term were enough for the time being.[293] He was generally very keen on the idea that Suleiman should oversee a transition to democracy.

The revolutionaries themselves were now faced by a growing contradiction between their rejection of piecemeal reforms, rooted in a deep suspicion of the promises made so far, and the lack of any real revolutionary alternative that could take power and manage the transitional period for itself. Ultimately, of course, it was not the revolutionary forces but SCAF that assumed this role.

Internationally, the EU struggled to articulate a single position on the Egyptian revolution. While the UK largely followed the US line, moving from an emphasis on urgent reform to the need for a rapid transfer of power as events unfolded, the French and German positions focused primarily on the need for 'self-restraint' and 'non-violence'. The Iranian revolution and the more recent memory of the 1990 elections in Algeria were very much at the forefront of policymakers' minds,[294] and many were wary of the consequences for the Middle East – and thus, of course, for Europe and Israel – if Mubarak

---

[292] Ibid.

[293] Within the campaign to support Baradei, there were two factions from the beginning. One, represented by Mostafa Alnagar, Abdel Rahman Youssef and Abdelmonem Emam, rejected opening to the left and Islamists and supported dialogue with Omar Suleiman. The other was represented by Zyad Elelaimy, Sally Touma, Basel Kamel and Mohamad Arafatt, all of whom could be described as leftists; they went on to be activists with the RYC, in cooperation with the left and Islamists, and later joined the Social Democratic Party.

[294] *Harper's Magazine*, Available online: https://bit.ly/3aN495o (accessed 17 October 2021).

was replaced by an Islamist government.[295] Thanks to this stereotyped image of the Arab revolutions, encouraged by a Western media that insisted on attributing all protest to the Muslim Brotherhood despite their near-absence from the first few days of revolutionary activity,[296] all European countries agreed that the priority was to put in place a stable and organized transitional government headed by Omar Suleiman, an experienced figure with well-established diplomatic links with the West and a close relationship with Israel. Nicolas Sarkozy, Angela Merkel and David Cameron were united in their praise for Suleiman's appointment and the prospective national dialogue process. When dialogue failed, they had nothing more to say.

XI The Revolutionary Youth Coalition (RYC) (4–5 February)

By the time hundreds of thousands of demonstrators poured into squares across Greater Cairo on 'the Friday of the Departure', the strength of the Egyptian regime was at a nadir. That Friday saw Tantawi make an official visit to Tahrir, where he tried to convince demonstrators that Mubarak was sincere and that he would not be standing for the presidency again. Various other prominent personalities followed his example, visiting Tahrir or organizing pro-Mubarak demonstrations in Mostafa Mahmoud. But the number of people flocking to Tahrir just kept rising, as did the number of people who camped out in the square overnight.

The revolutionaries had been busy thinking up ways to give greater coherence to the revolution's political character. One issue that arose on Friday morning was the question of who would lead Friday prayers in the square. After some debate, they eventually settled on the imam of the Omar Makram Mosque, Sheikh Mazhar Shahin, a neutral figure with no known associations with or sympathies for Islamism. Shahin was asked to lead the prayers and give the Friday sermon.

Of course, the revolutionaries had not been against forming a single political front earlier on in the revolution, but few concrete steps had been taken in this direction because of mutual suspicion and a lack of political experience, as well as the difficulties presented by the rapid pace of events.[297] Now that the opposition parties were signalling an openness to dialogue with Omar Suleiman, however – a development whose ultimate results were far from guaranteed, and which might well lead to

---

[295] *John Pilger*, 9 February 2011, Available online: https://bit.ly/3j6pZFd (accessed 17 October 2021).
[296] Ibid.
[297] Personal interviews with Khaled Elsayed, Khaled Abdel Hamid, Mahmoud Sami, Islam Lotfy and Mohammad Abbas.

the co-option and defeat of the revolution – the need for a united front assumed a fresh urgency.

This united front came with the formation of the RYC, which brought together the core group of young activists who had organized the demonstrations of 25 January and had continued to meet regularly ever since. At the moment of its establishment, the RYC included YJF, 6 April, the Brotherhood and DFP youth, and various independents (who made up the majority of members). The group's manifesto, which was distributed in paper form and read out over loudspeakers in front of the huge civil service complex on Tahrir, made four now-familiar demands: Mubarak's resignation; an end to the state of emergency, restrictions on civil liberties and police abuses; dissolution of both houses of parliament; and the formation of a national unity government (backed by the armed forces) that would oversee the handover of power and the process of constitutional reform. Its fifth demand was for the establishment of a committee of inquiry, including representatives of human rights organizations, which would investigate the breakdown of law and order and the killing of protesters.[298]

In the days before the official start of national dialogue, various symbolic messages were exchanged between the regime (represented by Omar Suleiman) and the opposition. Both were keen to rule out any possibility of participation by revolutionary youth as a third party, making liberal use of backhanded compliments – 'good intentions', 'simple', 'unpretentious' – that served to justify their exclusion from politics. The activists' inability to organize themselves into a single body that might have represented them facilitated this process. But this inability was not the product of any failure on their part: the opposition parties, which all had young members in Tahrir, were quick to act, while the emerging cross-party groups that appeared on the square itself simply did not have enough time to establish themselves as leaders of the revolution.

The parties themselves were marshalling their forces for the moment of truth. They knew instinctively that by intensifying their rhetoric against the regime and flirting with the demands being made by demonstrators, they could both increase their own popularity and guarantee themselves a seat at the post-revolutionary table. Meanwhile, they could use the opportunity to get a few kicks in against a regime that had consigned them to the political wilderness.

The Brotherhood was making a great deal of effort to deflate regime attempts to fall back on the old equation of 'Mubarak or the Brotherhood'. In a statement, it announced that its aim was 'to serve the people', and not to

---

[298] Ibid.

pursue its own presidential or governmental ambitions, emphasizing that its approach was 'gradual, peaceful, popular reform'. It also emphasized that it would be open to any 'serious' proposal for dialogue seeking a way out of the crisis, while warning the government against any attempt to ignore popular demands for an immediate Mubarak exit and new legislative elections.[299] Moreover, it maintained that it was in full agreement with the general consensus that Egypt should be a civil democratic state with an Islamic frame of reference – an ambiguous formulation that could mean almost anything at all – in which all citizens should enjoy freedom, equality and social justice. It further made it clear that it favoured a parliamentary system of government, a position that was not to survive contact with the presidency.[300]

Baradei, meanwhile, offered Mubarak a safe exit while continuing to argue for a presidential council (with military representation, of course) that would oversee a one-year transitional period ending with presidential and parliamentary elections under an amended constitution. The Committee of Wise Men likewise called on the army to 'carry out its patriotic function' and guarantee a safe transition to true democracy.[301]

On 4 February, Suleiman announced a new round of dialogue, reiterating that the 'brave' Mubarak would not be standing for the presidency again. In a telling reflection of the paternalistic framework within which senior regime figures operated, he emphasized that rebellion against the president was alien to Egyptian culture, maintaining that while the demonstrators were certainly Egyptian citizens, they were indisputably backed by foreign forces. He put off the implementation of full democracy to some future point after the development of a democratic 'culture' (meaning, in practice, never, since it is impossible for a democratic culture to develop under a non-democratic system). He also rejected out of hand any suggestion that Baradei might be included in dialogue.[302] The regime much preferred, if possible, to deal with the existing opposition parties (essentially part of the regime themselves) and was wary of Baradei's US connections, which drew on the regime's main source of foreign support.

As far as foreign support for the revolution was concerned, regime media now adopted a strategy of barefaced propaganda bordering on the surreal. A vast conspiracy linking Iran, Hezbollah, Hamas, Israel and the United States – the latter two allies with whom the regime was desperate to maintain good relations – was behind the protests, which represented a desperate attempt to undermine Egypt's national security. The complete lack

---

[299] *al-Wafd*, 4 February 2011, Available online: https://bit.ly/3mUEkWo (accessed 17 October 2021).
[300] *Youm7*, 4 February 2011, Available online: https://bit.ly/3bWviSU (accessed 7 July 2014).
[301] *Bet, 4 February 2011*, Available online: https://bet.us/3BiTDNP *(accessed 25 October 2021)*
[302] *ABC News*, 3 February 2011, Available online: https://abcn.ws/2DZ6RI0 (accessed 20 December 2014).

of logical coherence suggests that this was a deliberate attempt to confuse the public. The general message, however, could not have been clearer: the demands made by the young people are just, it suggested, but there are sinister forces at work. However, this propaganda was no longer addressing atomized individuals excluded from the public sphere. Egyptians were now standing shoulder to shoulder in their country's streets and squares, and the regime's attempts to win them over met with nothing but contempt.

Attempts to mediate between revolutionaries and regime continued throughout the next day. At a meeting at the Marriott, Ahmed Zewail sought to impress upon activists that the most that could be hoped for at this point was for Mubarak to essentially hand over power to Suleiman.[303] Amr Moussa likewise told demonstrators that their message had been received and understood by senior officials and that they should now go home.[304] Documents seized during the storming of SSIS headquarters were subsequently to reveal that Moussa had been selected and marketed as a popular figure who could be used to contain the revolution. The same strategy was behind the appointment of the known reformist Hossam Badrawi as NDP secretary general on 5 February.

XII The shortest dialogue in Egyptian history (6 February)

On 6 February, the 'Sunday of Martyrs', Tahrir was once again packed with people. Christian demonstrators, surrounded by a protective cordon of other revolutionaries, took communion at the nearby evangelical church of Kasr El Dobara; liturgical expressions intermingled with revolutionary slogans and affirmations of national unity, while Christian prayers for the souls of those killed during the revolution were followed by Muslim funeral prayers.[305] This church played a very important role during the demonstrations in Tahrir, providing first aid and shelter to the revolutionaries while acting as a physical embodiment of national unity between Egypt's different religious groups.

On symbolic occasions like this, the demonstrators in Tahrir took great pains to emphasize the importance of national unity against sectarianism. They were eager to make it clear that they represented the Egyptian people as a whole regardless of their religious, political or social background. The community assembled in the square was to serve as a model of the Egyptian society they wanted to build, a society enriched by its diversity.

---

[303] According to Khaled Elsayed, the activists believed that Zewail was speaking on behalf of the US.
[304] *Youm7*, 4 February 2011, Available online: https://bit.ly/3monU7F (accessed 7 July 2014).
[305] *Youm7*, 6 February 2011, Available online: https://bit.ly/3asXpJN (accessed 1 October 2021).

But ultimately this community proved fragile and ephemeral, unable to produce a unified movement, political party or leadership for the revolution.

The RYC's founding was officially announced at the home of Zyad Elelaimy's mother. In a subsequent step, the RYC released a list of members of its executive bureau, which included representatives from all the movements as well as independents; decisions were made by consensus.[306] So long as the movement had the single overarching aim of bringing down the regime, consensus was simple. But after Mubarak's fall, this would no longer be the case.

The representatives of the youth movements faced a great deal of pressure to negotiate or accept mediation with the regime. Efforts to win them over came from the elite opposition, in particular the Committee of Wise Men and the Brotherhood (specifically Morsi),[307] and ultimately from Omar Suleiman himself.[308] But all these efforts came to nothing, with the RYC adopting the basic principle of no negotiation prior to Mubarak's resignation.

Suleiman's national dialogue began at 12.00 pm and was over within three hours. Despite its failure to produce anything of substance, it was of great significance for the revolution in that it exposed the approach of the traditional parties for what it was. The leaders of the Wafd, Tagammu and the NDP, as well as representatives of the Muslim Brotherhood and various independent figures (some from the Committee of Wise Men) were all in attendance.[309] In a move not lacking in symbolism, the meeting was held in the cabinet office, overseen by an imposing portrait of President Mubarak hung on the wall. Despite Morsi's best efforts to convince them to send a representative, the RYC refused to attend.

The Brotherhood's representatives, Mohamed Saad Elkatatny and Mohamed Morsi, had already met with Suleiman privately.[310] This meeting remained a closely guarded secret kept even from members of the Brotherhood's Consultative Council, and caused a crisis within that body on 10 February when Abdel Moneim Aboul-Fotouh demanded to know what had happened (this set the reformist Aboul-Fotouh on his path out

---

[306] The RYC executive bureau included Khaled Elsayed and Mostafa Shawky (YJF); Ahmed Maher and Amr Ezz (6 April), Mohamed Al-Qasas, Mohammad Abbas, Islam Lotfy, Moaz Abdelkarim (Brotherhood youth); Zyad Elelaimy, Abdel Rahman Samir, Basem Kamel (Baradei campaign); Shadi Ghazali Harb and Amr Salah (DFP); and Nasser Abdel Hamid, Abdelrahman Fares and Sally Touma (independents).

[307] Islam Lotfy, personal interview.

[308] Personal interviews with Khaled Abdel Hamid and Zyad Elelaimy.

[309] *Youm7*, 6 February 2011, Available online: https://bit.ly/2H0GMtn (accessed 7 July 2014).

[310] It is no coincidence that these two pragmatic figures became president and speaker of the parliament after the elections.

of the Brotherhood). Suleiman also met young activists connected with the revolution privately.

According to contemporary media coverage, the opposition demanded protection for demonstrators, a national unity government, amendments to the constitution, separation of the NDP presidency and the national presidency, and accountability for those responsible for the bloodshed. The Brotherhood added a Mubarak exit, dissolution of the legislature and a provisional administration headed by the president of the SCC. This latter demand was rejected out of hand by Suleiman, who insisted that Mubarak serve out the remainder of his term.

It would be difficult to find a more accurate description of the situation than that given by Katatny to Mehwar TV. According to Katatny, the opposition made multiple attempts to identify acceptable compromises. When the opposition proposed that all political prisoners be immediately released, Suleiman said that this would require time, which was accepted by the opposition. When the opposition proposed ending the state of emergency, Suleiman said that the police had been completely defeated and that the army could not protect all areas of the country, and so the state of emergency remained crucial to maintain law and order for the time being. At this point, Katatny, now convinced that the opposition had been assured of the demonstrators' safety, said that if the Egyptian people received some of their rights, they would be patient on the rest. He also concurred that there might be some elements among the demonstrators with their own agendas seeking to undermine the dialogue. He additionally expressed his pleasure that pro-government news outlets had broadcast press statements from the Brotherhood without describing it as a 'banned' organization.[311] The media devoted most of its coverage of the dialogue to the interview with Katatny, who professed confidence in Suleiman's promises, justified delayed implementation of them until 'current circumstances' had been addressed and tried to persuade young people to leave Tahrir, 'which parties with their own special interests are preventing from taking place'. Abdel Moneim Aboul-Fotouh condemned Katatny's statements as reflecting 'the mentality of a persecuted organization'.

The opposition forces, in their press statement published the following day, maintained that there was general agreement on a battery of constitutional and legislative measures that needed to be taken in preparation for democratic elections when Mubarak stood down at the end of his term. Articles 76, 77 and 88 of the constitution had to be amended to facilitate the peaceful handover of power, the Court of Cassation's orders annulling the

---

[311] *YouTube*, 23 April 2012, Available online: https://bit.ly/3iz0GJY (accessed 7 July 2014).

results of the 2010 elections in various constituencies had to be implemented and those responsible for the breakdown of law and order following the 'uprising of the youth' had to be held to account. A judicial committee was to be set up (with political representation) to propose legislative changes, making its proposals in the first week of March. Restrictions on the media were to end and the state of emergency lifted as soon as the security situation allowed. The statement also made reference to 'the sincere patriotic role of our heroic armed forces in this delicate period'.[312]

The preliminary agreement produced by the second round of national dialogue proved very controversial in Tahrir and among the various political forces that had not participated. Baradei, who had not been invited, said that the talks lacked any credibility since those involved were 'the same people who have been running Egypt for thirty years', and that they were 'conducted entirely by the army'.[313] But more than anyone else it was the young people who were shocked by the talks and Katatny's comments. The Brotherhood leaders in Tahrir, Aboul-Fotouh and Mohamed El-Beltagy, stepped in to quell rumours that the organization was about to withdraw its constituency from the square, reiterating their commitment to remain in place until Mubarak fell.

Within a few hours, the Guidance Bureau had made a U-turn. Essam el-Erian announced that the Brotherhood was 'reassessing its position on dialogue with the regime, and did not agree with or put its name to the contents of the statement issued after political forces met with the vice-president'. Moreover, the final statement's 'partial reforms' fell far short of the popular demands.[314]

Various political forces defended the dialogue process as a political means of achieving the revolution's demands. Prominent voices included Mostafa Alnagar,[315] one of the coordinators of the Baradei campaign, as well as representatives of al-Gama'a al-Islamiyya, a former militant jihadi organization that had ceased its violent activities in the 1990s.[316]

In this context, it is worth returning to a key issue that Suleiman himself alluded to at various points and that has not been analysed in sufficient detail so far. Suleiman was constantly warning of the possibility of a military coup. This reflects, to my mind, a conflict within the regime itself –

---

[312] *Akhbar Al-Yom*, 6 February 2011, Available online: https://bit.ly/3b9nZYw (accessed 25 October 2021); *Addustour*, 7 February 2011, Available online: https://bit.ly/2SbQgnI (accessed 25 October 2021).
[313] *al-Ahram*, 6 February 2011, Available online: https://bit.ly/3kn3kD7 (accessed 8 July 2014).
[314] *al-Ahram*, 7 February 2011, Available online: https://bit.ly/2ZTcqzJ (accessed 8 July 2014).
[315] Alnagar, a doctor of moderate political opinions, was elected to parliament after the revolution. In September 2018, he disappeared without a trace. Like many others, he is thought to have been the victim of a regime kidnapping.
[316] *al-Ahram*, 7 February 2011, Available online: https://bit.ly/3bY2Ik3 (accessed 8 July 2014).

not between reformers and hardliners but between the presidency and the army. Suleiman presented the revolutionaries and the Brotherhood with a choice: dialogue or coup. Dialogue would mean accepting Mubarak's reform proposals and negotiating on the basis of Mubarak's six-month roadmap to democracy; a coup would mean the army taking power. Suleiman's predictions came true, once after Mubarak's resignation and again after Morsi had been elected president. But ultimately he could not win the trust of the opposition parties, the revolutionaries or even the army, as the 2012 presidential elections were to show.

The basic problem facing the revolutionaries, which only became worse after Mubarak stood down, was their inability to manage the transition period and their lack of any plan to this end. They had set out not as revolutionaries but as protesters. When they realized a revolution was within their grasp, they had resolved to bring down the regime. But they were only able to bring down Mubarak himself. They demanded reform, but refused to participate in any reform plan. They did not demand to be part of any government in order to implement the revolution's principles. They drove forward a revolutionary movement whose aim was to bring down the regime, but they did so with the purist mentality of demonstrators wary of getting their hands 'dirty' with the real business of politics. When some of them did decide to enter politics after the revolution, it was as individuals, who proved easy prey for organized political forces, including, ultimately, those of the counter-revolution.

XIII Independent decision making and overcoming stagnation (7–9 February)

Between 7 and 9 February, the regime's fate fell entirely into the hands of the newly organized revolutionaries and the army, which proved unwilling to protect the president. On 7 February, demonstrators prevented a planned resumption of government work by blockading the Mogamma, the vast civil service complex on Tahrir. After Ahmed Shafik announced on Tuesday that he would be beginning his work as prime minister, they also surrounded the Cabinet Building to prevent him from entering.[317] The army, meanwhile, evacuated the area and refused to intervene on the regime's behalf.

These moves were accompanied by a vast wave of strikes across Egypt and in Greater Cairo in particular. This development was very important: it torpedoed Suleiman and Shafik's attempts (with Mubarak behind them)

---

[317] Personal interviews with Islam Lotfy, Khaled Abdel Hamid, Zyad Elelaimy, Mostafa Shawky, Mahmoud Sami and Mohammad Abbas.

to isolate the demonstrators in Tahrir Square and return to normality in the rest of the country. The strikes obstructed their plan. The activists, including the freshly minted RYC, began to discuss further escalations and prepare for another *milyoniyya* on Tuesday.[318]

On Sunday, there was an attack on the gas pipeline connecting Egypt and Israel. On the evening of the same day, the recently released Wael Ghonim appeared on Egyptian TV, where he wept openly for those who had been killed in the course of the demonstrations. This interview touched many of those watching at home, who saw Ghonim as a successful middle-class, apolitical young man who had been badly mistreated by an unjust regime.[319]

Senior officials began to come out in support of the revolution, including the deputy president of Egypt's highest administrative court, Mohamed Gadallah. Gaber Asfour, the newly appointed culture minister, resigned after only ten days in office.[320] The rats were deserting the sinking ship. In politics, the opportunists are the best barometer of shifts in the atmosphere: the smart ones are the first to fall in line behind a strong regime and the first to abandon a losing bet.

On the same day, Egyptian media interviewed the families of those killed live on air for the first time. The day after saw the first of several marches from other areas of the city to the square, attracting many middle-class citizens and professionals. The Ghonim interview, the interviews with the families who had lost loved ones, the statements issued by senior officials – these developments had clearly resonated with Egyptians whose normal political behaviour certainly did not extend to sit-ins. The same Egyptians who were touched by the emotional speech of the president were now similarly moved by other emotional interviews and statements. Steven Cook tended to exaggerate the significance of this phenomenon, maintaining that the national dialogue had paralysed the square and created a sense of stagnation before the influx of fresh blood.[321] But while the developments of 6 and 7 February were certainly important, the revolution was never in any serious danger. In fact, there are many indications that having weathered the storm of Mubarak's second speech and the Battle of the Camel on the following day, it had been going from strength to strength. As we have seen, the national dialogue process had failed to have any real effect on the square, where there was very little confidence in the regime's promises.

---

[318] Ibid.
[319] The interview, with Mona Elshazly, was broadcast on *Ten PM*, [TV programme] Dream TV, 7 February 2014. See: *YouTube*, 7 February 2011, Available online: https://bit.ly/3vi5oCM (accessed 17 October 2021).
[320] *Al-Arabiya*, 10 February 2011, Available online: https://bit.ly/3bWOPCX (accessed 14 May 2014).
[321] Cook, *The Struggle for Egypt*, 290–1.

The regime had been backed into a corner, but the lack of a coherent international position on events in Egypt still afforded it some room for manoeuvre. On 7 February, Mubarak held a meeting with senior legislators and government officers and set up a constitutional committee to consider possible amendments, as well as a second committee to oversee the implementation of the 'points agreed upon during the national dialogue process'.[322] He also announced the formation of a committee of inquiry in an attempt to placate demonstrators, maintaining that he 'felt their pain'.[323] Ahmed Shafik, meanwhile, redoubled his efforts to convince the public that Mubarak should be allowed to serve out his term.[324] It was quite clear that as far as the regime was concerned, the second round of national dialogue was to be the last, and its results definitive. This came as a surprise to the opposition groups that had participated in what they had thought were preliminary discussions.

In an interview with Fox News, Obama expressed support for Mubarak's measures, stating that the United States would not push the president to leave now and that the important thing – given that Mubarak had already said he would not be standing for re-election – was that he 'start[ed] making a change'. He also described the Muslim Brotherhood as having anti-US 'strains' in their ideology, while emphasizing that it was important not to proceed as if 'our only two options are either the Muslim Brotherhood or a suppressed Egyptian people'.[325] The United States, at least, was clearly signalling that it considered the decision to hand over day-to-day administration of the country to Suleiman to constitute a 'peaceful transfer of power'. The EU, meanwhile, remained conspicuously silent.

Within the Arab world, Hezbollah secretary general Hassan Nasrallah congratulated Egypt's revolutionaries, characterizing their actions as a revolution against the regime's pro-Israel policy and locating it in a long history of 'resistance' against the 2006 invasion of Lebanon and the 2008–9 attack on Gaza. This was only to be expected given that Iran, Hezbollah's sponsor, had hailed the revolution as an 'Islamic resurgence'.[326] Of course, this position did not last very long when revolution spread to Syria. Soon enough Iran was arguing that all of the Arab revolutions were the product of a vast foreign conspiracy.

---

[322] The constitutional committee was head by the president of the Court of Cassation. See: *Youm7*, 9 February 2011, Available online: https://bit.ly/2ZFS0tH (accessed 8 July 2014).
[323] *Youm7*, 7 February 2011, Available online: https://bit.ly/35AoY2j (accessed 8 July 2014).
[324] *al-Ahram*, 7 February 2011, Available online: https://bit.ly/3AJeN7G (accessed 17 October 2021).
[325] For the full interview with Bill O'Reilly, see *YouTube*, 7 February 2011, Available online: https://bit.ly/3cX37p5 (accessed 25 October 2021).
[326] *Al-Manar*, 8 February 2011, Available online: https://bit.ly/3n14hnn (accessed 17 October 2021).

By 8 February, it was clear that the revolution's aspirations went far beyond the conclusions of Suleiman's national dialogue. The streets of Cairo were yet again teeming with people, including thousands of doctors, university professors and professionals.[327] Oil workers, some of the most important to the country's economy, went on strike to demand the resignation of Oil Minister Sameh Fahmy; they were joined by Red Crescent employees, factory workers and the staff of the Cairo sewage and street-cleaning authorities.[328] Members of the Journalists' Syndicate threw the pro-regime chair out of the building, while young journalists at *al-Ahram* added an unofficial supplement, Youth of Tahrir.

On 7 February, efforts began to establish a pro-revolutionary front of supportive parties, made up of thirty members: ten young activists and twenty representatives of various political currents, selected by the RYC executive committee.[329] But the political elite stymied this effort to establish a political entity that might have given the revolution a voice and a unified direction. At the front's first meeting on 9 February, the Brotherhood demanded that more leadership figures be added; the number of representatives then rose to forty-two. After a second meeting on 12 February, the number rose again to seventy-three, and after the third meeting on 14 February – which produced no other results because of disruption by secret police agitators – it had risen to 150. The continuous expansion of the front's leadership ranks indicated a lack of trust, and the opposition forces' inability to put the transition to democracy ahead of their own internecine struggles foreshadowed the problems of the transitional period.

The front's failure aside, however, these efforts made it clear that the entities outside the square – the Committee of Wise Men, the Popular Front for Change – were now obsolete. The RYC said as much in their statement issued on 9 February:

> We respect all the initiatives presented by the Committee of Wise Men and by other forces, but we would like to make it clear that they are not compatible with our proposal. We are not talking about reform or the appointment of a vice-president or compliance with the constitution, for which the NDP has never in its existence shown any respect. We are talking about a thoroughgoing revolution, not half measures; about comprehensive change, not petty reforms. It is our belief that the only guarantee of any reform is for the president to go.[330]

---

[327] *Youm7*, 8 February 2011, Available online: https://bit.ly/3mncfpW (accessed 8 July 2014).
[328] *Youm7*, 9 February 2011, Available online: https://bit.ly/2FxVc3N (accessed 8 July 2014).
[329] Personal interviews with Mohamed Al-Qasas, Islam Lotfy, Khaled Abdel Hamid, Khaled Elsayed, Zyad Elelaimy, Mostafa Shawky, Mahmoud Sami and Mohammad Abbas.
[330] *al-Ahram*, 9 February 2011, Available online: https://bit.ly/33t7aDM (accessed 8 July 2014).

The young revolutionaries had not yet realized that, first, overthrowing the president is not the equivalent of regime change and, second, democracy is not achieved by 'thoroughgoing revolution' but by gradual reform – even if revolution is the only means of bringing about such reform. They did not trust politicians, but at the same time they had no vision of their own that would have allowed them to lead a 'thoroughgoing revolution' to democracy. It took Mubarak's exit, the abrupt end of the revolution and their subsequent marginalization for them to realize this fact.

A sense of stalemate now began to fall over the revolutionary scene. The sit-in was firmly ensconced in Tahrir and not going anywhere. The various opposition forces continued their back and forth with the regime. Shafik, annoyed by the delay, issued a statement in which he mockingly suggested that 'we should hand meals out to [the sit-inners] – bring them some bonbons'. But on the revolutionary side, despite several efforts to get things moving again, nothing really seemed to be happening. The activists considered blockading the People's Assembly, but the continuing presence of the army made them reconsider. When members of the Cairo University faculty marched past the assembly building unmolested, the activists scrambled to set up another sit-in. But the People's Assembly, a good 600 metres away from Tahrir, was constantly haemorrhaging demonstrators who wanted to go back to the square itself.

At around the same time, Suleiman – by now the established face of the government – was telling a meeting of editors-in-chief that the only alternative to national dialogue was a coup. The opposition had largely swung into line behind the revolutionaries, with the DFP,[331] the Wafd[332] and the Brotherhood[333] all announcing their insistence on a Mubarak exit. Demands were also being made for the reclamation of illegally appropriated wealth.[334]

In the face of a mass popular mobilization that would not allow anyone to speak on its behalf, the regime's efforts to identify partners with which it could work out a settlement were doomed to failure. The new interior minister, Mahmoud Wagdy, signalled the regime's recognition of this when he met with Wael Ghonim.[335] This was a strong point so long as the revolutionary tide was high, since it meant that no elites were capable of brokering a deal in its name. But after Mubarak had been toppled, it was to become the complete opposite: political parties proliferated, all of them claiming to represent the 'revolutionary youth'.

---

[331] *Al Jazeera*, 8 February 2011, Available online: https://bit.ly/3bsipRb (accessed 31 October 2021).
[332] *al-Wafd*, 8 February 2011, Available online: https://bit.ly/3GBghVJ (accessed 17 October 2021).
[333] *Youm7*, 8 February 2011, Available online: https://bit.ly/3c2ZlbU (accessed 8 July 2014).
[334] *al-Wafd*, 8 February 2011, Available online: https://bit.ly/3FTegns (accessed 17 October 2021).
[335] Ghonim, *Revolution 2.0*, 298.

Before bringing this chapter to a close, it is worth noting that demonstrations on their own cannot topple a regime.[336] Even the sit-in in Tahrir Square, despite its vast size and its success in getting the world's attention and winning its sympathy, eventually lost momentum once Omar Suleiman began making the rounds of the opposition. The demonstrations were important. But had it not been for the army's intervention, the military's refusal to accept the new vice-president and the massive labour strikes, life might well have returned to normal under Suleiman and Shafik – a result that the United States and other Arab countries would have been quite happy with. Absent the high-profile regime defections and the army stepping in to force Mubarak to resign, the regime could have easily coexisted with the occupation of the square. Of course, without the demonstrations none of these things would have happened in the first place, but by themselves, demonstrations cannot bring down a regime. The military proved that indisputably in July 2013 when the Muslim Brotherhood launched its ill-fated sit-in in Raba'a Square, which remained isolated there.[337]

There were no significant changes in the international position on the revolution except for a slight refinement on the part of the White House, which set out four steps for Egypt to implement 'immediately': ending arrests, harassment, violence and the detention of journalists and civil society activists by the Interior Ministry; ensuring freedom of association and expression and an end to the state of emergency; expanding national dialogue; and inviting the opposition to put together a joint roadmap for the transitional period. The Emirati foreign minister[338] visited Egypt to express his solidarity with Mubarak.[339] More or less the same position was expressed by King Abdullah of Saudi Arabia, who warned Obama not to demean Mubarak, telling him that if the United States suspended aid to Egypt, then Riyadh would step in to the fill the gap.[340] Indeed, this period saw the emergence of a nascent counter-revolutionary front among regional powers, although as yet it did not take any clearly active form. The Saudi and Emirati positions – as expressed by the various media organizations supported with their money – would ultimately become a major impediment to the success of the revolutionary wave and the creation of democracies in the region.

---

[336] Atef Said, 'The Rise and Fall of the Tahrir Repertoire: Theorizing Temporality, Trajectory, and Failure', *Social Problems*, spaa024 (6 July 2020): 2, 10–11.
[337] Ibid., 11.
[338] Then US secretary of defence Robert Gates claims in his autobiography that the Emirati Crown Prince Mohamed Bin Zayed warned him that the alternative to Mubarak was a Sunni version of the Iranian Islamic Republic. Gates, *Duty*, 507.
[339] *Youm7*, 9 February 2011, Available online: https://bit.ly/2FDYTV4 (accessed 8 July 2014).
[340] *Reuters Arabic*, 10 February 2011, Available online: https://bit.ly/3pC06RU (accessed 8 July 2014).

XIV Endgame

1 The SCAF communiqué (10 February)

On 10 February, Egyptian state TV suspended normal programming in order to broadcast the first public statement issued by the SCAF. Despite its brevity, the timing of the message had important implications. No civilian official or political figure within the government, Mubarak included, were aware of the statement before it was broadcast. SCAF seem to have decided against a direct military coup against Mubarak. Nonetheless, there are many reasons to consider their move an *indirect* military coup.

Constitutionally, SCAF was chaired by the president. But on this occasion, it had met without either the president or his legal deputy being present, with Field Marshal Tantawi, the minister of defence, taking Mubarak's place. Its statement was issued as Communiqué No. 1, implying further statements to come. Moreover, it announced that it would be in 'permanent session' until further notice, suggesting that the armed forces were in it for the long haul. All this taken together was tantamount to a bloodless coup against the head of the regime.

The communiqué stated, 'The army is committed to protecting our great people and stands in solidarity with them. It is working to further their interests and achievements while at the same time protecting the nation.' It thus struck a balance between the revolutionaries' demands and what it believed to be in the interest of the state, and it unequivocally recognized the legitimacy of the square's demands, including the demand that Mubarak step down.

Not many realized at the time that a military coup was underway. Mubarak, after all, was still president. But he was president in name only: he no longer had any power.

2 A dose of emotion

The army's first communiqué represented a major shift in the revolution's trajectory. The army was aware that Mubarak's attempts to compromise had reached a dead end. If he was no longer capable of protecting the regime – in fact, had become a liability – then the military would have to take the initiative and save it instead.

In the hours that followed, Egypt waited with bated breath, expecting news to arrive any minute that Mubarak was handing power over to the army. When the president did appear, however, it was to make a third and final speech in which he announced that he was delegating all his powers to Suleiman, but that he would not be standing down until the end of his term.

Finally, abandoning his attempts to blame the revolution on Islamist plots or foreign conspiracies, he addressed the young revolutionaries directly, telling them that he was willing to meet all their demands short of his resignation. He called for a series of constitutional amendments concerning the state of emergency, presidential elections and term limits (although without any of the powers of the presidency being affected). He claimed that the only reason he wanted to stay in office was to protect the constitution and the country, and he swore that he would hold those who had caused the deaths of demonstrators to account. But he continued to deny any personal responsibility. The problem was not with the regime but with a few bad apples.

These promises and declarations of good faith were naturally accompanied by a heavy dose of sentimentality. Mubarak reminded listeners of his involvement in the 1973 war, which retains a great deal of symbolic power in popular Egyptian consciousness, claiming responsibility for having retaken Sinai. He also emphasized his successes in preventing further wars while refusing to bow down to foreign pressure, playing the role of the maligned and unappreciated hero.

The speech, of course, made no mention of the SCAF communiqué. Mubarak was trying to put the idea of his resignation to bed by appealing to the general population, hoping that he could establish himself as a mediator between them and the army, which had already effectively started to take power. But this bet did not pay off. The people sided with the army in the belief that the army was siding with them.

Mubarak's time was up. Other than the officers of the Republican Guard and a few close allies within the political establishment, he stood alone. Nonetheless, he made it quite clear that he would not be leaving Egypt and that he intended to die in the country in which he had been born. By doing so, he ruled out the Ben Ali option.

3 Behind the scenes

Hossam Badrawi, then the newly appointed secretary general of the NDP, maintained that Mubarak himself was willing to resign, but that others around him pressured him to stay on in order to preserve their own interests.[341] Menawy makes the same argument in his book, where he claims that Gamal Mubarak and various others uninvolved in the management of the crisis had prevented Mubarak from making concessions, including with his resignation. He eventually resigned when he was on his own in Sharm El-Sheikh or on his way there. Menawy bases his story on direct

---

[341] Menawy, *The Last Days*, 302.

impressions and conversations with security operatives and Information Minister Anas El-Fiqqi, who was supposedly very close to the family.[342]

On the same day that the speech was broadcast, the head of the CIA informed the US Senate that Mubarak would be resigning that day. The White House seems to have been convinced that this was what was going to happen, and when Mubarak did not announce his resignation as expected, the US administration released a statement saying that he had not gone far enough. The media reported that Obama had said as much to Mubarak that day.

Mubarak's speech was pre-recorded and showed unmistakable signs of having been cut and edited before being broadcast an hour and a half later than expected. Rumour had it that he had agreed with the army and the United States that he would resign, but had changed his speech at the last minute. On a visit to Michigan, Obama gave reporters a statement that suggested Mubarak would be stepping down.[343] In any case, Washington had certainly abandoned its former ally, and Obama took pains to emphasize that the United States stood with 'the Egyptian people', although that had manifestly not been the case.

Before giving his speech, Mubarak spoke to former Israeli defence minister Binyamin Ben-Eliezer, who has described himself as a friend of the Mubarak family. Ben-Eliezer claims that during their twenty-minute phone call, Mubarak told him:

> We see the democracy the US spearheaded in Iran and with Hamas, in Gaza, and that's the fate of the Middle East. [. . .] They may be talking about democracy but they don't know what they're talking about and the result will be extremism and radical Islam. [. . .] I have been serving my country, Egypt, for 61 years. Do they want me to run away? I won't run away. Do they want to throw me out? I won't leave. If need be, I will be killed here.[344]

Ben-Eliezer's comments reveal that Mubarak remained stubbornly convinced that he was in the right until the very end, refusing to believe he had made mistakes or had lost his legitimacy. He maintained that he had been the victim of a conspiracy and that democracy would only bring the Islamists to power. This reinforces my thesis: one, he did not resign; two, this was his own conviction; and three, he was toppled by a coup.

Most of the demonstrators stopped watching Mubarak's speech once it became obvious that he was not announcing his resignation. In the

---

[342] Ibid., 410–1, 417.
[343] *Radiosawa*, 10 February 2011, Available online: https://arbne.ws/2YWsbb8 (accessed 17 October 2021).
[344] *Ynet*, 11 February 2011, Available online: https://bit.ly/2RrlYwX (accessed 20 December 2014).

square, the chants rose up demanding his resignation, and the reality of the regime's weakness meant he was forced to. Within minutes of Mubarak's speech, Suleiman made another speech broadcast on state TV, praising the 25 January revolution and its 'success in bringing about an important change towards democracy'. He affirmed that he had accepted the powers of the presidency and that he would be putting into place the five points mentioned in Mubarak's speech: a peaceful handover of power, a full national dialogue, preserving the achievements of the youth's revolution, respect for the constitution and full implementation of the people's demands. He also reiterated his old claims about foreign incitement.

The young revolutionaries, and with them millions of other Egyptians, had put their faith in the revolutionary path – and their programme might have been implemented if they had managed to bring to power a revolutionary force capable of doing so. But it was the army that took power, and its approach did not differ from that set out by Mubarak in his speech. The army mounted a coup against not only Mubarak but the revolution itself.

4 The end (11 February)

Mubarak's last speech triggered a wave of anger in Tahrir and across Egypt's cities. The army had heavily implied that the president would be standing down, and senior officers like Hassan al-Roueini, commander of the Central Military Zone, had told demonstrators to prepare for a resignation during the speech. Expectations had been high. RYC members immediately met behind the field hospital, where they agreed to take immediate steps to escalate revolutionary activity. One suggestion was to surround the Egyptian broadcasting headquarters at Maspero and the presidential palace. After a long discussion, however, it was agreed that they would leave the presidential palace until Friday, so as not to empty the square of demonstrators and provide the regime with an opening.[345] The traditional parties mostly objected to this idea, afraid of clashes with the army. Marches nonetheless set off in both directions, but most of the marchers were picked up by the army and taken back to the square in military vehicles. Only a small vanguard of protesters managed to reach the presidential palace.

On Friday, 11 February, millions of Egyptians poured into the streets. The revolutionary forces, the traditional opposition parties and the labour unions joined forces to organize million-man marches across Egypt, with eight to twelve million citizens taking part countrywide. Regardless of the precise numbers, the vast protests that filled the streets and squares of

---

[345] Hany Mahmoud, personal interview.

Cairo and Alexandria in particular showed just how angry people were and how much they wanted to challenge the regime.

Demonstrators joined in Friday prayers, during which imams delivered sermons that cursed Mubarak openly. Those in Cairo then began to move towards the presidential palace in Qasr al-Uruba, where Mubarak and his family were. Those in Alexandria headed for Mubarak's official residence in Ras al-Tin. The army redeployed its troops around the presidential palace. These manoeuvrings and the unprecedented size of the protests meant that a confrontation with Mubarak was now entering its final stages. There was no longer any sign of support for the president anywhere – the pro-regime demonstrators had disappeared. In the absence of the security forces, the military was now under pressure to do something. A Republican Guard officer responded to the escalating chants after crowds were forced to allow cars to exit the palace by telling protesters, 'There's no need to get too excited – it's all over anyway.'

This was at 2.00 pm, by which time several officers and conscripts had joined the ranks of the demonstrators, meaning that the army itself was starting to lose control of its forces. The end had arrived for Mubarak. The army had expressed its willingness to protect him if he stood down, but instead he had chosen confrontation.

SCAF's response to the speech was to issue Communiqué No. 2, which sought to reassure the revolutionaries, some of whom had already called on the army to force Mubarak to step down. It was more detailed than the first communiqué, demonstrating quite clearly that the president's time was up. It cast the army as the guarantor of all Suleiman's promises, setting out a clear agenda: an end to the state of emergency 'as soon as the current conditions are overcome'; completion and implementation of the judicial challenges to the results of the 2010 elections; legislative amendments and free and fair presidential elections. The point of all this was specifically to make the transition to a democracy. At the same time, it emphasized the need for a return to normal life and an end to the demonstrations, while promising to protect those who had 'refused to accept corruption', implicitly conceding the presence of corruption within the regime.

The communiqué was released as protesters were still laying siege to the presidential palace.

At 6.00 pm, during this escalation, Suleiman appeared on state TV to read a short prepared statement – read from SCAF headquarters – announcing that Mubarak had resigned and handed over power to SCAF. A massive wave of pure, unadulterated joy swept the streets; the deposed president left with his family for Sharm El-Sheikh.

Despite calls from the stages to stay, to make sure that their demands were met, people began to leave the square.

5

Revolution in the provinces

In this chapter, we will look at the revolutionary mobilizations outside the capital city, an element of the Egyptian revolution that most studies have neglected. The participation of Egyptians from all over the country made the revolution a truly national affair. The narrative given here relies primarily on accounts given by participating activists, and is intended only to address this hole in the bigger picture. Of course, the role of the governorates was not restricted to the stories told by activists who remained outside Cairo. Many of those who filled the streets of the capital – especially after the Friday of Rage – had made their way there from elsewhere to participate in the demonstrations, well aware that it would be in Cairo that the fate of the revolution would be decided.

Nonetheless, while the main developments took place in Cairo, other areas also played an important role. Events in Suez were crucial to the first few days of the revolution, while Alexandria, Egypt's second-largest city, saw its fair share of revolutionary activity (and without the news that trickled in from Alexandria and the other governorates it seems unlikely that demonstrators in Tahrir Square could have maintained momentum for so long). Mahalla, bastion of the labour movement, also holds a special place in the history of the revolution for this reason.

I Mahalla Al-Kubra

1 25 January: Unions and politics in the Egyptian revolution

Mahalla Al-Kubra was one of the first cities to witness an organized popular mobilization on the eve of the revolution, aided by its long history of protest. As we have already seen in Chapter 3, the workers of the Spinning and Weaving Company had been central to the Egyptian protest movement for the last decade, and 6 April – born in Mahalla a few years before the revolution – was one of the most prominent of the new social movements.

Politically speaking, the attention of Mahalla's youth had largely been focused on pan-Arab issues; Ahmed Abdel Qader, a DFP member from the city, recalls that secondary school students had organized enormous demonstrations around the Second Intifada (2000), the US invasion of Iraq (2003) and the Israeli attack on Gaza (winter 2008–9). Their political consciousness had been shaped by critical voices coming from Al Jazeera, the more daring parts of the Egyptian private media, the activities of Kefaya and the possibilities for debate and discussion provided by Facebook.[1]

In the run-up to 25 January, the Mahalla Al-Kubra IPCC[2] issued a statement in support of planned protests, and on the evening of 21 January the IPCC and 6 April organized a conference with representatives of various political parties and activist groups from across the Nile Delta (held at the DFP HQ in Mahalla itself), encouraging locals to take part in the events planned for 25 January.[3] On the same day, a small group of activists (between thirty and fifty people) held a solidarity demonstration outside the city council building in support of the Tunisian revolution, joined by a number of passers-by; attendees took the opportunity to demand Habib el-Adly's dismissal. All of Mahalla's political forces were in favour of demonstrations, although the Wafd and the Brotherhood were wary of participating as institutions and instead decided to simply allow individual participation by members.[4]

On 22 January, more than 1,000 people joined a demonstration by horse-cart drivers against harassment by the traffic authorities, which regularly confiscated horses and goods and restricted the movement of carts around the city centre. A few days later, horse-cart drivers were to throw themselves enthusiastically into the National Police Day demonstrations.[5]

On 23 January, the IPCC met again to plan demonstrations for 25 January. As in Cairo, it was agreed that various small groups would converge on

---

[1] Ahmed Abdel Qader (DFP in Mahalla), personal interview, conducted by Ahmed Abd Rabou and Islam Hegazy in Mahalla, 19 December 2011. Most of the interviews that this section draws on were conducted during group discussions bringing together activists from various political movements and parties active in Mahalla, allowing for a lively debate. This has often allowed for a more accurate description of events without downplaying the role of any particular group.
[2] See the section on Mahalla Al-Kubra.
[3] The choice of location should not be taken to mean that the DFP was more central to the struggle than the other political parties. There were two main reasons why this party ended up being the host for much of Mahalla's activity: the DFP HQ is located on Bandar Square in the city centre, close to Shoun Square, and is easy to get to from almost anywhere in the city. It is also relatively spacious. These two qualities made it into a centre of activity for all political and social movements in Mahalla, including those parties that lacked premises of their own. The DFP had an unusually active and unusually intergenerational group of members, something which was immediately obvious during the interviews conducted for this book. The DFP's secretary general for Youth Abdelmonem Emam was a Mahalla local, and his presence galvanized youth activity in the city generally. Abdelmonem Emam, personal interview, conducted by Nerouz Satik over Skype, 17 November 2014.
[4] Alaa Bhlawan, personal interview.
[5] Ibid.

Shoun Square from multiple directions, and that activists would maintain a steady flow of people into the demonstration to give the impression of organic growth and encourage passers-by to join in.[6]

On the day, eleven young activists left the DFP headquarters and marched towards Shoun Square, where as planned they were joined by hundreds and then thousands of protesters from the surrounding area.[7] The demonstration included representatives of all the major political movements.[8] A video uploaded to YouTube shows a vast gathering of citizens tearing up pictures of Mubarak while chanting 'out, out with Hosni Mubarak!' and 'we don't want him!' A portrait of the president that hung over the main square was pulled down and ripped to pieces.[9] Some attendees brought pictures of Nasser and Sadat, although the latter proved very controversial and quickly disappeared.[10] (Nasser's pictures stayed: 'Mahalla people are generally very fond of Nasser,' says Abdel Qader.)[11]

Mahalla's long history of protest was key to the revolutionary activity in the city: the influence of union membership was clear from the outset. Despite the large Christian and Muslim communities living in the city, there have been no significant sectarian tensions of the kind witnessed elsewhere. As Abdel Qader said, 'When the Church of the Saints incident happened, we all went and celebrated the Coptic eid[12] at the Church of the Virgin, the biggest church in Mahalla. There were no tensions in the aftermath – and ever since, all the political movements have sent delegations to the Church of the Virgin on every Coptic holiday.'[13]

The security forces, supported by local thugs, attempted to contain the demonstration using various methods: a counter-demonstration, assaults on protesters, attempts to partially surround marchers and, finally, dialogue. All of these methods ultimately failed. There were simply too many people who had left their homes and workplaces to join in. That evening, encouraged by the news from Cairo, organizers decided to bring the sit-in to an end and reconvene the following day.[14]

The constant communication with demonstrators in Cairo was crucial. For the first time, protesters in Mahalla felt that they were part of a movement that extended far beyond the local region. 'We were in constant

---

[6] Ibid.
[7] Mohamed Fathi (Popular Socialist Coalition), personal interview, conducted by Ahmed Abd Rabou and Islam Hegazy in Mahalla, 20 December 2011.
[8] Ibid.
[9] *YouTube*, 25 January 2011, Available online: https://bit.ly/33uOWld (accessed 17 October 2021).
[10] Fathy Abdelhamid, personal interview.
[11] Ahmed Abdel Qader, personal interview.
[12] That is, Christmas.
[13] Ahmed Abdel Qader, personal interview.
[14] Alaa Bhlawan, personal interview.

phone contact with them. We encouraged them,' said one activist. 'For example, we told them that there were fifty thousand of us in Shoun Square – which there weren't! And in the same way, they told us that there were hundreds of thousands of people in Tahrir Square.'[15]

It is notable that in Mahalla the strength of union solidarity and the bonds produced by the city's history of protest allowed the movement to overcome the disappointment and disillusionment of the failed general strike of 6 April 2008. 'It would have made sense for participation in Mahalla to be limited, given the on-going effects of the demonstrations on 6 and 7 April 2008. On that occasion, it was the only [city] to revolt – and as a result, we had to work very hard to get people to come out onto the streets again,' Abdel Qader said.[16] But while the events of the strike had certainly left a bitter taste, they had also created a broad-based movement. Many young people had developed a new interest in politics and were now to form the backbone of the revolutionary activities in Mahalla. The 6 April Movement was not a party organization: 'We worked through the parties, independently of our leaders in Cairo.'[17]

There was another reason for the relative ease of the 2011 demonstrations compared to those of 2008. Abdel Qader explained: 'In April 2008, Mahalla was at the epicentre of events. Security reinforcements were brought in from five different directorates to put down [the protests]. But on 25 January, the security forces were spread out across several governorates.'[18]

The events of 25 January were marked by high participation from groups usually described as middle class, including students, recent graduates, and party and union officials. Some believe that this was the most important factor in the success of the demonstrations on this first day. Clashes with the security forces only began at midnight, when most demonstrators began to leave the area; ultimately, only twenty-five remained in place, many of whom were arrested.[19]

2 26 and 27 January: The security forces recover

Around noon on the following day, the security forces surrounded the headquarters of the DFP, arresting anyone who tried to enter or leave. Speaking by telephone to those inside – who, as noted, represented the various political groups and parties active in Mahalla – they offered to release detainees in exchange for signed guarantees that they would

---

[15] Ibid.
[16] Ahmed Abdel Qader, personal interview.
[17] Ibid.
[18] Ibid.
[19] Ibid.

organize no further demonstrations.[20] The cordon remained in place until midnight.[21] Meanwhile, activists' attempts to muster a fresh demonstration elsewhere in Mahalla were stymied by an intense security presence.[22] Several members of 6 April were arrested as part of a sweep carried out by the security forces in coordination with local NDP leadership.[23]

On 27 January, local lawyers held a demonstration that attracted many passers-by. No clashes with the security forces took place.[24]

3 28 January: The Friday of Rage

At Friday prayers on 28 January, preachers railed against demonstrators,[25] but nonetheless, once prayers were over, locals flowed into Shoun Square, where they were surrounded by large numbers of CSF men.[26] Before the communications blackout, activists worked hard to mislead the security forces by promoting alternative demonstration sites and discussing them in (likely tapped) phone calls, sending them careening off across the city in an effort to cover all possible protests.[27]

Tens of thousands of people took part in the Friday of Rage,[28] which in Mahalla was the biggest protest event of the revolution.[29] Local activists and their families provided the necessary materials,[30] and all political forces (including the Brotherhood) were in attendance.[31]

Despite a fairly raucous crowd keen to avenge those killed in Suez, there were no clashes with security forces early on in the day. Towards evening, however, the security forces fired tear gas into the crowds, setting off street fighting in the eastern and western parts of the city that continued until the following day.[32] One demonstrator was killed, and a group of angry protesters attacked a police station. No public property was destroyed, however, thanks to the establishment of popular committees by activists

---

[20] Alaa Bhlawan, personal interview.
[21] Hamdy Fakhrany (DFP/NAC and member of the people's parliament 2011–2), personal interview, conducted by Hani Awwad, 22 August 2012.
[22] Ahmed Abdel Qader, personal interview.
[23] Mohammad Fethy, personal interview.
[24] Alaa Bhlawan, personal interview.
[25] Some were direct employees of SSIS, while others were Salafists, according to Hamdy Fakhrany.
[26] Alaa Bhlawan, personal interview.
[27] Ahmed Abdel Qader, personal interview.
[28] Ibid.
[29] Various interviews.
[30] Shadi al-Rakhawy (DFP), personal interview, conducted by Ahmed Abd Rabou and Islam Hegazy, 19 and 20 December 2011.
[31] Alaa Bhlawan, personal interview.
[32] Ahmed Abdel Qader, personal interview.

and party leaders. These committees also prevented attacks on the houses of NDP officials.[33]

At around the same time, security personnel had completely lost control in Tanta – the administrative centre of the governorate – and were increasingly confused and angry.[34] That evening they withdrew from the streets of Mahalla and bunkered down in police stations, leading to direct attacks on the stations themselves. Some locals also attacked a shop selling alcohol, after which the Brotherhood warned its members to stay away from the area in order to avoid being blamed for the attack. This shop was the only one in the city to be damaged during the revolution.[35]

Late that evening, army forces also left Cairo for Mahalla, although they only arrived early the next day. As in Cairo, locals welcomed the army, with some of them spray-painting 'down with Mubarak!' on the sides of armoured cars without any objection from the drivers.[36] Nonetheless, the army's arrival made the political elite – still unsure of its position – quite anxious. Activists in Cairo reassured them that the army was not out to crush the revolution.[37]

Friday saw wide participation from all demographics, and produced several new leaders who would be prominent during the following days.

4 29–31 January

The Friday of Rage was decisive. The security forces had been completely defeated, just as in Cairo, and locals took on the responsibility of protecting private property while the army took up their stations around state institutions. One reserve officer called up during the crisis confirms that the army had not been given orders to fire on anyone.[38]

The day of 29 January saw an attack on a local police station intended to free prisoners, as security forces stood by and watched.[39] As news of the revolution in Cairo trickled in, a handful of officers with the SSIS with particularly bad reputations fled the station in government cars.[40] Angry young protesters stormed a police building, scattering its contents around the street. Other police stations were also set on fire, although the two main

---

[33] Alaa Bhlawan, personal interview.
[34] Mohammad Fethy, personal interview.
[35] Ahmed Sami (Muslim Brotherhood), personal interview, conducted by Ahmed Abd Rabou and Islam Hegazy in Mahalla Al-Kubra, 20 December 2011.
[36] Ahmed Abdel Qader, personal interview.
[37] Alaa Bhlawan, personal interview.
[38] Abdulhamid al-Basyuni (former air force engineer, retired 1987), personal interview, conducted by Islam Hegazy in Mahalla Al-Kubra, 20 December 2011.
[39] Ahmed Sami, personal interview.
[40] Mohammad Murad (IPCC member for the Labour Party), personal interview, conducted by Ahmed Abd Rabou and Islam Hegazy in Mahalla Al-Kubra, 20 December 2011.

security buildings in the city were protected by a popular committee set up by members of Salafist Islah Society. After ten rifles were stolen from a central armoury, a citywide appeal to return the weapons was launched via mosques and loudspeakers.[41]

With the security forces gone, demonstrators made use of their newfound freedom, gathering in Shoun Square – renamed 'Revolution Square' – and setting up placards and loudspeakers. Mohammad al-Abbasi, a local preacher, gave a speech in which he cast himself as the leader of the revolution in Mahalla (showing a sort of opportunism not uncommon among those who sought to take advantage of their eloquence and religious rhetoric as soon as the security forces were out of the picture), and the attendees prayed evening prayers together.[42] Organized popular committees were set up in almost every part of Mahalla,[43] alongside various party committees run by different local organizations, including the Brotherhood and the Salafists.[44] Once the communications blackout ended around midday, the IPCC acted as an essential interface between these different committees.[45]

On 30 and 31 January, local thugs were active in various areas of the city, making for a tense security situation; the army and the popular committees, however, managed to maintain order. The revolutionaries themselves, meanwhile, were considering their next move, agreeing that the sole guarantee against a regime reaction was to maintain a presence in the streets.[46] Some of those involved received death threats on their mobile phones, while their families faced attempts at intimidation from local NDP members.[47] In fact, even some non-affiliated locals shouted threats and insults at demonstrators from their balconies: the demonstrations still did not enjoy the unanimous support of the population.[48]

It seems likely that the local security forces, left without instructions by their superiors in the capital and taken completely by surprise, acted on their own initiative in this period. Falling back on the tried-and-tested technique of setting neighbourhood thugs on the protesters, they scrambled to burn and shred all documentary evidence of their activities in the city. It is quite plausible that the defeat of security forces in Cairo itself sent a wave of mass hysteria crashing over the security forces in the governorates.

---

[41] Ahmed Sami, personal interview.
[42] Ismail Abdelhafez, personal interview, 20 December 2011.
[43] Abdulhamid al-Basyuni, personal interview.
[44] Personal interviews with Ahmed Sami and Abdulhamid al-Basyuni.
[45] Abdulhamid al-Basyuni, personal interview.
[46] Various interviews.
[47] Ismail Abdelhafez, personal interview.
[48] Alaa Bhlawan, personal interview.

It is also worth noting that despite the deep roots of unionism in the city and the high level of education and familiarity with peaceful protest among those that first initiated the demonstrations, participation from those on the margins of society nonetheless brought with it considerable violence.

5 1–4 February: The countryside takes charge

The first day of February was a historic one in Mahalla: 200,000 people came out to demonstrate, packing Shoun Square and spilling out along the length of Bahr Street for the first time. A celebratory atmosphere prevailed among demonstrators.[49] This was the day of Mubarak's emotional speech, which won over many demonstrators and allowed pro-regime counter-demonstrators to make their first appearance.[50] Although the political elite refused to bring an end to the demonstrations since they knew that this would open the door to regime reprisals, there were many present who disagreed with this decision. Within half an hour of the speech being broadcast, some demonstrators were arguing that they had done what they had set out to achieve, even as others chanted, 'The regime hasn't gone away, this speech is nothing but a play!'[51]

The debates taking place in Mahalla were the same as those playing out across the country. As many of those in Shoun Square were considering going home in response to the speech, tens of thousands of demonstrators were leaving Tahrir Square for the same reason. And on 2 February, as the infamous pro-regime demonstration in Cairo was making its way across the city, a similar demonstration was taking place in Mahalla, organized by the local NDP. Most of those who participated in this demonstration were bussed in from the city's rural hinterland – agricultural and industrial labourers[52] – by NDP parliamentarians;[53] some of them were members of the Salafist organization Ansar al-Sunna or Salafist sheikhs.[54] Opposition figures received messages warning them to stay at home or risk being 'butchered'.[55]

Exploiting social tensions between city and countryside (where most of Mahalla's labourers reside) was a well-established regime strategy to keep political activity in Mahalla in check. The majority of security officers in the city, for example, were originally from rural areas, while prominent regime

[49] Ahmed Abdel Qader, personal interview.
[50] Alaa Bhlawan, personal interview.
[51] Abdulhamid al-Basyuni, personal interview.
[52] Alaa Bhlawan, personal interview.
[53] Hamdy Fakhrany, personal interview.
[54] Ahmed Sami, personal interview.
[55] Alaa Bhlawan, personal interview.

figures like businessman and NDP MP Mahmoud al-Shami maintained extensive patronage networks among village leaders.

Nonetheless, it was not only the regime that sought to exercise influence in the villages and the city's slums. The Brotherhood competed fiercely for the loyalty of these areas as well. In the 2010 elections, the rural vote was split between Shami (who took the seat thanks to an extensive campaign of violence) and the Brotherhood candidate Saad al-Husseini, a split which was to continue even after the revolution. The conflict between the Brotherhood and the NDP in these areas had less to do with ideology than with the fact that they were both popular movements – in the NDP's case, because of the vast resources made available to it by its position in government.

The arrival of the villagers and slum dwellers changed the leadership of the demonstrations completely. The first demonstrators of 25 January had been led by a range of political parties and union bodies active within the city itself.[56] After 1 February, however, the gatherings in Shoun Square took on a distinctly Brotherhood colouring. Dr Omar Amer, who treated many of those injured during the demonstrations, says that attendees were segregated by gender and that the platform set up for speakers was taken over by sheikhs linked to the organization, partially to encourage participants and partially to respond to the Salafist sheikhs who had condemned protesters.[57]

These developments, as well as the presence of many security officers from the countryside, helped Mahmoud al-Shami launch a propaganda counteroffensive against the revolutionaries, whom he branded Brotherhood stooges (foreshadowing the trajectory that the counter-revolution would take two years later). As well as spreading division among protesters already in two minds after Mubarak's speech, this counteroffensive mustered up enough support that on 2 February pro-regime demonstrators from the countryside were able to surround the DFP headquarters and pelt revolutionaries with stones and tiles from the roofs of nearby buildings; when members of the political elite ventured out onto the street, they were set upon with clubs and bats.[58] Attacks by thugs continued, with the army refusing to intervene to protect citizens. In fact, just like in Cairo in advance of the Battle of the Camel, the military contingents in Mahalla were ordered to withdraw from Shoun Square, suggesting less a spontaneous reaction to events and more a planned counter-revolutionary mobilization. Although

---

[56] Mohammed Mousa (Popular Socialist Coalition), personal interview, conducted by Ahmed Abd Rabou and Islam Hegazy in Mahalla Al-Kubra, 20 December 2011.
[57] Dr Omar Amer, personal interview, conducted by Hani Awwad, 22 August 2012.
[58] Alaa Bhlawan, personal interview.

this has not been so obvious to those scholars who have focused exclusively on Cairo, it is clear from Mahalla and elsewhere that the army had decided to give the NDP a chance to suppress the revolution.

Around nightfall and with pro-Mubarak demonstrations still ongoing, a defeated and down-cast opposition decided to delay further protests until 4 February.[59] Had the Battle of the Camel ended in victory for the counter-revolutionaries, similar scenes would likely have been seen in Cairo.

6 4–11 February: Joining Tahrir

On 4 February, Friday prayers were held in Shoun Square; all Brotherhood members were ordered to participate or face sanctions. Al Jazeera broadcast part of the sermon, which gave locals a significant morale boost.[60] After prayers ended, demonstrations set off from various mosques around the city, with huge numbers of people making their way towards Bahr Street. The revolution had regained its momentum.[61]

Participants say that 4 February also saw the first open participation by Mahalla's Copts. Participants interviewed attributed this relatively late arrival to the church's decision to encourage members not to take part. Of course, prominent Coptic activists like Sami Francisco of the IPCC were involved in the demonstrations,[62] but it was only when the clergy and the general congregation took part that people began to talk about 'Coptic participation' (although this runs contrary to the spirit of citizenship and indeed to a democratic understanding of the revolution).

The demonstrations continued throughout 6 and 7 February before beginning to shrink somewhat on Tuesday, 8 February, as revolutionaries from Mahalla began to make the trip to Cairo to join protesters in Tahrir. The armed forces, meanwhile, agreed to set times for demonstrations[63] in order to crack down on violence by pro-regime demonstrators – violence which continued until Mubarak's resignation on 11 February and included targeted assassinations of activists.[64] On 10 February, the Brotherhood gave its members permission to go and protest in Cairo, where they joined the sit-in in front of Maspero. And on 11 February, huge demonstrations were held to call once more for the fall of Mubarak, Omar Suleiman and the NDP.[65]

---

[59] Ibid.
[60] Ahmed Sami, personal interview.
[61] Personal interviews with Mohammad Murad and Fathy Abdelhamid.
[62] Ahmed Sami, personal interview.
[63] Ibid.
[64] Abdulhamid al-Basyuni, personal interview.
[65] Fathy Abdelhamid, personal interview.

II The Suez Uprising

1 Before the revolution

Suez has suffered more than other governorates since the time of Anwar Sadat, when massive corruption during the rebuilding of the city (80 per cent of which had been destroyed during successive clashes with Israel) left the inhabitants with sub-par housing despite their huge wartime sacrifices. In addition, the revenues from the canal, which make up a significant part of Egypt's GDP, have rarely been spent locally. The city itself faces a constant shortage of clean water, despite its ready availability in tourist villages nearby, and has received very little development funding at all since its Gulf-backed reconstruction in the 1980s. Moreover, the governorate suffered more than any other region in Egypt from the neoliberal restructuring pursued by the Mubarak regime: Suez is a city of labourers, and the sell-off of public companies produced a great deal of resentment. Politically, this translated into a strong sense of solidarity with Arab issues. Locals came out in force to protest in solidarity with the Second Intifada, for example, where demonstrators were heard chanting against Mubarak. Note here the similarity with marginalized areas in Tunisia, where pan-Arab protests likewise provided the opportunity to voice grievances against the regime itself.[66]

Most young people in Suez have only a secondary school education and are constantly haunted by the threat of unemployment.[67] Despite the Canal Zone, the various ports and harbours, the oil refineries and the many nearby resorts, there are not enough jobs for the city's many graduates. Workers from other areas of Egypt are often brought in to fill new positions. This has given rise to a pervasive sense of marginalization and neglect similar to that felt in areas like the Gafsa mining basin in Tunisia.[68] Social grievances in marginalized regions take the form of a heightened local identity and resentment towards outsiders. In 1997 it was announced, with a great deal of fanfare, that the government would be investing large sums of money to develop the northern Gulf of Suez,[69] providing a glimmer of hope to local inhabitants. But the project never materialized, and the 25 square kilometres of land set aside for it was redistributed to businessmen, including Ahmed Ezz and Naguib Sawiris, and a Chinese company that paid only 5 Egyptian pounds per square metre (then approximately $1.50).

---

[66] Bishara, *The Glorious Tunisian Revolution*, 195.
[67] Salah Amer Ahmed (YJF secretary), personal interview, conducted by Ahmed Abd Rabou in Suez, 17 November 2011.
[68] Bishara, *The Glorious Tunisian Revolution*, 197–8.
[69] *al-Wafd*, 14 February 2012, Available online: https://bit.ly/2RoP1kZ (accessed 19 November 2014).

After Cairo, Suez was the second centre of Kefaya activity in Egypt. The local political currents all came together, and in the 2005 parliamentary elections, 'Every NDP candidate failed – not a single one reached the second round. The Muslim Brotherhood won two seats and independent candidates another two seats, though the latter two then became MPs for the NDP seats.'[70] In 2010 there was an almost total boycott of the elections.

In both the 2005 and 2010 elections, local businessmen and factory owners forced their employees to vote for NDP candidates at the risk of losing their jobs. In Ramadan 2010, a few months before the revolution, relations between the city and the regime degenerated completely when those same NDP businessmen launched a media campaign in support of Gamal Mubarak. Local activists responded with a counter-campaign, distributing fliers with pictures of the president's son accompanied by the slogan 'Egypt is out of your league!'[71]

2 Preparing for 25 January

For Suez as for other regions, the Tunisian revolution was a major driver of change. The local political elite came out onto the streets en masse to celebrate Ben Ali's flight on 14 January, and on the same day decided to hold anti-Mubarak demonstrations four days later. The proposed date was then pushed back to 21 January, which would allow them to take advantage of the large numbers of people already out to perform Friday prayers. And on Friday, after prayers had been said in Arbaeen Square, the first demonstration of the Egyptian revolution began.[72] The demonstration was not a large one; although it included representatives of every major political movement in the city, participation was restricted to prominent members of the political elite, and the demonstrators (some 70–150 of them) were massively outnumbered by the security forces.[73] Those in attendance chanted pro-Tunisia slogans interspersed with more local calls for change like 'revolution in Tunisia, tomorrow in Egypt, revolution throughout the streets of Egypt!'[74]

---

[70] Ahmed Mahmoud, personal interview, 17 November 2011.
[71] Mohamed Abu Masr (Ghad Party), personal interview, conducted by Ahmed Abd Rabou in Suez, 17 November 2011. All the interviews in this section were conducted during two group discussions including activists and representatives of various political parties within the city.
[72] Arbaeen Square, or 'Martyrs' Square' as it was known after the revolution, is the largest public space in the city.
[73] Much the same as happened in Mahalla on the same day.
[74] Mohamed Abdel Razek (senior figure in the Nasserist Party in Suez), personal interview, conducted by Ahmed Abd Rabou in Suez, 17 November 2011.

On 22 January another demonstration took place in front of the Suez court complex, although less than twenty people attended.[75] Despite the small numbers, however, Brotherhood member Salah Amer Ahmed says that there was a marked tension in the air in these last days before the revolution.

3 25 January

As in other regions of Egypt, the various local organizations and political parties in Suez formed a committee to coordinate the demonstrations planned for 25 January. The committee agreed that demonstrations would begin at noon immediately after the afternoon prayer, hoping to attract as many worshippers as possible to the event. They also spoke to the city's security forces, agreeing that chants would be restricted to social and economic issues. Ahmed Mahmoud, who subsequently became the secretary of the Brotherhood's FJP, explained:

> We agreed that there would be no chants targeting Mubarak's family, but there were a lot of enthusiastic young people who didn't keep to the agreement. As 2.00 pm approached we started to whisper to one another about winding the demonstration down as had been agreed. At that point the security guys, some of whom we knew personally, were expecting us to finish and encouraging us to bring it to a close, since they'd been there since very early in the day and wanted to go home. But around 2.00 pm new faces appeared at the demonstration, faces we weren't used to seeing at demonstrations, people from poor and working-class areas in Suez. These weren't political people at all, and we hadn't expected them to take part. Then people who were usually passive bystanders started to join in, and the numbers just kept rising. When these new participants realized we were intending to bring the demonstration to an end at 2.00 pm, they were offended. The party representatives made it clear that they were against continuing the demonstration, since that was not what had been agreed [with the security services]. But the new people didn't accept that. They hadn't come just to go home straight away, they said. So they decided to continue the demonstration.[76]

Here we see the difference between the dynamism of the traditional political forces and that of the grassroots, the new element responsible for the success of the 25 January revolution. These marginalized, impoverished social groups had never been politically active before. They were not used

---

[75] Ibid.
[76] Ahmed Mahmoud, personal interview.

to the routine rhythm of party protests, but they immediately succeeded in changing that rhythm.

The influx of new protesters increased both the numbers and the ferocity of the demonstrations. Peaceful marches demanding justice, freedom and dignity gave way to violent clashes with the security forces, who used tear gas to try and disperse the protesters. Around 1.30 pm, a driver tried to set himself on fire, imitating Tunisia's Mohamed Bouazizi[77] – not the first self-immolation in Egypt after the Tunisian revolution, but thanks to its timing one of the most dramatic in terms of its effects.[78] 'In that moment, the mass of onlookers joined the demonstration, and that stirred in us a sort of revolutionary feeling that is difficult to describe now,' said local activist Ahmed El-Kelany.[79]

A column of protesters made its way to the Arbaeen Police Station. Having failed to keep the demonstration under control by normal means, the security forces now turned to violence to break it up. An attempt was made to arrest the ringleaders, in particular the activist Arabi Abdel Baset,[80] who was beaten up and dragged to the police station personally by Suez security chief Mohammed Abdel Hadi.[81] Kelany described the scene:

> After the demonstrations were broken up by the security forces and dissipated into the side streets, there were only about 300 people left in the square, and if the director of security hadn't used violence then by 7.00 pm there might only have been fifty of us. But when the security guys insulted us and beat us with truncheons, hundreds of people started pouring into the square from every direction to join us.[82]

Thanks to the fresh wave of popular participation, the demonstrations continued, and the violent police reaction changed the course of events completely. Mohamed Abu Masr calls those moments 'the beginning of open revolution in Suez', saying:

> We went back to Arbaeen Square, and at that moment the call to evening prayer went up, so we prayed in the street. When the imam finished speaking, there was a moment of silence, then all of a sudden the square was absolutely overflowing

---

[77] The driver was saved and prevented from dying.
[78] The man's name did not appear in the media, but all those present confirm that the incident took place.
[79] Ahmed El-Kelany, personal interview.
[80] A Nasserist and Quarrying Union activist involved in Kefaya and pro-Palestine demonstrations in Suez well known for his role in the composition of protest chants.
[81] Mohamed Abdel Razek, personal interview.
[82] Ahmed El-Kelany, personal interview.

with demonstrators. At exactly 6.25, the first shot was fired, and a war for the streets began.[83]

A demonstrator, Mohamed Ragab, had been shot dead by security forces, and over the course of the evening three others shared his fate. Gunfire and street fighting continued through to dawn on 26 January.

The coordination committee and the security forces had agreed on a limited two-hour protest for National Police Day, a march that would be allowed to gather in front of the governorate building so long as it avoided chants targeting the president or his family. But the unexpected involvement of thousands of new faces transformed this orderly protest into a much more ambitious demonstration willing to take on the police directly and protest outside security headquarters. Having never been involved in demonstrations before, of any kind, these new faces put the security forces on the back foot and they responded with live ammunition and tear gas. In turn, the subsequent deaths of four protesters galvanized popular opinion in Suez and elsewhere.

4 26–27 January

In the early hours of 26 January, the families of the four demonstrators killed the previous day attempted to pick up their bodies from the city morgue, but they were turned away by police, who had set up a cordon around the building. The young people present began throwing stones at police, and a scuffle ensued between the two sides. On the evening of the same day, activists and local demonstrators gathered outside the building after a rumour spread that security officials were 'bargaining' with the families over the release of the bodies. In the case of one of those killed, Gharib Aziz, police did in fact manage to pressure the family's to receive the body in secret and bury it without securing an autopsy report attesting to the cause of death.

At around 11.00 pm on 26 January, the police began to act erratically, firing randomly and driving armoured cars towards groups of protesters in the square. The subsequent confrontation lasted until dawn the next day, and on the afternoon of 27 January, thousands gathered in front of the Arbaeen Police Station. Local residents lowered bottles of water and packages of food down to the revolutionaries from their balconies. On both 26 and 27 January, the protests only gathered real momentum in the late

---

[83] Mohamed Abu Masr, personal interview. By 'a war for the streets', he means the fragmentation of the demonstrations into the narrow side streets surrounding the main road. Suez, like Alexandria, consists of a small number of large avenues surrounded by a warren of backstreets and alleyways.

afternoon because most of the city's inhabitants were still going to work or school during the day, only joining the demonstrators afterwards.

5 28 January: The Friday of Rage

Once the families of those killed had agreed to bury their loved ones in secret – an agreement brokered by Hafez Salama (a hero of the anti-colonial movement in Suez), the preacher Safwat Hegazy and the head of the local council, Mohamed Saad – there was no longer any reason to protest outside the morgue. The revolutionaries thus decided that the protest movements and political parties should return to demonstrating in Arbaeen Square.

The demonstrations of 28 January were not purely spontaneous. Egyptians active on Facebook spoke at length with their Tunisian counterparts, who advised them to get the organized movements to protest in the morning and preserve the strength of those more capable of engaging in sustained clashes until the evening; after a long day of policing protests, the security forces would struggle to engage demonstrators in the rabbit warren of backstreets and alleyways.[84] The protesters estimated that the security forces would not be able to maintain this pace for more than three nights without serious reinforcements. The Tunisians also explained how to use onions, vinegar and fizzy drinks to mitigate the effects of tear gas. The revolutionaries put all this advice into practice from the morning of 26 January onwards.[85]

Secondary school and university students took part in the Friday of Rage, as did the poor inhabitants of the working-class districts, including former arrestees who had escaped from Arbaeen Police Station. Young people from Farz, a low-income area adjacent to Arbaeen Square, handed out masks to those arriving to protect them from tear gas. The scene that played out in front of the police station in Arbaeen resembled those seen in Tunisia in preceding weeks: burning fences formed a barrier between protesters and the building, tuk-tuk drivers delivered stones for throwing, and the more protesters were killed or injured, the more first-time demonstrators flooded into the square.[86]

On the morning of 28 January, CSF reinforcements arrived from Ismailia (some 90 kilometres from Suez), but as they were approaching the security building, protesters set fire to their armoured cars and chased them away.[87]

---

[84] This tactic had been successfully used in Tunisia's Sidi Bouzeid throughout the first part of the demonstrations.
[85] Salah Amer Ahmed, personal interview, 17 November 2011.
[86] Interviews with Salah Amer Ahmed and Mohamed Abu Masr.
[87] Mohammed Abdul Latif Hamdan, personal interview, 17 November 2011.

According to the journalist Mohammed Abdul Latif Hamdan:

> At around 2.30 pm, the young people decided to get their revenge on the police for killing demonstrators and injuring dozens more. The guys from the slums were better at making Molotov cocktails than us, and they bombarded the CSF armoured cars parked in Ibrahim Farag Street with them. We were shocked to find that these cars were not, in fact, empty: there were lots of CSF men sleeping inside them, who leapt out and ran away as soon as the first bottle exploded, heading for the Arbaeen police station. Some of the demonstrators went after them, and when we got close to the building, we saw the staff coming out in total disarray. It reached the point that some locals took pity on the security guys and helped them get away.[88]

For the people of Suez, the burning of the Arbaeen Police Station was of huge significance: this was one of the bastions of Mubarak's regime, a symbol of despotism and humiliation. Its destruction meant that the regime was crumbling. Enthusiastic demonstrators surged towards the Suez security headquarters, hoping for a repeat performance there, although the police had managed to regroup there in such a way that this proved impossible, setting up a cordon around the building, even stationing officers on pro-regime businessman Ibrahim Farag's roof.[89] Some fourteen people died in the course of the demonstrations.

As the pressure on Suez increased, the revolutionaries coordinated further activities in Ismailia in an attempt to reduce it. On the Friday of Rage, tens of thousands of demonstrators came out onto the streets – an unprecedented number for the city and a turning point in its history. At around 7.00 pm, the police withdrew entirely as the army deployed around the Cairo road, and by 10.30 pm armoured vehicles had taken up positions on Arbaeen Square. As in Cairo, the demonstrators gave them an enthusiastic welcome.[90]

6 29 January

On 29 January, the Giza Security Directorate in Cairo sent a force of pro-regime thugs to its counterpart in Suez. These troublemakers were allowed to run riot in the streets of Suez throughout the evening, and a wave of theft and looting broke across the city. On the same day, popular committees

---

[88] Ibid.
[89] The Nasserist leader Mohamed Abdel Razek says that Farag came from humble origins before becoming rich by dubious means in the 1970s. He was a local symbol of corruption and the link between wealth and government.
[90] Ahmed Mahmoud, personal interview.

had been formed to protect citizens' property.[91] The army, meanwhile, does not seem to have intervened directly at all to prevent looting and rioting.

7 1–11 February

Just as elsewhere, many of Suez's inhabitants were genuinely affected by Mubarak's emotional speech broadcast on 1 February. A number concluded that the revolution had achieved most of its aims and that it was time to go home. On 2 February, thousands of pro-regime demonstrators, including many senior NDP figures and representatives from local and village councils, filled Arbaeen Square, waving pictures of Mubarak and shouting his name over loudspeakers.[92] As elsewhere, they were accompanied by security forces,[93] showing once again that the pro-regime demonstrations on this day were organized centrally throughout the country.

The remaining protesters decided to begin their counter-protest from Martyrs' Mosque instead of Arbaeen Square in order to avoid clashes with pro-regime demonstrators, but armed thugs were sent to their location deliberately and clashes broke out between the two sides. Just as in Cairo – where the Battle of the Camel was taking place at the same time – the ensuing violence did much to undermine the impact of Mubarak's second speech.

Further clashes took place on 3 February as demonstrators chanted against the Ahmed Shafik government and accused it of sending thugs to attack them; the army did not intervene. One proud son of Suez who had made his way to Cairo to join the protests there said:

> All across Tahrir, people were singing *O Houses of Suez*[94] [...] not to mention the incredible welcome they gave us as soon as we got there. People we didn't know were hugging us and kissing us – one guy was there with his twelve-year-old son, and after he'd greeted me enthusiastically he told his son to kiss my hand because I was from Suez![95]

The bloody confrontations and the killing of several demonstrators on the first day of the revolution gave Suez a special place in Egyptians' hearts, making it a symbol of resistance to the security forces. The city was already closely associated in the popular consciousness with the struggle against British colonialism and Israeli aggression, and in the wave of patriotic

---

[91] Mohamed Abu Masr, personal interview.
[92] See the entry on the same day in Mahalla for more examples.
[93] Mohamed Abu Masr, personal interview.
[94] A popular song about the city of Suez originally sung by Mohammad Hamam (1942–2007).
[95] Mohamed Abu Masr, personal interview.

feeling that accompanied the revolution it was only natural that it would take a prominent place in the revolutionary symbolic pantheon.

After Mubarak's unexpected refusal to step down in his speech of 10 February, demonstrators again gathered in front of the governorate building carrying placards with the names of those who had been killed. Several soldiers were sent by the army to help hang the placards, demonstrating its sympathy for demonstrators. After evening prayers, all those present waited expectantly for news that the president was standing down. Shortly thereafter, Omar Suleiman appeared on TV to announce Mubarak's resignation, and Suez celebrated like it had never celebrated before.[96]

III Alexandria

Alexandria was a protest hotspot on 25 January, and it was key to the broad, national character of the revolution.

Alexandria is distinct from other Egyptian governorates. It is a big city, with almost four million inhabitants, but unlike Cairo almost all of the working population is local – there is no significant 'outsider' presence except during holiday season. It has no vast slum districts of the kind found in Cairo. And it is no exaggeration to say that it has its own distinctive local identity.

Alexandria is built along a lengthy waterfront, which makes demonstrations quite difficult. The easternmost point of the city is almost 70 kilometres away from the westernmost, and it takes time and a great deal of planning to get the inhabitants of the various residential areas to gather in a specific spot. There is no single city centre, but rather 'various independent centres, as well as new suburbs out in the desert. . . . So there were individual spots of population density, exhaustion and protest scattered all over the place. The new suburbs are characterized by overcrowding, nothing but overcrowding and their position – the fact that they branch off the motorways'.[97]

The tourist road opened in 2002 had helped connect Alexandria with some of the Bedouin villages in its environs, but these suburbs could hardly be described as a 'poverty belt'. The security forces maintained a tight grip on Alexandria throughout the Mubarak era: the narrow margin of freedom won by Cairenes during the 2000s did not extend to their counterparts in Egypt's second city. Indeed, young people interested in politics often chose to relocate to Cairo.

[96] Mohammed Abdul Latif Hamdan, personal interview.
[97] Alaa Khaled, *Alexandrian Faces* [Arabic], 2nd edn (Cairo: Shorouk, 2013), 247–8.

But Alexandria also has another important distinguishing feature that may represent the key to understanding its political and social mobilization. According to Alaa Khaled, a local poet, Alexandrians feel:

> An ancient heritage has been lost, like the local notables who live on memories of the past. In the depths of their souls they feel mistreated – that there is no longer enough space for their ambitions, their sense of defeat, their new selves. These new selves were formed under the influence of another centre: the capital. They feel a secret attraction to [Cairo]'s people. They want to imitate Cairenes but also to take revenge on them. A sense of inferiority develops, not out of love or as a result of class distinctions within a single family, but from a broader sense that the city is weak.[98]

Alexandria is a city of ancient treasures, a city that like other great port cities was long characterized by a Mediterranean melange of cultures, religions and languages, and this has strongly affected its self-image vis-à-vis Cairo. The effect can be seen both in intellectual circles that trumpet the city's cosmopolitan heritage and in other circles (the Salafists, for example) that reject it outright.

Without understanding the effect of local identity, it is impossible to understand Alexandria's political, social or even religious movements. The city's liberals, leftists, nationalists and Islamists are invariably more radical in their positions on the regime; western Alexandria's famous Salafists are more Salafist than their counterparts elsewhere in Egypt. The same applies to unions, cultural movements and youth organizations, which have generally considered the elites of the capital to be more subservient and 'pragmatic' in their relationship with the regime. The Alexandrian elite has often felt that its desire to play the political role to which it is entitled is constantly running up against its distance from Cairo. It is for this reason that the revolutionary mobilization in Alexandria kept going until Mubarak's resignation, rather than petering out as demonstrators made their way to Cairo as happened in other areas of Egypt.

But just as local politics was more radical in Alexandria, so too were the security forces more repressive – or at least this was how Alexandrians felt. Kholoud Saeed, an activist, says:

> Alexandria was the torture capital of Egypt. The security forces in the city were famous for torturing activists and treating them brutally. And the public sphere was totally deprived of air – Alexandria University, for example, had an enormous security presence, unlike Cairo or Ain Shams, which enjoyed a certain margin

---

[98] Ibid., 16.

of freedom. [...] There was no forum or space whatsoever open to us, and if we wanted to do anything – whether journalism, cinema, writing or singing – we would go to Cairo.[99]

There is no way of knowing how different Alexandria's experience of security repression really was from other, more marginalized cities. But unlike the inhabitants of these cities, Alexandrians prefer to compare their experience with that of Cairo. They believed Cairo to be awash with media outlets, journalists and civil society organizations, which naturally subjected police activities to a certain kind of scrutiny. In Alexandria, meanwhile, there were many political movements but very little political space, the product of a growing middle class and a low poverty rate compared to other parts of the country.

The stability of the city's demographic make-up and the local roots of most of its inhabitants meant that the security forces were able to work with a familiar social map. This made it easier for them to identify sensitive areas, keep track of activists and establish ready contact with their leaders during crises.

Compared to Cairo, the political forces of Alexandria were already coordinating closely with one another by the revolution: an IPCC had existed since the Khaled Saeed protests in June 2010.[100] On the one hand, in a city where the security forces maintained an iron grip on all political activity, there was a sense that all political movements were all in the same boat. On the other, the 'Alexandrian character' – the elite's feeling of being 'one big family' – provided a framework within which it was possible to work together. And given the particular geography of the city and the omnipresence of the security forces, social media was of paramount importance.

Between 2008 and 2010, successive waves of tension swept through Alexandria. These tensions coincided with a rising poverty rate – from 6 to 11 per cent, according to the national statistics agency.[101] A series of major coastal storms hit the city, causing considerable damage, and in December 2010, a factory roof collapsed, killing dozens of workers.[102] These tensions

---

[99] Kholoud Saeed (translator and civil society activist), personal interview, conducted by Ahmed Abd Rabou and Aly El Raggal, Alexandria, 7 December 2011.
[100] Personal interviews with Mohamed Samir and Ahmed Fahmy.
[101] Central Agency for Public Mobilization and Statistics, *Select Poverty Indicators from Survey of Income, Expenditure and Consumption 2010/2011* [Arabic] (Cairo: CAPMAS, 2011), Available online: https://bit.ly/3pbOQeY (accessed 17 October 2021).
[102] The Moharram Bek textile factory was a six-storey building in the Hadra district. Its roof collapsed on 13 December 2010 after a heavy rainstorm, killing most of the thirty workers present in the building. See: *Al-Masry Al-Youm*, 16 December 2010, Available online: https://bit.ly/3pb1jzi (accessed 17 October 2021). The main reason for accidents like these in Egypt and in Alexandria in particular is widespread corruption in the construction sector and the failure of government

gave rise to unprecedented confrontations with the police, be it skirmishes between security forces and street peddlers or youth sit-ins in solidarity with detainees or against Mubarak's attempts to bequeath the presidency to his son.[103]

If not for social media, the killing of Khaled Saeed in custody would never have turned into the major public issue that it did. The same is true of Sayed Belal, who died under similar circumstances before being posthumously framed for the Church of the Saints bombing. Belal's Salafist background did not prevent Alexandria's varied political currents – Islamists, liberals, leftists – from rallying around his cause. Khaled Saeed's death had prompted the creation of a new public space allowing for unprecedented discussion of the political situation and the regime. Not only this, but in this new space the young people of Alexandria discovered that they were not an isolated minority, as they had believed, but that there were thousands of others just like them who shared their opinions and their desire for action. This was something that the traditional political parties had never imagined possible.

Mohamed Samir, a local activist,[104] said:

> Thanks to the Khaled Saeed page, we were able to hold two sessions with a range of different groups – liberals, socialists, independents in the Ghad Party – and as a result to organize two different actions. [. . .] After that, there was a clear need for on-going, consistent coordination. And that's how the Coordination Office came to be, which represented all the political forces in Alexandria, including the Brotherhood, the Baradei Campaign, 6 April, the socialists and Revolutionary Socialists, Hashd, the Karama Party, the Liberals, the Democratic Front [DFP] and the Ghad Party.[105]

The young people involved in the Coordination Office did not realize that they were in the process of becoming a political force in their own right. But thanks to their meticulous planning, their careful division of labour, their organization and their secrecy, that was exactly what was happening. Their bravery and willingness to engage in real-world action drew in all the other traditional forces, including the Brotherhood. This development was further encouraged by the fact that the office's members had no specific

---

policy in this area. For more on this see: *Al-Masry Al-Youm*, 1 January 2011, Available online: https://bit.ly/3iy0afd (accessed 15 December 2014).

[103] Ahmed Nagy (news photographer for *Shorouk* and civil society activist), personal interview, conducted by Ahmed Abd Rabou and Aly El Raggal, Alexandria, 7 December 2011.

[104] The interviews used in this section were conducted during two group discussions with members of a range of political movements.

[105] Mohamed Samir, personal interview.

factional identity – its purpose was to protest, fight against the regime and correct the course of corrupt state institutions. When they protested against torture and political detention irrespective of the identity of the victim, their credibility grew even more.[106] Acting mostly via the internet and operating on the basis of consensus and voluntary participation, this group of young people was able to tie together the activities of all the political parties.

One of the first things activists noticed when the office began operating was just how afraid of the police many people were. Mohamed Samir said, 'We decided to hold a sit-in at the train station to protest the power cuts. We were chanting, "They sell Israel gas while we live by lamplight!" People started to join in enthusiastically. But when we started chanting "down with State Security!" they got scared, went quiet and then disappeared.'[107]

On the eve of 25 January, the Baradei campaign, 6 April and the Ghad Party were all in favour of mobilizing and took responsibility for turning digital protest into real-life demonstrations. The Brotherhood, meanwhile, announced that it would not be taking part – just as it did everywhere else in Egypt – although it did not openly object to members participating as individuals. The composition of the protests over the next few days reflected the different levels of support evinced by the different parties.

The plan that the young leaders came up with was very similar to that of their counterparts in Cairo. Alexandria's activists had always protested in a handful of well-established locations – Raml Station, Haqqaniyya, Manshiyya – all of which are in wealthy, central areas of the city readily accessible to the media (and to the security forces). The point in these cases had been to ensure as much coverage as possible. But this time, they decided to begin their demonstrations in working-class areas, despite the risk that by doing so they would be crossing a line as far as the security forces were concerned. The plan was for small groups of activists to drum up as much support in the poor areas of eastern and western Alexandria as possible. It was agreed that no party symbols would be present, only the Egyptian flag. The night before, most of them spent the night at friends' houses in order to evade arrest by SSIS.[108]

The general sense was that the 25 January protests would, as usual, be the preserve of the activists. Some of the political parties were keen to maintain an 'escape route', coordinating their activities with the security forces.[109] They agreed to bring the demonstrations to an end at a particular time

---

[106] In August 2010, for example, they organized a sit-in in solidarity with Brotherhood detainees. Ibid.
[107] Ibid.
[108] Mohamed Samir, personal interview.
[109] Note the similarity to events in Suez, for which see the relevant section.

and to restrict themselves to social demands, avoiding any chants attacking the president or his family.[110] This seems to have reassured the security forces, because the Interior Ministry took no exceptional precautionary measures in Alexandria, dramatically underestimating activists' ability to rally support.

1 25 January: Struggling with Alexandria's geography

On 25 January everything seemed quite normal. Until 3.00 pm there were no demonstrations anywhere in Alexandria, and the members of the Coordination Office concluded that the city had decided not to get involved in popular political action.[111]

A demonstration marched in Sidi Bishr led by Safwan Mohamed, a member of the Baradei campaign responsible for the whole eastern section of the city at the Coordination Bureau. Demonstrators began with 'long live Egypt!' before moving on to chants expressing political demands. Alexandria's warren of narrow back streets meant that the security forces were unwilling to move in to crush the demonstration, allowing the organizers – like their counterparts in Cairo – to circulate locally and muster as many people as possible. By 3.00 pm, there were tens of thousands of demonstrators.[112]

Getting people out onto the streets in their local area, however, was only half the battle in a city with Alexandria's specific geography. Activists were very aware that bringing the demonstrations that had started in Mandara (in the east of the city) and Bahri (in the west) together in Sidi Gaber (the meeting point in the city centre) would require demonstrators to walk long distances along routes easily closed off by the security forces or the riot police – no less difficult a task than pushing through to Tahrir Square in Cairo. But given the importance of Sidi Gaber to the city – alongside the train station, it also hosts Alexandria's main police station whose staff and officers tortured and killed Khaled Saeed – thousands of locals were eager to make their way there. It was as if the whole city wanted to take its collective revenge against this symbol of the police state.

The security forces made several attempts to stop demonstrators from reaching Sidi Gaber, but after hundreds of young people proved themselves willing to stand firm in the path of the CSF armoured cars, they ultimately decided to leave the demonstrations alone.[113] The security forces' retreat

---

[110] Ahmed Nagy, personal interview.
[111] Ibid.
[112] Mohamed Samir, personal interview.
[113] Ibid.

gave participants a huge morale boost, banishing any vestiges of fear. In fact, the decision not to use violence against demonstrators had much the same effect as the decision to use ultra-violent means against their counterparts in Suez. In both cases, many locals with little prior interest in politics decided to participate. In the course of a popular mobilization, there are sometimes moments in which *any* action by the security forces can backfire.

With the security forces on the back foot, the demonstrations began to take on a more violent character, especially after the arrival of residents from east Alexandria's poorer and more marginalized areas. Demonstrators clashed with security forces, and the governorate security chief Mohamed Ibrahim was assaulted.[114] At this point, the security forces decided to disperse participants by force. It seemed as though 'the idea of peaceful protest had been forgotten'.[115]

Events now came thick and fast. Police positions near Raml were attacked, and the demonstrations turned into increasingly violent confrontations with the security forces. CSF reinforcements began to arrive in marked cars, some of which were set on fire by protesters.[116] At the same time, residents were shouting, 'out, out with Hosni Mubarak!' from their balconies,[117] and demonstrations were popping up across Raml Station and elsewhere.[118] In Victoria, in the east of the city, more than 20,000 people had gathered, and a huge picture of Gamal Mubarak was torn up in a symbolic rejection of the president's dynastic ambitions.[119] On Abu Qir Street in Bolkly, in front of a palace serving as an NDP office, other demonstrators tore up a picture of the president himself.

Consideration of the events of this first day of the revolution leads us to the conclusion that, while these demonstrations cut across different social groups, the fact that they set off from working-class or poorer areas proved decisive in solving the problem of Alexandria's geography. Previous protests in Alexandria had all run up against this basic problem: fighting off the security forces and reaching the centre of the city required large numbers of people willing to walk long distances.

---

[114] After the victory of the revolutionaries, Ibrahim was charged with the killing of eighty-three demonstrators, but was acquitted on 22 February 2014. See: *Al Jazeera*, 22 February 2014, Available online: https://bit.ly/3C4fQAJ (accessed 17 October 2021).
[115] Kholoud Saeed, personal interview.
[116] Mohamed Samir, personal interview; Aly El Raggal (activist in the Baradei campaign), personal interview, conducted by Ahmed Abd Rabou in Alexandria, 8 December 2011.
[117] Ahmed Nagy, personal interview.
[118] The Qaed Ibrahim Mosque, where later demonstrators gathered during the revolution, is also in Raml Station.
[119] Personal interviews with Ahmed Nagy and Abdulrahman Mahmoud (legal researcher), 8 December 2011.

The demonstrations continued until 1.00 am the next day, at which point most of the remaining protesters went home. At dawn, the backlash began, with a campaign of arrests against activists and journalists. Those who avoided arrest began to plan their next move.[120]

2 26–27 January

In the course of the morning of 26 January, the security forces released several of those arrested, including a number of journalists. At the same time, fresh protests were being organized on Facebook. For the most part, activists were inclined to save their energies for 28 January, the 'Friday of Rage'.

Nonetheless, the people of Alexandria did hold demonstrations on 26 January, albeit in smaller numbers than the day before. Whether from satellite TV, social media or mobile phones, they were aware that protests had not stopped in Cairo and that several people had been killed in Suez. 'So we couldn't just let things peter out in Alexandria when everything was still happening in Cairo and Suez,' as Mohamed Samir from the Baradei campaign told us.[121]

The security forces were much better prepared on 26 January than they had been the day before and had deployed in force in various strategic locations around the city. They had declared a general mobilization, and were arresting anyone suspected of calling for protests.

The day passed without any serious protests. The decision as to whether to organize any activities was left to individual activists in their own neighbourhoods, with the focus being on coordination ahead of the Friday of Rage. Protests against the killing of demonstrators in Suez were much discussed on social media and in text messages, but no concrete plans were made. Activists only began advocating *milyoniyya*s in Alexandria later, after 2 February.[122]

3 28 January

On the morning of 28 January, the Friday of Rage, the regime imposed a communications blackout on all internet and mobile services and jammed various satellite TV channels in order to cut Egyptians off from one another

---

[120] Mahienour El-Massry (Revolutionary Socialists, legal translator), personal interview, conducted by Ahmed Abd Rabou in Alexandria, 8 December 2011.
[121] Mohamed Samir, personal interview.
[122] Kholoud Saeed, personal interview.

and the outside world. For activists in Alexandria, this was a fundamental problem. Communication was now restricted to landlines.

Around noon, a great wave of spontaneous demonstrators surged out of most of the city's residential areas and made its way towards nearby squares and open spaces. By early evening, several police vehicles and buildings had been set alight or destroyed, particularly those in the poor interior of the city. Some demonstrations were highly organized, in large part thanks to major Muslim Brotherhood participation.[123]

That Friday, the streets of Alexandria were almost entirely empty of security officers and policemen – even the traffic police were conspicuously absent. Most of the CSF's available forces were deployed around the city's major mosques, where preachers (some on the government's payroll, some belonging to Salafist movements) condemned demonstrations as a threat to public order and the economy and in some cases showered praise on the regime. After midday prayers, most of these mosque attendees went home and did not participate in the demonstrations.

Nonetheless, it was clear that the security forces were on the back foot, incapable of accurately evaluating such unprecedented events. Their use of brute force had not cowed the demonstrators – in fact, their numbers had increased as a result. As yet, activists were still avoiding calls for the fall of the regime, hoping to encourage as many people as possible to participate. When security forces attacked devotees in Sidi Bishr Mosque, those present were angry but unable to fight back seriously. When a vast crowd of locals from nearby poor neighbourhoods arrived, however, everything changed: CSF deployed around Khaled bin al-Walid Street were stripped of their riot gear and truncheons.[124] Rather than use live ammunition, the CSF preferred to retreat. Huge masses of demonstrators made their way towards Sa'a Square via working-class areas, where they were joined by a mass of largely apolitical young men whiling away their hours in local coffee shops. As they got closer to the square, Mohamed Samir said:

> We started to see thick columns of smoke rising from the area around Sa'a Square, and we could hear the fire alarm of the Montazah security headquarters going off. We went towards the square, and we found five Interior Ministry armoured cars on fire. Before we'd even arrived at the square or Abu Suleiman Street, we came up against fierce security resistance. So we decided to turn around, and as we went past the security headquarters, we saw that it had been gutted by fire. Then, as we

---

[123] Ahmed Nagy, personal interview.
[124] Aly El Raggal, personal interview.

were making our way towards Abu Qir Street, we found that the villa belonging to the director of security had been looted.[125]

The 'organizers' were discovering demonstrations that they had not organized – in fact, a *popular uprising* they had not organized and could not control – and they were shocked. They could send out calls to protest, but they could not control what happened next. On 28 January, the number of demonstrators dwarfed the number on the previous days, including 25 January.

The destruction of the security buildings surprised Alexandrians almost as much as the mysterious disappearance of the security forces late that evening (with a few limited exceptions). The areas of Moharram Bek, Karmouz and al-Hadra had seen the fiercest clashes anywhere in the city. Demonstrators had attacked CSF armoured cars, and in the ensuing fighting some had been killed. Camp Caesar, on the other hand – a much older and largely middle-class area – saw no violence whatsoever from either side.[126] Mahienour El-Massry relates:

> The number of demonstrators we found there gave us an indescribable feeling. So we joined them, and the number just kept rising – many, many more than had been present on 25 January. [. . .] There was a big group of people coming from the other end of the waterfront, and we met by Mahrousa in Sidi Bishr. We decided to go down Iqbal Street, where the official residence of the director of security was. There people joined us who'd never participated in any political activity with us in the past. When we got to the security director's residence, it was empty. The guys with tattoos of ex-cons broke in and vandalized it, but when we chastised them for stealing some electrical goods they'd found inside, they tossed them aside and said that they represented the money stolen from the people. And then they carried demonstrating alongside us.[127]

People of very different class and cultural backgrounds came together in the demonstrations. Again we see that while the politicized demographics certainly organized actions on the day, they were also surprised to find huge gatherings of people they had nothing to do with; they did not lead these spontaneous demonstrations and were unable to control them. In fact, they were often taken by surprise.

All this shows the great difference between 25 January and the Friday of Rage in Alexandria. With the communications blackout and the news

---

[125] Mohamed Samir, personal interview.
[126] Mahienour El-Massry, personal interview.
[127] Ibid.

of repeated killings in Suez, many of the city's more comfortable residents were less eager to demonstrate – with the exception of the politically active group of organizers, who only succeeded in mustering a small number of people. What decided the course of events in Alexandria was the participation of large numbers of Brotherhood activists and young men from working-class districts. Together, they managed to break the grip of the Interior Ministry over the city.

Security centres were destroyed in Montazah, Bab Sharq and Raml. Interviews with the activists show that demonstrators regularly allowed CSF personnel to desert their posts or get out of their armoured cars unharmed before destroying them. Generally speaking, the CSF initially responded with live rounds and tear gas before quickly giving in, realizing they could not resist such a large mass of people. According to Massry's account, most middle-ranking and senior police and security officers simply went home, leaving their subordinates to their fate.[128]

By evening, demonstrators had control of most of eastern and central Alexandria, the corniche and the area around Qaed Ibrahim Mosque. At exactly 8.30 pm, the first army contingent arrived from Marsa Matruh. A curfew was announced and demonstrators were ordered to return to their homes. But nobody listened – and in fact, butane canisters were used to blow up the governorate building, in the last great symbolic gesture of the day.[129]

The army took up position around various important and sensitive areas of the city. Around 11.00 pm, groups of thugs were taking to the streets. Aly El Raggal tells us, 'Particular groups tried to loot some shops, but the demonstrators formed human shields to stop them. The popular committees hadn't been set up yet to protect public property. We started telling the army which areas were being looted, the areas that needed protection – they didn't know where the ideal places to deploy were.'[130]

As in other governorates, the army was welcomed with open arms by much of the local population, particularly when it became clear that they would not be fully enforcing the curfew. Demonstrators struck up warm relationships with the officers and the conscripts. Unlike Cairo, these relationships were not shaken by an event like the Battle of the Camel, where the army's refusal to intervene led many to question their intentions:

> The vehicles the army brought into Alexandria were in a really pathetic state, technically. I remember we were in the car and we heard the sound of tank tracks

---

[128] Ibid.
[129] Personal interviews with Kholoud Saeed and Mohamed Samir.
[130] Aly El Raggal, personal interview.

off to one side, but every few minutes or so one of the tanks would have to stop so someone could change the track or whatever. We really felt superior. If you'd seen pictures of the CSF formations in the city and how heavy-handed and violent they were before the revolution, or of the contingents in Manshiyya on 25 January out in force, all lined up like an occupying army, you'd understand why people felt like they'd proven themselves superior to the CSF, despite their numbers and their readiness to suppress the crowds.[131]

4 29 January–11 February

Mubarak's first speech fed the flames of popular anger. Most of the protests that followed took place around Qaed Ibrahim Mosque, as Alexandria lacks a single central location with the same symbolic valence as Tahrir Square. Sit-ins took place on 31 January and 1 February. But within an hour of Mubarak's second speech on 1 February, demonstrators were attacked near Cairo Station. It later emerged that the attackers had been encouraged by wealthy tradesmen, some of them closely linked to the NDP. Unlike in other cities, however, on 2 February there were no major attacks on demonstrators, and in the following days many of those activists and demonstrators who had been detained were released.[132]

Outside the realm of political activity, people busied themselves setting up popular committees to protect residences and commercial properties from looting. It is worth noting that these activities saw a certain amount of Salafist involvement in the revolution for the first time, albeit as individuals. The so-called Costa Salafists, young people more willing to consider resistance to the ruler than their older counterparts, played a particularly prominent role. Throughout the revolution, the Salafists maintained pressure on shopkeepers not to raise prices and even, in some cases, to lower them.[133]

On 4, 10 and 11 February, there were noticeable spikes in the numbers of demonstrators. The security forces had clearly given up on trying to suppress demonstrations, and people were eager to push Mubarak to resign.

After Mubarak's third and final speech, the Muslim Brotherhood called for a protest around Ras al-Tin, the president's official residence in Alexandria. The area, which also hosts Egypt's main naval base, was surrounded by both soldiers and internal security personnel. 'Demonstrators gathered in the north of the city, in Sidi Gaber, in Ras al-Tin and in front of Qaed Ibrahim

---

[131] Ibid.
[132] Personal interviews with Aly El Raggal, Mohamed Samir and Kholoud Saeed.
[133] Mohamed Samir, personal interview.

Mosque,' says Ahmed Nagy. 'It was clear that both the conscripts and the officers sympathized with protesters.'[134] It is worth noting that by this point the SCAF had convened 'indefinitely' and issued its first statement.

'We sang, we danced – the mood was one of acceptance of the other,' Mahienour El-Massry said. 'We were walking in the middle of a huge march made up of members of the Muslim Brotherhood, dancing while they clapped us on. They didn't tell us not to or express any kind of dislike. Those moments of acceptance had a very special character.'[135] There could be no better expression of the spontaneity of demonstrators during this period – and not just their spontaneity but also how far removed they were about any thought of political planning for the post-Mubarak era. They would prove unable to maintain this crucial spirit of cooperation between Islamists and secularists.

IV Aswan

Not all governorates experienced the sort of 25 January that we have described; the organized gatherings and spontaneous demonstrations cannot be generalized throughout the country. In other areas, although a mobilization did begin to take shape on this day, it did not succeed in bringing large numbers of people out onto the streets. Every city has its own peculiarities that made it more or less amenable to revolution. In this section, we will consider the case of Aswan.

1 Social background

The Aswan governorate sits at the southernmost extreme of the Arab Republic of Egypt. Known for its agriculture and simple industries, it has a marked tribal character in both the centre and periphery. Disputes are typically resolved by traditional means, and locals rarely have recourse to the judiciary. Its inhabitants can trace their origins back to areas all over Nubia and Upper Egypt, particularly Esna and Sohag.[136] The Nubian population, most of whom were displaced by the building of the Aswan Dam, are still waiting to be compensated for the loss of their homes, despite their constant demands for a just solution. Many Nubians work in Cairo as manual labourers.

---

[134] Ahmed Nagy, personal interview.
[135] Mahienour El-Massry, personal interview.
[136] Amir Mahmoud Amir (lawyer and activist in Aswan), personal interview, conducted by Ahmed Abd Rabou and Islam Hegazy, Aswan, 30 September 2011.

A shocking proportion of the Aswan governorate's population – some 50 per cent – live below the poverty line, according to official estimates.[137] Alongside low levels of education and strong sense of tribalism, this level of poverty made Aswan a stronghold of the Egyptian regime. Most of the local political elite belonged to the NDP, with only a modest showing for the Wafd, and in the 2005 elections the city returned more votes for Mubarak than any other.[138]

As I noted earlier, deteriorating living standards do not necessarily produce revolutionary conditions. Poverty can co-occur with depoliticization, marginalization and a lack of interest in public affairs. Where the only way of accessing state services is via the mediation of the political elite, and that political elite is loyal to the regime, this can play a significant role in containing protest. Such demonstrations as did take place on 25 January did not spring forth from the most economically underdeveloped neighbourhoods of the city.

Aswan had never witnessed any opposition demonstrations before 2011, despite a solid record of pro-Palestine and pro-Iraq demonstrations.[139] The only action organized by Kefaya and the NAC of any significance was a 6 January protest against the Church of the Saints bombing.[140] Local organizers complained of limited political consciousness in the governorate, even among themselves: when choosing slogans and chants for the 25 January protests, they had to seek the advice of more experienced activists on Facebook.[141] Many of them had only begun discussing public affairs on the Khaled Saeed page, and given the low level of internet access in the governorate, even this route into politics was limited to a small number of people.[142]

These activists handed out fliers encouraging locals to take part in demonstrations before 25 January, but they were met with mockery and disdain.[143] They attribute this not to fear of the security forces but a lack of interest in public affairs and an aversion to protest. Local shopkeepers even refused to sell demonstrators Egyptian flags or print fliers for them.[144]

Aswan was thus not very amenable to revolution, despite the unusually high levels of marginalization and unemployment experienced by the

---

[137] Central Agency for Public Mobilization and Statistics, *Select Poverty Indicators*.
[138] Personal interviews with Maysara Abdoun (Wafd, RYC) and Ahmed Abdelrazzaq (activist), conducted by Ahmed Abd Rabou and Islam Hegazy, Aswan, 30 September 2011.
[139] Maysara Abdoun, personal interview.
[140] Ahmed Ragab (Baradei campaign), personal interview, conducted by Ahmed Abd Rabou and Islam Hegazy, Aswan, 30 September 2011.
[141] Ahmed Abdelrazzaq, personal interview.
[142] Maysara Abdoun, personal interview.
[143] Ahmed Abdelrazzaq, personal interview.
[144] Ahmed Ragab, personal interview.

area, the near monopolization of jobs in the hydroelectric industry by 'outsiders',[145] the flagrant corruption that led to the closing down of whole sectors of the economy to reduce employment opportunities,[146] the contemptuous attitude of the security forces[147] and the despotic power of the city's business titans, led by Ahmed Ezz, who on one occasion had sabotaged the construction of an ironworks in the governorate because it did not suit them.[148] Aswan's political forces were weak.

The position of the Wafd in Aswan – the only party other than the NDP with a significant presence – was closely linked to that of the centre in Cairo, shifting from total rejection of the protests to willingness to allow individual members to participate. Those Wafdists who did take part played an important role in the arrangements for 25 January. Kefaya stepped in with the necessary materials (felt-tip pens, placards, flags) that local activists had been unable to source.[149]

On the eve of 25 January, the security forces warned activists against holding demonstrations, taking advantage of tribal bonds to pressure them via their relatives.

2 25 January

On 25 January, about thirty activists gathered at a café on Mahatta Square in the city centre.[150] Most of those present were members of the Wafd, Kefaya[151] or the NAC;[152] one Brotherhood member, two Salafist sheikhs, eight women[153] and a handful of independents were also in attendance. They did not have high expectations.[154] Nearly 1,000 locals had gathered nearby, some of whom tried to attack demonstrators while others chanted Mubarak's name.[155] Others still condemned the participation of women

---

[145] Muhyiddin Abdelhamid, personal interview, 30 September 2011.
[146] Mohammad Ali Badri (Wafd secretary general in Aswan, member of the Committee of Wise Men), personal interview, conducted by Ahmed Abd Rabou and Islam Hegazy, Aswan, 30 September 2011.
[147] Ibid.
[148] Construction of the ironworks, which would have created 3,000 jobs for locals, began in 1998, but was halted by the Atef Ebeid government; the CEO Mohammad Bahgat and his deputy were both imprisoned before having their sentences overturned. For more, see: *al-Ahram*, 22 March 2011, Available online: https://bit.ly/3kfroro (accessed 5 January 2015).
[149] Mohammad Ali Badri, personal interview.
[150] Ahmed Abdelrazzaq, personal interview.
[151] Muhyiddin Abdelhamid, personal interview.
[152] Personal interviews with Ahmed Ragab and Maysara Abdoun.
[153] Nagla Basyouni (TV producer from Aswan), personal interview, conducted by Ahmed Abd Rabou and Islam Hegazy, Aswan, 30 September 2011.
[154] Ibid.
[155] Ahmed Amer (TV producer), personal interview, conducted by Ahmed Abd Rabou and Islam Hegazy, Aswan, 30 September 2011.

alongside men, saying it was against local tradition.[156] The CSF were also present to film the demonstrators,[157] with some officers trying to convince them that the only alternative to the regime was chaos. Despite provocations from the demonstrators, however, including the chant 'State Security are the dogs of the state' – even more offensive in Arabic than in English – they did not attack them.[158]

After this unpromising start, the activists felt defeated,[159] and fell back on watching events in Cairo unfold on TV.[160] No disturbances took place in Aswan on 26 or 27 January.[161] Nonetheless, in the run-up to the Friday of Rage, they once again distributed fliers calling for protests in the city,[162] encouraged by the scenes in Tahrir Square. They were particularly affected by the violent response to demonstrators in Cairo and Suez.[163]

3 28 January (the Friday of Rage)

On the Friday of Rage everything suddenly changed. The Friday sermons focused, as elsewhere, on the dangers of unrest and the need for calm. Aswan's preachers went further than their counterparts elsewhere, branding the demonstrations 'sectarian strife', well aware of the weight such accusations carried in a city with a large Christian population. After some worshippers objected to these comments, preachers tried to prolong the prayer by adding extra sections. As soon as prayers were over, however, thousands of people poured out of the mosques and onto the streets to demonstrate,[164] and the general population of the city showed their solidarity with protesters.

Protesters tore up pictures of Mubarak[165] and chanted 'the people want the fall of the regime!' and 'Gamal, tell your dad the Egyptian people hate you!'[166] Elsewhere in the governorate, demonstrations were being held in Sohag and Luxor.

---

[156] According to activists' interviews, most of their families were affiliated with the NDP via tribal links. One Christian woman who participated was from an ultra-conservative background very hostile to demonstrations.
[157] Maysara Abdoun, personal interview.
[158] Personal interviews with Ahmed Amer and Nagla Basyouni.
[159] Muhyiddin Abdelhamid, personal interview.
[160] Maysara Abdoun, personal interview.
[161] Various interviews.
[162] Nagla Basyouni, personal interview.
[163] Maysara Abdoun, personal interview.
[164] Ibid.
[165] Ahmed Ragab, personal interview. Video footage of this is available on *YouTube*, 5 February 2011, Available online: https://bit.ly/3moly92 (accessed 1 October 2021).
[166] Maysara Abdoun, personal interview.

After Friday prayers, the security forces imposed an immediate communications blackout: mobile service was cut off and access to Facebook was blocked (although activists were able to get around this using techniques they had learnt from their Tunisian counterparts).[167] They also mustered a significant force of young men carrying stones who were tasked with breaking up the demonstrations or causing problems.[168] The director of security, meanwhile, was assaulted in Mahatta Square. Nonetheless, security forces did not react or use live ammunition for fear that things would spin out of control.[169] In any case, some of the officers were sympathetic to demonstrators, many of whom they knew personally.[170]

Demonstrators marched on the NDP headquarters, where some participants tried to force their way in and were repelled with fire hoses.[171] There was then an attempt to storm the security directorate,[172] sparking violent clashes; security forces were driven off by young men from poorer parts of the city armed with Molotov cocktails. Confrontations continued until the evening, when protesters withdrew from the square.[173] As security forces abandoned most of the city – banks, churches, parks (although not the TV building), locals formed popular committees to protect public property.[174] When demonstrators saw that the army had deployed in Cairo, they welcomed it as a defeat for the security forces and a victory for a 'patriotic' institution.[175]

4 29 January–1 February

On 29 January, the governor of Aswan issued a statement claiming that no demonstrations had taken place under his authority, prompting an ad hoc gathering in front of his headquarters to prove him wrong. This demonstration was forcibly broken up by police, but some participants then made their way to the city's military headquarters and blocked the road. This led to further attacks by the security forces, who beat demonstrators

---

[167] Ahmed Ragab, personal interview.
[168] Ahmed Amer, personal interview.
[169] Nagla Basyouni, personal interview.
[170] Ahmed Amer, for example, counts thirteen employees of the security forces among his relatives. He tells us they were ordered to kill those leading demonstrations, but that they agreed instead to break up the demonstration without firing live ammunition because so many of their family members were present (which, quite apart from anything else, might set off a major blood feud).
[171] Nagla Basyouni, personal interview.
[172] Maysara Abdoun, personal interview.
[173] Muhyiddin Abdelhamid, personal interview.
[174] Nagla Basyouni, personal interview.
[175] Amir Mahmoud Amir, personal interview.

and fired tear gas canisters into the crowd. After CSF personnel ended up brawling with soldiers, however, they withdrew.[176]

Activists and many other locals continued their protest until well into the night, after which many of them went off to do their shifts on the popular committees.

5 Mubarak's speech to endgame

Mubarak's second speech won him a great deal of sympathy from both loyalists and fence sitters in Aswan and was followed by pro-regime marches. At the same time, opposition demonstrations continued. Tribal factors played a key role in preventing any major confrontation between the two.[177] Limited opposition demonstrations continued in the square even after the pro-Mubarak marches came to an end. Protesters' main focus, however, was on events in Cairo and on their own political discussions. Mubarak's speech of 10 February, in which he was widely expected to announce his resignation, was met with major protests that lasted late into the night. Many activists from Aswan also made their way to the capital to join their compatriots in Tahrir.[178] After Mubarak did announce his resignation, everyone in Aswan – revolutionaries and otherwise – celebrated.

---

[176] Ahmed Amer, personal interview.
[177] Personal interviews with Ahmed Amer, Amir Mahmoud Amir, Muhyiddin Abdelhamid and Maysara Abdoun.
[178] Personal interviews with from Mohammad Ali Badri and others.

6

Revolutionary youth in numbers

In cooperation with activists who took part in the 25 January revolution,[1] we have put together a list of 333 people involved in the organizational networks behind the demonstrations. Their names are given along with their level of education, occupations and political affiliations. Together they constitute a (relatively large) representative sample of the young people who led the protests and who formed the organized core of activists at the heart of the revolution.

Most of these activists were either university graduates or students at the time. The majority are solidly middle class, for the most part from professional backgrounds. And most of them were already political before the revolution, belonging to a wide range of ideological currents, although the data demonstrate, as I have theorized elsewhere, that their ethical values and emphasis on cooperation and agreement allowed them to overcome these differences. Most of them were not party members, although a decent number were or had been at some point in the past. Of the rest, some were already involved in various youth organizations, while the others – who I refer to as 'independents' – were entirely unaffiliated. While classifying them, I have labelled some of these unaffiliated actors as 'Islamists' or 'leftists' because of their general intellectual interests, as identified by them or their fellow activists.

I have also distinguished between 'Brotherhood' and 'Brotherhood youth'. In both cases, the individuals in question were members of the Muslim Brotherhood organization. But those classified as 'Brotherhood youth' were also involved in the group that operated independently on the ground in the first days of the revolution without necessarily consulting the organization's leadership. Most of this group subsequently split or were expelled from the Brotherhood after the revolution. Those labelled simply 'Brotherhood', meanwhile, were also young activists, but they worked within the Brotherhood's established organizational channels and were not part of this independent group (Tables I.6.1 and I.6.2).

---

[1] This list was put together with the help of Abdelrahman Fares, Sameh al-Barqy, Khaled Elsayed and others, based on their personal knowledge and communications with other activists.

Table I.6.1 List of Revolutionary Youth Who Participated in the 2011 Revolution[a]

	Name	Affiliation (January 2011)	Home governorate	Occupation (January 2011)	Education (January 2011)
1.	Abdallah al-Saadawy	6 April	Giza	Student	Law
2.	Abdelmonem Emam	Baradei campaign	Al Gharbya	Trader	–
3.	Abdel Rahman Atef Marzouk[b]	6 April	Beni Soueif	Student	Secondary school
4.	Abdel Rahman Ezz[c]	6 April	Cairo	–	–
5.	Abdelrahman Fares[d]	Independent	Fayoum	Journalist	Secondary school, business
6.	Abdel Rahman Gadd	Independent	Assiut	Researcher	Economics and political science
7.	Abdel Rahman Helbawi	Islamist	Cairo	Businessman	–
8.	Abdel Rahman Youssef[e]	Baradei campaign	Cairo	Poet and author	BA in Islamic law
9.	Abdel Rahman Zidan[f]	YJF	Cairo	Student	Law
10.	Abdelmoneim Mahmoud[g]	Independent	Alexandria	Journalist	BA in law
11.	Abdelrahman al-Karbony[h]	Brotherhood	Cairo	Doctor	BA in medicine
12.	Abdullah Aoun	Independent	Giza	Student	Kuwait University
13.	Abdullah Modar	6 April	Assiut	Student	–
14.	Abdullah Taher	Independent	Fayoum	–	–
15.	Abdulrahman El Zaghimi	Leftist	Cairo	Engineer	BA in engineering
16.	Abdulrahman ElSayed	Independent	Cairo	Manager	BA in business
17.	Abdulrahman Horeidy	Brotherhood youth	Cairo	Manager of property company	BA in business
18.	Abdulrahman Mansour[i]	We Are All Khaled Saeed	Cairo	Student	BA
19.	Abdulrahman Samir	Baradei campaign	Cairo	–	–
20.	Abdulrahman Younes	Brotherhood youth	Beni Soueif	–	–
21.	Abeer El Saady	Independent	Cairo	Journalist	BA from Higher Institute for Computing
22.	Abeer Saad	Independent	Giza	Designer	–
23.	Afaf Mamdouh	6 April	Cairo	Student	–
24.	Ahmed Abdel-Gawad	Brotherhood youth	Cairo	Company manager	BA in business
25.	Ahmed Abdelhamid Hussein	Independent	Giza	Researcher	BA in science
26.	Ahmed Abu Heiba	Brotherhood youth	Cairo	Media	BA in engineering
27.	Ahmed Abu Khalil	Islamist Independent	Cairo	Documentary filmmaker	BA from Dar al-Ulum
28.	Ahmed Abu Zikry[j]	Independent	Beni Soueif	Sales representative	BA in business
29.	Ahmed Adel	Independent	Giza	Training consultant	BA in business

30.	Ahmed al-Gaaly		Brotherhood youth	Giza	Psychiatrist	BA in medicine
31.	Ahmed Aqil		Brotherhood youth	Cairo	Pharmacist	BA in pharmacology
32.	Ahmed Bahaa		Brotherhood youth	Giza	Engineer	BA in engineering
33.	Ahmed Bahaa el-Din		Brotherhood youth	Giza	Student	IT
34.	Ahmed Dawry[k]		Former police officer	Cairo	Sports sponsorship manager, tech company	BA in criminology
35.	Ahmed Douma[l]		YJF	El-Beheira	Student	Law
36.	Ahmed Eid		DFP	Cairo	–	–
37.	Ahmed Ezzat[m]		Revolutionary Socialists	Fayoum	Human rights lawyer	BA in law
38.	Ahmed Hamdy Farid		Brotherhood youth	Cairo	Sales representative	BA in business
39.	Ahmed Harara[n]		Independent	Giza	Dentist	BA in dentistry
40.	Ahmed Maher[o]		6 April	Cairo	Engineer	BA in engineering
41.	Ahmed Mahmoud Melad		Ghad Party	El-Beheira	Human rights lawyer	BA in law
42.	Ahmed Masry		Brotherhood youth	Alexandria	Student	Business
43.	Ahmed Mazroua		Independent	Al Gharbya (Tanta)	Student	–
44.	Ahmed Mohsen[p]		Brotherhood youth	Fayoum	Doctor	BA in medicine
45.	Ahmed Mustafa Naguib		Independent	Suez	University teaching assistant	–
46.	Ahmed Nezeily		Brotherhood youth	Cairo	Sales manager	BA in business
47.	Ahmed Osama		Brotherhood youth	Cairo	Engineer	BA in engineering
48.	Ahmed Ragab El Nady[q]		Brotherhood youth	Giza	Training consultant	BA in business
49.	Ahmed Saad		YJF	Fayoum	Student	Law
50.	Ahmed Salem		Brotherhood youth	Giza	Company manager	BA in science
51.	Ahmed Semir		Brotherhood youth	Cairo	Journalist	BA
52.	Ahmed Semir		YJF	Giza	Student	–
53.	Ahmed Shahin		Independent	Al Gharbya (Tanta)	Pharmacist	Engineering
54.	Ahmed Shawwaf		Independent	Giza	Student	BA in engineering
55.	Ahmed Shorbagy		Brotherhood youth	Giza	Engineer	BA in management
56.	Ahmed Zahran		Independent	Giza	Entrepreneur	BA from Dar al-Uhum
57.	Ahmed Zein'		Independent	Giza	Media	–
58.	Akram al-Irany		Labour Party	Cairo	Open source developer	BA in science
59.	Alaa Abd El Fattah[s]		Leftist independent	Giza	Education technology trainer and consultant	Business, MA in anthropology
60.	Alaa Shohba		YJF	Giza		
61.	Ali Abdelmoneim		Independent	Giza	Journalist	BA in media
62.	Ali Abdallah		Independent	Cairo	Pharmacist	BA in pharmacology

(*Continued*)

Table I.6.1 (Continued)

	Name	Affiliation (January 2011)	Home governorate	Occupation (January 2011)	Education (January 2011)
63.	Aly Khafagy[t]	Brotherhood youth	Cairo	Sales representative	BA in business
64.	Aly ElMashad[u]	Brotherhood youth	Cairo	Doctor	BA in medicine
65.	Aly El Raggal	Leftist	Alexandria	Researcher	–
66.	Amal Sharaf	6 April	–	–	–
67.	Ammar Atef	Independent	Fayoum	Student	–
68.	Ammar El-Beltagy[v]	Brotherhood youth	Cairo	Student	Dentistry
69.	Amr Ezz	6 April	Cairo	Lawyer	BA in law
70.	Amr Ezzat	Leftist	Giza	Journalist and human rights activist	BA in engineering
71.	Amr Magdi	Independent	Cairo	Researcher	BA in medicine
72.	Amr Qady	Independent	Cairo	Actor	Fine Arts Academy
73.	Amr Salahuddin	Brotherhood youth	Cairo	Doctor	BA in medicine
74.	Amr Saleh	DFP	Cairo	Journalist	–
75.	Anas al-Sultan[w]	Independent	Cairo	Azhari sheikh	BA in Islamic law
76.	Engy Hamdy	6 April	Cairo	Broadcaster	BA in media
77.	Arwa Marei	Sitt al-Banat	Cairo	Student	–
78.	Ashraf Mekky	Brotherhood youth	Cairo	Dentist	BA in dentistry
79.	Ashraf Saeed Hassan	6 April	Cairo	Workshop owner	–
80.	Asmaa Anwar Shehata	Brotherhood youth	Monofiya	Journalist	–
81.	Asmaa al-Beltagy[x]	Brotherhood youth	Cairo	Student	Secondary school
82.	Asmaa Mahfouz	6 April	Cairo	–	BA in business
83.	Awatef Saad[y]	Independent	Giza	Trainer	BA in science
84.	Bahaa Ibrahim	Brotherhood youth	Giza	Journalist	BA
85.	Bahaa Sanussi[z]	Independent	Alexandria	Accountant	BA in business
86.	Baho Bakhsh	Socialist Renewal	Cairo	–	Political science, AUC
87.	Baraa Ashraf[aa]	Independent	Giza	Entrepreneur	BA in media
88.	Baraa Magdy	6 April	Cairo	Student	–
89.	Basem Fathi	6 April	Cairo	Researcher	–
90.	Basem Kamel	Baradei campaign	Cairo	Engineer	BA in engineering
91.	Basem El Sherbiny[ab]	Brotherhood youth	Dakahliya	CEO	BA in science

92.	Bassem Sabry[ac]	Independent	Giza	Journalist	–
93.	Beesan Kassab	Revolutionary Socialists	Cairo	Journalist	–
94.	Belal Alaa	Tagammu	Dakahliya	Student	–
95.	Belal Diab	Ghad Party	Cairo	Student	–
96.	Belal Fadl	Independent	Giza	Writer	BA in media
97.	Beshoy Tamry	Independent	Cairo	Student	–
98.	Dalia Abd El-Hameed	Leftist	Cairo	Human rights activist	BA in pharmacology
99.	Dalia Moussa	Socialist Renewal	Cairo	–	BA from Dar al-Ulum
100.	Dalia Ridwan	6 April	Alexandria	Student	–
101.	Diyaa al-Sawi	Labour Party	Cairo	Journalist	BA in media
102.	Doaa al-Shamy	Independent	Giza	Chemist	BA in science
103.	Alsawy Mabrouk	Brotherhood youth	Monofiya	Entrepreneur	–
104.	Emad Arab	Independent	Giza	Entrepreneur	–
105.	Emad Moetazz	Brotherhood youth	Port Said	Human rights activist	BA in social services
106.	Enas Elmasarawy	Independent	Qalyobiya (Banha)	Human rights activist	–
107.	Esraa Abdel Fattah[ad]	Liberal	–	–	–
108.	Fady Iskandar	Karama Party	Cairo	Student	Media
109.	Faten al-Wakil	6 April	–	–	–
110.	Fatima al-Wakil	Labour Party	Cairo	Lawyer	BA in law
111.	Fatima Sarag	Leftist	Alexandria	Training consultant	BA in business
112.	Gaafar El-Zaafarani	Brotherhood youth	Cairo	–	–
113.	Ghada Naguib	Independent	Cairo	Journalist	Media
114.	Gihan Shaaban	Socialist Renewal	Cairo	Journalist	–
115.	Habiba Ahmed Abdelaziz[ae]	Brotherhood youth	Cairo	Researcher	Women's Faculty
116.	Habiba al-Awda	Independent	Cairo	Student	–
117.	Hadir Mohammad	6 April	Cairo	Student	Law
118.	Halem Henish[af]	YJF	Asyut	Student	–
119.	Hamed Sharit	Brotherhood youth	Cairo	–	–
120.	Hamada Al-Kashef	Egyptian Communist Party	Cairo	Economics journalist	Arabic language
121.	Hamada Fathi	Brotherhood	Giza	Journalist	–
122.	Hanan Kamal[ag]	Leftist	Cairo	Engineer	BA in engineering
123.	Hanan Magdy Alithy	Islamist independent	Cairo	Teaching assistant	Faculty of engineering
124.	Hani Gamal[ah]	Independent			

(Continued)

Table I.6.1 (Continued)

	Name	Affiliation (January 2011)	Home governorate	Occupation (January 2011)	Education (January 2011)
125.	Hany Mahmoud[ai]	Brotherhood youth	Giza	Director of al-Risala TV	BA from Dar al-Ulum
126.	Hani Mohammad al-Shenawy[aj]	Brotherhood	Giza	Entrepreneur	BA in science
127.	Hani Mohammad Taha	Independent	Ismailia	Schoolteacher	—
128.	Hashem Yahia	YJF	Cairo	Student	Economics and political science
129.	Hassan al-Banna	Brotherhood youth	Assiut	Student	—
130.	Hassan El-Banna Taher[ak]	YJF	Fayoum	Student	Media
131.	Hassan Ali	Independent	Cairo	Trader	Intermediate institute
132.	Hassan Khatiri	Brotherhood youth	Fayoum	Sales representative	BA in business
133.	Haytham Mohammadein[al]	Revolutionary Socialists	Cairo	Lawyer	BA in law
134.	Hazem Abdelhamid	Independent	Cairo	Photojournalist	—
135.	Heba Abdulljawad	Islamist independent	Giza	Engineer	BA in engineering
136.	Heidar Youssef	Brotherhood youth	Giza	Sales representative	BA in business
137.	Haitham Gabr	Socialist Renewal	Cairo	Journalist	Economics and political science
138.	Haitham Salah	YJF	Cairo	Student	Faculty of business
139.	Hend Magdy	Independent	Al Gharbya (Tanta)	Journalist	—
140.	Hend Mohsen[am]	Independent	Cairo	Journalist	BA in business
141.	Hossam Elhendy[an]	Independent	Cairo	Journalist	BA in science
142.	Hosam Elsyad[ao]	YJF	Cairo	Student	—
143.	Hossam Bahgat[ap]	Leftist	Cairo	Human rights activist	BA in law
144.	Hossam el-Hamalawy[aq]	Revolutionary Socialists	Cairo	Blogger and photographer	MA, political science
145.	Hossam Moanis[ar]	Karama Party	Cairo	—	—
146.	Hossam Sarhan[as]	Independent	Damietta	Designer	—
147.	Hossein Helmy[at]	YJF	Cairo	Worker	—
148.	Hussein Al-Galbana	Independent	El Arish	Journalist	Suez Canal University
149.	Ibrahim el-Houdaiby[au]	Islamist independent, left Brotherhood before the revolution	Giza	Researcher	BA in political science
150.	Ibrahim El-Yamani	Brotherhood	Cairo	Student	BA in medicine
151.	Ibrahim Saleh	Independent	Fayoum	Student	Engineering
152.	Eman Abdelmonem[av]	Independent	Giza	Journalist	Azhar degree in media

153.	Iman el-Baddiny	Islamist Independent	Cairo	Engineer	BA in engineering
154.	Iman Hassan	Baradei campaign	Alexandria	Owner of a beauty salon	–
155.	Iman Mohammad	Independent	Cairo	Student	–
156.	Islam Lotfy[aw]	Brotherhood youth	Cairo	Lawyer	BA in law
157.	Ismail Alexandrani[ax]	Independent	Alexandria	Journalist and researcher	BA
158.	Kareem Al Shaer	6 April	Cairo	Worker	–
159.	Karim Reda	Labour activist	Cairo	Director of IT centre	Secondary school certificate
160.	Khaled Abdel Hamid	Socialist Renewal	Cairo	Lawyer and human rights activist	–
161.	Khaled Ali	Leftist, Bread and Freedom Party			
162.	Khaled Elsayed[ay]	YJF	Cairo	Engineer, researcher	BA in engineering
163.	Khaled Fouda	6 April	Dakahliya	Student	Media
164.	Khaled Mansour	Salafist, independent Islamist	Cairo	Businessman	BA in engineering
165.	Khalid Tallima	PYC	Cairo	Journalist	–
166.	Khetab Sayyed Khateb	Brotherhood	Giza	Worker	Intermediate diploma
167.	Madiha Qarqar	Labour Party	Cairo	Engineer	BA in engineering
168.	Magdy Saad	Brotherhood youth	Cairo	Marketing investor	BA in business
169.	Mahienour El-Massry[az]	Revolutionary Socialists	Alexandria	Lawyer	BA in law
170.	Mahmoud Abou Fadl	Brotherhood youth	Giza	Film editor	BA from Dar al-Ulum
171.	Mahmoud El Shishtawy	Independent	Al Gharbya (Tanta)	Labourer	–
172.	Mahmoud Eleiba	Independent	Alexandria	Student	Law
173.	Mahmoud Moussa	6 April	Fayoum	Trainer	–
174.	Mahmoud Salah al-Garhy	Brotherhood	Beni Soueif	Sales manager	–
175.	Mahmoud Sami[ba]	6 April	Cairo	Accountant	BA in business
176.	Mahmoud Senoussi	Brotherhood	Giza	Student	–
177.	Mahmouc Yassin	YJF	Kafr El Shiekh	Student	Helwan University
178.	Mahmoud Zayed[bb]	YJF	–	Lawyer/human rights activist	–
179.	Malek Ady[bc]	Independent	Cairo	–	–
180.	Mamoud Afifi[bd]	6 April	Qalyobiya (Banha)	Lawyer	BA in law
181.	Marianne Fayeq	Independent	Cairo	Trainer	–
182.	Marwa Farouq	Socialist Renewal	Alexandria	Student	BA in science, al-Azhar
183.	Mariam El Zaafarani	Islamist	Assiut	Student	–
184.	Mariam Modr	Brotherhood	Giza	Labourer	–
185.	Medhat Snaker	6 April			

(Continued)

Table I.6.1 (Continued)

	Name	Affiliation (January 2011)	Home governorate	Occupation (January 2011)	Education (January 2011)
186.	Menna Shrfeldin	6 April	Cairo	Journalist	–
187.	Mina Daniel[be]	YJF	Cairo	Labourer	Intermediate diploma
188.	Moaz Abdelkarim[bf]	Brotherhood youth	Giza	Pharmacist	BA in pharmacology
189.	Mogahed Sharara	Islamist	Cairo	Journalist	BA in education
190.	Mohamad Ghazlan	Independent	Giza	Sales manager	BA in business
191.	Mohammad Abbas[bg]	Brotherhood youth	Giza	Businessman	BA in business
192.	Mohamed Al-Qasas[bh]	Brotherhood youth	Cairo	Media	BA from Dar al-Ulum
193.	Mohamed El-Baqer[bi]	Islamist	Cairo	Lawyer	BA in law
194.	Mohamed Salah[bj]	YJF	Cairo	Accountant	BA in business
195.	Mohammad Abdelsalam Agamy	Independent	Fayoum	Teaching assistant, al-Azhar	BA in business
196.	Mohammad Abdelsalam Feqhy	YJF	Alexandria	Student	BA in political science
197.	Mohamed Aboelgheit[bk]	Independent	Assiut	Journalist	BA in medicine
198.	Mohammad Adel[bl]	6 April	Dakahliya	Student	–
199.	Mohammad Affan[bm]	Brotherhood youth	Cairo	Doctor	BA in medicine
200.	Mohammad al-Baaly	Leftist	Cairo	Journalist	BA from Dar al-Ulum
201.	Mohammad al-Deeb	Association of Revolutionary Artists	El-Beheira	Actor	–
202.	Mohammad Ali Mobarak	Independent	Dakahliya	Carpenter	–
203.	Mohammad al-Khalifi[bn]	Brotherhood youth	Cairo	Civil servant	BA from Dar al-Ulum
204.	Mohammad al-Mohandes	Brotherhood youth	Cairo	Engineer	BA in engineering
205.	Mohammad al-Sayes[bo]	YJF	Al Gharbya	–	–
206.	Mohammad al-Sibai	Independent	Al Sharqia	Sales representative	BA in pharmacology
207.	Mohamad Arafatt	Baradei campaign	Cairo	–	–
208.	Mohammad Atia al-Shaer	Independent	Dakahliya	–	–
209.	Mohammad Awwad[bp]	YJF	Cairo	Labourer	Intermediate diploma
210.	Mohammad Badawi	YJF	Cairo	Dentist	BA in dentistry
211.	Mohammad Galal[bq]	Independent	Beni Soueif	Programmer	–
212.	Mohammad Gamal	Independent	Menia	Sales manager	–

#	Name	Affiliation	Location	Occupation	Education
213.	Mohammad Hassan Suleiman	Brotherhood youth	Cairo	Engineer	BA in engineering
214.	Mohammad Kheiry Gamil	Brotherhood	Fayoum	–	BA in computer science
215.	Mohammad Magdy	Islamist	Cairo	Azhari sheikh	–
216.	Mohammad Mahmoud	6 April	El-Beheira	Journalist	BA in media
217.	Mohammad Mostafa	Brotherhood	Cairo	Journalist	Business, Helwan University
218.	Mohammad Nagy[br]	YJF	Cairo	Student	BA in pharmacology
219.	Mohammad Osman	Brotherhood youth	Giza	Pharmacist	Institute of Cinema
220.	Mohammad Ramadan	Liberal	Cairo	Director	–
221.	Mohammad Reda	Independent	Damietta	Civil servant	–
222.	Mohammad Salah al-Gabaly	Brotherhood	Cairo	Engineer	BA in engineering
223.	Mohammad Sami	6 April	Cairo	Engineer	BA in engineering
224.	Mohammad Shams[bs]	Brotherhood youth	Giza	Engineer	BA in engineering
225.	Mohammad Souka	6 April	Cairo	Student	–
226.	Mohammad Waleed	Ahly Ultras	Cairo	Marketing investor	BA in medicine
227.	Mohammed Abdel Aziz[bt]	Kefaya	Cairo	–	–
228.	Mohammed ElSayed[bu]	Brotherhood	Giza	Tech entrepreneur	BA in engineering
229.	Mohebb Dous[bv]	Nasserist Thought Association	–	–	–
230.	Mona Seif	Leftist	Giza	Chemist, human rights activist	BA in science
231.	Mona Shaheen	Reform and Development Party (RDP)	Cairo	German embassy employee	–
232.	Mossab Ahmed	Independent	Giza	Software developer	–
233.	Mossab al-Gamal[bw]	Brotherhood youth	Giza	Engineer	BA in engineering
234.	Mossab Ragab	Brotherhood youth	Al Sharqia	Student	–
235.	Mostafa Alnagar[bx]	Baradei campaign	Cairo	Dentist	BA in dentistry
236.	Mostafa El Sawy[by]	Brotherhood youth	Giza	Designer, contracting company	BA in business
237.	Mostafa Fouad[bz]	6 April	Cairo	Student	–
238.	Mostafa Maher[ca]	6 April	Cairo	Student	–
239.	Mostafa Mahmoud	Independent	Giza	Singer and entrepreneur	BA in business
240.	Mostafa Shawky	YJF	Cairo	Engineer / Researcher	BA in engineering
241.	Mostafa Singer	Leftist	Sinai	Journalist	–
242.	Nada Teama	6 April	El-Beheira	–	–
243.	Nader ElSayed	Independent	Giza	Football player	BA in sports education
244.	Nagy Kamel[cb]	YJF	Cairo	Engineer	BA in engineering
245.	Nasama Zaghloul al-Ashmawy	YJF	Cairo	Student	–

(*Continued*)

Table I.6.1 (Continued)

	Name	Affiliation (January 2011)	Home governorate	Occupation (January 2011)	Education (January 2011)
246.	Nasser Abdel Hamid	Baradei campaign	Al Gharbya	Journalist/engineer	BA in engineering
247.	Nawwara Negm	Independent	Cairo	Journalist	BA
248.	Nehal al-Merghany	YJF	Cairo	Administrator	Higher Institute for Cooperation
249.	Nour Hamdy	YJF	Monofiya	Engineer	BA in engineering
250.	Noura Younes	Independent	Cairo	Journalist	–
251.	Omar Ahmed Moussa	Independent	Qalyobiya	Engineer	–
252.	Osama el-Mahdy	Brotherhood youth	Cairo	Trader	BA in business
253.	Osama Gamal Abdelhady	Brotherhood youth	Cairo	–	Economics and political science
254.	Osama Gaweesh[cc]	Brotherhood youth	Damietta	Dentist	BA in dentistry
255.	Osama Talaba[d]	Brotherhood youth	–	Student	Medicine
256.	Osman el-Sharkawy	Brotherhood	Monofiya	Engineer	BA in engineering
257.	Qassem Haroon	6 April	Fayoum	–	–
258.	Qotb Hassanein	Ghad Party	Alexandria	–	–
259.	Rabab El-Mahdi	Leftist	Giza	University professor	PhD in political science
260.	Rabha Seif Allam	Independent	Giza	Researcher	Economics and political science
261.	Ragia Omran	Leftist	Cairo	Human rights activist	BA in law
262.	Raida Naguib	Islamist	Giza	Journalist	BA
263.	Rami Sabry	Leftist	Fayoum	Pharmacist	BA in pharmacology
264.	Ramy Raoof	Leftist	–	Researcher, digital freedoms and security	–
265.	Rana Farouq	RDP	Cairo	–	–
266.	Rasha Azab	Leftist	Cairo	Independent journalist	–
267.	Rasha Saad	Independent	Giza	Student	Higher Institute for Computing
268.	Riham Atef Saoud	Independent	Cairo	Journalist	–
269.	Safwan Mohamed[ee]	Baradei campaign	Alexandria	–	–
270.	Salah al-Din Ayman	Brotherhood youth	Assiut	Student	Engineering
271.	Salah Galal	Brotherhood	Giza	Poet	Higher Institute for Social Services
272.	Sally Touma	Baradei campaign	Cairo	Psychiatrist	BA in medicine
273.	Salma Aql	Baradei campaign	Giza	Student	–

#	Name	Affiliation	Location	Occupation	Education
274.	Samar Salama	YJF	Cairo	Student	–
275.	Sameh al-Barqy[cf]	Brotherhood youth	Cairo	Human rights activist	BA in science
276.	Sameh Naguib	Revolutionary Socialists	Cairo	University professor	AUC
277.	Sameh Samir	Leftist	–	Lawyer	–
278.	Sanaa Seif[a]	Leftist	Giza	Student	Secondary school
279.	Sara Adel	6 April	El-Beheira	Student	–
280.	Sara Alaa	Brotherhood youth	Dakahliya	Student	–
281.	Sara Gamal	6 April	Cairo	Journalist	–
282.	Sara Mohammad	Independent	Cairo	Student	Media
283.	Sara Ramadan	YJF	Cairo	Student	Business
284.	Sayyed Abdullah	Brotherhood	Cairo	Entrepreneur	BA in science
285.	Sayyed Aboul Ela	–	Giza	Lawyer	BA in law
286.	Seham Shawada	Independent	Al Gharbya	Journalist	–
287.	Shadi Ghazali Harb[cb]	DFP	Cairo	Doctor	BA in medicine
288.	Shaimaa Hamdy	YJF	Cairo	Journalist	BA
289.	Shams El Fakhakhri	YJF	Alexandria	Schoolteacher	–
290.	Sherif Ayman	Brotherhood youth	Cairo	Student	Business
291.	Shawky Ragab	Labour Party	Al Gharbya	Civil servant	–
292.	Shaymaa Ahmed Mohamed	Brotherhood youth	Alexandria	Chemist	BA
293.	Shaymaa Hamed	Independent	Giza	Chemist	BA in science
294.	Shaymaa Rabie Khalifa	Independent	Giza	–	BA in science
295.	Shehab Abdelmagid	DFP	Cairo	–	Engineering
296.	Shorouk Alshawaf	Brotherhood youth	Giza	Journalist	–
297.	Solafa Magdy[cl]	YJF	Cairo	Lawyer	BA in law
298.	Sumayya Adel	Islamist independent	Alexandria	Student	Faculty of Arts
299.	Sumayya al-Shawwaf	Brotherhood youth	Giza	–	–
300.	Tahany Lesheen	Leftist	–	–	–
301.	Tamer Qenawy	Independent	Qena	Researcher	Economics and political science
302.	Tamer Wageeh	Socialist Renewal	Cairo	Sales manager	–
303.	Tareq Abdelgawad	Brotherhood youth	Cairo	Businessman	BA in business
304.	Tareq al-Deiry	Brotherhood	Beni Soueif	Lawyer	BA in law
305.	Tarek El Khouly[cj]	6 April	Cairo	Student	–
306.	Umniya Atallah	YJF	Cairo	Journalist	BA
307.	Wael Abbas	Independent	Cairo		

(Continued)

Table I.6.1 (Continued)

	Name	Affiliation (January 2011)	Home governorate	Occupation (January 2011)	Education (January 2011)
308.	Wael Adel	Change Academy	Cairo	Businessman	BA in engineering
309.	Wael Gamal	Revolutionary Socialists	Cairo	Journalist	Economics and political science
310.	Wael Ghonim	We Are All Khaled Saeed	Cairo	Regional director, Google	BA in engineering
311.	Wael Khalil	Revolutionary Socialists	Giza	IT consultant	BA in engineering
312.	Wafaa Saad	Independent	Giza	Student	BA in business
313.	Waleed Abd Elraouf[a,k]	YJF	Cairo	Lawyer	BA in law
314.	Walid Shawky[d]	6 April	Dakahliya	Dentist	BA in dentistry
315.	Walid al-Haddad	Brotherhood	Giza	Sales manager	BA in business
316.	Waleed Khairy	Nasserist	Cairo	Lawyer	BA
317.	Waleed Elsayed	Brotherhood	Cairo	Director of education centre	BA from Dar al-Ulum
318.	Wesam Atta	YJF	Al Gharbya	Student	Faculty of business
319.	Wesam Elbakry[e,m]	YJF	Cairo	Student	Faculty of business
320.	Yahya Metouali	Independent	Cairo	–	–
321.	Yasser Ahmed	Brotherhood	Giza	Businessman	BA from Dar al-Ulum
322.	Yasser El Hawary[e,n]	YJF	Cairo	Entrepreneur	BA in business
323.	Yasser ElSayed	Brotherhood	Giza	Engineer	BA in engineering
324.	Yasser Saber	Brotherhood	Giza	Journalist	–
325.	Yassmin al-Gayyoushy	YJF	–	Student	–
326.	Yosra Nagaty	Independent	Cairo	–	BA in agriculture
327.	Youssef Adel	YJF	Al Gharbya	Student	Engineering
328.	Youssef Mohammad Youssef	Independent	Fayoum		
329.	Youssef Ramez	Leftist	Alexandria	Journalist and researcher	Fine arts
330.	Youssef Shaaban[o,o]	Revolutionary Socialists	Alexandria	Journalist	Arabic language
331.	Zeinab Mahdy[e,p]	Independent	Cairo	Student	BA in Economics
332.	Ziad Ali	Liberal	Giza	Businessman	BA in law
333.	Zyad Elelaimy[c,q]	Baradei campaign	Cairo	Lawyer	

[a] Today many of these activists are either living outside Egypt; others are in prison or were killed by agents of the state.
[b] Lost his eye on 28 January 2011.
[c] Now living abroad.
[d] Now living abroad.
[e] Now living abroad.
[f] Arrested then released.
[g] Now living abroad.

h Now living abroad.
i Now living abroad.
j Now living abroad.
k Killed fighting with an anti-regime group in Iraq.
l Imprisoned since the coup with a total sentence of eighteen years.
m Now living abroad.
n Lost his right eye on the Friday of Rage and his left eye during the demonstrations of 19 November 2011.
o Imprisoned for three years before being released in January 2020.
p Now living abroad.
q Now living abroad.
r Now living abroad.
s Arrested and sentenced to imprisonment after the coup.
t Now living abroad.
u Now living abroad.
v Now living abroad.
w Now living abroad.
x Killed in the Rabaa Massacre.
y Now living abroad.
z Died during the events in Mohammed Mahmoud.
aa Died in September 2015.
ab Imprisoned for a period after visiting Egypt.
ac Died in April 2014.
ad Detained without charge since October 2019.
ae Killed in the Rabaa Massacre.
af Now living abroad.
ag Died in May 2019.
ah Detained then released.
ai Now living abroad.
aj Killed in the post-coup massacre of 6 October 2013. Known for his hot temper.
ak Detained for two years and three months then released.
al Detained without charge since May 2018.
am Now living abroad.
an Now living abroad.
ao Detained without charge since November 2019.
ap Living in Egypt but banned from travel.
aq Now living abroad.
ar Detained without charge since November 2019.
as Now living abroad.
at Lost one of his eyes during the revolution.
au Now living abroad.
av Now living abroad.
aw Now living abroad.
ax Imprisoned since 2015, serving a total sentence of ten years.
ay Now living abroad.
az Imprisoned after the coup, released and now detained without charge.
ba Detained then released.
bb Detained then released.
bc Arrested then released.
bd Now living abroad.
be Killed in the Maspero Massacre.
bf Now living abroad.
bg Now living abroad.
bh Detained without charge since February 2018.

Table I.6.2 Revolutionary Youth by Gender

Gender	Number	Percentage
Female	83	24.92
Male	250	75.08
Total	333	100

Table I.6.3 Revolutionary Youth by Profession

Profession	Number	Percentage
Student	67	20.1
Journalist	47	14.1
Engineer	23	6.9
Businessman	18	5.4
Manager	16	4.8
Lawyer	17	5.1
Doctor	14	4.2
Consultant and trainer	10	3.0
Researcher	10	3.0
Pharmacist/chemist	10	3.0
Media	8	2.4
Worker	7	2.1
Human rights activist	7	2.1
University professor/teacher	6	1.8
Artist	6	1.8
Sales representative	6	1.8
Civil servant	5	1.5
Accountant	3	0.9
Programmer	3	0.9
Other professionals/craftspeople	3	0.9
Designer	3	0.9
Azhari sheikh	3	0.9
Athlete	1	0.3
Not given	40	12.0
Total	333	100

Table I.6.3 shows the distribution of professional backgrounds among the individuals listed earlier. Note that the vast majority are university educated or students or have an obvious interest in public affairs due to their profession (lawyers and journalists, for example), and belong to the urban middle classes.

Looking at their political and organizational affiliations, we find that the largest single group, 26.7 per cent, consists of self-identifying independents, to which we can add the 5.7 per cent who described themselves as 'unaffiliated leftists' and the 2.7 per cent of 'unaffiliated Islamists'. If we also add those who belonged not to parties but to youth movements like 6 April or YJF, we find that the vast majority were not party members. Those who did have party affiliations, meanwhile, were largely Islamists and leftists, with less representation from the nationalist and liberal parties. Note, however, that the people listed here are those who came out either on their own initiative or as official liaisons with the young activists. As such, their numbers do not necessarily say much about the broader participation of these parties in the revolutionary mobilization.

The second-largest group after the independents (who actually cannot be treated as a group) were members of the independent youth movements (6 April, YJF, Baradei campaign, PYC, We Are All Khaled Saeed). The third largest was the Brotherhood youth (18.6 per cent), as distinct from categorized as 'Brotherhood' (6.3 per cent). Combining all members of the Muslim Brotherhood organization as a whole, their contingent represents 24.6 per cent of the sample.

Looking at broader ideological groupings, we find large numbers of Islamists, liberals and leftists. I am thoroughly convinced that the ideological divisions among the activists were not at all clear-cut and were in any case gradually broken down over the course of many joint actions. Their common belief in the aims of the revolution, which cut across their different ideological backgrounds, is indicative of the possibility of forming a single central political current across the Arab world – a current that would draw on both liberal (democracy, political rights and civil freedoms) and leftist thought (social justice), while simultaneously building on the traditions of Arab-Islamic history and remaining faithful to Arab-Islamic civilization and causes. This current would represent neither an extreme religious fundamentalism nor an extreme anti-religious type of secularism.

The young people who filled the squares of the Arab world in 2011 belonged to just this sort of current, or else were drawn towards it by their interactions with one another and their experiences of political reality. Its natural development, however, was brought to a premature halt by the old parties' squabble over the place of religion in the state, and the intervention of the army and all its consequences.

It has long been my view that isolated ideologies – Islamist, nationalist, leftist, liberal – are no longer capable of leading Arab society towards change. Although modern democracy must be liberal on issues of civil and political rights, and although it should be clear that in a modern democracy, the state cannot dictate religion or religious proscriptions, the alternative to authoritarianism will not emerge from an ideological stream but from the interaction of common cultural and ethical factors, and it will have to combine the useful aspects of all the different ideological currents.[2]

---

[2] See Bishara, *The Arab Question*.

Table I.6.4 Revolutionary Youth by Political Affiliation

Affiliation	Group/Party	Number	Percentage
Independent	They do not belong to any organized group/party	89	26.7
Independent youth movements	Youth for Justice and Freedom	38	11.4
	6 April	35	10.5
	We Are All Khaled Saeed	2	0.6
Leftist	Revolutionary Socialists	9	2.7
	Socialist Renewal	7	2.1
	Independent leftist	19	5.7
	Progressive Youth Coalition	1	0.3
	Bread and Freedom Party	1	0.3
Nasserist	Karama Party	2	0.6
	Nasserist Thought Association	1	0.3
Islamist	Brotherhood	21	6.3
	Brotherhood youth	62	18.6
	Independent Islamist	6	1.8
	Islamic Labour Party	5	1.5
Liberal	Independent liberal	3	0.9
	Baradei campaign	12	3.6
	Democratic Front	4	1.2
	Ghad Party	3	0.9
	Reform and Development	2	0.6
Nationalists	Ismatists (associated with Ismat Seif El Dawla)	1	0.3
Other (unidentified affiliation)		10	3.0
Total		333	100

The post-revolutionary polarization between secularists and Islamists, the negative role played by the army in the democratic transition and the failure of traditional parties during the transitional period are all likely to contribute to the re-emergence of this alternative.

We have not provided information about the religious backgrounds of the revolutionaries because this is not a category that they themselves used. Egyptian identity was the dominant factor, and the idea of citizenship was at the heart of revolutionary culture. Nonetheless, it is worth mentioning that our sample included six Christians, one Shi'I and one Baha'i. I say this only to show that the activist core always included Christians, as individual activists and citizens, and that their participation was not dependent on the attitude of the church. Note as well that the list included members of tiny minorities, so tiny that they are almost invisible in Egyptian society.

Table I.6.5 shows the price paid by activists during the revolution and its aftermath, especially after the military coup in 2013. Of course, this is nothing compared to the price paid by demonstrators as a whole, which is counted in thousands of deaths and injuries, many of them permanent and life-changing. But even among this hard core of activists, twelve have

Table I.6.5 Activists after the Revolution

Situation	Number	Percentage
In exile	39	11.71
Killed/died	12	3.60
Imprisoned (subsequently released or still in prison)	33	9.91
Permanent disability	4	1.2

Table I.6.6 Attitudes to the Coup

Position	Number	Percentage
Supported the coup	27	8.1
Initially supported the coup then reversed position	3	0.9
Opposed the coup	303	91.0
Total	333	100

been killed and 12 per cent are in exile, while some 10 per cent have been imprisoned;[3] others have been hounded or threatened with death, or are still facing prosecution. In addition to those who have been charged, many are nevertheless under investigation and in some cases banned from travel. Despite their struggle being entirely civil and entirely peaceful – to an exemplary degree recognized the world over – they have suffered and in some cases continue to suffer for their principles.

The majority of those who played organizing roles or took part in the revolution later opposed the military coup of 3 July 2013. Thirty of them who expressed some support for the coup were motivated by their opposition to the behaviour of the Brotherhood and the Morsi government, and of these, three subsequently changed their minds and became fierce public critics of the Sisi regime (Table I.6.6).

---

[3] When the Arabic edition of this book was first published in 2015, this number was only 3.3 per cent. Returning to the list to update it for the English edition, we discovered that the number of those imprisoned or forcibly disappeared had tripled.

7

Who took part in the revolution, and can revolutions be predicted?

Some conclusions can now be drawn. A revolution, in the sense of a broad popular movement seeking to change the political order, may occur when sustained protest activity involving a wide range of demographics makes the transition from piecemeal to political demands concerning the nature of the existing regime. Even if the protests themselves began spontaneously, this transition will require direction and leadership by politically conscious, influential groups. These groups may ultimately plan to take power themselves (generally after sidelining or purging their former allies in the struggle, a road which rarely leads to democracy), but this is a matter for the post-revolutionary period. What is important for our purposes is that both the broad popular dimension and the presence of an educated, politically conscious group are crucial to a revolution.

Two closely interconnected questions arise here. The first is: Does a political revolution depend on the middle class or on the poor? The obvious objection to this phrasing is that it is imprecise: middle-class participation is only relevant to revolutions with 'democratic ambitions'[1] – that is, revolutions against despotism. But since this is the kind of revolution that we are dealing with here – assuming the revolutions in Egypt and Tunisia were revolutions of this kind – the question stands. The second question is distinct, although clearly related: Do revolutions happen after a period of socio-economic decline and deterioration of rights and freedoms or after a period of recovery, economic growth and relative political liberalization? Some believe that answering this question will allow us to predict the exact timing of revolutions, but this idea can be dismissed out of hand: the timing is determined by a confluence of necessary and contingent factors and can never be predicted far in advance. Indeed, it is usually only after a revolution has occurred that articles are published explaining how predictable it was.

---

[1] I prefer this term to 'democratic revolution'.

I On participation in revolutions

Some academics have concluded, based on survey data, that high-income demographics are more open to joining a revolution. The World Values Survey, for example, shows a clear positive correlation between standard of living and 'emancipative values', leading the authors of one article to precisely this conclusion.[2] It is logical that the less a person has to worry about their material needs, the more interested they will be in meeting their moral and spiritual needs and the more emphasis they will place on freedoms as part of their ideal life. But this does not mean that they are more willing to participate in revolutions, and even if they say are, that does not mean that they will participate. All it means is that they will be indispensable to the subsequent process of building democracy. There is a very big difference between these two conclusions.

The only real statistical evidence that high-income individuals were the main participants in the Egyptian revolution comes from post-revolution opinion polls. The 2011 Arab Barometer, for example, suggests that demonstrators were disproportionately middle class and better educated, on average, than the general population.[3] That the middle class should be unusually well represented makes perfect sense, but this does not mean that they made up the majority of those who took part in the revolution – unless, of course, the middle class constitutes the majority of the population as a whole, and this is indeed the case in Egypt, according to the Arab Barometer's definitions. Even so, while it may be reasonable to characterize the majority of the population in Europe, Japan or the United States as middle class, this is not true in the Arab world (or most of South America, Asia or Africa, for that matter). The lower classes in the Arab world, defined as those who live in poverty, represent far more than the poorest 20 per cent of the population – probably more than the poorest 40 per cent[4] – among whom there are many educated people who feel a great sense of relative deprivation and injustice compared with their counterparts in the middle classes. These people are not middle class, but nor are they so poor that they have no time to think about rights and freedoms. Most company employees, civil servants and schoolteachers, for example – who would be solidly middle class in the West – number

---

[2] Fady Mansour, Tesa Leonce and Franklin G. Mixon, 'Who Revolts? Income, Political Freedom and the Egyptian Revolution', *Empirical Economics*, no. 3 (2021).
[3] Ibid.
[4] By 'live in poverty', of course, I do not mean those living under the poverty line, whose official definition varies from country to country, although in most Arab countries even this group accounts for more than the bottom quintile of the population.

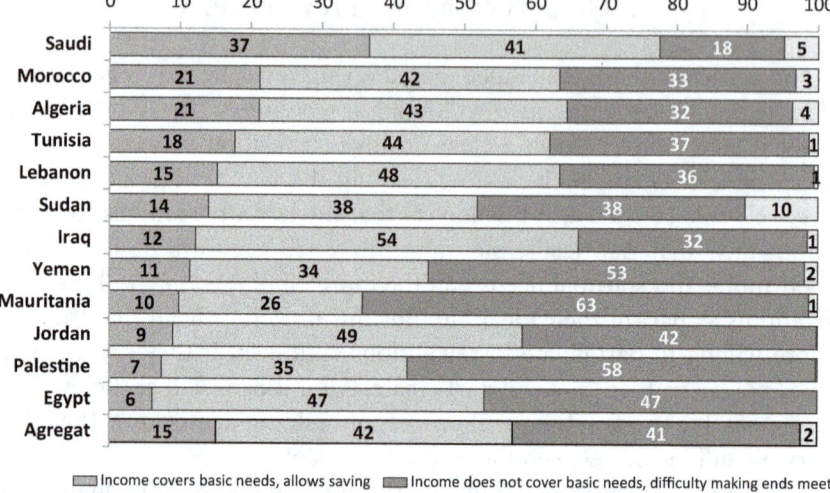

Figure I.7.1 Sufficiency of income for basic needs (all respondents to AOI).

among the poor in most of the Arab world, and certainly in Egypt, where their income barely covers basic needs.

Data and research on the Tunisian and Egyptian revolutions show that the politicized vanguard often come from the so-called middle class, where the level of education plays an important role and is more closely correlated to participation than income, especially since what is considered middle class in the West, such as civil servants, teachers and some technicians working in private institutions, are in the Arab world relatively poor, have a keen sense of deprivation and the class gap, and compare themselves with the upper classes. They are educated, but they are not middle class in the European sense.

Figures I.7.1 and I.7.2, taken from the AOI, shows that the majority of respondents in Egypt (and elsewhere) were either barely making ends meet or not making ends meet at all on their incomes.

Moreover, even revolutions for democracy depend on broad participation from groups with material grievances – shortages of food, clothing, shelter or medical care, for example. This book and my book on the Tunisian revolution[5] have shown that those revolutions were not imaginable without the poor classes. Whether a revolution is 'about democracy' or not depends not on the motivations and goals of those who take part, but the ability of the politically conscious elite or vanguard to direct the revolution not only

---

[5] Bishara, *Understanding Revolutions*.

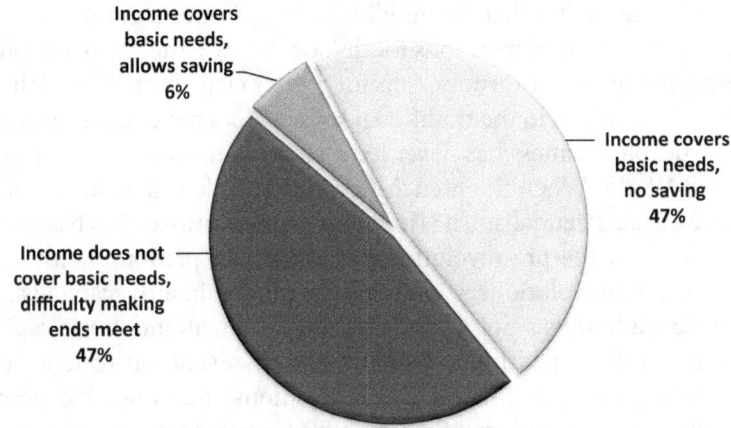

Figure I.7.2 Sufficiency of income for basic needs (Egyptian respondents to AOI).

towards regime change but towards civil liberties, free and fair elections and other such demands.

It is true that as a rule the core participants in a revolution are better educated and better off than the general population. This is only natural. The middle class was more resentful of the sense of stagnation embodied by Mubarak, the prospect of Gamal Mubarak succeeding to the presidency and the growing repression of the late Mubarak era after years of limited freedom and rising living standards. Nonetheless, there are two caveats. The first is that this group was generally planning to take part not in a revolution but in some kind of protest – a demonstration, a sit-in, a strike. The new social movements were primarily made up of university students, graduates and academics, but they only made the leap from 'elite' protest to revolution after the 'popular' classes joined them en masse, at which point they realized that regime change was possible and made it the central plank of their programme. It was this historical moment that made the events of 2011 into a revolution, whether in Egypt, Syria, Yemen or Tunisia.

This book has shown how that process played out in the case of Egypt specifically: waves of people from working-class districts (whether in Cairo, Suez or Alexandria) joined the organized demonstrations of 25 January, and then continued their own spontaneous demonstrations and clashes with the CSF on 26 and 27 January before taking part in force in the Friday of Rage on 28 January. The original organizers were shocked by the level of participation. Only later did professionals and university professors come out in large numbers – once international sympathy in the aftermath of the Battle of the Camel had given the sit-in legitimacy and it seemed safe to join in.

James Davies writes that the middle class plays a more important role in the emergence of and aspirations for democracy, whether by demanding a share in government or through calls for greater civil liberties,[6] and that big business – capitalism in the traditional sense – does not choose revolution. This is true: big business has never led a revolution, whether in Europe or the Third World. When the French Revolution is described as a capitalist revolution against feudalism, it is merely a theoretical assertion based solely on the fact that the pre-revolutionary period was predominantly feudal while the post-revolutionary period was predominantly capitalist. The French Revolution was not a capitalist revolution, although the capitalist system certainly gained much from a political revolution (one in which most of the participants had social motivations) that liberated peasants from feudal bonds, politically marginalized a parasitical aristocracy and opened the door wide to market freedoms.

Capitalism in Third World authoritarian states tends to fear democracy, especially since capital in these countries is typically closely linked to the regime by clientelism. With very few exceptions, business magnates have never been pro-democracy in Tunisia or Egypt.

In order to better understand public opinion on the Egyptian revolution, we will consider here the findings of the AOI[7] around two main survey areas: reasons for the revolution and participation in the revolution. These findings are worth reviewing and analysing because they provide a representative picture of how Egyptians felt about the revolution and involvement in it. (Note that the AOI was conducted three to four months after the revolution, meaning that it reflects attitudes after the victory of the revolution and not while it was still going on.) I present the data here disaggregated by specific variables:

- Demographic variables: citizens' attitudes were analysed by gender (male/female), age and level of education, as well as area of residence (urban/rural) and employment status (employed/unemployed).
- Family economic conditions: following methodologies that divide society into lower-income (poor), middle-income (middle class) and high-income (wealthy) brackets. This variable is based on self-reporting by respondents.[8]

---

[6] Ibid.; James C. Davies, 'Toward a Theory of Revolution', *American Sociological Review* 27, no. 1 (February 1962): 5–19.

[7] The 2011 AOI was conducted between May and June 2011 and was based on a sample of 1,200 respondents.

[8] The AOI is naturally based on the subjective impressions of respondents and may not reflect reality. This is especially true when it comes to questions about income and spending.

There are many methodologies available for dividing societies into classes according to economic conditions. The most common divides society into quintiles and orders them according to their total income. The poorest 20 per cent are then classified as 'poor' or 'vulnerable', the wealthiest 20 per cent 'rich', and the remaining 60 per cent middle class.[9] This methodology, however, sets the size of the middle class in advance in order to calculate changes in their income; since it does not consider changes in the size of the middle class itself, it has come in for criticism. It is even more problematic in developing countries, including Arab countries, for the reasons I have already noted.[10] There are many other methodologies, however, which attempt to solve this problem.

Perhaps one of the more popular is that which defines the middle class as those who make 75–125 per cent of the median income; those who earn less are classed as poor, while those who make more are considered rich.[11] Although this solves the problem of the predetermined middle class, it raises other issues. In Western countries it inflates the size of the rich stratum at the expense of the middle, leading economists to raise the upper limit of the middle class to 167 per cent or even 200 or 300 per cent of the median in some societies and thereby making the indicator methodologically useless for cross-societal comparisons.[12] In developing countries, meanwhile, using 75 per cent as the lower bound puts large portions of the population who should really be classed as poor in the middle class; some researchers using this model, for example, have described as much as 85 per cent of Egyptian society as middle class.[13]

Other researchers have thus developed new methodologies specifically for dealing with developing countries, including Egypt. There are two important examples worth considering here. The first sets the upper limit of the bottom class at the upper poverty line, which is calculated on the

---

[9] This is the methodology used by the EU. See: Anthony B. Atkinson and Andrea Brandolini, 'On the Identification of the "Middle Class"', *Society for the Study of Economic Inequality*, Working Paper 217, September 2011, 4. Available online: https://bit.ly/3kAVlII (accessed 25 October 2021).
See also: William Easterly, 'The Middle Class Consensus and Economic Development', *Journal of Economic Growth* 6, no. 4 (December 2001): 317–35.

[10] See, for example, the discussion here: *Arab Middle Class: Measurement and Role in Driving Change* (Beirut: Economic and Social Commission for Western Asia, 2014), 29–34.

[11] Carol Graham, Nancy Birdsall and Stefano Pettinato, 'Stuck In the Tunnel: Is Globalization Muddling the Middle Class?', *Centre on Social and Economic Dynamics*, Working Paper no. 14, August 2000, Available online: https://brook.gs/2FVpeyl (accessed 25 October 2021).

[12] Atkinson and Brandolini, 'On the Identification', 10.

[13] See: Ali Abdel Gadir Ali, 'The Middle Class in Arab Countries' [Arabic], *Jisr al-Tanmiya* 103 (May 2011); Ali Abdel Gadir Ali, 'The Political Economy of Inequality in the Arab Region and Relevant Development Policies', *Economic Research Forum*, Working Paper no. 502, August 2009, Available online: https://bit.ly/3kEuGEz (accessed 25 October 2021); Ali Abdel Gadir Ali, 'Social Justice and Public Spending Policies in Arab Revolution States' [Arabic], in *Development Policies and Challenges of the Revolution in the Arab Region* [Arabic], ed. Ibraheem Ahmad al-Badawi et al. (Doha and Beirut: ACRPS, 2017), 142–8.

basis of per capita spending on basic food items and non-food essentials.[14] Using this methodology, the lower-income stratum (poor and vulnerable to poverty) constituted 48.9 per cent of Egyptian society in 2011, while the middle class constituted 44 per cent and the upper class 7.1. per cent.[15]

The second important methodology divides Egyptian society into deciles, and then calculating each decile's share of public spending. This methodology defines the poor as any decile whose share of public spending falls below the national poverty line; any individual decile whose share of public spending is less than 8 per cent is considered 'poor', while those who account for between 8 per cent and 12 per cent are considered middle class. By this measure the middle class constitutes 40 per cent of the Egyptian population, the poor 51 per cent and the rich 9 per cent.[16]

The AOI relies on these two methodologies to classify respondents by income into three groups: poor, middle and rich. The sample was divided into ten deciles, after which each group's share of monthly household spending[17] was distributed by calculating an average of per capita spending in every decile based on the upper poverty line. Those groups, whose spending fell below the upper poverty line (less than 9 per cent of the group's total spending), were considered poor or vulnerable, while those whose spending accounted for more than 12 per cent were considered rich. Those who fell between these groups were considered to be middle class.[18]

Alongside household spending, the AOI also included another variable: respondents' own impressions of their economic situation. The survey asked respondents to choose which of the three following statements best described their situation: (1) our household income covers our basic needs, and we are able to save; (2) our household income covers our basic needs, and we are unable to save; or (3) our household income does not cover our basic, and we have difficulty making ends meet.[19]

---

[14] Khalid Abu-Ismail and Niranjan Sarangi, 'A New Approach to Measuring the Middle Class: Egypt', *ESCWA*, 26 December 2013, 14–16, Available online: https://bit.ly/33sk7h7 (accessed 25 October 2021). Average individual daily spending on the lower poverty line (individual needs to cover basic caloric intake) was $2.3 in 2011, while on the upper poverty line it was $3.

[15] Ibid.

[16] Kareema Kurayyem, 'Comparative Study of Poverty in Three Arab Low-, Medium- and High-Income Countries' [Arabic], in *Economic Growth and Sustainable Development in Arab Countries: Development Policies and Jobs* [Arabic], ed. Ashraf Abdelaziz Abdelqader et al. (Doha/Beirut: ACRPS, 2013), 281–6.

[17] As reported by respondents.

[18] Based on data published by the Egyptian statistical agency. See: Central Agency for Public Mobilization and Statistics, *Select Poverty Indicators*.

[19] Survey participants who gave this response were asked how they bridged the income gap. In repeated AOI surveys, respondents consistently said that they relied on traditional social solidarity networks (neighbours, relatives, etc.), charitable associations and/or government assistance, or borrowing.

Who Took Part in the Revolution?

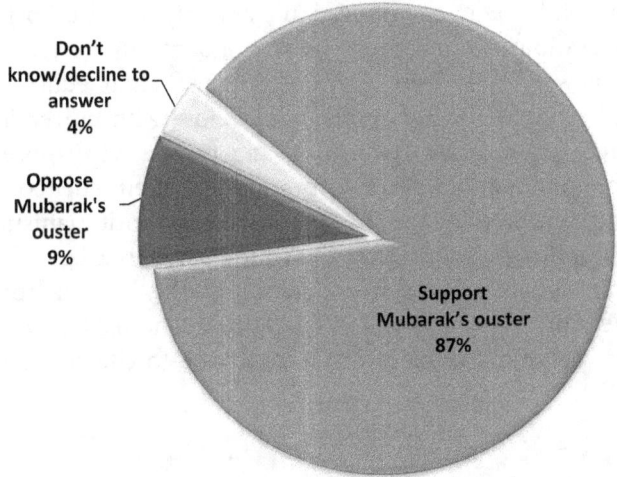

Figure I.7.3 Attitudes towards Mubarak's ouster.

1 Trends in public opinion: Why did the revolution erupt?

Before considering Egyptians' opinions of the causes of the revolution – which will contribute to an understanding of their attitudes towards it – it is worth noting that most respondents (some 87 per cent) supported the revolution, with only about 10 per cent opposing it. There is no clear correlation between demographic or economic variables (age, education, urban/rural or financial circumstances) and support for the revolution[20] (Figure I.7.3).

When asked what they believed the drivers of the revolution were, respondents generally gave one of four broad answers. The most cited was widespread corruption within the regime (40 per cent of respondents), emphasizing that Mubarak and his allies had 'robbed the people' and turned state property into private property. The second reason was poor economic conditions (30 per cent of respondents): poor living standards, high levels of unemployment and pervasive poverty. The third reason was injustice and oppression towards citizens (16 per cent). The fourth reason (9 per cent) was the dictatorial regime and its monopolization of power and suppression of freedoms, for which respondents listed a whole range of examples: the absence of political and civil freedoms, a lack of political pluralism and human rights violations (Table I.7.1).

An analysis of these opinions against demographic factors yielded considerable variation. Women focused more on economic factors and

---

[20] A one-way analysis of variance (OneWay ANOVA) test showed that demographic and economic variables had little to no impact on respondents' opinions on this question.

corruption, while men emphasized dictatorship and authoritarianism. Level of education had an impact on respondents' understanding of the revolution as well. Those with only a secondary school education or less emphasized economic factors more, while those with university degrees focused more on authoritarianism. Young people were more likely to mention economic conditions or corruption than their older counterparts. Similarly, urbanites were more likely to cite authoritarianism and the absence of political pluralism than their rural counterparts.

Economic variables were also significant. The lower a respondent's income, the more likely they were to mention economic factors, while the higher their income, the more likely they were to cite authoritarianism (Table I.7.2).

Table I.7.1 Causes of the Revolution[a]

Cause	Percentage (%)
Regime corruption	40
Economic deprivation	30
Oppression and lack of justice	16
Dictatorship/suppression of freedoms	9
Don't know/decline to answer	5
Total	100

[a] The actual question: In your opinion, what was the most important reason for the popular revolution in Egypt and the overthrow of Mubarak?

Table I.7.2 Causes of the Revolution by Gender, Age, Education, Residence and Income

Cause[a]	Gender (%)	
	Men	Women
Corruption	41	43
Economic deprivation	29	35
Oppression and lack of justice	20	14
Dictatorship/suppression of freedoms	10	8
Total	100	100

Cause	Age (%)				
	18–24	25–34	35–44	45–54	55+
Corruption	39	45	39	44	41
Economic deprivation	35	32	36	24	34
Oppression and lack of justice	18	16	17	22	15
Dictatorship/suppression of freedoms	8	7	8	10	10
Total	100	100	100	100	100

(*Continued*)

Table I.7.2 (Continued)

Cause[b]	Level of education (%)			
	Illiterate/some knowledge	Less than secondary	Secondary	Higher than secondary
Corruption	39	43	40	48
Economic deprivation	37	28	38	20
Oppression and lack of justice	20	20	15	17
Dictatorship/suppression of freedoms	4	9	7	17
Total	100	100	100	100

Cause	Place of residence (%)[c]	
	Urban	Rural
Corruption	42	42
Economic deprivation	28	36
Oppression and lack of justice	17	16
Dictatorship/suppression of freedoms	13	6
Total	100	100

Cause	Respondents' description of their household circumstances[d] (%)		
	Income covers basic needs, allows saving	Income covers basic needs, no saving	Income does not cover basic needs, difficulty making ends meet
Corruption	36	45	40
Economic deprivation	19	29	37
Oppression and lack of justice	27	17	16
Dictatorship/suppression of freedoms	18	9	7
Total	100	100	100

Cause	Income (%)		
	Low	Middle	High
Corruption	40	45	43
Economic deprivation	35	31	18
Oppression and lack of justice	18	15	23
Dictatorship/suppression of freedoms	7	9	16
Total	100	100	100

[a] A T-Test was carried out with a level of significance of 0.05. Gender proved to be of great relevance with regard to this question (0.00).
[b] An ANOVA test showed that education was a significant factor in this regard.
[c] A Chi-Square test with a level of significance of 0.05 showed that urban versus rural was a significant factor (0.3).
[d] A OneWay ANOVA test showed that income was a very significant variable.

2 Participation in the revolution

Respondents were asked a general question about whether they had taken part in the revolution between 25 January and 11 February. Some 16 per cent reported participating in some sort of revolutionary activity (including supporting the revolution on social media), while 84 per cent said that they had not (Figure I.7.4).

Disaggregating responses by demographic variables shows that men were around four times more likely to engage in all kinds of revolutionary activity than women. Young people also made up the majority of revolutionaries: most participants fell within the twenty-five to thirty-four age group (35 per cent) or the eighteen to twenty-four age group (24 per cent). Education also proved to be significant, with the largest number of participants holding a secondary certificate (37 per cent) and the second largest a university degree (34 per cent); those who described themselves as 'illiterate' accounted for only 10 per cent of participants. As expected, the majority of participants (70 per cent) were from urban rather than rural areas.

Economic status was also significant. There was an inverse correlation between household income and participation: the most likely to participate were those whose household income did not allow them to cover basic needs (44 per cent), followed by those who were able to provide basic necessities but could not save (41 per cent), with only a comparatively small number (16 per cent) from households whose income allowed them

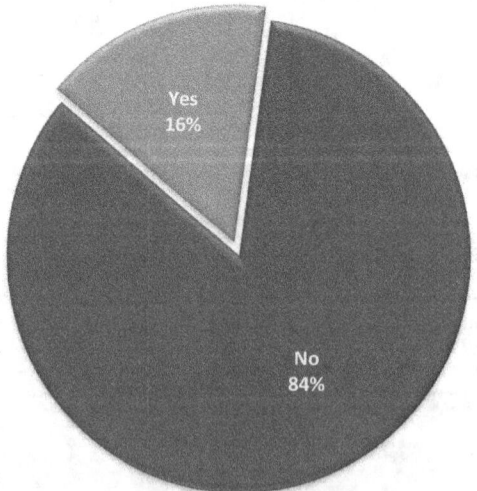

Figure I.7.4 Did you participate in the revolution?

to save. The same correlation applied with respect to income: 50 per cent of participants were from low-income strata, 36 per cent middle-income and only 14 per cent high-income.

It is thus clear that while the Egyptian revolution was truly popular – in that it brought together people from every part of Egyptian society – its backbone was made up of young urbanites of an average or above-average level of education who came from households that were either barely getting by or not making ends meet at all.

3 Types of participation

Of the 16 per cent of respondents who took part in the revolution in any sort of capacity, 51 per cent said they had attended at least one demonstration, whether in Tahrir or elsewhere, accounting for about 8 per cent of all respondents. Some 84 per cent (13 per cent of all respondents) said that they had been involved in the popular committees, 22 per cent (3 per cent of all respondents) that they had protected demonstrators, 19 per cent (3 per cent of all respondents) that they had only engaged online, and 13 per cent (2 per cent of all respondents) that they had provided demonstrators with food and water. Demonstrations were thus the activity that attracted most of those who said that they took part in some activity (note as well that taking part in popular committees did not necessarily mean participating directly in the revolution itself).

When we break down the different activities according to demographic data, we find that participation in demonstrations largely corresponds to participation in revolutionary activities overall: men were more likely to participate, as were people with a secondary certificate (39 per cent) or university degree (38 per cent).[21] Young people predominated, with the eighteen to twenty-four and twenty-five to thirty-four age groups accounting for 33 per cent each of demonstrators.

Economically, the largest number of demonstrators reported that their household income allowed them to cover basic needs but not to save (44 per cent), followed closely by those who could neither cover basic needs nor save (39 per cent). Those who reported being able to both cover basic

---

[21] An unpublished study based on Arab Barometer data suggests that university graduates made up a much higher proportion of participants (64 per cent). Review of the raw data, however, shows that this is an overstatement resulting from a number of factors, including a disproportionately high number of university graduates in the sample (with no compensatory weighting on the part of the authors) and the miscategorization of those who held standard or technical diplomas as university graduates. See: Mark R. Beissinger et al., 'Who Participated in the Arab Spring? A Comparison of Egyptian and Tunisian Revolutions', *Working paper presented at APSA Annual Meeting Paper, 2012*, Available online: https://bit.ly/3bvOsQ5 (accessed 25 October 2021) [Unpublished manuscript].

Table I.7.3 Participation by Revolutionary Activity

Activity	% of participants in revolution	% of all respondents
Demonstrations in Tahrir Square/other squares in the provinces	51	8
Protected demonstrators	22	3
Provided demonstrators with food and water	13	2
Popular committees to protect neighbourhoods	84	13
Distributing information and publications	5	1
Writing on the internet (e.g. Facebook and Twitter)	19	3
Organizational activity around protests, e.g. transport of protesters	5	1

needs and save, meanwhile, accounted for 16 per cent of demonstrators – which, while low, is around twice that cohort's size as a proportion of the population. Breaking down demonstrators by income, a slightly different picture emerges: 49 per cent of demonstrators fell into the low-income band, 34 per cent into the middle-income band and 17 per cent into the high-income band (showing once again the inverse correlation between income and participation). The disparity here arises from the fact that the first variable is self-reported, while the second is based on monthly household spending.[22]

It is also interesting to look more closely at those who only participated in the revolution digitally, even though there were relatively few of them (3 per cent of all respondents). The data shows that eighteen-to-twenty-four-year-olds were the most likely to take part through online activity, followed by twenty-five-to-thirty-four-year-olds, and that they were most likely to be university educated, with participation falling off in tandem with level of education. Moreover, supporting the revolution digitally correlates directly with reported household income: the majority of digital participants reported being able to both buy essentials and save. When compared with actual income, however, we found that the largest group (41 per cent) fell into the middle-income stratum, while only 32 per cent were from the higher-income stratum (Tables I.7.3 and I.7.4).

[22] The aforementioned study concluded that the middle classes were the group that participated in demonstrations in the largest numbers. This conclusion is based on their definition of the middle class as the middle three-fifths of the population by income. Review of the raw data, however, shows that some 55 per cent of the sample falls below the 2010–11 Egyptian national poverty line, and in any case, having the middle class account for 60 per cent of the Egyptian population is quite excessive. See: Beissinger, Jamal and Mazur, 'Who Participated'; Mansour, Leonce and Mixon, 'Who Revolts?'.

Table I.7.4 Participation in Revolutionary Activity by Gender, Age, Education, Residence and Income

Variable	Participated in all revolutionary activities (%)[a]	Participated in demonstration (%)	Supported revolution online (%)
Gender			
Men	83	84	78
Women	17	16	22
Age			
18–24	24	33	46
25–34	35	33	24
35–44	19	18	11
45–54	15	12	14
55+	7	4	5
Educational level			
Illiterate/some knowledge	10	9	0
Less than secondary	19	13	14
Secondary	37	39	31
Higher than secondary	34	38	56
Residence			
Urban	70	72	89
Rural	30	28	11
Respondents' description of their household circumstances			
Income covers basic needs, allows saving	16	16	37
Income covers basic needs, no saving	41	44	34
Income does not cover basic needs, difficulty making ends meet	44	39	29
Employment			
Working	70	70	57
Not working	30	30	43
Income			
Low	50	49	27
Middle	36	34	41
High	14	17	32

[a] A OneWay ANOVA test on self-reported economic circumstances and family income showed that these factors were very significant with regard to participation in the revolution.

II On timing

In theorizing revolution, Davies used not the example of the French Revolution but the Dorr Rebellion, an insurrection in the US state of Rhode Island caused by industrialization, urbanization and rising living standards and expectations followed by an economic slump between 1835 and 1840. The rebellion became a revolution that produced alternative institutions and demanded universal suffrage.[23] He also cites the Russian Revolution, where, within fifty-six years of the end of serfdom in 1861, a pattern of rising expectations followed by crisis caused by military defeat in 1904 and rebellion in 1905 gave way to political liberalization (an elected Duma), a security crackdown and ultimately another crisis with the First World War after a period of economic growth.[24] His final example is the Egyptian revolution of 1952, which was preceded by economic growth during the Second World War and a subsequent decline during the Korean War; the fruits of economic growth were not evenly distributed and were accompanied by periods of boom and bust tied to the changing demand for cotton. Defeat by Israel was followed by peasant uprisings in 1951 and forty-nine strikes in cities.[25]

I agree with Davies that the feeling of being deprived of rights or freedoms is tied both to aspirations for these things and living standards. Here we are beginning to find an answer to the second question raised earlier: the timing of revolutions. If such aspirations emerge only to be disappointed, they fuel greater anger and resentment. This is why revolutions typically take place after a period of high growth in which expectations rise, only to be dashed by a war, a global economic downturn or some other crisis. Of course, economic crisis or recession is not a necessary condition; revolutions may erupt at a time when economic growth is exacerbating inequality. This is not a new observation: de Tocqueville made a similar point in *The Ancien Régime and the French Revolution*.[26] He did not mean

---

[23] Davies, 'Toward a Theory', 8–9.
[24] Ibid., 11–13.
[25] Ibid., 14.
[26] I discuss de Tocqueville's account of social and political unrest and its relationship to rapid economic development in my most recent book on democratic transition. De Tocqueville argues that the French Revolution was preceded by rapid and continuous economic growth leading to prosperity and that the subsequent unrest was the product of non-economic causes – in fact, that it was most significant in areas that had seen the highest levels of development. Barrington Moore, meanwhile, argues that the French Revolution began not as a bourgeois revolution but as a peasants' uprising, only later attracting the urban poor and the middle classes critical of feudalism and the church. De Tocqueville's cultural-psychological account ties revolution to people's expectations and maintains that 'revolutions do not happen when things go from bad to worse. [. . .] The regime demolished by a revolution is usually better than that which preceded it.' See: Azmi Bishara, *The Issue of Democratic Transition*, 153–4, 184–5; Alexis de Tocqueville, *The Ancien Régime and the French Revolution*, trans. Arthur Goldhammer (Cambridge and New York: Cambridge University

that economic prosperity caused the revolution, but that people were driven to revolt for non-economic reasons (social or political) in economic conditions that encouraged aspirations for a better life.

Other academics have since made predictions based on Davies' article.[27] If quantitative data suggest a deteriorating economic situation after a period of growth or political liberalization, then this will produce the sort of popular resentment needed for a revolution. Under such conditions, the spark of revolution can spread from one country to another.[28] The point here is *relative* rather than *absolute* deterioration and deprivation. None of this suggests that most participants will be well off or even middle class.

Analysing socio-economic conditions prevailing before the 'Arab Spring', Campante and Chor find rising levels of education in a poor job market – that is, rising levels of unemployment in the countries which saw revolutions in the first year,[29] with no job opportunities for university graduates. Hassan Aly and Hany Abdel-Latif have noted that from 2002 to 2008, the countries of the region – including countries like Egypt in which revolutions took place – saw their average unemployment rate leap from 10 per cent to 25 per cent of graduates, despite average GDP growth of 5 per cent.[30] Others have reached similar conclusions. Among the twenty countries worldwide exhibiting the fastest growth in the average number of years of schooling, eight are Arab countries, including Egypt, Tunisia and Libya.[31] These countries have similarly limited job opportunities for graduates.[32]

According to Bassiouni's estimates, in 2009 roughly half of Egypt's eighty-five million people were under the age thirty, and of these some 60 per cent were unemployed. In 2011, it was estimated that 200 families owned 90 per cent of the Egyptian private sector.[33] It is not just economic growth that precedes revolutions then, but growth that does not create enough jobs for the growing numbers of young people capable of working, in particular graduates. As the class gap continued to widen, the sense of

---

Press, 2011), chapter III, 4, 152–9, 157; Barrington Moore Jr., *Social Origins of Dictatorship and Democracy: Lord and Peasant in the Making of the Modern World*, with a new foreword by Edward Friedman and James C. Scott (Boston, MA: Beacon Press, 1993), 68–9, 74–5, 81–2.

[27] Davies, 'Toward a Theory', 5–19.
[28] Simplice A. Asongu and Jacinta C. Nwachukwu, 'Revolution Empirics: Predicting the Arab Spring', *Empirical Economics* 51 (2016): 439–82.
[29] Filipe R. Campante and Davin Chor, 'Why Was the Arab World Poised for Revolution? Schooling, Economic Opportunities, and the Arab Spring', *Journal of Economic Perspectives* 26, no. 2 (Spring 2012): 167–88.
[30] Hany Abdel-Latif and Hassan Aly, 'Are Politically Connected Firms Turtles or Gazelles? Evidence from the Egyptian Uprising', *Social Science Research Network (SSRN) Electronic Journal* (15 April 2018), 2.
[31] Campante and Chor, 'Why Was the Arab World Poised', 168.
[32] Ibid., 169.
[33] Bassiouni, 'Egypt's Unfinished Revolution'.

deprivation grew – which is distinct from grinding poverty. A sense of deprivation implies an awareness of needs other than basic essentials, and here corruption is particularly relevant.[34] Anger at the existence of vast inequalities between the rich and the poor is further exacerbated when the source of that wealth is corruption. In such a case there is no possible moral justification for the disparity, and class resentments become tied up in political resentments, since corruption is a matter of the relationship between wealth and power.

Another reason for resentment may be the regime's attempts to roll back previous gains considered part of the country's way of life, which can spark a political crisis. Frerichs discusses the ethos that arose in Egypt around subsidies, which she calls the 'moral economy of bread', arguing that neoliberal policy in Mubarak's later years led to a 'loss of entitlements' and made bread into a political issue. When Sadat attempted to abolish bread subsidies in 1977, of course, it sparked the famous 'bread uprising'; Frerichs argues that the 2011 revolution was likewise a revolution of the hungry.[35] This is the opposite of Mansour's argument that it was a revolution of the middle classes and the educated.

In July 2010, the *Economist* published a special report celebrating Egypt's rising growth, shrinking public debt and growing participation in the world economy. According to the report, $46 billion was invested in the country from 2004 to 2009, while the national debt fell by one-third to the high, but more manageable figure of 76 per cent of GDP.[36] In the two years directly preceding the revolution, the rate of growth declined, coinciding with the global financial crisis after 2008, which affected Suez Canal tolls as well as tourism. Nevertheless, demand for housing continued to grow, with the rate of growth rising to 4.6 per cent.[37] The housing market's continued high growth is indicative of the distortion of an economy in which overall growth is not coupled with growth in other sectors, such as the labour market. The *Economist* agreed with Davies that the 1952 revolution happened during a time of high growth rates, but that the fruits of this prosperity generally fell to the bourgeois elite and the urban middle classes.[38]

The same applies to Egypt on the eve of Mubarak's fall. In the last decade of the twentieth century, growth was accompanied by rising levels

---

[34] Its dimensions are usually exaggerated, and it remains a favourite theme for populist politics after the revolution.
[35] Sabine Frerichs, 'Egypt's Neoliberal Reforms and the Moral Economy of Bread: Sadat, Mubarak, Morsi', *Review of Radical Political Economics* 48, no. 4 (2016): 610–32.
[36] 'Holding Its Breath: A Special Report on Egypt', *Economist*, 17 July 2010, 5, Available online: https://econ.st/2Rb7mld (accessed 25 October 2021).
[37] Ibid., 6.
[38] Ibid., 2.

Table I.7.5 Wages and Benefits as a Share of GDP (%)

Year	Egypt	Jordan	Tunisia	Morocco
2000	29	39	36	32
2010	25	40	36	30

Source: ESCWA, *Arab Middle Class: Measurement and role in driving change* (Beirut: United Nations, 2014), figure 45, at: https://bit.ly/3bstVvY (accessed 31 October 2021).

of poverty.[39] Poverty is also believed to have risen during the 1980s and the first half of the 1990s, but the second half of the 1990s saw a general reduction.[40] Frerichs argues that from 2000 to 2010, poverty increased despite higher growth: more than a quarter of the population were living under the national poverty line.[41]

The ESCWA report cited earlier compares the wage share as a percentage of GDP in Arab countries like Jordan, Tunisia or Morocco. In Egypt this figure fell from around 29 per cent in 2000 to 25 per cent in 2010, while in other countries it remained at 30–40 per cent, suggesting a bigger problem with social justice in Egypt (Table I.7.5).

The Gini coefficient shows rising inequality in the decade leading up to the revolution, although the ratio between the income share of the highest quintile and that of the lowest quintile remained the same. At the same time, the sense of deprivation and inequality increased.[42] In 1999, the Gini coefficient in Egypt reached 32.8 per cent, falling to 30.2 per cent in 2010.[43] The share of the bottom 20 per cent, however, stayed more or less constant from 1999 to 2010, at 8.9 per cent and 9.1 per cent, respectively. The same applies to the wealthiest quintile, whose share was 42.1 per cent in 1999 and 41.2 per cent in 2010 (Table I.7.6).

It is logical that protest will intensify during a time of rising growth in countries where the fruits of growth largely fall to the richest: capital and those linked by clientelism to the state. Whether that protest will become a revolution is something else entirely, dependent on the behaviour of

---

[39] Frerichs, 'Egypt's Neoliberal Reforms', 614.
[40] Ibid., 614; Samira Salem and Jane Gleason, 'An Examination of Poverty Reduction in Egypt: Contributing Factors, Sustainability, and Lessons', *Pro-Poor Economic Growth Research Studies*, March 2003, 6, Available online: https://bit.ly/36lVWUB (accessed 25 October 2021).
[41] Frerichs, 'Egypt's Neoliberal Reforms', 614; Heba El Laithy and Dina Armanious, 'The Status of Food Security and Vulnerability in Egypt, 2009', *World Food Programme*, December 2011, 49, Available online: https://bit.ly/35nhSyj (accessed 25 October 2021).
[42] Frerichs, 'Egypt's Neoliberal Reforms', 614; Vladimir Hlasny and Paolo Verme, 'Top Incomes and the Measurement of Inequality in Egypt', *World Bank*, Policy Research, Working Paper no. 6557, August 2013, Available online: https://bit.ly/2ZqIrih (accessed 25 October 2021); Paolo Verme, 'Facts vs. Perceptions: Understanding Inequality in Egypt', *World Bank Blogs*, 24 January 2013, Available online: https://bit.ly/2DJo1t0 (accessed 25 October 2021).
[43] World Bank, 'Gini index (World Bank estimate)—Egypt, Arab Rep.', Available online: https://bit.ly/2SfdpG2 (accessed 25 October 2021).

Table I.7.6 Income Distribution

Year	Poorest quintile	Second quintile	Middle quintile	Fourth quintile	Richest quintile
1990	8.7	12.5	16.3	21.4	41.1
1995	9.5	13	16.4	21.2	39.9
1999	8.9	12.5	15.8	20.7	42.1
2004	9	12.7	16.1	20.8	41.4
2008	9.2	13	16.2	20.8	40.8
2010	9.1	12.9	16.1	20.8	41.2

Source: World Bank, 'Income share held by lowest 20% – Egypt, Arab Rep.', at: https://bit.ly/3170BUF (accessed 25 October 2021); World Bank, 'Income share held by second 20% – Egypt, Arab Rep.', at: https://bit.ly/2K9Yrwv (accessed 25 October 2021); World Bank, 'Income share held by third 20% – Egypt, Arab Rep.', at: https://bit.ly/2Gxboj6 (accessed 25 October 2021); World Bank, 'Income share held by fourth 20% – Egypt, Arab Rep.', at: https://bit.ly/2YbcjAk (accessed 25 October 2021); World Bank, 'Income share held by highest 20% – Egypt, Arab Rep.', at: https://bit.ly/2JXFTRe (accessed 25 October 2021).

the regime and its repressive apparatus and other factors related to the consciousness of the protest movement's leaders.

But why is it that protest intensifies at moments of high growth? First, because middle-class expectations rise and, second, because although some of the benefits of growth may trickle down to the poorest in society, the well-off benefit far more, generating more opportunities for both conspicuous consumption and corruption. Growth, in short, produces greater inequality and a wider wealth gap. Absolute poverty may decrease, but relative poverty increases, and with it a sense of resentment. If a period of growth then gives way to slowdown and worsening living conditions, the likelihood of protest will naturally increase, but this likelihood is present, even absent, in a recession. Political crisis, war, a security crackdown or a revolution in a culturally similar country can all be the spark that set these resentments aflame. We are talking here about potentialities and not inevitabilities.

Another important element that emerged from the analysis of revolutions in Egypt, Tunisia and other Arab countries like Syria, Libya or Yemen is an awareness of human dignity. This developed in step with people's awareness of their nature as human beings who deserve to be treated with respect, and in particular not to be insulted or degraded or be treated as if their bodies were not their own (whether by physical assault or some other means). The significant development here is more intense police predation and a willingness to ride roughshod over citizens' dignity even as citizens themselves were no longer willing to tolerate this treatment. The security forces' reckless disregard for human dignity may be exacerbated by their lack of confidence in their coercive capacities or the polar opposite – their certainty that they are effectively unaccountable and that the populace will remain meek so long as they are afraid. In Egypt it is possible to observe a strong reaction to this increasing insensitivity on the part of the security services, exemplified in the torture of people detained arbitrarily. In Syria, the revolution implied a thoroughgoing rebellion against degrading treatment by the regime as a matter of daily routine, but in that case the rebellion did not result in dignity itself becoming a governing value of the revolution. In many cases, in fact, it led to imitation of the regime's own tactics as the revolution devolved into a civil war. This is not our topic here, however. What I want to emphasize is the importance of human dignity in understanding the psychology of the angry and rebellious. Rebellion against humiliation and efforts to reclaim human dignity should not be discounted as drivers of revolution, enabling people to overcome fear and push forward.

Concluding remarks

Part I

This first part of this book has been split into two main sections. Chapters 1 and 2 reviewed the social and political history of what I call the July Republic. Although there were basic continuities in the structure of the regime in this period that allow us to talk about a single republic, policies differed greatly under Nasser, Sadat and Mubarak. In particular, an economy in which the state played a central role in economic planning, industrialization and development was replaced by greater economic openness to the United States and the West more generally, a process driven by the Sadat-era realignment away from Moscow and towards Washington.

Privatization began under Sadat, but despite efforts to make the country more welcoming to foreign investment, the Egyptian economy remained dependent on the public sector throughout his tenure. It was only with Mubarak that real economic liberalization took place, in particular during the 2000s. However, liberalization did not produce a truly free market: the web of patron–client relationships linking the political to the economic sphere was too extensive for that. In fact, a new public economy was developing – a military economy built around the army which cemented its budgetary independence. At the same time, power was being centralized in the presidency at the expense of other state institutions. Despite Nasser's popularity and the force of his personality, the office of the president was stronger under Sadat than it was under him and was made stronger again under Mubarak. The autocratic element ultimately became so strong that it spread to the president's family and encouraged dynastic ambitions.

Although Nasser quickly emerged as the strongest of his erstwhile comrades, he was still obliged to make many compromises while in power, particularly with senior army officers. This ceased to be a problem after 1967 when he was able to place the blame for defeat at the army command's door. Sadat took advantage of this to subordinate the army entirely to the presidency, even during the 1973 war when the prestige of the institution was restored among the general population. Under Mubarak, a final accommodation was reached that granted the army broad autonomy in exchange for loyalty to the president, a compromise no doubt influenced by the growth of the military economy. During this period, the regime came to rely more on the various branches of the domestic security forces, but it was unable to do without the army in exceptional situations. And the army remained the strongest institution within the regime. It had no interest in putting this strength to work in politics, but this only increased its popularity by placing it above the 'corruption' of politics.

During the ascendancy of the public sector, the developmental state achieved a great deal. Among its significant achievements were land reform and free education, which facilitated the development of a new middle class of peasant origin within the state apparatus and encouraged a new culture that included higher expectations from the state. Financial shortfalls, administrative bloat and low productivity eventually conspired to limit the state's developmental role, but Egyptians could still be confident that they would be able to obtain essential items. Nonetheless, despite high growth rates under Sadat and Mubarak, frustration and despair ultimately became the order of the day for large portions of society. The poverty belts of unregulated slums that sprang up around cities and the yawning wealth gap attested to the regime's failure to translate economic growth into human development and were accompanied by endemic corruption and the rise of a crony capitalism based not on competition but on clientelism. The resentment that these developments found expression was in periodic outbreaks of social protest and in widespread opposition to the regime's foreign policy, especially with regard to Palestine and Iraq.

Economic liberalization came along with a degree of carefully controlled political liberalization. Licensed political parties were afforded a margin of freedom within which they were allowed to play the role of permanent opposition, thereby depriving them of any real opposition role, since an opposition that never has any opportunity to take power is simply part of the authoritarian regime's process of self-reproduction. Co-option of the official parties and limited press freedom, however, failed to contain social and political protest. Instead, true opposition to the regime migrated to the new social and protest movements.

The Egyptian regime launched several cosmetic reforms in response to domestic crises (the assassination of Sadat, for example) or foreign pressure (the rise of the neoconservatives in the United States). These reforms created some space for political action and union organizing as well as limited freedom within the private media. But the regime did not change its essentially authoritarian structure (combined with economic neoliberalism). Nor did the reforms bring about internal splits in the regime or escape its control.

Chapters 3 and 4 looked at the history of protest movements in Egypt in order to demonstrate that the revolution did not come out of the blue and that the Egyptian people were not meek and silent before 25 January. Most protests from 1952 onwards were driven by students and parts of the middle class on the one hand and labour activists on the other. The most significant outbreaks took place whenever student protests overlapped with those of broader society, the first signs of which appeared towards the end of Mubarak's tenure with the Mahalla strikes and other major labour mobilizations. The final break with the regime's 'competitive authoritarianism' took place after the flagrant abuses of the 2010 parliamentary elections, which were boycotted by most political parties. (The Muslim Brotherhood took part but did not win a single seat.) This followed a long period of social contention around the possibility of a dynastic succession within the Mubarak family, a prospect that went against the whole republican ethos. The question of succession was no less important to the general sociopolitical ferment than the neoliberalism pursued by the regime with particular vigour after the rise of Gamal Mubarak's technocrats and businessmen within the ruling NDP. The great paradox was that the more realistic it became that Mubarak's son would succeed him, the more people this possibility alienated within state institutions and the NDP. The army was particularly disturbed by the prospect of further economic reform that might target its own interests and by the growing prominence of big business within the state itself. Business had always been willing to accept a Bonapartist regime, staying out of politics in exchange for guaranteed stability and control of the economy. Indeed, most big businessmen had not only relied on the state for protection but benefited extensively from state contracts. The military did not want this to change. Opposition to a Gamal Mubarak presidency also galvanized political alliances of a new kind – alliances that cut across partisan boundaries and targeted the very heart of the regime, the presidency.

The domestic security forces, meanwhile, stepped up their repression. The violent and degrading treatment meted out to Egyptian citizens became another key issue of concern for many young people, who valued dignity no less than the necessities of daily life. This development was given expression by organized agitation against the regime's repressive practices and physical violence, which reached its peak after the killing of Khaled Saeed. Bread, dignity and social justice, which would later be the central planks of the January revolution, increasingly came to overlap.

The January revolution was not pre-planned. Had events followed the path set out by organizers in advance, it would certainly have been a social movement broader than those that had gone before, but it only became a revolution because of two factors. The first was the Tunisian revolution and the ouster of Ben Ali, which inspired young activists in Egypt to call openly, for the first time, for regime change. The second was the high turnout of people from new demographics on 25 January and, to a greater extent, 28 January. The two factors are related: the victory of the Tunisian revolution encouraged many of those who had not been involved in protests before to take part. Of particular importance here was the dialectical relationship between the spontaneous and the organized elements of the revolution, especially the transition from marches organized on social media (which the regime could only combat by cutting off internet access) to demonstrations driven by the people of working-class districts. Although today most of these people probably have Facebook accounts, this was not the case in 2011. They joined the revolution spontaneously, fuelled by the accumulated resentment of thirty-one years of political stagnation, violent treatment by the security forces and worsening economic and social conditions under Mubarak – as well as the glimpse of hope offered by Tunisia. This juncture between the organized and the spontaneous was the moment at which a protest movement with specific demands concerning the security forces became a revolution with demands that could only be achieved with the fall of the regime. Given their long experience of autocracy, for most of the population this meant getting rid of Mubarak.

The middle class alone does not make a revolution against the regime. Nor does poverty. The two must come together: a desire for freedom and social grievances. And although this itself is a necessary condition, it is not sufficient. There are many other contingencies that cannot be generalized into a standard model.

At the moment of revolution, the moment of broad popular participation, the use of violence only increased the number of people on the streets. The regime's gradual retreat before the forces of the revolution simply encouraged the latter to continue rather than containing it. Of course, we are not talking about maximum, unstinting violence of the kind used in Syria. Egypt did not see anything of this sort.

Nonetheless, it was an unusual revolution. It was broad based and sustained and managed to move beyond the basic demand-oriented struggle of the protest movements. It was a revolution that called for the regime to fall rather than toppling it itself, having no real understanding of how to topple the regime other than bringing Mubarak down. It had no plan of its own to take power or govern. Instead, it called for the regime to step aside and for other political and social forces to establish a new system. For this reason it has been referred to as a 'reformist revolution'. Millions of people from all parts of Egypt took part; the world looked on in awe at the unprecedented sight of tens and then hundreds of thousands of people (and on a few occasions, millions of people) occupying the central square of their capital city for more than two weeks. In the square itself confessional and social differences and the apparent irreconcilability of religious and secular views gave way to a sense of brotherhood and tolerance, a phenomenon often presented as an example of the revolutionary moment and its almost redemptive emotional immediacy. But after Mubarak stood down it quickly dissipated, leaving behind not a single organization or unified leadership – two weeks was not enough for a unified leadership to emerge – but a constellation of protest movements with very different post-revolutionary demands. It was a revolution that behaved like an enormous protest movement, breaking up as soon as Mubarak stood down as if it had achieved its aims. But it had not. The spirit of Tahrir proved unsustainable. The road was now clear for the organized parties and the army, which had taken over administration of the transitional period, to take centre stage.

The problem of the activists of 25 January was that they thought like a protest movement, which dissipates once its demands are met. They had no organization with plans to govern or even to influence or check those who governed. Some of them abandoned politics altogether, while others became part of the interminable squabbles of the established parties. Those who held fast to the revolutionary spirit, meanwhile, held protests and demonstrations on every issue imaginable, contributing to the general sense of post-revolution instability while failing to close ranks around the key task of building democracy.

Let us now try and draw out all these conclusions:

1. The January revolution was a popular revolution in every sense of the word. It expressed the aspirations and concerns of the people as a whole, and large numbers of people from every demographic participated. It could not have succeeded in bringing down Mubarak had the army not made the decision not to intervene and protect the regime by force. The army did give the regime a free hand in its attempts to suppress the revolution by the means it had available, including the security forces and mobs of thugs. But it was unable to do so, and in fact ended up encouraging the popular uprising and inviting international solidarity.
2. It would be wrong to imagine that this decision not to intervene – which ultimately became a military coup – arose from sympathy for the revolution. It was an expression of the army's independent will. The army was not planning a coup from the outset, but it was absolutely prepared to force Mubarak to step down and take power itself if he was unable to defeat the revolutionaries. Later on, it was to develop its own ambitions to rule. Although at first it did not act on these ambitions because of the popularity of revolutionary opposition to 'rule by soldiers', it was only too quick to fulfil them once the democratic transition ran into trouble.

3. The young activists of the new social and political movements, and indeed those who participated in the sit-in in Tahrir more generally, were able to overcome their ideological divisions. They maintained their distinct positions on various social issues, of course, but they were able to place values above ideology, allowing, most importantly, for bridges to be built between Islamists and secularists. This was a new development, one that points to a better future.
4. At the same time, however, the established political parties were divided by political, cultural and perhaps even emotional differences and split between their comfortable position within the regime and the possibilities presented by the new revolutionary space. As we have seen, they vacillated continuously between the revolution and dialogue with the regime. While they may have been forced to cooperate against the regime during the revolution, their conflicts and their fear of new competitors remained entrenched. Once the revolutionary fervour had subsided, they soon went back to fighting one another, unable to maintain this spirit of cooperation. In the second part of this book, we will see the disastrous consequences of this inability to put the transition to democracy above inter-party competition.
5. The young people in the square failed to realize that a revolution can bring down a regime but cannot build a democracy (although it would perhaps have been unreasonable to expect them to recognize this fact in the heat of the moment). A revolution can replace one regime with another if it has a revolutionary leadership that wants to take power and implement a comprehensive vision of how politics should work. Democracy, however, emerges only from a gradual process of transition and subsequent consolidation. This requires dialogue, compromise and consensus building. The revolutionaries were right to reject Omar Suleiman's offer of dialogue as a ploy that might have fatally undermined the revolution. I myself advocated a boycott of the national dialogue process during the revolution. But boycotting dialogue cannot be allowed to become an ideology, a form of revolutionary narcissism. During the transitional period, it is impossible to build democracy without dialogue with figures from within the regime. In this respect it is different from the revolutionary period. Democracy cannot be built from nothing. Egypt, like Tunisia, had one strength that many other countries in the region lacked: a stable state whose nature and borders were the subject of a genuine consensus among all sociopolitical forces. But unlike Tunisia, Egypt did not enjoy consensus among major political forces on the importance of democratic transition. When the main political forces believe that regime change is a zero-sum game they will lose, and when the army cannot at least be neutralized (if not won over), transition is not possible.

These issues and others will be covered in more detail in the following chapters of the second part of this book.

Part II

From Revolution to *Coup d'État*

1

In lieu of an introduction

I Transition to democracy in context

In the first part of the book we stopped at 11 February 2011. At this point an observer unfamiliar with later events might think that the story had reached a happy end. But looking more closely at the events described, they would find the potential for many different endings – reasons for hope to be sure, but equally reasons auguring setbacks and disappointment.

The story of the Egyptian revolution is one of a great hope which culminated in tragedy; a dream of generations turned into a nightmare. I myself witnessed scenes from the nightmare.[1] By the time I had begun writing this part, many of the revolutionaries I had met while preparing for the book, and Part I in particular, had been thrown in prison or scattered in exile.

---

[1] One of these nightmarish scenes was the ascent of a Military Intelligence officer of mediocre intellect and talent to the Egyptian presidency after a military coup and his subsequent iron-fisted rule of the country by the dissemination of a culture of hate and the construction of a political discourse based on fear and fear-mongering, ignorance and obscurantism.

    Introducing a book about a different military coup, Marx, in *The Eighteenth Brumaire of Louis Bonaparte*, writes, 'Victor Hugo confines himself to bitter and witty invective against the responsible publisher of the *coup d'état*. The event itself appears in his work like a bolt from the blue. He sees in it only the violent act of a single individual. He does not notice that he makes this individual great instead of little by ascribing to him a personal power of initiative such as would be without parallel in world history. Proudhon, for his part, seeks to represent the *coup d'état* as the result of an antecedent historical development. Unnoticeably, however, his historical construction of the *coup d'état* becomes a historical *apologia* for its hero.' See: Karl Marx, 'Author's Preface to the Second Edition' (1869), in Karl Marx, *The 18th Brumaire of Louis Bonaparte* (New York: International Publishers, 1969 [1852]), 10.

    This essay of Marx's is more a brilliant, biting satire than an authoritative analysis. I have presented this quote to demonstrate that the purpose of this part is not to launch scathing criticism against the organizer of the coup like some of the writers opposed to it, nor to justify it historically without holding those who carried it out responsible for their actions, but rather to cast some light on the road leading to the coup – including its concealed back-roads and hidden alleyways – and explain them as possibilities latent in the Egyptian post-revolution reality. These latent possibilities became realities because of people's choices and will, divisions in the ranks of the January revolution and the mismanagement of power, as well as the state apparatus turning against the revolution and the ambitions of a Military Intelligence officer of middling intellect and talent willing to do anything in order to rule.

What merits our study and consideration in this part is that this tragic outcome was not inevitable. It was generated by processes defined in part by human choice, in tandem with other factors. Events could have turned out very differently had the revolutionaries, political parties and other political forces, as well as the elites of the old regime had behaved differently.

Based on this conviction, I concur with scholars of the democratic transitions of the 1980s who concluded that the transition from an authoritarian regime does not necessarily lead to democracy. Like them, I believe that the role of political actors and their decisions and behaviour at the critical juncture of the transitional period are of crucial importance, though I do not adopt their model of the democratic transition. Indeed, I do not approach the historical phase examined here with any ready-made theoretical paradigm, particularly since the transition in this case began with a revolution rather than top-down reforms.

In their analysis, Linz and Stepan looked beyond structural factors that explained the breakdown of democratic regimes as the inevitable outcome of objective conditions, to focus instead on leadership practices and the behaviour of political elites in political life.[2] In particular, they explored how the elites' response to pressure from the extremist margins thwarts compromises between moderate forces, leading to the collapse of precarious democratic regimes under mounting pressures. It is not the democratic system itself that causes the collapse or gives rise to extremist forces, but rather the policies of regime actors. In their project on the democratic transitions of the 1980s, O'Donnell and Schmitter essentially adopt this approach to the study of collapse and apply it to the study of transitions, rejecting the premise that the transition from authoritarianism to democracy is conditional on structural factors deemed by modernization theory to be prerequisites for democracy. Granting such a premise would mean accepting the persistence of authoritarianism in most countries of the world, especially developing countries. In the concluding volume of their project,[3] they argue that elites' attitudes, proclivities, calculations and agreements as expressed in pacts determine the prospects of the democratic transition. 'Elites' here does not refer to an economic class, and their behaviour cannot be predicted based on conditions like economic structures, 'mainstream culture', economic growth rates, the size of the middle class, and levels of education.

---

[2] Juan J. Linz, *The Breakdown of Democratic Regimes: Crisis, Breakdown, and Reequilibration* (Baltimore, MD and London: The Johns Hopkins University Press, 1978). Although this work is Linz's alone, Stepan and Linz have reiterated this point in several of their jointly authored studies.
[3] Guillermo O'Donnell and Philippe C. Schmitter, eds, *Transitions from Authoritarian Rule: Tentative Conclusions about Uncertain Democracies*, vol. 4 (Baltimore: Johns Hopkins University Press, 1986).

O'Donnell and Schmitter find that the democratic transition is typically set in motion by reforms initiated under authoritarian rule to allow some measure of civil and political rights. That is, the process usually begins with an opening made possible by top-down reform, whatever the motives for such reforms may be. The opposition then grows more active, and fissures appear within the regime between moderates and hardliners. If the hardliners do not succeed in reversing the reforms, reformists have no choice but to seek allies for their struggle in the opposition. The process of transition may begin with a pact between regime moderates and the opposition,[4] or the regime may miscalculate by holding – and then losing – a genuine, fair election. Other trajectories are possible as well.

O'Donnell and Schmitter's emphasis on the role of the political leadership and elites and the decision-making process downplays the significance of structural and exogenous, international factors in the transitional period. When addressing internal factors, they begin with decision-makers. But if the Egyptian experience demonstrates the importance of political elites and their culture, it also shows, as we will see, that the role of the military and external factors cannot be ignored. Based on the theoretical discussions in O'Donnell and Schmitter's analysis, political actors seeking to supplant an authoritarian regime with a democracy would be advised to accept incrementalism and negotiate and cooperate with moderates within the existing regime. The authors do not offer such counsel explicitly, but it is implied by their conclusions, though they are extremely cautious in their articulation of them.[5] This implication also finds a place in the approaches of Linz and Stepan, Samuel Huntington and Seymour Martin Lipset, all of whom emphasize moderation and incrementalism in the transition process. Dahl, too, finds that the road to democracy runs exclusively through incremental phases, moderation and compromises in political behaviour.[6] O'Donnell and Schmitter do not pretend to offer a theory of or rules for democratization; rather, they attempt to capture the exceptional contingency of transitional processes.[7] They do not believe that toppling an authoritarian regime necessarily leads to democracy.

In Part I of this book, I showed that (1) the divide within the Egyptian regime did not appear due to top-down reforms, but a revolution from below; (2) the divide was between the military and the presidency, rather

---

[4] This requires the presence of organized forces capable of abiding by the agreed-upon terms and enforcing adherence to the pact by their bases, which can generate mutual trust. See: Barbara Geddes, 'What Do We Know about Democratization after Twenty Years', *Annual Review of Political Science* 2 (1999): 136.

[5] Nancy Bermeo, 'Rethinking Regime Change', *Comparative Politics* 22, no. 3 (April 1990): 362.

[6] Robert A. Dahl, *Polyarchy: Participation and Opposition* (New Haven: Yale University Press, 1971), 15, 33–4, 216.

[7] O'Donnell and Schmitter, *Transitions from Authoritarian Rule*, 3–4.

than between soft-liners and hardliners; and (3) the abdication of Mubarak – the linchpin of the authoritarian regime – led the military to assume the reins of power in the transitional phase. In other words, governance did not fall to a reformist wing within the regime or to a body formed by consensus between the regime and the opposition. The problem is that the military did not perceive itself as a faction – even when it negotiated over the nature of the coming regime and its own position within it – but rather saw itself as transcending all factions. It never considered itself a guarantor of democracy, even when, at the height of revolutionary legitimacy, it extolled 'the great revolution of Egypt's youth' and its commitment to the revolution's goals; rather, it saw itself as safeguarding 'the interests of the homeland and the nation'.

'Democratic transition' refers to that phase in which a country is run in pursuit of a specific goal: to lay the foundations of a democratic system. Agreement on these foundations is established through debate and other consensual mechanisms. This period is utilized to weaken the constituent parts of the old regime by breaking their monopoly on power and to strengthen the constituent parts of the new regime. The aim of the transitional period must be defined as the establishment of a democratic system – that is, there can be no period of transition towards the unknown. It is difficult to specify a duration for such a period because it depends on the maturity of political actors, society and the security apparatus, and on the state apparatus and its willingness to submit to or oppose democratization. An overly short or long transitional period may derail the whole process.

Opinions differ regarding the stability of a post-transition democracy. The test of democracy proposed by Lijphart is the establishment of a pluralist democratic regime operating in accordance with democratic processes, in which the regime is receptive to citizens' desires over a prolonged period of time that he estimates as a generation (thirty to thirty-five years by his criteria), after which he considers it a stable democracy.[8] Other scholars require at least two peaceful rotations of power through elections. Egypt did not reach this stage, whereas Tunisia has twice seen the peaceful rotation of power. While undoubtedly cause for optimism, it would be a mistake to consider Tunisia an established democracy, for reasons outside the scope of this study.

I am unsure as to whether I can agree with Lijphart's conclusions concerning the timeline for the consolidation of a democratic regime. We have no temporal measures for the transitional phase, only qualitative criteria. In the first phase of the transition, these are: (1) the breaking of the

---

[8] Arend Lijphart, *Democracies: Patterns of Majoritarian and Consensus Government in Twenty-One Countries* (New Haven: Yale University Press, 1984), 38.

monopoly on power held by the forces of the old regime; (2) a consensus around democratization processes between the main political forces opposed to the former regime and a large portion of the former regime elite; and (3) a lack of opposition from the military to the transition, which may be guaranteed by preserving some of its prerogatives. The details of the transitional period in Egypt presented in this part of the book lead to the conclusion that a majority government – 52 per cent in the case of the elected president – cannot lead a country to democracy if the army and state bureaucracy are still loyal to the old regime and if social and economic problems enable the excluded opposition to mobilize people against that government and produce polarization that threatens the transition process.

The first part of the transition phase does not require an agreement on democratic principles, whether expressed in the body of the constitution, in its preamble, or in a separate document. The important thing is a commitment to agreed-upon, democratic, institutional procedures. Yet a second phase of the transition is required before a democracy can be consolidated. In this phase, particularly when building institutions and holding elections, political elites representing a country's main forces must share, in addition to a commitment to procedures, a belief in a baseline of democratic principles, especially when it comes to legislating rights and liberties and taming the security and police apparatus.[9]

In my view, then, the transition comprises two stages: (1) the stage in which the old regime's monopoly on power is broken and a procedural consensus is reached and (2) the stage of building democratic institutions and enacting legislation, in which the culture of the political elite plays a significant role.

Some of the strengths of the January revolution became weaknesses in the transitional period. For example, the spontaneity and grassroots

---

[9] Standards for a successful democratic transition include civilian control of the security apparatus. In contrast, in Egypt we observe expanding military control of the security apparatus during the transitional period, as well as the autonomy enjoyed by the military itself. In summing up the standards for democratization in Eastern and Central Europe since 1989, two scholars of democratization in Eastern Europe enumerate eight criteria by which the success of the democratic transition can be judged from one state to the next: (1) full citizenship that does not exclude individuals or groups on the basis of race, ethnicity, gender or other factor; (2) the rule of law, meaning that government operates in accordance with the law, and there are laws protecting individuals and minorities from the tyranny of the majority; (3) the separation of powers and the independence of the judiciary; (4) those holding the reins of power, in both the legislative and executive authorities, are elected; (5) there are regular elections in which all adults have the right to vote without coercion or obligation; (6) freedom of expression and the existence of alternative sources of information; (7) the right to establish federations and organizations, including political parties and interest groups; and (8) civilian control of the security forces, meaning that the military and police are politically neutral, independent of domestic political pressure and subject to the oversight of civilian authorities. See: Mary Kaldor and Ivan Vejvoda, 'Democratization in Central and East European Countries: An Overview', in *Democratization in Central and Eastern Europe*, ed. Mary Kaldor and Ivan Vejvoda (London: Continuum, 2002), 54.

character of the revolution meant that the revolutionary forces striving for democracy in place of authoritarianism were unable to establish a political organization to demand inclusion in government and decision making during the transition.

In Egypt, as in Tunisia, there did exist one prerequisite for democracy: a consensus on the state.[10] But rather than the kind of ethnic divisions that hinder democratization in other states, in Egypt a division emerged between Islamist and secular political actors as a result of all actors' missteps during the transitional period. This division gradually acquired a cultural, identitarian nature, as both parties attempted to transform it into vertical rupture within Egyptian society. The problem was aggravated by the resurgence of the sectarian divide, which had been bridged in Tahrir Square during the revolution, but not in society at large. Political forces did not adhere to democratic procedures (to say nothing of principles) when they appealed to the military to resolve their disputes, having failed to do so through democratic means. With this, another strength of the January revolution – the military's neutrality in the struggle with the Mubarak regime – was subverted. This enabled the military to make inroads into the main competing political factions and ultimately to manipulate them by playing them against one another before reverting to an alliance with old regime forces.

Three different 'revolutions' overlapped during the transitional period. There was the popular January revolution and its forces, which remained unorganized amidst political parties' jockeying for power before the democratic transition could succeed. Then there was the 'revolution of expectations', which pressed for the fulfilment of the revolution's promises as quickly as possible. This occasioned growing recriminations and complaints related to bread-and-butter issues amidst continued instability, partly because of conflicts among political and revolutionary forces and partly due to people's rising expectations and the frequency of protests. Finally, there was the counter-revolution, which deployed the tools of the revolution – like mass rallies and mobilization – against the revolution itself. It also harnessed the institutions of the old regime, such as the judiciary, which was by then largely conservative following the Mubarak regime's battle with the judicial independence movement, and the state bureaucracy, which resisted change by sabotaging elected institutions.

---

[10] This seems an obvious condition but we must note that Rustow emphasizes it as a necessary condition in an article that became significant in the relevant scholarly literature. See: Dankwart A. Rustow, 'Transitions to Democracy: Toward a Dynamic Model', *Comparative Politics* 2, no. 3 (April 1970): 337–63.

The transitional period saw a gap open between political forces that had opposed the authoritarian regime but for divergent reasons. If a schism in the ruling elite is a precondition for the fall of an authoritarian regime (in Egypt's case, the impetus was a popular revolution), it follows that a prerequisite for a successful transition is for those forces opposed to the authoritarian regime to form a single front united behind the establishment of a democracy. Divisions within opposition forces may therefore impede the transition.

This unified democratic front entails both a shared belief in the possibility of managing political and ideological disputes within a democratic system and through respect for democratic procedures, and a willingness to accept uncertainty in the political process and the peaceful rotation of power. I shall return to this point later in the text. Many scholars identify mutual trust among leaders as the key element enabling such an agreement. Trust requires a common experience within a framework that provides for bargaining and consensus making, where each party can test other parties' fulfilment of their obligations. The Egyptian parliament could have functioned as such a framework but did not last long enough to do so;[11] it was dissolved by a court, as was another potential framework, the CA tasked with drafting the constitution. Trust cannot develop amidst totalizing, zero-sum ideological polarization, even given a history of shared struggle and even if the parties are able to reach tactical electoral bargains based on immediate interests.

In my view, before trust there must be a willingness to negotiate and make concessions for the sake of compromise, for it is through the negotiation process that trust is tested. For example, if one party is determined to resolve every issue with a vote, even during the transitional phase, simply because it has a majority, it suggests that party is not seeking consensus. By the same token, if the party that loses the vote pursues non-democratic methods in response, this precludes trust building. There must be a common threshold of faith in pluralistic democracy. Trust is impossible if political actors' commitment to democracy is tenuous, and this is made apparent through the process of negotiation itself and the willingness to make concessions in order to ensure a successful democratic transition.

The difference between Tunisian and Egyptian elites is not that trust existed among the former and did not among the latter; rather, the mindset of the al Nahda leadership in Tunisia differed from that of the Muslim Brotherhood in Egypt. Moreover, al Nahda was compelled to negotiate because it did not win a majority in parliament, even when it was the

---

[11] Mazen Hassan, Jasmin Lorch and Annete Ranko, 'Explaining Divergent Transformation Paths in Tunisia and Egypt: The Role of Inter-elite Trust', *Mediterranean Politics* 25, no. 5 (2019): 9, 17.

single largest party. Furthermore, if the transition in Tunisia had hinged on a bargain between al Nahda and the pro-revolution opposition secular parties, no deal would have been struck. It took a pragmatic secular elite coming out of the old regime, like the leadership of Nidaa Tounes, to reach an accommodation between Islamists and secularists.

Post-war political science in the West developed theoretical approaches attributing the fall of democracies in Italy, Germany, Poland and elsewhere prior to the First World War to severe ideological polarization between the left and the right in the wake of the Bolshevik revolution, coupled with the weakness of moderate forces, which made it impossible for political actors to find common ground[12] within a democratic, pluralistic framework such as parliament and other institutions. The same thing occurred in Latin America in the wake of the Cuban Revolution, driven by landowners, military leaders, some segments of the urban bourgeoisie and the right in general, which, like the United States, feared the spread of communism during the Cold War.

What is true for a democratic regime is even truer for a democratic transition, specifically when democratic institutions are still taking shape. Severe polarization and the heightened social agitation it brings may hinder institution building and give rise to a general sense of instability, insecurity and fear of the future. This is indeed what happened in Egypt when political elites fomented religious-secular polarization in the midst of their own conflicts, at the same time that broad swathes of Egyptians held high expectations of the new regime. Multiple social issues and legitimate grievances came to the fore simultaneously, which political elites attempted to harness in service of their conflict with one another.

Nancy Bermeo raises the important point that anti-democratic forces exploit social agitation in the streets, such as demonstrations and strikes, to take subversive steps to reconstitute authoritarianism. They do this by claiming that the activist bases of competing political forces represent a majority of citizens, intentionally conflating the general citizenry with its most activist, polarized segments which are prepared to take to the streets, typically under the influence of political elites. In contrast, the majority of citizens are not polarized, choosing to express themselves in different ways in elections.[13] Most people do not determine their identity or lifestyles and attitudes based on an ideological dichotomy of religious versus secular. The lack of polarization in Egyptians' attitudes will be addressed in the

---

[12] Nancy Bermeo, *Ordinary People in Extraordinary Times: The Citizenry and the Breakdown of Democracy* (Princeton and Oxford: Princeton University Press, 2003), 5. Giovanni Sartori is an important pioneer of this approach. See: Giovanni Sartori, *Parties and Party Systems: A Framework for Analysis* (New York: Cambridge University Press, 1976).

[13] Bermeo, *Ordinary People*, 228.

penultimate chapter of this book, which is based on surveys of Egyptians even after numerous attempts to polarize them, especially after the military coup. However, the elites who made the 'wrong' choices (calling on the military to intervene, for example), arguing that it was necessary to protect society from a possible civil war, justified their decisions by pointing to a deep rift in society; this rift, however, had no salience for the general population, but only for those who took part in demonstrations.

Furthermore, the fragmentation of the pro-January revolution forces and the freedom unleashed by the revolution gave anti-democratic Arab regional powers an opportunity to play a much more influential role than that which they had been able to play during the revolution itself, in particular by funding counter-revolutionary forces and investing in the media. Although the role of external actors was not the deciding factor in the Egyptian case, it was more significant in Egypt than in Tunisia due to Egypt's geostrategic importance. The inability of the forces that supported and joined the January revolution to form a united front committed to consensual democratic procedures and to the military's political neutrality also made the actions of external actors more consequential.

Linz and Stepan articulate five basic prerequisites for translating a promising transition into actual democracy:

1. Ascendant political elites must be convinced that democracy is the least bad choice because of their previous political experiences, and must be committed to protecting the democratic transition process.
2. The process of building institutions during the transition must be inclusive, so that no pivotal political force considers itself to have been excluded and everyone has a stake in the success of the process.
3. The military must be given serious incentives, allowing it to conclude that remaining in power will be more costly than stepping aside.
4. The political institutions established during the democratic transition period must not grant the majority exclusive power over another group, or prevent a particular group from obtaining a majority, and they must provide incentives for compromise and cooperation between opposing groups.
5. There must be a history of negotiation and bridge building between opposing forces, such that their shared commitment to the transitional political process is greater than what divides them.[14]

---

[14] Juan J. Linz and Alfred Stepan, *Problems of Democratic Transition and Consolidation: Southern Europe, South America, and Post-Communist Europe* (Baltimore: Johns Hopkins University Press, 1996), 7; Eva Bellin, 'A Modest Transformation: Political Change in the Arab World after the "Arab Spring"', in *The Arab Spring: Will It Lead to Democratic Transitions?* ed. Clement Henry and Ji-Hyang Jang (New York: Palgrave Macmillan, 2013), 39.

It seems to me that the Egyptian transition, even when it met these prerequisites, got decidedly mixed results, suggesting that this checklist offers a less-than-complete diagnosis of the problem. So, for example, Egyptian political elites had no problem answering the first question in the affirmative. Indeed, they affirmed that democracy was the least bad option, but their commitment to democratic procedures was at best dubious. Similarly, the military was provided with the right incentives by an elected parliament, but did not draw the 'right' conclusions from them. Finally, no pivotal forces were excluded from the democratic process, unlike Libya, for example. Although the NDP was dissolved, no political exclusion law was enacted and NDP elements were able to express themselves through other parties that competed in elections; their presidential candidate also won nearly half the votes.

Despite 'correctly' ticking the boxes, Egypt's transition failed for reasons related to (1) the culture of political elites; (2) the military's political ambitions; and (3) external actors who exploited schisms in the pro-revolution coalition. As is true everywhere, personal traits – spite, resentment and lust for position and power – undoubtedly contributed as well, in some cases making the struggle seem more like a petty student union leadership contest. Other issues, like the Muslim Brotherhood backtracking on their principled, correct position not to field a presidential candidate, cannot be explained without understanding their fear of losing their base to breakaway Islamists who decided to contest the election. Nor can we disregard Sisi's disgraceful character, his hunger for power and his willingness to do anything, including grovelling and feigning loyalty to the president against whom he was plotting a coup.

Alongside what I view as strengths of the Egyptian revolution, there were also the following weaknesses:

- The revolutionaries had no plan for what would happen after the fall of the regime. As I have shown in Part I, they were engaged in a mass protest movement that suddenly found itself in a revolutionary situation.
- The ouster of Mubarak – that is, the revolution itself – comprised two interrelated elements. The first was a broad, popular, civil revolution with a democratic character. The second was a military coup carried out by the army against Mubarak. We might say that the history of the post-revolutionary transitional period is the history of a struggle between the revolution and the covert coup. In the end, it was the coup that triumphed.

Mubarak's fall could have evolved into the fall of the regime rather than simply the fall of a dynasty. One of these possibilities won out over the other because of a programme, or lack thereof, for seeing such a transformation through on the part of those who took charge of the country. It happened that the military took over the country directly after the revolution, via the SCAF. The army was not a democratic force. Nor was it an army of professionals who believed that its mission was to protect the country and the constitution, and that it should leave governance to civil institutions led by elected officials.

Because revolutionary legitimacy forced the revolution's goals into the political arena, thereby limiting the influence of SCAF, there was an opportunity to arrive at a national pact or agreed-upon procedures for building democratic institutions and gaining access to power, along the lines of round-table negotiations between moderate regime elites and the opposition following the collapse of an authoritarian regime, as happened in Poland and Spain. But this did not take place. Political forces were divided between those who supported speedy elections to turn power over to civilians and those who opposed elections on the grounds of lack of preparedness, believing that if elections were hastily called, the NDP (Mubarak's party, reconstituted in another guise) and the Muslim Brotherhood would split the vote between them.

According to the aforementioned models of democratic transition, when an authoritarian regime fragments, it will typically divide into two camps: a moderate camp, which prefers liberalization, and a more dominant, hardliner camp, which opposes it. The hardliners oppose the political gamble of a partial or programmatic opening up of the regime and prefer instead to tighten the regime's grip. The moderates, on the other hand, generally believe that the crisis represents a real danger to the regime and that in order to shore up its popular base it must permit people to participate and play a role. Liberalization may lead to a backlash in the form of a military coup, as occurred in Greece in mid-1973 or Bolivia in November 1979,[15] or in the various Turkish coups d'état. In Egypt, however, this question was moot, as the revolution began from below and lopped off the head of the regime even as its basic structure remained in place and power shifted to the military.

The success of discussions to establish a pact between different political and social forces, laying the groundwork for democratic transition, is closely correlated with, on the one hand, the victory of the reforming force in the intra-regime conflict and, on the other, the unity of the opposition. It also depends on the popular social forces that can exert pressure on the negotiation process. When these negotiations lead to an agreement between different actors to hold elections, or to set a date for the regime to step down from power, it is customarily referred to

---

[15] Graeme Gill, *The Dynamics of Democratization: Elites, Civil Society, and the Transition Process* (New York: St. Martin's Press, 2000), 51.

by democratic transition theorists as a 'pact'. O'Donnell and Schmitter define this as 'an explicit, but not always publicly explicated or justified, agreement among a select set of actors which seeks to define . . . rules governing the exercise of power on the basis of mutual guarantees for the "vital interests" of those entering into it'.[16] In general, the regime splits during this period into moderates and hardliners, as does the opposition. The pact is an agreement between the moderates of each side, with both offering compromises to the hardliners on their own side to avoid angering them and having them turn against the process. In turn, these hard-line forces must offer concessions to be admitted to the democratic process. The political process therefore includes hardliners from both sides. This is how the opposition and the government came to an agreement in Colombia and Venezuela in 1957 and 1958, respectively, and similarly in Spain, on a constitutional framework for the new democracy. Round-table agreements are also a distinguishing feature of the transitions of many Eastern European states in the late 1980s.[17]

Both the Greek (1974) and Spanish (1977) regimes granted recognition to their communist parties. The Marxist parties of Brazil were officially recognized in 1985, and the Communist Party in Chile in 1989. The corollary of this, however, was that these parties recognized the political system, adopted peaceful political struggle, and agreed to work within official channels, in particular electoral ones, within a capitalist economic framework, and recognized the right to private property. This duly took place, and these countries' political parties moved towards the centre of the political spectrum. In my view, it is this that the Muslim Brotherhood in Egypt failed to do (they had achieved part of this in the 1990s, but were always in the opposition). They inscribed their own ideological conditions in the first post-revolution constitution through an alliance with the Salafists in the CA. This stands in contrast to the AKP in Turkey, for example, which recognized the secular nature of the state as a condition for joining the democratic process. In other words, the

[16] O'Donnell and Schmitter, *Transitions from Authoritarian Rule*, 37. For more on consensual pacts and the role of regime and opposition elites, both moderate and hardliners, in the process of negotiation during the transitional phase, see: Bishara, *The Issue of Democratic Transition*, 243–71. O'Donnell and Schmitter conclude that the transition from an authoritarian regime begins, directly or indirectly, with significant divisions within the regime itself, manifesting as a schism between moderates and hardliners. See: O'Donnell and Schmitter, *Transitions from Authoritarian Rule*. See also, Rustow, 'Transitions to Democracy', 355–6; Terry Lynn Karl, 'Petroleum and Political Pacts: The Transition to Democracy in Venezuela', in *Transitions from Authoritarian Rule: Latin America*, ed. Guillermo O'Donnell, Philippe C. Schmitter and Laurence Whitehead, vol. 2 (Baltimore and London: Johns Hopkins University Press, 1986), 196–218; Sujian Guo, 'Democratic Transition: A Critical Overview', *Issues & Studies* 35, no. 4 (1999): 136–7; Stephan Haggard and Robert R. Kaufman, 'The Political Economy of Democratic Transition', *Comparative Politics* 29, no. 3 (April 1997): 265.
[17] Gill, *The Dynamics of Democratization*, 53.

Brotherhood was less disposed to accept a common, national political pact. More importantly, the Brotherhood admitted to the democratic process Salafist forces that neither recognized nor accepted democracy, which introduced a dynamic of political one-upmanship that pulled the Brotherhood towards ideological extremism. Likewise, large parts of the other opposition parties continued to identify more closely with the old regime than the Brotherhood. Meanwhile, the old regime remained capable of forming coalitions with and against all opposition factions, and ultimately managed to disrupt the forces supporting the revolution and change, which were enervated by infighting.

Rather than taking time to secure a pact through discussion, Egypt's political actors instead rushed to resolve their conflicts through elections before the regime had actually changed. They behaved as if the regime had been defeated in a full-scale revolution, which was not the case, and so wanted to decide the question of which of them would rule via the elections – even as the regime remained in place, managing the transitional process through the military. Opposition parties wanted to resolve the question of *who* should rule before they had decisively settled the question of *how* to rule, and with the commitment to the agreed-upon response to the latter question still uncertain.

Immediately after the revolution, the broad national coalition that had brought it to victory splintered. The first division arose between those who wanted to continue with the old model of street protest (they were marginalized) and those who believed it was time to work within institutions. The latter were the political forces already organized into parties and those who wanted to organize in parties after it became more feasible. The second split came with the referendum on the constitutional amendments in March 2011, as will be discussed later in the text. Forces confident of themselves and their organizational strength wanted swift elections and supported the amendments; other forces deemed it best to delay elections until they were better able to compete, and they wanted to reach an agreement on constitutional principles binding on everyone prior to elections. This second, and more significant, division took the form of a religious-secular schism.

The pact that should have been reached with the forces of the old regime instead turned out to be a pact with the military, since it was overseeing the transitional phase. In general, pacts provide for guarantees to reassure actors who have much to lose in the democratic transition. Concessions were therefore made to the military. Both Islamist and non-Islamist forces offered such guarantees to the Egyptian army but ended up outbidding one other while simultaneously accusing one another of allying with the army.

It was the military that ultimately came out strongest from this process after its credibility had declined during its management of the transition.

The opposition did not accept the conditions that the old regime typically dictates in negotiations,[18] because the transition was not the outcome of regime-initiated reforms but of a popular revolution that only seemed to have toppled the regime. Behaving as if the revolution had defeated the regime, the opposition was therefore not prepared to bargain with any of its associated figures. But it was the military – not the opposition – that set the rhythm of the transition phase, forcing the opposition into the streets every time it wanted to challenge SCAF's right to determine the pace of change. Instead of offering guarantees to political forces of the old regime, the opposition offered them to the military. But those forces that found a refuge in an alliance with the military and the judiciary lost the democratic process, deepened the politicization of both of those institutions – neither one lacking in legitimacy and popular acceptance – and encouraged them to intervene to resolve contentious political issues.

Przeworski considers political actors' acceptance of democracy as tantamount to the acceptance of uncertainty. After all, in democracy there are no guaranteed outcomes, and a victory at one moment in time is no guarantee of future victories. In turn, political actors must agree to accept the uncertainty of election results. This is a prerequisite for political forces. Przeworski does not believe this acceptance is dependent on elites' political culture. Rather, it is based on a calculus of profit and loss: to lose with the possibility of winning in the future is preferable to losing everything under an authoritarian regime. In this, I believe he is mistaken, first because the acceptance of uncertainty derives from a culture that accepts bargaining and admits this sort of calculation in the first place and, second because other forces must be trusted to accept this same uncertainty. Dictatorships, Przeworski continues, despite their arbitrary nature and the difficulty of predicting their actions, accept no uncertainty when it comes to the rulers' interests. As such, a transition crosses the threshold into established democracy when it becomes unlikely that any one actor, particularly the military, will intervene to change the outcome of the democratic political process.[19] As long as there exists the possibility

---

[18] When beginning negotiations, the regime typically insists on conditions such as amnesty for officials' past crimes, the exclusion of radical parties from the coming government, etc. See: Gill, *The Dynamics of Democratization*, 58; Diane Ethier, 'Introduction: Processes of Transition and Democratic Consolidation: Theoretical Indicators', in *Democratic Transition and Consolidation in Southern Europe, Latin America and Southeast Asia*, ed. Diane Ethier (London: Macmillan, 1990), 11.

[19] Adam Przeworski, 'Democracy as a Contingent Outcome of Conflicts', in *Constitutionalism and Democracy*, ed. Jon Elster and Rune Slagstad (Cambridge: Cambridge University Press, 1988), 62.

of intervention by the military or security apparatus to change outcomes, one cannot speak of democracy.

Democracy is the process of subordinating all interests to competition, as well as the process of institutionalizing uncertainty, not only with respect to the individuals and groups who will occupy positions of power but also in regard to the uses of power. As such, the transition to political democracy generates not inevitabilities, but opportunities.[20] One who goes in search of inevitabilities will find himself a partner in the subversion of democracy. The democratic transition is the moment before which the apparatus of the authoritarian regime is capable of determining outcomes and after which no one is capable of doing so, as power passes from a clique to the people within a rule-based system. The transition to democracy takes place if two conditions are met: (1) the authoritarian regime is dismantled and (2) all political forces are committed to democratic institutions as the framework for competition to achieve their interests. Various forces allied against the authoritarian regime must be persuaded to pursue their interests in a pluralistic framework, convinced that they are not required to abandon them.

The struggle for democracy is therefore a struggle on two fronts: on the one side, to dismantle the authoritarian regime and, on the other, to establish the conditions necessary to achieve the interests of the group, party or current in the future, even in conflict with present-day allies. As such, the democratic task for the forces allied against the authoritarian regime is to come to a procedural accommodation, through which all these forces can pursue their interests within the framework of institutions. In the absence of such an accommodation, a new conflict arises among these actors, purging the weakest of them and giving rise to a new authoritarian regime. Institutions are thus the answer to the question of democratization.[21]

Here a question arises: Are rights, liberties and related accommodations a matter of procedure, or are they substantive issues? Following Dankwart Rustow's exclusion of principles from the consensus on rules and procedures, Przeworski writes that compromises on substantive issues are impossible because they cannot be enforced. When a political party wins, it may repudiate such pledges and prefer its own platform, and without mutual trust the other party will not compromise on a core issue fearing that the other party will not honour the compromise. Prior agreement on substantive matters is therefore impossible; what is needed is a consensus

---

[20] Adam Przeworski, 'Some Problems in the Study of the Transition to Democracy', in *Transitions from Authoritarian Rule: Comparative Perspectives*, ed. Guillermo O'Donnell, Philippe C. Schmitter and Laurence Whitehead, vol. 3 (Baltimore and London: The Johns Hopkins University Press, 1986), 47–63.

[21] Przeworski, 'Democracy as a Contingent Outcome of Conflicts', 63–4.

around the institutions that guarantee future adherence to agreements and ensure that no ruling majority can overstep a certain agreed-upon boundary.

My question is: Are rights and liberties an institutional question, or are they substantive matters not subject to prior agreement? In some Arab countries, among them Egypt, partisan, religious-secular polarization extended to the question of rights and freedoms, and such questions cannot be resolved with a procedural accommodation unless civil and political rights and liberties are considered no less than a part of the procedural consensus. In my view, some normative principles must be incorporated – forcefully inserted if necessary – in the procedural consensus of any prospective democratic regime. In exactly the way that scholars of transitions believe that an accommodation with the left required it to concede some of its positions on private property – a substantive rather than procedural concession – political actors with an ideology opposed to civil and political rights and liberties must similarly cede ground to reassure other actors that they will not impose this ideology in policies if they win an election.

Przeworski devotes some space to a discussion of concessions the left must make to prove that it is 'fit to rule', meaning that it will not threaten the existing socio-economic order. This is what the Socialist Party in Spain did when it rose to power under Felipe González, and Przeworski compares this to the case of the British Labour Party when it entered the government in 1924. In this sense, the transition put the left in a bind: a peaceful transfer of power becomes possible, but at the price of limiting the scope of the socio-economic transformations it wishes to bring about.[22] It is thus no longer possible to achieve what Marx thought it possible to achieve through democracy, which was to be a bridge to communism. In the case of Arab countries, democracy should not be a bridge to what Islamist movements call 'the rule of Shari'a', based on their own interpretation of Shari'a, just as democracy cannot be a bridge to the election of a secular fascist party that is not committed to democracy and does not respect rights and freedoms or to an atheistic regime that outlaws religious practices. For this reason, the democratic consensus must include non-procedural principles.

Motivating various forces to enter into institutional compromises is the conviction that they cannot prevail against the other party through conflict and that compromise is a better guarantor of their interests. It does not safeguard all interests, but it does ensure security and stability. The compromise is thus implicitly substantive, in the sense that groups

[22] Ibid., 80.

enter into it believing it to be a promising framework for the realization of their interests. The most important issue in the process of democratization are safeguards, which may take the form of institutions.[23] The Egyptian experience, however, shows that democratic institutions do not safeguard themselves if the military and security apparatus do not respect them. This is among the most significant conclusions to be drawn from the Egyptian case. Even if political forces honour the procedural agreement, the transition fails if the military and security apparatus do not. In contrast, if the latter do abide by the agreement, they can protect the transition even if a significant political force does not.

1 A note on methodology

In this part, I will continue to comprehensively document the history of the Egyptian revolution. This part is more difficult than the first, as the events concerned are still ongoing, and there is a dearth of secondary sources.[24] There has thus been no option except to rely on and shape the raw material after sifting through it, corroborating and confirming the events described therein in cooperation with researchers and observers who participated in them or experienced them up close, and applying critical thought, comparisons and an understanding of context. Analysis in this case must leave some questions without decisive answers, which may be provided later by unpublished documents. I have therefore relied on a few other studies of this period, where they exist. I have analysed the historical, economic and social background using both quantitative, statistical methods and qualitative methods. Reliance on a single methodology to study complex socio-historical phenomena is unacceptable, particularly when it comes to a still unfolding historical period. What is needed is an interdisciplinary methodology that draws on diverse theoretical approaches.

In this part, I have compared some premises and conclusions with the literature on democratic transition, in order to contribute to the theoretical debate and update it with data from the Egyptian Arab experience and theoretical conclusions drawn from it. The discussion is, ultimately, about how the democratic transition in Egypt failed.

Finally, I have tried to compose a compressed narrative of events without getting bogged down in the details, pausing at what I consider to be turning points and the most important factors affecting or related to them, in order to produce a composite picture drawn as much as is possible from different

---

[23] Ibid., 64.
[24] Some secondary sources appearing after the publication of this book in Arabic have been incorporated into the English translation.

perspectives. However, the author's point of view inevitably dominates. Alongside the narrative, or following just behind it, is an analysis in which I have tried to remain as objective as possible, in the sense of analysing data using scientific tools and siding with the truth, to the extent that it is ever possible to divorce oneself from one's bias for liberal democracy and social justice.

II The day after

Mubarak stood down on the evening of 11 February 2011. As activists set about cleaning Tahrir Square and the adjacent areas, in a symbolic assertion of a new approach to the public realm as a space for civic participation, Egypt – and the whole world with it – looked back over those powerful moments. Commentators and analysts lined up to praise the revolution and the young people who had carried it out. The overwhelming euphoria of victory at the toppling of the head of the regime overshadowed any talk of changing the regime itself.

The Egyptian army and the state apparatus bent with the revolutionary wind – indeed, to use it to oust Mubarak. On the evening of 10 February, the army carried out a 'bloodless' military coup, forcing Mubarak to withdraw completely from the political scene. The purpose of this step was pre-emptive: to keep the revolution from becoming a full-fledged confrontation with the regime, or the regime from advancing into a full-fledged confrontation with the people. It was also intended to put paid to any prospect of a succession within the Mubarak family and marginalize the coterie of business magnates around his son who had come to dominate government. The result was the weakening of three of the pillars of the regime – the NDP, the security forces and 'the ruling family' – and the strengthening of its fourth pillar, the army, which now held the reins of government.

By the early hours of the following Sunday (13 February), it was clear to everyone that the army was the key organization with the power to make and implement decisions during this period of institutional instability. With the head of the Egyptian state gone, SCAF assumed the duties of the presidency. The Egyptian revolutionary movement, for its part, had no head. No leadership with an aspiration to take over or participate in government had emerged from among its ranks, while the political forces that had supported the revolution were unable to come together under a single umbrella with a unified political agenda.

Due to the relatively short time they had spent together in the square, the revolutionary youth did not have the opportunity to organize themselves into a single body that could exclusively claim to represent revolutionary legitimacy. The RYC was established on 7 February, just four days before Mubarak stood down. It did not represent all the people who had staged the sit-in, and it did not have the time to prove that it represented them. This organization, which was born in Tahrir, neither attempted to establish alliances and cooperative relationships with other civil society organizations such as independent unions,[25] nor took it itself seriously in its dealings with political parties. The RYC included representatives of a number of parties, and the parties themselves tended to dismiss it as an ad hoc group of young people that had served its purpose now that Mubarak had stood down.

Since the coup of 3 July 2013, some two and a half years after the events in Tahrir, the assumption gained ground that the military leadership had a clear vision and agenda from the outset. Indeed, it is now commonly claimed that the 2013 coup was the culmination of a plan hatched when the army intervened openly in the revolution on 28 January 2011. This claim has been asserted by two antithetical parties. One, loyal to military rule, trumpets the ostensible farsightedness the army showed in its swift ousting of Mubarak in a masterful pre-emptive strike to contain the revolution and ultimately do away with the Muslim Brotherhood. The other, made up largely of Brotherhood members and supporters, sees a grand conspiracy that damns the army because it was already conspiring against the revolution at that moment when the youth in the square were chanting, 'The army and the people stand hand-in-hand'. Often this latter camp cites the hollow boasts of the former camp as evidence of the soundness of their charge.[26] The main problem with both claims is that they acquit the political players of their many mistakes, which helped pave the way for the coup and the return of authoritarianism. Even if there were such a grand conspiracy designed by the army, its accomplishment was not inevitable.

This does not preclude the existence of some politically ambitious army officers who entertained hopes to establish military rule after eliminating

---

[25] These independent unions proclaimed their defiance of the official state unions by launching a strike on the fifth day of the demonstrations in Tahrir, paralysing public transport in Cairo. Suez Canal Company workers staged a parallel strike on 7 February.

[26] For example, former deputy director of the GIS, Colonel Hussein Fouad appeared on the television programme *al-Qahira wa'l-Nas* to explain the army's perception of the situation during that period. When the 25 January revolutionary tide was high, he said, the army decided to absorb it and play along until the time was ripe to pounce. He claimed that the Muslim Brotherhood's ascent to power was part of the plan. The regime did not want to confront the Brotherhood directly because of their considerable popularity, so it gave the group an opportunity to govern and thereby expose their failures and destroy their popularity.
  Former Colonel Tharwat Fouad had previously made similar statements to *al-Watan* newspaper. He said that the intelligence agencies fed President Mohamed Morsi incorrect information. This is most probably true, but it does not prove the grand conspiracy, nor the inevitability of its success. See: *al-Araby al-Jadid*, 19 April 2015, Available online: https://bit.ly/3n29kTt (accessed 1 May 2015).

Mubarak and his would-be dynasty. But I believe – and this is corroborated by records and testimonies collected by the documentation project prepared for this study – that, after ousting Mubarak and taking control of government administration, the army then manoeuvred to manage the crisis in such a way as to safeguard its, not inconsiderable, interests regardless of whatever type of regime came along. Meanwhile, it engaged in various tugs of war with political forces, a game that included plenty of short-term planning and ad hoc alliances with forces that the army considered central and influential among the people – the Brotherhood one day, its adversaries the next – in order to advance what the army held to be the higher national interest and others claimed was the narrow interests of the army. Throughout it all, the generals maintained their condescending view of civilians, distaste for political parties, and aversion to the Brotherhood, and they held onto the conviction that, as the most disciplined force, they were the best qualified to run the country. But the army encountered some difficult and perplexing moments as it navigated the transitional phase, and it had to contend with pressures from diverse quarters: the legitimate demands of the 25 January revolution, international expectations of progress in democratization and widespread demands for the transfer of power to civilians.

The post-revolutionary Egyptian political scene featured a morally defeated ruling regime that had sacrificed its head and was now doing its best to turn its embrace of the revolution into a chokehold. This entailed lavishly praising the young revolutionaries and 'the revolution of the great people of Egypt' in SCAF communiqués and playing along with the revolutionary spirit by offering concessions that fell short of real change, while taking advantage of every opportunity to check revolutionary legitimacy in order to avoid having to make further sacrifices. Other players were the old opposition parties. Varying in their organizational health and the size of their grassroots bases, they struggled to pull themselves together and collect their feeble strength in a vain attempt to recover their lost youth. Towards this end, they summoned their legacy of expertise in political manoeuvring under the old regime in order to position themselves as mediators between the post-revolutionary extension of the regime and the forces of the revolutionary movement. Thus, as the latter remained set on issuing frequent reminders of the original demands by means of constant demonstrations and sit-ins, the traditional parties scrambled to rehabilitate their political prestige and the partisan cohesion that had disintegrated in Tahrir. But all the jostling and jockeying in the aftermath of Mubarak's departure could not conceal the two most salient features of the political landscape: the control of the military and the powerful entry of the Egyptian people into the public sphere and spaces.

This was a totally new variable. The question now was whether that force in the public sphere called 'the people' would support democratization or turn conservative, fearful of stability, repelled by the anarchy of change. To answer this question, and to understand why things turned out the way they did, we need to sketch out the transitional period as a whole.

Certain conditions needed to be met if the Egyptian people – or at least that part of them involved in public sphere life – were to become a force supportive of democratic transformation. First, there had to be a cohesive leadership with a clear and publicly stated goal, broad popular support and the ability to mobilize forces to attain that goal. When the struggle for democracy is marginalized in favour of identitarian and ideological divides that blur the boundary between what is and is not democratic, and when pro-revolutionary forces succumb to squabbling and dissension, this will inevitably confuse both the politically active grassroots forces and the 'silent majority' who sees nothing but anarchy. That bodes ill since, for the latter especially, a revolution means a revolution in expectations. They will expect a great many needs and demands to be fulfilled by the revolution – whose forces had not actually taken power – and they will fault the revolution when those expectations are not met.

Democratic forces also required a leadership capable of speaking to the people frankly about both the difficulties ahead and the gains to be made, and they needed to work to achieve some of the promised gains on bread-and-butter issues if they were to have credibility when talking about the difficulties. They also needed to avoid behaviours that would give the impression of anarchy. That meant minimizing demonstrations and sit-ins that obstruct daily life and refraining from mutual accusations of treachery, which only serve to cloud the agreed-on goal of the interim phase.

Since the deeply rooted bureaucratic and authoritarian structures of the Egyptian state remained unshaken after Mubarak's fall, the revolutionaries organized themselves into many disparate coalitions. These sustained pressure on the state apparatus to implement their legitimate demands and tried to keep the army from stemming the revolutionary tide and protecting, on the pretext of stability, the structures of the state the people had rebelled against. The 'achievements' scored after Mubarak's ouster (the dismissal of the Shafik government, dissolution of the State Security apparatus and the NDP, and reassessment of the selection process for provincial governors) reinforced a conviction among many who had participated in the 25 January demonstrations that their revolution was ongoing. However, they continued to lack a crucial ingredient: a unified political leadership that represented the revolution and simultaneously insisted on a share in the management of the transitional phase.

In an article published less than a week after Mubarak stood down, the historian Tarek El-Bishry wrote that the 25 January revolution had presented neither national nor social political aims but rather an exclusively organizational political aim: namely, to introduce a pluralist democratic system with free elections and to establish collective constitutional electoral institutions that would forestall opportunities for the resurgence of autocracy. Forfeiting or failing to achieve this goal would signify 'the total failure of the revolutionary act'.[27] In other words, Bishry maintained that democracy was the sole agreed-on demand of the 25 January revolution.

I second this view. If we look for a single common thread binding together the forces of the revolution – other than ousting Mubarak, which is subtractive rather than additive – we find it in the agreement on the idea of pluralist politics and political freedoms. This consensus was the direct product of the rejection of dictatorship. But it is precisely because I agree with Bishry's premise that I disagree with his later conclusions and his reduction of democracy to elections above all else. In my opinion, there should have been a joint declaration of the forces that supported the revolution establishing and clarifying the principles of a democratic system ready to hand as soon as Mubarak fell (perhaps, but not necessarily, in the form of a charter, a pact, between the key political forces, including those affiliated with the former regime); this could have provided the framework for the post-revolution elections. Elections alone do not dispense with the need for dialogue between political forces on the nature of the system of government. Nor should elections be held after a revolution for the purpose of choosing a system of government. They should be the product of the choice of a democratic system, which was the choice of the Egyptian revolution. This is not about whether a constitution should be written before or after elections, but about affirming political forces' commitment to participating in elections in accordance with a democratic system of government, of which elections are only one constituent part.

I agree with Bishry that a constitution reflects the living forces in society. As such, its provisions do not form the basis of social action, but vice versa; it is social action and daily reality that form the basis for the provisions, which should reflect this reality.[28] But this does not imply that democracy is subordinated to the will of a transient majority and fluctuating public

---

[27] Bishry, *Pages from the January 25 Revolution* 17, 28.
[28] Political culture helps explain the stability or durability of democracy, but not its emergence. A system of government – any system, not just a democratic one – will be more stable if it is compatible with prevailing values whether among the larger public or the elite. The central question here is whether it is possible to reconcile the prevailing culture with the political culture needed to support democracy. Ultimately, however, reconciliation is not enough. Democracy must be suffused into culture by means of direct and planned work in education, media and other fields. More crucially yet, institutions must truly adhere to democratic values so that they are taken seriously.

moods. True, when a constitution is drawn up for a particular state, the process should take into account that 'the organs of the state must emanate from a consensus among those deemed to represent the political and social forces that form the polity known as the nation'.[29] Of course, if this consensus conflicts with democracy, then there is no space for a democratic system to begin with, whether a constitution is drafted before or after elections. However, the revolution, which would presumably be the source of legitimacy for the forthcoming order, showed that there was no such contradiction. So, the need for the organs of the state to conform with the view of the majority, as Bishry believes, does not mean that democracy is equivalent to majority rule. The political culture of a majority that, in Egypt's case, had lived under a dictatorship for some seventy years is not going to be a democratic one. Accordingly, the elite should take the lead in defining the democratic system under which elections will be held. This will enable the general culture and political forces to evolve. After all, they are not static; they are influenced by the ruling order more than they influence it.

Overall, the transitional phase seemed to be governed by a fundamental question: Would this historical moment in Egypt produce a democratic transformation or, instead, social anarchy and a security breakdown that sociopolitical forces would be unable to contain? Chaos would result in either a greater political role for the military or a fragile democratic system.[30]

Problems were not long in coming. The dispute over constitutional amendments and supra-constitutional principles, the divide over whether the constitution should precede elections or vice versa, three changes of government within the transitional period, brutal police repression of mass demonstrations, the common attribution of violence to an unidentified (but manipulated) 'third party', groups among the marginalized urban populations ready to serve as the cudgels of political repression, various outbreaks of sectarian violence – all such phenomena made it clear that the transition would be long and complicated and littered with political, social, security-related obstacles, not to mention resistance from vested economic interests.

People's justified and understandable desire for security and stability after the revolution, and their inability to grasp the magnitude and multitude of the political and social factors that would determine the future of their revolution, meant that a long-term gradualist transition strategy was

---

[29] Bishry, *Pages from the January 25 Revolution*, 10–11.
[30] Shaimaa Hatab, 'Determinants of the Trajectory of the Democratic Transition in Egypt' [Arabic], in *The Egyptian Revolution: Motivations, Trends and Challenges* [Arabic], ed. Aya Nassar et al. (Beirut: Arab Centre for Research and Policy Studies, 2012), 464.

needed, though it might be maligned as 'unrevolutionary'. As the March referendum and the parliamentary elections showed, holding elections before changing the system merely brings the organizational capacity of parties extant before the revolution into the new era; it does not necessarily reflect the new political culture epitomized by the revolutionaries.

At a seminar titled 'Egypt in the Transitional Period' held about a month after the revolution, members of the RYC happily acknowledged that they had no unified political vision for the future of Egypt – because the RYC included political forces from across the political spectrum, from left to right and from Islamists to secularists.[31] Yet, democracy should not be a subject of controversy among diverse forces in a pro-democracy revolution. Nor, presumably, should the conceptualization of a democratic system be so involved as to spark dispute.

The strong points of the revolutionary movement became the very source of its weakness in the transitional period. The lack of a unified body representing the forces of the revolution and of an agreed-on, proactive working agenda limited their efficacy and influence, and all the more so when they fell into disarray as the so-called revolutionary youth coalitions proliferated. I believe that many of these coalitions were created specifically in order to disperse actual revolutionary forces across multiple, virtually indistinguishable organizations, some of which were fictional. On the whole, the transitional phase depleted rather than added to the assets of the revolutionary forces, which proved unable to convert the struggles they waged in that phase into political capital.

There was never a lack of people ready to use this fragmentation as a justification for excluding the revolutionary forces from actively participating in the formulation of the foundations and rules of the new order. The internal divisions in these forces first manifested itself clearly at the time of referendum on 19 March 2011. That was the critical moment when it became necessary to translate the grassroots power that overthrew Mubarak into representative democracy, but they were not yet equipped for political party work and electoral campaigning. This was the dilemma of the 25 January youth. There is a difference between the composition of Tahrir Square and the Egyptian people.

With the elections looming after the referendum, there was every reason to fear that the best organized and most experienced political forces – the Muslim Brotherhood and the now-disbanded but omnipresent rank and file of the NDP – would sweep the polls. There was also the worry that the elections would simply reproduce the influence of the traditional social

---

[31] *Al-Masry Al-Youm*, 28 March 2011, Available online: https://bit.ly/3m70nag (accessed 5 May 2015).

and economic elites. This explains why a coalition of democratic forces was keen to postpone elections for a while until they were better equipped to compete with the Muslim Brotherhood and NDP. Indeed, the election results would prove how well placed concerns about the electoral prospects of the revolutionary groups were. But they also showed that the fears of former NDP members' electoral performance were exaggerated, although there was no overstating the ongoing influence of these circles in the state bureaucracy or what might best be termed Egypt's 'deep state'.[32] On the other hand, delaying the polls would have done the revolutionary forces little good as long as they did not participate in government. That would have positioned them to take action against the old regime before the elections and to build their own solid grassroots bases.[33]

Appeals to political imagination, as exemplified by recourse to such unconventional methods as social media, are of no avail in such cases. Imagination cannot alter the balance of powers in the administration of the state. There was little to be gained from championing the methods that had mobilized the gatherings in Tahrir or declaring that the challenge facing the Arab revolutions and the Egyptian revolution in particular was 'to liberate the political and democratic imagination' in order to create institutions that allow for direct grassroots intervention, ensure the

---

[32] The term 'deep state' comes from modern Turkish politics and refers to an alliance embedded in the state bureaucracy. *Derin devlet* comprises the security apparatus, above all. The alliance is hostile to democracy and civil life, impedes democratization, engages in covert operations or covers up ultranationalist extremists' crimes against democracy, leftists, Islamists, the Kurds and anything perceived to threaten the conservative Kemalist structure of the Turkish Republic. The deep state is responsible for frustrating the work of civilian governments preparatory to staging military coups, which have occurred repeatedly in modern Turkish history. The term was borrowed by political activists in Egypt – correctly, in my view – to describe the state apparatus's obstruction of democratic transformation. It is important to bear in mind, however, that in Turkey the concept draws on a history of incidents – some factual, others fictitious – undertaken by tightly knit clandestine organizations inside the state apparatus since the Ottoman era. In other words, in Turkey, the term presumes the existence of an actual discrete organization that operates systematically, as opposed to mere collusion, whether or not it works in a planned manner in the pursuit of specific aims. I, on the other hand, use the term to refer to something else: the state bureaucracy and security apparatus which has been built up over several historical eras and become accustomed to serving and obeying sultans and autocrats. It is hard to make this apparatus obey outsiders unless they possess the power and strength to impose themselves on it. It can also develop its own agenda – this is what I mean by the deep state. Never in Egypt's history has this apparatus followed the orders of an elected popular government, with the sole exception of the Wafd Party, which consistently held the majority in the period from the 1919 revolution to the July 1952 revolution. Remember, however, that this party never ruled more than two years at any one time during this period. A more dangerous situation arises when the bureaucratic state shifts from passive resistance to democracy to support the architects of a coup.

[33] In a description of her visit to Egypt after the revolution, former US secretary of state Hillary Clinton relates a meeting she held with young students and activists and her impression that they lacked political experience and had no idea of how to organize parties, nominate candidates or run electoral campaigns. Likewise, they had no political programme and showed no interest in developing one, frequently argued among themselves, blamed the United States for any number of wrongs and cared little about the elections. See: Clinton, *Hard Choices*, 346.

sustainability of public participation in decision making and prevent the electoral process from reverting to a mechanism controlled by political money and old political elites. Much hay was made about the innovative potential of the youth who spearheaded the path to change, who could not be expected to stick to the tried-and-true 'recipe' for representative democracy, but were instead attuned to the possibilities of more direct forms of popular representation offered by modern technology, just as they had used this technology to challenge traditional mechanisms of oppression and to mobilize the masses.[34] This sort of talk is useful only for theoretical speculation or articulating a radical conception of democracy as a critique of the established mode of democracy. But this was not the task at hand in Egypt. The mission there was to build democracy. As for the 'Republic of the Square', it was a metaphor, not a system of government.

The post-revolutionary period cast into stark relief the vast difference between the ability to win on social media and the ability to win elections, that is, to channel people's political efficacy into the ballot box. It was as though the young revolutionaries had set themselves one specific task: to topple the president and then cede way to the older, established political forces (the Brotherhood, political parties and of course the army and the state apparatus). Most of these latter forces were not democratic in their world views. One might assert that they did not necessarily have to be democratic, but nor did they manage to organize the political game among themselves and to abide by agreed-on rules and procedures.

After the toppling of Ben Ali and Mubarak, conventional forces and regimes broke young people's monopoly on social media, which was quickly turned to the service of the regimes, their agencies and conventional forces, and against the youth and progressive forces. Since 2011, Arab security agencies have created armies of internet trolls who used fake social media accounts to spread rumours about the regime's political adversaries, disseminate propaganda and counter criticism with verbal abuse and slander. This was an important development that limited the efficacy of social networking platforms as an instrument against authoritarian regimes.

Still, the post-revolutionary political process should not be viewed solely from the perspective of the young revolutionaries and their groupings. It should also be seen from the perspective of the Egyptian people as a whole, since this was presumably their revolution. The revolution unleashed their energies and cleared the way for their self-expression in the public sphere.

---

[34] Walden Bello, 'The Arab Revolutions and the Democratic Imagination', *Foreign Policy in Focus*, 16 March 2011, Available online: https://bit.ly/3831McX (accessed 1 May 2015).

However, they did not enter that space with the culture of Tahrir Square alone, but also with the political cultural legacy of previous eras.

The revolutionary forces did not possess sufficient knowledge about how the state and its agencies worked, while for the army it was familiar territory. The traditional political parties were drawn to the organs of power and control – especially the army. Gradually, the fleeting admiration for the revolutionary youth faded. The established media helped considerably with this, consuming their youthful energies in news programmes, talk shows and commercial displays and playing on their frailties and lured them into treacherous terrains of rivalry, acrimony and mutual envy.

2

The army's return to politics

Neither a conspiracy nor just a contingency

I The military takes the reins

I have already discussed the military's behaviour in Tahrir Square in Part I. From the outset, it seemed to the revolutionaries that the army was sending mixed messages. Stories spread that the military police had supplied CSF deployed near the People's Assembly and Shura Council with ammunition when their stores were depleted on 28 January. On the other hand, soldiers let the revolutionaries graffiti 'down with Hosni Mubarak' on the sides of their tanks, a highly symbolic gesture. Lacking information about what was happening behind the scenes at the military high command, the revolutionaries made judgements based on their observations of the army's behaviour within a 2–3 kilometre radius of Tahrir Square.

Three days after the army descended on the Cairo streets, on 31 January 2011, the armed forces issued a statement. Tantamount to a declaration of good faith from the military establishment, the statement pledged that the army 'had not and would not resort to the use of force against the great people' and affirmed the 'legitimate demands of the demonstrators', who by then were already demanding the fall of the head of the regime. Scarcely a day later, however, on 2 February, the army's conduct in the Battle of the Camel raised questions among the confused demonstrators. Suspicions about its true leanings were fuelled after the military left the peaceful protesters vulnerable to pro-regime thugs brandishing knives and took no action to stop the ensuing, nearly day-long battle despite the casualties (10 people were killed and 1,500 injured). On the eve of the attack, and even during it, the military called on demonstrators to evacuate the square, after which it made successive attempts to surround demonstrators and confine them in Tahrir Square.

The military performed its duties in a partial, perfunctory fashion; for more than two weeks, it behaved as a regular army, ostensibly under the command of the president, albeit without obeying all the regime's orders. At the same time, it attempted to contain the revolutionaries as a threat not only to the president but to the institution of government as a whole. Unsure of how to manage the crisis, the military sought to avoid a conflict with the street in defence of the plan to engineer a hereditary presidential succession while also giving the regime an opportunity to put down the revolution by force. There is no doubt that Military Intelligence was aware of the preparations for the attack on Tahrir Square on 2 February.

Meanwhile, the military establishment itself, particularly the middle and lower ranks, grew increasingly restless, impatient with the generals' reluctance to make a decision, made evident when soldiers refused to obey orders to open fire on demonstrators. A major by the name of Ahmed Shoman soon joined the demonstrators in Tahrir, calling for the army to protect the people rather than the illegitimate regime. The fifteen-year veteran of the armed forces, who had been tasked with guarding the western entrance to Tahrir, claimed to speak for 'many of his colleagues' and said that fifteen officers – from the rank of major to lieutenant colonel – had joined the demonstrators. It should not automatically be concluded that this exceptional case helped push the military to make a choice. Nor is there any use in repeating the popular claim that the military deployed because the generals realized that getting ahead of the demand that Mubarak leave was their last chance to preserve their positions and privileges.[1] Similarly, there is no evidence that the root of the military's indecisiveness lay in its professionalism and popularity, which trumped its loyalty to the regime.[2]

It is important to note that the military's reluctance to quell the revolution at its inception encouraged many people to join in, and popular support for the demonstrations increased so dramatically that the grassroots participation in the revolution could no longer be ignored. Expressing an independent will, the military left the regime to suppress the revolution without its help. After domestic security forces and, later, paid thugs failed in this task and the revolution gained momentum, maintaining order might have brought the military into armed confrontation with millions of engaged citizens across the country, at a time when the revolution was winning greater sympathy internationally.

---

[1] Russ Wellen, 'Last Thing Washington Needs Is to Share Blame if Egypt Becomes Another Pakistan', *Institute for Policy Studies*, 17 February 2011, Available online: https://bit.ly/3m3IAAu (accessed 14 May 2015).
[2] Contra Eva Bellin's thesis in Eva Bellin, 'Lessons from the Jasmine and Nile Revolutions: Possibilities of Political Transformation in the Middle East?' *Middle East Brief*, no. 50 (May 2011): 4.

From the outset, two primary features of the military's behaviour were apparent. First, it did not wish to intervene, ostensibly because it was intent on exercising its constitutionally mandated authority and did not interfere in politics. The armed forces thus refused to be a tool for the suppression of demonstrators – at least this was what SCAF leaders told revolutionary youth.[3] Yet, in the transitional period, it did not hesitate to use armed force against unarmed demonstrators, indicating that, in fact, it had no qualms about using extreme violence against 'the great people' if it served the military's interest. Second, the rapid unfolding of events took the armed forces by surprise, as it did the revolutionary youth themselves. The military command found itself in an entirely unfamiliar situation: It was witnessing a protest movement spanning the entire country that demanded a change in the regime to which it owed fealty, and yet it was not part of that movement and had no hand in determining its course. Although military leaders feared revolutionary change, they were nevertheless dissatisfied with their diminishing share of power as Gamal Mubarak's influence peaked. As explicated in the first part, they were worried about Mubarak's attempt to bequeath the presidency to his son.

Although Mubarak officially turned the country's affairs over to the armed forces when he stepped down on 11 February, the military had already taken the reins a day earlier, after issuing Communiqué 1 on 10 February, announcing that SCAF was in permanent session pursuant to Article 180 of the constitution.[4]

The communiqué seemed to signal that the military was moving against Mubarak, leading Egyptians to believe that the military had played a historical role in settling the conflict with the regime in favour of the revolution, partly due to the somewhat romanticized regard in which the army was held.[5]

Despite apprehensions about the military assuming unilateral control of the transitional period, it was widely believed to be the sole remaining

---

[3] *Al-Masry Al-Youm*, 2 June 2011, Available online: https://bit.ly/3832Nlh (accessed 3 April 2015). Meetings between military leaders and youth were part of the army's strategy, at times seeking to contain them and at others misrepresenting them and fomenting discord and division within their ranks.

[4] *Shorouk*, 17 March 2011. Archived Copy Available Online: https://bit.ly/3m2ydwV (accessed 3 July 2015).

[5] Mohammad Taha Aliwa explicitly wrote that when the army was called to the streets, military leaders saw it as an opportune moment to remove the president and his clique in order to save the regime as a whole. The tone of the statement issued by SCAF on 1 February 2011 'encouraged the masses to stage sit-ins, which turned into a wave of civil disobedience that swept through nearly all of Egypt's cities'. Mohammad Taha Aliwa, 'Egypt on the Threshold of the Second Republic: Constitutional Changes before and after the 25 January Revolution' [Arabic], in *Constitutional Debate and the Transitional Phase in Egypt: Between 25 January and 30 June* [Arabic] (Beirut: Arab Centre for Research and Policy Studies, 2014), 48.

institution that could reliably safeguard the country during the democratic transition and that any deterioration in civilian-military relations would not serve the interest of the revolution[6] (the military was commonly described as 'the tent pole' in this phase). The forces which believed that the military coup of 10 February 2011 was motivated by a desire to preserve the regime after the ouster of Mubarak – and ensure that the military would be its backbone – were initially few in number with a barely audible voice. Soon enough, however, they grew louder.

The vast difference between the Egyptian army, its role and its aspirations and the structure of the Tunisian army – and the implications for the entirety of the democratic transition – became apparent after Communiqué No. 1.[7] Communiqués No. 2 and 3, issued on 11 February 2011, made the de facto reality of military rule official. In the second communiqué, the military pledged to issue necessary legislation, convoke free presidential elections and protect the interests of the people. Communiqué No. 4, issued on 12 February 2011, affirmed the armed forces' commitment to the previous communiqués, adding that the government of Ahmed Shafik would oversee the country's affairs pending the formation of a new government and that SCAF looked forward to ceding power to a civilian authority.

It may seem naive to some political scientists to wonder why the military intervenes in politics, as this depends on the type of governing system, the nature of the military credo and the kind of values disseminated within the military. In this regard, Samuel Finer writes that instead of asking what motivates the army to interfere in politics, 'we ought surely ask why they ever do otherwise'.[8] It is thus a political system's capacity to subordinate this powerful institution capable of organized violence to civilian rule that requires explanation.

---

[6] This was the line of argument of figures like Mohamed ElBaradei, who continued to call for 'civilian participation' in the transitional phase while affirming that 'the trust between the army and the people is a red line that must be preserved for the sake of the nation'. See: *Al-Masry Al-Youm*, 10 April 2011, Available online: https://bit.ly/3grVsPX (accessed 12 April 2015).

[7] Henry and Springborg say that, unlike the Tunisian case, Egypt under Hosni Mubarak was a military state. I have already shown this to be incorrect, insofar as it was less a military than a police state. Although the army was the primary power in the country, the Mubarak-era Egyptian regime was predicated on a historical compact that dictated that the military would not intervene directly in politics except in extreme cases. I concur, however, that although the Egyptian police outnumbered military personnel 3 to 1 (1.5 million police personnel to 450,000 soldiers), security and police forces in Egypt (unlike Tunisia) were inadequately equipped, poorly paid and held in contempt by the military. Contrary to Tunisia, the Egyptian military was permitted – even encouraged – to carve out its own economic empires. This reduced the burden of military spending on the government, and more importantly, it created a patronage network through which to buy officers' loyalty. See: *Foreign Affairs*, 21 February 2011, Available online: https://fam.ag/3a2I03w (accessed 30 June 2015).

[8] Samuel E. Finer, *The Man on Horseback: The Role of the Military in Politics*, with a new introduction by Jay Stanley (New Brunswick, NJ: Transaction, 2002), 6.

The military in Egypt, as elsewhere in the Third World, is the most powerful institution and most organized sociopolitical force, with previous experience in running the country's political affairs, particularly in the early stage of the July Republic, as discussed in Part I of this book.[9] More importantly, army officers in Egypt are akin to a fraternal league of a corporatist nature. The Egyptian military is an autonomous institution with diverse economic interests and investments that is resistant to any civilian oversight, especially in the wake of the peace agreement with Israel.

Using Finer's analytical framework, some scholars surmise that the Egyptian military intervened reluctantly. In fact, its desire to intervene changed over time based on the unfolding of events. In turn, this explains the shift in the army's attitude to intervention, from a defensive intervention on 28 January 2011 to more ambitious action on 10 February involving the direct administration of political affairs.[10] In effect, the military intervened when the opportunity presented itself. After the Egyptian political regime entered crisis mode, the military decided to remove the president. Aborting the revolution and simultaneously refusing to leave political power in the hands of Omar Suleiman – Mubarak's vice-president – it then opted to seize control itself,[11] thereby fulfilling Suleiman's 'prophecy' of a military coup, as discussed in Part I.

It should be emphasized that the military that had intervened in the January revolution was not a revolutionary band of junior officers who had staged a coup of their own accord, à la Portugal in 1974 or even Egypt in

---

[9] According to Henry and Springborg, the Egyptian army emerged as the winner after 11 February 2011, at least for the time being, but they predicted that it would be difficult for the military to maintain its victory: 'Although its size and strength are widely recognized, the Egyptian army is not the tight professional force that many consider it to be. It is bloated and its officer core is indulged, having been fattened on Mubarak's patronage. Its training is desultory, maintenance of its equipment is profoundly inadequate, and it is dependent on the United States for funding and logistical support.' See: Henry and Springborg, 'A Tunisian Solution for Egypt's Military'.

It seemed to the two scholars, then, that the army would not be able to capitalize on its win, and in fact, its performance in the first year of the transition was muddled in many respects. But it regrouped once the magnitude of the conflict between political and social forces became apparent, particularly among pro-revolution forces, and once it became evident how easy it was to disrupt the Muslim Brotherhood's administration of state and isolate the organization politically and socially from other political forces. The military used various means, including intelligence methods, to foment division, exploiting the fragility of the political elite and its susceptibility to division, polarization and infighting.

[10] Holger Albrecht and Dina Bishara, 'Back on Horseback: The Military and Political Transformation in Egypt', *Middle East Law and Governance* 3, nos. 1–2 (2011): 17.

[11] Looking at the evolution of the military's involvement in politics even after the coup of 3 July 2013 and following Eric Nordlinger's classification in his *Soldiers in Politics: Military Coups and Governments*, we might say that the Egyptian military alternated between the role of praetorian moderator, in which officers exercise a veto over government decisions; praetorian guardian, with the goal of upholding certain principles or the status quo, as is the case with the National Security Council in Turkey before the AKP extended its influence throughout civil institutions; and praetorian ruler, a pattern in which the military rules directly and leads the state towards radical socio-economic transformations, as was the case at the beginning of the July Republic.

1952. On the contrary, it was the conservative military leadership – a key component of the political regime and its interests, values and culture – that had intervened during the revolution. The army had not wanted to meet the demands of revolutionaries in Egypt's squares.[12]

The shift occurred gradually between 28 January and 10 February, when officers began to present themselves as 'serving the state rather than the government in power'. In other words, the military reframed its loyalties: Abandoning fealty to the regime, it expressed loyalty to 'society' and 'the nation'. We should be attentive here to the military's understanding of the nation as an abstract, uniform entity and its view of political parties as agents of division and fragmentation rather than vital national constituencies. We should also note the military's tendency to fluidly move from the idea of serving the people as a whole to the claim to embody and represent 'the nation' and its 'will'. That is, the military is naturally disposed to seeing itself as the genuine, authentic nation, unsullied by sectional interests.[13]

SCAF[14] defined its mandate in the fourth communiqué, issued on 12 February 2011, as 'ensuring the peaceful transition of power in a free democratic framework that allows an elected civilian authority to govern the country, defending the stability of the homeland and re-ordering priorities to achieve the legitimate demands of the people'. The fifth communiqué, issued as the country was still in a state of euphoria and shock following Mubarak's abdication, was the equivalent of a constitutional declaration, containing several important decrees affirming the military's responsibility for governing Egypt. Communiqué No. 5 suspended the constitution; charged SCAF with the temporary administration of the country's affairs for six months or until after the completion of elections for the People's

---

[12] Henry and Springborg wrote that the military as currently constituted would prove unable to meet protesters' demands: 'It cannot allow the core of the anti-Mubarak movement, such as the National Association for Change associated with Mohamed ElBaradei, to play a leading role in forming a new government. Nor can it allow a parliament to have real power. The anti-Mubarak opposition and an empowered legislative branch would seek at least an oversight role and ultimately try to subordinate the military to the civilian government.' See: Henry and Springborg, 'A Tunisian Solution for Egypt's Military'.

[13] On 4 November 2015, shortly before his visit to the UK, Egyptian President Abdel Fattah El-Sisi said during an interview with the BBC that 'the Egyptian people are part of the army'. (He meant to say, 'the army is a part of the people'.) This was an extremely telling slip of the tongue – a Freudian slip as it were – indicative of the military mentality I am describing here.

[14] SCAF was composed of twenty leading members of the armed forces, including chair Field Marshal Mohamed Hussein Tantawi, general commander of the armed forces and minister of defence and military production, and Lt General Sami Anan, chief of staff of the armed forces. See a list of all members in: *Shorouk*, 27 February 2011. Archived Copy Available Online: https://bit.ly/3833MBZ (accessed 5 October 2021).

It was noticed that the name of Abdel Fattah El-Sisi, the head of Military Intelligence, was subsequently added to the official sources, although his name was not mentioned in the initial coverage of the body, including by *Shorouk*. After Tantawi, Sami Anan was the most influential member of SCAF.

Assembly and Shura Council; tasked the chair of SCAF, Field Marshal Mohamed Hussein Tantawi, with representing SCAF before all domestic and foreign bodies; dissolved the People's Assembly and Shura Council; proclaimed SCAF's right to legislate in the transitional period through edicts with the force of law; formed a committee to amend some articles of the constitution and set the rules for a referendum on the amendments; provided for a caretaker government under Ahmed Shafik pending the formation of a new government; and required the state to enforce all international conventions and treaties to which it was a party. On 14 February 2011, SCAF issued its first law (Law 1/2011), the sole article of which stated: 'All provisions decreed by laws and regulations prior to the issuance of the constitutional declaration remain valid and enforceable provided they are not repealed or amended in accordance with the rules and procedures set forth in the constitutional declaration.'

With Communiqués No. 4 and 5, SCAF acquired both legislative and executive authority. This is of course understandable for a limited period of time during the transition. Yet, vesting so many vital powers in one body makes it an absolute authority – even Mubarak never held absolute executive and legislative power. The step came in response to the political vacuum created by Mubarak's departure and the dissolution of the People's Assembly, elected in a rigged process in 2010.

These decrees reassured the international community, particularly Egypt's allies in the United States, that Egypt would abide by its international agreements, most especially the peace accord with Israel. They also demonstrated that the military establishment was firmly in charge of Egypt's leadership and policies, which was the prime concern of the United States. As long as the army leadership was securely positioned, maintained the loyalty of the armed forces and adhered to Egypt's policies and its international alliances, it would be possible to control the trajectory of events and avoid the unknown.

The same day, Ahmed Shafik, the prime minister of the caretaker government who had been appointed by Mubarak as a replacement for Ahmed Nazif, underscored his government's commitment to restoring security and protecting investment, warning of a possible economic collapse, though he affirmed that there was no shortage of basic goods.[15] While it is true that, in effect, the Mubarak regime continued to run the country, the revolutionary phase was not yet over. A revolution had already toppled the dictatorship's figurehead, and the regime, including military

---

[15] Egyptian television broadcast the fifth communiqué on 14 February 2011, viewable at *YouTube*, Available online: https://bit.ly/3gFPFXb (accessed 5 May 2015). See also: *BBC Arabic*, 13 February 2011, Available online: https://bbc.in/3oFHLiX (accessed 5 May 2015).

leaders, was uneasily awaiting further developments. If political forces had continued to act on the spirit of the square, albeit using other methods, while showing a readiness to reach a consensus with old regime actors, it could have steered the transitional phase towards the overthrow of the entire regime.

But there are no ifs in history. Revolutionary forces were not adequately organized and prepared, and they did not understand that the battle with the Mubarak regime had not been won on 11 February 2011, but was only beginning, when the regime, newly lacking its leader, was at its weakest. The people had demonstrated their strength and will by toppling Mubarak, thereby clearing the way for concerted action for regime change, but veteran political forces preferred to disengage from the revolutionary movement to pursue their own struggle for power, which had not yet been wrested away from old regime forces. In February 2011, the NAC called on political parties to come together to articulate a shared vision for Egypt's future, but subsequent discussions came to naught. Although the Brotherhood initially agreed with other parties to press SCAF for a civilian presidential council to administer the transitional phase and begin the constitution writing process, it later withdrew from the initiative and began dealing with SCAF directly.[16]

SCAF's immediate post-revolution strategy was to indulge the prevailing revolutionary sentiment and the local and global revolutionary momentum while setting a ceiling on popular demands and simultaneously offering limited concessions supported by some political forces and opposed by others. In this way, it began to drive a wedge between revolutionary political forces and those circles that had adopted the revolution's discourse after Mubarak's abdication. Absent a comprehensive, consensual plan for systemic change, the former saw such piecemeal responses to specific demands as an abandonment of the revolution's goals; the latter viewed it as political pragmatism and saw opposition to such advances as reckless intransigence.

Hani Soliman cites cases of successful democratic transitions in the Philippines, Mexico, South Korea and Chile, where the main political forces reached a degree of consensus, leading to less military interference in politics.[17] (In Chile in the early 1970s, the right and the left became so polarized that the consensus was effectively annulled.[18]) Alternatively,

---

[16] Abd al-Fattah Madi, *Traces in the Square: How Was the January Revolution in Egypt Thwarted?* [Arabic] (Beirut: Arab Centre for Research and Policy Studies, 2020), 70–2, 77–81.

[17] Hani Soliman, *Civilian-Military Relations and the Democratic Transition in Egypt after the 25 January Revolution* [Arabic] (Beirut: Arab Centre for Research and Policy Studies, 2015), 30.

[18] See also: Arturo Valenzuela, *The Breakdown of Democratic Regimes: Chile* (Baltimore: Johns Hopkins University Press, 1978).

Rebecca Schiff posits that a concordance between military and political elites, along with civil society elites, leads to less military involvement in politics,[19] unlike the cases of Bangladesh, Pakistan and Thailand.[20] Egypt can now unequivocally be added to this list.

Pursuant to the item in Communiqué No. 5 to form a committee to amend the constitution, SCAF appointed a group of jurists, led by Judge Tarek El-Bishry, to draft amendments to a narrow set of articles from the 1971 constitution. These were defined by SCAF in the appointment decree as Articles 76, 77, 88, 93 and 189, all pertaining to the election of the president, People's Assembly and Shura Council; the committee was also to consider repealing Article 179. All except two of the articles were mentioned by Mubarak in his speech of 28 February 2011. In effect, then, SCAF initiative was an extension of the reforms Mubarak had proposed under pressure from the revolution. Indeed, the amendment committee itself was simply an updated version of the committee appointed by Vice-President Omar Suleiman to carry out Mubarak's pledged reforms.[21] From the outset, however, the committee members sought to rewrite other constitutional provisions as well.

Coming from on high, the decision to amend the 1971 constitution had nothing to do with the revolution and its forces and was made without their input, if not in opposition to them. The goal was certainly to allow for elections as soon as possible since the military clearly perceived that elections offered an exit from the revolutionary situation. Although fair elections are of course a democratic measure, the military sought elections before the regime had been transformed and without the participation of revolutionary forces, which had yet to organize their ranks. Yet, from that moment on, elections became everyone's overriding concern, even as groups of revolutionary youth believed street action should continue to topple the regime. (I discuss the constitutional amendments in more detail later.)

The same day that the fifth communiqué was issued (13 February 2011), the commander of the military police, Hamdy Badeen, asked protesters to remove the remaining tents in Tahrir Square. The army would subsequently deploy the military police to forcibly disperse protesters in the square, as

---

[19] Rebecca L. Schiff, 'Civil-Military Relations Reconsidered: A Theory of Concordance', *Armed Forces and Society* 22, no. 1 (Fall 1995): 7-9.
[20] Soliman, *Civilian-Military Relations*, 30-1.
[21] That committee had included Yehia El-Gamal, Ahmed Kamal Abul-Magd, Judge Serry Seyam and others. The new constitutional amendments committee chaired by Bishry comprised Atef Elbanna (professor of constitutional law at Cairo University), Mohammad Bahi Abu Younis (professor of constitutional law at Alexandria University), Sobhi Salih (Cassation Court attorney), Maher Sami (vice-president at SCC), Hassan al-Badrawi (vice-president of the SCC) and Hatem Bagato (president of the SCC's Commissioners' Authority and secretary of the committee).

it did, for example, on the Friday demonstration of 25 February on behalf of the revolution's martyrs, which saw scuffles between protesters and military police, and during Friday actions on 1 and 8 April.

Prior to the revolution, the Egyptian military operated independently, outside of parliamentary oversight; attempts had been made as well to immunize the security apparatus from judicial accountability. In addition to the near-permanent state of emergency that granted security forces extralegal authorities, the 2007 amendment of Article 179 of the constitution expanded their prerogatives to combat terrorism, even as they were not subject to the judicial restraints set forth in Articles 41, 44 and 45.[22] The military wanted to preserve its privileges.

The military did not repeal the emergency law, in effect since 1981, nor did it put an end to the prosecution of civilians in military courts or seek to dismantle the notorious security services. On the contrary, it allied with the security establishment for reasons of stability,[23] though the intent was to subordinate the internal security apparatus to military control. Perhaps we can say, then, that the military joined forces with the security establishment after first bringing the latter to heel. Although two democratic elections were held under SCAF – the parliamentary elections in late 2011 and the presidential election in mid-2012 – SCAF was always capable of controlling the outcome and result of electoral processes. The parliament was dissolved after the SCC declared the election law unconstitutional, and a constitutional declaration was issued granting SCAF legislative authorities, to ensure that the elected president could not exercise these powers. SCAF also claimed the right to form the Constituent Assembly while also retaining all prerogatives related to the affairs of the armed forces. The constitutional declaration, issued in August 2012, was tantamount to a second military coup under cover of law.[24] Though that one was ultimately thwarted by the election, the third coup of 3 July 2013 succeeded following the failed experiment of governance under the elected president.

Direct rule by SCAF spurred early debate and inquiry among numerous scholars. Hazem Kandil dismissed the possibility of the military reconstituting an authoritarian regime like that seen after the July 1952 coup, arguing that the military would reclaim its privileges and

---

[22] Bruce K. Rutherford, *Egypt after Mubarak: Liberalism, Islam, and Democracy in the Arab World* (Princeton, NJ: Princeton University Press, 2008), 248–50.
[23] Ibid., 57. See also: Hazem Kandil, 'Back on Horse? The Military between Two Revolutions', in *Arab Spring in Egypt: Revolution and Beyond*, ed. Bahgat Korany and Rabab El-Mahdi (Cairo, NY: The American University in Cairo Press, 2012), 245.
[24] Soliman, *Civilian-Military Relations*, 59–60; *Al Jazeera*, 15 August 2012, Available online: https://bit.ly/3qFgwac (accessed 5 October 2021).

interests after Mubarak's fall, but that it was not capable of restoring the regime. To support his argument, Kandil pointed to popular mobilization in the January 2011 revolution, which was lacking in 1952, as well as the military's long avoidance of politics and its transformation into a professional army. He also cited the power of the regime's security apparatus, which had kept the military out of politics, noting that this apparatus did not exist in the era of King Farouk, when army officers were steeped in partisan politics.[25] On the other hand, Javed Maswood and Usha Natarajan posited that despite the erosion of its mandates and capacities since 1952, the Egyptian military was still capable of instituting democratic reforms.[26] Though well reasoned and argued, both these theses were proven wrong by subsequent events. It turned out that the security apparatus was weakened by the revolution and the counter-revolution did not suffer a shortage of popular support; moreover, the army had no qualms about mounting a bloody coup against elected institutions, even when all that remained of them was an isolated president.

Only a united front of revolutionary or pro-democracy forces could have checked the military's ambitions to expand its prerogatives and privileges and enshrine them in the constitution, and brought the Defence Ministry's budget under civilian oversight. No single political actor in government was capable of this, and it became impossible as political forces proved willing to urge the army to take action against the elected president.

---

[25] Kandil, 'Back on Horse?' 217–47. I have already discussed the military's relationship to politics at length in Part I of this book, from its hold on government to its subordination to the presidency by the end of Nasser's tenure and particularly under Sadat, to the historic deal struck in the Mubarak era.

[26] Javed Maswood and Usha Natarjan, 'Democratization and Constitutional Reform in Egypt and Indonesia', in *Arab Spring in Egypt: Revolution and Beyond*, ed. Bahgat Korany and Rabab El-Mahdi (Cairo, NY: The American University in Cairo Press, 2012), 281–311.

In fact, Indonesia witnessed a popular revolution in 1998 marred by acts of violence, some of it arising from disputes between military leaders themselves, but the transition was more incremental than in Egypt. Vice-President Jusuf Habibie assumed the presidency for one year (1998–9), after which elections were held that brought Abdurrahman Wahid to power. The military retained explicit influence throughout the democratic transition. In the 2004 elections, General Susilo Bambang Yudhoyono beat opposition leader Megawati Sukarnoputri to win the presidency and was re-elected in 2009. Yudhoyono was one of the military officers who in 1997 persuaded Suharto to step down after 31 years of rule. See: Theodore Friend, *Indonesian Destinies* (Cambridge, MA: Belknap Press of Harvard University Press, 2003).

I tend to see some similarity with the Egyptian case. But what strikes me here is the consensus around democratic principles among Indonesian elites, including the main Islamist current, which was not the case in Egypt. See: Joshua Kurlantzick, 'Indonesia', in *Pathways to Freedom: Political and Economic Lessons from Democratic Transitions*, ed. Isobel Coleman and Terra Lawson-Remer (New York: Council on Foreign Relations, 2013), 151.

II The easy part: Dissolving the NDP

The easiest response to revolutionary demands in the wake of Mubarak's departure was to dissolve the NDP, the weakest pillar of the regime and, for the army, the least important; much like the state parties of other dictatorships towards the end of their eras, it had been eclipsed by the more important security apparatus and ruling family. The instrument used to dissolve the party – the judiciary – was not a dependably democratic institution on which the Egyptian revolution could rely. As discussed in Part I, NDP offices had already been torched; leading NDP figures had been imprisoned and the party's leadership had resigned. It was a simple matter to saddle the party with all the regime's corruption since it was, in fact, a patronage network, and many NDP leaders were already facing criminal charges of killing demonstrators or inciting it at the very least.

In its ruling dissolving the party, the court wrote that the fall of the regime and the party that corrupted it, seen in the abdication of the president, who was also the president of the ruling NDP, entails 'necessarily, as an inevitable, imperative outcome, the fall of the instruments through which it exercised its authorities, and the most important of these is the ruling party, which has been proven with certainty to have corrupted political, economic and social life, and it has become incumbent on the court to expose this fall'. The court added, 'It is established by general fact that the National [Democratic] Party grew under the wing of the ruling authority and was nurtured by its power, exploiting its assets. Indeed, state and party assets were intermingled.' In explaining the methods and means by which the NDP had corrupted political, economic and social life, and Egypt generally, the political parties circuit of the Supreme Administrative Court said, 'The unilateral exercise of governing powers by the former president, Hosni Mubarak, the former president of the party, regardless of the will of citizens, was one cause for the corruption of political life.' The court went on to say that the NDP majorities in both houses of parliament were manufactured and that the 2010 elections were rigged.[27]

The NDP was dissolved by a reasoned legal/political decision in which the court accused the party of corrupting political life, although this was not one of the charges in the indictment. Today the Egyptian judiciary cannot disavow its ruling, which I purposefully quoted at length because it encapsulates the courts' evaluation of the NDP at a time when the spirit of the 25 January revolution still prevailed. That the Egyptian courts could rule so decisively against the NDP and Mubarak – before the laws they

---

[27] *Al-Masry Al-Youm*, 17 April 2011, Available online: https://bit.ly/2IBoQGY (accessed 11 May 2015).

applied were changed to lead to completely opposite judgements – should come as no surprise. The same judiciary would later acquit Mubarak and issue the same kind of uncompromising rulings to advance the policies of the military coup after 3 July 2013, among them convictions and stiff sentences against revolutionary youth, journalists and others suspected of opposing the military rule. As for the court's claim that the NDP had corrupted political life, this charge was not repeated in the indictment of former officials, including Mubarak. The judiciary's approach shifted during Morsi's tenure, when it became more antagonistic towards elected institutions, and after the coup, which it in effect facilitated. It is clear that the judiciary's conduct shifted in line with the changing political situation, but overall it remained conservative and suspicious of popular participation.

The NDP was not a genuine ruling party, but rather a mechanism for organizing the regime's social base and a patronage network for personal, geographic and sectional interests, bound to the regime and loyal to it, and permeating the entire system. The campaign against the NDP apparatus and base continued, the party making a much easier target than the regime itself.

The same Administrative Court ruled in June 2011 that SCAF and the cabinet must issue a decree to dissolve the local councils. In suing for the dissolution of the councils, the petitioners cited 'their years-long corruption and because most positions on them were occupied by members of the dissolved National [Democratic] Party'.[28] And later, the Administrative Court welcomed cases arguing for the dissolution of the elected People's Assembly. What concerns us here is that the use of the Administrative Courts against the institutions of the old regime – of which they were a part – soon turned against revolutionary forces, whom the courts indulged only until the storm passed. The judiciary subsequently became a key party in the defence of the still-extant old regime and later the coup against elected institutions, in cooperation with the military leadership.

III SCAF and the revolutionary forces

As I explained in Part I, understanding the military establishment and its role in politics since 1952 is an essential prerequisite for understanding the nature and structure of the Egyptian state. Yet, it is simultaneously

---

[28] *BBC Arabic*, 28 June 2011, Available online: https://bbc.in/3gs3Sqt (accessed 11 May 2015). Note that the dissolution of the local councils left a vacuum, as no date was subsequently set for new local elections.

the most obscure aspect of the state, and the subject has yet to generate a sufficiently significant amount of empirical evidence to enable us to draw conclusions, or even generalizations, to build on. When the army stepped into the scene following the retreat of the internal security establishment during the clashes with protesters on 28 January 2011, in what became known as the 'Friday of Rage', it stirred a degree of confusion. How was one to deal with this? It was the first time the army had appeared publicly in politics since 1952.

The prevailing impression about the Egyptian armed forces in the Mubarak era and the dominant assumption in the literature on the army's role in decision making was that if the army was not a partner in government, it was at least a key instrument for supporting the regime's decisions. It was also presumed that the mutually beneficial relationship between the ruling regime and the military establishment was a good deal for the generals, who enjoyed financial profits, loyalty bonuses and positions in government or in industries connected with the army as a result. This laid the foundation for a system of protection in exchange for services rendered[29] and ensured that the army was content to play a supporting role for the regime and its main base, which in turn enjoyed considerable independence and autonomy. In this manner, the military establishment gradually shifted from the absolute hold on power after the 1952 revolution to protecting the regime from behind the scenes, where it remained from 1967 to the end of the Mubarak era.[30]

In Part I, I described how the army shifted its attention to economic activities after Egypt signed the Camp David Accords with Israel in 1979. Although we have already discussed this subject at some length, it is worth bearing it in mind in the context of the post-revolutionary interim phase and when considering studies published after the January revolution. It is difficult to draw an accurate map of the army's economic activity because it is not subject to oversight by any civilian body, including parliament.[31] Researchers offer varying and sometimes excessive estimates of the army's sway over the economy, with claims that it accounts for 25 to 40 or even 60 per cent of all economic activity. This makes the military the single-most powerful economic institution in the country. In addition to running major projects that produce goods not just for military but also for civilian

---

[29] Ian Williams, 'Ordinary Egyptians Have Little to Show For U.S. Military Aid to Egypt', *Foreign Policy in Focus*, 13 February 2011, Available online: https://bit.ly/33UFecS (accessed 12 May 2015).

[30] One can apply or dispense with Samuel Finer's thesis here. All that is needed is a knowledge of the specific history and common sense. To me, Finer's categorization of the phases of military control is not a theory, but a description that any average historian could articulate. See: Finer, *The Man on Horseback*, 164–84.

[31] Silvia Colombo, 'The Military, Egyptian Bag-snatchers', *Insight Egypt* (Istituto Affari Internazionali), no. 5 (November 2014).

consumption,[32] it manages partnerships with local and foreign private sector firms. It also has exclusive control over the defence budget and the $1.3 annual military aid package from Washington, most of which goes to purchasing arms from the United States.

Under Mubarak, three main military organizations were involved in profitable non-military transformative industries and services: the NSPO with its eleven factories and companies involved in infrastructure development, civil manufacture, agriculture, service industries and various other national economic sectors; the Ministry of Military Production, which operates more than fifteen factories that mostly manufacture or assemble weapons but also produce some civil sector goods such as electronic and sporting equipment; and the Arab Organization for Industrialization, which manages eleven factories around the country that manufacture equipment for both military and civilian use.[33]

The Ministry of Military Production owns eight factories outright, with 40 per cent of their output destined for the civilian consumer market. Some 70 per cent of the Arab Organization for Industrialization's production targets civilian markets. The military's industrial organizations produce a vast array of commodities and goods: steel, cement, chemicals, butane gas cylinders, cooking stoves, household appliances, gas piping, infant incubators, mineral water, pasta, olive oil and other foodstuffs, and much more. The army also owns a large number of petrol stations, hotels, reception halls, supermarket chains and transport and shipping companies.[34]

The army's economic organizations enjoy a significant competitive edge over civilian entrepreneurs, not only in terms of landownership but also in their ability to use conscripts as a low-cost workforce. Moreover, they are exempt from taxes under Law 47/2005 for security reasons. In some sectors, the army largely crowds out entrepreneurs, whose only choices are to cede way, enter into partnerships with it or accept work on a commission basis.

After Mubarak stepped down, military officials continued to deny that the army had relinquished political decision making under Mubarak in exchange for privileges.[35] They maintained that the armed forces had been

---

[32] Yezid Sayigh, 'Owners of the Republic: An Anatomy of Egypt's Military Economy', *Carnegie Middle East Centre*, 2019, 7; Zeinab Abul-Magd, 'The Egyptian Military in Politics and the Economy: Recent History and Current Transition Status', *CMI Insight* (Chr. Michelsen Institute), no. 2 (October 2013).

[33] Ahmed Morsy, 'The Military Crowds Out Civilian Business in Egypt', *Carnegie Endowment for International Peace*, 24 June 2014, Available online: https://bit.ly/36XpmZc (accessed 12 May 2015); Mahmoud Jaraba, 'The Egyptian Military's Economic Channels of Influence', *Middle East Institute*, 14 May 2014.

[34] Abul-Magd, 'The Egyptian Military in Politics and the Economy'.

[35] SCAF member Lieutenant-General Mohammad al-Assar stated that the armed forces 'have many roles that have not been announced yet'. They 'are the ones who halted the sale of Banque du Caire and the same applies to its position on the irresponsible sale of land belonging to public business

actively involved in setting certain policy orientations (on the economy in particular) and had pressured the regime to adopt certain policies. According to their statements, the armed forces had also been instrumental in the pushback against the plan to have Gamal Mubarak succeed his father as president. In fact, the military establishment's opposition to the hereditary succession scenario and the influence of the new business elites surrounding Gamal Mubarak was an open secret in Egypt before the outbreak of the revolution. Many researchers, in their discussions of the state's economic agenda, have shown how the army had opposed the government's privatization plans and economic liberalization policies on numerous occasions.[36] As I argued in Part I, it does not follow that the army was set on perpetuating the public sector at large; rather, it was determined to perpetuate its own public sector. Nor did this conflict in principle with a market economy, except insofar as monopolies, in general, conflict with the market economy. As long as the army's economy was accepted as the largest monopoly, there was room for private sector entrepreneurs to supply the army economy and capitalist ventures working with the army to carry out its projects.

On the army's role after 25 January, we should remember that it had never been committed to protecting a democratic system. While the army had been gradually subordinated to the political leadership, that leadership always consisted of former military officers. We should also bear in mind the history of the Egyptian army and the self-image it cultivated after 1952 as the 'Father of the Republic', a status that set it above other components of the political system. Add to this that the dominant mindset among the military elites abhorred political parties, had little regard for civilians, and saw the army as more dedicated to the state and better able to discern the country's security needs and interests. I believe that the army's long-standing self-image and culture influenced the policies of the military leadership that assumed control after the 25 January revolution and that, however positively or negatively one might assess that image, it was not supportive of democracy. Furthermore, although the army's self-conception is typically articulated in the language of patriotic duty and responsibility, it generally manifests itself in behaviours that betray a distaste for pluralism as a divisive and disintegrative force and a disdainful, custodial attitude towards society that includes the right to discipline it. And this is not to mention the army elites' tendency to resort to nationalist chauvinistic rhetoric and praise for the military's patriotic feats and

---

sector companies'. See: *Al-Masry Al-Youm*, 4 April 2011, Available online: https://bit.ly/2LkVspo (accessed 12 May 2015).

[36] Albrecht and Bishara, 'Back on Horseback', 19.

sacrifices in order to cover up their mismanagement of civilian life and, indeed, military life (including poor performance in combat), and their readiness to cast aspersions on all who criticize the armed forces.

A politically involved military and forces that utilize religion in politics have a basic trait in common: self-adulation. Both claim to represent something sacred that sets them above pluralism and diversity of opinion, that is beyond discussion and that only a heretic or traitor would dare question. This is antithetical to the very concept of democratic politics.

Clearly, SCAF did not use its powers to lay the foundations for a democratic transition after it assumed control on 11 February 2011. It used them to subordinate other security agencies, the media and the judiciary to the army and to increase the army's influence in the economy and the administrative structures of the state. Along the way, it played on patriotic sentiments and worked to the tune of the rally chant 'the army and the people stand hand-in-hand', while state-run media blared patriotic songs, some dating from the Nasserist era.

From February 2011 to June 2012 the army was both the executive and legislature. It appointed two of the weakest prime ministers in Egypt's modern history and had them appoint a large number of retired military brass, with ranks of colonel upwards, to various posts in government and the public sector. It also enacted a law granting army officers, including retired ones, immunity from prosecution in both military and civil courts (Law 45/2011).[37]

If at first the grassroots revolutionary movement revived the political reputation the army had enjoyed before the Sadat and Mubarak eras, the collision between the military establishment and the revolutionary activists who kept the movement alive in the streets soon chipped away at the patriotic aura that had placed the army beyond reproach. Initially, the army resisted bringing the leaders of the old regime to trial, even as more than 10,000 civilians, including revolutionary activists, were being brought before military tribunals.[38] Then, in the trials themselves, army commanders – Anan and Tantawi, above all – testified on behalf of Mubarak and his interior minister. Not only did they deny the possibility that Mubarak and Adly had issued orders to kill or were in any way directly responsible for the killing of demonstrators, they also dismissed the notion that security forces had opened fire on them at the orders of lower ranking security officials, fuelling the myth that 'outside elements' had killed the

---

[37] Abul-Magd, 'The Egyptian Military in Politics and the Economy'.
[38] Dina Shehata, 'Youth Movements and the 25 January Revolution', in *Arab Spring in Egypt: Revolution and Beyond*, ed. Bahgat Korany and Rabab El-Mahdi (Cairo, NY: The American University in Cairo Press, 2012).

demonstrators. The military commanders acted like part of the regime during the trials, and they defended it with the vocabulary that all regimes use to deny or justify acts of repression before a court. 'I don't know' was the consistent response to questions about what happened, while blame was deflected elsewhere, typically towards undefined 'foreign elements'. Using a type of syllogistic reasoning predicated on the regime's definition of itself as unimpeachable, army commanders repeatedly asserted that 'it does not stand to reason' or 'it is inconceivable' that the president or interior minister would issue an order to open fire, even if that was provably the case. The army commanders' testimonies offered plenty of literal and semiotic evidence that they were an extension of the regime, not an alternative to it. After the coup, military officers called to testify in court began to blame the violence on the Muslim Brotherhood.[39]

When the revolutionary forces demanded such trials, they had presumed that the army was not part of the regime. They thereby missed the opportunity to engage old regime forces in a dialogue in order to press for an organized transitional justice process as an integral part of the transition phase.

The army excluded civilians from decision making and refused to restructure the Ministries of Interior and Information. Such crucial issues became bones of contention with SCAF, which would only budge after persistent mass rallies. This, in turn, gave rise to the impression that the revolution was not over yet. On this point precisely, political forces split between those celebrating the revolution's victorious end and others – largely young people – who insisted on sustaining the same forms of protest until the revolution's aims were achieved.

The army showed no great political acumen at the time it assumed the reins of government. But this did not alter the fact that it was the one institution from the old era that was still intact and capable of unifying the country in the transitional phase. The only obstacles that checked any potential ambition to seize full control were the intensive presence of the Egyptian people in the public space after the revolution, the vitality of the

---

[39] See the testimonies in the case files of the first trial of Mubarak and Habib el-Adly in 2011, a part of which the court made available in its ruling in November 2014. Testimonies from the retrial, presided over by Judge Mahmoud al-Rashidi, were transcribed by lawyers present in closed sessions and made available to the author. I also consulted the court's judgement in the retrial of felony no. 1227/2011/Qasr al-Nil, acquitting Adly, Ahmed Ramzy, Adly Fayed, Hassan Abdel Rahman and Ismail el-Shaer from the charge of complicity in deliberate and premeditated murder (4–194 and 195–226), and felony no. 3642/2011/Qasr al-Nil, dismissing the charge of complicity between Mubarak and Adly in deliberate and premeditated murder (227–351), Judge Mahmoud al-Rashidi presiding, 29 November 2014. Some details of the secret testimonies of the big four in the Mubarak Trial (Tantawi, Anan, Mahmoud Wagdy and Mansour el-Essawy) were published in *Al-Masry Al-Youm*, on 2 and 3 June 2012.

very spirit of the 25 January revolution and its demands, and the endurance of its symbolic value during the period that followed the fall of Mubarak. However, this did not last long. Charisma must be institutionalized if it is to carry out its historic mission. Egypt's revolutionary forces lost their 'charisma' before it could be institutionalized and the revolution's aura was gradually tarnished in the tug of war between rival factions.

In their meeting with SCAF just after the revolution, the RYC presented two documents, one a list of pressing political demands and the other a list of less urgent economic and social demands. The first called for the creation of a civilian presidential council consisting of one military official and two civilians (possibly drawn from the judiciary), the dismissal of the Ahmed Shafik government, the lifting of the state of emergency, the amendment of the political parties law, the dissolution of the SSIS and the replacement of the editors-in-chief of state-owned newspapers. The coalition also demanded the release of all political prisoners and presented a list of their names.[40]

Despite the repeated calls for the creation of a civilian government that would include members from the military,[41] at no point did a unified umbrella of the political forces that took part in the January revolution emerge to demand the handover of rule or a rule-sharing arrangement with SCAF.

The RYC did not ask for a direct role in the arrangements. The group's inclination to defer to others from the judiciary or previous governments (such as Essam Sharaf) betrayed the lack of internal political, organizational and psychological structures necessary to transform such a loose coalition into an organized political movement with an aspiration to participate in the management of the transitional phase and the ability to forward delegates of their own. RYC leaders were organizers of a protest movement. The nature of protest movements is to press their demands and to end once their demands are met, even if they sometimes sprout political parties or nurture intellectuals, journalists and activists who go on to carry the torch on their own – which is what happened in this case. On 25 January 2011, a grassroots movement erupted and realized it was a revolution. However, it continued to operate with the mentality and practices of a protest movement whose grievance appeared to have been addressed when Mubarak stepped down. As for the question of regime change, it was left to a conflict that hinged on the balance of powers in the new phase.

[40] *Al-Masry Al-Youm*, 15 February 2011, Available online: https://bit.ly/3lDAJwO (accessed 13 October 2021).
[41] Numerous RYC statements reiterated this demand, which met with widespread controversy. Most media, which had begun to switch their allegiance from Mubarak to SCAF early on, were against the idea.

SCAF promised to dismiss the Shafik government, study how to restructure the state's security apparatus, lift the state of emergency before elections and ensure election monitoring by Egyptian and international civil society organizations. It tasked then deputy prime minister Yehia El-Gamal with reforming the management of the state-run newspapers and told the RYC to consult with him, and it pledged to engage in dialogue with the Independent Federation of Unions. But SCAF did not agree to the creation of a civilian presidential council, insisting that it would continue to manage the transitional phase on its own.

The RYC turned down the Shafik government's invitation to meet with members of the cabinet. Some of its activists objected to holding elections in six months, arguing that revolutionary forces were not yet equipped to form political parties and mount campaigns, and that this would leave the field open to the political forces that had dominated politics before the revolution. They had a point.

On 28 February 2011, as SCAF dragged its feet on its pledge to dismiss the Shafik government, the RYC issued a statement vowing that Friday marches would continue until the revolution's demands were met and calling for mass rallies on 4 March 2011 for the 'Friday of Defining Demands'.

Eleven days before this, on the eve of the 'Friday of Victory' rally on 18 February 2011, Public Prosecutor Abdel Meguid Mahmoud announced that his office had launched an investigation into complaints filed against Habib el-Adly, Zoheir Garana, Ahmed Ezz and Ahmed El Maghrabi. The media blazoned photos of their transfer to prison.[42] This was clearly a stopgap measure orchestrated by SCAF with little conviction, but it spoke to the strength of the revolutionary legitimacy at the time and the regime's weakness in the face of it.

The revolutionaries' main instrument of leverage was the mass rally called the *milyoniyya*, or million-man march. SCAF would cave to some of their demands in order to avert further pressure in this form, but it would also bargain and manoeuvre, taking advantage of the frequent quarrels between political factions. In addition to their function as a pressure card, the *milyoniyya*s also continued to serve as a form of collective action for diverse forces and a venue for them to agree on certain slogans and rallying cries. But before long, cracks began to show even in these venues. Activists split between those for or against the constitutional amendments that were put to a referendum in mid-March, and they split again over the supra-

---

[42] *Al-Arabiya*, 18 February 2011, Available online: https://bit.ly/34e2Byv (accessed 12 April 2015). The trials will be discussed in greater detail in the next chapter.

constitutional principles outlined in the Selmi Document. The division was visible in the *milyoniyya* of 18 November 2011.

Meanwhile, the Muslim Brotherhood leaders were focused on SCAF's promise to hold elections. They were so confident in their strength and so single-minded in the pursuit of that end that they ignored the demands of the revolutionary movements and committed numerous mistakes along the way. SCAF seized on the opportunity to lure the Brotherhood to its side, using the elections as bait. The other political forces' fear of and opposition to an early election was a key factor in orienting many of their actions and shaping the alliances they made.

On 19 February 2011, the Wasat Party won official recognition when the Political Parties Section of the Supreme Administrative Court ruled in favour of the party's appeal contesting the rejection of its application for a licence by the PPC. The date of the hearing had been set before the revolution. This was the party's fifth attempt to register since it was founded in 1996, but unlike the previous four times, the party's appeal was accepted. The laws had not changed; rather, the Egyptian judiciary had read the changing political winds and bent with them. The climate in February 2011 was steeped in revolutionary triumph and held the promise of many similar achievements. The ruling in favour of the Wasat Party was only the beginning. Numerous other new parties followed suit during the first half of 2011.

On 1 March, Field Marshal Tantawi announced grim news. The Egyptian economy was in peril, wheat reserves would last only a few weeks, Egypt was losing $320 million a day, there was not enough cash to pay public sector salaries and hard currency reserves had plunged to $20 billion. Tantawi's statement marked the beginning of a new approach by the army: it would stoke fear of the revolution and its consequences by sounding economic alarm bells warning of imminent bankruptcy and collapse, but without taking serious measures to curb the deterioration. From its perspective, SCAF had to contend with three major problems in managing the transitional phase: re-establishing civil peace and order, restoring security and remedying the economic problem. According to Tantawi, $6 billion of the Central Bank's reserves were consumed during the revolution. If that trend continued, the treasury's coffers would soon be depleted, he said. Worse yet, production had fallen to 20 per cent capacity and the stock exchange had lost 5 billion Egyptian pounds.

The revolutionaries' sole concrete achievement towards regime change was to force SCAF to dismiss the Shafik government. On 3 March 2011, SCAF tasked Essam Sharaf, a former minister of transport, with forming a new cabinet. Deputy Prime Minister Ali El-Selmi described the conditions under which the government was formed as follows:

> The Essam Sharaf government was formed on 3 March 2011 to be greeted by a spate of crimes, including the storming of State Security headquarters and the torching of its files and an unprecedented onslaught of thuggery and intimidation through acts of robbery, abductions of young women and men, the waylaying of motorists to force them to hand over their cars and sign bills of sale, and break-ins of people's homes and doctors' clinics to seize money and property. Such reception parties for the new prime minister were then crowned with the destruction of the Atfih church ... ushering in a new phase of sectarian tension.[43]

These were signs that the decline in state power in the transitional period and the security vacuum could descend further into security breakdown and social anarchy. However, at that point, revolutionary optimism and the confidence that change was in reach were still at their height. So, while conditions were rough, Selmi's description does not do justice to the prevailing spirit.

In a statement announcing that popular pressure had succeeded in ousting Shafik, the RYC said that it would continue to press the revolution's demands and vowed more mass rallies. With the announcement of the new government imminent, it said, it was necessary to immediately draw up a timetable for the realization of the aims of the revolution. Foremost of these were: the dismantlement of the State Security apparatus, the restructuring of the Ministry of Interior and the appointment of a civilian interior minister, the release of all political prisoners, the prompt and public prosecution of all state officials responsible for ordering or executing the orders to use violence and gunfire against the revolutionaries since 25 January 2011, the capture and prosecution of perpetrators of corruption, the convening of early municipal council elections, the implementation of the judicial ruling on a minimum and maximum wage (with the ratio set at 1:15), and the dissolution of the existing ETUF and the election of a federation representing Egyptian workers and their independent unions. But did all this need to be implemented in the transitional period? This and other declarations did not only demonstrate a confusion of priorities, but some of the demands united the forces of the old regime behind the army and against the democratic transition. The statement included other important demands such as extending the transitional period under the leadership of

---

[43] Ali El-Selmi, *The Democratic Transition and the Issue of Constitutional Principles* [Arabic] (Cairo: Al-Masry Press Foundation, 2012), 41–2.

a presidential council and postponing the date of the elections announced by SCAF.

Still, the revolutionaries' approach and actions remained limited to addressing demands to a component of the old regime – the army – relying on it to achieve the aims of the revolution, whereas the most crucial requirement for any pro-democracy revolutionary project is to participate directly in the management of the transition to democracy together with other political forces and moderate elements of the regime. Otherwise, even if some demands are met as a means to absorb the pressure of rallies and demonstrations, those who hold the power will continue to control how the demands are implemented. Take, for example, the demand for a civilian interior minister. What was to prevent the appointment of a civilian interior minister who was not committed to the revolution, its principles or its stances on the security apparatus and its relationship with the public?

Essam Sharaf's assumption of the premiership was proof of the power the January revolution had acquired. Though he was a former member of the NDP's Policies Committee – the seat of Gamal Mubarak's power – and had served as transportation minister in the Ahmed Nazif government, he supported the revolution and had taken part in the university professors' march from Cairo University to Tahrir to demand the departure of Mubarak. He was therefore perceived as a reformist figure, at least, and a suitable head of government in the transitional phase.

On 4 March, the day after he became the prime minister designate, Sharaf went to Tahrir Square, where demonstrators paraded him on their shoulders. No Egyptian prime minister had ever been celebrated in such a manner. He, in turn, delivered a speech to the crowds declaring that he derived his legitimacy from the revolutionary masses. The event was a symbolic landmark in the relationship between the government and the people, expressive of the ardent revolutionary climate at that time. Yet sponsored by the military, Sharaf then proceeded to form a government consisting mostly of Mubarak regime holdovers.

'The people want the fall of State Security' was another persistent demand. The revolutionary youth movements saw this apparatus as the greatest threat to the revolution, the most corrupt organ of the old regime and the most loyal to it. In this phase, this institution was no longer in control. The day after the Shafik government resigned, SSIS officials ordered a systematic burning and shredding of vast quantities of documents. The ensuing battle to storm the secret service's offices on 5 March 2011 acquired dual significance: it was both a symbol of the victory of the revolution and part of the process of overpowering a threat to democratization. The agency's offices in the Raml district of Alexandria were the first to fall to the demonstrators on 4 March, after a seven-hour siege. Hundreds of protesters rushed into the building to rescue documents and files only to find piles of shredded papers, according to eyewitnesses and videos filmed by demonstrators inside the building. That same day, thousands of demonstrators gathered outside the State Security's main headquarters in 6th October City in Cairo, galvanized by rumours about thick clouds of smoke rising from the building's garden. After storming the building, they found proof of the systematic burning of documents.[44] They also found large quantities of files in various offices, triggering rumours that some SSIS officers had left them there on purpose, though there was no way to confirm this.[45]

The army quickly regained control over the SSIS buildings and urged demonstrators to return the documents they had collected from the premises, and many did. There is considerable testimony that the army had initially facilitated the demonstrators' entry into the buildings. Undoubtedly, this process of re-securing the buildings and taking possession of documents furnished the army with resources previously unavailable to it for the purpose of dominating and controlling civil society and political circles. Lists of client networks, the results of the surveillance and wiretapping of tens of thousands of activists, politicians and journalists, and other such documents were among the instruments the army and Military Intelligence in particular used in order to assert its control over the country at a later stage.

The SSIS was dissolved ten days after the incursions despite SCAF's earlier objections that this would harm national security. According to Interior Minister Mansour el-Essawy's decree, the SSIS with all its directorates and offices throughout Egypt was abolished and replaced by the NSA (an already-existing department of the Interior Ministry), which would be responsible for preserving national security and fighting terrorism in accordance with the constitution, law and human rights principles, and without interfering in citizens' lives. The state-run Middle East News Agency reported that the officers who would staff the new agency 'will be chosen in the days ahead'.[46] The change had no immediate substantive or effective consequence, as the question of the ruling authority had not been

---

[44] A new interior minister had been brought in on the same day that several SSIS buildings were stormed, including the main headquarters in Cairo. See: *BBC Arabic*, 5 March 2011, Available online: https://bbc.in/2YkSUhG (accessed 11 April 2015).

[45] These include, for example, documents obtained by *Shorouk* newspaper, such as a notebook containing a list of citizen informants who worked for the agency, complete with their names, addresses, phone numbers and criminal status. See: *Shorouk*, 7 March 2011. Archived Copy Available Online: https://bit.ly/3qDXkcV (accessed 14 April 2015).

[46] *Al Jazeera*, 15 March 2011, Available online: https://bit.ly/3m2uNdo (accessed 14 April 2015).

settled yet. As would become clear after the military coup in 2013, this was nothing more than a name change.

Although the army helped demonstrators enter the SSIS buildings, it would prosecute many of them some years later.[47] This is all the more ironic in that the military police and Military Intelligence – the latter under the command of Abdel Fattah El-Sisi – did not move an inch to prevent the storming, though they had already begun to take repressive action against demonstrations and youth activists, many of whom were still detained or listed as missing years after 28 January 2011.

At the end of March 2011, investigations were launched into a large number of Egyptian political figures known for their opposition to the Mubarak regime. 'Case 250', as it was known in the press, was built on 12,000 pages of documents, 3,000 recordings of telephone conversations, 4,000 video tapes and the testimonies of the members of SCAF, former and current intelligence chiefs, officers with the NSA, and directors of the SSIS. Some 250 Egyptians working with NGOs were charged with the receipt of foreign funding and espionage after the revolution. Evidently, surveillance operations and wiretappings continued without interruption during this period.

After the coup of July 2013, more people were charged for the storming of the State Security buildings, an action that had been regarded as legitimate and revolutionary in 2011. Hassan Yousef later revealed that it was Omar Suleiman who had filed the complaint that initiated this case.[48] According to *Al-Masry Al-Youm*, the public prosecutor's office received successive complaints from lawyers, public figures and politicians, such as Mortada Mansour, most of whom were supporters of former president Hosni Mubarak.[49] The complaints accused some of the most prominent anti-Mubarak political activists, members of the 6 April Movement, some pro- and anti-Mubarak figures and, later, even members of the NSF that supported the coup of inciting the storming of security headquarters and/or espionage, receiving foreign funding and conspiring to overthrow the government. The authors of the complaints included a group of media personalities, politicians, prominent clerics and military figures who would be affiliated with the coup of 3 July 2013.[50] While Case 250 was initially directed against political and media figures who became prominent in the

---

[47] Ironically, four years later, an investigation was launched into Judge Zakaria Abdel-Aziz, to whom the demonstrators had turned in order to hand over documents to prevent them from being stolen or ending up in the wrong hands. Prosecutions also resumed against all those implicated in the 2011 storming of SSIS buildings.
[48] Yousef Hassan Yousef, *The Secrets of State Security Case 250* [Arabic] (Cairo: Dar Sama, 2015).
[49] *Al-Masry Al-Youm*, 28 June 2015, Available online: https://bit.ly/2X7dMIK (accessed 6 September 2015).
[50] *FJP Portal*, 2 July 2015, Available online: https://bit.ly/3oXRvsh (accessed 6 September 2015).

context of the 25 January revolution, it eventually expanded to include many individuals who supported the military coup. After 3 July 2013, Case 250 continued to hang over their heads like the sword of Damocles, a reminder of the peril they might face if they stepped out of line.

IV The discourse of SCAF and the debilitation of revolutionary movements

For the most part, a deep current of mistrust ran between the revolutionary forces and SCAF. There were three reasons for this. First, SCAF was slow to respond to demands that revolutionary forces considered essential to effecting a complete break with the former regime, leading them to suspect that SCAF was colluding with that regime.[51] Whenever SCAF did meet one of their demands, it did so grudgingly and after considerable grassroots pressure. Indeed, several actions early in the transitional phase were only initiated after a series of mass rallies, most notably the dismissal of the Shafik government, the dissolution of the SSIS and the prosecution of Mubarak and other symbols of corruption. The revolutionary forces tended to explain SCAF's behaviour in one of two ways: either it harboured the intent to preserve what remained of the old order and only feigned to bow to public pressure by sacrificing Mubarak, but no more, or it lacked a clear vision of how to manage the transitional phase, primarily because the military establishment was intrinsically rigid and conventional. It resisted change, and if changes had to be made, it would keep them to a minimum and consistent with the status quo, and SCAF, not the protesters, would set the pace.

To charges of foot-dragging, SCAF countered that its duty was to maintain order and security and to keep the country functioning, whereas making change was the business of an elected government. The effect of this was to focus the opposition's attention on elections, whether to call for them or fearmonger about the consequences of holding them too soon.

Second, numerous questions were raised about the real role of the military police during the revolution. News stories, activists' testimonies and reports by rights organizations implicated the military police in the torture of activists and the raids of the offices of Amnesty International and the Hisham Mubarak Law Centre on 3 February 2011. The military police also arrested many activists, including the lawyer Malek Adly on 30 January 2011 and the bloggers Wael Abbas and Kareem Amer on 4 February and 6 February, respectively, during the extended sit-in Tahrir. During the

---

[51] *Egypt Independent*, 11 April 2011, Available online: https://bit.ly/2K4hX1h (accessed 12 April 2015).

two weeks of the revolution, news outlets reported varying unconfirmed estimates of the number of activists detained by the military police, some of whom remained missing. *The Guardian* cited demonstrators who said they had been detained by members of the army and beaten in the Egyptian Museum in Tahrir Square. Such testimonies shook the prevailing image of the army and its role during the revolution.

SCAF persisted in denying the allegations outright, calling them attempts to drive a wedge between the army and the people. All proof that the military police detained and tortured revolutionaries was drowned out by the slogan 'the army and the people stand hand-in-hand'. Nevertheless, the military trials of several activists stirred widespread controversy, fuelled by the frequent clashes between the military police and demonstrators in Tahrir Square after the revolution. Grassroots movements against the prosecution of civilians in military courts gained momentum and the demand to abolish military trials of civilians persisted throughout the transitional period. This practice – a feature not just of the Mubarak era, but the entire July Republic – had been a major protest cry before and during the revolution.

The army's denial of acts of torture, opening fire at protesters and the resultant deaths, and its insistence on laying the blame for such incidents on unidentified parties aggravated the army's credibility crisis after the revolution. A 'third party' or other surreptitious elements such as 'remnants of the old regime' were handy boogeymen to blame for criminal actions, and SCAF and other officials invoked them liberally. The media's adoption of these terms served to cover up failure and negligence and to conceal the identity of groups and individuals that security forces or the military police used to attack protesters or instigate violence in demonstrations.

The first time a shadowy 'third party' was officially blamed was on 28 June 2011. That evening, a brawl erupted in front of the Balloon Theatre in Agouza when a crowd attempted to force their way into the theatre where the Ministry of Culture had organized a concert to commemorate the martyrs of the January revolution. According to the fact-finding report issued by the NCHR, the police resorted to excessive teargas causing many cases of asphyxiation. It also noted that organized gangs carrying knives and dressed similarly had deliberately provoked the violence. Afterwards, many public figures issued statements to the effect that the entire incident had been planned. After the 2013 coup, the 'third party' ruse would fall out of usage just as quickly as it had caught on.

In August 2012, Moataz El Fegiery, an Egyptian human rights researcher, was able to write that some 12,000 Egyptian civilians had been tried in military tribunals during the preceding eighteen months alone. Most of the trials involved ordinary crimes, but hundreds of political activists were among those brought before military courts. Although the elected parliament with an Islamist majority amended the Military Justice Code on 6 May 2012, the code still permitted civilians to be tried in military courts for crimes committed against the armed forces or in areas under the jurisdiction of the army, with jurisdiction determined by military prosecutors themselves.[52]

Egyptian security forces perpetrated innumerable gross human rights abuses during the transitional period, or had 'civilians' do it for them. The violations included killing protesters, excessive use of force to disperse demonstrators and the torture of demonstrators during arrest or detention. SCAF failed to investigate these crimes and identify the perpetrators. According to local and international human rights monitors, the armed forces were involved in a number of such crimes in order to silence critics, taking advantage of the fact that the civil public prosecutor did not have the jurisdiction to investigate crimes committed by members of the army. As Fegiery writes, 'On 10 May 2011, the SCAF amended the Code of Military Justice to provide military prosecutors with an exclusive jurisdiction over crimes committed by members of the military, even if investigation is initiated after their retirement.'[53]

Thirdly, some decrees infuriated the 25 January forces. Particularly galling was Law 34/2011 that SCAF introduced to re-criminalize labour strikes. SCAF then had the NSA (SSIS's successor) draw up lists of student activists in the universities. Another decree required organizers of university seminars to obtain prior approval from the service. The government then introduced and enforced an edict criminalizing sit-ins and disturbances that 'obstruct work'. Critics of the law, which SCAF had enacted in April 2011, described it as a return to the suppression of protest. The law carried penalties of imprisonment and a fine of up to 500,000 Egyptian pounds for anyone who, as long as the state of emergency was in effect, engaged in a protest or activity that prevented, obstructed or disrupted the operation of a governmental institution or public authority.

In general, SCAF's knee-jerk approach to crisis management was to notch up the nationalist populist rhetoric and accuse foreign forces and their agents of trying to drive a wedge between the army and the people. Such methods betrayed a lack of seriousness in handling crucial issues. A major example was the resurgence of incidents of sectarian strife, which

---

[52] *Eurasia Review*, 19 August 2021, Available online: https://bit.ly/3FdyUOF (accessed 26 September 2021).
[53] Ibid.

SCAF attributed to foreign conspiracies or other subversive elements. In addition to deflecting blame, the 'foreign conspiracy' ruse served as a ready-to-hand denunciation of revolutionary activity as a witting or unwitting service for the foreign schemers or, alternatively, as part of the groundwork for situations that SCAF had engineered but wanted to pass off as the work of a foreign conspiracy. Whatever the purpose, the media affiliated with the army increasingly exercised its disdain for the 'common people's' intelligence as it intensified the dissemination of rumours and conspiracy theories.

SCAF criticized calls for it to be held accountable as an entity independent of the army and involved in politics. Communiqué No. 24, posted on SCAF's Facebook page, sums up what it described as 'the fixed principles of working with the revolution'. Most importantly, it said, the army was on the side of the people and would never treat them with any form of violence, and embedded rogue elements were trying to undermine the revolution and provoke disputes between it and the army. Clearly keen to safeguard the military establishment's credibility and public image, SCAF opened channels of dialogue with diverse political, social and cultural elites and it held frequent meetings with writers, editors-in-chief and political forces.

Initially, SCAF maintained a certain public remoteness, relying on its communiqués, press releases and periodic meetings with cultural and political elites. Then, it adopted a more hands-on approach as it settled into its role and became more actively involved in politics and the media. In addition to holding more frequent press conferences to address recent developments or 'rumours', SCAF officials made themselves available for exclusive press interviews. SCAF also organized public relations campaigns that involved scheduling regular appearances for its officials on satellite television talk shows, funding the production of patriotic songs extolling the Egyptian army or posting large billboards showing military personnel helping people. Around this time, the Military Intelligence Service took over the networks of journalists, writers and media owners cultivated by the GIS and the SSIS, which became the foundation for a sprawling network of media operatives and allies at all levels of this sector. This network was put into operation with great efficacy from the second half of 2012 to the July 2013 coup.[54]

---

[54] Information leaked from Abdel Fattah El-Sisi's office following the coup revealed the nature of this network and how it was operated, and divulged that a number of well-known media professionals took their orders directly from the Military Intelligence Service. One of the leaks was a conversation between the official spokesman for the armed forces, Ahmed Ali, and Abbas Kamel, the director of the office of then defence minister Sisi. Kamel dictated a message for Ali to convey in order to counter the campaign to 'distort the image of Field Marshal Sisi during his election campaign'. Kamel then specified by name the media figures who would be tasked with disseminating the

SCAF's publicity campaign reiterated three basic messages: SCAF was the authority that was in charge of administering the affairs of the country in the period and would not accept dictates; it did not seek or ask for power, but was rather compelled to act in keeping with the people's trust in the armed forces; and it intended to complete its mission in six months so as to hand over government to a civil authority expressing the outlooks of the people and headed by a president elected through free and fair elections.[55]

SCAF spent a lot of time and effort refuting rumours. But when it started to use its media network to spread fictions to cover up crimes committed against civilians and to target adversaries, no one could compete. This resource would be put to its fullest use when the time came to assail an elected president with barrages of rumours and fabricated news. I will return to this later when discussing the short presidential term of Mohamed Morsi.

How SCAF deployed its rumour-mongering machine depended on its aims within a particular context. For example, initially, SCAF was determined to present an image of the armed forces consistent with revolutionary sentiments while it played along with the various parties and factions and set them against one another at the same time. We see this dynamic at play when, in a meeting with the editors-in-chief of the major newspapers, SCAF called on the people of Egypt and the youth of the revolution 'not to pay attention to, fall in with and repeat tendentious rumours that serve the enemies of the revolution and sow confusion at these historical moments the country is experiencing'. In the same meeting, it stressed that Egypt would never be ruled by 'another Khomeini'.[56] In effect, SCAF fed certain rumours and fears among many segments of Egyptian society and then addressed these same segments to reassure them.

It was obvious that SCAF lacked a clear vision for managing the transitional phase, and the extent of its confusion was reflected in a number of missteps. For example, it refused to create a presidential council. This betrayed a contradiction in its attitude. On the one hand, SCAF projected itself as intent upon a rapid transfer of civil authority within no more than six months. On the other, it was unwilling to let any non-military entity share in the administration of the country during the transitional period.

---

message. The recorded conversation can be heard on *YouTube*, 19 January 2015, Available online: https://bit.ly/2JRsCwr (accessed 12 April 2015).

[55] *Shorouk*, 6 March 2011. Archived Copy Available Online: https://bit.ly/37LoB4B (accessed 11 April 2015).

[56] *Al Riyadh*, 5 April 2011, Available online: https://bit.ly/2W9Gkxn (accessed 23 April 2015).

As a means to contain the power-sharing demand, it suddenly created a consultative council made up of civilians.[57]

Another error was its insistence on keeping the Shafik government. SCAF amended laws to prolong the tenure of this government that had been formed under Mubarak and that SCAF described as a 'caretaker' government. It also refused to dismiss highly unpopular ministers. Ultimately, however, it was forced to yield to the popular demands for the dismissal of the Shafik government and its replacement by one formed and led by someone acceptable to the youth of the revolution. Finally, it terminated the work of the constitutional amendment committee it had announced without citing cause. SCAF then replaced it with another committee, restricting its competencies to proposing limited amendments that would not serve the desired purpose or pave the way for the election of the most competent individuals as president or members of parliament. Then it set 19 March 2011 as the date for the referendum on the proposed constitutional amendments, forestalling any chance of improving or refining them through public debate.

This was the first time in the history of modern Egypt that the military establishment ruled the country directly. The revolution of 23 July 1952 was led by low- and mid-ranking officers who overthrew the old military establishment and then exchanged their military uniforms for civilian dress. In the period from the 25 January revolution to the presidential elections, the military establishment itself ruled overtly, in its original military capacity. The SCAF generals' irritated reactions to criticism showed that they were unused to hearing criticism from within the army itself, let alone from civilians.

SCAF had inherited a heavy legacy of Mubarak-era policies. As it assumed its new task unprepared, it needed the means to communicate much more than it needed means of repression. Initially, it built on the promises of reform that Mubarak had made in his last speeches and on the contacts that his vice-president, Omar Suleiman, had made during the revolution as he attempted to open up channels of dialogue with different political forces, including the Muslim Brotherhood. The army began to fulfil Mubarak's pledges and carry out Omar Suleiman's plan, after which it had no other plans. Under Tantawi, at least, the army did not oppose the transfer of authority to a civilian president. But it did insist on the continuation of four elements from the pre-revolutionary status quo:

---

[57] The council's authorities were defined in Decree 283/2011, but they remained unclear. It was made up of a mix of politicians close to SCAF and representatives of various political forces, and headed by the veteran politician Mansour Hassan. Hassan was effectively unable to supervise and monitor the work of the council, which collapsed upon the first major disagreement with the ruling officers.

the army's privileges, a package of reforms but no radical changes, the preservation of the peace agreement with Israel and preservation of the relationship with the United States.

After Mubarak was dismissed, SCAF released a communiqué outlining the features of the transitional phase and saying that the role of the current government would be limited to 'conducting business and carrying out the tasks required of it during the transitional phase'. It was clear that SCAF drew a distinction between a caretaker government and an interim government and that the government of Ahmed Shafik was the former. The Shafik government would only remain in office until an interim government was formed, and its functions would be restricted to ensuring the continuity of normal daily life. It would not have an influential part in determining Egypt's political future, as it did not have a mandate to introduce any changes by implementing new policies. This position came under harsh criticism from the revolutionary forces, which saw in it an attempt to reinstate the pre-revolutionary order because the Shafik government consisted of 'remnants of the former regime'.[58] Shafik, in an attempt to contain the criticisms, reshuffled the cabinet with an eye to creating a quasi-national coalition government, bringing on board affiliates of opposition parties and independents.[59]

On 22 February 2011, Tantawi, as head of SCAF, swore Shafik in for a second time as the prime minister of a government that included representatives of the Wafd Party, the Tagammu and the NFC. This step not only failed to reduce temperatures, but it triggered angrier protests led by the forces and parties that had not been consulted and included. The demonstrations reached their peak on 25 February 2011, which is to say three days after Shafik had taken office again. Hundreds of thousands of Egyptians amassed in Tahrir Square for the 'Friday of Purification and Salvation' in which the crowds reiterated their demand for the dismissal of the Shafik government and the purge of state institutions of old regime officials.

Numerous statements issued by such groups as the NAC, the People's Parliament and the Front to Support the Revolution called for Shafik's dismissal.[60] These statements did not include a demand for a government made up of political forces committed to the aims of the revolution and able to carry them out. These forces thought it more expedient to press for

---

[58] *Al-Masry Al-Youm*, 22 February 2011, Available online: https://bit.ly/2WCQz0O (accessed 22 April 2015).

[59] The new cabinet members were Yehia El-Gamal from the NFC, for the post of deputy prime minister; Mounir Fakhry Abdel Nour from the Wafd Party, as minister of tourism; and Gouda Abdel-Khalek of the Tagammu, as minister of solidarity and social justice. The other ministers remained in their posts. *al-Ahram*, 22 February 2011. Archived Copy Available Online: https://bit.ly/3mOg08T (accessed 13 October 2021).

[60] *al-Ahram*, 26 February 2011. Archived Copy Available Online: https://bit.ly/3FcZBSm (accessed 9 January 2022).

a government of technocrats, a demand that connotes an undemocratic aversion to politics. Such a government, by definition, cannot strive for radical change. It is not a decision-maker, and it does not set the aims it strives to achieve; it merely works to achieve the goals of those who appointed it.

As the protests escalated, the revolutionary coalitions called for the 'Friday of Persistence' demonstration on 3 March 2011. The day before the rally, SCAF announced Shafik's resignation and appointed Essam Sharaf to form a new government. The *milyoniyya* went ahead, but as a celebration of the triumph of one of the revolution's most important demands. The revolutionary momentum was still strong. The regime backed down before the revolutionaries' demands, and now there was a prime minister who addressed the nation in Tahrir Square. But such symbolic gestures did not create a government to carry out the aims of the revolution, a government capable of instituting radical change in the structure of the ruling order and pushing back against the deep state.

After the dismissal of the Shafik government, it was evident that the revolution's spontaneity would continue and that there had been no plan behind that demand. A change in prime ministers has never meant much in Egypt, including in this period. No serious thought had been given to the question of dialogue with any political exponent of the former regime. Essam Sharaf was a former member of the NDP Policies Committee, and his government consisted mostly of holdovers from that regime.

Within less than a year, the revolutionaries found themselves staring at a government headed by a former prime minister from the Mubarak era: Kamal Ganzouri. SCAF had assigned him to form a government on the grounds that its predecessor had failed. By this time, the revolutionary energies had largely dissipated, and the little that remained of it in the streets and squares moved spontaneously, with little forethought, in all directions. After a succession of disappointments, this movement of 'purists' was generally set against politics per se. The street movement did not trust politicians, and it continued to press demands that were not governed by a clear political programme, while the country needed someone to manage it. SCAF understood this. So, too, did some movements, such as the Muslim Brotherhood, which thought more about governance than revolution. They began to plan politically, which led them to support the steps SCAF took towards elections and to oppose measures that delay them. Unlike the revolutionaries, they entered the political fray. They had a project, and its goal was political power. After the revolutionary movements fragmented, the Muslim Brothers proved themselves more capable of organizing throngs in the squares when they wanted to. Other political forces also began to gear up for the political power game, but they feared the elections.

3

The lost opportunities and the deepening rift

I The constitutional amendments and referendum

A constitution sets forth the principles that govern a particular political order. The principles are in turn governed by basic values that are protected by the constitution and distinguish one system of governance from another. The constitution protects these principles from infringement by individuals, the authorities and even the legislature itself, if it enacts laws that contravene the letter of the constitution or the values it enshrines. At the same time, a constitution defines the governing authorities, their functions and their limits. Constitutions therefore typically comprise two basic parts, one concerned with normative principles and the other focused on the state administration and its regulatory systems. There may be other sections as well, but these two are indispensable, and constitutions usually make it harder to alter provisions in the first part than in the second.

In democratic systems, those who fear the majority can find refuge in the constitution, just as the majority does in many respects. This is not a flaw, but rather demonstrates the constitution's importance. It may give power to the democratic majority, but it constrains it as well, and in this sense it is 'undemocratic'. Its primary function is to place certain decisions beyond the democratic process by tying the hands of the majority and the public. How can a system that restrains the will of the majority be justified? We could consider the rights and liberties upheld by the constitution to be inherent and inalienable as democracy posits, or at least to reflect the fundamental principles of the democratic system along with other national values specific to a society's culture. As such, they stand above the inconstancy of the majority. We could also conceive of the constitution as limiting not only the will of government in defence of the people but the will of the people's representatives as well – a curb on the citizenry's propensity to sacrifice democratic principles for short-term interests, fleeting emotional satisfaction or temporary material benefit. In this case, the constitution offers a remedy for short-sightedness in the name of binding values. In this understanding, the citizenry needs the constitution.[1]

Another line of democratic thought holds that the constitution represents the will of previous generations, and the will of the dead should not govern that of the living. Since the will of each generation is binding only on itself, later generations should have the right to alter the constitution.[2] A third view sees the constitution not as an instrument for putting checks on democracy, but as a tool for implementing it. Democracy cannot be put into practice without tools, and in this case the tool is the constitution. Civil rights and liberties, and proscriptions on their infringements within certain limits, are the implementing instruments of democracy. Without them, the will of the majority cannot be realized, insofar as it is predicated on citizens forming their opinions by freely choosing among reasonable options, which in turn requires freedom of expression, the access to information, the right of assembly and the like. Ultimately these are all tools for shaping a majority capable of choosing. The majority does not have the right to assent to slavery, for a slave lacks will and cannot enter into free contracts. And while it is true that one generation constraining future ones is inconsistent with the spirit of democracy, the proper analogy is a legacy. A constitution handed down from one generation to the next is like inheriting the privileges of ownership; just as a person inherits a property with its debts and contractual claims, so citizens inherit a system of governance with its attendant obligations.[3] Later generations usually revise a democratic constitution such that the amendments do not conflict with the document's core values, such as equality, human dignity and freedom. Indeed, such amendments are typically made in pursuance of such values, and introduced to regulate aspects of life not conducted in accordance with them.

The constitution does not only constrain; it also grants prerogatives. A true constitutional government – that is, one that accepts the limitation of its powers, be it a republic or a monarchy – is a democratic government. Whether or not the constitution is a written document, it is difficult for it to endure in the short term absent a broad political, cultural and security elite that believes in it. It will likely not survive over the long term unless its values and even the structure of governance for which it provides are rooted in the culture of the broad public. Democratic values in transitional periods cannot rely on the culture that prevailed throughout decades of dictatorship; rather, influential elites who believe in them must actively

---

[1] Stephen Holmes, 'Precommitment and the Paradox of Democracy', in *Constitutionalism and Democracy*, ed. Jon Elster and Rune Slagstad (Cambridge: Cambridge University Press, 1993), 196.
[2] Ibid., 197.
[3] Ibid., 203–5.

defend them, especially in the case of regime change through revolution, when revolutionary legitimacy and popular antipathy to tyranny can be capitalized on.

The limits imposed by the constitution are not limits on the people. Rather, they are limits that the people set on the governing system and the majority, a majority of the people itself. The rules for a people's self-governance – namely, a constitution, written or unwritten – are what enables it to be constituted as an entity with a will – that is, a people – which is in turn capable of checking the authorities. This is precisely what prevents a fusion of the popular will and the leader into a single, sovereign will that dispenses with the need for a constitution to constrain politics, as critics of liberal constitutionalism like Carl Schmitt understood. In his many interwar works critiquing democracy, particularly his *Constitutional Theory* (1928), Schmitt vehemently opposed liberal constitutionalism, clinging to the myth of a fundamental contradiction between constitutional limits and democratic government and writing that 'the entire effort of constitutionalism was aimed at repressing the political'.[4]

The American constitution begins with the words 'We the people of the United States'. Bruce Ackerman asserts that we cannot begin to study the substance of the constitution without first appreciating the degree of authority needed to open with these words: though the constitution came out of secret, summertime meetings, the participants nevertheless claimed to speak for the people of the United States.[5] Ackerman tends to see the drafting of the constitution as a kind of 'counter-revolution' mounted to stop revolutionary action that might have led to a bloodbath or ended up eating its own. A constitution that establishes principles and procedures is the antithesis of a revolution that culminates in a Napoleon or Stalin rising to power in the revolution's name. In this sense, the constitution is a counter-revolution for Ackerman,[6] not in the way we understand it today – as a revolution by the old regime against the revolution – but as the culmination of a revolutionary process that simultaneously curtails it.

Andrew Arato, a scholar of democracy and civil society, writes that between the permanent revolution of the radicals who wish to press ahead with no endpoint in sight and the revolutionary amnesia of conservatives who seek to cement the status quo and erase all traces of its revolutionary origins, two issues must be resolved: first, the democratic origin of the new regime – that is, a recognition of the people as the source of the constitution

---

[4] Ibid., 231. See also: Carl Schmitt, *Constitutional Theory* [German] (Berlin: Duncker und Humblot, 1928), 41.
[5] Bruce A. Ackerman, 'Neo-federalism?' in *Constitutionalism and Democracy*, ed. Jon Elster and Rune Slagstad (Cambridge: Cambridge University Press, 1993), 156–7.
[6] Ibid., 158.

– and second, the protection and consolidation of freedoms against reversals and fluctuations, including the fickle will of the majority.[7] In the case of Egypt, no party rose to declare that they would write a democratic constitution in the name of the people after a democratic revolution. On the other hand, the Muslim Brotherhood and the military, as conservative forces, should ostensibly have been uninterested in permanent revolution and therefore keen to consolidate a regime via a constitution. But in fact they were interested in elections.

Constitutionalism is a political order based on a system of basic laws that simultaneously establish governing authorities and set limits on them. For liberals, these limits on the authorities are found primarily in political rights and civil liberties, the system of checks and balances between governing authorities, and a judiciary that operates independently of majority-minority shifts and is capable of imposing and defending these rights and liberties. That a judicial authority of this type – for example, a constitutional court – is not elected seems to run counter to democracy and infringe the authority of the legislator.[8] But there is no alternative to a body that is responsible for the constitution, whose objectivity and neutrality stems from its faithfulness to the constitution's provisions and is beholden to neither the majority nor the minority, but rather to the principles of the constitution.

Whether or not the body that drafts the constitution should be elected is a question that concerns solely the writing of the text. In contrast, the adoption of the constitution must be subject to some electoral process, be it approval in the parliament or constituent assembly by a special majority or a popular referendum, or both. Constitutions are typically fortified against legislative meddling to varying degrees. Some provisions are so foundational that they may be impervious to change even by a large majority, while others require a special majority or at least a majority of members, but no constitution can survive if a majority of the people persistently and diligently oppose its spirit and principles. Acceptance of the constitution as a given and the continuation of politics without civil wars or major social upheavals is therefore one form of democratic consent. Here I am speaking of democratic constitutions, meaning those documents that establish basic rights and civil liberties, and the peaceful transfer of power through free, periodic elections enumerate the governing procedures that establish the separation and limitation of powers and judicial independence, and define their terms of office.

---

[7] Andrew Arato, *Civil Society, Constitution and Legitimacy* (Lanham, MD: Rowman and Littlefield Publishers, 2000), 129.
[8] Ibid., 132.

After 1989, several Eastern European states adopted constitutions drafted by parliaments or bodies elected by them; other constitutions were written by sovereign councils like constituent assemblies or national conferences. In most cases, states that transitioned from one type of regime to another through negotiations and incremental settlements chose the first model, whereas states whose transition was spurred by a revolution largely favoured the second.[9]

1 The constitutional amendments

Communiqué No. 5, issued by SCAF on 13 February 2011 (which I earlier called the first constitutional declaration, preceding the amendments that were officially deemed as such), suspended the 1971 constitution, thereby transferring constitutional authorities to SCAF. With both executive and legislative powers in its grip, SCAF had the right to form and dismiss the government, issue decrees with the force of law, and repeal or amend existing laws or enact new ones. It then turned its attention to promoting a set of amendments to the 1971 constitution which would be issued as a constitutional declaration to govern the transitional phase and regulate subsequent political processes.

The amendments concerned the conditions for presidential candidacy, the duration of presidential terms, guarantees for the electoral process and rules for drafting a new constitution; they did not address the thirty-six articles in the 1971 constitution related to presidential prerogatives. The amendments also provided for the writing of the constitution subsequent to the People's Assembly elections rather than reaching a constitutional consensus prior to elections.

The decree forming the committee that would draft the amendments[10] defined its task as considering the repeal of Article 179 of the constitution, revised in 2007 to permit the enactment of two counterterrorism laws that eroded civil liberties, as well as changes to Articles 76, 77, 88, 93 and 189. Articles 76 and 77 define the procedures for the election of the president and his term in office; Article 88 concerns judicial supervision of elections; Article 93 addresses challenges to membership in the People's Assembly; and Article 189 lays out the procedures for amending the constitution. All told, then, the committee's mission focused on six articles. The decree also stated that related articles could be revised if 'the committee deems it

---

[9] Ibid., 139–40.
[10] I am relying on Tarek El-Bishry's account of the formation of the committee here rather than press reports because he was closely involved in the process and documented it, saving us the trouble of sorting through conflicting accounts and speculation. See: Bishry, *Pages from the January 25 Revolution*.

necessary to amend them to guarantee democracy and fair elections for the president, People's Assembly and Shura Council'. The committee was also tasked with revising statutes associated with the amended articles.[11]

The committee amended the procedures and timetable for constitutional amendments in Article 189 and then added what Tarek El-Bishry, the committee chair, believed to be the provision most critical to the constitutional situation and the entire system of governance: the newly written article required elected members of the People's Assembly and Shura Council, in their first convocation, to elect a constituent assembly to write a new constitution. A deadline of six months was set for the formation of the assembly and another six months was allotted to write the constitution; the referendum was to be held within fifteen days of its completion.[12]

Bishry writes that the disagreement among political forces centred not on the need to draft a new constitution, but rather on how it would be drafted. Should it be written by a SCAF-appointed committee of prominent political and media elites? Or by a committee of the people? Or should it be a committee selected from among the people's elected representatives?[13] He neglects to mention a fourth possibility: a national conference or a constituent assembly representing the forces that supported the revolution and moderate elements of the regime, which would put the product of its efforts to a popular referendum – a natural process following a revolution.

Bishry saw the demand for a constitution prior to elections as incoherent, motivated less by a lack of understanding than a fear of democracy (read: elections). Political forces that held this position, he opined, did not enjoy popular support and were wary of popular deliberation, much like the 'liberal constitutionalists' of old who stood against the Wafd Party from 1922 to 1952,[14] who, despite their name, were not liberals. This was true of some supporters of the 'constitution first' position. *In my view, the trajectory of the transitional period made it clear that the liberals in this case were not democrats and that democrats like Bishry were not necessarily liberals.* How, then, could a democratic constitution that preserved rights and liberties – in other words, a liberal democratic constitution – be formulated? It was not difficult to find this same phenomenon in the wider Arab world before the revolutions, but events since 2011 have demonstrated that many so-called liberals are in fact no such thing. The term 'liberal' came to be applied to any non-religiously observant person who favoured a market

---

[11] Ibid., 43.
[12] Ibid., 44.
[13] Ibid., 46.
[14] Ibid.

economy, even if they supported despotism and were unwilling to oppose the trampling of civil liberties and human rights.

At the same time, a fear of democratic principles (civil liberties, political rights, judicial independence, the peaceful rotation of power, etc.) was equally apparent among many who wanted elections first, among them the remnants of the NDP, the Salafist parties and the dominant faction within the Brotherhood after the revolution. Bishry did not address the other side of the argument: that liberal democrats were right to fear elections if their loss would mean the drafting of an undemocratic constitution. *If a genuinely democratic constitution were written, liberal democrats would need not worry about losing an election because the loss would not be final, and the same is true of those who were confident of electoral victory.*

In addition to the articles listed in the SCAF decree, the committee revised ten other provisions, including articles dealing with the emergency law and the new constitution. It also amended Article 75 on the conditions for presidential candidacy. Whereas it had previously required candidates to be Egyptian nationals born to two Egyptian parents, the committee specified that neither a candidate nor either of their parents could be dual nationals and that candidates could not be married to non-Egyptians!

Article 76 laid out three avenues to presidential candidacy: candidates could receive the endorsement of thirty members of the People's Assembly, collect endorsements from 30,000 citizens in fifteen governorates or be a member of a party holding at least one seat in the People's Assembly or Shura Council. The revised Article 77 limited the presidency to two four-year terms, compared to the previous six-year terms and no term limits. Article 88 provided for full judicial supervision of elections, from the preparation of voter rolls to the declaration of results. Article 93 granted the SCC jurisdiction over the resolution of disputes over the validity of parliamentary membership, a power previously held by the People's Assembly itself. Article 139 made the appointment of a vice-president obligatory while Article 148 barred the renewal of a state of emergency for more than six months without a popular referendum.

In writing these amendments, the committee was responding to demands that predated the revolution, such as calls for presidential term limits, a constitutional provision requiring the president to name a vice-president,[15] the certification of parliamentary membership by the courts rather than the assembly itself and judicial supervision of the electoral process. These very issues had once set the agenda for a genuine struggle

---

[15] Throughout three decades in power, Mubarak never appointed a vice-president. It was only on 29 January 2011, due to the breakout of the revolution, that he appointed Omar Suleiman, the head of the GIS, as a vice-president.

between the Mubarak regime on the one hand and the Egyptian political opposition and human rights organizations on the other.

Under the terms of the article 189(bis), a constituent assembly of 100 members, elected by a majority of members of both houses of parliament (exclusive of appointed members) in a joint session, would draft a constitution within six months of formation. The president would put the draft to a popular referendum within fifteen days of completion, and the constitution would enter into force from the date on which popular approval in the referendum was announced.

Also acting beyond the scope of the SCAF decree, the committee stripped the president of the unilateral, autocratic powers granted by the 1971 constitution. Namely, it removed the provision that made the president the arbiter among the branches of government, making the office of the presidency a coequal branch of government. Similarly, Article 73 had given the president the function of safeguarding the sovereignty of the people, respect for the rule of law and the protection of national unity. The committee scaled down this function to be exercised within the limits of the constitution and law and in the manner they specified.[16] These newly inscribed limits on presidential powers were not published in the constitutional declaration or voted on in the referendum. Additional provisions were tacked on to the constitutional amendments as well, including provisions on public rights and general popular guarantees, judicial independence and institutions enumerated in the 1971 constitution, and the competencies of SCAF and their transfer to the elected legislature. The constitutional declaration legitimated SCAF's authorities and set the terms for their transfer to elected civilian institutions.[17]

SCAF, then, issued a constitutional declaration that went beyond the amendments approved in the referendum. Explaining this decision, Bishry writes:

> The Supreme Council [of the Armed Forces SCAF] observed that the 1971 constitution would have transferred authority from it to the representative assembly upon or prior to its election, because according to the provisions of the constitution, if the president vacates his position or becomes permanently incapacitated, the president of the People's Assembly temporarily assumes the presidency. If the assembly is dissolved, it falls to the president of the Constitutional Court (Article 84). For this reason, SCAF decided to draft a constitutional declaration.[18]

---

[16] Ibid., 47–8.
[17] Ibid., 52.
[18] Ibid., 51.

2 The amendments' opponents

The constitutional amendments met with objections from constitutional scholars, civic associations, youth coalitions and political parties, among them the Tagammu Party and the Nasserist Party, while the Wafd did not take a definitive position until the eve of the referendum. Figures like Mohamed ElBaradei declared that putting a handful of amendments to a referendum while continuing to abide by 'Mubarak's constitution' was 'an insult to the revolution'. The 6 April Youth Movement launched the 'Know Your Rights' campaign to raise citizens' awareness of their rights under the amendments, and public meetings were organized to discuss their pros and cons.

Briefly, the opponents of the amendments made the following arguments:

- The constitution fell with the regime and was suspended by law with the SCAF decree. How, then, can a suspended constitution be amended?
- The amendments do not touch the absolute authorities enjoyed by the president, fuelling fears that the president (if presidential elections preceded parliamentary elections) would restore autocracy. In short, a president vested with enormous prerogatives could rule unilaterally in the absence of a parliament.
- The fifteen days allotted for a public discussion of the amendments prior to the referendum are not adequate time to allow broad popular participation in the debate.
- Yes, the proposed amendments do not preclude writing a new constitution. Indeed, they obligate state institutions to complete the constitution within eighteen months. However, a new constitution will not be written and enter into force until after legislative and presidential elections conducted in accordance with the old constitution.
- It was feared that early legislative elections would result in the Muslim Brotherhood and the remnants of the NDP splitting the seats in the assembly, since other political forces, particularly revolutionary forces, were not sufficiently organized to compete effectively in elections.

History did not vindicate all of these arguments, which were often politically motivated and did not rely on a rational diagnosis of problematic issues. The parliamentary election preceded the presidential election, and it was conducted in line with new laws. Opponents generally started from the premise that a new constitution, rather than amendments to the old text, was needed immediately, prior to any elections, and that elections should be conducted pursuant to the new document. This is an understandable, legitimate objection and can be explained without recourse to flimsy justifications, which ultimately interfered with a clear emphasis on this point and undermined the argument's credibility. This principled, reasonable objection should have been the focus.

Opponents generally asserted the need for SCAF to begin taking the steps necessary to choose a constituent assembly made up of legal and judicial bodies, politicians and intellectuals, and to give the committee adequate time to draft the document before soliciting public feedback, followed by a referendum. These proposals at least cohered around a clear plan:

- Issue a constitutional declaration, to include basic provisions for the administration of the country's affairs pending the adoption of a new constitution.
- Form a presidential council of two civilians and one military figure to administer the affairs of state for a maximum six-month transitional period; the council would have the authority to issue edicts with the force of law, including an edict governing the establishment of political parties.
- Form a committee of intellectuals and legal professors to write a draft constitution within a period of one month.
- Put the committee's draft constitution up for public debate and discussion by all political forces for a fifteen-day period.[19]
- Hold a referendum on the new constitution within fifteen days of the committee's completion of the final draft following public debate.
- Hold elections for the People's Assembly within two months (proposals were made to grant the Shura Council legislative powers like the upper house in parliaments in developed states or abolish it entirely).
- Hold elections for the president and vice-president within a month of the People's Assembly elections.

3 The amendments' supporters

The camp in favour of the constitutional amendments included several legal figures and political forces, most prominently the Muslim Brotherhood, which explicitly announced that it would vote for them. In effect, the Brotherhood turned the referendum into a test of its own strength, as if those who voted 'yes' at least agreed with, if not supported, the organization. This was not true of course, but the referendum gave it the chance to position itself as a positive political force seeking stability, just as the first signs of popular anxiety over the continued state of uncertainty or chaos had begun to appear.

Whether the amendments were approved or not, SCAF would be in a position to issue a constitutional declaration defining the terms for

---

[19] 'The Popular Referendum on the Amendments to the Constitution in Egypt', *Arab Centre for Research and Policy Studies*, Policy Analysis Unit, 21 March 2011, Available online: https://bit.ly/2YIeDk9 (accessed 1 October 2015).

the administration of the transitional period. Even so, it explicitly urged Egyptians to vote for the amendments. Conditions, according to one SCAF member, were not amenable to the drafting of a new constitution 'because the armed forces have other missions' and because approval of the amendments would lead to the abolition of the old constitution and the writing of a new one after elections.[20] This is indeed what happened, and the armed forces did not make false claims in this regard.

Supporters of the amendments generally advanced the following arguments:

- The amended provisions are the equivalent of an interim constitutional declaration to administer the transition period. There must therefore be a vote to approve the amendments as an independent constitutional document, not as part of a suspended constitution, with the goal of regulating the transfer of power.
- Setting presidential terms and term limits is essentially limiting presidential prerogatives.
- Current conditions do not allow for the drafting of a new constitution because the problem is not the writing of it, but forming a national consensus around its provisions, particularly Article 2, which states that Shari'a is a principal source of legislation,[21] and the shape of the political system (presidential or parliamentary?).
- The new constitution must be written by an elected body as stipulated in amended Article 189, not a body selected by SCAF.

The Muslim Brotherhood pushed hard for a yes vote in the referendum. Its official justification was the need to move ahead with other polls, especially parliamentary elections, since these presented a historic opportunity

[20] Al-Arabiya, 22 March 2011, Available online: https://bit.ly/3qDACBI (accessed 12 May 2015).
[21] In addition to the conventional formulation of past constitutions making Islam the state religion, the 1971 constitution added a provision making Shari'a a principal source of legislation. On 22 May 1980, Article 2 was amended to make Shari'a *the* principal source of legislation. According to Farahat and Farahat, 'This amendment accompanied another change to Article 77 of the constitution removing term limits on the presidency.' They add that it is accepted among scholars that the SCC, in narrowly interpreting the provision, prevented Egypt's transformation into a theocracy. See: Mohamed Nour Farahat and Omar Farahat, *Egyptian Constitutional History: A Reading from the Perspective of the January 2011 Revolution* [Arabic] (Beirut: Arab Scientific Publishers; Doha: Al Jazeera Centre for Studies, 2011), 79.
   One could see the history of the struggle between Islamist and secular forces in Egyptian society, and between reformist and dogmatic Islamists, as a conflict over the interpretation of this article – a response to the question of what it means for Islam to be the state religion and for Shari'a to be the primary source of legislation. The compromise reached was to purge laws of provisions contravening Shari'a, rather than adopt laws derived from it. In any case, Egyptian civil statutes rarely contradict Shari'a, according to a report of the parliamentary Religious and Social Affairs and Endowments Committee on 22 April 1985, which was heard by the People's Assembly on 4 May the same year. Not considering the constitutional amendment of Article 2 to be retroactive, the SCC subsequently denied numerous suits challenging the constitutionality of laws enacted prior to 1980. In other words, the court refused to alter the entirety of the statutory framework pursuant to the revision of Article 2. See: Aliwa, 'Egypt on the Threshold', 68–9.

to the most organized of revolutionary forces. The Brotherhood also had misgivings about prolonged military rule. The group attempted to dispel others' concerns by affirming its commitment to the principle of 'participation not disputation'. It further pledged not to field candidates for more than one-third of parliamentary seats (though it later backtracked[22]) and vowed not to field a presidential candidate (another broken promise). Indeed, Essam el-Erian, a member of the Brotherhood's Guidance Bureau, declared that the group was prepared to compete in elections on 'a single, unified national list' that would include 'revolutionary youth' and other interested political forces.

The Brotherhood waged the battle over the referendum on an identitarian basis, highlighting its Islamic identity and branding opponents of the amendments and others who wanted to amend Article 2 as Christians and secularists. As is often the case when Islamist movements act to rally their base and the devout public, their reformist discourse suddenly evaporated.

On 30 March 2011, a constitutional declaration was issued that included the articles voted on in the referendum along with many more provisions inserted by SCAF, some of them taken directly from the 1971 constitution and others written by SCAF itself. With these additional changes, the public was confronted with a new, SCAF-drafted constitution, which differed from the version put to a popular referendum. While revolutionary forces were split between those who insisted on a constitution first[23] and those who favoured elections first, the people who held actual power unilaterally drafted a constitution for the country in the form of a constitutional declaration of sixty-three articles, only eight of which were voted on by the people.

The SCAF-drafted constitutional declaration allowed the military to strengthen its role in political life and shore up its autonomy from civilian institutions. Quite early on, military officers expressed their desire to see an article in the coming constitution that would guarantee the armed forces' fiscal and administrative independence from the presidency and parliament. On 26 May 2011, Maj Gen Mamdouh Shahin, the deputy defence minister for constitutional and legal affairs, called for a special designation for the armed forces in the new constitution that would make

---

[22] Reversing its position, the Brotherhood announced upon forming the Freedom and Justice Party that it would contest 45–50 per cent of seats in the assembly. See: *France 24 Arabic*, 30 April 2011, Available online: https://bit.ly/2YGueQD (accessed 13 October 2021).

[23] According to Dina Shehata, this marked the beginning of the schism within youth movements, though most of them favoured the idea of a constitution before elections. See: Shehata, 'Youth Movements and the 25 January Revolution', 152–3. This is true, but she asserts that youth were divided between Islamists on the one hand and liberals and leftists on the other. This is not true. Many Islamist youth stood in opposition to the Brotherhood even before this stage and more clearly and stridently at this point and beyond.

them subordinate not to the government or the parliament, but directly to the people.[24] This made it clear that the military placed itself above politics – not in the sense of being non-partisan, but in a position above the government and parliament. In the common democratic understanding, being above partisanship means that the military is subordinate to the general policy direction of the government and parliament rather than to parties. In contrast, if the military is not answerable to the government and parliament, but rather to the people directly, it implies that the military enjoys actual sovereignty, a line of thought that leads to and justifies military fascism. This tendency, cloaked in claims of independence and subordination to the people, was visible early on and ultimately culminated in the coup of 3 July 2013, which was justified through a demagogic appeal to that same independence, which had ostensibly enabled the military to remain neutral from 28 January to 10 February 2011. The military, it was argued, staged the coup of 3 July in response to the popular will expressed on 30 June, the same way it had responded to the people after 25 January.

Since the Muslim Brotherhood was the leading supporter of the amendments drafted by the committee, and due to the composition of the committee itself, it was widely believed that SCAF and the Brotherhood had struck a political bargain. This is the origin of the division between what came to be called – wrongly, in my view – civil forces and Islamist forces. The severity of the polarization was apparent in the contentious debate surrounding and following the referendum. The recriminations extended to the constitutional amendments committee itself. Alleging that it had been dominated by the Brotherhood, opponents pointed to the presence of Brotherhood leader and lawyer Sobhi Salih and Bishry himself, who was known to have Islamist sympathies.

Though initially important, the public debate spurred by the amendments soon took a drastic turn for the worse, as it devolved from a discussion of which transitional phase should come first into accusations of foreign collaboration and ungodliness. Amendment supporters accused their opponents of receiving funds from the United States while their opponents branded them as Wahhabists seeking to 'Islamize' the revolution. The polarization reached its peak when some media outlets portrayed Islamists – the Brotherhood, Salafists and the Islamic Group – as the 'yes' group. It was at this point that discord began to impede the democratic transition. The situation could have been remedied if the dialogue that began with the referendum, about shared democratic principles among all parties, had continued, but that issue had not yet been resolved.

---

[24] Albrecht and Bishara, 'Back on Horseback', 20.

It was during the debate over the amendments and the mobilization for the referendum that the Salafists burst onto the political scene, their statements and declarations raising concerns among the general populace. Having been an inwards-looking, apolitical community under Mubarak, this marked their first public entry to post-revolution Egyptian politics. While their intentions were ambiguous, it seemed apparent that they sought to exploit the political opening offered by the revolution to impose their vision of Islam on society through legislation.[25]

On 31 March 2011, Ibrahim Ali, the lawyer for al-Gama'a al-Islamiyya, announced that 3,000 leaders and members of the IG and the Egyptian Islamic Jihad were returning to Egypt from abroad after their names had been removed from the travel ban lists. According to press reports, most of the returnees had been residing in Afghanistan, Chechnya, Bosnia and

---

[25] Salafist groups flourished after the collapse of Nasserism, while much of the Brotherhood was locked away in Egyptian prisons. Upon the release of Brotherhood members after the October 1973 war, they were shocked by the Salafists' strength and attempted to draw them into their own ranks, but a segment of Salafists had been influenced by the Qutbist strain of Brotherhood thought. As Salafism began to take shape in the early 1970s, branching into jihadi Salafism and a quietist Salafism that sought to remake society without rebelling against the ruler, the Religious Association (al-Gam'iyya al-Diniyya) was founded at Alexandria University, largely by medical students, some of whom remained prominent figures in the Salafist Call, and the Islamic Group was formed at Cairo University. The Islamist Group of Upper Egypt developed independently of the other two groups under the tutelage of Sheikh Omar Abdel-Rahman. See: Mohammad Yousri Salama, 'Salafists and the Copts of Egypt: A Look at Roots, Issues and Challenges' [Arabic], in *Egyptian Copts after the Revolution* [Arabic] (Dubai: al-Mesbar Centre for Studies and Research, 2012), 203–38. (The author was previously the official spokesman for the Nour Party.) The Salafist movement was initially influenced by the thought of Ansar al-Sunna al-Muhammadiyya. Established in 1926, that group evolved into a massive civic association rivalling other Salafist associations like the Shari'a Association. Salafist youth, among them medical students at Alexandria University like Said Abdel Azim, Yasser Borhamy, Mohammad Abdel Fattah Idris and Ahmad Farid, were heavily influenced by the Najdi strain of Wahhabi Salafism. As organized Salafist groups were taking shape, with the Alexandrian Salafists at the forefront, popular Salafist preachers emerged as well, most famously Mohammad Hassan, Mohammad Hussein Yaqoub and Abu Ishaq al-Heweny. The period from 1981 to 2005 is seen as the height of Salafist expansion. After 2008, security pressures on Salafists were eased and Salafist religious channels were allowed to appear on satellite television. This was interpreted as a move against the Brotherhood and the civil opposition like Kefaya, the NFC, the NAC and the 6 April Movement Ibid., 215. Some of the security establishment's approaches were premised on the belief that 'encouraging Salafists (non-violent of course) was one way of countering jihadi currents. For this reason, it never reached the point of total annihilation and eradication. The goal was always to keep Salafists under tight security control and surveillance' (Ibid., 212). This period saw severe sectarian tensions on several fronts, particularly visible in flashpoint issues like the construction of churches, alleged proselytization, and Christian claims that Coptic girls were being abducted and converted to Islam. Numerous anti-Christian fatwas were issued, particularly against the construction of churches. Some Salafist sheikhs even declared it permissible to kill Christians because they had broken the covenant and were no longer a protected minority (*ahl al-dhimma*) Ibid., 220. Symbolic fatwas were issued forbidding the construction of churches, asserting the need for the minority religious tax (*al-jizya*), declaring it permissible to fight Christians to force them to convert or pay the *jizya* as a subject population, prohibiting giving greetings to Copts or congratulating them on their holidays. These fatwas were published on the websites of Salafist preachers, in the pages of al-Tawhid or on the Sawt al-Salaf website. See: Wael Lutfi, 'Copts in Egypt and the Challenges of the Salafist Reality' [Arabic], in *Egyptian Copts after the Revolution* [Arabic] (Dubai: al-Mesbar Centre for Studies and Research, 2012), 241–72.

Herzegovina, Somalia, and Kenya, and some in Iran and London.[26] The news came at a time of seemingly greater state tolerance for and openness to Islamists, which allowed former jihadists to organize into small political parties.

Less than a week later, on 6 April 2011, the Interior Ministry removed the names of several leaders and members of Islamist groups, among them the Muslim Brotherhood, from the lists of banned and monitored travellers. Included in the names was that of Mohammed Badie, the general guide of the Muslim Brotherhood, and several members of the group's Guidance Bureau.[27]

For all intents and purposes, the transitional phase began to unfold in Egypt on 19 March 2011, the date of the referendum on the constitutional amendments, when for the first time in decades, Egyptians voted in a free, fair election.

Political forces that perceived in the amendments committee a budding alliance between SCAF and the Muslim Brotherhood advocated for a prolonged transition that would allow for the establishment of competitive political parties and coalitions. In the meantime, they wanted a joint civilian-military presidential council to govern, its members chosen by consensus, and a new constitution to be drafted. They thus urged the public to reject the constitutional amendments. Anti-amendment forces proved unable to persuade the public that the alternative to the constitutional amendments was not simply 'no', but rather 'yes' to a new constitution.

Despite some confusion in the voting process, turnout in the first poll after the revolution was unprecedented. Some eighteen million citizens participated, or 41.4 per cent of the electorate. The amendments were approved with 77 per cent of the vote.

For the first time, Egyptians voted using their national identity cards instead of the voting cards used to rig elections under Mubarak, a procedural measure instituted to ensure the integrity of the election. The Interior Ministry's role was limited to securing the voting process, while the judiciary alone – another first – staffed the committees overseeing every stage of the process.

The broad turnout for the referendum seemed less about the issue on the ballot than the general jubilation over the first free vote after the revolution and support for an electoral process that would put the Mubarak era firmly in the past. Even so, the constitutional amendments polarized Egyptian politics, drawing a line between supporters who viewed them as an interim

---

[26] *Al-Masry Al-Youm*, 31 March 2011, Available online: https://bit.ly/3m09OYM (accessed 11 May 2015).
[27] *Al-Masry Al-Youm*, 7 April 2011, Available online: https://bit.ly/2VWfgkT (accessed 11 May 2015).

measure for administering the transitional phase and opponents who saw in them a circumvention of the revolution's principles.[28]

There was a consensus even among the constitutional experts who sat on the amendments committee that the current constitution had to be replaced rather than amended because it was an expression of the pre-revolution political, economic and social climate. Yet, they asserted that writing a new constitution required an elected parliament – not SCAF – to form a constituent assembly, and so its work would not be completed in a year's time. Moreover, writing a new constitution would likely set off a contentious debate around 'sensitive articles' like Article 2, which affirms Islam as the state religion, Arabic as the official language and the principles of Shari'a as a primary source of legislation. Overall, Islamist forces favoured drafting the constitution after the elections in an elected assembly

The referendum exposed for the first time the chasm between the Egyptian people and its intellectual elite, with most opinion columns championing a no vote while the general population voted in favour of the amendments, and not necessarily for reasons related to the issues under public debate. Rather, the people voted in favour of the idea of a free election, out of joy at the success of the revolution and for the restoration of stability. A vote in favour of the amendments implied all of this, as if a 'yes' to the amendments was a 'no' to Mubarak. But the mass of people who turned out to vote was not divided over the issues that set political forces against one another. After all, the silent majority did not take part in the revolution. It sympathized with it, but when the referendum drove it to speak, it said 'yes', turning a deaf ear to the appeal of Tahrir Square youth.

The vote was also at least partly sectarian in nature. The prospect of a constitution written by an elected majority raised fears that such a body might not consider Coptic issues. Copts thus tended to vote against the amendments. Islamist religious forces were clearly attuned to this same possibility and so advocated a yes vote, as a vote against Copts. This was the most serious aspect of this dangerous political culture; devoid of the concept of equal citizenship, this sectarian culture began to express itself more freely during the referendum campaign.

Many people at this stage perceived an alliance between the military and the Brotherhood based on common interests and a power-sharing arrangement.[29] To support this view, they cited the Brotherhood-military consensus on the constitutional declaration, the composition of the

---

[28] The debate over 'supra-constitutional' principles began with Baradei's proposal. See: *Al-Masry Al-Youm*, 26 July 2011, Available online: https://bit.ly/3qGdHWu (accessed 25 May 2015).

[29] Some eighteen months later, many of these same people had no difficulty in throwing in their lot with the military against the Brotherhood.

amendments committee and their shared support for elections first, as well as cases in which soldiers at polling precincts had tolerated violations of election laws by Islamist parties, specifically the use of religious slogans and the distribution of religious flyers in and outside of polling places.[30] Zeinab Abul-Magd repeats this assertion of an opportunistic alliance or deal between the military and Islamists from summer 2012 to summer 2013, writing that it enabled the Brotherhood to sweep the People's Assembly and later take the presidency, but she ignores the Brotherhood's organizational strength. The ostensible alliance was not the sole factor in the group's success.[31]

The task of critics of the military-Brotherhood relationship can be made easier by adding that the military, as an institution with an interest in post-revolution stability, sought an understanding with organized social forces capable of mobilizing a broad public or controlling the street, and it found in the Brotherhood the force with the greatest grassroots influence. It was also the force best situated to act as a spoiler if the military chose to ally with other parties. Catering to the Brotherhood in order to contain it was thus initially a necessary tactic in SCAF's strategy, though the council was nevertheless hostile to partisanship in general and especially the Brotherhood.

The upshot was that SCAF advocated for the amendments in the lead up to the referendum to burnish its own legitimacy; then, afterwards it rejected them as it drafted a constitutional declaration containing provisions unrelated to the amendments put to a popular vote. It then began the process of sowing division and discord among civil political forces, pulling all political forces down this slippery slope.

II After the referendum

1 The trials of former regime leaders

Bringing former regime figures to trial was one of the revolutionaries' foremost demands after the fall of Mubarak – a demand that crucially was not advanced as a part of a broader push for transitional justice. When criticized for its foot-dragging on this front, SCAF countered that this was a matter for the public prosecutor and the judiciary. It did not meddle

---

[30] In the parliamentary and presidential elections of 2012, civic associations that monitored the elections documented cases in which the votes of poor citizens in rural and urban areas were bought with food. The military turned a blind eye to these infractions as well.

[31] Zeinab Abul-Magd, *Militarizing the Nation: The Army, Business, and Revolution in Egypt* (New York: Columbia University Press, 2017), 188.

in judicial investigations, its spokesmen would say, before intoning that no one was above the law and everyone implicated in crimes would be brought to justice. Only after months of sustained grassroots pressure were Mubarak and other regime figures brought to trial. But this development did not alter the composition of the courts and Public Prosecution or the nature of the testimonies given by military and security officials, and these figures and bodies – all part of the old regime – were the ones who determined the conduct and substance of the trials. In other words, this was not a new order prosecuting the old. It is little wonder, then, that once the popular pressure eased up, the judiciary sat back and relaxed – until after the 2013 military coup when it turned its attention to prosecuting 25 January revolutionaries with renewed vigour. So much of the revolutionary movements' time and energy was channelled into this single demand, rather than into transforming the regime to allow for transitional justice and national reconciliation.

Contrary to the opinion that political corruption carries no penalties under Egyptian law, the reverse is the case. When authorities are so inclined, they have laws they can turn to, some dating to the early years of the July Republic, for dealing with abuse of public funds, killing demonstrators and other types of political crimes, with penalties ranging from imprisonment to death. The real problem was that old regime figures were standing trial in old regime courts as defendants in ordinary felony cases and were therefore accountable only in a personal capacity under criminal law. They were not being brought to account as political authorities responsible for corrupting political life or ruling the country in accordance with emergency laws for thirty years, or for their complicity with Israel for the blockade and wars against Gaza. None of this falls in the jurisdiction of ordinary courts, criminal or otherwise.

Prosecuting Mubarak was a way to reassure the people. The prevailing mood at the time was that as long as Mubarak and sons remained at large, the revolution was not final and they were still free to pull strings and plot. The trials, when they occurred, addressed two main issues: financial corruption and the killing of demonstrators during the revolution. The public prosecutor took the first step on 12 February 2011 with the announcement that forty-three ex-ministers had been banned from travel. Moufed Shehab, Anas El-Fiqqi, Ahmed Aboul Gheit, Mamdouh Maree, Abdul Salam El-Mahgoub and Hatem El-Gabaly topped the list. Two days later, on 14 February 2011, the Cairo Appeals Prosecution launched an investigation into allegations related to the wealth accumulated by Mubarak and his family. Then the public prosecutor ordered the arrest of former interior minister Habib el-Adly, business tycoon Ahmed Ezz,

Minister of Tourism Zoheir Garana, Housing Minister Ahmed El Maghrabi and former housing minister Ibrahim Suleiman, pending investigations into abuse of public funds. At the same time, the Illicit Gains Authority launched an investigation into the wealth of Youssef Boutros Ghali, Rachid Mohamed Rachid, Ahmed Darwish, Ahmed El Maghrabi, Amin Abaza, Safwat El-Sherif, Zakaria Azmi, Gamal Mubarak and Moufed Shehab.[32]

The army had no qualms about crushing the business tycoons close to Gamal Mubarak and eliminating the competition they presented both to its economic activities in public sector companies and its private sector investments and international partnerships. It is evident that SCAF took advantage of its position in power to strengthen the army's economic role and prerogatives. In the process, it marketed its ability to use the armed forces to protect investments as one of the advantages of cooperating with it. At a later stage, the elected parliament took pains to avoid upsetting or provoking the army by encroaching on its economic domain and privileges. The constitution drafted by the CA was equally accommodating.[33]

The former minister of information Anas El-Fiqqi and the chairman of the ERTU were arrested on the order of the Public Prosecution's financial unit, which had launched an investigation into them on the charge of abuse of public funds. Ahmed Ezz, Maghrabi and Garana were referred to criminal court on the charges of profiteering and wilful harm to public assets. On 12 March 2011, a month after Mubarak was removed, the prosecution ordered the arrest of the four deputy interior ministers for fifteen days pending investigations into the killings of demonstrators.

On 1 April 2011, sensing that the procedures were taking too long, crowds assembled by the hundreds of thousands for the 'Friday for Rescuing the Revolution' to call for a speedy trial of Hosni Mubarak and the 'symbols of corruption' and to press the other demands of the revolution. They then planned for another *milyoniyya* the following week for the same purpose, called the 'Friday for the Purge and Prosecution'.

The mass rally of 8 April 2011 saw a qualitatively new phenomenon in the course of the Friday *milyoniyya*s. Over twenty army officers took part in the protests. The 8 April Officers,[34] as they were hailed in the media, presented a list of demands. They included the dissolution of SCAF, the arrest and trial of Hosni Mubarak and his family members and aides, the dismissal of

---

[32] *Al-Arabiya*, 17 February 2011, Available online: https://bit.ly/3oyZwAA (accessed 4 May 2015).
[33] Shana Marshall and Joshua Stacher, 'Egypt's Generals and Transnational Capital', *MERIP* 42, no. 262 (Spring 2012).
[34] The officers were arrested and sentenced to prison, which sparked a movement to demand their release. SCAF eventually released some of them but had them follow a rehabilitation programme. President Morsi granted an amnesty to the rest of the officers in 2013. See: *al-Wafd*, 9 January 2013. Archived Copy Available Online: https://bit.ly/3n3gJ4H (accessed 4 May 2015).

the public prosecutor[35] and the creation of an independent judicial body to try the members of the old regime. Other demands included the dismissal of Deputy Prime Minister Yehia El-Gamal, the dismissal and prosecution of the heads of the security apparatus and local government councils, the speedy release of all political prisoners and the payment of compensation, the dissolution of municipal councils and setting a date for democratic municipal elections, and the continued purge, and prosecution if warranted, of old regime figures from the state media and press institutions, ministries and other government agencies, and banks. The officers also called for the dismissal of SSIS appointed university presidents and faculty deans, the election of competent university presidents and deans, and the reform of the education system, as well as the rapid promulgation of a minimum and maximum wage law.

The army dispersed the demonstration in a midnight raid on 8 and 9 April and arrested the officers. One person was killed in the clashes, the first incident of its kind since the fall of Mubarak.

On 10 April 2011, Mubarak delivered a speech on Al-Arabiya TV, claiming he possessed no money or real estate abroad and denying the accusation of killing demonstrators. On 14 April, Mubarak and his two sons were arrested and detained pending investigations into charges related to killing demonstrators during the revolution and illicit gains.

Around this time, SCAF began to gather in a number of civilian elites who had played recurring roles in the July 1952 order, not just in the Mubarak era but also the Sadat and even Nasser eras. Their purpose was to give the generals a civilian face and help curb the revolutionary momentum. By joining them in the dialogue sessions arranged by SCAF, the revolutionaries conferred on these elites a status as mediators above the fray whereas, in fact, they were members of the old regime who had variously fallen in and out of favour in the course of their careers.

The dialogue tended towards limited reform that would leave the structures of the state intact and avoid the most important need: reform of the security apparatus. The civilians that SCAF had assembled did not represent a democratic culture or a pluralistic and inclusive legacy. They had served as instruments that carried out diverse tasks for the previous dictatorships. Under SCAF's sponsorship, they planted the seeds for the 'Committee of Fifty' and other such bodies that would lend the military coup a civilian facade after 3 July 2013 as well.

---

[35] In fact, the dismissal of the public prosecutor was a recurring demand in all the demonstrations. He had been one of the Mubarak regime's main instruments for striking at his political adversaries and acquitting regime members of charges of corruption.

Meanwhile, discord and mistrust intensified among the pro-January revolution forces. The tensions were epitomized in the call for a *milyoniyya* of secularist forces on 27 May 2011 without the Muslim Brotherhood. By this stage, the Brotherhood had withdrawn from the 25 January forces' Coordinating Committee, and its members confined themselves to representing their organization in a personal capacity in such entities as the RYC and the NAC, thus sparing the Muslim Brotherhood organization from the need to adhere to these entities' decisions. Although the second 'Friday of Rage' continued to voice the calls for justice for the martyrs of the revolution and the prosecution of the heads of the old regime, it was primarily informed by the participants' rejection of the roadmap agreed upon by SCAF and the Muslim Brotherhood, which called for parliamentary[36] elections before the adoption of a new constitution.

The Muslim Brotherhood released a statement declaring its refusal to participate in the rally and reproaching the demonstrators for harming the relationship between the army and the people. That day's *milyoniyya* was 'a revolution against the will of the people', the statement said and it warned against clashing with SCAF.[37] The Islamist organization had chosen to go its own way: to leave the street movement in order to attain power through the ballot box.

In fact, some Muslim Brotherhood youth from the RYC had taken part in the second 'Friday of Rage'. The following day, 28 May, Mahmoud Hussein of the Muslim Brotherhood's Guidance Bureau declared that the Muslim Brothers had no representatives in the RYC. Soon afterwards, the organization expelled a number of Muslim Brotherhood youth who had been members of the coalition. Then, under the leadership of Khairat el-Shater, the organization began to reassert the Muslim Brotherhood's distinct identity at the expense of the grassroots coalitions that the revolution had forged and that formed a sociopolitical foundation for democratization. At the same time, the Muslim Brotherhood renewed emphasis on organizational hierarchy and chain of command at the expense of field activists. The point was driven home with the expulsion of around a hundred youth from the organization. Before long, Abdel Moneim Aboul-Fotouh, a former member of the Guidance Bureau, would be expelled after he announced his candidacy for the presidency.

One of most significant ironies in the history of the Muslim Brotherhood in Egypt is that the January revolution offered the Muslim Brotherhood an opportunity to attain or share power democratically just after the hardliner

---

[36] *Deutsche Welle Arabic*, 27 May 2011, Available online: https://bit.ly/3BCdGbe (accessed 13 October 2021).

[37] *Al-Masry Al-Youm*, 28 May 2011, Available online: https://bit.ly/3gsCcBE (accessed 4 May 2015).

camp (led by Khairat el-Shater and Mahmoud Ezzat) had seized control of the movement and its hierarchical structures, resolving a battle with the reformist faction that had lasted since the 1990s.[38] This probably accounts for some of the Muslim Brotherhood's actions after Morsi became president. But the potential for such behaviour had existed long before the revolution and was evident in the rivalry between the hardliners and reformists (led by Aboul-Fotouh), as well as in the generational clash between the hardliners and a current of Muslim Brotherhood youth before, during and after the revolution.

From the moment that Abou Elela Mady left the Muslim Brotherhood to found the Wasat Party in 1996 to the recent pushback against Aboul-Fotouh, Ibrahim el-Zafarani and Khaled Dawoud, every Muslim Brotherhood reformist found himself totally isolated within the organization and then expelled. Other reformists were co-opted by the hardliners, such as Essam el-Erian and Helmy Elgazzar.[39]

At this stage, the Muslim Brotherhood adopted 'patriotic' rhetoric to defend SCAF. Opposition political forces met this with the charge that the two were colluding in order to marginalize the opposition. SCAF, intent on containing the grassroots movement, had aligned with the best-organized political force and the most able to control the street. The Muslim Brotherhood, for its part, had set its sights on a single goal since the announcement of the constitutional amendments on 30 March 2011: election day. They would make any deal with SCAF in order to reach that goal.

At that moment, they found an unexpected ally, at least for their most immediate objective. On 12 June 2011, the Nour Party was founded by the largest Salafist group in Egypt. Mohammad Nour, the party's spokesman, justified this sudden departure from the Salafists' long-held aversion to partisan politics (because democracy and political parties were heresies), saying that his movement wanted to protect Egypt from liberals and secularists who were working to abolish Egypt's Islamic identity.[40]

SCAF organized a series of dialogues with political forces, but the most important in terms of its attempts to contain the revolutionary youth movement was the one it held at Galaa Theatre on 1 June 2011. Representing SCAF were Ismail Etman, Mohammad al-Assar, Mamdouh

---

[38] Khalil Al-Anani, 'The "Anguish" of the Muslim Brotherhood in Egypt', in *Routledge Handbook of the Arab Spring: Rethinking Democratization*, ed. Larbi Sadiki (London and New York: Routledge, 2015), 237. Anani adds other factors that he claims explain the Muslim Brothers' failure to take 'more moderate' stances after they reached power, such as the suddenness of their inclusion in pluralistic politics and consequent lack of time to adjust, their immediate transition from officially banned opposition to the presidency and their intense partisan conflict with others, 234–5.

[39] Al-Anani, 'The Muslim Brotherhood in the Post-Morsi Period', 17–23.

[40] Al-Anani and Malik, 'Pious Way to Politics', 63.

Shahin and Mahmoud Hegazy. In a posting on its Facebook page, SCAF had invited representatives of 153 youth coalitions. According to some of the youth who withdrew from that dialogue, most of those who had succeeded in gaining admission to the theatre were members of the Muslim Brotherhood or the former NDP.[41]

This was clearly a bid to atomize the young revolutionaries and their organizations and leaderships. The invitation, itself, was suspicious. It appeared deliberately designed to diminish the leadership status of such basic movements as 6 April and the RYC and to bring affiliates with the old regime to the fore. Rather than address the invitation to the movements by name, SCAF opted for the vague category 'youth of the revolution'. The purpose was twofold: to hamper the activists' ability to organize in advance so as to present their demands as forcefully and systematically as possible and, second, to enable any young person to claim that he/she represents them. The majority of those 153 'coalitions' subsequently vanished.

Many media helped trivialize the term 'revolutionary youth', utilizing the fluidity of the revolutionaries' organization in the square and capitalizing on their eagerness to appear before the cameras in order to sow rivalry among them. Such treatment fed a general perception of revolutionary youth as something nebulous and encouraged the shift in the popular mood from admiration of noble spirited activists who were a source of national pride to weariness at their constant bickering and showing-off. The media also facilitated the infiltration of revolutionary ranks with young people who did not genuinely support the revolution or who were security agency moles. One of their functions was to dismiss well-known demands as the product of a privileged clique who had monopolized the role of revolutionary youth.

On 8 July 2011, Tahrir Square swarmed with tens of thousands of protesters calling for the 'Revolution First'. As the theme suggests, the rally was organized to pressure SCAF into carrying out the demands of the revolution. Not all the crowds went home at the end of the day. A large number of demonstrators decided to stage a sit-in, which lasted three weeks until, on 1 August, the army moved in to break it up. On the evening of 8 July, heated arguments erupted between those in favour and those opposed to an extended sit-in. The former camp had come to regard this protest mechanism as a reproducible magic formula they could apply to any problem and yield a triumph. Unfortunately, if the army set its mind against sit-ins and demonstrations and decided to use force to repress them, a massacre would result (as would occur in Raba'a Square two years

---

[41] *Al-Masry Al-Youm*, 1 June 2011, Available online: https://bit.ly/37MEbwW (accessed 4 May 2015).

later). Iterations of the sit-in formula have occurred in many countries. A famous example is Occupy Wall Street, which also met with a violent police response. Adherence to this formula reflects a tendency to idolize a revolutionary act and isolate it from the other factors that contributed to the success of the original act. In the Egyptian case, such factors include the broad spectrum of people that took part in the 25 January revolution, the widespread impression that the Mubarak regime had grown decrepit, and the army's refusal to repress the revolution, all of which were discussed in Part I.

A week before the break-up of the sit-in, on 23 July 2011, a protest march set off from Tahrir Square to Abbasiyya, bound for SCAF headquarters in the Ministry of Defence. The 6 April Movement spearheaded this march in response to a SCAF communiqué that accused the movement of sowing discord between the army and the people. Thousands of people joined in to express their solidarity with the movement, as well as their concern about the rhetoric of treachery and betrayal the army had begun to wield against activists and critics. Along the way, the marches were attacked in what many eyewitnesses described as 'an ambush'. One activist, Mohammad Mohsen, was killed, and dozens of others were wounded. The 'First Abbasiya Incident' acquired its particular notoriety from the fact that it was not the army, but gangs of thugs who attacked while the soldiers blocking the road to the Ministry of Defence looked on. Part of this orchestrated action involved inciting the public – referred to in the press as the 'local community'[42] or 'honourable citizens' – to take part in the onslaught. Some thugs arrested activists alleging they were spies. Not only did the authorities support that behaviour, some of the wrongfully arrested were detained in the headquarters of the military police and GIS despite the lack of any corroborative evidence.[43]

The 8 July 2011 sit-in marked the beginning of the call to arms against the demonstrators staging sit-ins in Tahrir on the grounds that they were 'saboteurs' who 'obstructed the wheel of production'.[44]

The ongoing protests forced Essam Sharaf to perform a cabinet reshuffle. Perhaps the main explanation for the harsh criticisms levelled

---

[42] Describing how the lumpenproletariat were organized to serve as a popular base for Louis Bonaparte, Marx writes, 'In his Society of December 10, he assembles ten thousand rascally fellows, who are to play the part of the people, as Nick Bottom that of the lion.' Marx, *The 18th Brumaire of Louis Bonaparte*, 76.

[43] Amr Gharbeia, 'An EIPR Researcher Tells the Story of His Journey from Military Police to General Intelligence to Al-Waely Police Department', *Egyptian Initiative for Personal Rights*, 28 July 2011, Available online: https://bit.ly/2WCGzof (accessed 15 April 2021).

[44] Footage of the beginning of the clashes can be seen on *YouTube*, 26 July 2011, Available online: https://bit.ly/3oOQ6kP (accessed 8 April 2015).

at his government was that it was the first to come to power after the revolution, and, so, broad segments of the population pinned very high expectations on it. But as much as it may have wanted to meet these hopes, it was hobbled by economic and security crises and general instability due to constant political upheaval. The second Sharaf government, unveiled on 21 July 2011, introduced fourteen new ministers, while retaining twelve from the previous cabinet. It is noteworthy that this was the first cabinet to include the eminent economist Hazem Beblawi and Ali El-Selmi as deputy prime minister; Beblawi would be appointed prime minister following the overthrow of the elected president Mohamed Morsi.

The revolutionary struggle had begun to transform into a struggle to force demands on a government unable to respond. As a result, one government was replaced by the next, but this could not quench the thirst generated by the limitless aspirations the revolution had unleashed. The only demand that could have worked would have been for a national conference that aimed to establish a revolutionary government around which the people could rally against the old regime in the framework of transitional justice. In the absence of this, a series of technocratic governments with no revolutionary component in them reeled beneath the weight of popular demands, including labour demands. Moreover, as these governments collapsed under such pressures, they furnished proof after proof of the failure of civilians in government. Also, as protesters turned their attention from the demand for justice and retribution to the demand to prosecute Mubarak regime leaders, the security agencies remained immune to change.

At this stage, as the country headed towards parliamentary elections, discussion began to focus on the question of supra-constitutional principles. Secularist forces were intent upon securing some legal safeguards for democratic principles, especially those related to liberties, in order to ensure that they continued to prevail even under a parliamentary majority or executive inimical to such principles. Rather than indicating their readiness to at least discuss the founding principles of the new order, the Islamists shrugged them off as the view of a minority unsupported by the majority of the population. To the Muslim Brothers, above all, popular majority outweighed democratic principles. Otherwise put, they reduced democracy to an instrument to reach power through the ballot box, free of a matrix of governing principles that all who attain power must uphold regardless of their ideology.

This is the fallacy of majoritarianism. It holds that democracy does not require a consensus, even on a minimum of fundamental principles, and that it only has to do with a set of agreed-on mechanisms and procedures for the peaceful rotation of authority. In the introductory chapter of this part, I criticized this view, which has its exponents among scholars of transition, and demonstrated that, without a minimal level of shared values, there cannot exist the necessary trust for the peaceful rotation of authority.[45]

On 29 July 2011, the Islamists, consisting primarily of the Muslim Brotherhood and the main Salafist organizations, held a *milyoniyya* called 'The Friday of Popular Will and Unity of Ranks'. Their main purpose was to demonstrate their opposition to supra-constitutional principles, though they also voiced the demands for the rapid purge of old regime figures from all state agencies, retribution against the murderers of revolutionaries and the abolition of military trials for civilians. Displays of Muslim religiosity dominated that day's activities, for which seven stages had been erected in Tahrir. The speeches mainly focused on condemning the civil state, the demand for rule by Shari'a and other catchphrases from the religious lexicon shared by all Islamist movements regardless of their diverse origins and trends. Similar demonstrations were held simultaneously in central squares in other main cities.

The event, subsequently dubbed the 'Friday of Shari'a' or, more caustically, 'Kandahar Friday',[46] both embodied and marked a turning point in the deep and growing rift among the political forces that had supported the January revolution. With its displays of Islamist extremism and fanatic rhetoric, it struck unprecedented dread into broad segments of the silent majority who had originally sympathized with the revolution but who were now alarmed at the course it was taking and, among urban middle classes in particular, at its implications for their lifestyles.

The Mubarak trial, which held its first hearing on 3 August, was an occasion to reunify ranks, but its attraction gradually faded. It had been generally presumed that was this would be less a trial of an individual than of an authoritarian regime,[47] but the reverse played out. As mentioned earlier, the charges were killing demonstrators and financial corruption, not responsibility for a full three decades of despotism. The trial was conducted

---

[45] Trust does not arise out of the blue without a common ground that includes a feeling of national belonging, an agreement on the state per se and a consensus around democracy, as well as shared historical experiences. Some researchers have discussed the lack of trust between Islamists and secularists, but without examining its roots, as this has no immediate bearing on the problem of consensus over procedural matters. See, for example, Juan J. Linz and Alfred Stepan, 'Democratization Theory and the "Arab Spring"', *Journal of Democracy* 24, no. 2 (2013): 23.

[46] It would subsequently be referred to as 'Kandahar One', as a 'Kandahar Two' would take place in November 2012. The committee charged with drafting a new constitution was meeting at the time, and the throng of Islamists in that demonstration voiced demands regarding the status of Shari'a in the constitution.

[47] As, for example, Hazem Beblawi had portrayed it. See: *Al-Masry Al-Youm*, 19 April 2011, Available online: https://bit.ly/2W0hW0I (accessed 13 April 2015).

like any ordinary criminal trial under the old regime, relying on the same laws and practices, the same unruly jumble of fractious lawyers and the same posturing from the judges. In deference to current public opinion, the latter paid lip service to the glorious 25 January revolution in their introductory remarks, and then worked against it when the opportunity arose. The media coverage, the clamour of the families of the victims and the loud pro-Mubarak supporters outside the court building may have initially suggested that this was indeed 'the trial of the century', as the press called it, but ultimately all of this merely disguised the ordinariness of the criminal hearings. Most of the key players in the Mubarak regime faced trials of this nature. Some were found guilty, others were tried in absentia and still others were released over the next three years; eventually all were acquitted of the most serious charges brought against them. Those found guilty of lesser crimes were penalized with fines or short prison terms after which they were released.

After all, it was their own regime that was trying them. The revolution might have brought the charges, but the process unfolded in accordance with the laws and dictates of the old regime and its extension into the post-revolutionary era, not under a consensual interim order pursuing transitional justice. This is the crucial takeaway from the forest of details around the trials. Furthermore, Public Prosecutor Abdel Meguid Mahmoud, a Mubarak appointee, was not interested in trying anyone from the old regime. So he prepared poorly and exerted little effort, even within the limits of the available legal framework. He approached his task grudgingly, resentful of the pressures from protesters and the public that sympathized with them, and assembled cases in which he had no personal conviction. Therefore, when the pressures subsided, he backtracked on or circumvented the measures he had taken. For these and other reasons, these were neither revolutionary tribunals to purge the system of members of the old order, as occurred in Iran after the revolution, or transitional justice courts convened to condemn those guilty of systematic human rights abuses and other crimes and to pardon those who did not commit such offences, in the framework of a national reconciliation in which all embrace the democratic system.[48] In the Egyptian case, the old regime officials in the defendants' dock and the judiciary were on the same side:

---

[48] The revolutionary tribunal proceedings conducted by officers like Abdel Latif Boghdadi and Anwar Sadat in Egypt after the 1952 revolution or by Fadel al-Mahdawi after the 1958 revolution in Iraq were early manifestations of the demagogic mob culture ushered in by the military coups and marked the beginning of the shift from the demand for democracy to military rule in the name of the revolution. Transitional justice, in contrast, is defined by a special set of laws and aims to help the transition to democracy. Governed by jurists who support democracy, it pursues measures to exact justice and promote reconciliation.

they agreed that the revolution was a deluge of unrest and rioting. The judges and prosecutors feared that they could become victims of the revolution just like the people they were trying, so they bent with the wind until the storm passed. They went through the motions, with no sincerity and dedication.

Still, we should stress that even if these trials were ordinary trials, they marked a major precedent for the Arab region. Never before had the head of state of an Arab country been brought to a trial of this sort. Previously, presidents or prime ministers overthrown by military coups (Abdul Karim Kassem, Abdul Salam Arif, Ahmed Ben Bella, Nureddin al-Atassi and Hosni al-Za'im) were executed or sentenced to long terms in prison following proceedings that were never made public.

The Mubarak trial – the nature of the charges against him and the competency and composition of the court – was another sign that the revolution had been steered towards cosmetic reforms as a means to absorb the popular anger. The 'reforms' were conducted from within the system, without the participation of the revolutionaries and beyond their control. It soon became clear that the government lacked both the will and the ability to implement the reforms.

The judicial proceedings for old regime figures spanned months. There were dozens of hearings for Mubarak, his two sons, his minister of interior and the deputy interior ministers, not to mention the many hearings in the trials of other Mubarak regime officials. In the forty-sixth session, which occurred on 2 June 2012, nearly a full year after the trial started, Judge Ahmed Rifaat sentenced Mubarak and Adly to life in prison, acquitted two deputy interior ministers of the charge of killing demonstrators, acquitted Mubarak of the charge of financial corruption, and acquitted Alaa and Gamal Mubarak of the charges against them. Eventually, the convictions were overturned on appeal.

2 The Israeli embassy incident

On 19 August 2011, an Egyptian officer and four conscripts were killed by Israeli forces near the Egyptian-Israeli border. The Multinational Force and Observers, the international peacekeeping force created to monitor the implementation of the terms of the peace treaty between Egypt and Israel, determined that Israel had committed two violations: first, its forces crossed the border into Egypt, and, second, they opened fire from inside Egyptian territory. The Egyptian Foreign Ministry formally protested the action, summoned the Israeli chargé d'affaires and demanded an inquiry into the incident.

This was not the first time the Israelis opened fire in the Sinai. Nor was it the first time that breaches of this sort had occurred since the signing of the peace treaty. However, in the climate of that time, the incident so outraged Egyptians that, on 20 August 2011, they staged a massive protest march which turned into an extended sit-in in front of the Israeli embassy. The military police broke it up the following Friday, 27 August 2011.

In my opinion, the weeklong Israeli embassy sit-in was a second wave of the 25 January revolution. It was led by the revolutionary youth, alone, while the other political forces and parties sat it out. The mobilization was organized through social media and included a call to march to Sinai. The crowd in front of the embassy featured the same diversity that characterized Tahrir Square in January 2011. They called for the expulsion of the Israeli ambassador.

On 9 September 2011, as popular anger and frustration mounted, a large number of protesters marched on the high-rise building that housed the embassy on an upper storey then destroyed portions of the concrete barrier that had been erected after the break-up of the sit-in two weeks earlier. Then, to the cheers of the crowd, one demonstrator scaled the facade of the high-rise, removed the Israeli flag from its pole and replaced it with the Egyptian flag. At one point, a group of demonstrators gained entrance into the building, stormed the embassy itself and grabbed documents and files, tore them up and tossed the shreds of paper like confetti from the balcony. The embassy staff, along with the ambassador, were evacuated from Egypt.

The army, which had watched from the sidelines, took advantage of the incident to stir alarm over the revolution and drive home the army's importance to the West and Israel. The incident met with harsh reactions from both government circles and established political parties. I believe that the reactions against what the demonstrators saw as a natural extension of the spirit of 25 January helped keep the question of Egypt's relations with Israel off the agenda of the discussions among political forces for a long time. This includes some Mubarak-era opposition forces that had built their 'glory' on their rejection of the peace accords with Israel. Suddenly, after the revolution in particular, they lost interest in the subject of peace with Israel, and they stopped raising the issue in their public discourse. The shift was reflected in their reactions to the revolutionaries' spontaneous protest act of storming the embassy, which they denounced as irresponsible and provocative. The political forces that had begun to vie for power and present themselves as candidates for government did not want to risk being pegged as 'radicals' who might want Egypt to rescind the peace accords with Israel.

III Registration of political parties and the law on the exercise of political rights

On 28 March 2011, SCAF introduced Law 12/2011 amending Law 40/1977 governing the establishment and operation of political parties. It rounded this out, on 20 July, with several amendments to Law 73/1956 on the exercise of political rights. The laws were both revised pursuant to the recent constitutional amendments. One of the most important provisions of the amended political parties law was that it made it possible to establish a party by a formal notification submitted to the PPC. If the committee did not reply within thirty days of notification, the party was automatically deemed legally registered as of the thirty-first day. This was a revolutionary change when compared to the law under Mubarak.

The newly amended Law 40/1977 also banned any party whose principles, programmes, activities or membership were founded on a religious basis or discriminated on the basis of gender, ethnic origin, language, religion or creed, as well as any party that operated a paramilitary organization. In addition, the law required parties to publicly disclose their principles, structures and sources of funding. The amendment abolished state funding of political parties. As a demonstration of its seriousness, a party had to demonstrate that it had at least 5,000 members from ten governorates and 300 members from all governorates.

In accordance with the new law, the PPC was reconstituted on a (theoretically) non-partisan basis by manning it with members of the judiciary. It was headed by the first vice-president of the Court of Cassation and included two other judges from the Court of Cassation, two appellate chief justices and two members of the State Council. Under the previous law, the speaker of the Shura Council (perforce a member of the ruling NDP) had chaired the PPC.

Against the backdrop of the new climate of freedom and openness, internal political and ideological disputes and tensions within the Muslim Brotherhood frothed to the surface and into public view as never before. The new freedom to establish political parties was tempting to anyone contemplating splitting off from the organization, which heightened internal tensions. Indeed, two of its most prominent members, Ibrahim el-Zafarani and Abdel Moneim Aboul-Fotouh, did exactly that, and a large number of middle-tier leaders and other members of the rank and file followed in their wake.[49]

---

[49] Zafarani said he resigned because of what he described as the Brotherhood's insularism and in response to Supreme Guide Mohammed Badie's instruction forbidding Muslim Brotherhood members from joining any party but the Brotherhood-linked FJP. Aboul-Fotouh's resignation was

The rupture sent shockwaves through the Islamist organization and strengthened the hand of the hardliners whose leaders who had not actively taken part preparing for the revolution, not least because most were in prison. Also, now there was the prospect of a rival Islamist alternative in the next presidential elections. Aboul-Fotouh had declared his intent to run early on, and, if the Muslim Brotherhood did not field a candidate, its members would probably vote for him, meaning that the breakaway member and his party might lure away a large segment of the base. After all, the Muslim Brotherhood members could not bring themselves to remain neutral in a competition between a former Muslim Brotherhood leader such as Aboul-Fotouh and Ahmed Shafik. This, I believe, was one of the main reasons, besides the intention of the Supreme Administrative Court, to invalidate the elected parliament in which the Islamists enjoyed a majority, that the Muslim Brotherhood would backtrack on its promise not to field a candidate in the presidential elections. The seeds for the nomination of Muslim Brotherhood Deputy Supreme Guide Khairat el-Shater a year later and then Guidance Bureau member Mohamed Morsi, after Shater's candidacy was invalidated, were planted in these early days.

Still, there were parliamentary elections to prepare for. Towards this end, the Muslim Brotherhood established its political wing, the FJP, in May 2011, and appointed Mohamed Morsi as its chairman, Essam el-Erian as deputy chairman and Mohamed Saad Elkatatny as secretary general.[50]

The SCAF edict amending the law on the exercise of political rights introduced a number of provisions that addressed demands the political opposition had been pressing since before the revolution, one of the most important being full judicial supervision of the electoral process. The amended law abolished voter registration methods that had facilitated electoral fraud in the past and called for the preparation of a national voter

---

connected with the decades-long tug of war between hardliners and reformists within the Muslim Brotherhood and, after the revolution, the dispute over his decision to field himself as president after the organization had decided not to nominate a candidate. See: *Al-Masry Al-Youm*, 1 April 2011, Available online: https://bit.ly/2VYSxF0 (accessed 13 October 2021).

[50] The establishment of the FJP was a great step forward. However, the Muslim Brotherhood's failure to register it opened it to charges of being an arm of the proselytizing organization and violating the law. The demand to register the party haunted Morsi throughout his presidency, as he was constantly accused of receiving orders from the Guidance Bureau, which precluded him from being a president for all Egyptians. One of the advantages of the FJP was that it made it possible for its members to evade criticism for aspects of the Muslim Brotherhood legacy, such as the fatwa opposed to the construction of churches and other fatwas inimical to Copts and women that were published in the organization's *al-Da'wa* magazine. The FJP was an opportunity to turn a new leaf. As though to demonstrate the break, Badie called on Copts to join the FJP, which included 100 Christians among its founding members who, moreover, had elected a Christian (Rafik Habib) as the party's deputy chairman. See: Abd al-Aziz Abd al-Qader, 'Egypt: Coptic Fears after the Rise of the Muslim Brotherhood' [Arabic], in *The Copts of Egypt after the Revolution* [Arabic] (Dubai: Mesbar Centre for Studies and Research, 2012), 139.

database generated from citizens' national ID numbers and associated information. An executive memo issued in pursuance of the decree established that the People's Assembly and Shura Council elections and the constitutional referendum would be supervised by the Supreme Election Committee, as stipulated in the constitutional declaration. The five-member body, all judges headed by the president of the Cairo Court of Appeals, would appoint an elections committee for each governorate headed by a chief appellate judge.

All that remained now were the tasks of implementing changes to important political rights and liberties, sorting out still-controversial details about the electoral system and lifting the state of emergency.

1 The political party map

The reconstitution of the PPC in compliance with the requirement of judicial supervision and the elimination of red tape flung open the doors for groups across the political spectrum to form new parties. Political forces that had once been barred from forming political parties seized the unprecedented opportunity.[51] But so did some of the more established political stakeholders, not least a large contingent of NDP politicians set on insinuating themselves into parliament under new brand names. The revolutionary youth movements, on the other hand, lacked a strong umbrella organization that could draw on their strength in the streets and a unified leadership capable of transforming the mass movement into a democratically oriented organizational force. Dozens of differently named groups carried the banners of the revolution's demands, but they were unable to merge into a larger political entity that would give the revolution a single address. There did emerge some liberal and leftist parties and coalitions that advocated ideas close to the revolution's ideology, but the hope of establishing democratic political entities with a chance of becoming viable contestants in the electoral race remained distant. The established movements and parties from before the revolution already had administrative and organizational structures that could easily be transformed into campaign structures. They had headquarters, lists of committed members, hierarchies and electoral experience.[52]

The New Wafd was a liberal party inspired by the pre-1952 Wafd Party. After its re-establishment under Sadat, it continued to operate in the margin available to it during the Mubarak era. With roots dating to the March

---

[51] *Al-Nahar* (Egypt), 28 March 2011, Available online: https://bit.ly/37Ns6Y7 (accessed 13 May 2015).
[52] *BBC Arabic*, 23 June 2011, Available online: https://bbc.in/370n1gb (accessed 11 July 2015).

1919 revolution, the Wafd originally rested on a large grassroots base, while its operations were dominated by a number of aristocratic families and prominent businessmen. The liberal-oriented New Wafd had made a mark for itself before the January revolution, when its former chairman Noaman Gomaa competed against Mubarak in the last presidential election in Egypt before the revolution. The 2005 presidential polls followed a relative political liberalization epitomized by an amendment to the presidential election law that allowed for a multi-candidate system. The change was nominal, however, as the security agencies still controlled the political game.

Shortly before the revolution, the party, now led by the business magnate El-Sayyid el-Badawi, tried to refurbish its image after a gruelling leadership crisis that had the marks of a generational clash. After the revolution, the Wafd called for the creation of an alliance of liberal parties that would work with the Muslim Brothers to forge an agreement on the nature of the post-Mubarak order. This consensus would appear during the lead up to the parliamentary elections at the end of 2011.

There were two other liberal parties: the DFP headed by Osama El-Ghazali Harb and the Ghad Party led by Ayman Nour. The youth of the former party were activists in the revolution, although both parties lost some of their younger members to the movements and coalitions that had emerged during the revolution. Representing the Arab nationalist left, the Karama (Dignity) Party was founded (though denied registration) before the revolution, in an attempt to revive the Nasserist camp, which catered to certain fringes in the old regime. Karama tried to stake a place for itself in Tahrir and the political arena, but its numbers were few. It drew on its leaders' history of activism in the student movement and its record of commitment to Arab causes and opposition to Israel and normalization.

The oldest left-wing party, dating to the introduction of the multiparty system under Sadat, originated, like the Wafd and NDP, in the period of the 'three platforms' of the ASU. The NPUP, commonly referred to as the Tagammu, evolved from the organization that represented the left-wing faction of the ASU. Before the revolution, the Tagammu was hard hit by schisms and the departure of its Marxist and Arab nationalist bases, who were repelled by the party chairman Refaat El-Saeed's right-leaning outlooks and his tendency to coordinate with the Mubarak regime.

The most remarkable developments following the amendment of the political parties law came from within the Islamist camp. The first newborn party after the January revolution and the first official Islamist party was the Wasat Party, which had been battling for recognition in the courts since the mid-1990s. Established as a breakaway faction from the Muslim

Brotherhood, the party succeeded in attracting moderate and democratic-leaning members of the organization and, thus, manifested an early convergence between Islamism and democracy. Its leaders, most notably Abou Elela Mady, were active in the EMC (Kefaya). Although the Wasat had a limited following before the revolution, it established credentials for itself as a mediator between Islamist forces and secularist parties.

The Muslim Brotherhood, which remained the strongest political organization after the revolution, founded the FJP. As the political wing of the Brotherhood, the FJP was able to utilize the group's huge organizational might and resources, and the political knowhow of its leaders and other members who had previously engaged in electoral battles for parliament, occupational syndicates and student unions during the Mubarak era. Such advantages raised questions about the boundaries between the mother organization as a proselytizing religious association with a history of covert operations and its new legitimate political party, required by law to act as such, not as a religious society. As mentioned earlier, internal tensions within the Muslim Brotherhood, especially those related to the organization's hierarchical rigidity and the lack of generational upward mobility, led many Brothers to defect. Still, these departures did little to diminish the organization's mobilizing capacities and social bases.

The FJP did not model itself after Turkey's AKP or, for that matter, the Moroccan JDP or the al Nahda movement in Tunisia. It did not separate itself as an autonomous entity from the Muslim Brotherhood movement, and the latter did not transform itself into a mere proselytizing association. The party remained the political arm of an Islamist movement that rejected the secular state (which the AKP has recognized and the JDP and al Nahda have accepted implicitly). The gulf between these two models became apparent during the visit of then Turkish prime minister Recep Tayyip Erdoğan to Cairo on 12 September 2011. Although hailed by Islamist movements upon his arrival, in interviews given during his visit he advised them to accept the secular state and denied that the AKP was an Islamist party. The Muslim Brotherhood felt let down, and some of its leaders regarded his remarks as interference in Egyptian affairs. This drove home the difference between a political party that set its sights on becoming a ruling party in a multiparty system and Islamist parties that aspire to power with the mentality of a religious opposition movement unable to delink political party work from religious proselytizing.

The next Islamist party born after the FJP raised multiple questions – to which we will return in greater detail later in the text – as it represented the Salafists who, throughout the Mubarak era, had remained aloof from politics. The Nour Party was the political wing of the Alexandria-based

Salafist Call movement and was able to capitalize on the successive waves of 'Salafization' and special relations with Saudi Arabia. The Nour Party, and the Authenticity (Asala) Party, another new Salafist party whose leadership was based largely in Cairo, decided to field candidates in the parliamentary elections. Both cases elicited considerable scepticism over their commitment to democratic frameworks and their potential inclusion in consensual processes for devising solutions to the complex social and economic issues that needed to be addressed after the revolution.

This was a major decision as it marked a precedent in the history of the Salafist movement, in Egypt at least, as the Kuwaiti Salafists preceded them in this regard. Karagiannis, Khosrokhavar and others assert that the Salafists' entry into electoral politics signalled a basic change in strategy, while Kamran Bokhari and Farid Senzai stressed that this did not signify an ideological evolution. All these authors agree that the Salafists saw an opportunity and seized it; they ran in the elections but they had no commitment to democracy.[53] This is true, of course, and none of the four aforementioned scholars or anyone else disputes it. It follows that allowing them to participate in determining the fate of the revolution, which they had opposed, and the transition to democracy, which they also opposed on principle, was one of the greatest mistakes made by political forces in this period. It would have a major impact on the course of the transition process, and it was instrumental in aggravating the polarization between the political players involved.

As for the Salafist parties themselves, they would go on to extend their newfound pragmatism to their methods of work and influence, but this would not bring them closer to democracy. If initially they thought their decision a sound one, in light of the amazing (to them) and alarming (to others) performance of their parties at the ballot box, that pragmatism would not necessarily prove beneficial to them in the long run. Their eventual conflict with the Muslim Brotherhood would ultimately lead them to support the military coup against elected institutions. This, in turn, would precipitate internal disputes in their parties and movements, losing them their once-significant grassroots support as evidenced in the post-coup 2015 elections and the loss of the respect they had once enjoyed among large swaths of the devoutly religious.

---

[53] Emmanuel Karagiannis, 'The Rise of Electoral Salafism in Egypt and Tunisia: The Use of Democracy as a Master Frame', *Journal of North African Studies* 24, no. 2 (2019): 212; Farhad Khosrokhavar, *The New Arab Revolutions That Shook the World* (London: Paradigm Publishers, 2012), 114; Kamran Bokhari and Farid Senzai, *Political Islam in the Age of Democratization* (New York: Palgrave Macmillan, 2013), 93.

Other parties with jihadist origins would follow, such as those formed by the ex-members of IG and the EIJ who had publicly revised their old positions.

New parties emerged on the secular side of the political spectrum. A number of businessmen threw their weight behind liberal initiatives in order to counter the Islamists' domination over the public sphere after the fall of Mubarak. The most prominent was Naguib Sawiris, who founded and invested considerable financial and media resources into the Free Egyptians Party and campaigned assiduously to recruit support among the Coptic community.

It is worth a brief pause, here, to consider how the term 'liberal' gained currency at this juncture and what it connoted. In the context of the polarization between secularists and Islamists, it was used to refer to anti-Islamist players, even if they were not necessarily liberal, in the sense of espousing civil rights and liberties. Often they were economically neoliberal but not necessarily politically liberal.

The foremost newly established entity that did, in fact, espouse a liberal ideological discourse was the ESDP led by university professor Mohamed Aboulghar, an activist in NAC and in the university professors' movement.[54] The party included an array of veteran politicians who enjoyed considerable respect among youth and individuals who themselves had been activists in their youth.

Among the Islamist youth was a significant contingent that had spearheaded the new generation movement in the Muslim Brotherhood, taken part in the January revolution from the outset and eventually resigned from that organization. They, too, formed a number of parties, most notably the Egyptian Current and Adl (Justice) Party. Both parties positioned themselves between Islamist and leftist or Arab nationalist ideas in an attempt to transcend the conventional secularist versus Islamist dichotomy.

Leftist youth also hastened to establish several parties, the most important of which were the SPAP and the Labour Party. Both included many veteran leftists and labour leaders, alongside leftist youth who, in addition to having taken part in the revolution, had been active in the labour

---

[54] Abou El-Ghar, like many other writers and intellectuals, abandoned his liberalism when he supported the coup, did not condemn the Raba'a massacre and called the protesters there terrorists. At the time, he justified his stances on the grounds of need to prioritize national security over human rights. Later, after 2015, when he fully understood the nature of the authoritarian regime, he would revise his views and become more consistently liberal. See: Daanish Faruqi and Dalia Fahmy, 'Egyptian Liberals, from Revolution to Counterrevolution, Introduction', in *Egypt and the Contradictions of Liberalism: Illiberal Intelligentsia and the Future of Egyptian Democracy*, ed. Daanish Faruqi and Dalia Fahmy (London: One World, 2017), 8–9.

movement, Kefaya, anti-globalization groups and other sociopolitical protest movements in the latter years of the Mubarak era. Some smaller socialist and Marxist parties also emerged, such as the renovated Egyptian Communist Party and the Socialist Party of Egypt.

The popular campaign to support Baradei as president and the NFC that he headed were also active at this stage. These would eventually converge and crystallize in their final form as the Constitution Party, founded in 2012. The party included a number of revolutionary youths who had become household names, but it was unable to field candidates in the elections because it filed its registration notification too late.

2 The list versus single-ticket system

The parliamentary election law, approved by the cabinet on 7 July 2011, triggered another controversy. It provided for a mixed system whereby half the parliamentary seats would be contested using electoral lists and the other half using the individual ticket system. In addition, individual candidates had to be independents unaffiliated with a political party. Most political parties and forces demanded the abolition of single tickets, arguing that the list system would provide for a more representative parliament; in contrast, the individual candidacy system favoured old regime affiliates and businessmen with wealth and influence and disadvantaged the newly established parties in particular.

On 1 October 2011, SCAF met with thirteen political parties (of which four were Islamist) in order to reduce tensions. Although there were many crucial bones of contention that needed to be addressed, such as the lifting of the state of emergency, a lustration law and the time frame for the transfer of authority, the participants at the meeting, which was chaired by SCAF Deputy Chairman Sami Anan, focused on changes to the electoral law. It was in this meeting that Anan agreed that the political parties could field candidates for seats allocated for the individual ticket system. Subsequently, the SCC would declare this unconstitutional and, on this basis, rule to dissolve the first elected parliament after the revolution. Participants in the meeting also pledged to cooperate with SCAF in the preservation of security and stability.

The agreement the participant parties reached in this meeting exposed their opportunism, their single-minded focus on the electoral law and their indifference to crucial issues of concern to other political forces. Indeed, no sooner was the agreement publicized than it triggered a public outcry. Then, in a further display of hypocrisy, the participants that had signed the agreement rushed to disavow it. On 5 October 2011, the Muslim

Brotherhood released a statement criticizing their party, the FJP, for signing the agreement.[55] A broad array of political movements assailed the Democratic Alliance (which began as a short-lived coalition between the Muslim Brotherhood and the Wafd Party) for flouting the will of all for the sake of their narrow electoral interests.

The 6 April Movement and the RYC called for a demonstration on 7 October 2011 to protest the pact between SCAF and the parties, the procrastination and circumvention of revolutionary demands, and any extension of SCAF's stay in power. Baradei also lashed out against the parties that took part in the 1 October meeting with SCAF. In a statement released by the NAC, he said that they had ignored the basic consensual demands that were essential to creating conditions conducive to the peaceful transfer of authority. The agreement that emerged from that meeting, he said, was nothing but a handful of limited gains that served the particular ends of the participants to the detriment of the public welfare, in exchange for their declaration of full allegiance to SCAF and praise for all the actions it had taken. The statement listed many demands the participants had ignored: a precise schedule for the transfer of power from SCAF to an elected civil authority, an end to the state of emergency bequeathed from the old era, an end to military trials of civilians, retrials before civil courts for civilians who had been sentenced by military tribunals, reform of security agencies, the purging of universities and media of old regime figures, an end to the suppression of the media and civil liberties by means of security-related administrative decrees, a law banning officials and other key members of the dissolved NDP from politics for at least five years.[56]

The controversy vividly threw into relief the difference, which we discussed in Part I, between the established opposition parties of the Mubarak era and the new social movements, such as the youth movements and the NAC, on the need to prioritize an agenda for revolutionary action to attain the revolution's aims. It also revealed how easy SCAF found it to work with those opposition parties – the very parties that the January revolution had caught by surprise – and to widen the gulf between them and the revolutionary and new social movements. Along the way, it worked to drive a wedge between the opposition parties themselves along the Islamist-secularist divide.

---

[55] Muslim Brotherhood statement on the SCAF meeting with political party heads, 5 October 2011. Although the Brotherhood website was subsequently suspended, a copy of the statement is available online: *Ikhwan Way Online*, Available online: https://bit.ly/2IvfLPK (accessed 13 July 2015).
[56] *Al-Arabiya*, 3 October 2011, Available online: https://bit.ly/2K57ouH (accessed 14 July 2015).

In the final years of the Mubarak era, political money had a fundamental say on the course of the electoral process. This continued after the revolution. Business magnates who felt jeopardized by the revolution and feared exposure of their connections with the former regime and how they made their fortunes spent lavishly to forge shields in the form of political parties and elected MPs. Huge sums of money were spent on media and campaign propaganda. Some customs endemic to the culture of political clientelism persisted as well, such as clan-based bloc voting and vote purchasing in poor and underprivileged areas. Political and businessmen's money played a major part in these processes as well as in covertly funding the establishment of new parties and financing the construction of their headquarters, the operations of their media mouthpieces and their electoral campaigns. For the most part, these processes lacked transparency in the absence of enforced funding regulations to prevent political parties from becoming vehicles catering to the interests of certain privileged groups or classes.

There were some well-known examples of the direct and open involvement of businessmen and corporate money in politics – the Free Egyptians Party and even the Wafd Party, which was headed by the business magnate El-Sayyid el-Badawi and whose steering committee included a number of prominent businessmen. But many parties obtained their founding capital from undisclosed sources. A prime example is the Nour Party, which, in the space of a few months, managed to open headquarters in every governorate and launch a massive parliamentary election campaign. It was widely suspected that the money came from the Gulf.[57] In the debates on foreign funding of political parties at the time, many alleged that the community associations operated by the Salafist Call (of which the Nour Party was the political wing) received huge sums of money from Gulf countries and individual donors from the Gulf who subscribed to Salafist ideology. The Salafists denied the allegations while Nour Party officials stated that the money was donated by businessmen who were members of the party and whose contributions had also been solicited to found the party's TV channel.

---

[57] *Elfagr*, 14 September 2011. Archived Copy Available Online: https://bit.ly/2IC5UrC (accessed 9 December 2020).

4

Sectarian strife, social protest and fears of instability

I Incidents of sectarian violence

On 4 March 2011 – that is, quite early in the transition – the flipside of the state's absence became apparent, as pre-existing tensions within Egyptian society came to the fore. Such social fissures in Arab countries are often papered over with glib talk of coexistence, Brotherhood and tolerance and platitudes about the 'goodness of the folk' who are 'peaceful by nature'. Any violence must therefore be the fault of foreign meddling or a domestic conspiracy to stir up trouble.

After a rumour spread of a romance between a Christian young man and young Muslim woman, a crowd of angry Muslims set upon the Church of the Two Martyrs in the town of Atfih in the Helwan governorate on Friday evening, 4 March, demolishing it. This was followed by a nine-day sit-in by Copts in front of the radio and television building in Cairo, known as Maspero, to protest the destruction of the church. The incident was seen as yet another mysterious attempt to foment sectarian strife, and it was widely suspected to be the work of a fifth column and counter-revolutionary militias.

The armed forces announced that it would rebuild the church 'at its own expense'. Forty-two rights organizations addressed a letter to SCAF demanding it takes the proper legal action in response to sectarian violence, while some Coptic voices accused the regime of giving free rein to Islamists to harass Copts.[1] The RYC issued a statement on 9 March accusing 'State Security officers on the loose and remnants of the regime' of inciting strife and criticizing the military for standing idly by 'as regime remnants toy with the security of the nation and citizens'. Joining in the condemnations, the Muslim Brotherhood held NDP remnants and State

---

[1] Federation of Maspero Youth, *Report on Incidents of Sectarian Violence in Egypt* [Arabic] (Cairo: 2012); 'Message to SCAF' [Arabic], *Arabic Network for Human Rights Information (ANHRI)*, 7 April 2011, Available online: https://bit.ly/39SDOU8 (accessed 1 May 2015).

Security responsible for fomenting sectarian strife between Muslims and Christians.[2] The Copts United website carried reports from local residents that a State Security informant had incited others to attack the church.[3] Similarly, members of a delegation of revolutionary youth who visited the village said that two former NDP representatives from the governorate were among the instigators. Soon after, a demonstration in solidarity with the Copts staging a sit-in in front of Maspero set off clashes between Christian protesters and Muslims, leaving 14 people dead and 140 injured, according to the Ministry of Health. The demonstrations at Maspero continued for several more days, and an attempt was made to occupy the area following the model of Tahrir Square.

The RYC called for a *milyoniyya* on 11 May 2011 to explicitly repudiate sectarian strife, organized around the slogan 'For Love of Egypt'. SCAF took immediate action, announcing that the village church would be rebuilt in its old location, villagers would be returned to their homes and those who had demolished and looted the church would be arrested.

Initially, the spirit of the revolution prevailed. The general public decried sectarian strife, blaming old regime remnants, and SCAF roundly condemned the strife and took swift measures to address it. Attempting to contain the Coptic response, Christian clerics moderated their tone, and Azhar scholars were notably resolute in condemning the incident, issuing a fatwa that prohibited the construction of a mosque on the site of a church. All of this overpowered the old pattern of behaviour that would transform an ordinary cross-confessional romance into an explosive sectarian crisis. This was the spirit of the 25 January revolution.[4] But the retreat of the values and culture of the revolution, SCAF's subsequent mishandling of the Maspero sit-in staged by Coptic youth demanding equality, the polarization of Egyptian society against the backdrop of the constitutional referendum, the so-called 'Kandahar Friday' demonstration and the contention over whether the constitution or elections should come first – all of this combined to push unresolved sectarianism, long addressed with a purely security-minded approach, to the forefront.

In the meantime, on 15 February 2011, in a world totally divorced from the events and aftermath of the revolution, various currents of Salafists, most of which had no active involvement in the revolution, met in the Al-Haram district where they agreed that Article 2 of the constitution, which designates Shari'a as a source of legislation, would be a red line. This

---

[2] Azmi Bishara, *Is There a Coptic Question in Egypt?* [Arabic] (Beirut: Arab Centre for Research and Policy Studies, 2012), 10–11.
[3] Ibid., 11.
[4] Ibid., 16.

was not surprising. The Salafist Call had organized rallies on 8 February, three days before Mubarak's abdication, to affirm the Islamic identity of the state and the need to enforce Article 2, and to respond to the rising voices demanding a citizenship-based, civil state. (The expression 'civil' here is a euphemism for 'secular'; though ambiguous and ill defined, it most certainly entails equal citizenship. The Islamists use the term as an antonym for military rule.) The meeting was the Salafist Call's response to Egyptians joining in the square heedless of sectarian barriers and Coptic youth slipping free of the political custodianship of the church.[5] In this way, there emerged a non-democratic political force from outside the revolution – one that adopted a generally quietist stance towards the old regime – making demands incompatible with the spirit of the revolution. This development exacerbated the incipient secular-Islamist divide between revolutionary forces that rejected Salafist ideas and warned about their rising influence and the Muslim Brotherhood, which, as the Salafists' rival, feared being outbid politically. The first manifestation of the counter-revolution in Egypt thus took the form of the Salafists, who took advantage of the recently opened public space in order to appeal to passions and fears, rekindle sectarianism, divert the revolution from its aims and push it down the path of communal conflict.

Concurrent with this, Prime Minister Essam Sharaf held several meetings that resulted in the formation of an important committee focused on national justice, one of whose top priorities was monitoring flashpoints of sectarian tension. Approaching sectarian strife as a social issue rather than security problem, the committee devised new methods of dealing with it, and concerned public intellectuals and political figures met with the committee in the Cabinet Building.

---

[5] Egyptian scholars, particularly Coptic scholars, are in near unanimous agreement that the dissolution of the Communal Council (al-Majlis al-Milli) after the July 1952 revolution excluded lay Copts from community representation. Nationalizations undertaken by the Nasserist regime further eroded the influence of the Coptic bourgeoisie and the role it had played in middle-class assimilation. Coptic representation in state institutions subsequently declined. With the rise of political Islam under Sadat, and as Pope Shenouda's charisma became apparent, the church became Copts' political representative, social haven and centre for educational, athletic and leisure activities, which were sponsored by the church and its affiliated associations. The Mubarak regime found this situation convenient, allowing it to control and manage the Coptic community through its direct relationship with church leaders. At the same time, interpersonal relations between Muslims and Copts were left to languish and fell victim to incitement by extremist forces: Salafists, some Coptic institutions in the diaspora and religious satellite channels – both Salafist and Christian – that were permitted to operate when tensions between the neoconservative administration in Washington and the Mubarak regime were at their height. The NDP's anti-Coptic demagoguery in the provinces during election campaigns was typically ignored. See: Bishara, *Is There a Coptic Question in Egypt?*; Andre Zaki Astafanus, 'Christian Forces in Egypt and Their Attitude to the Revolution' [Arabic], in *The Copts of Egypt after the Revolution* [Arabic] (Dubai: Mesbar Centre for Studies and Research, 2012) 106–11, and Abd al-Qader, 'Egypt: Coptic Fears', 133–6.

On 14 April 2011, twenty new governors were appointed. Residents of the Qena governorate rejected their new governor because 'he was a police officer who had taken part in acts in torture and also because he was a Christian'.[6] On 19 April, locals demonstrated in al-Sa'a Square in the city of Qena to protest Maj Gen Emad Michael's gubernatorial appointment, claiming that when another Copt was governor (Maj Gen Magdy Ayoub), the province had seen increased incidents of sectarian strife. Leaving aside the qualifications and character of Gen Michael, this was clearly a sectarian argument that equated the appointment of one Copt with that of another.

As the protests continued, demonstrators occupied the railroad tracks running south and brought train traffic to a halt. They then occupied government buildings in the governorate's capital, blocked the Cairo-Upper Egypt road and all roads leading into Qena, and threatened to cut supplies from the city's main water plant. Essam Sharaf's government responded that it would not yield to strong-arm tactics while SCAF tapped the interior minister to deal with the crisis. Salafist groups led the protest as the Muslim Brotherhood kept its distance and condemned the acts of vandalism and the disruption of citizens' daily lives.[7]

On 24 April 2011, Salafists in Alexandria, along with the Coalition to Support New Muslims (i.e. Christians who converted to Islam), organized a demonstration in front of the northern military zone headquarters, while well-known Salafist preacher Ahmed al-Mahalawy simultaneously led a bigger demonstration in front of the Qaed Ibrahim Mosque, both of them in defence of the rights of Christian women who had converted to Islam. A recurrent problem, the conversion of women is a sore point for Christians. They see it as the exploitation of a weakness and a violation of honour as conceived in the paternalistic, patriarchal culture shared by Muslims and Christians alike, especially since it is socially unacceptable and legally impossible for a Muslim (woman or man) to convert to Christianity or any other faith. For their part, the Muslim demonstrators were outraged that the church would dare detain what they claimed were Muslim women or prevent them from practising Islam. Of greater import than either party's grievance, however, is that these isolated incidents, the facts of which were often murky, generated significant sectarian resentment.

It began to seem to Coptic religious institutions and a sizeable segment of Copts at this time that the old regime had protected and guaranteed the safety of the Coptic minority. For Salafists, it looked more like the old regime had favoured Copts, and now the revolution and the weakness of the Mubarak regime offered an opportunity to change that situation. Yet

---

[6] Selmi, *The Democratic Transition*, 63–4.
[7] *BBC Arabic*, 21 April 2011, Available online: https://bbc.in/39X2mev (accessed 8 May 2015).

this was not a rebellion against the old regime, but the reproduction of its culture in mirror image.

On 14 May 2011, sectarian violence erupted in Imbaba following rumours that a Christian woman who had converted to Islam was being held against her will in the Mar Mina Church. As tensions escalated, Salafists surrounded the church and attempted to storm it. Copts responded by firing shots from the church rooftop. Salafists then attacked Coptic-owned homes and shops around the church, setting fire to dumpsters in front of the church and a nearby coffee shop owned by a Copt. Fingers were pointed at members of the old NDP who had taken part in the assault, and dozens of people involved in the violence were arrested.[8]

On 8 September 2011, the village of Marinab, located in the Edfu district of Aswan, witnessed violence between Muslims and Christians following the Friday prayer after several Muslims attempted to demolish an old building in town that Christians were converting into a church. Clashes between assailants and defenders of the building were broken up by security forces. A fact-finding report into the incident recommended dismissing the Aswan governor, building a church in the village and holding the perpetrators to account.[9] Though in keeping with the spirit of the revolution, these recommendations went unimplemented, remaining mere ink on paper. The failure to implement them, however, exacerbated related problems and fuelled the resentment and anger that ultimately culminated in the Maspero massacre on 9 October 2011.[10]

As Copts continued to protest the Marinab Church incident in Aswan following sectarian statements by the governor of Aswan,[11] tensions were

---

[8] According to a report from the NCHR, a governmental body, police and military forces had allowed events to unfold without intervening, leading to an escalation. See: *Al-Masry Al-Youm*, 13 May 2011, Available online: https://bit.ly/3gw7RST (accessed 3 May 2015).

[9] A report on the Marinab incident issued by the Egyptian Initiative for Personal Rights noted that SCAF was reluctant to address problems and that the sectarian issue was not being seriously dealt with, the better to exploit it politically. Criticizing this policy, the report states, 'What is so lamentable is not only the assault on Copts' homes, property, and place of worship and the state's failure to protect them; it is that we have seen these events unfold the same way and in nearly the same detail before. These crimes will continue to occur as long as there is no real change in how the authorities' deal with the issue.' See: Egyptian Initiative for Personal Rights, 'Report: Marinab Events a Flagrant Example of State's Bias towards Bigotry' [Arabic], 5 October 2011, Available online: https://bit.ly/3f7WTnY (accessed 13 October 2021).

[10] National Council for Human Rights, 'Final Draft of the Maspero Report from the National Council for Human Rights' [Arabic], 2 November 2011, Available online: https://bit.ly/3iUNbqc (accessed 13 October 2021).

[11] The governor's statements exemplified the conventional approach of the security bureaucracy and local executive leaders to sectarian issues: problems were downplayed; statements were biased to the Muslim majority and minimized the Christian presence; the presence of a house of worship was denied, or the construction of church was portrayed as an aggression and provocation to Islam, thereby sending a veiled threat to the Coptic minority; and the spectre of sectarian violence was raised. See: *Almesryoon*, 3 October 2011. Archived Copy Available Online: https://bit.ly/2JHPDlw (accessed 1 July 2015).

running high and the military began to lose patience with the incessant demonstrations. On 6 October 2011, the military police broke up a sit-in by Copts in front of Maspero, but the violent dispersion of the assembly did not deter the protesters. Indeed, it had the opposite effect. Three days later, on 9 October, the military police opened fire on another march of unarmed protesters in the vicinity of Maspero; as the crowd scattered, armoured personnel carriers pursued fleeing individuals, then ran over and crushed several people. A mob appeared seemingly from nowhere to assist the security forces in restoring order and began assaulting protestors, singling out Copts in particular. When the night was over, twenty-eight people were dead, according to the Ministry of Health and Population, among them twenty-six Copts, one Muslim and one soldier. Another 321 people were injured, the overwhelming majority of them civilians. It was described as the deadliest episode of sectarian violence in Egypt's modern history.[12]

Conflicting narratives of the day's events were offered. Some parties alleged a foreign conspiracy, while others accused NDP remnants of intentionally stoking tensions. Still others accused Maj Gen Abdel Fattah El-Sisi, then the director of Military Intelligence, of orchestrating events. These and other accounts differed depending on the narrator's view of the massacre.[13] Particularly striking was the flagrant sectarian incitement that day on official Egyptian television. One newscaster explicitly urged Muslims to come out and confront the Christians who were 'attacking the army' on the doorstep of Maspero. This met with severe censure from various quarters, and the day's events spurred angry reactions both at home and abroad.

The events at Maspero offered incontrovertible evidence that security forces (the military in this case) still adhered to a repressive method of policing that was indifferent to human life – exactly what the demonstrations of 25 January had turned out against – and that the old regime and its media continued to propagate a sectarianism that appealed to mob instincts, even at a time when the regime was more openly hostile to Islamist movements.

The sit-in at Maspero epitomized a new development that cannot be understood apart from the revolutionary climate. Coptic youth had begun to revolt against the Mubarak-era paradigm of state-Coptic relations mediated by the church, turning out to demonstrate for their rights as

---

[12] David D. Kirkpatrick, *Into the Hands of the Soldiers: Freedom and Chaos in Egypt and the Middle East* (New York: Viking, 2018), 92. The author reports a comment from one young Egyptian that night who said that the military was 'trying to start a civil war'.

[13] National Council for Human Rights, 'Final Draft of the Maspero Report'. It may be useful to compare this with the report issued by the military police. See: *Aswat Masr*, 27 February 2012, Available online: https://bit.ly/39WGUGQ (accessed 13 October 2021).

Egyptian citizens, though without abandoning their religious identity. A great many young people who had taken part in the January revolution side by side with Copts stood in solidarity with them.

The army opened fire on unarmed demonstrators, and a 'third party' was blamed. The media then embarked on a campaign of incitement, obfuscation and conspiracy-fuelled speculation that not only helped to obscure the real culprit but fuelled general anxiety and unease, which are always the prelude to demands for stability. The media and official and non-official spokespeople close to SCAF or other state agencies continually stoked the charged atmosphere, until rumours became standard fare and displays of contempt for people's intelligence the norm. In a sign of the fragmentation of revolutionary forces to come, the Islamists tended to sympathize with the military in the Maspero events. For its part, the Salafist Call issued a statement condemning 'the attack on the armed forces and Egyptian police'.[14]

Such reactions underlined the fact that a substantial segment of Islamists did not identify with the spirit of the January revolution and its demands, and particularly with the concept of citizenship deeply embedded in it, demonstrating a tendency to excuse injustice when it fell on Christian citizens. If there is such a thing as the cornerstone of modern democracy, it is to be found in a predisposition for equal citizenship. But democracy itself has no essence; it has, rather, values that can be cultivated or, to borrow the terminology of critics of democracy, what Tocqueville calls 'habits of the heart' or Hegel's 'ethical life' (*Sittlichkeit*).

Equality undergirds the idea that all citizens have the right to participate in politics by voting, exercising their right to express their opinions and the like. But this substantive core of democracy cannot be realized without procedural democracy since by itself this could lead to totalitarianism, in which the will of the individual is subsumed in the will of the people and the leader. By the same token, by themselves the procedures that guarantee rights and liberties, and define the prerogatives and terms of governing authorities, can be rendered meaningless, manipulated to serve the interests of the majority in compromises between interest groups and political parties and elites if the system does not protect citizens' civil and personal liberties. Absent these liberties, citizens would have no opportunity to determine the conditions of their lives through association, the free expression of opinions and grassroots initiatives. This is where the main value of liberalism – which is freedom – comes in. It is difficult to implement democracy – meaning citizens' participation in self-

---

[14] Lutfi, 'Copts in Egypt and the Challenges of the Salafist Reality', 264–5.

government – without guarantees for the political rights and civil liberties that give concrete expression to the principle of freedom.

Discrimination on the basis of religion, whether arising from political sectarianism or religio-ideological bigotry, is fundamentally incompatible with the principle of democracy. Amplifying sectarian fissures likewise impedes the democratic transition, and those with a stake in the success of the transition should unite to isolate those who play on these divisions. Procedurally, there was much that should have been done to guarantee equal citizenship and universalize a culture of citizenship, but partisan competition eclipsed this task, and no agreement was reached to isolate the forces that opposed equal citizenship.[15]

II Rising protest

In roughly this same period, in September 2011, social and labour protests were on the rise, with actions taking place simultaneously in eleven governorates. A significant feature of the late Mubarak years, labour protests were in a sense a dress rehearsal for the revolution, contributing to the development of a culture of protest among Egyptians in the years leading to the uprising. Starting on 5 February, labour actions also helped to cripple the state apparatus and institutions during the revolution. But after the revolution, labour activism gained steam. Although sectional labour actions were discouraged in the run-up to the coup in order to ensure the success of the period after 3 July 2013, initially counter-revolutionary forces had an interest in encouraging this kind of activism, in order to portray the revolution as an anarchic force and hinder the transition.[16] At the outset of the transition, some parties attempted to show that democratization was floundering by encouraging activists to make fair yet impossible demands given the circumstances, in order to derail the revolution and demonstrate that only a firm authoritarian hand was capable of reining in the chaos arising from 'undisciplined' social movements. The just social-economic demands could only be met through a negotiated long-term plan for social justice and human development under conditions of stability. Democratic forces also failed to focus the public's attention on the democratic transition

---

[15] Promoting the spirit of citizenship was a top item on the agenda of the Committee for National Justice. The committee had plans for raising cultural and educational awareness, but the focus on flashpoints of sectarian tension and the urgency of current events always delayed consideration of these issues and practical steps to implement them.

[16] *Al-Masry Al-Youm*, 12 September 2011, Available online: https://bit.ly/3gvcpZR (accessed 1 July 2015).

itself by channelling popular resentment into a purge of the old regime and the demand for transitional justice.

On 21 September 2011, labour activism reached a peak when public transit workers went on strike after negotiations with management stalled; the workers were seeking the disbursal of incentive pay, government-issued uniforms and an upgraded fleet of buses. The crisis lasted until 1 October. The 40,000-strong workforce of the Public Transit Authority had previously gone on strike in 2007 and 2009, as well as during the January revolution, before forming an independent union in March 2011. Strikes by public transport workers were seen in cities outside of Cairo as well. The armed forces dealt with the work stoppage by putting its own buses into circulation, driven by military personnel.[17]

The military was particularly angered by strikes in army-owned projects in the civil sector, where workers protested against both the military's management of factories and military rule more generally. Indeed, several strikes and demonstrations were organized against the military management of industrial facilities. Strikes in ports and airports – all of them managed by retired military officers – as well as army-run factories were particularly concerning. Workers demanded higher wages and also protested the prosecution of civilians in military courts.[18] This period also saw an uprising against governors in Suez and elsewhere, all of them retired generals.[19]

The frequency of protests increased under Morsi's tenure, particularly in 2013. In the first quarter of the year, some 2,400 labour actions were organized, ranging from strikes to demonstrations.[20] This created instability during the transition and generated a climate of chaos under Morsi. Joel Beinin writes that the Muslim Brotherhood, like the NDP, generally pursued neoliberal economic policies, engaging in what he calls the 'Salafization' of the market economy. Beinin and other writers, however, do not consider how the frequency of protests destabilized the transitional period, and they are not willing to admit the need to subordinate various struggles for the sake of a successful democratic transition, instead of exploiting the state's temporary weakness to win all demands in one go. In another article, Beinin writes that in the decade from 1998 to 2008, some two million Egyptians at 2,620 factories engaged in some form of protest action, whether a strike or demonstration. In Beinin's view, most of these protests were driven by the outcome of the neoliberal policies followed in

---

[17] *Shorouk*, 1 October 2011, Available online: https://bit.ly/3v4FhPO (accessed 13 October 2021).
[18] Abul-Magd, *Militarizing the Nation*, 189–93.
[19] Ibid., 195.
[20] Joel Beinin, 'Egyptian Workers after June 30', *MERIP*, 23 August 2013.

Egypt since 2004.²¹ The workers' demands were no doubt fair, but the drastic uptick in post-revolution actions cannot be explained without reference to the universalization of protests and strikes as part of the ethos of the revolution and the comparatively wider margin of freedom that opened up under President Morsi, as well as the politically motivated encouragement of strikes and demonstrations with the goal of fomenting instability.

Silvia Colombo writes that we can better understand the military's intervention in late June 2013 to depose Morsi, exploiting the dissatisfaction of millions of Egyptians who rallied around the Tamarod movement, if we consider the military's desire to protect its immense economic interests from the Brotherhood, which was busy replacing the neoliberal businessmen around Gamal Mubarak with its own clique of business cronies and alliances.²² The truth is that the military feared that a successful democratic transition would jeopardize its position. It therefore seized the opportunity presented by schisms in the opposition and the chaos of the transitional phase, gambling on the public's desire for stability. As for Morsi, he attempted to reconcile the existing market economy with economic populism, as evidenced by his performance and the decisions of his government and the Brotherhood. Morsi's campaign platform – dubbed the Nahda Project (*nahda* meaning renaissance or revival) – and the Brotherhood bloc's parliamentary performance suggest that Morsi had adopted neoliberalism, seeking to build on the status quo rather than overturn it.

Ironically, Morsi's programme combined a commitment to economic liberalization, the encouragement of the private sector, incentives for foreign investments and other right-wing policies with promises, programmes and the actual allocation of resources for redistributive policies that were more closely aligned with the centre-left's vision of the welfare state. This exacerbated the contradictions in public policies in the first part of Morsi's tenure, which will be addressed in more detail later in the text.²³

---

[21] Joel Beinin, 'Workers' Protest in Egypt: Neo-Liberalism and Class Struggle in 21st Century', *Social Movement Studies* 8, no. 4 (2009): 449.
[22] Silvia Colombo, 'The Military, Egyptian Bag-snatchers'.
[23] Ibid.

5

The Selmi Document, the events of Mohammed Mahmoud 1 and parliamentary elections

I The Selmi Document and the debate over the 'civil state'

Political parties were concerned that the Muslim Brotherhood and old NDP remnants were the best prepared for elections. Since the revolution had not taken power and imposed its principles, the elected parliamentary majority would thus be in a position to shape the country's constitution and system of government, and perhaps even its general way of life. The only solution was to formulate a set of foundational constitutional principles that would define the spirit and goals of the constitution, thereby denying any temporary majority undue control over the document. This is common practice in democracies, where such principles are articulated as a bill of civil or human rights or in the preamble to the constitution, as is the case with the French and American constitutions and more recently with those of post-transition South Africa and Brazil. Whether these core principles are articulated before or after elections is unimportant as long as it is agreed that they are not dependent on any temporary numerical majority.

In Egypt, secular forces attempted to retroactively stake out this position after it became clear that Islamists would use their electoral majority to impose constitutional dictates rather than pursuing dialogue and consensus. In contrast, in Tunisia an agreement around a democratic constitution was reached not through supra-constitutional principles prior to elections, but after the election of the National Constituent Assembly, which was tasked by a brief constitutional declaration with writing the constitution and acting as an interim legislature. The crucial issue, then, is not the timing of the constitution – should it be written before or after elections? – but rather the political culture of the main political and social forces and their willingness to compromise. This willingness was not evident in Egypt either before or after the elections, and the old regime and state bureaucracy weaponized this against the democratic transition.

The idea for a declaration of constitutional principles arose after the referendum settled the question of whether the new constitution would come before or after elections in the latter's favour. This necessitated the drafting of a document outlining the principles to govern the new constitution at the very least.

The National Accord Conference was held on 21 May 2011. Tasked by SCAF and the cabinet with presenting a comprehensive vision for the country's new constitution, the conference produced non-binding recommendations, generally favouring a constitution prior to elections. It further approved a declaration of constitutional principles for the new constitution, which were informed by the revolution and incorporated the basic demands of the revolution and the rights, liberties and principles to govern the new constitution, starting with the core principle that nationality and citizenship are fundamental, inalienable rights. Numerous documents formulating constitutional principles appeared at this time. The Muslim Brotherhood, for example, launched an initiative titled 'Together We Begin for the Sake of Egypt', based on discussions in meetings held on 16 and 22 March 2011.[1] There was also the 'For Egypt' initiative sponsored by the Democratic Alliance, which included the FJP and Wafd,[2] as well as the Azhar Document. All of these organizations and groups issued documents articulating their own constitutional principles, but they were unwilling to reach a consensus on a single binding document.

In a statement to the nation on 12 July 2011, SCAF asserted the need to draft a document of principles and rules for the selection of the CA, which was to be issued as a constitutional declaration pursuant to approval by political parties and forces.[3] This was also the stance of most participants in the national dialogue meetings and the National Accord Conference. The national dialogue, initially chaired by Yehia El-Gamal and from May 2011 by Abdel Aziz Hegazy, was held simultaneously with the National Accord Conference, also chaired by Gamal;[4] Maj Gen Mamdouh Shahin was the conference secretary.

At the initiative of Ali El-Selmi, the deputy prime minister for political development and democratization, a months-long dialogue process was begun on 6 August with the aim of compiling the desired document. Several versions were discussed throughout the process, which involved some 35 parties and 700 public figures. On 30 October 2011, Selmi called on political parties and forces to meet and discuss the draft document

---

[1] Selmi, *The Democratic Transition*, 111.
[2] Ibid., 139.
[3] Ibid., 150.
[4] The conference chaired by Yehia El-Gamal produced a document containing guidelines for constitutional rights that could not be amended or infringed in any democratic system.

resulting from these dialogues, later dubbed the Selmi Document,[5] on 1 November at the Egyptian Opera House in Cairo.[6] Most political forces and movements rejected the document on the grounds that it granted the armed forces broad authority to interfere in domestic affairs, particularly in its so-called supra-constitutional principles. Opposition forces argued that accepting the document would make the armed forces the de facto custodian of the Egyptian state. Selmi himself, however, told another story in his book, one barely heard through the ensuing clamour and partisan rivalry, during which the document's actual text was rarely explicitly addressed.

Selmi writes that various parties, most significantly the Wafd and the FJP, initially signed on to the document before it was released by the Sharaf government. The FJP had reservations about its description of Egypt as a 'civil state', although in the past the Brotherhood had agreed to this description. The party's reservations soon grew into opposition, and it began to insist that the document was merely a set of non-binding guidelines. According to Selmi, Islamist movements and some Islamist thinkers attacked the document without reading it. Among them was Mohamed Selim al-Awa, who published critical articles in *Shorouk* starting on 10 November 2011, arguing in effect that the document had been issued by a body without the right to do so. Tarek El-Bishry, describing it as 'the offence of the Selmi Document' in two articles on 11 and 21 November 2011 in *Shorouk*, asserted that it was an attempt by forces wary of elections to circumvent the constitutional amendments approved in the March referendum. Both critics belong to an intellectual stream that reduces democracy to majority rule, as an expression of the national will, unchecked by any restraints, except perhaps Shari'a principles. For them, the majority would therefore have the right to opt for a political system that applies Shari'a, adapted to the needs of the contemporary age and modern state.

At the same time, Mohamed ElBaradei and some intellectuals who helped write the document attacked it as well, although their objections concerned the prerogatives it granted to the military establishment. When the second constitutional declaration had finally been issued on 25 September 2011, it contained two articles (9 and 10) that were not previously discussed in the

---

[5] Ali El-Selmi was appointed deputy prime minister for political development and democratization in the government of Essam Sharaf. The official name of his eponymous document was the 'Document for the Declaration of Basic Principles of the New State Constitution and Standards for the Selection of the Constituent Assembly'. In his book documenting how the document came to be and responding to the recriminations it drew, Selmi says that religious parties called it 'the Selmi document for slander and calumny to bury constitutional principles'. Selmi, *The Democratic Transition*, 10.

[6] The text of the Selmi Document can be found at *Constitution Net*, Available online: https://bit.ly/3va3V1C (accessed 13 October 2021).

dialogues. These were added, Selmi writes,[7] to guarantee the integrity of the armed forces and the secrecy of Military Intelligence. Article 9 stated:

> The Supreme Council of the Armed Forces shall have exclusive jurisdiction to consider all matters pertaining to the armed forces and to discuss its budget, which shall be included as a single figure in the state budget. It shall have the exclusive authority to approve any legislation pertaining to the armed forces prior to issuance. The president of the republic is the supreme commander of the armed forces and the defence minister is the general commander of the armed forces. The president shall declare war pursuant to the approval of the Supreme Council of the Armed Forces and the People's Assembly.

This article does little to protect sensitive military information, as is the case in democratic states. Rather, it places the military above the constitution, making it a constitutional principle in and of itself, the equivalent of rights, liberties, citizenship and sovereignty.

Following meetings on 25 November 2011 with representatives of the FJP and the Democratic Alliance, Article 9 was amended to require only that the military be consulted on relevant legislation or before declaring war. But last-minute negotiations to save the document failed, and a mass rally was called to demand Selmi's dismissal.[8] A discussion of the document fell prey to partisan bickering, which is precisely the opposite of the consensus building that was needed around core constitutional principles. In my view, a consensus should have been reached through dialogue and pacts both prior and subsequent to elections, but the polarization made a thorough discussion of the document impossible. The contentious articles inserted by the military returned in similar form in the 2012 constitution after elections and again in the 2014 constitution after the coup, meaning that these dictates were not specific to a single document written prior to elections. Only a united democratic front could have countered, or at least modified them, but no transition to democracy was possible in Egypt without conceding some prerogatives to the army. Ironically, all the forces that rejected the military's special status to win partisan points later accepted it as a necessary compromise when it came time for them to govern. The problem was that Egyptian political forces did not know or trust one another, and their desire to power and/or fear of other parties' victory outweighed their commitment to democracy. The collapse of the Selmi Document in the public squares was the outcome of partisan point-

---

[7] Selmi, *The Democratic Transition*, 171–2.
[8] Ibid., 182.

scoring rather than a democratic dialogue on guiding principles for the constitution.

The Selmi Document defined Egypt as a civil state. This was the crux of the Islamists' objections, although the Muslim Brotherhood had incorporated the concept into its electoral platform in 2005, in the principles leaked from its 2007 platform under General Guide Mahdi Akef and in the platform published in 2011. The Democratic Alliance (the Brotherhood and its allies) presented an alternative document that was very similar to Selmi's except that it omitted the reference to a civil state.

Limor Lavie sees the civil state as a post-secular idea – a model poised between a secular state and a religious state that reconciles Islamic history and culture with modernity. In other words, it is a sort of compromise between the Iranian model and the secular European paradigm.[9] In fact, it is a pre-secular notion. It is the moderate secularism (though not named as such) that prevailed among the Arab political elite in the interwar period and even in the nationalist era. Most Arab nationalists adopted the formulation out of respect for the Islamic legacy, which was central to their disagreement with the communists. More recently, the adoption of this imprecise, ambiguous term ('the civil state') enabled secular and religious forces to sidestep a discussion of the prerequisites of a democratic state. When in the opposition, both forces embraced the term because, though vague, it entailed democracy in the sense of elections and the right to remove elected officials, referring to neither a military nor a religious state. Lavie states that in Tunisia there was a 'positive consensus' on what the civil state meant, which entailed al Nahda relinquishing its demands for an Islamic state governed by Shari'a in exchange for secular forces accepting al Nahda's participation in governance. In contrast, the agreement reached in Egypt was a 'dissensus': Everyone agreed on a civil state, but it turned out that no one agreed on what that actually meant. After the revolution, the Salafists naturally rejected the notion of a civil state, but even Islamists who had accepted the model, like the Muslim Brotherhood, refused to include the formulation 'civil state' in the constitution.[10] This debate within the political elite ultimately polarized a public that was not opposed to a civil state and equal citizenship, and was largely opposed to Shari'a-based government while simultaneously insisting on the importance of Islam as a legacy and framework of reference, as will be discussed in Chapter 9.

---

[9] Limor Lavie, 'Consensus vs. Dissensus over the "Civil State" Model: A Key to Understanding the Diverse Outcomes of the Arab Spring in Egypt and Tunisia', *British Journal of Middle Eastern Studies* 48, no. 3 (2019): 4.

[10] Ibid., 4, 7.

Lavie suggests understanding the conflict among various forces after the revolution as a struggle first over the definition of 'civil state' and second between supporters and opponents of the civil state, per se. This interpretation casts the 2013 coup as a response to popular demands for a civil state.[11] But Lavie ignores the conflict for power itself and over the military's privileges. Despite the importance she accords to the concept of the 'civil state', the term obscures more than it clarifies. Discussions of the relationship between religion and politics, Shari'a-based government and/or the acceptance of Shari'a as an authoritative reference – to say nothing of partisan power struggles – would be more productive if the term were neutralized or avoided entirely. A simple discussion of the principles underlying the constitution – should they be the principles of Shari'a? Or human and citizenship rights, which are not incompatible with the spirit of Shari'a if the latter is not understood as a system of enforceable laws? – sheds more light on positions and attitudes than viewing them through the lens of a consensus or dissensus over the 'civil state', which, unlike 'civil society', is a term defined by each party as it wished. It is not a concept with a universally accepted meaning or any established explanatory force.

If the civil state is taken to mean a modern state – not a polity representing a religious community but rather a people living in a territory defined by the state's borders – then all Arab states are civil states. In theory at least, their governments operate in the interest of their citizens rather than a specific religious group, even if the state claims religion as part of its identity or designates Shari'a as a source of legislation. When secularists adopted the term, they meant by it a secular state and made no bones about it. For them, the civil state was one that did not interfere in matters of religion. It was a state that separated religion from politics and refused to allow any party to claim to be a representative of religion or divine will, or to speak in the name of religion. And of course, it entailed a rejection of rule by divine right (which Islamists claim to reject as well).

During the debates between Egyptian secular intellectuals (liberals and leftists) and Islamists in the 1980s and 1990s, Islamists like Sheikh Yusuf al-Qaradawi initially dismissed the term 'civil state' as no more than a euphemism for secularism. But amidst fears that the revolution in Iran would spill over into the rest of the region, the Islamists were compelled to set themselves apart from the Islamic Republic. The Muslim Brotherhood, which had been sympathetic to the Iranian revolution, therefore explicitly rejected the idea of the religious state and theocratic government as an idea peculiar to Shi'ism. For Sunni Islamists such as the Brotherhood, an

---

[11] Limor Lavie, *The Battle over a Civil State: Egypt's Road to June 30, 2013* (Albany: SUNY Press, 2018), 93.

Islamic state is one governed not by clerics but by citizens responsible to the nation; they simply govern by Shari'a. In other words, Islamists narrowly defined a religious state (*dawla diniyya*) as one governed by the clerical class, a model that historically did not exist in Islam. This brings us back to the Islamists' conviction that secularism is a response to a specifically European need because the church governed as a state in the European Middle Ages, whereas there was no organized 'church' or clerical hierarchy in Islam.

By adopting the term 'civil state', the Brotherhood was able to distinguish itself from the rule of the mullahs in Iran and the jihadist movements engaged in a deadly conflict with the Egyptian regime in the 1990s following assassinations of intellectuals and terrorist attacks on tourists. It was in this same context that Islamists like Brotherhood General Guide Omar el-Telmesany began to reconcile themselves to democracy and elections, concluding that Islamists accept elections and do not advocate a religious state provided that elected officials govern in accordance with Shari'a. This accommodation also allowed General Guide Hudaybi to use the term 'civil state',[12] with the proviso that the source of authority for the civil state is Islam,[13] which secularists found unacceptable.

The adoption of a term open to multiple interpretations forestalled any chance for the debate over religion and state to become a productive discussion about democracy. In an authoritarian context, the more important issue is the relationship of both religion and secularism with democracy. After all, a conceptualization of the civil state as merely the opposite of the 'religious state' is compatible with authoritarianism. Furthermore, the stipulation that governing officials are elected in a civil state is insufficient and was not adequately elaborated. Nor was there any debate around the conditions for democracy and its relationship with religion, the meaning of an Islamic frame of reference for the state or how to interpret the constitutional provision making Shari'a a source of legislation. Would the interpretation of Shari'a be subordinate to democratic principles, or would majority rule be subordinate to a literal conception of Shari'a? A declared commitment to a civil state answered none of these questions, allowing all parties to sidestep thorny issues. Islamists' abandonment of the term only exposed the unproductiveness of the entire discussion.

Although the Muslim Brotherhood adopted the idea of a civil state for pragmatic reasons, some of its intellectuals and leaders adopted it in principle, which led them to important conclusions about equal

---

[12] Ibid., 18–9, 24.
[13] Ibid., 6–7, 24.

citizenship and the interpretation of Shari'a as values and principles rather than enforceable laws. These figures gradually found their way out of the Brotherhood, as the organization lost members in waves of defections and slow attrition. Yet even before the Brotherhood unofficially adopted the idea of the civil state in the 1990s and then officially in its 2005 electoral platform, it had gradually given up its demands for the strict enforcement of the *hudud* punishments, the literal application of Shari'a and the return of the caliphate since being allowed to operate openly after Nasser's death. These were not tactical shifts; they were motivated by a realization of the impossibility of achieving these demands in the modern state, coupled with a desire to participate in governance in the framework of the nation state. Many secularists failed to understand this, seeing every change in Islamists' positions as a mere tactical shift or, more accurately, a ruse.

The conflict outlined earlier took the form of a battle over constitutional or supra-constitutional principles. I therefore do not consider the idea of constitutional principles to be the problematic aspect of the Selmi Document. The topic merited discussion among all various political forces. Rather, the document's primary defect was the provisions inserted by the armed forces that placed the military establishment above civilian institutions and beyond accountability, leading to partisan wrangling that brought together both opponents and supporters of the constitutional principles. These same privileges were ultimately accepted in the constitution after the military coup. This fact helps shed light on the conflicts that ultimately led to the military coup, foregrounding the main plot points obscured amidst the thicket of events that transpired from 25 January 2011 to 3 July 2013. The main story of that period is the military's struggle (and behind it the deep state) against democratization and political forces' inability to unite behind the democratic transition as a joint undertaking that entails negotiating with the military over its prerogatives. The army's alliances shifted throughout until it found the opportunity to reverse the whole process in a military coup, after civil forces had been fractured by their differences. There is a distinction between recognizing the military's privileges as part of a compromise in the transitional phase and giving it custodianship over civilian institutions. The latter is not a supra-constitutional principle honoured in any democratic system. Indeed, such a 'principle' can be used to subvert democracy because it makes the military an autonomous sovereign body.

In democratic systems, elected institutions have the power of the purse – it is one of their most significant prerogatives and an important policymaking tool, as demonstrated by both history and theory. The British parliament originated in demands by representatives of the upper class to have a say in the levying and spending of taxes, particularly when raising an army and prosecuting a war. In other words, state institutions are kept in check through budget oversight. The lack of such oversight was one of the prime markers of the toothlessness of the Egyptian National Assembly under the monarchy, and later the People's Assembly after the 1952 revolution. Both assemblies were denied any detailed information about the state budget, particularly the military budget. In fact, budgetary oversight by parliament has been an animating cause for Egyptian constitutionalism and sovereignty since the Urabi revolt on 9 September 1881. At that time, France and Britain intervened with the cabinet and Prime Minister Sherif Pasha, who subsequently created a new ministry specifically to deny budgetary oversight to the Chamber of Deputies. In contrast, the 1923 constitution granted no privileges to the Egyptian army. Parliamentarians subjected the military budget to critical scrutiny[14] and discussed other internal military affairs, making independent proposals.[15] Things changed radically after 1952, but even under Mubarak the regime did not enshrine the de facto lack of parliamentary budgetary oversight in the constitution.

After the January revolution, the army sought to codify its privileges in the constitution prior to any democratic process whose outcome it could not control, fearing an unmanageable democratic parliament. But the revolutionary fervour in the streets and the high expectations of Egyptians and others around the world made it impossible for the military to impose its will. It manoeuvred instead, testing the waters and then retreating while waiting for an opportune moment. Its primary weapon was the fear of Islamist control among much of the middle class and intelligentsia and a segment of the working class and their concomitant readiness to see military custodianship as a form of protection. This was the social base that was mentally prepared to accept the conflation of constitutional principles with military privileges.

Much like Turkey, Egypt required a temporary accommodation with the military establishment that gave it certain prerogatives and a degree of autonomy in the transitional period in order to win its trust and neutralize it, to ensure that a core component of the regime did not feel it was losing everything to the democratic transition. A historic bargain like this may be needed to make reform and a gradual transition to democracy possible, but it does not entail sovereignty over elected institutions. Such

---

[14] Abd al-Azim Ramadan, *The Egyptian Army in Politics 1882–1936* [Arabic] (Cairo: Dar al-Maarif, 1977), 220.
[15] Salah Eissa, *A Constitution in the Trash Bin* [Arabic] (Cairo: Ahram Centre for Translation and Publication, 2011), 96–8.

a bargain is not a democratic, supra-constitutional principle, but rather a pragmatic, legitimate compromise in a transitional period, pending the consolidation of democracy, the transformation of the military's ethos and the construction of a professional military.

The Selmi Document was subsequently amended, but a majority of political forces continued to reject it. One might say that it went down in a popular defeat in the first round. The military was therefore obliged to bide its time until the revolutionary tide receded. Although the Selmi Document was ultimately shelved, I discuss it here at length because the conflict around it illuminates critical dynamics in this period.

Islamist movements objected to the document not because of its inclusion of military privileges, but because they opposed the very idea of constitutional principles. Some secular forces opposed it because of the military privileges while others supported it because they feared the electoral majority. (The document provided for parliamentarians to make up one-fifth of the CA.) Meanwhile, the army, and behind it the deep state, sought to preserve its prerogatives. As for the revolutionaries, they were excluded from this three-player game entirely.

A *milyoniyya* was called in Tahrir and other squares around Egypt on 18 November 2011, known as 'the Friday of the Single Demand'. The demonstration was part of the political mobilization organized by forces opposed to the document and demanding the transfer of power to civilians. Although many political factions took part, the event was dominated by Islamists, most prominently the Muslim Brotherhood, the Salafist Nour Party and the followers of Sheikh Hazem Salah Abu Ismail.

II Street politics: The events of Mohammad Mahmoud

The protests rendered the Selmi Document a dead letter, and its author soon declared the document to be a non-binding guide.[16] After the demonstrators cleared Tahrir Square at sunset that day, groups of revolutionary youth who also opposed the Selmi Document – because of the privileges it granted to the military – remained in the square after the stages had been dismantled and the protest was over. Enraged by the opportunism of the parties that had sidelined them, revolutionaries were in the mood to protest and set themselves apart from political parties. They had no plan or centralized leadership to answer the question of what to do. This spontaneity was a weakness in a period of complex alignments

---

[16] *Al-Masry Al-Youm*, 19 November 2011, Available online: https://bit.ly/3m7PXXW (accessed 15 August 2015).

that differed fundamentally from the situation on 25 January 2011. The military leadership was angry as well because its prerogatives had been the subject of derision and protest. That the army was able to single out these revolutionary youth for repression in the bloody battle in Mohammed Mahmoud Street demonstrated that the latter were on their own.

These events began the next morning, 19 November 2011, and came to be known as the second wave of the revolution because of the ferocity of the conflict between the protestors and security forces and the heavy casualties that ensued. The demands motivating the action were also the most strident heard since Mubarak's fall: the speedy conclusion of the transitional phase, the transfer of power to an elected civilian government by mid-next year, expedited trials of old regime figures, and compensation for the revolution's dead and injured and an end to delaying tactics on this front (the families of victims were staging a sit-in because of official stalling). Though the demands were just, they were championed by a group of revolutionary youth who waded into the battle alone, divorced from the larger popular movement.

Revolutionary youth, along with a great number of young people who were not affiliated with any political movement, faced off against security forces in a confrontation that lasted from 19 to 24 November. Although the Muslim Brotherhood had taken its political demands to the square the day before these events began, the organization refused to become involved in the confrontation. 'The Brotherhood sold us out at Mohammed Mahmoud' became a common refrain among the young people who participated in the clashes, among them Islamist youth, leading many of them to conflate the Brotherhood's position with responsibility for the killing. When later given the chance, many of them punished the Brotherhood by allying with the party actually responsible for the bloodbath – namely, the army.

The confrontation began when soldiers violently attacked a few hundred people occupying the square, most of them young people and the families of the revolution's martyrs. Initially, small crowds joined them in solidarity, and that first day 500 people were injured. The high number of casualties exposed the army's brutality and its mismanagement of demonstrations compared to the CSF. More revolutionaries were galvanized into action and the numbers grew to a few thousand in the following days, which exacerbated the fighting.[17]

---

[17] The Nadeem Centre estimated the casualties at 90 people dead and more than 8,000 injured. See: 'Look, Citizens: It's Crimes of Genocide [Arabic], available at: *Facebook*, 31 November 2011, Available online: https://bit.ly/3mWPhpk (accessed 30 May 2015).

A report from the Egyptian Initiative for Personal Rights examined the type of gas used in the events and the resulting heavy casualties. See: Egyptian Initiative for Personal Rights, 'Report on

The scene of events on those tumultuous days were the streets around Tahrir Square, particularly Mohammed Mahmoud Street, which runs parallel to the Downtown campus of the American University in Cairo and ends a block away from the Interior Ministry. Security forces used a degree of violence unprecedented in demonstrations during and before the revolution. Particularly outrageous was that security forces targeted demonstrators with intent to cause permanent disability. Snipers aimed for protestors' eyes using rubber-coated bullets, live ammunition and shotgun pellets. The carnage prompted Amnesty International to call for a moratorium on the export of crowd control weaponry to Egypt until the security services could be restructured. Video footage caught images of corpses tossed in garbage cans. The crackdown by security forces resulted in 5,000–8,000 injuries, including hundreds of permanent injuries, and some 90 deaths. The episode showed the Egyptian people the magnitude of the military's violence and brutality and its reckless disregard for the lives of civilians, features that became even clearer after the coup.

The events of Mohammed Mahmoud threw into relief another division that had crystallized over the past months between advocates of formal politics pursued through institutional channels and exponents of informal politics and popular action as a means to bring change. Broadly speaking, the opposition was split between those who wanted to remain in the street using the tactics of the revolution and those who wanted to move ahead with parliamentary elections.[18] (Others did not want to remain in the streets, but nevertheless feared parliamentary elections.) Arguments over the efficacy of formal versus informal politics raised larger questions about the role of civil society in this period and in general.

In this context, 'civil society' typically does not refer to the original meaning of the term as a contractual society or bourgeois society that

---

the Use of Riot Control Gas during the November Events' [Arabic], January 2012, Available online: https://bit.ly/3ixUW5g (accessed 30 May 2015).

See also the statement from five human rights organizations: Egyptian Initiative for Personal Rights, 'After Three Days of Brutal Violence against Demonstrators: Egyptian Rights Organizations Demand Indictment of Leading Security Officers', 22 November 2011, Available online: https://bit.ly/2YgI3VJ (accessed 15 May 2021).

The National Society for Human Rights and Law offered further documentation in a report following up on the implementation of the recommendations of the fact-finding committee formed in the wake of the events. The report calls the episode 'a state crime'. See: 'Mohammad Mahmoud Is a State Crime' [Arabic], the National Community for Human Rights and Law (NCHRL), November 2013. A copy of the report of the fact-finding committee created by Presidential Decree 10/2012, headed by Judge Ezzat Sharbash, can be found at: *ISSUU, Inc.*, Available online: https://bit.ly/2Ldjmmu (accessed 13 October 2021).

[18] Ketchley, *Egypt in a Time of Revolution*, 10–11. Overall, Ketchley restates Charles Tilly's thesis that protest repertoires are typically limited. Protests that follow a successful action tend to repeat more than adapt and adapt more than innovate. The result is that the regime learns from experience how to deal with protests.

depends on market economy and reproduces itself outside the state. Nor does it refer to the community inherent in the elected legislature. Rather, it usually refers to grassroots activism as expressed through civic associations, federations, unions, social movements and spontaneous popular action with the goal of exercising oversight and participating in public life outside the electoral process. One tradition associated with Joseph Schumpeter sees civil society as a burden on democracy, a type of pressure on elected institutions that could hinder their operation and lead to their collapse or the rise of a pernicious populism. This tradition believes that the role of the people should end at the ballot box.[19] Western scholars of democracy developed a negative attitude towards social activism in politics and its impact on democratic institutions following the student and labour movements of the 1960s and 1970s in Western Europe, but the notion that civil society plays a decisive role in equipping citizens for democracy and limiting authoritarian practices made a resurgence in the wake of the labour activism in socialist Poland in the late 1980s, when civil societies in Eastern Europe were seen as dependable opponents of communist regimes.

In fact, there is a distinction between grassroots political action in an established democracy and a fragile one. Similarly, the role of activism differs when toppling an authoritarian regime and when building democratic institutions in the critical, precarious phase following regime collapse. The research on democratic transitions finds that popular activism plays an important role in pressuring the old regime for expanded reforms on the way to democracy. When building democracy, however, street activism can be counterproductive, undermining the stability needed for a successful transition, creating a volatile climate that turns a broad swathe of the silent public off democracy and acting as a drag on the economy. In this sense, the Brotherhood did things by the book so to speak, retreating from street action once it became possible to work within the framework of democratic institutions and elections. In pursuing this tack, however, it split the alliance of January revolution forces, withdrawing unilaterally without consulting other parties.[20] It was more important to preserve the alliance that supported the revolution and achieve consensus within it before negotiating elections with the army.

In his book on his tenure as finance minister in this period, Hazem Beblawi wrote that after the events of Mohammed Mahmoud the cabinet met 'and the head of the ministry addressed the assembled parties and

---

[19] Joseph A. Schumpeter, *Capitalism, Socialism and Democracy* (London and New York: Routledge, 1996 [1942]), 232–302, esp. 269; Max Weber, *Essays in Sociology*, ed. and trans. H. H. Gerth and Wright Mills (New York: Oxford University Press, 1946), 294–5.
[20] Ketchley, *Egypt in a Time of Revolution*, 81.

explained the impossibility of continuing at the ministry, saying he had tendered his resignation. He also expressed regret and distress that measures had been taken to disperse the sit-ins, including by the use of force, without consulting the prime minister and even absent his knowledge'.[21]

In response to local and international criticism, Tantawi appeared in public attempting to justify the crimes committed on Mohammed Mahmoud, claiming that the armed forces had shown restraint in dealing with the sit-ins and 'sectional demands' that were hindering production and warning of impending economic collapse. He added that the military was working to reconcile political forces and was committed to a political process that would culminate in the transfer of power. He further accused unknown forces of trying to bring down the Egyptian state, asserting that they were 'working in secret to drive a wedge between the people and the armed forces'. These accusations were adopted by the SCAF-aligned media.[22] Even before Tantawi made a statement, the Sharaf government resigned. (The next day, veteran apparatchik Kamal Ganzouri was tasked with forming a new government.) Tantawi also affirmed that parliamentary and presidential elections would take place as scheduled, both before 30 June 2012, which was welcomed by the Brotherhood and other forces who were well prepared for elections. But the break between Brotherhood and youth forces had already taken place.

The Mohammed Mahmoud episode concluded on 25 November 2011 with a large demonstration in Tahrir, a defined date for the transfer of power from SCAF and the fall of a weak, inept government that was nevertheless not responsible for the unfolding of events. These events were truly a second revolutionary wave. Set in motion by revolutionary youth acting alone, they put paid to the dilatory tactics used to prolong SCAF rule. It is worth pausing at what 'acting alone' means here: Youth acted without other parties and absent the solidarity of the street, which stood by and watched the crackdown. By that time, the silent majority was turning into the anxious majority, frightened of instability – a factor that would be decisive in determining the status of revolutionary forces after Mohammed Mahmoud.

The same day, the US administration said in an official statement that 'the full transfer of power to a civilian government must take place in a just and inclusive manner that responds to the legitimate aspirations of the

---

[21] Hazem Beblawi, *Four Months in the Cage of Government* [Arabic] (Cairo: Dar al-Shorouk, 2012), 155.
[22] Tantawi's speech was aired the evening of 21 November. See the CBC YouTube page: *YouTube*, Available online: https://bit.ly/2VZ2DFU (accessed 30 May 2015).

Egyptian people, as soon as possible'.[23] Up to that point, the administration had voiced no objections to the military's hold on power in Egypt.

The new government formed by Kamal Ganzouri was sworn in on 7 December 2011. The so-called Government of National Salvation included thirteen holdovers from the Sharaf government and sixteen new ministers. The appointment of a prominent Mubarak-era functionary as prime minister demonstrated the ability of the old regime and the July Republic to place its own people in positions of power in perilous moments. Ganzouri had previously served as minister of planning in the government of Atef Sedky and as prime minister in the second half of the 1990s. His government was known for the anaemic economy at the time and national megaprojects like the Toshka project, which squandered billions of pounds for a negligible return. But he was a veteran bureaucrat with experience in the ways of the Egyptian deep state. He was summoned in a moment of crisis that had ravaged the state itself, leaving the bureaucracy flailing and fragmented in the face of street action. His cabinet was a U-turn instead of a step forward and aptly demonstrated SCAF's ability to persistently leave revolutionary forces on the back foot.

III Formal politics: Parliamentary elections

The first round of the three-stage parliamentary elections began on 28 November, the first since the revolution.[24] The last elections, which had taken place in 2010 just three months before the revolution, saw widespread rigging, generating popular resentment and ushering in the January revolution.

The alliances forged during the election campaign revealed a new partisan map dominated by Islamists. One of the most significant electoral coalitions was the Democratic Alliance of the Wafd, the FJP and several other parties, reminiscent of the old Brotherhood-Wafd alliance of the 1980s. But the Wafd soon withdrew from the coalition, choosing to compete on its own list in order to field more candidates. The Nour Party

---

[23] 'Statement by the Press Secretary on Recent Developments in Egypt', *The White House*, 25 November 2011, Available online: https://bit.ly/3uqI4Cm (accessed 30 September 2021).

[24] The parliamentary elections, organized in accordance with procedures laid out in a constitutional declaration, proceeded using a proportional list system for two-thirds of the assembly's seats and a single-ticket system in the remaining one-third. As discussed earlier, after Sami Anan met with political parties, an amendment was introduce to permit parties to compete for the seats allotted to individuals, which had been limited to independent candidates. The elections were staggered over three stages, each two days long and covering nine governorates. The first stage began on 28 November 2011, the second on 14 December and the third on 3 January 2012. Runoff elections took place a week after the first day of voting in each stage. Expatriate Egyptians were given the chance to vote at Egyptian embassies and consulates abroad.

and the Nasserist Party followed suit shortly before the election, while the Nasserist Karama Party led by Hamdeen Sabahi remained in the coalition along with the Ghad Party led by Ayman Nour and several smaller parties.

Against the Democratic Alliance stood the Egyptian Bloc, and behind it prominent businessman Naguib Sawiris and his Free Egyptians Party, joined by the leftist Tagammu and the recently formed ESDP. The traditional left thus united with the neoliberal right against an Islamist-led coalition, showing clearly that the salient divide was no longer a left-right split on the economy, but rather a religious-secular one that revolved around the nature of the state and quickly devolved into identity politics. The Egyptian Bloc assembled under the banner of 'defending the civil state', and it was alleged that their lists included former members of the dissolved NDP, prompting defections similar to those that plagued the Democratic Alliance. Most significantly, a leftist bloc of the Popular Socialist Alliance, the Communist Party and the Egyptian Socialist Party withdrew from the Egyptian Bloc. The DFP decided to go the elections alone.

The Free Egyptians Party, founded by Sawiris, received support from the business community and Christians and won seventeen seats in the 2011 elections; after supporting the coup, it won sixty-five seats in the 2015 parliamentary elections, more than any other single party, but it subsequently lost everything when it purged all regime critics from the party ranks, thereby relinquishing its independence.[25] While the Egyptian Bloc was a secular alliance that affirmed the separation of religion and state, it apparently coordinated with Coptic churches to turn out the Coptic vote. Instead of the secular-religious divide working for the party, the Egyptian Bloc was thus perceived to be representing Copts and the sectarian polarization damaged its prospects. Of course, it also lacked the electoral experience of the Wafd and the Muslim Brotherhood.[26]

In addition to the Egyptian Bloc and the Democratic Alliance, Salafist parties like Nour and the Authenticity Party formed their own coalition. The BDP, led by former jihadists, campaigned for an Egyptian renaissance on the basis of Islamic identity, articulating a national project that would involve all Egyptians.

For revolutionary youth, the most important coalition was The RCA, which included the Popular Socialist Alliance (after it withdrew from the Egyptian Bloc), the Egypt of Freedom Party, the Egyptian Current and the

---

[25] Michele Dunne and Amr Hamzawy, 'Egypt's Secular Political Parties: A Struggle for Identity and Independence', *Carnegie Endowment for International Peace*, March 2017, 10–1, Available online: https://bit.ly/3ayOhmO (accessed 13 October 2021).

[26] Ibid., 13.

Egyptian Alliance Party. This coalition campaigned on the familiar Tahrir slogan: bread, freedom, social justice and human dignity.

In addition to the four main coalitions, the Third Way List, founded by the self-proclaimed moderate Justice Party, positioned itself between the Democratic Alliance and the Egyptian Bloc, while the Wasat Party allied with the Islamist Pioneer and Renaissance Parties to form the Centre Coalition. A group of small leftist parties banded together as the Coalition of Socialist Forces.

In short, secular parties were fragmented in the 2011 elections, which left voters confused. The Wafd won thirty-six seats on its own in the first free elections in Egypt. Rather than seeing the seats they won as an achievement to build on, the parties in the Egyptian Bloc instead saw the Islamist majority in the People's Assembly as a defeat, and unlike the Wafd, they were unwilling to reconcile themselves to this reality. Faced with the secular alignment against it, the Muslim Brotherhood (FJP) grew closer to the Salafists they had previously seen as adversaries, thus replicating the dynamic around the constitutional amendments in March 2011.[27] In fact, it was not only the secular forces arrayed against it that pushed the Brotherhood towards the Salafists. As the Salafists raised the stakes, the Brotherhood feared they would draw away some of its own social base, a concern heightened by the Nour Party's surprisingly strong showing in the parliamentary elections.

The elections made the FJP the dominant party in parliament, with 44 per cent of seats. It was followed by the Nour Party, which won half that amount. That is, the two parties combined came away with two-thirds of the parliament. The liberal and leftist parties combined won no more than 25 per cent of seats, and one-third of these went to the Wafd. Revolutionary youth not aligned with the Islamists suffered a resounding defeat, showing them in stark terms the gulf between the world of protest and that of the ballot box. The Islamists claimed a clear majority in the People's Assembly: the FJP held 127 seats and the Salafist Nour Party held 96. They were followed by the Wafd (thirty-six seats), the Egyptian Bloc Alliance (thirty-three seats), the Wasat Party (ten seats), the RDP (eight seats), the RCA (seven seats), the Freedom Party (four seats), the Nationalist Party of Egypt (four seats), the Egyptian Citizen Party (three seats), the Union Party (two seats), the Egyptian Arab Union Party (one seat) and the Democratic Peace Party (one seat).

The Islamist victory at the polls in Egypt provided much fodder for theories about a new chapter in the region's political history. But the Islamist victory was expected, and the spectre of just such an outcome had

---

[27] Ibid., 16.

long been exploited to heighten fears of democracy. Indeed, the Algeria scenario[28] was widely cited as a reason to delay democratic reforms across the Arab world in the static period that preceded the revolutions of 2011. Some observers predicted darkly that the Islamists' victory would defeat the democratic values of the Arab revolutions, while others asserted that the Muslim Brotherhood assuming power through democratic means would spell the end of jihadist movements. All of this speculation was premature. Numerous possibilities presented themselves: once in government, the Islamists might change, amending their platform and political culture as required of a ruling party, or they might fail at governance. Either way, nothing would remain the same. Similarly, religious political violence typically does not end and perhaps intensifies, particularly at the margins, as state authority is weakened by major cataclysms.[29]

Eva Bellin saw the FJP's parliamentary plurality and its absolute majority with the Salafists, whose commitment to democratic principles was uncertain, as a problem for the democratic transition in Egypt, making majority rule and the exclusion of others a possibility. The bridges among anti-Mubarak forces were also weak, meaning that secular parties tended to avoid an alliance with the Brotherhood. Even so, the common experience of oppression under the old regime could have generated a shared commitment to political reform, Bellin asserted, which, with luck, might allow these forces to overcome the divide between them, at least in the short term.[30] But the shared commitment was not to be. Enjoying a comfortable majority with the Salafists, the Muslim Brotherhood had no real incentive to reconcile with secularists. It erred in choosing to reach an understanding with the Nour Party and others, thereby deepening the political rift. The organization also misjudged the significance of its majority: a parliamentary majority is not everything in a transitional phase in which the position of influential elites, the state apparatus and other parties matter.

The very fact of a new parliament dominated by Islamist parties set off successive political conflagrations, all exploited by SCAF, as we shall see.

The postponement of presidential elections angered many political forces, raising doubts about the eventual transition of power to a civilian president. SCAF sought to contain their ire by establishing a consultative council, announced on 8 December 2011. Bringing in many public and

---

[28] Following reforms in the 1980s, Algerian Islamists swept the municipal elections of 1990 and later the first round of the parliamentary elections, prompting a military coup that cancelled the elections and forestalled further reform.

[29] On this topic see, Lin Noueihed and Alex Warren, *The Battle for the Arab Spring: Revolution, Counter-Revolution and the Making of a New Era* (New Haven: Yale University Press, 2012), 280–3.

[30] Eva Bellin, 'A Modest Transformation', 43–5.

political figures, the council was to assist SCAF in managing the country's affairs. In its first meeting on 11 December, Mansour Hassan was elected chair. Abou Elela Mady (president of the Wasat Party) and Sameh Ashour (the president of the Nasserist Party and head of the Bar Association) were elected vice-chairs, while law professor Mohamed Nour Farahat was chosen as secretary.

The Consultative Council's mandate was defined as offering an opinion on domestic affairs, issues and events, as well as matters brought to its attention by SCAF and proposed laws and international conventions, pending the convocation of the People's Assembly and Shura Council. The council was to issue its opinion within a week of receiving matters for consideration, and it could make suggestions for dealing with crises that might arise or matters of concern to the citizenry in any area.[31]

Lacking any real authority, the council saw successive resignations in the weeks after its formation. The resignations were occasioned by several new political crises, especially the Cabinet Building events, which will be discussed later in the text, as well as differences of opinion on the council that precluded any final decision and the fact that SCAF did not solicit the council's opinion when it came to state management.

IV The cabinet incident, the 'military liars' campaign and the People's Assembly debacle

After the events at Mohammed Mahmoud, some protestors continued to stage a sit-in in Tahrir. But after Kamal Ganzouri was appointed prime minister, they moved their sit-in to a street nearby in front of the Cabinet Building, where they were joined by groups of Ultras, the organized football fan clubs that had become active during the revolution. At dawn on 16 December 2011, clashes erupted between the demonstrators and security forces. A SCAF communiqué blamed the demonstrators, claiming that some of them had attacked vital facilities using stones, shotguns and Molotov cocktails, injuring several people on the premises. The statement said that security forces had not taken any steps to break up the sit-in and that communications were in progress with some of the youth who were helping to maintain security and stability in that area.

In fact, security forces had already reverted to the use of severe violence against demonstrators, including live ammunition. But the particularly excessive force seen in these clashes made them stand out in the memory

---

[31] *al-Tahrir*, 8 December 2011. Archived Copy Available Online: https://bit.ly/3oFrtGO (accessed 30 May 2015).

of the revolution. That morning, security forces grabbed a young female demonstrator by her *abaya* and dragged her on the ground, exposing parts of her body and undergarments, and brutally kicked her. The incident with '*sitt al-banat*' (the best of girls), as she came to be known after video footage of the attack went viral, sparked widespread outrage, and not just because of the brutality. Censure was also directed against the Muslim Brothers, Salafists and other Islamists who blamed the young woman for the violence and degradation inflicted on her. Snide remarks like, 'And what was she doing there to begin with?'[32] – insinuating that only a woman of loose morals would have attended a sit-in – epitomized the Islamists' attitude towards that incident and women activists in general.

During those events, the nearby Institute of Egypt, a research academy founded at the time of the Napoleonic expedition to Egypt at the turn of the nineteenth century, caught fire, resulting in the loss of priceless manuscripts, books and other historical treasures.[33] Sheikh Emad Effat, an Azhar scholar and a senior official at the Dar al-Ifta (the institution responsible for issuing fatwas), was subsequently killed during the break-up of the sit-in in front of the Cabinet Building. Sheikh Effat had been the most prominent religious figure who had supported the revolution from the outset.

On Friday, 23 December 2011, tens of thousands turned out in Tahrir for the 'Free Women of Egypt' *milyoniyya* in defence of Egyptian women. Demonstrators staged processions carrying empty coffins to symbolize the activists killed since the beginning of the Cabinet Building events. A march set off from Azhar Mosque to Tahrir in commemoration of Sheikh Emad Effat.[34]

The abuse of the *sitt al-banat* brought to mind one of the most painful and sensitive issues for women in Egypt: the virginity tests the military police performed on arrested female activists. Emblematic of the brutality and ruthlessness security forces unleashed against the revolution, the practice constitutes a degradation of human dignity and an offence to honour in the prevalent culture not only in Egypt. In that charged climate, the activist Samira Ibrahim, a victim of the practice, filed a suit against the military physician alleged to have performed these tests. Although a military court acquitted the officer and sentenced a conscript under his

---

[32] The expression was first used by the Salafist preacher and show host Khaled Abdullah on his programme, *The New Egypt*, aired on the Islamist al-Nas satellite TV station. Other Islamists picked it up and reiterated it to express their reaction to that incident.

[33] *Deutsche Welle Arabic*, 18 December 2011, Available online: https://bit.ly/39W2Bqg (accessed 30 May 2015).

[34] Several video clips captured the abuses committed by the army and police during the cabinet incident. See: *Rassd News Network*, 13 December 2014, Available online: https://bit.ly/3FKGErG (accessed 2 June 2015).

command, the Administrative Court subsequently ruled that the military should ban virginity tests. The military court rejected the ruling on the grounds that the military had never authorized the practice,[35] signalling that the army had no intention to reform its behaviour towards civilians.[36]

SCAF then held a press conference in which Major General Adel Emara defended the military and denied that the army had ever used force, from the Maspero massacre through the Mohammed Mahmoud and Cabinet Building clashes. Incensed at the press conference, especially as it came on top of the media's constant airing of SCAF's aspersions against activists, the National Front for Democracy and Justice, the People's Committee for the Defence of the Revolution, 6 April and other revolutionary movements launched the audacious Askar Kazeboon (Military Liars) awareness-raising campaign. Activities included video screenings in public spaces around the country to expose the falsehood of the military's denials of its use of violence.

It was a bold and controversial move. Screenings were attacked by gangs of thugs and in Alexandria, by Salafists as well. They also met with criticism from ordinary members of the public who merely longed for stability. Even so, the screenings drew large audiences, which rankled with SCAF, forever fretting about its public image. The Military Liars campaign was another salient example of an initiative that relied entirely on the autonomous resources of the revolutionary youth and their ability to organize spontaneously at the level of the street, without the involvement of, or regardless of opposition from, the established parties and movements.[37]

Mounting tensions between the revolutionary youth movements and the Muslim Brotherhood would flare into skirmishes during the celebrations of the first anniversary of the 25 January revolution in Tahrir Square in Cairo and Qaed Ibrahim Square in Alexandria. The Muslim Brothers, who now openly sided with SCAF and against the revolutionaries, insisted on celebrating the victory of the revolution while the revolutionaries were determined to remind the public that the revolution had not yet attained

---

[35] Al-Masry Al-Youm, 17 December 2011, Available online: https://bit.ly/2JOa0gN (accessed 3 May 2015).

[36] Ironically, Samira Ibrahim, who gained international repute for her fight against these practices, would later announce her support for the presidential candidacy of Abdel Fattah El-Sisi, even though Sisi had served as director of the Military Intelligence Service at the time she filed her suit and thus bore direct responsibility for those practices in that capacity, as well as for the harassment and arrest of activists. Indeed, he was the first to acknowledge the virginity tests after SCAF's initial denials.

[37] This was not the revolutionary youth's first such campaign. Before this they launched 'No to Military Trials' and then '7akemouhom' (Bring 'em to Trial). The latter was in response to a bill proposed by Muslim Brotherhood MPs to grant SCAF members immunity from judicial investigations and proceedings.

its aims. The Islamists' triumph in the parliamentary elections also fed the tensions, all the more so because the Muslim Brothers began to make common cause with the Salafists in parliament instead of, at the very least, following an even-handed approach towards the Salafist parties and the non-Islamist parties.

The newly elected parliament was sworn in on 23 January 2012. To the surprise and consternation of many, the Salafist MPs added a phrase to the constitutionally stipulated oath of office, swearing to uphold the constitution 'in a manner that does not violate the Law of God'. In breaching the constitution in this manner, the Salafists, who had recently dug in their heels against a set of democratic supra-constitutional principles, had just sworn to uphold a completely different set of supra-constitutional principles, a theocratic one derived from Shari'a – as they interpreted it, of course. In the very first session of parliament, they proclaimed their refusal to pledge allegiance to democracy.

One might have expected the Muslim Brotherhood to develop a more sophisticated conception of democracy out of a sense of responsibility inspired by their newly won capacity as the majority party. Instead, pietistic rivalry with the Salafists would drive them in the opposite direction: to backpedalling on their pro-democratic stances. The ostentatious religiosity that the Salafists brought with them into parliament inspired jokes among Egyptians and schadenfreude among those inclined to marvel at the oddities that democracy washes up onto parliamentary shores. But the Salafists' discourse, with its refusal to commit to democracy, was instrumental in deepening the lethal secularist-Islamist polarization in the transitional process, as the Muslim Brotherhood gave into religio-political one-upmanship. The Salafist discourse had thrown the Muslim Brotherhood off-balance during the electoral campaigns, because they had never had to deal with political competition from that quarter during the Mubarak era, and it continued to taunt them in the context of the party rivalry beneath the parliamentary dome. A year and a half later, when the moment of choice came, the Salafists – above all, the Nour Party, which represented the mainstream of that movement – backed the military coup against the Muslim Brotherhood and the elected president. After their hardliner stances on the nature of the constitution drove secularists to withdraw from the CA, the Salafists allied with the coup supported by the secularists.

Disorder and confusion carried the day in the People's Assembly. The antics of some Salafists MPs seemed calculated to make a mockery of the government body to which they had been elected. A more important, yet less visible, source of the problem was that Samy Mahran still served as secretary general of the People's Assembly and Shura Council, a post he had held since the Mubarak era and from which he actively obstructed the parliament's work. The inexperienced speaker of the assembly was frequently compelled to solicit the advice of this Mubarak-era holdover. A long-serving guardian of parliamentary bylaws tailored to the NDP, Mahran had no intention to help change them.

Lawmaking was an essential means to clip the wings of the institutions of the old order, including the judiciary, which would soon serve as a main tool to hem in, paralyse and then oust elected bodies. But the People's Assembly was never given much of a chance to devote itself seriously to legislating. Parliament and the judiciary locked horns early on, with the SCC and chairman of the Judges' Club Ahmed Al-Zend leading the charge. The battle would culminate in the dissolution of the parliament.

At the outset of the last decade of his rule, Mubarak moved to restructure and realign the SCC, which had grown too liberal in his view. In 2002, he appointed a chief justice from outside the court to chair it. Justice Fathi Naguib, in turn, increased the number of justices on the court from nine to fifteen, selecting the new members from outside the State Council.[38] This was the SCC bequeathed to the transitional period: anti-liberal and loyal to the former regime. When it wrestled with parliament or the executive for judicial independence, it was driven not by liberal principles but by self-preservation as an institution that felt threatened by democracy from below. Not long after appointing Naguib, Mubarak initiated a sweeping purge of reformist judges, replacing dismissed judges with ones more focused on perks and benefits or more amenable to bribes. Then, in 2009, regime loyalist Zend was elected chairman of the Judges' Club.

The political parties that were represented in the People's Assembly in 2012 would have been wise to ally with the revolutionary forces outside the chamber, but they did not. So when the first post-revolutionary legislative body faced the conspiracy to dissolve it within less than six months after it was sworn in, it found no one among the revolutionaries or the larger masses to come to its defence. The dissolution of parliament on 14 June 2012 was the first coup against the process of democratization, and it was greeted with an eerie silence.

The SCC, chaired by Justice Farouk Sultan, justified its ruling to dissolve parliament on the grounds that it had been elected on the basis of invalid procedures. In its reasoning, it cited Article 38 of the constitutional declaration of 30 March 2011, as amended on 25 September 2011, providing for the election of parliament via a system that combined electoral lists (for

---

[38] Sahar Aziz, '(De)liberalizing Judicial Independence', in *Egypt and the Contradictions of Liberalism: Illiberal Intelligentsia and the Future of Egyptian Democracy*, ed. Daanish Faruqi and Dalia Fahmy (London: One World, 2017).

two-thirds of the seats) with individual tickets (for one-third of the seats). The court further cited the provision that the seats reserved for individual tickets could only be contested by independents. As noted earlier, the political parties held that this provision violated the principle of equal opportunity, so SCAF had agreed that they could nominate candidates for these seats. But not only did the SCC refuse to take this into account; it also refused to permit a re-election for the one-third of seats in question. Instead, it dissolved the first parliament elected in the first fair polls since the 1952 revolution, leaving Egypt without a parliament from June 2012 to January 2016. The SCC would go on to obstruct every effort by President Mohamed Morsi to amend the law to permit for new parliamentary elections.[39] It would also dissolve the CA – twice.

There was no outcry against the dissolution of the People's Assembly, no grassroots actions taken to defend the authority elected as a manifestation of the will of the people. This did not bode well for any elected body.

The dominant political forces in the People's Assembly made a number of mistakes that facilitated its dissolution as well as the overthrow of the elected president a year later. More immediately, their actions exposed and intensified partisan power conflicts at a time when the democratization process needed unity and the ability to compromise. One of the first mistakes of the FJP and its allies was to push for the dismissal of the current cabinet so that it could form one dominated by the parliamentary majority. Their insistence on this point was odd, in that only a few weeks remained until 30 June 2012 when the elected president would assume office and all the powers that came with it. As Tarek El-Bishry observed, 'This strange action from it [i.e. the FJP/Muslim Brotherhood] drove all political forces in Egyptian society to rally against it. This included forces in government agencies, influential players in the media and others with popular appeal who shape public opinion.'[40]

It helped little that the People's Assembly did not throw its weight behind the revolutionary demand to try Mubarak and his coterie. The lawmakers could have drafted legislation pertaining to the practice of dictatorship. This was, after all, the new parliament's first legislative duty, and it might have altered the course of the trials. But it only started to introduce legislation against the old regime after the FJP nominated a presidential candidate. It was not until after the Muslim Brothers became rivals in the race for the presidency that a lustration bill to bar former regime members from holding office entered the parliamentary agenda.[41] Similarly, the lawmakers did not

---

[39] Ibid., 105, 107.
[40] Bishry, *Pages from the January 25 Revolution*, 215–6.
[41] Ibid., 217–18.

move to amend the laws governing the structure of the SCC until after the court began to deliberate on the legitimacy of the People's Assembly.

Revolution means changing the system of government through an extra-constitutional process. No revolution in the world has ever sought recourse to an already-extant constitutional court. One of the first tasks of a revolution is to change the constitution. This cannot be done while recognizing the court that was created to uphold the old constitution and the old regime, and that obstructs and prohibits the instruments to change them. But the People's Assembly and Shura Council did not act as though it was their duty to follow through legislatively on the revolution's aims and to rally the revolutionary forces behind the first popularly elected governing body. Instead, they immersed themselves in the tugs of war between rival blocs as though they were a parliament governing a deeply rooted democracy. One of the strangest acts of that assembly was its declaration of a weeklong strike when it failed to have the cabinet dismissed, though it did not have the constitutional authority to do so.

Opponents of the SCC's interference in parliamentary actions on the election law and the lustration law proceeded from the principle of the separation of powers.[42] In fact, their stance was not only weak but was undemocratic in principle, which strengthened the hand of the pro-SCC jurists. Constitutional courts have the jurisdiction to intervene in the decisions of parliament if they conflict with the constitutional principles in a democratic order. This is why such courts are established to begin with: to interpret the constitution and safeguard it against fluctuations in the nature of the political majority and attempts to circumvent the principles of the social contract enshrined in the constitution. A hallmark of a democratic system is its prioritization of political rights and civil liberties, which is why it has no problem with a constitutional court intervening in the work of elected bodies. The real problem, in this case, was not the principle of judicial intervention per se, but the fact that the constitution at hand was that of the old regime, as was the court that rose to the defence of the old constitution and itself. The jurists' motives for interfering in the work of elected bodies were far from liberal and democratic. They were bent on obstructing change that might be detrimental to their interests.

The opponents of the SCC's interference in parliament, who for the most part belonged to the Islamist parliamentary majority, clung implacably to a weak argument. To them, democracy essentially meant majority rule and

---

[42] Yousri Mohammad al-Assar, 'The Status of the Constitutional Court in the Constitutional and Legal Systems in Egypt' [Arabic], in *Constitutional Debate and the Transitional Phase in Egypt: Between 25 January and 30 June* [Arabic] (Beirut: Arab Centre for Research and Political Studies, 2014), 170. Assar defends the rulings of the SCC against the arguments of its critics.

they applied it everywhere, including in the CA. This was less a tactical error than a declaration of principle that flew in the face of democracy as democrats understand it. If it had been genuine democrats speaking here, they would have argued that they had no problem with a constitutional court's powers to check the legislature, but rather with the SCC itself, because they rejected the constitution that established it. They would have further stressed that the only instruments that had the right to check the majority in a democratic parliament were a new democratic constitution that enshrined the values of the revolution and a constitutional court committed to democratic values and safeguarding them.

The SCC overturned Law 120/2011 and Decrees 108 and 123 of 2011, which amended Law 38/1972, and on this basis it ruled that the People's Assembly was illegitimate. In my view, the court's intervention in the designation of electoral constituencies exceeded its jurisdiction, but as long as it had been given the right to intervene, its ruling against the electoral law did, indeed, invalidate the People's Assembly.

Perhaps the court's ruling to overturn the lustration law, thereby making it possible for old regime officials to run in the presidential elections, better illustrates my point. The lawmakers had introduced an amendment to Law 17/2012 on the exercise of political rights to strip individuals who had held senior posts in the old regime of their right to hold office and take part in elections for a period of ten years. The Presidential Election Commission referred this text to the SCC, which found that the political ban inflicted a punishment without a court ruling, retroactively, for unspecified deeds, and in violation of the principle of equality under law.[43] In his reasoning, Judge Yousri Mohamed Al-Assar rested his argument on existing constitutional texts and principles which, perforce, did not preclude the possibility of a return to dictatorship. In form, the court was right to abide by the old constitution. But any court that expressed the values and principles of the revolution would have regarded a political ban on members of the former regime as a principle of the new order, which would presumably want to prevent former collaborators in dictatorship from holding key government offices again.

History had performed its sleight of hand. The advocates of elections prior to a new constitution wanted to take advantage of their majority before the adoption of a new constitution, then the SCC came along to rule against the majority in accordance with the old constitution. There are no ifs in history, but for the sake of argument we can reckon that if the FJP and its allies had supported the 'constitution first' principle, the SCC would not have been able

---

[43] Ibid., 194.

to impose its will on the majority because the new constitution would have upheld the values of the revolution and prevented a return to dictatorship. The majority's determination to evade the adoption of a democratic constitution or, at the very least, a set of constitutional principles, before the elections ultimately backfired. They imagined this would free them of constitutional restrictions. Instead, they found themselves shackled to the old constitution and its chief instrument, the SCC.

On 14 January 2012, Mohamed ElBaradei announced that he would not field himself in the presidential elections. His decision surprised many Egyptians who had come to see him as one of the strongest contenders for that office. In addition to his considerable political clout, he was a symbol of the revolution. He had returned to Egypt before the revolution to find the ground already prepared for him to play a major role in the opposition to the Mubarak regime, and after the overthrow of Mubarak, he remained a powerful presence in the political fray. He was particularly outspoken in his opposition to SCAF's actions and decrees and vehemently denounced the coordination between SCAF and the Muslim Brotherhood. He was among the many who suspected that the Muslim Brotherhood and SCAF had struck a pact and he called for unity against it.

Baradei's decision not to run for president crowned his rejection of the entire course the interim process had taken since 11 February 2011. Undoubtedly, his decision was informed by the dominance of the pre-revolutionary opposition parties, the decline in the influence of the revolutionary forces and their exclusion from the ménages à trois of SCAF, the Islamists and the new/old secularist parties. He would also have sensed the collusion between SCAF and old regime forces against the new faces who rose to prominence on the wave of the hope for change embodied in the 25 January revolution. Baradei's withdrawal from the contest may have benefited others, such as Amr Moussa and Hamdeen Sabahi, who were not affiliated with the Islamist movement. However, they were not symbols of the January revolution.

On the other hand, Baradei did launch a political party (the Constitution Party) as the presidential campaigns were heating up. He announced this in a statement released by his press office on 9 April 2012, adding that he would serve as the party's founding secretary. After Morsi's election, it became a hub for the secularist opposition to his administration. It then evolved into the core of the NSF, the source of the front's grassroots legitimacy and the banner of the coalition of opposition parties that would play a key role in organizing the mass demonstrations that Morsi triggered with his constitutional declaration in late November 2012. The party continued to spearhead opposition stances and activities until Morsi's ouster, after which it began its decline.

6

The Constituent Assembly, presidential elections in a chaotic climate and the elected president

I The Constituent Assembly (CA)

In its first meeting to discuss the creation of the CA on 3 March 2012, the parliament formed technical committees to receive suggestions from both MPs and the public for creating a mechanism to select members of the assembly. On 17 March, it convened again to adopt a method; after a vote, it was decided that MPs would fill half the seats in the assembly.

In a third meeting on 24 March, the People's Assembly and Shura Council approved the 100 members of the assembly by majority vote. The FJP and Salafist Nour Party claimed thirty-six of the fifty seats allotted to MPs, with the remaining fourteen going to other parties and independents, among them the Wafd, the ESDP, RDP, the Free Egyptians, the Wasat Party, Karama and BDP. The remaining fifty seats in the assembly included twelve Islamists and thirty-eight non-Islamists. Some thirty-five members later resigned from the assembly, among them the representatives of Azhar and Egyptian churches,[1] the SCC and civil parties, objecting that it did not include adequate representation for young people, women, Christians, other minorities and peripheral areas. Several demonstrations were organized to protest the Islamist dominance of the assembly.

The Islamist parliamentary majority approached the contest over the CA that would write the country's constitution after a popular revolution

---

[1] After the revolution, the Muslim Brotherhood made several attempts to win the trust of Copts by visiting the church on Christian holidays, as both a group and a party, led by Morsi before his election to the presidency. Mohammed Badie also met with a delegation from the evangelical church at the Brotherhood's central offices on 28 February 2012 and issued a significant statement focusing on partnership during the revolution and the principle of citizenship. Unfortunately, this type of meeting did not become routine and did not evolve into community dialogue on the grassroots level. See: Abd al-Qader, 'Egypt: Coptic Fears', 156–7. The Brotherhood did not succeed in winning Copts' trusts sufficiently to bridge the gap between them. This was due in part to its tactical alliance with the Salafists in parliament and the CA and in part to the constant mobilization against the Brotherhood by other parties and some diaspora Coptic organizations.

like a syndicate or student council election, as if one additional seat here or there would determine the fate of the entire movement. They did not understand that having clearly demonstrated their strength in the People's Assembly election, they could be more modest in their claims on the CA: everyone understood that the number of seats they held did not reflect their might or the influence they could wield over contentious articles. But Islamists did not act responsibly to ensure the success of the democratic transition by drawing all Egyptian social constituencies into a dialogue to reach a consensus. Competition from the Salafists, the zealotry of the FJP's parliamentary bloc and a degree of post-election hubris all served to reinforce the Brotherhood's intransigence.

Several petitions were filed with the Administrative Court seeking the annulment of the decree establishing the assembly. Finally, on 10 April 2012, the Supreme Administrative Court ruled to invalidate the entire assembly, finding that the decree authorizing it was an administrative, rather than legislative decision, and the court thus had jurisdiction in the matter.

A new CA was formed. While Islamist forces maintained a slight majority, civil society and other political forces were better represented in the new assembly. In the meantime, the SCC had accepted Ahmed Shafik's challenge to the decision barring him from presidential candidacy. Court rulings dissolving the elected People's Assembly and allowing Shafik to run for president were issued the same day, on 14 June 2012.

The dissolution of the People's Assembly was soon overshadowed by the presidential election, which SCAF had committed to holding on schedule, chastened by popular pressure brought to bear in protests in Tahrir Square, the bloody events of Mohammed Mahmoud Street and the Cabinet Building, and successive manifestations of its mismanagement of the transitional period.

II The Port Said massacre

Following a football game between the Port Said-based Masry Club and the Cairo-based Ahly Club, a massacre at the Port Said Stadium took place on 1 February 2012, the eve of the first anniversary of the Battle of the Camel. Thousands of spectators attacked Ahly Ultras and fans with sticks and knives resulting in the deadliest episode in the history of Egyptian sports, a tragedy that claimed the lives of 74 people and injured another 254. Forensic medical reports found that most of the deaths were caused by gunfire, bladed weapons and asphyxiation by tear gas.[2] I do not exclude

---

[2] *Shorouk*, 3 April 2012. Archived Copy Available Online: https://bit.ly/2VZzeeK (accessed 8 June 2015).

the possibility that the incident involved reprisals by the security apparatus against the Ultras, who had actively clashed with security forces since 25 January 2011, for example during the Cabinet Building events, in which they played a leading role.

The catastrophe sparked a public outcry and political protests from several quarters. Trying to allay popular anger, SCAF chair Tantawi promised to punish those responsible. The People's Assembly convened in an emergency session, where accusations were bandied about with much vehemence, some pointing fingers at NDP remnants, others alleging involvement by the security forces and still others blaming 'a third party' for the calamity.

Many Masry fans were arrested, along with others suspected of involvement in the incident. It is imperative to understand the dynamic of evolving popular anger in this period. There can be no doubt that the eruption of violence and random fires on many occasions was not entirely spontaneous, and certain forces most certainly exploited these incidents to demonstrate that the January revolution had led to outright anarchy and that a restoration of stability was required.

On 10 March 2012, the Egyptian Football Federation cancelled all league games in the new season after a meeting with several sports clubs.[3] This was a natural consequence of the increasingly intertwined relationship between politics and sports, two arenas bridged largely by the organized football fans known as Ultras. Historically, the game of football, the massive state and media attention devoted to it and the cultivation of loyal fan bases was seen as a way to distract the general public from politics, by supplanting political partisanship with team spirit. But the football pitch was also a place for the expression of popular grievances and sentiments on domestic and foreign policies. Fan chants from the bleachers provided an early sign of political trends, a more accurate barometer than the media for measuring the popular political mood. Mass sports, and especially football, is a complex phenomenon with its own particular dynamic in which mass psychology – particularly relatively free, collective self-expression and the expression of social frustration in an area outside the state's political control – overlaps with business, market laws, and marketing and advertising.

The final years of Hosni Mubarak's presidency set the stage for this changing relationship between sport and politics in Egypt. During this period, football and the national team's pan-African victories acted to reinforce patriotic sentiment and conflate it with satisfaction with the regime, in a general climate of national political frustration. Football was psychological compensation for a vast swathe of the public, especially

---

[3] *BBC*, 10 March 2012, Available Online: https://bbc.in/3aK7mTe (accessed 8 May 2015).

youth, and it was treated as such by the regime and its media. Memories of the events surrounding the matches between Egypt and Algeria for the African Championship, and the magnitude of chauvinistic mobilization they saw, were still fresh on the eve of the revolution. But this overlap between politics and sport is a double-edged sword: clashes between police and Ultras soon morphed into protests against the regime.

When the revolution erupted, football fans were primed for politicization, and the antagonistic relationship between Ultras and police facilitated the fans' involvement in the revolution, which in turn deepened the gulf between Ultras and the management of football clubs. Cheers were politicized, and sports events became occasions to score political points against the authorities through fan and political activities and rioting.

At the same time, the decision to suspend league play shut down one of the few remaining sources of entertainment, fuelling frustration with the revolution and the unstable, unnatural and unsettling conditions it had generated. Registration for presidential candidacy – an important step towards the transition to civilian power – officially began on 10 March 2012 against the backdrop of this deadly chaos.

III The run-up to the presidential election

Ahmed Shafik was the first person to throw his hat into the presidential ring, soon after the candidacy period officially opened. In March 2012, the Muslim Brotherhood's Consultative Council reconsidered its decision of May 2011 not to field a presidential candidate.[4] The May meeting was the same one in which a majority of the council, for what it deemed exigent reasons, abandoned its decision to compete for just one-third of parliamentary seats, to allow for greater political diversity after the revolution, and resolved instead to run for more than half of the parliament's seats. Since then, the Brotherhood's declared position had been that it would not nominate one of its own members for the presidency.[5] Nevertheless, the Brotherhood backed

---

[4] *New York Times*, 31 March 2012, Available Online: https://nyti.ms/3vlbUcd (accessed 18 October 2021). See also Azmi Bishara, 'Revolution against Revolution, the Street against the People, and Counter-Revolution', Arab Centre for Research and Policy Studies, September 2013. The Brotherhood's decision to field a presidential candidate took three meetings of the Consultative Council. The first option was to support a non-Brotherhood candidate. Judge Tarek El-Bishry was approached, but he declined to run. A simple majority of the council decided on 1 April 2013 to nominate Shater. See: *Ikhwan Online*, 1 April 2012, Available Online: https://bit.ly/3gvqKFl (accessed 18 October 2021).

[5] In an interview with the Middle East News Agency in April 2011 – that is, before the parliamentary elections and after the 8 April sit-in involving a group of military officers who accused the Brotherhood of reneging on revolutionary demands and joining forces with SCAF – the Brotherhood General Guide, Mohammed Badie, said in response to a question about other political forces' fears that the Brotherhood would win a majority in the parliament, 'The Brotherhood will

Khairat el-Shater for president, with Mohamed Morsi designated the alternate. The decision, approved by a slim margin in the Guidance Council, had serious implications for Egypt's future. The Brotherhood reversed itself after the dissolution of the People's Assembly became likely, which would leave the organization without representation, and after most political parties had withdrawn from the first CA. The decision also followed a bitter media exchange between the Brotherhood and SCAF, during which the latter advised the Brotherhood to remember the lessons of history 'to avoid repeating mistakes of a past we do not wish to see return'.[6]

According to first-hand accounts, the Brotherhood mulled the decision internally in light of new developments on the ground, most importantly its mounting conflict with SCAF since the parliamentary elections, in particular SCAF's support for the Ganzouri government against the parliament wish to form a new government. In addition, the CA was facing legal hurdles, which served SCAF's designs to meddle with the writing of the constitution in order to curtail the powers of the presidency, enable a parliamentary majority to nominate the prime minister and secure for itself a privileged position in the document. Moreover, many of the independent figures whom the Brotherhood had considered backing were not running for president, among them Tarek El-Bishry, Judge Ahmed Mekki and Judge Hossam El Gheriany, and it was not convinced that other Islamist candidates were capable of managing the next phase. The Brotherhood's Consultative Council considered two options: either the organization would reverse its decision not to field a candidate or it would back the best Islamist candidate from outside the group. Various names were discussed as possibilities, such as Abdel Moneim Aboul-Fotouh (newly independent of the Brotherhood after the revolution), Mohamed Selim al-Awa (a lawyer close to the Brotherhood) and Hazem Salah Abu Ismail (a Salafist whom the Brotherhood had backed as a parliamentary candidate in the Mubarak era). It was feared that leaving the matter up to the Brotherhood's base would have adverse consequences for the organization.[7]

---

compete for one-third of the seats in the People's Assembly, under the slogan of "participation not domination". If these fears were well placed, why wouldn't we say we're going to take 60, 70, or 80 per cent of the seats, or with God's help, we've decided to take 75 per cent of seats and we'll win them?' Ultimately, the Brotherhood fielded candidates for more than 40 per cent of the seats. In the same interview, Badie added that the Brotherhood would not object if the FJP selected a woman or Copt for its president, explaining that in keeping with Islamic jurisprudence and Shari'a the Brotherhood would not field a woman or a Copt for president, but others had the right to do so, and if the people elected one of these, the Brotherhood would accept it. *Shorouk*, 13 April 2011. Archived Copy Available Online: https://bit.ly/3m376BZ (accessed 1 June 2015).

[6] *Shorouk*, 25 March 2012, Available Online: https://bit.ly/3BTQq8K (accessed 18 October 2021).

[7] Based on information collected by the author from numerous sources in and around the Brotherhood.

SCAF waited expectantly for the Brotherhood's Consultative Council to meet. The vote on the question was postponed until 3 April 2012 – that is, until after Mohamed Morsi met with SCAF leaders to demand the dismissal of the Ganzouri government and raise the issue of the CA. Morsi put the results of his meeting with SCAF to the Consultative Council, which debated for several hours before finally deciding to vote, first on the question of whether to field a candidate at all and, then, if warranted, on a candidate. According to informed parties, the degree of disagreement was striking, indicating that the council members well understood the gravity of the step they were considering. In the final accounting, the decision to field a Brotherhood candidate passed by a margin of just four votes (fifty-six to fifty-two). When the time came to vote on nominees, Khairat el-Shater received a majority, followed by Morsi, who was designated an alternate. When the decision was announced to the organization, it stirred heated discussion and prompted several resignations. It also raised the spectre of a possible confrontation with the military, which was preparing to back a candidate it could deal with and whose loyalty it trusted.

In choosing this course, the Brotherhood began treating the transitional period as a means to insert themselves into state institutions and take power. Capitalizing on the fact that they were the most organized and prepared party, the Brotherhood made this their central goal, to which all alliances were subordinated.

It could be argued that the Brotherhood leadership believed at the time that once in power they could implement the goals of the revolution, but this depended on winning over the state apparatus, which proved impossible. The state apparatus paid no heed to the organization as it fought and competed with other political forces, nor when it formed a parliamentary majority, nor when it reached the seat of power through an elected president. Gradually, the Brotherhood found itself isolated, facing down the state bureaucracy alone, as the latter led initially an covert and then overt mutiny against the elected president Morsi. When opposition forces allied with the state apparatus and media against the Brotherhood, isolating the organization did not prove a difficult task. There was a structural dilemma underlying the Brotherhood's organization, strategy and performance as it approached power and at the moment it claimed the presidency: It had not yet shed its old self-conception, which was less that of a political party than a sect. The Brotherhood saw itself as a homogenous 'us'; everyone else was 'them'.

It could also be argued that the Brotherhood's decision to field a presidential candidate was the ideal way to prevent a coup against the revolution – one being plotted by laying the groundwork for Shafik to sweep the presidential election – especially since other forces were scattered, weak and unable to thwart such a plan if carried out against one of their own candidates.[8] And this may indeed be one of the factors considered by the Brotherhood. Nevertheless, the question remains: Why did the organization not support a revolutionary candidate and defend that candidate against such a plot? Why did it need to be a Brotherhood candidate to merit the organization's defence? In any case, it was clear that when the Brotherhood chose to field its own candidate, SCAF still held many cards that would allow it to impede the revolution's course. Most importantly, it could dissolve parliament; if the Brotherhood candidate won, it could thereby hold on to legislative authority in the absence of a parliament, to prevent the Islamists from simultaneously controlling both legislative and executive authority. This would also prevent the elected president from winning the support of the elected parliament to confront the state apparatus with a united front. Some believe that the Brotherhood resolved to field its own candidate after the intention to dissolve the People's Assembly became clear to the leadership.[9]

After Khairat el-Shater declared candidacy, Omar Suleiman filed his candidacy papers. Some observers believe that SCAF urged Suleiman to act, hoping the gambit would culminate in a deal that saw both Shater and Suleiman withdraw their candidacy. But I doubt SCAF backed Suleiman, whom they had objected to as Mubarak's vice-president. The application period was closed on 8 April 2012, after ten candidates had been disqualified, among them Suleiman, Shater, Hazem Salah Abu Ismail, Ayman Nour and Mortada Mansour; thirteen presidential candidates remained.

At the last moment, the Brotherhood attempted to push through the lustration law proposed by lawyer Essam Sultan, a Wasat Party leader, in order to bar Suleiman and other old regime figures from candidacy. Brotherhood leader Mahmoud Ghozlan asked Tantawi to approve 'the political exclusion law passed by the elected People's Assembly, which expresses the will of 85 million Egyptians and publish it in the Official Gazette'.[10] But SCAF refused to ratify the law, instead referring it to the SCC, which declared it unconstitutional. With this ruling, the court blocked attempts to exclude top officials from the old regime from returning to power. The Brotherhood declared it would take part in the Friday demonstration 'to protect the revolution', called by numerous forces. Some revolutionary forces believed that the renewed talk of the political

---

[8] See the interview on *Witness to the Age*, [TV programme] Al Jazeera, 2 March 2014, Available Online: https://bit.ly/2JOsrlu (accessed 9 June 2015).
[9] Ibid.
[10] *Akhbar el-Yom*, 15 April 2012. Archived Copy Available Online: https://bit.ly/3n1zLst (accessed 5 May 2015).

exclusion law (which was one reason Tahrir had been newly occupied) offered a chance to unite revolutionary ranks against SCAF and old regime remnants. Speaking for the Brotherhood, Mahmoud Ezzat, a member of the Guidance Bureau, said that the organization would participate in the demonstration because it felt that the people's will was being subverted and the revolution hijacked, adding that a coup against it was underway with the goal of reconstituting the old regime with the same old faces. The Brotherhood's about-turn was met with some suspicion.

Mohamed El-Beltagy, the Brotherhood leader closest to revolutionary movements since the occupation of Tahrir and the Mohammed Mahmoud events, proposed an initiative of three urgent, necessary tasks: first, the need for national revolutionary forces to unite and make the *milyoniyya* of 20 April its signal moment; second, reforming the CA to underscore a broad national consensus, absent majority dictates or minority obstruction. This was tantamount to a concession from the Brotherhood following the severe contention over membership in the CA between Islamist and civil forces. The third task was to build a consensus around a single presidential candidate to confront the old regime. This, Beltagy said, would be difficult, but not impossible.[11] The 6 April Movement backed the action, while the NAC, led by Mohamed ElBaradei, announced its support for the political exclusion law targeting Mubarak regime remnants adopted by the People's Assembly, though it added that the law was late in coming and should be expanded. The 20 April demonstration was a success, forcing SCAF's hand, and Tantawi ratified the law on 27 April 2012, again pledging that power would be turned over to the elected authority on the appointed date of 30 June 2012. (The political exclusion law was subsequently overturned by the SCC.)

The judiciary assisted SCAF in excluding worrisome presidential candidates, disqualifying both Shater and Abu Ismail, the most popular Islamist candidates. The disqualification of Omar Suleiman was more understandable. Not seeing in Morsi a threat comparable to Shater, SCAF accepted the Brotherhood's alternate. Abu Ismail's supporters protested, launching an open-ended sit-in in front of the Defence Ministry on 28 April 2012 after a demonstration in Tahrir.

Though the official reason for Abu Ismail's disqualification was that his mother had obtained US citizenship – which violated the provisions of the 2011 constitutional amendments – the decision remained the subject of public controversy for months. His supporters believed he was disqualified because of his successful campaign. Their sit-in in front of the Defence Ministry was unusual at the time, and the protestors expressed

---

[11] *Al Riyadh*, 15 April 2012, Available Online: https://bit.ly/3oEevcE (accessed 25 May 2015).

their readiness to challenge the authorities' violence, which had been demonstrated on numerous occasions during SCAF's tenure.[12] On 4 May 2012, security forces broke up the sit-in following two days of clashes between the protestors and unknown armed assailants (the clashes ended with the interference of military forces, who had previously declared they would not forcibly break up the assembly). An estimated eleven people were killed, along with one member of the security forces. The protestors then organized two large demonstrations in Abbasiya Square and Tahrir, broken up by military police following clashes with protestors. After Abbasiya Square was cleared, a three-day, night-time curfew was imposed on the surrounding area.

Military forces used water hoses and tear gas to disperse the demonstrators, kettling and then arresting several of them. The demonstrators captured several of the unknown armed assailants and turned them over to military forces, which released them, suggesting that they were on the same side. Abu Ismail himself urged the demonstrators to go home and abandon the sit-in. He had not been present at the sit-in from the beginning, which provoked a wave of criticisms and disappointment among his supporters.[13] On 5 May 2012, military forces also stormed the Nour Mosque, arresting dozens of demonstrators, men and women, who had gathered to protest Abu Ismail's disqualification.

On 6 May, prominent businessman Naguib Sawiris, speaking at the annual dinner of the WINEP, criticized what he deemed the US administration's support for Islamists, citing the US tolerance of Islamist control of the People's Assembly, Shura Council and CA and referring to the Egyptian military as a safety valve.[14] Not all businessmen were as ideological as Sawiris, however. Some looked beyond their political preferences to their interests, which encouraged them to seek an understanding with whoever ruled Egypt. In general, recognizing that it does not operate in a well-entrenched, free-market economy, the Egyptian bourgeoisie understands the significance of the state's role in the economy and the importance of placating the authorities.[15]

---

[12] *al-Ahram*, 28 April 2012. Archived Copy Available Online: https://bit.ly/39WyFuk (accessed 25 May 2015).
[13] A compilation of video footage of the sit-in is available at the blog *Mella5er*, 5 May 2012, Available Online: https://bit.ly/3neQ70E (accessed 26 June 2015).
[14] During the long wait for announcement of presidential election results, Naguib Sawiris, along with other secularists, expressed concerns that the Brotherhood would impose 'an Islamic state . . . where Christians don't have the same rights'. See: Jane Kinninmont, 'New Socio-Political Actors: The Brotherhood and Business in Egypt', *German Marshall Fund of the United States*, 18 July 2012, 3–4, Available Online: https://bit.ly/3B3BUKt (accessed 15 June 2015).
[15] For example, businessman Mohamed Abou El Enein, a prominent former member of the NDP and the ceramic titan of Egypt who headed the parliamentary industry committee, said in an interview with *al-Ahram*, 'We have to support the new president, whether it is Mursi or

The first round of the two-day presidential election kicked off on 23 May 2012. Expatriate Egyptians had already voted on 11 May over a period of seven days. The runoff between the top two candidates was held on 16 and 17 June. Egyptians abroad voted in the second round for seven days starting on 3 June.

During the campaign, old regime forces raised the alarm about the possible election of an Islamist candidate. In an interview with *Al Hayat* published on 19 and 20 May 2012, Omar Suleiman spoke of three dangers of an Islamist victory:[16] first, he said, the Islamists did not possess the personnel to administer state institutions, and 40 per cent of Egyptians are poor and easily deceived with promises of assistance such as maternity benefit and offers of rice, sugar and other foodstuffs; second, an Islamist president would head a religious state of a kind Egyptians have never known, and jihadist groups may again become active; third, there was the Palestinian issue and its implications for Egypt's ties with the United States. Suleiman opined that Egypt's strategic relationship with the United States might deteriorate:

It would be worse off than Pakistan or Afghanistan, seen as a country that exports terrorism without any sovereign decision-making authority. It would thus lose its role and its army, 70 per cent of whose weapons come from the United States. The economy would crash. There were 500 factories that are part of QIZ and which export goods to the United States, and this should increase.

He went on to speculate that there could be a military coup against the Brotherhood. The Brotherhood would thus militarize itself as a revolutionary guard against the army, at which point Egypt could spiral into civil war like Iraq. None of these predictions came to pass, save the military coup, which the Brotherhood did not meet with a militia as he had expected. All of it was no more than fear-mongering.

Before the first round of the election, pro-revolution forces made efforts to bring together Abdel Moneim Aboul-Fotouh and Hamdeen Sabahi, both seen as representatives of revolutionary forces, although the overwhelming majority of revolutionary youth supported Aboul-Fotouh. Sabahy was the

---

Shafiq.... We need... investments to grow and closed factories to re-open'. See: Kinninmont, 'New Socio-Political Actors'. Abou El Enein was also the owner of the television channel Sada al-Balad, which later became a major mouthpiece for the military coup, inciting against all critics through its main programme, hosted by Ahmed Moussa, himself a former security official known for his vulgar language against all of Sisi's opponents. Since economic liberalization, Egyptian capitalists have always accommodated themselves to the authorities in power; they have never constituted a critical force against the regime, let alone a democratic force. This applies to Sawiris, Abou El Enein and others.

[16] For part one of the interview, see: *Rasseen*, 20 May 2012. Archived Copy Available Online: https://bit.ly/2Z43da9 (accessed 18 October 2021).

option for revolutionary forces that did not wish to support an Islamist candidate, even a reformist one. There were several proposals for them to join tickets as president and vice-president, but ultimately neither candidate would cede to the other. It was yet another example of the division in revolutionary ranks, which seemed incapable of uniting. Revolutionary forces thus bear some responsibility for their own marginalization and the subsequent polarization between the Brotherhood and the old regime candidate. It should be noted that Aboul-Fotouh threw his support behind Morsi in the second round; Sabahy, on the other hand, abstained from endorsing either candidate, even as the majority of revolutionary forces supported Morsi against the regime candidate in the runoff despite their disagreement with the Brotherhood.

Thirteen candidates participated in the first round of the election. Of the nearly 51 million eligible voters, roughly 23.5 million voted, bringing turnout to 46 per cent.[17] Morsi and Shafik received the most votes, qualifying them for the runoff, which Morsi won with 51.73 per cent of the vote compared to 48.27 per cent for his 'independent' opponent.[18] SCAF turned power over to the elected president at the appointed time at the end of June 2012.[19]

Table II.6.1 shows the results of the first round of the election, demonstrating the real strength of the candidates: Shafik received 23.66 per cent of valid votes, while Morsi received 24.78 per cent. All combined, candidates opposed to the old regime, even if not all of them were aligned with revolutionary forces, received 70 per cent of the vote in the first round. There is no better illustration of the magnitude of the opportunity lost by opposition forces due to their failure to unite than the results of the first free and fair presidential election after the revolution.

The results of the election, held after more than a year of SCAF rule and coming after a period of unrest and uncertainty, can be considered a victory for the revolution. It required a special talent on the part of opposition

---

[17] Full election results for the first round can be found on the website of the *Supreme Election Committee*, Available Online: https://bit.ly/37V74am (accessed 10 July 2015).

[18] Morsi's campaign announced his victory before the official results were declared, thwarting any attempt to rig the outcome. His campaign director Ahmed Abdel Aty explained that the near-final tally indicated that Morsi had received about thirteen million votes, nearly one million more than his competitor, or 52.5 per cent for Morsi compared to 47.5 per cent for Shafik. *France 24 Arabic*, 18 June 2012, Available Online: https://bit.ly/3n1urW0 (accessed 26 May 2015). The final official results were very close to the figures released by the Morsi campaign when 97 per cent of the votes had been counted. For the full election results for the second round, see the *Supreme Election Committee*, Available Online: https://bit.ly/2Z7t8xY (accessed 10 July 2015).

[19] Hillary Clinton, then US secretary of state, wrote that when Tantawi's favoured candidate lost to the Muslim Brotherhood candidate by a slim margin, Tantawi allowed the result to stand. See: Clinton, *Hard Choices*, 347.

Table II.6.1 Final Results of the First Round of the Presidential Election, 2012

Candidate	Number of votes	Percentage of vote
Mohamed Morsi	5,764,952	24.78
Ahmed Shafik	5,505,327	23.66
Hamdeen Sabahi	4,820,273	20.72
Abdel Moneim Aboul-Fotouh	4,065,239	17.47
Amr Moussa	2,588,850	11.13
Mohamed Selim al-Awa	235,374	1.01
Khaled Ali	134,056	0.58
Other candidates	151,445	0.65
Total	*23,265,516*	*100*

Source: Official website for the 2012 presidential election, at: https://bit.ly/37V74am (accessed 10 July 2015).

Table II.6.2 Final Results of the Presidential Runoff, 2012

Candidate	Number of votes	Percentage of votes
Mohamed Morsi	13,230,131	51.73
Ahmed Shafik	12,347,380	48.27
Total	*25,577,511*	*100*

Source: Official website for the 2012 presidential election, https://bit.ly/2Z7t8xY (accessed 10 July 2015).

political forces to waste the opportunity suggested by the aforementioned figures, and yet opportunities continued to be missed in the second round.

But before turning to the runoff between Morsi and Shafik, it may be useful to consider their respective bases of support. Shafik, the candidate of the old regime, led other candidates only in rural areas, where his main competition was Morsi. He came in second in Cairo after Sabahy.[20] The three main opposition candidates were competitive in all areas and led in urban areas, particularly Sabahy, whereas the strength of the old regime candidate was concentrated in NDP strongholds in the first round (see Tables II.6.2 and II.6.3).

The aforementioned data illustrates one very basic fact: whereas opposition votes accounted for 70 per cent of votes in the first round, they made up only 52 per cent in the second round, which suggests that the opposition began to disintegrate. Clearly, some share of Sabahy and Moussa voters cast their votes for Shafik in the runoff, while some Sabahy voters abstained altogether after he announced he would do the same. But I believe that a small share of his votes went to Morsi in the runoff. Voter turnout was also greater in the second round.

---

[20] Official website for the 2012 presidential election: *Supreme Election Committee*, Available Online: https://bit.ly/37V74am (accessed 10 July 2015).

Table II.6.3 Comparison of Votes Cast

Valid votes cast in the first round	Valid votes cast in the runoff	Difference in valid votes cast
23,265,516	25,577,511	2,311,995

The difference between Morsi's vote totals in the first and second rounds was more than seven million, meaning that he received votes that had gone to Aboul-Fotouh and part of the votes of Sabahy, as well as the votes from people who did not vote in the first round. Shafik received some of Sabahy and Moussa's votes, as well as those of some first-time voters.

Table II.6.4 shows the results of the runoff disaggregated by governorate and rural and urban areas. It demonstrates that Shafik received many of Sabahy's votes in major cities like Cairo and Alexandra and that Morsi's hard majority – critical for the transition to democracy – did not include the major cities, which went to Shafik. These results point to the precariousness of Morsi's hold on power, illustrating several key facts. First, opposition forces were not united behind him. Second, the majority of the urban middle class did not support Morsi, which would make it difficult for him to govern during the transition to democracy. Thirdly, Egyptian society in the election was not divided between pro- and anti-democracy forces, with the former aligned behind the opposition candidate. Rather, Morsi's slim majority included a substantial percentage of people who were not committed to democracy, while some supporters of democratization threw their support to Shafik in fear of the Islamists.

On 14 June 2012, the minister of justice gave military police and Military Intelligence personnel the right to detain civilians.[21] Three days later, on 17 June – that is, after the election but shortly before the results were announced – SCAF issued a constitutional declaration containing several articles that limited the new president's authority. Article 60(bis) affirmed SCAF's right to intervene in the composition of the CA if there was some impediment to its work and gave it the right to veto the constitution. It reasserted SCAF's jurisdiction over all matters concerning the armed forces, making it independent of the government, and gave the SCAF chair several other authorities pending the adoption of the constitution. In essence, the declaration made the elected president a SCAF

---

[21] Justice Minister Decree 4991/2012 gave officers and non-commissioned officers with Military Intelligence and the military police judicial police powers in crimes committed by civilians. Published in the Official Gazette on 13 June 2012, the decree triggered angry reactions. Rights organizations issued a joint statement condemning the measure. See: Cairo Institute for Human Rights Studies, 'Welcome to the Military State of Egypt: Minister of Justice Decree More Repressive than State of Emergency', 13 June 2012, Available Online: https://bit.ly/3cKvd7a (accessed 15 May 2021).

Table II.6.4 Final Results of the Presidential Runoff, 2012, by Governorate and Urban Population

Governorate	Urban population (%)	Eligible voters (millions)	Valid votes cast (millions)	Turnout (%)	Morsi votes (millions)	Shafik votes (millions)
Total	42.73	50.96	25.58	51.85	13.23 (51.73%)	12.35 (48.7%)
Cairo	100	6.49	3.40	54.83	1.50 (44.28%)	1.89 (55.72%)
Giza	58.73	4.28	2.26	54.81	1.35 (59.71%)	0.91 (40.29%)
Al Sharqia	23.10	3.49	1.93	56.64	0.88 (45.72%)	1.05 (54.28%)
Dakahliya	27.95	3.66	1.90	53.39	0.85 (44.38%)	1.06 (55.62%)
El-Beheira	19.13	3.22	1.55	49.48	0.91 (58.38%)	0.64 (41.39%)
Menia	18.91	2.66	1.33	51.80	0.86 (64.42%)	0.47 (35.58%)
Qalyobiya	44.69	2.59	1.46	58.03	0.61 (41.71%)	0.85 (58.29%)
Alexandria	99.05	3.29	1.69	53.67	0.97 (57.50%)	0.72 (42.50%)
Al Gharbya	29.86	2.90	1.58	55.81	0.58 (37%)	0.99 (62.96%)
Sohag	21.38	2.34	0.91	40.12	0.53 (58.24%)	0.38 (41.76%)
Assiut	26.45	2.08	0.90	44.65	0.55 (61.51%)	0.35 (38.49%)
Monofiya	20.49	2.20	1.32	61.56	0.38 (28.47%)	0.95 (71.53%)
Kafr El Shiekh	23.08	1.86	0.77	42.65	0.43 (55.41%)	0.34 (44.59%)
Fayoum	22.51	1.55	0.76	50.64	0.59 (77.76%)	0.17 (22.24%)
Qena	19.76	1.60	0.51	33.06	0.29 (55.61%)	0.23 (44.39%)
Beni Soueif	23.22	1.42	0.77	55.92	0.51 (66.47%)	0.26 (33.53%)
Aswan	42.49	0.86	0.32	37.90	0.16 (51.93%)	0.15 (48.07%)
Damietta	38.68	0.85	0.46	55.89	0.26 (56.02%)	0.20 (43.98%)
Ismailia	45.34	0.70	0.38	55.50	0.20 (54.25%)	0.17 (45.75%)
Luxor	37.9	0.67	0.26	40.30	0.12 (46.95%)	0.14 (53.05%)
Port Said	100	0.44	0.24	58.14	0.11 (45.76%)	0.13 (54.24%)
Suez	100	0.38	0.21	56.00	0.13 (62.74%)	0.08 (37.26%)

(*Continued*)

Table II.6.4 (Continued)

Governorate	Urban population (%)	Eligible voters (millions)	Valid votes cast (millions)	Turnout (%)	Morsi votes (millions)	Shafik votes (millions)
Matrouh	70.25	0.20	0.08	40.60	0.07 (80.12%)	0.02 (19.88%)
North Sinai	60.28	0.21	0.09	46.95	0.06 (61.51%)	0.04 (38.49%)
Red Sea	95.31	0.22	0.09	43.49	0.047 (49.37%)	0.048 (50.63%)
New Valley	47.75	0.14	0.06	45.44	0.04 (63.38%)	0.02 (36.62%)
South Sinai	50.60	0.06	0.02	40.82	0.012 (49.66%)	0.012 (50.34%)
Egyptians abroad	N/A	0.59	0.30	52.29	0.23 (74.87%)	0.08 (25.13%)

Source: Ibid.

subordinate. This constitutional coup preceded the military coup by a year, signalling that military leaders intended to retain not only their privileges but their political role as well. SCAF argued that the declaration filled the legislative vacuum left by the dissolution of the People's Assembly, but in fact, in preserving SCAF's powers, it made the council a coequal head of government, even after the election of a new president, rendering the ceding of power to the president a merely formal measure without real substance.[22] When the declaration was issued, SCAF was aware that Morsi had already won the election. Having dissolved the parliament, it sought to deprive the president of his authorities, making him dependent on SCAF in the absence of an elected parliament.

So, Morsi won the election, but he did not win power; instead, he had to seize it after his election. Relying on his legitimacy as Egypt's first elected president, he annulled the constitutional declaration, much to the satisfaction of many political forces that viewed it as cementing military custodianship of the political system.

In the week after the runoff vote but before the release of results, and amidst fears that the election was being rigged on Shafik's behalf, independent liberal democrats and representatives of some opposition forces met with Morsi on 21 June 2012 at the Fairmont Hotel in Cairo to hammer out an agreement to stand against SCAF's attempted circumventions.[23] The meeting offered the chance to create a broad democratic front of 25 January forces that could form a sociopolitical network of support around the institution of the elected president. Figures in attendance included Seif al-Din Abdel Fattah, Hassan Nafaa, Sekina Fouad, Ahmed Maher, Wael Khalil, Hamdi Qandil, Alaa Al Aswany, Mohamed Elsaeed Idries and Wael Kandil. Known as the 'Fairmont Group', the coordinator was Seif al-Din Abdel Fattah. But the potential of the group to become a working framework for revolutionary forces was not realized. The first three meetings of Fairmont Group held before the announcement of election results came to naught after Morsi failed to follow through on commitments he made.

The most significant outcome of the first meeting was a statement that SCAF's constitutional declaration established a military state, deprived the president of his powers and usurped legislative authority.[24] The Fairmont Group met on a weekly basis, discussing how to reverse the dissolution of the parliament, where the president would take the oath of office (it was the

---

[22] *al-Watan*, 17 June 2012, Available Online: https://bit.ly/2JSCvtN (accessed 27 May 2015).
[23] Ahmed Emam from Strong Egypt and Khaled Hanafi from the FJP, both of whom attended the meeting, appeared on Yosri Fouda's television programme to discuss the meeting with Morsi, the goal of which was to open a dialogue with all major forces in Egypt. *The Latest*, [TV programme] ONTV, 7 November 2012.
[24] *Shorouk*, 7 July 2012, Available Online: https://bit.ly/3lRvQQM (accessed 27 May 2015).

group's idea for Morsi to take the oath in the square after being sworn in by the court), the selection of the prime minister, ministers and members of the second CA, and whether or not to join Morsi's presidential team.[25]

The attitude of some of the Brotherhood personnel around the president, and the president's failure to abide by the Fairmont agreement were early indicators that the presidency would be isolated from non-Brotherhood intellectuals and a sociopolitical base. Many members of the Fairmont Group later joined in the call for demonstrations on 30 June 2013. The Brotherhood's conduct in this context is symptomatic of totalitarian political movements that are unable to genuinely engage with allies, treating them as means to an end, to be cast aside when the organization no longer has any use for them.

Certain 'theories' about the presidential election circulated even among scholars, some of whom could not believe that the revolution had forced free elections for the second time or assumed the military's omnipotence. One of these theories held that SCAF feared that if Shafik won the election, the Brotherhood would revolt, possibly taking up arms. This would force the military to intervene, which in turn could set off communal violence. The military thus thought it better for the Brotherhood to win and be brought down by their failures of governance.[26] Such theories read events backwards as the outcome of a conscious plan or conspiracy. The plain fact is that the Muslim Brotherhood won a fair election without SCAF's help. Indeed, the constitutional declaration was drafted in anticipation of Morsi's victory. Espousers of theories like these believe that since Mubarak's fall in February 2011, democracy had lost to a deal between the Brotherhood and military. The military needed just six months to realize that the deal was unworkable because the Brotherhood was committed to a theocracy and the idea of the Islamic nation rather than the Egyptian nation state.

Cherif Bassiouni speculates that Tantawi and SCAF knew the results and operated on the basis of the following assumptions: first, that what happened on 25 January was a popular revolution that could not be quelled without killing thousands of people, in which case the military would lose all legitimacy. It was therefore necessary to depose Mubarak. This supposition is supported by the military's opposition to the presidential succession plan as well as Mubarak's appointment of Omar Suleiman as vice-president, which the military rejected due to long-standing antagonism between the military and the intelligence service. Second, the best option for SCAF was to back a presidential candidate representing the military establishment in

---

[25] Seif al-Din Abdel Fattah, personal interview, conducted by the author in the offices of the Arab Centre for Research and Policy Studies, Doha, 6 September 2015.
[26] Bassiouni, 'Egypt's Unfinished Revolution', 64.

its conflict with the Brotherhood in order to gauge the popularity of the Brotherhood and pro-democracy forces. Shafik's candidacy was thus a test, but in the end the military pulled the rug out from under him. (Bassiouni does not explain how. Did they need to rig the elections for him to win?) If the military had supported Shafik as it supported Sisi in 2014, it would have been successful, but this would also have led to communal conflict.[27]

The problem with this analysis is that it views the military as the all-powerful protagonist of events. While it is true that the army preferred removing Mubarak to suppressing the revolution, it was in an essentially reactive, rather than proactive, stance at that point. Moreover, for several months it was on the defensive against the revolutionary momentum that directly followed Mubarak's abdication, when many revolutionary forces, backed by revolutionary legitimacy, began demonstrating against SCAF. In short, the military was unable to ensure the success of its preferred candidate in the first free and fair presidential elections in Egypt. It did not pull the rug out from under Shafik, and when it was able to do so with the elected Brotherhood president a year later, it did not hesitate to seize the opportunity. In 2014, Sisi was not simply the army's preferred candidate; he was its overt candidate in the wake of a military coup. The 2014 election was neither fair nor democratic, and Sisi had to pressure politicians like Hamdeen Sabahi to run in order to maintain a façade of competition.

IV The elected president who never ruled

The president-elect was sworn in on 30 June 2012. Given the absence of a parliament, SCAF had him perform this formality before the SCC, which had recently dissolved the elected parliament. The significance of SCAF's insistence on this will become clear later in the text. Afterwards, Morsi delivered his inaugural address at Cairo University before a large audience of representatives of revolutionary groups, government bodies and businessmen and others affiliated with the old regime. Tantawi and Anan arrived late. This was intentional, of course, an attempt to slight Morsi and display their disregard for his status. The moment Tantawi and Anan made their entry, chants of 'down with military rule!' echoed throughout the hall. The brass and officials in the front rows sat rigid, stony gazes fixed forward. It was an awkward moment. Suddenly Ahmed Abdel Aty, a Muslim Brotherhood leader who was acting as master of ceremonies that day, shot up and shouted, 'The army and people stand hand-in-hand!'

---

[27] Ibid., 65–6.

The front rows repeated the chant. Then, as Morsi entered, the room once again filled with choruses of 'down with military rule!'

On 8 July 2012, just over a week after his inauguration, President Morsi issued Decree 11/2012 reinstating the People's Assembly so that it could resume its duties until the next legislative elections, which were to be held within sixty days. Two days later, the reinstated parliament reconvened. Addressing fellow MPs, People's Assembly Speaker Mohamed Saad Elkatatny reaffirmed the principles of respect for the rule of law and non-intervention in the affairs of the judiciary. Referring to the one-third of the MPs who had been elected on the basis of the single-ticket system, he said that the Court of Cassation had the jurisdiction to rule on the validity of their membership. He then adjourned parliament until the court resolved the matter.

And with that another opportunity was lost. Just before this, the various revolutionary coalitions had assembled in front of Maspero preparing to march over to the People's Assembly in a show of solidarity. They felt that Morsi's decree to reinstate the parliament was a bold and democratic move. However, the speaker of parliament had told them not to bother, as the session would only last a few minutes.[28] The leader of the FJP bloc thereby prevented popular democratic forces from rallying around the elected parliament to bolster it against the devices of the old regime. This was an early manifestation of an approach that would ultimately leave Muslim Brotherhood leaders alone and defenceless in their facedown with the old regime. After allying with the Nour Party in parliament and the CA, and after sidling up to SCAF and trying to curry favour with the old regime, even after parliament was dissolved, the Muslim Brotherhood leadership would be hard put to find allies later on.

The SCC overturned the presidential decree reinstating the People's Assembly and ordered the execution of its original ruling without modification. Morsi's decree would have been a sound move had it had the solid backing of revolutionary and popular alliances capable of challenging the SCC. But the other political parties in parliament did not side with Morsi, contrary to his expectations. Rather, they accused him of infringing upon the remit and independence of the judiciary. They had chosen to act as opposition parties even if this entailed siding with a constitutional court bent on obstructing democratic transformation. They evidently failed to realize that, in a time of transition, being a partner in a process of democratization outweighed thwarting a ruling party. Meanwhile, SCAF cast itself as the ever vigilant and ardent defender of judicial independence.

---

[28] Seif al-Din Abdel Fattah, personal interview.

When Morsi ordered the dismissal of the public prosecutor, there was nothing to prevent the same scenario from recurring: the judiciary remained a party to the conflict, and there was no transitional justice process underway with an extraordinary prosecutorial component compatible with the revolutionary aspiration for radical transformation based on revolutionary legitimacy. The ongoing battles with the judiciary in the absence of a serious transitional or revolutionary alternative angered many legal experts at the time.

The lack of a strong and broad-based sociopolitical coalition continued to cast its shadow over Morsi's actions and battles. We see it in evidence, again, in his choice of a technocrat to form a government rather than a charismatic political figure who could serve as a powerful ally in the fight against the deep state. On 24 July 2012, Morsi tasked Hisham Qandil with forming a new cabinet to succeed the Ganzouri government. After a week of consultations, it was sworn in on 2 August 2012, with President Morsi administering the oath of office.

The Qandil government subsequently underwent several reshuffles in order to absorb popular anger or to resolve internal disputes. The most salient instances occurred in January and May 2013. For the most part, the members of his cabinets were independents, which is to say unaffiliated with a political party. Qandil himself had served as minister of water resources and irrigation in both the Sharaf and Ganzouri governments. He became the youngest prime minister in the history of Egypt and remained in his post until Morsi was overthrown. His government acted in a caretaker capacity from the outset, but it quickly found itself reeling beneath the deluge of demands and high expectations. This was not a government designed to lead the political confrontation that this phase required. It did not even conceive of itself as a spearhead in the struggle to secure the foundations of democracy against the resistance of the old regime.

A good place to start, and one that would have won widespread support, was the reform of the internal security apparatus, which remained as central a demand as it had been since the outset of the revolution. The police force itself had been thrown into upheaval and internal division following the outbreak of the revolution. On 29 July 2012, the Interior Ministry underwent the most sweeping shake-up in that institution's history. In the course of extensive transfers and promotions, 454 generals were pensioned off, 6 new assistant interior ministers were appointed, 6 security directorate chiefs were appointed at the governorate level and a new director was assigned to the General Administration of Elections.[29]

---

[29] *Al-Masry Al-Youm*, 29 July 2012, Available Online: https://bit.ly/2K2PEjD (accessed 2 July 2015).

But the changes were purely cosmetic. The ministry's outlook had not changed, as was palpably clear in the way the ministry challenged the elected president himself.

On 5 August 2012, shortly before Qandil's cabinet met for the first time, armed men attacked a military post at the Karam Abu Salem border crossing in Rafah. It was the middle of Ramadan. Sixteen Egyptian servicemen were killed and seven were wounded while breaking their fast after sunset. The gunmen then seized two armoured vehicles from a security checkpoint and attacked the Israeli border. The Israeli army intercepted the attackers and announced it had killed eight of them.[30] Morsi, the defence minister and the army chief of staff flew to Sinai. Before an investigation could even begin, media and certain political quarters began to blame the president for the incident, although the attack occurred in a border zone that fell under the responsibility of the army. Two days later, Qandil was assailed with verbal abuse from the crowds during the funeral procession for the slain soldiers, even though the army had organized the ceremony. Morsi did not attend the funeral, evidently having been warned that a similar reception awaited him. Instead, he went to the Qubba Military Hospital to visit the injured soldiers. Afterwards, he returned to his office and called an emergency meeting of party and military officials to discuss the latest developments.

Held later that same day, the meeting was attended by Mohamed Saad Elkatatny, Essam el-Erian (FJP), Emad Abdel Ghafour (Nour Party), Abou Elela Mady (Wasat), Safwat Abdel Ghany (BDP) and Ayman Nour (Ghad). The most important military figures present were Military Intelligence Director Abdel Fattah El-Sisi and Interior Minister Ahmed Gamal El Din; Defence Minister Mohamed Tantawi and Chief of Staff Sami Anan were exempted. I had the opportunity to interview one of the attendees, Seif al-Din Abdel Fattah, who related that Morsi asked Sisi and Gamal El Din to explain to those present what had happened. Their accounts were so ambiguous and lacking in detail that, at one point, Mady turned to the president and said, 'We didn't come here to listen to the type of generalities we read in the press. He hasn't said anything.' Also according to Seif al-Din, Sisi only addressed Morsi when he spoke, barely even looking at the other participants. When Morsi interrupted him to ask him to 'speak to the people here', Sisi would soon turn back to the president and act as though no one else were present in the room.[31] I included this observation here because it is indicative of Sisi's attitude towards civilians.

[30] CNN Arabic, 6 August 2012, Available Online: https://cnn.it/3phjFim (accessed 2 July 2015).
[31] Seif al-Din Abdel Fattah, personal interview. I believe that this description is remarkable for its visible semiotic embodiment of Sisi's attitudes towards political parties and civilians in general and

Henceforward, the new rules of play became increasingly apparent. The old regime forces and the media owned by Egyptian businessmen (outright or as facades for entrepreneurs from the Gulf) took advantage of the nearly limitless climate of freedom of expression to blame the president for every problem. The opposition parties, including the ones that had supported the revolution, acted as if it were their main duty to oppose Morsi and make him fail. It was as though they had lost all sense of a higher national duty to ensure a successful transition to democracy. At the same time, despite the fact that Morsi was elected by a very narrow majority, he and the Muslim Brotherhood

> hastened to behave like any ruling coalition that makes decisions and governs alone, as if it were in a firmly established democracy. In response to its critics, the ruling party would reiterate, on a daily basis, that it is the opposition's right to oppose, and it is their [the ruling party's] right to rule. The new ruling party did not in any way understand the importance of partnership in periods of transition, something it sorely needed in the face of the old state apparatus.[32]

Both sides behaved as though Egypt were an entrenched democracy with at least a century's worth of democratic traditions. So, while one side focused on staying in power and the other side focused on staying the course in opposition, unity against an implacable enemy to democratization got lost in between.

The repercussions of the Karam Abu Salem terrorist attack operated at two levels. The first and most immediate was the political contest between SCAF and Morsi, who seized the opportunity to transfer or dismiss several senior military leaders. The second was the military response, which entailed a sweeping counterterrorist campaign against militant Islamist groups and organizations in Sinai. Never before, since the Egyptian-Israeli peace treaty was signed, had the Egyptian armed forces moved such quantities of heavy military equipment into Sinai, heedless of the protocols which barred any Egyptian militarized presence in the border zone.

On 7 August 2012, Morsi dismissed General Intelligence Director Murad Mowafi and replaced him with Mohammad Raafat Shehata, who came from within the agency.[33] He also dismissed Abdel Wahab Mabrouk as governor of North Sinai and appointed Mohamed Ahmed Zaki as

---

his deference to the highest-ranking person present. He added that the next day he spotted General Sisi, who had become defence minister, walking down a long corridor in the presidential palace towards President Morsi in order to kiss the president's head.

[32] Bishara, 'Revolution against Revolution', 13–14.
[33] Shehata remained the director of GIS throughout the Morsi era without actually running the agency. The deep state had no intention of taking orders from someone appointed by Morsi. Shehata was one of the first Morsi appointees removed from his post after the coup. He was appointed adviser

commander of the Republican Guard; ironically, Zaki would be the person to arrest Morsi after the coup. In the following days, Morsi made a series of surprise decisions that sent shockwaves across the country and shifted the balance of power between the presidency and the army in favour of the former. He retired both Defence Minister Mohamed Hussein Tantawi and Chief of Staff Sami Anan, replacing them, respectively, with General Abdel Fattah El-Sisi[34] and Major General Sedki Sobhy.[35] One credible source asserts that Sisi personally negotiated the dismissals with Morsi.[36]

Hellyer posits that Morsi was not strong enough on his own to overthrow the army leadership. He would have needed a coup from within the army hierarchy staged by ambitious officers. According to him, that is precisely what happened: Morsi acted not as president but as a collaborator who stood to benefit from the internal coup and was happy to help camouflage it. Morsi and SCAF both wanted Tantawi and his circle out of the army, so they worked out a mutually beneficial arrangement towards that end. Given the strong ties between SCAF members and the United States, they would have most likely notified Washington of this arrangement, and, in fact, there were reports that the United States had received some advance notice that there would be changes in SCAF.[37]

I do not support this reading. I am more inclined to believe that the ouster of Tantawi, Anan and others came at the initiative of Morsi, but likely involved pledges of appointments to ambitious officers like Sisi, who, in his capacity as director of the Military Intelligence Service, was in a position to furnish Morsi with sufficient information on the potential impact on the army of such a move. This was a presidential decree coordinated with the officers who would replace the outgoing generals. Also arguing against the internal coup hypothesis is that Tantawi was treated with respect and that Sisi and Tantawi remained close after 2013.

Morsi also appointed Judge Ahmed Mekki as his vice-president and rescinded the constitutional declaration that SCAF issued only days before the results of the presidential elections were announced, in a bid

---

on strategic affairs to interim president Adly Mansour, but he never exercised the functions of that post either.

[34] Gilbert Achcar reminds us how Sisi, when he was director of Military Intelligence, 'had distinguished himself in June 2011 by justifying the "virginity tests" that the SCAF had inflicted, among other humiliations, on 17 female demonstrators who had been arrested on Tahrir Square in March'. Achcar adds, 'Sisi's declarations were such an embarrassment that the SCAF was forced to publicly disavow him.' See: Gilbert Achcar, *The People Want: A Radical Exploration of the Arab Uprising*, trans. G. M. Goshgarian (Beirut: Saqi, 2013), 225–6.

[35] *BBC Arabic*, 8 August 2012, Available Online: https://bbc.in/3pcCpPW (accessed 6 June 2015).

[36] David Ottaway and Marina Ottaway, 'Egypt's Leaderless Revolution', *Cairo Review of Global Affairs*, no. 17 (Spring 2015).

[37] H. A. Hellyer, 'Military or President: Who Calls the Shots in Egypt', *Brookings*, 24 August 2012, Available Online: https://brook.gs/3lVNbYY (accessed 19 October 2021).

to limit the powers of the elected president. However, Hellyer overlooked this in his assessment. It does not stand to reason that a constitutional declaration issued by the military would be repealed by the same military after an internal coup. The military's constitutional declaration sparked a widespread outcry when it was announced on 17 June 2012, and its repeal met with equally widespread relief. Morsi's shake-up of the armed forces leadership was similarly welcomed due to the deterioration of the army's public image as the result of its role during the transitional phase under SCAF.

The steps Morsi took that day marked the true founding moment of his legitimacy, precisely because of the popularity of these measures, which, moreover, spoke to the general yearning for a strong president capable of ending an extended period of anarchy and confusion. Morsi was at the height of his power at that point. A collection of forces led by former MP Mohamed Abu Hamed tried to mobilize a *milyoniyya* on 24 August 2012 to call for the overthrow of Morsi and Muslim Brotherhood rule. The turnout was very low compared to the mass demonstrations seen in Egypt in the year and a half since the January revolution.[38]

That moment of power and revolutionary legitimacy offered an unprecedented window to implement a package of reforms and hem in old regime forces. The pro-revolutionary forces were certainly keen to work with a president ready to lead the way. But Morsi did not pursue that route. He shrugged off the revolutionary coalitions out of the belief that he had found a reliable ally in the head of Military Intelligence.

In his search for a powerful ally among the generals, Morsi proved willing to turn a blind eye to the crimes Military Intelligence had committed during the revolution and afterwards. But perhaps his failure to bring Sisi to account for these offences and the apparent ease with which he fell for the hype about Sisi's religious devoutness, as though piety was a sufficient job qualification, were the least of Morsi's mistakes when he decided to make Sisi his minister of defence. Here was a man who knew the most intimate secrets and weaknesses of army officers. Moreover, Military Intelligence had taken control of the SSIS after demonstrators had stormed its offices the previous year. So, Sisi had access to the SSIS's network of contacts and intelligence, complete with reams of information on the press, political parties, activists and political life in general. According to my interviews with politicians and activists who had met with Sisi directly

---

[38] But the pattern would continue. Leaks from the defence minister's office after the coup and before Sisi became president revealed that such actions received encouragement from Sisi and his office. They would escalate until Morsi's overthrow. Less than a year later, a similar campaign launched in Spring 2013 would gain momentum and succeed.

after the revolution and early in the transition, he was something of a political chameleon. Nasserists took him to be a Nasserist and Islamists thought of him as one of theirs, but at heart he believed in military rule. Sisi also excelled in playing the faithful soldier to his commander-in-chief, as attested by the accounts of ministers who took part in cabinet and security council meetings he attended.[39] In short, Morsi's appointment of Sisi as defence minister would cost him the presidency and compel Egypt to pay an incalculable price.

In mid-October 2012, legal proceedings were initiated against Anan and Tantawi on charges related to the killing of demonstrators during the revolution. In a revealing sign of his desire to reconcile with the old regime, Morsi leapt to their defence.[40] This was a stratagem, not an inadvertent blunder. Another significant example of this strategy was his decision to withhold publication of the report by the fact-finding committee he had formed to investigate rights abuses committed during the 2011 uprisings. Such attempts to play up to the army would subsequently contradict arguments Morsi made in his own defence during the so-called 'Hamas espionage' case. During that trial, he accused Sisi and other military officials of responsibility for 'the bloodshed after 25 January 2011 and until he became president'. Morsi further testified that armed civilians in the employ of Military Intelligence, which was under Sisi's command, commandeered rooms in various buildings in Tahrir Square and that the report released by the fact-finding committee in late 2012 confirmed this. As to why he had not ordered the arrest of Sisi and the other officers responsible for the murders, Morsi responded that he wanted to avoid harming the military establishment: 'I didn't want it to be put about that it was headed by a criminal, so I waited until the results of the investigations to ensure that the institution would remain safe.' He also accused Sisi of a conspiracy to stage a coup in collusion with SCC chief justice Adly Mansour and Interior Minister Mohamed Ibrahim to oust him from power.[41]

---

[39] Former minister of state Mohamed Mahsoob revealed many aspects of this conspiracy in an interview on *Witness to the Age*, [TV programme] Al Jazeera, 30 March 2014, Available Online: https://bit.ly/3n6diu4 (accessed 6 June 2015).

The Egyptian historian Mohamed Al-Gawadi told me in an interview on 7 September 2015, that the sycophancy was genuine, not conspiratorial playacting. He said that a person of Sisi's character held no ambition beyond serving his president as a defence minister like any other, such as Tantawi, for example. However, Sisi seized the opportunity when he saw the president besieged and driven into a corner by other political forces. I felt it important to add this here because Gawadi's statement conflicts with many other views. It suggests that Sisi pretends to manifest others' attitudes is an attempt to win their admiration.

[40] This occurred on 18 October 2012. See: *al-Ahram*, 18 October 2012, Available Online: https://bit.ly/3m1dOvD (accessed 3 July 2015). It is noteworthy that the former Muslim Brotherhood official Kamal al-Helbawi, who would subsequently support the coup, criticized Morsi for defending Tantawi and Anan and demanded they be brought to trial.

[41] *BBC Arabic*, 18 January 2015, Available Online: https://bbc.in/3715wMq (accessed 7 July 2015).

The results of the fact-finding committee were damning. But Morsi's foot-dragging on publicizing the report is surprising and his justification that he was motivated by concern for the reputation of the military establishment is incomprehensible – that is, unless that concern was informed by his eagerness to win the army to his side. Morsi's behaviour would prove disastrous as the clouds of an impending coup began to loom in March 2013. It also throws into relief Morsi's naiveté as a politician whose office required him to take critical decisions under extremely complicated circumstances.

On 30 August 2012, which is to say two months after taking office, Morsi flew to Tehran to take part in the summit of non-aligned nations. It was the first visit of an Egyptian president to Iran since the revolution that overthrew Shah Pahlavi in 1979. The rupture between the two countries had been cemented by President Sadat's offer to host the deposed shah, and it continued throughout the Mubarak era. Morsi, in his speech at the summit, sustained the long-held Egyptian stances on Iranian policies. In fact, he was so critical that the official Iranian translator was compelled to soften the tone in the Persian version that was aired on Iranian state television. At the same time, Morsi was determined to signal a shift towards a less-dependent, more diversely oriented foreign policy. He would do so again at the international level in his visit to China.

An important prelude to the president's Iranian visit occurred a year earlier when an Egyptian 'people's delegation', which included a number of well-known public figures, visited Iran in June 2011. The GIS had its own opinion on this popular diplomatic venture, choosing this occasion to deport the third secretary of the office of the Iranian Interests Section in Cairo, who had been arrested on suspicion of espionage, on the same flight that the delegation took to Tehran. The deep state was not keen on a policy shift towards Iran. Realizing this helps us appreciate the limited strategic impact of Morsi's visit to Tehran on Egyptian-Iranian bilateral relations. It yielded no substantial breakthrough capable of withstanding the wider regional turbulence. Therefore, after Morsi's ouster, Egyptian-Iranian relations remained tepid, despite some attempts by the post-coup government to open channels of communication with the Nouri al-Maliki government in Iraq and some attempts to do the same with the Bashar al-Assad regime in Syria. Given this context, Morsi's visit never transcended its symbolic significance, and the same applies to Iranian president Mahmoud Ahmadinejad's visit to Cairo in February 2013.

Closer to home, Morsi's reception of Ismail Haniyeh,[42] then president of the Hamas governing authority in Gaza, triggered sharply divergent reactions. If it met with a large and enthusiastic welcome by many, it

---

[42] Former Hamas-affiliated Palestinian prime minister who was elected in 2006. He is currently the chairman of the Hamas Political Bureau.

infuriated some quarters of the political elite.⁴³ Haniyeh himself took the occasion to say, 'The new Egypt under the leadership of the Muslim Brotherhood has altered the equation in the region.... Egypt is returning to its prime thanks to the full support the Egyptian people give to the Palestinian cause.'⁴⁴ The Palestinian ambassador to Cairo, on behalf of Palestinian Authority President Mahmoud Abbas, demanded a formal explanation for the Hisham Qandil government's reception of Haniyeh, whom Abbas had dismissed as prime minister and therefore had no official standing as a head of state. Morsi ignored the complaint and merely reaffirmed Egypt's commitment to an active role in the Palestinian reconciliation process.⁴⁵ Morsi's gesture to Hamas and his pledge to promote reconciliation and help end the blockade on Gaza angered the Israelis as well.

The anniversary of the Egyptian military victory in the 1973 war occasioned the display of a reorientation of a different kind. A large number of Islamist and jihadist leaders attended the celebrations in Cairo Stadium that year. This was an unprecedented and peculiar sight at an event meant to pay tribute to the armed forces, given the state's decades-long war against Islamist extremist groups, some of which had openly declared war on the state and damned it and its rulers as heretics. The opposition did not interpret that scene as a gesture of Islamist reconciliation with and assimilation into the state, but rather seized on it to fan indignation among the public. Against the backdrop of that visibly Islamist crowd, the absence of former defence minister Tantawi and former chief of staff Anan – both of whom had fought in the 6 October war – was all the more glaring. The general impression was that the course of events after the revolution had taken a turn contrary to the normal order. To make matters worse, Morsi did not mention Sadat's name once during his approximately two-hour-long speech, feeding the sensationalist reportage on the 'snub to Sadat' and the presence of 'Sadat's murderers' at the 6 October festivities.

Within less than a year, the state locked horns with Islamist movements in Sinai, the theatre of the October War. A struggle to purge the peninsula of terrorism now unfolded on the same terrain as the struggle against the Israeli occupation four decades earlier. By then, the presence of an Islamist movement in power had been consigned to history as an aberration, which defied sound logic.

The source of the confusion surrounding the 6 October Day celebrations was that the elected president had not acted as a representative of a revolution with a mission to overturn the regime and its entire apparatus.

---

⁴³ Al Jazeera, 27 July 2012, Available Online: https://bit.ly/37Mm765 (accessed 7 June 2015).
⁴⁴ Watan News, 31 October 2012, Available Online: https://bit.ly/2W0p3X3 (accessed 7 June 2015).
⁴⁵ Al Akhbar (Egypt), 19 September 2012. Archived Copy Available Online: https://bit.ly/36Zk8w0 (accessed 7 June 2015).

He was a far cry from Khomeini whose public prosecutor passed death sentences wholesale while he proceeded to enforce a complete overhaul of the state, with its judiciary, parliamentary, executive and security bodies, and its symbols, rites and national holidays. Khomeini had no interest in the emblems of the past. He swept all that aside and introduced new and different symbols, rhetoric and culture, and he asserted an iron grip on the press. But nor was Morsi an inclusive reformist whose goal was to lead the transitional phase to democracy with the support of the broadest possible sociopolitical consensus and without effecting a rupture with history. Morsi was not able and probably not willing to use brute force to break the back of the old regime like Khomeini did. Nor was he prepared to enter into broad-based popular alliances in order to impose reforms. He was therefore attacked by revolutionaries and reformists alike. The old regime quickly perceived his vulnerability and proceeded to weaken him soon after that moment of strength and electoral legitimacy epitomized by the dismissal of Tantawi and Anan.

On 10 October 2012, the Cairo Criminal Court, with Judge Hassan Abdullah presiding, acquitted all the defendants in the Battle of the Camel case.[46] The twenty-four defendants had been accused of killing peaceful demonstrators, in collusion with the old regime and the NDP, in the melee that erupted in Tahrir Square and its vicinity on 2 February 2011. The judges escaped censure as criticism focused on the public prosecutor's poor preparation and the consequent insufficient evidence and conflicting testimonies.

This was not the first case in which defendants – police officers and old regime personnel – were acquitted of similar charges. Most of these trials had been set into motion under pressure from revolutionary forces when their strength in the street was at its height. The acquittals occurred after that strength had abated. Subsequently, as the balance of power between the revolution and the counter-revolution shifted in favour of the latter, the regime and its judiciary, which remained intact, turned the tables and began to prosecute numerous figures associated with the 25 January revolution. In these cases, the majority were found guilty. It is thus true that in terms of the identity of the defendants and the rulings, political trials after the revolution were contingent on the balance of powers between the key players in the political conflict. Even so, the courts remained intrinsically biased in favour of the old regime throughout. Thus, no sooner had the revolutionary forces fallen into disarray and the judiciary felt that the

---

[46] *Al-Arabiya*, 10 October 2012, Available Online: https://bit.ly/3FXL1Qh (accessed 19 October 2021).

security forces and the army had regained their strength than the courts became the sharpest weapon in the old regime's fight against change.

On 12 October, in response to the outcry against the court's ruling on the Battle of the Camel case, Morsi dismissed the public prosecutor, Abdel Meguid Mahmoud, whom he appointed as ambassador to the Vatican, and replaced with Talaat Ibrahim. These decisions were framed in a constitutional declaration.[47]

Mahmoud refused to comply with Morsi's decision and declared he would remain in his post.[48] This was not an act of personal defiance, in my view, but a stance emboldened by the support and encouragement of the deep state. Ahmed Al-Zend, the chairman of the Judges' Club and a key figure of the Mubarak-era judiciary, convened an emergency meeting of the club to declare solidarity with the dismissed public prosecutor. This was neither Zend's first nor last action against an elected body. It would not be inaccurate to say that he was the judiciary's spearhead in its resistance to democratization. Let us recall that it was Zend who had mobilized the judges against the now-dissolved People's Assembly, which he had described as a thorn in Egypt's back.[49]

Revolutionary forces had long called for the dismissal of the public prosecutor. Yet once the step was taken – and after the acquittal of the defendants on the Battle of the Camels case no less – some pro-revolutionary forces joined the chorus of critics of his dismissal. They described it as a step to assert the Muslim Brotherhood's control over the prosecution – to 'Brotherhoodize' the prosecution as they put it. A number of prominent figures, such as Hamdeen Sabahi, paid solidarity visits to Mahmoud. Morsi caved into the pressures and retracted the dismissal. This marked the old regime's first victory in its direct confrontation with the elected president and the dawn of a full-fledged counter-revolution with the aim to overthrow him.

---

[47] Tarek El-Bishry rightfully faulted the president for dismissing and appointing an official not just in accordance with a law but on the basis of something greater: a constitutional declaration. Such instruments should not be promulgated for a single person or issue, but to establish a general rule or principle. See: Tarek El-Bishry, *The January Revolution and the Conflict for Power* [Arabic] (Cairo: Dar el Basheer, 2014), 107.

[48] *France 24 Arabic*, 12 October 2012, Available Online: https://bit.ly/33VReuA (accessed 7 June 2015).

[49] Zend was a kingpin of the judicial wing of the 'deep state' and an exponent of the judges who did not subscribe to judicial independence and saw no problem with being subordinate to the executive. They operated from the standpoint that the judiciary could serve as a weapon in a political conflict and that it should function as part of the Egyptian political regime to defend it and punish its opponents through rulings issued 'in the name of the people'. This perspective enables us to understand why a judge like Zend would continue to defend the Mubarak regime after the revolution that overthrew it and why, before then, he had turned a blind eye to the flagrant electoral fraud in the 2005 and 2010 parliamentary elections. He was nothing, if not consistent, in being among the first and foremost proponents of the mass demonstrations on 30 June 2013. See: *al-Araby al-Jadid*, 20 May 2015, Available Online: https://bit.ly/2LeNiyE (accessed 21 June 2015).

The polarization mounted between the Muslim Brotherhood and their few allies versus the rest of the political parties and forces. On 12 October, violent brawls erupted in Tahrir Square between pro-Muslim Brotherhood and pro-revolutionary forces during the mass demonstration the latter camp had organized to mark the first 100 days of Morsi's rule. The protestors dubbed the rally 'Account Statement Friday' and drew up a balance sheet of what he had and had not achieved in terms of the pledges he had made in his electoral platform. Some Muslim Brothers also wanted to hold a rally that day, but in order to protest the acquittal of the defendants in the Battle of the Camel case and to support Morsi in his battle against the public prosecutor. They chose to assemble near the Egyptian Museum, so as to leave the square itself to their adversaries, even though the Muslim Brotherhood's Party, the FJP, was now the ruling party. This did not forestall the clash. According to the Ministry of Health, forty-two people were injured that day, many due to wounds received from flying stones, bottles and other projectiles. Subsequent estimates placed the number of wounded at over 140.

The anti-Morsi revolutionary forces had been the first to call for a *milyoniyya* that day. They held that the Muslim Brothers' rally was an attempt to 'Brotherhoodize' the agenda of that Friday's demonstration and claimed that the Brothers were the first to attack. They called for another demonstration the following Friday, which they dubbed 'Egypt's not your country estate'. Further skirmishes between Morsi supporters and his opponents would follow over the coming months, with gradually increasing frequency and acrimony until his ouster in mid-2013. The marches and rallies also became opportunities for gangs of hoodlums, widely suspected to be in the pay of security agencies and former ruling party officials, to instigate brawls, sow turmoil and fuel the sharpening polarization. The most significant clash between the two sides occurred on 5 December 2012, when pro-Morsi supporters broke up the sit-in in front of the Ittihadiyya Presidential Palace. That would seal the total rupture between Morsi and the Muslim Brotherhood, and their erstwhile allies in the January revolution.

As a final note here, it is worth mentioning a statement that Wasat Party chairman Abou Elela Mady made on the subject of systematic thuggery. I believe he and his party ended up paying dearly for this remark after the coup. In a public symposium organized by the Wasat Party on 24 March 2013,[50] Mady said that Morsi had told him that as president he came to discover that years earlier the GIS had formed a militia of 300,000 thugs of whom 80,000 operated in Greater Cairo.

---

[50] A video clip of that symposium is available on the *Yqeen* YouTube channel: *YouTube*, 24 March 2013, Available Online: https://bit.ly/36XZ88S (accessed 5 September 2015).

The deterioration

Unlike a Greek tragedy, it was not fate but politics

I The battle over the constitution and Morsi's constitutional declaration

On 3 November 2012, Morsi held three separate meetings with Amr Moussa, Hamdeen Sabahi and Abdel Moneim Aboul-Fotouh, his former electoral competitors, in an attempt to forge a national consensus that could resolve the disputes within the CA responsible for drafting the constitution, according to a statement from the official presidential spokesman. Nothing concrete came out of the meetings.

The CA was riven by sharp disagreements between Islamists – particularly Salafists with their zealotry – and other forces, reflecting incompatible views on contentious issues like the status of Shari'a in the constitution. Salafists staged a demonstration on the Friday following Morsi's meetings (9 November 2012). As two of the most prominent political figures opposed to the Morsi government, Moussa and Sabahy joined with Mohamed ElBaradei and several other figures to form the NSF, which acted as an umbrella for various anti-Brotherhood forces.

In attempting to write a democratic constitution, the framers referred to some of the better provisions in past Egyptian constitutions, particularly the 1923 text and the draft constitution submitted by a fifty-member civilian committee in 1954 to the Revolutionary Command Council, which rejected it. Discussions in the CA were made more difficult by opposition political forces' obstructionism, which put partisan conflict before the responsibility to establish a post-revolution democracy, as well as the Salafists' excesses and the Brotherhood's desire not to be outflanked by them. Also problematic was the Brotherhood's desire to cede to the wishes of the military to enshrine their privileges and immunities in the constitution. Article 195, for example, was a concession to the army, making the defence minister the general commander of the armed forces and requiring the minister to be appointed from among the military's ranks. This provision was not found in the 1971 constitution, although it was customary practice. Article 198 recognized the military justice system as an independent judicial body, and the constitution did not provide for parliamentary oversight of the military budget, although it did not exclude the possibility either.[1]

On 9 November 2012, thousands of Islamists descended on Tahrir to demand the application of Shari'a, an event dubbed 'Kandahar Two'.[2] The action took place against the backdrop of the fierce arguments in the CA over the status of Shari'a in the constitution. The Brotherhood and the Nour Party chose not to participate in the Friday demonstration, which its organizers had called 'the Friday for the Application of Shari'a', wanting to find some consensus within the assembly. Meanwhile, representatives of civil political forces threatened to withdraw from the assembly because of Islamist dominance, and Baradei declared that the CA did not represent all segments of the Egyptian people.[3] Soon representatives of the three churches pulled out, followed by representatives of civil forces.

Morsi's opponents did not engage in an objective discussion of the constitution or address its actual weaknesses. Rather, they saw a successful constitution as a success for Morsi rather than for the democratic transition itself, ultimately abandoning their duty and derailing the process. The drafting process in the assembly was open to the media, which published

---

[1] Elected officials' oversight of executive actions, including in matters of defence, is a prerequisite for democracy and civilian political control, but the constitutional articles immunizing the military hindered civilian oversight of the defence and security sectors. The 1971 constitution did not provide for such oversight, noting only that the military budget should be submitted to the People's Assembly as a single figure without further detail. The authors of that constitution cited the need for secrecy to justify the provision, arguing that the armed forces' budget revealed sensitive information about armaments and military readiness and so they preferred to withhold it from the people's representatives, disregarding entirely the risk of corruption absent any external oversight. It is true that some items in military budgets are confidential even in democracies, but these account for no more than 5–10 per cent of the budget, and even these confidential items are discussed in closed parliamentary committees. The 2012 constitution kept the workings and budget of the armed forces hidden from popular oversight as exercised by parliament. Instead of oversight, the constitution created the National Defence Council, an unelected, executive council formed by the president pursuant to Article 197. Two-thirds of the council's seats were dedicated to military personnel with the remaining third going to the prime minister, the heads of the House of Representatives and the Shura Council (both elected), and the ministers of finance, foreign affairs and the interior. The article tasked the council with a discussion of the armed forces' budget and required the council's input on any draft laws related to the armed forces. The provision was retained in the constitutional amendments of 2013 in Article 203, which also reverted to the 1971 provision about the inclusion of the military's budget as a single-line item in the state budget, thereby denying the House the right to discuss the workings of the armed forces and crippling parliament in one of its main tasks. A discussion of the military budget was to take place exclusively within the NDC.

[2] This followed Kandahar One on 29 July 2011.

[3] *France 24 Arabic*, 10 November 2012, Available online: https://bit.ly/3aSHWmu (accessed 9 June 2015).

the various drafts. Hundreds of experts and representatives from various constituencies participated in discussions. It was a democratic process, but was not valued as such. The failure of the process, despite its flaws, was catastrophic in every sense of the word.

Despite media coverage, broad public participation and many members' commitment to a responsible, sincere debate, the process of writing the constitution took place in a climate that was polarized along identity and partisan lines, in both the wider public sphere and the CA itself.

Appeasing various political forces with this or that article took the place of dialogue, leaving the constitution without a coherent character governed by a set of mutually agreed principles, despite the zealous preoccupation with provisions specific to Egypt's identity. Unlike constitutions that formed the basis for democratization in countries like Spain, Brazil and South Africa, the new Egyptian constitution did not put rights and liberties front and centre. Instead, the focus was on identity-related issues of little legislative import.

On 16 November 2012, the opposition gathered in Tahrir Square with the goal of bringing down Morsi, at least according to some of its representatives. This was a premature move against a president elected after a democratic revolution. On 20 November, the CA was surrounded, and security forces informed members that they could not be responsible for their safety. The members refused to evacuate.[4]

During the commemoration of the events of Mohammed Mahmoud the previous year, clashes erupted between demonstrators and police; during the skirmishes Gaber Salah (known as Jika), a well-known member of the 6 April Movement, was shot in the head and killed. The incident further stoked public anger at the Morsi regime and police practices. Jika's funeral procession drew a large crowd, turning it into a veritable demonstration and lending symbolic political importance to his death. The scene recalled for many the funeral processions of other icons of the revolution, like Sheikh Emad Effat (shot and killed during the Cabinet Building sit-in) and Mina Daniel (run over by an armoured personnel carrier in the Maspero massacre). Jika joined their ranks in the revolutionary movement's collective memory.

The incident had implications for how the regime dealt with violence on the ground, which became clear during the Ittihadiyya events, when Interior Minister Ahmed Gamal El Din refused to obey Morsi's orders to use force against violent demonstrators in front of the presidential Ittihadiyya Palace. Fearing the political and criminal repercussions of such

---

[4] *Witness to the Age*, [TV programme] Al Jazeera TV, 20 April 2014, Available online: https://bit.ly/37HX044 (accessed 9 June 2015).

conduct, the minister demanded written authorization from Morsi. Morsi refused, which had consequences for later events, as we will see.

On 22 November, Morsi issued a constitutional declaration as part of his efforts to prevent the SCC from dissolving the Shura Council and the CA, the matter of which was indeed coming before the court. Having already dissolved the People's Assembly, the court seemed to be methodically setting siege to elected institutions, forcing Morsi's hand. Looking for a way to stop the SCC's obstruction of democratically elected institutions, Morsi issued the declaration, which put presidential decrees beyond judicial oversight at a time when the opposition, acting irresponsibly, stood with the court's actions. The declaration fuelled controversy and rage at Morsi of a kind unprecedented since he had assumed office. The criticisms focused on several specific provisions, most importantly those making Morsi's decrees unchallengeable and immunizing the Constituent Assembly and Shura Council against dissolution, as well as the provisions for the appointment of the public prosecutor.

The declaration was issued immediately after the Israeli war on Gaza, during which Egypt and the United States had mediated a ceasefire between Israel and Hamas. Egyptian efforts met with the praise of the US administration,[5] leading the opposition to attribute the timing of the constitutional declaration to American and Israeli satisfaction with the Morsi administration and their certainty that he would not deviate from the broad lines of the Arab-Israeli conflict drawn by the United States. Relying on such conspiratorial thinking, the opposition (or at least several of its leading figures) concluded that by toeing the line when it came to Israel, Morsi had secured American support for his presidency and a green light for his domestic actions. This demagoguery was easily turned in the opposite direction when needed. In the West, some observers warned of the collaboration between Morsi and Hamas. For the Egyptian public, however, Morsi was accused of having received the blessing of the United States.

The reaction to the constitutional declaration played out across multiple levels. Regarding the judiciary, which had become a tool for crippling

---

[5] Hillary Clinton writes that she began mediating a ceasefire with the permission of the president, after it became clear that Israel intended to launch a ground invasion of Gaza within forty-eight hours. See: *Hard Choices*, 479. Israeli military leaders harboured doubts about such a ground invasion, but Prime Minister Netanyahu's Likud base was enthusiastic. Clinton portrayed Morsi as an inexperienced politician thrust by circumstances from the backbench to the presidency, but she writes that he was not a demagogue when it came to the Gaza War and showed a readiness to make political deals Ibid., 448. She also discusses how he scrutinized the details of the agreement and refused to speak with Netanyahu by phone, despite the Egyptian-Israeli peace accord, preferring to use her as a go-between Ibid., 485. This paints quite a different portrait of Morsi than that drawn by the Egyptian opposition.

elected institutions and undermining the democratic transition, the general assembly of the Judges' Club announced a protest against the declaration, while the Cassation Court suspended proceedings and the SCC called the declaration 'extortion'. A motley assortment of old regime remnants and opposition political forces teamed up to mobilize and demonstrate, spurring counter-mobilization and demonstrations. Some Morsi supporters set siege to the SCC, setting off another wave of criticisms, even from within the pro-Morsi ranks.

When the protests began, Mohammad Fouad Gaballah, Morsi's legal adviser who helped draft the declaration, announced that 'there will be no retreat from the constitutional declaration issued by President Mohamed Morsi'.[6] The exceptional circumstances would be addressed by temporarily immunizing his decisions until the new constitution entered into force and institutions were fully operative, thereby protecting the Shura Council and CA from dissolution.

The objective justification for the constitutional declaration was sound: to protect the democratic transition from the constant, systematic assault of the SCC, which was loyal to the old regime.[7] But the declaration was poorly formulated, and the public was not apprised of it in advance. In retrospect, the constitutional declaration cannot be compared to even one of the undemocratic measures taken after the coup, which were far worse, though they did not provoke an outcry by the same circles opposed to Morsi's declaration. This raises a question: Was the opposition in fact concerned about a democracy under threat by the elected president? The constitutional declaration, or perhaps its specific formulation, was a mistake, but much of the opposition was motivated by considerations that had nothing to do with democracy. The mobilization against Morsi was not triggered by his constitutional declaration of 22 November 2012, as was later claimed; it began days earlier.

In response to the declaration, a group of political parties formed the NSF, which brought together the Constitution Party (led by Mohamed ElBaradei), Strong Egypt (led by Aboul-Fotouh, who later parted ways with the front), the Wafd, the Popular Current, the ESDP, the Popular Socialist Alliance, the Revolutionary Democratic Coalition (consisting of ten small parties and movements) and the Nasserist parties, as well as the Egypt of Freedom Party, the Free Egyptians, the Farmers' Syndicate,

---

[6] *Al-Masry Al-Youm*, 23 November 2012, Available online: https://bit.ly/33Umzhm (accessed 8 June 2015).

[7] Justifying Morsi's constitutional declaration, one scholar argues that he tried to protect elected institutions from the judiciary's ongoing efforts to dissolve them. This was especially urgent since the courts had dissolved the first elected People's Assembly in Egypt's history on a technicality. See Ketchley, *Egypt in a Time of Revolution*, 78.

the Independent Federation of Farmers and the Women's National Front. The Salvation Front was led by Baradei and two other former presidential candidates, Hamdeen Sabahi and Amr Moussa.

Announcing that it refused to speak with the president until he rescinded the constitutional declaration, the NSF urged Egyptians to mobilize in the public square. It reiterated its support for any grassroots action by revolutionary youth and expressed support for the judges and jurists opposed to the declaration, seeing the issue as a matter of judicial independence.[8]

Morsi called for political dialogue to contain the crisis, but the broad opposition and charged atmosphere – which was tense even before the declaration was issued – did not work in his favour. On the ground, the crisis evolved quickly, resulting in watershed moments like the Ittihadiyya events of 5 December 2012 and significant realignments on the political map effected through the NSF. Morsi was thus compelled to retract the declaration, issuing another on 9 December 2012 that backtracked on provisions in the previous declaration.

On 1 December, a crowd of Morsi supporters surrounded the SCC on the Almaadi Corniche, in advance of the hearing for petitions seeking the dissolution of the Constituent Assembly and Shura Council. The hearings, scheduled for the next day, were postponed because of the protest, and judges were forced to enter the building through the back doors or stay away entirely. The siege lasted about a month,[9] breaking up after the CA had completed its task and the constitution was approved in a popular referendum.

The crisis also jeopardized judicial supervision of the referendum for the constitution, with judges divided on participation.[10] Some judges made supervision conditional on an end to the siege of the SCC. Although the protestors at the court did thwart the court's dissolution of the CA, the action, despite its importance, was not a universally popular one. We can only imagine what a revolutionary front could have done if it had united against the forces of the old regime that were impeding the democratic transition. These old regime forces included the SCC and

---

[8] As the NSF was taking shape, there was another public outcry after Muslim Brotherhood lawyers filed legal complaints against several critics of the constitutional declaration, among them Hossam Eissa, a law professor who would become justice minister in the post-coup transition government. At the same time, several Brotherhood offices were vandalized. The Brotherhood therefore believed that the NSF had exceeded the bounds of acceptable opposition and veered into a tacit endorsement of violence in the name of the revolution.

[9] *CNN Arabic*, 1 January 2013, Available online: https://cnn.it/3pduhib (accessed 8 June 2015).

[10] *Ahram Online*, 11 December 2012, Available online: https://bit.ly/2YVTXol (accessed 19 October 2021).

the deep state, which continued to obstruct the transition and ultimately helped derail it entirely.

Amidst the political conflict set in motion by Morsi's constitutional declaration, some opposition forces organized marches to the Ittihadiyya Presidential Palace in Heliopolis. On 4 December 2012, crowds joined the marches in numbers far exceeding the organizers' expectations. Security forces removed the barriers that had blocked traffic on the streets leading to the presidential palace as hundreds of thousands of people assembled. When the demonstrations were over, several demonstrators decided to stage a sit-in by the palace walls. At around noon the next day, a group of Morsi supporters headed there as well to demonstrate in support of the president, raising the prospect of clashes between the two sides. And in fact, as the pro-Morsi crowd grew into a few thousand people, some of them attacked and removed the tents set up by Morsi opponents, beating up the protestors and journalists present. Photos and video footage of the clash between Morsi supporters and a handful of anti-Morsi protestors began to circulate, showing Morsi supporters assaulting well-known leftist activist Shahenda Maklad and several other male and female activists. As the news spread, a counter-mobilization was organized and began heading to the scene. By the evening, the two sides were involved in large-scale clashes that left ten people dead (most of them with the Brotherhood, according to subsequent reports) and 748 injured, according to the Ministry of Health. Forensic medical reports showed that both Morsi supporters and opponents were killed.[11] The events spread to other governorates, which saw similar anti-Morsi demonstrations. Opposition protestors in Mahalla Al-Kubra even managed to take control of the City Council building.[12]

According to statements from FJP leaders, seeing the dereliction of the security forces, Brotherhood leaders sent their own people to break up the sit-in to protect the presidential palace from possible attacks. Interior Minister Gamal El Din's refusal to obey Morsi's order to disperse the sit-in, and his request for written authorization to use gunfire led to his dismissal the next month. Yet, the Muslim Brotherhood's deployment of violence, whatever the justifications offered, evoked past episodes in the Brotherhood's relations with other political forces, recalling its tendency to smear opponents as unbelievers and its willingness to use violence in political competition.

At this point, on 8 December 2012, the military issued a statement, taking a position of neutrality and implicitly referring to the president, to

---

[11] For video documentation of events at the Ittihadiyya Palace from an activist's point of view, see the *Mella5er*, 6 December 2012, Available online: https://bit.ly/39YdQ1E (accessed 9 June 2015).
[12] *Dostor*, 17 November 2012, Available online: https://bit.ly/39TGgK4 (accessed 9 June 2015).

whom it was ostensibly subordinate, and the protestors as equal 'parties'. For the first time since Tantawi's removal, the military thus appeared to signal that it was not under the president's control, raising the same questions about its loyalties asked after 25 January. Given the statement's importance, I quote it at length here:

> With growing sorrow and concern, the armed forces are following current developments and the divisions that have beset the country. . . . The continuation of such divisions poses grave risks, threatening the pillars of the Egyptian state and battering its national security. As such . . . the armed forces affirms the following: the great Egyptian people, who impressed the world with their peaceful revolution of 25 January 2011 and thwarted everyone who wished to steer the revolution from its peaceful course, is capable with their awareness and perspicacity of continuing to express their opinions peacefully, far from the violence the country is currently witnessing. The course of dialogue is the best and only way to reach a consensus that serves the interests of the nation and citizens. Anything else will lead us into a dark tunnel with catastrophic consequences, something we will not permit. The military establishment is always on the side of the great Egyptian people and cares for their unity, and it is an essential part of the national fabric and the nation's sacred soil. . . . In this context, we affirm and support serious, sincere national dialogue and the democratic path to deal with contentious issues and points, in order to reach a consensus among all parties of the nation.[13]

On 12 December 2012, Sisi, the minister of defence, unbeknownst to Morsi, invited party leaders and other public figures to meet with him. He later cancelled the meeting after Morsi objected, but no action was taken against him. Moreover, no serious investigation into the Ittihadiyya events was conducted, and no one was held responsible. With the benefit of hindsight, I believe that these events and the political manoeuvring and military statements that followed were a rehearsal for 30 June 2013. The statement from the military was a rough draft of the one it issued after the coup of 3 July 2013.

The Ittihadiyya events marked the beginning of Defence Minister Sisi's persistent interference in politics. Always positioning himself as independent of the president's authority, he claimed to be a neutral party, setting the military above all parties and their demands, among them the president himself, and assuming responsibility for addressing issues facing the nation. This was the posture he adopted on 29 January 2013

---

[13] *Youm7*, 8 December 2012, Available online: https://bit.ly/3oAM3Z6 (accessed 8 June 2015).

when speaking to students at the War College.¹⁴ That meeting was the first time Sisi mentioned the potential for 'state collapse'. In his speech, he portrayed the military as a neutral arbiter above all other parties and spoke of the president himself as a mere 'party' to the disagreement. At this time, too, the defence minister began cultivating relationships with Egyptian celebrities and artists, ostentatiously inviting them to celebrations hosted at the Defence Ministry and taking photographs with them. The objective of this public relations offensive is clear. Photos with celebrities not only effectively marketed him to the public; they also portrayed the man in uniform as a refuge for those who feared Islamist control.

Some opposition demands were accepted – for example, the revocation of the constitutional declaration and the creation of a new ministry that included national forces – in an attempt to persuade figures like Baradei and other NSF leaders to abandon the goal of toppling Morsi and find ways to cooperate. But every time one of their conditions was met, they formulated a new one, according to the personal testimony of Mohamed Mahsoob, former minister of legal affairs and a leading figure in the Wasat Party.¹⁵ There can be no doubt that for NSF leaders, things had moved beyond specific demands of the president to an aspiration to topple him and a willingness to cooperate with the old regime to do so.

Just seven days after Morsi issued his revised constitutional declaration, the referendum on the new constitution took place. (The CA had approved the text in a nineteen-hour marathon session from 19 to 20 November 2012.) The result was released ten days later: the constitution had been approved.¹⁶ The referendum was conducted in a period of heightened political division, not only between pro- and anti-Morsi forces but also within the ranks of the opposition itself, between those who called for a boycott of the referendum and those who advocated a 'no' vote.

The referendum was held over two days: on 15 December 2012 in ten governorates and on 22 December¹⁷ in the remaining seventeen governorates, in addition to expatriate votes. The turnout was notably low, with only 32.9 per cent of the electorate casting a ballot. The constitution

---

[14] *Al Akhbar*, 29 January 2013. Archived Copy Available Online: https://bit.ly/2JQCRAX (accessed 8 June 2014).
[15] *Al Jazeera*, 27 April 2014, Available online: https://bit.ly/2VXLk81 (accessed 9 June 2015). As of this writing, I consider Mahsoob the most important, comprehensive source for this period.
[16] Morsi revoked the original constitutional declaration on 9 December 2012. See: *Shorouk*, 9 December 2012, Available online: https://bit.ly/3BXpNzN (accessed 8 June 2015).
[17] The same day, Vice-President Mahmoud Mekki announced his resignation. The crisis created by the constitutional declaration spurred several presidential aides and advisers to resign, along with members of the CA. See: *al-Watan*, 22 December 2012, Available online: https://bit.ly/2W0xd1D (accessed 9 June 2015).

was approved by a majority of 63.8 per cent of voters in a fair, democratic process. The result was announced on 25 December 2012.

In the 2011 referendum on the constitutional amendments, the anti-Islamist vote came to approximately 20 per cent. Its share increased in this referendum, to 36.2 per cent, as did the percentage of non-voters. Even so, secularists did not consider this an achievement and continued to rely on the military to bring Brotherhood rule to an end.[18] If they had seen both the boycott and the no vote as an accomplishment that could be built on democratically, they would have realized that they were capable of voting out Morsi in democratic elections. At that point, the presidency was too weak to tamper with the election result, even if it had wanted to. Even in this case, however, I doubt that secular forces would have been able to unite around a single candidate against Morsi. In the most well-known incident between the referendum in December 2012 and the coup of July 2013, the NSF, comprising most secular parties, rebuffed Morsi's invitations to sit down and talk, or even discuss possible amendments to the constitution.

The constitution was approved by a little less than two-thirds of voters, who themselves constituted only one-third of the electorate. Turnout was thus lower than for the referendum on the constitutional amendments conducted by SCAF in 2011 (41 per cent), the presidential elections (50 per cent) and the People's Assembly elections from 28 November 2011 to 11 January 2012 (60 per cent).[19] In other words, the constitution was not the object of consensus among the major social and political forces in Egypt and so did not embody a set of commonly held principles. The polarization therefore grew even starker after the referendum. As noted earlier, the process of writing the constitution took place in 'an overall climate of polarization, which produced a constitution outside the bounds of agreement, consensus and accord'.[20] The debates were also articulated in terms of a majority versus a minority. While such an adversarial mind-set is acceptable in parliament, it has no place in discussions relating to the whole of society and its ideals,[21] which is what consensus-based constitutions are. These require an entirely different climate and compromise, at least among the forces that have agreed to build a democracy. In contrast, the vote on this constitution involved alliances of a different sort. The Brotherhood allied with the Salafists, who were explicitly hostile to democracy; on the

---

[18] Michelle Dunne and Amr Hamzawy, 'Egypt's Secular Political Parties', 20.
[19] Seif al-Din Abdel Fattah, 'The Egyptian Constitution between Interpretation, Amendment and Enactment: A View from the Perspective of Political Consensus' [Arabic], in *Constitutional Debate and the Transitional Phase in Egypt: Between 25 January and 30 June* [Arabic] (Beirut: Arab Centre for Research and Political Studies, 2014), 134.
[20] Ibid., 122.
[21] Ibid., 128.

other side, the opposition began to legitimize their alliance with the old regime and the military, which were also undemocratic forces. Amidst such polarization, there could be no dialogue that would lead to concessions for the sake of concluding a pact founded on democratic principles.

In any case, we cannot ignore the fundamental weaknesses of the new constitution, which rightly should have been the focus of the debate. I have already mentioned how rights and liberties, as governing principles for the constitution, took a backseat to identity issues.

During the debate, Islamist forces attempted to amend Article 2 – 'Islam is the state religion and Arabic is its official language. The principles of Shari'a are the primary source of legislation' – to strike the word 'principles', thereby making Shari'a itself the main source of legislation. The article ultimately remained unchanged, and Article 3 was added in an attempt to allay Christians' concerns, stating, 'The principles of the religious laws of Egyptian Christians and Jews are the primary source of legislation regulating their personal status matters, religious affairs and the selection of their spiritual leaders.' In fact, this was already standard practice and gave Christians and Jews no new rights; it was simply a form of psychological reassurance.[22] The Islamists were appeased with the addition of Article 4 on Azhar and Article 219 in Section 2 of Chapter 5, titled 'General Provisions', which defines the principles of Shari'a to include 'its general evidence, its foundational rules and rules of jurisprudence, and credible sources accepted in orthodox Sunni schools of law'.[23] The provision also circumscribed the jurisdiction of courts, setting the authority of Islamic jurists above that of the constitution.[24]

Constitutional scholars saw Article 219 as tantamount to a revision of Article 2. Though it was not explicitly articulated as such, it was an explanatory provision to guide scholars as they interpreted the principles of Shari'a to determine whether legislation was consistent with it, in contrast to conventional practice in which laws interpret the constitution. Moreover, while the principles of Shari'a are well established and accepted, Shari'a-derived judgements change depending on time and place and are not subject to a consensus among jurists.[25]

Article 4 also set an unelected body – the institution of Azhar – above the legislative and judicial branches, making it the interpreter of the constitution, which should be the function of the SCC.[26] This provision

---

[22] Aliwa, 'Egypt on the Threshold of the Second Republic', 78.
[23] Ibid., 77–8.
[24] Ibid., 78.
[25] Seif al-Din Abd al-Fattah, annexes to part two of *Constitutional Debate and the Transitional Phase in Egypt*, 292.
[26] Ibid., 293.

undermined the credibility of those who claimed that the SCC was interfering in the province of elected institutions, showing that the claims of interference were not a principled position. After all, the new constitution permitted an unelected body to review laws passed by the elected People's Assembly. In contrast, in a democratic system based on democratic principles, constitutional courts are necessary to ensure that the legislature adheres to these principles, which are considered the bedrock values of the constitution.

In Egypt, then, the democratic transition was beset from one side by an activist constitutional court that stepped in not in defence of democratic values, but against democracy and in defence of the old regime on the grounds of legal formalism, and from the other side by a legislative authority that wanted an unelected religious body to interfere in its work, not in pursuance of democratic principles, but of Shari'a.

Democratic forces, particularly youth forces, hotly contested Article 197 on the National Security Council, which barred parliament from reviewing the budget of the armed forces. Going further than the 1971 constitution, the article codified what had previously been an unwritten norm – and an undemocratic one at that – in an attempt to appease the military leadership at a time when doing so was neither possible nor advantageous.

The constitution ultimately favoured a presidential system rather than the mixed presidential-parliamentary system that it ostensibly enshrined. Under Article 139, the president selected the prime minister without the input of the parliamentary majority and was responsible for appointing governors and political state officials. The final version of the text also gave the president the right to appoint SCC justices.

Democrats were also wary of Article 81, which stated, 'The citizen's inalienable rights may not be suspended or diminished. No law may regulate the exercise of rights and liberties in a way that infringes their origin and essence. Rights and freedoms shall be exercised in a way that does not contravene the components set forth in the chapter on the state and society in this constitution.' Noting that the third sentence contradicted the first two, they argued that it imposed restrictions derived from the fundamental, yet legally undefined components of state and society, which could be interpreted to restrict rights and liberties.[27] This debate took place at a time when genuine democratic critique overlapped with incitement against elected institutions and the rise of old regime forces that were hostile to the principles of the January revolution.

---

[27] Ibid., 84.

These were the most substantive criticisms of the constitution, but they were often lost amidst the vapid and slanderous media coverage. The need to reach a consensus on democratic values and principles and domesticate the state apparatus and army took a back seat to partisan sparring. A constitution remains mere ink on paper if it is not buttressed by a democratic culture in state institutions. And as for the task of cultivating a broad democratic public, the opposite occurred. The forces that should have supported the democratic transition were extremely fragmented along political and partisan lines, and so no broad front of party-backed intellectuals emerged to promote constitutional values as a key component of Egyptian national identity in the coming phase. On the eve of and after the constitutional referendum, Morsi vowed as president to adopt amendments agreed upon by political forces, which would be put to the parliament after the election of a new assembly, but the climate was not conducive to consensus. Meanwhile, the forces that led the CA and wrote the constitution could do nothing but talk about a majority-approved constitution and promise that it could be amended later. This in itself undermined the legitimacy of the constitution, highlighting the lack of consensus around it.

On 6 January 2013, Prime Minister Hisham Qandil undertook a cabinet shuffle, appointing ten new ministers, three of them from the Muslim Brotherhood and seven independents. Among the new faces was Interior Minister Mohamed Ibrahim,[28] who would later be a main partner in the coup against the elected president.

Against this charged backdrop, on 10 January 2013, the presidency announced the resignation of Central Bank Governor Farouk El Okdah and the appointment of Hisham Ramez in his stead. The change came as Egypt's foreign currency reserves continued to dwindle and the value of the Egyptian pound plummeted.

II The economy in the transitional phase and under Morsi's presidency

Economically, it is impossible to draw a line between the SCAF and Morsi eras. True, the latter distinguished itself somewhat with an attempt to devise an economic policy, though it lacked the time to refine and carry it out. In contrast, the economic policy of the early transitional phase was in a shambles: ad hoc crisis management and no long-term planning, as

---

[28] For a good treatment of Ibrahim's work serving Morsi versus his service to the coup, see *Mada Masr*, 16 December 2013, Available online: https://bit.ly/3pcqwtj (accessed 9 June 2015).

Table II.7.1 Per Capita Income: Investment and Savings (2010–14)

	2010	2011	2012	2013	2014
GDP per capita (current US$)	2,646	2,792	3,230	3,263	3,380
GDP growth (%)	5.15	1.76	2.23	2.19	2.92
Gross domestic savings (% of GDP)	14.26	12.98	8.11	7.87	5.21
Gross capital formation (formerly gross domestic investment) (% of GDP)	19.5	17.1	16.03	14.21	13.64
Foreign direct investment (% of GDP)	2.92	−0.2	1	1.45	1.51
Inflation – per cent change in the Consumer Price Index (%)	11.27	10.06	7.11	9.47	10.07
Egyptian population size (millions)	82.76	84.53	86.42	88.4	90.42
Population growth (%)	1.98	2.11	2.21	2.27	2.26
EGP to USD exchange rate	5.7	5.9	6.1	6.1	7.1

Source: World Bank, 'GDP per capita (current US$) – Egypt, Arab Rep.', at: https://bit.ly/3vNdp31 (accessed 26 October 2021); World Bank, 'GDP growth (annual %) – Egypt, Arab Rep.', at: https://bit.ly/3bb2SVE (accessed 26 October 2021); World Bank, 'Gross domestic savings (% of GDP) – Egypt, Arab Rep.', at: https://bit.ly/3mfAIzt (accessed 26 October 2021); World Bank, 'Gross capital formation (% of GDP) – Egypt, Arab Rep.', at: https://bit.ly/2XRbONa (accessed 26 October 2021); World Bank, 'Foreign direct investment, net inflows (% of GDP) – Egypt, Arab Rep.' at: https://bit.ly/3mg69tb (accessed 26 October 2021); World Bank, 'Inflation, consumer prices (annual %) – Egypt, Arab Rep.' at: https://bit.ly/3vJwnrn (accessed 26 October 2021); World Bank, 'Population, total – Egypt, Arab Rep.' at: https://bit.ly/3mf0xPQ (accessed 26 October 2021); World Bank, 'Population growth (annual %) – Egypt, Arab Rep.' at: https://bit.ly/3nodJBu (accessed 26 October 2021); UN Economic and Social Commission for Western Asia (ESCWA), External Trade Bulletin of the Arab Region, Issue no. 25 (New York: UN, 2017), xiii, at: https://bit.ly/2XQLKS7 (accessed 26 October 2021).

SCAF kept its eyes the clock waiting for its shift to end. But apart from this, the whole period from SCAF rule to the Morsi presidency was one long continuum of political instability, plummeting investments, dwindling tourism and shrinking production. Despite claims to the contrary, the economy remained the same as it was before the revolution, shackled by decades-old structural problems, regardless of the mutual recriminations between rival political forces. Given the lack of sufficient time to make the necessary reforms and the lack of a unified plan the revolutionary forces could rally behind in a constructive and mutually supportive spirit, the old order would inevitably prevail over the new.

Table II.7.1 illustrates the most important structural problems in the Egyptian economy, showing how basic, underlying trends continued until 2014.

As the aforementioned figures indicate, there was no major change in growth between the SCAF and Morsi periods and no reduction in per capita income (GDP divided by population). On the other hand, gross domestic savings took a plunge and the same applies to the gross domestic investment. The figures were low to begin with, but by the end of this period they dropped to rates that would be ominous for any economy. The decline was an important indicator of the instability and uncertainty that

Table II.7.2 GDP Growth (%)

	2010	2011	2012	2013	2014
Egypt Statistical Yearbook	1.8	2.2	2.2	2.1	–
United Nations ESCWA Data	5.15	1.77	2.21	2.18	2.92
World Bank Data	5.15	1.76	2.23	2.19	2.92

Source: Arab Republic of Egypt Central Agency for Public Mobilization and Statistics (CAPMAS), *Statistical Yearbook* (Cairo: CAPMAS, 2014), Table 19-1; United Nations ESCWA, 'National Accounts Database', at: https://bit.ly/3md4CEq (accessed 26 October 2021); World Bank, 'GDP growth (annual %) – Egypt, Arab Rep.', at: https://bit.ly/3bb2SVE (accessed 26 October 2021).

cast their shadow over the transitional phase. This can also be seen through the decline in the rate of the Foreign Direct Investment in 2011, though it witnessed a slight increase in the following years (Table II.7.1).

In 2014, the CAPMAS put real GDP growth at about 5.1 per cent for 2009–10.[29] In Part I, I discussed what this growth signified with respect to the state of the economy before the revolution. In the first year after the revolution, growth plunged to around 2 per cent and stayed at that level until 2014 (Table II.7.2).[30] There was thus no difference between SCAF and Morsi in terms of economic performance, and both struggled to meet rising expectations after the revolution amidst declining state resources and capacities. The population grew by around 2.5 per cent in the same period,[31] meaning that GDP growth was less than population growth. This is an indicator of declining standards of living which is a strain on any economy, all the more so when more than half of those able to work are not in the workforce, women in particular (employment rates in 2010–14 ranged between twenty-seven and thirty million of the working-age population of between fifty-two and fifty-six million (62–63 per cent of the total population). In the same period, the rate of working women ranged only between 22 and 23 per cent of the total labour force).[32]

Equally significant is the decline in wages to GDP, as observed by the UN ESCWA, in a report released in 2014.[33] In addition to deteriorating living standards, this indicator reflected the growing disparity in income

---

[29] Arab Republic of Egypt CAPMAS, *Statistical Yearbook* (Cairo: CAPMAS, 2014), Table 22-6.
[30] Ibid.; World Bank, 'GDP Growth (Annual %) – Egypt, Arab Rep.', Available online: https://bit.ly/3bb2SVE (accessed 26 October 2021).
[31] World Bank, 'Population Growth (Annual %) – Egypt, Arab Rep.', Available online: https://bit.ly/3nodJBu (accessed 26 October 2021).
[32] World Bank, 'Labor Force, Total – Egypt, Arab Rep.', Available online: https://bit.ly/3BkjaX8 (accessed 26 October 2021); World Bank, 'Population Ages 15–64 (% of Total Population) – Egypt, Arab Rep.', Available online: https://bit.ly/3vMtmqh (accessed 26 October 2021); World Bank, 'Labor Force, Female (% of Total Labor Force) – Egypt, Arab Rep.', Available online: https://bit.ly/3bfaXZF (accessed 26 October 2021).
[33] UN ESCWA, National Account Studies of the Arab Region, bulletin no. 34 (Beirut: UN, 2014), Available online: https://bit.ly/3mikZ2n (accessed 26 October 2021).

Table II.7.3 GDP and Expenditure at Current Rates

	2009	2010	2011	2012	2013
Employee compensation (in millions of EGP)	259,257	303,567	364,719	440,278	489,963
Operating surplus (profits) (in millions of EGP)	734,778	847,023	945,187	1,068,222	1,187,389
GDP (in millions of EGP)	1,042,135	1,206,640	1,371,078	1,575,500	1,753,252
Employee compensation to GDP (%)	24.9	25.1	26.6	27.93	27.95
Profits to GDP (%)	70.5	70.2	68.9	67.8	67.7

Source: UN Economic and Social Commission for Western Asia (ESCWA), National Account Studies of the Arab Region, bulletin no. 34 (Beirut: UN, 2014), Table II-5, p. 26, at: https://bit.ly/3mikZ2n (accessed 26 October 2021).

distribution between labour and capital and, accordingly, a decline in the level of social justice. This area saw a slight improvement in the Morsi era due to wage hikes in 2012 and 2013 Table II.7.3).

According to the World Bank estimates, unemployment stood at 8.76 per cent of the labour force in 2010, then climbed to 13.15 per cent in 2014.[34]

However, it is widely believed among specialists that the official figures did not reflect reality and could not withstand an empirical test. Table II.7.4 illustrates how the population and employment problems are intertwined According to the Egypt Statistical Yearbook produced by CAPMAS, an estimated 3.2 million new entries into the labour market, which consists of around 50 per cent of working-age people able to work, between 2011 and 2014. The market absorbed only 1.77 million of them, meaning that some 1.4 million remained without work during those four years, augmenting the already burgeoning ranks of the unemployed (unemployment rate increased from 9 per cent in 2010 to 13.2 per cent in 2013).[35] A portion of these young people found work abroad, alleviating some of the pressures of unemployment. But the actual unemployment rate is still much higher than the official one.

Foreign trade declined under both SCAF and Morsi. According to the *Joint Arab Economic Report* 2014, exports covered about 53.9 per cent of the value of imports in 2009 and this fell to 42.4 per cent by 2014 (as in Table II.7.5).[36]

---

[34] World Bank, 'Unemployment, Total (% of Total Labor Force) (National Estimate) – Egypt, Arab Rep.', Available online: https://bit.ly/3vN2MNw (accessed 26 October 2021).
[35] CAPMAS, *Statistical Yearbook*, Table 4-1.
[36] Arab Monetary Fund, *Joint Arab Economic Report 2014* (Abu Dhabi: Arab Monetary Fund, 2014), Table 8-1, Available online: https://bit.ly/3pPY2pk (accessed 26 October 2021).

Table II.7.4 Population Growth and Labour Force

	2010	2011	2012	2013	2014
Population of Egypt (millions)	78.7	80.5	82.5	84.6	86.8
Population growth (millions)	1.7	1.8	2	2.1	2.2
Population growth (%)	2.28	2.44	2.57	2.52	2.54
Estimated working-age population (millions)	1.57	1.55	1.54	1.63	1.67
Estimated new entries into the labour market (which consists of around 50% of working-age people able to work) (thousands)	786	778	773	817	838
New jobs (thousands)	--	350	490	600	330
Newly unemployed per year (thousands)	--	428	283	217	508

Source: CAPMAS, *Statistical Yearbook*, Table 2-4.

Table II.7.5 Import Coverage of Exports (million USD)

Year	2009	2010	2011	2012	2013
Exports	24.34	28.03	32.35	31.08	30.61
Imports	45.21	54.36	63.79	73.55	70.88
Import coverage through exports (%)	53.9	51.6	50.7	42.25	42.2

Source: Arab Monetary Fund, *Joint Arab Economic Report 2014* (Abu Dhabi: Arab Monetary Fund, 2014), Table 8-1, at: https://bit.ly/3pPY2pk (accessed 26 October 2021).

The trade deficit after the revolution was huge by any standard. The most salient aspect of the weakness of Egyptian exports is that raw materials and light industrial products account for most of the value of the exports. This is a chronic structural flaw in Egyptian exports, as is the case with most Third World countries. Manufactured goods with a high added value do not constitute a significant proportion of exports.

Fiscal health can be summed up in two points: the balance of trade and payments, and foreign reserve levels. First, Egypt's balance of payments at the end of the 2013/14 fiscal year was relatively even, but fragile due to its reliance on foreign assistance.[37] The CBE report for that fiscal year recorded a foreign trade deficit of $33.7 billion. But it also registered a significant rise in current unrequited transfers from $19.3 billion in 2012–13 to $30.4 billion in 2013–14 (of which $18.5 billion were private transfers, mostly in the form of remittances from Egyptian workers abroad in the Gulf, and $11.9 billion in official transfers in the form of cash and commodity grants

---

[37] CAPMAS, *Statistical Yearbook*, Table 22-6.

Table II.7.6 Foreign Reserves (billion USD)

Year	2009	2010	2011	2012	2013
Reserves	32.3	33.8	15.4	11.7	13.6

Source: Arab Monetary Fund, *Joint Arab Economic Report 2014* (Abu Dhabi: Arab Monetary Fund, 2014), Table 9-4, at: https://bit.ly/3pPY2pk (accessed 26 October 2021).

and donations to Egypt after the coup from Gulf countries compared to $835.6 million in official transfers in the year 2012–13).[38]

Regarding foreign reserves, the Central Bank's report for the 2013–14 fiscal year lists the government's hard currency reserves (NIR), at $16.7 billion, covering only 3.3 months of merchandise imports at end of June 2014. Also, as noted earlier, it was contingent on Gulf countries' aid to the Egyptian government (the Sisi regime at the time). The same report indicates that the reserves were on a downward trajectory. During the period when the report was being prepared, they fell to $15.9 billion, as of November 2014, down from about $35 billion in 2010.[39] The *Joint Arab Economic Report 2014* also depicts the steady attrition of hard currency reserves during the interim period from 2011 to 2013 (see Table II.7.6). During the transitional phase, no support was forthcoming from either Western democratic nations or from Arab Gulf countries, apart from Qatar.

Adding further details to the grim picture, the national budget for 2013–14 showed a huge deficit that would be unacceptable in any healthy economy in which the deficit would never range beyond 3–5 per cent. Revenues and expenditures that year clocked in at 22.9 per cent and 35.1 per cent of GDP, respectively, producing a deficit of 12.5 per cent.[40]

National tax revenues from 2010 to 2013 came to around 14 per cent of GDP.[41] Such a low tax burden is indicative of widespread tax evasion, poor government capacity to levy taxes, and large informal economic sectors (Table II.7.7).

Just three items in the Egyptian budget – wages, debt service and subsidies of basic goods – came to $687.7 billion in 2014, or 149 per cent of revenues. Nothing was left over for investment and funding government operations. Expenditures, which came to over 178 per cent of revenues that

---

[38] Central Bank of Egypt, *Press Release: Performance of the Balance of Payments During FY 2013/14*, Available online: https://bit.ly/2Zv1xaj (accessed 26 October 2021).
[39] Central Bank of Egypt, *Annual Report 2013/2014*, 20, Available online: https://bit.ly/3EpSard (accessed 26 October 2021).
[40] Ibid., 61.
[41] Arab Monetary Fund, *Joint Arab Economic Report 2014*, Table 6-3; The World Bank estimates for the years 2012 and 2013 differs than the estimates of the Arab Monetary Fund report. See: *World Bank*, 'Tax Revenue (% of GDP) – Egypt, Arab Rep.', Available online: https://bit.ly/3vM0BtK (accessed 26 October 2021).

Table II.7.7 Tax Burden

Year	2010	2011	2012	2013
Tax burden (revenues as % of GDP) – estimates of the Arab Monetary Fund	14.1	14.0	13.2	14.3
Tax revenue (% of GDP) – estimates of the World Bank	14.13	14.01	12.39	12.22

Source: Arab Monetary Fund, *Joint Arab Economic Report 2014*, Table 6-3; World Bank, 'Tax revenue (% of GDP) – Egypt, Arab Rep.', at: https://bit.ly/3vM0BtK (accessed 26 October 2021).

Table II.7.8 National Budget Deficit

Year	2009	2010	2011	2012	2013
Deficit (billion USD)	−12.99	−17.74	−23.09	−27.75	−37.11
As % of GDP	−6.9	−8.1	−9.8	−10.6	−13.7

Source: Arab Monetary Fund, *Joint Arab Economic Report 2014* Table 6-10.

year, were being financed by the deficit. This, too, is a chronic structural problem in the Egyptian economy. Also, these figures do not support the government's published data on low inflation and unemployment rates (8.2 per cent and 13 per cent, respectively).[42] Domestic sources (Egyptian banks) covered 86 per cent of the deficit for 2013–14. This generates inflation. The government lowered the required reserve ratio to enable banks to extend loans to the government, and it borrowed from abroad. Table II.7.8 shows the increase in government deficit from the pre-revolutionary period through the transitional phase.

Morsi came to the presidency with a vision for rescuing the economy through autonomous development. He would often say that the aim of his economic policy was 'for Egypt to produce its own food, its own medicine and its own weapons'.[43] He could certainly not achieve an economic boom in the short time he would be president, given the seemingly insurmountable obstacles he faced. In addition to the cumulative structural problems inherited from the Mubarak era, production had ground to a halt in many sectors, sectorial strikes proliferated, and instability and turmoil drove away foreign investment and tourism.

Morsi also had to address popular expectations, which soared the moment he entered the presidential palace. However, he did not form a revolutionary government that might work to lower the ceiling of these

---

[42] This would become apparent in retrospect with the steady fall of the Egyptian pound against the dollar after the coup, especially from 2016 to 2019.

[43] Morsi said this frequently, for example during his visit to Brazil and in his speech to workers at the Iron and Steel Company. See: *Youm7*, 9 May 2013, Available online: https://bit.ly/3pfadvE (accessed 11 June 2015).

expectations by directing attention towards revolutionary political tasks such as implementing transitional justice, restructuring the Interior Ministry and other steps needed to change the old regime.

During his year in power, the economy continued to deteriorate, as was reflected in all macroeconomic indicators. True, the Morsi government did not implement a comprehensive reform or development plan during that turbulent period. But it is equally true that the counter-revolutionary forces persistently cast him as responsible for economic troubles inherited from the SCAF period and the old regime before that, and they also worked to obstruct his attempts to solve the problems.

From the left, in particular, came the charge that the Muslim Brotherhood espoused a right-wing, neoliberal economic ideology. As proof, they pointed to such business magnates as Khairat el-Shater and Hassan Malek, both key Muslim Brotherhood figures. However, just as the Muslim Brotherhood had no comprehensive social justice theory, it had never forged a comprehensive neoliberal economic theory either. Amr Adly rightfully rejects the criticism as an oversimplification. The Muslim Brotherhood was not Egypt's equivalent to the British Tories or the American Republican Party. Rather, he writes,[44] the fusion between the Muslim Brotherhood's conservatism and its businessmen essentially stemmed from practical concerns related to what the Muslim Brotherhood identified as its political interests, which included the need to ensure economic stability. It was also informed by the nature of the transitional phase and the seething conflicts of that period, Adly asserts, to which I would add the types of alliances the Muslim Brotherhood made while it was in power.

The Muslim Brothers took Egypt's floundering market economy as the starting point for their policy. Shater, backed by fellow businessmen, campaigned to encourage others in the business community to invest in and boost the economy. Accordingly, they tried to persuade them that market stability was in reach and that their investments and business interests would be safe. They also sent out reassuring signals about the nature of the new regime to counter the well-known scaremongering surrounding it.

There was nothing inherently wrong with this behaviour from the standpoint of democratization. Historical experiences show that, in the bargaining process of democratization, the elite of the former authoritarian regime should not have to lose everything. They need to be reassured that the new institutional order will ensure some of their interest at least, even if it will not guarantee them a share in political power. The transition to

---

[44] *Jadaliyya*, 8 August 2012, Available online: https://bit.ly/3maNYlH (accessed 10 June 2015).

democratic institutions is not a subversion of the class order. Class conflict is a matter left to those who criticized the bargaining process from this perspective and who will have the opportunity to fight for their viewpoint at a subsequent phase, from within the democratic system.[45] However, the Muslim Brotherhood's problem did not reside in the bargaining process per se, but in its inability to win the confidence of the classes with which it wanted to conclude a historical pact and in its loss of the trust of the bulk of the revolutionary forces.

After the legislative elections that handed the Islamists a parliamentary majority, the Muslim Brotherhood approached the business community. Shater, the Muslim Brotherhood second in command, gave a speech at the AmCham in which he stressed the need to sustain strong economic relations with the West. He also spoke of the economic strains that hampered the government's ability to finance development projects and the need for private investment in important infrastructure works in particular (roads, water and sewage lines, electricity grids, etc.).[46]

For the first time in its history, the Muslim Brotherhood created an economic organization to propel Islamists to the centre of economic life. In February 2012, the wealthy Muslim Brotherhood business magnate Hassan Malek[47] founded the EBDA to bring together prominent Islamist businessmen who shared a desire to reach outside Muslim Brotherhood circles to forge new business alliances. The board of directors included such businessmen as Safwan Thabet of Juhayna Food Industries and Mohammad Mo'men of the Mo'men Group.[48]

EBDA aimed to promote investment and economic growth and to support small and medium enterprises (SMEs). According to Minister of Industry and Foreign Trade Hatem Saleh, 'The Muslim Brotherhood-dominated government allocated 20 per cent of state land for industrial investment projects to SMEs. In addition, the state planned to help SMEs by providing technical support, training programs, and necessary funding.'[49]

The immediate economic agenda of the FJP included such items as expanding the tax base by increasing business investments, streamlining bureaucratic procedures and making them more efficient, stimulating foreign investment and creating an Islamic charity fund for the poor financed by a voluntary 2 per cent alms tax (*zakat*).[50] The latter point reflects the Muslim Brotherhood's charity-oriented approach to caring

---

[45] Przeworski, 'Democracy as a Contingent Outcome of Conflicts', 80.
[46] Kinninmont, 'New Socio-Political Actors', 3–4.
[47] *Islamweb*, 22 May 2011, Available online: https://bit.ly/33UWlLx (accessed 5 September 2015).
[48] Jaraba, 'The Egyptian Military's Economic Channels of Influence'.
[49] Ibid.
[50] Kinninmont, 'New Socio-Political Actors', 3.

for the poor, as opposed to an economic policy-oriented approach that perceives a structural relationship between poverty and the economy.

Morsi's government tried to channel investment away from the centres in Cairo and Alexandria. An example was the Suez Canal Corridor, a project that focused on developing the governorates of Suez, Ismailia and Port Said with a target date set for 2017. One of the mega projects in the corridor initiative was Technology Valley in Ismailia, which entailed, in addition to a variety of technological programmes, constructing a tunnel linking the Sinai to the west bank of the canal. The initiative also envisioned creating an industrial zone and a major seaport on the Mediterranean. The Egyptian government anticipated that the initiative could attract $100 billion in investments and create a million jobs as a direct result of its projects. However, the plan rankled with the army brass, who saw the three Suez Canal governorates as key strategic zones and, hence, their own turf; they also realized that they would be marginalized in the project.[51]

The canal corridor proposal is a salient example of concern for development and promoting the business sector at the same time. The initiative would presumably have been a leading engine for investment, as it would have secured both investment and financial support from Qatar. However, as it would probably have excluded the army from a key profitable venture in an area it saw as its own sphere of influence, the army, journalists connected with the Office of the Defence Minister (as subsequent leaks would reveal), and some opposition figures began to spread rumours that cast the project as a plot to sell the Suez Canal. In fact, the military saw that area as the preserve for its own corporate investments,[52] as would become apparent when it set that project into full swing after the coup.

It is almost incredible how Morsi was held responsible for the economic deterioration so early on in his presidency. It was as though he had created the structural problems inherited from the Mubarak era and then topped them off with the financial burdens and market turmoil in the violent and unstable period after the revolution. Since the beginning of the revolution in January 2011, a million Egyptians had lost their jobs due to the upheaval and the consequent fall-off in investment and tourism. The diminishing revenues from investments and tourism contributed to the erosion of hard currency reserves, which plunged to less than half their level on the eve of Mubarak's overthrow, even if aid from Saudi Arabia (during the SCAF era) and Qatar helped stanch the depletion. The plummeting reserves fed speculation about a possible devaluation of the Egyptian pound. But the new government was reluctant to take such action because it would

[51] Jaraba, 'The Egyptian Military's Economic Channels of Influence'.
[52] Colombo, 'The Military, Egyptian Bag-snatchers'.

trigger higher inflation and further diminish the purchasing power of the poor. Bear in mind that 40 per cent of Egyptians lived on less than two dollars a day.[53]

Some of the economic problems at the time stemmed from the climate of anxiety and uncertainty after the revolution. Theoretically, the handover of power to an elected president could help remedy that uncertainty, at least in terms of the country's political orientation and forthcoming economic policy. A tangible sign of such a possibility occurred the day after Morsi was declared the winner in the presidential elections: the Egyptian stock exchange shot up 7.5 points,[54] the largest single-day increase since the 2008 global financial crisis. It was natural for people to worry about rising unemployment rates, inflation, budgetary deficit, the declining value of the local currency, the problem of how to service the national debt and the decline in foreign investment from over $30 billion to under $1 billion. It was also natural to expect Morsi, as president, to address these problems. But to blame him for causing them was nothing less than scurrilous. Perhaps the best proof that the accusations and rumour-mongering were orchestrated is to be found in the fact that the authors of the accusations and rumours fell silent when the same problems persisted and even worsened precipitously during the first year after the 3 July 2013 coup.

The reluctance of businessmen to invest was part of the crisis that Morsi was accused of creating. There was no sign of it abating. The figures, in general, pointed to the persistence of the structural problems in the Egyptian economy while no genuine plan to grapple with specific issues stood a chance of succeeding in face of the lack of cooperation and, indeed, the outright defiance from of the state bureaucracy.

It cannot be denied that all economic data and reports gave a generally negative picture of the economy under Morsi. In his year in power, Egypt's credit rating was downgraded for the fourth time, reflecting the international concern over the instability and the precarious state of the economy.[55] Exchange rates for foreign currencies spiked as never before and the dollar broke the 7.00 Egyptian pound barrier for the first time. The rate had been 6.07 per dollar before Morsi took office.

I have previously discussed the 'expectations revolution' in Egyptian society after the January revolution. The term signifies that people had become more demanding on bread-and-butter issues. This meant that any government that came to power after a revolution that championed

---

[53] Doaa S. Abdou and Zeinab Zaazou, 'The Egyptian Revolution and Post Socio-Economic Impact', *Topics in Middle Eastern and African Economies* 15, no. 1 (May 2013): 103.
[54] *Financial Times*, 25 June 2012, Available online: https://on.ft.com/3pfwuJX (accessed 20 October 2021); *Al Arabiya*, Available online: https://bit.ly/3n3Jwaw (accessed 20 October 2021).
[55] Colombo, 'The Military, Egyptian Bag-snatchers'.

social justice had to work to improve the lives of the people in concrete and tangible ways, even at the expense of budgetary figures and against the advice of economists. Progress towards this end was essential to the stability of the post-revolutionary regime. Therefore, while more long-term policies were being drawn up, social policy had to be prioritized when shaping short-term economic policies precisely because of the emphasis it gives to people's livelihoods at this stage. However, CAPMAS statistics show that the poverty rate in Egypt during this period climbed to 25.2 per cent of the population, up from 22 per cent before the revolution. According to an unofficial report by the EFB, 42 per cent of Egyptians lived below the poverty line in 2013.[56] I believe that this figure more vividly expresses the social conditions in Egypt both after and before the revolution.

At the same time, we should bear in mind that the poverty rate in Egypt is very high to begin with and that official statistics have always been misleading, making it hard to speak empirically of an increase in poverty during the two years after the revolution. According to CAPMAS, unemployment rose to 13.2 per cent in the first quarter of 2013, up from 13 per cent in the last quarter of 2012. Unemployment had stood at 9.1 per cent in the first quarter of 2010. However, such figures are inaccurate – unemployment has always been much higher than reported rates, perhaps as much as twice as high. Recall that the employment rate, in general, is 28 per cent of the populace, or half the working-age population. In other words, each breadwinner supports three other people. When you have an annual 2.5 per cent population growth, a low savings rate that dropped to 5 per cent of GDP in 2013–14, a consequently low investment rate of no more than 14 per cent (which does not even permit for 2 per cent economic growth, below the rate of population growth), plus an investment climate plagued by such major disincentives as the red tape, corruption and crony capitalism that controls the gateways into the Egyptian economy, and then add to the mix heavy doses of political instability and turmoil, you are bound to get far larger numbers of unemployed and a more severe deterioration of living standards than official figures let on.

---

[56] Lipset famously said that 'the more well-to-do a nation, the greater the chances that it will sustain democracy'. Certainly, the higher the per capita income, the more stable a democratic system is, and the higher the level of education, the more the people will demand political participation. To me, Lipset's maxim seems generally correct (albeit with respect to the consolidation of democracy, but not as a prerequisite for a successful transition), despite the criticism it has met with. Lipset, here, is concerned with the factors that sustain the stability of the democratic system. See: Seymour Martin Lipset, 'Some Social Requisites of Democracy: Economic Development and Political Legitimacy', *American Political Science Review* 53, no. 1 (March 1959): 75. In subsequent articles, he attempted to extend the requisites he posited to the transition process, adding to them other conditions related to the prevalent democratic culture.

Egypt's foreign debt climbed to $45.5 billion during the Morsi era, up from $34.4 billion in the previous year. However, GDP growth rose from 1.8 to 2.4 per cent, according to some estimates.[57] Morsi's endeavours to stimulate investments and reverse economic trends had begun to bear fruit. In addition to seeking assistance from Gulf countries, which met with remarkable support from Qatar, he sought closer cooperation with countries outside the traditional list. So he visited India, China and various European countries for this purpose, and it paid off. During his period in office, gross implemented investments rose from 170.4 billion Egyptian pounds to 181.4 billion pounds. In addition, the agricultural sector recorded some improvement, especially in wheat production and a simultaneous decrease in wheat imports.[58]

Nevertheless, the cumulative crises that Morsi had inherited became the instrument to undermine this progress, while a series of fuel shortages, frequent electricity blackouts and other such crises were used to notch up pressures on him and chip away at his popularity. Meanwhile, he continued to clash with other political forces, as the components of the deep state banded together to set into motion a systematic drive to topple him, involving the creation of the Tamarod movement and the organization of anti-Morsi demonstrations.

Perhaps tourism offers the best illustration of the malicious hyperbole used to attribute all economic woes to Morsi. This is a sector that is notoriously hypersensitive to security and stability, and suffered considerably since the revolution and the spread of unrest and violence. Tourism was Egypt's largest hard currency earner before 2011. Some fifteen million tourists came to the country in 2010, yielding around $12.5 billion in revenues. After the revolution, the numbers of tourists and revenues dropped by a third, and they stayed at that level. Later, however, the sector began to pick up again, bolstered by the rising anticipation of stability as the country embarked on a democratic stage. Minister of Tourism Hisham Zazou[59] was optimistic on its prospects for recovery. In May 2013, he announced that the influx of tourism had increased and that he anticipated the figure to reach thirteen million by the end of the year, a 17 per cent increase from the year before. The boom did not last. The series of crises in 2013, including terrorist attacks against tourists in Sinai and protests in Luxor, drove the numbers down again. Many leaders in the tourist sector, among whom were former military officials, figured prominently in the 30 June alliance against Morsi.

---

[57] *Al Jazeera*, 27 June 2013, Available online: https://bit.ly/3uGAqUH (accessed 10 June 2015).
[58] Ibid.
[59] Zazou was a minister in the Qandil government who was not affiliated with the Islamist movement. He supported the demands of the 30 June demonstrations and resigned from the cabinet in protest.

Egyptians looked to Morsi to remedy their economic difficulties, and he had no comprehensive development plan. But he was not to blame for the problems. It is impossible to understand the economy of his year in power without understanding the structural problems that hobbled the economy, whether those bequeathed from the Mubarak era or those that set in after the revolution. Above all, it is impossible to understand the economic deterioration in the transitional period without taking into account the political turmoil and instability in both the SCAF and Morsi eras.

III The state-directed media

The second anniversary of the revolution saw large-scale violence between Morsi's opposition and the Muslim Brotherhood that left more than 200 people injured. Demonstrations were also organized in front of Morsi's family home in Al Sharqia, and a fire was set nearby. Crowds assembled in the governorates of Cairo, Alexandria, Suez, Ismailia, Port Said, El-Beheira, Menia and Al Gharbya, and in many instances attacked the offices of the Brotherhood and its political party, as well as other public buildings. Morsi's opponents blocked the railroad between Cairo and the Nile Delta and the railway line linking the south to the governorate of Beni Soueif and Menia; the Cairo-Nile Delta Agricultural Road was also cut.

Rumours about Morsi were deftly deployed to foment chaos. The impact of the rumour mill is well illustrated by a ridiculous story that was repeatedly and firmly denied, but which nevertheless damaged Morsi's image after it was endlessly hyped, circulated and recycled through a network of intelligence-affiliated media: the lie that Morsi wanted to lease out Egypt's antiquities. The rumour was started by *Youm7*, one of several media outlets that do the bidding of their funders and take orders from the intelligence services, regularly publishing fabrications.[60] The goal was to assassinate the character of the elected president, vilify him and portray him as conspiring against Egypt. *Youm7* along with a well-known set of other newspapers and satellite programmes tirelessly targeted Morsi with falsehoods and groundless speculation, in this case with the story of a Qatari plan to lease Egypt's antiquities for $2 billion.[61]

Talk of 'leasing antiquities' quickly morphed into headlines touting 'the sale of the Pyramids', which were splashed across multiple newspapers

---

[60] *Youm7* is an exemplar of the yellow press that rents out its services to the regime, security services and capital and has no qualms about publishing outright falsehoods. Arab authoritarian regimes have long-established platforms like these to slander their critics, and *Youm7* in particular was funded by Gulf States and local capital hostile to the post-2011 transition.

[61] *Youm7*, 27 February 2013, Available online: https://bit.ly/3n6zKmV (accessed 9 July 2015).

connected to the intelligence services. The fiction was backed up with several 'documents'. On 28 February 2013, the day after the rumour first appeared, the official whom *Youm7* had quoted by name in support of its story publicly declared the documents to be forged and denied that Qatar or any other country was seeking to lease Egypt's antiquities. Saying that the exposé 'flies in the face of facts', he called it entirely baseless. The finance minister, too, said the documents published in the journalist's 'investigation' were not authentic and denied that he had brought any such Qatari offer to the cabinet for consideration. The antiquities minister confirmed that another topic had been under discussion,[62] saying that *Youm7* had intentionally misrepresented an old story and threw Qatar's name into the mix. The original story came from an Egyptologist by the name of Mohammad El-Bialy, who said that the CSA had discussed a proposal submitted by an Egyptian citizen to the Finance Ministry to increase state revenues. The citizen suggested auctioning off usufruct rights in well-known antiquity zones – the Al-Haram and Sphinx, Abu Simbel and the Luxor temples – to global tourism firms for a period of three to five years; the minister and members of the council unanimously rejected the idea.

Yet, the story remained live, snowballing between March and June 2013 and popping up in different guises. At the same time, the denials were given less and less coverage as part of a deliberate strategy of scaremongering directed by the intelligence apparatus or, more likely, an alliance of intelligence agencies and local and Arab businessmen. I say this with near certainty based on subsequent leaks from Defence Minister Sisi's office that exposed the linkages and networks working to spin a particular narrative during Morsi's tenure and after the coup as well. As was true in many other cases, official denials were ignored and the original fiction was expanded, fed and inflated. Media outlets solicited opinions from pundits about falsehoods, and experts, political figures, and intellectuals were asked to comment on events that never happened. Amidst the general media uproar, lawyers and figures connected to the intelligence services filed lawsuits and complaints with the public prosecutor asking for an investigation. These lawsuits were covered as straight news stories about actual charges, backed up with comments that declared the president a traitor. The media subsequently published analyses that purported to prove the Brotherhood's hatred of Egypt and its history. The fabrications of the yellow press became facts, prompting further speculation about why Morsi was selling antiquities sites to Qatar. From the time the false story was first circulated and up until the coup, it was regularly reported that Qatar had

---

[62] *al-Ahram*, 28 February 2013, Available online: https://bit.ly/3DXaJTo (accessed 9 July 2015).

made an offer of $2 billion, Morsi had accepted and objections from the Supreme Council of Antiquities and experts had put an end to the project.

With the splintering of revolutionary forces, the regime's attempts to hold any newspaper accountable for defamation could be spun into a free-speech issue, and the deep state with its apparatus and media exploited the divisions within the revolutionary ranks to this end. The so-called electronic committees run by the security apparatus – essentially, state-managed trolls – spread these sensationalist stories on social media, circulating the false narrative more broadly and creating the impression of a massive public revolt against Morsi.[63]

The fabrication of the lie, the fraudulent documents and statements that gave it depth, and the reiteration of the lie in talk shows, opinion columns and journalistic 'exposés' created an echo chamber where widely held, but nevertheless false beliefs flourished. This same mechanism was used to circulate a laundry list of lies that gained currency between the spring and summer of 2013, among them that Morsi had agreed to the establishment of a Palestinian state in Sinai; that Morsi and Shimon Peres were personally close; and that Morsi had supplied oil to Hamas in Gaza even as Egypt was experiencing a major fuel crisis.

As the political crises mounted, Morsi attempted to counter the slander and tendentious rumours that were severely eroding his popularity, but he could not make his voice heard above the media hubbub.

These political and personal rumours were not bound by any standard of decorum, reason or shame. They spread and mutated with abandon, defying all logic and the common sense of both their purveyors and the broader public. The most trivial of these was that the Brotherhood's Guidance Bureau controlled Morsi's decisions and his every action. In fact, he made decisions independently; the real problem was that he did not truly govern. Unable to exercise any authority over state institutions and unwilling to take on the old regime, he instead attempted to contain it. At the same time, his aides from within the Brotherhood leadership treated other political forces with disdain. Intoxicated by power, they felt strong enough to ignore allies, and from the beginning they were exasperated by the need to cultivate and manage alliances, as demonstrated by their conduct during the Fairmont meetings. As Morsi surrounded himself with a group of Brotherhood aides and marginalized all others, he came to seem like a figurehead, not in charge of even himself.

When a handful of satellite channels associated with the January revolution proved successful, other satellite channels proliferated, seeking

---

[63] *CNN Arabic*, 24 December 2012, Available online: https://cnn.it/3vro4jy (accessed 9 July 2015).

to take advantage of the upswing in viewership, as well as protect the interests of their owners and funders, rehabilitate them amidst fears that they were targeted by the revolution and influence the course of the revolution. In this, they exploited the lack of a clear media regulatory framework governing registration and the relationship between media owners and editors.

A variety of channels appeared, among them religious and religio-political outlets, all offering platforms for political influence through the talk show format. Because most channels were openly partisan – their ownership being the prime determinant of their editorial slant – it was only natural that the polarization of the political landscape would migrate to the media and be reflected in satellite channels' content and editorial stance. Given the lack of any public oversight that could objectively assess media content, a subset of the media became tools for character assassination and political incitement, and even a platform for settling political and personal differences. Thanks to the enormous increase in funding from domestic and foreign parties who wanted to influence events in Egypt, as well as a surge of popular interest in public affairs, the power and political influence of the media was magnified.

The media free-for-all, the lack of professional standards and private channels' support for the counter-revolution cannot be understood without an understanding of media ownership and the ties between media owners and anti-democratic political forces, domestic and foreign. The pattern of media ownership encouraged unprofessionalism, flagrant bias and propagandistic practices, turning the media into the arena for a propaganda war and a dumping ground for misinformation – a sensationalism machine designed to obscure genuine issues and conflicts and public awareness of them.[64]

---

[64] A set of names loom large in private media in Egypt, all of them with clear political and partisan commitments. One category includes Naguib Sawiris (the founder of the Free Egyptians Party) and El-Sayyid el-Badawi (president of the venerable liberal Wafd Party). A second category includes businessmen associated with the Mubarak regime, like Ahmed Bahgat and the Daabas family. The third and most dubious category comprises newcomers who typically act as fronts for foreign funders. The exemplar of the latter is Mohammad al-Amin. A complete unknown in the media industry, he had made a name for himself in the agricultural sector. Yet in the space of a year, Amin acquired a sprawling media empire, starting with the CBC network, which included various news and variety channels, and going on to acquire a stake in other media properties, most significantly al-Nahar and its network of influential satellite channels. He also bought a controlling stake in the Arab News Agency and *Youm7* and *Fagr* newspapers, founded *al-Watan* newspaper and bought shares in *Al-Masry Al-Youm*. Amin doubled the pay of journalists at his new stations, making jobs at his outlets highly competitive, and numerous politicians and activists were brought into his empire's fold. Amin had previously worked largely in business in Kuwait, where he spent sixteen years; it later emerged that he was a partner of Mansour Amer, a prominent businessman close to Mubarak and his son and the owner of the Porto chain of tourist resorts, which has branches in Arab states (the Porto Tartus in Syria, for example). After the revolution, he entered media partnerships with Mubarak regime figures like Safwat El-Sherif, who was a partner in *Youm7*. In an interview, Amin stated that he had no ties to officials in Egypt prior to the revolution and that no one knew anything about him

The substantial investment that flowed into satellite television following the revolution stands in sharp contrast to investors' general reluctance to invest in other sectors given the alarming economic indicators at the time, which led to a broad economic recession. Investments in media were motivated not by investors' interest or expertise, but by politics. Defying economic or financial logic, they sought to mobilize the public by steering the media at a time when it truly was a mass media.

Businessmen were linked to the media through the nexus of capital and funding, which in turn drove multiple pernicious trends: the unprofessional editorial interference of media owners, the wilful violation of professional standards that subordinated facts to politics, the practices of obfuscation, sensationalism, the publication of lies and slander, and the blurring between news and opinion. More importantly, some businessmen may have served as fronts for capital from rich Gulf States acting through various corporate vehicles. Some also dedicated their media outlets to the service of various agencies with which they wished to cultivate a relationship for the sake of both their personal interests and political alliances.

The new climate of media freedom after the revolution, the citizenry's heightened interest in public affairs and a growing understanding on the part of social and political forces, both domestic and regional, of the importance of public opinion all led to the proliferation of print and digital outlets with mass readership. Many of these outlets soon overstepped professional standards in service of the interest groups and constituencies they represented. It began with tenuous steps and gradually slid into outright disregard for professional norms and the wholehearted adoption of sensationalism, bald-faced lies, misinformation, rumours and slander.

The margin of media freedom had begun to expand in the late Mubarak era, which saw the establishment of several private outlets, most significantly *Al-Masry Al-Youm*, *Shorouk* and *Dostor*, independent newspapers that broke with the official and quasi-official state press. While they were given some latitude for criticism, they were nevertheless subject to hard red lines and hosted both regime loyalists and critics on their pages. This was before social media and new digital formats reshaped the landscape.

In general, the private media reflected the rise of businessmen and their growing power in the regime in the last fifteen years of Mubarak's rule,

(despite his partnership with Mansour Amer, a close associate of Gamal Mubarak). See: *Youm7*, 2 December 2011, Available online: https://bit.ly/3n3WKDh (accessed 13 June 2015). See also: *al-Nahar* (Egyptian), 20 May 2012, Available online: https://bit.ly/39XCUG3 (accessed 13 June 2015); *al-Ayam al-Masria*, 29 December 2012. Archived Copy Available Online: https://bit.ly/3gvmPZr (accessed 13 June 2015). Although the latter source makes unsupported claims, it nevertheless contains details about the questions surrounding Amin and the legal complaints filed against him.

relying as it did on funding by businessmen and revenue from corporate advertisers. What concerns us here is that the old regime permitted this class to establish media outlets that were more open and liberal than the state bureaucracy, and the difference between this private press and the state-owned media quickly became apparent.

The new press made room for a new generation of analysts and writers, which greatly expanded its readership. In turn, this encouraged private newspapers, which first emerged in the mid-1990s, to rapidly expand into the digital sphere as well as conventional print media. In the space of a few months, these outlets established websites and social media accounts.

The private press ultimately grew to include more than twenty-five dailies and weeklies. After the revolution, media openness at times tipped into unprofessionalism, but this was initially a side effect of the new unrestrained exercise of media freedom made possible by the revolution and the masses of people who rejected the political propaganda of the Mubarakist media. It soon became apparent, however, that part of raucousness was intentional, purposefully created by social and political forces, both domestic and regional, that used the media to protect their anti-revolutionary interests. Now forced to consider public opinion after the revolution, these forces realized that if they could not win the public over, they at least needed to turn it against the revolution and its supporters.

The CIHRS, in collaboration with other rights organizations,[65] published a comprehensive report on the media's performance during the parliamentary elections of 2011–12. Those elections took place under SCAF rule and were punctuated by pivotal events that had a significant impact on the unfolding of the revolution and the roles of various players.[66] The report concluded that as a whole the media failed to act as a source of objective information meant to guide the public and help them understand the election, instead devoting much of its coverage of the positions of Islamist currents to provocative fatwas about the bikini, alcohol and the guardianship of women. The state-owned media was more subdued, still chastened by its former support for Mubarak in the early days of the revolution, and so in the election it was overall less biased, though it, too, tended to laud SCAF and attacked the council's critics. In contrast, in private media, funding sources determined its biases to a certain degree, the report concludes.

---

[65] Cairo Institute for Human Rights Studies, 'Media and Parliamentary Elections in Egypt: Evaluation of Media Performance in the Parliamentary Elections, 12 October 2011–15 January 2012', 2012. The report relies on principles affirmed by the UN special rapporteur on freedom of expression, the Council of Europe, and media monitoring organizations like the Pavia Observatory (Italy) and International Media Support (Denmark).

[66] Ibid., 7–27.

8

The coup

I Anarchy and how to sow it

On 9 March 2013, over a year after the Port Said Stadium massacre in which seventy-two Ahly Club fans were killed, the Port Said Criminal Court pronounced its final verdicts on the seventy-three defendants, among whom were several Interior Ministry officials. It confirmed the death sentences it had previously issued against twenty-one defendants, and sentenced five years to life imprisonment, ten to fifteen years in prison and six to ten years in prison. Others received shorter sentences, and twenty-eight were acquitted. The twenty-one death penalties had triggered emotional reactions when they were first announced several weeks earlier in the preliminary sentencing on 26 January 2013. In Port Said, angry crowds converged on the Port Said Central Prison but were intercepted by the army, which had sealed the area off. Over thirty people, including members of the police, were killed in clashes between demonstrators and police in Port Said, Ismailia and Suez. Tensions were already fraught in the area, like in the rest of the country, against the backdrop of the second anniversary of the 25 January revolution. In the course of the demonstrations and clashes on that occasion, police stations and other government buildings in the Suez Canal cities came under attack. In response to the escalating violence over the next few days, the army deployed and Morsi declared a state of emergency in the three cities and imposed a curfew. Many in Port Said and Ismailia defied the curfew.

The state of emergency strengthened the position of the army and gave it administrative tasks related to the circumstances. On 26 January 2013, Morsi convened an NDC meeting to review the recent political and security developments. Afterwards, the council released a statement containing several resolutions on how to handle the crisis.[1] It was the first time Morsi

---

[1] *Reuters Arabic*, 26 January 2013, Available online: https://reut.rs/3irfZpV (accessed 13 June 2015).

had met with the council;[2] prior to this, he had let it operate on its own amidst the turbulent conditions.

Neither Morsi nor his aides and advisers had the power to control the courts' rulings – not because the judiciary was independent but because it was set against them. This also applied to a large extent to the security forces, which were uncooperative. Indeed, security officials were likely plotting the anarchy as a means to undermine the Morsi government. It was easy to turn popular rancour and discontent against the elected president and his government. Journalists affiliated with the security establishment and many prominent businessmen were ready to heap blame on their political adversary, the Muslim Brotherhood, and the secular opposition parties and intellectuals helped.

As the unrest continued over the following days and spread beyond the Suez Canal cities to other urban centres, the situation seemed about to spin out of control. On 30 January 2013, the Azhar published a Declaration on the Renunciation of Violence. According to its preamble, it was drafted by a committee of representatives of the 25 January revolutionary youth, Azhar and the church. It was signed by representatives of political parties and youth movements. The ten-point document affirmed the sanctity of life, condemned violence and stressed the need to preserve the national fabric and uphold the state and its institutions. It also underscored the government's responsibility to do what was necessary to maintain security and protect public property without prejudice to human rights and freedoms.[3]

Instead of doing their duty, police staffs in several governorate security directorates staged protests and strikes. On 10 February 2013, they chained shut security directorate headquarters and police stations and called for the dismissal of Interior Minister Mohamed Ibrahim, who had barely completed his first month in that post, accusing him of 'throwing himself into the embrace of the Muslim Brotherhood'. They demanded more arms, the repeal of the new protest law and a halt to the 'Brotherhoodization' of the Interior Ministry. Some months from then, at the time of the coup, that minister would have the chance to show how 'Brotherhoodized' he had become.

The police protests and sit-ins spread to the governorates of Al Sharqia, Alexandria, Kafr El Shiekh, Qalyobiya, Damietta, Beni Soueif, Assiut, Red Sea, Giza, New Valley and Luxor, as well as to the port security sector. The mounting popular unrest and demonstrations in Port Said since 26 January

---

[2] *al-Ahram*, 26 January 2013, Available online: https://bit.ly/341x8PT (accessed 14 June 2015).
[3] For text of the declaration see: *Reuters*, 31 January 2013, Available online: https://reut.rs/3G6yJVI (accessed 20 October 2021).

segued into a civil disobedience campaign declared on 17 February and lasting more than three weeks.[4]

During this period, the first 'people's notary bureau' was opened in the city to issue civilian 'powers of attorney' authorizing the army to govern on the signatory's behalf. It was the beginning of a petition drive demanding Morsi's resignation or, more accurately, asking the army to overthrow him. Also around the beginning of the civil disobedience movement, rumours, fed by the press in the manner I discussed earlier, started to circulate that Morsi might dismiss Sisi and other senior ranking army officers.[5] Other rumours spoke of clashes between members of the police and members of the army.

The scales had begun to tip in favour of the army, which barely lifted a finger to enforce the curfew Morsi had imposed in the Canal Zone cities.

The media campaign against Morsi and the Muslim Brotherhood was gaining momentum. The systematic instigation of unrest and disorder was generating a stronger yearning for security and stability. The pro-revolutionary political parties and forces had torn themselves apart with mudslinging and factionalism. Against this acrimonious backdrop, there was no organized force left apart from the army and the unaltered state apparatus. Egyptians here furnished conclusive evidence of societies' short memories and their greater inclination to forget when their fears and instincts are triggered.

On 1 March 2013, a march to support the armed forces was staged in Nasr City in the area in front of the Manassa, the reviewing stand where Sadat was assassinated, located on Nasr road near the Cairo International Convention Centre. The main purpose of 'Support the Army Friday', as the occasion was called, was to reject any interference with the military command and the 'Brotherhoodization' of the army. Yes, this rumour, too, had taken hold, despite the lack of a shred of evidence that the Muslim Brotherhood was scheming to assert its hegemony over the army. Obviously, the army had orchestrated that day's march through its connections with the media, security agencies, thugs and the like. Newly formed political alliances, which would disappear afterwards without a trace, furnished the grassroots facade for the organizers. They were given names that spoke to the longing for stability and evoked constructiveness (as opposed to destruction), patriotism and reverence for the army, such as 'Protection Movement', 'National Initiative for Positive Interaction', 'Native Son', 'Silent Majority Coalition' and 'Military Retirees'. A nod was given

---

[4] *Aswat Masriya*, 1 March 2013, Available online: https://bit.ly/37J764I (accessed 14 June 2015); *Al Riyadh*, 18 February 2013, Available online: https://bit.ly/2VZgdZJ (accessed 14 June 2015).

[5] *Youm7*, 18 February 2013, Available online: https://bit.ly/2IzGYRx (accessed 14 June 2015).

to the revolution with the 'People's Committee to Protect the Revolution' and some political activists were on hand.⁶ Many of the members of these previously unknown groups had obviously been recruited by security agencies, affiliates of the former NDP and some business magnates. They were basically rent-a-crowds that could be called in to play their part, like a song-and-dance troupe, wherever required.

Suddenly a scandal threw the Muslim Brotherhood onto the defensive. As it was reported in portions of the press, a member of its Consultative Council insulted the army in a poem he recited during a gathering at the FJP headquarters. The poet reportedly described Sisi as a 'rat'.⁷ Tempers flared between the army and the Brotherhood, culminating in a statement in which the armed forces spokesman warned, 'Our patience will not last. Our response will be harsh and it will rest on military law.'⁸ Most news outlets that day chose to play up the rumour that Morsi planned to fire Sisi. *Al-Masry Al-Youm* blazoned, 'The Army's Message Has Reached the Ittihadiyya', the message being, according to political party leaders, that any move on the military establishment would be seen as an attempt on the part of the Muslim Brotherhood to control and alter the identity of the army. Another article in the same newspaper, 'The Army Bares its Teeth', cited a military source as saying that if the government dismissed Sisi it would be committing 'political suicide'.⁹ *Shorouk* borrowed the term for its headline – 'Interfering with Sisi Would Be an Act of Political Suicide for the Regime' – from a military source who informed the paper that a wave of anger had spread through the rank and file of the armed forces following the publication of leaks about the military establishment and the likelihood of dismissals of some of its senior leaders, foremost among whom was Sisi. 'The military establishment will never allow, under any circumstances, a repetition of the Field Marshal Hussein Tantawi and Lt. Gen. Sami Anan scenario with Lt. Gen. Abdel Fattah El-Sisi', the source said.

Then another front opened against Morsi before he could catch his breath. On 21 April 2013, the Supreme Administrative Court issued a stay on Presidential Decree 134/2013 calling for new People's Assembly elections on the basis of the parliamentary elections law (Law 2/2013), which had

---

⁶ *Akhbar el-Yom*, 1 March 2013, Available online: https://bit.ly/3DdZ3va (accessed 15 June 2015).
⁷ Mostafa Bakry, a journalist and press conduit for the Egyptian security agencies since the Mubarak era and subsequently close to Sisi, wrote that the incident was 'a new provocative attempt, on top of previous ones, to extort and deliberately offend the military leadership. But the army still stands strong against Brotherhoodization and remains a powerful obstacle to the Brotherhood's drive to control the Egyptian state and trap it in their clutches'. See: *al-Watan*, 10 April 2013, Available online: https://bit.ly/3D58TiD (accessed 14 June 2015).
⁸ Ibid.
⁹ *Al-Masry Al-Youm*, 19 February 2013, Available online: https://bit.ly/3oxEd2i (accessed 16 June 2015).

been recently passed by the Shura Council. Morsi had previously called for new polls in order to replace the elected People's Assembly that had been dissolved in 2012 following an SCC ruling. The Administrative Court, in its ruling, argued that the new electoral law had first to be referred to the SCC in keeping with Article 177 of the 2012 constitution, which required prior judicial review of bills regulating presidential, legislative and local elections to ascertain their constitutionality.[10]

Had elections gone ahead, the opposition parties would have scored major gains in the People's Assembly due to the Muslim Brotherhood's rapidly shrinking popularity, and their criticism could have been channelled into a democratic, institutional avenue. Morsi and the Muslim Brotherhood could not have rigged elections at that point because they did not control either the judiciary or the security agencies. But the judiciary continued to act as an instrument to obstruct democratization, undermine elected bodies and abort the January revolution, and the opposition parties blindly supported its actions.

On 16 March 2013, demonstrations were staged in Sohag during Morsi's visit to the governorate. Central squares filled with large crowds chanting anti-Morsi and anti-Muslim Brotherhood slogans. Morsi was forced to cancel a scheduled meeting with students and staff of Sohag University.[11]

That same day marked the beginning of a new wave of clashes in the capital after a protest rally outside the Muslim Brotherhood Guidance Bureau headquarters in the Al-Mokattam district. Anti-Muslim Brotherhood graffiti spray-painted on nearby walls provoked the headquarters' guards. The ensuing scuffle quickly escalated into mutual barrages of stones, Molotov cocktails and other projectiles. During the melee, some Muslim Brother youth assaulted several journalists who were covering the incident.

As tensions and mutual recriminations continued to build, opposition forces called for another rally in front of the Guidance Bureau. The event, held on 22 March 2013, was dubbed the 'Friday of Restitution of Dignity'. It, too, descended into fierce clashes between the Muslim Brothers and demonstrators, during which 210 people were injured.[12] Skirmishes also erupted in front of FJP headquarters in Cairo, Alexandria and Mahalla Al-Kubra. The Muslim Brotherhood had never been so isolated. With virtually no allies left to help defend it, it had to bus in members and supporters in other governorates to help protect the Guidance Bureau in Al-Mokattam. The threat was palpable. Some anonymous groups had

---

[10] *BBC Arabic*, 6 March 2013, Available online: https://bbc.in/2W0ZaXa (accessed 16 June 2015).
[11] *Alhurra*, 16 March 2013, Available online: https://arbne.ws/3jlvYGB (accessed 20 October 2021).
[12] *France 24 Arabic*, 23 March 2013, Available online: https://bit.ly/3jkD3qH (accessed 20 October 2021); *al-Ahram*, 23 March 2013, Available online: https://bit.ly/30KBgVB (accessed 20 October 2021).

set fire to four Muslim Brotherhood offices elsewhere in the country. The Interior Ministry deployed the CSF to cordon off the vicinity around the headquarters in Al-Mokattam. In a speech two days later, Morsi warned of insidious designs against Egypt and vowed to cut off the hands of the conspirators.[13]

A resurgence of sectarian tensions then added to the brew. On 5 April 2013, armed clashes erupted between Muslims and Christians in Khosos in the Nile Delta governorate of Qalyobiya. It was not this city's first experience with sectarian strife. It had flared there before the 2011 revolution. On this occasion, graffiti spray-painted on a mosque triggered exchanges of gunfire between local Muslims and Christians. Two Christians and a Muslim were killed and six Muslims and a Christian were injured in the violence. During the funeral procession for the Christian victims at the Coptic Cathedral in Abbasiyya, a fight broke out between some Christian youth and an officer and three soldiers at the main gate of the cathedral. The violence quickly spiralled, resulting in two more Christians killed and numerous injuries.[14]

On 19 April, Morsi supporters rallied in front of the SCC to demand an overhaul of the judiciary in order to purge it of old regime personnel. Towards this end, they called for the implementation of the judiciary law, which reduced the age of retirement for judges to sixty, thereby making way for a large injection of fresh blood. With the implementation of the new law, 3,500 judges would be pensioned off.[15] The demonstrators also called for the dismissal of the minister of justice, the prosecution of Ahmed Al-Zend (president of the Judges' Club) and Abdel Meguid Mahmoud (the former public prosecutor) and trials of other old regime figures. In addition to Muslim Brotherhood and FJP supporters, members of other Islamist parties, movements, coalitions and organizations attended the rally.

On 21 April 2013, Minister of Justice Ahmed Mekki tendered his resignation to Morsi against the backdrop of the controversy over the judiciary law. The former People's Assembly had been scheduled to debate it before the SCC ruled to dissolve the assembly in June 2012. When the Shura Council took up the bill, some members of the Judges' Club

---

[13] The video of Morsi's speech on the incidents was posted on *YouTube*, 25 March 2013, Available online: https://bit.ly/3gvuLd7 (accessed 17 June 2015).

[14] Egyptian Initiative for Personal Rights, 'Khusous: A History of Sectarian Tension and Violence' [Arabic], 11 April 2013, Available online: https://bit.ly/37N8Av6 (accessed 20 October 2021).

[15] Abdel Khalek Farouk believes that the law was part of the attempts by the Muslim Brotherhood and their allies to gain control over the judicial authority, just as Morsi's constitutional declaration was a step in his siege of the SCC. Farouk holds that the 30 June 2013 marches were a response to the Muslim Brothers' encroachment against the judiciary and other transgressions. However, he also faults SCAF for using the SCC in its conflict with the revolutionary forces. See: Abdel Khalek Farouk, *The Crisis of the Egyptian Judiciary, Freedom of the Press and Human Rights* [Arabic] (Rabat: Mominoun Without Borders, 2014), 285–6.

staged a strike in May 2013 in protest, claiming that the law threatened to subordinate the judiciary to the executive authority.[16]

The demands of the demonstration of 19 April had once been among the rallying cries of all the forces that supported the January revolution. By this stage, only the Islamists were advocating them. Morsi could have accomplished these aims when he was at the peak of his power after dismissing Tantawi and Anan and when he could have mustered a broad-based coalition of revolutionary forces to stand with him in his battle to take on the deep state. At that time, however, his priority had been to find allies in the military establishment. He had avoided the confrontation only for it to be forced on him later on when his support had dwindled to the Islamist movement. Before long, support from that direction would shrink as well.

Morsi was no Erdoğan, who recognized the existing secular democratic state and undertook to reform an established system of government. Erdoğan had nothing to do with the founding of the Turkish republic and its system of government. He came to power through a multiparty electoral system that had been in place and liberalized long before that (since the Bülent Ecevit government in 1974, which included Islamists), and his electoral success rested on a broad coalition that included the non-Islamist bourgeoisie and middle class. Nor was Morsi a Khomeini, a charismatic leader at the head of a clerical network who commandeered a democratic revolution and turned it into a theocratic one that eliminated opponents through sweeping purges and executions. Morsi operated under different conditions and he had to find his own way. He had not inherited a democratic system, but nor did he have access to the kind of power that could enable him to rule by force and eliminate the Muslim Brotherhood's opponents.[17]

As skirmishes picked up between pro- and anti-Morsi forces, the mysterious Black Bloc entered the fray. This seeming leaderless collection of anonymous mask-wearing activists appeared as suddenly as they would vanish after the coup. They clashed with Morsi supporters in Abdel Moneim Riad Square, in Talaat Harb Street and then in the vicinity of the High Court Building where the pro-Morsi demonstrations were demanding a purge of the judiciary.[18]

That spring, an unprecedented wave of fuel shortages in petrol stations, scarcity in butane gas canisters for household appliances and electricity

---

[16] *Shorouk*, 31 May 2013, Available online: https://bit.ly/2W2n30u (accessed 21 October 2021).
[17] For another perspective on the difference between Erdoğan and Morsi, and between Khomeini and Morsi, see: Achcar, *The People Want*.
[18] *al-Ahram*, 20 April 2013, Available online: https://bit.ly/2Z5mZBY (accessed 20 July 2015).

blackouts seemed calculated to focus attention on government ineptness and weakness. On 24 April 2013, US secretary of state John Kerry and US secretary of defence Chuck Hagel met with Morsi and tried to persuade him to lift fuel subsidies and take other measures so that Egypt could receive a $5 billion loan. Hagel, during that visit, brought Ambassador Anne Patterson with him to sit in on a separate meeting with Sisi. Patterson knew Sisi quite well. '[A]nd she noticed a change in his tone: Sisi signaled for the first time in her hearing that the military was considering intervening to oust Morsi.'[19]

II Tamarod and its dubious origins

The new Tamarod youth movement that suddenly burst onto the scene was one of the most prominent vehicles for grassroots mobilization against Morsi and evolved into the popular backdrop for the military coup. Though short-lived, it generated major publicity collecting signatures for a petition demanding that Morsi step down and hold early presidential elections. Tamarod was at the centre of the wave of anger at Morsi and the Muslim Brotherhood from the beginning of May until the coup on 3 July 2013, successfully uniting and mobilizing Egyptians against Morsi's presidency and energizing angry young people and the coalition of opposition secular parties that had come together in the NSF.

A week after Tamarod announced its existence, the NSF on 9 May 2013 officially threw its support behind the movement and its petition drive. The NSF had already expressed its opposition to participating in legislative elections and rejected Morsi's cabinet shuffle, which he had undertaken in an effort to mollify their objections to the composition of the government.[20]

Even if we accept for argument's sake that Tamarod grew out of the coordinated efforts of some revolutionary youth, though with the backing of old regime forces – whether businessmen who felt that their privileged monopoly position was in jeopardy or the military and security apparatus – this still does not explain the movement's development and its ability to mobilize the enormous crowds seen on 30 June 2013.[21] While we cannot ignore the initiative involved, the planning, and the conspiring, the important questions remain: How did these forces come

[19] Kirkpatrick, *Into the Hands of the Soldiers*, 213–14.
[20] *Elnashra*, 8 May 2013, Available online: https://bit.ly/3B3aKEg (accessed 5 September 2015).
[21] Regardless the inflated numbers in the Tamarod estimations of the turn out on that day (fifteen million people or twenty-two million), there can be no doubt that the size of the crowds rivalled the numbers seen in Egyptian squares during the January revolution.

together to form a diverse coalition of democratic revolutionaries, old losing opposition parties, remnants of the old regime, the deep state, the military leadership and the broad, non-political public that was angry with the current state of affairs and concerned about the future? How were the ranks of the revolutionary forces penetrated? What explains the broad response to the Tamarod movement? Answering these questions requires an analysis of the dynamics of the conflict that determined the trajectory of the Egyptian revolution after the fall of Mubarak and the polarization that peaked in the second half of Morsi's presidency, which is what this book has attempted to do.

There is no secret here. The political and social situation was extremely fraught – a tinderbox that needed only a spark (or a conspiracy, if you prefer) to set off an explosion. Capacities, organization and a publicity machine that these young Tamarod activists did not possess were nevertheless marshalled in support of the initiative. Unlike the January revolution youth, the organizers of this initiative did not rely on social media alone, and they did not take on the state and its institutions. On the contrary, the conventional media was pressed into service and state institutions cooperated with Tamarod. We should call the state apparatus colluding with political forces against an elected president what it is – the prelude to a coup – even knowing nothing about what would happen on 3 July 2013.

Initially, Tamarod's rise, structure and methods of operation seemed no different from many other movements and initiatives that had captured the public eye and proved capable of mobilizing crowds and organizing demonstrations in the two and a half years between the revolution and the coup, many of which I have discussed in this book. Going back to late 2012, we can see that the NSF was a strong opposition force well equipped to play a positive role in forcing fundamental changes, even though elements associated with the old regime had joined its ranks. Its activism was a warning bell, alerting the new regime to the gravity of national divisions and the need to take serious measures to address the crisis, particularly since many of the roots of this crisis were to be found in the legacy of the Mubarakist state and challenging them required a national consensus. Instead, both sides fuelled the political polarization, while the media further magnified problems, giving the public an inflated sense of their seriousness. Old regime forces exploited these conditions, drawing on their political and media investments to paint themselves as revolutionaries and ingratiate themselves to the public. These forces waged a war of attrition against an elected president who had not been in office long enough to justify calls for his ouster, though he had made errors that his government had recognized.

Tamarod's emergence gave added impetus to the NSF, generating a movement that outwardly resembled that of the January revolution in its demands for far-reaching change and its reliance on 'the legitimacy of the square'. In fact, however, it was calling for a coup against the democratic transition set in motion by the 25 January revolution. The declared demand was early presidential elections, but many of the old regime forces that mobilized and supported the movement were not interested in moving up the date of elections, but in tightening their grip on the country and stopping the democratic transition in its tracks. Some forces aligned with Tamarod did seek to return to the revolution's principles and blamed Islamists for their style of governance and their abandonment of the revolution; others sought to quash the January revolution entirely and took advantage of the public's weariness with revolution and 'chaos' and its fear of instability to do so.

The Tamarod movement spoke to a latent anger. The campaign against President Morsi was launched in early 2013 with the following slogans: 'Because there's still no security, because the martyrs' rights still haven't been vindicated, because there's no dignity for me and my country, because the economy's collapsed and it's founded on begging, because it's dependent on America – because of this, we don't want you.' In its mode of operation, Tamarod was peaceful, collecting signatures for a petition demanding that Morsi step down and transfer power to the chief justice of the SCC. It defined its objective as the collection of fifteen million signatures by 30 June 2013, which would mark exactly one year of Morsi's presidency.

The movement's discourse combined the lexicon of the 25 January revolutionaries with an angry populism. Its petition form included the name and national identity number of the signatory, and the forms were widely distributed by youth volunteers and other citizens furious with Morsi's policies. Leaders in the field coordinated efforts and collected the signed forms to forward to the movement's headquarters, where the information was entered into a database. Later the movement allowed the public to sign the petition through its website.

Three young men affiliated with the Nasserist movement became the face of Tamarod: Mahmoud Badr, Hassan Shaheen and Mohammed Abdel Aziz[22] (David Kirkpatrick describes them as three journalists who 'appeared out of nowhere').[23] Acting as the movement's spokesmen, they

---

[22] Abdel Aziz's name is one of the 330 revolutionary youth activists included in Part I of this book. But the most prominent of the three spokesmen, Mahmoud Badr, was not identified as an activist by any well-known revolutionaries.

[23] Kirkpatrick, *Into the Hands of the Soldiers*, 216. He adds that Sisi confidante Mohamed Hassanein Heikal trained all three.

steered the movement's heated discourse over two stormy months. The press called them the movement's leaders, and initially they claimed to have been part of the Kefaya movement before the revolution.[24]

Tamarod proceeded as if collecting signatures from more Egyptians than voted for Morsi in the presidential election would be sufficient to strip him of legitimacy. The campaign was similar to previous initiatives in which Egyptians had launched petition drives, most significantly the campaign in support of Baradei in 2010, which mandated him to speak on behalf of Egyptians and bring reform demands to Mubarak. But the real godfather of the Tamarod movement was the shadowy campaign that had been launched in Port Said just a few months earlier, which sought to collect signatures in support of Defence Minister Abdel Fattah El-Sisi. That campaign was suspended by an oral order from the Public Notary Office, which barred its employees from notarizing the signatures.

Initially, Tamarod's petition drive did not meet with a broad response, but the campaign gained momentum with the persistence of political unrest, the exacerbation of the economic crisis and the media's scaremongering, as well as the unmistakable collusion of the state bureaucracy and old regime forces. In addition to the petition drive, Tamarod leaders floated Sisi's name as a possible national saviour, effectively downplaying the NSF and its associated parties as potential civil alternatives. On the other hand, when Mahmoud Badr, an unknown journalist who had not been active in the January revolution, insisted on headlining the campaign with Sisi's name, the other two founders balked.[25] The attempt to combine an appeal to Sisi to 'save' the country with the collection of signatures from citizens angry about Morsi's policies set off a dispute within Tamarod that divided its leadership after the coup and then led to angry recriminations in the media during the post-coup presidential campaign. Shaheen and Abdel Aziz supported former presidential candidate Hamdeen Sabahi, whereas Badr backed Sisi in that race. Then with the help of the coup alliance in support of Sisi's presidential candidacy, Badr led his own mini-coup within the organization on 7 February 2014, announcing that the

---

[24] Kefaya, which brought together Egyptian political and intellectual elites in 2004 to oppose the Gamal Mubarak succession, peaked from 2005 and 2008, after which the movement shrank markedly. Though it remained on the political landscape, it no longer had any real impact, and most of its youth members joined new movements demanding change. It faded away after the revolution, as its most prominent activists joined other parties and coalitions, although some claimed that the movement continued to exist after the revolution. The adoption of the name of the venerable, nationally known Kefaya movement by the young men leading Tamarod was a clear falsehood and they soon abandoned it. See: *Shorouk*, 28 April 2013, Available online: https://bit.ly/3mijHDn (accessed 11 June 2015).

[25] Things unfolded in accordance with Badr's wishes (or what was wished for him), raising many questions about him.

Tamarod general assembly had suspended the membership of Shaheen and Abdel Aziz.

At that point, events unfolded the way they typically do with such movements: personal disputes erupted as both sides slung accusations that in turn spilled various secrets such as alleged ties with businessmen and rumours of in-kind payments, some of which were subsequently confirmed. Indeed, several pertinent facts would come to light. Tamarod may have begun as an opposition youth movement, but its rapid rise and well-funded petition drive were not entirely its own doing. Ties between the movement and the security establishment were proven. Even early on, a liberal activist who had initially joined Tamarod posted a comment on her Facebook page in October 2013 saying that she had left the movement after discovering it had received funds from Mubarakist businessmen (Hussein Salem was mentioned) and the Cairo front for the Kuwaiti Kharafi Group – the same front that had hired lawyers to defend Mubarak. The movement's leaders had not denied 'indirect' coordination with the Egyptian intelligence and security services, the activist said, which had been mediated by Diaa Rashwan and Hamdeen Sabahi.[26] Later, leaked phone conversations involving Abbas Kamel, then Sisi's chief of staff and currently director of the Egyptian Intelligence Service, revealed that the military had received Emirati funding for its political activities, including for financing Tamarod.[27]

The petition drive was supported by parties, unions and political movements, which helped to print, distribute and collect the petition forms or submit and store them. The movement also rented offices in the governorates in order to collect the signature forms and forward them to the main headquarters in Cairo.

One scholar cites Tamarod as an example of how ruling forces can orchestrate and control seemingly grassroots actions, similar to the demonstrations against Nawaz Sharif in Pakistan, organized by Imran Khan's military-backed party, or the yellow-shirts movement in Thailand, where conservative forces allied with the military and king to organize protests to bring down the government.[28] Numerous sources confirm Tamarod's ties to the military and Interior Ministry. The testimony of Ahmed Maher, a founder of the 6 April Youth Movement, is particularly

---

[26] For Ghada Naguib's statement, see her two-episode interview: *The Testimony*, [TV programme] Al Jazeera, 10 March 2019, Available online: https://bit.ly/3vrsiI9 and *The Testimony*, [TV programme] Al Jazeera, 11 March 2019, Available online: https://bit.ly/2Z8co9h (accessed 20 October 2021).

[27] *al-Araby al-Jadid*, 1 March 2015, Available online: https://bit.ly/3n5O3In (accessed 23 June 2015). See also: Kirkpatrick, *Into the Hands of the Soldiers*, 217–8, where he writes that he concluded in April 2013 that Sisi stood behind Tamarod. Kirkpatrick also covered this period and the intelligence leaks about Emirati funding for Tamarod as the correspondent for the *New York Times*.

[28] Ketchley, *Egypt in a Time of Revolution*, 108.

pertinent here. Maher says he was contacted to encourage his movement to do exactly what Tamarod did, but he refused.²⁹

III 'We're one people, you're another'

By 30 June 2013, groups of young people standing in squares and on the roadside distributing petition forms had become a common sight. During this phase, in a departure from the peacefulness of the 25 January revolution, violent clashes between Islamists and others became more frequent, as Egypt entered a low-intensity civil conflict between two opposition camps or identities. This 'us versus them' mentality was ably captured by a new song titled 'We're One People, You're Another'. The division was the natural outcome of the transformation of political debate and competition between political forces with different platforms into a religious-secular conflict. This sort of polarization can easily be converted into an identity conflict that does not serve democracy, but rather creates new sociopolitical vertical fractures in society.

The division of Arab societies between secularists and the religiously observant, or between political forces that claim to be secular and others that claim to be religious – and this is more accurate since the public itself is not divided into opposing secular and religious camps – does give rise to political pluralism. On the contrary, it generates social fissures that preclude pluralism. Vertical communal divisions that are antithetical to pluralism divide the community into 'us' and 'them', whereas democratic political pluralism refers to diversity within the 'us' itself, rather than setting it against a 'them'. Regardless of factors for social cohesion, the 'us' for a democratic system is the entire citizenry. Within it, competing political forces vie to win its trust, each with divergent views about the interests of this common 'us'.³⁰

The media waged the Cold War, while quasi-militias and gang-like bands assumed responsibility for the hot war. The two combined – the gang activity coupled with media incitement – added a violent dimension to communal tensions, even as the police approach to the growing security vacuum raised questions. The Muslim Brotherhood's involvement in these incidents further heightened the growing unease, and it was no longer

---

[29] Ibid., 112–13.
[30] Azmi Bishara, 'Us and Them and the Dilemma of Democratic Culture in the Age of Revolution' [Arabic], in *On Revolution and the Propensity for Revolution* [Arabic], 2nd edn (Beirut: Arab Centre for Research and Policy Studies, 2014), 144.

difficult to see the groundwork being laid to authorize the armed forces to step in to prevent the eruption of a civil war.

In the meantime, the media and political parties increasingly urged the armed forces to confront the Islamists' capacity for mobilizing crowds amidst unrest and fear-mongering that undermined any opportunity for mediation, dialogue or rapprochement between political opponents. This climate similarly gave forces that until recently had been silenced by the January revolution the chance to surface and foment a military coup. The sequence of events indicates that this was more than a surge of legitimate anger at failed governance. It was a movement gaining steam in parallel to another project hatched by the military establishment to assume control, some of whose outlines had become apparent the moment Mubarak was removed.

As for Tamarod's effectiveness, the movement claimed to have collected more than twenty-two million signatures as of 29 June 2013 – many times more than the actual number collected.[31] The media not only covered the movement's impressive performance; it also inflated these figures, while the image of the movement's spokesmen was burnished in the press and their press conferences were organized in newspapers' offices.[32]

Tamarod was the object of much suspicion from the Muslim Brotherhood, intellectuals and independent figures who questioned the veracity of their claims to have collected millions of signatures. The forces aligned behind the campaign channelled their efforts into mobilizing huge crowds on 30 June, conscious of the need to visibly show that those who had signed the Tamarod petition had turned out to demonstrate (or voted with their feet, one might say). In the era of revolution and revolutionary legitimacy, a revolutionary spectacle was required. The campaign therefore relied heavily on the media and the capacities made available by the armed forces. The display on 30 June, which was aired live on television, proved a fitting culmination of the Tamarod campaign, demonstrating the extraordinary resources that had been marshalled to produce it, all under the direct aegis of the armed forces.[33]

---

[31] Mohamed Fawzi, a member of the campaign's steering committee, confirmed that no more than 8.5 million signatures were collected (in any case, a huge number), casting doubt on the statements of the movement's spokesmen, Badr and Abdel Aziz. *al-Araby al-Jadid*, 22 May 2014, Available online: https://bit.ly/3gyYK3D (accessed 22 May 2015).

[32] This cast further doubts on the impartiality of the independent press in Egypt and its role in supporting the war of attrition against the government and fuelling anger. See: *al-Watan*, 3 July 2013, Available online: https://bit.ly/39XlOI5 (accessed 22 May 2015).

[33] In a television interview, former Information Minister Salah Abdel Maqsoud revealed that the armed forces hired director Khaled Youssef to film the crowds from a helicopter furnished by the military. *Private Meeting*, [TV programme] Al Jazeera, 27 March 2014, Available online: https://bit.ly/3uxXPaM (accessed 22 June 2015).

The aforementioned leaks regarding Emirati funding for the Defence Ministry, unbeknownst to the president, proved that the defence minister's office had begun planning the coup and its aftermath in communication with Gulf States. Tamarod was the 'revolutionary' tool used to portray the military coup against the elected president as a response to popular demands, similar to the January revolution with one key difference: this time, the army, along with other deep state forces, was directly involved in orchestrating the grassroots action by fomenting chaos and sabotaging elected institutions.

As the Tamarod campaign gained momentum, neither government reforms nor cabinet shuffles were of interest to anyone; the downfall of the president was the sole demand. Even so, Prime Minister Hisham Qandil did undertake a cabinet shuffle, bringing on nine new ministers.[34]

In mid-May 2013, armed militants in Sinai abducted seven Egyptian soldiers.[35] Morsi intervened to stop a military operation against the kidnappers and worked to free the soldiers through negotiations, thus saving their lives. For many, however, the soldiers' rescue was not the important point, and, remarkably, no one but Morsi celebrated their return. (The lack of celebration for the living is merely the flipside of the lack of interest in the dead, as demonstrated by the indifference to the repeated killings of soldiers in Sinai. No investigations have been conducted to determine responsibility, and terrorist operations continue to be used to mobilize opinion against all opponents and dissidents.) Amidst the heightened antipathy to Morsi, his achievement became yet another cause for incitement against him after the crisis was defused. Several former generals asserted that the Muslim Brotherhood was sheltering jihadists in Sinai and had enabled criminals detained by the security force to escape, and it was claimed that the Brotherhood and Hamas were responsible for the abduction of several Egyptian soldiers in Sinai. None of this was true, and no evidence was offered to support it.

The appointment of Alaa Abdel Aziz as culture minister in the last cabinet shuffle occasioned objections from many intellectuals and artists. A professor at the Fine Arts Academy with a specialty in film criticism, he was relatively unknown in cultural circles, but his dismissal of many senior ministry employees sparked protests, and his severe criticisms stoked fears of the 'Brotherhoodization' of the Culture Ministry among some intellectuals, despite Abdel Aziz's own nationalist leanings. The crisis persisted for weeks, during which staff at the Opera House and its music troupes demonstrated in front of the Culture Ministry building. This

---

[34] *Shorouk*, 7 May 2013, Available online: https://bit.ly/3mi3EWj (accessed 22 June 2015).
[35] *Al Jazeera*, 16 May 2013, Available online: https://bit.ly/3gvyI1r (accessed 22 June 2015).

was followed by a sit-in by numerous artists and intellectuals. Following attempts to disperse the assembly on 11 June 2013, clashes erupted between Brotherhood supporters of the minister and the protestors, after which the latter staged a sit-in in front of the minister's office.

On 2 June, the SCC, nearly a year after overturning the People's Assembly elections, invalidated the Shura Council elections and the Constituent Assembly, although the ruling did permit the Shura Council to continue with its legislative functions pending the election of a new House of Representatives. (Notably, two days earlier, some members of the Judges' Club had protested the Shura Council debate of a new judiciary law.) In short, in a scene unprecedented in either democratic or undemocratic systems, the judicial branch ultimately exercised near full control over the political trajectory of the transition and the fate of elected institutions.

Two weeks before he was deposed, Morsi took part in a rally in the Cairo Stadium in support of the Syrian revolution, attended by tens of thousands of Islamists of all stripes. In his speech, he declared that the Egyptian people and military would back Syrian revolutionaries to help liberate the country from its despotic regime. To be clear, this was neither a policy statement nor a presidential decree, but a rhetorical affirmation of solidarity with the Syrian revolution. Even so, obviously Morsi had not consulted the military before making his stance public. In other conditions, the speech may not have raised any hackles or been taken literally,[36] but in his shaky position, with political forces following his every statement looking to pounce, it triggered a public uproar. Moreover, the conference itself was a disaster. Several preachers addressed the crowds with incendiary anti-Shi'i rhetoric; a few days later, eight Shi'i Egyptians were killed by a mob in a town close to Cairo.[37]

On 19 June 2013, Ahmad al-Tayyeb, the grand sheikh of al-Azhar, issued a fatwa allowing Muslims to oppose the ruler: 'Peaceful opposition to the legitimate ruler is permissible and lawful and has no relationship to belief or unbelief,' he wrote. Despite appearances, the fatwa was not revolutionary or progressive, as it may have been were it issued in a revolutionary situation; rather, it was consistent with the mobilization by the deep state, its media

---

[36] Regarding the semiotics of the crisis of governance for the Islamist current in this phase, note that at the end of the conference participants sang 'In Your Sanctuary, Lord', a hymn that draws on and alludes to the tribulations of the Islamist movement. This took place in an enormous stadium filled with tens of thousands of people, Egyptians and non-Egyptians. Outside the stadium, however, Egyptians were not familiar with this song sung by their president with his allies – they may not have ever even heard of it. Sometimes semiotics is more illuminating than analysis, and this encapsulates exactly what I meant when I said that the Brotherhood acted more like an insular sect, though a large one, than a political party.

[37] *BBC Arabic*, 23 June 2013, Available online: https://bbc.in/2VZwqy7 (accessed 23 June 2015).

apparatus and Tamarod. The sheikh of al-Azhar had not issued a similar fatwa against Mubarak or SCAF – indeed, quite the opposite.[38]

Tayyeb's *fatwa* came in response to inquiries from some opposition forces about the permissibility of demonstrating against Morsi, and it ran counter to some preachers who had forbidden rebellion against the ruler (Morsi) during the coming demonstrations on 30 June and declared participants to be unbelievers.[39] On 21 June, the Muslim Brotherhood called for a demonstration under the banner 'No to Violence', during which Tayyeb was attacked for his fatwa. After Tayyeb's appearance as a representative of the religious establishment on the stage from which the first coup announcement was made, any political analyst should have assumed that his fatwa was part of the groundwork for the military coup.

On 26 June, as the military began deploying throughout Cairo, Reuters, quoting SCAF, reported the outlines of a roadmap: the suspension of the constitution, the dissolution of the Shura Council, the formation of a civilian transitional council and the drafting of a new constitution in the coming months. The same day, Morsi gave a lengthy speech to a group of state representatives, among them the ministers of defence and interior, Prime Minister Hisham Qandil and a crowd of his supporters.[40] He adopted an aggressive tone as he addressed those who were casting his legitimacy into doubt and undermining him, but he defended the armed forces and lavished compliments on the military as Sisi sat in the

---

[38] Fatwas and counter-fatwas were used to stake out political positions, giving them religious legitimacy and support and thus helping to promote them among pious segments of society. Tayyeb swung between, on the one hand, urging prudence, rejecting declarations of unbelief (*takfir*) as a political tool and supporting peaceful action and, on the other, attempting to rein in the opposition to Mubarak during the 25 January revolution. On 3 February 2011, he issued a statement calling on revolutionary youth to embrace prudence instead of 'fragmenting Egypt', urging them to return to their homes in keeping with Mubarak regime rhetoric. Hours before Mubarak's abdication was announced, he told state television that demonstrations were now forbidden since the president had met the revolution's demands. His later fatwa on the permissibility of peaceful protest, while correct, was issued in the context of his declared support for a possible military coup. As anti-coup protests gained steam, and some of them were organized at Azhar and its university, Tayyeb described the action of holding Qurans aloft at demonstrations as 'a trick to capture the minds of simple folk'.

[39] Generally, Salafists hold that rebellion against the ruler is forbidden as long as he adheres to Shari'a and does not enjoin sin. During the crisis, several fatwas were issued by Yasser Borhamy, Muhammad Said Raslan, Omar Abd al-Kafi and several other Salafists.

[40] In a speech to the armed forces, Sisi stated that he dictated the basic outlines of Morsi's speech in light of the military's proposals for defusing the crisis, but Morsi rejected his counsel. See: *YouTube*, 13 April 2015, Available online: https://bit.ly/3DXJU1o (accessed 20 October 2021). He confirmed this in interviews during his election campaign a year after the coup, including in an interview with the Hayat channel. See *YouTube*, 4 February 2018, Available online: https://bit.ly/3vwjAbn (accessed 20 October 2021). In that interview, Sisi clarified that Morsi was already embattled when he gave the speech and had asked Sisi about the military planes flying overhead. According to Sisi, Morsi wanted other military commanders to attend the speech to ensure that the military would hear and understand what he said.

front row. 'We've got men as good as gold in the armed forces,' Morsi memorably commented.[41]

On 28 June 2013, the Muslim Brotherhood and Morsi supporters began a sit-in at Raba'a al-Adawiyya Square in advance of the demonstrations of 30 June called by Tamarod and opposition political forces. The occupation of the square lasted for six weeks, extending beyond Morsi's removal and drawing in growing crowds, particularly after the coup.[42] Between 18 June and 3 July, demonstrators and Morsi partisans clashed and seventy-four Brotherhood offices and headquarters were torched, most of them in the three-day period from 28 June to 1 July.[43]

Millions of Egyptians in many cities participated in the demonstrations of 30 June 2013, demanding that Morsi step down. The state apparatus and the opposition united against the Brotherhood; the armed forces and police, as well as Azhar and the Coptic Church, had declared their neutrality in the political crisis.

The demonstrations continued the next day, during which ten people were killed in front of the Brotherhood's Guidance Bureau headquarters in Al-Mokattam. The same day, five ministers resigned in solidarity with the protestors' demands. The demonstrations were concentrated in Tahrir Square and the area around the Ittihadiyya Presidential Palace, as well as the main squares of other Egyptian cities.

On 1 July 2013, and against the backdrop of the slander that Morsi had embroiled the country in a civil war, the minister of defence issued a statement on behalf of the armed forces giving 'political forces' forty-eight hours to resolve the crisis. If no agreement could be reached that met the people's demands, the minister said, the armed forces would announce a roadmap and take measures to enact it. Once more, the minister of defence treated the president as just one of many political forces, rather than the legitimate, elected executive.

The presidency responded to the statement on the morning of 2 July 2013 with its own statement, which noted that the military's words 'carry connotations that may disrupt the already complex national landscape'. Later that same day, the Court of Cassation invalidated the appointment of a new public prosecutor, further confusing matters.

More cabinet members resigned, among them the foreign minister and Sami Anan, appointed as Morsi's security adviser (in reality, a figurehead

---

[41] *Al-Masry Al-Youm*, 27 June 2013, Available online: https://bit.ly/2ZpIAFe (accessed 26 October 2021).
[42] The sit-in ended in an unprecedented bloodbath on 14 August 2013, leaving some 1,500 people dead. It began primarily with Morsi supporters' calls for a *milyoniyya* under the banner of 'Legitimacy Is a Red Line'.
[43] Ketchley, *Egypt in a Time of Revolution*, 115.

position that was more of a face-saving gesture for Anan, who had been dismissed by Morsi); thirty members of the Shura Council also resigned.

Strangely, until 2 July 2013, it seems that Morsi and his office were certain that no coup was in the works.[44] Only then, Morsi gave a speech,[45] broadcast on state television, during which he attempted to stop the coup that was quickly bearing down on him. Rejecting Sisi's dictates, Morsi said he continued to 'cling to this legitimacy and stand in guard over it'. He reiterated this later in the speech declaring that 'there is no alternative to electoral constitutional and legal legitimacy', vowing 'to preserve legitimacy at the cost of my life' and saying that 'he who strives for illegitimacy will find this aim turned against him'.

Attempting to blunt the discourse of the putschists who accused the Brotherhood of seeking to destroy the military, Morsi addressed members of the armed forces directly: 'I want to preserve the army, which we have built with our blood, our sweat and our resources. Beware of offense to the armed forces. Do not confront the army with violence or use it against it. Preserve the military for it is our major reservoir. Violence and bloodshed are a trap that brings joy to our enemies.'

Morsi seemed to offer a final concession, speaking of 'an initiative from the government and armed forces' to form a national coalition government and an independent legal committee to draft constitutional amendments and a media code of ethics. He did not forget to blame the media. 'We say to the media: enough' – while admitting that he had made errors during his tenure: 'I confess that I have made mistakes. . . . The cause of the problems is the past and some failure on my part.' But the speech did not derail the plot coming together against him in the streets and within the military. It was too late, and every concession he made at this point looked like weakness.

The crisis culminated in Morsi's arrest by the military on 3 July 2013. Adly Mansour, the chief justice of the SCC, assumed the duties of the president and appointed Mohamed ElBaradei as his vice-president. The candidate of revolutionary forces, Baradei had refused to stand in the presidential election, but this did not prevent his supporters from attempting to persuade SCAF to appoint him president after the revolution. This, the council refused to do, but it did ultimately agree to his appointment as

---

[44] Seif al-Din Abdel Fattah told me that he contacted the president's office on the afternoon of 2 July for reassurance and was told that Sisi was then present with the president and everything was fine. He was informed that an agreement had been reached, which he would hear about that evening, and that he would be dispatched to NSF leaders to apprise them of it and secure their agreement.

[45] The speech was televised on 2 July 2013 and can be found on *YouTube*, Available online: https://bit.ly/3C0Rg3y (accessed 20 October 2021).

vice-president, without elections and after a military coup.[46] He resigned six months later in the wake of the massacre at Raba'a Square.

The coup took place on the evening of 3 July 2013. After the deadline for a resolution came and went, the defence minister announced that the SCC chief justice had assumed the duties of the president pending early presidential elections and that the constitution had been suspended. Announcing the coup, Sisi was surrounded on a stage by a carefully chosen cast of political and military leaders designed to demonstrate support for the coup by diverse political factions, social constituencies and religious institutions.[47]

The roadmap he announced seemed to meet the demands of the demonstrators and the Egyptian people more broadly:

- The constitution was temporarily suspended.
- The chief justice of the SCC would take the oath of office before the court's general assembly.
- Early presidential elections would be held with the chief justice assuming presidential power in the interim period, pending the election of a new president.
- The interim president would have the power to issue constitutional declarations during the transitional phase.
- A strong, capable, technocratic government would be formed, vested with the authorities necessary to administer the transition.
- A committee representing all parties and areas of expertise would be formed to consider amendments to the suspended constitution.
- The SCC was called on to swiftly approve an electoral law for the House of Representatives and begin preparations for parliamentary elections.
- A code of media ethics would be drafted to guarantee media freedom while ensuring professionalism, credibility and neutrality and the prioritization of the nation's supreme interests.
- Executive measures would be taken to empower youth and integrate them into state institutions as decision-making partners, aides to ministers and governors, and in various positions of executive authority.
- A supreme national interest committee would be formed of figures who enjoyed the trust and acceptance of all national elites and represented diverse outlooks.

---

[46] Ottaway and Ottaway, 'Egypt's Leaderless Revolution'.
[47] The figures assembled on the platform included military commanders as well as the sheikh of al-Azhar and the Coptic patriarch, political leaders (most prominently Baradei) and Tamarod leaders Mahmoud Badr and Mohammed Abdel Aziz, Nour Party leader Galal al-Morra, and writer Sekina Fouad. Lined up in rows flanking Sisi, the seating arrangement suggested that the military and civilian figures shared in the moment and would share governance as well. But the military soon claimed exclusive power.
See Sisi's speech on BBC News Arabic channel on *YouTube*, 3 July 2013, Available online: https://bit.ly/3C1fgDJ (accessed 20 October 2020).

After the announcement, several other attendees briefly spoke, among them the Sheikh of al-Azhar Ahmad al-Tayyeb, Pope Tawadros II, Baradei, Galal al-Morra and Mahmoud Badr. Employing their specific rhetorical lexicons – alternately Islamic, Christian and liberal – they laid out their view of the developments and their reasons for supporting the coup.

Pro-Morsi broadcast media were suspended immediately after the statement, and a broad arrest campaign was initiated against the Muslim Brotherhood. The country had entered a new era.

One might rightly ask: Why did the military mount a coup against Morsi, who had recognized and indeed expanded their privileges, instead of exploiting the presidency's weakness for its own ends? The answer is inevitably complex. We cannot ignore the personal ambitions of a person like Sisi or the ever-present temptation of a coup for SCAF, all of whose members question civilians' ability to run the country and hold a deep-seated aversion to the Muslim Brotherhood. Nor can we disregard the idea that concern within the military establishment about possible chaos near the end of Morsi's tenure spurred it to act. But the military and police cultivated this state of chaos, as previously shown. The shortest answer is that the military seized an opportune moment to take power amidst the failures of civilian forces and their inability to rise above their differences for the sake of a successful transition.

In his first speech to the nation after assuming the presidency, Morsi had thanked and saluted the Egyptian military, saying, 'God alone knows the degree of esteem I hold for you in my heart.' Morsi maintained the military's privileged position within the state administrative apparatus by appointing military officers as ministers, governors and senior administrators. But he did dismiss Tantawi in August 2012, appointing Sisi in his stead, later promoting the latter to field marshal after an incident in Sinai in which armed militants killed several soldiers. Initially, Sisi cooperated so closely with the Morsi government that rumours spread that he was a member of the Brotherhood, which could not have been further from the truth.

Morsi and his government granted the military benefits that exceeded the norm in a healthy civilian-military relationship, while the legislature helped the military to expand its commercial empire. For example, the Manpower Development Committee in the Shura Council transferred ownership of a state-owned car factory to the Ministry of Military Production. The military was also permitted to obtain more land for building new shopping centres and a medical college for the staff of its for-profit hospitals that treat civilians. In addition, the military establishment was able to preserve the secrecy of the budgets of many of its commercial institutions.

Under Morsi, many of the military's exceptional political and economic advantages were enshrined in the new constitution.[48] Sisi was quite pleased with this and invited Morsi to several military functions, such as the graduation ceremony for new officers and the inauguration of new military enterprises. Some scholars take seriously Sisi's assertion – repeated on many occasions – that the military would not involve itself in politics and would devote its efforts to protecting the country at home and abroad. Indeed, in justifying the coup, researchers conclude that in taking a stand against Morsi, and siding with youth and opposition groups that had repeatedly railed against the military's privileges, the military acted recklessly, sacrificing its own interests for those of the country and risking serious losses in the future as a result. In short, they argue, in abandoning Morsi the military abandoned its own interests for the sake of the country![49]

On the contrary, it was young people and civilian politicians who took a risk in siding with the military. In doing so, they ceded a core part of their identity and lost the initiative, and the military ultimately turned against them as well. Very quickly, the military shifted its sights to shutting down the public square altogether, clearing it of all political actors save for the state itself. It is true that in opting to mount a coup against the elected president, the military risked a temporary loss of American aid, part of which was briefly suspended by the Obama administration after the coup.[50] But in exchange, it won the entire country, securing its interests and realizing its old ambitions to rule Egypt. The military knew that ultimately the United States and Europe would deal with whoever was in charge in an allied state and would not stand on principles or values. It understood that America's strategic ties to Egypt are, in fact, its ties to the Egyptian military.

It should be remembered that the military was prepared to cooperate with the Muslim Brotherhood against secular parties earlier in the transition, and that its current leadership coordinated with Morsi to

---

[48] Scholars emphasize the importance of granting a politicized military privileges and benefits, including material rewards and immunity for past crimes, in order to persuade it to relinquish its political role and return to the barracks. This may be true in some cases, as in post-revolution Indonesia, but in Egypt the military was given all the privileges it desired, but still seized the first opportunity to return to power amidst social and political unrest. Moreover, it did not trust the elected civilian president. For the case of Indonesia, see: Kurlantzick, 'Indonesia', 148.

[49] Abul-Magd, 'The Egyptian Military in Politics and the Economy'.

[50] The Egyptian armed forces receive military assistance from the United States. Indeed, most of the $1.5 billion given to Egypt annually is military aid. The United States froze this aid in the wake of the coup in July 2013 and the violence that followed, but Congress resumed aid to Egypt after the presidential election that brought Sisi to power, although the election was widely considered an illegitimate farce. A substantial part of military aid to Egypt comes in the form of arms and military equipment purchased from US manufacturers with US aid. See: Walaa Ramadan, 'The Egyptian Military Empire', Middle East Monitor, 9 July 2014, Available online: https://bit.ly/3mdjYaG (accessed 1 June 2015).

replace the old command with itself. It then cooperated with opposition parties against Morsi. But the military disdains civilians in general and does not trust them. At no stage, however, was the Brotherhood a terrorist movement, by any definition. The army designated the group as such after the coup to criminalize it and justify the crackdown and the violence it employed. In short, the military 'risked' something to gain everything because the opportunity to rule the entire country presented itself.[51] In this sense, it risked nothing. In his *The Man on Horseback*, Samuel Finer writes that for the military to interfere in politics against the government, it must find an opportunity and be disposed to intervene. For him, the disposition consists of two elements: first, a conscious motive and, second, the will to act. I believe that both the opportunity and the willingness were present in this coup.

IV The role of the Nour Party

The Salafist Nour Party was present on the stage when Sisi announced the coup, represented by its Secretary General Galal al-Morra. Morra completed the job begun by the religious leadership of the Salafist Call in promoting the coup and persuading the Salafist Islamist base of its necessity. As discussed earlier, Salafist forces, particularly the Nour Party, participated only marginally in the January revolution. Indeed, some Salafist religio-political leaders attempted to dissuade the public from acting against Mubarak, considering a popular uprising to be 'strife', which it was better to sit out.

The relationship between the Nour Party and the Muslim Brotherhood and Morsi's presidency evolved over three stages. The first began with the mushrooming of Islamist parties, when a few religious leaders with cross-Islamist appeal sought to build a broad Islamist bloc that could act effectively in the post-Mubarak landscape. During the debates on the constitution, the Salafists went on the offensive against 'secular forces', which in their view included revolutionary youth and nationalist, liberal and leftist forces; at this point, they merely coordinated with the Brotherhood on matters constituting a threat to the Islamist current as a whole. Also in this phase, the Salafists constantly raised the religious stakes in parliament and the CA, spurring the Brotherhood to take more unyielding positions on constitutional issues they had previously conceded or resolved in dialogue with secularists. At the end of this phase, the Nour Party's true position

---

[51] Finer, *The Man on Horseback*, 23.

was revealed when it appeared on stage in support of the coup. In the third, post-coup phase, the Nour Party began displacing the Brotherhood on the political stage, attempting to supplant the organization as a religious party looked on with favour by the new military rulers.

We cannot understand the transformation of the Nour Party and its shifting position on the Islamist partisan spectrum without understanding the parameters of its sphere of action as an organization that combined advocacy for the 'Salafization' of Egyptian society and 'correct religion' with political quietism and obedience to the ruler. The January revolution had challenged its way of operating in the public sphere in a way that could no longer be ignored.

The significance of the Nour Party should not be underestimated. It built up an impressive popular base,[52] and acted shrewdly in elections, adopting a discourse that looked more open than expected given the long-established image of the Salafist as a close-minded zealot. The party was fronted by political faces with public appeal[53] and promoted a discourse that accepted democracy – provided it respected Shari'a – after having declared it forbidden by religion prior to 25 January. But the party did not adhere to the values and principles of the revolution nor did it count itself as part of it in any way that would suggest it was committed to it, or even pay lip service to it. Indeed, it consistently pushed the religious envelope in the People's Assembly and CA, and its conduct and discourse were a principal cause of the widening gulf between religious and secular forces.

In February 2013, the Nour Party proposed an initiative to address the violent political polarization and the crisis facing Morsi. To the powerful security bureaucracy, which was looking for a chance to waylay the presidency and political institutions, the Nour Party appeared to be a pragmatic alternative to the Brotherhood, a party with grassroots strength and an international presence. The Nour Party also helped to spread the notion of the 'Brotherhoodization' of the state bureaucracy, and indeed it was the first to use the phrase in that context.[54] Even so, the party publicly rejected the action of 30 June 2013 and let some of its most prominent

---

[52] *Aswat Masriya*, 19 February 2012, Available online: https://bit.ly/3m2pevF (accessed 26 June 2015).
[53] For example, the party's spokesman, Nader Bakkar, who became the youngest MP in 2012, and Younes Makhioun, the party chair. The former party chair, Emad Abdel Ghafour, broke with Nour to form the Nation Party and became a presidential aide to Morsi.
[54] The Nour Party raised the issue of 'Brotherhoodization' in a party report. Public opinion was inflamed when the press quoted Makhioun as saying that 13,000 Brotherhood members had been appointed to the civil service. Party Vice-President Ashraf Thabet later denied this number, saying that in the report Makhioun had noted that Brotherhood members had been appointed to government jobs in numerous governorates, and the report referred to 13 governorates, not 13,000 appointees. It should also be noted that at this time Morsi's attempts to reach a rapprochement with Iran inspired a whirlwind PR campaign against the move by Salafist forces, led by the Salafist Call and the Nour Party. See: *Al-Masry Al-Youm*, 28 February 2013, Available

figures cast doubt on Tamarod. The subject set off a schism within the Salafist current: a number of prominent sheikhs viewed the conflict through the traditional prism of Islamists versus secularists, or Islam versus its foes, and these figures ultimately broke with the party and the Salafist Call to join various coalitions that supported Morsi's legitimacy; another faction believed in the need to avert harm resulting from demonstrations, which could end in widespread clashes given the enormous popular mobilization against Morsi.

At the moment of the coup, the rhetoric of the Nour Party was focused on avoiding bloodshed and averting a civil war, as articulated in Galal al-Morra's statement. This is the classic justification for a military coup – one used by the military itself – a security discourse par excellence that claims to be about 'saving the nation', a locution that al-Morra used in his statement more than once.[55] This rhetoric invoked the cases of Syria and Iraq to make Egyptians fearful of democracy. The Nour Party claimed it was making efforts that required raising the alarm about the dangers of strife and 'the destruction of the state' and ended up claiming that its efforts at reconciliation had been broken on the rocks of the Brotherhood's intransigence.

Even worse was the flagrant hypocrisy of the Salafists' decision to stand next to the Coptic patriarch on the coup stage after having actively promoted an anti-Christian sectarian discourse that helped to destabilize the transitional period – like killers crying at their victim's funeral. Even here, they used sectarian arguments to justify the decision. Prominent Salafists called on the movement to confront the 'Nasara'[56] and challenge the church's attempts to favourably position itself by supporting the army's actions, especially since Islamists would not be able to withstand the severe public pressure they were facing. This partially echoed the Brotherhood's claims that Tamarod and the wave of violence that preceded 30 June was all orchestrated by the church.[57] In the end, the advocates of obedience to the ruler (unless, it seems, he is elected) and 'might makes right' hid behind claims that they were mitigating possible harm, minimizing the chances of civil war and strife, seeking reform and standing with the military to prevent the church from monopolizing such an influential position.

---

online: https://bit.ly/39Y6riE (accessed 26 June 2015); *al-Watan*, 1 March 2013, Available online: https://bit.ly/3n893OL (accessed 25 June 2015).

[55] Posted on *YouTube*, 3 July 2013, Available online: https://bit.ly/3B02qUW (accessed 25 June 2015).
[56] Literally, 'Nazarenes', the term is extremely offensive to Egyptian Christians.
[57] *Facebook*, 7 October 2013. Archived Copy Available Online: https://bit.ly/3lYbxkP (accessed 20 October 2021).

The moment was a turning point within the Nour Party, spurring many members to break with the party[58] and leading to the collapse of alliances across the Salafist spectrum. Some described the position of the Salafist Call in Alexandria as divisive, saying it had overstepped the bounds of the permissible.[59] Indeed, some leading Salafists considered the Nour Party the 'faction of hypocrites' and 'a thorn in their brothers' throats who will get their just desserts from God'.[60] In the 2015 elections, the party's fortunes declined, and it took just eleven seats in parliament.[61]

Nour was not a real political party in the conventional sense of the word. Decisions were made by a set of sheikhs, and it was naturally predisposed to authoritarianism, with a demagogic focus on a single issue – the position of Shari'a in laws and social life – and an affirmation of Islamic identity that took sectarian forms. So, when its leaders put forth initiatives for accord and reconciliation, other political forces did not take them seriously. The Nour Party took wholly contradictory positions: it spoke about unity while inciting sectarianism; it withdrew its support for the roadmap announced by the coup following massacres by security forces when dispersing sit-ins in front of the Republican Guard headquarters and in Raba'a al-Adawiyya Square, but then participated in the fifty-member committee drafting a new constitution after the coup.

Those who said that Morsi's removal was not a coup, but a second wave of the 25 January revolution, argued that the army acted in solidarity with the street to prevent a civil war and that the new roadmap included safeguards that would restore democracy and civic life. This quickly proved to be a lie. The demonstrations of 30 June brought together Morsi opponents that supported the principles of the January revolution with others who supported the Mubarak regime. On the eve of the coup and afterwards, there was much debate about the 'legitimacy of the street' versus the 'legitimacy of the regime'. In fact, in this case, relying on the military to act against the people's vote at the ballot box was not 'street legitimacy', but part of the coup. If 30 January must be considered a revolution given its

---

[58] Ibid. Several members of the party's governing body resigned, among them Ahmed Abu al-Einein, as well as a number of outreach officials in the governorates, while many influential religious leaders associated with the party fell silent.
[59] Party leader and president of the Salafist Call, Yasser Borhamy, attempted to promote the narrative that the party accepted what had happened after the army had already deployed around the country and detained the president and that party leaders had no knowledge of what was going on. The party also tried to dissuade members from resigning, but failed.
[60] These were the words of Mohammad Abdel Maqsoud, a leading preacher with the Salafist Call. See: *YouTube*, 31 July 2013, Available online: https://bit.ly/33ZE7ZH (accessed 31 June 2015).
[61] The Sisi regime reduced the number of seats elected by party lists to 120 of 596 seats, increasing the proportion of single-ticket seats. The president also appointed twenty-eight parliamentarians. Turnout was much reduced, and Salafist voters punished the Nour Party for its pro-coup stance. See: Karagiannis, 'The Rise of Electoral Salafism in Egypt and Tunisia', 213.

undeniable popularity, it was a counter-revolution against the democratic transition.[62] This became apparent very soon as talk of the legitimacy of the street, the legitimacy of January, and 'the second revolution' evaporated, replaced by acclamations for the sincere leader and the sanctification of the military and the uniform. The 25 January revolution was denigrated and its leading figures tossed in prison, exposing the true nature of the counter-revolution. Despite the good intentions of many who took part in the 30 June demonstrations, the popular movement was shown to be purely instrumental for military leaders and counter-revolutionary forces.

V Mediation attempts and covert international support

In an interview in July 2015, former Muslim Brotherhood leader Ashraf Abdel Ghaffar said that US secretary of state John Kerry had told Khairat el-Shater in a meeting that the United States had no objections to the Brotherhood contesting the presidential election. Calling Kerry's position a trap for the Brotherhood, Abdel Ghaffar compared it to the trap set for Saddam Hussein with the occupation of Kuwait, portraying the Brotherhood as being unwittingly seduced by power.[63] This is conspiratorial thinking unsupported by any evidence. If the Brotherhood erred in fielding a presidential candidate, 'blinded by the lure of power', it does not follow that the candidacy was part of an American plot. The Brotherhood discussed the issue at length internally. I do not give credence to this trap business; rather, I see in American policy a pragmatic guarantee of US interests. The United States was less interested in the fact of the Brotherhood fielding a candidate than in the future president's policies. It is worthwhile noting here that after the coup against Morsi, Kerry himself accused the Brotherhood of hijacking the revolution. He did not oppose the Brotherhood fielding a candidate when the organization was strong, but he quickly adopted the language of its counterforces when the Brotherhood was weak. Indeed, Kerry opined that with its actions, the Egyptian army was 'restoring democracy' in the country,[64] and so he opposed the United States considering what happened in Egypt on 3 July 2013 a coup.[65] Since the US administration is obligated by law to deal differently with a military coup regime, the refusal to officially label it a coup precluded punitive measures or sanctions against the new Egyptian regime.

[62] Bishara, 'Revolution against Revolution', 29–30.
[63] *al-Sharq*, 22 July 2015, Available online: https://bit.ly/3l5dY4B (accessed 20 October 2021).
[64] 'Interview With Hamid Mir of Geo TV', US Department of State, 1 August 2013, Available online: https://bit.ly/3BgunbK (accessed 20 October 2021).
[65] Bishara, 'Revolution against Revolution', 8.

The subsequent furore over whether the 3 July action was or was not a coup was an attempt to obfuscate long-established terminology and concepts. After prolonged popular campaigns against Western-backed coups and coup regimes in the Third World – most notoriously, Augusto Pinochet's coup against elected Chilean President Salvador Allende – various laws in Western states were enacted that defined a coup as a military coup against an elected government and subsequently barred Western governments from providing any assistance to coup regimes.[66]

The new rulers in Egypt therefore strove to persuade the US government that what happened was not a coup, but a revolution, the proof being the mass popular mobilization on 30 June 2013.

In a speech before the twenty-eighth annual briefing of the Overseas Security Advisory Council in Washington, Kerry said:

> And those kids in Tahrir Square, they were not motivated by any religion or ideology. They were motivated by what they saw through this interconnected world, and they wanted a piece of the opportunity and a chance to get an education and have a job and have a future, and not have corrupt government that deprived them of all of that and more. And they tweeted their ways and Facetimed their ways and talked to each other, and that's what drove that revolution. And then it got stolen by the one single-most organized entity in the state, which was the Brotherhood.[67]

In just a few words, Kerry ably encapsulates the shallowest Western understanding of the revolution and projects Western assumptions on to Egypt's youth; he also doubles down on the long-standing hypocrisy in US foreign policy, which is based on calculations of pure interest, and the condescension common to Western liberals when it comes to the choices of peoples of the Third World.

Mohamed ElBaradei explained his position in support of the coup in an interview two years later, after he had become opposed to what was happening in the Egypt in the wake of the dispersal of the Muslim Brotherhood sit-in in Raba'a Square. In the process, he disclosed important information that raised questions about the role of Catherine Ashton, the foreign affairs representative for the EU, and the EU envoy to Egypt,

---

[66] Other international bodies provide for similar legal sanctions against coup regimes. The African Union, for example, imposes limits on the recognition of governments that come to power through a coup. Ibid., 167–8.
[67] 'Remarks at the Overseas Security Advisory Council's 28th Annual Briefing', US Department of State, 20 November 2013, Available online: https://bit.ly/3a1Mk1Q (accessed 20 October 2021).

Bernardino León.⁶⁸ Baradei said that he accepted the 'plan' drafted by Ashton after the coup, but, he said, 'The military manipulated the situation and opened fire on the Muslim Brotherhood's sit-ins, although there were good intentions to end the conflict peacefully. With the turn to violence, there was nothing else I could offer,' after which he withdrew from the post-coup coalition.⁶⁹

Ashton's plan involved the release of prisoners in exchange for an end to the demonstrations, including the Brotherhood's sit-in in Raba'a al-Adawiyya Square, followed by early elections and a return to the democratic path. But the military, which would have been the instrument for implementing such a plan, rejected this role. Having been given the chance to return to power by civilian political forces, the military would not waste it in order to appease Baradei or anyone else. It shifted course and evaded the initiative, likely in coordination with supportive Arab states like the UAE and Saudi Arabia.

The Muslim Brotherhood believed that Baradei's admission exposed a European role in the coup preparations, as represented by Ashton.⁷⁰ But Europe was involved in mediation efforts long before the coup and even after it, during which early elections were proposed. While this was not what the Brotherhood wanted at the time, it does not constitute conspiring with the military to organize a coup. The coup itself unleashed an international outcry and was widely dubbed a coup by the global public. In the wake of this, Baradei, other Egyptian (and Gulf) officials and even some revolutionary youth who supported the action of 30 June launched an international public relations offensive to clarify that in siding with the street the military acted no differently than it had during the 25 January revolution; at worst, the action could be considered 'a reformist coup', if not a revolutionary position, by the military in support of the masses who had turned out in Egypt's squares on 30 June 2013.

In this climate, Ashton sought to assess the situation. She visited Cairo and met with Morsi in his secret jail,⁷¹ and she asked to meet with several groups, among them the NASL or the Anti-Coup Alliance, which included, among others, former prime minister Hisham Qandil and Brotherhood leader Mohammed Ali Beshr (both later arrested). Ashton

---

⁶⁸ *Ahram Online*, 8 July 2015, Available online: https://bit.ly/3aVFATO (accessed 20 October 2021). Also see Al Jazeera's report on Baradei's statement and the role of León on *YouTube*, 7 July 2015, Available online: https://bit.ly/3C1q9p5 (accessed 20 October 2021).
⁶⁹ *Rassd*, 27 January 2015, Available online: https://bit.ly/3E2FDK7 (accessed 20 October 2021).
⁷⁰ Al Jazeera's report on León's role, *YouTube*, 7 July 2015, Available online: https://bit.ly/3C1q9p5 (accessed 20 October 2021).
⁷¹ *Al Jazeera*, 30 July 2013, Available online: https://bit.ly/33ZmzwO (accessed 25 June 2015).

also met with representatives from Tamarod and 6 April, as well as with Sisi and Adly Mansour.

Ashton's visit took place just two days after more than eighty pro-Morsi demonstrators were shot and killed by security forces at the Republican Guard building. The Muslim Brotherhood and its supporters clung to their demands – a rejection of the coup and its consequences, and an end to the crackdown and arrests – while the pro-coup camp, including then vice-president Baradei, attempted to persuade international parties of a viable democratic alternative – namely, the roadmap. Baradei claimed that there were genuine guarantees for the implementation of the roadmap and that the coup authority was committed to turning the country over to a civilian authority. The EU tended to support this camp on pragmatic grounds. Ashton told the Council of the EU that the restoration of democracy and support for civil society motivated her actions.

Ashton had met with Morsi shortly before he was deposed and informed him that both he and Egypt were in crisis and that economic and political failure would spur popular unrest and demonstrations against him.[72] In published statements, Ashton said that Morsi's performance contributed to the crisis that had led to 30 June. Ashton's initiative, which she denied publicly, called for Morsi's supporters to end their sit-ins in Raba'a and Nahda and other protests in exchange for a 'safe exit', the end of legal action against them and the release of Brotherhood and Islamist detainees, followed by early elections and a return to the democratic course. The initiative was accepted by Khairat el-Shater, then in prison, but the meetings between the European delegation and Sisi were cancelled shortly thereafter. The military subsequently denied that there was any agreement, and it used lethal force in Raba'a and many other Egyptian squares.

Ashton seemed to have accepted Europe's recognition of events as a fait accompli while putting faith in a transitional period defined by a roadmap that would guarantee a swift transition, as Baradei and other sources claimed. But in seeing the coup as the armed forces siding with a revolution against Morsi, pro-January revolution supporters of the 30 June action deceived themselves even before the Europeans. In contrast, the military knew what it wanted and imposed a new reality, relying on Ashton and her peers in Europe to accept the new facts on the ground and strongman rule.

Amr Darrag, who was responsible for foreign relations in the FJP, said that in her repeated visits – four by his count – Ashton tried to persuade party leaders that 'it was all over' and that 'there are going to be (new) elections under a roadmap'. Ashton refused to divulge details of her

---

[72] *EU Newsroom*, 11 November 2013, Available online: https://bit.ly/3AU9KBf (accessed 8 July 2015).

conversation with Morsi, but his son, who accompanied her on the visit to his father, said that she tried to persuade Morsi to 'accept the situation' and step aside for new elections. Attempting to be more convincing, she told Morsi that millions had turned out against him while only 50,000 people were in the streets to support him. 'If there were only 50,000 people on the street', Morsi replied, 'you wouldn't have come to see me,' demonstrating his faith in the pressure being exerted by anti-coup forces.[73]

The United States and EU worked in unison to push for what they deemed the pragmatic position, though in fact they helped to consolidate the coup even as popular opposition to it was growing. The US seized on Ashton's initiative, and American envoy to Egypt William Burns, tasked with reviving it after several failed rounds of mediation, pursued the same tack as Ashton and León before him. But the plan again ran up against the rejection of the military. Those who had appeared on the stage with Sisi when he first announced the coup, among them Baradei, had been sidelined, used as a 'cover' for a full-fledged coup, according to Baradei. León and the Americans again announced that the 'plan' had been rejected. León said that he had made a last-ditch effort to persuade the generals before the bloody dispersal of Morsi's supporters at the Raba'a sit-in.[74] The rejection of the plan and the failure of European and American efforts were followed by the break-up of the sit-in, the suppression of demonstrations and a broad wave of violence, the European response to which was far more tepid than its earlier statement might have suggested.

Although it quickly revealed its true nature after the dispersal of the Raba'a sit-in and two days later in the events at Ramses Square, the coup regime faced no real sanctions. After the Raba'a massacre and marginalization of the ostensibly democratic faction of the coup, the United States decided to freeze military aid to Egypt while encouraging all Egyptian parties to adhere to and implement the roadmap.[75]

Despite the deteriorating situation and the exposure of the roadmap as a kind of rhetorical ornament to cover up the coup, no effective Western countermeasures were taken. At the first sign of armed jihadist activity targeting American interests, the well-worn imperialist discourse again reared its head, dictating the need to sacrifice democracy if that was the cost of protecting US interests. Soon enough, the largely cosmetic pressures and sanctions against the coup, both European and American, were lifted.

---

[73] *Independent*, 5 May 2015, Available online: https://bit.ly/2IzzPk1 (accessed 7 July 2015).
[74] *EU Observer*, 15 August 2013, Available online: https://bit.ly/3oFtDGw (accessed 7 July 2015); for a narrative on how US efforts ended in failure, see: *New York Times*, 17 August 2013, Available online: https://nyti.ms/3gzCK9a (accessed 8 July 2015).
[75] The freeze was soon lifted, and under Trump, US-Egyptian relations became warmer than ever.

VI After the coup: Reading a book by its cover

Although this study set its endpoint at 3 July 2013, after giving due consideration to the limitations on the study or writing of current history, I felt it appropriate to dedicate some pages to the aftermath of the coup. Already then, the signs of the new order were visible, so much so that, even at that early stage, there was no excuse for not being able to read the nature of the form of rule to come.

On 4 July 2013, Judge Adly Mansour was sworn in as acting president. According to the roadmap, he would serve in this capacity until presidential elections were held. Mansour had served on the SCC since 1992. He was appointed chief justice on 30 June 2013 – the same day the *milyoniyya* marches set off to demand Morsi's overthrow. He took his oath of office as SCC chief justice on 4 July, just minutes before he was sworn in as acting president.

The moment Morsi was ousted, rioting erupted across the country, resulting in dozens of dead and hundreds of wounded. Fingers pointed to the Muslim Brotherhood and Morsi supporters. That same day brought synchronized attacks against five police and army checkpoints in North Sinai, including at the El Arish airport. The Brotherhood was accused of being behind these attacks, even though the extremist militant organizations active in Sinai, such as Ansar Bait al-Maqdis, were known to hate the Muslim Brotherhood almost as much as they did the state. Also, churches were attacked in various parts of the country. Muslim Brotherhood members and Morsi supporters were implicated in those as well.

Over the next few days, security forces arrested Muslim Brotherhood Deputy Supreme Guide Khairat el-Shater and former presidential candidate Hazem Salah Abu Ismail. Clashes erupted between the Republican Guard and Morsi supporters who had staged marches from Raba'a al-Adawiyya Square. Fights broke out between Morsi supporters and opponents in and around Tahrir Square. Twelve people were killed in Alexandria and one in Assiut during skirmishes between Muslim Brothers and the police and locals. Several Coptic homes were attacked in Menia.[76]

At dawn on 8 July 2013, pro-Morsi demonstrators marched on the Republican Guard headquarters in Heliopolis, Cairo, to demand his reinstatement. They had been led to believe that the deposed president was being held there. Numerous and diverse eyewitness testimonies and other accounts from political sources or ordinary people have documented

---

[76] *Al-Masry Al-Youm*, 6 July 2013, Available online: https://bit.ly/33VEuUU (accessed 20 October 2021).

the events as they unfolded.[77] The security forces 'defending' the building opened fire into the demonstrators. The Department of Forensic Medicine reported that 61 people were killed and more than 435 wounded that morning. Henceforward, the architects of the coup would pursue the course of bloodshed to the end. Every passing day brought further vilification of the Muslim Brotherhood and increasing violence in suppressing opponents of the coup. This was the prelude of the security apparatus's reversion to its practices in the Mubarak era, but with even more brutality. They had lifted all restraints against the use of live ammunition, physical abuse during arrest and torture in prison. According to some, this is also when the security agencies went on the offensive to exact revenge for the criticisms and insults they had endured after the January revolution.

There are three main reasons why they were able to get away with such heinous practices. The first was the division of political forces into 'us' and 'them'.[78] This inserts the friend-versus-enemy dialectic into domestic politics, which eliminates moral compunctions when dealing with the enemy. (To Carl Schmitt, this was the essence of politics: states at war with other states foster a friend-versus-foe mentality whereby the same moral, ethical and cultural standards do not apply to both sides.) Politics that cleave society into two imagined, antithetical cultures reduce the political arena to a state akin to a civil war and numb sensitivities towards the abuse, torture, rape and murder of fellow citizens.

The second reason was the authoritarian revival. In asserting its return after a counter-revolution, authoritarianism is generally fiercer in its violence and repression than the regime the revolution had overthrown, because a resurgent authoritarianism is strongly motivated by rancour and revenge.

The third and final reason was that the new authoritarian regime had learned its lesson, acting on the belief that the security agencies of the overthrown regime had been too lenient with its opponents. By not suppressing demonstrations, they had encouraged growing participation in the protest movement. For Sisi, this was a 'mistake' that must never happen again.

The desensitization towards the repression of some alien 'them' had already occurred in post-revolutionary Egypt. The Muslim Brothers were indifferent to the crimes committed by security agencies against

---

[77] Human Rights Watch, 'All According to Plan: The Rab'a Massacre and Mass Killings of Protesters in Egypt', 12 August 2014, Available online: https://bit.ly/3qTBLFw (accessed 25 June 2015).

[78] Robert Dahl defines the point of transition away from autocracy with the maxim: 'The more the costs of suppression exceed the costs of toleration, the greater the chance for a competitive regime.' Dahl, *Polyarchy*, 15. To this we should add: the threshold of tolerance for suppression and intolerance of plurality rises the more that society cleaves into 'us' versus 'them' identities.

protestors in Maspero, Mohammed Mahmoud and other clashes. Later on, at the height of the animosity between the Muslim Brotherhood and its opponents, the latter ignored the tear gassing, beatings and shootings the security forces had inflicted and sided with the same lethal agencies against the Muslim Brotherhood. The images of police officers paraded on shoulders in Tahrir Square on 30 June 2013 were iconic (and probably orchestrated by the security agencies themselves). The police wanted such scenes to be perceived as an apology to them, freeing them of the need to reform. The Interior Ministry took it as a green light not just to continue the same practices but also to employ them more extensively against the Muslim Brothers, other Islamists and all opponents of the coup.

On 16 July 2013, interim president Adly Manour swore in the government of Hazem Beblawi, replacing the Hisham Qandil cabinet. The Beblawi government included several ministers affiliated with the NSF, the main umbrella of opposition forces before Morsi's overthrow. Some were activists in the January revolution who had helped organize protests against Morsi. They included Ziad Bahaa El-din (deputy prime minister for economic affairs and minister of economic cooperation), Hossam Eissa (minister of higher education), Ahmed El Borai (minister of social solidarity), Kamal Abou Eitta (minister of labour),[79] Mounir Fakhry Abdel Nour (minister of industry), Taher Abou Zeid (minister of sports) and Khalid Tallima (deputy minister for youth). Beblawi retained five members of the Qandil cabinet: Abdel Fattah El-Sisi (defence minister), Mohamed Ibrahim (interior minister), Ahmed Emam (minister of electricity), Hisham Zazou (minister of tourism) and Atef Helmy (communications minister). The number of women in the cabinet fell to three: Maha El Rabbat (minister of health), Laila Iskandar (minister of environment) and Dorria Sharaf El Din (minister of information).[80]

Almost two years earlier, SCAF had offered the premiership to Beblawi after the Essam Sharaf government resigned on 21 November 2011, in the aftermath of the Mohammed Mahmoud Street events. Beblawi relates that his friend Hossam Eissa, a well-known Nasserist university professor, phoned him at the time to tell him he was the only person being considered to replace Sharaf and that someone from SCAF was going to phone him.

---

[79] Workers looked forward to better treatment after Morsi and under Sisi, especially after Kamal Abou Eitta, a leading activist for the creation of independent labour unions, was appointed as minister of labour. Their hopes were dispelled within a month. Abu Eita had stood by and watched as security forces moved to break up a labour strike at the Suez Steel Company in Suez, a city that had been in the vanguard of the January revolution. Beinin cites Abu Eita's proclamation after Morsi's removal: 'Workers who were champions of the strike under the previous regime should now become champions of production.' The remark signalled that Abu Eita had renounced his labour activist role. Beinin, 'Egyptian Workers after June 30'.

[80] Al Jazeera, 16 July 2013, Available online: https://bit.ly/3neVxdg (accessed 25 June 2015).

In response to Beblawi's question as to how he had learned this, Eissa answered that SCAF member Maj Gen Hassan al-Roueini had told him. Barely had Beblawi hung up than Chief of Staff Sami Anan called him up with a job offer.[81] The information, which appeared in a memoir that Beblawi published before he became prime minister, is significant because it is indicative of a certain continuity in SCAF's thinking and decisions, especially as concerned potential appointees to head the government or steer the economy and people it turned to for advice. That Hossam Eissa, who had been in contact with SCAF since the beginning of the transitional period, was given a seat on the Beblawi cabinet indicates that a contingent of Nasserists had thrown their lot in with the army from the outset. Some were in direct contact with Sisi, according to Beblawi's memoir.

A segment of the political opposition which had supported the January revolution was included in the first government after 3 July 2013, as a means to camouflage the coup against an elected president and democratic transition. These politicians took part in a government that hunted down, arrested and abused the dignity of colleagues with whom they had sat together in numerous meetings during the preceding year.

Although the secular parties were strongly represented in the government and in the first elected parliament after the coup, this would be short-lived. It was initially necessary to keep the Muslim Brothers isolated and deprived of support as the coup regime rounded up their leaders and laid the groundwork for the break-up of the Raba'a and Nahda sit-ins. Once the regime felt strong and secure enough, it dispensed with all the secular parties apart from its firmest supporters.

The Wafd and the Free Egyptians Party backed Sisi's nomination for president in 2014. The ESDP was reluctant to officially back a candidate, but many of its members openly supported Sisi. The process of divide and conquer from within the parties had begun, reviving a tradition from the Mubarak era. The parties dispensed with the search for a leadership with any distinct and independent views that might jar with the general mania of adulation for the army and Sisi. The resultant party leaderships were puppets in the hands of the security agencies, even more blatantly so than during the Mubarak era. As the next electoral cycle approached, new parties emerged. As they were merely parliamentary lists backed by the presidency, they are of no concern to us here.

In including a considerable number of opposition politicians in the first post-coup government, rather than opting for a government of technocrats, the putschists demonstrated their growing astuteness.

---

[81] Beblawi, *Four Months in the Cage of Government*, 157–8.

The stratagem enabled them to rally broad swaths of the public around them as they proceeded to establish the legitimacy of the new regime by packaging it as an extension of the 30 June demonstrations, which were billed as a revolution. Perhaps some of those who joined that government acted out of the conviction that it was a prelude to the return to democracy after a brief detour. The generals and security chiefs would not let those civilians indulge in that fantasy for long. As the military asserted total control over the country, relying on Mubarak-era loyalists, it threw countless 25 January revolutionaries into prison, including those who took part in the 30 June marches, and stifled all criticism and opposing views. Before long, the military dispensed with the NSF and its ministers and marginalized the political movements that had flourished while in the opposition to Morsi.

After the Beblawi government resigned, politicians from the secular parties were excluded from government. Businessmen were also politically marginalized. They were given a free hand in the market, but not in power, although even in the marketplace they could not exceed the ceiling set by the army's monopolies.[82] In Bonapartist military dictatorships of this sort, the state is independent from the movement of society and social classes. The bourgeoisie resigns from politics, leaving the affairs of state to the dictator who secures their interests without any say on their part on how he does so.

In his speech on the occasion of the naval and air force academy graduation ceremonies on 24 July 2013, Sisi called on the people to rally in the streets and squares to grant him a 'mandate' to confront terrorism

---

[82] Marx describes the struggle of the bourgeoisie outside and inside parliament, the struggle that overthrew its own rule and compelled it to cede to Napoleon III and his militia, which the army joined, as follows: 'Thus the industrial bourgeoisie applauds with servile bravos the *coup d'etat* of December 2, the annihilation of parliament, the downfall of its own rule, the dictatorship of Bonaparte. The thunder of applause on November 25 had its answer in the thunder of cannon on December 4, and it was on the house of Monsieur Sallandrouze, who had clapped most, that they clapped most of the bombs.' Marx, *The 18th Brumaire of Louis Bonaparte*, 115.

Even those who cheered the dictator were not spared if they were suspected of entertaining political ambitions of any sort. Marx goes on to explain the nature of the Bonapartist separation of the state from society and how it can represent itself vis-à-vis society through a leader of its choice from outside that society who has not arisen through the social power conflicts as a representative of one social force in its rivalry with another. He writes, 'Only under the second Bonaparte does the state seem to have made itself completely independent. As against civil society, the state machine has consolidated its position so thoroughly that the chief of the Society of December 10 suffices for its head, an adventurer blown in from abroad, raised on the shield of a drunken soldiery, which he bought with liquor and sausages, and to which he must continually ply with sausage anew. Hence the down-cast despair, the feeling of most dreadful humiliation and degradation that oppresses the breast of France and makes her catch her breath. She feels dishonored.' Ibid., 122–3.

However, for this very reason – the sense of humiliation and shame – the mechanisms of flag-waving patriotism and chauvinism kick in, producing jingoistic ravings and adulations of the unmatched genius of the dictator, defeater of conspiracies and defier of world powers, even if he secretly courts their blessings. Such is the official discourse in the Sisi era.

and potential violence. It was a curious request given that the fight against terrorism is, inherently, a part of the work of the armed forces. The army did not need a popular mandate to do its duty to fight terrorism when and where it exists. Clearly, this was a consummately political appeal for popular cover to sanction the use of violence for purposes that do not fall under the remit of the armed forces. It was a mobilization drive to generate mass desensitization towards, if not public applause for, the maltreatment of political adversaries, now recast as terrorists. On 26 July 2013, dubbed 'Mandate Friday', enormous throngs filled the squares for the *milyoniyya*-turned plebiscite on the use of violence against the Muslim Brothers and other political opponents branded as terrorists. It was a spectacle of mass frenzy in a rite to glorify a military saviour[83] who was accorded a stature no less than that of Nasser.

The celebratory atmosphere of that day was punctuated by violent clashes between pro- and anti-Morsi forces in various parts of the country. At least 6 people were killed and more than 215 people wounded. About a quarter of these casualties occurred in the governorates of Cairo, Damietta, Al Sharqia and Alexandria.

At dawn the following day (27 July 2013), hundreds of demonstrators set off from the Raba'a encampment on a protest march in the direction of the Manassa, or military reviewing stand, on Nasr Street. They were intercepted by security forces, which opened live fire into the demonstrators, killing ninety-five. The clashes continued through the night and into the following day.

Tens of thousands of Muslim Brotherhood supporters and their families had been staging a sit-in next to Raba'a al-Adawiyya Mosque for many weeks, during which they had demonstrated a great ability to remain firm in a hostile environment. The stage set up in the square was a place where they could listen to speeches by their leaders and supporters from various sectors of society. The long sit-in, as steadfast as it was, also displayed the Muslim Brotherhood's weakness. What good was a sit-in some hundred thousand strong if they were alone among millions and the state apparatus stood against them? In that encampment with their families, they looked more like a cult that had barricaded itself off against

---

[83] Marx opens the *The Brumaire* with the words, 'Hegel remarks somewhere that all facts and personages of great importance in world history occur, as it were, twice. He forgot to add: the first time as tragedy, the second as farce. [...] Men make their own history, but they do not make it just as they please; they do not make it under circumstances chosen by themselves, but under circumstances directly encountered, given and transmitted from the past. The tradition of all the dead generations weighs like a nightmare on the brain of the living.' Ibid., 15.
Sisi dressed up as – or his supporters, uncomfortable with the way he spoke and acted, dressed him up as – Nasser in order to convince themselves and others to accept him as a leader on top of the ruins of democracy and the corpses of the victims of the counter-revolution.

the world than a political party staging a protest. With every passing day, the political horizons of the sit-in shrank, as did its chances of transitioning from a defensive to an offensive posture capable of scoring a political win.

On 14 August 2013, after the protestors in Raba'a and Nahda squares had endured for an extraordinary month and a half in the open air, security forces moved in to clear them away. The operation began at about 6.30 am. Security forces sealed off all roads leading to the squares and used bulldozers to raze the brick barriers the protestors had built. Then they opened fire with teargas and guns. Hundreds were killed and thousands were wounded that morning, despite the purported creation of safe corridors by police to enable the protestors to leave peacefully.

The casualty estimates vary greatly. The Ministry of Health reported 670 dead and 4,400 wounded on both sides. Muslim Brotherhood sources claimed that 2,200 protestors were killed and many more thousands wounded. Protestors accounted for the majority of the dead. In a press conference that evening, the interior minister announced, without batting an eyelid, that 43 policemen and 149 civilians had been killed by the Muslim Brotherhood.[84] That same day, rioting and vandalism erupted in several governorates. According to press reports, twenty-one police stations and four churches were set on fire on 14 and 15 August.[85]

Human Rights Watch condemned the violence used in the break-up of the Raba'a sit-in as a crime against humanity.[86] In *The Weeks of Killing*,[87] one of the most objective treatments of that six-week period, the EIPR described three forms of violence. One was the communal violence involving non-state civilian groups, such as affiliates of a political party or faction, armed gangs for hire (termed *baltagiyya* or thugs), and unorganized groups. Although the report described this type of violence, which mainly occurred in Cairo and other urban centres, as 'low intensity', it nevertheless killed dozens, wounded hundreds and destroyed considerable amounts of property. I believe that this mode of violence was, for the most part, driven

---

[84] Wiki Thawra reports, '932 people were killed according to a fully documented body count, another 133 people were killed according to counting initiatives without official documents, and 29 unidentified individuals were killed according to a preliminary count by human rights agencies, though there exists a possibility of double-counting. . . . As for the injury count, as it is impossible to make a complete and accurate count of all injuries during the incident due to the intertwined circumstances, the Ministry of Health inventory was used. This lists 1,492 injured across 23 hospitals.' *Wiki Thawra*, 3 September 2013, Available online: https://bit.ly/33Z4vCF (accessed 27 June 2015).

[85] *Wiki Thawra*, 25 August 2013, Available online: https://bit.ly/3BVmpFs (accessed 27 June 2015).

[86] Human Rights Watch, 'All According to Plan'.

[87] Egyptian Initiative for Personal Rights, 'The Weeks of Killing: State Violence, Communal Fighting, and Sectarian Attacks in the Summer of 2013', June 2014, Available online: https://bit.ly/2Yls7BK (accessed 20 April 2021).

by security agencies bent on disseminating chaos and fear of impending civil war. Much of it was attributed to 'third parties', the Black Bloc and other unidentifiable persons.

The second form was systematic state violence used to disperse demonstrators, clear sit-ins or break up brawls between civilians. State violence was responsible for the great majority of casualties during those bloody weeks due to the excessive force that killed dozens and wounded hundreds of Morsi supporters in front of the Republican Guard building at dawn on 8 July 2013, killed dozens and wounded hundreds more in the Manassa massacre on 27 July and killed around a thousand people in the break-up of the Raba'a and Nahda sit-ins. This carnage was not the result of some inadvertent failure to limit the use of lethal force to cases of extreme necessity. It was deliberate, intended to establish the new mode of repression and deterrence of opposition. It was reminiscent of Pinochet's crackdown on the left and democratic forces in Chile after his coup.

Sectarian attacks, the third type of violence covered in the EIPR report, targeted their victims on the basis of their religious affiliation. Often the purpose was to exact revenge out of the belief that the targets were responsible for certain political situations (whether real or imagined) and their consequences. Egyptian Copts and their property and Coptic churches were subjected to frequent attacks during this period by diverse non-state actors, including Morsi supporters, resulting in fifteen dead and dozens injured. This type of violence was the product of the spike in hate speech and incitement against Copts and other religious minorities on the part of Islamist religious and political leaders after Morsi's overthrow. Those movements did not carry out attacks against the Azhar and its affiliated mosques and organizations, even though Azhar had backed the coup as well.

In response to the flare-up in violence, the government declared a month-long state of emergency, introduced a 9.00 pm–6.00 am curfew in several governorates, halted some train services and tightened security nationwide. On 24 November 2013, the government passed a new law that was more restrictive of the rights of protest and free assembly than anything that had existed under Mubarak. On 22 December 2013, Ahmed Maher, founder of the 6 April Movement, and fellow activists Mohammad Adel and Ahmed Douma were arrested and ultimately sentenced to three years in prison on the charge of illegal demonstrations. Those who organized and took part in demonstrations marking the third anniversary of the revolution, on 25 January 2014, met with the unrestrained wrath of the security apparatus: 49 people were killed, 247 were wounded and more than 1,000 were arrested. The previous day, improvised explosive devices detonated in four different places in Cairo killed six civilians while eight activists were killed in protest demonstrations.[88]

The number of political detainees skyrocketed after Sisi took over. According to a Human Rights Watch report, an Interior Ministry official estimated that 22,000 people had been arrested in 2013. The ECESR estimated as many as 41,000 detainees as of May 2014. The Muslim Brotherhood, at the time, held that 29,000 of its supporters were in jail. The Arab Network for Human Rights Information placed the figure as high as 60,000 political prisoners, among whom were opposition activists, journalists and Muslim Brotherhood members (or alleged members).[89]

The closure of the public sphere made it easier for the military command to tighten its grip on the economy and expand the army's economic activities in collaboration with Gulf States that backed the political direction Egypt was taking. Large sums of economic assistance and investments from Saudi Arabia, the UAE and Kuwait were funnelled into economic activities and development projects operated by the Egyptian army and its companies.

The military's attempts to advance the economic involvement and welfare of its companies and officers had continued without interruption since the fall of Mubarak. With Sisi's rise to the presidency in June 2014, it could unify its economic activities and operations. From late 2013 to the early months of 2014, the Defence Ministry was given $1 billion worth of contracts from the Ministries of Health, Transport, Housing and Youth to carry out major infrastructure projects such as constructing new highways and residential complexes, and rebuilding hospitals and youth recreation centres.[90]

In May 2014, the director of the Armed Forces Engineering Authority announced that the military had executed 473 strategic and service projects since the middle of 2012. A salient example was the agreement that Emaar Misr, a subsidiary of the UAE-based Emaar Properties company, signed in February 2014 with the Ministries of Defence, Housing, and Local Development to build a shopping centre, Emaar Square, as part of the Uptown Cairo housing project.[91]

As explained previously, the army is not subject to any form of oversight. Three NSPO contracts for the construction of new highways raised further concerns over accountability when they were signed in 2014.

---

[88] Bassiouni, 'Egypt's Unfinished Revolution', 68.
[89] Human Rights Watch, 'Egypt's Political Prisoners', 6 March 2015, Available online: https://bit.ly/35DQNqM (accessed 9 September 2020); Barbara Zollner, 'Surviving Repression: How Egypt's Muslim Brotherhood Has Carried On', *Carnegie Middle East Centre*, 11 March 2019, Available online: https://bit.ly/3kiq5rz (accessed 9 September 2020).
[90] Colombo, 'The Military, Egyptian Bag-snatchers'.
[91] Morsy, 'The Military Crowds Out Civilian Business in Egypt'.

These agreements, signed between the Ministries of Transportation and Defence, stated that the NSPO company responsible for the construction, development and management of roads would build, manage and lease two of the roads for ninety-nine years and the third for fifty years.[92] These contracts were signed after April 2014 when the government passed a law restricting the right of third parties to challenge business and real estate contracts signed with the state.

Since then, the army's companies have continued their aggressive expansion. The army can take possession of any portion of non-agricultural and unexploited land it sets its sights on. That puts 87 per cent of the country at its disposal. Disparate patches of land have gradually coalesced into vast properties, some in very profitable locations, marked off by fences with signs identifying them as military zones and prohibiting photography, with watchtowers to guard them. The UAE-based Emaar company began construction of a large commercial and residential complex on a 4.5 million square metre plot of land belonging to the army overlooking Greater Cairo after signing an agreement during a ministerial economic meeting in February 2014.[93]

The military's drive to expand its economic activity encountered no serious opposition, not even from the secular parties that had demanded a civil state during Morsi's year in power. In fact, quite to the contrary, they welcomed the army's economic role, especially in infrastructure development, hailing the military as the trustworthy saviour who rescued the economy and the state from the brink of collapse.

Until the end of 2013, Sisi maintained the posture that he had no intention to run for president and that the army had no designs on power. On 27 January 2014, interim president Adly promoted him to field marshal. At that point, Sisi signalled a shift, saying he would only run for office if the people asked him to and the army authorized it.[94] As though on cue, an orchestra of media fanfare and popular festivals struck up to trumpet his praises until, on 26 March 2014, Sisi resigned as defence minister and announced his candidacy. He handily won the presidential election, held on 26 and 27 May (and extended for another day), and was sworn in on 3 June. At the moment, there is no sign of him stepping down anytime soon. The constitution was amended in 2019 to enable him to run for re-election until 2034.[95]

[92] Ibid.
[93] *Middle East Monitor*, 9 July 2014, Available online: https://bit.ly/2YlYjVl (accessed 12 July 2015).
[94] *Ahram Online*, 27 January 2014, Available online: https://bit.ly/3obQAlh (accessed 20 October 2020).
[95] For the full text of the amendments, see the State Information Service, Available online: https://bit.ly/34eCnMq (accessed on 20 October 2020); for more details, see: 'Egypt: New Constitutional Amendments Proposed', *Library of Congress*, 13 February 2019, Available online: https://bit.ly/3jonOKQ (accessed 20 October 2020).

The dawn of the Sisi presidency set into motion the comprehensive revision of the media narrative of the 25 January revolution. Now that the putschist regime had secured its position and assembled its troops of old regime intellectuals and pundits and new regime journalists directly linked to army and Military Intelligence, there was nothing to keep them from openly tarnishing the revolution they once had once praised while they furtively pursued their designs. They could also settle scores with the 25 January revolutionaries, including those who had taken part in the 30 June marches against Morsi to call for early elections or even military intervention against the Muslim Brothers. The time had come as well not just to rehabilitate members of the old regime but also to induct and train new faces for the new order. By this point, the coup had completed its transformation from a political act performed at a certain historical juncture into a full-fledged political regime. The future of the democratization movement is contingent on how it frames and organizes its response to this. Principled opposition to the coup itself is insufficient for mounting a viable and potentially successful opposition to the authoritarian regime that arose from it.

This subject is beyond the scope of this study. However, history tells us that civilians do not stand up against their national armies and that peaceful demonstrations recede before repression or, in some cases (as in Syria), cede way to the armed opposition. It has also taught us that, even in the case of strong armies, the rule of officers cannot last as long as bureaucratically entrenched totalitarian or authoritarian regimes. After all, other officers, like them, could rebel, or gradual reforms in response to a spate of crises could forestall the perpetuation of the same mode of rule. This is why autocrats change their military uniforms for civilian dress and create bureaucratized dictatorships, which are more durable once loyalty is assured. Sisi, however, unlike Nasser and others, did not form a political party. He received the absolute support of a number of pseudo-parties, but his main party remained the army. Then, as he implemented a development strategy that steered away from the policy of subsidizing basic commodities, he used coercion and intimidation to go where previous regimes had feared to tread in order to meet IMF and World Bank conditions.

9

Egyptian public opinion during the transition and after the coup

With the failure of the democratic transition in Egypt, some theorists of political culture again took up the idea of the Arab and Islamic democratic exception. As stated previously, it is my belief that a mass democratic political culture does not emerge under dictatorship but under democracy and that the political culture of the influential political elite therefore carries greater weight as a determinant of the success or failure of democratization.

That said, this chapter will explore trends in Egyptian public opinion on the eve of the revolution, during the transition and after the coup on issues like democracy, the Arab revolutions and other attitudes related to political culture, confidence in the democratic process and an understanding of the causes of the failed transition. Four opinion surveys conducted in Egypt throughout this eventful period give us a rare chance to examine these trends directly over several years.[1] They also allow us to make systematic comparisons that are difficult to do based on the kind of rapid polls typically conducted by policy analysts and the media. The goal of this exploration is twofold: first, to lay bare the enormous gulf between claims about the popular will made by politicians and other public actors in order

---

[1] The analysis in this chapter relies on the Arab Opinion Index, an annual survey conducted by the Arab Centre for Research and Policy Studies and designed with the participation of the author. The index was launched in Egypt in 2011 immediately after the revolution. The first survey was conducted between 30 May and 7 June 2011 and polled 1,200 men and women. The second poll was conducted between 26 December 2012 and 11 January 2013, and is referred to throughout this chapter as the 2012 poll or 2012 findings. That survey polled 1,970 Egyptians. The third poll was conducted between 18 March and 22 May 2014, with a survey sample of 2,297 Egyptians. The fourth and final poll discussed here was conducted between 13 May and 3 June 2015 and surveyed 2,400 Egyptians. All surveys were conducted through face-to-face interviews.

Polling samples were selected through a randomized, multistage, self-weighted, clustered approach, with an overall margin of error of ±2–3 per cent. Samples were selected with consideration for the relative weight of rural/urban residence and the major administrative divisions in Egypt, such that every individual in Egypt is equally likely to appear in the sample. The sample was designed to allow an analysis of findings disaggregated by region, governorate and the major administrative divisions in Egypt.

The Arab Opinion Index has been conducted since 2011. For more information, see https://bit.ly/3pylEwL.

to justify their own stances and people's actual attitudes as reflected in their answers to direct questions, and, second, to refute the common claim that the Egyptian people developed a negative attitude to democracy when the longing for stability became a primary motivation for political behaviour.

Unfortunately, there is virtually no direct, sustained and broad examination of public opinion in research on Arab societies, and comprehensive, cross-disciplinary research cannot rely on the media alone to accurately convey opinions in society. Economic, business, political, media and cultural elites can express themselves through state and private media, create hype, and manufacture what seem to be popular trends purporting to reflect public attitudes. But in fact elites tend to project their own views onto the broader public. Comparative statistical data offers an utterly different picture of the public than such elite portrayals suggest. Although elites certainly have an influence on people's attitudes and ideas, these attitudes are inconsistent with the stereotypical portrait of 'the people' or 'the masses'. Moreover, quantitative research does not ignore the impact of the media on public opinion. On the contrary, a longitudinal comparison of data makes the media's influence quite clear. Indeed, one of the most important conclusions gleaned from a comparative study of the survey findings is that the Egyptian public's views about the revolution, the transitional period and democracy shifted *after* the coup, not before it, in contrast to claims made in the pro-coup media. In other words, the coup was not a response to shifts in public opinion.

This chapter will focus on Egyptian public opinion on three central issues: the 25 January revolution, the Arab revolutions and the Arab Spring; democratic values (the understanding of democracy, the attitude towards it and the evaluation of the level of actually existing democracy in Egypt); and political Islamist and non-Islamist movements.

I Egyptian public opinion on the 25 January revolution, the Arab revolutions and the Arab Spring

When Egyptians were asked in late 2012 and early 2013 – that is, when unrest in Egypt was at its peak – how they viewed the Arab revolutions of 2011, including the Egyptian January revolution, 61 per cent said they had a positive or very positive view. In other words, despite multiple disappointments, a large majority of the population was pro-revolution, compared to just 20 per cent who had a negative or somewhat negative view of the revolution. In contrast, in 2014, following the military coup, the dissolution of elected institutions and a full year of intense media mobilization, respondents with a favourable view of the January revolution dropped to 43 per cent, while

32 per cent now had a negative view; 25 per cent of respondents answered 'don't know' or declined to respond, up from 20 per cent. In 2015, amidst increased polarization, 47 per cent of respondents had a positive view of the January revolution, up from 43 per cent, while 44 per cent held a negative view, up from 32 per cent from the previous year. This increase was drawn largely from the bloc of respondents who were reluctant to answer, which fell to 9 per cent in 2015 from 25 per cent in 2014. The swing in Egyptian public opinion on the Arab revolutions, including the January revolution, was statistically significant, falling from 30 per cent of respondents who viewed the revolutions very favourably in 2012 to 14 per cent in 2014 and 2015. It should also be noted that opinions shifted in two directions over the three polls. Those with a positive view of the revolutions declined in favour of those who described them as 'somewhat negative'. The 2015 survey found that 14 per cent of respondents unhesitatingly evaluated the Arab revolutions and the 25 January revolution as very positive while 11 per cent were strongly against the revolutions (Figure II.9.1).

An analysis of views of the Arab revolutions and the January revolution disaggregated by various demographic variables shows that men were more favourably inclined towards the revolution than women, though by slim margins. In contrast, support for the revolution was inversely correlated with the respondent's age: young people ages eighteen to thirty-four were more positive about the revolution than other age cohorts.

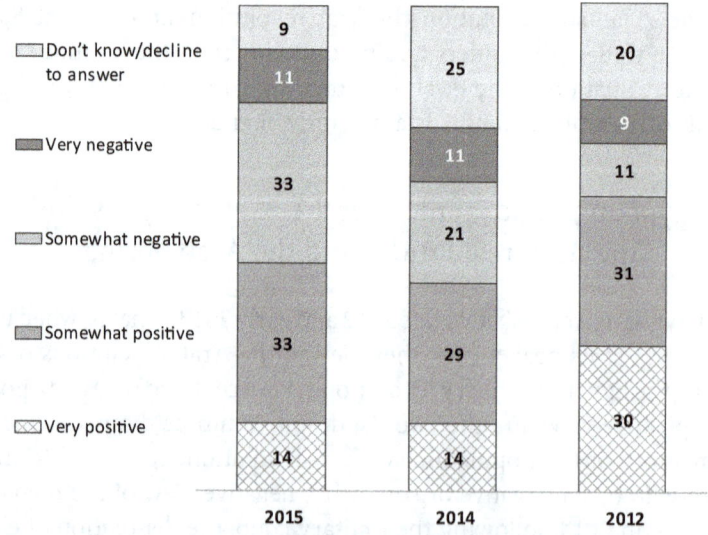

Figure II.9.1 Attitudes towards the Arab revolutions and the Arab Spring (2012, 2014, 2015).

Table II.9.1 Attitudes towards the Arab Revolutions by Age, Education, Rural/Urban Residence and Religiosity (2015)

Respondent's view of the Arab revolutions	Age (%)				
	18–24	25–34	35–44	45–54	55+
Very/somewhat positive	53	55	49	48	46
Very/somewhat negative	47	45	51	52	54
Total	100	100	100	100	100
Respondent's view of the Arab revolutions	Level of education (%)				
	Illiterate/some knowledge	Less than secondary	Secondary	Higher than secondary	
Very/somewhat positive	44	50	54	62	
Very/somewhat negative	56	50	46	38	
Total	100	100	100	100	
Respondent's view of the Arab revolutions	Place of residence (%)				
	Urban		Rural		
Very/somewhat positive	50		53		
Very/somewhat negative	50		47		
Total	100		100		
Respondent's view of the Arab revolutions	Self-identified level of religiosity (%)				
	Very religious		Somewhat religious		Not religious
Very/somewhat positive	52		53		44
Very/somewhat negative	48		47		56
Total	100		100		100

A favourable view of the revolution increased with educational level, with respondents with a university education or higher holding the most positive attitudes towards the revolutions. Respondents in rural areas gave a more positive assessment of the revolutions than their urban peers. Looking at the intersection between respondents' attitudes and their level of religiosity shows that self-described non-observant people had a more negative assessment of the revolution; the most positive were respondents who described themselves as somewhat religious, followed by respondents who said they were very religious. Educational attainment and age were the variables that most clearly correlated with Egyptians' views of the revolution: the more educated and younger the respondent, the greater is their support for the revolution (Table II.9.1).

When respondents who viewed the Arab revolutions and the January revolution favourably were asked why, most gave answers related to domestic politics, such as the revolution's opposition to injustice, tyranny and corruption, and support for democracy and freedoms. In 2015, the

Table II.9.2 Reasons Cited for Positive View of the Arab Revolutions (2012, 2014, 2015)

Reasons cited for the positive view	% 2012	2014	2015
Toppled corrupt regimes and are against corruption	19	14	24
Toppled dictatorships and established democratic rules	15	13	15
People demanded their rights and liberties and claimed some of them	0	5	12
Ended injustice and laid foundation for justice and equality	15	9	11
Gave citizens freedom of opinion and expression	7	0	10
Positive, but did not achieve all their ambitions	5	6	10
People restored their will and dignity	8	6	8
Will change Arab world for the better	3	5	7
Realized some or all of people's demands	3	5	2
Improvement of economic conditions	1	1	1
Gave citizens freedom and rights	10	6	0
Other reasons	1	4	0
Don't know/decline to answer	14	26	0
Total	100	100	100

share of respondents who cited democracy, freedom and a rejection of injustice and corruption as major factors for their positive view of the revolution increased markedly, at the expense of respondents who gave no reason, who had increased from 14 per cent of respondents in 2012 to 25 per cent in 2014. Significantly, respondents who had positive views of the revolution focused on factors like the removal of corrupt regimes, an end to injustice and the granting of freedom of expression in the poll of late 2012. These factors were cited less frequently in the 2014 survey, conducted nine months after the coup, before again increasing in the 2015 poll to nearly the level of the 2012 poll. In other words, there was a shift in Egyptian public opinion between 2012 and 2014 towards a more negative view of the revolution, but this trend reversed in 2015 (Table II.9.2).

In contrast, respondents who held somewhat or very negative views of the revolutions largely explained their position by citing instability, 'the spread of chaos', and similar terms expressing a desire for stability and security; they also expressed doubts that the revolution would achieve its goals. These are classic justifications for resisting change, often appearing in the discourse of opponents of change more generally. No doubt some of these respondents supported the old regime or had some interest in its perpetuation, but such sentiments are usually not made explicit; rather, they are expressed in terms of stability and fear of anarchy.

Nevertheless, I tend to believe that a large share of people who were not favourably disposed to the revolution after having lived through it did, in fact, long for security and stability. This is a prime motivator for people's

Table II.9.3 Reasons Cited for Negative View of the Arab Revolutions (2012, 2014, 2015)

Reasons cited for the negative view	(%)		
	2012	2014	2015
Spread of chaos and insecurity	22	20	25
Major human casualties	2	2	19
Destruction of states and their institutions	4	14	14
Revolutions did not achieve goals	16	25	11
Crises and instability in some states	15	6	11
Deteriorating economic conditions	1	1	8
It is a foreign conspiracy or fomented from abroad	1	1	8
Opposed to revolution generally	2	0.2	2
Served interest of narrow group	0	1	1
Religious currents assumed power	6	2	0
Other reasons	0	3	0
Don't know/decline to answer	7	12	0
Total	100	100	100

behaviour and in their relationship to the state generally. In times of instability and heightened fears of chaos, the desire for security becomes a prime determinant of people's attitudes and actions. Moreover, Egyptians' shifting focus on different reasons over several polls is another indication of the extent to which they were influenced by unfolding events and the official and mainstream media discourse. In 2015, 69 per cent of the reasons cited for a negative view of the revolutions were related to security and stability (e.g. the spread of chaos, the lack of security, major human casualties and critical domestic conditions), as opposed to 43 per cent in 2012. Another significant indicator is the increase in respondents who stated that the Arab revolutions were a foreign conspiracy: this number reached 8 per cent in 2015, compared to 1 per cent in the polls of 2012 and 2014. These shifts demonstrate the impact of the media discourse in this period, which pointed to conditions in Libya, Syria and Yemen as evidence of a foreign conspiracy to divide Arab states and foment chaos in the Arab world (Table II.9.3).

Deeply held attitudes were made clearer when respondents were asked which of two sentences best described their view of the Arab revolutions of 2011: (1) the Arab Spring is over and the old regimes are returning; (2) although the Arab Spring revolutions are stalled, they will ultimately achieve their aims. We read support for the second sentence as reflective of a positive attitude towards the Arab revolutions. Some 51 per cent of respondents chose the second option, even in 2015, or two years after the coup (very near the 47 per cent of respondents who viewed the revolutions favourably), despite the intensive anti-revolution propaganda broadcast by state-friendly media and near-total dearth of dissenting opinion. In 2015,

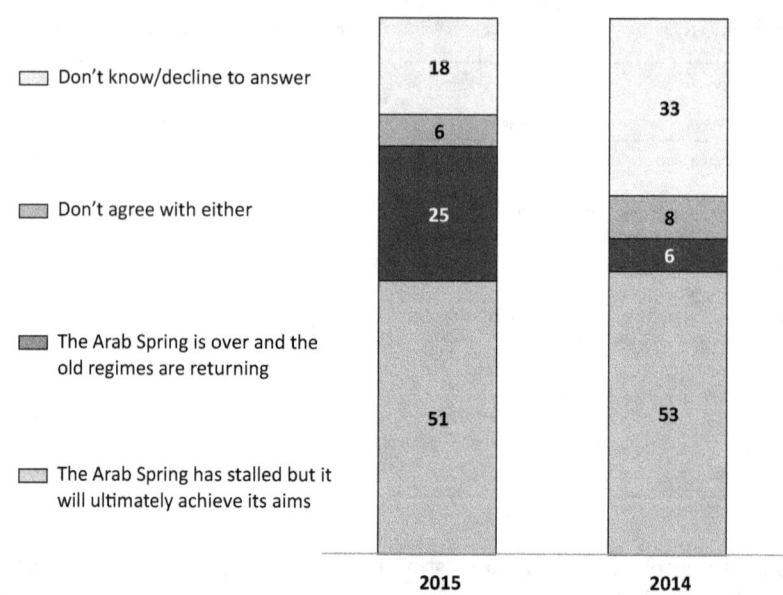

Figure II.9.2 Views on the future of the Arab Spring (2014, 2015).

25 per cent of respondents said that the Arab Spring had failed and was over, compared to 6 per cent in 2014. This sharp increase in respondents who believed that the revolutions had failed and old regimes had returned reflects an important swing in Egyptian public opinion, indicating that Egyptians in 2014 were still uncertain about the outcome of their revolution and maintained hope that the first year of the coup would end with the restoration of political pluralism. This hope appears to have evaporated for a large segment of the Egyptian public by 2015 (Figure II.9.2).

Asked why the Arab revolutions had stalled and had not achieved their aims, 60 per cent of respondents cited security instability and deteriorating economic and living conditions; only 7 per cent cited foreign intervention as the main reason, despite widespread talk of foreign conspiracies. Just 15 per cent of respondents gave this as the second most significant cause of the thwarted revolutions. In what I believe would come as a shock to 'opinion makers' in politics and the media, only 4 per cent said that the conduct of Islamist parties was the main reason the Arab revolutions had failed, while 13 per cent cited it as the second most important cause. The public also contradicted Islamist movements that accused non-Islamist parties of conspiring against them when they were in power, with just 2 per cent of respondents saying that the conduct of non-Islamist parties was the principal reason for the failed revolutions and 7 per cent citing it as a secondary cause. Nor did respondents give much weight to media

Table II.9.4 Top Three Reasons the Arab Revolutions Stalled and Failed to Meet Their Aims (2015)

Factor	Most important (%)	Second most important (%)	Third most important (%)
Deteriorating security in some states	40	8	5
Deteriorating economic and living conditions	20	22	3
Foreign interference	7	15	13
Incitement by old regime forces	7	10	11
Emergence of extremist movements	4	9	12
Conduct of Islamist political parties	4	13	7
Conduct of non-Islamist political parties	2	7	6
Media incitement	2	6	8
Political conflict between revolutionary forces	2	5	10
Lack of deeply rooted culture of democracy among people	2	2	6
Stances of Arab militaries and/or security apparatus	1	2	5
Frequency of sit-ins and labour strikes	0	1	6
Sectarian, tribal, geographic or ethnic divisions	0	1	4
Don't know/decline to answer	10	1	3
Total	100	100	100

incitement, with 2 per cent citing it as a main cause and 7 per cent as a secondary cause. On the contrary, respondents focused largely on factors related to living conditions and security (Table II.9.4).

The following graph illustrates Egyptians' shifting attitudes to Mubarak's ouster, showing for comparison's sake the mood in the country just a few months after the revolution in 2011, when 87 per cent of Egyptians polled supported his removal (Figure II.9.3).

II Egyptian public opinion on democratic values

1 The concept of democracy

The surveys make it clear that most Egyptians have a reasonable understanding of democracy; less than one-fifth of respondents were unable to provide a definition or substantive description of democracy or said they did not know the most important conditions for democracy. A

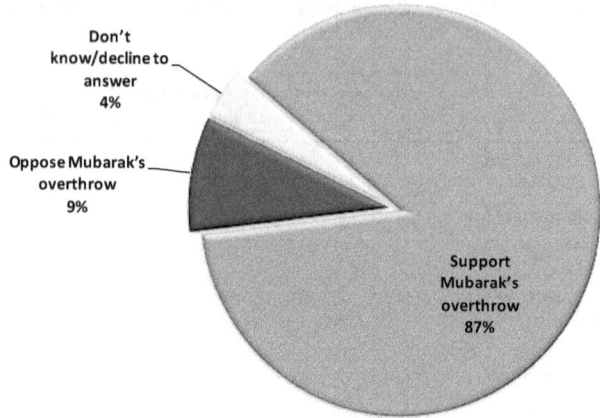

Figure II.9.3 Attitudes towards the 25 January revolution and the removal of Hosni Mubarak (2011).

comparison of four surveys shows that Egyptians understand democracy in terms of political and civil rights, the idea of justice and equal citizenship or the structure of government. In their definition of democracy, 60 per cent of respondents mentioned guarantees for political and civil liberties, guarantees for equality and justice or the nature of a democratic system of governance. In contrast, 21 per cent said that the primary condition for democracy is economic prosperity or guarantees for security, safety and stability, although guaranteeing security and stability is the state's function regardless of whether the regime is democratic or not.

A comparison of the findings of the four surveys shows a shift in the Egyptian public's understanding of democracy. Respondents associating it with guarantees for political and civil liberties declined from 34 per cent in 2011 to 20 per cent in 2015; the share of respondents who could not define democracy also declined. At the same time, more respondents identified democracy with equality and justice, improved economic conditions or a guarantee of security, safety and stability. Only 4 per cent of respondents defined it as the establishment of a democratic system of government in 2011, but this share jumped to 13 per cent in 2012 and remained fairly steady at 11 per cent in the 2014 and 2015 surveys. This increase from 4 per cent in 2011 to 11 per cent in 2015 indicates the wider public currency of concepts such as the separation of powers, checks and balances, the rotation of power and political pluralism after the January revolution. Respondents' citing citizen equality and justice, rather than liberties, as the primary condition for democracy in the 2015 poll may also reflect a desire to give the new regime positive marks on the democratic scorecard despite the erosion of liberties (Table II.9.5).

Table II.9.5 Most Important Condition to Consider a Country a Democracy (2011, 2012, 2014)

Prerequisites for democracy	2011 (%)	2012 (%)	2014 (%)	2015 (%)
Guarantees for political and civil liberties	34	28	24	20
Citizen equality and justice	20	19	17	29
Democratic system of governance and institutions	4	13	11	11
Improved economic conditions	6	4	7	12
Security, safety and stability	10	6	5	9
Application of religious laws	–	–	–	0.1
Associated with positive values	–	1	2	0.4
Other	4	2	0	1
Don't know/decline to answer	22	27	34	18
Total	100	100	100	100

2 Attitudes towards democracy

Respondents were asked whether they agreed or disagreed with statements expressing negative attitudes towards democracy, for example that democracy is associated with anarchy, tensions and disagreement (a common opinion among the military establishment and supporters of the military regime), poor economic performance (a common opinion in both some leftist and conservative quarters) or opposition to Islam (the position of some Islamist movements and radical secularists). That respondents overwhelmingly disagreed with these propositions demonstrates their support for democracy. A small minority – no more than one-quarter of respondents – agreed with one of four of these statements, but a larger percentage believed that 'our society' is not ready for democracy. Egyptian society's ill preparedness for democracy, however, was not related to Islam: more than 70 per cent of respondents in 2015 strongly disagreed that Islam and democracy were incompatible.

We asked respondents their opinion of five statements. Less than 1 per cent agreed with all five statements, while 3 per cent agreed with four of them; 10 per cent agreed with three of the statements and some 15 per cent agreed with two. These respondents constitute the hard core of democratic opposition. Some 27 per cent of respondents opposed four of the statements while agreeing with one of them (Table II.9.6).

Political attitudes were again assessed by directly asking respondents their opinion of democracy. A persistent majority believed democracy to be better than other systems of government despite its problems, while a small minority disagreed with this sentiment.

It can be concluded that most Egyptians were not influenced by common anti-democratic ideologies or that the influence exerted by media hostile to democracy and political pluralism was marginal. The greatest support

Table II.9.6 Attitudes towards Anti-Democratic Sentiments (2011, 2012, 2014, 2015)

To what extent do you agree with the following statements?		Agree or strongly agree (%)	Disagree or strongly disagree (%)	Don't know/ decline to answer (%)	Total (%)
Economic performance is poor in a democratic system	2015	24	63	13	100
	2014	12	59	29	100
	2012	19	66	15	100
	2011	21	53	26	100
A democratic system is not good at maintaining order	2015	18	67	16	100
	2014	12	59	30	100
	2012	18	66	16	100
	2011	26	47	27	100
A democratic system is indecisive and contentious	2015	26	60	14	100
	2014	21	51	28	100
	2012	25	58	16	100
	2011	27	48	26	100
A democratic system is incompatible with Islam	2015	12	71	17	100
	2014	7	65	29	100
	2012	13	72	15	100
	2011*	–	–	–	–
Our society is not ready for democracy	2015	46	38	16	100
	2014	32	39	29	100
	2012	41	44	15	100
	2011*	–	–	–	–

* This statement was not given in the 2011 Arab Opinion Index.

Table II.9.7 Attitudes towards Democracy (2011, 2012, 2014, 2015)

To what extent do you agree with the following statement?		Agree or strongly agree (%)	Disagree or strongly disagree (%)	Don't know/ decline to answer (%)	Total (%)
Democracy, despite its problems, is better than other systems of government	2015	60	23	16	100
	2014	57	13	30	100
	2012	66	18	16	100
	2011	56	18	27	100

for democracy was seen in the 2012 poll, when two-thirds of respondents agreed that it was the best system, compared to 18 per cent who disagreed. The highest level of opposition to democracy was seen in the 2015 poll, when nearly one-quarter of respondents disagreed (Table II.9.7).

Respondents' democratic values were put to the test when they were asked whether human rights should be subordinated to security and could be justifiably infringed for reasons of security – a difficult test to pass for citizens in democratic countries as well. We found that Egyptians overwhelmingly opposed or strongly opposed infringements of human rights in order to maintain security. In other words, a majority opposed

Table II.9.8 Attitudes towards the Infringement of Human Rights for the Sake of Security (2012, 2014, 2015)

To what extent do you agree with the following statement: Maintaining security justifies infringements of human rights in Egypt?	2012 (%)	2014 (%)	2015 (%)
Strongly agree	6	10	19
Agree	2	5	6
Disagree	27	24	37
Strongly disagree	55	38	30
Don't know/ decline to answer	9	23	8
Total	100	100	100

a coup against democracy in principle (as a normative value), with 67 per cent of respondents in 2015 and 62 per cent in 2014 opposed to infringing human rights in the name of security. This was down from 82 per cent in 2012, but even when the security situation deteriorated, support for rights over security remained relatively high (62 per cent).

The strong consensus around this view in the Morsi era should be underscored, as both his supporters and opponents were in agreement. In the final analysis, in the two surveys conducted after the coup, those who held the unwavering position that human rights should not be subordinated to security concerns outnumbered sixfold those who strongly supported the opposite proposition; in the 2012 poll, about six months before the coup, they outnumbered the latter camp more than 27-fold. In other words, the non-negotiable, principled position lost 20 per cent points after the coup. This substantial swing demonstrates that the coup regime's media discourse and supporters successfully convinced some 20 per cent of the public to turn a blind eye to human rights violations in the service of security. Some 25 per cent of Egyptian respondents supported infringements of human rights for the sake of security in 2015 – virtually the same share of respondents who opposed democracy or agreed with statements disparaging the democratic system (Table II.9.8).

An overwhelming majority of Egyptians persistently believed that a democratic system was suitable for Egypt: 80 per cent of respondents held this opinion in 2015, compared to 60 per cent in 2014 and 82 per cent in 2012. Support clearly faltered in 2014 immediately after the coup, but returned to its previous high level in 2015. Notably, a large majority (65 per cent in 2015) rejected a political system in which only non-religious parties compete or some religious parties are excluded; this share declined to 46 per cent in 2014, down from 60 per cent in 2012. A growing majority also considered a Shari'a-based system of government inappropriate, reaching 65 per cent in 2015.

Table II.9.9 Views on the Appropriate System of Government for Egypt (2012, 2014, 2015)

System		Suitable (%)	Not suitable (%)	Don't know/ decline to answer (%)	Total (%)
Pluralist political system in which all parties compete in regular elections (democratic system)	2015	80	9	11	100
	2014	59	9	32	100
	2012	82	5	13	100
A political system in which only non-religious parties compete in elections	2015	20	65	15	100
	2014	19	46	36	100
	2012	23	60	17	100
A political system in which only Islamist parties compete in elections	2015	31	56	12	100
	2014	10	56	35	100
	2012	33	51	15	100
A Shari'a-based system without elections or political parties	2015	21	65	14	100
	2014	10	56	34	100
	2012	30	54	16	100
A political system with formal elections in which an undemocratic authority makes decisions without regard to opposition opinions (authoritarian system)	2015	16	70	13	100
	2014	6	61	34	100
	2012	21	63	15	100

A persistent majority similarly opposed a system that limited political competition to religious parties and excluded secular parties; a minority of one-third at most believed that a system that only includes religious parties would be best for Egypt (Table II.9.9).

When respondents were asked directly what kind of system they would prefer to govern Egypt, a persistently large majority (about 75 per cent) chose democracy in the three years this question was polled (Figure II.9.4).

An analysis of political preferences by various demographic variables shows that men were more inclined to democracy than women, while women preferred a political system limited to religious parties at slightly higher rates than men, though the difference is statistically insignificant. Age was a determining factor to some extent, with the greatest support for democracy voiced by young people ages 18–24. Support for democracy also increased with education and was higher in urban than rural areas (Table II.9.10).

3 Assessing the level of existing democracy in Egypt

Answers shifted when respondents were asked to evaluate the current state of democratic conditions in Egypt. When it comes to translating support

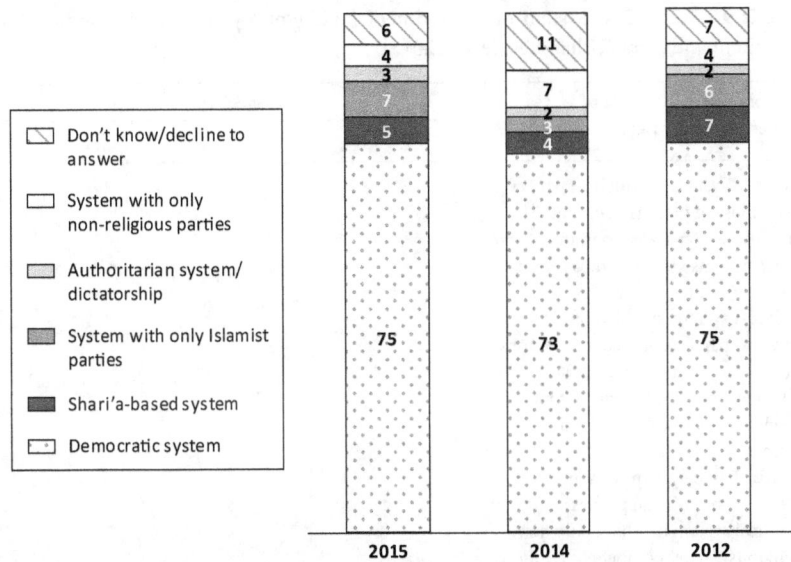

Figure II.9.4 The best system of government for Egypt (2012, 2014, 2015).

for democracy into a current assessment of undemocratic conditions, other factors like national pride or fear of instability come into play. A slim majority of respondents believed that political freedoms were guaranteed in Egypt, with the exception of the freedom to pursue legal action against the government and its institutions and, in 2015, the freedom to demonstrate. Overall, over the three surveys conducted in two very different political eras, there was very little change in the degree to which Egyptians believed that freedom of press and the freedom to join political parties or civil society organizations were guaranteed. There was, however, a marked increase in respondents who said that the freedom to sue the government was not guaranteed in 2015 compared to the 2014 and 2012 polls. The same is true of freedom of expression of opinion, with 38 per cent of respondents saying it was not guaranteed in 2015, compared to 28 per cent in 2012 and 27 per cent in 2014. Public opinion was divided on the freedom to demonstrate: 42 per cent of respondents said it was not guaranteed in 2015, a significant jump from 25 per cent in 2012.

Of course, one's view of guarantees for democratic freedoms is linked to one's experience of exercising these freedoms. Whether there exists respect for the rotation of power, or the freedom to join a political party or civil society organization is an abstract question if a citizen has not witnessed the rotation of power or attempted to join a party or civic association. In contrast, guarantees for petitioning the government for redress, participating in a demonstration or expressing an opinion are felt more

Table II.9.10 The Best System of Government for Egypt, by Gender, Age, Educational Attainment and Rural/Urban Residence (2015)

The most suitable system of government for Egypt	Gender (%)	
	Men	Women
A political system in which all parties regardless of platform compete in representative elections and governments are formed based on election results	81	78
A political system in which only Islamist parties compete in elections	6	9
A political system ruled by an authority that makes decisions without regard to election results or opposition opinion	3	4
A Shari'a-based system without elections or political parties	5	5
A political system in which only non-religious parties compete in elections	5	3
Total	100	100

The most suitable system of government for Egypt	Age (%)				
	18–24	25–34	35–44	45–54	55+
A political system in which all parties regardless of platform compete in representative elections and governments are formed based on election results	82	79	78	79	79
A political system in which only Islamist parties compete in elections	7	7	9	8	8
A political system ruled by an authority that makes decisions without regard to election results or opposition opinion	3	4	2	5	4
A Shari'a-based system without elections or political parties	5	6	5	4	5
A political system in which only non-religious parties compete in elections	3	3	6	4	4
Total	100	100	100	100	100

The most suitable system of government for Egypt	Level of education (%)			
	Illiterate/some knowledge	Less than secondary	Secondary	Higher than secondary
A political system in which all parties regardless of platform compete in representative elections and governments are formed based on election results	79	83	78	81
A political system in which only Islamist parties compete in elections	8	5	8	8

(Continued)

Table II.9.10 (Continued)

A political system ruled by an authority that makes decisions without regard to election results or opposition opinion	4	3	3	4
A Shari'a-based system without elections or political parties	5	5	6	4
A political system in which only non-religious parties compete in elections	4	4	4	3
Total	100	100	100	100

The most suitable system of government for Egypt	Place of residence (%)	
	Urban	Rural
A political system in which all parties regardless of platform compete in representative elections and governments are formed based on election results	82	78
A political system in which only Islamist parties compete in elections	5	10
A political system ruled by an authority that makes decisions without regard to election results or opposition opinion	3	4
A Shari'a-based system without elections or political parties	6	5
A political system in which only non-religious parties compete in elections	4	4
Total	100	100

concretely as these are situations citizens might confront in their daily lives. Opinions about these issues are therefore more significant than those about abstract questions (Table II.9.11).

When it comes to assessing the freedom to criticize the government, there is a significant difference between 2012 and 2014. In 2012, 88 per cent of respondents said they could do so without fear, compared to 8 per cent who were afraid to criticize the government. In 2015, only 41 per cent said they could criticize without fear. Respondents were more tentative after the coup in 2014, when their attitudes were still influenced by the instability of the transitional period and the coup regime had not yet tightened its grip. Some 51 per cent felt they could criticize the government while 25 per cent were uncertain and 24 per cent said they could not. This suggests that citizens saw 2014 as a transitional phase and believed that the exceptional circumstances would change once the roadmap was fully implemented.

By 2015, more than half of respondents were afraid to criticize the government, reflecting their belief that the system had been consolidated, and this was the most that they could expect in terms of the political

Table II.9.11 Evaluation of Guarantees for Political and Civil Liberties (2012, 2014, 2015)

To what extent do you believe that the following freedoms are guaranteed in Egypt?		Year	Somewhat or fully guaranteed (%)	Somewhat or fully not guaranteed (%)	Don't know/decline to respond (%)	Total (%)
Democratic principles	Freedom to pursue legal action against the government and its institutions	2015	48	45	8	100
		2014	46	35	19	100
		2012	47	38	14	100
	Regular, free and fair representative elections	2015	64	29	6	100
		2014	49	31	19	100
		2012	54	33	13	100
	Respect for the rotation of power	2015	60	30	9	100
		2014	49	32	20	100
		2012	54	32	14	100
Freedom of assembly and association	Freedom to join political parties	2015	62	28	10	100
		2014	59	22	20	100
		2012	63	24	14	100
	Freedom to join civil society organizations	2015	64	25	11	100
		2014	59	17	23	100
		2012	59	25	17	100
	Freedom to participate in demonstrations	2015	48	42	10	100
		2014	57	26	17	100
		2012	65	25	11	100
Freedom of opinion	Freedom of expression of opinion	2015	58	38	4	100
		2014	58	28	13	100
		2012	66	27	8	100
	Freedom of the press	2015	68	26	6	100
		2014	64	22	15	100
		2012	63	28	9	100

Table II.9.12 Assessment of the Freedom to Freely Criticize the Government (2012, 2014, 2015)

Do you think that people these days can criticize the government without fear?	Yes (%)	No (%)	Don't know/decline to answer (%)	Total (%)
2015	41	51	8	100
2014	51	24	25	100
2012	88	8	5	100

process. Fear of criticizing the government increased sixfold from late 2012 – six months before the coup – to 2015. It should be noted that the question focused on criticism of the government rather than the regime, ruler or president, which would no doubt engender greater fear (Table II.9.12).

Shifts in public opinion on democracy and the evaluation of democracy in Egypt can be further illustrated by looking at how Egyptians evaluate the application of the principle of equality on the ground. This comparison is particularly salient since roughly one-third of Egyptians associated democracy with equality and justice. The surveys found that a majority of Egyptians believed that the principle of equal citizenship regardless of citizens' political influence or social status was not applied in Egypt. Opinion was divided on the question of equality on the basis of wealth, gender, religion and geographic residence. Overall, 40–50 per cent of respondents believed that certain segments of Egyptian society are discriminated against; in some cases – for example, citizens without political influence or the poor – this discrimination affects the overwhelming majority of the citizenry. A comparison of poll data for 2015 and 2012 reveals negligible differences in respondents' feelings of discrimination (Table II.9.13).

III Egyptian public opinion on Islamist and non-Islamist political movements

With the exception of 2014, the surveys found that a majority of respondents would agree to be governed by a political party with which they disagreed politically if it came to power through free and fair elections; support for this proposition fell below 50 per cent in 2014 and 2015 when the party was identified as Islamist or non-Islamist. The findings demonstrate that some segment of supporters of Islamist parties would not submit to governance by a non-Islamist party even if it were elected in a free and fair election; similarly, some opponents of Islamist parties would not accept governance by an elected Islamist party. The findings also capture the degree of

Table II.9.13 Assessment of the Application of the Principle of Equal Citizenship (2012, 2014, 2015)

To what extent do you believe that the following principles are applied in your country?	Year	Somewhat or fully applied (%)	Somewhat or fully not applied (%)	Don't know/ decline to answer (%)	Total (%)
Equality of all citizens regardless of wealth or poverty	2015	44	52	4	100
	2014	28	61	11	100
	2012	38	54	8	100
Equality of all citizens regardless of gender	2015	52	43	5	100
	2014	52	36	12	100
	2012	47	45	8	100
Equality of all citizens regardless of religion	2015	51	44	5	100
	2014	53	34	12	100
	2012	48	44	9	100
Equality of all citizens regardless of social status	2015	32	61	7	100
	2014	29	58	13	100
	2012	36	54	9	100
Equality of all citizens regardless of cultural, linguistic, ethnic or racial background	2015	38	50	13	100
	2014	36	43	22	100
	2012	32	51	18	100
Equality of all citizens regardless of political influence	2015	29	61	10	100
	2014	27	57	16	100
	2012	31	56	13	100
Equality of all citizens regardless of place of residence	2015	41	47	12	100
	2014	36	46	18	100
	2012	34	52	14	100

polarization in Egyptian society during this period. In contrast, in 2011, there was majority support for an opponent's party even when the party was identified, although it declined slightly when the party was named as Islamist, indicating that some opponents of Islamist parties rejected governance by an elected Islamist party even in 2011. Among supporters of Islamist parties, rejection of governance by non-Islamists increased after the coup (Table II.9.14).

Fears of governance by an Islamist party increased markedly from 2014 to 2015, reaching 60 per cent in 2015, up from just 39 per cent in 2014. In 2012, 52 per cent of respondents said they had no concerns about an Islamist party assuming power, compared to 35 per cent who did (Table II.9.15).

Table II.9.14 Attitudes towards Governance by Various Political Parties

Would you support or oppose governance by a political party you do not agree with if it came to power in free and fair elections?	Year	Support (%)	Oppose (%)	Don't know/ decline to answer (%)	Total (%)
A political party whose ideas and platform I disagree with	2015	52	34	14	100
	2014	41	19	39	100
	2012	64	23	12	100
	2011	58	28	14	100
An Islamist political party	2015	48	34	18	100
	2014	29	31	41	100
	2012*	–	–	–	–
	2011**	51	35	14	100
A non-Islamist political party	2015	40	42	18	100
	2014	32	24	44	100
	2012*	–	–	–	–
	2011**	56	30	15	100

*This question was not asked in the 2012 poll.
**In the 2011 poll, the question specified 'a religious party' rather than an Islamist party.

When respondents who said they had concerns were asked why in the 2015 survey, 17 per cent said they feared unilateral Islamist rule, while 8 per cent said they feared Islamists' incompetence and inability to assume responsibility; 9 per cent feared they would pursue their partisan interests. The most common reason cited (by 48 per cent of respondents) was the fear of Islamists' fanaticism, the imposition of their lifestyles, opinions and beliefs, and the restriction of liberties or discrimination against women and Copts.

Egyptians' concerns about Islamist political movements assuming power are shaped by several factors, the most significant in my view being that they are not confident that Islamists would respect the lifestyles of other citizens and cultural and social diversity – that is, Islamists would impose what they feel are religious dictates on people's everyday lives. Propaganda must also be considered as a factor, as concerted efforts were made to foment fear of Islamists' lack of respect for the rules of democracy, the Brotherhoodization of the state, and their incompetence. But regardless of the source of these impressions, they are reflected in the opinions of some 60 per cent of Egyptians. Moreover, these fears are likely to grow and become more firmly embedded if Islamist movements do nothing to dispel them by making programmatic and practical changes (Table II.9.16).

Table II.9.15 Attitudes towards the Rising Influence of Islamist Political Movements (2012, 2014, 2015)

Given the rise of political Islamist movements in the wake of the Arab Spring, do you have any concerns about them assuming power?	Yes (%)	Somewhat (%)	No (%)	Don't know/decline to answer (%)	Total (%)
2015	27	33	31	9	100
2014	17	22	20	41	100
2012	22	13	52	13	100

Table II.9.16 Reasons for Concern about Islamist Political Movements' Rise to Power (2015)

Most significant concern	Percentage (%)
Authoritarianism and unilateral rule	17
Fanaticism, intolerance and militancy	12
They will use religion to achieve their goals and interests	10
Spread of extremism and chaos	10
They will pursue their partisan and personal interests at the expense of the public interest	9
Incompetence and inability to take responsibility	8
They will impose their opinions and beliefs	6
Discrimination and lack of justice and equality	6
Erosion of women's rights	6
They will not apply religion correctly	6
Restriction of citizens' personal freedoms	4
Religious and sectarian discrimination	4
They will adversely impact relations with Western states	2
They are beholden to foreign bodies	1
Don't know/decline to answer	1
Total	100

Some 56 per cent of respondents in 2015 said they had some or many concerns about governance by non-Islamist (secular) political parties, while 34 per cent harboured no fears of these parties. Notably, virtually the same percentage of respondents were at least somewhat concerned by Islamist and non-Islamist movements, with a difference of just 4 percentage points in 2015, whereas in 2014, just 24 per cent of respondents feared non-Islamist political movements. In other words, respondents' concerns about non-Islamist movements doubled in the space of a little over a year, a shift that may be attributable to the ineffectiveness of non-Islamist parties that continued to exist after the military coup but were marginalized.

Table II.9.17 Attitudes towards the Rising Influence of Non-Islamist Political Parties (2014, 2015)

Given the rise of non-Islamist (secular) political movements in the wake of the Arab Spring, do you have any concerns about them assuming power?	Yes (%)	Somewhat (%)	No (%)	Don't know/decline to answer (%)	Total (%)
2015	17	39	34	10	100
2014	8	16	28	48	100

In the final analysis, 60 per cent and 56 per cent of Egyptians expressed concerns about Islamist and secular political parties respectively. This is indicative of the lack of trust in political parties generally and the success of efforts to demonize parties across the ideological spectrum under the military coup regime (Tables II.9.15 and II.9.17).

Some 42 per cent of those who feared the rise of non-Islamist movements were concerned that these parties were not religious; these respondents' concerns centred on Islamic identity, the overturning of Shari'a, changes to customs and traditions, and moral decay. The remaining respondents – the majority – expressed fears of the type that might be held by citizens in any democracy. It should also be noted that respondents cited similar fears about Islamist and secular political movements and with virtually the same frequency for concerns such as authoritarianism, discrimination, incompetence and pursuit of their partisan interests. This may reflect this bloc of citizens' desire for a democratic state and effective, non-corrupt governance regardless of ideological affiliation. This finding may also be interpreted as evidence of the coup regime's successful efforts to make citizens suspicious and fearful of political parties in general. Of course, the record of most existing parties supports this impression (Table II.9.18).

In 2015, the Arab Opinion Index asked respondents a direct question: Do you support a civil or religious state? Some 45 per cent of respondents stated that they wanted a civil state, accepting the distinction between the two concepts; 19 per cent supported a religious state. Some 30 per cent said it did not matter, indicating that other factors aside from religion were more important in determining their attitude to the system of governance (Figure II.9.5).

An analysis of opinions on the civil versus the religious state by various demographic variables shows that men supported a civil state more than women. Age is not correlated with respondents' opinions, but more than

Table II.9.18 Reasons for Concern about Non-Islamist Political Movements' Rise to Power (2015)

Most significant concern	Percentage (%)
They will pursue their partisan and personal interests at the expense of the public interest	11
Moral decay and corruption	10
Authoritarianism and unilateral rule	8
Deteriorating security and the spread of chaos	8
Lack of respect for religion or people's religious values	8
Discrimination and lack of justice and equality	7
They will not preserve Islamic and Arab identity	7
They are beholden to foreign bodies	6
They will impose their ideas and opinions on society	6
Elimination of Islam as a source of legislation	5
Their goals and platforms are unclear	4
Incompetence and inability to govern	4
Restriction of freedoms, especially religious freedoms	3
Because they are not religious, they will discriminate against religious people	3
Imposition of values incompatible with our values, customs and traditions	2
I don't trust them	4
Don't know/decline to answer	0
Total	100

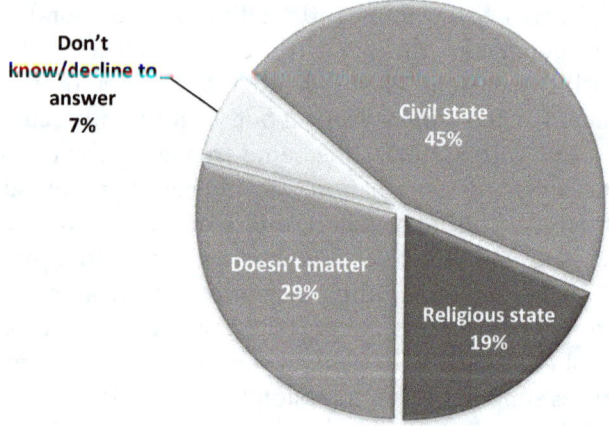

Figure II.9.5 Attitudes towards the civil and religious state (2015).

one-third of respondents aged eighteen to twenty-four said it did not matter. Support for a civil state increased with educational attainment, and respondents in urban areas favoured a civil state more than rural dwellers (Table II.9.19).

When given a choice of definitions of the religious state in 2015, 43 per cent of respondents said it was a state in which all civil, criminal and

Table II.9.19 Attitudes towards the Civil and Religious State by Gender, Age, Education and Urban/Rural Residence (2015)

Would you prefer a civil or religious state?	Gender (%)	
	Men	Women
Civil state	50	47
Religious state	20	22
Doesn't matter	30	31
Total	100	100

Would you prefer a civil or religious state?	Age (%)				
	18–24	25–34	35–44	45–54	55+
Civil state	41	52	51	50	52
Religious state	21	19	25	18	20
Doesn't matter	38	29	24	32	29
Total	100	100	100	100	100

Would you prefer a civil or religious state?	Level of education (%)			
	Illiterate/someknowledge	Less than secondary	Secondary	Higher than secondary
Civil state	42	41	54	59
Religious state	23	18	21	18
Doesn't matter	34	41	25	24
Total	100	100	100	100

Would you prefer a civil or religious state?	Place of residence (%)	
	Urban	Rural
Civil state	52	46
Religious state	17	23
Doesn't matter	30	31
Total	100	100

contractual legislation is based on Shari'a. Respondents choosing this definition included many opponents of the religious state. In contrast, the 33 per cent who defined the religious state as one in which Islam constituted a cultural and civilizational frame of reference most certainly included many supporters of the religious state. The responses thus underscore the many points of agreement among supporters and opponents of a religious state whenever they are asked to actually define it (Table II.9.20).

There is notable overlap in the responses to the next question, which asked respondents about their definition of a civil state. Some 26 per cent of respondents defined it as a de facto secular state, while 48 per cent said that it was a state that recognized the value of citizenship independent of religion (secular or near-secular state), but they simultaneously believed that Islam would constitute a cultural and civilizational reference for such a state (Table II.9.21).

Table II.9.20 The Definition of a Religious State (2015)

Which of the following statements best describes your understanding of a religious state?	Percentage (%)
A religious state is one in which all social, economic, political and criminal laws are based on Shari'a	43
A religious state is one in which the people are the source of authority; it is governed by the constitution and recognizes the value of citizenship, and Islam is a civilizational and cultural reference	33
A religious state is one based on the rotation of power through elections in which only Islamist parties compete	5
Don't know/decline to answer	18
Total	100

Table II.9.21 The Definition of a Civil State (2015)

Which of the following statements best describes a civil state in your view?	Percentage (%)
A civil state is one in which the people are the source of authority; it is governed by the constitution and recognizes the value of citizenship independent of religion	26
A civil state is one in which the people are the source of authority; it is governed by the constitution and recognizes the value of citizenship independent of religion, and Islam is a civilizational and cultural reference	48
A civil state is one in which the people are the source of authority; it is governed by the constitution and recognizes the value of citizenship independent of religion, and secularism is a cultural and civilizational reference	7
Don't know/decline to answer	19
Total	100

IV Concluding observations

Consistent polling reveals that Egyptian public opinion is much more nuanced than researchers would conclude by relying on Egyptian media or than journalists might surmise from personal encounters, whether with a taxi driver on the way to their hotel or even with civil society and political activists at a café.

Egyptian public opinion is complex. Most Egyptians support democracy and understand what it means. When asked more specific questions about the components of democratic culture and a democratic system, they seem less supportive – whether motivated by fear or caution or because the situation becomes more immediate and less abstract – but they do not fundamentally change their stance. The restive transitional phase clearly made citizens less willing to unconditionally accept governance by a party with which they fundamentally disagree. In this respect, both supporters and opponents of religious parties became more intolerant of one another. Even so, a majority continued to support democracy and sees no contradiction between it and Islam. The polls also found that support for the revolution and democracy is substantially higher among youth and citizens with a university education.

Although some people's professed commitment to human rights over security concerns proved flimsy in the Morsi era, when they justified human rights abuses for the sake of security after the military coup, a majority of Egyptians did not accept such justifications. Polls show that Egyptians do not conform to the clichés about the democratic transition and the January revolution propagated by the media after the coup. Clearly, the pro-coup media did not speak for a majority of Egyptians, who proved to be more democratic than both the media and the cultural elite (which, as this book has shown, was highly polarized). Nevertheless, the media did have a negative influence on Egyptians' attitudes to democracy; instead of educating the public about it, it propagandized and scaremongered.

The coup was not a response to the leanings and attitudes of most Egyptians. The product of orchestrated media campaigns, justifications for the coup came subsequent rather than prior to it. In undemocratic countries – and perhaps democracies as well – public opinion is clearly influenced by events more than it influences them. Polling immediately after the January revolution found that more than 80 per cent of Egyptians supported Mubarak's ouster in a revolution. I believe that respondents who expressed fears of democratization were influenced by the coup, particularly in the 2014 survey, whose findings diverged from those of both 2012 and 2015. This was also clearly evident in support for human rights over security concerns, which fell from 80 per cent to 60 per cent after the coup, as well as in other issues explored above. A comparison of respondents' evaluations of existing democracy and equality in 2015 and 2014 (two years and one year after the coup respectively) show that Egyptians were less influenced by concerted media mobilization in 2015 and more inclined to state things as they were.

A majority of Egyptians believe that the main reason for the failure of the Arab revolutions, including the Egyptian revolution, was the unstable security and living situation. This comports with what I identified as a primary determinant of Egyptians' behaviour towards the military coup: to the extent that they played a direct role in events, they were motivated by a desire for stability after a disorienting, tumultuous transition.

The Egyptian public is not sharply divided along secular-religious lines. Although there are secularists and religious people who sharply distinguish a religious from a civil state, the definition of a religious state for a large minority (33 per cent) is extremely similar to the plurality's conception of the civil state (48 per cent). In both cases, respondents associated their conception of civil or religious state with the rule of law and the constitution and the value of citizenship, while also recognizing Islam's position as a cultural and civilizational reference.

10

International reactions from the fall of Mubarak to the coup

Despite Egypt's regional and international significance, external players had no remarkable and certainly no definitive impact during the revolution. Internal factors prevailed, most importantly the broad-based national coalition that coalesced around the revolution, the rise of revolutionary legitimacy, the role of the army and the brevity of the actual uprising. This situation could have continued through the transitional phase had it not been for the fact that the weight of the most critical factor – the unity of diverse political forces over the revolution – declined in favour of (a) the unified, organized factor (the army) and (b) the external factor (primarily countries opposed to democratization in Egypt). There were many areas where international and regional powers could assert their influence during the interim phase, an inherently unstable period in which economic deterioration and reduced standards of living typically engender a growing need for foreign economic assistance and investment. It is also a period in which the media plays a pivotal role. In a general climate of uncertainty, the public becomes more politicized and takes a greater interest in the press. It is simultaneously more susceptible to propaganda and rumour-mongering. The greater the ability of external actors to take advantage of such circumstances, the greater impact they will have. In Egypt, external actors gained in influence due to internal conditions. Above all, the mounting acrimony and discord arising from the failure of political forces to agree to make the democratic transition work provided the opening foreign powers needed. Those powers unwilling to invest in Egypt during the stage of governance by democratically elected bodies seized on opportunities to actively invest in media opposed to those institutions, strike up alliances with opposition factions and fund political actions organized by the army, such as ostensibly grassroots movements against the elected government. Such circumstances also put world powers like the United States in a position to green-light a coup if they deemed the conditions ripe.

I The United States: Trying to please all and pleasing none

The shifting American stances during the uprising, as discussed in Part I, betrayed a sharp disagreement within the Obama administration over whether or not to abandon a trusted ally and uncertainty over the alternatives. Obama initially asked Mubarak to introduce a package of reforms and start a transitional phase to implement them; then he changed his mind and said it was time for Mubarak to step aside.

As already discussed in Part I, Chapter 4, the US administration foreign policy makers were not on the same page concerning the reaction to the revolution and the message to Mubarak. Former US secretary of defence Robert M. Gates writes in his memoirs that when demonstrations began to widen in Egypt, the US administration was divided on how to respond. As some conservatives and human rights activists were already criticizing Obama's cautiousness regarding Tunisia, the NSS thus urged strong support for the demonstrators in Egypt. On 28 January 2011, Mike Mullen told Gates that NSS members Denis McDonough, John Brennan and Ben Rhodes favoured the option of changing the leadership in Egypt. On the other hand, Mullen added that Biden, Clinton and Donilon had urged caution regarding the consequences of abandoning Mubarak. Meanwhile, Obama, as reported by Mullen to Gates, was clearly leaning towards proclaiming an aggressive posture and issuing public statements. Gates notes that he felt concerned that 'the president couldn't erase the Egyptians' memory of decades-long [US] alliance with Mubarak with a few public statements'. Gates supported a call for an 'orderly transition' and preventing a power vacuum because it likely would be filled by radical groups. Gates, Donilon, Biden and Clinton shared the same concern that the president and the White House and NSS staffs were stressing on the need for regime change.[1]

Throughout the uprising, Washington was in daily contact with the Egyptian military command, as evidenced by statements made by State Department spokesperson Philip Crowley in a press briefing on 4 February 2011.[2] Secretary of State Hillary Clinton was among the US officials opposed to Mubarak standing down, citing as one concern the potential rise of the Muslim Brothers to power. After the revolution, when asked what her government's position would be if the Muslim Brotherhood came to power through democratic elections, she said, 'Any party that is committed to nonviolence, committed to democracy, committed to the rights of all Egyptians, whoever they are, should have the opportunity to compete for

---

[1] Gates, *Duty*, 503–4.
[2] *NPR*, 4 February 2011, Available online: https://n.pr/2YfaljX (accessed 21 October 2021).

Egyptian votes.'³ Her shift had less to do with her views on the Muslim Brotherhood organization per se than it did with her own political agenda and practices. The day after the first round of parliamentary elections concluded on 28 November 2011, Clinton issued a congratulatory message to the Egyptian people,⁴ even though the Islamists had just secured a parliamentary majority.

The American position on domestic developments in Egypt from SCAF rule through the Morsi presidency was pitched to satisfy all sides. Officials' statements remained general and focused on supporting democratization and the renunciation of violence by all parties.⁵ For example, when President Barack Obama phoned Morsi to congratulate him on his presidential victory, he also phoned the losing candidate, Ahmed Shafik, to urge him to stay active in Egyptian politics, help unify the Egyptian people and continue to support democratic transition.⁶ In tandem with their communications with the Egyptian presidency after Morsi took office, US diplomats took pains to speak with diverse political forces and NGO activists, as was evidenced during the visit of US deputy secretary of state William Burns to Cairo on 6–8 July 2012 and Secretary of State Clinton's visit to Egypt on 14 July 2012. Against the backdrop of mounting polarization after the constitutional declaration crisis of November 2012 and escalating pro- and anti-Morsi demonstrations, new US secretary of state John Kerry arrived in Cairo on 2 March 2013, meeting with opposition parties and representatives of the business community before seeing Morsi.⁷ Then he met with Defence Minister Sisi and a number of NGO activists. The visit focused on the need to form a national unity government in Egypt.⁸ The text of Obama's phone call with Morsi on 7 December 2012⁹ is another

---

3   'Social Media Dialogue with Dr Ahmed Ghanim of Egypt's Masrawy.com', *US State Department*, 23 February 2011. Transcript Available Online: https://bit.ly/3DVHGzo (accessed 1 October 2021).
4   For Secretary Clinton's statement on the Egyptian elections, see: 'Statement on Egyptian Elections', *US Department of State*, 30 November 2011, Available online: https://bit.ly/3C1Giup (accessed 21 October 2021).
5   See the website of the US embassy in Egypt, which commented on events and published statements issued by US officials. Most statements gave equal status to both sides (revolutionary youth vs. security forces or pro- and anti-Morsi forces). For 2011, see: 'Press Releases 2011', *Embassy of the United States Cairo – Egypt*, Available online: https://bit.ly/3jxP5xd (accessed 26 October 2021); and for 2012, see 'Press Releases 2012', *Embassy of the United States Cairo – Egypt*, Available online: https://bit.ly/3pAKVZ5 (accessed 26 October 2021).
6   *BBC Arabic*, 24 June 2012, Available online: https://bbc.in/2W2uwwx (accessed 1 October 2015).
7   Kerry met with opposition figures before meeting Morsi because the opposition had accused the United States of being biased in favour of him. Some opposition leaders, such as Baradei and Sabahy, refused to meet Kerry. See: *BBC Arabic*, 2 March 2012, Available online: https://bbc.in/3pjV6RT (accessed 8 August 2015).
8   *Shorouk*, 2 March 2012, Available online: https://bit.ly/2Z8l0Ng (accessed 8 August 2015).
9   'Readout of the President's Phone Call with Egyptian President Morsi', *The White House*, 6 December 2012, Available online: https://bit.ly/3C1Nyqt (accessed 11 April 2021).

instance of the American attempt to take the middle ground between opposing forces in Egypt in this period.

The US position on the transitional phase during the Morsi government may best be summed up in Obama's remarks in an interview with Telemundo TV network in September 2012, following the attacks on the US embassies in Egypt and Libya: 'I don't think that we would consider them [the Egyptian government] an ally, but we don't consider them an enemy.'[10] That epitomized a fundamental decline in Washington's relationship with the Egypt government, which previous US administrations had regarded as an ally when it was under Mubarak.

1 US economic and military aid to Egypt after the revolution

Towards the end of 2011, Washington created special funds to channel additional economic assistance to Egypt, Jordan and Tunisia to stimulate their economies and promote democratization. For Egypt, this took the form of the EAEF. Approved by Congress in November 2012, the fund aimed to develop the private sector, especially in agriculture, by supporting SMEs with facilitated loans and technical assistance. The federal government earmarked $60 billion for the project in 2012.[11] However, Congress froze the fund after the Egyptian army ousted Morsi. It then released the funds on 13 December 2014, after the ratification of the new Egyptian constitution. The freeze on US arms exports to Egypt was also lifted, even though progress towards democracy required more than the mere promulgation of a constitution. In 2015, a Congressional Research Service assessment report on the efficacy of the EAEF found that the allocations had not been properly invested in Egypt and did not attain their desired results.[12]

Congress maintained the Economic Support Fund component of aid to Egypt at $250 million for the 2012 and 2013 annual budgets,[13] then it reduced it to $200 million in 2014 and $150 million in 2015; it maintained this same level in 2016.[14] In 2018 and 2019, Donald Trump's administration allocated $1.4 billion per year in bilateral assistance for Egypt, most of which ($1.3 billion) went to military assistance while the next largest chunk was dedicated to economic support. In its budgetary proposal for 2021, the

---

[10] *Foreign Policy*, 13 September 2012, Available online: https://bit.ly/300bY5m (accessed 21 October 2021).
[11] The board overseeing this fund consisted of three Egyptian citizens, three US citizens and three US-Egyptian dual nationals, and it was chaired by James Harmon. See: *Al-Masry Al-Youm*, 25 March 2013, Available online: https://bit.ly/2JQpyk9 (accessed 26 July 2015).
[12] Jeremy M. Sharp, 'Egypt: Background and U.S. Relations', *Congressional Research Service*, 30 September 2021, Available online: https://bit.ly/3lYFqOw (accessed 21 October 2021).
[13] Ibid., 20.
[14] Ibid., 20.

Trump administration requested congressional approval for a $1.4 billion aid package to Egypt.[15]

Some congressional members voiced frequent demands for a freeze or reduction in economic aid to Egypt in response to the many crises during the interim period, the Morsi presidency and after the coup, but their appeals fell on deaf ears. The United States did not allocate aid to support democratic transition or the elected government. The amount of overall support remained considerably less than it had been during the Mubarak era, and it would increase again after the coup. The Israeli lobby and direct Israeli diplomacy was instrumental in convincing the United States to accept and ease its pressures on the Sisi government. It is noteworthy that the level of US foreign military assistance to Egypt has remained a nearly constant $1.3 billion since the January revolution.[16]

2 The military coup

As the Egyptian military command was secretly preparing to oust the elected president, Egyptian defence minister Sisi told US secretary of defence Chuck Hagel, in a meeting at the Defence Ministry, that 'Muslim Brotherhood rule in Egypt is over'.[17] US-Egyptian relations were more focused on military affairs at this point. Hagel, who had become the most important channel of communications between Washington and Egypt,[18] arrived in Cairo on 24 April 2013 to discuss the fight against terrorism and smuggling, mainly in Sinai, and the democratic transition. Only after his meeting with Sisi did he meet with President Morsi.[19]

While the United States supported the 30 June 2013 protests, it continued to call for constructive dialogue between Egyptian political forces.[20] Addressing the impending demonstrations the day before, President Obama told the press that the United States did not take sides with the government or the opposition in Egypt.[21] In a subsequent press conference

---

[15] Jeremy M. Sharp, 'Egypt: Background and U.S. Relations', *Congressional Research Service*, 27 May 2020, Available online: https://bit.ly/37rDUB1 (accessed 20 October 2020).
[16] Ibid., 16–18.
[17] Sisi said this in a television interview aired on CBC and ONTV, see: *Daily Motion*, 6 and 7 May 2014, Available online: https://bit.ly/3jnz3G2 (accessed 21 October 2021).
[18] Mohammed al-Manshawi, 'Washington and Cairo: From the January Revolution to the Election of Sisi: The Reality of Interests and the Illusion of Change' [Arabic], in *The Arabs and the US: Interests, Concerns and Issues in a Changing Environment* [Arabic], ed. Marwan Kabalan (Beirut: Arab Centre for Research and Policy Studies, 2017), 510.
[19] *Atlantic Council*, 25 April 2013, Available online: https://bit.ly/3b0ISFn (accessed 21 October 2021).
[20] *al-Ahram*, 30 June 2013, Available online: https://bit.ly/2JQbJSM (accessed 16 August 2015).
[21] *Washington Post*, 29 June 2013, Available online: https://wapo.st/2FPEcGs (accessed 20 October 2020).

on 1 July 2013, he stressed that while Morsi was the elected leader, he now had to respect the opposition and minority groups:

> [T]he U.S. government's attitude has been we would deal with a democratically elected government. What we've also said is that democracy is not just about elections, it's also about how are you working with an opposition; how do you treat dissenting voices; how do you treat minority groups. And what is clear right now is that although Mr. Morsi was elected democratically, there's more work to be done to create the conditions in which everybody feels that their voices are heard, and that the government is responsive and truly representative.[22]

That same day, the State Department spokesperson told a press briefing that Secretary of State Kerry was in contact with Egyptian opposition leaders Amr Moussa and Mohamed ElBaradei, as well as the army, the Egyptian government and Morsi, in his capacity as the elected president of Egypt. The spokesperson declined to comment on the forty-eight-hour ultimatum that the army had given political forces to resolve their differences.[23] At this point, Obama was not receiving daily updates on Egypt, and Hagel was inclined to encourage the army to take over; for his part, Kerry had given up on Morsi.[24]

On the evening of 1 July 2013, Obama phoned Morsi, but did not express a clear position on the situation in Egypt. While the United States was committed to the democratic process, he said, it did not take sides,[25] and it was unable to control the army.[26] Meanwhile, unofficial US sources reported that Obama had warned the Egyptian army against staging a

---

[22] Obama identified the United States's main priority that day as the need to protect its embassy in Cairo. See: 'Remarks by President Obama and President Kikwete of Tanzania at Joint Press Conference', *The White House*, 1 July 2013, Available online: https://bit.ly/37RmjRp (accessed 16 August 2015).

[23] *The Wall Street Journal*, 2 July 2013, Available online: https://on.wsj.com/3khHfWT (accessed 20 October 2020).

[24] Kirkpatrick, *Into the Hands of the Soldiers*, 228.

[25] The US embassy in Egypt posted excerpts of the readout of the phone call:
'The President told President Morsy that the United States is committed to the democratic process in Egypt and does not support any single party or group. He stressed that democracy is about more than elections; it is also about ensuring that the voices of all Egyptians are heard and represented by their government, including the many Egyptians demonstrating throughout the country. President Obama encouraged President Morsy to take steps to show that he is responsive to their concerns, and underscored that the current crisis can only be resolved through a political process.'
'President Obama also underscored his deep concern about violence during the demonstrations, especially sexual assaults against female citizens. He reiterated his belief that all Egyptians protesting should express themselves peacefully, and urged President Morsy to make clear to his supporters that all forms of violence are unacceptable.' 'Readout of the President's Call with President Morsy of Egypt', *The White House*, 2 July 2013, Available online: https://bit.ly/3oHof9e (accessed 21 October 2021).

[26] Kirkpatrick, *Into the Hands of the Soldiers*, 234.

coup if it wanted to continue to receive US military aid.[27] Hagel made two phone calls to Sisi in the space of two days, one only a few hours before the coup, though no details were disclosed.[28] Undoubtedly, by this time the pragmatists in the Obama administration had gained ground.

After the coup, Obama issued a brief statement urging Egyptians to renounce violence and to elect a new civilian government as soon as possible. He expressed his 'deep concern' over the army's decision to remove Morsi but asked it to safeguard the rights of the Egyptian people. 'The voices of all those who have protested peacefully must be heard – including those who welcomed today's developments, and those who have supported President Morsy [sic],' he said.[29] He added that his government would be studying whether the army's action was a coup and the actions it would have to take accordingly.[30] Or, as he put it, 'I have directed the relevant departments and agencies to review the implications [of that day's developments] under U.S. law for our assistance to the Government of Egypt.'[31] Ben Rhodes reported that a 'tortured debate' erupted in Washington about whether to label what had clearly been a coup. Naming it a coup would entail restrictions on the type of assistance that the United States provides to the Egyptian government. Rhodes was among few who supported labelling it a coup for the sake of the US credibility. Rhodes ultimately lost the argument.[32]

US officials were divided between those who supported Morsi's removal as the culmination of a grassroots revolution similar to the 25 January revolution and those who saw it as a military coup. The division did not follow party lines, whether among government officials or in the US press.[33] In a joint statement released on 5 July 2013, Chairman Ed Royce and Ranking Member Eliot Engel of the House of Representatives' Committee

---

[27] The same sources cited the US ambassador to Egypt Anne Patterson and two other State Department officials as saying that the demands Egyptians were voicing in their protests were largely consistent with the reforms that Washington and its allies had been urging for weeks. See: *al-Joumhouria*, 2 July 2013, Available online: https://bit.ly/3aUamwm (accessed 16 August 2015).

[28] al-Manshawi, *America and the Egyptian Revolution*, 309.

Kirkpatrick wrote, 'The White House received reports on the calls [between Hagel and Sisi] and saw that Hagel had coddled instead of scolded.' Hagel told Kirkpatrick that 'he had been besieged by complaints about Morsi from Israel, Saudi Arabia, and the United Arab Emirates' and added that 'MBZ and other leaders in the Middle East were warning me then that the Muslim Brotherhood is the most dangerous element afoot in the Middle East today'. Kirkpatrick, *Into the Hands of the Soldiers*, 226.

Even after the coup, 'Hagel talked to Sisi nearly every other day that summer, for a total of seventeen calls over five weeks, sometimes for as long as ninety minutes.' Despite Hagel warning Sisi that he would lose support if he abused the military takeover, Hagel's tone was still conciliatory (Ibid., 265).

[29] 'Statement by President Barack Obama on Egypt', *The White House*, 3 July 2013, Available online: https://bit.ly/3BCDPX6 (accessed 21 October 2021).

[30] Manshawi, *America and the Egyptian Revolution*, 310–11.

[31] 'Statement by President Barack Obama on Egypt'.

[32] Ben Rhodes, *The World as It Is* (New York: Random House, 2018), 205–6.

[33] For more detail, see: Ibid.; Manshawi, *America and the Egyptian Revolution*, 305–38.

on Foreign Affairs held that the Muslim Brotherhood failed to understand what democracy really means. The statement gave the impression that the events were a positive development towards democracy, rather than a coup. There was no hint of a possible suspension or review of US aid to Egypt.[34] In the other congressional chamber, the camp that labelled these events as a coup submitted a proposal to cut off US aid to Egypt. The bill, submitted by Republican senator Rand Paul on 31 July 2013, was defeated in a vote eighty-six in favour and thirteen against.[35] The vote on Paul's proposal was taken after a fellow senator read out a letter from the AIPAC opposing a cut-off of US assistance to Egypt, as it could increase instability, undermine important US interests and jeopardize Israel's security.[36] AIPAC had become a pro-coup lobby, joining ranks on this matter with the lobbies of some Gulf countries such as the UAE.

Washington continued its attempts to work with Egypt to promote the formation of a national unity government and curb the escalating civil strife. Deputy Secretary of State William Burns visited Cairo on 15 July and again on 2 August 2013.[37] Military coordination continued between the defence ministers, who exchanged thirty phone calls between 3 July 2013 (the coup) and 19 December 2013 (when Morsi was charged with espionage).[38] The contacts did nothing to forestall the Raba'a and Nahda Square massacres. Afterwards, Obama issued a statement on 15 August, during his summer holiday, strongly condemning the steps taken by Egypt's interim government and security forces against civilians. He called on Egyptian authorities to respect universal human rights, lift martial law which denies those rights and initiate a process of national reconciliation. He reiterated his country's neutrality towards the political players in Egypt, pointing to how both sides in Egypt had accused the United States of supporting the other side. Although Obama, in that statement, announced the cancellation of the biannual Bright Star joint military manoeuvres with Egypt, in fact these had been suspended since the outbreak of the Arab revolutions in 2011 due to the deteriorating security situation.[39]

The US government is required by law to suspend military aid to any military that carries out a coup against a democratically elected government.

---

[34] 'Chairman Royce and Ranking Member Engel Release Joint Statement on Ongoing Events in Egypt', *US House of Representatives, Committee on Foreign Affairs*, 5 July 2013, Available online: https://bit.ly/37PWGR4 (accessed 9 December 2020).
[35] *CNN*, 31 July 2013, Available online: https://cnn.it/39XIPdX (accessed 17 August 2015).
[36] *Jewish Telegraphic Agency*, 1 August 2013, Available online: https://bit.ly/3mb8CCc (accessed 17 August 2015).
[37] *Anadolu Agency*, 4 August 2013, Available online: https://bit.ly/2XADSUQ (accessed 18 August 2015).
[38] Manshawi, *America and the Egyptian Revolution*, 350.
[39] Gilad Wenig and Eric Trager, 'Bring Back Bright Star', *Washington Institute for Near East Policy (WINEP)*, 21 August 2015, Available online: https://bit.ly/2Xw9M4H (accessed 3 September 2015).

So, US officials avoided using the term 'coup' to refer to Morsi's ouster, however harsh their repeated criticisms of the actions of the Egyptian army and the human rights situation in Egypt.[40] Through this circumlocution, Washington could circumvent the law, demonstrating that political expediency could trump the rule of law in democratic countries as well. However, Egyptian military and security forces were so excessive in their clampdowns on protests and arrests of political activists, Islamist or otherwise, that the US government was forced to take concrete action. In August 2013, it suspended major components of US military aid to Egypt, such as scheduled deliveries of F-16s, Apache helicopters and tanks. The freeze was lifted in March 2015 despite the worsening human rights situation in Egypt.[41]

The ongoing repression of protests did not keep Secretary of State Kerry from visiting Cairo on 3 November 2013[42] and from stating, on 20 November 2013, after his return to Washington, that the Muslim Brothers had hijacked the 25 January revolution and that the Egyptian army acted to restore democracy to Egypt.[43] It would not take long for US-Egyptian relations to revert to the pre-revolution status quo. On 25 September 2014, President Obama met President Sisi on the sidelines of the UN General Assembly inaugural session. It was the first meeting between an American and Egyptian president since Hosni Mubarak's visit to the White House in 2010. Although Morsi had asked for a meeting with Obama during the inaugural session in 2012, it never took place.[44] Congress, for its part, added certain exceptions to the appropriations laws governing the release of foreign military appropriations to Egypt, enabling Kerry to waive the required democracy certification.[45] Congress had granted a similar power to former secretary of state Condoleezza Rice in 2008.

In general, the United States cared about domestic developments in Egypt only insofar as they affected the structure of the Middle Eastern regional order or jeopardized US-Israeli interests or other strategic issues of mutual concern. The United States was able to accommodate the Egyptian army's conduct of domestic affairs while criticizing it at the diplomatic level. However, Kerry's portrayal of the coup as a step towards democracy was a declaration of support if not a form of collusion. It is also hard to think of an acceptable rationale for Obama to avoid meeting with the elected

[40] *CNN*, 23 August 2013, Available online: https://cnn.it/3n5lI4R (accessed 17 August 2015).
[41] *BBC Arabic*, 1 April 2015, Available online: https://bbc.in/3jiwbu7 (accessed 9 August 2015).
[42] *Al-Arabiya*, 2 November 2013, Available online: https://bit.ly/373SmOU (accessed 18 August 2015).
[43] *Alhurra*, 21 November 2013, Available online: https://arbne.ws/3G6F6Zo (accessed 18 August 2015).
[44] *Shorouk*, 26 September 2014, Available online: https://bit.ly/3nc8kNW (accessed 18 August 2015).
[45] Human Rights Watch, 'World Report 2015: Egypt, Events of 2014', Available online: https://bit.ly/3oQhwdj (accessed 21 October 2021).

president Morsi while agreeing to meet the president who staged a violent coup against him.

During the post-revolutionary interim phase, the United States maintained varying relationships with most Egyptian political forces while its strategic relationship with the Egyptian army remained a constant. Washington's strategic ally in Egypt was hardly a liberal force and certainly not an Islamist one. It was the military. Nothing illustrates this more than the continued influx of military aid throughout the transitional phases despite the steady reductions in economic aid, as shown above. In addition, Egyptian-US dialogue shifted from the political track to military channels. What mainly brought military leaders from both countries together was the United States's need to discuss the situation in Egypt in terms of its repercussions on regional security. The United States didn't mind a coup against an elected civilian president. Its actions did not go beyond rhetorical appeals to Egyptian political forces to engage in dialogue and reconciliation. It continued in the same mode after the removal of Morsi and despite the repression of civil liberties. The quick return to the norm in US-Egyptian relations ultimately gave the coup Washington's seal of approval.

After a brief hiatus that ended with the overthrow of Egypt's first elected civilian president, Washington and Egypt resumed their strategic partnership, dating from the Egyptian-Israeli peace treaty in 1979. As always, the need to guarantee Israel's security set the agenda. Sisi has proven this by sustaining the blockade against Gaza, destroying the underground border tunnels, coordinating with the United States and Israel on the security of the Gulf of Aden and cooperating on other issues related to the structure of the regional order.

II European-Egyptian relations after 25 January

After the 25 January revolution, EU policymakers hastened to recalibrate their positions and adapt to the Egyptian protestors' demands for freedom, democracy and change. EU High Representative for Foreign Affairs Catherine Ashton visited Egypt twice in the first half of 2011: on 22 February and 18 June. On the first occasion, it was to discuss the EU finance ministers' decision to consider freezing the assets of key Mubarak regime figures.[46] On the second occasion,[47] she asked the Egyptian government to

---

[46] *BBC Arabic*, 16 February 2011, Available online: https://bbc.in/2Lj9xU5 (accessed 1 September 2015); *Politico*, 9 February 2011, Available online: https://politi.co/3aYPOTq (accessed 1 September 2015).

[47] 'Catherine Ashton visits Jordan, Egypt, Israel and Occupied Palestinian Territory', *European Union*, 15 June 2011, Available online: https://bit.ly/3G6Iaom (accessed 1 September 2015).

meet its obligations to lift the state of emergency and present a clear time frame and schedule for introducing constitutional reforms.[48] President of the European Commission José Manuel Barroso delivered a message to the Egyptian people ahead of his visit to Cairo on 14 July 2011, affirming the EU's and the new Egypt's partnership for freedom and Europe's solidarity with the protestors in Tahrir Square and the entire region.[49] During his visit, Barroso met with SCAF head, Tantawi, representatives of NGOs, the Grand Mufti of Egypt Ali Gomaa and the Coptic Patriarch Pope Shenouda III.[50]

In May 2012, the EU Commission released its progress report on the implementation of the agreed-upon EU Neighbours political action plan for Egypt for 2011. The report concluded that under SCAF, Egypt had made inroads in implementing reforms in the framework of the agreed-upon plan. The electoral system had been reformed, free parliamentary elections had been held in two rounds, and SCAF had pledged to hand over power to a civilian authority after presidential elections. On the other hand, the report noted that SCAF's record of respect for basic human rights and democratic standards had not been satisfactory. It cited the use of excessive force during demonstrations, especially against women, and the persistence of arbitrary arrests, military trials, torture and degrading treatment in prisons. The report also criticized the Egyptian authorities' incitement of public opinion against civil society organizations that receive foreign funding and the lack of progress in the establishment of a joint free trade zone due to the Egyptian authorities' lack of commitment.[51]

EU officials and reports repeatedly condemned the violence in Egypt under SCAF and reiterated their calls for an end to the state of emergency and a transfer of power to civilian rule as soon as possible.[52] The EU, as well as individual member states, stressed the need to hold elections on time. When they were held, it sent a delegation to monitor the process.[53] To mark the inauguration of the first post-revolutionary People's Assembly, Ashton issued a congratulatory statement, on 23 January 2012, expressing her 'hope that the Parliament will drive on the democratic reforms to meet the expectations of the Egyptian people for social rights, economic growth

---

[48] See Ashton's statements archived at the European External Action Service: *European External Action Service*, Available online: https://bit.ly/3m41UB7 (accessed 1 September 2015).
[49] *al-Ahram*, 13 July 2011, Available online: https://bit.ly/3ajJ8yX (accessed 1 September 2015).
[50] *al-Ahram*, 14 July 2011, Available online: https://bit.ly/3bdFEi1 (accessed 1 September 2015).
[51] 'Implementation of the European Neighbourhood Policy in Egypt Progress in 2011 and Recommendations for Action', *European Commission*, 15 May 2012, Available online: https://bit.ly/3DooyKi (accessed 21 October 2021).
[52] See the archive of the EU Delegation to Egypt at: *European External Action Service*, Available online: https://bit.ly/3aijzhL (accessed 21 October 2021).
[53] 'The EU's Response to the "Arab Spring"', *European Commission*, 16 December 2011, Available online: https://bit.ly/300iI3a (accessed 21 October 2021).

and fundamental freedoms'.⁵⁴ Individual European governments did not release statements welcoming the results of the Egyptian parliamentary elections. Perhaps many shared a view commonly held in France. French minister of state for youth affairs Jeannette Bougrab told the press on 2 December 2011 that she was very worried the Islamists would win the parliamentary elections in Egypt and other Arab Spring countries.⁵⁵

After the presidential elections, Barroso sent a congratulatory message to Morsi on 25 June 2012 and Ashton lauded the elections while taking part in an EU-sponsored conference in Cairo.⁵⁶

The EU increased its financial assistance to Egypt to help it through the rocky straits of the transition. In 2011, it offered a €20 million aid package to support civil society,⁵⁷ and on 17 August 2011, the EU Commission allocated €100 million to help improve the standard of living of the poor in Cairo.⁵⁸

During Morsi's visit to Brussels in September 2012, the EU pledged €500 million from EU financial institutions in the form of an additional comprehensive package of long-term assistance to Egypt.⁵⁹ On 14 November 2012, Egypt hosted the first EU-Egypt Task Force, which was jointly headed by EU High Representative for Foreign Affairs Catherine Ashton and Egyptian foreign minister Mohamed Amr.⁶⁰ The EU Commission followed through on its pledge with €300 million in grants, €90 million in the framework of the SPRING programme, €50 million for macro-financial assistance and €160 million in investment.⁶¹ In addition, the EU offered €450 million in the framework of the macro-financial assistance linked with Egypt's agreement with the IMF.

Also in November 2012, the EIB announced that it could lend Egypt €1 billion a year in 2012 and 2013, with the possibility of this reaching €2 billion a year. Of this, the bank had already signed a €200 million loan

---

54 'Statement by High Representative Catherine Ashton on the Opening Session of the Egyptian Parliament', *EU Delegation to Egypt*, 23 January 2012, Available online: https://bit.ly/3ajQnqv (accessed 15 April 2021).
55 *Le Parisien*, 2 December 2011, Available online: https://bit.ly/3mv3qeg (accessed 21 October 2021).
56 Remarks by Ashton at the 'Egyptian Women: The Way Forward' conference, European Commission, 19 July 2012: *European Commission*, Available online: https://bit.ly/3oyowrE (accessed 6 September 2015).
57 'The EU's Response to the "Arab Spring"'.
58 'New Commission Support to Improve Living Conditions and Create Jobs in Egypt', *EU Delegation to Egypt*, 17 August 2011, Available online: https://bit.ly/3E39jGR (accessed 1 October 2021).
59 'Statement by President Barroso Following his Meeting with Mr Mohamed Morsi, President of Egypt', *European Commission*, 13 September 2012, Available online: https://bit.ly/2KfOhhO (accessed 8 September 2015).
60 'First meeting of EU-Egypt Task Force to Support the On-Going Reforms in Egypt', *European Commission*, 13 November 2012, Available online: https://bit.ly/3gynoS1 (accessed 8 September 2015).
61 'EU-Egypt: True Partnership for People and Transformation', *European Commission*, 14 November 2012, Available online: https://bit.ly/3m5PIfU (accessed 8 September 2015).

for the Cairo metro project and another €45 million loan for community development. In like manner, the EBRD announced plans to increase its loans to Egypt to €1 billion a year in 2012 and 2013.[62] EU Council president Herman Van Rompuy summed up the scale of European investments in Egypt during his visit to Cairo on 13 January 2013: they totalled €5 billion in the form of grants and loans in 2012 and 2013 from the EU and European states and institutions,[63] of which the EIB provided €2 billion, the EBRD another €2 billion, plus €1 billion in aid provided by individual European countries.[64]

On the other hand, the EU share in overall foreign direct investment in Egypt fell from 81 per cent in the 2011/2 financial year to 52 per cent in 2012–23.[65] In 2011, Egypt received €5.4 billion in FDI in 2011, up from €3 billion in 2010. However, this fell to €4.1 billion in 2012 (in which SCAF governed the first half and Morsi the second).[66]

On 13 September 2011, Germany signed two financial and technical cooperation agreements with Egypt, one for €72 million to support development projects and another €17 million in-kind grant to fund public service improvement projects. On 23 September 2012, an EU/French Development Agency signed a €940 million deal with Egypt to fund the third line of the Greater Cairo Metro.[67] In 2011, Prime Minister David Cameron pledged £110 billion to Egypt and Tunisia over four years.[68] Most of these aforementioned pledges never bore fruit.

Morsi received British foreign secretary William Hague in Cairo on 11 September 2011. Egypt's foremost concern, at the time, was to recuperate Egyptian assets smuggled abroad to the UK and the extradition of former regime figures wanted for prosecution in Egypt.[69] Morsi also visited EU headquarters on his first official visit to Europe. He flew to Brussels in September 2012 with the dual aim of encouraging European investments

---

[62] 'Egypt: EIB Lends EUR 200m for the Cairo Metro Line and EUR 45m for Community Development', *European Commission*, 14 November 2012, Available online: https://bit.ly/340DUoX (accessed 8 September 2015).
[63] *Reuters Arabic*, 13 January 2013, Available online: https://reut.rs/3Gbgbnl (accessed 7 September 2015).
[64] *al-Wafd*, 13 January 2013, Available online: https://bit.ly/2Ze7fNv (accessed 3 September 2015).
[65] On EU Trade policies, see the website of the EU delegation in Egypt, Available online: https://bit.ly/2YyDRAF (accessed 6 September 2015).
[66] Ibid.
[67] It is noteworthy that the procedures for the funding were implemented in December 2014 (after the coup). *Al-Masry Al-Youm*, 18 February 2015, Available online: https://bit.ly/3n5rmUB (accessed 10 September 2015).
  Also see: 'Signature of a €940 Million European Financing Package for the Construction of the Third Phase of Greater Cairo Metro Line 3', *Embassy of France in Egypt*, 23 September 2012, Available online: https://bit.ly/2ZaI3HQ (accessed 10 September 2015).
[68] *Youm7*, 20 October /10/2011, Available online: https://bit.ly/2VZ5tdI (accessed 8 September 2015).
[69] *Shorouk*, 12 September 2012, 5.

in Egypt and garnering EU support for Egypt's democratization process.[70] He then flew to Rome where most of his meetings with Italian officials focused on economic cooperation.[71]

On 17 December 2012, against the backdrop of the escalating violence and demonstrations in Egypt after Morsi's constitutional declaration, Berlin suspended talks with Cairo on a partial cancellation of Egypt's debt to Germany because it feared another dictatorship was emerging in Egypt under Morsi.[72] Just hours ahead of Morsi's arrival in Germany on 30 January 2013, German foreign minister Guido Westerwelle told ARD television that economic aid to Egypt was contingent on advances in democratic development[73] (he did not lay down the same condition when Sisi visited Germany after the coup). In her joint press conference with Morsi, German chancellor Angela Merkel identified two key determinants of Cairo's relationship with Berlin: openness to dialogue with all political forces in Egypt and respect for civil liberties and human rights, inclusive of the religious freedoms of minorities. Morsi came away from that meeting empty-handed.[74] Due to the mounting turmoil back home, Morsi had to cut his visit to Germany short and cancel a scheduled visit to France. Still, he was able to receive French foreign minister Laurent Fabius in Cairo on 18 February 2013 and secure a pledge for increased French investments in Egypt.

On the whole, the policies of the EU and individual European states did not obstruct the democratic transition in Egypt after the revolution. EU countries offered aid and presented encouraging economic initiatives as a matter of principle. Nevertheless, Europe quickly adjusted to the reversal in democratization and the coup, essentially shrugging it all off as a return to business as usual in Egypt. The EU, like the United States, refrained from using the term 'coup' and stressed the need to include all political forces in the roadmap. It did not denounce, as a matter of principle, the military's removal of Egypt's first elected civilian president, but it did denounce the military's repressiveness and exclusionist attitudes afterwards.

On 3 July 2013, EU High Representative for Foreign Affairs Ashton urged 'all sides to rapidly return to the democratic process, including the

---

[70] *Anadolu Agency*, 12 September 2012, Available online: https://bit.ly/3ncvtj3 (accessed 6 September 2015).
[71] *Al-Masry Al-Youm*, 13 September 2012, Available online: https://bit.ly/2LpBrxW (accessed 6 September 2015).
[72] These views were voiced by Minister for Economic Cooperation and Development Dirk Niebel in remarks to the *Berliner Zeitung*. See *Deutsche Welle Arabic*, 17 December 2012, Available online: https://bit.ly/3oISr0z (accessed 6 September 2015).
[73] *France 24 Arabic*, 30 January 2013, Available online: https://bit.ly/3oFLdug (accessed 6 September 2015).
[74] *Al Jazeera*, 31 January 2013, Available online: https://bit.ly/3nagmFG (accessed 6 September 2015).

holding of free and fair presidential and parliamentary elections and the approval of a constitution, to be done in a fully inclusive manner, so as to permit the country to resume and complete its democratic transition'.[75] European governments followed suit in official statements released on 3 July and the following days. They too avoided calling Morsi's removal a coup while stressing the need for the avoidance of violence and inclusiveness. Effectively, they bowed to the fait accompli. German foreign minister Westerwelle deplored the 'severe setback for democracy' and urged the restoration of the constitutional order as quickly as possible.[76] British foreign secretary Hague appealed to 'all sides to show restraint and avoid violence'. He added, 'The United Kingdom does not support military intervention as a way to resolve disputes in a democratic system.'[77] French foreign minister Fabius did not address Morsi's removal directly and instead focused on the need to press forward with the promised elections.[78]

On the other hand, the foreign ministers of Norway and Sweden were more principled and outspoken in their criticism of the Egyptian army as well as in their criticism of the EU's position on the steps it had taken.[79] On 7 July 2013, Swedish foreign minister Carl Bildt praised the African Union's 'stand of principle'[80] on events in Egypt and faulted the EU for not doing the same.[81] Norwegian foreign minister Espen Barth Eide said on 15 August that the situation in Egypt 'has all the characteristics of a military coup'.[82] He added, that despite whatever the generals said regarding their plan for a swift return to civilian rule, almost everything that had happened in Egypt since they took control was going in the wrong direction.[83] One cannot help but to observe a pattern: the further removed a democratic European country was from the realm of strategic interests, the more explicitly it voiced its negative reaction towards the coup. Naturally, this does not hold for countries with no interests in Egypt, as is the case with some Eastern European countries, nor are they characterized by the prevalence of a deeply rooted democratic culture.

---

[75] 'Statement by EU High Representative Catherine Ashton on Developments in Egypt', *European Union*, 3 July 2013, Available online: https://bit.ly/3uUjnyw (accessed 10 September 2015).
[76] *Deutsche Welle Arabic*, 4 July 2013, Available online: https://bit.ly/2JHFbuj (accessed 10 September 2015).
[77] 'Foreign Secretary Statement on the Situation in Egypt', *United Kingdom Government*, 3 July 2013, Available online: https://bit.ly/3nitUQy (accessed 10 September 2015).
[78] *Spiegel International*, 4 July 2013, Available online: https://bit.ly/39UIV68 (accessed 9 December 2020).
[79] *al-Ahram*, 30 June 2015, Available online: https://bit.ly/3B2b1GC (accessed 10 September 2015).
[80] He expressed this on *Twitter*, 7 July 2013, Available online: https://bit.ly/3FuCjIZ (accessed 10 September 2015).
[81] *Rassd*, 7 July 2013, Available online: https://bit.ly/3G7ossI (accessed 10 September 2015).
[82] *Livemint*, 15 August 2013, Available online: https://bit.ly/3DshCeS (accessed 10 September 2015).
[83] *Al Jazeera*, 15 August 2013, Available online: https://bit.ly/37LHNPG (accessed 10 September 2015).

The EU tried to mediate between the post-coup regime and the Muslim Brotherhood. Ashton held numerous meetings with Egyptian military officials and various political forces during her two visits to Cairo in the space of two weeks in the second half of July,[84] and she repeatedly called for the inclusion of all political forces in the government. However, as discussed in Chapter 8, this did not imply the need to return to the pre-coup order, but rather the need to convince the Muslim Brotherhood to bow to reality, engage in the political process and take part in parliament and government.

In a way, the EU could be said to have implicitly condoned the coup. Former interim vice-president Mohamed ElBaradei revealed, during a seminar at the European University Institute in May 2015, that the EU envoy Bernardino León was the one who had worked out the plan that Sisi announced on 3 July 2013[85] and that Baradei had hoped Sisi would commit to. Whether or not one regards the roadmap as rhetorical cover for a coup and a means to win friends and allies while ignoring its substance and building a new military dictatorship in Egypt, Baradei's remarks are telling. He exposed the EU's role, its advanced knowledge of the coup, its fear of Islamist movements and its wariness of the democratic process after the revolutionary wave that swept the Arab region.

European institutions condemned the break-up of the Raba'a and Nahda sit-ins without taking any diplomatic other steps aimed at stopping the regime's severe repression policies. On 14 August 2013, the EU issued a statement urging Egyptian authorities to exercise the utmost restraint.[86]

The statements of European foreign ministers, all issued the same day, were little more than expressions of embarrassment and mere lip service to condemning the human rights abuses. They reflected no substantial change in the European relationship with Egypt.

After Sisi's 'win' in the presidential elections in 2014, European powers treated him as a legitimately elected head of state, turned the page on the Raba'a massacre and subsequent repressions of protests, random arrests and collective death sentences, and welcomed him in their capitals. All the aforementioned statements stressing the need for inclusive democratization and European support for this process proved to be rhetorical exercises unsupported in practice.

[84] *Deutsche Welle*, 30 July 2013, Available online: https://bit.ly/2YBt6OA (accessed 10 September 2015).

[85] *Ahram Online*, 8 July 2015, Available online: https://bit.ly/3Fx0Ddi (accessed 10 September 2015); *CNN Arabic*, 7 July 2015, Available online: https://cnn.it/3n77nVE (accessed 10 September 2015).

[86] 'Statement by EU High Representative Catherine Ashton on the Situation in Egypt', *European External Action Service*, 14 August 2013, Available online: https://bit.ly/3nivkus (accessed 10 September 2015).

The European powers were too keen on stability to support the Arab revolutions. They did not stand in the way of democratization in Egypt, if only because of the force of the revolutionary tide in the region. Nor did they regret the overthrow of an elected government by a military coup. European financial policies remained the same during the period of democratic transformation and after the coup against it. The EBRD opened its first permanent office in Egypt on 4 November 2014.[87] The European institutional support programmes that existed before the revolution continued their operations. On 31 March 2014, the Egyptian government signed a $190 million loan agreement with the EBRD to upgrade the electricity plants of Shabab and Damietta West.[88] Soon afterwards, the bank offered another €126 million loan to modernize Egypt's railway system.[89]

Ironically, the SPRING programme, which aimed to support democracy in Egypt and Tunisia, continued after the coup against democracy in Egypt. The EU and Egypt signed an agreement in the framework of this programme on 26 November 2013 to carry out joint cooperative projects worth €90 million.[90] True, the funding was for infrastructural projects, so it was not strictly political assistance. However, when the programme was introduced, its goal was to meet the needs of an elected Egyptian government and help it through the democratic transition.

In a statement issued at the twenty-seventh session of the UN Human Rights Council in Geneva in September 2014, the EU criticized the deteriorating human rights situation in Egypt.[91] It was reminiscent of the European approach to Mubarak. The EU would release intermittent statements criticizing the state of human rights and lack of democratic freedoms and processes in Egypt in order to please European human rights organizations and lobbies and for the sake of the self-image, while European capitals gave warm welcomes to Mubarak, supported him politically and avoided exerting any effective pressure on him.

The major European powers give precedence to geostrategic considerations in the Mediterranean basin in which some of them are located. They care, first and foremost, about stability, preventing northward-bound illegal migration across the Mediterranean, combatting

---

[87] *Youm7*, 28 October 2014, Available online: https://bit.ly/3C29iSU (accessed 10 September 2015).
[88] *Egypt Independent*, 31 March 2014, Available online: https://bit.ly/3FugZDB (accessed 21 October 2021); *Dostor*, 25 May 2014, Available online: https://bit.ly/3nLNWU4 (accessed 10 September 2015).
[89] *EBRD*, 22 May 2014, Available online: https://bit.ly/3neOjGl (accessed 21 October 2021).
[90] *Asharq al-Awsat*, 26 November 2013, Available online: https://bit.ly/2ZhWE4b (accessed 10 September 2015).
[91] Ibrahim Manshawi, 'Contradictory Positions: EU-Egyptian elations after 30 June', [Arabic] *Arab Centre for Research and Studies (ACRSEG)*, 25 October 2014, Available online: https://bit.ly/343lsMy (accessed 10 September 2015).

terrorism and peace with Israel. Human rights are important at the level of public opinion. Rarely have European governments understood that geostrategic issues are intrinsically related to the realization of Arab and Palestinian peoples' rights. Generally, this matter of principle gets lost in the rush of events and the need to take stances on the issues of the moment. Also, European countries' general fear of Islamist movements coming to power in the Arab region often overrides their belief, acquired through experience, in the need not to exclude Islamists from the political process and the public sphere.

Apart from such prominent exceptions as Sweden, European countries returned to their customary coexistence with dictatorships that ensured stability along the eastern and southern shores of the Mediterranean. They had only deviated from custom when forced to by the grassroots uprisings. Ultimately, Arab democratic forces were unorganized and failed to do enough to address public opinion in Europe.

III Russia and the interim phase

Russia was leery of the Egyptian revolution and the other Arab revolutions, for fear of two possible outcomes: (1) democratization, which Russia considers an expansion of Western political culture and American influence, and (2) the Islamists' assumption to power, ushered in by the revolution. In general, Russia's contacts with Egyptian political elites were limited, as was Russian diplomatic and media interest in domestic developments in Egypt since the Sadat's policy turn. Its main focus was on developments in the Syrian revolution. Moscow sent no diplomatic envoys to Cairo during the period of SCAF rule with the sole exception of the Russian foreign minister Sergey Lavrov's visit on 10 March 2012, when he met with Tantawi on the sidelines of a Russian meeting with Arab League officials to discuss the Syrian crisis.

Russia adapted to the democratization process in Egypt as it evolved. It could not have opposed the results of the free and fair democratic elections if only because, as an emergent global power, it had to work closely with a regional power such as Egypt. Russian president Vladimir Putin congratulated Morsi on his victory in the polls on 25 June 2012.[92] Russia also declared its support, in principle, for the Islamic Quartet initiative to resolve the Syrian crisis that Morsi launched soon after coming to power.[93]

---

[92] *RT Arabic*, 25 June 2012, Available online: https://bit.ly/3lZ5egM (accessed 14 September 2015).
[93] *Ahram Online*, 5 March 2014, Available online: https://bit.ly/2YqPOZj (accessed 14 September 2015).

Morsi flew to Moscow on 18 April 2013. The focus was on economic relations and cooperation in energy. The two sides signed a deal to supply Egypt with liquefied natural gas and agreed to explore a linkup between Russian and Arab natural gas pipelines, restructure Egyptian steel and coal manufacturing plants with the assistance of Russian firms, monitor the establishment of the Egyptian-Russian Business Council and study future joint projects in energy, agriculture and transportation.[94] They also agreed to negotiate the creation of a free trade zone between Egypt and the Eurasian Customs Union (which, at the time, consisted of Belarus, Kazakhstan and Russia).[95]

President Morsi ignored Russia's designation of the Muslim Brotherhood as a terrorist organization and Moscow's support for Mubarak during the 25 January revolution. He was more intent on breaking free of the foreign relations straightjacket of the Mubarak era and pursuing a policy less-dependent on the United States. Russia picked up on these signals and took advantage of the opening in order to improve its image in the Arab and Islamic world. Exploring potential for economic and energy cooperation afforded opportunities for dialogue and a way to test the horizons of a bilateral relationship that acknowledged political differences. Still, Moscow remained apprehensive of the Muslim Brotherhood's ideological orientation and the growing closeness between Cairo and Ankara. Therefore, after the coup, once assured that the system of government had reverted to the Mubarak-era order, Moscow returned to the stance it had adopted during the revolution.

On 5 July 2013, the Russian Foreign Ministry issued a statement referring to a phone call between the Egyptian and Russian foreign ministers, in which Lavrov 'confirmed the unchanged principal position of Russia in support of lawful aspirations of the Egyptian people to better life in conditions of freedom and democratic renewal'.[96] Two days later, Putin warned that Egypt was on the verge of a civil war like that in Syria.[97] Moscow never spoke out against the use of excessive force in the break-up of the Raba'a and Nahda sit-ins.

In practical terms, Russia fell in with the Egyptian military regime's narrative on Morsi's removal and subsequent events. Russian policy adopted the Egyptian army's discourse as it evolved until, eventually, it reached full conformity in rhetoric, outlooks and policies. Egyptian-

---

[94] *al-Ahram*, 22 April 2013, Available online: https://bit.ly/3m3qe2D (accessed 10 September 2015).
[95] Ibid.
[96] 'About Phone Conversation of Russian Foreign Minister Sergey Lavrov with the Acting Minister of Foreign Affairs of Egypt Mohamed Kamel Amr', *Ministry of Foreign Affairs for the Russian Federation*, 5 July 2013, Available online: https://bit.ly/3ndJUDy (accessed 14 September 2015).
[97] *RT Arabic*, 7 July 2013, Available online: https://bit.ly/2VXtIt0 (accessed 14 September 2015).

Russian relations in the post-coup era experienced a quantum leap in cooperation in various domains, far exceeding the levels that had existed in the Mubarak era. Symbolic of this development was the arrival of the Russian missile cruiser *Varyag* in the port of Alexandria on 11 November 2013,[98] two days ahead of the arrival of Russian defence minister Sergei Shoigu and foreign minister Sergey Lavrov in Cairo, on a joint visit that Egyptian officials described as 'historic'.

The Egyptian defence and foreign ministers, Abdel Fattah El-Sisi and Nabil Fahmy respectively, reciprocated with a visit to Moscow on 13 February 2014. This was after Washington had trimmed its annual allocation of military aid to Egypt.[99] Sisi, although still the defence minister, was accorded the welcome of a head of state. Putin even offered Sisi his endorsement as such: 'I know that you, mister defence minister, have decided to run for president of Egypt. I wish you luck both from myself personally and from the Russian people.'[100] Russian diplomacy was growing less reserved in demonstrating its full support for the Egyptian army and its narrative, as was also evidenced by frequent praises of the Egyptian army's role in protecting Egypt and safeguarding its stability. The reciprocal, top-level visits took place in accordance with the Treaty on Strategic Partnership signed by Hosni Mubarak and then Russian president Dmitry Medvedev during the latter's visit to Cairo in 2009.[101] However, it was not until after the 2013 coup that the terms of the treaty were put into effect, showing once again that a tough authoritarian regime is the kind of government Putin likes best.

After becoming president in June 2014, Sisi would visit Moscow three more times in just over a year. In September 2014, Russia announced a massive arms deal with Egypt, estimated at $3.5 billion.[102] During Putin's visit to Cairo on 9–10 February 2015, he and Sisi signed a memorandum of understanding to build a nuclear energy plant.[103] Meanwhile, Russia continued to include the Muslim Brotherhood in its list of terrorist organizations, which it updated in February that year.

---

[98] *Ahram Online*, 11 November 2013, Available online: https://bit.ly/3lrCoFD (accessed 14 September 2015).
[99] *BBC Arabic*, 12 February 2013, Available online: https://bbc.in/3n910kE (accessed 14 September 2015).
[100] *BBC*, 13 February 2014, Available online: https://bbc.in/30OKmkb (accessed 15 September 2015).
[101] Alaa al-Gadidi, 'Interests Not Axes: The Opportunities and Limitations of Russian-Egyptian Relations after 30 June' [Arabic], *al-Siyassa al-Dawliya*, 9 February 2015, Available online: https://bit.ly/30MDVOC (accessed 15 September 2015).
[102] *Reuters*, 17 September 2014, Available online: https://reut.rs/2ZhRkOf (accessed 14 September 2015).
[103] The Egyptian president took advantage of Putin's visit to produce an extravaganza with the grandeur, pomp and ceremony reminiscent of the era of the grand potentates.

Russia and Egypt began to coordinate more closely on various regional issues in the Levant, not least the Syrian crisis. Under Sisi, the Egyptian stance on the Syrian revolution would gradually shift. As consistent with the domestic agenda, Cairo was inclined to sympathize with authoritarian regimes and against any grassroots uprising, an attitude that was also informed by a phobia of Islamists of all stripes. Egypt pushed to form a Syrian opposition that would serve as an alternative to the National Coalition for Syrian Revolution and Opposition Forces and that would agree to a political solution that accepted the principle of the survival of the Bashar regime. The post-coup regime in Egypt would naturally be averse to the overthrow of existing Arab regimes

Although the strategic frameworks of the Egyptian regime's alliance with the United States remained unchanged, Sisi tried to diversify his alliances, and he found in Russia a partner that supported dictatorships around the world without compunction, in contrast to Western powers with their incessant human rights caveats raised by their parliaments and public opinion. From the Russian perspective, Moscow's support for the Sisi regime suited its general strategy in the region. The Putin and Sisi regimes shared the fondness for filling the ideological vacuum with nationalist chauvinism and venerating past glories. Russia also feared that the wave of democratization might strike the Muslim countries to its southeast. Moscow projects its experience in Eastern Europe and the former Soviet Republics onto its conceptualization of democratization, for which it is synonymous with the expansion of Western influence.

Russia, like China, is free to conduct foreign policy unencumbered by the pressures of domestic public opinion. The Putin regime has managed to stem the tide of public opinion towards democratic pluralism and rally it behind jingoistic slogans that draw on the popular yearning for the days of its superpower pre-eminence. This has allowed Moscow to pursue foreign policies based on geostrategic calculations free of Soviet-era ideological considerations and unhampered by pressures from public opinion. The same applies to a large extent to Chinese foreign policy, with the difference that for China economic considerations outweigh geostrategic ones except within its immediate, constantly expanding, regional sphere.

IV China's position on the January revolution and the SCAF phase

Beijing's reaction to the fall of the Ben Ali regime in Tunisia and then the Mubarak regime in Egypt is exemplified by its decision to tighten social media surveillance and block such expressions as 'Tunisian uprising', the 'Jasmine Revolution' and, later, 'Tahrir Square'.[104] Totalitarian regimes like Russia and China, though they laud their own historic revolutions that shape their founding myths, fear the revolutions of the present day. Their discourse at home is therefore tuned to the key of 'order' and 'stability' while their discourse abroad shifts to the key of 'non-intervention in the domestic affairs of other nations'. They disapprove of the spread of the idea of democracy in the Third World and people's admiration for it. So, they launch propaganda campaigns to show how unsuitable it is to cultures outside Europe and the United States, and their media dwells in elaborate detail on the problems and crises that arise in democratic states. Although some Arab revolutions rose against regimes allied to the West, as was the case with the Mubarak regime, China, like Russia, regarded them with a leery eye. For the Chinese regime, the revolutions were a breach of the traditional principles and foundations upon which the international order was built – above all, the principle of sovereignty, which, making no distinction between the regime and the state, meant the sovereignty of the existing regime.

China made no secret of its anxiety over the participation of Islamist movements in the Arab revolutions and their subsequent rise to power. After all, it could influence Chinese Muslim minorities in Xinjiang, Ningxia and Gansu.[105] From this perspective, Beijing was naturally suspicious of Turkey's support for the Arab revolutions and the Egyptian revolution in particular. It feared that the success of these revolutions would increase Turkey's influence in the Middle East, which, in turn, would feed the nationalist and secessionist sentiments of Turkic peoples, especially in East Turkestan, where an independence movement made several attempts to establish an independent state in the first half of the twentieth century.[106]

China said little during the Egyptian revolution until 10 February 2011 when, in response to Western calls for Mubarak to step down, it objected to 'foreign intervention in Egyptian affairs'.[107] Then, on 12 February 2011, the day after Mubarak stepped down, the Chinese Foreign Ministry avoided welcoming the step, in contrast to many Western and regional powers. It merely said that '[China] believes that recent developments in the situation

---

[104] Paul Salem, 'Future of the Arab Order and Regional and International Stances on the Revolution' [Arabic], *al-Mustaqbal al-Arabi* 34, no. 3098 (April 2013), 152.
[105] Mohammed Fayez Farhat, 'Chinese and Russian Conduct towards the Arab Spring Wave: A Reading Beyond Economic Interests' [Arabic], *Siyasa Arabiya*, no. 1 (March 2013), 43.
[106] Ibid.
[107] Sharif Fadel Mohammed, 'Egyptian-Chinese Relations between Continuity and Change: 2003–2013' [Arabic], *al-Mustaqbal al-Arabi* 36, no. 420 (February 2014), 42.

in Egypt could help restore stability and social order in the country as soon as possible'.[108]

But Chinese officials were too pragmatic to let their disapproval of the turn of events in Egypt keep them from communicating with SCAF and strengthening political and economic cooperation. Acknowledging the new realities, they worked to ensure the continuity of Chinese exports to and investments in Egypt, which accounted for a significant portion of the bilateral balance of trade. In this spirit, Chinese foreign minister Yang Jiechi visited Cairo on 3 May 2011 and met with SCAF chief Tantawi. On the economic track, China dispatched to Egypt a delegation headed by the Chinese minister of trade and including representatives of twenty financial and economic institutions in order to boost economic cooperation and trade between Beijing and Cairo.[109] The Chinese ambassador to Egypt, Song Aiguo, described the Chinese foreign minister's visit to Egypt as proof that relations between the two countries 'have not changed and that they will rise to a higher level after the January revolution'. The ambassador added that his government had offered a 60 million yuan, or about $9 million, grant to Egypt.[110] Also, by the end of May 2011, China had cancelled its travel warning to Chinese tourists for a number of Egyptian cities, including Hurghada, Sharm El-Sheikh, Luxor and Aswan.[111]

After becoming president, Morsi moved to recalibrate Egypt's foreign relations within its established strategic spheres (the Arab, African, Islamic, Mediterranean and international spheres). This entailed an 'eastward orientation' in order to strengthen Egypt's relations with emerging international and regional powers, such as China, India and Pakistan, and to reduce dependency on the West. China was his first stop in his tours outside the Arab region. Heading a delegation of several ministers and eighty businessmen, he arrived in Beijing on 28 August 2013, with the dual goal of stimulating Chinese investment in Egypt and increasing the volume of trade with China.[112] He came back with eight agreements which provided for a non-refundable $70 million grant to launch joint projects in infrastructure and electricity, a gift of 300 police cars, cooperative projects in solid waste treatment and other areas of environmental protection, closer cooperation in tourism and agricultural research,[113] plus a facilitated loan of $200 million from the CDB to support SMEs. In addition, Egyptian

---

[108] *People's Daily*, 12 February 2011, Available online: https://bit.ly/3gFlUFJ (accessed 2 October 2015).
[109] *al-Ahram*, 1 September 2015, Available online: https://bit.ly/37RQIiv (accessed 2 October 2015).
[110] *Saudi Press Agency*, 3 May 2011, Available online: https://bit.ly/3G93I3F (accessed 21 October 2021).
[111] *al-Ahram*, 31 May 2011, Available online: https://bit.ly/3qHtSTj (accessed 2 October 2015).
[112] *Al Jazeera*, 28 August 2012, Available online: https://bit.ly/3B26Oml (accessed 21 October 2021).
[113] *al-Ahram*, 22 December 2014, Available online: https://bit.ly/39VEHeE (accessed 2 October 2015).

and Chinese businessmen signed various agreements yielding a total of $4.9 billion worth of investments.[114]

Despite the upheaval in Egypt during Morsi's presidency, the volume of bilateral trade with China during the first four months of 2013 totalled $3.45 billion, or 32 per cent more than in the same period in 2012. Chinese investments in non-financial sectors in Egypt exceeded $600 million.[115]

Beijing did not take a clear position on the 3 July coup. On 4 July, the Chinese Foreign Ministry spokeswoman said, 'China respects the choice of the Egyptian people.' She also appealed to calm: 'We also hope that all parties concerned in Egypt can avoid using violence and properly solve their disputes through dialogue and consultation and realize reconciliation and social stability.'[116] China issued a similar appeal in the aftermath of the break-up of the Raba'a and Nahda sit-ins. On 15 August 2013, its Foreign Ministry spokesperson said China hoped all parties would put the interests of the country and people first and exercise restraint to avoid more casualties.[117]

Once the post-coup order took root and began to win international acceptance, China gradually showed its preference for the new government. The first tangible example of this was its invitation to the Egyptian foreign minister to visit Beijing on 14 December 2013.[118] The visit paved the way to re-energized bilateral economic ties. Soon afterwards, on 22 February 2014, a delegation of Chinese businessmen arrived in Egypt on the first official Chinese visit after the coup. Prior to this, China condemned the bombing of the security directorate building in Mansoura on 24 December 2013.[119]

Sisi made his first visit to China after becoming president on 23 December 2014. Less than a year later, in early September 2013, he paid a second visit upon the invitation of the Chinese president to attend the seventieth anniversary celebrations of China's victory in the Second World War.

---

[114] Essam Abdel Shafie, 'Looking East: Shifts in Egyptian Foreign Policy towards Asian States' [Arabic], *al-Siyassa al-Dawliya*, 4 April 2013. Archived Copy Available Online: https://bit.ly/3BrDjKY (accessed 30 October 2021).

[115] *Sada Elbalad*, 29 May 2013, Available online: https://bit.ly/2Z5krns (accessed 21 October 2021).

[116] *Ahram Online*, 4 July 2013, Available online: https://bit.ly/3m54LXy (accessed 20 October 2015)

[117] *People's Daily*, 15 August 2013, Available online: https://bit.ly/3mzaTsR.

[118] 'Egyptian Foreign Minister Nabil Fahmy Visits China' [Arabic], *Chinese Embassy in Egypt*, 11 December 2013, Available online: https://bit.ly/3oG46Nv (accessed 2 October 2015).

[119] 'Foreign Ministry Spokesperson Hua Chunying's Regular Press Conference on December 24, 2013', *Ministry of Foreign Affairs of the People's Republic of China*, 24 December 2013, Available online: https://bit.ly/3E8j2ff (accessed 21 October 2021).

V The Gulf Cooperation Council (GCC) countries and Egypt after the revolution

During the January revolution, Saudi Arabian King Abdullah bin Abdul Aziz phoned President Hosni Mubarak on 29 January 2011 to declare his support:[120] 'The attempt to undermine security and stability in Egypt on the part of infiltrators in the name of freedom of expression is unacceptable.'[121] He also asked Washington to prevent the 'humiliation of Mubarak' and offered to replace the United States as a source of economic aid to Egypt.[122]

Ben Rhodes referred to the stance of the ambassadors from Saudi Arabia and the UAE, who announced in the press during the revolution that Obama had been badly advised by younger people 'who were more interested in preserving Obama's brand than listening to the wise hands who understood that democracy couldn't work in the Middle East'. Rhodes felt they meant him by these words, because he was one of those 'younger people'.[123]

Riyadh had to reconcile itself with the fall of Mubarak. 'The government of the Kingdom of Saudi Arabia welcomes the peaceful transition to the authority in Egypt and hopes that the efforts of the Egyptian armed forces will succeed in restoring peace, stability and tranquillity to the brotherly Arab Republic of Egypt,' the Saudi Press Agency reported, citing an official source.[124] Saudi Arabia quickly moved to establish ties with the Egyptian army command, which it saw as an acceptable replacement and probably hoped it would last. To Riyadh, the transition to SCAF could be seen as a decision that Mubarak had taken and, accordingly, not a revolutionary one.

The UAE reacted similarly. In a joint press conference in Baghdad with the Iraqi foreign minister on 3 February 2011, the UAE foreign minister Abdullah bin Zayed Al Nahyan acknowledged the rightfulness of demands for reform in Egypt, but he condemned the attempts by 'certain parties' to exploit these demands. What was happening in Egypt was 'abhorrent and shameful exploitation', he said.[125] Nahyan went a step further. He flew to Cairo on 8 February 2011, while the demonstrations in Tahrir were at their height, as a gesture of solidarity with Mubarak. After Mubarak stepped down, Abu Dhabi released a statement expressing its 'confidence in the

---

[120] *The Guardian*, 29 January 2011, Available online: https://bit.ly/2Y2CavI (accessed 30 October 2021).
[121] *BBC Arabic*, 11 February 2011, Available online: https://bbc.in/3jcCEXl (accessed 21 October 2021).
[122] *Elaph*, 21 April 2011, Available online: https://bit.ly/340nTzq (accessed 20 August 2015).
[123] Rhodes, *The World as It Is*, 107.
[124] *Al Bayan*, 13 February 2011, Available online: https://bit.ly/2W3hGOE (accessed 20 August 2015).
[125] *BBC Arabic*, 3 February 2011, Available online: https://bbc.in/3jcCEXl (accessed 21 October 2021).

ability of SCAF to administer the affairs of the country in these delicate circumstances in a manner that achieves the hopes and aspirations of the Egyptian people'.[126]

In Chapter 3 of Part II, we discussed the revolutionaries' storming of the Israeli embassy on 9 September 2011.[127] The clashes between demonstrators and security forces spilled over to the Saudi embassy, a few blocks away, and some protestors attempted to set fire to it.[128] Saudi Arabia did not close its embassy at the time. But it would less than nine months later against the backdrop of the case of Ahmed El-Gizawy, the Egyptian human rights lawyer and activist who was arrested upon arrival at King Abdulaziz Airport in Saudi Arabia on the charge of smuggling illicit prescription drugs into the country. According to Egyptian activists, the real reason for his arrest was because he had filed a suit against the Saudi government for the maltreatment and torture of Egyptian detainees in Saudi prisons. Gizawy's arrest and subsequent sentencing to twenty lashes triggered outrage in Egypt, precipitating mass demonstrations in front of the Saudi embassy. On 29 April 2012, Saudi Arabia shuttered its embassy and would not reopen it until 1 June 2012, after an Egyptian delegation flew to Riyadh to sort things out.[129] Then followed a Saudi-Egyptian protocol accord yielding a $1.5 billion package of Saudi economic aid to Cairo of which $1 billion was to be deposited into the CBE.[130]

The Saudi embassy had to smooth over other controversies that surfaced in Egypt when Saudi officials were found to have come to the service of Mubarak cronies. An example is the case of Prince Mansour bin Muqrin bin Abdul Aziz, the son of the head of Saudi Intelligence, and his sister Princess Lamia bint Muqrin, both of whom were implicated in helping the Egyptian business tycoon Hussein Salem smuggle his assets from Egypt to Saudi Arabia in early 2011, for which Salem had a warrant out for his arrest. The Saudi embassy hastened to establish backchannels with the Egyptian judiciary and intelligence services in order to bury the case. It was difficult, given the political climate at the time, but they eventually succeeded.[131]

---

[126] *CNN Arabic*, 7 February 2013, Available online: https://cnn.it/3E33Ik0 (accessed 21 October 2021).
[127] *Al Jazeera*, 10 September 2011, Available online: https://bit.ly/3oCjv1p (accessed 22 August 2015).
[128] *Alrai*, 11 September 2011, Available online: https://bit.ly/3aVKWOO (accessed 21 October 2021).
[129] The delegation was headed by People's Assembly Speaker Mohamed Saad Elkatatny and Shura Council Speaker Ahmed Fahmy. See: *CNN Arabic*, 1 June 2012, Available online: https://cnn.it/3m755Vo (accessed 22 August 2015).
[130] *CNN Arabic*, 10 June 2012, Available online: https://cnn.it/3B3euVx (accessed 21 October 2021).
[131] Wikileaks revealed many details about the case in the Saudi Cables, published in collaboration with *Mada Masr*. See: The Saudi Cables no. 117617, *WikiLeaks*, Available online: https://bit.ly/37W54P7 (accessed 25 October 2021) and The Saudi Cables no. 118521, *WikiLeaks*, Available online: https://bit.ly/3acoqlR (accessed 24 May 2015). For a fuller discussion of the case, see: *Mada Masr*, 24 June 2015, Available online: https://bit.ly/3b1LAdQ (accessed 1 October 2021).

Gulf countries said little about the elections, the constitutional drafting process and the Islamists' parliamentary victories under SCAF rule. Saudi Arabia and King Abdullah, personally, were more interested in securing Mubarak's release from prison. The Egyptian GIS proposed an initiative whereby the Gulf countries would offer $10 billion in economic aid to Egypt in exchange for the former president's release. Intelligence chief Murad Mowafi negotiated the deal with a Muslim Brotherhood leader, who agreed on the condition that $1 billion would be paid to the families of the victims of the 25 January revolution.[132]

The Kingdom of Saudi Arabia was also keen to improve its image among the Egyptian public. Towards this end, Saudi officials approached influential media figures and paid them to produce programmes portraying Saudi Arabia in a positive light and praising its services to Egypt.[133] More important to Riyadh at the time was to block Iranian access to religious and media channels. None other than Mostafa Bakry, now a strident supporter of the Bashar regime in Syria, offered his services, and the Saudi embassy transmitted his application to the Saudi Foreign Ministry to launch a satellite channel that would 'be a powerful voice against the Shi'a and support the positions of the Kingdom'.[134] In addition to offsetting the Iranian drive to draw closer to government and religious institutions in Egypt, Saudi Arabia forged close relations with Egyptian Salafist leaders whom it funded 'to confront the Shi'a tide by publishing books and periodicals on Islamic jurisprudence and holding seminars and conferences in youth clubs and gatherings to warn of that sectarian danger'.[135]

The UAE, like Riyadh, rushed to Mubarak's defence, using various types of leverage with SCAF to keep him from going to trial and implicating Emirati businessmen in the illegalities of the former regime. Abu Dhabi stopped issuing work permits to Egyptians employed in the Gulf, and it suspended visa services for Egyptians.[136] It postponed Prime Minister Essam Sharaf's visit to Abu Dhabi several times, and then, when it received him on 5 July 2011, it pledged a $3 billion economic aid package to Egypt,[137]

---

[132] For more details, see *Mada Masr*, 21 July 2015, Available online: https://bit.ly/30Nm7Tv (accessed 21 October 2021).

[133] *Mada Masr*, in collaboration with Wikileaks, published many of the communications between Egyptian media figures and the Saudi embassy in Cairo. All involve requests for financing in exchange for singing the Kingdom's praises. See: *Mada Masr*, 5 July 2015, Available online: https://bit.ly/3vwz3IJ (accessed 1 October 2021).

[134] The Saudi Cables, no. 120797, *WikiLeaks*, Available online: https://bit.ly/3gDGt5l (accessed 23 May 2015).

[135] For a discussion of Riyadh's response to Iranian policies in Egypt, see: *Mada Masr*, 9 July 2015, Available online: https://bit.ly/3m0pONQ (accessed 1 October 2021).

[136] The Saudi Cables, no. 83686, *WikiLeaks*, Available online: https://bit.ly/2IBUJPv (accessed 24 August 2015).

[137] *Al-Arabiya*, 5 July 2011, Available online: https://bit.ly/2K89fPs (accessed 20 August 2015).

which would never materialize. As UAE-Brotherhood tensions intensified, so too did Abu Dhabi's relations with SCAF because of 'the Egyptian army's lack of zeal for restraining the Muslim Brotherhood' in response to the UAE's request.[138]

Qatar, which felt that SCAF had protected and sided with the 25 January revolution, took steps to support democratization in Egypt. On 3 May 2011, Sheikh Hamad bin Khalifa, then the ruling emir of Qatar, visited Cairo (in the first visit by an Arab ruler to Egypt since the revolution), where he would meet with Field Marshal Tantawi to discuss implementing a number of joint economic and development programmes to support the Egyptian economy.[139] Qatar followed through with a pledge to invest $10 billion in Egypt,[140] and soon afterwards Crown Prince Tamim bin Hamad Al Thani (now the current emir) came to Egypt on 30 June 2011 in order to meet with Tantawi. While in Egypt, he met with a delegation of 25 January activists. In March 2012, Brotherhood leader Khairat el-Shater visited Qatar during a tour of Gulf countries following the parliamentary elections in Egypt. One purpose was to reassure Doha that 'Qatari investments that will flow into Egypt will be safeguarded by the investment laws that the elected People's Assembly will pass'. Shater also met with Egyptian religious figures, such as Qaradawi, and asked them to support him in the presidential elections or at least not to back the presidential candidate Abdel Moneim Aboul-Fotouh.[141]

Gulf countries made frequent pledges to support the Egyptian economy through aid and investment. But whereas Abu Dhabi was unwilling to commit direct investments until after the presidential elections,[142] CBE reports show that, from January 2011 to July 2012 (just after Morsi took office), direct Qatari investments increased rapidly. Saudi and Emirati direct investments steadily decreased during this period. Despite the inverse trajectories, Qatar continued to rank fourth in the volume of Arab direct investment in Egypt after the UAE, Saudi Arabia and Kuwait because of their influxes from earlier periods.[143] Still, Qatar was the only Arab

---

[138] The Saudi Cables, no. 84947, *WikiLeaks*, Available online: https://www.wikileaks.org/saudi-cables/doc84947.html.
[139] *al-Ahram*, 3 May 2011, Available online: https://bit.ly/3nyifO3 (accessed 20 August 2015).
[140] *Reuters*, 24 May 2011, Available online: https://reut.rs/3mzbz1n.
[141] The Saudi Cables, no. 83201, *WikiLeaks*, Available online: https://bit.ly/375qwlm (accessed 23 May 2015).
[142] *Mada Masr*, 26 July 2015, Available online: https://bit.ly/2ZhjHMu (accessed 1 October 2021).
[143] The Gulf States were the third largest investors in Egypt after the EU and the United States. Among them, the UAE ranked first, although its investments fell to $176.9 million from $186 million in the second quarter of the previous year. Saudi Arabia, with investments of around $79.6 million (down from $109.2 million), came second, followed by Kuwait ($15.5 million down from $17.3 million). Qatar came fourth, but its investments followed a reverse trajectory, jumping from $9.8 million to $13.2 million compared to the same quarter the previous year.
See: *Al Raya*, 13 July 2012, Available online: https://bit.ly/30DOwv2 (accessed 21 October 2021); *Asharq al-Awsat*, 11 July 2012, Available online: https://bit.ly/3nfyOxN (accessed 21 October 2021).

country, apart from Saudi Arabia, to offer financial gifts and deposits to Egypt after the revolution.

As the presidential elections approached, Saudi Arabia's ambassador to Cairo met several of the candidates. Its foreign minister, Saud bin Faisal, forwarded the minutes to King Abdullah. Most of the meetings were with candidates who were not well-favoured in the polls, apart from Ahmed Shafik.[144] Meetings were not held with Morsi, Aboul-Fotouh or Hamdeen Sabahi. The minutes revealed the rivalry between Shafik and Amr Moussa to win Saudi Arabia's good graces. Shafik accused Morsi, Aboul-Fotouh and Moussa of receiving funding from Qatar, while Moussa told the Saudi ambassador that a Shafik win would be disastrous because of his affiliation with the old regime. Another rival, Mohamed Selim al-Awa promised that if he won, he would never permit Iranian expansion in Egypt. Awa had good relations with Tehran.[145]

The UAE backed Shafik and provided him with considerable political and media support. It would also host him while he was being tried for corruption in absentia after Morsi came to power. In 2017, he decided to field himself for president again, this time challenging President Sisi, who was running for a second term in 2018.[146] He then appeared in a video, broadcast on Al Jazeera on 29 November 2017, saying that he was blocked from leaving the UAE 'for reasons he could not understand and did not want to understand'. He said that he was grateful to the UAE for hosting him, but he criticized the travel ban that deprived him of his constitutional right to take part in the elections and that was, therefore, an unacceptable interference in Egypt's domestic affairs.[147] On 2 December 2017, he was deported to Egypt on a private plane and was placed under heavy guard, while his family told the press they did not know where he was.[148] A month later, on 7 January 2018, he withdrew his candidacy saying he 'would not be the best person to steer the country during the coming period'.[149]

Kuwait and Bahrain followed the Saudi lead in their policies towards Egypt while Oman retained its customary neutrality towards the rivalries in Egypt and the crises in the region as a whole.

---

[144] The other candidates were Amr Moussa, Mohamed Selim al-Awa, Hisham Bastawisy and Hossam Khairallah.
[145] For further details, see the Saudi Cables, no. 36100, *WikiLeaks*, Available online: https://bit.ly/3aeI8gG (accessed 23 May 2015); *Mada Masr*, 6 July 2015, Available online: https://bit.ly/3pnb1Pe (accessed 21 October 2021).
[146] Ahmed Shafik, *Twitter*, 29 November 2017, Available online: https://bit.ly/3m6uvma (accessed 20 October 2020).
[147] *Al Jazeera*, 29 November 2017, Available online: https://bit.ly/3m4tw62 (accessed 20 October 2020).
[148] *Reuters Arabic*, 2 December 2017, Available online: https://reut.rs/3kdZgW5 (accessed 20 October 2020).
[149] Ahmed Shafik, *Twitter*, 7 January 2018, Available online: https://bit.ly/2T6T9H2 (accessed 20 October 2020).

1 Gulf policies towards the Morsi presidency

Although Gulf capitals officially welcomed Morsi's electoral victory, their statements hinted at their concerns and fears. Riyadh, in a letter from the Saudi monarch to the new Egyptian president, offered its congratulations to the Egyptian people.[150] The Emirati Foreign Ministry issued a statement welcoming Morsi's victory and calling for stability in Egypt.[151] Qatar's emir and prime minister sent congratulatory telegrams to the president-elect and lauded the 'democratic method in the first presidential elections in Egypt'. They also praised 'the role that SCAF and the Egyptian judiciary played in safeguarding and ensuring the success of the experience'.[152]

The new administration took pains to win the good will of the Gulf countries and reassure them that it had no intent of exporting the revolution or interfering in the domestic affairs of other countries.[153] Morsi made Saudi Arabia his first destination abroad as president.[154] The agenda of the visit, which took place on 11 July 2011, was dominated by customary protocol and diplomatic formalities. There was little substance. The kingdom did not respond to the Morsi administration's initiatives and showed little interest in its policies towards the Syrian revolution even though Riyadh and Cairo shared the same position on the Syrian regime. When Morsi unveiled his plan, in August 2012, for an 'Islamic Quartet' to resolve the Syrian crisis, it was received coolly in Riyadh,[155] which then frowned on his participation in the summit of the Non-Aligned Movement that was held in Tehran later that month.[156] The criticisms Morsi levelled at Tehran's policies in the Levant did not assuage the disapproval.

Riyadh took no official positions on subsequent developments in Egypt, but the Saudi-funded media was clear in its antipathy for the Morsi presidency and its support for the opposition, especially during the protests sparked by Morsi's constitutional declaration in late 2012.[157] During the first half of 2013, there were no developments of note in the Saudi-Egyptian relationship, although Riyadh continued to monitor the mounting tensions between the Egyptian army and the presidency.[158]

---

[150] *Al-Arabiya*, 25 June 2012, Available online: https://bit.ly/3r33Rhv (accessed 25 May 2015).
[151] *Asharq al-Awsat*, 25 June 2012, Available online: https://bit.ly/3Cvpix6 (accessed 25 August 2015).
[152] *Al Jazeera*, 25 June 2012, Available online: https://bit.ly/37qFS3T (accessed 25 May 2015).
[153] *Fekr Online*, 11 March 2015. Archived Copy Available Online: https://bit.ly/3CxVccq (accessed 25 May 2015).
[154] *Al Riyadh*, 11 July 2012, Available online: https://bit.ly/2WnDXXB (accessed 25 August 2015).
[155] *Fekr Online*, 11 March 2015, Available online: https://bit.ly/3CyGpOA (accessed 31 October 2021).
[156] Seif al-Din Abdel Fattah, personal interview, 5 September 2015, Doha.
[157] For more insight into the Saudi media coverage of these events, see: Al Jazeera, 7 December 2012, Available online: https://bit.ly/3nnWqPL (accessed 25 August 2015).
[158] A Saudi Foreign Ministry cable contains an update in late 2012 on these tensions and their causes. Among the causes it lists the failure of the presidency to engage in the dialogue with political forces that the army had called for on 11 December 2012 and Muslim Brotherhood Supreme Guide

The UAE put on a positive public face when Morsi was elected and adopted a covert hostility towards his administration. The UAE foreign minister praised the inaugural address Morsi delivered at Cairo University on 30 June 2012, homing in on his vow that Egypt would not intervene in the domestic affairs of other countries and would not export the Egyptian revolution.[159] Meanwhile, well-known Emirati activists unleashed broadsides against the Egyptian Muslim Brotherhood on social media, leading the Egyptian Foreign Ministry to summon the Emirati ambassador in Cairo to lodge a formal protest against some of those activists. Abu Dhabi also suspended its pledges of economic support to Egypt. On 21 August 2012, the Egyptian minister of finance Momtaz El-Saeed announced, 'The UAE will not be offering financial assistance to Egypt at this stage.'[160]

In a related development, UAE authorities arrested sixty Emirati citizens in September 2012 and charged them with 'creating and operating a secret organization with a paramilitary wing that threatens security and the founding principles of the state'. It added that the organization was 'linked with foreign agencies, from which it received instructions and funding in order to seize power and establish a theocratic government in the UAE'.[161] Then, on 8 October 2012, the Emirati Foreign Ministry launched a broadside: 'Muslim Brotherhood ideology does not believe in the nation state or in the sovereignty of nations. This is why it is not odd that the international Muslim Brotherhood organization has been making contacts and working to undermine the dignity, sovereignty and laws of states.' The statement urged Gulf countries to work together 'to prevent the Muslim Brotherhood from conspiring to destroy governments in the region'.[162]

The UAE furnished enthusiastic support in the press for the wave of protests against the November 2012 constitutional declaration.[163] On

---

Mohammed Badie's remarks on 21 December 2012, in which he said: 'The soldiers of Egypt are obedient. But they need a wise leadership to raise their awareness after the corrupt command that had been responsible for them.' The cable states that the first concrete translation of the army's anger at this was Defence Ministerial Decree 203/2012 prohibiting private ownership, lease, the granting usufruct rights or any disposition of any portion of the land adjacent to Egypt's eastern borders in the area referred to in the Camp David Annex as Area C. The decree also required the approval of the army, Interior Ministry and the intelligence agencies for any project in the area. See: the Saudi Cables, no. 3839, *WikiLeaks*, Available online: https://bit.ly/3p3UZGq (accessed 27 August 2015).

[159] *al-Ahram*, 30 June 2012, Available online: https://bit.ly/37rZe93 (accessed 27 August 2015).
[160] *Anadolu Agency*, 21 August 2012, Available online: https://bit.ly/3E3x8yc (accessed 25 August 2015).
[161] *Al Sbah*, 5 February 2013, Available online: https://bit.ly/3CgwyMY (accessed 21 October 2021).
[162] *Reuters Arabic*, 8 October 2012, Available online: https://reut.rs/3B5aILb (accessed 26 August 2015).
[163] In December 2012, Mohammed Musaad Yaqout of the FJP charged that a 'Gulf cell' was conspiring to topple Morsi and overthrow the legitimate government in collusion with the NSF in Egypt. He added that Ahmed Shafik and former Fatah leader Mohammed Dahlan were also involved, along with the Dubai police chief Dahi Khalfan. The remark infuriated Abu Dhabi. See: *Almal News*, 18 December 2012, Available online: https://bit.ly/3AWC85S (accessed 21 October 2021).

2 January 2013, it arrested a number of Egyptians whom it accused of being Muslim Brotherhood members who were 'conspiring' with Emirate citizens to found a branch of their organization in the UAE.[164] Morsi sent a delegation of officials, including the director of the GIS, to secure the release of the detained Egyptians,[165] but the visit failed to improve relations.[166] In early January 2013, it was reported that a Muslim Brotherhood women's cell had been rounded up in the UAE.

Against the backdrop of continuing attacks against Morsi and the Muslim Brotherhood in Emirati social media, the Brotherhood's Consultative Council met on 10 January 2013 to discuss the crisis with Abu Dhabi. Opinion was divided between those who argued that the presidency and Foreign Ministry should be given more time to handle the problem and others who thought that Deputy Supreme Guide Khairat el-Shater should fly to the UAE with an envoy from Qatar to offer guarantees to Emirati officials that the Brotherhood would not intervene in Emirati affairs and not export Egypt's democratization experiment to the UAE.[167] The Brotherhood did send an envoy, but only a middle-tier official whose visit failed to achieve a breakthrough towards an entente.[168]

There are no reports of any economic support from Gulf countries to Egypt during Morsi's year in office, with the exception of Qatar.[169] Doha deposited $2 billion in the CBE during Sheikh Hamad bin Khalifa's visit to Cairo on 11 August 2012.[170] It then announced a package of $18 billion worth of investments on the occasion of the visit of Qatari prime minister Hamad bin Jassim Al Thani to Cairo on 6 September 2012, during which he drew up the first five-year timetable for implementing the agreements.[171] Some $8 billion of the investments were earmarked for power plants, liquefied natural gas projects and other industries in eastern Port Said, while the other $10 billion would be dedicated to tourist projects on the northwest Mediterranean coast.[172]

---

[164] *Al-Manar*, 2 January 2013, Available online: https://bit.ly/3G3GlIR (accessed 21 October 2021).
[165] *al-Quds al-Arabi*, 2 January 2013, Available online: https://bit.ly/3GaadTW (accessed 21 October 2021).
[166] *Al Jazeera*, 22 January 2013, Available online: https://bit.ly/3mwZQhH (accessed 27 August 2015).
[167] *Mada Masr*, 26 July 2015.
[168] Seif al-Din Abdel Fattah, personal interview.
[169] *Aswat Masriya*, 23 January 2014, Available online: https://bit.ly/37tXsEu (accessed 21 August 2015).
[170] *Arab48*, 12 August 2012, Available online: https://bit.ly/3rdiRtt (accessed 21 August 2015). Al-Ahram, in its coverage, mentioned that this was the Qatari emir's first visit to Egypt since the January revolution, suggesting that Doha had deliberately refrained from an official visit until the Muslim Brothers won the elections. In fact, the emir had paid an earlier visit during the SCAF era. See: *Masrawy*, 11 August 2012, Available online: https://bit.ly/3vAu1uF (accessed 21 October 2021).
[171] *al-Ahram*, 6 September 2012, Available online: https://bit.ly/37s7YMf (accessed 20 August 2015).
[172] *Kuwait News Agency*, 6 September 2012, Available online: https://bit.ly/2WoyCPU (accessed 20 August 2015).

The CBE received the first Qatari deposit in early October 2012, which brought up hard currency reserves from $14.42 to $15.127 billion. The reserves had fallen by 7 per cent in September.[173] On 8 January 2013, Doha extended Egypt another $2.5 billion to help prevent the slide of the Egyptian pound.[174]

Doha met all its economic pledges to Egypt, as Egyptian finance minister Morsi El Sayed Hegazy, confirmed in a press conference on 20 January 2013.[175] By that time, it amounted to a $1 billion grant, a $1.5 billion deposit with the CBE and $2.5 billion in purchased bonds.[176] On 10 April 2013, at the time of Egyptian prime minister Hisham Qandil's visit to Qatar, Doha added $3 billion more in the form of purchased bonds or long-term deposits. It then offered to supply Egypt with natural gas to help offset the shortage in the summer of 2013, and it allowed Egyptian firms to operate in Qatar directly, without need for a local sponsor.[177]

The intersection between the domestic polarization in Egypt and the contradictions between the Gulf countries' policies and positions towards Egypt was neither pronounced nor especially visible during the first half of 2013. Only after the 3 July coup did it become explicit. At that point, it also became clear that the divide was not just about Islamist rule in Egypt but also about democratization generally.

The GCC countries, with the exception of Qatar, converged into an increasingly shrill choir of anti-Morsi rhetoric after the Tamarod movement announced the countdown to the 30 June 2013 marches to demand early presidential elections. They depicted Morsi as a dictator challenged by a grassroots uprising similar to the 25 January revolution. Ironically, the media touting the coming marches were the same news outlets that had worried about the 25 January revolution while it was happening and that only began to cover it clearly after its victory. The reason they equated the 30 June marches with 25 January was to confer legitimacy on the former as a revolution, regardless of their true feelings about revolution. All was fair in the battle between Arab powers that supported the revolution and the opposing axis that championed the counter-revolution. Ben Rhodes wrote that in June 2013, when the protests against the Egyptian elected president were again mounting, the United States received indications that the Egyptian military, backed by the Saudi and Emirati governments, was behind the unrest, and was going to overthrow the deeply flawed yet

---

[173] *CNN Arabic*, 2 October 2012, Available online: https://cnn.it/3vzZY6A (accessed 21 October 2021).
[174] *Reuters Arabic*, 8 January 2013, Available online: https://reut.rs/3b0yAoO (accessed 21 October 2021).
[175] *Al-Ittihad*, 21 January 2013, Available online: https://bit.ly/3vBPinJ (accessed 21 October 2021).
[176] *Al Raya*, 20 January 2013, Available online: https://bit.ly/2XBO0g6 (accessed 21 October 2021).
[177] *Al Riyadh*, 10 April 2013, Available online: https://bit.ly/2IWLhq4 (accessed 21 August 2015).

democratically elected government. Those parties were also supporting an information campaign against Anne Patterson, the American ambassador, in demonstrating her as an accomplice of the Muslim Brotherhood.[178]

Leaked cables from the office of Defence Minister Abdel Fattah El-Sisi, made public in 2015, revealed that the UAE helped fund the Tamarod movement in collaboration with Egyptian intelligence,[179] as discussed previously. When we add to this that Saudi and Emirati media chimed in with local Egyptian media owned by prominent business magnates to urge the Egyptian army to oust Morsi as it did Mubarak, we are left with no room to doubt that the Gulf lent a financial, political and media hand to the preparations for the coup. Gulf countries opposed to democratization in Egypt took advantage of the press freedoms after the revolution to invest in media hostile to elected institutions because the latter were staffed with Islamists. Rumour-mongering and scare campaigns played an important role in generating instability. In addition to funding Tamarod, the UAE funded the political activities of the Office of the Defence Minister who aspired to power.

On 3 July 2013, the Saudi monarch sent a congratulatory letter to Adly Mansour, who had just been named interim president. He took the occasion to salute 'the men of all the armed forces, represented in the person of General Abdel Fattah El-Sisi, who led Egypt at this phase out of a tunnel the dimensions and repercussions of which only God knows'.[180] Gulf leaders, without exception, congratulated Mansour after he was sworn into office on 4 July 2013. On 8 July 2013, a delegation from the UAE arrived in Cairo to offer 'support that has never been interrupted under any circumstances, as we see Egypt as much of a supporter of the UAE as the UAE is a supporter of Egypt'.[181] By 9 September 2013, four high-level Emirati delegations had visited Cairo.[182]

The Qatari media were among the first to call the events of 3 July 2013 a military coup. As vehement as the opposition was, Emir Tamim bin Hamad, in keeping with the protocol between Qatar and other Arab states, congratulated Mansour after he was sworn in.[183]

---

[178] The Emirati ambassador in the United States, Yousef Al Otaiba, sent Rhodes 'a photo of a poster that cast Patterson in this light with no other message attached'. Rhodes describes this as 'one of the more brazen acts that I'd experienced in my job'. Rhodes, *The World as It Is*, 204.

[179] *al-Araby al-Jadid*, 1 March 2015, Available online: https://bit.ly/3mvZ6JM (accessed 27 August 2015).

[180] *Al Riyadh*, 4 July 2013, Available online: https://bit.ly/3ahnEE0 (accessed 27 August 2015).

[181] I adduce this quote by then Emirati ambassador to Cairo, Mohammed Bin Nakhira Al-Dhaheri Al Dhaheri, simply to underscore the misinformation: As I have shown, the UAE cut its support to Egypt during the Morsi era. See: *al-Ahram*, 9 July 2013, Available online: https://bit.ly/3gTkIPg (accessed 27 August 2015).

[182] *Assabeel*, 9 September 2013, Available online: https://bit.ly/3B6nkl8 (accessed 21 October 2021).

[183] *Al Jazeera*, 4 July 2013, Available online: https://bit.ly/2LEVHvr (accessed 28 August 2015).

A comparison between Gulf countries' reactions to the 25 January revolution and the events of 3 July 2013 shows that those that supported the revolution opposed the coup and vice versa. One can only conclude that support for the coup was informed not only by opposition to the Islamists but also to the grassroots movement and democratization, for fear that the contagion would spread to the Gulf and elsewhere in the Arab region, especially given Egypt's weight and influence.

Gulf countries rushed to embrace the military regime in Egypt and to shower it with urgent economic aid. By 11 July 2013, they had pledged $12 billion: $5 billion from Saudi Arabia, $4 billion from Kuwait and $3 billion from the UAE. Of this amount, $3 billion were in non-repayable grants. The rest was in deposits in the CBE or petroleum derivatives.[184] Two years later, Saudi Arabia, Kuwait and the UAE offered $12 billion more ($4 billion each) on the occasion of the Egyptian Economic Development Conference in Sharm El-Sheikh in March 2015.[185] Oman chipped in $500 million.[186]

Qatar continued to fulfil its end of the agreements it had signed with Egypt under Morsi. On 2 August 2013, it delivered the first shipment of natural gas after Morsi's removal. Four more shipments would be delivered over the next six weeks to help Egypt contend with the fuel shortage.[187] Doha also offered to mediate between the government and the pro-Morsi camp in order to avert the break-up of the Raba'a and Nahda sit-ins.[188]

Regardless of how regional and international powers truly felt about the violent clearing of the sit-ins on 14 August, their general reaction was to call for restraint and dialogue and avoid taking sides. The exception was some Gulf countries that openly supported the dispersal as a sovereign right of the state. On 16 August 2013, King Abdullah stated that the Saudi government and people 'stand with Egypt against terrorism, lawlessness and strife . . . and their legitimate right to deter all who manipulate and mislead simple people among our brethren in Egypt'.[189] The statement was unequivocal in its support for the actions the Egyptian regime took to clear the sit-ins. The speed with which this statement followed that action suggests that Riyadh had given its blessing in advance. The communiqué from Abu Dhabi followed immediately afterwards. It echoed the Saudi monarch's statement, including the claim that the dispersal of the sit-ins

---

[184] *CNN Arabic*, 11 July 2013, Available online: https://cnn.it/3plXQ17 (accessed 21 October 2021).
[185] *BBC Arabic*, 13 March 2015, Available online: https://bbc.in/3ntDnDK (accessed 28 August 2015).
[186] *Alwasat*, 13 March 2015, Available online: https://bit.ly/34lb42Q (accessed 28 August 2015).
[187] *al-Ahram*, 12 September 2013, Available online: https://bit.ly/3b1tfxe (accessed 21 October 2021).
[188] *Al Jazeera*, 4 August 2013, Available online: https://bit.ly/37oAdeS (accessed 30 August 2015).
[189] *Al-Arabiya*, 16 August 2013, Available online: https://bit.ly/388d7bw (accessed 29 August 2015).

was an exercise of the sovereign right of the Egyptian state.[190] Manama, too, fully endorsed the Saudi stance and the need 'to fight acts of violence, extremism and terrorism'.[191]

Kuwait also supported the actions taken by the Egyptian government to preserve security and stability. However, in a statement the Kuwait News Agency attributed to a Kuwaiti Foreign Ministry source, Kuwait expressed 'its sorrow for such a large number of lives lost among the Egyptian people'. The source also urged political forces in Egypt 'to respond to the Egyptian government's repeated appeals for serious dialogue between all sectors of Egyptian society' and to proceed with the roadmap as scheduled.[192] Oman issued no official comment.

The statements from the Gulf were not only alike in substance; they also used similar terminology. For example, they referred to the dispersal of the sit-ins as the 'current incidents', as though to suggest that clashes had erupted between two equally matched sides requiring state intervention to stop the violence. The statement from Abu Dhabi emphasized the sovereignty of the Egyptian state and the principle of non-intervention in its affairs. Reports by Western officials have revealed that Emirati officials had urged Egyptian authorities to break up the Raba'a sit-in.[193]

After the coup, Qatar called for Morsi's release and condemned the ban on protests, arguing that it jeopardized the accomplishments of the 25 January revolution.[194] On 14 August 2013, the Qatari Foreign Ministry issued a statement denouncing the break-up of the Raba'a and Nahda sit-ins and urging 'whoever holds power and authority in Egypt to refrain from the security option in confrontations with peaceful sit-ins and demonstrations'. It also urged Egyptian political forces to engage in dialogue.[195]

Some Gulf countries rushed to the defence of the post-coup order in Egypt and campaigned to improve its image. UAE foreign minister Abdullah bin Zayed flew to Washington on 24 July 2013 to persuade officials there not to cut off US aid to Egypt.[196] On 18 August 2013, Saudi foreign minister Saud al-Faisal went to France 'to reveal the full facts, unify efforts and furnish support for Egypt'.[197]

Meanwhile, tensions between Egypt and Qatar soared. A main reason for this was Al Jazeera's coverage of the repression of demonstrations in Egypt. As Qatari deposits with the CBE reached maturity and neither side

---

[190] *Al Bayan*, 16 August 2013, Available online: https://bit.ly/34jGu9y (accessed 29 August 2015).
[191] *Alwasat*, 16 August 2013, Available online: https://bit.ly/3jlmWsT (accessed 21 October 2021).
[192] *al-Watan*, 16 August 2013, Available online: https://bit.ly/3aX49zR (accessed 21 October 2021).
[193] Manshawi, *America and the Egyptian Revolution*, 317.
[194] *Al Jazeera*, 23 July 2013, Available online: https://bit.ly/37wV9R7 (accessed 30 August 2015).
[195] *Al Jazeera*, 14 August 2013, Available online: https://bit.ly/3p3nNPI (accessed 30 August 2015).
[196] Manshawi, *America and the Egyptian Revolution*, 320.
[197] *al-Ahram*, 19 August 2013, Available online: https://bit.ly/387vGN2 (accessed 27 August 2015).

asked to renew their terms, Egyptian authorities returned the money to Doha.[198] By November 2014, this amounted to $6 billion out of the original $6.5 billion.[199]

The differences between the Qatari position towards Egypt and that of Saudi, the UAE and Bahrain evolved into an internal GCC crisis. The latter camp, which opposed any foreign policy line from the Gulf in support of democracy in Egypt, withdrew their ambassadors from Doha in March 2014, after previous pressures failed to persuade it to change its stance towards Egypt.[200] Over the next few years, relations between Qatar and the Saudi-led camp plus Egypt worsened until they reached breaking point. In 2017, these four countries imposed a blockade on Qatar.

Riyadh and Abu Dhabi were instrumental in the siege against the elected government in Egypt and in mobilizing its overthrow, primarily through the media. In addition to investing in Egyptian media outlets, they gave their own media a green light to use the term 'revolution' with a positive connotation when referring to the 30 June 2013 marches that culminated in Morsi's ouster on 3 July 2013. Amazingly, these media were suddenly glorifying Nasser – historically, Saudi Arabia's arch-enemy – now that it had become useful to liken Sisi to Nasser as a means to paint the coup against democracy as something else.[201]

Whereas Gulf countries had little influence on the revolutionary uprising, I believe they played a pivotal role in the transitional phase. They were then crucial to the campaign against the Morsi presidency and to engineering the coup. During the revolution, the Gulf countries had disapproved of Washington's withdrawal of its support for Mubarak, which they thought bode ill for the United States's relations with its other allies in the region. As their subsequent actions would make clear, these countries feared the changes the revolution could bring, not just because they opposed the Islamists' assumption to power but because they opposed the democratization process in the Arab region as a whole. In their minds, democratization posed a threat to stability. That it should occur in such an influential and central country as Egypt meant that the process had to be thwarted at all costs. Hence, these countries' determination to marshal enormous financial, media and diplomatic resources against Morsi and

---

[198] *Al-Arabiya*, 11 October 2014, Available online: https://bit.ly/3vynz7q (accessed 21 October 2021).
[199] *Reuters Arabic*, 6 November 2014, Available online: https://reut.rs/3nkdwPN (accessed 21 October 2021).
[200] *BBC Arabic*, 6 March 2014, Available online: https://bbc.in/2Z6uVmy (accessed 21 October 2021).
[201] 'Recalling GCC Ambassadors from Doha: A Background and Future Predictions', *Arab Centre for Research and Policy Studies*, 9 March 2014, Available online: https://bit.ly/3B1UQcs (accessed 21 October 2021).

the 25 January revolution in general and to fund for the coup, support the post-coup order and lobby on its behalf in Western capitals.

VI The Iranian position during SCAF rule

Iran saw the 25 January revolution as an opportunity to improve its relations with Egypt, efforts which, it believed, had been previously obstructed by American and Israeli pressures on the former regime. In view of Egypt's geopolitical centrality in the Arab region and the Middle East as a whole, Iran was convinced that building a new and robust relationship with Cairo would serve its national interests, especially given that the fall of Mubarak could precipitate a shift in regional power balances in Tehran's favour.[202] With this consideration in mind, Iran notched up its support for the Palestinian resistance in Gaza, taking advantage of the deterioration of security in Sinai to increase arms shipments to Hamas.[203]

The Egyptian-Iranian relationship was one of the thorniest issues for Egyptian foreign policy in the post–25 January period. SCAF, at the time, was keen to depart from the polarized alignments Egypt had been party to under Mubarak and open up to diverse regional and international powers. In this spirit, Egyptian foreign minister Nabil Elaraby met with the director of the Iranian Interests Bureau in Cairo on 4 April 2011, and told him that Egypt was willing to revive diplomatic relations with Tehran.[204] A month later, Iranian foreign minister Ali Akbar Salehi phoned his Egyptian counterpart. Then, the following day, in a press conference during his visit to Qatar on 4 May 2011, he said that Iranian-Egyptian relations were improving after the removal of Mubarak and that Iran hoped to develop them further.[205] That this came soon after the SCAF gave permission to two Iranian warships to pass through the Suez Canal for the first time since the diplomatic rupture between the two countries[206] confirmed the general impression that Egypt was in the process of implementing a foreign policy reorientation.

Seizing on such overtures, Tehran took further steps towards a rapprochement with Egypt. Salehi announced that his government planned to change the name of Khaled Islambouli[207] Street to 'Martyrs of Egypt' and

---

[202] Farah al-Zaman Abu Sha'ir, 'Determinants of Iran's Position on Egypt after the Revolution' [Arabic], *Al Jazeera Centre for Studies*, 8 January 2013, Available online: https://bit.ly/3E3v2OZ (accessed 30 September 2015).

[203] 'The Assault on Gaza Leaves Israeli Objectives Unachieved', *Arab Centre for Research and Policy Studies*, 22 November 2012, Available online: https://bit.ly/3GbVUhu (accessed 30 September 2015).

[204] *BBC Arabic*, 4 April 2011, Available online: https://bbc.in/3p0HZSe (accessed 30 September 2015).

[205] *Alwasat*, 4 May 2011, Available online: https://bit.ly/3mB80pH (accessed 1 October 2015).

[206] Ibid.

[207] Islambouli led the group of officers who assassinated Sadat.

that he looked forward to official and non-official exchanges of visits with Egypt. However, various factors would intervene to slow the courtship. Not least of these was Cairo's fear of provoking Gulf countries against the backdrop of rising tensions between Riyadh and Tehran after the GCC sent the Peninsula Shield Forces into Bahrain. After Egypt arrested Qassem Hosseini, a diplomat at the Iranian embassy in Cairo, on charges of espionage, Cairo's management of its relations with Tehran reverted to the security and intelligence agencies.[208] Morsi's election in June 2012 revived Tehran's hopes. 'The revolutionary movement of the Egyptian people . . . betokens the beginning of a new era of changes in the Middle East,' the Iranian foreign minister declared on 24 June 2012 after the results of the polls were announced.[209]

While the Muslim Brotherhood in Egypt and the regime in Tehran had had their differences, there was no history of bad blood between them. The Brotherhood had welcomed the Islamic revolution in Iran as a manifestation of the 'Islamic awakening' in the 1980s. After coming to power, the Morsi administration and the Muslim Brotherhood, as well as some other political forces, felt that normalizing relations with Iran was integral component of a diplomatic drive to revive Egypt's regional role. They simultaneously stressed that renewed relations with Tehran would never come at the expense of Egypt's relations with the Gulf countries, and they pointed to the fact that GCC countries had embassies in Tehran. It did not stand to reason, they argued, for Egypt to maintain diplomatic relations with Israel while perpetuating the break with Iran, a member of the Organization of Islamic Cooperation (OIC) and a regional actor that influences some important issues, not least the Palestinian cause. Moreover, Egypt would not be able to reclaim its regional role in resolving Middle East crises and the Syrian conflict, in particular, without opening channels of communication with Iran.

Despite the discomfort Morsi caused his Iranian hosts[210] with his remarks at the Non-Aligned Movement summit in Tehran in August 2012, his attendance created the much-needed opening for an Egyptian-Iranian entente. This was, after all, the first visit by an Egyptian president to Tehran since the Islamic revolution in Iran in 1979.[211] Cairo's announcement, in early September, of the creation of a liaison committee for the Islamic Quartet to resolve the Syrian crisis widened the opening. Tehran welcomed

---

[208] *al-Ahram*, 29 May 2011, Available online: https://bit.ly/2LK7IQu (accessed 30 September 2015).
[209] *RT Arabic*, 24 June 2012, Available online: https://bit.ly/2KDa7M0 (accessed 30 September 2015).
[210] *Al Jazeera*, 1 September 2012, Available online: https://bit.ly/38gFbJI (accessed 1 October 2015).
[211] 'Breaking the Ice: Political Implications of President Morsi's Visit to Iran' [Arabic], *al-Siyassa al-Dawliya*, 28 August 2012. Archived Copy Available Online: https://bit.ly/3bnxBPx (accessed 30 October 2021).

the initiative, which was tantamount to official Egyptian recognition of Iran's regional role and the need to communicate with Tehran in order to reach understandings on regional crises. It was even more enthusiastic about attending the Quartet's first meeting in Cairo on 17 September 2012, even though Saudi foreign minister Saud al-Faisal would not attend.[212] Despite the vast gap between Tehran and the other Quartet members on the Syrian crisis, Iranian officials were eager to take advantage of the initiative in order to draw closer to Cairo. Therefore, they assiduously attended the committee's periodic meetings even though they realized how difficult it would be for the participants to reach the necessary consensus to attain their stated aim of resolving the Syrian crisis.[213]

Within a few months, the stage was set for Iranian president Mahmoud Ahmadinejad's visit to Cairo, to attend the fifty-seventh session of the OIC.[214] Ahmadinejad was the first Iranian president to visit Egypt in thirty-four years.[215] The visit, on 5 February 2013, mixed politics with religion. Ahmadinejad visited al-Azhar after meeting with Morsi. However, his meeting with Sheikh Ahmad al-Tayyeb ended up exposing divergences and antipathies rather than the cultural and religious commonalities that the Iranian delegation had hoped to showcase. The Grand Imam of al-Azhar did not attend the scheduled joint press conference, delegating his adviser Hassan Shafie to stand in for him. Shafie vehemently lashed out against 'Iran's attempts to spread Shi'ism in Sunni countries', 'to malign the Companions of the Prophet'[216] and to meddle in the internal affairs of Arab nations. The Iranian president and his aides were visibly taken aback and forced to protest in front of the cameras that were broadcasting the event live.[217]

Most GCC countries appeared at a loss as to how to handle the thaw in relations between Iran and Cairo, whether under SCAF or Morsi. Officially they expressed no reservations, but their state-owned media made their irritation quite clear. Saudi Arabia had no enthusiasm for the Islamic Quartet initiative and skipped several meetings. Nor could Morsi manage to bring the four heads of state together on the sidelines of the OIC summit. The Saudi delegate to the summit had pointedly left Egypt ahead

---

[212] *Sky News Arabic*, 23 September 2012, Available online: https://bit.ly/3p2e9Na (accessed 1 October 2015).
[213] *Al-Alam*, 9 January 2013, 15, Available online: https://bit.ly/2KwnT3k (accessed 1 October 2015).
[214] *BBC Arabic*, 5 February 2013, Available online: https://bbc.in/3qZtcJ8 (accessed 1 October 2015).
[215] *Al Jazeera*, 5 February 2013, Available online: https://bit.ly/2Wr6X0N (accessed 1 October 2015).
[216] Available on *YouTube*, 5 February 2015, Available online: https://bit.ly/37su7Kl (accessed 1 October 2015).
[217] *Asharq al-Arabi*, 6 February 2013, Available online: https://bit.ly/3m3xyyp (accessed 21 October 2021).

of the scheduled gathering of the Quartet members.[218] Therefore, contrary to Morsi's intent, Ahmadinejad's visit to Cairo ended up heightening tensions between Egypt and the Gulf. It did not help that the Egyptian Foreign Office took pains to note, in the OIC summit's closing statement, Iran's 'reservation' on the point that criticized the Syrian regime and held it responsible for the violence in Syria.[219] Egypt also included a point in support of the Islamic Quartet initiative.[220]

Tehran's hopes that Muslim Brotherhood rule in Egypt would pave the way to a new and solid relationship with Egypt quickly faded against the backdrop of the unrest that preceded the coup. When Morsi severed diplomatic relations with Damascus on 13 June 2013[221] and Islamist voices in Cairo called for 'jihad' in Syria,[222] the distance between the two sides over that conflict broadened into a breach. Iranian media and the Iranian-aligned Arab media suddenly changed their tone towards Morsi and the Muslim Brotherhood. He and the Islamist organization were now US puppets and agents of Israel, no less.[223] This became a steady refrain in the Iranian-affiliated Lebanese media, which habitually accuses all who disagree with it of working for Israel.

Iranian decision-makers were of two minds as to how to respond to the events in Egypt after 30 June 2013, as a result of which it took them several days to release an official statement after the coup. On the one hand, the overthrow of the first elected Egyptian president who represented the Islamist trend was embarrassing for Iran. The 'Islamic awakening' had become a frequently reiterated term in its diplomatic lexicon,[224] and Supreme Leader Ali Khamanei had described the Egyptian and Tunisian revolutions as extensions of that awakening that were inspired by the Iranian revolution.[225]

On the other hand, Tehran must have felt a certain schadenfreude at the protests against Morsi, who had recently begun to stir trouble for Iran on the Syrian question. He was also a rival in championing the Palestinian

---

[218] *al-Quds al-Arabi*, 6 February 2013, Available online: https://bit.ly/3joGbPA (accessed 1 October 2015).
[219] *al-Wafd*, 7 February 2013, Available online: https://bit.ly/30TfTSd (accessed 21 October 2021).
[220] *Asharq al-Awsat*, 8 February 2013, Available online: https://bit.ly/3E3hCCB (accessed 21 October 2021).
[221] *al-Ahram*, 13 June 2013, Available online: https://bit.ly/3C5YfrR (accessed 21 October 2021).
[222] *Al-Arabiya*, 13 June 2013, Available online: http://bit.ly/38bMoLb (accessed 1 October 2015). See also the video of the conference of Muslim scholars and their stances on the Syrian cause, *YouTube*, 13 June 2013, Available online: https://bit.ly/2XzzrJP (accessed 21 October 2021).
[223] *Asharq al-Awsat*, 20 July 2012, Available online: https://bit.ly/3pqw0Rs (accessed 21 October 2021).
[224] Suzanne Maloney, 'Tehran's Take On Egypt's Revolutionary Coup', *Brookings*, 12 July 2013, Available online: https://brook.gs/31m7tQG (accessed 19 October 2015).
[225] *Christian Science Monitor*, 4 February 2011, Available online: https://bit.ly/2Tl8Jz7 (accessed 19 October 2015).

cause. In addition to opening his arms to the Hamas leaders who left Syria, he monopolized (in coordination with Qatar and Turkey) the management of the crisis of the Israeli invasion of Gaza in 2012. However, he was the first Egyptian president to want to revive bilateral relations with Iran and to include Iran in efforts to resolve complex regional conflicts. Plus, there was the uncomfortable fact that Iran's adversaries, Saudi Arabia and the UAE, backed the coup economically and politically.

In light of such contradictory feelings, it is not surprising that the statements issued by the Iranian Foreign Ministry Spokesman Abbas Araghchi on 7 July 2013 – four days after the coup – were so ambiguous and open to interpretation: 'We believe it inappropriate for the army to intervene in politics to overthrow someone who was democratically elected,' he said. But then he seemed to blame Morsi for his fate: 'Egypt faced two major questions. The first was that the demands of the people had to be fulfilled and the second was President Morsi's incompetence in managing the country, especially foreign affairs.' The statement seemed to suggest that Morsi was ousted because he did not see eye to eye with Tehran on foreign policy.

Araghchi, in his remarks, also addressed Islamists in Egypt: 'Every spring is followed by a hot summer and a cold winter. We must tolerate them. Islamists and revolutionaries must not imagine that everything is over. This is all part of the continuous movement.' With regard to that movement, he said he hoped that developments in Egypt 'will have a positive effect on the Islamic Awakening'. He added that his government would continue to monitor closely 'how the developments in Egypt affect the Syrian arena'.[226]

Although the Iranian Foreign Ministry statement was not as harsh as many others (from the United States, the United Nation and the United Kingdom, for example), the Egyptian foreign minister, keen to curry favour with Gulf donors, released a statement on 11 July 2013 condemning Iran's 'unacceptable' interference in Egypt's domestic affairs.[227] Fearful that Araghchi's statement might set Iranian-Egyptian relations back to their pre-revolution status, Salehi phoned Mohamed ElBaradei, who was serving as vice-president at the time, to affirm Iran's respect for the will of the Egyptian people and their demands concerning their political future. He urged political forces and elites to participate in the national political process to realize these demands.[228]

The Egyptian military regime's dependency on economic assistance from the Gulf influenced its foreign policy orientations – negatively in the case of the

---

[226] *BBC Arabic*, 7 July 2013, Available online: http://bbc.in/3p0Cd2N (accessed 1 October 2015).
[227] *Almasdar Online*, 11 July 2013, Available online: https://bit.ly/2XEoyqk (accessed 21 October 2021).
[228] *Al-Alam*, 13 July 2013, Available online: https://bit.ly/30Q4QJp (accessed 21 October 2021).

Iranian-Egyptian bilateral relationship. After the break-up of the Raba'a and Nahda sit-ins, contacts broke off entirely and a war of words flared between the two sides. The Iranian Foreign Ministry and parliament condemned the 'massacre' against the Egyptian people and accused the Egyptian army of 'slaughtering Muslims' with American support and cover.[229] Afterwards, they condemned the army's repression of demonstrators. The Egyptian Foreign Ministry countered with numerous statements denouncing Iranian interference in Egyptian domestic affairs and frequently summoned the Iranian chargé d'affaires in Cairo to the ministry.[230]

After Sisi launched his campaign for the presidency, he frequently broached the subject of Egyptian-Iranian relations in interviews with Gulf-based news channels like Al-Arabiya and Sky News. The security of the Gulf was the portal for the Iranian relationship with Egypt, he said, the key as to whether this relationship would be positive or negative.[231] He would continue in the same vein after becoming president. But such utterances were more rhetorical than practical, said primarily to please the Gulf countries. He did not comply with Saudi and Emirati requests to commit Egyptian troops to the war in Yemen, and he shifted to a reconciliatory tack towards the Syrian regime.

The weight of the Gulf (Saudi-UAE) factor in Egyptian-Iranian relations after the coup manifested itself in many ways. A prime example is the invitation Egypt sent to the Iranian president to attend Sisi's inauguration as president on 8 June 2014. The gesture came as a surprise to many, especially given the spate of angry exchanges between Tehran and Cairo during the Adly Mansour presidency. But, in the interim, Iranian-Gulf relations had experienced a brief thaw after Iranian foreign minister Mohammad Javad Zarif undertook a tour of several Gulf States in an attempt to defuse tensions over various regional controversies. In keeping with such developments, Cairo invited Rouhani to Egypt and began to express a desire to develop a 'just' relationship with Tehran as it had with other countries in the Gulf region.[232] Tehran accepted the invitation, which it called a 'positive step',[233]

---

[229] *Al-Arabiya*, 14 August 2013, Available online: http://bit.ly/3r4xvTy (accessed 1 October 2015).
[230] *BBC Arabic*, 6 January 2014, Available online: http://bbc.in/3mn3ScA (accessed 1 October 2015).
[231] *Al-Arabiya*, 21 May 2014, Available online: http://bit.ly/37shWx9 (accessed 1 October 2015).
[232] *Elbadil*, 8 June 2014, Available online: https://bit.ly/3kaH55J (accessed 1 October 2015). *Elbadil* was founded by Mohamed El-Sayed Said before the Egyptian revolution as a liberal, pro-democracy newspaper. With Iranian funding, channelled through Arab intermediaries, it became a mouthpiece for supporters of the Syrian regime. Despite its leftwards-leaning origins, it went the way of many other newspapers and media outlets that changed hands and found new funders after the revolution.
[233] *Al-Akhbar* (Lebanon), 10 June 2014, Available online: http://bit.ly/2Ws0ySM (accessed 1 October 2015).

but in the end, Rouhani had the Iranian chargé d'affaires in Cairo attend on his behalf.[234]

One possible reading of Iran's lukewarm response was that Tehran rejected Egypt's approach to the bilateral relationship. It saw the invitation as part of Sisi's drive to win regional and international legitimacy for the coup and was unwilling to play into that, even if it acknowledged the fait accompli. Sisi, for his part, took advantage of Tehran's preference for the middle-of-the-road course to extort the Gulf countries by hinting that if they did not give him sufficient financial support, he would move closer to Iran.

The desire to improve relations with Egypt is perhaps a constant in Iranian foreign policy thinking. Iran wanted to end the animosity and draw Cairo away from the anti-Iranian axis in the region, thereby weakening that axis and strengthening Iran's hand in Syrian and Iraq. Therefore, once the circumstances were propitious in the interim phase, it began to court Egypt. It then rejoiced at the Islamist victories in Egyptian elections since they held the promise of more room for dialogue and interaction free from the dictates of the Egyptian army.

Iranian-Gulf relations remain the main determinant of Egyptian-Iranian ties. Nevertheless, Cairo and Tehran have been moving closer in their outlooks on various regional issues and crises, most notably the Syrian conflict. Egypt is (like the UAE) inclined to open up to the Syrian regime. Indeed, it is on this precise point that Egypt and Iran converge on the Syrian question. It offers considerable scope for security and political cooperation, while acknowledging differences on other strategic issues. The formula could work as long as nothing leads them to significantly change their regional outlooks.

VII Turkey against the coup

The revolution and transitional period presented Turkey with an opportunity to open a new page in its relationship with Cairo. It sought a complete break with the generally fraught – or at best cool – pre-revolutionary bilateral climate, and it looked forward to increasing and diversifying trade and Turkish investments in Egypt, taking advantage of the country's economic straits after the revolution. Turkish president Abdullah Gül's visit to Egypt on 17 March 2011 was a concrete translation of these hopes.[235] The Turkish stance was shaped in large measure by developments in Syria after

---

[234] *Bawaba News*, 7 June 2014, Available online: https://bit.ly/3joSrCE (accessed 21 October 2021).
[235] Gül was the first head of state to visit Egypt after the revolution.

the outbreak of the revolution there. As tensions between Damascus and Ankara escalated, the former withdrew from the Turkish-Syrian High Level Strategic Cooperation Council and suspended their free trade agreement in December 2011. Syria also restricted the movement of Turkish goods through Syria to Jordan and the Gulf. Accordingly, Ankara set into motion plans to use Egypt rather than Syria as Turkey's portal to the Arab world and as a transit hub for the movement of Turkish goods to the Gulf. Towards the latter end, the Egyptian Ministry of Transport and the Turkish Ministry of Economy signed a memorandum of understanding for the passage of Turkish freight to the Gulf via Egyptian ports. The Roll-on Roll (Ro-Ro) Agreement, as it was called, went into effect on 23 April 2012.[236]

Also indicative of Egypt's greater importance for Turkey was then foreign minister Recep Tayyip Erdoğan's decision to break with Turkish diplomatic custom and choose Cairo as the first stop for his foreign tours at the outset of his third term as prime minister, instead of Northern Cyprus and Azerbaijan. Arriving in Cairo on 12 September 2011, he brought with him six ministers, a large team of advisers and diplomats, and more than 250 businessmen and investors, with the purpose of expanding cooperation with Egypt in diverse fields.[237] During his three-day trip, the two sides launched the Egyptian-Turkish economic forum which aimed to increase bilateral trade to $5 billion over the next two years. More than 500 businessmen attended the event.[238]

The Turkish decision to develop relations with Egypt was motivated by pragmatic considerations shaped by mutual interests. Even if the golden era of bilateral relations under the Morsi government lay ahead, this decision preceded the arrival of the Muslim Brotherhood to power and thus puts paid to the simplistic analyses put forward by Egyptian research centres keen to reduce this bilateral relationship after the revolution to the ideological dimension.

When he came to power, Morsi devoted much of his attention to foreign policy despite the difficult domestic circumstances. He set the restoration of Egypt's regional role as one of his foremost priorities. Towards this end, he pursued a proactive policy that he translated into several foreign tours that included Saudi Arabia (12 July 2012), Iran (12 August 2012) and China (28 August). However, his hopes ran up against an array of obstacles, not least the Saudi antagonism towards the Egyptian revolution and democratic transition. As Western nations were waiting to see how

---

[236] *CNN Arabic*, 25 April 2012, Available online: https://cnn.it/3aXBhr9 (accessed 21 October 2021).
[237] *Al-Masry Al-Youm*, 22 November 2012, Available online: https://bit.ly/3njb5N9 (accessed 21 October 2021).
[238] Ibid.

the situation unfolded in Egypt before opening up to and supporting the new government, Morsi found only two countries willing to support Egypt during his presidency: Qatar and Turkey. Still, the ideological factor was certainly a plus for the latter.

After Morsi visited Turkey on 30 September 2012, Ankara offered Egypt $2 billion in aid of which $1 billion was in the form of a five-year renewable deposit to bolster Egypt's hard currency reserves, and the other $1 billion was to fund Egyptian imports from Turkey and infrastructure projects.[239] Ankara and Cairo also agreed to implement a memorandum of understanding on renewable energy development. According to its terms, Turkey would increase investments in this sector and Egypt would engage the expertise of Turkish firms in partnership with the private sector in the construction of power plants. While Morsi's visit to Turkey was primarily economic, it included political dimensions that aggravated polarization regionally and in Egypt. Morsi delivered a speech to the general congress of the ruling party (AKP) in which he outlined his administration's positions on regional crises, in particular the Syrian conflict.[240]

A series of reciprocal visits, meetings, MoUs and cooperation protocols followed. On 17 November 2012, Erdoğan paid his second visit to Cairo during which the two sides discussed opening a shipping line to Egypt, transit and transport services, and other facilities that would make Egypt the gateway for Turkish trade to the Gulf and Asia. During that visit, Egypt signed twenty-seven agreements with Turkey in health, transport, heritage preservation, trade, economic cooperation and other areas. Erdoğan announced his government's intent to increase Turkish investments in Egypt to $10 billion over the next three years.[241] Turkey soon became the second-largest importer of Egyptian exports after Saudi Arabia.[242] Sisi, in his capacity as defence minister, took part in the International Defence Industry Fair in Istanbul during 7–10 May 2013.[243]

After all that, it is little wonder that Turkey was outraged by Morsi's ouster, which it called a military coup against a legitimate and democratically elected president.[244] Apart from the abrupt interruption to the strong relation Turkey had developed with Cairo, Ankara's position was also informed by the permanently looming danger of a military coup at home. In his denunciation of the action undertaken by the Egyptian

---

[239] *Al Jazeera*, 28 July 2013, Available online: https://bit.ly/3C7RohQ (accessed 21 October 2021).
[240] Viewable on *YouTube*, 30 September 2012, Available online: https://bit.ly/3gXmzm0 (accessed 6 September 2015).
[241] *al-Ahram*, 18 November 2012, Available online: http://bit.ly/3nscHmU (accessed 11 September 2015).
[242] *al-Ahram*, 8 October 2013, Available online: https://bit.ly/34n3Dbd (accessed 11 September 2015).
[243] *al-Watan*, 8 May 2013, Available online: http://bit.ly/3msDA8T (accessed 11 September 2015).
[244] *Al Jazeera*, 4 July 2013, Available online: http://bit.ly/3ntN1pW (accessed 11 September 2015).

army, the Turkish prime minister appealed to Egyptians to heed the lessons of Turkey's history of military coups. If Morsi made mistakes, he could pay for them in the ballot box in the next elections, Erdoğan said. He also criticized Western governments for not openly calling the Egyptian army's removal of Morsi a military coup.[245]

Turkey's condemnations increased in vehemence in tandem with the mounting violence used to suppress protests in Egypt. In response to the dispersal of the Raba'a sit-in on 14 August 2013, Erdoğan called on the UN Security Council and the Arab League to halt the 'massacre', which he held was the outcome of the international community's inaction towards the coup. In remarks to the press the same day, he reiterated his condemnation of the break-up of the sit-in and expressed his concern that the situation in Egypt could turn into another Syria.[246]

On 23 November 2013, the Egyptian government recalled its ambassador to Turkey and reduced the level of its diplomatic representation in Turkey to chargé d'affaires. The Turkish ambassador to Cairo was summoned to the Foreign Ministry, informed that he was persona non grata and told to leave the country.[247] From then on,[248] the Turkish prime minister took every occasion to criticize the new order in Egypt, and lash out at Sisi personally and remind him of the fate of coup-makers in Turkey. At the same time, Istanbul became the new base for most leaders of the Egyptian Islamist opposition and their organizations.

Ankara's hard-line stance towards the new order in Egypt can be attributed to several causes, the most important being the Turkish sensitivity to military intervention in politics. During the second half of the twentieth century, the country experienced five military coups or indirect military interventions (in 1960, 1971, 1980, 1993 and 1997). The AKP itself experienced several coup attempts that were exposed (in the Ergenekon and Sledgehammer cases), not to mention the attempted coup of 15 July 2016, whose masterminds must have been inspired by the success of the coup in Egypt. Military coups and military intervention in politics in general are the main threat to the democratic process and elected institutions in Turkey. On the other hand, the AKP was also convinced that the 3 July 2013 coup in Egypt was part of a foreign conspiracy that had set its sights on all supporters of the Arab Spring revolutions, or what Prime Minister

---

[245] *RT Arabic*, 5 July 2013, Available online: https://bit.ly/3gUd0V5 (accessed 13 September 2015).
[246] *Al Jazeera*, 14 August 2013, Available online: http://bit.ly/2KDdPoU (accessed 13 September 2015).
[247] *Asharq al-Awsat*, 24 November 2013, Available online: https://bit.ly/3jpIgxA (accessed 21 October 2021).
[248] The year 2021 seems to be the year of reconciliation between the two countries.

Ahmet Davutoğlu called the 'axis of democracy'.[249] It was such thinking that led Erdoğan to link the 30 June 2013 marches to the Gezi Park protests on 28 May 2013, which he also described as a 'coup attempt' similar in context and motive to events in Egypt.[250] This was hyperbole of course.

On 15 August 2013, Egypt cancelled the joint naval manoeuvres with Turkey that were held annually in October,[251] and it suspended most of the economic agreements that Egypt had signed with Ankara since 2011, most notably the Ro-Ro shipping line.[252]

VIII Egyptian-Israeli relations after 25 January

Israel prefers 'moderate' authoritarian regimes it can deal with, even if they do not have formal peace agreements with it. Despite all its talk about being the sole democracy in the region, it does not want democracies to emerge, not out of concern for this distinction but out of fear of Arab public opinion and how it would be reflected in democratically determined foreign policies. It dreads the inherent uncertainty of democracy and the prospect of waiting for election results in an Arab state every four years, preferring instead that Arabs anxiously await the results of Israeli elections. The Israeli anxiety over the spectre of democratization in Arab societies speaks of a colonialist relationship with the region that is antithetical to the aspirations of its peoples. Even if Israel has signed peace agreements with Arab governments, it nevertheless keeps a vigilant eye on political currents and shifts in popular moods in the vicinity. Israel was, therefore, alarmed by the Egyptian revolution, as it would be by any Arab grassroots uprising. But the Egyptian case was special because of the particular sensitivity of Egypt's relationship to Israel. When one reviews Israeli officials' statements, speeches and writings during and after the Egyptian revolution, one cannot help but observe the magnitude of apprehension among the Israeli ruling elite over the prospect of change in Egypt.[253]

The first concrete manifestation of change after the revolution, as far as the relationship with Israel was concerned, was the Egyptian government's decision, on 28 May 2011, to open the Rafah crossing between Sinai and

---

[249] *Al Jazeera Centre for Studies*, 10 January 2015, Available online: https://bit.ly/3nh1tCL (accessed 21 October 2021).
[250] Ibid.
[251] *Al Jazeera*, 16 August 2013, Available online: http://bit.ly/34m9jCB (accessed 13 September 2015).
[252] *Dostor*, 23 April 2015, Available online: https://bit.ly/3G5U55M (accessed 21 October 2021).
[253] Mahmoud Muharib, 'Israel and the Egyptian Revolution', *Arab Centre for Research and Policy Studies*, 21 April 2011, Available online: https://bit.ly/3jr7MTf (accessed 21 October 2021).

Gaza to women, children and men over age forty. Israel strongly objected to the decision.[254]

Another litmus test of change occurred a few months later. Cases of Israeli shootings Egyptian soldiers near the border with Gaza had occurred before the revolution. One such incident occurred on 18 November 2004, killing three CSF conscripts, and another occurred on 2 June 2006, resulting in the death of two Egyptian army officers.[255] The Mubarak regime managed to contain the domestic repercussions of these incidents, first, through closer coordination with Israel and, second, by blaming Hamas. But the revolution and its aftermath brought new variables and uncertainties into play. On 18 August 2011, the Israeli air force killed five Egyptian soldiers near the border with Israel while in pursuit of gunmen in Sinai.[256] Two days later, the Egyptian Foreign Ministry summoned the Israeli ambassador to protest the Israeli attack and Israel's violation of Egyptian airspace in breach of the peace treaty between the two countries.[257] On the other hand, the incident led to closer security coordination and to an agreement, at the end of August 2011, to increase the number of Egyptian forces in Sinai. Egypt also launched an extensive security sweep targeting 'armed elements' in the area.[258]

The revolutionary-spirited Egyptian public refused to take the deaths of Egyptian soldiers so stoically. On 9 September 2011, a throng of demonstrators split off from that Friday's 'Correcting the Path' *milyoniyya* in Tahrir in order to march on the Israeli embassy in Giza. A large contingent of them stormed and trashed the embassy, and threw files and documents out the window. The siege ended only after Egyptian Special Forces intervened to free six Israeli security personnel who had been trapped inside the premises and after President Obama, his secretary of defence Leon Panetta and other US officials intervened with Egyptian officials,[259] after which the eighty Israelis who staffed the embassy were evacuated from Egypt, leaving only the deputy chief of mission.[260]

Israel launched its first assault against Gaza after the Egyptian revolution on 9 March 2012, killing dozens of Palestinian civilians over the next

---

[254] *BBC Arabic*, 6 August 2012, Available online: http://bbc.in/3mtoWhN (accessed 24 September 2015).
[255] Ibid.
[256] That pursuit occurred after eight Israelis were killed by unidentified gunmen in two separate attacks against two Israeli buses in Eilat, near the border with Israel.
[257] *Al-Ittihad*, 21 August 2011, Available online: https://bit.ly/3h392td (accessed 25 September 2015).
[258] *Addustour*, 27 August 2011, Available online: https://bit.ly/3aYjAaG (accessed 21 October 2021).
[259] *BBC Arabic*, 10 September 2011, Available online: http://bbc.in/34ma2DP (accessed 29 September 2015).
[260] *BBC Arabic*, 10 September 2011, Available online: http://bbc.in/38dHDkf (accessed 25 September 2015).

four days.²⁶¹ The day after attack began, Egypt tried to broker a ceasefire between Israel and the Palestinian resistance factions. After intensive talks with Hamas and other Palestinian parties, and with Amos Gilad, director of the Political-Military Affairs Bureau at the Israeli Defence Ministry, and Amir Eshel, head of the IDF's Planning Directorate, the GIS eventually succeeded. The ceasefire went into effect at dawn on 14 March 2012. Although the two sides disputed some of the conditions – for example, Israel opposed ending targeted assassinations in Gaza – the truce brought the military operations to a halt.²⁶²

On the whole, the Egyptian attitude towards Israeli aggressions against Gaza changed somewhat after the revolution. At one level, Cairo became a more impartial mediator, pivoting away from its bias in favour of Israel, which was not greatly perturbed. What did trouble it was the statement issued by the Egyptian parliament's Arab Affairs Committee on 12 March 2012, calling for the expulsion of the Israeli ambassador from Egypt and a halt to normalization with Israel.²⁶³ The statement outlined what the committee believed should be the general contours of Egyptian policy towards Israel. It held that Israel was 'the main enemy threatening Egyptian national security', rejected recognition of the legitimacy of Israel and called on the government to assist the Palestinian people in their armed struggle against it.²⁶⁴ This was not an official government position, but the statement did issue from a People's Assembly committee in the first elected parliament after the revolution.

Economically, according to figures from the Israel Export and International Cooperation Institute, Egyptian exports to Israel in 2011 dropped to half the volume of the previous year, or by around $180 million.²⁶⁵ The main reason was the interruptions in the export of Egyptian natural gas to Israel following repeated bombings of the pipeline. On the other hand, Egyptian imports from Israel more than tripled, twice, jumping from $12 million to $46 million and then to $210 million. This was due to Egypt's commitment under the QIZ agreement requiring a certain percentage of Israeli components in Egyptian products in the petrochemical, food and textile industries, thereby qualifying these products for tariff-free access to US markets. Egyptian imports from Israel during that period were concentrated in the QIZ-designated sectors.

---

²⁶¹ *BBC Arabic*, 10 March 2012, Available online: http://bbc.in/2Kh3lvH (accessed 26 September 2015).
²⁶² 'The Israeli Aggression on the Gaza Strip', *Arab Centre for Research and Policy Studies*, 17 March 2012, Available online: https://bit.ly/2XyB7mS (accessed 21 October 2021).
²⁶³ *Al Bayan*, 13 March 2012, Available online: http://bit.ly/34hhmR1 (accessed 26 September 2015).
²⁶⁴ *al-Ahram*, 12 March 2012, Available online: https://bit.ly/30OKss5 (accessed 21 October 2021).
²⁶⁵ *Al-Masry Al-Youm*, 3 May 2012, Available online: http://bit.ly/3r57hQW (accessed 27 September 2015).

By 22 July 2012, armed groups in Sinai had sabotaged the gas pipeline to Israel fifteen times. On 22 April 2012, out of the deference to public opinion that the revolution dictated at the time, Egyptian authorities rescinded the natural gas agreement with Israel. Israeli prime minister Benjamin Netanyahu tried to attribute this to commercial disputes. However, former minister Binyamin Ben-Eliezer, who had signed the agreement in 2005 as the minister of industry, refuted the prime minister's claim. The cause was political, he said, and it had to do with the shifting Egyptian mood on the relationship with Israel.[266]

Israel reaped enormous gains from the natural gas it received from Egypt (this was before Israel itself became a natural gas producer in the eastern Mediterranean). Egypt began its gas exports to Israel in 2008, in accordance with an agreement signed with Israel three years earlier. Israel saved billions of dollars thanks to the huge difference between the agreed on price ($3 per cubic metre) and the price the gas fetched in the international market ($12 per cubic metre).[267] To Israeli decision-makers, the cancellation of that agreement was another harbinger of a strategic turning point in the Egyptian-Israeli relationship. Shortly before the Egyptian government issued that decision, it came to light that a camp in the Israeli government, led by Foreign Minister Avigdor Lieberman, advocated treating post-revolutionary Egypt as a threat greater than the Iranian nuclear programme. Lieberman was quoted as saying that the situation with Egypt would become so dangerous that Israel would have to restructure its army so as to reprioritize and rebuild the Southern Command.[268] In fact, much of this was scaremongering. Israel was certain that the Egyptian army command would continue to fulfil its obligations under existing agreements.

A central theme of Israeli official discourse was its alarmism about Islamist movements in the Arab region. Its argument was that if the current dictatorships fell, they would be replaced by Islamist rule, which is another kind of dictatorship. But Israel still had to deal with a new reality in Egypt, and it could not afford to appear anti-democratic. It thus praised the democratization process, and when Morsi emerged the victor, it asked him to preserve the peace treaty with Israel.[269] At the same time, it made sure to keep its other channels to Egypt open, namely its relations with

---

[266] *Al Jazeera*, 23 April 2012, Available online: https://bit.ly/3vwTgy9 (accessed 21 October 2021).
[267] 'The Significance and Implications of the Israeli Stance on the Termination of the Egyptian Gas Export Deal', *Arab Centre for Research and Policy Studies*, 22 May 2012, Available online: https://bit.ly/3E08f6H (accessed 21 October 2021).
[268] *Makor Rishon*, 22 April 2012, Available online: https://bit.ly/34lTj3k (accessed 25 September 2015).
[269] *Al Riyadh*, 24 June 2012, Available online: http://bit.ly/2K3AN99 (accessed 1 October 2015).

the Egyptian military and security establishments.[270] In July 2012, just after Morsi was sworn in, Netanyahu dispatched his adviser and special envoy Yitzhak Molcho to Cairo to notify Egyptian military authorities that Israel would oppose any amendment to the military annex of the Camp David Accords, should the new president want that.[271]

In Israel, two factions locked horns over how Morsi's election might affect Israel's 'freedom' to undertake military actions against Gaza. One camp held that if Israel was to sustain a minimum level of cooperative relations with Egypt, it had to exercise restraint and avoid a major operation such as the war it unleashed against Gaza in 2008. The other side argued that while it was essential to maintain a positive relationship with Egypt, it was best to try to familiarize the new administration in Cairo with the reality of the balance of forces on the ground, albeit not to the point of provoking a rupture. The Israeli assault against Gaza on 14 November 2012 was an occasion to show the new rulers in Egypt that Israel would not hesitate to retaliate against any missile attack.

During the Israeli invasion of Gaza in late 2008, the Israeli-Egyptian blockade never eased, and the official Arab order remained indifferent to Arab public opinion on the matter. Arab leaders could not even agree to meet in order to condemn that aggression. Some Arab powers, especially Egypt, openly campaigned to undermine a 'Gaza Summit' held in Doha. After the Arab Spring revolutions, Arab governments understood that they had better pay closer attention to public opinion, and this was all the more the case in the countries where the revolutions had succeeded. In the wake of the Israeli assault on Gaza in November 2012, Arab delegations visited Gaza with the active assistance of Egyptian authorities and the Arab League. Egyptian prime minister Hisham Qandil headed the first such delegation on 16 November 2012.[272] Tunisian foreign minister Rafik Abdessalem arrived the next day.[273] Then, on 20 November, a delegation of Arab foreign ministers headed by the Arab League secretary general and including the Turkish foreign minister paid an unprecedented visit to Gaza.[274] During the period of elected governing bodies in Egypt, Arab officialdom broke the blockade against Gaza for the first time.

In the past, Israel had counted on the Mubarak regime to use its control of the border and other means to pressure the Palestinian resistance to

---

[270] *al-Ahed News*, 30 July 2012, Available online: https://bit.ly/3aXEYgv (accessed 27 September 2015).
[271] *Arab48*, 3 July 2012, Available online: http://bit.ly/3mv6B3L (accessed 27 September 2015).
[272] *Al Jazeera*, 16 November 2012, Available online: http://bit.ly/3mtBpBK (accessed 25 September 2015).
[273] *al-Madenah News*, 16 November 2012, Available online: https://bit.ly/3nkjX5p (accessed 21 October 2021).
[274] *Anadolu Agency*, 21 November 2012, Available online: https://bit.ly/3DY8xuG (accessed 21 October 2021).

yield to Israel conditions. This time, the Egyptian reaction to the Israeli military operation was radically different. It supported Gaza morally and politically. It mounted an energetic diplomatic and political drive, regionally and internationally, to build up pressure on Israel to halt the attack. Then it brokered a truce that guaranteed the fulfilment of essential needs and demands in Gaza.[275] Moreover, Egypt recalled its ambassador from Israel, reopened the Rafah crossing full-time, allowed convoys of food and medical relief into Gaza and made hospitals in El Arish available for treating wounded Palestinians. The Egyptian government also permitted pro-Palestinian grassroots activism in Egypt, which had previously been prohibited.[276]

Israel still tried to maintain good ties with Egypt during the Morsi presidency, and its prime minister asked cabinet members to avoid commenting on the system of government there. However, in practical terms, the relationship remained limited to the security dimension and the direct communications between Egyptian and Israeli security officials. Although the Morsi administration did not pursue a revolutionary policy towards Israel and upheld the peace treaty to the letter, Israel enthusiastically welcomed the coup, as evidenced by official and media reactions to developments in Egypt. The overwhelming view was that military rule in Egypt was best for Israel.[277] Accordingly, Israel hastened to help furnish a cloak of international legitimacy for the new military regime, and it countered voices that condemned the coup and called for the restitution of constitutional legitimacy in Egypt. AIPAC lobbied Congress to lift the freeze on US military aid to Egypt,[278] while Netanyahu, his defence minister Moshe Ya'alon and his National Security Adviser Yaakov Amidror spearheaded the Israeli diplomatic drive to secure US recognition of the post-coup regime.[279]

Soon after the coup, Israel and Egypt upped the level of their coordination over border security. In October 2013, for the first time since the Camp David Accords, Israel allowed Egypt military aircraft to fly over the area near the border with Gaza – beyond what even the Mubarak regime was permitted.[280]

---

[275] 'The Assault on Gaza Leaves Israeli Objectives Unachieved'.
[276] *Al Jazeera*, 20 November 2012, Available online: http://bit.ly/2LGNDdH (accessed 27 September 2015).
[277] For a comprehensive documentation of Israeli positions on the military coup and its aftermath, see: *The Israeli Stance on Events and Changes in Egypt in One Year: Mid-June 2013–Mid-July 2014* [Arabic], Malaff Ma'lumat, no. 21 (Beirut: Zaytouna Centre for Studies and Consultations, 2014).
[278] Manshawi, *America and the Egyptian Revolution*, 350.
[279] Saleh al-Na'ami, 'What's behind the Israeli Celebration of the Military Coup in Egypt?' [Arabic], *Siyasat Arabiyya*, no. 4 (September 2013), 43.
[280] *The Israeli Stance on Events and Changes in Egypt*, 82.

As we have seen, Egyptian reactions to Israeli military operations in Gaza are an important barometer for assessing the tenor of the Egyptian-Israeli bilateral relationship and its evolution in line with political developments in Egypt in the Mubarak, SCAF and Morsi eras. So, how did the Egyptian position change in response to the first Israeli assault against Gaza after the coup (7 July–24 August 2014)?

Israeli launched that offensive on 7 July 2014, just hours after GIS Director Mohamed al-Tuhami left Tel Aviv. One was reminded of how Israeli foreign minister Tzipi Livni announced the offensive against Gaza in December 2008 while standing next to Egyptian foreign minister Ahmed Aboul Gheit. In 2014, the Egyptian government showed little interest in mediating a ceasefire. It shared the Israeli aim of making Gaza pay very dearly, because it saw this as an extension of its war against the Muslim Brotherhood, to which Hamas belongs. The United States and UN calls for restraint and calm were therefore relayed to Hamas by Qatar, not Egypt.[281]

The Egyptian stance towards the Israeli war on Gaza in 2014 set a precedent in the history of the Arab-Israeli conflict. For the first time, Egypt officially sided with Israel against a US truce proposal. US secretary of state John Kerry flew to Cairo on 21 July 2014 on the first leg of a shuttle tour in the region, to include Tel Aviv, in order to broker a truce between the Palestinian resistance and Israel. Tel Aviv rejected all his ideas and proposals. On 27 July, Netanyahu told American television news networks that the only initiative Israel would accept was the Egyptian initiative.[282] More significantly, the Egyptian presidency and Foreign Ministry made it clear on several occasions during that period that Egypt would not accept any modifications to its original ceasefire proposal.[283] The harmony with Israel was striking.

Soon after the coup, Egypt and Israel began to explore joint economic ventures and renewed cooperation in energy. This time, however, it worked in the opposite direction: Cairo now imported gas from Israel in accordance with a deal signed with Tel Aviv in 2014.[284]

---

[281] 'Operation Protective Edge: Israel's July 2014 Assault on Gaza', *Arab Centre for Research and Policy Studies*, 10 July 2014, Available online: https://bit.ly/3G90tZU (accessed 21 October 2021).

[282] 'The Israeli Assault on Gaza: Another International Test Failed by the Obama Administration', *Arab Centre for Research and Policy Studies*, 7 August 2014, Available online: https://bit.ly/3vxDzXt (accessed 21 October 2021).

[283] *Alhurra*, 21 July 2014, Available online: https://arbne.ws/3G66ve5 (accessed 21 October 2021).

[284] *The Wall Street Journal*, 3 March 2015, Available online: https://on.wsj.com/2XLxcmV (accessed 26 October 2021); *Al-Masry Al-Youm*, 4 March 2015, Available online: http://bit.ly/37pKmrA (accessed 29 September 2015).

Final observations

In the experiences of top-down reforms leading to democratization in Spain, Latin America and some Eastern European countries, the ruling elites who launched the reform process lost exclusive control of their own initiative and were forced to go further, due to the reaction of regime hardliners and/or by a rising popular movement that demanded more. The best way forward was to first come to terms with the opposition – or more precisely, the 'moderate' opposition – in order to transition to a pluralistic system that permitted for the peaceful rotation of authority. The compromises they reached towards this end guaranteed that neither side lost everything and that the moderates from both the regime and the opposition could work together to ensure the success of the transition. In the Arab countries that initiated political reforms in the 1980s and the beginning of this century, the reins never slipped from the regimes' hands. They thus remained in a position to backtrack, which they generally did. In any event, the reforms were cosmetic while the chances of schism and defection among the ruling elite were low in the bureaucratic dictatorships in the Arab world. Therefore, it would be mistaken to regard the revolutions that occurred in these countries as complementary to or emanating from the top-down reform processes. In these cases, it was bottom-up revolutions, not reforms, that split the ruling elites.

A revolution is a grassroots drive to change a system of government from the outside. Reforms come from within. In the case of the Egyptian revolution, we have a grassroots movement that rammed the outer ramparts of the regime in order to force the regime to reform itself. The revolution brought forth no outside alternative force to seize power, as is the purpose of revolutions, and it found no reformist faction on the inside that it could trust to institute reforms gradually.

As long as the revolutionary spirit prevailed in the street during the final days of Mubarak and in the period immediately after his overthrow, the movement could dictate reforms by mobilizing protests. But it could never penetrate the regime's outer walls. It did not even try to manage or even participate in the management of the transitional phase. The revolutionary forces dissipated their energies in the street in attempts to reiterate the 25–28 January model – that is, peaceful mass protests and sit-ins – and they gradually dissipated their unity when the main political forces cast their lot with the existing institutions of the state. Then the organized political forces and pro-revolutionary elites split over which should come first, completing the transitional phase reforms or holding elections. Underlying this break lay a seething current of mistrust between the key political forces and a sharp difference over the nature of the state.

After the parliamentary elections, no revolutionary force emerged with the resolve, let alone the ability, to uproot the old regime and dismantle its stays. This was not a Bolshevik or Iranian revolution, a model which does not lead to democracy. Nor was there sufficient impetus for the logic and dynamics of democratic transition, which requires a consensus among the key political forces, including moderate circles from the old regime. Instead, the movement that won the parliamentary majority behaved as though its function was to rule and the function of the opposition was to oppose, as if it were exercising the prerogatives of a ruling party in one of the longest established democracies in the world. This was not the case, obviously. So, the government-versus-opposition dynamic played out in the absence of a common commitment to the success of the democratic transition. As a result, the only aim they shared was to make the other side fail. In the process, mutual suspicion between political forces deepened while the state bureaucracy remained sympathetic to the old regime; the judiciary resisted the emergence of a new order for fear it might lose its privileges, and the army had zero commitment to democracy and entertained political ambitions of its own.

No democratic transition could succeed under such conditions, not without the unity of pro-democracy forces acting with the force of revolutionary legitimacy and equipped to bargain with pro-regime forces so as to neutralize most of them by convincing them that they would not lose everything and that democracy was the best option for them too. That phase must also engage transitional justice to bring to account members of the old regime responsible for major crimes. This cannot be done in the old regime's courts. Transitional justice combines judicial and reconciliatory mechanisms into a larger process that aims to unify the largest possible portion of society behind democratization, but without neglecting the injustices perpetrated by the old regime.

In Egypt, old regime forces, which included the power-seeking army, used their judiciary to obstruct and undermine the work of the elected parliament and eventually to dissolve it. Liberals joined non-democratic forces in exploiting the liberal principle that it is the duty of the judiciary to defend the constitution from the tyranny of the majority, even though the constitution in question was not a liberal one, but one that served an authoritarian regime. Such are history's ironic twists: constitutional principles from the old regime's constitution were used to fight the political forces that made up the first democratically elected majority. These very forces had adamantly opposed the promulgation of a new constitution before the elections, thinking that they would be able to bend the old constitution to their will afterwards. Instead, they fell victim to the old constitution and its courts. They then sidelined the minority, which consisted of secularist parties, rather than reach an accommodation with them. So that minority, which had little commitment to democracy and democratization and which doubted the democratic commitment of the Islamist majority, sided with the SCC and the military against the elected parliament and then against the elected president.

An important debate took place ahead of the parliamentary elections about the need to agree on a set of supra-constitutional principles before the elections rather than wait until the elected parliamentary majority adopted a constitution tailored to its principles and its conception of a democratic system. The main impetus for that discussion was a deep mistrust between the key political players. Had there existed the trust that all sides would commit to a successful transition to democracy, they would have agreed that it was in their common interest to reach a consensus after the elections. But this essential condition did not exist. So, the secular forces pushed for a set of supra-constitutional principles and for parliamentary elections to be delayed in order to give the new political forces, which, thanks to revolutionary pressures, had recently been granted the opportunity to form political parties, time to prepare for the elections. The Islamist forces opposed supra-constitutional principles on the grounds that they would restrict the will of the majority (even though this is one of the main points of a constitution and even though they had their own supra-constitutional principles). They opposed any delay in the elections, and thus contributed to fragmenting the coalition forged by the revolution, thereby depleting the force of revolutionary legitimacy in its confrontation against the old regime. Ultimately, they proved that they could not rule by parliamentary majority alone. It was an important lesson.

Many scholars have discussed how democracy is not just about elections and majority rule grounded in the moral equality between citizens and the peaceful rotation of authority. They have shown that the concept also embraces rights and freedoms as essential values in their own right and indispensable conditions to the exercise of democracy through electoral processes and the peaceful rotation of authority. Indeed, rights and freedoms historically preceded the expansion of suffrage in established democracies. However, the Egyptian experience showed that a majority could not rule if the state bureaucracy was uncooperative, if no effort were made to reach a consensus with the majority of the middle class, influential elites and technocrats who had voted for the minority in parliament, and, last but not least, if the army was uncommitted to serving democracy and was not only undeterred by a unified national front from interfering in politics but, in fact, was actively encouraged by some political forces to do so.

The Egyptian case also demonstrated that, in the matter of democratic culture in a time of transformation, the determinant is not mass culture, as important as it is in the direct transition from authoritarianism to democracy. More significant is the culture of the elites who took over the rudder from disorganized revolutionary youths, who, rather than insisting on a role in government, demanded reform of government and left the details to political elites. The latter proved unable to organize the political game democratically, including consensus on the rules of the game before the rotation of power between them. Instead of agreeing and adhering to democratic procedures and constitutional principles, they split along a religio-political versus secularist divide. This reflected nothing that existed in Egyptian society at large. Egyptians, like other Arab peoples, are not either politically secularist or politically religious. But the elites endeavoured to cleave society along that divide with their methods of political mobilization and propaganda. The entry of the Salafists, a socially fringe and dogmatically extremist religious movement, into politics and the parliamentary electoral race was instrumental to generating this polarization as they lured the Muslim Brothers into pietistic one-upmanship. On the other side, some secular opposition forces, fearful of the elections, ratcheted up the alarmism and fear-mongering over Muslim Brotherhood rule and the Islamist organization's designs to assert its hegemony over the state.

In *The Arab Question* (2007), I discussed theories that hold that democratization is the product of a negotiating and bartering process between non-democratic forces for reasons that have nothing to do with democracy. I demonstrated that it would be difficult to foster democratic transition in Arab and Third World countries in general without democratically minded elites committed at least to the democratization process. Political institutions in old established democracies reproduce themselves independently of the stakeholders and their political culture. This is not the case in the transition from authoritarian rule. As the saying goes, you can't have democracy without democrats or, more accurately, democratically oriented elites. This is because the transition proceeds from authoritarianism to democracy directly, not via a gradual expansion of suffrage. A popular democratic culture cannot prevail under a dictatorship, so any direct transition from dictatorship to democracy will perforce occur before a democratic culture can take root among society at large. In the absence of democratically oriented elites, the transition is likely to run aground on the shoals of self-serving deals with old regime forces to the detriment of democracy and democratization. The Egyptian case illustrates this dynamic. The bartering between the elites or between them and the components of the old regime in the post-revolutionary period did not produce rules for a democratic game that could effectively regulate their relationship and organize the smooth and peaceful rotation of power between them in the future.

Instability and uncertainty worsened in the transitional phase due to an albeit anticipatable inability to meet the high expectations of the people, the intensive protest activity, a decline in economic growth, the deterioration in public services, mounting sectarian strife and escalating terrorist activity in the Sinai. A spiralling tug of war between government and opposition compounded the impact of all of this.

In Egypt, the army played an undemocratic role. However, it could have been compelled to submit to democracy had the revolutionary forces preserved their unity behind a democratic programme. The people, for their part, celebrated the revolution's victory in toppling Mubarak, and they enthusiastically participated in the electoral processes that followed. However, they grew increasingly perturbed and angered by the anarchy as political forces locked horns in a partisan struggle, stopped drawing a clear distinction between democratic and non-democratic forces and even allied with the army against their political adversaries. When you find political elites who advocate for democracy against an undemocratic regime that excludes them, and then turn against democracy if they are not included in a government, you have glaring proof of the shallowness of their democratic culture. A political elite whose support for democratization depends solely on the size of its share in power and who will withdraw their support if they do not get a slice of the pie is not a democratic elite. Here, consociationalism might serve as a stopgap to forestall their antagonism to democratization.

Elections are not a sufficient gauge of the success of democratic transition. Elections should mean that the necessary conditions have been met to enable government by the people through their representatives elected in multiparty polls.[1] According to the case examined in this work,

---

[1] Robert A. Dahl, *Democracy and Its Critics* (New Haven, CT: Yale University Press, 1989), ch. 12. In *Polyarchy*, Dahl holds that elections are, realistically, the minimum threshold for manifesting the achievement of democratic principles in a system of government.

if elections are held under conditions of extreme ideological or cultural/identitarian polarization, the elections will lead to a crisis that can only be defused if a broad-based coalition steps in to mend the rift.

Nor are elections, per se, sufficient for a democratic transformation. They must be held in a framework of minimal acceptable principles agreed upon by at least the key forces. Otherwise, the division during elections will be over these principles themselves, which could jeopardize the cause of democracy and the transition to it. Without a set of minimal agreed upon principles, democracy is unattainable. For example, if some key parties believe majority rule means one thing and their adversaries believe it means something else entirely, the elections will precipitate a gulf akin to cultural and ethnic divides that inhibit democratic pluralism. In the event that the two sides cannot arrive at a mutually acceptable definition of the concept, it is preferable to circumvent majority rule by means of agreed upon national unity arrangements during the interim phase, or even after an election, in order to safeguard the democratization process.

On the other hand, it is equally dangerous when pro-democracy forces trivialize elections as 'ballotocracy' and do not respect their results, as such thinking might encourage some democratic contingents to ally with undemocratic forces. While the motive may be to uphold liberal values threatened by a majority parliamentary bloc that might impose policies inimical to basic freedoms, such alliances ultimately backfire, facilitating the re-emergence of authoritarian regimes that crush the very liberal values those forces tried to protect.

It is impossible to achieve a democratic transition in a country in which the army is the sole institution with the strength and ability to maintain security and stability after a revolution if the army does not side with the demand for democracy and has ambitions to rule. Therefore, either the army must back democratic demands or political forces must negotiate a deal with it whereby the army maintains some of its prerogatives and accepts a pluralistic order that gradually reduces the military's political influence. If this does not happen, and if a significant contingent of the regime does not enter into a pact with a united opposition front, then even if the army does not protect a current ruling regime, it can ultimately prevail by dividing and subsequently repressing the revolutionary forces (as we have seen in the Egyptian case after the fall of the Mubarak regime). Alternatively, the army could actively side with the authoritarian regime, in which case a predominantly peaceful revolution could degenerate into an armed conflict between the army and militant forces and then spiral into a full-fledged civil war, the outcome of which is contingent on balances of power and other domestic and external factors. In countries like Syria, where the army's loyalty to the regime is guaranteed due to bonds of identity or other such affiliations, a civil war erupted. In cases where the army had its sights set on ruling the country, the democratic transition failed.

Where the army is the main protector of security and stability, there can be no progress towards democracy if the military command believes its role exceeds national defence and outweighs the need to obey elected civil leaders committed to the constitution and who might change from one election to the next. In such a case, democratic forces can only try to neutralize the army by persuading it to agree to compromise solutions that aim to depoliticize and professionalize the army gradually through hierarchical restructuring and reforming the army creed. In Egypt, the moment the army took control after Mubarak stepped down, it exceeded the bounds of the autonomy to which it had reconciled itself under his regime. It took control of other security agencies that it saw as rivals, governed the country exclusively during the transition and eventually advanced one of its own to serve as president after staging a military coup against an elected president.

This discussion must not overlook the role of the media as a mediator between elite and mass culture. The media is a crucial component that may either advance or obstruct democratization. An unprofessional army could become a part of this component by forming its own propaganda corps and media machine or utilize existing media that perceives it as an alternative to 'democratic anarchy'.

Any discussion and research on the failure of the transition to democracy must also consider Islamist movements and their impact on the process. It is not in the scope of this study to recount the historical background of these movements or the causes that led to their rising political power. But it is its duty to give pause to the formidable obstacle that arose due to the role played by these movements and the attitudes of their adversaries. In this context, it is important to focus on the Muslim Brotherhood in particular, as it was the most organized political force and one of the opposition forces from the Mubarak era that supported the January revolution.

The Muslim Brotherhood is not a revolutionary force. Generally speaking, it is a movement that subscribes to gradually reforming society to lay the foundation for an Islamic system of government, which is its ultimate aim. Discussions have taken place among its rank and file and leading thinkers over whether or not democracy could be used as an instrument to attain power. They identified democracy as a means rather than an end. But there is always a possibility that the means could alter and control their aim if they became convinced that democracy was the only system of government that would allow them to stand in the opposition legally and even access a share in power. This would have to come at a price, however: namely, the organization would have to accept all the components of a democratic order, instead of just taking the idea of elections and majority rule and leaving the rest. It would also mean that it cannot use the state to force its vision of religion and way of life on the people. In return, it would have the right to work to establish a just order, in keeping with its Islamic values, as long as it respected these conditions. According to many Islamic jurists, any just order is an Islamic one.

After some wavering, the Muslim Brotherhood joined the revolution to overthrow a regime that had marginalized and tried to eliminate it. It hoped to play a greater political role in Egypt after the revolution. The Muslim Brotherhood was never a democratic movement but, at its latest stage of evolution, it was ready to adapt to democracy. More accurately, it was set on getting democracy to adapt to it by custom fitting public freedoms to its conception of Shari'a. This is why the Muslim Brotherhood could not be depended on to steer democratization. It had not yet resolved itself in favour of democracy and its requirements. The chances of it progressing further in that direction lessened after the revolution when the multiparty system opened the political realm to Salafist forces that were explicitly averse to democracy and which, during electoral campaigns, sparred with the Muslim Brothers over religious credentials. Extremist forces opposed to democracy in principle, such as the Salafists, should have been barred from running in elections. On the other hand, excluding a major political force such as the Muslim Brotherhood would impede the transition. Yet, the secular political forces were unprepared to ally with the Muslim Brothers to ensure a successful transition. They were more willing to ally with the old order to forestall a Muslim Brotherhood monopoly on power.

This brings us to one of the most important premises of this study: it is impossible to continue talking about democratization until Islamist movements revise their positions on the fundaments of democracy, as opposed to democratic procedures. The fear of Islamists in power related less to whether or not they would abide by democratic processes than with the spectre of their monopolization of power; it was feared that they would then utilize the state apparatus to force a particular way of life on everyone in both the public and private spheres under the banner of Shari'a and, moreover, to impose a particular interpretation of who is or is not a true believer. The latter was one of the greatest sources of mistrust. On the other side of the equation was the Muslim Brothers' fear that exclusion from power would lead them not back into the legitimate opposition but towards clampdowns and prison. In the event of another transition phase, progress can only be attained if non-Islamist forces revise their attitudes on excluding the Islamist movement and reconcile themselves to the need to reach an agreement with it on how to make the democratization process succeed.

The Egyptian experience should have given rise to processes of introspection, self-criticism and evaluation, leading to conclusions about the future of political action against authoritarianism in Egypt. There have, indeed, been some efforts of this sort, but they have occurred on the fringes of the main political movements, and they generally led their authors to split off from their movements or abandon politics and the public sphere entirely. The movements, themselves, have issued no statements openly acknowledging the mistakes they made. Naturally, after the shock they received and under the conditions of security crackdowns and sweeping arrests, one can understand why they might go on the defensive, lay the blame on others, monopolize the role of victim and attribute failure to conspiracy. However, maintaining this stance leads nowhere and deepens the mistrust, which only worsens when secular and religious political forces are inclined to fulminate, denounce opposing views as treason or heresy, and spout other such fanatical rhetoric. Such behaviour only confirms the apprehensions about these movements' assumption to power: if this is how they behave when in the opposition, imagine what they will do in government.

I hope this work has contributed to an understanding of a crucial period in the history of the Arab region and to documenting the course of its grassroots uprisings against dictatorship. Equally, if not more importantly, I hope it has helped shed light on some crucial theoretical issues by offering a study of a concrete case. Reality is the laboratory of the social sciences, and their core methodology is the historical method which examines phenomena in their unfolding.

Bibliography

Arabic Books

Abd al-Fadil, Mahmoud. *Crony Capitalism: A Study of Social Economy* [Arabic]. Cairo: Dar al-Ain, 2011.

Abd al-Qader, Abd al-Aziz. 'Egypt: Coptic Fears after the Rise of the Muslim Brotherhood' [Arabic]. In *The Copts of Egypt after the Revolution* [Arabic]. Dubai: Mesbar Centre for Studies and Research, 2012.

Abdel Fattah, Seif al-Din. 'The Egyptian Constitution between Interpretation, Amendment and Enactment: A View from the Perspective of Political Consensus' [Arabic]. In *Constitutional Debate and the Transitional Phase in Egypt: Between 25 January and 30 June* [Arabic]. Beirut: Arab Centre for Research and Political Studies, 2014.

Abdel Karim, Shadi et al. *Potential Risk: Corruption in Egypt* [Arabic]. Said Abdelhafiz (ed.). Cairo: Multaqa al-Hiwar li'l-Tanmiya wa-Huquq al-Insan, 2007.

Abdel Nasser, Gamal. *The Philosophy of the Revolution and the Pact* [Arabic]. Beirut: Dar al-Qalam, 1970.

Abdelfattah, Izzeddin. *Workers and Businessmen: Transformations of Political Opportunities in Egypt* [Arabic]. Cairo: Centre for Political and Strategic Studies, 2003.

Abdelrahim, Hafez. *Political Clientelism in the Arab Society: A Socio-Political Reading of the National Structure in Tunisia* [Arabic]. Beirut: Centre for Arab Unity Studies, 2006.

Abdelsalam, Sheima and Hoda Salaheddin. *Blogs* [Arabic]. Cairo: International Centre for Future and Strategic Studies, 2010.

Abdullah, Ahmad. 'The Armed Forces and the Development of Democracy in Egypt' [Arabic]. In *The Army and Democracy in Egypt* [Arabic]. Ahmad Abdullah (ed.). Cairo: Sina Publishing, 1990.

Abdullah, Thana Fuad. *The Future of Democracy in Egypt* [Arabic]. Beirut: Centre for Arab Unity Studies, 2005.

Abu al-Naga, Shirin. *From the Papers of Shahenda Maklad* [Arabic]. Cairo: Merit, 2006.

Abu'l-Ala, Sayyid Fawzi. *Charged with Supporting Gaza* [Arabic]. Cairo: HIsham Mubarak Law Centre, 2010.

Al Aswany, Alaa. *Essays by Alaa Al Aswany* [Arabic]. 2nd edn. Cairo: Shorouk, 2010.

Al Tuhami, Ahmed. 'Youth and Politics: Experience of Student Activism' [Arabic]. In *The Future of Society and Development in Egypt: Youth Perspective* [Arabic]. Abdelaziz Shadi (ed.). Cairo: Cairo University Faculty of Economics and Political Science, 2002.

al-Assar, Yousri Mohammad. 'The Status of the Constitutional Court in the Constitutional and Legal Systems in Egypt' [Arabic]. In *Constitutional Debate and the Transitional Phase in Egypt: Between 25 January and 30 June* [Arabic]. Beirut: Arab Centre for Research and Political Studies, 2014.

al-Husseini, Ishaq Mousa. *The Muslim Brotherhood: The Largest Modern Islamic Movement* [Arabic]. 2nd edn. Beirut: [Dar Beirut], 1955.

Ali, Ali Abdel Gadir. 'Social Justice and Public Spending Policies in Arab Revolution States' [Arabic]. In *Development Policies and Challenges of the Revolution in the Arab Region* [Arabic]. Ibraheem Ahmad al-Badawi et al. (eds.) Doha/Beirut: ACRPS, 2017.

Ali, Said Ismail. *Culture of the Oppressed* [Arabic]. Cairo: Alam al-Kutub, 2008.

al-Isawi, Ibrahim. *Social Justice and Development Models: With Special Attention to Egypt and its Revolution* [Arabic]. Beirut: ACRPS, 2014.

al-Isawi, Ibrahim. *The Egyptian Economy in Thirty Years: An Analysis of Macroeconomic Developments since 1974 and a Discussion of its Social Repercussions with an Alternative Development Outlook* [Arabic]. Cairo: al-Maktaba al-Akadimiyya, 2007.

al-Khodeiri, Mahmoud. 'How Does Law 46/1972 on the Judicial Authority Legitimize the Infringement of Judicial Independence?' [Arabic]. In *Judges and Political Reform* [Arabic]. Nabil Abdel Fattah (ed.). Cairo: Cairo Institute for Human Rights Studies, 2006,

al-Manshawi, Mohammed. 'Washington and Cairo: From the January Revolution to the Election of Sisi: The Reality of Interests and the Illusion of Change' [Arabic]. In *The Arabs and the US: Interests, Concerns and Issues in a Changing Environment* [Arabic]. Marwan Kabalan (ed.). Beirut: Arab Centre for Research and Policy Studies, 2017.

al-Manshawi, Mohammed. *America and the Egyptian Revolution from 25 January to 3 July and Beyond: Testimony from Washington* [Arabic]. Cairo: Shorouk, 2014.

al-Naggar, Ahmed al-Sayyed. 'Socialist Experiments in Egypt, the Impact of Egypt's Turn to Market Policies, and the Impact of Globalization and Structural Adjustment' [Arabic]. In *The Social Welfare State and Discussion of the Seminar Organized by the Centre for Arab Unity Studies in Cooperation with the Swedish Institute in Alexandria* [Arabic]. Beirut: Centre for Arab Unity Studies, 2006.

al-Naqib, Khaldoun Hasan. *The Authoritarian State in the Contemporary Arabian East: A Constructivist Comparative Study* [Arabic]. 3rd edn. Beirut: Centre for Arab Unity Studies, 2004.

al-Rafi'I, Abderrahman. *23 July 1952 Revolution: Our National History in Seven Years 1952–1959* [Arabic]. 2nd edn. Cairo: Dar al-Ma'arif, 1989.

al-Rafi'I, Abderrahman. *The 1919 Revolution: The National History of Egypt from 1914 to 1921* [Arabic]. 4th edn. Cairo: Dar al-Ma'arif, 1987.

al-Sayyed, Nariman. 'The New Media and Opportunities for Democratization of Authoritarian Regimes: A Study of the Vision and Practices of Politically Active Youth, the Case of Egypt' [Arabic]. In *The Egyptian Revolution: Motivations, Trends and Challenges* [Arabic]. Aya Nassar et al. (eds.). Beirut: Arab Centre for Research and Policy Studies, 2012.

al-Shahhat, Atef. 'The Role of the Judges' Club in Strengthening Judicial Independence and Political Reform' [Arabic]. In *Judges and Political Reform* [Arabic]. Nabil Abdel Fattah (ed.). Cairo: Cairo Institute for Human Rights Studies, 2006.

al-Shatti, Ismail et al. *Corruption and Righteous Governance in Arab Countries* [Arabic]. Beirut: Centre for Arab Unity Studies, 2004.

al-Shourbagi, Manar. 'Kefaya: Redefining Politics in Egypt' [Arabic]. In *The Return of Politics: New Social Movements in Egypt* [Arabic]. Dina Shehata (ed.). Cairo: Ahram Centre for Political and Strategic Studies, 2010.

Amin, Galal. *Egypt and the Egyptians under Mubarak, 1981–2011* [Arabic]. 2nd edn. Cairo: Shorouk, 2011.

Ashmawi, Sayyed. *Peasants and Power in Light of the Egyptian Peasants' Movement* [Arabic]. Cairo: Merit, 2000.

Astafanus, Andre Zaki. 'Christian Forces in Egypt and Their Attitude to the Revolution' [Arabic]. In *The Copts of Egypt after the Revolution* [Arabic]. Dubai: Mesbar Centre for Studies and Research, 2012.

Ayubi, Nazih. *The Centralized State in Egypt* [Arabic]. Beirut: Centre for Arab Unity Studies, 1989.

Beblawi, Hazem. *Four Months in the Cage of Government* [Arabic]. Cairo: Dar al-Shorouk, 2012.

Bernard-Maugiron, Natalie. 'Evolution of the Relationship between Judges and Human Rights Organizations during 2005' [Arabic]. In *Judges and Political Reform* [Arabic]. Nabil Abdel Fattah (ed.). Cairo: Cairo Institute for Human Rights Studies, 2006.

Beshir, Mohamed Gamal. *The Ultras: When the Masses Challenge Nature* [Arabic]. 4th edn. Cairo: Dar Dawwen, 2012.

Bishara, Azmi. *From the Jewishness of the State to Sharon: A Study on the Contradiction of Israeli Democracy* [Arabic]. 2nd edn. Cairo: Shorouk, 2010).

Bishara, Azmi. *Is There a Coptic Question in Egypt?* [Arabic]. Beirut: Arab Centre for Research and Policy Studies, 2012.

Bishara, Azmi. *The Arab Question: Introduction to an Arab Democratic Declaration* [Arabic]. Beirut: Centre for Arab Unity Studies.

Bishara, Azmi. *The Glorious Tunisian Revolution: The Structure and Unfolding of a Revolution through Its Daily Happenings* [Arabic]. Beirut: ACRPS, 2012.

Bishara, Azmi. *The Issue of Democratic Transition: A Comparative Theoretical and Applied Study* [Arabic]. Beirut: ACRPS, 2020.

Bishara, Azmi. 'Us and Them and the Dilemma of Democratic Culture in the Age of Revolution' [Arabic]. In *On Revolution and the Propensity for Revolution* [Arabic]. 2nd edn. Beirut: Arab Centre for Research and Policy Studies, 2014.

Boghdadi, Abdel Latif. *Memoirs of Abdel Latif Boghdadi* [Arabic]. vol. 1. Cairo: al-Maktab al-Misri al-Hadith, 1977.

Desouky, Assem. *Large Landowners and Their Role in Egyptian Society, 1914–1952* [Arabic]. Cairo: Shorouk, 2007.

Diab, Mohammed Hafez. *Uprisings or Revolutions in the Modern History of Egypt* [Arabic]. Cairo: Shorouk, 2011.

Eissa, Salah. *A Constitution in the Trash Bin* [Arabic]. Cairo: Ahram Centre for Translation and Publication, 2011.

El Agati, Mohammad. 'Protest Movements in Egypt: Phases and Evolution' [Arabic]. In *Social Movements in the Arab World: Egypt, Lebanon, Bahrain* [Arabic]. Amr El-Shobaki (ed.). Beirut: Centre for Arab Unity Studies, 2011.

El Agati, Mohammad. 'The Left and Protest Movements in Egypt: Ajeej – Popular Committee for Supporting the Uprising – March 20 Movement' [Arabic]. In *The Return of Politics: New Social Movements in Egypt* [Arabic]. Dina Shehata (ed.). Cairo: Ahram Centre for Political and Strategic Studies, 2010.

El-Bishry, Tarek. *Egypt: Between Insubordination and Disintegration* [Arabic]. 2nd edn. Cairo: Shorouk, 2010.

El-Bishry, Tarek. *Muslims and Copts in the Framework of the National Community* [Arabic]. 4th edn. Cairo: Shorouk, 2004.

El-Bishry, Tarek. *Pages from the January 25 Revolution* [Arabic]. Cairo: Shorouk, 2012.

El-Bishry, Tarek. *Political Movement in Egypt, 1945–1952* [Arabic]. 2nd edn. Cairo: Shorouk, 1983.

El-Bishry, Tarek. *The Egyptian Judiciary between Independence and Containment* [Arabic]. 2nd edn. Cairo: Shorouk, 2006.

El-Bishry, Tarek. *The January Revolution and the Conflict for Power* [Arabic]. Cairo: Dar el Basheer, 2014.

El-menawy, AbdelLatif. *The Last Days of Mubarak's Regime: 18 Days* [Arabic]. Cairo: al-Dar al-Misriyya al-Lubnaniyya, 2012.

El-Selmi, Ali. *The Democratic Transition and the Issue of Constitutional Principles* [Arabic]. Cairo: Al-Masry Press Foundation, 2012.

El Shazly, Saad. *The October War* [Arabic]. Paris: Arab Nation Foundation, 1980.

El-Shobaki, Amr. 'The Property Tax Collectors' Protests: From Sectional Strike to Independent Union'. In *The Return of Politics: New Social Movements in Egypt* [Arabic]. Dina Shehata (ed.). Cairo: Ahram Centre for Political and Strategic Studies, 2010.

Farahat, Mohammad Nour and Omar Farahat. *Egyptian Constitutional History: A Reading from the Perspective of the January 2011 Revolution* [Arabic]. Beirut: Arab Scientific Publishers; Doha: Al Jazeera Centre for Studies, 2011.

Farouk, Abdel Khalek. *The Crisis of the Egyptian Judiciary, Freedom of the Press and Human Rights* [Arabic]. Rabat: Mominoun Without Borders, 2014.

Fawzi, Mohamed. *The Three-Year War 1967–1970: Memoirs of Former Minister of Defence General Mohamed Fawzi* [Arabic]. 5th edn. Cairo: Arab Future, 1990.

Galal, Isamuddin. *The National Street: The School and Model, 1924–2008* [Arabic]. Cairo: Merit, 2009.

Ganzouri, Kamal. *My Way: The Years of Patience, Confrontation and Solitude: From the Village to the Premiership* [Arabic]. Cairo: Shorouk, 2014.

Ghonim, Wael. *Revolution 2.0: If, One Day, the People Wanted to Live* [Arabic]. 2nd edn. Cairo: Shorouk, 2012.

Ghunaym, Adel Hassan. 'The Other Face of Gamal Abdel Nasser' [Arabic]. In *Gamal Abdel Nasser and His Age* [Arabic]. Adel Hassan Ghunaym (intro). Cairo: Dar al-Ma'aref, 2013.

Hammad, Magdy. 'The Military Establishment and the Egyptian Political Regime, 1952–1980' [Arabic]. In *The Army and Democracy in Egypt* [Arabic]. Ahmed Abdullah (ed.). Cairo: Sina Publishing, 1990.

Hammada, Amal. '25 January 2011: Leader, Agent, Regime' [Arabic]. In *The Egyptian Revolution: Motivations, Trends and Challenges* [Arabic]. Aya Nassar et al. (eds.). Beirut: Arab Centre for Research and Policy Studies, 2012.

Hammouda, Hussein Muhammad Ahmed. *Secrets of the Free Officers Movement and the Muslim Brotherhood* [Arabic]. 2nd edn. Cairo: Zahra Arabic Media, 1985.

Hamroush, Ahmed. *The Story of 23 July Revolution* [Arabic]. 3rd edn. Cairo: Madbouli, 1983.

Hamroush, Ahmed. *Witnesses to the July Revolution* [Arabic]. 2nd edn. Cairo: Madbouli, 1984.

Hassanein, Muhammad Ahmad Ali. *Internal Migration in Egypt: a Study in Human Geography* [Arabic]. Beirut: Centre for Arab Unity Studies, 2010.

Hatab, Shaimaa. 'Determinants of the Trajectory of the Democratic Transition in Egypt' [Arabic]. In *The Egyptian Revolution: Motivations, Trends and Challenges* [Arabic]. Aya Nassar et al. (eds.) Beirut: Arab Centre for Research and Policy Studies, 2012.

Heshmat, Mohammad Gamal. *Rigging Is a State Crime and an MP's Experience* [Arabic]. Tanta: Dar al-Bashir li'l-'Thaqafa wa'l-'Ulum, 2011.

Hilal, Ala al-Din. *The Egyptian Political System: Between Past Legacy and Future Prospects, 1981–2010* [Arabic]. Cairo: al-Dar al-Misriyya al-Lubnaniyya, 2010.

Howeidi, Amin. *Lost Opportunities: the Resolute Decisions in the Attrition War and October* [Arabic]. Beirut: Matbu'at Publishing and Distribution, 1992.

Hussein, Ahmed Abdelhamid. *Diary of the Egyptian Revolution, January 2011* [Arabic]. Doha: Al Jazeera Institute for Studies, 2011.

Imam, Abdallah. *Memoirs of Salah Nasr* [Arabic]. vol. 1. Cairo: Dar al-Khayal, 1999.

Ismail, Hamada. *The 1935 Uprising between the Rise of Cairo and Outrage of the Provinces* [Arabic]. Cairo: Shorouk, 2005.

Jayyed, Ramzi Mikhail. *The Crisis of Democracy and the Dilemma of the 'Nationalist' Press, 1952–1984* [Arabic]. Cairo: Madbouli, 1987.

Khaled, Alaa. *Alexandrian Faces* [Arabic]. 2nd edn. Cairo: Shorouk, 2013.

Kurayyem, Kareema. 'Comparative Study of Poverty in Three Arab Low-, Medium- and High-Income Countries' [Arabic]. In *Economic Growth and Sustainable Development in Arab Countries: Development Policies and Jobs* [Arabic]. Ashraf Abdelaziz Abdelqader et al. (eds.). Doha/Beirut: ACRPS, 2013.

Leila, Ali. 'Why Did the Revolution Break Out? A Study on the Status of State and Society' [Arabic]. In *The Egyptian Revolution: Motivations, Trends and Challenges* [Arabic]. Aya Nassar et al. (eds.). Beirut: Arab Centre for Research and Policy Studies, 2012.

Lutfi, Wael. 'Copts in Egypt and the Challenges of the Salafist Reality' [Arabic]. In *Egyptian Copts after the Revolution* [Arabic]. Dubai: al-Mesbar Centre for Studies and Research, 2012.

Madi, Abd al-Fattah. *Traces in the Square: How Was the January Revolution in Egypt Thwarted?* [Arabic]. Beirut: Arab Centre for Research and Policy Studies, 2020.

Mahdi, Rabab. 'The Workers of Mahalla: The State of a New Labour Movement' [Arabic]. In *The Return of Politics: New Social Movements in Egypt* [Arabic]. Dina Shehata (ed.). Cairo: Ahram Centre for Political and Strategic Studies, 2010.

Mansouri, Nadim. *Sociology of the Internet* [Arabic]. Beirut: Muntada al-Ma'arif, 2014.

Mekki, Ahmed. 'The Clash between Judges and the Nasserist Regime' [Arabic]. In *Judges and Political Reform* [Arabic]. Nabil Abdel Fattah (ed.). Cairo: Cairo Institute for Human Rights Studies, 2006.

Menissi, Ahmed. *New Social Movements in the Arab Region: The Egyptian Case* [Arabic]. Abu Dhabi: Emirati Centre for Strategic Studies and Research, 2010.

Mohieddin, Khaled. *And Now I Speak* [Arabic]. Cairo: Ahram Centre for Translation and Publishing, 1992.

Muhafaza, Ali. *Britain and Arab Unity 1945–2005* [Arabic]. Beirut: Centre for Arab Unity Studies, 2011.

Naguib, Mohamed. *I Was a President of Egypt* [Arabic]. Cairo: al-Maktab al-Misri al-Hadith, 1984.

Nassar, Aya. 'The Symbolism of Tahrir Square' [Arabic]. In *The Egyptian Revolution: Motivations, Trends and Challenges* [Arabic]. Aya Nassar et al. (eds.). Beirut: Arab Centre for Research and Policy Studies, 2012.

Oshti, Fares. 'Historical Roots of Social Movements in Arab Countries' [Arabic]. In *Social Movements in the Arab World: Egypt, Lebanon, Bahrain* [Arabic]. Amr El-Shobaki (ed.). Beirut: Centre for Arab Unity Studies, 2011.

Ouda, Gihad. 'The Military Establishment and Foreign Policy under President Mubarak, 1981–1987' [Arabic]. In *The Army and Democracy in Egypt* [Arabic]. Ahmad Abdullah (ed.). Cairo: Sina Publishing, 1990.

Raggal, Ali. 'A Revolution Patterned after Others: An Attempt to Understand the Nature and Type of the Egyptian Revolution' [Arabic]. In *The Egyptian Revolution: Motivations, Trends and Challenges* [Arabic]. Aya Nassar et al. (eds.). Beirut: Arab Centre for Research and Policy Studies, 2012.

Ramadan, Abd al-Azim. *The Egyptian Army in Politics 1882–1936* [Arabic]. Cairo: Dar al-Maarif, 1977.

Ramadan, Abdelazim. *The Story of Abdel Nasser and the Communists* [Arabic]. Cairo: Egyptian Book Authority, 1998.

Sadat, Anwar. *In Search of Self: My Autobiography* [Arabic]. Cairo: al-Maktab al-Misri al-Hadith, 1978.

Said, Atef Shehat. *Torture in Egypt, 1981–2008: A Crime Against Humanity* [Arabic]. Cairo: Dar al-Iltizam, 2010.

Salama, Mohammad Yousri. 'Salafists and the Copts of Egypt: A Look at Roots, Issues and Challenges' [Arabic]. In *Egyptian Copts after the Revolution* [Arabic]. Dubai: al-Mesbar Centre for Studies and Research, 2012.

Shaqra, Gamal. 'The Modern State in Egypt (3) (1952–1970)' [Arabic]. In *The Reference for Egypt's Modern and Contemporary History* [Arabic]. Yunan Labib Rizq (ed.). Cairo: Higher Council for Culture, 2009.

Shehata, Dina. 'Introduction: The New Protest Movements in Egypt' [Arabic]. In *The Return of Politics: New Social Movements in Egypt* [Arabic]. Dina Shehata (ed.). Cairo: Ahram Centre for Political and Strategic Studies, 2010.

Shehata, Dina. 'Youth Protest Movements: Youth for Change, Tadamon, and 6 April Youth Movement' [Arabic]. In *The Return of Politics: New Social Movements in Egypt* [Arabic]. Dina Shehata (ed.). Cairo: Ahram Centre for Political and Strategic Studies, 2010.

Shibli, Ali. *The Crisis of the Global Great Recession and its Repercussions for Rural Egypt, 1929–1934* [Arabic]. Cairo: Shorouk, 2006.

Shokr, Abdel Ghaffar. *The Struggle for Democracy in Egypt* [Arabic]. Cairo: Centre for Arab and African Research, 2009.

Siyam, Imad. 'Map of Peaceful Protests in Egypt: Preliminary Indications of the Emergence of a New Kind of Civil Society' [Arabic]. In *The Return of Politics: New Social Movements in Egypt* [Arabic]. Dina Shehata (ed.). Cairo: Ahram Centre for Political and Strategic Studies, 2010.

Tammam, Hossam (ed.). *Abdel Moneim Aboul-Fotouh: A Witness to the History of the Islamic Movement in Egypt, 1970–1984* [Arabic]. Tarek El-Bishry (intro.). Cairo: Shorouk, 2010.

Tammam, Hossam. *The Muslim Brotherhood: Before the Revolution* [Arabic]. Cairo: Shorouk, 2012.

The Israeli Stance on Events and Changes in Egypt in One Year: Mid-June 2013–Mid-July 2014 [Arabic]. Malaff Ma'lumat, no. 21. Beirut: Zaytouna Centre for Studies and Consultations, 2014.

Yassin, Abdul Qader. 'Nasser and the Egyptian Communist Movement' [Arabic]. In *Gamal Abdel Nasser and His Age* [Arabic]. Adel Hassan Ghunaym (into.). Cairo: Dar al-Ma'arif, 2013.

Yousef, Yousef Hassan. *The Secrets of State Security Case 250* [Arabic]. Cairo: Dar Sama, 2015.

Zahran, Farid. *The New Social Movements* [Arabic]. Cairo: Cairo Institute for Human Rights Studies, 2007.

Zahran, Gamal. 'Regional Trends in Egypt and their Relations with the Center' [Arabic]. In *The Egyptian Revolution: Motivations, Trends and Challenges* [Arabic]. Aya Nassar et al. (eds.) Beirut: Arab Centre for Research and Policy Studies, 2012.

Zohri, Ayman. *Conditions of Egyptian Society* [Arabic]. Shibin al-Kom, Egypt: [self-published], 2006.

Foreign Language Books

Abdel-Malek, Anouar. *Egypt: Military Society; the Army Regime, the Left, and Social Change Under Nasser*. Charles Lam Markmann (trans.). New York: Random House, 1968 [1962].

Abul-Magd, Zeinab. *Militarizing the Nation: The Army, Business, and Revolution in Egypt*. New York: Columbia University Press, 2017.

Achcar, Gilbert. *The People Want: A Radical Exploration of the Arab Uprising*. G.M. Goshgarian (trans.). Beirut: Saqi, 2013.

Ackerman, Bruce A. 'Neo-federalism?'. In *Constitutionalism and Democracy*. Jon Elster and Rune Slagstad (eds.). Cambridge: Cambridge University Press, 1993.

Aidi, Hisham D. *Redeploying the State: Corporatism, Neoliberalism, and Coalition Politics*. New York: Palgrave Macmillan, 2009.

Al-Anani, Khalil. 'The "Anguish" of the Muslim Brotherhood in Egypt'. In *Routledge Handbook of the Arab Spring: Rethinking Democratization*. Larbi Sadiki (ed.). London; New York: Routledge, 2015.

Al-Gawadi, Muhammad. *Police Commanders in Egyptian Politics 1952–2000* [Arabic]. Cairo: General Egyptian Book Organization, 2008.

Aliwa, Mohammad Taha. 'Egypt on the Threshold of the Second Republic: Constitutional Changes before and after the 25 January Revolution' [Arabic]. In *Constitutional Debate and the Transitional Phase in Egypt: Between 25 January and 30 June* [Arabic]. Beirut: Arab Centre for Research and Policy Studies, 2014.

Arab Republic of Egypt Central Agency for Public Mobilisation and Statistics (CAPMAS). *Statistical Yearbook* (Cairo: CAPMAS, 2014).

Arato, Andrew. *Civil Society, Constitution and Legitimacy*. Lanham, MD: Rowman and Littlefield Publishers, 2000.

Ayubi, Nazih N. *Over-stating the Arab State: Politics and Society in the Middle East*. London and New York: I.B. Tauris, 2001.

Aziz, Sahar. '(De)liberalizing Judicial Independence'. In *Egypt and the Contradictions of Liberalism: Illiberal Intelligentsia and the Future of Egyptian Democracy*. Daanish Faruqi and Dalia Fahmy (eds.). London: One World, 2017.

Bassiouni, M. Cherif. 'Egypt's Unfinished Revolution'. In *Civil Resistance in the Arab Spring: Triumphs and Disasters*. Adam Roberts et. al. (eds.). Oxford: Oxford University Press, 2016.

Batatu, Hanna. *The Old Social Classes and the Revolutionary Movements of Iraq*. Princeton: Princeton University Press, 1978.

Beattie, Kirk J. *Egypt during the Sadat Years*. New York: Palgrave, 2000.

Beinin, Joel. *Workers and Peasants in the Modern Middle East*. Cambridge: Cambridge University Press, 2001.

Bellin, Eva. 'A Modest Transformation: Political Change in the Arab World after the "Arab Spring"'. In *The Arab Spring: Will it Lead to Democratic Transitions?* Clement Henry and Ji-Hyang Jang (ed.). New York: Palgrave Macmillan, 2013.

Bermeo, Nancy. *Ordinary People in Extraordinary Times: The Citizenry and the Breakdown of Democracy*. Princeton, Oxford: Princeton University Press, 2003.

Berque, Jacques. *Egypt: Imperialism and Revolution* [French]. Paris: Gallimard, 1967.

Bishara, Azmi. *Syria 2011–2013: Revolution and Tyranny before the Mayhem*. London and New York: I.B. Tauris, 2022.

Bishara, Azmi. *Understanding Revolutions: Opening Acts in Tunisia*. London and New York: I.B. Tauris, 2021.

Bokhari, Kamran and Farid Senzai. *Political Islam in the Age of Democratization*. New York: Palgrave Macmillan, 2013.
Cherif M. Bassiouni, 'Egypt's Unfinished Revolution', in *Civil Resistance in the Arab Spring: Triumphs and Disasters*, ed. Adam Roberts et al. (Oxford: Oxford University Press, 2016).
Clinton, Hillary Rodham. *Hard Choices: A Memoir*. New York: Simon and Schuster, 2014.
Cook, Steven A. *Ruling but not Governing: The Military and Political Development in Egypt, Algeria, and Turkey*. Baltimore: Johns Hopkins University Press, 2007.
Cook, Steven A. *The Struggle for Egypt: From Nasser to Tahrir Square*. Oxford and New York: Oxford University Press, 2013.
Copeland, Miles. *The Game of Nations: The Amorality of Power Politics*. New York: Simon and Schuster, 1970.
Cottrell, Philip L. 'A Survey of European Investments in Turkey, 1854–1914: Banks and the Finance of the State and Railway Construction'. In *East Meets West: Banking, Commerce and Investment in the Ottoman Empire*. Philip L. Cottrell, Monica Pohle and Iain L. Fraser (eds.). Aldershot, Hampshire, UK: Ashgate, 2008.
Dahl, Robert A. *Democracy and Its Critics*. New Haven, CT: Yale University Press, 1989.
Dahl, Robert A. *Polyarchy: Participation and Opposition*. New Haven: Yale University Press, 1971.
Davis, Eric. *Challenging Colonialism: Bank Misr and Egyptian industrialization 1920–1941*. Princeton, NJ: Princeton University Press, 1983.
de Tocqueville, Alexis. *The Ancien Régime and the French Revolution*. Arthur Goldhammer (trans.). Cambridge/New York: Cambridge University Press, 2011.
El Houdaiby, Ibrahim. 'Islamism in and after Egypt's Revolution'. In *Arab Spring in Egypt: Revolution and Beyond*, Bahgat Korany and Rabab El Mahdi (eds.). Cairo/New York: The American University in Cairo Press, 2012.
el-Nawawy, Mohammed and Sahar Khamis. *Egyptian Revolution 2.0: Political Blogging, Civic Engagement, and Citizen Journalism*. New York: Palgrave Macmillan, 2013.
Ethier, Diane. 'Introduction: Processes of Transition and Democratic Consolidation: Theoretical Indicators'. In *Democratic Transition and Consolidation in Southern Europe, Latin America and Southeast Asia*. Diane Ethier (ed.). London: Macmillan, 1990.
Fahmy, Ninette S. *The Politics of Egypt: State-Society Relationship*. London and New York: Routledge, 2012.
Farah, Nadia Ramsis. *Egypt's Political Economy: Power Relations in Development*. Cairo: American University in Cairo Press, 2009.
Faruqi, Daanish and Dalia Fahmy. 'Egyptian Liberals, from Revolution to Counterrevolution, introduction'. In *Egypt and the Contradictions of Liberalism: Illiberal Intelligentsia and the Future of Egyptian Democracy*. Daanish Faruqi and Dalia Fahmy (eds.). London: One World, 2017.
Finer, Samuel E. *The Man on Horseback: The Role of the Military in Politics*. Jay Stanley (intro.). New Brunswick, NJ: Transaction, 2002.
Friend, Theodore. *Indonesian Destinies*. Cambridge, MA: Belknap Press of Harvard University Press, 2003.
Gates, Robert. *Duty: Memoirs of a Secretary at War*. New York: Alfred A. Knopf, 2014.
Gill, Graeme. *The Dynamics of Democratization: Elites, Civil Society, and the Transition Process*. New York: St. Martin's Press, 2000.
Gotowicki, Stephen H. 'The Military in Egyptian Society'. In *Egypt at the Crossroads: Domestic Stability and Regional Role*. Phebe Marr (ed.). Washington DC: National Defense University Press, 1999.

Handoussa, Heba et al. *Egypt Human Development Report 2010: Youth in Egypt: Building our Future*. Cairo: UN Development Programme, 2010.

Henry, Clement M. and Robert Springborg. *Globalization and the Politics of Development in the Middle East, Contemporary Middle East*. 2nd edn. New York: Cambridge University Press, 2010.

Herrera, Linda. *Revolution in the Age of Social Media: The Egyptian Popular Insurrection and the Internet*. London and New York: Verso, 2014.

Hinnebusch, Raymond A. 'The Formation of the Contemporary Egyptian States from Nasser and Sadat to Mubarak'. In *The Political Economy of Contemporary Egypt*. Ibrahim M. Oweiss (ed.). Washington, DC: Centre for Contemporary Arab Studies, Georgetown University, 1990.

Hinnebusch, Raymond A. *Egyptian Politics under Sadat: The Post-Populist Development of an Authoritarian-Modernizing State*. Cambridge, Cambridgeshire; New York: Cambridge University Press, 1985.

Holmes, Stephen. 'Precommitment and the Paradox of Democracy'. In *Constitutionalism and Democracy*. Jon Elster and Rune Slagstad (eds.). Cambridge: Cambridge University Press, 1993.

Huntington, Samuel P. *Political Order in Changing Societies*. New Haven: Yale University Press, 1968.

Ivecovic, Ivan. 'Egypt's Uncertain Transition', In *Egypt's Tahrir Revolution*. Dan Tschirgi, Walid Kazziha and Sean F. McMahon (eds.). Boulder, CO.: Lynne Rienner Publishers, 2013.

Jr., Barrington Moore. *Social Origins of Dictatorship and Democracy: Lord and Peasant in the Making of the Modern World*, with a new foreword by Edward Friedman and James C. Scott. Boston, MA: Beacon Press, 1993.

Kaldor, Mary and Ivan Vejvoda. 'Democratization in Central and East European Countries: An Overview'. In *Democratization in Central and Eastern Europe*. Mary Kaldor and Ivan Vejvoda (ed.). London: Continuum, 2002.

Kandil, Hazem. 'Back on Horse? The Military between Two Revolutions'. In *Arab Spring in Egypt: Revolution and Beyond*. Bahgat Korany and Rabab El-Mahdi (eds.). Cairo, New York: the American University in Cairo Press, 2012.

Kandil, Hazem. *Soldiers, Spies, and Statesmen: Egypt's Road to Revolt*. London and Brooklyn, NY: Verso, 2012.

Kandil, Hazem. *The Power Triangle: Military, Security, and Politics in Regime Change*. Oxford, New York: Oxford University Press, 2016.

Karl, Terry Lynn. 'Petroleum and Political Pacts: The Transition to Democracy in Venezuela'. In *Transitions from Authoritarian Rule: Latin America*. vol. 2. Guillermo O'Donnell, Philippe C. Schmitter and Laurence Whitehead (eds.). Baltimore/London: Johns Hopkins University Press, 1986.

Kassem, Maye. *Egyptian Politics: The Dynamics of Authoritarian Rule*. Boulder, Colorado: Lynne Rienner Publishers, 2004.

Kazziha, Walid. 'Egypt under Mubarak: A Family Affair'. In *Egypt's Tahrir Revolution*. Dan Tschirgi, Walid Kazziha and Sean F. McMahon (eds.). Boulder, CO: Lynne Rienner Publishers, 2013.

Ketchley, Neil. *Egypt in a Time of Revolution: Contentious Politics and the Arab Spring*. Cambridge: Cambridge University Press, 2017.

Khosrokhavar, Farhad. *The New Arab Revolutions That Shook the World*. London: Paradigm Publishers, 2012.

Kienle, Eberhard. *A Grand Delusion: Democracy and Economic Reform in Egypt*. London and New York: I. B. Tauris, 2001.

Kirkpatrick, David D. *Into the Hands of the Soldiers: Freedom and Chaos in Egypt and the Middle East*. New York: Viking, 2018.
Kurlantzick, Joshua. 'Indonesia'. In *Pathways to Freedom: Political and Economic Lessons from Democratic Transitions*. Isobel Coleman and Terra Lawson-Remer (eds.). New York: Council on Foreign Relations, 2013.
Lavie, Limor. *The Battle over a Civil State: Egypt's Road to June 30, 2013*. Albany: SUNY Press, 2018.
Lijphart, Arend. *Democracies: Patterns of Majoritarian and Consensus Government in Twenty-One Countries*. New Haven: Yale University Press, 1984.
Linz, Juan J. and Alfred Stepan. *Problems of Democratic Transition and Consolidation: Southern Europe, South America, and Post-Communist Europe*. Baltimore: Johns Hopkins University Press, 1996.
Linz, Juan J. *The Breakdown of Democratic Regimes: Crisis, Breakdown, and Reequilibration*. Baltimore, MD/London: The Johns Hopkins University Press, 1978.
Louis, Wm Roger and Avi Shlaim. *The 1967 Arab-Israeli War: Origins and Consequences*. Cambridge: Cambridge University Press, 2012.
Marx, Karl. 'Author's Preface to the Second Edition' (1869). In Karl Marx, *The 18th Brumaire of Louis Bonaparte*. New York: International Publishers, 1969 [1852].
Maswood, Javed and Usha Natarjan. 'Democratization and Constitutional Reform in Egypt and Indonesia'. In *Arab Spring in Egypt: Revolution and Beyond*. Bahgat Korany and Rabab El-Mahdi (eds.). Cairo, New York: the American University in Cairo Press, 2012.
McMahon, Sean F. 'Egypt's Social Forces, the State, and the Middle East Order'. In *Egypt's Tahrir Revolution*. Dan Tschirgi, Walid Kazziha and Sean F. McMahon (eds.). Boulder, CO.: Lynne Rienner Publishers, 2013.
Mitchell, Richard Paul. *The Society of the Muslim Brothers*. New York and Oxford: Oxford University Press, 1993 [1969].
Mitchell, Timothy. *Rule of Experts: Egypt, Techno-Politics, Modernity*. Berkeley, Los Angeles and London: University of California Press, 2002.
Noueihed, Lin and Alex Warren. *The Battle for the Arab Spring: Revolution, Counter-Revolution and the Making of a New Era*. New Haven: Yale University Press, 2012.
O'Donnell, Guillermo and Philippe C. Schmitter (eds). *Transitions from Authoritarian Rule: Tentative Conclusions about Uncertain Democracies*. vol. 4. Baltimore: Johns Hopkins University Press, 1986.
Obama, Barack. *A Promised Land*. New York: Viking, Penguin Books, 2020.
Osman, Tarek. *Egypt on the Brink: From Nasser to Mubarak*. New Haven: Yale [University Press, 2010.[
Owen, Roger. *The Middle East in the World Economy, 1800–1914*. rev. ed. London and New York: I. B. Tauris, 1993.
Paczyńska, Agnieszka. *State, Labor, and the Transition to a Market Economy: Egypt, Poland, Mexico, and the Czech Republic*. University Park, PA: Pennsylvania State University Press, 2009.
Palmer, Monte, Ali Leila and El Sayed Yassin. *The Egyptian Bureaucracy*. Syracuse, NY: Syracuse University Press, 1988.
Pommier, Sophie. *Egypt: Behind the Scenes* [French]. Paris: Editions la Découverte, 2008.
Przeworski, Adam. 'Democracy as a Contingent Outcome of Conflicts'. In *Constitutionalism and Democracy*. Jon Elster and Rune Slagstad (eds.) Cambridge: Cambridge University Press, 1988.

Przeworski, Adam. 'Some Problems in the Study of the Transition to Democracy'. In *Transitions from Authoritarian Rule: Comparative Perspectives*. vol. 3. Guillermo O'Donnell, Philippe C. Schmitter and Laurence Whitehead (eds.). Baltimore/London: The Johns Hopkins University Press, 1986.

Rhodes, Ben. *The World as It Is*. New York: Random House, 2018.

Rutherford, Bruce K. *Egypt after Mubarak: Liberalism, Islam, and Democracy in the Arab World*. Princeton, NJ: Princeton University Press, 2008.

Sartori, Giovanni. *Parties and Party Systems: A Framework for Analysis*. New York: Cambridge University Press, 1976.

Schmitt, Carl. *Constitutional Theory* [German]. Berlin, Duncker und Humblot, 1928.

Schumpeter, Joseph A. *Capitalism, Socialism and Democracy*. London/New York: Routledge, 1996 [1942].

Shahin, Emad El-Din. 'Democratic Transformation in Egypt: Controlled Reforms… Frustrated Hopes'. In *The Struggle over Democracy in the Middle East: Regional Politics and External Policies*. Nathan Brown and Emad el-Din Shahin (eds.). London and New York: Routledge, 2010.

Shehata, Dina. 'Youth Movements and the 25 January Revolution', in *Arab Spring in Egypt: Revolution and Beyond*. Bahgat Korany and Rabab El-Mahdi (eds.). Cairo/New York: The American University in Cairo Press, 2012.

Sirrs, Owen L. *A History of the Egyptian Intelligence Service: A History of the Mukhabarat, 1910–2009*. Milton Park [England] and New York: Routledge, 2010.

Soliman, Hani. *Civilian-Military Relations and the Democratic Transition in Egypt after the 25 January Revolution* [Arabic]. Beirut: Arab Centre for Research and Policy Studies, 2015.

Soliman, Samer. *The Autumn of Dictatorship: Fiscal Crisis and Political Change in Egypt under Mubarak*. Peter Daniel (trans.). Stanford, California: Stanford University Press, 2011.

Stacher, Joshua. *Adaptable Autocrats: Regime Power in Egypt and Syria*. Stanford, California: Stanford University Press, 2012.

Valenzuela, Arturo. *The Breakdown of Democratic Regimes: Chile*. Baltimore, Johns Hopkins University Press, 1978.

Weber, Max. *Essays in Sociology*. H.H. Gerth and Wright Mills (eds. and trans.). New York: Oxford University Press, 1946.

Arabic Journal Articles

Abdelhafiz, Ahmed. 'The Judiciary and Political Reform in Egypt' [Arabic]. *Kirasat Istratijiyya* (Cairo) 17, no. 181 (November 2007).

Al-Anani, Khalil. 'The Muslim Brotherhood in the Post-Morsi Period' [Arabic]. *Siyasat Arabiya*, no. 4 (April-September 2013).

Ali, Ali Abdel Gadir. 'The Middle Class in Arab Countries' [Arabic]. *Jisr al-Tanmiya* 103 (May 2011).

al-Na'ami, Saleh. "What's behind the Israeli Celebration of the Military Coup in Egypt?' [Arabic]. *Siyasat Arabiyya*, no. 4 (September 2013).

Dirbala, Nagi [et al.]. 'Diary of a Sit-in' [Arabic]. *Qudah* 21 (April-September 2006).

Farhat, Mohammed Fayez. 'Chinese and Russian Conduct towards the Arab Spring Wave: A Reading Beyond Economic Interests' [Arabic]. *Siyasa Arabiya*, no. 1 (March 2013).

Hammada, Amal. 'Defiers of Authority: The Ultras as a Force for Redefining the Relationship between the Street and State' [Arabic]. *al-Siyasa al-Duwaliyya* (supplement on theoretical trends), 187 (January 2012).

Mohammed, Sharif Fadel. 'Egyptian-Chinese Relations between Continuity and Change: 2003–2013' [Arabic]. *al-Mustaqbal al-Arabi* 36, no. 420 (February 2014).
'Palestinian Sources to Ahram: Hamas prevents the delivery of Egyptian Aid to Gaza Strip, 26 December 2008'. [Arabic] *Palestine Today: Alzaytouna*, no. 1273 (2008).
Salem, Paul. 'Future of the Arab Order and Regional and International Stances on the Revolution' [Arabic]. *al-Mustaqbal al-Arabi* 34, no. 3098 (April 2013).
Shaaban, Ahmad Bahauddin. 'Lucky Is He Who Lives the Moment of Revolution!' [Arabic]. *al-Adab* 59, no. 4–6 (April/June 2011).
'The Judges' Statement: Eventful Days and a New Ministry' [Arabic]. *al-Qudah* 21 (April–September 2006).

Foreign Languages Journal Articles

Abdel-Latif, Hany and Hassan Aly. 'Are Politically Connected Firms Turtles or Gazelles? Evidence from the Egyptian Uprising'. *Social Science Research Network (SSRN) Electronic Journal* (15 April 2018).
Abdou, Doaa S. and Zeinab Zaazou. 'The Egyptian Revolution and Post Socio-Economic Impact'. *Topics in Middle Eastern and African Economies*, vol. 15, no. 1, (May 2013).
Abul-Magd, Zeinab. 'The Egyptian Military in Politics and the Economy: Recent History and Current Transition Status'. *CMI Insight* (Chr. Michelsen Institute), no. 2 (October 2013).
Ahmed, Amel and Giovanni Capoccia. 'The Study of Democratization and the Arab Spring'. *Middle East Law and Governance* 6, no. 1 (2014).
al-Anani, Khalil and Maszlee Malik. 'Pious Way to Politics: The Rise of Political Salafism in Post-Mubarak Egypt'. *Digest of Middle East Studies* 22, no. 1 (Spring 2013).
Albrecht, Holger and Dina Bishara. 'Back on Horseback: The Military and Political Transformation in Egypt'. *Middle East Law and Governance* 3, nos. 1–2 (2011).
Alterman, Jon B. 'American Aid to Egypt in the 1950s: From Hope to Hostility'. *Middle East Journal* 52, no. 1 (Winter 1998).
Asongu, Simplice A. and Jacinta C. Nwachukwu. 'Revolution Empirics: Predicting the Arab Spring'. *Empirical Economics* 51 (2016).
Beinin, Joel. 'Workers' Protest in Egypt: Neo-Liberalism and Class Struggle in 21st Century'. *Social Movement Studies* 8, no. 4 (2009).
Bellin, Eva. 'Lessons from the Jasmine and Nile Revolutions: Possibilities of Political Transformation in the Middle East?'. *Middle East Brief*, no. 50 (May 2011).
Bermeo, Nancy. 'Rethinking Regime Change'. *Comparative Politics* 22, no. 3 (April 1990).
Campante, Filipe R. and Davin Chor. 'Why Was the Arab World Poised for Revolution? Schooling, Economic Opportunities, and the Arab Spring'. *Journal of Economic Perspectives* 26, no. 2 (Spring 2012).
Colombo, Silvia. 'The Military, Egyptian Bag-snatchers'. *Insight Egypt* (Istituto Affari Internazionali), no. 5 (November 2014).
Cooper, Mark. 'The Demilitarization of the Egyptian Cabinet'. *International Journal of Middle East Studies* 14, no. 2 (May 1982).
Davies, James C. 'Toward a Theory of Revolution'. *American Sociological Review* 27, no. 1 (February 1962).
Easterly, William. 'The Middle Class Consensus and Economic Development'. *Journal of Economic Growth* 6, no. 4 (December 2001).
Eaton, Tim. 'Internet Activism and the Egyptian Uprisings: Transforming Online Dissent into the Offline World'. *Westminster Papers* 9, no. 2 (April 2013).

Frerichs, Sabine. 'Egypt's Neoliberal Reforms and the Moral Economy of Bread: Sadat, Mubarak, Morsi'. *Review of Radical Political Economics* 48, no. 4 (2016).

Geddes, Barbara. 'What Do We Know about Democratization after Twenty Years'. *Annual Review of Political Science* 2 (1999).

Guo, Sujian. 'Democratic Transition: A Critical Overview'. *Issues & Studies* 35, no. 4 (1999).

Haggard, Stephan and Robert R. Kaufman. 'The Political Economy of Democratic Transition'. *Comparative Politics* 29, no. 3 (April 1997).

Harb, Imad. 'The Egyptian Military in Politics: Disengagement or Accommodation?'. *Middle East Journal* 57, no. 2 (Spring 2003).

Hassan, Mazen, Jasmin Lorch and Annete Ranko. 'Explaining Divergent Transformation Paths in Tunisia and Egypt: The Role of Inter-elite Trust'. *Mediterranean Politics* 25, no. 5 (2019).

Karagiannis, Emmanuel. 'The Rise of Electoral Salafism in Egypt and Tunisia: The Use of Democracy as a Master Frame'. *Journal of North African Studies* 24, no. 2 (2019).

Kechichian, Joseph and Jeanne Nazimek. 'Challenges to the Military in Egypt'. *Middle East Policy* 5, no. 3 (September 1997).

Kurtzer, Daniel and Mary Svenstrup. 'Egypt's Entrenched Military'. *The National Interest*, no. 121 (September/October 2012).

Lavie, Limor. 'Consensus vs. Dissensus over the "Civil State" Model: A Key to Understanding the Diverse Outcomes of the Arab Spring in Egypt and Tunisia'. *British Journal of Middle Eastern Studies* 48, no. 3 (2019).

Linz, Juan J. and Alfred Stepan. 'Democratization Theory and the "Arab Spring"'. *Journal of Democracy* 24, no. 2 (2013).

Lipset, Seymour Martin. 'Some Social Requisites of Democracy: Economic Development and Political Legitimacy'. *American Political Science Review*, vol. 53, no. 1 (March 1959).

Mansour, Fady, Tesa Leonce and Franklin G. Mixon. 'Who Revolts? Income, Political Freedom and the Egyptian Revolution'. *Empirical Economics*, no. 3 (2021).

Marshall, Shana and Joshua Stacher. 'Egypt's Generals and Transnational Capital'. *MERIP* 42, no. 262 (Spring 2012).

'Nafisa al-Marakibi: A Farmer Who Paid Her Life to Defence of Her Land'. *al-Ard*, no. 7 (April 2010).

Ottaway, David and Marina Ottaway. 'Egypt's Leaderless Revolution'. *Cairo Review of Global Affairs*, no. 17 (Spring 2015).

Richter, Thomas and Christian Steiner. 'Politics, Economics and Tourism Development in Egypt: Insights into the Sectoral Transformations of a Neo-Patrimonial Rentier State'. *Third World Quarterly* 29, no. 5 (2008).

Rustow, Dankwart A. 'Transitions to Democracy: Toward a Dynamic Model'. *Comparative Politics* 2, no. 3 (April 1970).

Said, Atef. 'The Rise and Fall of the Tahrir Repertoire: Theorizing Temporality, Trajectory, and Failure'. *Social Problems*, spaa024 (6 July 2020).

Schiff, Rebecca L. 'Civil-Military Relations Reconsidered: A Theory of Concordance'. *Armed Forces and Society* 22, no. 1 (Fall 1995).

Springborg, Robert. 'The President and the Field Marshal: Civil-Military Relations in Egypt Today'. *MERIP* 17, no. 147 (July/August 1987).

Stramer-Smith, Janicke and Ian M. Hartshorn. 'Securitising the New Egypt: Partisan vs. Revolutionary Demands'. *The Journal of North African Studies* 26, no. 1 (April 2020).

Youssef, Samir M. 'The Egyptian Private Sector and the Bureaucracy'. *Middle Eastern Studies* 30, no. 2 (1994).

Zhuo, Xiaolin, Barry Wellman and Justine Yu. 'Egypt: The First Internet Revolt?'. *Peace Magazine* (July/September 2011).

Interviews

Abdelmonem Emam, 3 January 2012 and 17 November 2014.
Abdelrahman Fares, 24 February 2014.
Abdelrahman Mansour, 24 April 2012.
Abdulhamid al-Basyuni, 20 December 2011.
Abdullah El Tahawey, 8 October 2012.
Abdulrahman Gadd, 13 May 2012.
Abdulrahman Mahmoud, 8 December 2011.
Abou Elela Mady, 6 October 2012.
Ahmed Abdelrazzaq, 30 September 2011.
Ahmed Abu Khalil, 6 April 2014.
Ahmed Amer, 30 September 2011.
Ahmed El-Kelany, 17 November 2011.
Ahmed Fahmy, 7 December 2011.
Ahmed Iraqi Nassar, 24 April 2012.
Ahmed Mahmoud, 17 November 2011.
Ahmed Nagy, 7 December 2011.
Ahmed Ragab, 30 September 2011.
Ahmed Ragheb, 19 April 2012.
Ahmed Saleh, 24 April 2012.
Ahmed Sami, 20 December 2011.
Alaa Bhlawan, 19 December 2011.
Albert Shafik, 9 April 2012.
Ali al-Din Hilal, 8 May 2012.
Aly El Raggal, 8 December 2011.
Amir Mahmoud Amir, 30 September 2011.
Ammar El-Beltagy, 9 October 2019.
Amr Farag, 12 April 2014.
Amr Guevara, 23 April 2012.
Amr Salah, 7 May 2012.
Ashraf El Enani, 22 October 2011.
Former Brotherhood member (anonymous), 22 November 2012.
George Ishaq, 22 May 2012.
Hamdy Fakhrany, 22 August 2012.
Hany Mahmoud, 5 September 2015 and 15 September 2015.
Hozaifa Aboul-Fotouh, 6 February 2014.
Islam Lotfy, 9 October 2012.
Ismail Abdelhafez, 20 December 2011.
Kamal Abou Eitta, 12 April 2012.
Kareem el-Beheiri, 3 January 2012.
Khaled Abdel Hamid, 27 May 2014.

Khaled Elsayed, 10 November 2015.
Khalid Tallima, 2 May 2012.
Kholoud Saeed, 7 December 2011.
Mahienour El-Massry, 8 December 2011.
Mahmoud Afifi, 14 April 2012.
Mahmoud Sami 23 March 2014.
Maysara Abdoun, 30 September 2011.
Moaz Abdelkarim, 2 May 2011.
Mohammad Abbas, 9 October 2012.
Mohamed Abdel Razek, 17 November 2011.
Mohamed Abu Masr, 17 November 2011.
Mohamed Al-Gawadi, 7 September 2015.
Mohamed Al-Qasas, 14 February 2014.
Mohamed Fathi, 20 December 2011.
Mohamed Naim, written statement.
Mohamed Salah, 23 January 2014.
Mohamed Samir, 7 December 2011.
Mohammad Ali Badri, 30 September 2011.
Mohammad Awwad, 2 May 2014.
Mohammad Badawi, 21 February 2014.
Mohammad Murad, 20 December 2011.
Mohammed Abdul Latif Hamdan, 17 November 2011.
Mohammed Mousa, 20 December 2011.
Mostafa Shawky 4 May 2014.
Mostafa Singer, 22 October 2011.
Muhyiddin Abdelhamid, 30 September 2011
Nagi Muris, 25 April 2012; 24 April 2012 and 28 May 2012.
Nagla Basyouni, 30 September 2011.
Omar Amer, 22 August 2012.
Sa'id Uteil, 22 October 2011.
Salah Amer Ahmed, 17 November 2011.
Salah El-Buluk, 21 October 2011.
Sally Touma, 21 May 2014.
Seif al-Din Abdel Fattah 6 September 2015 and 5 September 2015.
Shadi al-Rakhawy, 19 December 2011 and 20 December 2011.
Taher Abu'l-Nasr, 21 April 2012.
Waleed Abd Elraouf, 24 June 2014.
Zakaria Abdel-Aziz, 30 November 2012.
Zyad Elelaimy, 11 May 2014.

Online Articles, Working Papers and Seminars

Abdel Shafie, Essam. 'Looking East: Shifts in Egyptian Foreign Policy towards Asian States' [Arabic]. al-Siyassa al-Dawliya. 4 April 2013. Archived copy available online: https://bit.ly/3BrDjKY (accessed 30 October 2021).
Abu Sha'ir, Farah al-Zaman. 'Determinants of Iran's Position on Egypt after the Revolution' [Arabic]. Al Jazeera Centre for Studies. 8 January 2013. At: https://bit.ly/3E3v2OZ (accessed 30 September 2015).

Bibliography

Abu-Ismail, Khalid and Niranjan Sarangi. 'A New Approach to Measuring the Middle Class: Egypt'. ESCWA. 26 December 2013. At: https://bit.ly/33sk7h7 (accessed 25 October 2021).

al-Gadidi, Alaa. 'Interests Not Axes: The Opportunities and Limitations of Russian-Egyptian Relations after 30 June' [Arabic]. al-Siyassa al-Dawliya. 9 February 2015. At: https://bit.ly/30MDVOC (accessed 15 September 2015).

Ali, Ali Abdel Gadir. 'The Political Economy of Inequality in the Arab Region and Relevant Development Policies'. Economic Research Forum, Working Paper no. 502. August 2009. At: https://bit.ly/3kEuGEz (accessed 25 October 2021).

al-Sahari, Ibrahim. '25 and 26 February 1986: Twenty Years after the CSF Uprising' [Arabic]. Centre for Socialist Studies. 2006. At: https://bit.ly/32qa6BL (accessed 17 February 2014).

Atkinson, Anthony B. and Andrea Brandolini. 'On the Identification of the "Middle Class"'. Society for the Study of Economic Inequality, Working Paper 217. September 201. At: https://bit.ly/3kAVllI (accessed 25 October 2021).

Beinin, Joel and Hossam el-Hamalawy. 'Strikes in Egypt Spread from Center of Gravity'. MERIP. 5 September 2007. At: https://bit.ly/35yjzJb (accessed 25 October 2021).

Beinin, Joel. 'Egyptian Workers after June 30'. MERIP. 23 August 2013.

Beissinger, Mark R. et al. 'Who Participated in the Arab Spring? A Comparison of Egyptian and Tunisian Revolutions'. Working paper presented at APSA Annual Meeting Paper. 2012. At: https://bit.ly/3bvOsQ5 (accessed 25 October 2021) [Unpublished manuscript].

Bello, Walden. 'The Arab Revolutions and the Democratic Imagination'. Foreign Policy in Focus. 16 March 2011. At: https://bit.ly/3831McX (accessed 1 May 2015).

Bishara, Azmi. 'Can We Speak of a "Coptic Question" in Egypt?'. Arab Centre for Research and Policy Studies. May 2011. At: https://bit.ly/3A2rM45 (accessed 25 October 2021).

Bishara, Azmi. 'Revolution against Revolution, the Street against the People, and Counter-Revolution'. Arab Centre for Research and Policy Studies. September 2013.

'Breaking the Ice: Political Implications of President Morsi's Visit to Iran' [Arabic]. al-Siyassa al-Dawliya. 28 August 2012. Archived copy available online: https://bit.ly/3bnxBPx (accessed 30 October 2021).

Copp, John W. 'Egypt and the Soviet Union: 1953–1970'. PhD diss., Portland State University, Portland, 1986.

Dunne, Michele and Amr Hamzawy. 'Egypt's Secular Political Parties: A Struggle for Identity and Independence'. Carnegie Endowment for International Peace. March 2017. At: https://bit.ly/3ayOhmO (accessed 13 October 2021).

El Laithy, Heba and Dina Armanious. 'The Status of Food Security and Vulnerability in Egypt, 2009'. World Food Programme. December 2011. At: https://bit.ly/35nhSyj (accessed 25 October 2021).

Gharbeia, Amr. 'An EIPR Researcher Tells the Story of His Journey from Military Police to General Intelligence to Al-Waely Police Department'. Egyptian Initiative for Personal Rights. 28 July 2011. At: https://bit.ly/2WCGzof (accessed 15 April 2021).

Graham, Carol, Nancy Birdsall and Stefano Pettinato. 'Stuck In the Tunnel: Is Globalization Muddling the Middle Class?'. Centre on Social and Economic Dynamics, Working Paper no. 14. August 2000. At: https://brook.gs/2FVpeyl (accessed 25 October 2021).

Hellyer, H. A. 'Military or President: Who Calls the Shots in Egypt'. Brookings. 24 August 2012. At: https://brook.gs/3lVNbYY (accessed 19 October 2021).

Hlasny, Vladimir and Paolo Verme. 'Top Incomes and the Measurement of Inequality in Egypt'. World Bank, Policy Research, Working Paper no. 6557. August 2013. At: https://bit.ly/2ZqIrih (accessed 25 October 2021).

Jaraba, Mahmoud. 'The Egyptian Military's Economic Channels of Influence'. Middle East Institute. 14 May 2014.

Kinninmont, Jane. 'New Socio-Political Actors: The Brotherhood and Business in Egypt'. German Marshall Fund of the United States. 18 July 2012. At: https://bit.ly/3B3BUKt (accessed 15 June 2015).

Maloney, Suzanne. 'Tehran's Take On Egypt's Revolutionary Coup'. Brookings. 12 July 2013. At: https://brook.gs/31m7tQG (accessed 19 October 2015).

Manshawi, Ibrahim. 'Contradictory Positions: EU-Egyptian elations after 30 June'. [Arabic] Arab Centre for Research and Studies (ACRSEG). 25 October 2014. At: https://bit.ly/343lsMy (accessed 10 September 2015).

Morsy, Ahmed. 'The Military Crowds Out Civilian Business in Egypt'. Carnegie Endowment for International Peace. 24 June 2014. At: https://bit.ly/36XpmZc (accessed 12 May 2015).

Muharib, Mahmoud. 'Israel and the Egyptian Revolution'. Arab Centre for Research and Policy Studies. 21 April 2011. At: https://bit.ly/3jr7MTf (accessed 21 October 2021).

'Operation Protective Edge: Israel's July 2014 Assault on Gaza'. Arab Centre for Research and Policy Studies. 10 July 2014. At: https://bit.ly/3G90tZU (accessed 21 October 2021).

Ottaway, David B. 'Egypt at the Tipping Point?'. Woodrow Wilson International Centre for Scholars, Middle East Program Occasional Paper Series. Summer 2010. At: https://bit.ly/33CzLGX (accessed 20 December 2014).

'Politicians and Activists: 6 April created a new Political Map in Egypt'. Cairo Institute for Human Rights Studies. 23 April 2008. At: https://bit.ly/3b5avwW (accessed 25 October 2021).

Ramadan, Walaa. 'The Egyptian Military Empire'. Middle East Monitor. 9 July 2014, at: https://bit.ly/3mdjYaG (accessed 1 June 2015).

'Recalling GCC Ambassadors from Doha: A Background and Future Predictions'. Arab Centre for Research and Policy Studies. 9 March 2014. At: https://bit.ly/3B1UQcs (accessed 21 October 2021).

Roll, Stephan. 'Gamal Mubarak and the Discord in Egypt's Ruling Elite'. Carnegie Endowment for International Peace. 1 September 2010. At: https://bit.ly/3iypiEy (accessed 16 December 2020).

Salem, Samira and Jane Gleason. 'An Examination of Poverty Reduction in Egypt: Contributing Factors, Sustainability, and Lessons'. Pro-Poor Economic Growth Research Studies. March 2003. At: https://bit.ly/36lVWUB (accessed 25 October 2021).

Saqr, Bashir. 'News Report on Farmers' Movements in Egypt in Recent Years' [Arabic]. Contemporary Worker Research Centre. 3 May 2009. At: https://bit.ly/32BsHed (accessed 23 July 2014).

Sayegh, Yezid. 'Above the State: The Officers' Republic in Egypt'. Carnegie Endowment for International Peace. 1 August 2012. At: https://bit.ly/3CmtHSI (accessed 12 November 2014).

Sayigh, Yezid. 'Owners of the Republic: An Anatomy of Egypt's Military Economy'. Carnegie Middle East Centre. 2019.

Taha, Yassin. 'The Socialism of 23 July and the Battles of Small Landholders in Kamshish' [Arabic]. Centre for Socialist Studies. September 1997. Archived copy available at: https://bit.ly/2ZDmmA7 (accessed 28 October 2021).

Taha, Yassin. 'The Socialism of 23 July and the Battles of Small Landholders in Kamshish' [Arabic]. Centre for Socialist Studies. September 1997. Archived copy available at: https://bit.ly/2ZDmmA7 (accessed 28 October 2021).
'The Assault on Gaza Leaves Israeli Objectives Unachieved'. Arab Centre for Research and Policy Studies. 22 November 2012. At: https://bit.ly/3GbVUhu (accessed 30 September 2015).
'The Israeli Aggression on the Gaza Strip'. Arab Centre for Research and Policy Studies. 17 March 2012. At: https://bit.ly/2XyB7mS (accessed 21 October 2021).
'The Israeli Assault on Gaza: Another International Test Failed by the Obama Administration'. Arab Centre for Research and Policy Studies. 7 August 2014. At: https://bit.ly/3vxDzXt (accessed 21 October 2021).
'The Popular Referendum on the Amendments to the Constitution in Egypt'. Arab Centre for Research and Policy Studies. Policies Analysis Unit. 21 March 2011. At: https://bit.ly/2YIeDk9 (accessed 1 October 2015).
'The Significance and Implications of the Israeli Stance on the Termination of the Egyptian Gas Export Deal'. Arab Centre for Research and Policy Studies. 22 May 2012. At: https://bit.ly/3E08f6H (accessed 21 October 2021).
Verme, Paolo. 'Facts vs. Perceptions: Understanding Inequality in Egypt'. World Bank Blogs. 24 January 2013. At: https://bit.ly/2DJo1t0 (accessed 25 October 2021).
Wellen, Russ. 'Last Thing Washington Needs Is to Share Blame if Egypt Becomes Another Pakistan'. Institute for Policy Studies. 17 February 2011. At: https://bit.ly/3m3IAAu (accessed 14 May 2015).
Wenig, Gilad and Eric Trager. 'Bring Back Bright Star'. Washington Institute for Near East Policy. 21 August 2015. At: https://bit.ly/2Xw9M4H (accessed 3 September 2015).
Williams, Ian. 'Ordinary Egyptians Have Little to Show For U.S. Military Aid to Egypt'. Foreign Policy in Focus. 13 February 2011. At: https://bit.ly/33UFecS (accessed 12 May 2015).
Zaghloul, Naeem Saad. 'Digital Media in Egypt: Reality and Challenges' [Arabic]. Egyptian Cabinet Information and Decision Support Centre. February 2010.
Zollner, Barbara. 'Surviving Repression: How Egypt's Muslim Brotherhood Has Carried On'. Carnegie Middle East Centre. 11 March 2019. At: https://bit.ly/3kiq5rz (accessed 9 September 2020).

Documents and Reports

'About Phone Conversation of Russian Foreign Minister Sergey Lavrov with the Acting Minister of Foreign Affairs of Egypt Mohamed Kamel Amr'. Ministry of Foreign Affairs for the Russian Federation. 5 July 2013. At: https://bit.ly/3ndJUDy (accessed 14 September 2015).
'Arab Middle Class: Measurement and role in driving change'. Economic and Social Commission for Western Asia (ESCWA). Beirut: United Nations, 2014. At: https://bit.ly/3bstVvY (accessed 31 October 2021).
'Behind the Walls of Fear: Police Siege on Fayyoum Governorate' [Arabic]. Arabic Network for Human Rights Information. At: https://bit.ly/3ixHYSN (accessed 5 October 2014).
'Catherine Ashton visits Jordan, Egypt, Israel and Occupied Palestinian Territory'. European Union. 15 June 2011. At: https://bit.ly/3G6Iaom (accessed 1 September 2015).

'Chairman Royce and Ranking Member Engel Release Joint Statement on Ongoing Events in Egypt'. US House of Representatives, Committee on Foreign Affairs. 5 July 2013. At: https://bit.ly/37PWGR4 (accessed 9 December 2020).

'Egypt: EIB Lends EUR 200m for the Cairo Metro Line and EUR 45m for Community Development'. European Commission. 14 November 2012. At: https://bit.ly/340DUoX (accessed 8 September 2015).

'Egypt: New Constitutional Amendments Proposed'. Library of Congress. 13 February 2019. At: https://bit.ly/3jonOKQ (accessed 20 October 2020).

'Egyptian Foreign Minister Nabil Fahmy Visits China' [Arabic]. Chinese Embassy in Egypt. 11 December 2013. At: https://bit.ly/3oG46Nv (accessed 2 October 2015).

'EU-Egypt: True Partnership for People and Transformation'. European Commission. 14 November 2012. At: https://bit.ly/3m5PIfU (accessed 8 September 2015).

'First meeting of EU-Egypt Task Force to Support the On-Going Reforms in Egypt'. European Commission. 13 November 2012. At: https://bit.ly/3gynoS1 (accessed 8 September 2015).

'Foreign Ministry Spokesperson Hua Chunying's Regular Press Conference on December 24, 2013'. Ministry of Foreign Affairs of the People's Republic of China. 24 December 2013. At: https://bit.ly/3E8j2ff (accessed 21 October 2021).

'Foreign Secretary Statement on the Situation in Egypt'. United Kingdom Government. 3 July 2013. At: https://bit.ly/3nitUQy (accessed 10 September 2015).

'Holding Its Breath: A Special Report on Egypt'. Economist. 17 July 2010. At: https://econ.st/2Rb7mld (accessed 25 October 2021).

'Implementation of the European Neighbourhood Policy in Egypt Progress in 2011 and Recommendations for Action'. European Commission. 15 May 2012. At: https://bit.ly/3DooyKi (accessed 21 October 2021).

'Message to SCAF' [Arabic]. Arabic Network for Human Rights Information. 7 April 2011. At: https://bit.ly/39SDOU8 (accessed 1 May 2015).

'Mohammad Mahmoud Is a State Crime' [Arabic]. The National Community for Human Rights and Law (NCHRL). November 2013.

'National Fact-Finding Commission Summary Report on the Events of the 25 January Revolution' [Arabic]. At: https://bit.ly/3BPS8Id (accessed 17 October 2021).

'New Commission Support to Improve Living Conditions and Create Jobs in Egypt'. EU Delegation to Egypt. 17 August 2011. At: https://bit.ly/3E39jGR (accessed 1 October 2021).

'Press Conference Statement by Secretary Acheson'. *Department of State Bulletin* 27, no. 690 (July/September 1952). At: https://bit.ly/3jkcpMH (accessed 25 October 2021).

'Press Releases 2011'. Embassy of the United States Cairo – Egypt. At: https://bit.ly/3jxP5xd (accessed 26 October 26, 2021).

'Press Releases 2012'. Embassy of the United States Cairo – Egypt. At: https://bit.ly/3pAKVZ5 (accessed 26 October 26, 2021).

'Remarks at the Overseas Security Advisory Council's 28th Annual Briefing'. US Department of State. 20 November 2013. At: https://bit.ly/3a1Mk1Q (accessed 20 October 2021).

'Signature of a €940 Million European Financing Package for the Construction of the Third Phase of Greater Cairo Metro Line 3'. Embassy of France in Egypt. 23 September 2012. At: https://bit.ly/2ZaI3HQ (accessed 10 September 2015).

'Social Media Dialogue with Dr Ahmed Ghanim of Egypt's Masrawy.com'. US State Department. 23 February 2011. Transcript available online: https://bit.ly/3DVHGzo (accessed 1 October 2021).

'Statement by EU High Representative Catherine Ashton on Developments in Egypt'. European Union. 3 July 2013. At: https://bit.ly/3uUjnyw (accessed 10 September 2015).

'Statement by EU High Representative Catherine Ashton on the Situation in Egypt'. European External Action Service. 14 August 2013. At: https://bit.ly/3nivkus (accessed 10 September 2015).

'Statement by High Representative Catherine Ashton on the Opening Session of the Egyptian Parliament'. EU Delegation to Egypt, 23 January 2012. At: https://bit.ly/3ajQnqv (accessed 15 April 2021).

'Statement by President Barroso Following his Meeting with Mr Mohamed Morsi, President of Egypt'. European Commission. 13 September 2012. At: https://bit.ly/2KfOhhO (accessed 8 September 2015).

'Statement On Egyptian Elections'. US Department of State. 30 November 2011. At: https://bit.ly/3C1Giup (accessed 21 October 2021).

'The EU's Response to the "Arab Spring"'. European Commission. 16 December 2011. At: https://bit.ly/300iI3a (accessed 21 October 2021).

Amnesty International. 'Arms Transfers to the Middle East and North Africa: Lessons for an Effective Arms Trade Treaty'. 2011. At: https://bit.ly/3nC0BJ3 (accessed 25 October 2021).

Amnesty International. 'Egypt Rises: Killings, Detentions and Torture in the "25 January Revolution"'. 19 May 2011.

Amnesty International. 'Egypt Rises: Killings, Detentions, and Torture in the "25 January Revolution"'. 19 Match 2011. At: https://bit.ly/3lLX9fi (accessed 17 October 2021).

Amnesty International. '"We are not dirt": Forced evictions in Egypt's informal settlements'. 23 August 2011. At: https://bit.ly/2Z6kgbI (accessed 17 October 2021).

Arab Middle Class: Measurement and Role in Driving Change. Beirut: Economic and Social Commission for Western Asia, 2014.

Arab Monetary Fund. *Joint Arab Economic Report 2014*. Abu Dhabi: Arab Monetary Fund, 2014. At: https://bit.ly/3pPY2pk (accessed 26 October 2021).

Cairo Institute for Human Rights Studies. *Bastion of Impunity, Mirage of Reform: Human Rights in the Arab Region, Annual Report 2009*. Cairo: CIHRS, 2009. At: https://bit.ly/3Ecbpo0 (accessed 1 October 2021).

Cairo Institute for Human Rights Studies. 'Media and Parliamentary Elections in Egypt: Evaluation of Media Performance in the Parliamentary Elections, 12 October 2011–15 January 2012'. 2012.

Cairo Institute for Human Rights Studies. *Roots of Unrest: Human Rights in the Arab Region, Annual Report 2010*. At: https://bit.ly/3vHGY5R (accessed 1 October 2021).

Cairo Institute for Human Rights Studies. 'Welcome to the Military State of Egypt: Minister of Justice Decree More Repressive than State of Emergency'. 13 June 2012. At: https://bit.ly/3cKvd7a (accessed 15 May 2021).

Central Agency for Public Mobilization and Statistics. *Select Poverty Indicators from Survey of Income, Expenditure and Consumption 2010/2011* [Arabic]. Cairo: CAPMAS, 2011. At: https://bit.ly/3pbOQeY (accessed 17 October 2021).

Central Bank of Egypt. *Annual Report 2013/2014*. At: https://bit.ly/3EpSard (accessed 26 October 2021).

Central Bank of Egypt, *Press Release: Performance of the Balance of Payments During FY 2013/14*. At: https://bit.ly/2Zv1xaj (accessed 26 October 2021).

Egyptian Initiative for Personal Rights. 'After Three Days of Brutal Violence Against Demonstrators: Egyptian Rights Organizations Demand Indictment of Leading Security Officers'. 22 November 2011. At: https://bit.ly/2YgI3VJ (accessed 15 May 2021).

Egyptian Initiative for Personal Rights. 'Khusous: A History of Sectarian Tension and Violence' [Arabic]. 11 April 2013. At: https://bit.ly/37N8Av6 (accessed 20 October 2021).

Egyptian Initiative for Personal Rights. 'Report on the Use of Riot Control Gas during the November Events' [Arabic], January 2012, at: https://bit.ly/3ixUW5g (accessed 30 May 2015).

Egyptian Initiative for Personal Rights. 'Report: Marinab Events a Flagrant Example of State's Bias towards Bigotry' [Arabic]. 5 October 2011. At: https://bit.ly/3f7WTnY (accessed 13 October 2021).

Egyptian Initiative for Personal Rights. 'The Weeks of Killing: State Violence, Communal Fighting, and Sectarian Attacks in the Summer of 2013'. June 2014. At: https://bit.ly/2Yls7BK (accessed 20 April 2021).

Federation of Maspero Youth, *Report on Incidents of Sectarian Violence in Egypt* [Arabic]. Cairo: 2012.

Human Rights in the Arab World: Report from the Arab Organization for Human Rights on the State of Human Rights in the Arab World, Annual Report 2009-2010 [Arabic]. Beirut: Centre for Arab Unity Studies/Arab Organization for Human Rights, 2010.

Human Rights Watch. 'All According to Plan: The Rab'a Massacre and Mass Killings of Protesters in Egypt'. 12 August 2014. At: https://bit.ly/3qTBLFw (accessed 25 June 2015).

Human Rights Watch. 'Egypt's Political Prisoners'. 6 March 2015. At: https://bit.ly/35DQNqM (accessed 9 September 2020).

Human Rights Watch. 'World Report 2012: Egypt - Events of 2011'. At: http://bit.ly/2CyCR4r (accessed 25 October 2021).

Human Rights Watch. 'World Report 2015: Egypt, Events of 2014'. At: https://bit.ly/3oQhwdj (accessed 21 October 2021).

International Republican Institute. 'Egyptian Public Opinion Survey April 14-April 27, 2011'. At: https://bit.ly/30ctO2s (accessed 25 October 2021).

Ministry of Communications and Information Technology and UNCTAD. 'ICT Policy Review, Egypt'. 2011. At: https://bit.ly/30bwdKP (accessed 25 October 2021).

Nashwa Nashat (ed.). *The State of Human Rights in Egypt: Annual Report 2008* [Arabic]. Cairo, Egyptian Organization for Human Rights, 2008.

National Council for Human Rights. 'Final Draft of the Maspero Report from the National Council for Human Rights' [Arabic]. 2 November 2011. At: https://bit.ly/3iUNbqc (accessed 13 October 2021).

Open Net Initiative. 'Internet Filtering in Egypt'. 2009. At: https://bit.ly/3kVcIxI (accessed 20 January 2020).

Ragai, Ghada. *Report on the Conditions of Workers in Spinning, Weaving, and Garment Manufacture* [Arabic]. Land Centre for Human Rights. November 2008.

Sayed, Hussein. *Review of the Executive Plan 2015-2020 in the Context of the National Population and Development Strategy 2015-2030*. Cairo: UNFPA, August 2020. At: https://bit.ly/3p0K9B9 (accessed 17 December 2020).

Sharp, Jeremy M. 'Egypt: Background and U.S. Relations'. Congressional Research Service. 27 May 2020. At: https://bit.ly/37rDUB1 (accessed 20 October 2020).

Sharp, Jeremy M. 'Egypt: Background and U.S. Relations'. Congressional Research Service. 30 September 2021. At: https://bit.ly/3lYFqOw (accessed 21 October 2021).

Sharp, Jeremy M. 'Egypt: Background and U.S. Relations'. *CRS Report for Congress*. 27 May 2020. At: https://bit.ly/33nAfAk (accessed 25 October 2021).

The Arab Opinion Index. Arab Centre for Research and Policy Studies. At: https://bit.ly/3r6tCh6 (accessed 17 December 2020).

UN Economic and Social Commission for Western Asia (ESCWA), National Account Studies of the Arab Region, bulletin no. 34 (Beirut: UN, 2014), at: https://bit.ly/3mikZ2n (accessed 26 October 2021)

US Department of State. 'Memorandum of Conversation, Prepared in the Embassy in Cairo'. *Foreign Relations of the United States, 1952-1954, The Near and Middle East, Volume IX, Part 1*, Document 5. At: https://bit.ly/32gc0ok (accessed 20 December 2014).

US Department of State. 'The Ambassador in Egypt (Caffery) to the Department of State'. *Foreign Relations of the United States, 1952-1954, The Near and Middle East, Volume IX, Part 2*, Document 1006. At: https://bit.ly/3niahs2 (accessed 20 December 2014).

News Networks and Websites

ABC News: Online website of a news division of Walt Disney Television's ABC broadcast network.
Addustour: Online website of an Arabic daily newspaper published in Jordan.
Akhbar Al-Yom: Online independent political news website.
Akhbar el-Yom: Arabic language weekly newspaper published in Egypt.
Al Akhbar (Egypt): State-owned semi-official Arabic daily newspaper based in Egypt.
Al Bawaba: A news, blogging and media website headquartered in Amman.
Al Bayan: Arabic language newspaper in the United Arab Emirates which is owned by Government of Dubai.
Al Jazeera Media Network: A public media conglomerate based in Qatar. It is the parent company of International Arabic news channel Al Jazeera and other similarly branded factual media operations.
Al Raya: Arabic daily newspaper published in Doha, Qatar.
Al Riyadh: Riyadh-based, pro-government Saudi daily newspaper.
Al Sbah: Palestinian daily, political news website.
al-Ahed News: News site based in Beirut Lebanon and owned by Hezbollah.
al-Ahram: Online website of an Egyptian daily newspaper founded on 5 August 1875.
Al-Akhbar (Lebanon): Online Website of a Daily Arabic language newspaper.
Al-Alam: Online website of the Arabic news channel broadcasting from Iran and owned by the state-owned media corporation Islamic Republic of Iran Broadcasting.
Al-Arabiya: Online website of the Pan Arabi TV news channel Al-Arabiya based in Dubai.
al-Araby al-Jadid: Pan-Arab media outlet headquartered in London. It was first launched in March 2014 as an online news website.
al-Ayam al-Masria: Independent, daily, and electronic Egyptian newspaper.
al-Gomhuria: State-owned Egyptian Arabic language daily newspaper.
al-Hiwar al-Mutamaddin: Online website of a non-governmental, non-profit organization concerned with issues of culture, media, and politics.
Alhurra: Arabic-language satellite TV channel that broadcasts news and current affairs programming to audiences in the Middle East and North Africa. It also has a website.
Al-Ittihad: Arabic language newspaper published daily in the United Arab Emirates.
al-Joumhouria: Lebanese daily newspaper founded in 1924.
al-Madenah News: Online website that publishes news on Jordan and the Arab world.
Almal News: Daily business source for board range of business information.
Al-Manar: Online website of a Lebanese satellite television station owned and operated by the political party Hezbollah, broadcasting from Beirut, Lebanon.

Almasdar Online: Independent Yemeni news organization paving the way forward for informed, impartial content on Yemen and the region.

Al-Masry Al-Youm: Online website of an Egyptian privately owned daily newspaper that was first published in June 2004.

Almesryoon: Egyptian press website effective since 2004 in Arabic.

Al-Nahar (Egypt): Independent Egyptian newspaper that publishes since 2007, and has a website.

al-Quds al-Arabi: Independent pan-Arab daily newspaper, published in London since 1989.

Alrai: Kuwaiti daily newspaper.

al-Sharq: Arabic daily newspaper published in Doha, Qatar.

al-Tahrir: Privately owned Classical Arabic daily published in Egypt. It also publishes online.

al-Wafd: Online website of a daily newspaper published by the Wafd party in Giza, Egypt.

Alwasat: Arabic-language daily newspaper in Manama, Bahrain.

al-Watan (Egypt): Online news portal that provides the latest news from Egypt, the Arab countries and the world.

Anadolu Agency: State-run news agency headquartered in Ankara, Turkey.

Arab48: Online website dedicated to Arab, Palestinian and Israeli news.

Asharq Al-Awsat: Online website of an Arabic international newspaper headquartered in London.

Assabeel: Arabic weekly newspaper in Amman, Jordan.

Aswat Masr: Egyptian website dedicated to opinion surveys.

Aswat Masriya: Website concerned with Egyptian political, economic, social, and cultural affairs.

Atlantic Council: Online website of The Atlantic Council; an American think tank in the field of international affairs founded in 1961

Bawaba News: Online website dedicated to publishing news from Egypt and the Arab world.

BBC: The British Broadcasting Corporation responsible for the gathering and broadcasting of news and current affairs and has several divisions such as BBC News TV channel that also owns a website. It also has an Arabic Language version of its branded factual media operations.

Bet: Online news website.

Bibliotheca Alexandria: Online website of a library and cultural center located in Alexandria, Egypt.

Central Agency for Public Mobilization and Statistics: Online website of the official statistical agency of Egypt that collects, processes, analyses, and disseminates statistical data and conducts the census. CAPMAS was established by a Presidential Decree 2915 in 1964.

Christian Dogma: Online Coptic Christian Egyptian website.

Christian Science Monitor: Online website of a non-profit news organization that publishes daily articles in electronic format as well as a weekly print edition.

CNN: The Cable News Network, a multinational news-based pay television channel headquartered in Atlanta, United States. It has websites in both Arabic and English.

Constitution Net: A project created to support legislators, constitutional lawyers and other constitutional practitioners in finding useful and relevant information, sharing knowledge and building a community of best practice.

Daily News Egypt: English-language daily Egyptian newspaper established in 2005 and relaunched in June 2012.

Dailymotion: Video-sharing technology platform.
Dostor: Independent Daily Egyptian opposition newspaper
Dotmsr: Online News Portal that provides the latest news from Egypt.
Deutsche Welle Arabic Arabic: Online website of a German public state-owned international broadcaster funded by the German federal tax budget.
EBRD: Official website of the European Bank for Reconstruction and Development; an international financial institution founded in 1991.
Egypt Independent: Online newspaper that formerly published a weekly 24-page English-language edition of the Egyptian newspaper, Al-Masry Al-Youm.
Egyptian Initiative for Personal Rights: Online website of an independent Egyptian human rights organization, established in 2002.
Elaph: Daily Arabic independent online newspaper and is not associated with any established print or broadcast medium.
Elbadil: Privately owned Egyptian newspaper known for its left-wing orientation.
Elfagr: Egyptian independent weekly newspaper, based in Cairo.
Elnashra: Independent electronic newspaper that published news of Lebanon and the Middle East.
EU Newsroom: Website that gathers briefings from press rooms of EU institutions.
EU Observer: European online newspaper launched in 2000 by the Brussels-based organisation EUobserver.com ASBL.
Eurasia Review: Independent journal that provides a venue for analysts and experts to disseminate content on a wide range of subjects.
European Commission: Official website of the executive branch of the European Union, responsible for proposing legislation, enforcing EU laws and directing the union's administrative operations.
European External Action Service: Website of the diplomatic service and combined foreign and defence ministry of the European Union.
Facebook: Online social media and social networking service.
Fekr Online: Online magazine dedicated to spreading awareness and knowledge through the analysis of social and political aspects.
Financial Times: Daily newspaper printed in broadsheet and published digitally that focuses on business and economic current affairs.
FJP Portal: Freedom and Justice Portal is an online news website concerned with local, social, international, sports, cultural, and other news.
Foreign Affairs: Online website of an American magazine of international relations and U.S. foreign policy published by the Council on Foreign Relations.
Foreign Policy: Daily website and glossy print magazine, with podcasts, events, and readers all over the globe.
France 24 Arabic: The Arabic TV channel of the French state-owned international news television network, France24.
Global Fire Power: Online platform that provides analytical display of data concerning 140 modern military powers.
Guardian: Online website of a British daily newspaper founded in 1821.
Harper's Magazine: Online website of a monthly magazine of literature, politics, culture, finance, and the arts, launched in New York City in June 1850.
Ikhwan Online: The official website of the Muslim Brotherhood.
Ikhwan Way Online: Intellectual, educational and advocacy online Blog.
Ikhwan Wiki: Online official historical encyclopaedia of the Muslim Brotherhood.
Independent: British online newspaper established in 1986.

Islamweb: Islamic website that publishes fatwas, Quran, articles, fiqh, lectures, prayer times, and other Islamic-related content.
ISSUU, Inc.: Danish-founded American electronic publishing platform based in Palo Alto, California, United States.
Jadaliyya: Free ezine founded in 2010 and features English, Arabic, French, and Spanish-language content by academics, journalists, activists, and artists from and/or on the Middle East and is produced by the Arab Studies Institute.
Jewish Telegraphic Agency: International news agency and wire service serving Jewish community newspapers and media around the world.
John Pilger: Personal online website of the Australian journalist John Pilger.
Khaberni: Online Jordanian daily news website.
Kuwait News Agency: Online website of the official state news wire service based in Kuwait.
Le Parisien: French daily newspaper covering both international and national news, and local news of Paris and its suburbs.
Livemint: Indian Delhi-based financial daily newspaper published by HT Media.
Mada Masr: Independent, liberal Egyptian online newspaper, founded in June 2013.
Makor Rishon: Israeli newspaper associated with Religious Zionism and the conservative right-wing.
Masrawy: Arabic Egyptian news web portal that operates under the ONA institution for press and media.
Mella5er: Blog website of activist Marianne Magdy.
Middle East Monitor: A not-for-profit press monitoring organisation founded on 1 July 2009.
Muntada al-Mohamoon al-'Arab: Online website of a cultural, humanitarian and awareness project that was launched in 1999, aiming to spread legal awareness among the people of the Arab nation.
New York Times: American daily newspaper founded in 1851 and based in New York City. It also publishes its news online.
NPR: National Public Radio is an American privately and publicly funded non-profit media organization headquartered in Washington, D.C.
People's Daily: Website of the official newspaper of the Central Committee of the Chinese Communist Party.
Politico: Political journalism company based in Arlington County, Virginia, that covers politics and policy in the United States and internationally. It primarily distributes content online.
Radiosawa: Online website of a Middle Eastern radio station broadcasting in the Arab world.
Rassd News Network: Alternative media network based in Cairo, Egypt, and was launched as a Facebook-based news source on 25 January 2011.
Rasseen: Electronic news website that publishes updates from Jordan and the Arab world.
Reuters: Online website of an international news organization owned by Thomson Reuters.
Revolutionary Socialists: Blog published by Ayman Abdul-Mo'ti.
RT Arabic: Online website of a Russian state-controlled international television network funded by the federal tax budget of the Russian government.
Sada Elbalad: Egyptian news website and satellite television channel established in 2011.
Sama News: An independent Palestinian news agency.
Saudi Press Agency: Website of the official news agency of Saudi Arabia.
Shabab 6 April: Online website of 6 April Youth Movement.

Shorouk: An independent Arabic newspaper that also publishes its news online.
Sky News Arabic: Online website of the Arabic 24-hour rolling news channel broadcast mainly in the Middle East and North Africa.
Spiegel International: German news website founded in 1994.
State Information Service: Website of the State Information Service; nation's main public relations agency.
Supreme Election Committee: Official website of the presidential elections dedicated to providing all information related to the elections and Egyptian votes inside and outside Egypt.
Telegraph: Online website of an American magazine of international relations and U.S. foreign policy published by the Council on Foreign Relations.
The Jerusalem Post: Online website of a newspaper based in Jerusalem, founded in 1932 during the British Mandate of Palestine by Gershon Agron as The Palestine Post.
The Wall Street Journal: American business-focused, English-language international daily newspaper based in New York City.
The White House – Office of the Press Secretary: A governmental agency responsible for gathering and disseminating information to three principal groups: the President, the White House staff, and the media.
The World Bank Group: A family of five international organizations that make leveraged loans to developing countries. It has an open-data website that provides a listing of available World Bank datasets, including databases, pre-formatted tables, reports, and other resources.
Twitter: American microblogging and social networking service.
Washington Post: American daily newspaper published in Washington, D.C.
Wiki Thawra: Website that is a statistical data base of the Egyptian Revolution and documents all the events with direct links.
WikiLeaks: International non-profit organisation initiated in 2006 and publishes news leaks and classified media provided by anonymous sources.
Workers of Egypt: Blog published by Kareem el-Beheiri in Mahalla al-Kubra.
Ynet: Israeli news and general-content websites, and is the online outlet for the Yedioth Ahronot newspaper.
Youm7: Online website of an Egyptian privately owned daily newspaper. It was first published as a weekly paper in October 2008 and has been published daily since May 2011.
YouTube: Online video platform owned by Google.

Index

6 April Movement   124, 131, 138,
   143, 145–9, 151–2, 154, 157,
   168, 196, 197, 232, 252, 272,
   318, 402, 419, 434, 448, 480,
   519, 559, 586
6 October Bridge   242, 244
6 October Day celebrations   513
6 October war   513
6th October City   227, 401
9 March Independent Universities
   Movement   164
11 September attacks   163
20 March Movement   119
25 January demonstrations
   26–28 January   194–7
   day of   183–94
   defeat of security forces   208–12
   Egyptian army   212–20
   elite mobilization   197–201
   Friday of Rage   201–8
   preparing for   166–78
1919 revolution   11, 110, 122
1935 uprising   122
1948 war   15, 16, 70
1952 revolution   127, 338, 391, 468, 483
1961–3 laws   161
1971 constitution   56, 415, 528
   Article 2   421, 422, 426, 451
   Article 56   58
   Article 73   418
   Article 75   417
   Article 76   256, 415
   Article 77   256, 415, 417
   Article 78   57
   Article 88   256, 415, 417
   Article 93   256, 415, 417
   Article 139   417
   Article 148   417
   Article 189   256, 415, 417, 421
   Article 198   518
1990 elections   250
2010 elections   138, 166, 268, 277, 389

Aal, Sayed Abdel   217
Abaza, Amin   429
Abbas, Essam Hassan   210
Abbas, Mohammad   170, 184, 513
Abbas, Wael   150, 403
Abbas Bridge Massacre (1946)   14, 112
al-Abbasi, Mohammad   275
Abbasiya Square   207, 434, 495
ABC channel   246
Abdel Al, Kamal   132
Abdel Aziz, Alaa   562
Abdel-Aziz, Zakaria   162
Abdel Fattah, Seif al-Din   7, 502, 507
Abdel Ghaffar, Ashraf   574
Abdel Hady, Aisha   126
Abdelkarim, Moaz   171
Abdel-Latif, Hany   337
Abdel-Mageed, Waheed   174
Abdel Moneim Riad Square   169, 186
Abdel Nour, Mounir Fakhry   581
Abdelrahim, Hafez   88
Abdel Rahman, Mohamed Galal   211
Abdel-Rahman, Omar   85
Abdessalem, Rafik   668
Abdin Palace affair (1942)   15
Abd Rabou, Ahmed   6
Abdul Aziz, Abdullah bin   233, 263, 641,
   643, 645, 651
Abdul Aziz, Mansour bin Muqrin
   bin   642
Abdullah, Ahmad   75
Abdullah, Hassan   514
Abou Eitta, Kamal   126, 190, 581
Aboul-Fotouh, Abdel Moneim   115, 139,
   185, 248, 255–7, 432, 441, 491, 497,
   499, 517, 521, 644, 645
Aboul-Fotouh, Hozaifa   139
Aboulghar, Mohamed   174, 446
Aboul Gheit, Ahmed   223, 428, 670
Abou Zeid, Taher   581
Abu al-Nasr, Muhammad Hamid   84
Abu Dhabi   643–4, 647, 648, 651, 652

Index

Abu Fajr, Massaad 150
Abu Ghazala, Abdel Halim 71–2, 76, 78, 82
Abu Hamed, Mohamed 510
Abu Ismail, Hazem Salah 469, 491, 493–5, 579
Abu Khalil, Ahmed 207
Abul-Magd, Ahmed Kamal 235
Abul-Magd, Zeinab 427
Abu Simbel 543
Abu Taleb, Youssef Sabri 73
Account Statement Friday 516
Ackerman, Bruce 413
Adel, Mohammad 586
Adl (Justice) Party 446
Adly, Amr 536
Adly, Malek 403
el-Adly, Habib 166, 178, 183, 190, 205, 208, 210, 225, 230, 244, 270, 395, 397, 428, 438, 588
Administrative Control Authority (ACA) 78
Administrative Court 209, 480, 488
Afghan Arabs 83, 85
African Championship 490
agrarian aristocracy 45
agrarian reform 22, 23
Ahlawi firm 132
Ahly Club 488, 548
Ahly Ultra 132, 175, 189, 202, 478, 488
Ahmadinejad, Mahmoud 512, 656, 657
Ahmed, Salah Amer 281
Ahmed Abdel Aziz Street 185
Ahmed Helmy Tunnel 207
Ahmed Urabi Bridge 203
Aid Committee 131
Ain Shams University 114, 131
Akef, Mahdi 137, 139, 464
al-Ahram 10, 173, 178, 183, 242, 261
al-Akhbar 173
Al-Arabiya TV 239, 430
al-Azhar University 118, 245, 549, 565, 586
al-Dostor 134
Alexandria 9, 134, 138, 155, 156, 160, 195, 268, 269, 287–92, 400, 480, 538, 552, 573
  26–27 January 294

  28 January 294–8
  29 January–11 February 298–9
  struggling with geography 292–4
Alexandria Businessmen's Association (ABA) 97
Alexandria Investigations Bureau 31
Alexandria protests (2010) 149
Alexandria Salafist movement 158, 177
Alexandria University 288
Algeria 250, 490
Al-Haram 198, 543
Al-Haram Street 203
Al-Haram Tunnel 203
AlHayah network 201
Al Hayat 496
al-Hilal 10
Ali, Ibrahim 424
Ali, Kamal Hassan 69
Ali, Muhammad 9
alienation 38, 107, 117, 140
Al Jazeera 175, 201, 229, 234, 236, 244, 270, 278, 645, 652
Al Jazeera Mubasher 197, 234
Allende, Salvador 575
al-Masa' 25
Al-Masry Al-Youm 134, 163, 174, 176, 402, 446, 451
Al-Mokattam 552–3, 565
alms tax (zakat) 537
Alnagar, Mostafa 197, 257
al Nahda movement 357, 444, 464
al-Tawhid wa'l-Jihad 130
Aly, Hassan 337
Amer, Abdel Hakim 27, 36–7, 60, 62–3, 67
Amer, Ali 41
Amer, Kareem 403
Amer, Omar 277
American Chamber of Commerce (AmCham) 97, 98, 537
American Civil War (1861–5) 11
American Israel Public Affairs Committee (AIPAC) 624, 669
American University 471
Amidror, Yaakov 669
Amin, Galal 174
Amin, Samir 44
Amnesty International 248, 403, 471
Amr, Mohamed 628

Anan, Sami   220, 222, 231, 236, 237, 248,
    394, 447, 504, 507, 509, 511, 513,
    514, 551, 554, 565, 582
anarchy   29, 209, 212, 214, 224, 227, 246,
    548–55
*Ancien Régime and the French Revolution,
    The* (de Tocqueville)   336
Anglo-Egyptian Treaty (1936)   13, 15,
    17, 112
Angry Ones youth movement   132
Ankara   635, 661
Ansar al-Sunna   276
Ansar Bait al-Maqdis   130, 579
anti-authoritarian movements   146
anti-colonial policies   111
Anti-Coup Alliance. *See* National Alliance
    to Support Legitimacy and Reject
    the Coup (NASL)
anti-democracy   30, 358, 545
anti-liberal populism   19
anti-Mubarak demonstrations   280, 383
anti-sectarian rallies   135
anti-terrorism   166
Arab Affairs Committee   666
Arab-African summit (1977)   123
Arab Barometer   323
Arab Centre for Research and Policy
    Studies (ACRPS)   5, 6
Arab Cold War   38
Arab countries   3, 26, 70, 88, 117, 174,
    263, 327, 337, 339, 340, 366, 438, 450
Arab-Islamic civilization   319
Arab-Israeli conflict   52, 520, 670
Arab League   55, 235, 663, 668
Arab League Street   169, 184, 204
Arab Network for Human Rights   587
Arab Opinion Index (AOI)   7, 324, 326,
    611
Arab Organization for
    Industrialization   392
Arab Question, The (Bishara)   674
Arab Republic of Egypt   57
Arab revolutions   5, 251, 260, 375, 590–3,
    595, 596, 615, 624, 633, 634, 638
Arab socialism   36–43
Arab Socialist Union (ASU)   36, 37, 40,
    43, 47, 49, 50, 54, 56, 57, 60, 62, 67,
    159, 443
Arab societies   319, 560, 591

Arab Spring   337, 591–7, 628, 663, 668
Elaraby, Nabil   654
Arafat, Yasser   55, 117
Araghchi, Abbas   558
Arato, Andrew   413
Arbaeen Police Station   281–5
Arbaeen Square   280, 282, 284–6
Arif, Abdul Salam   438
aristocracy   29, 59, 326
armed forces   61–3, 67, 74, 76, 153, 164,
    208, 211, 219, 228, 231, 237, 242,
    247, 252, 257, 264, 278, 378–81,
    384, 387, 391–4, 405, 407, 421, 422,
    429, 450, 456, 458, 462, 467, 473,
    499, 508, 510, 513, 518, 550, 551,
    561–6, 577, 584, 587, 641, 650
Armed Forces Engineering
    Authority   587
Artists and Authors for Change   120
Asfour, Gaber   259
Ashour, Sameh   478
Ashton, Catherine   245, 575–8, 626–8,
    630
al-Assad, Bashar   186, 209, 512
al-Assad, Hafez   49
al-Assar, Mohammad   132, 185
Assiut University   131
Aswan   167, 299–304, 454
    25 January   301–2
    29 January–1 February   303–4
    Friday of Rage   302–3
    Mubarak's speech   304
    social background   299–301
Aswan Dam   26
Aswan governor   454
Aswan negotiations (1974)   70
Al Aswany, Alaa   101, 502
Ataba Square   114
al-Atassi, Nureddin   438
Atta, Wesam   183
Aty, Ahmed Abdel   504
Austria   10
Authenticity (Asala) Party   445, 475
authoritarianism   26, 30, 36, 42, 44, 47,
    48, 75, 81, 86–8, 90, 91, 94, 96, 153,
    214, 319, 326, 330, 343, 344, 352–4,
    356–8, 361, 364, 365, 369, 371, 376,
    387, 436, 457, 465, 466, 472, 536,
    573, 580, 589

autocracy 28, 29, 75, 345, 372
al-Awa, Mohamed Selim 462, 491, 645
Awwad, Hani 6
'axis of democracy' 664
Ayoub, Magdy 453
Azhar Document 461
Aziz, Abdel 557, 558
Aziz, Gharib 283
Azmi, Zakaria 429

Bab al-Louq Square 228
el-Badawi, El-Sayyid 196, 201, 217, 235, 443, 449
Badeen, Hamdy 386
Badie, Mohammed 232, 239, 425
Badr, Mahmoud 557, 558, 568
Badr, Zaki 84
Badrawi, Hossam 254, 265
Baghdad Pact 33, 34
Bahrain 645, 653
Bahr Street 143
El-Bakoory, Ahmed Hassan 23
Bakry, Mostafa 643
Balloon Theatre 404
al-Banna, Hassan 12, 15, 24
Banque Misr 12
El Baradei, Mohamed 151–4, 157, 169, 197–9, 202, 203, 216, 219, 223, 229, 232, 239, 245, 248, 250, 253, 257, 291, 292, 294, 319, 419, 447, 448, 462, 486, 494, 517, 522, 525, 566, 575–8, 622, 632, 658
Baradei campaign 153, 169, 171, 197, 198, 245, 257, 291, 292, 294
Bar Lev line 69
Barout, Jamal 7
al-Barqy, Sameh 190
Barroso, José Manuel 627, 628
Basateen 198
Basset, Abdel Maseeh 177
Bassiouni, Cherif 218, 503
Bassiouni, M 337
Bastawisy, Hisham 164
Battle of the Camel 236, 240–7, 249, 259, 277, 278, 286, 297, 325, 378, 488, 514–16
Bayoumi, Rashad 243
BBC Media Action 193

Beblawi, Hazem 435, 472, 581–3
Bedaya movement 234
el-Beheiri, Kareem 142, 150
Beijing 537–40
Beinin, Joel 458
Belal, Sayed 158, 290
Bella, Ahmed Ben 438
Bellin, Eva 477
El-Beltagy, Mohamed 176, 191, 192, 242, 244, 257, 494
Ben Ali, Zine al-Abidine 92, 167, 173, 175, 212, 214, 265, 280, 344, 376, 637
Ben-Eliezer, Binyamin 266, 667
Beni Soueif cultural centre 104
Bermeo, Nancy 358
Beshr, Mohammed Ali 231, 576
El-Bialy, Mohammad 543
Biden, Joe 215, 221, 618
bilateral relationship 635, 659–61
Bildt, Carl 223, 631
bint Muqrin, Lamia 642
El-Bishry, Tarek 372, 373, 386, 416–18, 423, 462, 483, 491
Black Bloc 554, 586
blogosphere 172
blogs/bloggers 149–51
board elections (2009) 165
Boccaccio al-Salam 104
Boeing 737 104
Boghdadi, Abdel Latif 22
Bokhari, Kamran 445
Bolshevik revolution 358
El Borai, Ahmed 581
Borhamy, Yasser 177
Bouazizi, Mohamed 156, 167, 282
Bougrab, Jeannette 628
Boulos, Maged 243
bread riots (1977) 55, 72, 81, 114, 118, 338
Brennan, John 618
Britain. *See also* United Kingdom (UK)
  mass protest against (1946) 14, 112
  occupation of Egypt (1882) 10, 15, 17, 19, 21
British Labour Party 366
British Protectorate 11
British tutelage 17, 59
Brotherhoodization 549, 550, 562, 571, 609

Brotherhood youth   155, 170, 229, 305, 319
brutality   104, 119, 120, 133, 137, 156, 167, 176, 193, 213, 470, 471, 479, 580
Brzezinski, Zbigniew   70
Building and Development Party (BDP)   475, 487
bureaucracy   37, 46, 47, 54, 62, 88–90, 92, 94, 96, 97, 102, 104, 161
Burns, William   578, 619, 624
Bush, George W.   86
business associations   97
businessmen   96–101, 105

Cabinet Building   478–86, 488
Caffery, Jefferson Thomas   21
Cairo   9, 17–18, 22, 30, 33–5, 37, 38, 40, 45, 49, 50, 55, 65, 67, 70, 78, 90, 99, 100, 104–8, 110, 112, 116–17, 119, 120, 122, 123, 128, 131, 132, 134, 138, 143, 152, 155, 160, 167, 169, 176, 186, 192–9, 203, 205–7, 209, 212, 218, 226, 234, 236, 240, 251, 258, 261, 262, 268–72, 274–8, 280, 285–9, 291, 292, 294, 297, 301–4, 378, 401, 428, 444, 445, 450, 458, 462, 471, 480, 499, 502, 512, 513, 559, 563, 576, 585, 587, 588, 619, 625, 627–30, 632, 639–48, 650, 654–62
Cairo Appeals Prosecution   428
Cairo cigarette rollers' strike (1899)   110
Cairo Court of Appeals   442
Cairo Institute for Human Rights Studies (CIHRS)   547
Cairo International Convention Centre   550
Cairo Stadium   563
Cairo University   24, 103, 111, 112, 118, 131, 138, 151, 155, 176, 262, 400, 504, 647
Cameron, David   251, 629
Campante, Filipe R.   337
Camp Caesar   296
Camp David Accords (1979)   52, 55, 69, 115, 391, 668, 669
Canal Zone   35
capitalism   12, 36, 47, 48, 57, 74, 81, 103, 326, 343

capitalist transition   161
capitalization   94
caretaker government   212, 384, 408, 409
Central Agency for Public Mobilization and Statistics (CAPMAS)   531, 532, 540
Central Auditing Organization (CAO)   106
Central Bank of Egypt (CBE)   533, 642, 644, 648, 649, 651, 652
Central Intelligence Agency (CIA), US   31, 36, 266
Central Military Zone   267
Central Security Forces (CSF)   68, 72, 73, 76, 116, 119, 149, 175, 176, 186, 191–7, 199, 203–12, 219, 273, 284, 292, 293, 295–7, 302, 304, 325, 470, 665
Centre for Trade Union and Workers Services   125
Chamber of Deputies   468
Children of Egypt (website)   150
China   22, 34–5, 637–40
China Development Bank (CDB)   639
Chinese Foreign Ministry   638, 640
Chinese Muslim   638
Chor, Davin   337
Christians   58, 135, 172, 177, 198, 254, 527
Christian women   453
church construction   134–5, 149
Church of the Saints bombing (2010)   135, 149, 157, 158, 166, 290
Church of the Saints protests   168
Church of the Two Martyrs   450
Church of the Virgin Mary   177, 271
citizen journalism programmes   168
citizenship   9, 320, 426, 456, 457, 461, 463, 465, 466, 494, 598, 607
civil courts   448
civil disobedience   111, 550
civil liberties   252, 325, 326, 414, 415, 417, 448, 457, 484, 598, 626, 630
civil rights   353, 366, 412, 446, 598
civil service   9, 13, 37, 44, 78
civil society   154, 161, 164, 263, 289, 369, 386, 397, 401, 413, 465, 471, 472, 488, 577, 603, 614, 627
civil state   460–9, 475, 588, 611–13
class conflict   537

class gap 324, 337
class struggle 36, 62
clientelism 57, 87–96, 326, 339, 343, 449
Clinton, Hillary 178, 215, 216, 233, 245, 618, 619
Coalition of Socialist Forces 476
Coalition to Support New Muslims 453
Cold War 21, 23, 24, 34, 38, 358, 560
Colombia 362
Colombo, Silvia 459
colonialism 41, 45, 110, 112, 286
Committee for State Security (KGB) 36
Committee of Fifty 430
Committee of Wise Men 249, 250, 253, 255, 261
Committee on Foreign Affairs 624
communal divisions 560
communal violence 585
communications blackout 143, 189, 198, 224, 273, 275, 294, 296, 303
communications infrastructure 89, 150
communism 21, 22, 24, 36, 358, 366
Communist Party 362, 447
competitive authoritarianism 344
conciliatory policies 95
Congress 620
Congressional Research Service 620
Constituent Assembly (CA) 357, 362, 429, 461, 469, 481, 483, 485, 487–8, 491, 494, 495, 499, 503, 505, 517–22, 529, 570, 571
constitutional amendments 58, 111, 137, 149, 150, 217, 265, 363, 373, 386, 397, 408, 411–15, 432, 525
    opponents 419–20
    supporters 420–7
constitutional courts 414, 484, 485, 505, 528
constitutional declaration 383, 384, 387, 415, 418, 420, 422, 426, 427, 442, 460–2, 482, 486, 499, 502, 503, 509, 510, 515, 517–29, 619, 630, 646, 647
constitutional principles 398, 460, 461, 463
constitutional referendum 31, 34, 56, 67, 150, 163, 363, 374, 384, 397, 408, 411–15, 442
Constitutional Theory (Schmitt) 413
Constitution Party 447, 486, 521

Consultative Council 139, 255, 408, 477, 478, 490–2, 551, 648
Cook, Steven 74, 75, 259
Coordinating Committee 431
Coordination Bureau 292
Coordination Office 154, 155, 290
Coptic Christians 134, 149, 426, 450, 451, 453–5, 475, 553, 586
Coptic Christmas 149
Coptic Church 475, 565, 586
Coptic Evangelical Organization 177
Copts United 451
corporatism 57, 87–96
corruption 16, 27, 47, 59, 66, 78, 88, 91, 94, 96, 99, 100, 104, 120, 121, 134, 150, 157, 174, 214, 235, 268, 279, 301, 329, 330, 338, 340, 343, 389, 390, 399, 403, 428, 429, 436, 438, 540, 594, 645
cosmetic reforms 343, 438
Costa Salafists 298
counter-revolution 4, 64, 229, 231, 258, 263, 277, 356, 359, 388, 413, 450, 457, 514, 515, 536, 545, 574, 580, 649
counterterrorism laws 415
Court of Cassation 160, 164, 165, 233, 235, 256, 440, 505, 565
Crimean War (1853–6) 10
criminal law 428
cross-party alliance 235, 252
Crowley, Philip 618
CSF mutiny (1986) 116–17, 175, 236
Cuban Revolution 358
cultural revival (*nahda*) 10
Culture Ministry 562
curfew 205, 213, 223, 228, 235, 297, 495, 548, 550, 586
Czech arms deal 33
Czechoslovakia 33
Czech Republic 25

Daniel, Mina 172, 519
Daniel, Peter 8
Darrag, Ahmed 197
Darrag, Amr 577
Darwish, Ahmed 429
Davies, James 326, 336–8
Davutoğlu, Ahmet 664
Dawoud, Khaled 432

al-Dawwar, Kafr 25
Dawwen 151
'Day of Rage: Make a Commotion' campaign 155
Debates 118
de Beauvoir, Simone 127
decision making 47, 75, 84, 139, 258–63, 353, 356, 376, 391, 392, 395
Declaration on the Renunciation of Violence 549
Decree 11/2012 505
Decree 35/1979 71
Decree 108 485
Decree 123 485
Decree 134/2013 551
Decree 162/1962 63
Decree 367/1966 63
Decree 1956/1966 63
Decree 2878 63
Defence Academy 61
Defence Ministry 77, 242, 388, 494, 525, 562, 587, 621, 666
democracy 25, 28, 29, 67, 84, 178, 224, 233, 247, 250, 253, 258, 261, 262, 266, 319, 322–4, 326
  assessing existing 602–7
  attitudes towards 599–602
  concept of 597–9
Democratic Alliance 448, 461, 463, 464, 474–6
democratic elections 224, 256, 387, 526, 618, 634
Democratic Front Party (DFP) 142, 154, 176, 199, 245, 248, 252, 262, 270–2, 277, 443, 475
democratic government 412, 413
democratic institutions 355, 358, 361, 365, 367, 389, 472, 537, 552
Democratic Movement for National Liberation (HADITU) 16, 17, 24–7
Democratic Peace Party 476
democratic pluralism 637, 676
democratic politics 145, 364, 394
democratic principles 527, 528
democratic reforms 86, 99, 235, 388, 477, 627
democratic system 154, 253, 352, 354, 357, 372–4, 393, 411, 437, 467, 484, 528, 537, 554, 560, 563, 598, 601, 614, 631, 673
democratic transition 5, 6, 79, 84, 86, 87, 247, 320, 346, 347, 352–9, 361–3, 365, 367, 381, 385, 394, 399, 423, 457–60, 467, 468, 472, 477, 478, 518, 521, 522, 528, 529, 557, 574, 582, 590, 615, 617, 619, 621, 630, 631, 633, 661, 672, 674–7
democratic values 412, 477, 485, 528, 529, 591, 600
democratization 353–6, 365, 367, 370, 371, 400, 431, 457, 461, 467, 482, 483, 499, 505, 508, 515, 519, 536, 552, 589, 590, 615, 617, 619, 620, 630, 632–4, 637, 644, 648–51, 653, 664, 667, 671–9
demographics 94, 105, 148, 193, 274, 296, 322, 323, 345
Department of Forensic Medicine 580
depoliticization 66, 174, 300
deprivation 323, 324, 337–9
Deraa 108
despotism 7, 90, 322, 417, 436
de Tocqueville, Alexis 456
dictatorship 153, 330, 372, 384, 483, 484, 589, 632, 637, 667
digital protest 291
digital revolution 193
El Din, Dorria Sharaf 581
El-din, Ziad Bahaa 581
al-Din Hilal, Ali 222
direct confrontation 95, 137
discrimination 607, 611
Doctors for Change 120
Doctors' Syndicate 131, 173
Doha 644, 648, 649, 651, 653
Dokki Square 185
domestic politics 81, 222, 580
Donilon, Tom 215, 618
Dorr Rebellion 336
Dostor 153, 174, 546
Douma, Ahmed 132, 586
'Dreamland' 93
Dream TV 149
dual economy 93
Dulles, John Foster 22
Duweiqa 104

Eastern Europe 25, 44, 146
economic activity 71, 73, 76, 80, 96, 587
Economic and Social Commission for
 Western Asia (ESCWA) 339, 531
economic crisis 53, 114, 336, 337
economic growth 37, 92–5, 106, 322,
 336, 337, 343, 352, 537, 540
economic inequality 239, 337
economic liberalization 46, 76, 78,
 80–90, 94–6, 103, 342, 343,
 393, 459
economic policy 44, 46, 529, 535, 538
economic reforms 161, 214, 344
economic status 12, 332
Economic Support Fund 620
Economist 338
Eden, Anthony 21
education 324, 337
Effat, Emad 479, 519
Egypt Air hijacking (1985) 76
Egypt Human Development Report 102
Egyptian Alliance Party 476
Egyptian-American Enterprise Fund
 (EAEF) 620
Egyptian Arab Union Party 476
Egyptian army 212–20, 368, 381, 393,
 406, 574, 620, 623, 625, 631, 635
 official responses 214–20
 and revolutionaries 212–14
Egyptian army transformation 59–79
 army subordinated to president
  66–72
 historic pact and independent
  army 72–9
 military hegemony and overlap of
  army and president 59–66
Egyptian Bar Association 90, 117, 130,
 165, 195, 478
Egyptian Bloc 475, 476
Egyptian Business Association 97
Egyptian Business Development
 Association (EBDA) 537
Egyptian Center for Economic and Social
 Rights (ECESR) 248, 587
Egyptian Center for Economic Studies
 (ECES) 98
Egyptian Centre for Social and Economic
 Rights 196
Egyptian Citizen Party 476

Egyptian Communist Party 23, 24, 154,
 447
Egyptian Consciousness (blog) 150
Egyptian constitution 519
 Article 2 527
 Article 4 427
 Article 9 463
 Article 38 482
 Article 41 387
 Article 44 387
 Article 45 387
 Article 76 386
 Article 77 386
 Article 81 528
 Article 88 386
 Article 93 386
 Article 139 528
 Article 158 101
 Article 177 552
 Article 179 386, 415
 Article 180 380
 Article 197 528
 Article 219 527
Egyptian Current 446, 475
Egyptian Economic Development
 Conference 651
Egyptian Football Federation 489
Egyptian Foreign Ministry 438, 634,
 647, 658
Egyptian government 60, 142, 178, 196,
 216, 236, 245, 538, 623, 627, 633,
 652, 663
Egyptian history 3, 7, 68, 77, 101, 218,
 254–8
Egyptian identity 320
Egyptian Initiative for Personal Rights
 (EIPR) 586, 587
Egyptian Intelligence Service 559
Egyptian Islamic Jihad (EIJ) 84, 424,
 446
Egyptian Movement for Change
 (EMC) 119–23, 130, 135, 136,
 145–9, 165, 169, 173, 175, 270, 279,
 300, 301, 444, 447, 558
Egyptian Museum 213, 404, 516
Egyptian National Assembly 468
Egyptian Popular Committee 118
Egyptian Radio and Television Union
 (ERTU) 429

Egyptian revolution   326, 351, 360, 367,
    372, 375, 389, 556, 633, 671
  2011   3, 5, 6, 7, 18, 56, 67–9, 77, 79,
    84–7, 95, 98, 107, 110, 18, 147, 148,
    157, 158, 165, 266, 270, 306, 338,
    345, 346, 356, 359, 369, 370, 383,
    387, 390, 394, 396, 402, 408, 431,
    433, 436, 438, 442, 443, 451, 469,
    471, 475, 477, 480, 486, 503, 511,
    531, 538, 539, 546, 547, 553, 564,
    581, 590, 591, 595, 597, 598, 600,
    609, 618–20, 624, 626–9, 638–9,
    641–4, 654 (see also 25 January
    demonstrations)
  middle-class participation   323–34
  timing   336–41
  unions and politics in   269–72
Egyptian-Russian Business Council   635
Egyptian Social Democratic Party
    (ESDP)   446, 475, 487, 521, 582
Egyptian Socialist Party   475
Egyptian society   30, 36, 55, 102, 134,
    141, 150, 170, 233, 254, 327, 328,
    333, 356, 408, 450, 451, 483, 499,
    539, 571, 599, 607, 652
Egyptian Trade Union Federation
    (ETUF)   127, 241, 399
Egyptian women   479
Egyptian Women for Change   154
'Egypt in the Transitional Period'   374
Egypt of Freedom Party   475, 521
Egypt Statistical Yearbook   532
Egypt Today   119
Eid, Ahmed   199
Eisenhower, Dwight   33, 36
Eissa, Hossam   581, 582
Eissa, Ibrahim   153
Elelaimy, Zyad   190, 198, 199, 255
El Arish   129
Elbadil   134
election law   387, 427, 443, 447, 484, 551
electoral commission   83
electoral fraud   91, 162, 163, 167, 441
electoral politics   83, 445
electoral process   154, 387, 414, 417, 425,
    441, 449, 472
Emaar Properties   587
Emam, Abdelmonem   197
Emam, Ahmed   581

Emara, Adel   480
Emara, Mahmoud   174
Emirati Foreign Ministry   646, 647
endowments (*Awqaf*)   23
El Enei, Mohamed Abou   242
Engel, Eliot   623
Engineers Against Receivership   121
equality   135, 149, 253, 412, 451, 456,
    485, 598, 607
Erdoğan, Recep Tayyip   444, 554, 661–4
el-Erian, Essam   115, 139, 173, 176, 191,
    197, 257, 422, 432, 441, 507
Eshel, Amir   666
el-Essawy, Mansour   401
Etman, Ismail   242, 432
EU-Egypt Task Force   628
EU/French Development Agency   629
EU High Representative for Foreign
    Affairs   628
Eurasian Customs Union   635
Europe   10, 250
European Bank for Reconstruction and
    Development (EBRD)   629, 633
European-Egyptian relations   626–34
European Investment Bank (EIB)   629
European Union (EU)   250, 260, 577,
    578, 626–34
European University Institute   632
Ezz, Ahmed   99, 218, 221–4, 236, 244,
    279, 301, 399, 429
Ezz, Amr   171
Ezzat, Mahmoud   191, 230, 243, 432, 494

Fabius, Laurent   630
Facebook   193, 194, 197, 199, 218, 270,
    284, 294, 300, 303, 345, 559
Facebook activism   136
Facebook revolution. *See* digital
    revolution
factionalism   13, 26, 550
Faculty of Agriculture   132
Faculty of Engineering   114
Faculty of Medicine   111
al-Fadil, Abd   108
Fahmy, Nabil   636
Fahmy, Sameh   261
Fairmont Group   502, 503
al-Faisal, Saud   652, 656
Farag, Ibrahim   285

Farahat, Mohamed Nour 478
Fares, Abdelrahman 6, 170
Farmers' Syndicate 521-2
farm tenancy contracts 94
Farouk (king) 12, 15-18, 26, 331
Fattah, Esraa Abdel 143
fatwa 451, 563
Fawzi, Mohammed 37-40, 42, 62, 64, 66
El-Fayoumi, Kamal 142
Fayoum University 132
Federation of Egyptian Students 115
El Fegiery, Moataz 404
El Feki, Mostafa 163
feudalism 326
field officers testimony 210-11
Finance Ministry 126, 543
financial crisis 89, 558
Finer, Samuel 381, 570
El-Fiqqi, Anas 220, 266, 428
Fiqqis 127
First World War 11, 14, 336, 358
Foda, Farag 85
food committees 188
Food for Peace programme 39, 46
football match 488-90
'For Egypt' 461
Foreign Affairs 218
foreign conspiracy 243, 260, 406, 455, 595, 596
foreign currency 54, 89, 529, 539
foreign debt 90, 541
foreign direct investment 531, 638
foreign investment 25, 80, 133, 161, 342, 459, 537, 539
foreign policy 35, 46, 74, 343, 618, 637, 654, 658
foreign trade 36, 45, 95, 532, 533
formal politics 471, 474-8
Fouad, Ahmed 20, 502
Fouad, Sekina 197
Fox News 260
France 10, 35, 223
Francisco, Sami 278
fraternization 213
Freedom and Justice Party (FJP) 281, 441, 444, 448, 461, 462, 474-7, 483, 485, 487, 488, 505, 516, 523, 537, 551-3, 577

Freedom House courses 168
Freedom Now. *See* Popular Campaign for Change (PCC)
freedom of expression 214
Freedom Party 475
free education 44, 46, 343
Free Egyptians Party 446, 475, 487, 545, 582
Free Egyptian Youth 231-3
free elections 372, 407, 426
free market 74, 342
Free Officer Command Cell 16, 26
Free Officers 13, 16-21, 23-36, 43, 56, 59, 61
freer electoral system 86
Free Union of Egyptian University Students 139
'Free Women of Egypt' 479
Free Youth of Egypt 171
French Revolution 326, 336
Frerichs, Sabine 338, 339
'Friday for Rescuing the Revolution' 429
'the Friday for the Application of Shari'a' 518
'Friday for the Purge and Prosecution' 429
Friday of Defining Demands (2011) 397
Friday of Persistence (2011) 410
'The Friday of Popular Will and Unity of Ranks' 436
'Friday of Purification and Salvation' 409
Friday of Rage 139, 186, 187, 193, 196, 197, 199-208, 214, 216-20, 224, 269, 273-4, 284-5, 294, 296, 302-3, 317, 325, 391, 431
  Cairo 205-8
  Galaa Bridge 203-5
  Imbaba and Talebiyya 202-3
'Friday of Restitution of Dignity' 552
'the Friday of the Single Demand' 469
Friday of Victory (2011) 397
Front for the Defence of Egyptian Demonstrators (FDEP) 155
funding 34, 73, 92, 359, 402, 406, 440, 449, 545, 547, 559, 562, 627, 633, 647
funeral processions 224-8
Future, The 118
Future Generation Foundation (FGF) 98

Gaballah, Mohammad Fouad   521
El-Gabaly, Hatem   101, 428
Gadallah, Mohamed   259
Gaddafi, Muammar   186, 233
Galaa Bridge   203–5
Gama'a al-Islamiyya   85, 86, 257
El-Gamal, Yehia   397, 430, 461
Gamal El Din, Ahmed   507, 519, 523
Gamal Mansour Group   16
al-Gamasy, Abdel Ghani   69, 71
Ganzouri, Kamal   410, 473, 478, 491, 492, 506
Garana, Zoheir   244, 397, 429
gas pipeline attack   259
Gates, Robert   215, 220, 236
Gates, Robert M.   618
Gaza blockade   130–2
Gaza Strip   33, 35, 39, 130, 131, 664, 668–70
Elgazzar, Helmy   432
General Administration for Conscript Affairs   210
General Administration of Elections   506
General Intelligence Service (GIS)   31, 58, 66, 69, 77, 85, 138, 144, 157, 209, 210, 242, 254, 275, 291, 393, 399–404, 406, 430, 512, 513, 516, 643, 666
General Investigations Service   31, 64
General Security Division   209
General Security Forces   211
Germany   11, 629, 630
Ghad Party   58, 143, 147, 154, 176, 197, 226, 235, 249, 290, 291, 443, 475
Ghafour, Emad Abdel   507
Ghali, Youssef Boutros   221, 429
Ghany, Safwat Abdel   507
El-Ghazali Harb, Osama   197, 443
El Gheriany, Hossam   491
Ghonim, Wael   152, 157, 167, 168, 197, 200, 259, 260, 262
Ghozlan, Mahmoud   192, 493
Gibbs, Robert   216
Gilad, Amos   666
Gini coefficient   339
Giza   114, 131, 135, 191, 198, 199, 202–8
Giza Security Directorate   285
El-Gizawy, Ahmed   642
global financial crisis (2008)   539

Gomaa, Ali   627
Gomaa, Shaarawi   65
González, Felipe   366
Google   200
Government of National Salvation   474
grassroots movement   396, 404, 432, 617, 651
Greater Cairo   194, 196, 203, 206, 207, 226, 251, 258
Gross Domestic Product (GDP)   45, 71, 73, 78, 92, 98, 102, 103, 337, 339, 530, 531, 534, 540
Guardian   404
guerrilla attacks   17, 33, 35, 112
Guevara, Che   127
Guidance Bureau   191, 217, 229–32, 243, 257, 422, 425, 431, 441, 494, 544, 552, 565
Guidance Council   491
Guidance Office   176
Gül, Abdullah   660
Gulf Cooperation Council (GCC) countries   641–56
Gulf of Aqaba   40, 64
Gulf War (1991)   80, 85, 90
Gurion, David Ben   41

Hadi, Ibrahim Abdel   28
Hadi, Mohammed Abdel   282
Hagel, Chuck   555, 621, 622
Hague, William   629, 631
half-per cent society   13
Hamad, Emir Tamim bin   233, 650
el-Hamalawy, Hossam   150
Hamas   200, 229, 253, 512, 520, 544, 562, 652, 665, 666, 670
Hamas espionage case   511
Hamedi, Zoheir   6
Hamid, Nasser Abdel   171–2
Hamzawy, Amr   174
Haniyeh, Ismail   512
Harb, Shadi Ghazali   199
Harb, Talaat   12
Al-Hariri, Abu Al-Izz   222
Hassan, Ammar Ali   175
Hassan, Mansour   478
Hassan II (king)   96
El Hawary, Yasser   197
Hawwa, Huda   6

Hebron battle (2002)   118
Hegazy, Abdel Aziz   461
Hegazy, Mahmoud   433
Hegazy, Safwat   244, 284
Hegel, Georg Wilhelm Friedrich   456
Heikal, Mohamed Hassanein   62, 175
Hellyer, H. A.   509
Helmy, Atef   581
Henish, Halem   183, 188
Henry, Clement   87
Heshmat, Gamal   163
Hezbollah   200, 253, 260
High Court   173, 176, 185, 192
higher education reform   138
Higher Executive Committee   40, 43
Higher Policy Committee   71
Hinnebusch, Raymond   68
Hisham Mubarak Law Centre   155, 171, 188, 284, 403
Hitchcock, Chris   8
Hosseini, Qassem   655
household spending   328, 334
House of Representatives   563, 567, 623
housing crisis   106
Housing Ministry   587
Howeidi, Amin   34, 39, 40, 42, 64–6
al-Hudaybi, Hassan   24, 466
al-Hudaybi, Mamun   84
hudud punishments   467
human dignity   4, 7, 340, 341, 412, 476, 479
humanitarian aid   132
human rights   41, 120, 146, 192, 248, 252, 329, 401, 404, 417, 437, 601, 615, 624, 625, 627, 630, 633, 637
Human Rights Watch   248, 585, 587
Huntington, Samuel   353
Hurshid Pasha   110
Hussein (king)   41, 96
Hussein, Magdy Ahmed   119, 132
Hussein, Mahmoud   431
Hussein, Salahuddin   127
al-Husseini, Saad   277
Hussein Tawfiq Group   16

Ibrahim, Hassan   22
Ibrahim, Mohamed   293, 511, 529, 549, 581
Ibrahim, Samira   479

Ibrahim, Talaat   515
ideological polarization   357, 358
Idries, Mohamed Elsaeed   502
Illicit Gains Authority   429
Imam, Sheikh   42
Imbaba   198, 199, 202–3
imperialism   22, 24
income   324–9, 334, 531
incrementalism   353
Independent Federation of Farmers   552
Independent Federation of Unions   397
Independent Universities Movement   121
industrialization   32, 37, 44, 47, 53, 336, 342, 392
inflation   535, 539
Institute of Egypt   479
intergenerational tensions   138, 139
interim government   409
Interior Ministry   23, 68, 72, 76, 77, 85, 121, 136, 146, 147, 167, 176, 178, 183, 186, 190, 191, 193, 194, 201, 206, 208–11, 213, 225, 226, 228, 230, 233, 234, 263, 292, 295, 297, 401, 425, 471, 506, 536, 548, 549, 553, 559, 581, 587
Internal Security Directorate   31
international agreements   125
International Atomic Energy Agency (IAEA)   151
International Bank for Reconstruction and Development (IBRD)   34
International Defence Industry Fair   662
International Federation of Journalists   168
International Labour Organization (ILO)   126
international military campaigns   10
International Monetary Fund (IMF)   53, 81, 82, 90–2, 589
International reactions and fall of Mubarak
  China's position on January revolution and SCAF phase   637–41
  European-Egyptian relations   626–34
  Gulf Cooperation Council (GCC) countries   641–54
  Iranian position during SCAF rule   654–60
  Israel   564–70

Russia and interim phase 634–7
Turkey 660–4
United States 617–26
international support 574–8
internet 193–4, 197, 209, 300
inter-party cooperation 155
Inter-Party Coordination Committee (IPCC) 270, 275, 278, 289
IP tracking 209
Iran 253, 260, 437, 512
Iranian Foreign Ministry 658
Iranian Interests Bureau 654
Iranian Interests Section 512
Iranian revolution 250, 465
Iraq 25, 26, 55, 117, 119, 175, 224, 343, 572
Iraq-Iran war (1980–8) 78
Iraq war (2003) 117, 118, 136
Iron Guard 16, 18
al-Isawi, Ahmed 92, 93
Ishaq, George 152
Iskandar, Laila 581
Iskander, Amin 119
Islam 12, 13, 38, 85, 466
Islamic awakening 655, 657
Islamic charity fund 537
Islamic Group (IG, al-Gama'a al-Islamiyya) 84, 423, 424, 446
Islamic identity 422, 452, 573, 611
Islamic Labour Party 119, 132
Islamic Quartet 633, 646, 655, 657
Islamic Republic 465
Islamic revolution 655
Islamism 36, 444
Islamist movements 3, 83, 366, 422, 436, 444, 455, 462, 469, 486, 513, 554, 591, 596, 607–13, 632, 633, 638, 667, 678
Islamist parties 444, 596, 607
Islamist Pioneer and Renaissance Parties 476
Islamists 12, 43, 51, 57, 64, 73–6, 89, 113, 118, 130, 131, 162, 305, 347, 358, 360, 363, 374, 423, 425, 426, 436, 443, 446, 450, 455, 460, 464, 465, 476, 478, 511, 563, 572, 651
Islamization 85
Ismail, Ahmed Tawfiq 69
Ismail, Al Nabawi 72
Ismail, Mamdouh 100, 104
Israel 34, 35, 39–41, 54, 55, 60, 64, 69, 70, 115, 116, 126, 128, 131, 138, 146, 215, 250, 251, 253, 391, 409
 agreement and relations with Egypt 42, 70, 71, 133, 438, 439, 508, 626, 654, 663–70
 attack on Gaza and Sinai 64, 65, 132, 260, 270, 520, 658, 665, 668
 embassy incident 438–40
 invasion of Lebanon (2006) 260
Israel Export and International Cooperation Institute 666
Istiqama Mosque 198, 199
Italy 10
Ittihadiyya events (2012) 516, 519, 522–4, 565

January revolution. *See* Egyptian revolution, 2011
Jews 257
jihadi Salafism 38, 85
jihadist movements 466
jihadists 425, 562
Johnson, Lyndon 40
Joint Arab Economic Report 532, 533
Joint Defence Council 41
Jordan 215, 339, 620, 661
Journalists for Change 120
Journalists' Syndicate 145, 149, 165, 172, 195
Judges' Club 42, 158–65, 521, 553, 563
judges' massacre (1969) 42, 159, 162
judicial reforms 160, 161
judiciary movement 158–65
Juhayna Food Industries 537
July Republic 3, 20–55, 68, 342, 382, 404, 428, 474
 Arab socialism and Nasserism 36–43
 consolidating power within Free Officers 26–36
 Nasser's legacy 43–7
 presidential system and president's party 55–9
 social mobilization 23–6
July revolution 100, 112
Justice and Development Party (AKP, Turkey) 362, 444, 662, 663

Justice and Development Party (JDP, Morocco)   444
Justice Conference   162
Justice Party   422

Kafr al-Dawwar incident   113, 122
Kamel, Abbas   559
Kamel, Basem   171, 198
Kamshish   128
Kandahar Friday   436, 451
Kandahar Two   518
Kandil, Hazem   68, 79, 225, 387
Kandil, Wael   174, 502
Karam Abu Salem terrorist attack   507, 508
Karama (Dignity) Party   119, 154, 172, 176, 443, 475, 487
Karmouz and al-Hadra   296
Kasr El Dobara church   254
Kassem, Abdul Karim   25, 83, 85, 438
Elkatatny, Mohamed Saad   197, 229, 255, 441, 505, 507
Kazziha, Walid   135
Kefaya. *See* Egyptian Movement for Change (EMC)
keffiyeh   117
El-Kelany, Ahmed   282
Kerry, John   555, 574, 575, 619, 622, 625, 670
Khaled, Alaa   288
Khaled bin al-Walid Street   295
Khaled Islambouli Street   654
Khaled Saeed protests (2010)   289
Khalifa, Hamad bin   644, 648
Khalil, Wael   502
Khamanei, Ali   657
Khan, Imran   559
al-Khazen, Jihad   223
al-Khazindar, Ahmed   15
Khrushchev, Nikita   26
Kirkpatrick, David   557
Kissinger, Henry   43
Know Your Rights campaign   419
Korean War   336
Kuwait   574, 587, 644, 645, 651
Kuwait News Agency   652
Kuwait War   117
Kuwaiti Foreign Ministry   652
Kuwaiti Kharafi Group   559

labour activism   457, 472
Labour and Unions Observatory   125
labour market   338, 532
labour mobilizations   110, 113, 120–2, 124, 344
labour movement   104, 120–3
Labour Party   117, 154, 176, 446
labour protests   457–9
Labour Rights and Freedoms Coordinating Committee   125
labour unions   110, 267
land reform   32, 36, 44, 45, 94, 106, 127, 343
land reform law (1952)   45
Land Reform Peasants' Solidarity Committee   129
Latif Hamdan, Mohammed Abdul   285
Latin America   358
Lavie, Limor   464, 465
Lavon, Pinhas   31
Lavon affair (1954)   31
Lavrov, Sergey   634, 635
Law 1/2011   384
Law 2/2013   551
Law 4/1968   67
Law 12/2011   440
Law 17/2012   485
Law 25/1966   63
Law 34/2011   405
Law 35/1976   125
Law 38/1972   485
Law 39/1979   78
Law 40/1977   440
Law 43/1974   80, 81
Law 45/2011   394
Law 46/1972   160
Law 47/2005   392
Law 48/1979   161
Law 65/1971   80
Law 69/1974   161
Law 73/1956   440
Law 96/1992   94, 127
Law 120/2011   485
Law 127/1980   71
Law 150/1964   161
Law 162/1958   38
Law 179/1953   32
Law 203/1991   98
Lebanon   175

leftists 19, 25, 50, 51, 112–14, 123, 305, 319, 446, 465, 476
legislative elections 164, 253, 419, 555
  1995 86
  2010 148
León, Bernardino 575, 578, 632
lethal force 186, 205, 209–11
liberal democracy 23, 368
liberalism 456
liberalization 92, 361
liberal parties 443
liberals 86, 117, 288, 290, 313, 432, 465, 476
Liberation Rally 23, 24, 60
Libya 337, 340, 595
Libyan revolution 225
Lieberman, Avigdor 667
Lijphart, Arend 354
Linz, Juan J. 352, 353, 359
Lipset, Seymour Martin 353
list vs. single-ticket system 447–9
live ammunition 113, 192, 197, 210, 211, 283, 303, 471, 478, 580
living standards 98, 214, 300, 323, 325, 336, 531
Livni, Tzipi 670
Lotfy, Ali 97
Lotfy, Islam 172, 190, 191, 199
Luxor massacre (1997) 85
Luxor temples 543

Mabrouk, Abdel Wahab 508
McClure, Mandy 8
McDonough, Denis 618
Mady, Abou Elela 115, 119, 432, 444, 478, 507, 516
El Maghrabi, Ahmed 244, 397, 429
al-Mahalawy, Ahmed 453
Mahalla Al-Kubra 120, 122–5, 142, 144–7, 150, 155, 269–78, 344, 523, 552
  29–31 January 274–6
  countryside takes charge 276–8
  Friday of Rage 273–4
  Joining Tahrir 278
  security forces recover 272–3
  unions and politics in Egyptian revolution 269–72
Mahalla Weavers' Association 142
Mahatta Square 301, 303

el-Mahdy, Osama 183, 191
Maher, Ahmed 14, 168, 232, 502, 559, 586
Maher, Aly 20, 59
Mahfouz, Naguib 85
El-Mahgoub, Abdul Salam 428
el-Mahgoub, Rifaat 84
Mahmoud, Abdel Meguid 244, 397, 437, 515, 553
Mahmoud, Ahmed 281
Mahmoud, Hany 6, 191, 197, 213, 234, 235
Mahmoud, Mohammed 14, 223
Mahmoud, Mostafa 171
Mahmoud, Sedky 41
Mahran, Samy 481
Mahsoob, Mohamed 525
Maklad, Shahenda 197, 523
Malek, Hassan 536, 537
al-Maliki, Nouri 512
Manassa massacre (2013) 586
Mandate Friday 584
Man on Horseback, The (Finer) 570
Manour, Adly 581
Manpower Development Committee 568
Manshiyya Square 156
Mansour, Abdelrahman 157, 166
Mansour, Adly 511, 566, 577, 579, 650
Mansour, Mohamed 101, 167, 338
Mansour, Mortada 242, 402, 493
Maoism 22
March 1919 revolution 442–3
Maree, Mamdouh 428
marginalization 71, 107, 129, 262, 279, 300, 497, 578
Marinab Church incident 454
market economy 87, 103, 393, 458, 459, 472, 536
Mar Mina Church 454
Martyrs' Mosque 286
Marxism 36
Marxist left 112
Marxist parties 362
Marx, Karl 366
Maspero 450, 451
Maspero massacre (2011) 172, 454, 480
Masr, Mohamed Abu 282
Masry Club 488

El-Massry, Mahienour 296
Maswood, Javed 388
Matariyya 205
media discourse 213, 595, 601
media freedom 84, 546, 547, 567
media ownership 406, 545, 546
Medvedev, Dmitry 636
Mehwar 207
Mekki, Ahmed 491, 509, 553
Mekki, Mahmoud 164
El-menawy, AbdelLatif 222, 241, 265
Merkel, Angela 251, 630
Michael, Emad 453
middle class 12, 13, 15, 19, 36, 37, 59, 61, 78, 101–3, 107, 120, 174, 259, 272, 305, 337, 338, 340, 344, 345
Middle East 250
Middle East Defence Organization (MEDO) 22
Middle East News Agency 401
military behaviour 378, 379
military-Brotherhood relationship 427
military budget 71, 73
military college 13, 15
military coup 5, 6, 18, 19, 24, 59, 75, 130, 218, 249, 264, 320, 321, 359, 360, 381, 382, 390, 402, 403, 502, 504, 555, 621–6, 663
military courts 63, 64, 86, 132, 387, 404, 405, 479, 480
Military Criminal Police 64
military dictatorship 60, 593
military economy 79, 342, 343
military establishment 12, 59, 220, 228, 378, 379, 384, 390–4, 403, 406, 408, 462, 467, 468, 551, 554, 561, 568
military hegemony 59–66
Military Intelligence Service 39, 64, 242, 245, 379, 402, 406, 463, 499, 509–11, 589
Military Justice Code 405
military leadership 369, 382, 390, 393, 470
military liars (Askar Kazeboon) campaign 478–86
military organizations 392
military police 378, 386, 403, 439, 455, 499
military politics 59–65

Military Prosecution 211
military regime 35, 79, 88, 635, 658
military service 9, 62, 63, 71, 78
million-man march (*milyoniyya*) 200, 231, 245, 294, 397, 410, 429–31, 436, 451, 469, 494, 510, 516, 579, 584, 665
Ministry of Culture 404
Ministry of Defence 434
Ministry of Health 451, 516, 523, 585
Ministry of Health and Population 455
Ministry of Information 233
Ministry of Justice 160
Ministry of Labour 125
Ministry of Local Government 63, 125
Ministry of Military Production 392, 568
Ministry of National Guidance 37
Ministry of War 63
Misr, Banque 35
Misr, Emaar 587
al-Misri, Aziz 17
Misr Spinning and Weaving strike 113, 114, 122–5
Mitchell, Timothy 93
mobile phones 95, 103
modernization 10–12, 22, 32, 36, 43, 45, 88, 352
Mogamma 258
Mohamed, Safwan 292
Mohamed, Taha 170
Mohammed Mahmoud events 469–74, 488, 494, 519, 581
Mohammed Mahmoud Square 208
Mohammed Mahmoud Street 187, 230, 233, 488
Moharram Bek 296
Mohieddin, Khaled 25–7, 35, 42, 65
Mohieddin, Zakaria 27, 64
Mohsen, Mohammad 434
Molcho, Yitzhak 668
Mollet, Guy 34
Molotov cocktails 197, 225, 242, 303, 478, 552
Mo'men, Mohammad 537
Mo'men Group 537
Moneim, Abdo Abdel 167
Monofiya 127
monopolization 43, 229, 300–1, 329
monopoly capitalists 74, 95

Morale Department 231
Morocco 339
Morqos, Anba 177
al-Morra, Galal 568, 570, 572
Morsi, Mohamed 3, 56, 73, 170, 191, 219, 229, 242, 248, 249, 255, 258, 321, 390, 407, 432, 435, 441, 458, 459, 483, 486, 490, 492, 494, 497–8, 502, 542, 544, 548, 550, 551, 553–8, 562, 564–6, 568–73, 576–9, 581, 583, 586, 588, 589, 601, 619–26, 629, 631, 634, 635, 639, 645, 646, 655–8, 661, 662, 668, 669
  constitutional declaration 517–29
  economy in transitional phase 529–42
  as elected president 504–16
  gulf policies 646–54
  visit to Brussels (2012) 628–9
Moscow 634–7
Mossad attacks (1954) 31
Mostafa Mahmoud Square 171–3, 183, 184, 204, 236, 238, 251
Moussa, Abdo 6, 498, 622
Moussa, Amr 235, 254, 486, 517, 522, 645
Moustafa, Tamir 161
Mowafi, Murad 508
Mubarak Alaa 438
Mubarak, Gamal 79, 81, 82, 87, 89, 91, 94, 95, 98–100, 135, 138, 152, 178, 221–3, 233, 240, 244, 247, 265, 280, 293, 325, 344, 380, 392, 428, 438, 459
Mubarak, Hosni 3–6, 55–8, 68, 71–3, 76–91, 94–7, 100–10, 116–17, 120, 123, 125–8, 132, 133, 135, 137, 141, 143, 148, 151, 152, 158, 161, 162, 166, 169, 175, 178, 183, 186, 190, 195, 205, 207, 212, 214, 216–24, 228–31, 233–40, 243–59, 262–8, 271, 276–8, 281, 285, 286, 290, 298, 300, 301–4, 325, 329, 338, 342–6, 354, 356, 360, 368–72, 374, 376–80, 382–96, 400, 402, 403, 408, 410, 417, 419, 424–30, 434–8, 442–8, 451, 453, 457, 468, 470, 482, 483, 486, 489, 493, 503, 535, 538, 546, 556, 558, 561, 564, 570, 580, 582, 586, 587, 597, 615–21, 625, 626, 633–8, 641–3, 650, 653, 654, 665, 668, 669, 671, 676, 677

Mubarak and Sons, Inc. 101
Mullen, Mike 236, 618
Multinational Force and Observers 438
multiparty system 443, 444, 554, 678
municipal elections 430
Muslim Brotherhood 12–16, 21, 23–6, 31, 38, 41, 58, 64, 76, 82–6, 89, 91, 114, 135–41, 148, 151, 154–6, 163, 164, 168, 170–3, 176, 184, 186, 191, 195, 197–200, 203, 217, 218, 221, 226, 228–32, 239, 243, 247, 248, 250–2, 255–7, 260–3, 270, 275–7, 280, 281, 290, 291, 295, 297, 298, 301, 305, 319, 321, 344, 357, 360–3, 369, 370, 374–6, 385, 395, 398, 408, 410, 414, 417, 419–23, 425–7, 431–2, 436, 440–7, 450, 453, 458, 460–7, 469, 470, 472, 474–7, 480–3, 486, 488, 490–4, 496, 503–5, 508, 513, 515, 516, 523, 529, 536, 537, 549–55, 560–2, 564, 565, 569, 570, 574–81, 584, 585, 587, 618, 619, 624, 632, 635, 636, 644, 647, 648, 655, 657, 661, 670, 677, 678
Muslims 450, 451, 453, 454, 553
Mustafa, Abdel Galil 154, 197
'My Name Is Khaled Saeed' (Facebook page) 157
My Right 155

Nafaa, Hassan 152, 154, 502
Naguib, Fathi 482
Naguib, Mohamed 17, 18, 23–4, 26–30, 59–60
Nagy, Ahmed 299
Nahda Project 459
Nahda square 577, 582, 585, 586, 624, 632
al-Nahhas, Mustafa 12–13, 17, 30, 112
Nahia approach 202
Nahia demonstration 184–5, 196, 198
Nahia Street 169–71, 173, 176, 183–5
Al Nahyan, Abdullah bin Zayed 641
Naim, Mohamed 7
Naim, Sameer 108
Nasr, Mahmoud 77
Nasr, Salah 31, 39, 60, 64, 65
Nasrallah, Hassan 260
Nasr City 198, 199, 206, 207, 550

Index

Nasr Street 584
Nasser, Gamal Abdel 16, 20–47, 56–68, 78, 82, 91, 94, 100, 112, 117, 122, 127, 141, 159–61, 271, 342, 400, 430, 467, 653
Nasserist movement 577
Nasserist Party 419, 475, 478, 521
Nasserists 48, 51, 52, 82, 83, 113, 119, 123, 131, 142, 154, 173, 217, 235, 249, 511, 582
Natarajan, Usha 388
National Accord Conference (2011) 461
National Alliance to Support Legitimacy and Reject the Coup (NASL) 576
National Assembly 40, 63
National Association for Change (NAC) 135, 136, 138, 151, 154, 171, 176, 186, 197, 216, 222, 223, 300, 301, 385, 409, 431, 446, 448, 494
National Coalition for Syrian Revolution and Opposition Forces 637
National Constituent Assembly 460
National Council for Human Rights (NCHR) 404
National Crisis Management Committee 232
national debt 338, 539
National Defence Council (NDC) 67, 548
National Democratic Party (NDP) 54, 57, 58, 72, 75, 79, 82, 83, 86, 92–9, 135–7, 162–4, 178, 201, 207, 218, 221, 222, 230, 233, 236, 238, 241, 244–6, 248–50, 254–6, 261, 265, 273–8, 280, 286, 293, 298, 300–2, 344, 360, 361, 368, 371, 374, 375, 389, 390, 400, 410, 413, 417, 419, 433, 440, 442, 443, 448, 450, 451, 454, 455, 460, 475, 482, 489, 498, 514, 551
national dialogue 214, 221, 245, 248–51, 255, 257, 259–63, 267, 347, 461, 524
   parties 248
   struggle between elites 249–51
National Front for Change (NFC) 409, 447
National Front for Democracy and Justice 480
National Guard 28, 63

national identity 10, 110, 125, 529, 557
nationalism 74, 117
Nationalist Party of Egypt 476
nationalists 17, 36, 42, 51, 60, 112, 114, 115, 186, 288, 319, 464
nationality 461
nationalization 25, 32, 34–7, 44, 45, 60, 88, 122
National Police Day 17, 166, 167, 173, 270, 283
National Progressive Unionist Party (NPUP) 117, 443
national reconciliation 428, 624
National Salvation Front (NSF) 402, 486, 517, 521, 522, 525, 526, 555–8, 581, 583
national security 40, 122, 152, 209, 215, 250, 253, 401
National Security Agency (NSA) 401, 402, 405
National Security Council 528
National Security Staff (NSS) 618
National Service Projects Organization (NSPO) 392, 587, 588
National Union 60, 159
national unity 26, 32, 254
national unity government 196, 223, 232, 252, 256, 619, 624
National Workers' and Students' Committee 14, 112
Nawwar, Salah 128
Nazif, Ahmed 49, 89, 150, 190, 209, 221, 384, 400
NDP Policies Committee 83, 89, 178, 223, 410
neoconservatives 58, 86, 138, 163
neocons' policy 136
neoliberal government 95
neoliberalism 92, 105, 343, 344, 459
neoliberal policy 79, 124, 174, 338, 458, 536
Netanyahu, Benjamin 667–70
New Wafd 442
New York Times 102
Nezeily, Ahmed 191, 192, 230
Nidaa Tounes 358
Non-Aligned Movement 33, 646
Non-Aligned Movement summit (2012) 655

non-aligned nations summit 512
non-capitalist model 26
non-democratic forces 452, 672, 674, 675
non-democratic methods 357
non-Islamist movement 591, 607–15
non-Islamist parties 596, 607
non-Muslim poll tax (*jizya*) 9
Norway 631
'No Surrender: Egypt's Youth Will Take It Back' (Facebook page) 143
Nour, Ayman 58, 151, 226, 443, 475, 493, 507
Nour, Mohammad 432
Nour Party 432, 444, 445, 449, 469, 474–7, 481, 487, 505, 518, 570–4
Nubia 299
al-Nuqrashi, Mahmoud Fahmi 15, 28

Obama, Barack 215–16, 220, 233, 240, 246, 260, 263, 266, 569, 618–25, 641, 665
Obama administration 175, 216, 569, 618
Occupy Wall Street 434
October War 69
O'Donnell, Guillermo 352, 353, 362
Office of the Commander-in-Chief for Political Guidance 60
Office of the Defence Minister 538
Officers' Club 18
Officers' Republic 76–9
Official Gazette 493
oil exports 92
oil revenues 55, 81, 82, 103
El Okdah, Farouk 529
Old Security Directorate 158
ONTV 200, 236
opening up (*infitah*) 80, 81, 105
Operation Black Arrow (1955) 33
Order of the Nile 152
Organization of Islamic Cooperation (OIC) 655–7
Osman, Osman Ahmed 97
al-Oteifi, Bassem 211
Othman, Amin 14
Ottaway, David 100
Ottoman Empire 10–12
Ouda, Ziyad 115
Overseas Security Advisory Council 575

Palestine 15, 17, 18, 20, 41, 52, 117, 119, 120, 130–3, 300, 343, 665–6, 668
Palestinian solidarity committee 119
pan-Arabism 37, 38, 60, 117–19, 130, 270
Panetta, Leon 665
Paris Peace Conference 111
parliamentary elections 249, 253, 374, 419, 421, 435, 445, 449, 471, 474–8, 480, 547, 567, 627, 630, 672–3
  2005 280
  2010 155, 221, 222, 280, 344
  2011 363, 443
  2015 475, 573
parliamentary system 15, 253
partisan politics 11, 32, 136, 138, 388, 432
party affiliations 319
patriotism 76, 200, 212
patron-client relationships 83, 87, 88, 342
Patterson, Anne 555, 650
Paul, Rand 624
peaceful protest (2001–8) 134
peace treaty 54, 71, 409, 438
peasantry 23, 45
Penal Code 86
Pentagon 220
People's Assembly 56–8, 67, 84, 114, 126, 131, 162, 233, 262, 378, 383–4, 386, 390, 415–18, 420, 427, 442, 463, 468, 478–88, 491, 493–5, 502, 505, 515, 520, 526, 528, 553, 571, 627, 644, 666
People's Assembly elections 86, 118, 415, 420, 526, 551, 563
People's Committee for the Defence of the Revolution 480
People's Committee to Protect the Revolution 551
People's Court 27, 31
People's Parliament 232
People's Party 111
Peres, Shimon 544
petty thugs (*baltagiyya*) 68, 194, 199
Philosophy of the Revolution (Nasser) 30
Pinochet, Augusto 575, 586
pluralism 30, 75, 87, 393
  intra-elite 75
  party 48, 87, 94

pluralistic democracy 23, 355, 357, 372
pluralistic party system 19
police abuses 102, 150, 166, 252
police stations, attack on 205–8, 212
police violence 28, 90, 112, 132, 143, 150, 156, 157, 166, 175
political activism 144, 145
political activists 123, 156, 178
political activity 137, 139, 298
political blogging 149
political change 118, 120, 134, 135, 139
political culture 118, 364, 373, 374, 377, 412, 426, 590, 634
political discourse 22, 122, 145
political elites 40, 45–7, 55, 82, 148, 185, 249, 261, 274, 276, 277, 280, 300, 352, 353, 355, 358–60, 376, 386, 464, 513, 590, 674, 675
political forces 4–6, 154, 165, 170, 200, 216, 218, 257, 270, 273, 281, 301, 347, 356–8, 361, 363–5, 372–5, 395, 397, 409, 410, 416, 420, 425, 426, 432, 439, 442, 463, 467, 473, 477, 483, 497, 517, 519, 521, 556, 560, 565, 576, 580, 621, 626
political freedom 37, 81, 87, 91, 218
political leadership 39, 62, 66, 160, 353
political liberalization 163, 322, 336, 337, 343, 443
political movements 16, 19, 114, 136, 146, 175, 192, 195, 271, 280, 289, 396, 448, 583
political parties 23–6, 29, 32, 119, 124, 130, 141, 142, 155, 156, 168, 195, 217–20, 248, 249, 262, 270, 277, 281, 343, 344, 347, 352, 356, 362, 369, 370, 376, 377, 383, 385, 389, 393, 396–8, 419, 420, 425, 432, 439, 440, 442, 443, 447, 456, 460, 461, 469, 482, 483, 490, 505, 510, 516, 521, 526, 549, 550, 561, 603, 610, 611, 673
Political Parties Committee (PPC) 398, 440, 442
Political Partics Section 398
political pluralism 32, 44, 329, 330, 560, 596, 598
political polarization 556, 571
political revolution 20, 232, 322, 326

political rights 32, 87, 134, 148, 319, 353, 366, 414, 417, 440–9, 598
political system 9, 22, 148, 153, 170, 393
politicization 144, 364
Popular Campaign for Change (PCC) 120, 235, 249
Popular Campaign to Support Baradei 154, 157
Popular Coalition for Change 235, 249
Popular Committee to End the Blockade 130
Popular Current 521
Popular Democratic Movement for Change (HASHD) 176
Popular Front for Change 261
popular movements 5, 12, 277, 322
Popular Socialist Alliance Party (SPAP) 446, 475–6, 521
population growth 105, 531
Port Said Central Prison 548
Port Said coal heavers' strike (1882) 110
Port Said Criminal Court 548
Port Said massacre (2012) 488–90, 548
post-revolutionary period 109, 322, 326, 376, 675
post-revolution constitution 362
poverty 101–3, 107, 289, 300, 323, 329, 338, 339, 343, 538, 540
poverty line 106, 300, 327, 328, 339, 540
pre-Islamic paganism ('new Jahiliyya') 38
Presidential Council 62
Presidential Election Commission 485
presidential elections 163, 175, 216, 252, 265, 268, 381, 419, 441, 477, 485, 526, 528, 557, 558, 566, 567, 579, 588, 627, 631, 644
  2000 86
  2005 443
  2011 151
  2012 258, 387
  run-up to 490–9, 502–5
private press 200, 270, 547
private property 161, 183, 274, 329, 362, 366
private-public partnerships 80
private sector 45, 53, 56, 78, 83, 92, 124, 125, 337, 392, 393, 429, 459, 620, 662

privatization   79, 81, 87, 88, 90–3, 95, 96, 98, 342, 393
procedural democracy   456
Progressive Youth Coalition (PYC)   319
'Project for a Nation'   151
property rights   129, 161
property tax clerks' strike   125–7
protest in modern Egypt   110–65
  6 April Movement and general strike   145–7
  1919 uprising   110
  bloggers and technological upsurge   149–51
  against British forces   111
  Cairo cigarette rollers' strike (1899)   110
  death of Saeed   156–8
  in final years of Mubarak   133–5
  Judges' Club and independent judiciary movement   158–65
  labour mobilizations in Kafr al-Dawwar (1952)   113
  labour movement and social movements   142–4
  under Mubarak   116–17
  Mubarak's last decade and social movements   117–21
  Muslim Brotherhood and social movements   135–41
  National Association for Change (NAC) and political participation   151–6
  Palestine issue   130–3
  Port Said coal heavers' strike (1882)   110
  protests against Sidqi   111
  rebellion against Hurshid Pasha (1805)   110
  resistance against Napoleon (1798–1801)   110
  social protests (see social protests)
  student occupation of Tahrir Square (1972)   113, 118
  Urabi revolt (1881–2)   110
protest movements   5, 91, 134, 136, 140, 141, 145–8, 152, 172, 189, 195, 196, 269, 284, 340, 343, 345, 360, 380, 396, 447
Przeworski, Adam   364–6

Public Debt Administration   10
public funds   428, 429
Public Notary Office   558
public opinion   35, 85, 150, 156, 326, 329–31, 437, 483, 546, 590, 633, 637, 667
  on 25 January revolution, Arab revolutions and Arab Spring   591–7
  assessing existing democracy   602–7
  attitudes towards democracy   599–602
  concept of democracy   597–9
  on Islamist and non-Islamist political movements   607–14
public property   273, 297, 303
Public Prosecution   159, 428, 429
public sector   32, 37, 45–7, 53, 56, 61, 74, 76, 78, 79, 81, 83, 89, 98, 143, 342, 394, 429
Public Transit Authority   458
Putin, Vladimir   634–7

Qader, Abdel   271, 272
Qader, Ahmed Abdel   270
Qaed Ibrahim Mosque   297, 298, 453
Qaed Ibrahim Square   480
Qandil, Hamdi   502, 529, 562, 564, 581, 668
Qandil, Hisham   506, 507, 513
al-Qaradawi, Sheikh Yusuf   465
Al-Qasas, Mohamed   172, 184, 225
Qasr al-Aini Street   187
Qasr al-Nil Bridge   185, 204, 205, 246
Qatar   534, 538, 541–3, 644, 649, 652
Qatari Foreign Ministry   652
El-Qazzaz, Omar   168
Qorqor, Magdy   119
Qualifying industrial one (QIZ)   496, 666
Qubba Military Hospital   507
Qutb, Sayyid   38

Raba'a al-Adawiyya Square   565, 573, 575–9, 582, 632, 652
Raba'a massacre   578, 632
El Rabbat, Maha   581
Rachid, Rachid Mohamed   429
radical Islamists   90
Radwan, Fathi   30
Ragab, Mohamed   283

El Raggal, Aly   195, 297
Rahman, Hassan Abdel   6, 137
Ramez, Hisham   529
Raml district   400
Ramses Square   132, 136, 207, 578
Elraouf, Waleed Abd   171
Rasd network   155
Rashad, Youssef   16
Rashwan, Diaa   559
Rassd News Facebook page   168, 197
Rateb, Hassan   201
rational bureaucracy   88
Red Crescent   131, 261
Reform and Development Party (RDP)   476, 487
reformist revolution   5, 345
regime leaders, trials of   427–38
religious education   139
religious-secular conflict   560
religious state (*dawla diniyya*)   466
rentier economy   81
rentier income   89
repression   26, 38, 68, 90, 94, 102, 160, 325, 373, 395, 408, 580
Republican Guard   27, 205, 265, 268, 579
Republic of Tahrir   220, 236
   army and people   237
   Brotherhood declaration   230
   creation   233–6
   emotional speech   237–40
   Ezz, Ahmed   221–4
   Free Egyptian Youth   231–3
   funeral processions for martyrs   224–8
   sit-in continues   228–9
resistance against landlords   127
Revolutionary Command Council (RCC)   22, 24, 25, 27–30, 56, 65, 517
Revolutionary Democratic Coalition   521
revolutionary movements   4, 62, 148, 196, 198, 258, 398, 400, 403–10, 428, 433, 480, 481, 494
Revolutionary Socialists   154, 172, 176
Revolutionary Youth Coalition (RYC)   6, 190, 251–4, 258, 261, 267, 369, 374, 396–7, 399, 431, 433, 448, 450, 451
revolutionary youths   252, 262, 305–21, 380, 432, 433, 447, 469, 473, 475, 522
Revolution Continues Alliance (RCA)   476

Revolution Square. *See* Shoun Square
Rhodes, Ben   618, 623, 641, 649
Rifaat, Ahmed   438
El Rifai, Yahya   160, 162
Riyadh   641–3, 646, 653, 655
Rogers, William   43
Rogers Plan (1970)   43
Roll-on Roll Agreement (Ro-Ro, 2012)   661
Rommel, Erwin   17
Rompuy, Herman Van   629
Roosevelt, Kermit   21
al-Roueini, Hassan   267, 582
Rover Scouts (*gawwala*)   14
Royce, Ed   623
Rushdi, Ahmed   76, 84
Russia   634–6
Russian Foreign Ministry   635
Russian Revolution   336
Rustow, Dankwart   365

Saad, Mohamed   284
Sabahi, Hamdeen   115, 119, 226, 239, 475, 486, 496, 498, 504, 515, 517, 522, 558, 559, 645
Sabri, Ali   21
Sadat, Anwar   17, 27, 31, 46–58, 61, 65–72, 76, 78, 82, 85, 87, 88, 92, 96, 97, 113–16, 122, 123, 128, 160, 161, 271, 279, 338, 342, 343, 394, 430, 442, 443, 512, 513, 550, 634
Saddam Hussein   574
Sadek, Mohamed   39, 69
Saeed, Khaled   139, 149, 155–8, 166–8, 194, 197, 289, 290, 292, 300, 344
El-Saeed, Momtaz   647
El-Saeed, Refaat   173, 177, 443
Salafist Call   177, 445, 449, 452, 456, 570, 572, 573
Salafist Islah Society   275
Salafist parties   417, 445, 475
Salafists   158, 275, 288, 298, 362, 423, 424, 432, 444, 445, 451–3, 464, 475–7, 480, 481, 488, 517, 526, 570, 572, 573
Salafist sheikhs   276, 277, 301
Salafization   445, 458, 571
Salah, Gaber (Jika)   519
Salama, Hafez   284

Salam Camp   147
Saleh, Amr   199
Saleh, Hatem   537
Salehi, Ali Akbar   654, 658
Salem, Hussein   642
Salem, Mamdouh   30, 72
Salem, Salah   30, 38
Salih, Sobhi   423
Salvation Front   552
Sami, Mahmoud   157, 168, 169, 171, 196
Samir, Mohamed   290, 291, 294, 295
al-Sanhuri, Abdel Razzaq   22
Sarkozy, Nicolas   251
Sartre, Jean-Paul   127
satellite television   406, 546
Satik, Nerouz   6
Saudi Arabia   33, 34, 38, 40, 233, 263, 445, 538, 576, 587, 641–6, 651, 653, 656, 658, 661, 662
Saudi Foreign Ministry   643
Saudi Press Agency   641
Sawiris, Naguib   279, 446, 475, 495
El Sawy, Mostafa   225
Sayed, Daoud Abdel   107
El-sayed, Khaled   6, 170, 184, 231
El Sayed Hegazy, Morsi   649
Sayigh, Yezid   77, 78
Sayyida Zeinab   205
Schiff, Rebecca   386
Schmitt, Carl   413, 580
Schmitter, Philippe C.   352, 353, 362
school education   106, 279, 330
Schumpeter, Joseph   472
Second Intifada (2000)   117, 118, 270, 279
Second World War   13, 14, 24, 122, 336, 640
Secret Apparatus   16
Secret Section   31
sectarian attacks   586
sectarianism   149, 254, 451, 452, 455, 457, 573
sectarian violence   135, 373, 450–7, 553
Secular Copts   177
secularism   464–6
secularists   85, 299, 320, 347, 358, 374, 422, 432, 444, 446, 570, 572
secular parties   476, 526, 583, 588, 602
securitization   122

security forces   36, 37, 44, 47, 48, 50, 51, 57, 59, 68, 72, 75, 77–9, 82–4, 87, 95, 96, 104, 107, 108, 113, 114, 118–20, 123–6, 128–32, 134–6, 138, 142–4, 146, 147, 149, 153, 156–8, 162, 164, 167–9, 172, 173, 175, 176, 178, 183–8, 193, 194, 196, 200, 202, 204–6, 208–12, 218, 225, 226, 228, 244, 248, 268, 271–5, 280–4, 286–96, 298, 300, 301, 303, 340, 343–6, 368, 379, 387, 394, 404, 405, 454, 455, 470, 471, 478, 479, 489, 495, 515, 519, 523, 549, 565, 573, 577, 579–81, 584, 585, 624, 625, 642
Seddik, Youssef Mansour   19
Sedky, Atef   82, 474
Seifan, Samir   6
El-Selmi, Ali   399, 435, 461
Selmi Document   460–70
Senzai, Farid   445
Serageddin, Fouad   28
Al Shaer, Karim   150
Shafie, Hassan   656
el-Shafie, Hussein   31
Shafik, Ahmed   221, 222, 239, 245, 258, 260, 262, 263, 286, 381, 384, 396–400, 403, 408–10, 441, 488, 490, 492, 497–9, 502–4, 619, 645
el-Shahat, Abdel Moneim   158
Shaheen, Hassan   557–9
Shahin, Mamdouh   422, 432–3, 461
Shahin, Sheikh Mazhar   251
Shah Pahlavi   512
al-Shami, Mahmoud   277
Sharaf, Essam   398, 400, 410, 434, 452, 462, 473, 506, 581, 643
Sharaf, Sami   65, 241
Shari'a   57, 94, 366, 421, 426, 436, 451, 462, 464–7, 517, 518, 527, 528, 571, 573, 611, 613, 678
Shari'a Association   131
Sharif, Nawaz   559
Sharm El-Sheikh   39, 102, 108, 265, 268
Sharon, Yitzhak   40
El Sharqawy, Mohamed   150
el-Shater, Khairat   137, 140, 431, 432, 491–3, 536, 574, 577, 579, 644, 648
Shawky, Mostafa   190, 226
El Shazly, Saad   69

Shehab, Moufed   429
Shehab Street   184
Shehata, Mohammad Raafat   508
Sheikh Zuweid   129
Shenouda III (Pope)   233, 627
El-Sherif, Safwat   76, 136, 244, 429
Sherif Pasha   468
Shi'a   643
Shi'i Egyptians   563
Shi'ism   465, 656
El-Shobaki, Amr   174
Shoigu, Sergei   636
Shoman, Ahmed   379
Shorouk   174, 177, 232, 462, 546, 551
Shoun Square   142, 144, 271, 273, 275–7
Shubra al-Kheima   168, 172, 176, 177, 186–7, 198, 205–7, 244
Shura Council   58, 378, 381, 386, 416, 417, 420, 440, 442, 478, 481, 484, 487, 495, 520–2, 552, 553, 563, 564, 566, 568
Sidi Bouzid   108
Sidi Gaber   292
Sidqi, Ismail   111
Sidqi, Mustafa Kemal   16
Simon Bolivar Square   208
Sinai   35, 39, 41, 50, 51, 55, 64, 65, 67, 69, 70, 89, 113, 122, 128–30, 150, 265, 439, 507, 508, 513, 538, 541, 544, 562, 568, 579, 621, 654, 664, 665, 667, 675
Sirri, Hussein   18
Sirrs, Owen   33, 36
El-Sisi, Abdel Fattah   62, 245, 321, 360, 402, 455, 504, 507, 509–11, 524, 525, 534, 543, 550, 551, 555, 558, 559, 564, 566–70, 577, 578, 580–3, 587–9, 619, 621, 623, 625, 626, 630, 632, 636, 637, 640, 645, 650, 653, 659, 660, 662, 663
sitt al-banat (the best of girls)   479
Six-Day War   61, 64
small and medium enterprises (SMEs)   537, 620, 639
SMS text messages   193, 194, 197, 209, 218, 294
Sobhy, Sedki   509
social activism   472
social conditions   101–9
social forces   361, 373, 427
socialism   32, 74
Socialist Party   366, 447
Socialist Renewal   171, 231
social justice   4, 7, 368, 457, 532, 536, 540, 607
social media   143, 146, 152, 156, 157, 172, 175, 198, 289, 290, 294, 345, 375, 376, 439, 544, 546, 547, 556, 647, 648
social movements   95, 117–21, 130, 131, 133, 136, 142–5, 148, 159, 176, 269, 325, 344, 448, 457
social protests   122–30, 174, 343
  Misr Spinning and Weaving strike   122–5
  property tax clerks' strike and first independent union   125–7
  protests on periphery   128–30
  provincial protest   127–8
social security   46, 90, 121
Society of Muslim Brothers   141
socio-economic conditions   132, 194, 337
Sohag University   552
solidarity movement   117
Soliman, Abdel Kareem (Kareem Amer)   150
Soliman, Hani   385
Song Aiguo   639
Sorour, Fathy   233
Soviet Union (USSR)   22, 24, 26, 33–5, 39, 40, 42, 43, 67
Sphinx   543
Spinning and Weaving Company   269
Springborg, Robert   76, 87
SPRING programme   628, 633
state bureaucracy   47, 62, 88, 92, 355, 356, 375, 460, 547, 558
State Council   131, 160, 440, 482
State Department   22, 622
state-directed media   542–7
state of emergency   56, 57, 86, 94, 116, 154, 160, 162, 173, 176, 190, 216, 230, 234, 249, 252, 256, 257, 263, 265, 268, 387, 396, 397, 405, 417, 442, 447, 448, 548, 586, 627
State Security   86, 162, 371, 399, 401, 402, 450
State Security Investigations Service (SSIS). *See* General Intelligence Service (GIS)

Stepan, Alfred   352, 353, 359
Stockholm Peace Appeal (1950)   22
street politics   469–74
student activism   115
Student Bureau   172
student movement   115, 147, 443
student revolution   67
Students for Change   120
student union elections   115
student unions   115, 444
student uprising (1972)   118
subsidies   53, 55, 81, 91, 98, 114
Sudan   11
Suez, deaths in   196
Suez Canal   9–11, 13, 17, 25, 32–5, 43, 45, 60, 69, 70, 90, 338, 538
Suez Canal cities   279, 548, 549
Suez Canal Company   10, 34
Suez Canal Corridor   538
Suez uprising   279–87
  1–11 February   286–7
  25 January   281–3
  26–27 January   283–4
  29 January   285–6
  Friday of Rage   284–5
  preparing for 25 January   280–1
  before revolution   279–80
Sulayman, Sedki   64
Suleiman, Ibrahim   429
Suleiman, Omar   85, 138, 196, 221–3, 231, 233, 235, 239, 245–58, 260–4, 267, 268, 278, 287, 347, 382, 386, 402, 408, 493, 494, 496, 503
Sultan, Essam   493
Sultan, Farouk   482
Sunday of Martyrs   254
Sunni Islamists   465
'Support the Army Friday'   550
supra-constitutional principles   373, 397–8, 435, 436, 460, 462, 467, 469, 481, 673
Supreme Administrative Court   389, 398, 441, 488, 551
Supreme Constitutional Court (SCC)   86, 161, 162, 256, 387, 417, 447, 482–8, 493, 504, 505, 511, 520–2, 527, 528, 552, 553, 557, 563, 566, 567
Supreme Council of Antiquities (CSA)   544
Supreme Council of the Armed Forces   463
Supreme Council of the Armed Forces (SCAF)   65, 67, 77, 237, 249, 250, 264, 265, 268, 299, 361, 364, 368, 370, 380, 381, 383–7, 390–410, 415–23, 425–7, 429–34, 440, 441, 447, 448, 450, 451, 453, 454, 456, 461, 473, 474, 477, 478, 480, 483, 486, 488–95, 497, 499, 502–5, 508–10, 526, 529–32, 536, 542, 547, 564, 566, 568, 581, 582, 619, 627, 629, 634, 637–44, 646, 654–60
  discourse of   403–10
  and revolutionary forces   390–403
Supreme Election Committee   442
Supreme Judicial Council (SJC)   160, 162
Sweden   631
Syria   25, 26, 33, 36, 37, 39–41, 96, 260, 340, 345, 572, 595, 659–61
Syria 2011-2013: Revolution and Tyranny before the Mayhem (Bishara)   6
Syrian revolution   6, 225, 563, 634, 637, 646

Taba bombings   129
El Tafahny, Ahmed   234
Tagammu Party   129, 143, 154, 155, 172, 173, 177, 217, 222, 235, 248, 255, 409, 419, 443, 475
Taher Plan   64
Tahhan, Gehad   142
Tahrir Square   51, 109, 113, 118, 119, 130, 131, 135, 147, 149, 169, 170, 178, 185–7, 194, 196, 199, 205–7, 210, 213, 215, 221, 223, 226, 234, 236, 238, 239, 259, 263, 269, 272, 276, 292, 298, 302, 356, 368, 374, 377–9, 386, 400, 404, 409, 410, 426, 433, 434, 439, 451, 469, 471, 480, 488, 511, 514, 516, 519, 565, 575, 579, 581, 627
Talebiyya   198–9, 202–3
Tallima, Khalid   581
Tamarod movement   459, 555–60, 572, 577, 649, 650
Tammam, Husam   141
Tantawi, Mohammed Hussein   73, 77, 78, 219, 220, 222, 231, 236, 237, 251, 264, 384, 394, 398, 408, 409, 473,

489, 493, 494, 503, 504, 507, 509, 511, 513, 514, 524, 551, 554, 568, 627, 634, 639
Tanzimat reformers 10
Tawadros II (Pope) 568
Tawfiq Pasha (Khedive of Egypt and Sudan 1879-1892) 10
tax base 537
tax revenues 534
al-Tayyeb, Ahmad 245, 563, 564, 568, 656
technocrat government 249
Technology Valley 538
Tehran 512, 645, 646, 654–60
Tel Aviv 670
el-Telmesany, Omar 84, 466
terrorism 86, 162, 210, 401, 584
Tewfik Pasha 10
Thabet, Safwan 537
Al Thani, Tamim bin Hamad 644, 648
Thant, U 39
Third Way List 476
Third World 23, 26, 44, 45, 59, 326, 382, 533, 575, 674
Tiran Straits 35, 39, 40, 42, 64
'Together We Begin for the Sake of Egypt' 461
Toshka project 474
totalitarianism 456
tourism 81, 85, 89, 101, 103, 338, 530, 535, 538, 541
Trager, Eric 218
transitional justice 395, 427, 435, 458
Transportation Ministry 588, 661
Treaty on Strategic Partnership (2009) 636
tribal culture 129
tried-and-tested technique 275
Tripartite Aggression 34, 35, 39
Trump, Donald 620, 621
al-Tuhami, Mohamed 670
Tunisia 5, 10, 55, 108, 147, 156, 157, 167, 170, 173–5, 178, 209, 212, 224, 279, 284, 322, 325, 337, 339, 340, 345, 354, 357, 359, 444, 460, 618, 620, 629, 633, 637
Tunisian revolution 169, 172, 175, 176, 178, 183, 194, 270, 280, 282, 324, 344, 345
Turkey 638
Turkish Ministry of Economy 661
Turkish-Syrian High Level Strategic Cooperation Council 661
Twitter 193, 194

unaffiliated Islamists 318
unaffiliated leftists 318
undemocratic constitution 149, 411, 417
Understanding Revolutions: Opening Acts in Tunisia (Bishara) 5–6
unemployment 105, 106, 120, 199, 214, 235, 279, 300, 329, 337, 532, 535, 539, 540
UN General Assembly 625
UN Human Rights Council 633
Union Party 476
United Arab Command 41
United Arab Emirates (UAE) 576, 587, 641, 643, 645, 647, 648, 650, 653, 658
United Arab Republic (UAR) 25, 36, 37, 41, 45, 62
United Kingdom (UK) 10, 11, 14, 33, 34, 60, 111, 223, 250, 631. *See also* Britain
United States 11, 21, 30, 33–5, 38, 40, 42, 46, 54, 58, 70, 73, 75, 80, 86, 90, 126, 138, 163, 178, 215, 220, 221, 224, 237, 253, 260, 263, 266, 342, 358, 392, 409, 413, 423, 520, 569, 578, 617, 637, 641, 649, 653
  administration 233, 266, 473, 520, 574, 618, 620
  attack on embassies (2012) 620
  commercial relations with Egypt 97
  constitution 413
  economic and military aid to Egypt 620–1
  foreign policy 575
  government 40, 236, 575, 624
  invasion of Iraq (2003) 117, 118, 136, 137, 151, 163, 270
  military 77, 220
  relations with Egypt 22, 132, 220, 383, 496, 620–6
  and SCAF 509
United States Agency for International Development (USAID) 92
unregulated slums 105, 107, 108, 343
UN Security Council 663
Urabi, Ahmed 10

Urabi revolt (1881–2)   12, 110, 468
US Senate   266

Varyag   636
Venezuela   362
'Victory for Gaza' festival   132
Voice of the Mahalla Workers   142
voting process   425

Wadi Natroun Prison   228
Wafd Party   12–14, 16–18, 23, 24, 28, 30, 58, 111, 112, 117, 122, 135, 143, 154, 176, 196, 201, 217, 222, 235, 239, 248, 249, 255, 262, 270, 300, 301, 409, 416, 419, 442, 443, 448, 449, 461, 462, 474–6, 487, 521, 545, 582
Wagdy, Mahmoud   212, 262
Wahhabi Salafism   38
Wali, Yousef   92, 94, 100
War College   525
War of Attrition (1967)   42
War on Terror   130
Wasat (Centre) Party   115, 118, 119, 154, 398, 432, 433, 476, 478, 487, 516
Washington   618, 620, 624–6, 641, 653
Washington Post   100
wealth gap   53, 76, 96, 98, 101, 340, 343
We Are All Khaled Saeed campaign   155–7, 166–8, 194, 197, 319
Weavers' Union   124
Weber, Max   88
Weeks of Killing, The   585
Western government   575
Western media   219, 251
Westerwelle, Guido   245, 630, 631
We Want to Live (blog)   150
We Want To Live movement   129
White House Situation Room   215
White Knights firm   132
WikiThawra (website)   206
wildcat strike (1975)   114
Wisner, Frank   236
women activists   479
women rights   58
Women's National Front   522
Workers' Committee for National Liberation   112
Workers of Egypt (blog)   142
Workers' Vanguard   24

working class   12, 91, 93, 103, 135, 169, 186, 468
working-class districts   192–4, 197, 218, 284, 297, 325, 345
Working Group on Egypt   99
working women   531
work stoppages   123, 124, 133
World Bank   91, 92, 103, 107, 532, 589
World Values Survey   323

Ya'alon, Moshe   669
Yang Jiechi   639
Yassin, Ossama   232
Yedioth Ahronoth   73
Yemen   33, 35, 37, 46, 340, 595
Yemen War   37
Yom Kippur War (1973)   43, 70, 71, 81, 114, 342, 513
Youm7   542–3
Young Brothers   138–40, 171, 196, 198
Young Brothers' Facebook group   172
Young Egypt Society   14, 112
Yousef, Hassan   402
Youssef, Abdel Rahman   197
Youth for Change movement   120, 145, 164
Youth for Justice and Freedom (YJF)   147–9, 151, 168, 169, 171, 172, 176, 183, 188, 202, 226, 231, 252, 318
youth movements   169, 171, 183, 196, 220, 231, 234, 247, 255, 318, 319, 400, 432, 448, 480
Youth of Tahrir   261
youth politics   168
YouTube   175, 199, 271

el-Zafarani, Ibrahim   432, 440
Zaghloul, Samy Saad   11–13, 209
al-Za'im, Hosni   438
Zakher, Kamal   177
Zaki, Andrea   177
Zaki, Mohamed Ahmed   508, 509
Zamalek Ultra   132, 175, 189, 202, 478
Zarif, Mohammad Javad   659
Zayed, Abdullah bin   641
Zazou, Hisham   541, 581
Zein, Ahmed   234
el-Zeini, Noha   163
Al-Zend, Ahmed   162, 165, 482, 515, 553
Zewail, Ahmed   235, 254

www.ingramcontent.com/pod-product-compliance
Lightning Source LLC
Chambersburg PA
CBHW071700300426
44115CB00010B/1266